Kaplan Publishing are constantly finding new ways to make a difference to your exciting online resources really do offer something different to students looking for exam success.

This book comes with free MyKaplan online resources so that you can study anytime, anywhere. This free online resource is not sold separately and is included in the price of the book.

Having purchased this book, you have access to the following online study materials:

CONTENT	ACCA (including FFA,FAB,FMA)		FIA (excluding FFA,FAB,FMA)	
	Text	Kit	Text	Kit
iPaper version of the book	✓	✓	✓	✓
Interactive electronic version of the book	✓			
Check Your Understanding Test with instant answers	✓			
Material updates	✓	✓	✓	✓
Latest official ACCA exam questions*		✓		
Extra question assistance using the signpost icon**		✓		
Timed questions with an online tutor debrief using clock icon*		✓		
Interim assessment including questions and answers	✓		✓	
Technical answers	✓	✓	✓	✓

* Excludes F1, F2, F3, F4, FAB, FMA and FFA; for all other papers includes a selection of questions, as released by ACCA

** For ACCA P1-P7 only

How to access your online resources

Kaplan Financial students will already have a MyKaplan account and these extra resources will be available to you online. You do not need to register again, as this process was completed when you enrolled. If you are having problems accessing online materials, please ask your course administrator.

If you are already a registered MyKaplan user go to www.MyKaplan.co.uk and log in. Select the 'add a book' feature and enter the ISBN number of this book and the unique pass key at the bottom of this card. Then click 'finished' or 'add another book'. You may add as many books as you have purchased from this screen.

If you purchased through Kaplan Flexible Learning or via the Kaplan Publishing website you will automatically receive an e-mail invitation to MyKaplan. Please register your details using this email to gain access to your content. If you do not receive the e-mail or book content, please contact Kaplan Flexible Learning.

If you are a new MyKaplan user register at www.MyKaplan.co.uk and click on the link contained in the email we sent you to activate your account. Then select the 'add a book' feature, enter the ISBN number of this book and the unique pass key at the bottom of this card. Then click 'finished' or 'add another book'.

Your Code and Information

This code can only be used once for the registration of one book online. This registration and your online content will expire when the final sittings for the examinations covered by this book have taken place. Please allow one hour from the time you submit your book details for us to process your request.

ACCA

Paper P6

Advanced Taxation

Complete Text

Finance Act 2016
for June 2017 to March 2018
examination sittings

British library cataloguing-in-publication data

A catalogue record for this book is available from the British Library.

Published by:
Kaplan Publishing
Unit 2 The Business Centre
Molly Millars Lane
Wokingham
Berkshire
RG41 2QZ

ISBN 978-1-78415-687-9

The text in this material and any others made available by any Kaplan Group company does not amount to advice on a particular matter and should not be taken as such. No reliance should be placed on the content as the basis for any investment or other decision or in connection with any advice given to third parties. Please consult your appropriate professional adviser as necessary. Kaplan Publishing Limited and all other Kaplan group companies expressly disclaim all liability to any person in respect of any losses or other claims, whether direct, indirect, incidental, consequential or otherwise arising in relation to the use of such materials.

Printed and bound in Great Britain.

Acknowledgements

We are grateful to the Association of Chartered Certified Accountants for permission to reproduce past examination questions. The answers have been prepared by Kaplan Publishing.

Contents

		Page
Chapter 1	Income tax: Computation	1
Chapter 2	Employment income and related NICs	39
Chapter 3	Property and investment income	97
Chapter 4	Pensions	131
Chapter 5	Income tax planning	157
Chapter 6	CGT: Computations and stamp duty land tax	175
Chapter 7	CGT: Variations to computations	199
Chapter 8	CGT: Shares and securities for individuals and stamp duty	227
Chapter 9	CGT: Reliefs for individuals	261
Chapter 10	Overseas aspects of income tax and capital gains tax	341
Chapter 11	An introduction to inheritance tax	403
Chapter 12	IHT: special valuation rules, reliefs, and the death estate	449
Chapter 13	IHT: overseas, administration and tax planning	503
Chapter 14	The taxation of trusts	537
Chapter 15	Personal financial management	557
Chapter 16	Ethics and personal tax administration	569
Chapter 17	New and ongoing unincorporated businesses	607
Chapter 18	Cessation of an unincorporated business	691
Chapter 19	Partnerships: income tax and capital gains tax	723
Chapter 20	VAT: outline	743
Chapter 21	VAT: administration and overseas aspects	781

Chapter 22	Corporation tax: computations and administration	795
Chapter 23	Calculation of corporation tax: income and gains	821
Chapter 24	Corporation tax losses	869
Chapter 25	Business financial management	885
Chapter 26	Family companies and related planning scenarios	901
Chapter 27	Groups and consortia	943
Chapter 28	Overseas aspects of corporation tax	993
Chapter 29	Planning for companies	1021
Chapter 30	Questions and Answers	1043

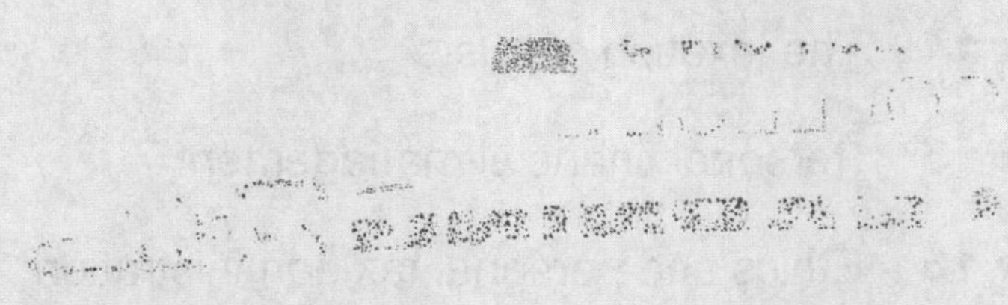

Paper Introduction

How to Use the Materials

These Kaplan Publishing learning materials have been carefully designed to make your learning experience as easy as possible and to give you the best chance of success in your examinations.

The product range contains a number of features to help you with the study process. They include:

(1) Detailed study guide and syllabus objectives

(2) Description of the examination

(3) Study skills and revision guidance

(4) Tax rates and allowances

(5) Complete text or essential text

(6) Question practice

The sections on the study guide, the syllabus objectives, the examination and study skills should all be read before you commence your studies. They are designed to familiarise you with the nature and content of the examination and give you tips on how to best approach your learning.

The **complete text or essential text** comprises the main learning materials and gives guidance as to the importance of topics and where other related resources can be found. Each chapter includes:

- The **learning objectives** contained in each chapter, which have been carefully mapped to the examining body's own syllabus learning objectives or outcomes. You should use these to check you have a clear understanding of all the topics on which you might be assessed in the examination.
- The **chapter diagram** provides a visual reference for the content in the chapter, giving an overview of the topics and how they link together.
- The **content** for each topic area commences with a brief explanation or definition to put the topic into context before covering the topic in detail. You should follow your studying of the content with a review of the examples. These are worked examples which will help you to understand better how to apply the content for the topic.
- **Test your understanding** sections provide an opportunity to assess your understanding of the key topics by applying what you have learned to short questions. Answers can be found at the back of each chapter.

- **Summary diagrams** complete each chapter to show the important links between topics and the overall content of the paper. These diagrams should be used to check that you have covered and understood the core topics before moving on.
- **Questions to practice** are provided at the back of the text.

Quality and accuracy are of the utmost importance to us so if you spot an error in any of our products, please send an email to mykaplanreporting@kaplan.com with full details, or follow the link to the feedback form in MyKaplan.

Our Quality Co-ordinator will work with our technical team to verify the error and take action to ensure it is corrected in future editions.

Icon Explanations

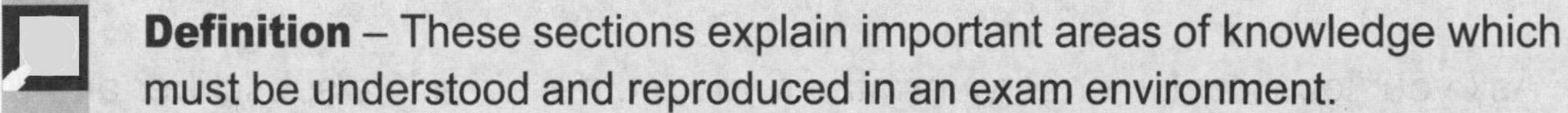

Definition – These sections explain important areas of knowledge which must be understood and reproduced in an exam environment.

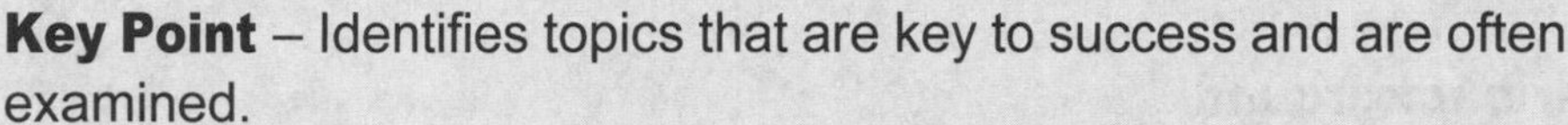

Key Point – Identifies topics that are key to success and are often examined.

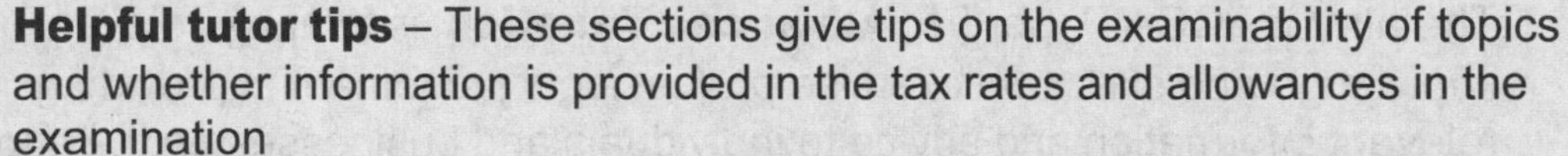

Helpful tutor tips – These sections give tips on the examinability of topics and whether information is provided in the tax rates and allowances in the examination

Expandable Text – Within this complete text and in the online version expandable text provides a more detailed explanation of key terms. These sections are printed in the text, and appear hidden in the online version but can be shown on screen. They will help to provide a deeper understanding of core areas. Reference to this text is vital when self studying.

Test Your Understanding – Following key points and definitions are exercises which give the opportunity to assess the understanding of these core areas. Within the text the answers to these sections are at the end of the chapter; within the online version the answers can be hidden or shown on screen to enable repetition of activities.

Example – To help develop an understanding of topics the illustrative examples and the test your understanding (TYU) exercises can be used.

New topic – This symbol indicates new areas of study, building on knowledge gained from previous studies or the introduction of a completely new topic.

Online subscribers

Our online resources are designed to increase the flexibility of your learning materials and provide you with immediate feedback on how your studies are progressing.

If you are subscribed to our on-line resources you will find:

(1) Online reference material: reproduces your Complete or Essential Text on-line, giving you anytime, anywhere access.

(2) Online testing: provides you with additional online objective testing so you can practice what you have learned further.

(3) Online performance management: immediate access to your on-line testing results. Review your performance by key topics and chart your achievement through the course relative to your peer group.

Ask your local customer services staff if you are not already a subscriber and wish to join.

Paper background

The aim of ACCA Paper P6, **Advanced Taxation**, is to apply relevant knowledge and skills and exercise professional judgement in providing relevant information and advice to individuals and businesses on the impact of the major taxes on financial decisions and situations.

Objectives of the syllabus

On the successful completion of this paper candidates should be able to:

- Apply further knowledge and understanding of the UK tax system through the study of more advanced topics within the taxes studied previously and the study of stamp taxes.
- Identify and evaluate the impact of relevant taxes on various situations and courses of action, including the interaction of taxes.
- Provide advice on minimising and/or deferring tax liabilities by the use of standard tax planning measures.
- Communicate with clients, HM Revenue and Customs and other professionals in an appropriate manner.

Syllabus objectives

We have reproduced the ACCA's syllabus below, showing where the objectives are explored within this book. Within the chapters, we have broken down the extensive information found in the syllabus into easily digestible and relevant sections, called Content Objectives. These correspond to the objectives at the beginning of each chapter.

Syllabus learning objective	Chapter reference
A APPLY FURTHER KNOWLEDGE AND UNDERSTANDING OF THE UK TAX SYSTEM THROUGH THE STUDY OF MORE ADVANCED TOPICS WITHIN THE TAXES STUDIED PREVIOUSLY AND THE STUDY OF STAMP TAXES	
(1) Income and income tax liabilities in situations involving further overseas aspects and in relation to trusts, and the application of exemptions and reliefs	
(a) The contents of the Paper F6 study guide for income tax and national insurances, under headings: [2]	
– B1 The scope of income tax	
– B2 Income from employment	
– B3 Income from self employment	
– B4 Property and investment income	
– B5 The comprehensive computation of taxable income and the income tax liability	
– B6 National insurance contributions for employed and self-employed persons	
– B7 The use of exemptions and reliefs in deferring and minimising income tax liabilities	
The following additional material is also examinable:	
(b) The scope of income tax: [3]	
(i) Explain and apply the concepts of residence and domicile and advise on the relevance to income tax	**1,10**
(ii) Advise on the availability of the remittance basis to UK resident individuals [2]	**10**
(iii) Advise on the tax position of individuals coming to and leaving the UK	**10**
(iv) Determine the income tax treatment of overseas income	**10**

	(vi) Understand the relevance of the OECD model double tax treaty to given situations	10
	(vii) Calculate and advise on the double taxation relief available to individuals	10
(c) Income from employment: [3]		
	(i) Advise on the tax treatment of share option and share incentive schemes, including employee shareholder shares	2
	(ii) Advise on the tax treatment of lump sum receipts	2
	(iii) Advise on the overseas aspects of income from employment, including travelling and subsistence expenses	10
	(iv) Identify personal service companies and advise on the tax consequences of providing services via a personal service company	26
(d) Income from self employment: [3]		
	(i) Advise on a change of accounting date	17
	(ii) Advise on the relief available for trading losses following the transfer of a business to a company	18
	(iii) Recognise the tax treatment of overseas travelling expenses	10
	(iv) Advise on the allocation of the annual investment allowance between related businesses	17
	(v) Identify the enhanced capital allowances available in respect of expenditure on green technologies [2]	17
(e) Property and investment income: [3]		
	(i) Advise on the tax implications of jointly held assets	5
	(ii) Recognise the tax treatment of savings income paid net of tax	1
	(iii) Income from trusts and settlements: Understand the income tax position of trust beneficiaries	14

(f) The comprehensive computation of taxable income and the income tax liability: [3]

(i) Understand the allocation of the personal allowance to different categories of income 1

(ii) Advise on the income tax position of the income of minor children 1

(g) The use of exemptions and reliefs in deferring and minimising income tax liabilities:

(i) Understand and apply the rules relating to investments in the seed enterprise investment scheme and the enterprise investment scheme [3] 3

(ii) Understand and apply the rules relating to investments in venture capital trusts [3] 3

(2) **Chargeable gains and capital gains tax liabilities in situations involving further overseas aspects and in relation to closely related persons and trusts together with the application of additional exemptions and reliefs**

(a) The contents of the Paper F6 study guide for chargeable gains for individuals under headings: [2]

- C1 The scope of the taxation of capital gains
- C2 The basic principles of computing gains and losses
- C3 Gains and losses on the disposal of movable and immovable property
- C4 Gains and losses on the disposal of shares and securities
- C5 The computation of capital gains tax
- C6 The use of exemptions and reliefs in deferring and minimising tax liabilities arising on the disposal of capital assets

The following additional material is also examinable

(b) The scope of the taxation of capital gains: [3]

(i) Determine the tax implications of independent taxation and transfers between spouses 6

(ii) Identify the concepts of residence and domicile and determine their relevance to capital gains tax 10

(iii) Advise on the availability of the remittance basis to non-UK domiciled individuals [2] **10**

(iv) Determine the UK taxation of foreign gains, including double taxation relief **10**

(v) Conclude on the capital gains tax position of individuals coming to and leaving the UK **10**

(vi) Advise on the UK taxation of gains on the disposal of UK residential property owned by non-residents **10**

(vii) Identify the occasions when a capital gain would arise on a partner in a partnership on the disposal of a partnership asset **19**

(c) Capital gains tax and trusts:

(i) Advise on the capital gains tax implications of transfers of property into trust [3] **14**

(ii) Advise on the capital gains tax implications of property passing absolutely from a trust to a beneficiary [2] **14**

(d) The basic principles of computing gains and losses: [3]

(i) Identify connected persons for capital gains tax purposes and advise on the tax implications of transfers between connected persons. **6**

(ii) Advise on the impact of dates of disposal and conditional contracts **6**

(iii) Evaluate the use of capital losses in the year of death **6**

(e) Gains and losses on the disposal of movable and immovable property: [3]

(i) Advise on the tax implications of a part disposal, including small part disposals of land **7**

(ii) Determine the gain on the disposal of leases and wasting assets **7**

(iii) Establish the tax effect of capital sums received in respect of the loss, damage or destruction of an asset **7**

(iv) Advise on the tax effect of making negligible value claims **6**

(v) Determine when capital gains tax can be paid by instalments and evaluate when this would be advantageous to taxpayers **6**

(f) Gains and losses on the disposal of shares and securities: [3]

(i) Extend the explanation of the treatment of rights issues to include the small part disposal rules applicable to rights issues **8**

(ii) Define a qualifying corporate bond (QCB), and understand what makes a corporate bond non-qualifying. Understand the capital gains tax implications of the disposal of QCBs in exchange for cash or shares **8**

(iii) Apply the rules relating to reorganisations, reconstructions and amalgamations and advise on the most tax efficient options available in given circumstances **8,27**

(iv) Establish the relief for capital losses on shares in unquoted trading companies **8**

(g) The use of exemptions and reliefs in deferring and minimising tax liabilities arising on the disposal of capital assets: [3]

(i) Understand and apply enterprise investment scheme reinvestment relief **3,9**

(ii) Understand and apply seed enterprise investment scheme reinvestment relief **3,9**

(iii) Advise on the availability of entrepreneurs' relief in relation to associated disposals **9**

(iv) Understand and apply the relief that is available on the transfer of an unincorporated business to a limited company **9**

(v) Understand the capital gains tax implications of the variation of wills **13**

(3) **Inheritance tax in situations involving further aspects of the scope of the tax and the calculation of the liabilities arising, the principles of valuation and the reliefs available, transfers of property to and from trusts, overseas aspects and further aspects of administration**

(a) The contents of the Paper F6 study guide for chargeable gains under headings: [2]

- D1 The basic principles of computing transfers of value
- D2 The liabilities arising on the chargeable lifetime transfers and on the death of an individual
- D3 The use of exemptions in deferring and minimising inheritance tax liabilities
- D4 Payment of inheritance tax

The following additional material is also examinable

(b) The scope of inheritance tax:

(i) Explain the concepts of domicile and deemed domicile and understand the application of these concepts to inheritance tax [2] **11,13**

(ii) Identify excluded property [2] **11**

(iii) Identify and advise on the tax implications of the location of assets [3] **13**

(iv) Identify and advise on gifts with reservation of benefit [3] **13**

(v) Identify and advise on the tax implications of associated operations [2] **13**

(c) The basic principles of computing transfers of value:

(i) Advise on the principles of valuation [3] **12**

(ii) Advise on the availability of business property relief and agricultural property relief [3] **12**

(iii) Identify exempt transfers [2] **11**

(d) The liabilities arising on chargeable lifetime transfers and on the death of an individual [3]

(i) Advise on the tax implications of chargeable lifetime transfers	**11**
(ii) Advise on the tax implications of transfers within seven years of death	**11**
(iii) Advise on the tax liability arising on a death estate	**12**
(iv) Advise on the relief for the fall in value of lifetime gifts	**11**
(v) Advise on the operation of quick succession relief	**12**
(vi) Advise on the operation of double tax relief for inheritance tax	**13**
(vii) Advise on the inheritance tax effects and advantages of the variation of wills	**13**

(e) The liabilities arising in respect of transfers to and from trusts and on property within trusts:

(i) Define a trust [2]	**14**
(ii) Distinguish between different types of trust [3]	**14**
(iii) Advise on the inheritance tax implications of transfers of property into trust [3]	**14**
(iv) Advise on the inheritance tax implications of property passing absolutely from a trust to a beneficiary [2]	**14**
(v) Identify the occasions on which inheritance tax is payable by trustees [3]	**14**

(f) The use of exemptions and reliefs in deferring and minimising inheritance tax liabilities: [3]

(i) Advise on the use of reliefs and exemptions to minimise inheritance tax liabilities, as mentioned in the sections above	**11,12,13 14**

(g) The system by which inheritance tax is administered, including the instalment option for the payment of tax:

(i) Identify the occasions on which inheritance tax may be paid by instalments.[2] **13**

(ii) Advise on the due dates, interest and penalties for inheritance tax purposes.[3] **13**

(4) **Corporation tax liabilities in situations involving further overseas and group aspects and in relation to special types of company, and the application of additional exemptions and reliefs**

(a) The contents of the Paper F6 study guide, for corporation tax, under headings: [2]

- E1 The scope of corporation tax
- E2 Taxable total profits
- E3 Chargeable gains for companies
- E4 The comprehensive computation of the corporation tax liability
- E5 The effect of a group structure for corporation tax purposes
- E6 The use of exemptions and reliefs in deferring and minimising corporation tax liabilities

The following additional material is also examinable:

(b) The scope of corporation tax: [3]

(i) Identify and calculate corporation tax for companies with investment business. **23**

(ii) Close companies:

- Apply the definition of a close company to given situations **26**
- Conclude on the tax implications of a company being a close company or a close investment holding company **26**

(iii) Identify and evaluate the significance of accounting periods on administration or winding up **22**

(iv) Conclude on the tax treatment of returns to shareholders after winding up has commenced **26**

(v) Advise on the tax implications of a purchase by a company of its own shares **26**

(vi) Identify personal service companies and advise on the tax consequences of services being provided via a personal service company **26**

(c) Taxable total profits: [3]

(i) Identify qualifying research and development expenditure, both capital and revenue, and determine the reliefs available by reference to the size of the individual company/group **23**

(ii) Recognise the relevance of a company generating profits attributable to patents **23**

(iii) Identify the enhanced capital allowances available in respect of expenditure on green technologies, including the tax credit available in the case of a loss making company **23**

(iv) Determine the tax treatment of non trading deficits on loan relationships **23**

(v) Recognise the alternative tax treatments of intangible assets and conclude on the best treatment for a given company **23**

(vi) Advise on the impact of the transfer pricing and thin capitalisation rules on companies **23**

(vii) Advise on the restriction on the use of losses on a change in ownership of a company **24**

(d) The comprehensive calculation of corporation tax liability: [3]

(i) Assess the impact of the OECD model double tax treaty on corporation tax **28**

(ii) Evaluate the meaning and implications of a permanent establishment **28**

(iii) Identify and advise on the tax implications of controlled foreign companies **28**

(iv) Advise on the tax position of overseas companies trading in the UK **28**

(v) Calculate double tax relief **28**

(e) The effect of a group structure for corporation tax purposes: [3]

(i) Advise on the allocation of the annual investment allowance between group or related companies **23**

(ii) Advise on the tax consequences of a transfer of intangible assets **27**

(iii) Advise on the tax consequences of a transfer of a trade and assets where there is common control **27**

(iv) Understand the meaning of consortium owned company and consortium member [2] **27**

(v) Advise on the operation of consortium relief **27**

(vi) Determine pre-entry losses and understand their tax treatment **27**

(vii) Determine the degrouping charge where a company leaves a group within six years of receiving an asset by way of a no gain/no loss transfer **27**

(viii) Determine the effects of the anti-avoidance provisions, where arrangements exist for a company to leave a group **27**

(ix) Advise on the tax treatment of an overseas branch **28**

(x) Advise on the relief for trading losses incurred by an overseas subsidiary **27**

(f) The use of exemptions and reliefs in deferring and minimising corporation tax liabilities: [3] **24,27,29**

(i) Advise on the availability and the application of disincorporation relief **26**

(ii) Determine the application of the substantial shareholdings exemption **23**

(5) Stamp taxes (stamp duty, stamp duty reserve tax, and stamp duty land tax)

(a) The scope of stamp taxes [3]

(i) Identify the property in respect of which stamp taxes are payable. **6,8**

(b) Identify and advise on the liabilities arising on transfers. [3]

(i) Advise on the stamp taxes payable on transfers of shares and securities **8**

(ii) Advise on the stamp taxes payable on transfers of land **6**

(c) The use of exemptions and reliefs in deferring and minimising stamp taxes [3]

(i) Identify transfers involving no consideration **6,8**

(ii) Advise on group transactions **27**

(d) Understand and explain the systems by which stamp taxes are administered [2] **6,8**

(6) Value added tax, tax administration and the UK tax system

(a) The contents of the Paper F6 study guide for value added tax (VAT) under headings:

- F1 The VAT registration requirements
- F2 The computation of VAT liabilities
- F3 The effect of special schemes

The following additional material is also examinable:

(i) Advise on the impact of the disaggregation of business activities for VAT purposes [3] **20**

(ii) Advise on the impact of divisional registration [3] **20**

(iii) Advise on the VAT implications of the supply of land and buildings in the UK **20**

(iv) Advise on the VAT implications of partial exemption **20**

(v) Advise on the application of the capital goods scheme **20**

(b) The contents of the Paper F6 study guide for the UK tax system and its administration under headings:

- A1 The overall function and purpose of taxation in a modern economy
- A2 Principal sources of revenue law and practice
- A3 The systems for self assessment and the making of returns
- A4 The time limits for the submission of information, claims and payment of tax, including payments on account
- A5 The procedures relating to compliance checks, appeals and disputes
- A6 Penalties for non-compliance

(i) Advise on the increased penalties which apply in relation to offshore matters [2] **16**

B THE IMPACT OF RELEVANT TAXES ON VARIOUS SITUATIONS AND COURSES OF ACTION, INCLUDING THE INTERACTION OF TAXES

(1) **Identify and advise on the taxes applicable to a given course of action and their impact. [3]** **13,15,17 18,26,29**

(2) **Identify and understand that the alternative ways of achieving personal or business outcomes may lead to different tax consequences.** **17,18,26 29**

(a) Calculate the receipts from a transaction, net of tax and compare the results of alternative scenarios and advise on the most tax efficient course of action. [3] **5,15,17 18,13**

(3) **Advise how taxation can affect the financial decisions made by businesses (corporate and unincorporated) and by individuals**

(a) Understand and compare and contrast the tax treatment of the sources of finance and investment products available to individuals. [3] **15**

(b) Understand and explain the tax implications of the effect of the raising of equity and loan finance. [3] **15,25**

(c) Explain the tax differences between decisions to lease, use hire purchase or purchase outright. [3] **15,25**

(d) Understand and explain the impact of taxation on the cash flows of a business. [3] **15,25**

(4) **Assess the tax advantages and disadvantages of alternative courses of action.[3]** **5,13,17 18,26,29**

(5) **Understand the statutory obligations imposed in a given situation, including any time limits for action and advising on the implications of non-compliance. [3]** **16,17,24 25,26,27 29**

C MINIMISE AND/OR DEFER TAX LIABILITIES BY THE USE OF STANDARD TAX PLANNING MEASURES

(1) **Identify and advise on the types of investment and other expenditure that will result in a reduction in tax liabilities for an individual and/or a business.[3]** **3,15,17 25,29**

(2) **Advise on legitimate tax planning measures, by which the tax liabilities arising from a particular situation or course of action can be mitigated. [3]** **5,13,17 18,24,26 27,29**

(3) **Advise on the appropriateness of such investment, expenditure or measures given a particular taxpayer's circumstances or stated objectives.[3]** **5,17,25 26,27,29**

(4) **Advise on the mitigation of tax in the manner recommended by reference to numerical analysis and/or reasoned argument.[3]** **5,17,24 26,27,29**

(5) **Be aware of the ethical and professional issues arising from the giving of tax planning advice.[3]** **5,15,16 26,29**

(6) **Be aware of and give advice on current issues in taxation.[3]** **5,16,26 29**

D COMMUNICATE WITH CLIENTS, HM REVENUE AND CUSTOMS AND OTHER PROFESSIONALS IN AN APPROPRIATE MANNER

(1) **Communicate advice, recommendations and information in the required format:[3]** **5,16,29**

For example the use of:

- Reports
- Letters
- Memoranda
- Meeting notes

(2) **Present written information, in language appropriate to the purpose of the communication and the intended recipient.[3]**

(3) **Communicate conclusions reached, together, where necessary with relevant supporting computations.[3]**

(4) **State and explain assumptions made or limitations in the analysis provided; together with any inadequacies in the information available and/or additional information required to provide a fuller analysis.[3]**

(5) **Identify and explain other, non-tax, factors that should be considered.[3]**

The superscript numbers in square brackets indicate the intellectual level at which the subject area could be assessed within the examination.

Level 1 (knowledge and comprehension) broadly equates with the Knowledge module.

Level 2 (application and analysis) with the Skills module.

Level 3 (synthesis and evaluation) to the Professional level.

However, lower level skills can continue to be assessed as you progress through each module and level.

The Examination

Examination format

The paper consists of two sections:

Section A consists of two compulsory questions.

Question 1 has 35 marks, including 4 professional marks.

Question 2 has 25 marks.

Section B consists of three 20-mark questions, two of which must be answered.

Questions will be scenario based and will normally involve consideration of more than one tax, together with some elements of planning and the interaction of taxes. Computations will normally only be required in support of explanations or advice and not in isolation.

Tax rates, allowances and information on certain reliefs will be given in the examination paper.

	Number of marks
Section A	
Two compulsory questions	60
Section B	
Choice of two from three questions	40
	100

Total time allowed: 3 hours and 15 minutes.

The pass mark is 50%.

Paper-based examination tips

Spend time reading the examination paper carefully. We recommend that 15 minutes should be spent reading and planning.

Where you have a choice of questions (section B), decide which ones you will do.

If 15 minutes are spent reading the examination paper, this leaves three hours to attempt the questions:

- **Divide the time** you spend on questions in proportion to the marks on offer.
- One suggestion **for this examination** is to allocate a maximum of 1.8 minutes to each mark available (180 minutes/100 marks), so a 20 mark question should be completed in approximately 36 minutes. If you plan to spend more or less time than 15 minutes reading the paper, your time allocation per mark will be different.

Unless you know exactly how to answer the question, spend some time **planning** your answer. Stick to the question and **tailor your answer** to what you are asked. Pay particular attention to the verbs in the question (e.g. calculate, explain, advise, state).

Spend the last five minutes reading through your answers and making any additions or corrections.

If you **get completely stuck** with a question, leave space in your answer book and **return to it later**.

If you do not understand what a question is asking, state your assumptions. Even if you do not answer in precisely the way the examining team would hope for, you should be given some credit, if your assumptions are reasonable.

You should do everything you can to make things easy for the marker. The marker will find it easier to identify the points you have made if your answers are legible.

Computations: It is essential to include all your workings in your answers. Many computational questions require the use of a standard format. Be sure you know these formats thoroughly before the examination and use the layouts that you see in the answers given in this book and in model answers.

Adopt a logical approach and cross reference workings to the main computation to keep your paper tidy and organised.

Reports, memos and other documents: some questions ask you to present your answer in the form of a report or a memo or other document. So use the correct format – there could be easy marks to gain here.

Communication of information

It is important to use the appropriate format for the communication of information, both in real life and in the examination.

In the compulsory Section A scenario-type exam questions, the examining team will tell you if they wish you to present your answer in a specific format, for example: as a report, a letter, briefing notes, or a memorandum. There will be marks available for using the appropriate format and style.

The scenario questions are often open-ended, and will usually require you to analyse information, work through a series of steps and provide advice. Sometimes you may be advising a client directly, or you may be providing information to your manager in preparation for a meeting with a client.

You may have to state assumptions if incomplete information is provided, and may have to identify further information to be requested from your client. If you are asked to come to a conclusion, it is important that you do so.

Extracts from answers to past exam questions are shown below, to help you to see what the various formats could look like. These presentations do not have to be followed exactly, but give suggested layouts for you to follow in the examination.

The questions provided in chapter 30 at the end of this material are not full examination standard questions, but will enable you to build up to answering such questions. Most 'real' examination questions are multi-tax questions, as you can see from the extracts below.

Full examination questions and answers with detailed guidance on how to approach each individual scenario, 'walk through' answers with tips and tutorial notes can be found in the Kaplan Publishing exam kit.

Report format

If you are asked to write a report in the exam, you should set it up as shown below.

The report should be broken down into clearly labelled sections, and you should write in full sentences. However, you should still try to use short paragraphs, and avoid showing lengthy calculations within the body of the report.

REPORT

To	**Mr Daube**
From	**Tax advisers**
Date	**6 December 2017**
Subject	**Various corporate matters**

Sale of shank Ltd

Use of trading losses

Loss brought forward

The loss brought forward of £35,000 can only be set against future trading profits of the same trade within Shank Ltd.

However, there is a possible restriction on the use of this loss as Shank Ltd will change its owners when it is sold to Raymond Ltd on 1 February 2018.

If there is a major change in the nature or conduct of trade within three years of this change in ownership, the loss will not be allowed to be carried forward past 1 February 2018.

A major change would include a change in products or services offered, markets or customers.

As Mr Daube is of the opinion that the company will only become profitable if there are fundamental changes to its commercial operations, it seems likely that the restriction will apply.

Current year loss

The loss for the year ended 31 March 2018 cannot be set against current year profits or previous year profits of Shank Ltd, as there are none available. Shank Ltd has no other source of income.

All or part of this loss could be surrendered to other companies within Shank Ltd's 75% losses group. This group contains Hock Ltd, Shank Ltd, Rump Ltd and Brisket Ltd, but not Knuckle Ltd.

The loss available for surrender must be time apportioned, as Shank Ltd will only be part of the losses group for part of the year. For the purposes of group relief, Shank Ltd is deemed to leave the group once 'arrangements' for sale are in place. The contract for sale will represent such an 'arrangement', therefore Shank Ltd can only surrender losses up to 1 November 2017.

The maximum loss available for surrender to Hock Ltd and Rump Ltd is therefore £31,500 (7/12 × £54,000) from 1 April 2017 to 31 October 2017.

Brisket Ltd has only been part of the losses group since 1 May 2017, therefore the maximum loss available for surrender to Brisket Ltd is £27,000 (6/12 × £54,000), from 1 May 2017 to 31 October 2017.

The maximum loss that can be claimed by group companies will be limited to their taxable total profits for the corresponding period.

Any remaining losses will be carried forward by Shank Ltd along with its £35,000 brought forward loss and the loss incurred between 1 November 2017 and 31 January 2018, as described above.

Loss on sale of Shank Ltd

The sale of Shank Ltd will be covered by the substantial shareholding exemption, as Hock Ltd is disposing of shares and has held at least 10% of the shares in Shank Ltd for 12 months in the two years before the sale, and both companies are trading companies.

Accordingly, there will be no relief for the capital loss on the disposal of the shares.

Threshold for payment of corporation tax by instalment

Companies are related 51% group companies where one company controls another, or where companies are under the common control of another company.

Companies that join during the accounting period are deemed to be part of the group from the beginning of the following accounting period. Companies that leave during the accounting period are deemed to still be part of the group until the end of the current chargeable accounting period.

Knuckle Ltd has no related 51% group companies, so the threshold for Knuckle Ltd will be £1,500,000.

All of the Hock Ltd group companies except Brisket Ltd are related 51% group companies for the year ended 31 March 2018.

Accordingly the threshold for Hock Ltd and Rump Ltd for the year ended 31 March 2018 is £500,000 (£1,500,000 ÷ 3).

Brisket Ltd will be related to its previous owner and any other companies related to its previous owner. The threshold for Brisket Ltd will therefore be different from that shown above.

Sales of buildings

Gains/losses on sale

Gar building

The sale of the Gar building to Hock Ltd will be at no gain, no loss, as Shank Ltd and Hock Ltd are part of the same 75% capital gains group.

Cray building

	£
Proceeds	420,000
Less: Cost	(240,000)
Unindexed gain	180,000
Less: Indexation allowance (£240,000 × 0.250)	(60,000)
Chargeable gain	120,000

Monk building

	£
Proceeds	290,000
Less: Cost	(380,000)
Capital loss	(90,000)

Letter format

If you are asked to write a letter in the examination, be mindful of whom you are writing to. If you are writing to a client, try to avoid using technical language that the client may not understand.

You should still try to break down your letter into short paragraphs and use headings to clearly label what you are writing about.

Calculations should generally be shown in a separate appendix, as in the letter below.

Generally, your letter should start with 'Dear [Name]' and finish with 'Yours sincerely'.

LETTER

C & D Co
High Street
Manchester

Sushi
3 The Avenue
Manchester

6 December 2017

Dear Sushi

Further to our recent meeting, I set out below my advice in connection with the assets you inherited from your mother.

UK inheritance tax and the statue

On the death of your mother

Your mother was not UK domiciled, and would therefore only be subject to UK inheritance tax on UK assets.

As your mother had no UK assets, there will be no UK inheritance tax due on her death.

On your death

UK assets

Your UK assets will be subject to UK inheritance tax, regardless of your domicile status.

Overseas assets

However, your overseas assets will only be subject to tax if you are UK domiciled or deemed to be UK domiciled.

Domicile

Your domicile is the country in which you have your permanent home.

At birth, your domicile of origin is inherited from your father. You would therefore have inherited the domicile of Zakuskia.

Even though you have been living in the UK for a number of years, you will remain domiciled in Zakuskia unless you acquire a domicile of choice in the UK.

To do this, you must acquire a permanent home in the UK and sever all ties with Zakuskia.

However, even if you have not chosen to be UK domiciled, you will be deemed to be domiciled in the UK, for inheritance purposes only, once you have been resident in the UK for 17 out of the last 20 tax years (ending with the tax year in which any assets are transferred).

As you have been resident in the UK since May 2003, you will be deemed domiciled in the UK from 2019/20 onwards.

This means that from 2019/20 onwards, both your UK assets and your overseas assets will be subject to UK inheritance tax.

Should you die before 2019/20, your overseas assets will only be subject to UK inheritance tax if you have acquired a domicile of choice in the UK.

The Zakuskian income

Remittance basis

Under the remittance basis, overseas income is only taxed in the UK when it is remitted, or brought in, to the UK.

The remittance basis is only available to individuals who are not UK domiciled. Accordingly, it will only be available to you if you have not chosen to acquire UK domicile.

Meaning of remittance

The most obvious example of a remittance is when income is brought directly into the UK.

However, the definition of remittance also includes:

- Using overseas income to settle debts in the UK
- Using overseas income to purchase goods and services which are subsequently bought into the UK with the exception of:
  - Personal items (e.g. clothes, shoes, jewellery)
  - Items brought to the UK for repair
  - Items costing no more than £1,000

Conclusion

If you remit £100,000 to the UK, it would be beneficial for you to claim the remittance basis, if it is available.

Your UK income tax liability will increase by £88,108 if the remittance basis is claimed, but by £70,000 if it is not (see Appendix).

Please call me if you require any further explanations or advice.

Yours sincerely

Tax manager

APPENDIX:

Increase in UK tax liability due to Zakuskian income

Remittance basis not available

		£
Gross Zakuskian income		200,000
UK income tax (45% × £200,000)		90,000
Less:	Double tax relief for Zakuskian tax (lower than UK tax) (£200,000 × 10%)	(20,000)
Additional UK tax payable		70,000

Remittance basis available and claimed (Note 1)

		£
Gross Zakuskian income remitted		100,000
UK income tax (45% × £100,000)		45,000
Less:	Double tax relief for Zakuskian tax (lower than UK tax) (£100,000 × 10%)	(10,000)
		35,000
Plus:	Remittance basis charge (Note 2)	50,000
Plus:	Loss of capital gains tax annual exempt amount (Note 3) (£11,100 × 20%)	2,220
Additional UK tax payable		87,220

Memorandum format

A memorandum is usually set out as shown below. Short sentences and bullet points can be used. Calculations can be included within the body of the memorandum, and should be clearly labelled as always.

MEMORANDUM

To	Tax manager
From	Tax assistant
Date	3 December 2017
Subject	Adam Snook

This memorandum considers the external finance required by Adam Snook (AS) to start his new business together with a number of related matters.

External finance required

	£	£
Total cost of project		310,000
Sale proceeds of shares/loan stock (£104,370 + £29,900)	134,270	
CGT on sale of shares/loan stock (W1)	(5,063)	
		(129,207)
External finance required		180,793

Assumptions:

AS has made no other disposals for the purposes of capital gains tax in 2017/18.

AS has no capital losses brought forward.

Workings: Capital gains tax

(W1) Capital gains tax on sale of shares/loan stock

		£
Gains realised (£36,114 (W2) + £8,616 (W3))		44,730
Less: Annual exempt amount		(11,100)
Taxable gains		33,630
Capital gains tax	£	
Gains in basic band (£32,000 – £15,370 (W5))	16,630 × 10%	1,663
Balance of gains (£33,630 – £16,630)	17,000 × 20%	3,400
	33,630	5,063

(W2) Gain on sale of shares

	£
Sale proceeds	104,370
Less: Deemed cost (W4)	(68,256)
Chargeable gain	36,114

Study skills and revision guidance

This section aims to give guidance on how to study for your ACCA exams and to give ideas on how to improve your existing study techniques.

Preparing to study

Set your objectives

Before starting to study decide what you want to achieve – the type of pass you wish to obtain. This will decide the level of commitment and time you need to dedicate to your studies.

Devise a study plan

Determine which times of the week you will study.

Split these times into sessions of at least one hour for study of new material. Any shorter periods could be used for revision or practice.

Put the times you plan to study onto a study plan for the weeks from now until the exam and set yourself targets for each period of study – in your sessions make sure you cover the course, course assignments and revision.

If you are studying for more than one paper at a time, try to vary your subjects as this can help you to keep interested and see subjects as part of wider knowledge.

When working through your course, compare your progress with your plan and, if necessary, re-plan your work (perhaps including extra sessions) or, if you are ahead, do some extra revision/practice questions.

Effective studying

Active reading

You are not expected to learn the text by rote. However, you do need to learn the tax rules and have a firm grasp of a considerable amount of detail (e.g. the conditions to be satisfied). You must also understand what you are reading and be able to use the rules to pass the exam and develop good practice.

A good technique to use is SQ3Rs – Survey, Question, Read, Recall, Review:

(1) **Survey the chapter** – look at the headings and read the introduction, summary and objectives, so as to get an overview of what the chapter deals with.

(2) **Question** – whilst undertaking the survey, ask yourself the questions that you hope the chapter will answer for you.

(3) **Read** – through the chapter thoroughly, answering the questions and making sure you can meet the objectives. Attempt the exercises and activities in the text, and work through all the examples.

(4) **Recall** – at the end of each section and at the end of the chapter, try to recall the main ideas of the section/chapter without referring to the text. This is best done after a short break of a couple of minutes after the reading stage.

(5) **Review** – check that your recall notes are correct, and make sure you have retained the facts and sufficient level of detail.

You may also find it helpful to re-read the chapter to try to see the topic(s) it deals with as a whole.

Note taking

Taking notes is a useful way of learning, but do not simply copy out the text. The notes must:

- be in your own words
- be concise
- cover the key points
- be well organised
- be modified as you study further chapters in this text or in related ones.

Trying to summarise a chapter without referring to the text can be a useful way of determining which areas you know and which you don't.

Three ways of taking notes:

(1) **Summarise the key points of a chapter.**

(2) **Make linear notes** – a list of headings, divided up with subheadings listing the key points. If you use linear notes, you can use different colours to highlight key points and keep topic areas together. Use plenty of space to make your notes easy to use.

(3) **Try a diagrammatic form** – the most common of which is a mind map. To make a mind map, put the main heading in the centre of the paper and put a circle around it. Then draw short lines radiating from this to the main sub-headings, which again have circles around them. Then continue the process from the sub-headings to sub-sub-headings, advantages, disadvantages, etc.

Highlighting and underlining

You may find it useful to underline or highlight key points in your study text – but do be selective. You may also wish to make notes in the margins.

Revision

The best approach to revision is to revise the course as you work through it. Also try to leave four to six weeks before the examination for final revision. Make sure you cover the whole syllabus and pay special attention to those areas where your knowledge is weak. Here are some recommendations:

Read through the text and your notes again and condense your notes into key phrases. It may help to put key revision points onto index cards to look at when you have a few minutes to spare.

Review any assignments you have completed and look at where you lost marks – put more work into those areas where you were weak.

Practise examination standard questions under timed conditions. If you are short of time, list the points that you would cover in your answer and then read the model answer, but do try to complete at least a few questions under examination conditions.

Also practise producing answer plans and comparing them to the model answer.

If you are stuck on a topic find somebody (a tutor) to explain it to you.

Read good newspapers and professional journals, especially ACCA's Student Accountant – this can give you an advantage in the exam.

Ensure you **know the structure of the exam** – how many questions and of what type you will be expected to answer. During your revision attempt all the different styles of questions you may be asked.

Further reading

You can find further reading and technical articles under the student section of ACCA's website.

Tax rates and allowances

Supplementary instructions

1 **You should assume that the tax rates and allowances for the tax year 2016/17 and for the financial year to 31 March 2017 will continue to apply for the foreseeable future unless you are instructed otherwise.**

2 **Calculations and workings need only to be made to the nearest £.**

3 **All apportionments should be made to the nearest month.**

4 **All workings should be shown.**

INCOME TAX

		Normal rates	Dividend rates
		%	%
Basic rate	£1 – £32,000	20	7.5
Higher rate	£32,001 – £150,000	40	32.5
Additional rate	£150,001 and over	45	38.1
Savings income nil rate band	– Basic rate taxpayers		£1,000
	– Higher rate taxpayers		£500
Dvidend nil rate band			£5,000

A starting rate of 0% applies to savings income where it falls within the first £5,000 of taxable income.

Personal allowances

	£
Personal allowance	11,000
Transferable amount	1,100
Income limit	£100,000

Residence status

Days in UK	Previously resident	Not previously resident
Less than 16	Automatically not resident	Automatically not resident
16 to 45	Resident if 4 UK ties (or more)	Automatically not resident
46 to 90	Resident if 3 UK ties (or more)	Resident if 4 UK ties
91 to 120	Resident if 2 UK ties (or more)	Resident if 3 UK ties (or more)
121 to 182	Resident if 1 UK tie (or more)	Resident if 2 UK ties (or more)
183 or more	Automatically resident	Automatically resident

Remittance basis charge

UK resident for:	Charge
7 out of the last 9 years	£30,000
12 out of the last 14 years	£60,000
17 out of the last 20 years	£90,000

Child benefit income tax charge

Where income is between £50,000 and £60,000, the charge is 1% of the amount of child benefit received for every £100 of income over £50,000.

Car benefit percentage

The relevant base level of CO_2 emissions is 95 grams per kilometre.

The percentage rates applying to petrol cars with CO_2 emissions up to this level are:

	%
50 grams per kilometre or less	7
51 grams to 75 grams per kilometre	11
76 grams to 94 grams per kilometre	15
95 grams per kilometre	16

Car fuel benefit

The base level figure for calculating car fuel benefit is £22,200.

Individual Savings Accounts (ISAs)

The overall investment limit is £15,240.

Pension scheme limits

Annual allowance	
2014/15 – 2016/17	£40,000
2013/14	£50,000
Minimum allowance	£10,000
Threshold income limit	£110,000
Income limit	£150,000
Lifetime allowance	£1,000,000

The maximum contribution that can qualify for tax relief without any earnings is £3,600.

Authorised mileage allowances: cars

Up to 10,000 miles	45p
Over 10,000 miles	25p

Capital allowances: rates of allowance

Plant and machinery

Main pool	18%
Special rate pool	8%

Motor cars

New cars with CO_2 emissions up to 75 grams per kilometre	100%
CO_2 emissions between 76 and 130 grams per kilometre	18%
CO_2 emissions above 130 grams per kilometre	8%

Annual investment allowance

Rate of allowance	100%
Expenditure limit	£200,000

Cap on income tax reliefs

Unless otherwise restricted, reliefs are capped at the higher of £50,000 or 25% of income.

CORPORATION TAX

Rate of tax	20%
Profit threshold	£1,500,000

Patent box – deduction from net patent profit

Net patent profit × ((main rate – 10%)/main rate)

VALUE ADDED TAX

Standard rate	20%
Registration limit	£83,000
Deregistration limit	£81,000

INHERITANCE TAX: Nil rate bands and tax rates

	£
6 April 2016 to 5 April 2017	325,000
6 April 2015 to 5 April 2016	325,000
6 April 2014 to 5 April 2015	325,000
6 April 2013 to 5 April 2014	325,000
6 April 2012 to 5 April 2013	325,000
6 April 2011 to 5 April 2012	325,000
6 April 2010 to 5 April 2011	325,000
6 April 2009 to 5 April 2010	325,000
6 April 2008 to 5 April 2009	312,000
6 April 2007 to 5 April 2008	300,000
6 April 2006 to 5 April 2007	285,000
6 April 2005 to 5 April 2006	275,000
6 April 2004 to 5 April 2005	263,000
6 April 2003 to 5 April 2004	255,000
6 April 2002 to 5 April 2003	250,000

Rate of tax on excess over nil rate band	– Lifetime rate	20%
	– Death rate	40%

Inheritance tax: taper relief

Years before death	Percentage reduction
Over 3 but less than 4 years	20%
Over 4 but less than 5 years	40%
Over 5 but less than 6 years	60%
Over 6 but less than 7 years	80%

CAPITAL GAINS TAX

		Normal rates	Residential property
Rates of tax	– Lower rate	10%	18%
	– Higher rate	20%	28%
Annual exempt amount		£11,100	
Entrepreneurs' relief	– Lifetime limit	£10,000,000	
	– Rate of tax	10%	

NATIONAL INSURANCE CONTRIBUTIONS
(Not contracted out rates)

Class 1 Employee	£1 – £8,060 per year	Nil
	£8,061 – £43,000 per year	12%
	£43,001 and above per year	2%
Class 1 Employer	£1 – £8,112 per year	Nil
	£8,113 and above per year	13.8%
	Employment allowance	£3,000
Class 1A		13.8%
Class 2	£2.80 per week	
	Small profits threshold	£5,965
Class 4	£1 – £8,060 per year	Nil
	£8,061 – £43,000 per year	9%
	£43,001 and above per year	2%

RATES OF INTEREST (assumed)

Official rate of interest	3%
Rate of interest on underpaid tax	3%
Rate of interest on overpaid tax	0.50%

STAMP DUTY LAND TAX
Non-residential properties

£150,000 or less	0%
£150,001 – £250,000	2%
£250,001 and above	5%

Residential properties

£125,000 or less	0%
£125,001 – £250,000	2%
£250,001 – £925,000	5%
£925,001 – £1,500,000	10%
£1,500,001 and above	12%

Note: These rates are increased by 3% in certain circumstances

STAMP DUTY

Shares	0.5%

chapter

1

Income tax: Computation

Chapter learning objectives

Upon completion of this chapter you will be able to:

- prepare an income tax computation for an individual given a range of different types of income/payments
- allocate the personal allowance to different categories of income
- determine the taxability of the income of minor children
- calculate the child benefit charge and explain when it arises.

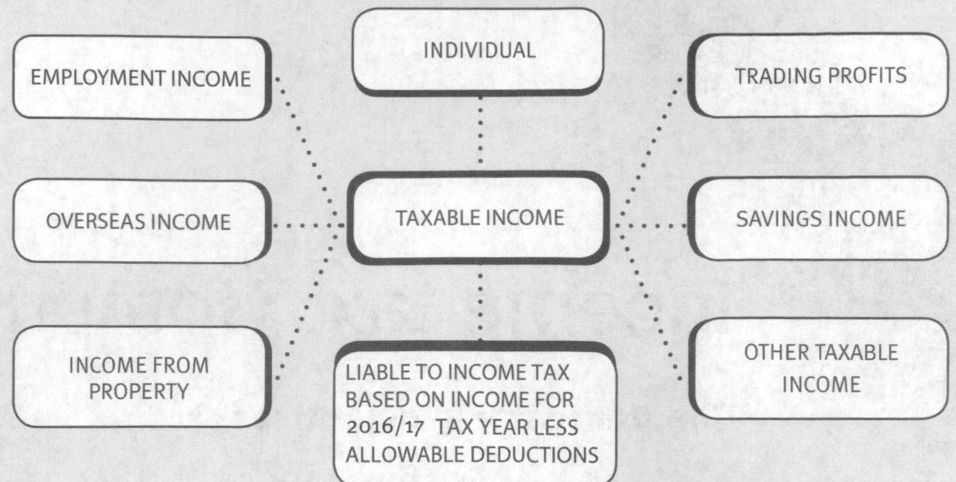

Introduction

This and the following two chapters deal with the basic charge to income tax and national insurance, concentrating on an employed individual with property and investment income.

Much of this chapter is a revision of rules covered at F6 but there are some significant changes to the taxation of savings and dividend income in the Finance Act 2016 that affect the operation of the income tax legislation.

A reminder of the F6 rules is given in expandable text and revision examples are provided to check your retention of the required F6 knowledge. You will need to review these thoroughly as part of your P6 studies.

1 Income tax computation

Basis of assessment

Income tax is payable on an individual's taxable income for a tax year.

The June 2017, September 2017, December 2017 and March 2018 examinations are based on the tax year 2016/17, which is from 6 April 2016 to 5 April 2017.

Individual taxpayers, married or single, are taxed separately on their own taxable income.

Taxable income

A reminder of the computation of taxable income, the classification of income and the rates of income tax is given in the pro forma income tax computation below.

Pro forma income tax computation

Name of individual
Income tax computation – 2016/17

	Notes	£
Earned income		
Employment income		x
Trading profits		x
Other earned income	1	x
Savings income		
Interest received gross	2	x
Interest received net (× 100/80)	3	x
Investment income		
Property income		x
Other types of investment income	4	x
Dividend income		
Dividends received from UK companies		x
Other dividends	5	x
Total income		x
Less: **Reliefs**	6	
Qualifying loan interest (gross amount paid)		(x)
Loss reliefs		(x)
Net income		x
Less: Personal allowance (PA)	7	(x)
Taxable income		x

		£
Income tax (calculated at relevant rates)	8	x
Less: Marriage allowance (MA)	9	(x)
EIS, SEIS and VCT relief (30%/50%/30%)	10	(x)
Double taxation relief (DTR)	11	(x)
Income tax liability		x
Less: Tax credits	12	(x)
Income tax payable by self-assessment		x

Remember that in the taxable income computation:

- all income is included **gross**
- any exempt income is excluded.

Exempt income

The following income is exempt from income tax:

- income from Individual Savings Accounts (ISAs)
- NS & I savings certificate interest
- interest on repayment of tax
- redundancy payments
- scholarship income
- gaming, lottery and premium bond winnings
- state benefits paid in the event of accident, sickness, disability or infirmity.

Notes to computation:

(1) **Other earned income** includes:

- pensions from former employment
- state pensions
- profits from furnished holiday lettings (Chapter 3).

(2) **Interest received gross** includes:

- bank and building society interest, gilt-edged security interest, NS & I bank interest, interest from quoted corporate bonds issued by UK resident companies
- foreign interest (gross of overseas tax suffered) (Chapter 10)

(3) **Interest received net** includes:

- interest from unquoted corporate bonds issued by UK resident companies to individuals (e.g. loan note interest)
- interest from an 'interest in possession' (IIP) trust (Chapter 14).

(4) **Other types of investment income** includes:

- annuity income (income element only)
- non-savings income from an IIP trust (× 100/80) (Chapter 14)

- discretionary trust income (× 100/55) (Chapter 14)
- other foreign income (gross of overseas tax suffered) (Chapter 10)
- dividends from a real estate investment trust (REIT) (× 100/80) (Chapter 3)

(5) **Other dividend income** includes:

- dividends from an IIP trust (× 100/92.5) (Chapter 14)
- foreign dividends (gross of overseas tax suffered) (Chapter 10)

(6) **Qualifying loan interest** is covered later in this Chapter.
Loss reliefs are covered in detail in Chapters 17 and 18.
The maximum amount allowed to be deducted from total income is the greater of:

- £50,000, or
- 25% of adjusted total income

More detail of the maximum restriction is given in Chapter 17.

(7) The PA is normally £11,000, but could be abated to £Nil.

(8) The following **rates of income tax** apply in 2016/17:

Income level	**Band**	**Income non-savings**	**Savings** (see below)	**Dividends** (see below)
First £32,000	Basic rate (BR)	20%	20%	7.5%
£32,001 – £150,000	Higher rate (HR)	40%	40%	32.5%
£150,001 and over	Additional rate (AR)	45%	45%	38.1%

The above rates of income tax and associated bands are included in the tax rates and allowances provided to you in the examination.

Remember to:

- tax income in the following order:
  (1) non-savings income
  (2) savings income
  (3) dividend income

  - extend the basic rate and higher rate bands by the **gross amount paid** in the tax year of:
    - **personal pension scheme** contributions (PPCs) and free standing additional voluntary contributions (AVCs) paid into a registered pension scheme (Chapter 4), and
    - **gift aid donations**
      However, note donations to charity by an individual are not examinable at P6.

(9) Subject to conditions, a maximum of 10% of the PA (i.e. £1,100 for 2016/17) can be transferred to a spouse or civil partner (see section 3).

(10) Relief under EIS, SEIS and VCTs is covered in Chapter 3.

(11) Double taxation relief (DTR) and the treatment of overseas income is covered in Chapter 10.

(12) From 2016/17 most types of savings income and all dividend income are received gross with no income tax deducted at source. Therefore, PAYE is the only tax credit that will commonly be deductible to calculate income tax payable.

Rates of tax on savings

- Savings income is normally taxed in the same way as 'non-savings income' at the basic, higher and additional rates of tax (20%, 40% and 45%).
- However, a starting rate of tax of 0% will apply to savings income where it falls into the first £5,000 of taxable income.

In addition, basic rate and higher rate taxpayers are entitled to a savings income nil rate band.

- The savings income nil rate band is:

– Basic rate taxpayer	£1,000
– Higher rate taxpayer	£500
– Additional rate taxpayer	£Nil

The savings income nil rate bands are included in the tax rates and allowances provided to you in the examination.

Savings income is taxed as the next slice of income after non-savings income. Therefore the rates of tax applicable to savings income depend on the level of taxable non-savings income. The procedure to follow is:

(1) Calculate income tax on non-savings income

(2) Apply the different rates of tax on savings income in the following order:

(i) Starting rate

(ii) Savings nil rate band

(iii) Normal rates (i.e. basic, higher and additional rates)

(i) **Starting rate**

This only applies in fairly limited situations i.e. where taxable non-savings income is less than £5,000. If:

- No taxable non-savings income – the first £5,000 of taxable savings income is taxed at 0% (i.e. it is tax free)
- Taxable non-savings income below £5,000 – savings income falling into the rest of the first £5,000 is taxed at 0%
- Taxable non-savings income in excess of £5,000 – the 0% starting rate is not applicable.

(ii) **Savings nil rate band**

If there is further savings income to tax, consider the savings nil rate band. If the taxpayer is:

- A **basic rate** taxpayer – the next **£1,000** falls in the savings nil rate band and is taxed at 0%
- A **higher rate** taxpayer – the next **£500** falls in the savings nil rate band and is taxed at 0%
- An **additional rate** taxpayer i.e. taxable income is £150,000 or more – **not applicable**

To determine whether the taxpayer is a basic, higher or additional rate taxpayer, ascertain the highest tax band that their taxable income falls within.

For example, a taxpayer with taxable income of £45,000 is a higher rate taxpayer as he has taxable income falling into the higher rate band of £32,001 to £150,000.

(iii) **Normal rates**

If there is further savings income to tax, apply the normal savings rates as follows:

- The basic rate of 20% applies to savings income falling within the basic rate band (BRB) i.e. the first £32,000 of taxable income.
- The higher rate of 40% applies to savings income falling within the higher rate band (HRB) i.e. income in the range £32,001 to £150,000 of taxable income.
- The additional rate of 45% applies to savings income where taxable income exceeds £150,000.

Note that the BRB and HRB are first reduced by non-savings income and savings income that has been taxed at the starting rate and the savings income nil rate.

The above procedure may seem complicated but if you use the columnar layout of the income tax computation (see below) it will be relatively easy to determine which rates to apply.

Test your understanding 1

Eugenie received bank interest of £6,000 during the tax year 2016/17.

Calculate Eugenie's income tax payable assuming she also had employment income in the tax year 2016/17 of:

(a) £14,200 (PAYE of £640 deducted)

(b) £29,000 (PAYE of £3,600 deducted)

(c) £41,000 (PAYE of £6,300 deducted)

In the examination always indicate the rate at which income is taxed, even if the rate is 0%. This shows that you understand that the income is taxable and that you know how to apply the different rates.

Rates of tax on dividends

- The first £5,000 of dividend income falls in the dividend nil rate band and is therefore tax-free.
- The following rates of tax apply to any remaining dividend income:

Dividends falling into the:	Dividend rates
Basic rate band (first £32,000)	7.5%
Higher rate band (£32,001 – £150,000)	32.5%
Additional rate band (over £150,000)	38.1%

The rates and thresholds applicable to dividends are included in the tax rates and allowances provided to you in the P6 examination.

Applying the appropriate rates of tax to dividend income

Dividend income is taxed as the top slice of income (i.e. after non-savings income and savings income).

(1) The dividend nil rate band applies to the first £5,000 of dividend income.

  (i) Unlike the savings starting rate (which only applies in certain limited circumstances) and the savings income nil rate band (which depends on the tax position of the individual) the dividend nil rate band **always applies** to the first £5,000 of dividend income.

  (ii) The dividend income taxed at the dividend nil rate reduces the basic rate and higher rate bands when determining the rate of tax on the remaining dividend income.

(2) Any remaining dividend income is taxed at the special dividend rates set out above.

Example 1

Andy received the following income in the tax year 2016/17:

Employment income	£50,000 (PAYE of £9,200 deducted)
Dividends received	£6,000

Calculate Andy's income tax payable for 2016/17.

Solution

Andy's income tax liability 2016/17

	Total	Non-savings income	Dividend income
	£	£	£
Employment income	50,000	50,000	
Dividend income	6,000		6,000
Total income	56,000	50,000	6,000
Less: PA	(11,000)	(11,000)	
Taxable income	45,000	39,000	6,000

Income tax		£
£		
32,000 × 20% BR (Non-savings income)		6,400
7,000 × 40% HR (Non-savings income)		2,800
5,000 × 0% DNRB (Dividend income)		0
1,000 × 32.5% HR (Dividend income)		325
45,000		
Income tax liability		9,525
Less:	Tax credits	
	PAYE	(9,200)
Income tax payable		325

Test your understanding 2

For the tax year 2016/17, Kei had the following income:

Property income	£31,000
Bank interest received	£2,000
Dividends received	£10,500

Calculate Kei's income tax liability for the tax year 2016/17.

Qualifying loan interest

A reminder of the types of loan interest qualifying for relief as an allowable deduction in an income tax computation is given in expandable text and is summarised in the diagram in section 4.

A maximum deduction restriction applies to these payments and loss relief. However, it is more likely to be examined in the context of losses, therefore the detailed rules are in Chapter 17.

Qualifying loan interest

Relief is given for interest paid on loans incurred to finance expenditure for a qualifying purpose but only interest paid at a reasonable commercial rate. Amounts paid in excess are not allowable.

Note that qualifying loan interest is **paid gross** and the gross amount paid in the tax year is an allowable relief against total income (subject to the maximum deduction).

The main types of qualifying purposes to which the loan must be applied:

(1) **Partnerships**

- The contribution of capital into a partnership (including limited liability partnerships).
- A loan made by a partner for the purchase of plant or machinery for use in the partnership – year of purchase and next 3 years.

(2) **Close companies**

The purchase of ordinary shares in, or loans to, a 'close' trading company (Chapter 26) or a company in the EEA which would be a 'close' trading company if it were situated in the UK.

The following conditions must be satisfied:

- the individual (with associates) owns at least 5% of the ordinary share capital at the time the interest is paid; or
- they own some shares in the company at the time the interest is paid and, during the period from the purchase of the shares until the payment of the interest, they must have worked for the greater part of their time in the actual management of the company, or an associated company.

(3) **Employee-controlled companies**

Relief is available to full-time employees for loans taken out to acquire ordinary shares in an employee-controlled, UK or EEA resident, unquoted trading company.

(4) **Personal representatives**

The payment of inheritance tax on the deceased's personal estate. Relief is available for one year only.

The treatment of royalties paid by an individual

Patent and copyright royalties payable for trading purposes (calculated on an accruals basis) are an allowable deduction in calculating the adjusted trading profits of a business.

Copyright royalties are paid gross and patent royalties continue to be paid net of the basic rate of income tax (20%).

The collection of the basic rate tax on patent royalties is not examinable.

2 Personal allowances

The personal allowance is included in the tax rates and allowances provided in the examination.

Every taxpayer (including children) is entitled to a personal allowance.

- The amount for the tax year 2016/17 is £11,000.
- There is no restriction to the PA where the individual is only alive for part of the tax year (i.e. full allowance available in the tax year of birth or death).

- The basic PA is deducted from the taxpayer's net income from the different sources of income in the most beneficial order. In the majority of cases, this will be:

  (1) Non-savings income

  (2) Savings income

  (3) Dividend income

However, there are some cases where this will not be the most beneficial order (see below).

Surplus personal allowances are normally lost, they cannot be set against capital gains nor can they be transferred to any other taxpayer.

However, subject to conditions, a maximum of 10% of the PA (i.e. £1,100 for 2016/17) can be transferred to a spouse or civil partner (see section 3).

Reduction of personal allowance – high income individuals

- The basic PA is gradually reduced for individuals with income in excess of £100,000.
- The reduction of the basic PA is based on the taxpayer's adjusted net income (ANI) which is calculated as follows:

	£
Net income	X
Less: Gross gift aid donations	(X)
Less: Gross personal pension contributions (PPCs)	(X)
Adjusted net income (ANI)	X

- Where the taxpayer's ANI exceeds £100,000, the basic PA is reduced by:
  - **50% × (ANI – £100,000)**
  - If necessary, the reduced PA is rounded up to the nearest pound (although in the examination, rounding up or down is acceptable).
- A taxpayer with ANI in excess of £122,000 will therefore be entitled to no basic PA at all, as the excess above £100,000 is twice the PA.
- The effective rate of tax on income between £100,000 and £122,000 is therefore 60%. This is made up of:
  - higher rate income tax = 40%
  - lost PA (½ × 40%) = 20%
- Taxpayers at or near this margin may therefore wish to consider making additional gift aid or personal pension contributions in order to reduce their ANI below £100,000.

Test your understanding 3

Lorna has an annual salary of £130,000 and made gross personal pension contributions in the tax year 2016/17 of £19,000.

Calculate Lorna's taxable income for the tax year 2016/17.

Test your understanding 4

Tristan earned employment income of £137,500 and received bank interest of £22,500 and dividends of £17,000 in the tax year 2016/17.

Calculate the income tax payable for the tax year 2016/17.

Prior to the 2016/17 tax year, a higher personal allowance (often referred to as the personal age allowance (PAA)) was available for older taxpayers.

This has been abolished with effect from 6 April 2016 and therefore is no longer examinable.

Allocation of the personal allowance

For the majority of individuals it will be most beneficial to deduct the personal allowance (PA) from non-savings income first, then deducting any remaining PA from savings income and finally dividend income.

However, the tax legislation requires the PA to be offset in the most beneficial manner, which may mean deducting the PA from the different sources of income in a different order, for example offsetting the PA against dividend income prior to savings income.

This may be necessary in order to take advantage of the savings rate nil rate band, or the starting rate for savings income.

Example 2 – allocation of the personal allowance

Bernard has the following income for the tax year 2016/17:

Pension income	£7,500
Savings income	£5,000
Dividend income	£12,000

Calculate Bernard's income tax liability for the tax year 2016/17, allocating the personal allowance to the different sources of income in the most beneficial order.

Solution

	Total	Non-savings income	Savings income	Dividend income
	£	£	£	£
Pension income	7,500	7,500		
Savings income	5,000		5,000	
Dividend income	12,000			12,000
Total income	24,500	7,500	5,000	12,000
Less: PA	(11,000)	(7,500)		(3,500)
Taxable income	13,500	0	5,000	8,500

Income tax		
£		
5,000 × 0% SR (Savings income)		0
5,000 × 0% DNRB (Dividend income)		0
3,500 × 7.5% BR (Dividend income)		262
13,500		
Income tax liability		262

Notes:

(1) Deducting the personal allowance in the most beneficial manner is automatic and is not a matter of choice or tax planning for the taxpayer.

(2) The starting rate for savings is available as saving income falls within the first £5,000 of taxable income

Bernard will save £263 by allocating his PA to dividend income in preference to savings income. This is because £3,500 of income is covered by the starting rate for savings and taxed at 0% rather than being taxed at 7.5% as dividend income (£3,500 × 7.5% = £262).

The income tax computation below shows the income tax liability that would have arisen if the PA was allocated to savings income in preference to dividend income.

	Total	Non-savings income	Savings income	Dividend income
	£	£	£	£
Pension income	7,500	7,500		
Savings income	5,000		5,000	
Dividend income	12,000			12,000
Total income	24,500	7,500	5,000	12,000
Less: PA	(11,000)	(7,500)	(3,500)	
Taxable income	13,500	0	1,500	12,000

Income tax		
£		
	1,500 × 0% SR (Savings income)	0
	5,000 × 0% DNRB (Dividend income)	0
	7,000 × 7.5% BR (Dividend income)	525
13,500		
Income tax liability		525

Test your understanding 5

Ana has the following income for the tax year 2016/17:

Employment income	£6,800
Savings income	£4,200
Dividend income	£12,000

Calculate Ana's income tax liability for the tax year 2016/17, allocating the personal allowance to the different sources of income in the most beneficial order.

3 The taxation of families

The taxation of married couples

Each spouse in the marriage is taxed separately.

Civil partners (same-sex couples registered as a civil partnership) are treated in the same way as married couples.

However, there are special rules governing:

- the allocation of income between the spouses where assets are jointly owned
- transfer of unused personal allowance (the marriage allowance).

In addition, married couples can transfer income-generating assets between them to minimise their joint income tax liability.

Jointly owned assets

- Generally, income generated from assets owned jointly will be split 50:50 regardless of the actual percentage ownership.
- Where jointly owned assets are held other than in a 50:50 ratio, an election can be made to HMRC for the income to be taxed on the individual partners according to their actual ownership, with the exception of jointly held bank accounts, which are always split 50:50.
- Where the jointly owned asset is shares in a close company, income is automatically taxed on the individual partners according to their actual ownership.

Marriage allowance

A spouse or civil partner can elect to transfer a fixed amount of the PA to their spouse/civil partner. This is commonly known as the marriage allowance (MA).

The MA is available provided neither spouse/civil partner is a higher rate or additional rate taxpayer.

In practice, however, it will only be beneficial to make the election provided the transferor spouse/civil partner does not fully utilise their PA of £11,000 but the recipient spouse/civil partner does, so that their total income tax liability as a couple will be reduced.

Electing for the MA allows the transfer:

- to the other spouse (or civil partner)
- of a fixed amount of PA (regardless of the amount of unused PA)
  = 10% × the individual personal allowance
  = £1,100 for the tax year 2016/17.

Note that there is no provision for transferring less than this amount.

The transferable amount of £1,100 will be included in the tax rates and allowances provided to you in the examination.

The effect of the election is that the:

- transferring spouse's PA is reduced by the fixed amount of £1,100 (for 2016/17)
- the recipient spouse's income tax liability is reduced by a maximum of £220 (£1,100 MA × 20% BR income tax).

Note that:

- the transferring spouse makes the election
- the relief is given as an income tax reducer in the recipient's income tax liability computation
- the recipient's own PA is not increased
- the maximum benefit from the MA is £220
- if the recipient's income tax liability is less than £220, a tax repayment is not possible but the amount by which the transferor's PA is reduced remains £1,100
- at best the relief reduces the recipient's income tax liability to £Nil
- in the year of marriage the full allowance is available
- relief is usually given by adjusting the individual's tax code under PAYE (or through self-assessment if they are not employed).

Example 3 – Marriage allowance

Kevin and Judy are married. Kevin is employed and earns a salary of £35,000 per annum. Judy spends most of her time looking after their two children but works on a Saturday, earning an annual salary of £6,000. They do not have any other income.

Judy makes an election to transfer the marriage allowance to Kevin.

Calculate Kevin and Judy's income tax liabilities for the tax year 2016/17.

Solution

Income tax computation – 2016/17

	Kevin	**Judy**
	£	£
Employment income = net income	35,000	6,000
Less: PA (Note)	(11,000)	(6,000)
Taxable income	24,000	0
Income tax liability (£24,000 × 20%)	4,800	0
Less: MA (£1,100 × 20%)	(220)	
Income tax liability	4,580	0

Note: Judy's personal allowance is reduced to £9,900 (£11,000 – £1,100).

This is still more than her total income of £6,000, so she has no tax liability.

If one spouse (or civil partner) has unused PA of ≥ £1,100:

- the maximum tax saving of £220 will be achieved

If one spouse (or civil partner) has unused PA of < £1,100:

- the fixed amount of £1,100 must still be transferred
- however, the transferring spouse will have to pay some tax, and
- the maximum total tax saving for the couple will be = (unused PA × BR income tax)

Test your understanding 6

Katie and Emily are civil partners. Katie is a basic rate taxpayer and her only source of income is from self-employment. Emily is studying in the tax year 2016/17 and does not utilise her personal allowance.

Emily makes an election to transfer the marriage allowance to Katie.

Calculate Katie and Emily's income tax liabilities for the tax year 2016/17 assuming they have the following amounts of income:

	Katie	Emily	
(a)	**£30,000**	**£Nil**	
(b)	**£11,900**	**£Nil**	
(c)	**£30,000**	**£9,960**	**from part-time employment**

To be effective for the tax year 2016/17, the election can be made:

- **in advance**
  - by 5 April 2017
  - the election will remain in force for future tax years, unless
  - the election is withdrawn, or
  - the conditions for relief are no longer met
- **in arrears**
  - by 5 April 2021
(i.e. within 4 years of the end of the tax year)
  - in this case the election will only apply to the tax year 2016/17 in isolation.

The taxation of children

Income of a child is assessable to income tax.

- The child has their own income tax computation.
- The child also has full entitlement to a PA, even in the year of birth.
- If required, returns and claims are completed on behalf of the child by a parent or guardian.

Where the child has received taxed income, a repayment of tax will probably arise.

Income derived from a source set up by a parent (a parental disposition) is:

- assessed on the parent, not the child
- unless
  - the gross income received in the tax year is £100 or less, and
  - the child is under 18 (and unmarried).

Parental disposition

- Where a child under the age of 18 (and unmarried) has investment income that is derived from capital provided by a parent:
  - the income is treated as belonging to the parent (if the parent is still alive), rather than the child
- the capital could be provided by:
  - setting up a formal trust or settlement, or
  - a gift of money (e.g. opening a bank account in the child's name) or shares
- if the gross income does not exceed £100 in the tax year, then it is not taxed on the parent and is taxed as the child's income.
- the legislation does not apply to a Child Trust Fund.

The child benefit charge

Child benefit is a tax-free payment from the Government that can be claimed in respect of children.

However a child benefit income tax charge arises where:

- an individual receives child benefit, and
- they, or
  - their spouse/civil partner, or
  - their partner with whom they are living with as if they were married or in a civil partnership
- have 'adjusted net income' (ANI) of £50,000 or more.

'ANI' is calculated in the same way as for the restriction of personal allowances for high income individuals.

The tax charge is as follows:

Income	Tax charge
Between £50,000 and £60,000	1% of child benefit for each £100 of income over £50,000
Over £60,000	The amount of child benefit received

In calculating the tax charge both the appropriate percentage and the tax charge are rounded down to the nearest whole number.

The charge effectively removes the benefit for high income individuals.

Where the charge applies the taxpayer must complete a tax return and the charge is collected through the self-assessment system (Chapter 16).

Child benefit claimants, or their partner, can avoid the tax charge if they choose not to claim child benefit.

Where both partners have ANI in excess of £50,000, the charge is levied on the person with the higher income. However, at P6 this scenario will not be examined.

Example 4 – Child benefit tax charge

Helen's only source of income is her salary of £57,000 per year. She pays a personal pension contribution of £2,000 per year.

Her husband, Andy, has no income as he looks after the couple's three children.

Andy received child benefit of £2,501 during the tax year 2016/17.

Calculate Helen's income tax liability for the tax year 2016/17.

Solution

Income tax computation – 2016/17

	£
Employment income	57,000
Less: PA	(11,000)
Taxable income (all = 'non-savings income')	46,000
Income tax:	
£	
34,500 × 20% (W1)	6,900
11,500 × 40%	4,600
46,000	
Add: Child benefit charge (W2)	1,125
Income tax liability	12,625

Note: Although Andy has no income, it is not possible to elect for the marriage allowance of £1,100 to be transferred as Helen is a higher rate taxpayer.

Workings

(1) **Extension of basic rate band**

	£
Current basic rate threshold	32,000
Add: Gross PPCs (£2,000 × 100/80)	2,500
Revised threshold	34,500

(2) **Child benefit tax charge**

	£	£
Child benefit received		2,501
Net income	57,000	
Less: Gross PPC (£2,000 × 100/80)	(2,500)	
Adjusted net income	54,500	
Less: Lower limit	(50,000)	
	4,500	
1% per £100 of £4,500 = 45%		
Child benefit charge = 45% of £2,501 (round down)		1,125

Test your understanding 7

Sanjay and Nisha live together with their two children. Nisha has no income in the tax year 2016/17 but Sanjay has taxable trading profits from his building business of £61,000, and paid £1,500 into his personal pension.

Nisha received child benefit of £1,788 during the tax year 2016/17.

Calculate Sanjay's income tax liability for the tax year 2016/17.

Comprehensive example – taxation of families

Test your understanding 8

Kate has the following income, outgoings and allowances for the year ended 5 April 2017. She is married to Norman.

	£
Salary	37,200
Benefits, assessable as employment income	1,875
Allowable expenses of employment	(95)
Bank interest received	650
Building society interest received	2,115
Interest from an ISA account	500

Norman and Kate have a daughter, Ashleigh, aged 10. Ashleigh was given £5,000 of 3½% War loan on 6 April 2016 as a birthday present by Kate. Interest is received gross.

On 15 November 2016 Norman and Kate jointly bought a property that has been let out as unfurnished accommodation. The assessable property income for the tax year 2016/17 is £4,100. No declaration has been made in respect of this source of income.

Calculate the income tax payable by Kate for the tax year 2016/17.

4 Chapter summary

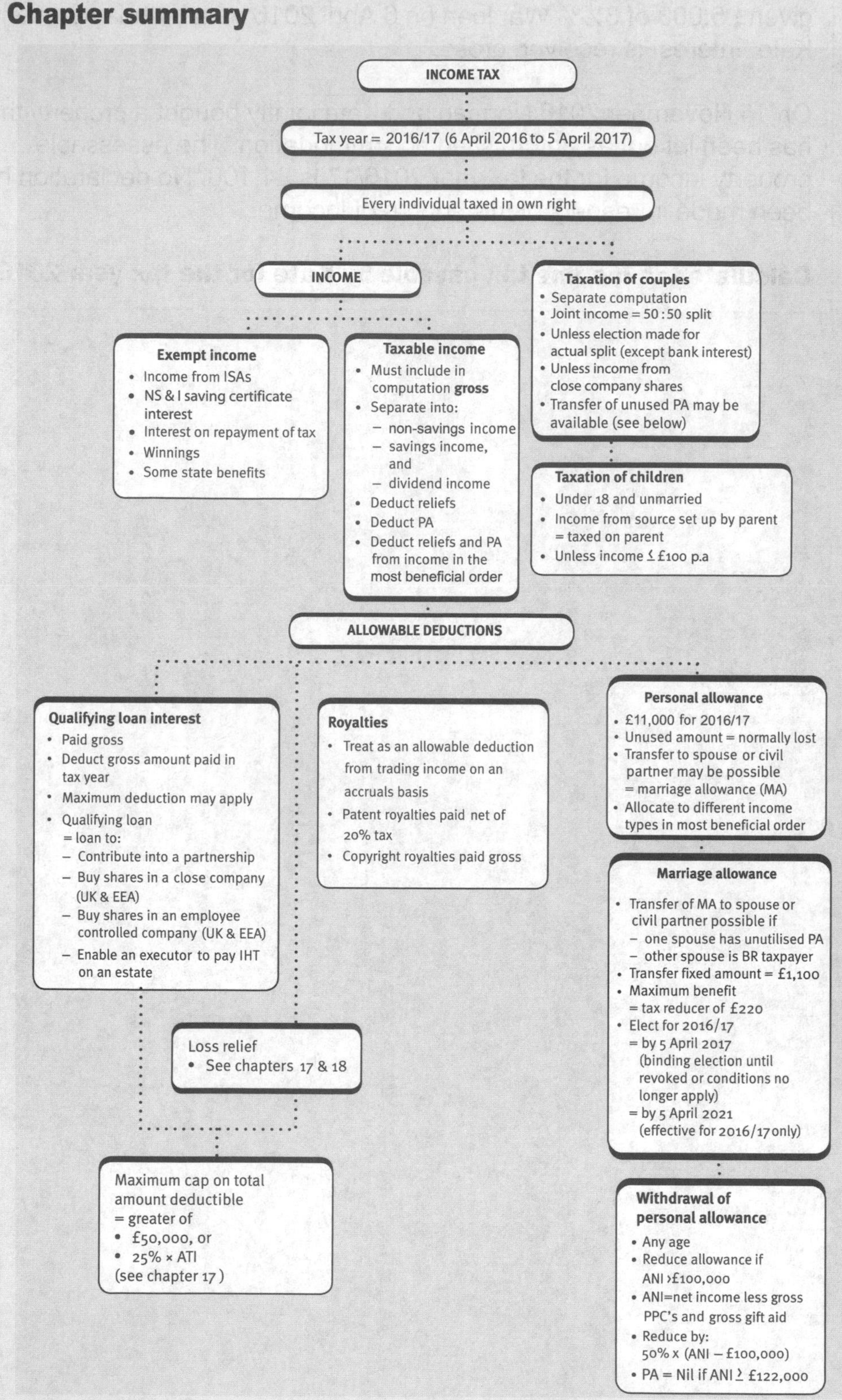
INCOME TAX
Tax year = 2016/17 (6 April 2016 to 5 April 2017)
Every individual taxed in own right
INCOME
Taxation of couples
• Separate computation
• Joint income = 50 : 50 split
• Unless election made for actual split (except bank interest)
• Unless income from close company shares
• Transfer of unused PA may be available (see below)
Exempt income
• Income from ISAs
• NS & I saving certificate interest
• Interest on repayment of tax
• Winnings
• Some state benefits
Taxable income
• Must include in computation gross
• Separate into:
– non-savings income
– savings income, and
– dividend income
• Deduct reliefs
• Deduct PA
• Deduct reliefs and PA from income in the most beneficial order
Taxation of children
• Under 18 and unmarried
• Income from source set up by parent = taxed on parent
• Unless income ≤ £100 p.a
ALLOWABLE DEDUCTIONS
Qualifying loan interest
• Paid gross
• Deduct gross amount paid in tax year
• Maximum deduction may apply
• Qualifying loan = loan to:
– Contribute into a partnership
– Buy shares in a close company (UK & EEA)
– Buy shares in an employee controlled company (UK & EEA)
– Enable an executor to pay IHT on an estate
Royalties
• Treat as an allowable deduction from trading income on an accruals basis
• Patent royalties paid net of 20% tax
• Copyright royalties paid gross
Personal allowance
• £11,000 for 2016/17
• Unused amount = normally lost
• Transfer to spouse or civil partner may be possible = marriage allowance (MA)
• Allocate to different income types in most beneficial order
Marriage allowance
• Transfer of MA to spouse or civil partner possible if
– one spouse has unutilised PA
– other spouse is BR taxpayer
• Transfer fixed amount = £1,100
• Maximum benefit = tax reducer of £220
• Elect for 2016/17
= by 5 April 2017 (binding election until revoked or conditions no longer apply)
= by 5 April 2021 (effective for 2016/17 only)
Loss relief
• See chapters 17 & 18
Maximum cap on total amount deductible
= greater of
• £50,000, or
• 25% × ATI
(see chapter 17)
Withdrawal of personal allowance
• Any age
• Reduce allowance if ANI >£100,000
• ANI=net income less gross PPC's and gross gift aid
• Reduce by: 50% x (ANI – £100,000)
• PA = Nil if ANI ≥ £122,000

Test your understanding answers

Test your understanding 1

Income tax computation – 2016/17

(a) **Employment income of £14,200**

	Total	Non-savings income	Savings income
	£	£	£
Employment income	14,200	14,200	
Bank interest	6,000		6,000
Total income	20,200	14,200	6,000
Less: PA	(11,000)	(11,000)	
Taxable income	9,200	3,200	6,000

Income tax £		
3,200	× 20% BR (Non-savings income)	640
1,800	× 0% SR (Savings income)	0
5,000		
1,000	× 0% SNRB (Savings income)	0
3,200	× 20% BR (Savings income)	640
9,200		
Income tax liability		1,280
Less: Tax credits	PAYE	(640)
		640
Income tax liability		

Notes:

(1) The starting rate applies to £1,800 of the savings income as it falls within the first £5,000 of taxable income.

(2) Eugenie is a basic rate taxpayer as her taxable income (£9,200) is less than £32,000. Her savings nil rate band is therefore £1,000.

(b) **Employment income of £29,000**

	Total	Non-savings income	Savings income
	£	£	£
Employment income	29,000	29,000	
Bank interest	6,000		6,000
Total income	35,000	29,000	6,000
Less: PA	(11,000)	(11,000)	
Taxable income	24,000	18,000	6,000

Income tax £		£
18,000	× 20% BR (Non-savings income)	3,600
1,000	× 0% SNRB (Savings income)	0
5,000	× 20% BR (Savings income)	1,000
24,000		
Income tax liability		4,600
Less: Tax credits PAYE		(3,600)
Income tax payable		1,000

Notes:

(1) The starting rate does not apply as savings income does not fall within the first £5,000 of taxable income.

(2) Eugenie is a basic rate taxpayer as her taxable income (£24,000) is less than £32,000. Her savings nil rate band is therefore £1,000. The balance of her savings income of £5,000 (£6,000 – £1,000) is taxed at the basic rate.

(c) **Employment income of £41,000**

	Total	Non-savings income	Savings income
	£	£	£
Employment income	41,000	41,000	
Bank interest	6,000		6,000
Total income	47,000	41,000	6,000
Less: PA	(11,000)	(11,000)	
Taxable income	36,000	30,000	6,000

Income tax £		
30,000	× 20% BR (Non-savings income)	6,000
500	× 0% SNRB (Savings income)	0
1,500	× 20% BR (Savings income)	300
32,000		
4,000	× 40% HR (Savings income)	1,600
36,000		
Income tax liability		7,900
Less: Tax credits		
PAYE		(6,300)
Income tax payable		1,600

Note: Taxable savings income falling in the starting rate band or savings nil rate band reduces the basic rate band of £32,000.

Test your understanding 2

Kei income tax liability 2016/17

	Total	Non-savings income	Savings income	Dividend income
	£	£	£	£
Property income	31,000	31,000		
Bank interest	2,000		2,000	
Dividend income	10,500			10,500
Total income	43,500	31,000	2,000	10,500
Less: PA	(11,000)	(11,000)		
Taxable income	32,500	20,000	2,000	10,500

Income tax		
£		
20,000	× 20% BR (Non-savings income)	4,000
500	× 0% SNRB (Savings income)	0
1,500	× 20% BR (Savings income)	300
5,000	× 0% DNRB (Dividend income)	0
5,000	× 7.5% BR (Dividend income)	375
32,000		
500	× 32.5% HR (Dividend income)	162
32,500		
Income tax liability		4,837

Note: Taxable savings income falling in the savings nil rate band reduces the basic rate band of £32,000.

Test your understanding 3

Lorna

Taxable income computation – 2016/17

	£
Employment income = total income	130,000
Less: PA (W)	(5,500)
Taxable income	124,500

Working: Adjusted PA

	£	£
Basic personal allowance		11,000
Net income (Note)	130,000	
Less: Gross pension contributions (PPCs)	(19,000)	
Adjusted net income	111,000	
Less: Income limit	(100,000)	
	11,000	
Reduction of PA (50% × £11,000)		(5,500)
Adjusted PA		5,500

Note: In this question, as there are no other sources of income and no reliefs:

Employment income = total income = net income.

The question only requires the taxable income figure, not income tax payable.

Test your understanding 4

Tristan

Income tax computation – 2016/17

	Total	Non-savings Income	Savings Income	Dividend Income
	£	£	£	£
Employment income	137,500	137,500		
Savings	22,500		22,500	
Dividends	17,000			17,000
Total income	177,000	137,500	22,500	17,000
Less: PA (Note)	0	0		
Taxable income	177,000	137,500	22,500	17,000

Income tax:	£		£
Non-savings income – basic rate	32,000	× 20%	6,400
Non-savings income – higher rate	105,500	× 40%	42,200
	137,500		
Savings income – higher rate	12,500	× 40%	5,000
	150,000		
Savings income – additional rate	10,000	× 45%	4,500
Dividend income – DNRB	5,000	× 0%	0
Dividend income – additional rate	12,000	× 38.1%	4,572
	177,000		
Income tax liability = income tax payable			62,672

Note: As total income = net income = ANI, and this exceeds £122,000 (£100,000 plus more than double the PA), the PA is reduced to £Nil.

Test your understanding 5

Ana
Income tax computation 2016/17

	Total	Non-savings income	Savings income	Dividend income
	£	£	£	£
Employment income	6,800	6,800		
Savings income	4,200		4,200	
Dividend income	12,000			12,000
Total income	23,000	6,800	4,200	12,000
Less: PA	(11,000)	(6,800)		(4,200)
Taxable income	12,000	0	4,200	7,800

Income tax		
£		
4,200	× 0% SR (Savings income)	0
5,000	× 0% DNRB (Dividend income)	0
2,800	× 7.5% BR (Dividend income)	210
12,000		
Income tax liability		210

Note: The PA is deducted from dividend income in preference to savings income to utilise the starting rate for savings, whilst still fully utilising the dividend nil rate band.

Ana will save £315 by allocating her PA to dividend income in preference to savings income. This is because £4,200 of income is covered by the starting rate for savings and taxed at 0% rather than being taxed at 7.5% as dividend income (£4,200 × 7.5% = £315).

Test your understanding 6

(a) **Income tax computation – 2016/17**

	Katie	Emily
	£	£
Trading income = net income	30,000	0
Less: PA	(11,000)	(0)
Taxable income	19,000	0
Income tax liability (£19,000 × 20%)	3,800	0
Less: MA (£1,100 × 20%)	(220)	
Income tax liability	3,580	0

Note: All of Emily's PA is unused.
Maximum benefit of election = £220.

(b) **Income tax computation – 2016/17**

	Katie	Emily
	£	£
Trading income = net income	11,900	0
Less: PA	(11,000)	(0)
Taxable income	900	0
Income tax liability (£900 × 20%)	180	0
Less: MA (£1,100 × 20%) restricted	(180)	
Income tax liability	0	0

Note: All of Emily's PA is unused.
Maximum benefit of election = restricted as Katie's income is not sufficient to obtain the full benefit.

(c) **Income tax computation – 2016/17**

	Katie	Emily
	£	£
Trading income = net income	30,000	9,960
Less: PA	(11,000)	(9,900)
Taxable income	19,000	60
Income tax liability		
(£19,000 × 20%)	3,800	
(£60 × 20%)		12
Less: MA (£1,100 × 20%)	(220)	
Income tax liability	3,580	12

Note: Only £1,040 (£11,000 – £9,960) of Emily's PA is unused, however if the election is made, the fixed amount of £1,100 must be transferred.

The couple's total income tax liability would be:

With the election £3,592

Without the election £3,800

Tax saving from the election = (£3,800 – £3,592) = £208

Alternative calculation = (£1,040 unused PA × 20%) = £208

Test your understanding 7

Sanjay

Income tax computation – 2016/17

		£
Taxable trading profits		61,000
Less: PA		(11,000)
Taxable income (all = 'non-savings income')		50,000
Income tax:		
	£	
	33,875 × 20% (W1)	6,775
	16,125 × 40%	6,450
	50,000	
Add: Child benefit charge (W2)		1,627
Income tax liability		14,852

Note: Although Nisha has no income, it is not possible to elect for the marriage allowance of £1,100 to be transferred as Sanjay is a higher rate taxpayer.

Workings

(1) **Extension of basic rate band**

	£
Current basic rate threshold	32,000
Add: Gross PPCs (£1,500 × 100/80)	1,875
Revised threshold	33,875

(2) **Child benefit tax charge**

	£	£
Child benefit received		1,788
Net income	61,000	
Less: Gross PPC (£1,500 × 100/80)	(1,875)	
Adjusted net income	59,125	
Less: Lower limit	(50,000)	
	9,125	
1% per £100 of £9,125 = 91.25% rounded down to 91% Child benefit charge = 91% of £1,788 (rounded down)		1,627

Test your understanding 8

Kate
Income tax computation – 2016/17

	£	£
Employment income (£37,200 + £1,875 – £95)		38,980
Bank interest	650	
Building society interest	2,115	
War loan interest (Note 2) (3.5% × £5,000)	175	
Interest from an ISA account (exempt)	0	
		2,940
Property income (Note 1)		2,050
Total income		43,970
Less: PA		(11,000)
Taxable income		32,970

Analysis of income:

Dividends	**Savings**	**Non-savings income**
£0	£2,940	(£32,970 – £2,940) = £30,030

Income tax:

£		£
30,030	× 20% (non-savings income)	6,006
500	× 0% (SNRB)	0
1,470	× 20% (savings)	294
32,000		
970	× 40% (savings)	388
32,970		
Income tax liability = income tax payable		6,688

Notes:

(1) The property income, being joint income, is divided between Norman and Kate on a 50:50 basis (£4,100 ÷ 2 = £2,050).

(2) The war loan interest is assessed on Kate because her daughter is under 18 and unmarried and the income is derived from capital provided by the parent, and the income is more than £100 in the tax year.

(3) Kate is entitled to a savings nil rate band (SNRB) of £500 as she is a higher rate taxpayer. The SNRB reduces the basic rate band.

chapter

2

Employment income and related NICs

Chapter learning objectives

Upon completion of this chapter you will be able to:

- recognise the factors that determine whether an engagement is treated as employment or self-employment and state the differences in the tax treatment
- given details of a remuneration package calculate the employment income assessable taking into account any allowable deductions
- explain when reimbursed expenses are exempt
- distinguish between the structure of a share option scheme and other share awards to employees
- differentiate between the taxation consequences of unapproved and approved share option schemes
- describe the operation of the various share incentive schemes and identify the key requirements for approval
- identify how an employer would choose which approved scheme to offer
- explain the tax treatment of employee shareholder shares
- identify the income tax and NIC treatment of lump sum receipts from employment
- summarise the different classes of national insurance relevant to employers and employees and calculate amounts due.

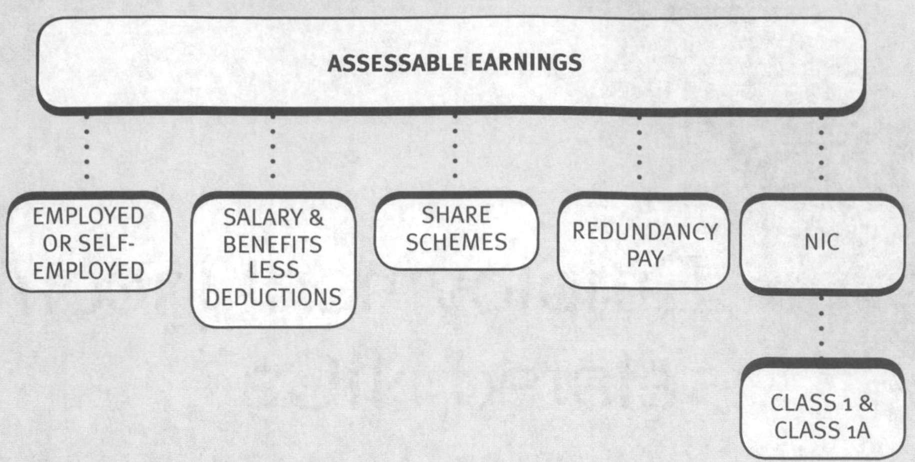

Introduction

This chapter is mainly a revision of the income tax implications of being employed covered in F6.

A brief reminder of F6 content is given in expandable text and revision examples are provided to check your retention of the required F6 knowledge.

The main new topics introduced are the tax implications of shares schemes and the treatment of termination payments.

1 Employment status

The distinction between employment and self-employment is fundamental:

- an employee is taxable under the employment income provisions
- a self-employed person is assessed on the profits derived from his trade, profession or vocation under the rules governing trading income.

HMRC look at various factors, laid down by statute and case law decisions, to decide whether an individual is employed or self-employed.

The factors considered to determine employment or self-employment status are frequently examined.

Factors of employment or self-employment

The primary test to consider is the nature of the contract that exists:

- Employment contract of service
- Self-employment contract for services

However, even in the absence of a contract of service the following factors would be taken into account when deciding whether an employment exists:

- **Obligation** – by the 'employer' to offer work and the 'employee' to undertake the work offered. An 'employee' would not normally be in a position to decline work when offered.
- **Control** – the manner and method of the work being controlled by the 'employer'.
- **Fixed hours** – the 'employee' being committed to work a specified number of hours at certain fixed times.
- **Integration** – the work performed by the 'employee' is an integral part of the business of the 'employer' and not merely an accessory to it.
- **Risk** – the economic reality of self-employment is missing (namely the financial risk arising from not being paid an agreed, regular remuneration).
- **Equipment** – the use of equipment can be a useful factor in determining 'employee' status.
- **Rights** – if the person has rights under employment legislation, or has the right to receive regular remuneration, holiday pay, redundancy pay or benefits.
- **Source of work** – how many different sources of income does the individual have.

Consequences of status

The tax status of an individual is very important in determining how earnings are taxed. A summary of the key differences is set out below.

	Self-employed	Employee
Income tax	• Trading profits: current year basis • Expenses: 'wholly and exclusively'	• Employment income: receipts basis • Expenses: 'wholly exclusively and necessarily'
Payment of income tax	• Self-assessment	• Monthly – PAYE
NICs	• Class 2 – flat weekly rate • Class 4 – based on profits	• Class 1 primary – based on cash earnings
Payment of NICs	• Class 2 and 4 – with income tax under self-assessment	• Monthly – PAYE
Pensions	• Personal pension scheme	• Occupational pension scheme and/or, • Personal pension scheme
VAT	• Register • Reclaim input VAT	• Suffer input VAT

2 Calculation of employment income

Pro forma – Employment income computation

	£	£
Salary		X
Bonus/Commission		X
Benefits		X
Reimbursed expenses		X
Cash vouchers		X
		X
Less: Allowable deductions		
– Expenses incurred wholly, exclusively, necessarily		(X)
– Contributions to employer's pension scheme		(X)
– Subscriptions to professional bodies		(X)
– Charitable donations: payroll deduction scheme		(X)
– Travel and subsistence expenses		(X)
– Deficit on mileage allowance		(X)
– Cost of any shares acquired in an approved SIP		(X)
		X
Add: Redundancy payment	X	
Less: Exemption	(X)	
		X
Employment income		X

Basis of assessment

Directors and employees are assessed on the amount of earnings received in the tax year (the **receipts basis**).

Earnings

The term 'earnings' includes cash wages or salary, bonuses, commission and benefits made available by the employer.

Earnings

Cash vouchers

- A voucher that can be exchanged for an amount of cash that is greater than, equal to, or not substantially less than the cost of providing it. For example, premium bonds.

State benefits

The following state benefits are subject to income tax:

- Statutory sick pay (SSP).
- Statutory maternity pay (SMP).
- Retirement pension and bereavement benefits.

Earnings can include amounts paid for services rendered in the past or to be rendered in the future.

'Golden hellos'

- A payment made to induce an individual to enter into employment will be taxable unless it represents compensation paid for giving up something received under their previous employment in order to enter into the current employment.

Third party payments

- Payments made by persons other than the employer if they relate to the provision of services. This would include, for example, tips received by a taxi-driver or waiter.

'Golden handshakes' and restrictive covenant payments

- A payment made to an employee in return for an undertaking to restrict his activities. An example would be where the employee agrees not to work for a competitor within a set period of time after leaving his current employment.

The receipts basis

The date of receipt is the **earlier** of:

- the actual date of payment, or
- the date the individual becomes entitled to the payment.

In the case of directors who are in a position to manipulate the timings of payments there are extra rules.

They are deemed to receive earnings on the **earliest** of four dates:

- the actual date of payment

- the date the individual becomes entitled to the payment
- when sums on account of earnings are credited in the accounts
- where the earnings are determined:
  - before the end of a period of account = the end of that period
  - after the end of a period of account = date the earnings are determined.

Test your understanding 1

Broadfoot, a director of RIK Ltd, received a bonus of £25,000 on 1 September 2016.

The bonus related to the results of the company for the year ended 31 March 2016. It was credited to Broadfoot in the accounts on 15 July 2016 following a board meeting on 30 June 2016.

Advise when the bonus is assessable as employment income.

Allowable deductions

The general rule is that expenditure will only be deductible if it is incurred **wholly, exclusively** and **necessarily in the performance** of the duties.

The other types of allowable expenditure shown in the pro forma computation are specifically permitted by statute law.

A reminder of the rules for travel expenses and the mileage allowance deduction is given in expandable text and is summarised in the diagram below.

Travel expenditure

Travelling expenses may be deducted only where they:

- are incurred necessarily in the performance of the duties of the employment, or
- are attributable to the necessary attendance at any place by the employee in the performance of their duties.

Relief is not given for the cost of journeys that are ordinary commuting or for the cost of private travel.

- Ordinary commuting is the journey made each day between home and a permanent workplace.
- Private travel is a journey between home and any other place that is not for the purposes of work.

Relief is given where an employee travels directly from home to a **temporary** place of work.

- A temporary workplace is defined as one where an employee goes to perform a task of limited duration, or for a temporary purpose.
- However, a place of work will not be classed as a temporary workplace where an employee works there continuously for a period that lasts, or is expected to last, more than 24 months.

Where an employee passes their normal permanent workplace on the way to a temporary workplace, relief will still be available provided the employee does not stop at the normal workplace, or any stop is incidental (e.g. to pick up some papers).

Where an employee's business journey qualifies for relief, then the amount of relief is the full cost of that journey. There is no need to take account of any savings the employee makes by not having to make his or her normal commuting journey to work.

Approved mileage allowance payments

Employees who use their own vehicles for work will normally be paid a mileage allowance.

There are approved mileage allowance payment (AMAP) rates set by HMRC as follows:

Cars and vans	
First 10,000 miles p.a.	45p
Over 10,000 miles p.a.	25p
Passenger rate	5p
Motorcycles	24p
Bicycles	20p

- The car and vans rate is given in the examination, but not the other rates.
- Provided the mileage allowance received is within these rates; no assessable benefit arises.

- Where the mileage allowance received is:

	Effect on employment income:
> AMAP rates	Excess = assessable benefit
< AMAP rates, or no allowance received	Difference = allowable deduction

- However, no deduction claim is allowed for any shortfall on the passenger rate where less than 5p a mile is paid.

Summary

Employment income

Allowable deductions

- Expenses incurred wholly, exclusively and necessarily
- Contributions to employer's pension scheme
- Subscriptions to professional bodies
- Travel expenditure
- AMAPs

AMAPs

- Tax free mileage allowance for use of own vehicle for work
- If mileage allowance received > AMAP:
  - Excess = benefit
- If mileage allowance received < AMAP:
  - Difference = allowable deduction

Travel expenditure

- Must be necessarily incurred in performance of duties
- Relief available for travel to temporary workplace
- No relief for
  - Ordinary commuting
  - Private travel
- Do not reduce travel to temporary workplace for travel from home to normal place of work

Test your understanding 2

Bernard uses his own car for business purposes for which his employer pays an agreed allowance. Bernard drives 12,000 business miles in 2016/17.

Bernard took a work colleague on some business trips totalling 5,000 miles for which he received an extra 4p per mile from his employer.

Calculate the assessable benefits on Bernard, or the mileage expenses claims, for the tax year 2016/17 assuming Bernard's employer pays a mileage allowance for the car of:

(a) 20p per mile or (b) 50p per mile.

3 Employment benefits

The benefit rules were covered in detail at F6. This section provides a reminder of the key rules that need to be retained for P6.

Employment benefits can be divided into two catagories:

- Exempt benefits
- Taxable benefits

Exempt benefits

A reminder of the rules relating to the types of exempt benefits is given in expandable text and the examples include some exempt benefits to check your retention of the required F6 knowledge.

Exempt benefits

- Employer's contribution to a registered pension scheme
- Pensions advice up to £150 per employee per year
- Subsidised canteen, unless part of a salary sacrifice scheme
- Car parking space
- Provision of work buses, bicycles, subsidies for public transport
- One mobile phone per employee (including smart phones)
- Work related training provided by employer
- In-house sports and recreational facilities
- Staff parties of up to £150 p.a. per employee
- Entertainment from a third party to generate goodwill and gifts from a third party up to £250 from any one source in a tax year
- Welfare counselling
- Workplace nurseries run by employer at the workplace or at other non-domestic premises (including facilities run jointly with other employers or local authorities)
- Child care costs up to £55 per week (reduced to £28 for higher rate taxpayers and £25 for additional rate taxpayers)
- Contribution towards home worker expenses up to £4 per week or £18 per month without documentation, more with documentation
- Job related accommodation
- Relocation and removal expenses up to £8,000

- Overnight expenses up to £5 per night in UK and £10 per night overseas
- Employer liability insurance, death in service benefits and permanent health insurance
- Medical insurance and treatment while working abroad
- Eye care tests
- Long service awards up to £50 per year of service to mark employment of 20 years or more.
- Loans with a beneficial interest rate, provided the loan is ≤ £10,000 throughout the year (see later).

Recommended medical treatment

An exemption applies:

- for expenditure incurred by employers on recommended medical treatment
- by a health care professional
- for an employee assessed as unfit for work due to injury or ill health
- after a period of sickness absence of at least 28 consecutive days
- for the purpose of assisting the employee's return to work.

The exempt benefit is a maximum of **up to £500 per employee per tax year**.

Any amount incurred in excess of the £500 exemption limit is assessed to income tax and NICs as a benefit of employment in the normal way.

Trivial benefits

From the tax year 2016/17, a new exempt benefit has been introduced in respect of 'trivial' benefits provided by employers to employees. A benefit is trivial if it meets the following conditions:

- the cost of providing the benefit does not exceed £50
- it is not cash or a cash voucher
- it is not provided in recognition of services

If any of these conditions are not met, the benefit is taxed in the normal way.

Taxable benefits

Prior to the tax year 2016/17, certain taxable benefits were only assessed on employees earning £8,500 or more ('P11D exmployees') and not on employees earning less than this amount. This distinction has now been abolished and taxable benefits are now assessed on all employees regardless of amount of earnings in the tax year.

Note that a benefit is taxable if

- it arises 'by reason of employment', and
- is provided either to the employee or to a member of his family or household
- either directly by the employer or by a third party.

The following table summarises the key taxable benefits:

General rule = Assessed on:
• Cost to the employer • Marginal cost to the employer if an 'in house' benefit
Specific valuation rules for some benefits: • Non-cash vouchers • Credit cards • Living accommodation • Expenses relating to living accommodation • Use and gift of assets • Cars, fuel and vans • Beneficial loans • Scholarships • Payment of a director's liability

Remember that:

- Where a benefit is only available for part of the year; the assessable amount is time apportioned.
- Where an employee contributes towards the benefit; the employee contribution is an allowable deduction (exception = the provision of private fuel).
- Where employers provide in-house benefits (such as free air tickets for employees of an airline) the measure of the benefit is the additional or marginal cost incurred by the employer, not a proportion of the total cost.

A reminder of the rules relating to these benefits is given in expandable text and the rules are summarised in the diagram in section 4. Revision examples are provided to check your retention of the required F6 knowledge.

Non-cash vouchers and credit cards

Non-cash vouchers

Employees provided with non-cash vouchers are taxed on the cost to the employer of providing the voucher. Non-cash vouchers are vouchers that can be exchanged for goods or services (e.g. retail vouchers) and includes transport vouchers (e.g. travel season tickets).

Credit cards

Employees provided with credit cards by their employer will be taxed on the value of any costs charged to the card for personal use.

Living accommodation

	Taxable benefit
Basic charge	Higher of • Annual value of property • Rent paid by employer, if any (only applicable if property rented on behalf of employee)
Additional charge for expensive accommodation	• Only applicable if property purchased by employer (not rented) and the property 'cost' in excess of £75,000 • Benefit = ('Cost' of accommodation less £75,000) × ORI% • 'ORI' is the official rate of interest, currently 3%. The official rate of interest will be provided in the examination • 'Cost' = purchase price of property plus the cost of capital improvements made before the start of the tax year • If property is owned by the employer for more than 6 years before providing it to the employee: Use MV of property when first provided (not purchase price)

Job related accommodation (JRA)

No benefit arises where the property is job-related accommodation.

- To qualify as JRA, the property must be provided:
  - where it is necessary for the proper performance of the employee's duties (e.g. a caretaker)
  - for the better performance of the employee's duties and, for that type of employment, it is customary for employers to provide living accommodation (e.g. hotel-worker)
  - where there is a special threat to the employee's security and the employee resides in the accommodation as part of special security arrangements (e.g. prime minister).
- A director can only claim one of the first two exemptions if:
  - they have no material interest in the company (i.e. holds no more than 5% in the company's ordinary share capital), and
  - they are a full-time working director or the company is a non-profit making organisation.

Living accommodation expenses

Expenses connected with living accommodation (i.e. ancillary benefits), such as lighting and heating, and use of assets provided in the accommodation are taxable on an employee where the cost is met by the employer as follows:

Benefit	**If not JRA**	**If JRA**
Expenses in connection with living accommodation	Cost to employer	Total benefits = limited to 10% rule (see note below)
Use of assets	20% rule (see below)	

Notes

- The 10% JRA limit applies to the following types of expense:
  - heating, lighting and cleaning
  - repairing, maintaining or decorating the premises, and
  - the use of furniture/goods normal for domestic occupation.
- The total accommodation benefits taxed on an employee for JRA is limited to 10% of 'net earnings'
  - 'net earnings' = employment income (including all assessable benefits other than the living accommodation ancillary benefits).

Use of assets

Where the ownership of the asset is retained by employer, but the employee has private use of the asset, the taxable benefit is:

- 20% × open market value when first made available (usually cost).
- Where the employer rents the asset made available to the employee instead of buying it, the employee is taxed on the higher of:
  - the rent paid by employer
  - 20% rule.
- The provision of one mobile phone to an employee is an exempt benefit. However, the 20% rule will apply to any additional mobile phones provided.

Example 1 – Living accommodation

Mr X, a director of X Ltd, lives in a furnished company flat that cost the company £105,000 on 1 June 2012. He occupied the property from 15 June 2012. The accommodation is not job related.

The annual value of the flat is £2,500 and Mr X pays X Ltd rent of £150 a month. Furniture was worth £6,000 in June 2012. The company pays £2,000 for the running costs of the flat and £1,500 in council tax.

Calculate Mr X's total taxable benefits for 2016/17.

Solution

Total taxable benefits – 2016/17	£
Basic charge (annual value)	2,500
Additional charge (£105,000 – £75,000) × 3%	900
	3,400
Less: Contribution (£150 × 12)	(1,800)
Accommodation benefit	1,600
Use of furniture (20% × £6,000)	1,200
Living expenses benefit	2,000
Council tax	1,500
Total taxable benefits	6,300

Gift of assets

- If an employer purchases a new asset and gives it to an employee immediately, the employee is taxed on the cost to the employer.
- Where an employee has had the private use of an asset which is then given to him, the employee is taxed on the higher of:

	£	£
(i) MV of asset when gifted		X
(ii) MV of asset when first made available to the employee	X	
Less: Benefits already taxed on employee for private use	(X)	
		X

- Any employee contribution can be deducted from the taxable amounts computed according to the rules above
- Where the asset being given to an employee is a used car or van or bicycle provided for work:
  Benefit = method (i) above (i.e. ignore method (ii)).

Example 2 – Use and gift of asset

Rooney was provided with a new video camera by his employer on 6 October 2014 costing £2,000. He was allowed to keep the camera on 5 January 2017 when its value was £500.

Show the benefit taxable on Rooney for all years.

Solution

Taxable benefits

		£
2014/15	Use of asset: (£2,000 × 20% × 6/12)	200
2015/16	Use of asset: (£2,000 × 20%)	400
2016/17	Use of asset: (£2,000 × 20% × 9/12)	300
	Plus	
	Gift of asset: (working)	1,100
	Total amount taxable in 2016/17	1,400

Working: Gift of asset

		£	£
2016/17	Further benefit on gift of asset – higher of		
	(i) MV at date of gift		500
	(ii) MV when first made available	2,000	
	Less: Taxed to date (£200 + £400 + £300)	(900)	
			1,100

Motor cars

- Where a car is made available for private use, the taxable benefit is:

	£
Appropriate % × List price of car when first registered	X
Less: Employee contributions for private use of car	(X)
Taxable benefit	X

- The list price of the car is the price when first registered
  - includes the cost of extras, both those provided with the car and any made available subsequently
  - can be reduced by any capital contribution made by the employee, subject to a maximum of £5,000
- The appropriate percentage:
  - depends on the rate at which the car emits carbon dioxide
- The rules can be summarised as follows:

CO_2 emissions per km	Petrol car %	Diesel car %
50 grams or less	7	10
51 – 75 grams	11	14
76 – 94 grams	15	18
95 grams	16	19
Each complete additional 5 grams emission above 95 grams	An additional 1% is added to the 16% or 19% up to a maximum % of 37%	

- The benefit
  - is reduced by periods for which the car was unavailable for more than 30 consecutive days.
  - is reduced if the employee makes contributions towards the running costs.
  - takes into account all running expenses of the vehicle. Therefore, there is no additional charge for insurance, repairs, car tax, etc.
- A separate benefit applies if private fuel is provided.
- If more than one car is provided to employee/relative, then separate benefits for the car and private fuel are calculated for each car.
- No benefit on pool cars.
- The maximum % that can be applied to any car is 37%.

Private fuel

- Where an employer provides private fuel the benefit is:

  (same percentage used for car benefit × £22,200).

- The £22,200 is given in the tax rates and allowances in the examination.
- Contributions made by the employee towards the private fuel are ignored unless **all** private fuel is reimbursed in full (in which case no benefit arises).
- The benefit charge is reduced for periods of non-availability, unless non-availability during the tax year is only temporary.

Test your understanding 3

Charles took up employment with Weavers Ltd on 1 July 2016.

His remuneration package included a two-year old petrol-driven car, list price £24,000. He took delivery of the car on 1 July 2016. The CO_2 emission rating is 229 g/km.

As a condition of the car being made available to him for private motoring, Charles paid £100 per month for the car and £50 per month for petrol during 2016/17.

Weavers Ltd incurred the following expenses in respect of Charles' car:

	£
Servicing	450
Insurance	780
Fuel (of which £1,150 was for business purposes)	2,500
Maintenance	240

Calculate Charles' taxable car and fuel benefits for 2016/17.

Van benefit

Where a van is made available for private use to an employee the taxable benefit is:

- £3,170 p.a. for unrestricted private use of the van.
- £598 p.a. if private fuel is provided by the employer.
- These benefits are time apportioned if the van is unavailable to the employee for 30 consecutive days or more during any part of the tax year.
- Taking the van home at night is not treated as private use and incidental private use is also ignored if insignificant.
- Contributions by the employee towards the van (not the fuel) reduce the benefit chargeable.
- Where employees share the private use of the van, the scale charge is divided between the employees, on a just and reasonable basis (e.g. by reference to the amount of private use).

Example 3 – Company car vs. van

A plc is offering Tom, a higher rate taxpayer, two possible new vehicles for his private use. The first vehicle on offer is a petrol engined car with a list price of £15,000 including VAT and CO_2 emissions of 94 g/km.

The second vehicle is a petrol engined van with the same list price and CO_2 emissions. Private use of the van is not considered to be insignificant.

A plc will pay for all running costs including fuel for both vehicles.

Calculate the benefit taxable on Tom in 2016/17 for the two vehicles and advise him which one he should select.

Solution

Option 1 – Provision of company car		£
Car benefit	(£15,000 × 15%) (W)	2,250
Fuel benefit	(£22,200 × 15%)	3,330
Total benefits		5,580

Option 2 – Provision of company van

	£
Van benefit	3,170
Fuel benefit	598
Total benefits	3,768

Conclusion: The company van would be more tax efficient.

Working: Appropriate percentage for company car

CO_2 emissions = between 76 – 94 g/km, the appropriate % = 15%.

Beneficial loan

- Beneficial loans are loans made to an employee with an interest rate below the official rate of interest (3% for 2016/17).
- The benefit is calculated as follows:

	£
Interest at the official rate (using either the average or precise method)	X
Less: Interest actually paid in the tax year	(X)
Taxable benefit	X

- A small loan exemption applies where the total of an employee's beneficial loans is ≤ £10,000 throughout the tax year.
- Two methods of calculating the interest at the official rate:
  - Average method = charge is based on the average capital

    average capital = (opening balance + closing balance) × ½

  - Precise method = calculate interest on a day to day basis on the balance of the loan outstanding
- Either the taxpayer or HMRC can elect for the precise method.
- HMRC will only elect where it appears that the average method is being exploited and the precise method gives a materially higher figure.

Example 4 – Beneficial loan

Daniel was granted a loan of £35,000 by his employer on 31 March 2016 to help finance the purchase of a yacht. Interest is payable on the loan at 2% per annum.

On 1 June 2016 Daniel repaid £5,000 and on 1 December 2016 he repaid a further £14,000. The remaining £16,000 was still outstanding on 5 April 2017. Daniel earns £30,000 per annum.

Calculate the taxable benefit for 2016/17 using both the average method and the precise method.

Solution

Average method		£	£
(£35,000 + £16,000) × ½ × 3%			765
Less: Interest paid			
06.04.16 – 31.05.16	£35,000 × 2% × 2/12	117	
01.06.16 – 30.11.16	£30,000 × 2% × 6/12	300	
01.12.16 – 05.04.17	£16,000 × 2% × 4/12	107	
			(524)
Taxable benefit			241

Precise method		£
06.04.16 – 31.05.16	£35,000 × 3% × 2/12	175
01.06.16 – 30.11.16	£30,000 × 3% × 6/12	450
01.12.16 – 05.04.17	£16,000 × 3% × 4/12	160
		785
Less: Interest paid – as above		(524)
Taxable benefit		261

The taxable benefit will be the average method of £241 unless an election is made.

Daniel will not make the election for the precise method.

It is unlikely that HMRC will elect for the precise method in this example.

Scholarships

If a scholarship is provided to a member of an individual's family or household, the cost of it is taxable as a benefit on the individual.

No taxable benefit arises where:

- the scholarship is awarded from a separate trust scheme, and
- the person receiving it is in full-time education at a school, college or university, and
- not more than 25% of payments made in the tax year from the scheme are made by reason of a person's employment.

Scholarship income is exempt in the hands of the recipient.

Payment of director's tax liability

- Where tax should have been deducted from a director's earnings under the PAYE system, but was not, and the tax is paid over to HMRC by the employer, the director is treated as receiving a benefit.
- The benefit is the amount of tax accounted for, less any amount reimbursed by the director (if any).
- Note that this rule applies only to directors.

Comprehensive example

Test your understanding 4

Vigorous plc runs a health club. The company has three employees who received benefits during 2016/17 and it therefore needs to prepare forms P11D for them. Each of the three employees is paid an annual salary of £35,000. The following information is relevant:

Andrea Lean

(1) Andrea was employed by Vigorous plc throughout 2016/17.

(2) Throughout 2016/17 Vigorous plc provided Andrea with a petrol powered company motor car with a list price of £19,400. The official CO_2 emission rate for the motor car is 245 g/km. Vigorous plc paid for all of the motor car's running costs of £6,200 during 2016/17, including petrol used for private journeys. Andrea pays £150 per month to Vigorous plc for the use of the motor car.

(3) Vigorous plc has provided Andrea with living accommodation since 1 November 2014. The property was purchased on 1 January 2012 for £130,000. The company spent £14,000 improving the property during March 2013, and a further £8,000 was spent on improvements during May 2016. The value of the property on 1 November 2014 was £170,000, and it has an annual rateable value of £7,000. The furniture in the property cost £6,000 during November 2014. Andrea personally pays for the annual running costs of the property amounting to £4,000.

(4) Throughout 2016/17 Vigorous plc provided Andrea with a mobile telephone costing £500. The company paid for all business and private telephone calls.

Ben Slim

(1) Ben commenced employment with Vigorous plc on 1 July 2016.

(2) On 1 July 2016 Vigorous plc provided Ben with an interest free loan of £120,000 so that he could purchase a new main residence. He repaid £20,000 of the loan on 1 October 2016.

(3) During 2016/17 Vigorous plc paid £9,300 towards the cost of Ben's relocation. His previous main residence was 125 miles from his place of employment. The £9,300 covered the cost of disposing of Ben's old property and of acquiring his new property.

(4) During the period from 1 October 2016 until 5 April 2017 Vigorous plc provided Ben with a new diesel powered company motor car which has a list price of £11,200. The official CO_2 emission rate for the motor car is 104 g/km. Ben reimburses Vigorous plc for all the diesel used for private journeys.

Chai Trim

(1) Chai was employed by Vigorous plc throughout 2016/17.

(2) During 2016/17 Vigorous plc provided Chai with a two-year old company van, which was available for private use. The van has CO_2 emissions of 123 g/km and the private use was not considered to be insignificant. The van was unavailable during the period 1 August to 30 September 2016. Chai was also provided with private fuel for the van.

(3) Vigorous plc has provided Chai with a television for her personal use since 6 April 2014. The television cost Vigorous plc £800 in April 2014. On 6 April 2016 the company sold the television to Chai for £150, although its market value on that date was £250.

(4) Throughout 2016/17 Vigorous plc provided Chai with free membership of its health club. The normal annual cost of membership is £800. This figure is made up of direct costs of £150, fixed overhead costs of £400 and profit of £250. The budgeted membership for the year has been exceeded, but the health club has surplus capacity.

(5) On 1 January 2017 Vigorous plc provided Chai with a new computer costing £1,900. She uses the computer at home for personal study purposes.

Calculate the benefit figures that Vigorous plc will have to include on the forms P11D for Andrea, Ben and Chai for 2016/17.

4 Summary

Employment benefits

Exempt benefits

- Non-work benefits up to £50 per gift
- Employer's contribution to pension
- Pensions advice (up to £150)
- Subsidised canteen
- Car parking space
- Work buses, bicycles, subsidies for public transport
- One mobile phone per employee
- Work related training
- Sports and recreational facilities
- Staff parties (up to £150 p.a)
- Welfare counselling
- Workplace nurseries
- Child care costs up to £55/£28/£25 per week
- Home worker expenses (up to £4 per week or £18 per month)
- Job related accommodation
- Relocation expenses (up to £8,000)
- Overnight expenses (up to £5 per night in UK and £10 per night overseas)
- Employer liability insurance, death in service benefits and PHI
- Beneficial loans totalling ≤ £10,000
- Medical treatment up to £500 per year

Taxable benefits

- Valued at:
  - General rule: Cost to employer (in house benefits = marginal cost)
  - Specific rules for certain benefits
- Always:
  - deduct employee contributions (except private fuel)
  - time apportion if not available all year

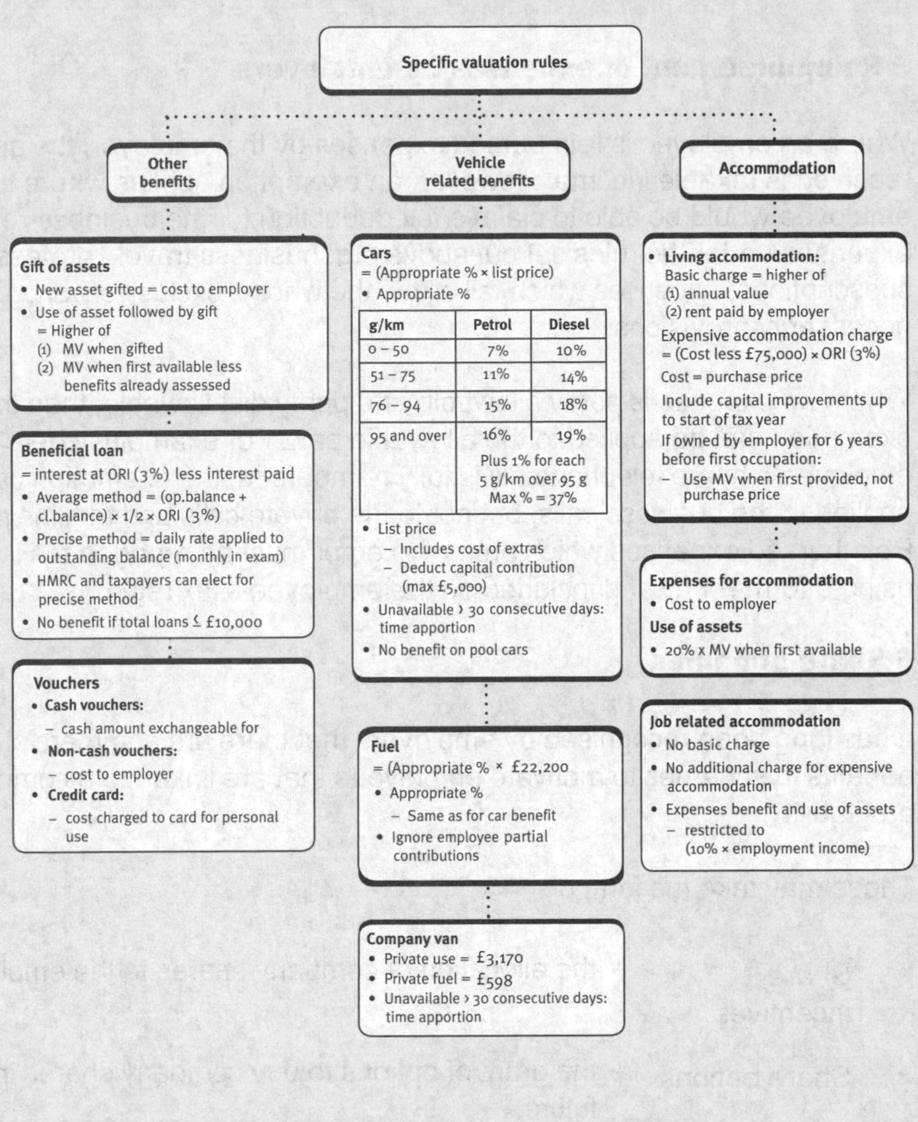
Specific valuation rules
Other benefits
Vehicle related benefits
Accommodation
Gift of assets
• New asset gifted = cost to employer
• Use of asset followed by gift = Higher of
(1) MV when gifted
(2) MV when first available less benefits already assessed
Beneficial loan
= interest at ORI (3%) less interest paid
• Average method = (op.balance + cl.balance) × 1/2 × ORI (3%)
• Precise method = daily rate applied to outstanding balance (monthly in exam)
• HMRC and taxpayers can elect for precise method
• No benefit if total loans ≤ £10,000
Vouchers
• Cash vouchers:
– cash amount exchangeable for
• Non-cash vouchers:
– cost to employer
• Credit card:
– cost charged to card for personal use
Cars
= (Appropriate % × list price)
• Appropriate %
g/km | Petrol | Diesel
0 – 50 | 7% | 10%
51 – 75 | 11% | 14%
76 – 94 | 15% | 18%
95 and over | 16% | 19%
Plus 1% for each 5 g/km over 95 g Max % = 37%
• List price
– Includes cost of extras
– Deduct capital contribution (max £5,000)
• Unavailable › 30 consecutive days: time apportion
• No benefit on pool cars
Fuel
= (Appropriate % × £22,200
• Appropriate %
– Same as for car benefit
• Ignore employee partial contributions
Company van
• Private use = £3,170
• Private fuel = £598
• Unavailable › 30 consecutive days: time apportion
• Living accommodation:
Basic charge = higher of
(1) annual value
(2) rent paid by employer
Expensive accommodation charge = (Cost less £75,000) × ORI (3%)
Cost = purchase price
Include capital improvements up to start of tax year
If owned by employer for 6 years before first occupation:
– Use MV when first provided, not purchase price
Expenses for accommodation
• Cost to employer
Use of assets
• 20% x MV when first available
Job related accommodation
• No basic charge
• No additional charge for expensive accommodation
• Expenses benefit and use of assets
– restricted to (10% × employment income)

5 Reimbursement of expenses by employers

Where an employee is reimbursed expenses by the employer, the amount received is taxable income. However, an exemption applies where the employee would be able to claim a tax deduction for the business-related expenses under the rules set out above e.g. business travel, professional subscriptions, expenses which fall within the wholly, exclusively and necessarily provisions.

Where an expense is partly allowable and partly disallowable, then the exemption can be applied to the allowable part. For example, where an employee's home telephone bill is fully reimbursed, the exemption can be applied to the business calls, but not to the private calls and the line rental. Reimbursed expenses which are not exempt must be reported to HMRC using a form P11D and included on the employee's tax return.

6 Share schemes

It has long been recognised by employers that there are commercial benefits in schemes to motivate employees that are linked to a company's profitability.

These may take the form of:

- Share incentives – the allocation of company shares to the employee.
- Share options – the grant of options to buy company shares in the future.

Successive governments have encouraged these incentives by giving tax privileges to schemes, provided that they meet the relevant requirements.

Schemes that satisfy conditions have significant tax advantages and those that do not are not tax-advantaged.

Formal HMRC approval used to be required to establish a tax-advantaged scheme, however such approval is no longer needed. Nevertheless, the two types of scheme are often still referred to as 'approved' schemes and 'unapproved' schemes and you could see either term used in the P6 examination.

Share options

A share option is an offer to an employee of a right to purchase shares at a future date at a predetermined fixed price set at the time the offer is made.

The taxation consequences of share options depends on whether or not they are approved by HMRC as follows:

Event	Unapproved (i.e. not tax-advantaged)		Approved (i.e. tax-advantaged)	
Granting of option.	No tax.		No tax.	
Exercise of option.	**Income tax charge:**	£	No tax.	
	MV @ exercise date	X	(Note 2)	
	Cost of option	(X)		
	Cost of shares	(X)		
	Employment income	X		
	NIC charge if shares readily convertible into cash. (Note 1)			
Disposal of shares.	**Capital gain arises:**	£	**Capital gain arises:**	£
	Sale proceeds	X	Sale proceeds	X
	MV @ exercise date	(X)	Cost of option	(X)
			Cost of shares	(X)
	Gain (Note 3)	X	Gain (Note 3 + 4)	X

Notes:

(1) In the P6 exam, class 1A NIC will be payable by the employer unless the shares are quoted, in which case class 1 will apply, which means the employee will also be liable.

(2) For approved enterprise management incentive (EMI) schemes there may be an income tax charge on exercise, if the options are issued at a discount to the MV at grant.

(3) Entrepreneurs' relief (ER) will be available if:

- the company is a trading company
- the employee owns ≥ 5% interest in the ordinary share capital of the company, and
- the employee has owned the shares for at least 12 months.

(4) For approved EMI schemes, for ER:

- there is no requirement to hold ≥ 5% shareholding, and
- the 12 month ownership period can be counted from the date the option was granted (not when the shares acquired).

Test your understanding 5

Alan is employed by Sugar Ltd, a trading company. On 1 July 2012 he was granted the option to buy 1,000 shares in Sugar Ltd for £2, their market value at that time.

He exercises the option on 17 October 2016 when the shares are worth £4.50. On 20 October 2016 he sells them for £5 each.

The shareholding represents less than a 5% interest in the company.

Explain the tax implications of the above events assuming the scheme is approved or unapproved.

Share incentives

An employer may gift shares in the employing company to an employee or allow the employee to buy them at a discounted price.

Where this happens the employee will include in their earnings:

(Value of the shares less price paid (if any) for the shares)

In the P6 exam, if the shares are quoted they are 'readily convertible' and so this amount will also be liable to class 1 NIC.

Where they are unquoted, and not 'readily convertible' class 1A NIC will apply.

7 Approved share option and incentive schemes

There are four types of scheme that receive favourable tax treatment:

- Savings-related share option schemes (SAYE)
- Company share option plans (CSOP)
- Enterprise management incentive scheme (EMI)
- Share incentive plans (SIP)

The detail of how each scheme operates and the conditions which must be satisfied is given in expandable text.

The conditions and key rules are summarised in the tables below.

	CSOP	**EMI**	**SAYE**
Participation	Employer chooses	Employer chooses	All employees
Maximum value	£30,000 per employee	£250,000 per employee Scheme max £3m	£500 per month
Exercise period	3 – 10 years	Up to 10 years	3 or 5 years
Issue price	MV	Issue at MV to avoid IT charge on exercise	Not < 80% of MV
Base cost of shares for CGT	Price paid	Price paid plus discount (if any) taxed as income on exercise	Price paid
Other	If own > 30% of company = excluded from scheme	Gross assets ≤ £30m Employees < 250 ER period of ownership runs from date of grant, and no need to own ≥ 5% of OSC.	

Share incentive plan (SIP)	
Participation	**All employees**
Awarded free shares	Max £3,600 per year
Purchase partnership shares (cost = allowable deduction against employment income)	Max = lower of: • £1,800, and • 10% salary
Awarded matching shares	Max 2 per partnership share
Dividends	Tax free if invested in further shares
Holding period	5 years for full benefit
Base cost of shares	MV when removed from plan

SAYE option scheme

There is favourable tax treatment for share option schemes that are linked to a SAYE (Save As You Earn) contract.

How the scheme operates

- The employees pay a maximum of £500 per month into a SAYE scheme, for a period of 3 or 5 years.
- Interest on the scheme is exempt from income tax.
- At the end of the scheme the money can be used to exercise the share options or the employee may just withdraw the money for their own use.

As an approved scheme:

- No income tax will be charged on the grant or exercise of the option.
- On the subsequent disposal of the shares, a capital gain may arise.

Conditions for the SAYE scheme

- All employees must be able to participate in the scheme on similar terms although it is acceptable to exclude employees who have worked for the company for less than a qualifying period, as long as the period chosen does not exceed five years.

- The purchase price of the shares is usually met by the employee out of the SAYE accumulated savings.
- The price at which options are offered is not less than 80% of market value of the shares when the option was granted.
- The costs of setting up such a scheme are allowable as a trading expense for the company.

Company share option plan (CSOP)

- This type of approved share option scheme differs from the SAYE schemes described above in that:
  - the aggregate value of options granted is potentially much higher
  - the company has much greater discretion in allocating options to employees.

How the scheme operates

- The company grants the employee the right to buy shares at some time in the future, at a price fixed at the time of the grant of the option.
- Some time later the employee will pay the required amount and the shares are issued to them.
- As an approved scheme:
  - There is no income tax or NIC charge on the grant of the option.
  - On the exercise of an option there is no charge to tax.
  - On the final disposal of scheme shares, CGT will be charged on any gain arising.

Conditions for the CSOP scheme

- Eligible employees must be either full-time directors (i.e. working at least 25 hours per week) or full-time or part-time employees.
- Close company directors with a material interest (> 30%) are ineligible. Subject to the above, the company has complete discretion as to participants.

- The option must be exercised between 3 and 10 years of the grant.
- The price payable for the shares on exercise of the option must not be materially less than their market value at the time.
- There is a £30,000 limit to the value of shares for which a participant may hold unexercised options at the time.
- Employees owning more than 30% of the company are ineligible to participate.
- The costs of setting up such a scheme are allowable as trading expenses.
- Participation in the scheme need not be extended to all employees nor be on equal terms to all participants.

Enterprise management incentive scheme (EMI)

The EMI scheme was introduced to enable options to be granted to selected employees in smaller companies. The rules are more generous than for CSOPs.

How the scheme operates

- Enterprise management incentive schemes enable options worth up to £250,000 to be granted to **selected** employees.
- As an approved scheme:
  - There is no income tax or NIC charge on the grant of the option.
  - No income tax or NIC is charged on the exercise of the option if the option price at the time of grant was at least MV at that time.
  - If the exercise price was granted at a discount, the charge is based on the difference between the market value at the date of the grant and the exercise price (if any).
  - The CGT base cost of the shares is the price paid plus the discount (if any) that has been treated as income on exercise.
  - On sale of the shares, the period for which the option is held can be counted as part of the 12 months ownership period for entrepreneurs' relief.

Conditions for the EMI scheme

- There is no limit on the number of employees who may benefit, although the total value of options granted by the company may not exceed £3 million.
- Qualifying companies must have < 250 full-time employees.

- An employee must work for the company for at least 25 hours per week, or for at least 75% of his working time if less, and must not have a material interest in the company (i.e. > 30%).
- The company must be a qualifying trading company. Certain trades, such as property development, are excluded. The company's gross assets must not exceed £30 million.
- An employee may not be granted options over shares worth more than £250,000 at the time of grant. Options granted under a company share option plan must also be taken into account.
- Options must be capable of being exercised within ten years of grant, and may be granted at a discount, or at a premium.
- The company must not be a 51% subsidiary or otherwise controlled by another company and persons connected with that company.

Share incentive plans (SIPs)

A SIP is a scheme that allows the employer to give shares to their employees, and for the employees to buy further shares, without an income tax charge.

On disposal CGT will apply to any profit made.

How the scheme operates

A SIP can involve the employees acquiring shares in 3 different ways.

- The employer may gift up to £3,600 shares to the employee each year. The amount received is usually dependent on the financial performance of the company. These are referred to as free shares.
- Depending on the terms of the specific scheme an employee **may** be allowed to buy up to £1,800 of partnership shares. The cost is deducted from their pre-tax salary (up to a maximum of 10% of salary).
- Depending on the terms of the specific scheme the employer **may** choose to issue further free shares on a 2:1 basis to the partnership shares, so if the employee buys £1,800 the employer may issue a further £3,600 of shares at no cost to the employee. These are referred to as matching shares.
- Not all schemes offer partnership or matching shares.
- Dividends paid on employee's shares held under the plan can be reinvested tax free in further shares. There is no limit to the amount of dividends that can be reinvested in the SIP.

- As an approved scheme:
  - There is no income tax or NIC charge on the acquisition of the shares.
  - On the final disposal of scheme shares, CGT will be charged on any gain arising.

Conditions for the SIP

- The plan must be available to all employees of the company or a group company.
- The plan must have no arrangements for loans to employees.
- For the tax-free advantages, the plan shares must be held for at least 5 years.

Taxation consequences of the value received

The taxation consequences of the value received from an approved SIP are as follows:

Income tax and NICs

- Shares held in the plan for 5 years

  If free, partnership or matching shares are held in a plan for five years, there is no income tax or NIC charge at the time the plan shares are awarded.

  Dividend income used to acquire shares is tax-free as long as the shares are held in the plan for 3 years.
- Shares held in the plan for 3 to 5 years

  If the shares have been held for between 3 and 5 years, income tax and NIC will be charged on the lower of:

  (i) the initial value of the shares, or

  (ii) the value at the date of withdrawal.
- Shares held in the plan for less than 3 years

  Income tax and NIC will be payable on their value at the time when they cease to be held in the plan.

Capital gains

- If employees take the shares out of the plan and sell them later, there is a capital gain arising on the increase in value after the shares were withdrawn.
- To calculate the gain, the cost of the shares is their value when taken out of the plan.

  Accordingly, if the shares are sold on the same day they are taken out of the plan, no gain arises.

Choice of approved scheme

In order to decide which scheme is most appropriate, the conditions of each scheme should be compared to the employer's requirements.

Key factors to consider are:

- Does the employer want to reward all employees, or just key employees?
- What size is the employer's business?

  EMI is only available to smaller companies.

- Does the employer want to award shares or offer share options?
- How much does the employer want to offer?
- What holding period for the shares/options does the employer want to impose?

Example 5 – Unapproved vs. Approved share option schemes

Claire is granted share options in her employing company, a fully listed plc. Claire has an annual salary of £50,000.

The planned arrangements are as follows:

(1) The cost of the option is 5p per share.

(2) 10,000 shares can be acquired for £1.60 per share (= market value at grant of option).

(3) The share option can be exercised at any point after 3 years but before 10 years has expired. Claire will exercise her options in November 2016.

(4) The MV of shares at the exercise date in November 2016 will be £3.80.

(5) The shares are sold in January 2017 for £4.20 per share.

Other capital transactions by Claire during 2016/17 have utilised her annual exempt amount.

Assuming the share option scheme is either an unapproved scheme or an approved company share option plan:

(i) **Prepare a table of the tax charges for Claire arising on the above events.**

(ii) **State the overall net cash position of the transaction, including the preferred option.**

Solution

(a) **Tax charges**

	Unapproved scheme	**Approved CSOP**
	£	£
IT (W1)	8,600	0
NICs (W1)	430	0
CGT (W1) (W2)	800	5,100
Total	9,830	5,100

(b) **The net cash position:**

	Unapproved scheme	**Approved CSOP**
	£	£
Receipt on disposal	42,000	42,000
Less:		
Costs to acquire shares	(16,500)	(16,500)
Tax charges	(9,830)	(5,100)
Net cash flow	15,670	20,400

Clare will therefore be £4,730 (£20,400 – £15,670) better off if the share options are organised through a CSOP scheme. This is clearly due to the lower tax charge of £4,730 (£9,830 – £5,100).

Note: If the requirement had just asked for the tax saving or the cash benefit of the CSOP scheme, the answer could be calculated more quickly at the margin.
As £21,500 will be taxed at 20% to CGT instead of 42% (40% income tax and 2% NICs), the tax saving will be:
£21,500 × (42% – 20%) = £4,730.

Workings

(W1) **Unapproved scheme**

- No tax charge @ grant
- Exercise

	£
MV at date of exercise (10,000 × £3.80)	38,000
Less:	
Cost of option (10,000 × 5p)	(500)
Cost of shares	(16,000)
Employment income	21,500
Income tax charged (£21,500 × 40%) (Note)	8,600
Employee's NICs (2% × £21,500) (Note)	430

Note: Claire's employment income already means she is a HR taxpayer and the NIC upper limit threshold is exceeded. Therefore she will be taxed at 40% on additional employment income and 2% NICs.

- Sale of shares

	£
Sale proceeds (10,000 × £4.20)	42,000
Less: MV at date of exercise	(38,000)
Chargeable gain = Taxable gain (Note)	4,000
CGT (£4,000 × 20%) (Note)	800

Note: Claire has already used all of her AEA, therefore her additional chargeable gain is all taxable. As her taxable income is greater than £32,000, her gain is taxed at 20%.

(W2) **Approved scheme**

- No tax charge @ grant.
- No tax charge @ exercise.
- With an approved scheme the whole profit is charged to CGT on the ultimate disposal of the shares.

	£
Sale proceeds	42,000
Less:	
Cost of option	(500)
Cost of shares	(16,000)
Chargeable gain = Taxable gain	25,500
CGT (£25,500 × 20%)	5,100

8 Employee shareholder shares

'Employee shareholder' status is an employment status that applies to employees with an equity-linked employment contract.

In exchange for giving up certain employment rights, such as statutory redundancy pay and protection against unfair dismissal, employees will be awarded shares in the company they work for or the parent company.

To obtain tax relief on the award of the employee shareholder shares in the employer company:

- the awarded shares must be worth at least £2,000, and
- there must be no consideration paid for the shares other than the surrender of employment rights.

Tax relief

	Employee does not own a material interest (Note 1)	Employee owns a material interest
Income tax and NIC	Income tax charge: £ Value of shares awarded X Less: Tax free amount (Note 2) (2,000) — Employment income X — NIC charge: if shares readily convertible into cash. (as for unapproved share options)	Income tax and NIC charges: • Full value of shares awarded = treated as employment income • taxable in the normal way
Capital gains tax	On the disposal of the first £50,000 value of shares awarded (Note 3): • Chargeable gains arising = exempt • Losses arising = not allowable If the employee owns both employee shareholder shares and other shares in the company: • the employee can decide the proportion of shares disposed of that is to be treated as employee shareholder shares	• no exemption available • disposal of shares taxed in the normal way

Notes:

(1) The employee has a material interest if they own at least 25% of the voting rights in the company.

(2) The employee is deemed to have paid £2,000 for the shares and only the excess in value of shares received is taxed.

(3) The value of shares awarded for the purposes of the £50,000 exemption is based on the value at the time of acquisition (not disposal). The exemption is subject to a lifetime limit of £100,000 of chargeable gains.

9 Lump sum payments on termination or variation of employment

Lump sum payments from employment may be:

- partially exempt
- wholly exempt, or
- wholly chargeable.

The tax treatment of a lump sum payment made to an employee on the cessation of employment depends on whether or not the payment is a genuine redundancy payment on the cessation of employment.

Taxation treatment

The position is summarised in the table below:

Wholly exempt	Partially exempt	Wholly chargeable
• Statutory redundancy payments • Payments for injury, disability or death • Lump sum payments from a registered pension scheme	• Genuine discretionary (ex gratia) termination payments (see below) – first £30,000 exempt – limit reduced if statutory redundancy payments received	• Any payment which is contractual (e.g. restrictive covenants) • Any other payment received which is expected, usual employer practise (e.g. gardening leave, customary payments in lieu of notice)

Genuine ex gratia termination payments include:

- redundancy payments
- compensation for loss of office
- some payments made in lieu of notice
- damages for breach of contract or wrongful dismissal.

Note the first £30,000 exempt rule also applies to any benefits received as part of the termination package (e.g. the company car).

Taxable amounts are:

- Assessed in the year of receipt
- Paid net of PAYE if paid before leaving and P45 issued
- Paid net of 20%/40%/45% income tax if paid after leaving and P45 issued
- Taxed as the top slice of the individual's taxable income (after dividend income) at the individual's highest marginal rate of income tax. This will preserve the preferential dividend tax rates.
- Exempt from NICs (if a genuine ex-gratia payment), but liable to class 1 NICs if a wholly chargeable payment.

Test your understanding 6

Albert, age 40 years, received an ex gratia lump sum of £80,000 from his employers following his redundancy in December 2016.

He has other remuneration of £35,000, income from furnished accommodation of £2,745 and dividends received of £2,000 for 2016/17.

Albert also received £5,000 statutory redundancy pay.

Calculate Albert's income tax liability for 2016/17.

Unapproved retirement benefits

- Where an ex-gratia payment is made to an employee approaching retirement age, HMRC may deem the payment to be made under an unapproved retirement benefit arrangement and thereby assessable in full (i.e. without the £30,000 exemption).
- Retrospective approval can be given for the sum to be fully exempt.

10 National Insurance Contributions (NICs)

The main classes of NIC paid in respect of an employed individual and the persons who are liable to pay are summarised as follows:

Class of contribution	**Basis of assessment**	**Person liable**
Class 1 primary	A percentage based contribution based on employee earnings in excess of £8,060 per year for 2016/17.	Employee
Class 1 secondary	A percentage based contribution based on employee earnings in excess of £8,112 per year for 2016/17. Employers obtain £3,000 relief to offset against class 1 secondary NICs (see below).	Employer
Class 1A	A percentage based contribution based on assessable benefits provided to employees.	Employer

The rules for NICs payable in respect of a self-employed individual are covered in Chapter 17.

A reminder of the rules for class 1 and class 1A contributions covered at F6 is given in expandable text and are summarised in the diagram below.

Class 1 NICs

Class 1 contributions – employed persons

A liability for class 1 contributions arises where an individual:

- is employed in the UK; and
- is aged 16 or over; and
- has earnings in excess of the earnings threshold.

Employee (primary) contributions

- Employee class 1 NICs are paid at 12% and 2%.
- Contributions are calculated as a percentage of **gross earnings** with **no allowable deductions**.
- There is no liability where gross earnings do not exceed the earnings threshold of £8,060 p.a.

- Employee class 1 contributions, at the rate of 12%, are paid on earnings in excess of the threshold but below the upper earnings limit (UEL) of £43,000.
- Earnings in excess of the UEL are subject to a rate of 2%.
- Class 1 NICs are calculated on an 'earnings period' basis (i.e. if paid weekly, 1/52 of the limits are used, and if paid monthly, 1/12 of the limits are used).
- However, in the examination, the annual limits are supplied and it is acceptable to calculate the liabilities on an annual basis.
- Employee class 1 contributions cease when the employee reaches state pension age. Up until 5 April 2010 the state pension age was 65 for men and 60 for women. Between 2010 and 2018 the state pension age for women is gradually increasing to 65. From 2018 onwards the state pension ages for both men and women will be aligned and are further increasing.
- The employer is responsible for calculating and accounting for the Employee class 1 contributions to HMRC under the PAYE system.
- The gross earnings on which class 1 contributions are calculated comprise any remuneration derived from employment paid in cash or assets which are readily convertible into cash.
- Gross earnings includes:
  - Wages, salary, overtime pay, commission or bonus.
  - Sick pay, including statutory sick pay.
  - Tips and gratuities paid or allocated by the employer.
  - Payment of the cost of travel between home and work, or on any profit element where business travel is reimbursed.

    For example, where the payment of a mileage allowance is in excess of the HMRC approved rate of 45p per mile, the excess above 45p per mile is subject to class I NICs.
  - Remuneration, such as bonuses, made by using financial instruments such as shares, unit trusts, options, gilts, gold, precious stones, fine wines and 'readily convertible' assets. An asset is 'readily convertible' if arrangements exist for its purchase.
  - Remuneration in the form of non-cash vouchers (e.g. M&S vouchers but not tax exempt vouchers such as vouchers for child care of no more than £55/£28/£25 per week).

- The following are disregarded in calculating gross earnings for primary contributions:
  - Most benefits (see above regarding use of financial instruments and vouchers).
  - Redundancy payments.
  - Payments of any pension.

Employer's (secondary) contributions

- The rate of employer's class 1 NICs is 13.8% on gross earnings above £8,112 p.a.
- The contributions are a deductible expense for the employer when calculating taxable profits.
- There is no liability where gross earnings do not exceed the earnings threshold of £8,112.
- Where earnings exceed the threshold then contributions are paid on earnings in excess of the threshold. There is no reduced rate when earnings exceed the UEL.
- Employer's class 1 contributions cease when the employee leaves the employment. There is no upper age limit, the employer is liable in full even if the employee is above state pension age.
- The exemption from employer's class 1 NICs for employees aged under 21 is not examinable.

NIC employment allowance

Employers are able to claim up to £3,000 relief p.a. from their employer's class 1 NIC contributions.

Note that the allowance:

- cannot be used against any other classes of NICs (e.g. class 1A)
- is claimed through the real time information (RTI) PAYE system
- will be provided in the tax rates and allowances in the exam.

The allowance is not available to companies where a director is the only employee.

Class 1A contributions

- Employers are required to pay class 1A contributions on taxable benefits provided to P11D employees.
- There is no class 1A charge in respect of any benefits that are already treated as earnings for class 1 contribution purposes (e.g. cash vouchers).
- The rate of class 1A NICs is 13.8%.
- The contributions are a deductible expense for the employer when calculating taxable profits.

Employees reaching state pension age

- An employee who continues to work after attaining state pension age has no liability for employee class 1 NIC contributions.
- The employer is still liable for full employer's class 1 NIC contributions.

Deduction and payment by the employer

- The employer calculates the employee and employer's class 1 contributions at each weekly or monthly pay date.
- At the end of each PAYE month (5th) the total contributions become payable along with income tax deducted under PAYE, not later than 14 days thereafter (i.e. by 19th each month). However, most businesses now pay electronically and are allowed an extra 3 days. Therefore, the usual payday **is 22nd of each month**.
- The class 1A contributions are payable annually in arrears to HMRC by **22nd July** following the end of the tax year.

Persons with more than one job

- A person with more than one job is separately liable for employee class 1 NIC contributions in respect of each job falling within the scope of class 1 contributions (where earnings are over the earnings threshold of £8,060 p.a.).
- Each employer is also separately liable for Employer's class 1 NIC contributions.
- The total employee class 1 contributions from all employments is subject to an overall annual maximum.
- Employees with more than one job can prevent overpayment of contributions by applying for deferment of contributions, or claiming a refund after the end of the tax year.

Company directors

- Where a person is a company director he or she is deemed to have an annual earnings' period.
- The annual earnings thresholds and the UEL therefore apply.
- The rules prevent directors avoiding NICs by paying themselves a low monthly salary, and then taking a large bonus.

Summary

NICs PAYABLE IN RESPECT OF AN EMPLOYED PERSON

- PAID BY EMPLOYEE
  - CLASS 1 EMPLOYEE
- PAID BY EMPLOYER
  - CLASS 1 EMPLOYER'S
  - CLASS 1A

	CLASS 1 EMPLOYEE	CLASS 1 EMPLOYER'S	CLASS 1A
Payable on:	• gross cash earnings – no allowable deductions – includes vouchers	• gross cash earnings – no allowable deductions – includes vouchers	• taxable benefits – excludes exempt benefits and vouchers
Payable when:	• aged 16 - state pension age	• aged 16 or over	• aged 16 or over
Rate:	• 12% on earnings between £8,060 and £43,000 • 2% thereafter	• 13.8% on earnings above £8,112 • £3,000 relief available	• 13.8% on the value of taxable benefits
Due date:	• payable under PAYE by 22nd of each month	• payable under PAYE by 22nd of each month	• payable by 22nd July following the end of the tax year

Example 6 – NICs

Janet is paid a salary of £18,000 p.a. She was also paid a bonus of £10,000 in the first week of March 2017.

Calculate Janet's class 1 employee NICs for 2016/17 if she is an employee or a director.

Solution

(i) **An employee**

If Janet is an employee she will pay NICs on earnings of £1,500 per month for 11 months and earnings of £11,500 for the month in which the bonus was paid as follows:

	£
(£1,500 – £672 (Note)) × 12% × 11 months	1,093
(£3,583 – £672) × 12% × 1 month	349
(£11,500 – £3,583 (Note)) × 2% × 1 month	158
	1,600

Note: Monthly limits

Primary threshold = (£8,060 ÷ 12) = £672

Upper threshold = (£43,000 ÷ 12) = £3,583

(ii) **A director**

If Janet is a director, she will pay NICs by reference to her total earnings in the year as follows.

Annual remuneration = (£18,000 + £10,000) = £28,000

Class 1 employee NICs = (£28,000 – £8,060) × 12% £2,393

Test your understanding 7

Alex is paid £9,300 and Betty £46,400 in the tax year 2016/17.

Betty also receives £9,600 taxable benefits of employment.

Calculate the employee's and the employer's class 1 and class 1A NIC payable for the year.

11 Chapter summary

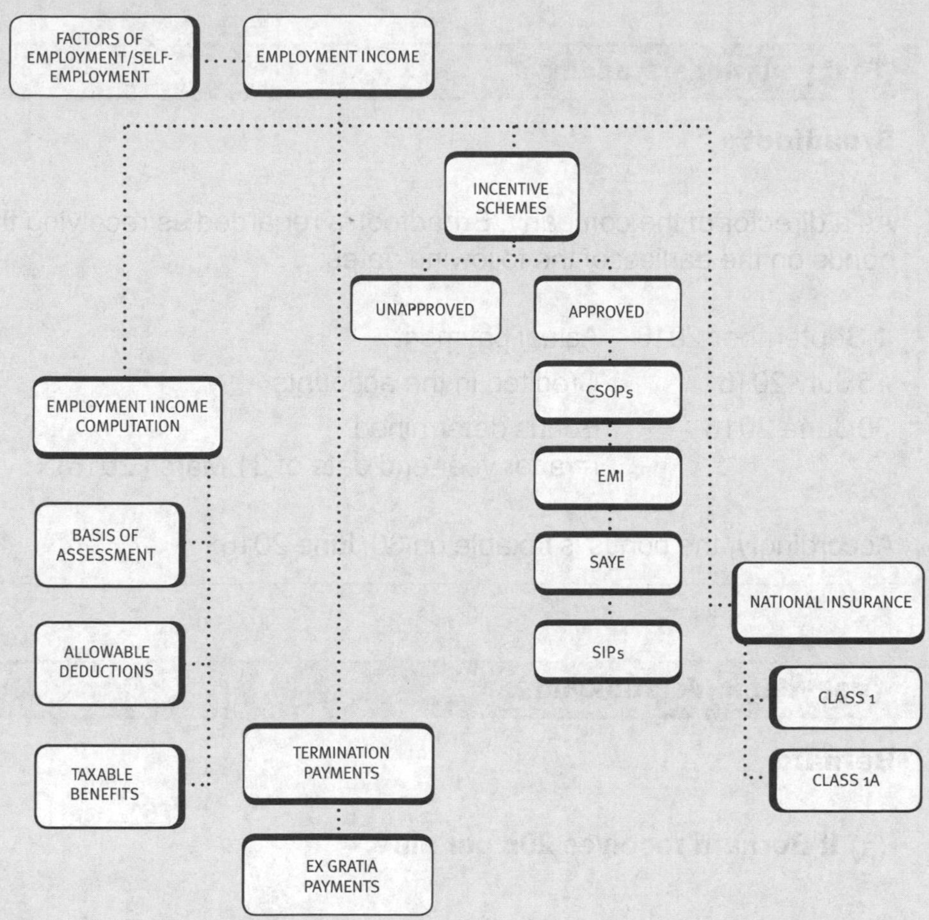

Test your understanding answers

Test your understanding 1

Broadfoot

As a director of the company, Broadfoot is regarded as receiving the bonus on the earliest of the following dates:

1 September 2016	Actual payment
15 July 2016	Credited in the accounts
30 June 2016	Bonus determined (= after year end date of 31 March 2016)

Accordingly, the bonus is taxable on 30 June 2016.

Test your understanding 2

Bernard

(a) **If Bernard receives 20p per mile**

			£
Mileage allowance claimed		12,000 × 20p	2,400
AMAP	First 10,000 miles	10,000 × 45p	(4,500)
	Remaining 2,000 miles	2,000 × 25p	(500)
Mileage expense claim = allowable deduction			(2,600)

(b) **If Bernard receives 50p per mile**

			£
Mileage allowance claimed		12,000 × 50p	6,000
AMAP	First 10,000 miles	10,000 × 45p	(4,500)
	Remaining 2,000 miles	2,000 × 25p	(500)
Mileage allowance assessable benefit			1,000

Note: The passenger allowance is tax free as it is < 5p per business mile.
Bernard cannot make an expense claim for the shortfall in the passenger AMAP of 1p (5p – 4p) per mile.

Test your understanding 3

Charles

Charles has the use of the car and fuel for 9 months of 2016/17 (1 July 2016 to 5 April 2017).

	£
Car benefit (£24,000 × 37% (W) × 9/12)	6,660
Less: Payment for use (£100 × 9 months)	(900)
	5,760
Fuel benefit (£22,200 × 37% × 9/12)	6,160
Taxable benefit	11,920

Note: No reduction for contributions towards private fuel.

There is no additional charge for any running costs of the car with the exception of the fuel provision.

Working: Appropriate % = 16% + (225 – 95) × 1/5 = 42%, but restricted to 37% maximum.

Test your understanding 4

Vigorous plc

Andrea Lean

		£
Car benefit (£19,400 × 37%) (Note 1)		7,178
Less: Contribution by Andrea (£150 × 12)		(1,800)
		5,378
Fuel benefit (£22,200 × 37%)		8,214
Living accommodation	– Annual rateable value	7,000
	– Additional benefit (Note 2)	2,070
	– Furniture (£6,000 at 20%)	1,200
Mobile telephone (Note 3)		0

Notes:

(1) The relevant percentage for the car benefit is 46% (16% (245 – 95 = 150 × 1/5)), but this is restricted to the maximum of 37%.

(2) The living accommodation cost in excess of £75,000 so there will be an additional benefit.

Since the property was purchased within six years of first being provided, the benefit is based on the purchase price of the property plus improvements prior to 6 April 2016.

The additional benefit is therefore £2,070 ((£130,000 + £14,000) – £75,000 = £69,000 at 3%).

(3) The provision of one mobile telephone does not give rise to a taxable benefit, even if there is private use.

Ben Slim

	£
Beneficial loan (Note 1)	2,400
Relocation costs (£9,300 – £8,000) (Note 2)	1,300
Car benefit (£11,200 × 20% × 6/12) (Note 3)	1,120

Notes:

(1) The benefit of the beneficial loan using the average method is £2,475 ((£120,000 + £100,000) × ½ = £110,000 at 3% × 9/12).

Using the precise method the benefit is £2,400 ((£120,000 at 3% × 3/12) + (£100,000 at 3% × 6/12)).

Ben will therefore elect to have the taxable benefit calculated according to the precise method.

(2) Only £8,000 of relocation costs are exempt, and so the excess is a taxable benefit.

(3) The relevant percentage for the car benefit is 20% (16% + 3% (charge for a diesel motor car) + 1% ((100 – 95) = 5 × 1/5).

The motor car was only available for six months of 2016/17.

There is no fuel benefit as Ben reimburses the company for the full cost of private diesel.

Chai Trim

	£
Van benefit (£3,170 × 10/12) (Note 1)	2,642
Fuel benefit (£598 × 10/12) (Note 1)	498
Television (Note 2)	330
Health club membership (Note 3)	150
Computer (£1,900 × 20% × 3/12) (Note 4)	95

Notes:

(1) The van and private fuel was only available for ten months of 2016/17 so the benefit is time apportioned.

(2) Chai will have been assessed to a benefit of £160 (£800 at 20%) in respect of the television for both 2014/15 and 2015/16.

The benefit on the sale of the television is £330 (£800 – £160 – £160 – £150), as this is greater than £100 (£250 – £150).

(3) In-house benefits are valued according to the marginal cost. The taxable benefit in relation to the health club membership is therefore the direct costs of £150.

(4) The computer was only available for 3 months so the benefit is time apportioned.

Test your understanding 5

Alan

(i) **Approved share options**

1 July 2012	Grant of option = No tax	
17 October 2016	Exercise of option = No tax	
20 October 2016	CGT on disposal:	
		£
	Sale proceeds	5,000
	Less: Cost	(2,000)
	Chargeable gain – 2016/17	3,000

ER is available on this gain if it is an EMI approved scheme as there is no requirement to hold ≥ 5% interest, the options were granted > 12 months pre disposal of shares, Alan works for the company and it is a trading company.

(ii) **Unapproved share options**

1 July 2012	Grant option = No tax	
17 October 2016	Exercise of option:	
	Employment income	
	= 1,000 × (£4.50 – £2)	£2,500
	Assessed to income tax and NICs.	
20 October 2016	CGT on disposal:	
		£
	Sale proceeds	5,000
	Less: MV @ exercise	(4,500)
	Chargeable gain – 2016/17	500

ER is not available as Alan does not hold ≥ 5% interest in the ordinary share capital and does not own the shares > 12 months pre disposal.

Test your understanding 6

Albert

Income tax computation – 2016/17

	£	£	£
Remuneration			35,000
Lump sum		80,000	
Less: Exempt amount	30,000		
Less: Statutory redundancy pay	(5,000)		
		(25,000)	
Taxable amount			55,000
Employment income			90,000
Property business income			2,745
Dividends			2,000
Total income			94,745
Less: Personal allowance			(11,000)
Taxable income			83,745

Analysis of income:

Dividends	**Termination payment**	**Non-savings income**
£2,000	£55,000	(£83,745 – £55,000 – £2,000) = £26,745

Income tax:

£		£
26,745	× 20% (Non-savings income)	5,349
2,000	× 0% (DNRB)	0
3,255	× 20% (termination payment)	651
32,000		
51,745	× 40% (termination payment)	20,698
83,745		
Income tax liability		26,698

Test your understanding 7

Alex

		£
Employee class 1 NICs = (£9,300 – £8,060)	× 12%	149
Employer's class 1 NICs = (£9,300 – £8,112)	× 13.8%	164

Betty

		£
Employee class 1 NICs		
(£43,000 – £8,060)	× 12%	4,193
(£46,400 – £43,000)	× 2%	68
		4,261
Employer's class 1 NICs = (£46,400 – £8,112)	× 13.8%	5,284
Employer's class 1A NICs = £9,600	× 13.8%	1,325

Total employer's class 1 NICs

	£
Employer's class 1 NICs (£164 + £5,284)	5,448
Less: Employment allowance	(3,000)
	2,448

chapter

3

Property and investment income

Chapter learning objectives

Upon completion of this chapter you will be able to:

- calculate the assessable income arising from the letting of property
- define when a letting qualifies as furnished holiday accommodation and explain the differences compared to normal lettings
- explain when rent-a-room relief will apply
- calculate the amount assessable when a premium is received for the grant of a short lease
- demonstrate the reliefs available for a property business loss
- recognise the tax free income products
- explain the key features of an ISA
- identify the circumstances when accrued income provisions apply and calculate taxable amounts
- list the key conditions and purpose of an EIS scheme, SEIS scheme and VCT scheme and recognise what IT relief is available to an investor and how it is given
- identify the circumstances for withdrawal of relief for the above schemes and how this is affected.

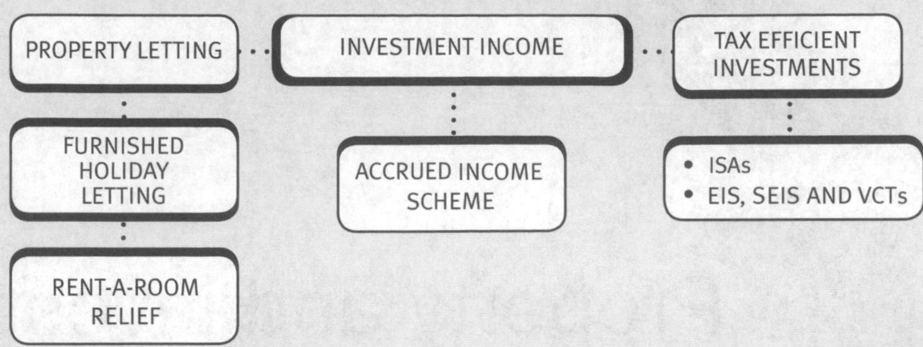

Introduction

This chapter is mainly a revision of the main types of exempt income and the income tax implications of letting property covered at F6.

A brief reminder of the F6 content is given in expandable text and revision examples are provided to check your retention of the required F6 knowledge.

The new topics introduced at P6 are the accrued income scheme, real estate investment trust income and tax efficient investments such as EIS, SEIS and VCT investments.

1 Property income

All income from land and buildings is taxed on individuals as property income.

Property income includes:

- rental income under any lease or tenancy agreement less allowable expenses
- the premium received on the grant of a short lease
- profits arising from the commercial letting of furnished holiday accommodation
- rental income received under the rent-a-room scheme.

Rental income

A reminder of the rules for computing assessable rental income under a lease or tenancy agreement covered at F6 is given in expandable text and is summarised in the diagram in section 5.

Rental income

Basis of assessment

If an individual lets out a property or several properties, the profits from renting the properties is calculated as if the individual had a single trade:

	£
Rental income from all properties	X
Less: Related expenses (see below)	(X)
Assessable property income	X

- the rental income is assessable on an accruals basis
- the related expenses are deductible on an accruals basis
- although treated as a trade, the income is investment income and taxed at 20%/40%/45% as 'non-savings income'.

Allowable deductions

The expenses allowable against the rental income are computed under the normal rules for a business.

- To be allowable, the expenses must be incurred wholly and exclusively in connection with the business.
  This covers items such as:
  - insurance
  - utility costs
  - agents fees and other management expenses
  - repairs
  - interest on a loan to acquire or improve the property
  - irrecoverable debts.
- Any expenditure incurred before letting commences is allowable under the normal pre-trading expenditure rules.
- **Where property is not let at a full rent** (e.g. to a relative) a portion of the expenses incurred will be disallowed as not being wholly and exclusively incurred for the business.

  For example, if rent charged is £250 p.a. but a commercial rent would be £1,000 p.a., only 25% of expenses will be allowed.

  In practice HMRC would allow the expenses but only up to the amount of the rent on that property.

- **If property is occupied for part of the year by the owner**, any expenses relating to the private use will not be allowed as a deduction.
- There is no deduction allowed for capital expenditure on the property or the initial cost of furnishings.
- Repairs are allowed when incurred, providing they relate to the letting.
- Depreciation may be charged in the accounts but is not an allowable deduction for tax purposes.
- Normal capital allowances are not available for plant and machinery in a dwelling house.

Replacement funiture relief

Prior to the 2016/17 tax year, landlords could claim a 'wear and tear allowance' in respect of furnished property. This has now been abolished. From the tax year 2016/17, a deduction for replacement furniture relief is given instead.

The cost of replacing furnishings (e.g. beds, televisions, fridges, freezers, carpets, floor coverings, curtains, crockery and cutlery) is allowable, even if the property is not fully furnished.

There is no relief for the initial cost of purchasing the furnishings.

The amount of relief available is reduced by any proceeds from the sale of the asset being replaced.

Relief is only available for a like-for-like replacement. No deduction is available for any costs which represents an improvement. For example if a washing machine is replaced with a washer-dryer, only the cost of a replacement washing machine would qualify for relief.

Test your understanding 1

Giles owns a cottage which he lets out furnished at an annual rate of £3,600, payable monthly in advance. During the tax year 2016/17 he incurs the following expenditure:

		£
May 2016	Cost of new garage	2,000
June 2016	Insurance for year from 5 July (previous year = £420)	480
Nov 2016	Replacement freezer	380
May 2017	Redecoration (work completed in March 2017)	750

The tenant had vacated the property during June 2016 without having paid the rent due for June. Giles was unable to trace the defaulting tenant, but managed to let the property to new tenants from 1 July 2016.

Calculate the property business profit for the tax year 2016/17.

2 Furnished holiday accommodation

Profits arising from the commercial letting of furnished holiday accommodation (FHA) are:

- assessable as property business income, but
- treated as though the profits arose from a separate trade, and
- treated as earned income, not investment income.

The conditions and rules for FHA are given in expandable text and summarised in the diagram in section 5.

Furnished holiday accommodation

Qualifying conditions

In order to qualify as a FHA, the accommodation must satisfy all of the following conditions:

- the property is situated in the UK or the EEA, **furnished** and let on a **commercial basis**
- it is **available** for commercial letting, to the public generally, as holiday accommodation for not less than **210 days** a year

- the accommodation is **actually let** for at least **105 days** a year (excluding periods of long term occupation)
  - Where a taxpayer owns more than one property, the 105 days test is satisfied if the average number of days for which the properties are let in the year is at least 105.
- the accommodation is normally **not let for > 31 consecutive days** to the same person. However, if during a 12 month period there are periods of letting to the same person in excess of 31 consecutive days, the aggregate of these long periods **must not exceed 155 days** in total.

Losses

Losses from FHA cannot be set against any other income, they can only be carried forward and offset against profits from the same FHA business.

UK losses can only be set against future UK FHA income, and EEA losses can only be set against future EEA FHA income.

The advantages of FHA treatment

The profits will be treated as earned income arising from a single trade carried on by the landlord.

The advantages of being treated as earned income include:

- profits treated as relevant earnings for pension relief purposes (see Chapter 4)
- normal capital allowances (e.g. annual investment allowance) are available on all plant and machinery including furniture provided, instead of replacement furniture relief (Chapter 17)
- property treated as business asset for CGT purposes and consequently on the disposal of FHA the following reliefs are available (Chapter 9):
  - entrepreneurs' relief
  - rollover relief, and
  - gift relief.
- Business property relief for IHT may be available (Chapter 12) but only if:
  - it is run as a business (for example, a caravan park or estate)
  - there is substantial involvement by the owner, and
  - additional services are provided (e.g. cleaning, laundry, TV, light and heat, activities).

3 Rent-a-room relief

When an individual lets furnished accommodation in their main residence, a special exemption applies.

A reminder of the rules is given in expandable text and is summarised in the diagram in section 5.

Rent-a-room relief

- If the gross annual receipts (before expenses or capital allowances) are £7,500 or below:
  - the income will be exempt from tax
  - can elect to ignore the exemption for that year if a loss is incurred.

- If the gross annual receipts are more than £7,500:
  - the individual may choose between:

    (i) paying tax on the excess of the gross rent over £7,500; and

    (ii) being taxed in the ordinary way on the profit from letting (rent less expenses less replacement furniture relief).

Married couples

A married couple (or civil partners) who take in lodgers can either have:

- all the rent paid to one spouse (who will then have the full limit of £7,500), or
- have the rent divided between them (and each spouse will then have a limit of £3,750).

4 Property business losses

Profits and losses on all the properties are aggregated.

- If there is an overall loss, the property income assessment for the year will be £nil.
- The loss is carried forward and set against the first available future property income.

Example 1 – Property business losses

Sheila owns three properties which were rented out. Her assessable income and allowable expenses for the two years to 5 April 2017 were:

Property	**1**	**2**	**3**
Income	£	£	£
2015/16	1,200	450	3,150
2016/17	800	1,750	2,550
Expenses			
2015/16	1,850	600	2,800
2016/17	900	950	2,700

Calculate Sheila's property income or losses for 2015/16 and 2016/17.

Solution

Property income/losses	**2015/16**	**2016/17**
	£	£
Income		
(£1,200 + £450 + £3,150)	4,800	
(£800 + £1,750 + £2,550)		5,100
Less: Expenses		
(£1,850 + £600 + £2,800)	(5,250)	
(£900 + £950 + £2,700)		(4,550)
Profit/(loss) in year	(450)	550
Less: Loss b/f	–	(450)
Property income	0	100
Loss c/f	450	0

5 Summary

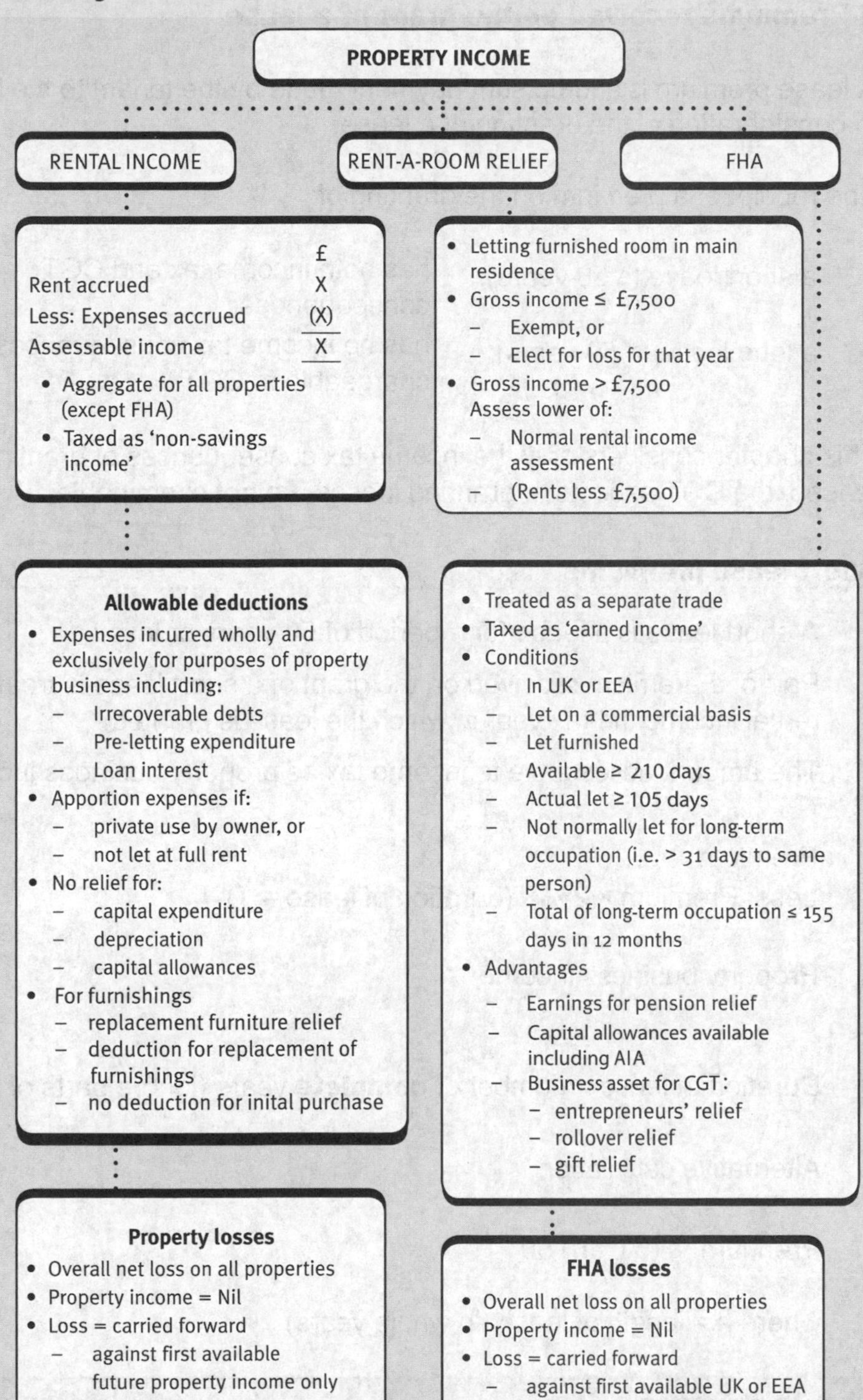
PROPERTY INCOME
RENTAL INCOME
RENT-A-ROOM RELIEF
FHA
£
Rent accrued X
Less: Expenses accrued (X)
Assessable income X
• Aggregate for all properties (except FHA)
• Taxed as 'non-savings income'
• Letting furnished room in main residence
• Gross income ≤ £7,500
– Exempt, or
– Elect for loss for that year
• Gross income > £7,500
Assess lower of:
– Normal rental income assessment
– (Rents less £7,500)
Allowable deductions
• Expenses incurred wholly and exclusively for purposes of property business including:
– Irrecoverable debts
– Pre-letting expenditure
– Loan interest
• Apportion expenses if:
– private use by owner, or
– not let at full rent
• No relief for:
– capital expenditure
– depreciation
– capital allowances
• For furnishings
– replacement furniture relief
– deduction for replacement of furnishings
– no deduction for inital purchase
• Treated as a separate trade
• Taxed as 'earned income'
• Conditions
– In UK or EEA
– Let on a commercial basis
– Let furnished
– Available ≥ 210 days
– Actual let ≥ 105 days
– Not normally let for long-term occupation (i.e. > 31 days to same person)
– Total of long-term occupation ≤ 155 days in 12 months
• Advantages
– Earnings for pension relief
– Capital allowances available including AIA
– Business asset for CGT:
– entrepreneurs' relief
– rollover relief
– gift relief
Property losses
• Overall net loss on all properties
• Property income = Nil
• Loss = carried forward
– against first available future property income only
FHA losses
• Overall net loss on all properties
• Property income = Nil
• Loss = carried forward
– against first available UK or EEA FHA profits only (UK and EEA are separate trades)

6 Premiums received on the grant of a lease

A lease premium is a lump sum payment made by the tenant to the landlord in consideration of the granting of a lease.

The receipt of a premium on the granting of:

- a short lease (≤ 50 years): has both income tax and CGT consequences
- a long lease (> 50 years): has no income tax consequences but is chargeable to CGT.

This chapter considers only the income tax consequences of granting leases, the CGT aspects of granting leases are not examinable.

Short lease premiums

- A short lease is a lease for a period of 50 years or less.
- Part of a premium received on the grant of a short lease is treated as rental income the tax year in which the lease is granted.
- The amount assessable to income tax as property business income is:

	£
Premium	X
Less: Premium × 2% × (duration of lease – 1)	(X)
Property business income	X

Duration of lease = number of **complete** years (ignore parts of a year).

- Alternative calculation:

Premium × (51 – n)/50

where n = length of lease (in whole years)

Length of lease

To avoid income tax it would be a simple matter to grant a lease for over 50 years, but to give the landlord the right to end the lease before the expiration of 50 years.

Anti-avoidance legislation provides that where the lease can be terminated at some date during the lease, the period of the lease is taken to the **earliest** date on which the lease **may** be terminated.

Test your understanding 2

Rodney granted a 21 year lease of business premises to Charles on 1 July 2016 for a premium of £10,500.

He also granted a lease for another building with 14 years and 2 months left to run to Alice for a premium of £30,000.

Calculate Rodney's property income assessment for the tax year 2016/17.

Comprehensive example

Test your understanding 3

John Wiles acquired two houses on 6 April 2016.

House 1 is let as furnished holiday accommodation. House 2 is let furnished.

House 1 was available for letting for 42 weeks during 2016/17 and was actually let for 16 weeks at £200 per week. During the 10 weeks that the house was not available for letting, it was occupied rent free by John's sister. Running costs for 2016/17 consisted of council tax £730, insurance £310 and advertising £545.

House 2 was unoccupied from 6 April 2016 until 31 December 2016 due to a serious flood in May 2016. As a result of the flood £7,465 was spent on repairs.

On 1 January 2017 the house was let on a four year lease for a premium of £4,000 and a rent of £8,600 per annum.

Immediately after the purchase, John furnished the two houses at a cost of £5,200 per house. During 2016/17 John also rented out one room of his main residence. He received rent of £7,850 and incurred allowable expenditure of £825.

(i) Briefly explain whether House 1 will qualify to be treated as a trade under the furnished holiday accommodation rules.

State the tax advantages of the house being so treated.

(ii) Calculate John's property business loss for the tax year 2016/17 and advise him of the possible ways of relieving the loss.

7 Real estate investment trusts

A real estate investment trust (REIT) gives investors the opportunity to invest in a quoted property business set up as an investment trust.

Dividends received by an individual out of the profits of a REIT are not treated like other dividend income. Instead the income is:

- treated as property income
- taxed as non-savings income (i.e. not savings and not dividend income)
- received net of 20% tax.

Illustration 1 – Real estate investment trusts

An individual who receives dividends of £1,200 from a REIT will include gross property income in their tax return of £1,500 (£1,200 × 100/80).

The income will be taxed at the rates of 20%, 40% or 45% depending on whether they pay tax at the basic, higher or additional rate.

A tax credit of £300 (£1,500 × 20%) is available to reduce the actual tax payable, and can be repaid if relevant.

8 Tax free investments

The main types of investment giving tax free or exempt income are as follows:

- interest on NS & I savings certificates
- income from individual savings accounts (ISAs)
- dividends from shares held in a venture capital trust (VCT)
- income tax repayment supplement
- premium bond, national lottery and betting winnings.

Individual savings accounts (ISAs)

An ISA can be opened by any individual aged 18 or over (16 for cash ISAs) who is resident in the UK.

An ISA offers the following tax reliefs:

- Income (interest and dividends) received is exempt from income tax.
- Disposals of investments within an ISA are exempt from CGT.

There is no minimum holding period, so withdrawals can be made from the account at any time.

A reminder of the rules for the type of investment allowed through an ISA is given in expandable text.

Types of investments

An ISA can be made up of either of the following components:

- Cash and cash-like equity products

  These include bank and building society accounts, as well as those NS&I products where the income is not exempt from tax.

  16 and 17 year olds may only invest cash ISAs.

- Stocks, shares and insurance products

  Investment is allowed in shares and securities listed on a stock exchange anywhere in the world.

  Unlisted shares and shares traded on the Alternative Investment Market (AIM) do not qualify.

Subscription limits

For the tax year 2016/17 the annual subscription limit and maximum amount that can be invested by an individual in a NISA is £15,240.

Note that spouses and civil partners each have their own limits.

This ISA limit is included in the tax rates and allowances provided in the examination.

Any combination of cash and shares can be invested, up to the total of £15,240.

Savers can also withdraw money from a cash ISA and replace it in the same tax year without the replacement contributing to their maximum investment.

Savers have a choice of account providers.

ISAs and the income tax nil rate bands

The tax advantages of ISAs have been removed for many taxpayers by the introduction of the savings nil rate band (SNRB) and the dividend nil rate band (DNRB):

Cash ISAs

- For many basic and higher rate taxpayers, the introduction of the savings nil rate band (SNRB) investing in a cash ISA no longer provides a tax benefit. This is because their savings income is within the SNRB and is therefore taxed at 0%.
- ISAs will still be beneficial for additional rate taxpayers (who are not entitled to a SNRB) and all taxpayers whose SNRB is already fully utilised.

Stocks and shares ISAs

- For many individuals, the introduction if the dividend nil rate band (DNRB) means that investing in a stocks and shares ISA no longer provides an income tax benefit. This is because their dividend income is within the DNRB and is therefore taxed at 0%.
- Stocks and shares ISAs will still be beneficial for taxpayers whose DNRB is already fully utilised. In addition, chargeable gains made within a stocks and shares ISA are exempt from capital gains tax and will therefore be advantageous to taxpayers who make chargeable gains in excess of the annual exempt amount.

Innovative Finance ISAs

Investment is allowed in peer to peer lending platforms. Peer to peer lending platforms match individuals who have funds to lend with individuals who require a personal loan. **The innovative finance ISA is not examinable**.

Transfer of ISA allowance to spouse/civil partner on death

In relation to deaths on/after 3 December 2014, an additional allowance can be claimed for the surviving spouse or civil partner.

- The amount of the allowance will be equal to the value of the deceased person's ISA savings at the time of death.

  This means that ISA savings can be transferred to the surviving spouse and retain their beneficial tax treatment.

Note that:

- spouses will be entitled to the allowance even if the ISA assets are left to someone else
- a claim must be made for the additional allowance.

9 The accrued income scheme

This topic has been added to the F6 syllabus with effect from the FA2016 examinations. If you have studied for the F6 examination under the FA2016 syllabus, this topic may not be new to you

The accrued income scheme was introduced to prevent the practice of 'bond washing'.

Interest is normally paid on securities at regular intervals. As the interest payment date gets nearer, the capital value of the securities increases as any purchaser is buying the accrued income in addition to the underlying capital value.

When the securities are sold they are usually exempt from CGT so this element of growth relating to the interest escapes tax.

Background – Bond washing

This scheme applies to marketable securities such as gilts and loan notes.

Interest is paid to the registered holder on a certain date. However, an individual who sells the security before that date will not receive the interest payment due on that date as by then it would be no longer owned.

However, the price the vendor receives for selling the security will be inflated to take account of the fact that the purchaser is due to receive the next interest payment.

By this time, the vendor has received a capital receipt in relation to the sale of the security, and as there is no income paid out, there is no charge to income tax in respect of the increased selling price.

As gilts and loan notes are exempt from CGT, any gain arising on the disposal will also escape capital gains tax. Overall therefore, any interest due to be paid out and included in the selling price of the security will escape tax.

How the scheme operates

- Under the scheme, interest is deemed to accrue on a daily basis (but computations in the exam are to be calculated on a monthly basis unless the question says otherwise).
- The purchase price (or disposal price) of the security is therefore apportioned between the income element and the capital element.
- The income element is assessed as interest income.
- The scheme does not apply unless the total nominal value of securities held by an individual exceeds £5,000 at some time during the year of assessment.
- The scheme does not apply if the securities are transferred on death.

Example 2 – Accrued income scheme

Ahmed sold £15,000 6% loan stock cum interest on 31 October 2016 for proceeds of £20,000. He originally acquired the loan stock on 1 May 2014. Interest is payable on 30 June and 31 December each year.

Calculate the amount assessed on Ahmed as interest income for the tax year 2016/17.

Solution

Interest income – 2016/17

	£
Interest received – 30 June 2016 (£15,000 × 6% × 6/12)	450
Accrued interest included in SP of loan stock (from 1 July 2016 – 31 October 2016) (£15,000 × 6% × 4/12)	300
Total interest assessable to income tax	750

Note: For CGT purposes the SP are £19,700 (£20,000 – £300). However, any gain arising is exempt as the loan stock is a qualifying corporate bond (QCB).

10 Enterprise investment scheme

The enterprise investment scheme (EIS) is intended to encourage investors to subscribe for new shares in unquoted trading companies.

- Since the investor is committing the whole investment to one company, which may well not yet have a track record, this is a high risk investment.
- Furthermore, unless the shares become quoted, the investor may not be able to realise their investment easily. A successful company, however, may carry high returns.

To qualify for the scheme:

- the **investor** must:
  - subscribe, in cash, for new ordinary shares in a qualifying company
  - **not** be an **employee** or director of the company
  - be independent of the company at the time of the first share issue (i.e. **not** already hold shares in the company at the time of investment, unless the shares held by the investor are qualifying EIS or Seed EIS shares)
  - have an **interest of 30% or less** in the company's ordinary share capital (OSC)
- the **company,** at the date the shares are issued, must:
  - be an **unquoted trading company** with a permanent establishment in the UK
  - be no more than 7 years old when first using the scheme or has raised qualifying funds in its first 7 years unless
    - the total investment represents more than 50% of turnover averaged over the preceding five years
- shares listed on the AIM count as unquoted for this purpose, although arrangements to obtain a quotation must not exist when the shares are issued
- an **effective 90% interest** trading subsidiary (i.e. through an indirect interest) will also qualify for relief
- the company must be carrying on a qualifying trade, or research and development intended to lead to such a trade, and
- have no excluded activities. There are a number of **investment activities** which are **excluded**, and therefore do not constitute a qualifying trade. These activities include:
  - financial activities
  - legal and accountancy services
  - dealing in commodities, futures, shares, securities and other financial instruments
  - property backed activities such as farming and market gardening and property development
  - shipbuilding
  - coal and steel production
  - energy generation activities
- the company must be in sound financial health
- have **250 or fewer full-time employees**

- have **gross assets** of:
  - **less than £15 million** before the share issue, and
  - no more than **£16 million** after the issue.
- the funds must be used:
  - within two years of the issue of the shares or, if later, two years from commencing qualifying activities
  - for the purposes of the qualifying trade
  - with the intention to grow and develop the business
- the funds cannot be used
  - to finance the purchase of another existing company or trade
- the **maximum investment** that can be raised by an EIS company:
  - **£5 million in any 12 month period**, and
  - **£12 million lifetime total** (from EIS, Seed EIS and VCT schemes).

Tax consequences

Income tax

- **Income tax relief = 30% × (cost of the shares subscribed for)**
  - Maximum investment = **£1 million per tax year**
  - Therefore maximum tax reducer = £300,000
  - **Deduct from** the individual's **income tax liability**
  - Can reduce liability to £Nil, but cannot create a tax repayment.
- An investor may elect to carry back the amount invested to the previous year, but cannot get relief on more than £1 million in any one tax year.
- Note that dividends received from an EIS investment are taxable in the normal way.

Test your understanding 4

Tom is not an employee of A Ltd and does not currently own any shares in A Ltd. Tom subscribes for 10,000 new ordinary shares in A Ltd (a 1% interest) for £30,000 on 30 June 2016.

A Ltd is an unquoted trading company set up 4 years ago.

Tom's income tax liability in 2016/17 is £14,000.

Show the amount of EIS relief allowable for 2016/17, assuming Tom does not wish to carry back the relief to 2015/16.

Capital gains tax

- Capital gains on the disposal of shares in qualifying companies are exempt provided the shares have been held for **three years**, but capital losses are allowable.
- An election can be made for capital losses to be relieved against total income in the same way as trading losses (see Chapter 8).
- It is also possible to obtain EIS reinvestment relief in respect of EIS shares, which defers the gain where the proceeds from the disposal of an asset are reinvested (see Chapter 9).
- Although the CGT on the disposal is only deferred, the initial relief is effectively 40% or 50% (30% income tax on the EIS investment, and 10% or 20% CGT deferred).

Inheritance tax

- Shares in an EIS scheme qualify for business property relief (BPR) as they are unquoted shares, provided they have been owned for two years. (see Chapter 12).

11 The Seed enterprise investment scheme (SEIS)

This scheme, similar to EIS, is designed to encourage investment in smaller start-up companies.

To qualify for the scheme:

- the **investor** must:
  - subscribe, in cash, for new ordinary shares in a qualifying company
  - **not** be a current **employee** (but can be a director or previous employee)
  - have an **interest of 30% or less** in the company's OSC
- the **company**, at the date the shares are issued, must:
  - be an **unquoted trading company** with a permanent establishment in the UK
  - be carrying on a qualifying trade that is less than two years old, or it is preparing to carry on a qualifying trade
  - have no excluded activities (as for the EIS scheme)
  - be in sound financial health
  - have **fewer than 25 full-time employees**
  - have **gross assets** of **£200,000 or less**
  - not previously have used the EIS or VCT schemes

- the funds must be used:
  - within three years of the issue of the shares
  - for the purposes of the qualifying trade
  - with the intention to grow and develop the business
- A company cannot raise more than **£150,000 of investment** through the SEIS scheme in any **three year period**.

Tax consequences

Income tax

The reliefs available for the investor are as follows:

- **Income tax relief = 50% × (cost of the shares subscribed for)**
  - Maximum investment = **£100,000 per tax year**
  - Therefore maximum tax reducer = £50,000
  - **Deduct from** the individual's **income tax liability**
  - Can reduce liability to £Nil, but cannot create a tax repayment.
- An investor may elect to carry back the amount invested to a previous year, but cannot get relief on more than £100,000 in any one tax year.

Capital gains tax

- Like the EIS scheme:
  - **gains** on shares held for at least **three years** will be **exempt,** and
  - an election can be made for capital losses to be relieved against total income in the same way as trading losses (see Chapter 8).
- It is possible to obtain SEIS reinvestment relief in respect of SEIS shares, which exempts some of the gain where the proceeds from the disposal of any asset are reinvested (see Chapter 9).

Inheritance tax

- Shares in an SEIS scheme qualify for business property relief as they are unquoted shares, provided they have been owned for two years. (see Chapter 12).

Test your understanding 5

Imran subscribes for qualifying SEIS shares costing £60,000 in 2016/17 and has an income tax liability of £37,000.

Show the SEIS relief available for the tax year 2016/17 assuming Imran does not wish to carry back the relief to 2015/16.

12 Venture capital trusts

Relief for investment in venture capital trusts (VCTs) was introduced to encourage individuals to provide capital for unquoted trading companies.

The VCT buys shares in EIS companies and so an individual is able to invest in a **spread** of unquoted companies, thus reducing their risk.

Qualifying conditions for a VCT

The qualifying conditions for a VCT are similar to the conditions for the EIS. The key rules are given in expandable text.

Venture capital trust

- A VCT has to be quoted on a recognised stock exchange in the EEA.
- At least **70%** of the investments of a VCT have to be in unquoted trading companies, with not more than **15%** in any one company.
- At least **70%** of this investment must be in the form of new ordinary shares (as opposed to shares that carry preferential rights).
- The **unquoted trading companies** that are invested in must:
  - have a permanent establishment in the UK
    - include companies quoted on the AIM
    - include an **effective 90% interest** trading subsidiary (i.e. through an indirect interest)
  - be less than 7 years old when first using the scheme or has raised qualifying funds in its first 7 years
  - not be carrying on an excluded activity (as defined for EIS)
  - be in sound financial health

  - have **250 or less full-time employees** at the time the investment is made
  - have **gross assets** of:
    - **less than £15 million** before the share issue, and
    - no more than **£16 million** after the issue.
- the **maximum investment** that can be raised by a VCT:
  - **£5 million in any 12 month period**, and
  - **£12 million lifetime total** (from EIS, Seed EIS and VCT schemes).

Tax consequences

Income tax

- **Income tax relief = 30% × (cost of the shares subscribed for)**
  - Maximum investment = **£200,000 per tax year**
  - Therefore maximum tax reducer = £60,000
  - **Deduct from** the individual's **income tax liability**
  - Can reduce liability to £Nil, but cannot create a tax repayment.
- No carry back facility.
- **Dividend** income from a VCT = **exempt** from income tax for investments up to £200,000 p.a.

Capital gains tax

- Capital gains on the disposal of shares in a VCT are exempt for investments of up to £200,000 p.a.
- No relief for capital losses.
- No deferral relief available.

Inheritance tax

- Shares in a VCT do **not** qualify for business property relief.

Comparison of VCT, EIS and SEIS

<table>
<tr><th></th><th>Enterprise investment scheme
(EIS)</th><th>SEED EIS
(SEIS)</th><th>Venture capital trust
(VCT)</th></tr>
<tr><td>Level of risk</td><td colspan="2">• High
• Only one company invested in</td><td>• Not as high
• Risk spread over a number of investments</td></tr>
<tr><td rowspan="2">Qualifying individual</td><td colspan="2">• Subscribes in cash
• New ordinary shares
• Qualifying company
• Owns ≤ 30% of ordinary share capital</td><td rowspan="2">• Subscribes in cash
• Newly issued shares</td></tr>
<tr><td>• Not employee or director
• Independent of company prior to first issue</td><td>• Not current employee
(can be director or previous employee)</td></tr>
<tr><td rowspan="2">Qualifying company / VCT</td><td colspan="2">• Unquoted trading company
• Have permanent establishment in UK</td><td rowspan="2">• VCT must be quoted on a stock exchange in EEA
• Qualifying investments
= in EIS qualifying companies
• Approved by HMRC</td></tr>
<tr><td>• Carrying on a trade ≤ 7 years old when first use scheme
• Full time employees ≤ 250
• Gross assets
≤ £15m before, and
≤ £16m after subscription</td><td>• Carrying on a trade < 2 years old, or preparing to carry on a trade when first use scheme
• Full time employees < 25
• Gross assets
≤ £200,000 before subscription
• Not previously used EIS or VCT</td></tr>
<tr><td rowspan="2">Funds used</td><td>• Within 2 years of issue of shares</td><td>• Within 3 years of issue of shares</td><td>• Within 2 years of issue of shares</td></tr>
<tr><td colspan="3">• For purposes of qualifying trade
• With the intention to grow and develop the business
• Cannot be used to purchase another existing company or trade</td></tr>
</table>

	Enterprise investment scheme (EIS)	SEED EIS (SEIS)	Venture capital trust (VCT)
Max funds company can raise	• £5 million in any 12 months • £12 million lifetime total	• £150,000 in any 3 year period	• £5 million in any 12 months • £12 million lifetime total
Max investment by individual	• £1 million p.a.	• £100,000 p.a.	• £200,000 p.a.
Retention period for IT relief	• IT relief withdrawn if sold within 3 years		• IT relief withdrawn if sold within 5 years
IT relief: deduct from IT liability	30% of amount subscribed	50% of amount subscribed	30% of amount subscribed
Carry back amount to previous year	• Any amount invested • no relief on an investment of > £1 million in any one tax year	• Any amount invested • no relief on an investment of > £100,000 in any one tax year	• No carry back
Dividend income	• Taxable		• Exempt
CGT on disposal	• Gain – exempt if held > 3 years • Loss – allowable – can elect to convert into an IT loss		• No gain or loss • regardless of when sold
CGT deferral relief (see Chapter 9)	• Gain on any chargeable asset deferred if proceeds reinvested in EIS shares • Gain crystallises when EIS shares disposed of	• Up to max of 50% of the gain on any chargeable asset = exempt • Relief withdrawn if SEIS shares sold within 3 years	• No relief
IHT – BPR	• 100% if owned ≥ 2 years		• No BPR

Withdrawal of tax relief

- The income tax relief is withdrawn if the shares are not held for a minimum period of three years for EIS and SEIS, and five years for VCT.
- If the investor sells the shares within three years for EIS and SEIS and five years for VCT they must repay the income tax relief given to HMRC as follows:

	Not at arm's length	**At arm's length**
IT relief withdrawn (i.e. amount of IT that becomes payable)	**All** original IT relief given	Lower of: • original IT relief given • (% relief × SP received for shares)

For the SEIS scheme, if the disposal within three years is:

	Not at arm's length	**At arm's length**
CGT relief withdrawn (i.e. previously exempted gain that becomes chargeable) (Chapter 9)	**All** of the gain previously exempted	• A proportion of the gain previously exempted • Proportion $= \frac{\text{Amount of IT relief withdrawn (above)}}{\text{Original IT relief given}}$

An example covering both the income tax and CGT consequences of a withdrawal of the relief is given in Chapter 9.

13 Comprehensive example

Test your understanding 6

Matthew has the following investment income in addition to a salary of £90,000:

- Dividends from VCT investment of £3,000
- Dividend from REIT of £4,992
- Dividend from IIP trust of £2,205
- Discretionary trust income of £3,300

Both trusts comprised quoted shares only. He also invested £50,000 in a qualifying EIS scheme during the tax year.

He also sold 11% £10,000 Government stock on 31 May 2016 which he originally acquired on 1 July 2015. Interest is payable on 31 December and 30 June each year and the proceeds were £12,000.

He has paid private pension contributions during the period of £13,260.

Calculate the income tax liability for the tax year 2016/17.

14 Chapter summary

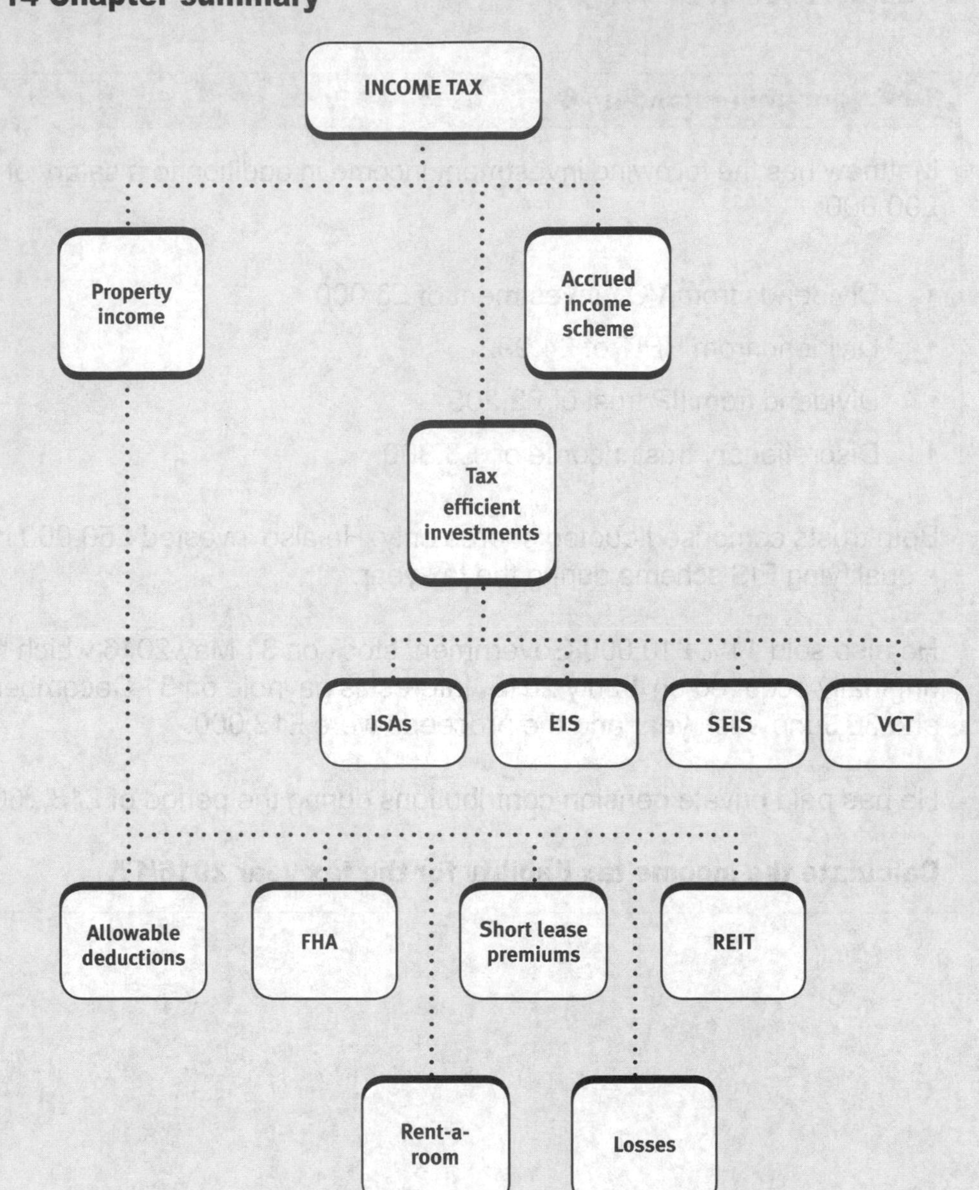

Test your understanding answers

Test your understanding 1

Giles

Property business profit – 2016/17

	£
Rent accrued	3,600
Expenses:	
Irrecoverable debt – June 2016 rent (1/12 × £3,600)	(300)
Insurance (3/12 × £420 + 9/12 × £480)	(465)
Replacement freezer	(380)
Redecoration	(750)
Property income	1,705

Notes:

(1) The new garage is classified as capital and is not deductible for property income purposes. It will be added to the cost of the property when calculating any gain on the disposal.

(2) Replacement furniture relief is available for the cost of the replacement freezer.

Test your understanding 2

Rodney

	£	£
21 year lease:		
Premium	10,500	
Less: £10,500 × 2% × (21 – 1)	(4,200)	
		6,300
14 year lease:		
Premium	30,000	
Less: £30,000 × 2% × (14 – 1)	(7,800)	
		22,200
Property income		28,500

Alternative calculation

	£
21 year lease:	
[(51 – 21)/50] × £10,500	6,300
14 year lease:	
[(51 – 14)/50] × £30,000	22,200
Property income	28,500

Test your understanding 3

John Wiles

(i) **House 1**

It is likely that House 1 will be regarded as a furnished holiday accommodation (FHA) as it meets the following conditions:

- Situated in the UK or EEA, furnished and let on a commercial basis
- Available for letting to the public for not less than 210 days in 2016/17
- Actually let at least 105 days in that 210 day period
- It is not clear how long each person occupied the house for. However, in 2016/17, assuming there were no single lettings of > 31 days, the house will be a FHA.

Advantages of the house being FHA

- Capital allowances will be available on plant and machinery, such as furniture and kitchen equipment. The annual investment allowance (AIA) of 100% is available (see Chapter 17). This will be more beneficial than replacement furniture relief.
- The FHA income will qualify as earnings for pension purposes
- On disposal, the house will qualify for entrepreneurs' relief, ROR or gift relief if the conditions for the reliefs are met.

(ii) **UK property income/loss – 2016/17**

FHA		£
Rent receivable (House 1) (16 × £200)		3,200
Less: Allowable expenses		
Council tax (£730 × 42/52)		(590)
Insurance (£310 × 42/52)		(250)
Advertising		(545)
AIA (£5,200 × 42/52)		(4,200)
FHA loss (Note 1)		(2,385)
Other property income		£
Rent receivable (House 2) (£8,600 × 3/12)		2,150
Lease premium (W)		3,760
Less: Allowable expenses		
Repairs		(7,465)
		(1,555)
Rent from furnished room	7,850	
Less: Rent-a-room relief	(7,500)	
		350
Property loss (Note 2)		(1,205)

Working: Lease premium

£4,000 × [(51 – 4)/50] = £3,760

Notes:

(1) The loss incurred in letting the FHA must be carried forward and offset against the first available future UK FHA income.

(2) The net loss incurred in letting House 2 and the furnished room in John's main residence must be carried forward and offset against the first available future property income.

Test your understanding 4

Tom

Tom can reduce his income tax in the tax year in which he buys the EIS shares by 30% of the amount invested.

	£
Income tax liability	14,000
Less: EIS relief (30% × £30,000)	(9,000)
	5,000

Tom must repay the income tax saving to HMRC if he sells the shares within **three** years.

Test your understanding 5

Imran

Imran can reduce his income tax for 2016/17 by 50% of the amount invested.

	£
Income tax liability	37,000
Less: SEIS relief (50% × £60,000)	(30,000)
	7,000

Imran must repay the income tax saving to HMRC if he sells the shares within **three** years.

Test your understanding 6

Matthew

Income tax computation – 2016/17

	£
Employment income	90,000
Accrued income (W1)	458
Income from REIT (£4,992 × 100/80)	6,240
Discretionary trust income (£3,300 × 100/55)	6,000
IIP trust income (£2,205 × 100/92.5) (dividends)	2,384
VCT dividends – exempt	0
Total income = Net income	105,082
Less: PA (W2)	(11,000)
Taxable income	94,082

Analysis of income

Dividends	**Savings**	**Non-savings income**
£2,384	£458	(£94,082 – £458 – £2,384) = £91,240

Income tax:

£		£
48,575	× 20% (Non-savings income) (W3)	9,715
42,665	× 40% (Non-savings income)	17,066
91,240		
458	× 0% (SNRB)	0
2,384	× 0% (DNRB)	0
94,082		26,781
Less: EIS relief (£50,000 × 30%)		(15,000)
Income tax liability		11,781

Workings

(W1) **Accrued interest**

The selling price includes interest accrued from 1.1.2016 to 31.5.2016 = 5 months.

Accrued interest = (£10,000 × 11% × 5/12) = £458.

(W2) **Personal allowance**

As Matthew's net income is greater than £100,000, his personal allowance may be reduced.

However, the net income is reduced by the gross pension contribution of £16,575 (£13,260 × 100/80) to give adjusted net income of £88,507 (£105,082 – £16,575).

Therefore the full PA is available.

(W3) **Extended basic rate band**

Matthew's basic rate band is extended by the gross pension contribution of £16,575.

Extended basic rate band = £48,575 (£32,000 + £16,575).

chapter

4

Pensions

Chapter learning objectives

Upon completion of this chapter you will be able to:

- explain the different types of pension schemes that can be registered with HM Revenue & Customs (HMRC)
- explain the basis for calculating the maximum annual contributions to a registered pension scheme for an individual
- calculate the tax relief available for pension contributions
- explain the concept of the lifetime allowance and the implications of the allowance being exceeded.

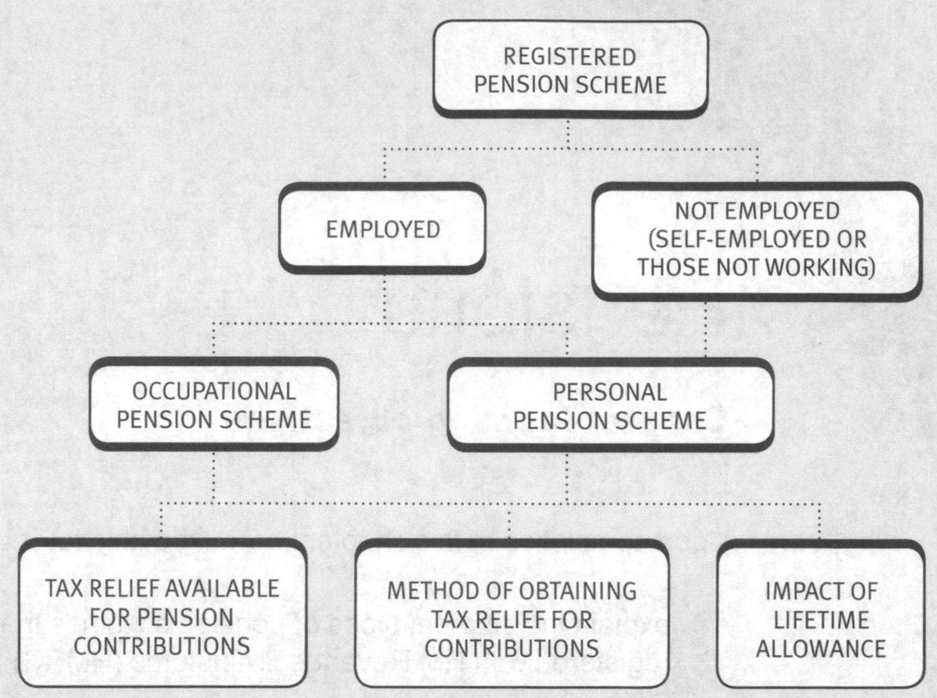

Introduction

This chapter is a revision of the tax consequences of investing in a registered pension scheme covered in F6.

A brief reminder of F6 content is given in expandable text and revision examples are provided to check your retention of the required F6 knowledge.

The main new topics introduced are the spreading of employer contributions, prohibited assets and benefits received on retirement and on death.

1 Registered pension schemes

An individual can set up an investment of funds to provide an income during their retirement in a tax efficient way by making payments into a registered pension scheme.

A pension scheme is a savings plan for retirement that enjoys special tax privileges, but only if the scheme is registered with HMRC.

Investing in a registered pension scheme is a long-term investment and is very tax efficient for the following reasons:

- The individual obtains tax relief on the contributions made into the scheme.
- Where an employer contributes into the scheme, tax relief for the employer contributions is available with no taxable benefit for the employee.
- Registered pension scheme funds can grow tax-free as the scheme is exempt from income tax and capital gains tax.
- On retirement, part of the funds can be withdrawn as a tax-free lump sum.

Types of registered pension schemes

The two main types of registered pension scheme available are:

- occupational pension schemes – applicable to employees only
- personal pension schemes – applicable to all individuals.

A reminder of the types of registered pension schemes is given in expandable text and is summarised in the diagram in section 3.

Occupational pension schemes

An occupational pension scheme is a scheme set up by an employer for the benefit of its employees.

An employer may use an insurance company to provide a pension scheme for its employees, or it may set up its own self administered pension fund.

Employees may:

- be automatically enrolled depending on the size of the employer
- choose not to join the employer's scheme and set up a personal pension plan, or
- contribute into both the employer's occupational scheme and set up a personal pension scheme.

Contributions into occupational schemes may be made by the employer, and the employee.

Registered occupational pension schemes may be 'defined benefit' or 'money purchase' schemes.

Under a defined benefit scheme the benefits obtained on retirement are linked to the level of earnings of the employee.

Under a money purchase scheme (also known as 'defined contribution' scheme) the benefits obtained depend upon the performance of the investments held by the pension fund.

Personal pension schemes

Personal pension schemes can be established by **any** individual including those not working (including children).

Contributions into personal pension schemes may be made by:

- the individual, and
- any third party on behalf of the individual e.g. the employer, a spouse, parent or grandparents.

Personal pension schemes are usually 'money purchase' schemes administered by financial institutions on behalf of the individual.

Overview of the tax relief rules for registered pension schemes

- The **amount** of tax relief available for pension contributions is the same regardless of whether the scheme is an occupational or personal pension scheme.
- The **method** of obtaining tax relief for the contributions is different depending on the scheme.
- Once the funds are invested in the scheme, **all** registered pension schemes are governed by the same rules.

2 Tax relief for pension contributions

A reminder of the maximum annual contributions eligible for tax relief is given in expandable text and is summarised in the diagram in section 3.

Relief for contributions made by individuals

Tax relief is available for pension contributions if:

- the pension scheme is a registered scheme, and
- the individual is resident in the UK and aged under 75.

Regardless of the level of earnings, an individual may make pension contributions of **any amount** into:

- a pension scheme, or
- a number of different pension schemes.

However, tax relief is only available for a **maximum annual amount** each tax year.

The total maximum annual gross contribution for which an individual can obtain tax relief is the **higher** of

- £3,600, and
- 100% of the individual's 'relevant earnings', chargeable to income tax in the tax year.

Relevant earnings includes trading profits, employment income, and furnished holiday accommodation income but not investment income.

Note that:

- The maximum limit applies to the total gross contributions made into all schemes where:
  - An employee contributes to both an occupational and a personal pension scheme, or
  - An individual contributes into more than one personal pension scheme.
- An individual with no relevant earnings can obtain tax relief on gross contributions of up to £3,600 p.a.

3 The method of obtaining tax relief for pension contributions

The method of obtaining tax relief for pension contributions is different depending on the type of pension scheme.

A reminder of the method of obtaining relief for pension contributions is given in expandable text and is summarised in the diagram in section 3.

Relief for contributions made by an individual

Personal pension contributions

The method of obtaining tax relief for contributions into a personal pension scheme (PPCs) is the same whether they are made by an employee, a self-employed individual or an individual who is not working.

Relief is given as follows:

- For a basic rate taxpayer, basic rate tax relief is automatically given by deduction at source when contributions are paid, as payments are made to the pension fund net of 20% tax. The payment is ignored in the IT computation.
- For higher rate and additional rate taxpayers, 40% or 45% tax relief is given as follows:
  - 20% at source.
  - 20% or 25% through the income tax computation, obtained by extending the basic rate and higher rate bands by the gross payment (so that more income is taxed at 20% and less at 40% or 45%).

Occupational pension scheme contributions

Where employees make pension contributions into an occupational pension scheme:

- payments are made gross, and
- tax relief is given through the PAYE system by reducing the earnings subject to tax (i.e. the payment is an allowable deduction from employment income).

Test your understanding 1

The following individuals made gross pension contributions into a personal pension scheme in the tax year 2016/17 and had the following trading profits:

	Pension contributions (gross)	Trading profits
	£	£
Cindy	25,000	20,000
Don	40,000	85,000

Explain how tax relief for the pension contributions will be given in the tax year 2016/17 for each individual and calculate the income tax liability of Don for 2016/17.

Test your understanding 2

Henry is employed by Lloyd Ltd on a salary of £80,000 p.a. He is a member of the company's occupational pension scheme.

Henry pays 3% of his salary into the scheme each year. He has no other income.

Calculate Henry's income tax liability for the tax year 2016/17, showing how tax relief is obtained for his pension contributions.

Relief for contributions by employers

Contributions paid by an employer into a registered pension scheme are:

- tax deductible in calculating the employer's taxable trading profits, provided the contributions are paid for the purposes of the trade, and
- an exempt employment benefit for the employee, and
- added to the pension contributions paid by the employee on which tax relief is given to determine whether the annual allowance has been exceeded and an income tax charge levied.

The deduction against the employer's trading profits is given in the accounting period in which the contribution is **paid**; the accounting treatment is not followed.

Example 1 – Relief for contributions

Hugh is a self-employed builder who prepares accounts to 30 September each year. His recent tax adjusted trading profits have been:

Year ended 30 September 2015	£80,000
Year ended 30 September 2016	£90,000

Hugh's wife, Holly, has employment income from a part-time job of £13,500 p.a. and property income of £20,000 p.a.

They also have a joint bank account on which they earned interest of £5,000 in the tax year 2016/17.

During the year to 5 April 2017, Hugh paid £19,400 into his registered personal pension scheme. Holly paid £2,600 into her employer's registered occupational pension scheme and Holly's employer contributed a further £2,000.

Calculate how much of the pension contributions made by Hugh, Holly and Holly's employer in the tax year 2016/17 will obtain tax relief and explain how the tax relief will be obtained.

Solution

Hugh

- Hugh can obtain tax relief for a pension contribution of up to a maximum of 100% of his earnings in 2016/17.
- His earnings are his assessable trading profits for 2016/17 = £90,000 (year ended 30 September 2016).
- Investment income such as bank interest is not included.
- Hugh will have paid the pension contribution net of basic rate tax of £4,850 (£19,400 × 20/80).
- The gross pension contribution is £24,250 (£19,400 × 100/80).
- Higher rate tax relief is obtained by extending the basic rate band by £24,250 from £32,000 to £56,250.

Holly

- Holly can obtain tax relief for a gross pension contribution of up to a maximum of the higher of £3,600 or 100% of her employment earnings in 2016/17 (i.e. £13,500).
- Her gross pension contribution of £2,600 is less than £13,500, therefore she can obtain tax relief for all £2,600 contributions paid.
- Holly's employer will deduct the gross contribution of £2,600 from her employment income before calculating her income tax liability under PAYE.
- Holly's employer's contribution of £2,000 is an exempt benefit.

Holly's employer

- Holly's employer will obtain tax relief for all of the £2,000 contribution made into the occupational pension scheme.
- Relief is given as an allowable deduction in the calculation of the employer's taxable trading profits.

Contributions in excess of annual allowance

There is no limit on the amount of contributions that may be made into pension schemes by an individual, his employer or any other party.

However, tax relief for pension contributions made by an individual is restricted to the maximum annual amount.

A tax charge is levied on the individual if the total of all contributions (by the individual, their employer and third parties) on which relief has been obtained exceeds the **annual allowance** (AA).

The AA for the tax year 2016/17 is £40,000.

- This can be increased by **bringing forward** any unused annual allowances from the **previous three tax years**.

  The AA for 2014/15 and 2015/16 was also £40,000. However, for tax years up to and including 2013/14, the AA was £50,000.

- An unused amount can only be carried forward if the individual was a member of a registered pension scheme for that tax year, otherwise it is lost.
- The AA for the **current year is used first**, then the unused AA from earlier years **starting with the earliest tax year** (i.e. on a FIFO basis).

- The AA figures for the tax year 2016/17 and the three prior years are given in the tax tables provided in the examination.

Test your understanding 3

Steve and Mike made gross personal pension contributions as follows:

	Steve	**Mike**
	£	£
2013/14	52,000	0
2014/15	35,000	5,000
2015/16	17,000	6,000

Steve has been a member of a registered pension scheme since the tax year 2007/08. Mike joined a registered pension scheme in the tax year 2014/15. Both have relevant earnings of £200,000 per annum.

State the maximum gross contribution that Steve and Mike could make in the tax year 2016/17 without incurring an annual allowance charge.

Test your understanding 4

Ahmed made the following gross contributions to his personal pension:

	£
2013/14	22,000
2014/15	36,000
2015/16	33,000
2016/17	58,000

He has relevant earnings of £200,000 each year.

State the amount of unused allowances to carry forward to the tax year 2017/18.

Calculation of annual allowance charge

Where the total of all contributions on which relief has been obtained exceeds the AA (including brought forward annual allowances) there is a tax charge on the excess.

The tax charge is calculated as if the excess is the individual's top slice of income (i.e. taxed last after all sources of income, including dividends) but is taxed at non-savings income rates.

The excess is therefore taxed at 20/40/45% and added to the individual's total tax liability, and is either paid through the self-assessment system or, in some cases, may be taken from the individual's pension fund.

Test your understanding 5

Marcus has been employed for many years and set up his personal pension scheme ten years ago.

In the tax year 2016/17 Marcus earned £100,000 and made a gross contribution of £50,000 into his personal pension scheme in 2016/17.

Marcus has regularly contributed £50,000 (gross) to his pension since the tax year 2005/06.

His employer contributed a further £30,000 into his personal pension scheme in the tax year 2016/17.

Calculate Marcus' income tax liability for the tax year 2016/17.

Restriction of annual allowance – high income individuals

- The annual allowance is gradually reduced for individuals with high income.
- The restriction applies to individuals with a 'threshold income' exceeding £110,000 and 'adjusted income' exceeding £150,000.
- The annual allowance is reduced by:
  (Adjusted income – £150,000) × 50%

- If necessary, the reduction is rounded down to the nearest pound (although in the examination rounding up or down is acceptable).
- The maximum reduction to the annual allowance is £30,000, which means that the minimum annual allowance an individual will be entitled to is £10,000.

Note that the definitions of the key terms 'threshold income' and 'adjusted income' are complicated in practice, but for P6 purposes can be simplified as shown below.

Approach to questions

- Calculate 'threshold income' as follows:

	£
Net income (from the income tax computation)	X
Less: Individual's **gross personal pension** contributions	(X)
Threshold income	X

- If threshold income exceeds £110,000, calculate the individual's adjusted income as follows:

	£
Net income (from the income tax computation)	X
Plus: Individual **employee's occupational pension** contributions	X
Employer's contributions into any scheme for that individual	X
Adjusted income	X

If threshold income ≤ £110,000	The annual allowance for the tax year is £40,000 (no restriction).
If threshold income > £110,000 and adjusted income ≤ £150,000:	
If threshold income is > £110,000 and adjusted income > £150,000:	The annual allowance for the tax year must be reduced by (adjusted income – £150,000) × 50%

- Note that if the individual's adjusted income is £210,000 and a restriction is necessary, the annual allowance will be reduced to the minimum of £10,000.

Note that the term 'adjusted income' for pension purposes is not the same as 'adjusted net income' for the purposes of restricting the personal allowance. For the 'adjusted income' figure, there is no deduction for gross gift aid donations nor the individual's gross personal pension contributions, and the employers pension contributions need to be added to net income.

However, as the adjustments to net income to calculate adjusted income all relate to employment, for the purposes of the P6 exam, adjusted income for self-employed individuals will be the same as net income.

Test your understanding 6 – Annual allowance for high income

The following are details of pension contributions made by, and on behalf of, four individuals during the tax year 2016/17:

	Gross contributions made by the individual		Employer's contributions	Net income
	Occupational pension	Personal pension		
	£	£	£	£
Ann	11,000	23,000	20,000	120,000
Belinda	0	2,000	0	125,000
Carol	12,000	0	20,000	160,000
David	20,000	0	28,000	165,000

Calculate the annual allowance for the tax year 2016/17 for each individual assuming they have no unused allowances brought forward.

Spreading of employer contributions

Where there is an increase in the level of employer contributions from one period to the next of over 210%, HMRC require the tax relief to be spread evenly over a number of years.

Spreading provisions

The first 110% is relievable in the current year. The excess is dealt with as follows:

Excess (over 110% of previous year)	**Tax relief obtained**
Less than £500,000	All in current year
Between £500,000 and £1,000,000	Spread evenly over 2 years
Between £1,000,000 and £2,000,000	Spread evenly over 3 years
£2,000,000 or more	Spread evenly over 4 years

Additional contributions for existing pensioners are deductible when made.

Summary

PENSION CONTRIBUTIONS
Paid by the individual
Paid by the employer
Tax relief available each tax year on contributions up to lower of:
• Gross contributions paid
• Maximum annual amount = the higher of:
– £3,600, and
– 100% of the individual's relevant earnings (e.g. employment income, trading income and/or FHA)
Tax relief on amount paid
PERSONAL PENSION SCHEME
OCCUPATIONAL PENSION SCHEME
Occupational pension scheme or personal pension scheme
Paid net of 20% income tax
Paid gross
Paid gross
• Basic rate relief (20%) given at source
• Higher rate and additional rate relief given by extending the basic rate and higher rate band thresholds by the gross contributions paid.
• Tax relief given via PAYE as an allowable deduction against employment income
• Tax relief to employer = an allowable deduction in calculating taxable trading profits
• An exempt benefit.
If total pension inputs › annual allowance:
= income tax charge on individual
• Annual allowance £40,000 for 2016/17
• Include annual allowance charge as 'non-savings income'
• but does not affect ANI
• Unused allowance can be c/f 3 tax years
• Annual allowance = £40,000 for 2015/16 and 2014/15 and £50,000 for years prior to 2014/15

4 Accessing the pension

Benefits on retirement

The funds in the pension scheme cannot be accessed by the individual until they reach pension age. Each pension scheme will have its own scheme rules regarding when an individual can access the scheme funds.

However, the minimum pension age can never be below 55.

For individuals in **defined benefit schemes** (principally occupational pension schemes) the benefits on reaching pension age are **linked to the level of earnings** of the employee.

For individuals in **money purchase schemes** (principally personal pension schemes) the benefits on pension age are **dependent on the amount of funds accumulated** in the pension fund (i.e. contributions plus investment income/gains).

Following recent changes to the pension rules, individuals with money purchase schemes now have complete flexibility in the way in which they can access the accumulated funds in their pension scheme when they reach pension age.

All or part of the pension fund can be taken to provide a pension at any time above this pension age.

It is therefore possible to receive a pension and still continue to work.

On reaching pension age, the individual may:

(i) receive a tax free lump sum payment

Maximum = 25% of the lower of

- the value of the fund
- the lifetime allowance (see below)

(ii) withdraw the balance of the pension fund at any time.

The part of the fund not withdrawn can continue to grow in a relatively tax-free environment.

Any withdrawals from the balance of the fund are treated as taxable income and are liable to income tax at the normal rates of tax (i.e. 20%, 40% or 45%).

The part of the fund not withdrawn can continue to grow in a relatively tax-free environment.

The lifetime allowance charge

There is no restriction on the **total** contributions that an individual can make into a registered pension scheme. However, if the funds in the scheme exceed the lifetime allowance when a benefit is taken there will be a tax charge on the excess.

The lifetime allowance for the tax year 2016/17 is £1 million.

If the fund exceeds £1 million and the excess is to be used to fund a larger annuity the tax charge will be 25% of the excess.

Where the taxpayer chooses to take the excess in cash the tax charge will be 55% of the excess.

Benefits on death

On the death of the individual, the pension scheme may provide:

- a pension income, and/or
- lump sums for dependants (e.g. spouse, civil partner, child under the age of 23 or other dependant).

Further tax charges may arise depending on:

- the individual's age
- their marginal rate of income tax
- whether the scheme is a money purchase or a defined benefit scheme
- whether any of the fund has already been utilised to provide benefits.

Summary

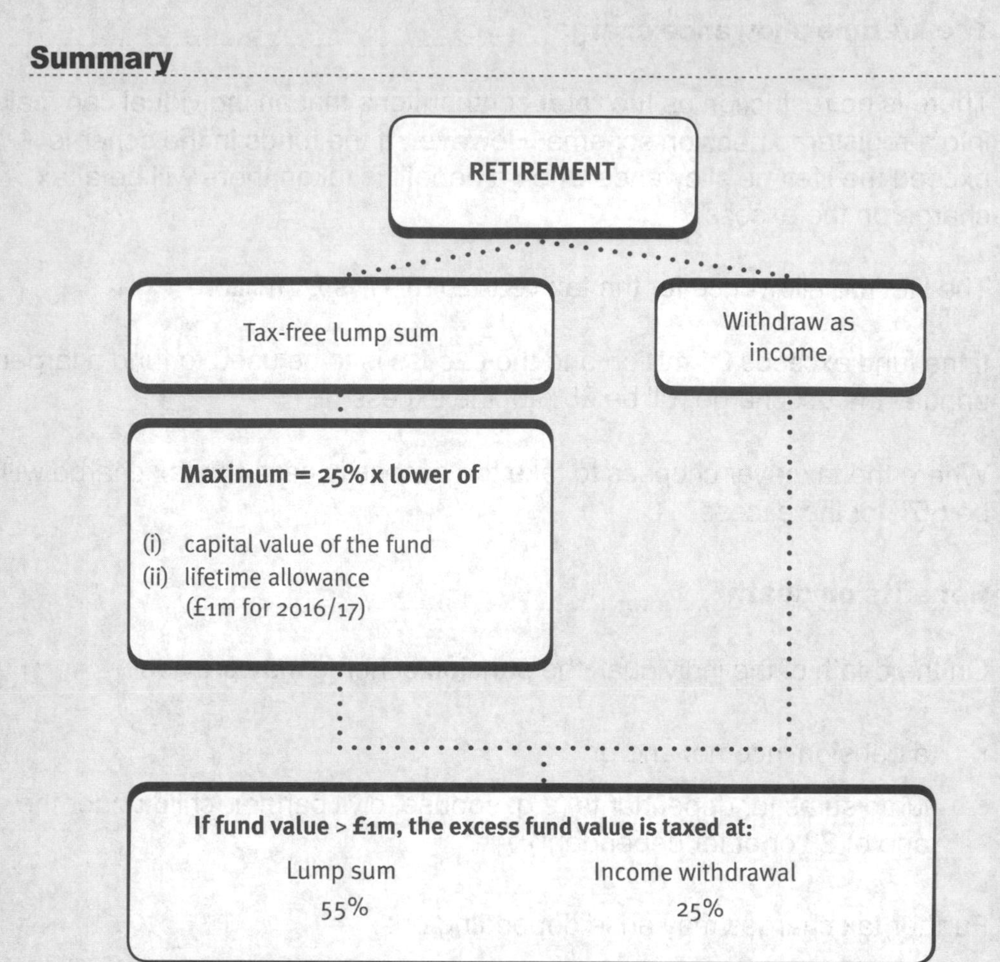
RETIREMENT
Tax-free lump sum
Withdraw as income
Maximum = 25% x lower of
(i) capital value of the fund
(ii) lifetime allowance (£1m for 2016/17)
If fund value > £1m, the excess fund value is taxed at:
Lump sum
55%
Income withdrawal
25%

5 Chapter summary

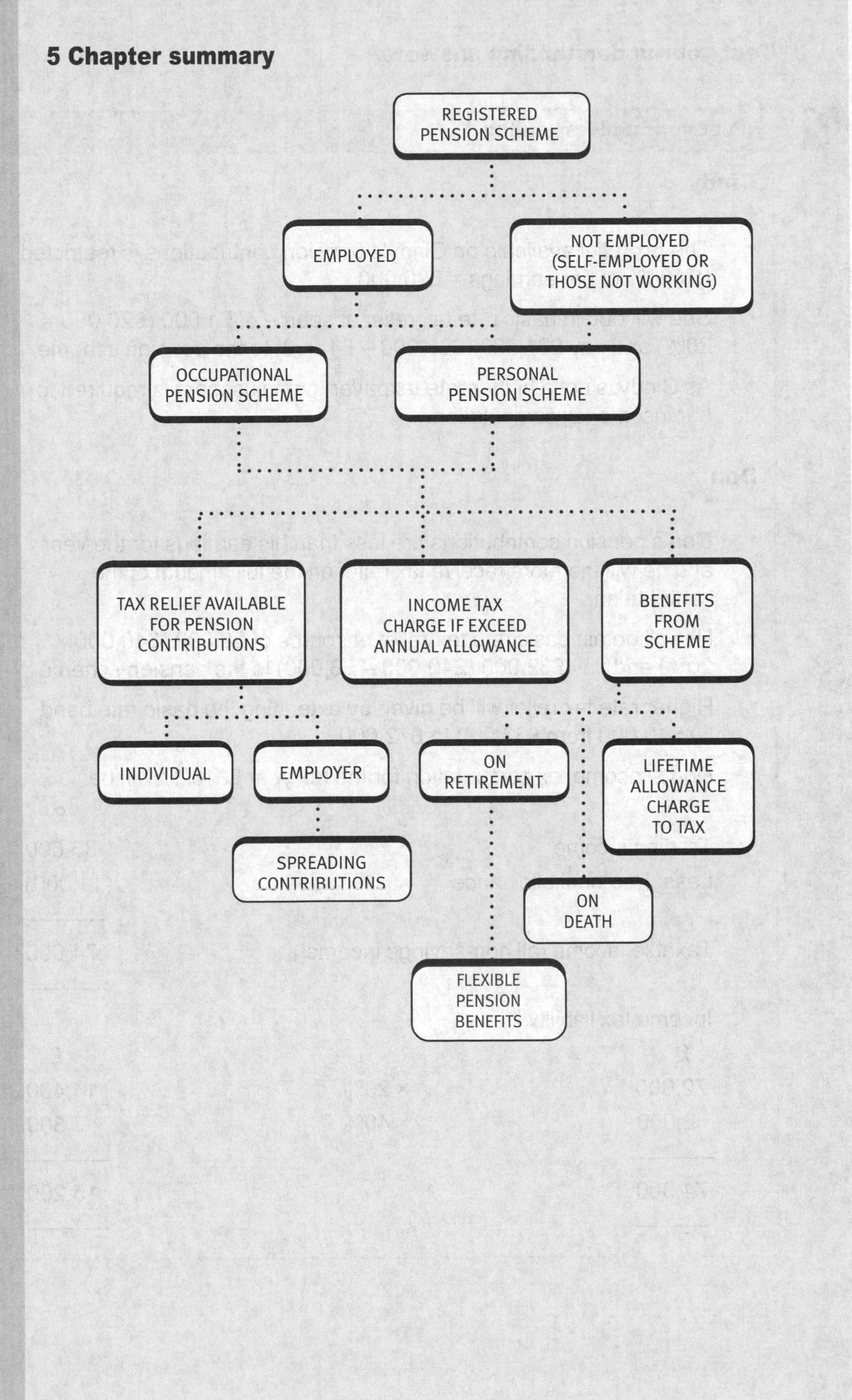

Test your understanding answers

Test your understanding 1

Cindy

- The tax relief available on Cindy's pension contributions is restricted to 100% of her earnings = £20,000.
- She will obtain basic rate tax relief at source of £4,000 (£20,000 × 20%) and pay £21,000 (£25,000 – £4,000) to the pension scheme.
- As Cindy is not a higher rate taxpayer, no adjustment is required to her income tax computation.

Don

- Don's pension contributions are less than his earnings for the year and he will therefore receive tax relief on the full amount of the contribution.
- He will obtain basic rate tax relief at source of £8,000 (£40,000 × 20%) and pay £32,000 (£40,000 – £8,000) to the pension scheme.
- Higher rate tax relief will be given by extending the basic rate band by £40,000 from £32,000 to £72,000.
- Don's income tax computation for the tax year 2016/17 will be:

	£
Trading income	85,000
Less: Personal allowance	(11,000)
Taxable income (all non-savings income')	74,000

Income tax liability

£		£
72,000	× 20%	14,400
2,000	× 40%	800
74,000		15,200

Test your understanding 2

Henry

Income tax computation – 2016/17

		£
Salary		80,000
Less: Employee's pension contributions (3%)		(2,400)
Employment income		77,600
Less: PA		(11,000)
Taxable income		66,600
Income tax:	£	£
Basic rate	32,000 × 20%	6,400
Higher rate	34,600 × 40%	13,840
	66,600	
Income tax liability		20,240

Note: The employer's contribution into his pension scheme is an exempt employment benefit and is therefore not taxable income for Henry.

Henry's occupational pension scheme contributions have reduced his taxable income by £2,400 and thus the amount of tax that he has paid at the 40% rate. He has therefore obtained tax relief at 40% for his pension contributions. Lloyd Ltd will deduct the £2,400 from the amount of taxable pay from which income tax is deducted through the PAYE system.

Test your understanding 3

Steve

	£
Unused allowances:	
2013/14 Contributions in excess of £50,000	0
2014/15 (£40,000 – £35,000)	5,000
2015/16 (£40,000 – £17,000)	23,000
Total unused allowances b/f	28,000
Add: Allowance for 2016/17	40,000
Maximum gross contribution for 2016/17 to avoid charge	68,000

Mike

	£
Unused allowances:	
2013/14 Not a member of registered pension scheme	N/A
2014/15 (£40,000 – £5,000)	35,000
2015/16 (£40,000 – £6,000)	34,000
Total unused allowances b/f	69,000
Add: Allowance for 2016/17	40,000
Maximum gross contribution for 2016/17 to avoid charge	109,000

Test your understanding 4

Ahmed

	Allowance available	Used 2016/17	c/f
	£	£	£
Allowance for 2016/17	40,000	(40,000)	0
Unused allowances b/f			
2013/14 (£50,000 – £22,000)	28,000	(18,000)	0
2014/15 (£40,000 – £36,000)	4,000		4,000
2015/16 (£40,000 – £33,000)	7,000		7,000
	79,000	(58,000)	
Unused allowances c/f to 2017/18			11,000

Note: The allowance for the current tax year must be used first, then the unused allowance b/f from the previous three years, starting with the earliest tax year.

The remaining allowance from 2013/14 of £10,000 (£28,000 – £18,000) cannot be c/f to 2017/18 as it is more than three years ago.

Test your understanding 5

Marcus

- Marcus can obtain tax relief for a gross pension contribution of up to a maximum of 100% of his earnings = £100,000 in the tax year 2016/17. Therefore relief will be available for the gross £50,000 paid.
- Marcus will have paid the pension contributions net of basic rate tax of £10,000 (£50,000 × 20%) and paid £40,000 (£50,000 × 80%) into the pension scheme.
- Higher rate relief is obtained by extending the basic rate band threshold by £50,000 from £32,000 to £82,000.
- Relief on £30,000 is given as an allowable deduction in computing the employer's taxable trading profits.
- The total gross contributions paid into the scheme in the tax year 2016/17 will be £80,000 (£50,000 + £30,000) which exceeds the annual allowance of £40,000.
- There is no annual allowance b/f as contributions of £50,000 in the previous three years were greater than the AA for each of those years.
- Marcus will therefore have an additional income tax liability in the tax year 2016/17 on £40,000 (£80,000 – £40,000).
- Marcus' income tax computation for 2016/17 will be:

	£
Employment income = net income	100,000
Less: PA (Note)	(11,000)
Taxable income	89,000

Income tax

	£		£
Extended basic rate band	82,000	× 20%	16,400
Higher rate band	7,000	× 40%	2,800
	89,000		
Annual allowance charge:			
Higher rate band	40,000	× 40%	16,000
	129,000		
Income tax liability			35,200

Note: There is a normal PA available as the ANI is £50,000 (£100,000 – £50,000)

Test your understanding 6 – Annual allowance for high income

Threshold income:

	Ann	Belinda	Carol	David
	£	£	£	£
Net income	120,000	125,000	160,000	165,000
Less: Individual's gross PPCs	(23,000)	(2,000)	(0)	(0)
Threshold income	97,000	123,000	160,000	165,000

Ann's threshold income is ≤ £110,000, therefore she will be entitled to the full AA in the tax year 2016/17.

For Belinda, Carol and David threshold income is > £110,000 and adjusted income needs to be calculated.

Adjusted income:

	Ann	Belinda	Carol	David
	£	£	£	£
Net income		125,000	160,000	165,000
Plus: Employee OPCs		0	12,000	20,000
Employer's contributions		0	20,000	28,000
Adjusted income	n/a	125,000	192,000	213,000

Belinda does not have any occupational pension contributions or employer contributions so net income = adjusted income. Her adjusted income is < £150,000 and therefore no restriction of the AA is required.

For Carol and David, it is necessary to restrict the AA as adjusted income is > £150,000.

Annual allowance for 2016/17:

	Ann	Belinda	Carol	David
	£	£	£	£
Annual allowance	40,000	40,000	40,000	40,000
Less: Reduction in allowance				
(192,000 – £150,000) × 50%			(21,000)	
(213,000 – £150,000) × 50% = £31,500 (restricted)				(30,000)
Revised annual allowance	40,000	40,000	19,000	10,000

chapter

5

Income tax planning

Chapter learning objectives

Upon completion of this chapter you will be able to:

- identify and advise on the types of tax efficient investments and other expenditure that will result in a reduction in income tax liabilities for an individual
- identify suitable tax planning measures in a given scenario to mitigate tax liabilities for an individual.

Introduction

This chapter is the first of a number of chapters contained in the text book aimed at introducing tax planning measures to minimise tax liabilities.

This chapter only considers personal income tax aspects but later you will be expected to consider multi-taxation scenarios from both a personal and business tax aspect.

The main areas to consider for income tax planning are:

- tax efficient types of income and expenditure
- allowances available
- tax efficient remuneration.

1 Mitigating income tax liabilities

Tax efficient income

As there are different forms of income the areas of consideration will vary, however some of the key aspects to consider are:

- the range of exempt sources of income, as outlined in Chapter 3
- the range of tax exempt benefits, as covered in Chapter 2
- the different tax rates on alternative sources of taxable income, as revised in Chapter 1.

Example 1 – Tax efficient income

Danka is a higher rate tax payer. She has recently inherited various investment assets with a projected annual income comprising:

£10,000 UK dividends from quoted and unquoted shares.

£5,000 building society interest.

She wishes to minimise her income tax liability through a consideration of alternative forms of similar investments.

Identify two suitable investments that will reduce Danka's future income tax liability.

Solution

As a higher rate taxpayer, Danka will be entitled to a £500 savings nil rate band (SNRB). All taxpayers are entitled to a £5,000 dividend nil rate band (DNRB). Danka's savings and dividend income exceeds these nil rate bands. Therefore she should consider investing assets generating income in excess of the nil rate bands in an ISA account.

An individual has the opportunity each tax year to invest in an ISA account. The maximum annual investment is £15,240 in stocks and shares or cash, in any combination.

All income, both dividend and interest, is tax free. Therefore, use of this facility each tax year could be recommended as it means the income will become tax free.

She could also consider using the venture capital trust scheme. This quoted investment provides both tax free dividends and income tax relief at a rate of 30% on investments up to £200,000 p.a.

Tax efficient expenditure

An individual can obtain tax relief on certain types of expenditure. The rate of the relief and the precise treatment of each varies in the income tax computation, but the key types are summarised below:

Type	Maximum tax relief	Treatment in IT computation	Details in:
Personal pension scheme	45%	For HR and AR payers only – extend BR and HR bands	Chapter 4
Occupational pension contributions	45%	Relief through PAYE	Chapter 4
Qualifying loan interest	45% on up to greater of: – £50,000 or – 25% of ATI	Deduct from total income	Chapter 1
EIS/SEIS	30%/50% on up to £1 million/ £100,000 investment	Tax reducer – deduct from IT liability	Chapter 1 and 3
VCT	30% on up to £200,000 investment	Tax reducer – deduct from IT liability	Chapter 1 and 3

2 Income tax planning scenarios

Earlier chapters have established the technical rules for computing income tax liabilities for an individual. This section considers some possible examination scenarios where you should consider basic income tax planning techniques.

Maximising use of allowances

Individuals should ensure they use their personal allowance and nil rate bands as fully as possible, for example:

- Increasing their non-savings income in order to fully utlilise their PA, if their savings and/or dividend income is going to be fully taxed at 0%. They could do this by withdrawing more from a pension scheme or generating more earned income or property income.
- Taking advantage of the savings and dividend nil rate bands if they have significant investment income.
- Shareholders of owner-managed businesses may wish to extract £5,000 of profits as dividends to take advantage of the dividend nil rate band. This will be more tax-efficient than extracting profits as further salary/bonus which would be subject to income tax and national insurance (see Chapter 26).

Married couples and civil partners

Married couples and civil partners should consider the following techniques:

- equalising income and maximising use of nil rate bands
- use tax-free investments
- maximising pension contributions.

Equalisation of income

Spouses are taxed separately. They may choose to own assets in sole ownership or jointly.

The income from jointly owned assets is taxed in equal shares. Where the underlying ownership of the asset is not equal an election can be made to apportion the income using the proportion in which the investment is owned, with the exception of joint bank accounts, which are always taxed 50:50.

In addition, married couples can transfer income-generating assets between them, at no tax cost, to minimise their joint tax liability.

In particular, married couples should aim to utilise where possible both individuals:

- Personal allowances
- Starting rate bands
- Savings and dividend nil rate bands
- Basic rate bands

If one spouse is a basic rate taxpayer and the other is a higher rate/additional rate taxpayer, the couple should aim to utilise the basic rate taxpayers savings nil rate band of £1,000, which will be higher than the nil rate band available to the higher rate (£500) or additional rate (£Nil) taxpayer.

The dividend nil rate band is £5,000 regardless of the amount of income an individual has. However, if one spouse has dividend income in excess of £5,000 they may wish to transfer some shares to their spouse to utilise their dividend nil rate band.

These rules and advice also apply to partners within a civil partnership.

It may also be possible to make a marriage allowance election to transfer a fixed amount of the personal allowance from one spouse/civil partner to the other (see Chapter 1).

It is important to recognise that the transfer of the interest in the asset to the spouse/civil partner must be a genuine gift to be effective for income tax purposes. There is no immediate CGT/IHT implication.

Example 2 – Equalisation of income

Kyria and Spence are a married couple. In the tax year 2016/17 Kyria had earned income of £2,000 and Spence £41,000.

They own a property in joint names but the cost was provided 80% by Spence and 20% by Kyria.

A declaration is in force to support the ownership percentage. The annual income from the property is £10,000.

In addition, they also have a joint investment bank account with a cash balance of £35,000 that earns interest of £800 gross per annum.

Calculate the taxable income for Kyria and Spence respectively and advise them of any income tax planning measures they should consider to reduce their liabilities for the future.

Solution

	Kyria	Spence
	£	£
Earned income	2,000	41,000
Investment income	400	400
Property income (20:80)	2,000	8,000
Total income	4,400	49,400
Less: PA (restricted)	(4,400)	(11,000)
Taxable income	0	38,400

Tax planning

Kyria has unused PA, and basic rate band, whilst Spence is a higher rate tax payer with £6,400 (£38,400 – £32,000) taxed at 40%.

The marriage allowance cannot be used as Spence is a higher rate taxpayer.

Spence will not pay income tax on his investment income as he is entitled to a £500 savings nil rate band. There is therefore no benefit in transferring this income to Kyria.

The following could be considered:

- Transfer of a larger percentage ownership of the property to Kyria.
- Neither appear to be making any payments into a pension.

Effect

- A transfer of a larger percentage of the property to Kyria would save Spence tax at 40% and enable Kyria's surplus personal allowance and 20% basic rate tax band to be utilised.
- £15,240 cash each invested in a cash ISA (the maximum contribution per year) would result in tax-free earnings.
- Provided that Kyria remains a basic rate taxpayer, savings income up to £1,000 would be covered by the savings nil rate band.
- In addition, if Kyria's taxable non-savings income remained below £5,000, the remaining investment income would be taxed at 0% up to the £5,000 limit.
- In Spence's case, any pension contributions would provide tax relief at 40% for contributions above the basic rate band.

Test your understanding 1

Stan and Karrie are a married couple. For the tax year 2016/17 they expect to have the following income:

Stan	£	**Karrie**	£
Employment income	170,000	Employment income	20,000
Savings income	2,000	Savings income	0
Dividend income	0	Dividend income	7,000

Advise the couple of any beneficial tax planning measures they should make to minimise their combined income tax liabilities.

Pension contributions

Spouses and civil partners should both be looking to make pension contributions. If the contributions are not to be made equally, the higher rate taxpayer should make the contributions.

Note that pension contributions made by a higher rate taxpayer with dividend income may achieve a saving in excess of 40%, as they receive higher rate relief for the contributions and, due to the extension of the basic rate band, dividends could fall into the basic rate band and achieve further tax savings.

Also, a taxpayer with income in excess of £100,000 may consider making pension contributions to avoid the reduction of the personal allowance.

Example 3 – Pension contributions

Julie is self-employed and made profits of £40,000 in the year ended 31 March 2017.

Her only other income is dividends received of £10,000.

Calculate the tax saving that will be achieved if Julie pays £4,680 into her personal pension in the tax year 2016/17.

Solution

		£
Trading income		40,000
Dividend income		10,000
Total income		50,000
Less: Personal allowance		(11,000)
Taxable income		39,000

Analysis of income:

Dividends	Non-savings income
£10,000	£29,000

Income tax – with no pension contributions

£			£
29,000	× 20%	(Non-savings income)	5,800
3,000	× 0%	(Dividend income)	0
32,000			
2,000	× 0%	(Dividend income)	0
5,000	× 32.5%	(Dividend income)	1,625
39,000			
Income tax liability			7,425

Income tax – with pension contributions

Gross pension contribution = (£4,680 × 100/80) = £5,850
Higher rate threshold = (£32,000 + £5,850) = £37,850.

£			£
29,000	× 20%	(Non-savings income)	5,800
5,000	× 0%	(Dividend income)	0
3,850	× 7.5%		289
37,850			
1,150	× 32.5%	(Dividend income)	374
39,000			
Income tax liability			6,463

Tax saving

Tax saved in computation (£7,425 – £6,463)	962
Tax saved at source (£5,850 – £4,680)	1,170
	2,132

Alternative calculation

The tax saving can be calculated very quickly without doing full income tax computations, simply by using Julie's marginal rates of tax.

The extension of the basic rate band will mean that dividends previously taxed at 32.5% will now be taxed at just 7.5%, as follows:

	£
Tax saved by gross pension contribution:	
At source (payment made net of 20% tax) (20% × £5,850)	1,170
By extension of basic rate band (32.5% – 7.5%) × £3,850	962
Total saving (as above)	2,132

Where possible, you should always try to calculate tax savings using marginal rates in the exam.

Test your understanding 2

Emily has an annual salary of £122,000, and is considering making a contribution to her personal pension to avoid losing her personal allowance.

Calculate the tax saving that will be achieved if Emily pays £17,600 cash into her personal pension in the tax year 2016/17.

Tax efficient remuneration

The technical details on employment income were covered in Chapter 2. This is another possible scenario for income tax planning through the comparison of different remuneration packages.

A selection of areas to consider are:

- the provision of a company car compared to using the individual's own car and claiming mileage allowance
- comparison of approved and unapproved share schemes
- using a range of exempt benefits.

Test your understanding 3

Workout plc runs a nation-wide chain of health clubs, with each club being run by a manager who is paid an annual salary of £42,500. The company has a flexible remuneration policy in that it allows managers to enhance their salary by choosing from a package of benefits.

Gareth Step is to be appointed as a manager of Workout plc on 6 April 2016 and he has asked for your advice regarding the tax implications arising from each aspect of the benefits package.

The package is as follows:

Motor car

Option 1:

Workout plc will provide a new petrol car with a list price of £19,200 and CO_2 emissions of 147 g/km, and will pay for all running costs, including private fuel. Gareth will make a capital contribution of £3,000 towards the cost of the car, and will also be required to contribute a further £50 per month towards its private use. He will drive a total of 1,750 miles per month, of which 60% will be in respect of journeys in the performance of his duties for Workout plc.

Option 2:

Alternatively, Workout plc will pay Gareth additional salary of £500 per month, and he will lease a private motor car. Workout plc will then pay an allowance of 30 pence per mile for business mileage.

Accommodation

Option 1:

Gareth currently lives 140 miles from where he is to be employed by Workout plc. The company will pay £7,500 towards the cost of relocation, and will also provide an interest free loan of £90,000 in order for Gareth to purchase a property. The loan will be repaid in monthly instalments of £1,000 commencing on 15 April 2016.

Option 2:

Alternatively, Workout plc will provide living accommodation for Gareth. This will be in a house that the company purchased in 2001 for £86,500. The house has a rateable value of £7,700 and is currently valued at £135,000. The furniture in the house cost £12,400. Workout plc will pay for the annual running costs of £3,900.

Telephone

Option 1:

Workout plc will provide Gareth with a mobile telephone costing £500, and will pay for all business and private telephone calls.

Option 2:

Alternatively, Workout plc will pay Gareth £75 per month towards the cost of his fixed telephone at home. The total annual cost will be £1,400, of which £300 is for line rental, £650 for business telephone calls and £450 for private telephone calls.

Explain the tax implications for Gareth arising from each aspect of the benefits package.

You should assume that benefits are provided on 6 April 2016.

VAT and the tax implications for Workout plc should be ignored.

3 Chapter summary

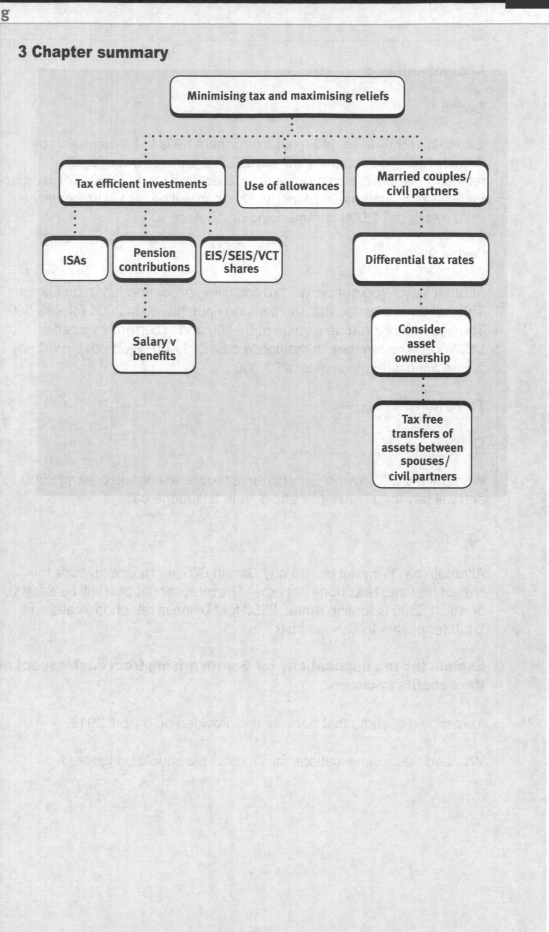

Minimising tax and maximising reliefs

- Tax efficient investments
  - ISAs
  - Pension contributions
    - Salary v benefits
  - EIS/SEIS/VCT shares
- Use of allowances
- Married couples/ civil partners
  - Differential tax rates
    - Consider asset ownership
      - Tax free transfers of assets between spouses/ civil partners

Test your understanding answers

Test your understanding 1

Stan and Karrie – income tax planning measures

Stan is an additional rate taxpayer, so he is not entitled to a savings income nil rate band (SNRB). His savings income will be subject to income tax at a rate of 45%. Karrie is a basic rate taxpayer, and is currently not utilising her £1,000 SNRB. Stan should transfer his savings to Karrie; £1,000 would be taxed at 0% (SNRB) and the remaining £1,000 would be taxed at 20% (basic rate), saving tax of £700 ((£1,000 × 45%) + (£1,000 × (45% – 20%))).

Karrie has fully utilised her dividend nil rate band (DNRB) of £5,000. Her dividend income in excess of this will be taxed at 7.5% She should transfer sufficient shares to Stan to generate dividend income of £2,000 (£7,000 – £5,000). This income would be taxed at 0% as it would be covered by Stan's DNRB and would save tax of £150 (£2,000 × 7.5%).

Test your understanding 2

Income tax computation – 2016/17 with no pension contributions

		£
Employment income = total income		122,000
Less: Adjusted PA (Note)		(0)
Taxable income		122,000
Income tax	£	£
Non-savings income – basic rate	32,000 × 20%	6,400
Non-savings income – higher rate	90,000 × 40%	36,000
	122,000	
Income tax liability		42,400

Note: In this example, as total income = net income = ANI, and this is £122,000 (£100,000 plus more than double the PA), the PA is reduced to £Nil.

Income tax computation – 2016/17 with pension contributions

		£
Employment income = total income		122,000
Less: PA (W)		(11,000)
Taxable income		111,000

Gross pension contribution = (£16,000 × 100/80) = £22,000
Higher rate threshold = (£32,000 + £22,000) = £54,000

Income tax	£	£
Non-savings income – basic rate	54,000 × 20%	10,800
Non-savings income – higher rate	57,000 × 40%	22,800
	111,000	
Income tax liability		33,600

Tax saving	£
Tax saved in computation (£42,400 – £33,600)	8,800
Tax saved at source (£22,000 – £17,600)	4,400
Total saving	13,200

Working: Adjusted PA	£	£
Personal allowance		11,000
Net income	122,000	
Less: Gross pension contribution	(22,000)	
Adjusted net income	100,000	
Less: Income limit	(100,000)	
	0	
Reduction of PA		0
Adjusted PA		11,000

Alternative calculation

The tax saving can be calculated very quickly without doing full income tax computations, simply by using Emily's marginal rate of tax.

The extension of Emily's basic rate band will mean that income previously taxed at 40% will now be taxed at 20%, as follows:

	£
Taxed saved by personal allowances (£11,000 × 40%)	4,400
Tax saved by gross pension contribution:	
At source (payment made net of 20% tax) (20% × £22,000)	4,400
By extension of basic rate band (40% – 20%) × £22,000	4,400
Total saving (as above)	13,200

Where possible, to save time, you should always try to calculate tax savings using marginal rates in the examination.

Test your understanding 3

Workout plc

Tutorial note: You are required to explain the tax implications for Gareth only, but not required to advise him which options to choose.

Company car

Gareth will be assessed on employment income on a car benefit of £3,612 (W1) and a fuel benefit of £5,772 (W1).

The additional income tax liability is £3,754 ((£3,612 + £5,772) × 40%).

Cash alternative

The additional salary of £500 per month will be taxed as employment income, with 40% income tax and 2% NIC.

This will leave cash of £3,480 (£500 × 12 = £6,000 × 58%) after tax and NIC.

Gareth will be paid an allowance of 30p per mile for 12,600 (1,750 × 12 × 60%) business miles.

The mileage allowance received will be tax free (exempt IT and NICs) and Gareth can make the following expense claim which will reduce his IT liability:

	£
10,000 miles at 45p	4,500
2,600 miles at 25p	650
AMAP	5,150
Less: Mileage allowance received (12,600 at 30p)	(3,780)
Expense claim against employment income	1,370

Gareth needs to consider whether the cash salary is preferable to the company car. If he accepts the cash he will receive:

	£
Cash – additional salary	3,480
Mileage allowance	3,780
Income tax relief on shortfall (40% × £1,370)	548
	7,808
Plus: Total tax no longer payable on benefits	3,754
Increase in cash	11,562

He needs to consider whether this is enough to buy and run his car personally. If it is, the cash alternative would appear to be better.

Relocation costs

As the £8,000 limit is not exceeded, there should not be a taxable benefit in respect of the relocation costs paid for by Workout plc. This is because Gareth does not live within a reasonable daily travelling distance of where he is to be employed.

The exemption covers such items as legal and estate agents' fees, stamp duty land tax, removal costs, and the cost of new domestic goods where existing goods are not available in the new residence.

Beneficial loan

Gareth will be assessed on the difference between the interest paid on the loan and the official rate of interest as earnings. The 'average' method of calculation gives a taxable benefit for the tax year 2016/17 of £2,520 (W2).

The additional income tax liability is therefore £1,008 (£2,520 at 40%).

The balance at 5 April 2017 is after taking account of 12 monthly repayments of £1,000.

Living accommodation

Gareth will be assessed on the provision of the living accommodation provided to him. There will be an additional benefit based on the market value of £135,000, since the house cost in excess of £75,000 and it was purchased more than six years before first being provided.

The taxable benefit will be:

	£
Rateable value	7,700
Additional benefit (£135,000 – £75,000) × 3%	1,800
Furniture (£12,400 × 20%)	2,480
Running costs	3,900
Total accommodation benefits	15,880

The income tax liability is £6,352 (£15,880 × 40%).

Mobile telephone

The provision of one mobile telephone per employee does not give rise to a taxable benefit, even if there is private use.

Fixed telephone

If Gareth receives £75 per month towards his home telephone, he will assessed on a taxable employment benefit of £900 (12 × £75). However he will be able to make an expense claim of £650 in respect of the expenditure on business calls.

The additional income tax liability is therefore £100 (£900 – £650 = £250 × 40%).

Workings

(W1) **Car and fuel benefit**

CO_2 emissions = 147 g/km, available all year

Appropriate % = 16% + ((145 – 95) × 1/5) = 26%

Cost = (£19,200 – £3,000 capital contribution) = £16,200

	£
Car benefit (£16,200 × 26%)	4,212
Less: Monthly contribution (£50 × 12)	(600)
Car benefit	3,612
Fuel benefit (£22,200 × 26%)	5,772

(W2) **Beneficial loan**

	£
Loan at start of year	90,000
Loan at end of year	78,000
	168,000
Average loan = (£168,000 ÷ 2) = £84,000	
Assessable benefit (£84,000 × 3%)	2,520

chapter

6

CGT: Computations and stamp duty land tax

Chapter learning objectives

Upon completion of this chapter you will be able to:

- compute the capital gains tax payable, given a variety of basic transactions for an individual including the treatment of losses
- recognise when a disposal is effective for capital gains tax purposes
- recognise when a negligible value claim can be made and the effect thereof
- determine when capital gains tax can be paid by instalments and evaluate when this would be advantageous to taxpayers
- identify the capital gains tax position for an individual at death and the additional relief available for capital losses
- advise on the capital gains tax implications of transfers of property into a trust
- explain the different types of stamp duty, identify when stamp duty land tax is payable on the transfer of land and calculate the amount of stamp duty payable.

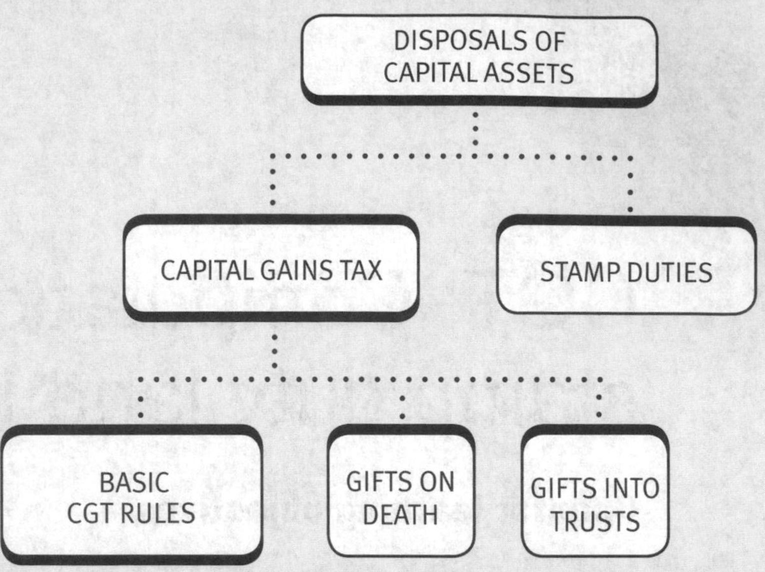

Introduction

This and the following three chapters deal with the way in which individuals are subject to capital gains tax on their chargeable gains.

Much of this chapter is a revision of the rules covered in F6. A brief reminder of F6 content is given, and revision examples are provided to check your retention of the required F6 knowledge.

The main new topics introduced include the implications of putting assets into a trust and stamp duty land tax.

1 Basic capital gains tax rules

The scope of capital gains tax

Capital gains tax (CGT) is charged on gains arising from **chargeable disposals** of **chargeable assets** by **chargeable persons**.

A reminder of these important terms is given below.

A **chargeable person** includes individuals, companies and business partners in a partnership.

This chapter covers the CGT implications of disposals by individuals.

Chargeable disposal	**Exempt disposal**
The following are treated as chargeable disposals: (i) sale or gift of the whole or part of an asset (ii) exchange of an asset (iii) loss or total destruction of an asset (iv) receipts of a capital sum derived from an asset, for example: • compensation received for damage to an asset • receipts for the surrender of rights to an asset.	Exempt disposals include: (i) disposals as a result of the death of an individual (ii) gifts to charities.
Chargeable assets	**Exempt assets**
All forms of capital assets, wherever situated, are chargeable assets. Common examples include: • Freehold land and buildings • Goodwill • Short lease • Long lease • Unquoted shares • Quoted shares • Unit trusts • Chattels bought and sold > £6,000. (Chattels are tangible movable assets e.g. furniture, plant and machinery)	Exempt assets include: • Motor vehicles (including vintage cars) • Main residence (subject to occupation) • Cash • Wasting chattels (e.g. racehorses and greyhounds) • Chattels bought and sold ≤ £6,000 • Investments held within an ISA • Qualifying corporate bonds (QCBs) • Gilt-edged securities • National savings certificates • Shares in a VCT • Endowment policy proceeds • Foreign currency for private use • Receivables • Trading inventory • Prizes and betting winnings.

The basis of assessment

Individuals are assessed to CGT:

- under self-assessment
- on actual disposals of capital assets between 6 April and 5 April.

The date of disposal

Determining the date of disposal is very important as it determines the tax year in which a chargeable gain is assessed or an allowable loss arises.

Event	Date of disposal
Lifetime transfer:	
• normally	• Date of the contract/agreement to transfer the asset (not necessarily the same date as the actual date of transfer)
• conditional contract	• Date when all of the conditions are satisfied and the contract becomes legally binding
Transfers on death:	• Date of death of the individual (although no CGT payable on death) – see section 3

Example 1 – Date of disposal

Emily decided to sell an investment property to Joe. Contracts were exchanged on 13 February 2017 with an intended completion date of 25 March 2017, but the contract was conditional on planning permission being obtained.

Planning permission was granted on 29 March 2017 and completion took place on 8 April 2017.

State, with reasons, the tax year in which the gain will be taxed.

Solution

Emily will be taxed on the gain in the tax year 2016/17.

The completion date is not relevant. The sale agreement was a conditional contract and the disposal takes place when the condition is satisfied (i.e. 29 March 2017).

The capital gains tax computation

Step 1 Calculate the chargeable gains/allowable loss arising on the disposal of each chargeable asset separately

Step 2 Consider the availability of any CGT reliefs (Chapter 9)

Step 3 Calculate the net chargeable gains arising in the tax year = (capital gains less allowable losses)

Step 4 Deduct capital losses brought forward

Step 5 Deduct the annual exempt amount = taxable gains

Step 6 Calculate the CGT payable for the tax year.

Pro forma capital gains tax payable computation – 2016/17

	£
Net chargeable gains for the tax year	X
Less: Capital losses brought forward (see Note)	(X)
	X
Less: Annual exempt amount (AEA)	(11,100)
Taxable gains	X
CGT payable (taxable gains × appropriate rate))	X

The calculation of the individual chargeable gains/allowable losses

	Notes	£
Consideration	1	X
Less: Incidental costs of sale	2	(X)
Net disposal proceeds		X
Less: Allowable expenditure		
– Acquisition cost	3	(X)
– Incidental costs of acquisition	2	(X)
– Enhancement expenditure		(X)
Chargeable gain/(allowable loss)		X/(X)

Notes

(1) The consideration is normally:

- **disposal proceeds actually received** for a sale to an unconnected person
- **market value** for gifts and sales to connected persons.

(2) Allowable incidental costs of sale and acquisition include:

- legal expenses
- valuation fees, estate agent fees, auctioneer's fees
- advertising costs
- stamp duty (on shares) and stamp duty land tax (on land and buildings).

(3) The acquisition cost is normally:

- **actual cost** if the asset was purchased
- **market value** when acquired if the asset was gifted
- **probate value** at the date of the donor's death if the asset was inherited.

Capital losses

Current year capital losses

Capital losses arising on assets in the current tax year are set off against chargeable gains, arising in the same tax year:

- to the maximum possible extent
- they cannot be restricted to avoid wasting all or part of the AEA.

Any unrelieved capital losses are carried forward to offset against gains in future years.

Brought forward capital losses

Brought forward losses:

- are set against chargeable gains **after** any current year losses have been deducted
- will be restricted to preserve the AEA of £11,100
- any unused loss is then carried forward for use in the future.

Negligible value claims

If the value of an asset becomes negligible for whatever reason, the owner may claim relief.

They are then treated as having disposed of, and immediately reacquired, the asset at its negligible value. This treatment crystallises a capital loss.

The deemed disposal is treated as occurring:

- at the date of the claim, or
- up to two years before the start of the tax year in which the claim was made.

The back dating of the capital loss applies only if the asset was actually of negligible value at both the date of the claim and the earlier date.

Annual exempt amount

An individual is entitled to an annual exempt amount (AEA) each tax year.

- For the tax year 2016/17 the AEA is £11,100.
- If the AEA is not utilised in any particular tax year, then it is wasted.

Computation of CGT payable

CGT is payable on the taxable gains arising in a tax year as follows:

- The rate of CGT is dependent upon the amount of a taxpayer's total taxable income (i.e. after deduction of the personal allowance) and the type of asset being disposed of.
- Taxable gains are taxed **after** taxable income (i.e. as the top slice) but do not combine income and gains in one computation.
- Generally where total taxable income and gains are less than the upper limit of the basic rate band, CGT will be at 10%.
- Generally to the extent that any gains (or any part of gains) exceed the basic rate band they will be taxed at 20%.
- If the basic rate band is extended due to gift aid donations or personal pension contributions the extended basic rate band will also be used to establish the rate of CGT.
- Any unused income tax personal allowance cannot be used to reduce taxable gains.

Rates of CGT

CGT is paid at the normal rates, unless the gain arises on the disposal of a residential property.

	Falling in basic rate band	In excess of basic rate band
Normal rates	10%	20%
Residential property rates	18%	28%

In practice, a taxpayer's main residential property (i.e. their home) will be exempt from CGT under the principal private residence relief rules (PPR). However, where the gain on the disposal of a residential property is not fully exempt (e.g. on an investment property which is let out) it is taxed at the higher rates.

Offset of AEA and capital losses

The taxpayer can offset the AEA and capital losses against whichever gains he chooses. In order to maximise the reliefs they should be offset firstly against residential property gains, as they are taxable at higher rates than other gains.

The unused basic rate may also be offset in the most beneficial way. The tax saving will be the same regardless of the gains against which it is used (as switching gains tax at 28% to 18% or switching gains taxed at 20% to 10% produces the same result).

However, for simplicity in the P6 examination the unused basic rate band should be used in the same way as the AEA and capital losses i.e. firstly against residential property gains.

Test your understanding 1

Julie sold the following assets in the tax year 2016/17:

- an investment property on 1 July 2016 for £650,000. She had acquired the building for £80,000 in June 2002 and had extended it at a cost of £30,000 in June 2004
- a painting on 1 August 2016 for £20,000, incurring auctioneer's fees of 10%. She had acquired the painting for £35,000 in April 2004.
- a rare comic book on 1 December 2016 for £30,000. The comic book had been purchased on 1 December 2001 for £5,000.

Julie had capital losses brought forward of £16,000. Julie's only source of income in the tax year 2016/17 was trading income of £40,000.

Calculate Julie's capital gains tax payable for the tax year 2016/17 and state the due date for payment.

A summary of the basic CGT rules

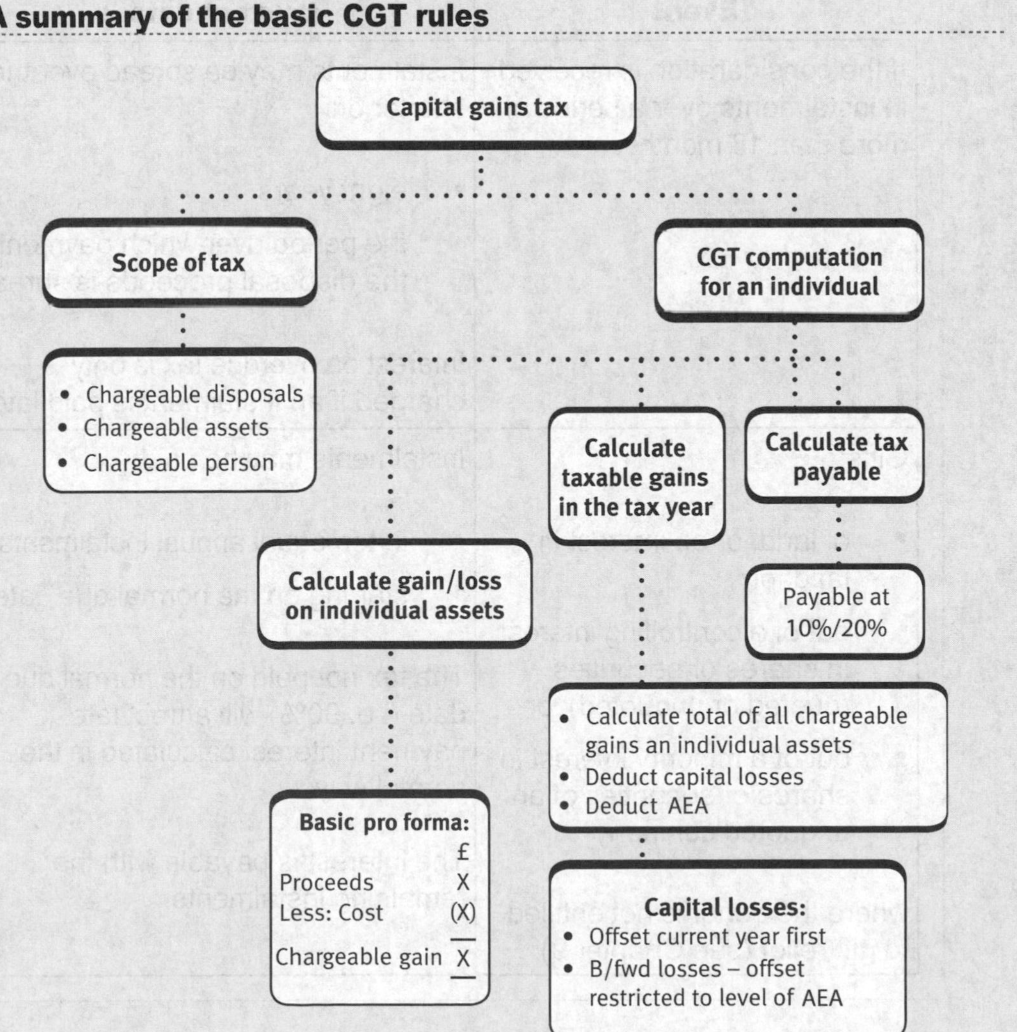

2 The payment of capital gains tax

Payment under self-assessment

CGT is normally payable:

- under self-assessment
- in one payment along with the balancing payment of income tax
- 31 January 2018 for the tax year 2016/17.

Payment by instalments

CGT may be paid by instalments:

- where consideration is received in instalments, and
- on certain lifetime gifts.

Payment by instalments

Event	Payment details
If the consideration is received in instalments over a period of more than 18 months.	Instalments may be spread over the shorter of: • eight years • the period over which payment of the disposal proceeds is spread. Interest on overdue tax is only charged if an instalment is paid late.
Gifts: • of land, or an interest in land; or • out of a controlling interest in shares or securities (quoted or unquoted); or • out of a minority interest in shares or securities of an unquoted company where the donor is not entitled to gift relief (see Chapter 9).	Instalments may be paid: • in ten equal annual instalments • starting on the normal due date. The tax not paid on the normal due date (i.e. 90%) will attract late payment interest calculated in the normal way. The interest is payable with the remaining instalments.

3 Capital gains tax on the death of an individual

The CGT consequences of the event of death

CGT is a 'lifetime tax'. Transfers on the death of an individual are therefore exempt disposals.

The CGT consequences of death are as follows:

- no capital gain or allowable loss arises as a result of the death
- the beneficiaries inherit the assets of the deceased and are deemed to acquire the assets:
  - with a base cost equivalent to the market value of the asset at the date of death (i.e. at probate value)
  - on the date of death, regardless of the date they actually receive the asset.

Note that whilst the increase in the capital value of an asset from acquisition to the date of death is not liable to CGT, there are inheritance tax (IHT) implications arising from the death of an individual (see later chapters).

Example 2 – Death of an individual

John bought an asset on 16 August 1993 for £300 and died on 10 December 2016 when the asset was worth £1,000,000. The asset is left to Malcolm, his son. The executors gave the asset to Malcolm on 24 March 2017.

Malcolm sold the asset for £1,200,000 on 16 March 2018.

Explain the CGT consequences arising from the above events.

Solution

John's death

On John's death the following consequences arise:

- the increase in the value of the asset of £999,700 (£1,000,000 – £300) is exempt from CGT
- Malcolm is deemed to acquire the asset at a base cost of £1,000,000 on 10 December 2016
- the fact that Malcolm actually received the asset on 24 March 2017 is not relevant.

Sale of asset by Malcolm

On the disposal of the asset by Malcolm: a chargeable gain of £200,000 (£1,200,000 – £1,000,000) will arise.

Valuation of quoted shares on death

Note that the probate value of quoted shares (and therefore the base cost for CGT purposes) is:

- where a valuation was obtained on death

  = the lower of the quarter up or the average marked bargains method using the IHT valuation rules (see Chapter 12)

- where a valuation was not obtained on death

  = the mid-price value using the CGT valuation rules (see Chapter 8)

  (this will be the case where the value of the estate falls below the IHT threshold and no IHT was payable).

Tax planning

It is possible to change the terms of an individual's will after they have died by entering into a deed of variation.

A deed of variation can have both CGT and IHT consequences. See Chapter 13 for details.

Capital losses in the year of death

Losses in excess of gains arising in the tax year of death can be:

- carried back three tax years
- on a LIFO basis
- and set against the remaining net gains in those years.

Note that the set off must be restricted to preserve the AEA, as for brought forward losses.

As a result of carrying back losses, a repayment of CGT will be obtained from HMRC. This repayment will be an asset at the date of the individual's death, to be included in his death estate (see Chapter 12).

Transfer of ISA on death

Remember that on death, an ISA allowance equal to the deceased individual's ISA savings can be claimed by the surviving spouse/civil partner (Chapter 3).

As a result, the deceased individual's ISA savings will retain their beneficial tax treatment (i.e. exemption from income tax and capital gains tax) in the future, in the hands of the surviving spouse/civil partner.

4 Transfers of assets into a trust

An individual may gift assets into a trust fund during their lifetime or on their death under the provisions of their will.

The following CGT consequences will arise in respect of a gift into a trust:

Lifetime gift by the donor	Gift on death of the donor
• Chargeable disposal at full market value • Gift relief is available on any asset (Chapter 9) as there is an immediate charge to IHT	• No chargeable gain or allowable loss arises as a result of the death • The trustees acquire the assets at probate value on the date of death

Trusts are covered in more detail in Chapter 14.

5 Stamp duty land tax

There are two types of stamp taxes:

	Transactions
Stamp duty	Transfers of shares and other marketable securities
Stamp duty land tax	Transfers of UK land and property

Stamp duty is covered in detail in Chapter 8. This section covers stamp duty land tax.

Stamp duty land tax (SDLT) is payable on transactions involving land, unless the transaction is specifically exempt.

SDLT is payable:

- by the purchaser
- on the transfer of land and property, lease premiums and rent paid under leases
- in England, Wales and Northern Ireland
- based on the value of the property transferred and the type of property.

SDLT is charged on premiums paid in respect of a lease and the rent paid on leases. However, this aspect of SDLT is not examinable.

In Scotland, land and buildings transaction tax (LBTT) replaces SDLT from 1 April 2015, however LBTT is not examinable.

Purchases of UK land and property

SDLT is charged as follows:

Non-residential property

Value	
£150,000 or less	0%
£150,001 – £250,000	2%
£250,001 and above	5%

Residential property

Value	
£125,000 or less	0%
£125,001 – £250,000	2%
£250,001 – £925,000	5%
£925,001 – £1,500,000	10%
£1,500,001 or more	12%

Note: the rates applying to residential property are increased by 3% in certain circumstances (see below).

SDLT is calculated on a stepped basis on the value falling within each band.

The rates payable are included in the tax rates and allowances provided in the examination.

Consideration paid

The consideration subject to duty is any money or money's worth provided by the purchaser.

Where the consideration is unascertainable at the time of the transaction it must be estimated. Any changes to the consideration caused by future events must be notified to HMRC and duty will be paid or repaid as appropriate.

Example 3 – Stamp duty land tax

Peter Robinson purchased the following in September 2016.

(a) A terraced house costing £110,000.

(b) A town house costing £275,000. Peter will use this house as his main residence.

(c) A retail shop costing £140,000.

(d) A office building costing £200,000.

Calculate the amount of stamp duty land tax payable.

Solution

(a) SDLT on the purchase of a terraced house (residential property): £Nil, as the price paid is ≤ £125,000. An additional 3% SDLT will not be levied provided Peter does not own any other residential property (see below).

(b) SDLT on the purchase of town house (residential property):

£		£
125,000 ×	0%	0
125,000 ×	2%	2,500
25,000 ×	5%	1,250
275,000		
SDLT payable		3,750

(c) SDLT on the purchase of a shop (commercial property): £Nil, as the price is ≤ £150,000

(d) SDLT on the purchase of a freehold office (commercial property):

£		£
150,000 ×	0%	0
50,000 ×	2%	1,000
200,000		
SDLT payable		1,000

Test your understanding 2

Wayne purchased a non-residential property for £420,000.

Ray sold some residential land to Margaret for £385,000. Margaret then sold some non-residential land to Beth for £145,000.

Assuming all transactions took place in the tax year 2016/17, calculate the amount of SDLT payable and state who is liable to pay on each transaction.

Higher rates for residential property

Higher rates than the rates in the table above apply in respect of the acquisition of residential property by the following:

- an individual who already owns a residential property (and who is not simply replacing a main residence, or
- any other taxable person (e.g. a company).

In these circumstances the standard rates of SDLT will be increased by 3%. The amount of the percentage increase is included in the tax rates and allowances provided to you in the examination. However, the circumstances in which the increase applies are not.

Exemptions from stamp duty land tax

There is no SDLT payable if the transfer is exempt.

The main exempt transfers are as follows:

- gifts, provided no consideration is given
- divorce arrangements
- variation of a will
- transfers of assets between members of a 75% group of companies.

Transfers between 75% companies

There is no charge to stamp duty or SDLT where assets are transferred between two group companies.

Two companies are in a group where one is a 75% subsidiary of the other or they are both 75% subsidiaries of a third company. This definition may be regarded as the same as that for chargeable gains.

This relief is not available where, at the time the assets are transferred, arrangements exist for the purchasing company to leave the group.

Any relief given in respect of SDLT is withdrawn, with duty becoming payable, if the transferee company leaves the group within three years of the transfer whilst still owning the land transferred.

Administration of stamp duty land tax

SDLT is payable:

- by the purchaser
- with the return which should be submitted within 30 days of the completion date (i.e. the date on which the contract for the land transaction is legally completed).

Late payment interest is charged on late paid tax.

Penalties may be charged.

Administration of SDLT

The purchaser will receive a certificate from HMRC which must be submitted to the Land Registry in order to register ownership of land.

In a manner similar to self-assessment, HMRC will issue the certificate immediately but will then have nine months in order to make an enquiry into the return.

Penalties may be charged in respect of:

- incorrect returns (this follows the penalty regime for all other taxes, see Chapter 16)
- failure to provide information requested by HMRC
- assisting in the preparation of an incorrect return.

The fraudulent evasion of SDLT is an offence which may result in a fine and/or prison.

Summary

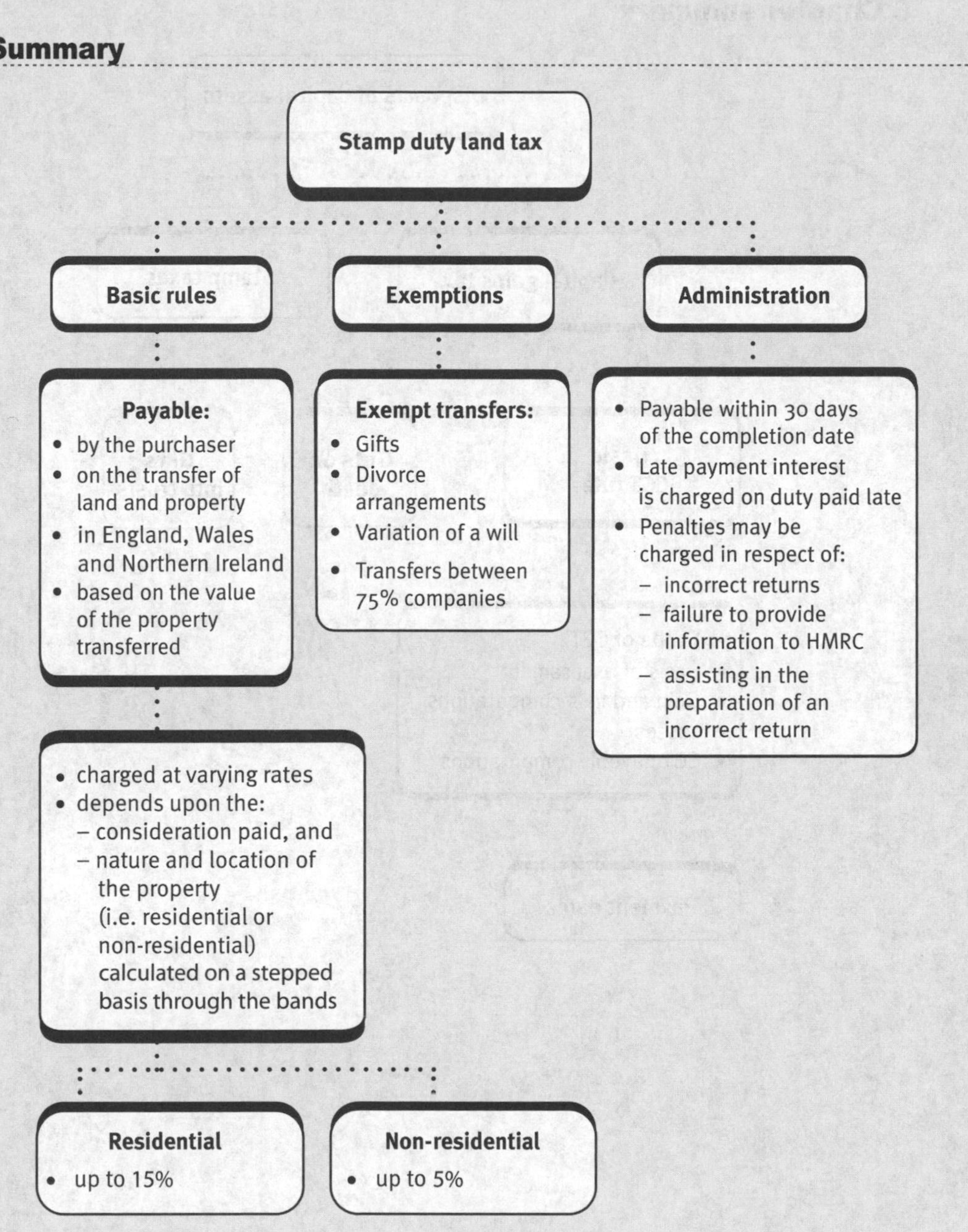

Stamp duty land tax
Basic rules
Exemptions
Administration
Payable:
• by the purchaser
• on the transfer of land and property
• in England, Wales and Northern Ireland
• based on the value of the property transferred
Exempt transfers:
• Gifts
• Divorce arrangements
• Variation of a will
• Transfers between 75% companies
• Payable within 30 days of the completion date
• Late payment interest is charged on duty paid late
• Penalties may be charged in respect of:
– incorrect returns
– failure to provide information to HMRC
– assisting in the preparation of an incorrect return
• charged at varying rates
• depends upon the:
– consideration paid, and
– nature and location of the property (i.e. residential or non-residential) calculated on a stepped basis through the bands
Residential
• up to 15%
Non-residential
• up to 5%

6 Chapter summary

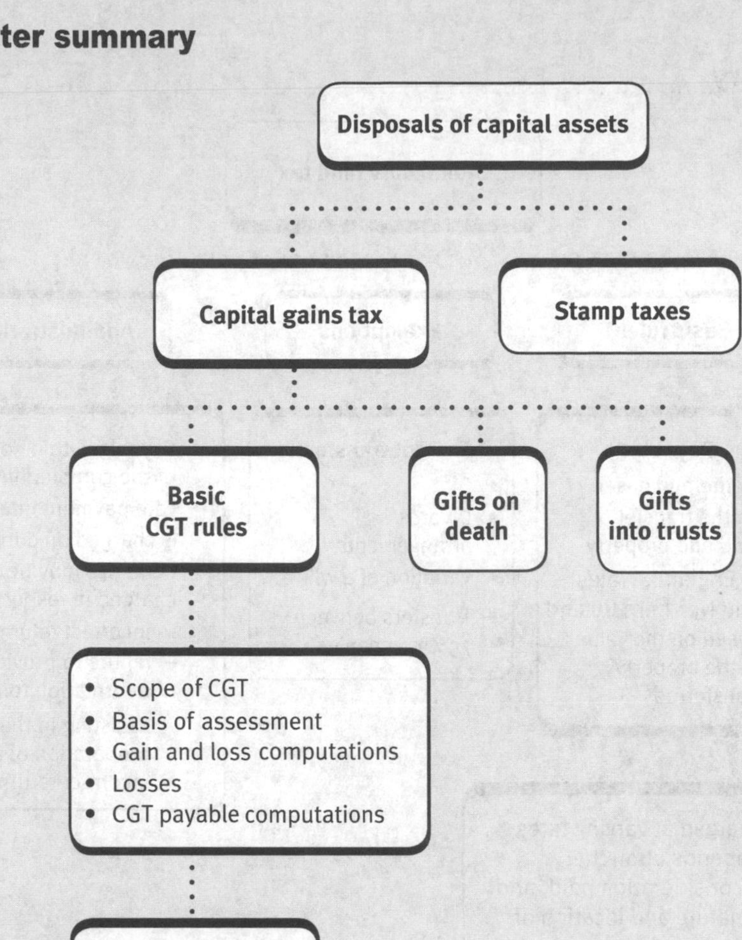
Disposals of capital assets
Capital gains tax
Stamp taxes
Basic CGT rules
Gifts on death
Gifts into trusts
• Scope of CGT
• Basis of assessment
• Gain and loss computations
• Losses
• CGT payable computations
Payment dates

Test your understanding answers

Test your understanding 1

Julie
Capital gains tax computation – 2016/17

		Total	Residential property	Other gains
	£	£	£	£
Investment property				
Disposal proceeds	650,000			
Less: Cost of acquisition	(80,000)			
Enhancement expenditure	(30,000)			
		540,000	540,000	
Comic book				
Disposal proceeds	30,000			
Less: Cost of acquisition	(5,000)			
		25,000		25,000
Painting				
Disposal proceeds	20,000			
Less: Allowable selling costs	(2,000)			
Net proceeds	18,000			
Less: Cost of acquisition	(35,000)			
		(17,000)	(17,000)	
Net chargeable gains arising in tax year		548,000	523,000	25,000
Less: Capital losses brought forward		(16,000)	(16,000)	
Annual exempt amount		(11,100)	(11,100)	
Taxable gains		520,900	495,900	25,000

	£			
Basic rate (W)	3,000	×18%	(residential)	540
Higher rate	492,900	× 28%	(residential)	138,012
Higher rate	25,000	× 20%	(other gains)	5,000
	520,900			
Capital gains tax liability				143,552
Due date				31.1.2018

Note: Losses and the AEA are allocated to residential property gains in preference to other gains as they are subject to CGT at higher rates.

Working: Basic rate band remaining

	£	£
Basic rate band		32,000
Trading income	40,000	
Less: PA	(11,000)	
Taxable income		(29,000)
Basic rate band remaining		3,000

Test your understanding 2

Wayne

£		£
150,000	× 0%	0
100,000	× 2%	2,000
170,000	× 5%	8,500
420,000		
SDLT payable		10,500

Margaret

£		£
125,000	× 0%	0
125,000	× 2%	2,500
135,000	× 5%	6,750
385,000		
SDLT payable		9,250

		£
Beth	(under £150,000) = commercial	0

chapter

7

CGT: Variations to computations

Chapter learning objectives

Upon completion of this chapter you will be able to:

- identify connected persons for CGT purposes and advise on the implications of transfers between them
- recognise how capital transactions are treated for transfers between spouses and registered civil partners and identify tax planning opportunities for spouses and civil partners
- calculate the CGT payable, given a variety of transactions including part disposals, chattels and plant and machinery
- state the effect for capital gains on the disposal of a wasting asset including those used in a trade
- identify the appropriate capital gains tax treatment of a small part disposal of land
- calculate the gain on the disposal of both long and short leases
- explain the capital gains tax treatment where an asset is lost or destroyed and the effect of capital sums received
- explain the capital gains tax treatment where an asset is damaged and the effect of capital sums received.

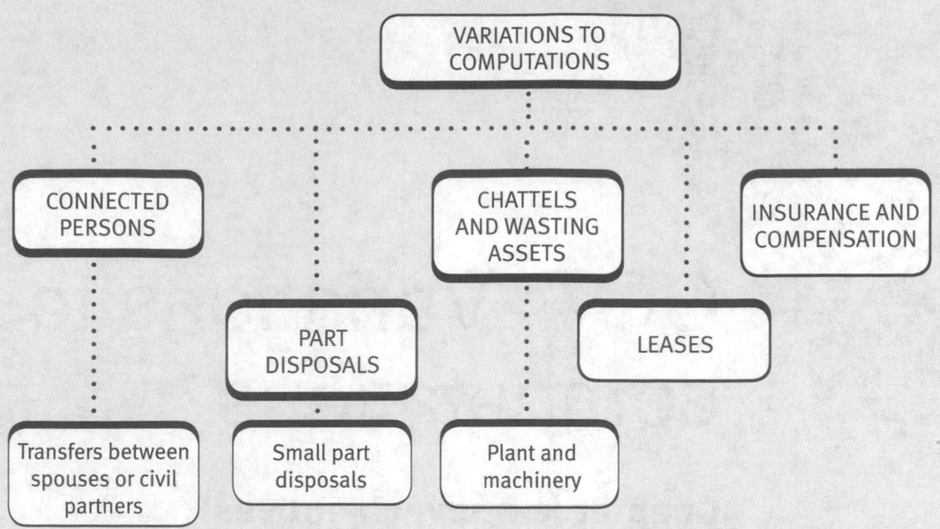

Introduction

The basic pro forma for calculating chargeable gains/(allowable losses) can be used for all disposals of any assets. However, in certain circumstances, additional special rules are needed.

This chapter is mainly revision of topics covered at F6. A brief reminder of F6 content is given and revision examples are provided to check your retention of the required F6 knowledge.

The main new topics introduced at P6 include tax planning aspects, connected persons and the assignment of leases.

1 The treatment of disposals between connected persons

The definition of connected persons

An individual is connected with their:

- spouse or civil partner
- relatives (and their spouses or civil partners)
- spouse's or civil partner's relatives (and their spouses or civil partners)
- their business associates
- a company they control.

The term '**relative**' means:

- brothers and sisters

- parents, grandparents and other ancestors
- children, grandchildren and other descendants.

The term '**business associate**' means:

- partners in business
- a business partner's spouse or civil partner
- relatives of the business partner.

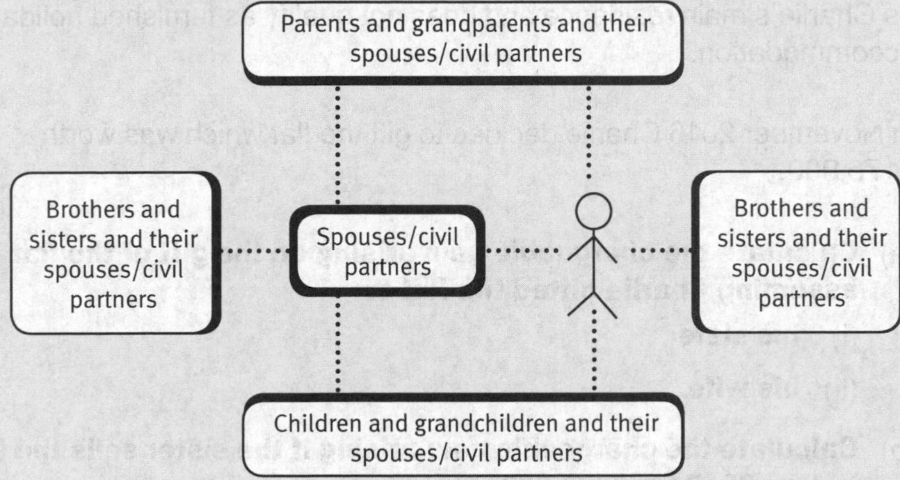

The implications of disposals to a connected person

The CGT implications of making a disposal to a connected person **other than to the spouse or civil partner** are as follows:

Consideration used in the gain computation	• **Market value** at the date of the disposal (regardless of any consideration actually received).
Capital loss on a disposal to a connected person	• Can **only** be set off against current or future gains arising from disposals to the same connected person.

The implications of transfers between spouses or civil partners

Inter spouse transfers and transfers between civil partners are treated as: 'nil gain/nil loss' (NGNL) transfers.

- The transfer is deemed to take place for a consideration which will give rise to neither a gain nor a loss, regardless of any actual consideration which may have been received.

- The transferor is therefore deemed to have disposed of the asset at its acquisition cost.

Note that these rules only apply whilst the couple are living together (i.e. not separated).

Test your understanding 1

Charlie bought a seaside flat in Cornwall in December 1993 for £23,600 to use when he was on holiday from work. The flat has never been used as Charlie's main residence and does not qualify as furnished holiday accommodation.

In November 2016 Charlie decided to gift the flat which was worth £175,000.

(a) **Calculate the chargeable gain arising on the gift of the flat assuming Charlie gifted the flat to:**

(i) **his sister**

(ii) **his wife.**

(b) **Calculate the chargeable gain arising if the sister sells the flat in May 2017 for £200,000.**

(c) **Calculate the chargeable gain arising if the wife sells the flat in May 2017 for £200,000.**

Married couples and civil partners – tax planning

A married couple and civil partners can use the nil gain/nil loss (NGNL) transfer rule to their advantage to save tax in some situations.

For the purposes of this section reference made to spouses also applies to partners in a civil partnership.

Utilising capital losses

Capital losses cannot be transferred between spouses.

Where one spouse will make a chargeable gain and the other a capital loss, it is possible to transfer the asset (or a part share in an asset) before the disposal on a NGNL basis, so one spouse makes both disposals and the loss can be used to reduce the chargeable gain.

Utilising annual exempt amounts

Each spouse is entitled to an annual exempt amount (AEA).

The couple can also utilise the NGNL transfer rule to ensure each spouse fully utilises:

- any capital losses they may have from earlier years
- their AEA (£11,100 for the tax year 2016/17).

Utilising basic rate band

Generally taxable gains in the basic rate band are only taxed at 10%, whereas taxable gains in the higher rate band are taxed at 20%.

Where residential property is sold and the resulting gain is not fully exempt under the PPR exemption, the gain is taxed at 18% in the basic rate band and 28% in the higher rate band (see Chapter 6).

If any taxable gains remain after utilising capital losses and AEAs, the couple can use the NGNL transfer rule to ensure that these gains are left with the spouse paying tax at the lowest rate.

Delaying disposals until the following tax year

Tax saving

- If the AEA has already been utilised in a particular tax year, delaying the disposal of an asset until the following year will:
  - allow the offset of the later year's AEA against any gain arising
  - thereby saving tax on a further £11,100.
- If the individual is a basic rate tax payer, and taxable income is lower in a subsequent tax year, delaying the disposal would mean that:
  - more of the basic rate band would be available, and
  - therefore more of the resulting taxable gain could be taxed at 10% (or 18% if it is a residential property gain).

Cash flow advantage

- Gains realised on disposals up to and including 5 April 2017 are assessable in the tax year 2016/17 and the associated CGT is payable by 31 January 2018.
- If disposals later in the tax year can be delayed until 6 April 2017 or later:
  - the gain is realised in the tax year 2017/18, and
  - any CGT is payable one year later, by 31 January 2019.

Selling assets in tranches

Where assets can be split and sold piecemeal (e.g. shares), selling them in tranches in different tax years can allow the use of more than one AEA and a lower total taxable gain overall.

Impact on income tax

Inter spouse transfers of capital assets do not give rise to a CGT liability. However, care should be taken in advising which assets are transferred between spouses.

A transfer of:

- non-income generating assets (e.g. a painting, antiques) will have no impact on the couple's income tax position
- income generating assets (e.g. shares, letting property) will result in the income being taxed on the recipient spouse in the future.

The couple should ensure that assets generating income are owned by the spouse paying income tax at the lowest rate.

The couple can jointly own assets in equal or unequal proportions. However, it is important when giving advice to remember that:

- even if owned in unequal proportions, any income generated from jointly owned assets will normally be split 50:50 between the spouses
- unless the couple make a joint election to split the income based on beneficial ownership.

Exceptions are:

- dividends from shares in a close company, which are always split on a beneficial ownership basis
- interest from joint bank accounts, which is always split 50:50.

Test your understanding 2

Alex owns a residential investment property that would realise a chargeable gain of £32,000 if sold in the tax year 2016/17. Alex has taxable income of £60,000.

His wife, Vanessa, has capital losses brought forward of £6,200. Vanessa has taxable income of £15,000.

Explain the tax planning measures you would recommend and the taxation effect with supporting calculations as necessary.

2 Part disposals

The problem with part disposals is identifying how much of the original cost of the asset relates to the part disposed of.

A reminder of the rules is given in expandable text and is summarised in the diagram in section 5.

Part disposals – the allowable expenditure calculation

The appropriate proportion is calculated as follows:

Cost × A/(A + B)

Where: A = gross consideration of the part disposed of
B = market value of the remainder (at the time of the part disposal)

The appropriate proportion formula is applied to:

- the original cost (including any incidental acquisition costs)
- enhancement expenditure where the enhancement applies equally to the whole asset.

Note that if the enhancement relates:

wholly to the part disposed of:	• deduct in full in the part disposal computation.
wholly to the part retained:	• do not deduct any in the part disposal computation.

Small part disposals of land and buildings

Where the proceeds received on the part disposal of land and buildings are 'small', a part disposal gain arises unless an election is made.

The effect of making an election is that:

- there will be no part disposal at the time
- the gain is deferred until the disposal of the remainder

- the gain is deferred by deducting the proceeds received on the small part disposal from the original cost of the asset
- the base cost of the part retained is therefore reduced and the gain arising on the subsequent disposal of the remainder will be higher.

Definition of 'small'

Proceeds of the part disposal:

(i) ≤ 20% of the value of land and buildings before the part disposal, and

(ii) total of all land sales in the year ≤ £20,000.

Test your understanding 3

Edward bought a 12 acre plot of land for £30,000 in March 2007 for investment purposes.

In July 2016, Edward sold two acres of the land for £9,500. The remaining 10 acres were worth £80,000.

In September 2017 Edward sold the remaining 10 acres for £135,000.

Calculate the chargeable gains arising from the disposals of the land assuming:

(i) **an election is made to defer the gain on the part disposal.**

(ii) **an election is not made.**

3 Chattels and wasting assets

A reminder of the special rules for calculating the gain or loss arising on a chattel or a wasting asset is given in expandable text and is summarised in the diagram in section 5.

Chattels

A chattel is defined as tangible movable property.

Chattels may be wasting assets (i.e. with a predictable life not exceeding 50 years) or non-wasting.

The CGT consequences of chattels can be summarised as follows:

Wasting chattels	**Non-wasting chattels**
Expected life 50 years or less.	Expected life more than 50 years.
Examples: racehorse greyhound boat, caravan	Examples: antiques jewellery paintings
• Exempt. • Exception: plant and machinery (see below).	• If bought and sold for £6,000 or less: – exempt. • If bought and sold for more than £6,000: – chargeable in the normal way • Otherwise: special rules apply – but not examinable at P6.

Wasting chattels

Wasting assets have a predictable life of 50 years or less.

For CGT purposes, wasting assets can be split into three key categories.

- Chattels not eligible for capital allowances = exempt from CGT (see above).
- Chattels eligible for capital allowances (e.g. plant and machinery).
- Other wasting assets.

Plant and machinery

Plant and machinery is **always** deemed to be a wasting asset.

- Sold at a gain – normal calculations apply
- Sold at a loss – no gain/no loss as relief for loss is given in the capital allowances computation.

Other wasting assets

This category covers wasting assets which are not chattels as they are not tangible and/or not movable (for example, immovable plant and machinery, copyrights and licences).

The allowable expenditure on these assets is deemed to waste over the life of the asset on a straight line basis.

Accordingly, when a disposal is made:

- the allowable expenditure is restricted to take account of the asset's natural fall in value
- the asset's fall in value is deemed to occur on a straight line basis over its predictable useful life
- the allowable cost is calculated as:

  C less [P/L × (C – R)]

  where:

  P = the disposer's period of ownership.
  L = the asset's predictable life.
  C = the cost of the asset.
  R = the residual value of the asset.

Example 1 – Wasting assets

On 16 March 2009 Nicholas bought an asset at a cost of £45,000. It had an estimated useful life of 25 years and an estimated scrap value of £6,000. He sold the asset on 17 March 2017.

Calculate the chargeable gain or allowable loss arising from the sale in March 2017 assuming:

(i) **the asset is a wasting asset and was sold for £34,000**

(ii) **the asset is plant and machinery eligible for capital allowances and was sold for £34,000**

(iii) **the asset is plant and machinery eligible for capital allowances and was sold for £63,000.**

Solution

(i) Wasting asset – sold for £34,000

	£	£
Sale proceeds		34,000
Less: Cost	45,000	
Less: Wasted cost		
8/25 × (£45,000 – £6,000)	(12,480)	
Allowable element of acquisition cost		(32,520)
Chargeable gain		1,480

(ii) P&M eligible for capital allowances – sold for £34,000

Nicholas has sold the machinery for a loss of £11,000 (£45,000 – £34,000).

He is compensated for this loss through the capital allowances system as he receives net capital allowances of £11,000 during his period of ownership of the machinery.

The allowable capital loss computation is therefore adjusted to reflect the relief for the loss already given through the capital allowances system and results in an NGNL situation as follows:

	£	£
Sale proceeds		34,000
Less: Cost	45,000	
Less: Net capital allowances	(11,000)	
		(34,000)
Allowable loss		0

(iii) P&M eligible for capital allowances – sold for £63,000

Normal chargeable gain computation required as any capital allowances given will be claimed back with a balancing charge in the capital allowances system.

	£
Sale proceeds	63,000
Less: Cost	(45,000)
Chargeable gain	18,000

4 Leases

There are two situations relating to leases that are examinable:

- the assignment of a long lease
- the assignment of a short lease.

The assignment of a lease means the complete disposal of the leasehold interest in the property and is usually by way of a sale or a gift.

The calculation of the chargeable gain

The CGT treatment on the assignment of a lease is as follows:

Long lease	Short lease
(i.e. a lease with > 50 years to run at the date of disposal)	(i.e. a lease with 50 years or less to run at the date of disposal)
• Normal gain computation applies.	• Disposal of a wasting asset • The allowable expenditure is adjusted to take account of the depreciating nature of the asset • The cost is multiplied by the fraction: $\frac{\text{\% for life of the lease left on disposal date}}{\text{\% for life of the lease left on acquisition}}$ • If required, HMRC's lease depreciation percentages will be given in the examination question.

Leases depreciate on a curvilinear basis: the lease loses value gradually at first, however at a much quicker rate nearer to the end of the life of the lease.

Test your understanding 4

Frank sold a leasehold shop for £90,000 on 30 September 2016. He had acquired the lease for £50,000 on 1 October 2015 when the lease had 40 years to run.

Lease percentages are as follows:

40 years	95.457%
39 years	94.842%

Compute the chargeable gain arising on the assignment of the short lease in the tax year 2016/17.

The lease percentage calculation

The length of time remaining on a lease at the time of disposal and acquisition is normally straightforward to calculate.

However, there are two situations to look out for:

- Where there are options within the lease to terminate the lease before expiry. The end of the lease is taken to be:
  - the earliest date when either the landlord or the tenant has the option to terminate the lease.
- The length of time remaining on the lease may not always be a whole number of years. Where this is the case:
  - calculations are performed to the nearest month
  - depreciation in between each year is deemed to occur on a straight line basis
  - $1/12^{th}$ of the difference between the percentages for the years either side of the actual duration is added for each extra month.

Test your understanding 5

Geoffrey purchased a lease with 48 years to run on 1 September 2011 for £62,000. On 28 January 2017 he sold the lease for £75,000.

Calculate the chargeable gain arising on the sale.

Lease percentages are as follows:

48 years	99.289%
43 years	97.107%
42 years	96.593%

5 Summary of variations to the basic computations

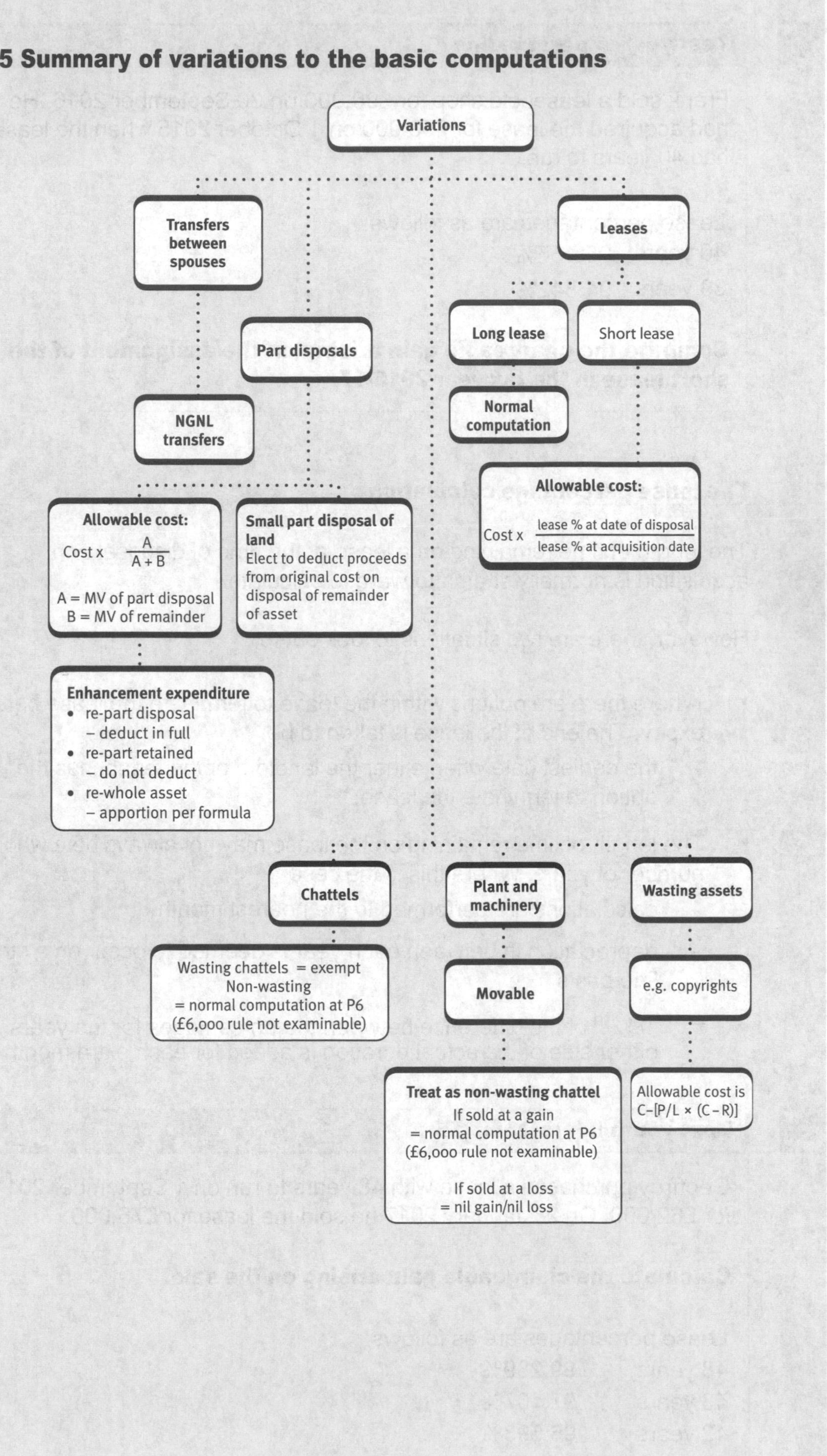

6 Compensation and insurance

Introduction

Most capital transactions have two parties; a buyer and a seller.

However, when an asset is damaged, destroyed or lost and the asset's owner receives compensation (usually from an insurance company):

- the owner has received a capital sum without disposing of the asset
- the payer has received nothing in return.

Consequently a special set of rules is required.

The rules vary according to whether the asset has been:

- completely lost/destroyed or merely damaged
- whether the owner has replaced or restored the asset.

These rules were covered at F6 and are summarised in the following sections with diagrams and examples.

Asset is totally destroyed or lost

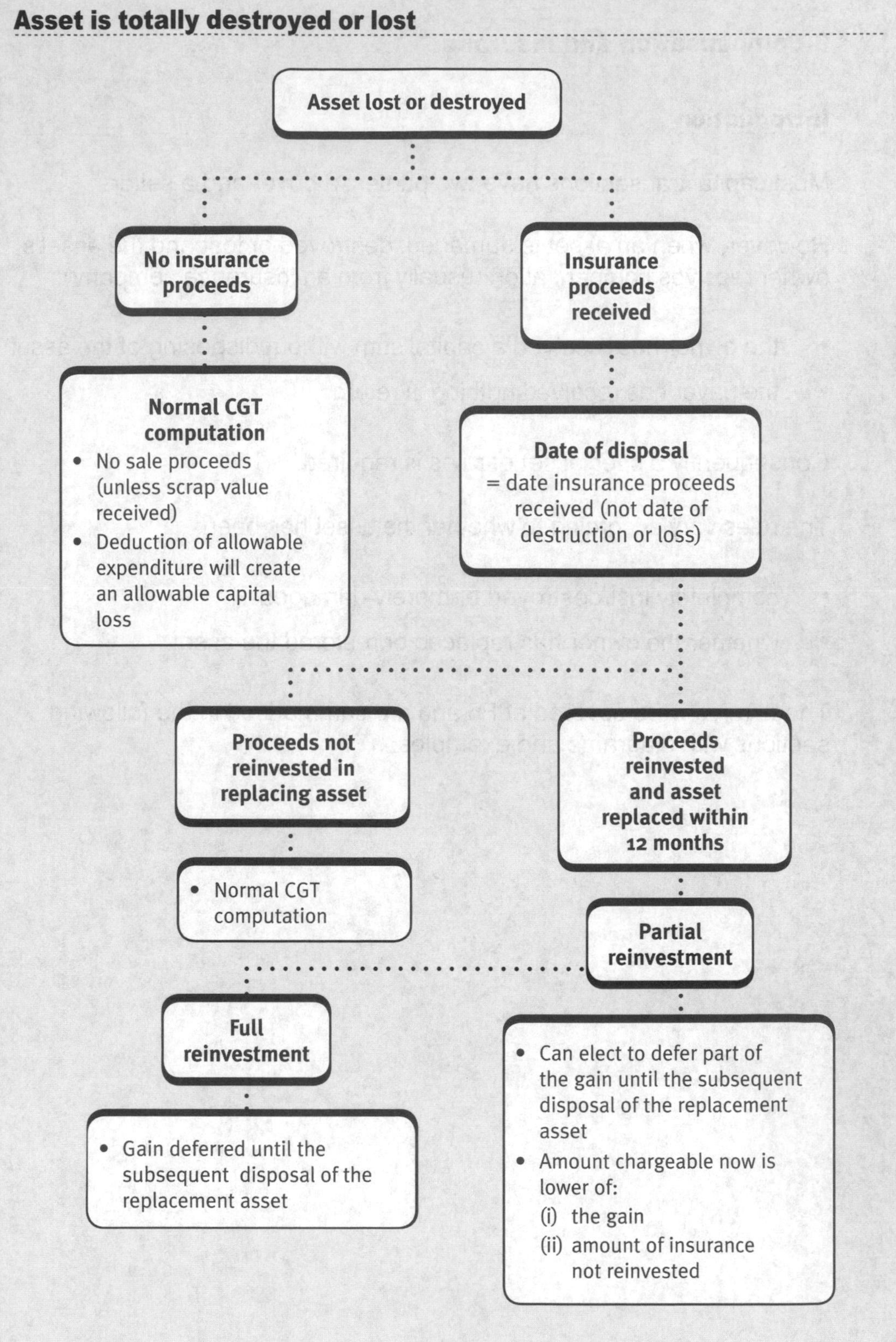

Example 2 – Asset destroyed

Nadir purchased a capital asset for £15,000 on 1 April 1997 which was destroyed by fire on 31 July 2016. She received scrap proceeds of £1,000. The asset was not insured.

Calculate the allowable capital loss arising in the tax year 2016/17.

Solution

	£
Proceeds (scrap proceeds)	1,000
Less: Cost	(15,000)
Allowable loss	(14,000)

Example 3 – Asset destroyed

Bill purchased an asset for £25,000 on 1 October 1998 which was destroyed by fire on 30 September 2016. He received scrap proceeds of £1,000 and compensation of £35,000 from his insurance company on 1 January 2017.

He purchased a replacement asset for £40,000 on 1 February 2017.

Assuming that Bill claims the loss by fire to be a no gain/no loss disposal, calculate the allowable expenditure (base cost) of the replacement asset.

Solution

	£	£
Cost of replacement asset		40,000
Less: Compensation	35,000	
Scrap proceeds	1,000	
	36,000	
Less: Cost of old asset	(25,000)	
		(11,000)
Replacement asset base cost		29,000

Test your understanding 6

Belinda purchased an antique necklace for £21,140 on 1 October 2004 which she lost on 30 June 2016. She received compensation of £45,000 from her insurance company on 1 October 2016 and purchased a replacement necklace for £50,000 on 1 November 2016.

She sold the replacement necklace for £65,000 on 1 March 2017.

Assuming that Belinda claims the loss to be a no gain/no loss disposal, calculate the chargeable gain arising on the sale of the replacement necklace on 1 March 2017.

Asset is damaged but not totally destroyed or lost

Where an asset is damaged there are no implications for CGT purposes unless compensation (e.g. insurance proceeds) is received.

Where an asset is damaged and compensation is received there is a part disposal for CGT purposes. However, the computation is varied depending on whether or not the insurance proceeds are used to restore the asset.

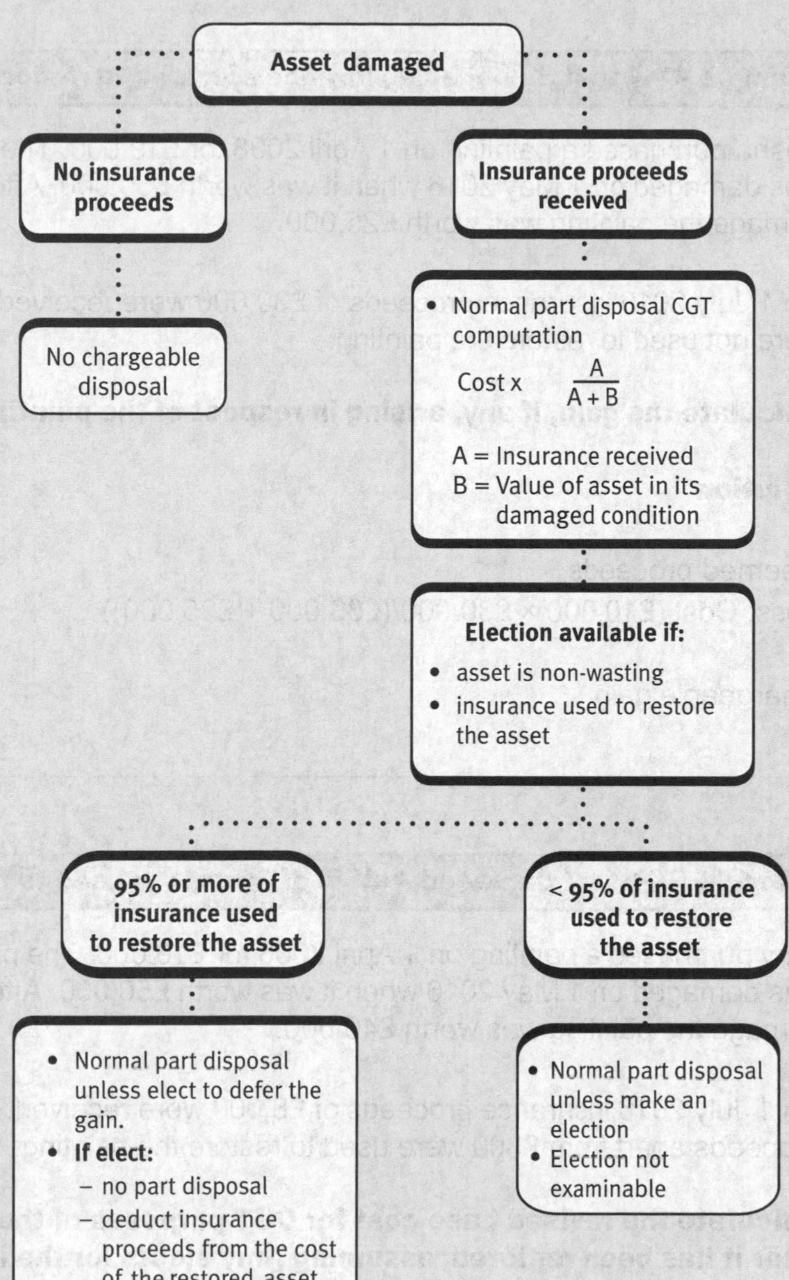

Asset damaged
No insurance proceeds
No chargeable disposal
Insurance proceeds received
• Normal part disposal CGT computation
Cost x $\frac{A}{A + B}$
A = Insurance received
B = Value of asset in its damaged condition
Election available if:
• asset is non-wasting
• insurance used to restore the asset
95% or more of insurance used to restore the asset
• Normal part disposal unless elect to defer the gain.
• If elect:
– no part disposal
– deduct insurance proceeds from the cost of the restored asset
< 95% of insurance used to restore the asset
• Normal part disposal unless make an election
• Election not examinable

Example 4 – Asset damaged, insurance not used to restore asset

Sasha purchased a painting on 1 April 2008 for £10,000. The painting was damaged on 1 May 2016 when it was worth £50,000. After the damage the painting was worth £25,000.

On 1 July 2016 insurance proceeds of £30,000 were received, which were not used to restore the painting.

Calculate the gain, if any, arising in respect of the painting.

Solution

	£
Deemed proceeds	30,000
Less: Cost (£10,000 × £30,000/(£30,000 + £25,000))	(5,455)
Chargeable gain	24,545

Example 5 – Asset damaged, > 95% of insurance used to restore

Amy purchased a painting on 1 April 2008 for £10,000. The painting was damaged on 1 May 2016 when it was worth £50,000. After the damage the painting was worth £40,000.

On 1 July 2016 insurance proceeds of £8,000 were received. All of the proceeds apart from £300 were used to restore the painting.

Calculate the revised base cost for CGT purposes of the painting after it has been restored, assuming Amy elects for the insurance proceeds to be rolled over against the cost of the painting.

Solution

As more than 95% of the proceeds are used to restore the asset and Amy has elected for the proceeds to be rolled over against the cost of the painting, there is no part disposal and the revised base cost of the painting is as follows:

	£
Original cost	10,000
Less: Insurance proceeds	(8,000)
	2,000
Plus: Cost of enhancement	7,700
Revised base cost	9,700

7 Chapter summary

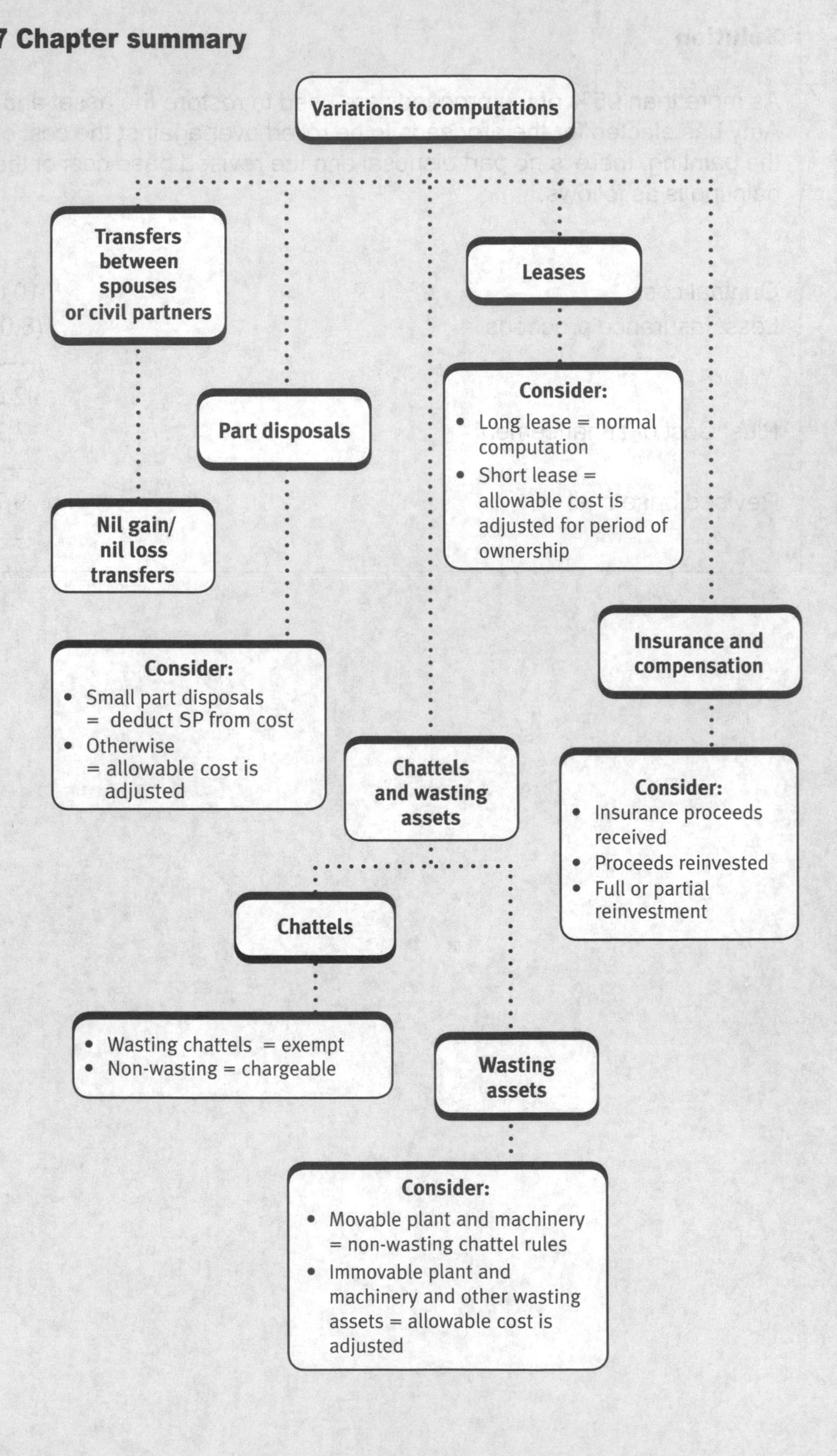

Variations to computations
Transfers between spouses or civil partners
Nil gain/ nil loss transfers
Part disposals
Consider:
• Small part disposals = deduct SP from cost
• Otherwise = allowable cost is adjusted
Leases
Consider:
• Long lease = normal computation
• Short lease = allowable cost is adjusted for period of ownership
Insurance and compensation
Consider:
• Insurance proceeds received
• Proceeds reinvested
• Full or partial reinvestment
Chattels and wasting assets
Chattels
• Wasting chattels = exempt
• Non-wasting = chargeable
Wasting assets
Consider:
• Movable plant and machinery = non-wasting chattel rules
• Immovable plant and machinery and other wasting assets = allowable cost is adjusted

Test your understanding answers

Test your understanding 1

Charlie

(a) (i) **Gift of flat to sister – November 2016**

	£
Market value	175,000
Less: Cost (December 1993)	(23,600)
Chargeable gain	151,400

(ii) **Gift of flat to wife – November 2016**

This is a NGNL for Charlie

(b) **Sale of flat by sister – May 2017**

	£
Sale proceeds	200,000
Less: Deemed cost = market value at the date of the gift	(175,000)
Chargeable gain	25,000

(c) **Sale of flat by wife – May 2017**

	£
Sale proceeds	200,000
Less: Deemed cost	(23,600)
Chargeable gain	176,400

Note: The rate of CGT applicable to the taxable gain in each of these circumstances would be 18% to the extent that the taxpayer has any basic rate band remaining and 28% on any gain in excess of the remaining basic rate band. This is because the asset being disposed of is residential property which is not fully exempt under the PPR exemption.

Test your understanding 2

Alex and Vanessa

Recommendations

Both husband and wife should consider making use of the CGT AEA. This can be achieved if Alex transfers part of the ownership of the property to Vanessa prior to the disposal to a third party. The transfer between spouses is treated as a NGNL transaction.

As Vanessa has capital losses brought forward these could be used to offset any gain arising that belongs to her.

Vanessa also has part of her basic rate band remaining, so this should be used. As the asset being disposed of is a residential property and the gain arising will not be fully covered by the PPR exemption, gains in the basic rate band will be taxed at 18% whereas Alex will be taxed at 28%.

Current position

	Alex	**Vanessa**
	£	£
Chargeable gains	32,000	0
Less: Capital loss b/f	(0)	(c/f again)
	32,000	0
Less: AEA	(11,100)	(not used)
Taxable gain	20,900	0
BRB remaining £0/(£32,000 – £15,000)	0	17,000
CGT payable (£20,900 × 28%)/(£0× 18%)	5,852	0

Vanessa could receive gains of up to:

- £17,300 (£6,200 capital losses b/f + £11,100 AEA) and have no CGT to pay, and
- a further £17,000 (remaining basic rate band) and only pay CGT at 18%.

The taxation effect

The % which needs to be transferred to obtain the optimum position on disposal is calculated as follows:

Alex requires a gain of £11,100 to use his AEA. He will then pay no CGT.

The balance of the gain of £20,900 (£32,000 – £11,100) should be realised by Vanessa to use her AEA of £11,100, capital losses of £6,200 and the remainder is taxed at the basic rate.

A gain of £20,900 for Vanessa out of a total of £32,000 is 65%, therefore 65% ownership of the asset should be transferred to Vanessa pre sale.

Revised position

	Alex	**Vanessa**
	£	£
Chargeable gains	11,100	20,900
Less: Capital loss b/f	(0)	(6,200)
	11,100	14,700
Less: AEA	(11,100)	(11,100)
Taxable gain	0	3,600
CGT payable (£0 × 28%)/(£3,600 × 18%)	0	648

Tax saving

CGT saving is £5,204 (£5,852 – £648).

Alternative calculation:

	£
Utilisation of Vanessa's AEA and capital loss b/f Tax saving (£17,300 × 28%)	4,844
Remaining gain taxed at a lower rate Tax saving (£3,600 × (28% – 18%))	360
	5,204

Test your understanding 3

Edward

(i) **An election to defer the gain on the part disposal is made**

Disposal in July 2016

In July 2016, the whole 12 acres are worth £89,500 (£9,500 + £80,000).

This is the only sale of land in the tax year, and the sale proceeds received of £9,500 are

- ≤ £17,900 (20% × £89,500), and
- ≤ £20,000.

Therefore an election can be made to defer the gain.

No gain arises on the part disposal, the base cost of the remaining 10 acres becomes £20,500 (£30,000 – £9,500).

Disposal in September 2017	£
Sale proceeds	135,000
Less: Base cost	(20,500)
Chargeable gain	114,500

(ii) **No election is made**

Disposal in July 2016	£
Sale proceeds (2 acres)	9,500
Less: Cost (2 acres)	
= £30,000 × £9,500/(£9,500 + £80,000)	(3,184)
Chargeable gain	6,316

Disposal in September 2017	£
Sale proceeds	135,000
Less: Remaining cost (£30,000 – £3,184)	(26,816)
Chargeable gain	108,184

Note: The total chargeable gains = £114,500 (£6,316 + £108,184) which is the same total as part (i).

However, with the election the gain is deferred until the later disposal of the remainder. Whether or not this is beneficial will depend on the availability of AEAs, the level of taxable income and the tax rates applicable when the disposals are made.

Test your understanding 4

Frank

	£
Sale proceeds	90,000
Less: Deemed cost	
$£50,000 \times \frac{94.842 \text{ (\% for 39 years)}}{95.457 \text{ (\% for 40 years)}}$	(49,678)
Chargeable gain	40,322

Test your understanding 5

Geoffrey

	£
Disposal proceeds	75,000
Less: Deemed cost (W)	(60,504)
Chargeable gain	14,496

Working: Deductible lease cost

Years left to run at acquisition: 48 years
Years left to run at disposal: 42 years 7 months

The percentage for 42 years 7 months is:

96.593 + 7/12 × (97.107 – 96.593) = 96.893

The allowable cost to deduct in the computation is therefore:

$$£62,000 \times \frac{96.893 \text{ (\% for 42 years 7 months)}}{99.289 \text{ (\% for 48 years)}}$$

= £60,504

Test your understanding 6

Belinda

	£
Proceeds	65,000
Less: Cost (W)	(26,140)
Chargeable gain	38,860

Working: Replacement asset base cost

	£	£
Cost of replacement necklace		50,000
Insurance proceeds	45,000	
Less: Base cost	(21,140)	
		(23,860)
Replacement asset base cost		26,140

chapter

8

CGT: Shares and securities for individuals and stamp duty

Chapter learning objectives

Upon completion of this chapter you will be able to:

- calculate the gain on the disposal of shares by an individual including situations which involve bonus and rights issues
- define a qualifying corporate bond (QCB), understand what makes a corporate bond non-qualifying and identify the capital gains tax implications of the disposal of QCB's
- identify the alternative capital gains tax treatment of the sale of rights issues
- identify the capital gains tax implications for an individual of a takeover or reorganisation of a shareholding in exchange for other shares, and where there is cash consideration received
- identify the capital gains tax implications for an individual of a takeover involving an exchange of shares for shares, cash and/or QCBs
- explain the capital gains tax implications arising from the liquidation of a company
- recognise the relief available for a capital loss on unquoted trading company shares
- identify when stamp duty is payable on the transfer of shares and securities and calculate the amount of stamp duty payable.

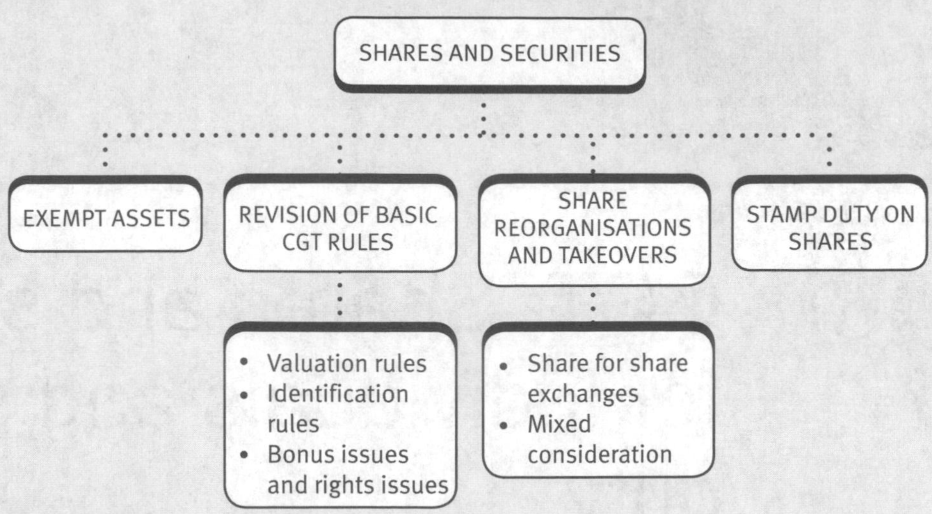

Introduction

This chapter revises the CGT rules as they apply to shares and securities, which were covered at F6.

A brief reminder of F6 content is given, and revision examples are provided to check your retention of the required F6 knowledge.

New topics introduced at P6 include the treatment of the sale of rights nil paid, share reorganisations with mixed consideration, the liquidation of a company and stamp duty which is levied on transactions in shares.

1 A revision of basic shares and securities rules

Exempt shares and securities

All shares and securities disposed of by an individual are subject to CGT except for the following, which are exempt:

- listed government securities (i.e. gilt-edged securities) (e.g. Treasury stock, Exchequer stock)
- qualifying corporate bonds (QCB) (e.g. company loan stock)
- shares held in an ISA.

Note that gilt-edged securities and QCBs are exempt assets only when disposed of by an individual or a trust (but not when disposed of by a company, see Chapter 22).

Definition of a QCB

A QCB is a security (loan note) which:

(a) represents a normal commercial loan

(b) is expressed in sterling and has no provision for either conversion into, or redemption in, any other currency; and

(c) was issued after 13 March 1984 or was acquired by the disposer after that date (whenever it was issued)

(d) it cannot be converted into shares.

Valuation rules for shares

For the purposes of the rest of this chapter, the rules described apply to both shares and securities which are not exempt. However, for simplicity the term 'shares' will be used to denote both shares and securities.

On the sale of shares to an unconnected person, the actual sale proceeds are used in the chargeable gain computation.

On a lifetime gift of shares, or the transfer to a connected person, the market value must be used.

The market value of shares for lifetime gifts, for CGT purposes, is calculated as follows:

Quoted Shares	Value = the mid-price quoted on the Stock Exchange (i.e. the simple average of the lowest and highest closing prices of the day)
Unquoted Shares	In the examination the appropriate value will usually be given.

Test your understanding 1

The closing prices of shares in ABC plc are quoted in the Stock Exchange Daily Official List at 230p – 270p.

Calculate the value of ABC plc shares for capital gains tax purposes.

For the valuation rules for shares gifted on death, see Chapter 6, section 3.

Identification rules for individuals

Disposals of shares are matched in the following order with acquisitions:

(1) on the same day as the date of disposal

(2) within the **following** 30 days on a first in, first out (FIFO basis)

(3) in the share pool
(i.e. shares acquired before the date of disposal are pooled together).

The share pool simply keeps a record of the number of shares in the same company acquired and sold, and the cost of those shares.

When shares are disposed out of the share pool the appropriate proportion of the cost that relates to the shares disposed of is calculated. The shares are disposed of at their average cost.

Bonus issues and rights issues

	Bonus issue	**Rights issue**
Explanation	A bonus issue is: • the distribution of free shares • to existing shareholders only • in proportion to their existing shareholding.	A rights issue is: • the offer of new shares • to existing shareholders only • in proportion to their existing shareholding • usually at a discount on the current market value.
For identification purposes	Bonus and rights shares are included in the share pool.	
For the purposes of calculating the gain on the shares	As bonus shares are free: • the number of shares are included in the pool, but no cost • the total cost of the shares purchased is shared between all of the shares in issue after the bonus issue.	As there is cost involved in purchasing the rights shares: • the number of shares are included in the pool, and the cost is added in the same way as a normal purchase • the total cost is shared between all of the shares in issue after the rights issue.

Example 1 – Bonus and rights issues

Carmichael had the following transactions in Rudderham Ltd shares.

January 2014	purchased 1,800 shares for £5,400
March 2015	bonus issue of 1 for 2
May 2015	purchased 600 shares for £1,500
June 2015	took up 1-for-3 rights issue at £2.30 per share
August 2016	sold 4,000 shares for £14,000

Assume that Rudderham Ltd is not Carmichael's personal trading company.

Calculate the chargeable gain or allowable loss on the disposal in August 2016.

Solution

		Number	Cost
			£
January 2014	Purchase	1,800	5,400
March 2015	Bonus issue (1:2)	900	0
May 2015	Purchase	600	1,500
		3,300	6,900
June 2015	Rights issue (1:3) × £2.30	1,100	2,530
		4,400	9,430
August 2016	Sale	(4,000)	(8,573)
Balance c/f		400	857

	£
Sale proceeds	14,000
Less: Cost	(8,573)
Chargeable gain	5,427

Test your understanding 2

Tom Chalk purchased the following shares in A plc:

	Number	Cost
		£
18.04.94	1,500	900
14.06.97 Rights issue (70p each)	1:3	
31.05.06	1,000	2,000
31.07.06 Bonus issue	1:4	
31.08.10	900	1,500
28.01.17	1,500	3,000

Tom disposed of 4,500 shares in A plc on 31 December 2016 for £22,500. Assume A plc is not Tom's personal trading company.

Identify which shares are sold and calculate the total taxable gains arising in the tax year 2016/17.

Sale of rights nil paid

If the shareholder who is offered the rights issue does not wish to purchase more shares in the company they can sell the right to buy the new shares to another person. This is known as a 'sale of rights nil paid'.

The treatment of a 'sale of rights nil paid' for CGT purposes depends on the amount of sale proceeds (SP) received as follows:

If SP received are:	(i) > 5% of the value of the shares on which the rights are offered; **and** (ii) > £3,000.	(i) ≤ 5% of the value of the shares on which the rights are offered; **or** (ii) ≤ £3,000 if higher.
CGT treatment:	• deemed part disposal of original shares held. • normal part disposal computation required.	• no chargeable disposal at the time of the sale of rights nil paid. • SP received are deducted from the cost of the original shares.

Test your understanding 3

Ernest acquired 12,000 shares in Pickford plc on 22 July 1996 for £24,000.

On 13 August 2016 there was a 1 for 5 rights issue at £2.30 per share. The market value of the shares after the issue was £2.65 per share.

Ernest did not take up the issue, but sold his rights nil paid on 25 August 2016.

He sold 10,000 of his shares in Pickford plc for £37,000 on 23 June 2017.

Assume that Pickford plc is not Ernest's personal trading company.

Calculate the chargeable gains arising assuming the rights are sold nil paid for:

(a) **£6,000**

(b) **£1,500**

Summary

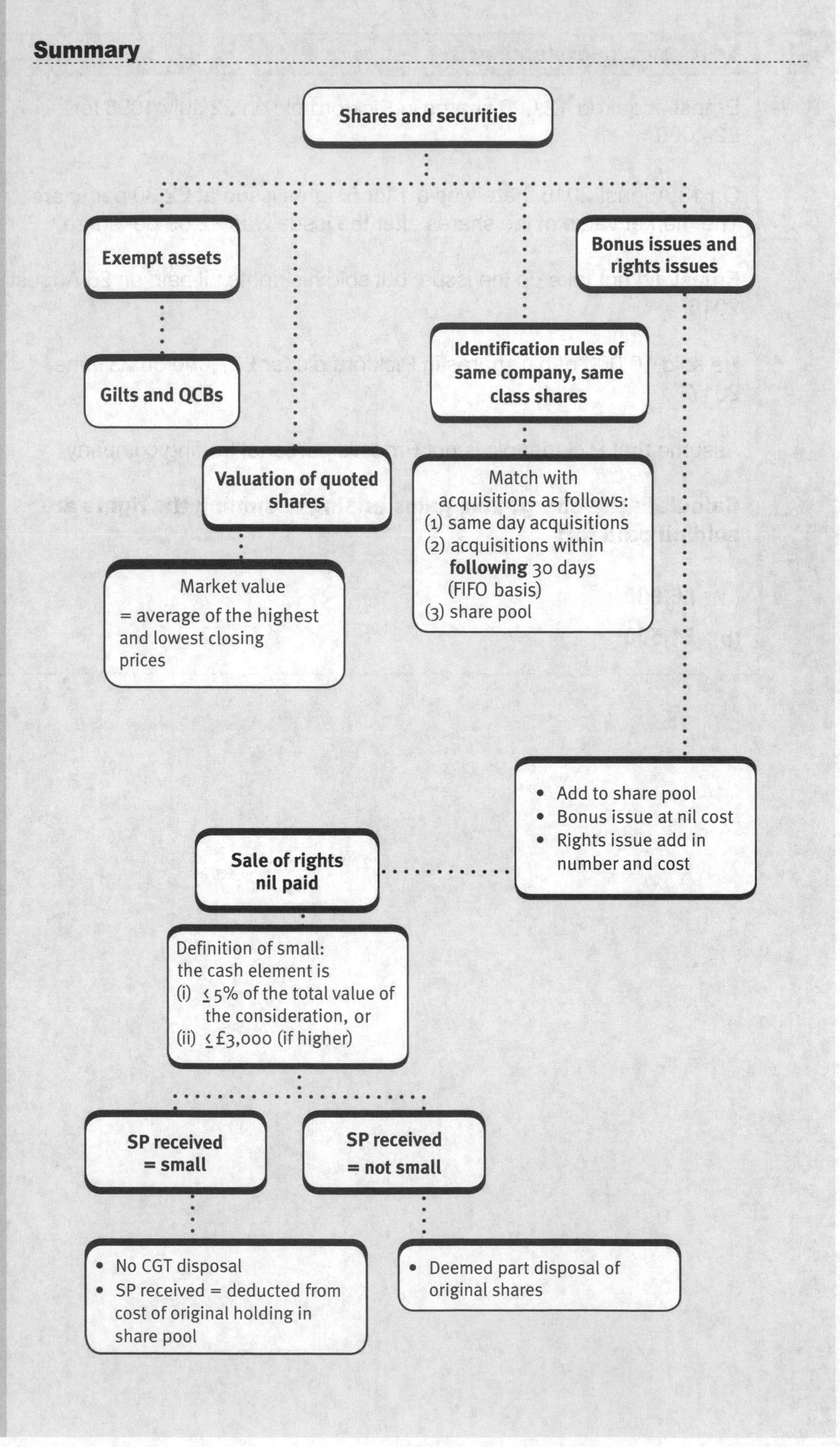
Shares and securities
Exempt assets
Gilts and QCBs
Valuation of quoted shares
Market value
= average of the highest and lowest closing prices
Identification rules of same company, same class shares
Match with acquisitions as follows:
(1) same day acquisitions
(2) acquisitions within **following** 30 days (FIFO basis)
(3) share pool
Bonus issues and rights issues
• Add to share pool
• Bonus issue at nil cost
• Rights issue add in number and cost
Sale of rights nil paid
Definition of small: the cash element is
(i) ≤ 5% of the total value of the consideration, or
(ii) ≤ £3,000 (if higher)
SP received = small
SP received = not small
• No CGT disposal
• SP received = deducted from cost of original holding in share pool
• Deemed part disposal of original shares

2 Reorganisations and takeovers

Introduction

A reorganisation involves the exchange of existing shares in a company for other shares of another class in the same company.

A takeover occurs when a company acquires shares in another by issuing:

- shares
- loan notes
- cash.

Share for share exchanges

Where the consideration for a reorganisation or takeover only involves the issue of shares in the acquiring company, the transaction is referred to as a 'paper for paper' transaction.

A reminder of the share for share exchange rules covered at F6 is given in expandable text and is summarised in the diagram below.

Share for share exchange

The tax consequences are as follows:

- No CGT is charged at the time of the reorganisation/takeover.
- The new shares acquired are treated as if they were acquired at the same time and at the same cost as the original shares.
- The new shares 'stand in the shoes' of the old shares (i.e. the date of purchase and the cost of the original shares become the deemed date of purchase and cost of the new shares acquired).

- Where the shareholder receives more than one type of share in exchange for the original shares, the cost of the original shares is apportioned to the new shares by reference to the **market values** of the replacement shares and securities as follows:
  - quoted shares: **on the first day of quotation**
  - unquoted shares: **at the time of the first disposal** of those shares.

For this treatment to apply where Company A is taking over Company B, the following qualifying conditions must be satisfied:

- Company A obtains more than 25% of Company B's ordinary share capital as a result of the offer; or
- there is a general offer to members of Company B which would give control to Company A if accepted; or
- Company A can exercise more than 50% of the voting power in Company B.
- The exchange is for a bona fide commercial reason.
- The exchange is not part of a scheme or arrangement which has as its main purpose the avoidance of CGT or corporation tax.

The acquiring company can obtain advance clearance from HMRC that the transaction comes within these rules and that the qualifying conditions have been met.

Test your understanding 4

Major purchased 2,000 ordinary shares in Blue plc for £5,000 in June 2013.

In July 2016 Blue plc underwent a reorganisation and Major received two 'A' ordinary shares and one preference share for each ordinary share. Immediately after the reorganisation 'A' ordinary shares were quoted at £2 and preference shares at £1.

In December 2016 Major sold all his holding of 'A' ordinary shares for £8,000.

Assume that Blue plc is not Majors' personal trading company.

Calculate the chargeable gain or allowable loss arising on the disposal in December 2016.

The individual taxpayer may choose to disapply the normal share for share rules if they want to.

Interaction with entrepreneurs' relief

- Entrepreneurs' relief will only be available on a future disposal of the replacement shares if the replacement shares meet the necessary conditions (see Chapter 9).

- It therefore may be more beneficial to choose to disapply the normal share for share exchange rules, so that any gain on disposal of ordinary shares is chargeable to CGT immediately and may be covered by the AEA and/or the gain arising is taxed at 10% to take advantage of entrepreneurs' relief available now.

Takeovers: Consideration in cash and shares

If the consideration for the takeover consists of a mixture of cash and shares, the tax consequences depend on whether the cash element of the transaction is small.

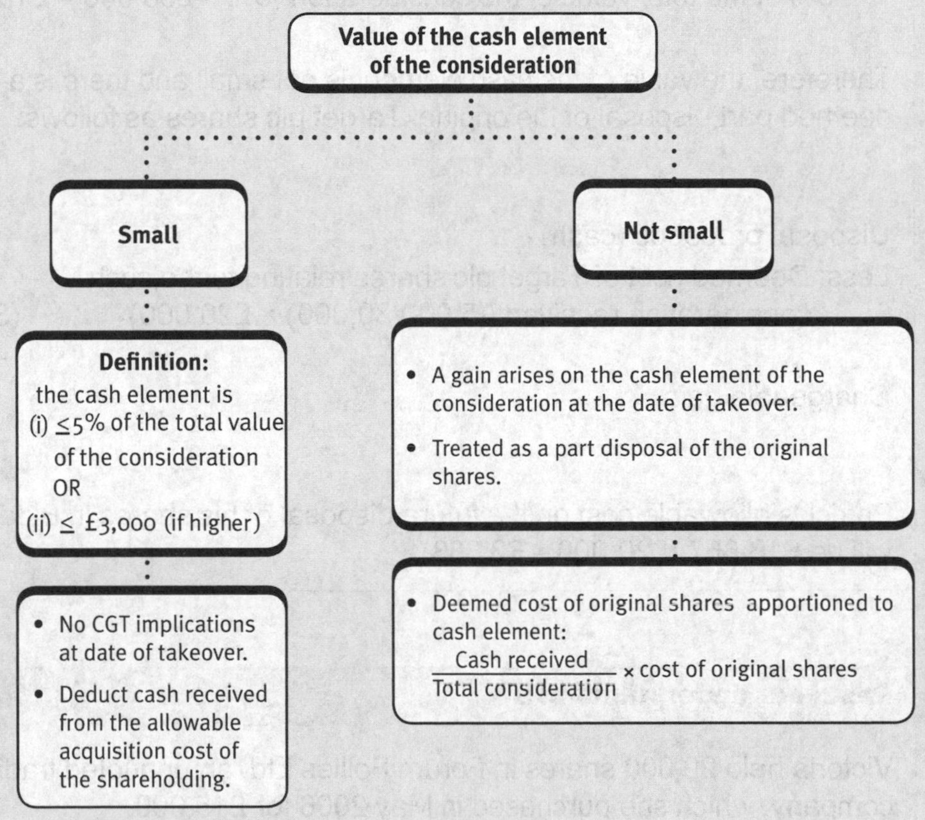

Example 2 – Takeovers

Patrick bought 10,000 shares in Target plc in May 2011 for £20,000.

On 3 November 2016 the entire share capital of Target plc was acquired by Bidder plc. Target plc shareholders received 2 Bidder plc shares and £0.50 cash for each share held. Bidder plc shares were quoted at £1.25.

Calculate the chargeable gain accruing to Patrick as a result of the takeover in November 2016.

Solution

	£
Shares (20,000 × £1.25)	25,000
Cash (10,000 × £0.50)	5,000
Total consideration from Bidder plc	30,000

The cash Patrick has received of £5,000 exceeds higher of:

- £3,000; and
- 5% of the total value of the consideration (5% × £30,000 = £1,500).

Therefore, the value of the cash element is not small and there is a deemed part disposal of the original Target plc shares as follows:

	£
Disposal proceeds (cash)	5,000
Less: Deemed cost of Target plc shares relating to the cash consideration received ((5,000/30,000) × £20,000)	(3,333)
Chargeable gain	1,667

Patrick's allowable cost on the future disposal of his shares in Bidder plc will be £16,667 (£20,000 – £3,333).

Test your understanding 5

Victoria held 20,000 shares in Forum Follies Ltd, an unquoted trading company, which she purchased in May 2006 for £15,000.

In January 2017 Exciting Enterprises plc acquired all the share capital of Forum Follies Ltd.

Under the terms of the takeover, shareholders in Forum Follies Ltd received three ordinary shares and one preference share in Exciting Enterprises plc, plus £1 cash for every two shares previously held in Forum Follies Ltd.

Immediately after the takeover, the shares in Exciting Enterprises plc are quoted at £3 each (ordinary shares) and £1.50 each (preference shares).

Victoria has never worked for Forum Follies Ltd and has taxable income of £40,000 for the tax year 2016/17.

Calculate Victoria's capital gains tax liability for the tax year 2016/17.

Takeovers: Mixed consideration, including QCBs

If consideration for the takeover consists of a mixture of shares, cash and QCBs (e.g. company loan notes), there are CGT consequences relating to:

- the cash element of the consideration
- the QCBs received.

At the time of the takeover

The tax consequences relating to the cash element of the consideration are the same as summarised in the previous section above.

The tax consequences of receiving QCBs in exchange for shares as part of the takeover consideration are as follows:

- a chargeable gain is computed at the time of the takeover, as if the corporate bond were cash
- the gain is not taxed at that time
- the gain is 'frozen' and is not charged until the corporate bond is disposed of at a later date.

Subsequent disposal of corporate bond

When the corporate bond is disposed of:

- no gain arises on the bond itself as QCBs are exempt assets
- the 'frozen' gain becomes chargeable and will be taxed at 10%/20%.

Interaction with entrepreneurs' relief

- If entrepreneurs' relief is available on the gain computed at the time of the takeover, the taxpayer may elect for entrepreneurs' relief (see Chapter 9), and the gain eligible will be taxed at 10% at that time.

- Any remaining gain above the lifetime limit can be 'frozen' and will crystallise when the QCB is disposed of. This gain will be taxed at the appropriate rate when it crystallises in the future.
- If entrepreneurs' relief is not claimed, the gain at takeover will be deferred, as described above, and will be taxed at the appropriate rate when the QCB is disposed of in the future.

Tax planning

These rules provide a tax planning opportunity as the individual:

- can choose when they will dispose of the QCBs
- can dispose of the QCBs in small amounts on a piecemeal basis.

They can plan to ensure that, as far as possible, the deferred gain is crystallised and matched against:

- any unused annual exempt amount each year
- any available capital losses

so that no CGT arises on the disposal of the QCBs.

Example 3 – Mixed consideration

On 26 May 2016, Mike sold 200 £1 ordinary shares in Café plc for £5,500 and all of his loan notes in Café plc for £9,600.

Mike originally bought 1,500 shares in Joe's Café Ltd in July 2011 for £1,215 when he started to work for the business.

Joe's Café Ltd was taken over by Café plc in August 2012.

For every 20 ordinary shares held in Joe's Café Ltd a shareholder received:

- £100 in cash
- 10 ordinary shares in Café plc
- £1 loan notes in Café plc.

Immediately after the takeover the value of Café plc's shares and securities were:

£1 ordinary shares	£12
Loan notes	£55

Assume Joe's Cafe Ltd is not Mikes' personal trading company.

Calculate the capital gains arising in the tax years 2012/13 and 2016/17.

Solution

Apportionment of cost of Joe's Café Ltd 1,500 ordinary shares to the consideration received August 2012.

	Purchase consideration	Cost allocation
Cash	£	£
(£100 × 1,500/20)	7,500	
(£1,215 × £7,500/£20,625)		442
750 ordinary shares in Café plc		
(10 × £12 × 1,500/20)	9,000	
(£1,215 × £9,000/£20,625)		530
Loan notes		
(£55 × 1,500/20)	4,125	
(£1,215 × £4,125/£20,625)		243
	20,625	1,215

Cash consideration of £7,500 exceeds £3,000 and exceeds £1,031 (5% of £20,625).

Therefore cash consideration is not small. A part disposal would have arisen in 2012/13 on the cash consideration as follows:

Disposal of Joe's Café Ltd shares for cash – August 2012

	£
Cash received	7,500
Less: Deemed cost	(442)
Chargeable gain in 2012/13	7,058

Disposal of Joe's Café Ltd shares for QCBs (loan notes) – August 2012

	£
Value of loan notes received	4,125
Less: Deemed cost	(243)
'Frozen' gain	3,882
Taxable at time of takeover in 2012/13	0
Total chargeable gains in 2012/13 (£7,058 + 0)	7,058

Disposal of 200 Café plc shares – 26 May 2016

	£
Proceeds	5,500
Less: Deemed cost (£530 × 200/750)	(141)
Chargeable gain	5,359

Disposal of Café plc loan notes – 26 May 2016

The gain on the disposal of the loan notes of £5,475 (£9,600 – £4,125) is exempt from CGT, as the loan notes are QCBs.

However, the frozen gain that arose at the time of the takeover in 2012/13 becomes chargeable in 2016/17 on the disposal of the loan notes.

	£
Chargeable gain in 2016/17 when the loan notes are sold	3,882
Total chargeable gains in 2016/17 (£5,359 + £3,882)	9,241

Test your understanding 6

On 31 March 2017, Jasper sold 400 £1 ordinary shares in Grasp plc for £3,600.

Jasper had acquired the Grasp plc shares as a result of a successful takeover bid by Grasp plc of Cawte plc on 5 December 2016.

Prior to the takeover Jasper had owned 12,000 £1 ordinary shares in Cawte plc (not his personal trading company), which he had acquired for £15,700 on 3 May 2014.

The terms of the take-over bid were:

- one £1 ordinary share in Grasp plc, plus
- two 10% loan notes in Grasp plc, plus
- 40p in cash

for every £1 ordinary share in Cawte plc.

The following are the quoted prices for the shares and loan notes of Grasp plc at 5 December 2016:

£1 ordinary shares	350p
10% loan notes	110p

(a) **Calculate the chargeable gains arising in 2016/17.**

(b) **Explain the CGT consequences that would arise if Jasper were to sell all of his loan notes in Grasp plc in June 2018 for £32,000.**

Summary

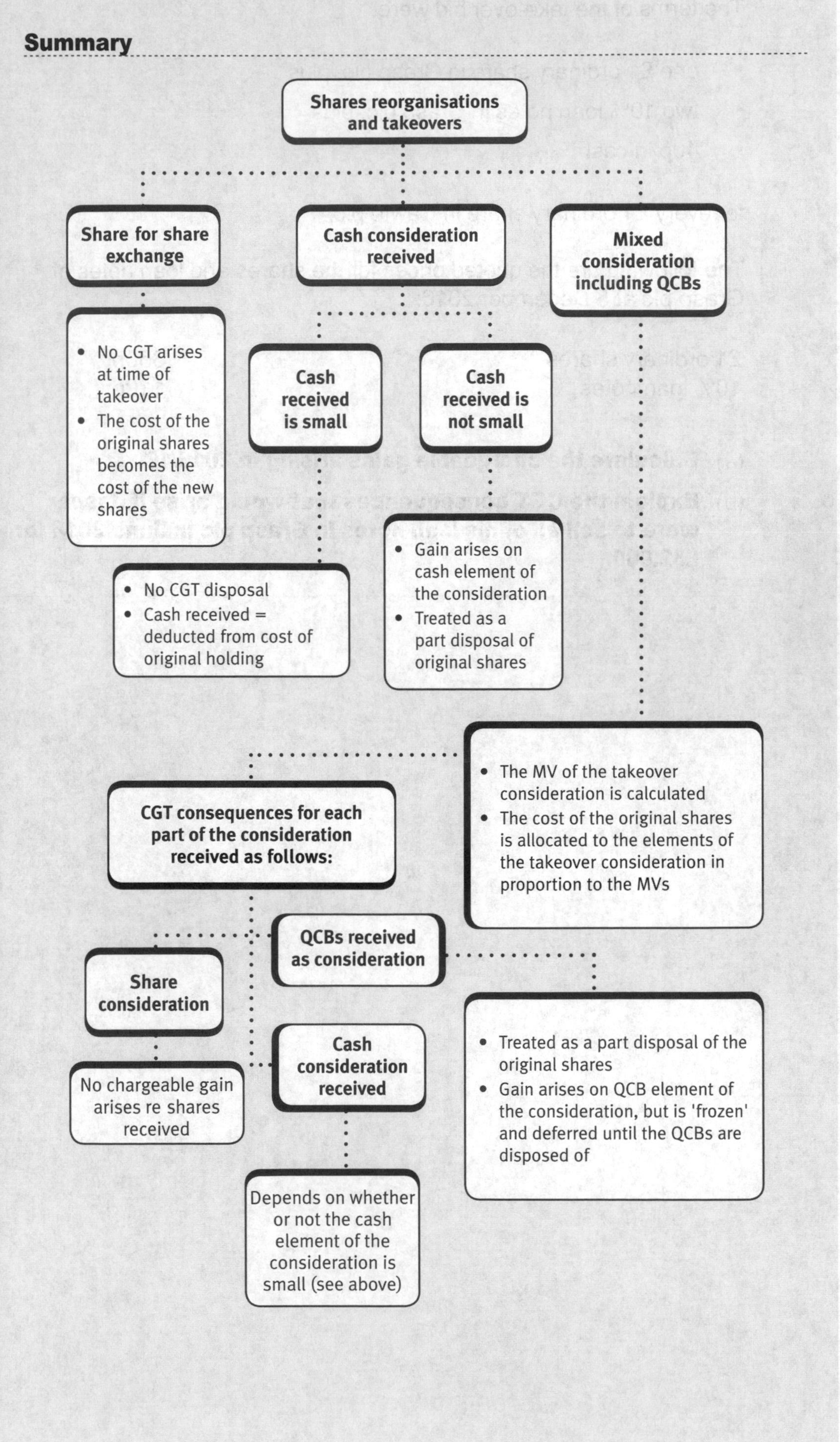

Shares reorganisations and takeovers
Share for share exchange
Cash consideration received
Mixed consideration including QCBs
• No CGT arises at time of takeover
• The cost of the original shares becomes the cost of the new shares
Cash received is small
Cash received is not small
• No CGT disposal
• Cash received = deducted from cost of original holding
• Gain arises on cash element of the consideration
• Treated as a part disposal of original shares
• The MV of the takeover consideration is calculated
• The cost of the original shares is allocated to the elements of the takeover consideration in proportion to the MVs
CGT consequences for each part of the consideration received as follows:
QCBs received as consideration
Share consideration
No chargeable gain arises re shares received
Cash consideration received
Depends on whether or not the cash element of the consideration is small (see above)
• Treated as a part disposal of the original shares
• Gain arises on QCB element of the consideration, but is 'frozen' and deferred until the QCBs are disposed of

3 The liquidation of a company

On the liquidation of a company, the liquidator will distribute cash or other assets to the shareholders once the company's liabilities have been paid.

The CGT implications are as follows:

- the shareholders are treated as having sold their shares for proceeds equal to the amount received on the liquidation
- a chargeable gain on the disposal of shares must be computed in the normal way.

Loss relief against income

Capital losses are normally carried forward and used to reduce future chargeable gains. However, an alternative use of the capital loss can be claimed.

Relief against income is available if:

- the loss arises on **shares subscribed for** in an **unquoted trading company,** and
- conditions are satisfied.

A claim for relief against income enables the individual:

- to use the capital loss to reduce total income
- of the tax year in which the loss arose and/or the preceding tax year.

Therefore, the claim effectively converts a capital loss into a trading loss which can be utilised in the same way as trading loss relief against total income (see Chapter 17).

As a result, it is possible that higher tax savings can be achieved and relief for the losses obtained earlier.

Conditions for loss relief against income

Relief against income is only available if:

- the loss arose on the disposal of:
  - unquoted ordinary shares
  - in an eligible trading company (defined in the same way as for EIS purposes).
- the shares must have been subscribed for, not purchased; and

- the disposal must have:
  - been an arm's length transaction for full consideration, or
  - occurred on the winding-up of the company, or
  - been because the value of the shares has become negligible.

Test your understanding 7

Bob subscribed for 5,000 shares in W Ltd, an unquoted trading company, in August 2009 for £3 per share.

On 1 December 2016, Bob received a letter informing him that the company had gone into receivership. As a result, the shares are almost worthless.

The receivers dealing with the company estimate that on the liquidation, he will receive 10p per share.

Bob has non-savings income £45,000 in the tax year 2016/17.

State any reliefs Bob can claim regarding the fall in value of his shares in W Ltd and describe the operation of any reliefs which could reduce Bob's taxable income.

4 Stamp duty and stamp duty reserve tax

Introduction

Stamp duty land tax is covered in detail in Chapter 6. This section covers stamp duty, which is payable on the transfer of shares and other marketable securities unless the transfer is specifically exempt.

Stamp duty is payable:

- normally by the purchaser
- on the transfer of shares and securities when transferred by a formal instrument (e.g. a written document known as a stock transfer form)
- not on newly issued shares
- based on the consideration payable for the shares/securities (note that this is not necessarily the market value of the shares)

Where shares and securities are transferred without a written document, for example where shares are transferred electronically, stamp duty reserve tax (SDRT) applies.

The rate of duty payable

Stamp duty is normally:

- charged at a rate of ½% of the consideration payable for the shares/securities
- rounded up to the nearest £5
- levied on the date of the transfer document
- there is no charge if the consideration is £1,000 or less.

SDRT is normally:

- charged at a rate of ½% of the consideration payable for the shares/securities
- rounded to the nearest pence
- levied on the date of the agreement.

Exemptions from stamp duty

The main exemptions from stamp duty relate to either the type of transfer or the type of security being transferred as follows:

- exempt transfers:
  - gifts, provided no consideration is given
  - divorce arrangements
  - variation of a will
  - change in composition of trustees
  - takeovers and reconstructions where the new shareholdings mirror the old shareholdings
  - transfers between 75% group companies (see Chapter 7)
  - investment transfers.
- exempt securities:
  - government stocks
  - most company loan stock (but not convertible loan stock)
  - unit trusts
  - shares quoted on growth markets (e.g. AIM shares).

To qualify for exemption, the transfer document must state which exemption is being claimed.

Company loan stock exempt from stamp duty

Most company loan stock is exempt from stamp duty provided it:

(a) cannot be converted into shares or other securities; and

(b) does not carry interest at more than a commercial rate or at a rate linked to the company results; and

(c) does not carry the right to the repayment of more than the nominal amount of the capital, unless the premium is reasonable in relation to other loan stock listed in the Stock Exchange Daily Official List.

Example 4 – Stamp duty

Harry made the following purchases in the tax year 2016/17:

(a) 5,000 shares in a quoted company for £10,000

(b) £8,000 8% convertible loan stock of a quoted company for £12,000

(c) £10,000 5% Treasury Stock 2020 for £9,000

(d) 5,000 units in Growbig unit trust for £6,250

(e) 10,000 £1 ordinary shares in an unquoted company for £75,000. The shares had a market value of £250,000 at that time.

Show how much stamp duty is payable by Harry on each of these transactions.

Solution

(a) 0.5% × £10,000 = £50

(b) 0.5% × £12,000 = £60

(c) Nil – there is no stamp duty on the purchase of government securities

(d) Nil – there is no stamp duty on the purchase of units in a unit trust

(e) 0.5% × £75,000 = £375 (the market value of the shares is not relevant)

Test your understanding 8

In February 2017, Hooker purchased the following:

(a) 5,000 shares in Summit plc for £10,230.

(b) the whole of the issued share capital of Harcourts Ltd for £125,000 plus an additional payment of £35,000 if the company's profits for the year ending 31 December 2016 exceed £80,000.

(c) £10,000 5% Treasury Stock 2022 for £9,500.

Calculate the amount of stamp duty payable.

Administration of stamp duty

Where stamp duty is due, a stock transfer form must be presented to HMRC and duty must be paid at the same time.

A penalty may be imposed if a document is not stamped within 30 days:

- of its execution; or
- being brought into the UK if it was executed outside the UK (and does not relate to UK).

Interest is charged from 30 days after the date of execution, whether the document was executed in the UK or not.

A penalty for an incorrect return may be imposed in line with the penalty regime for all taxes (see Chapter 16).

Summary

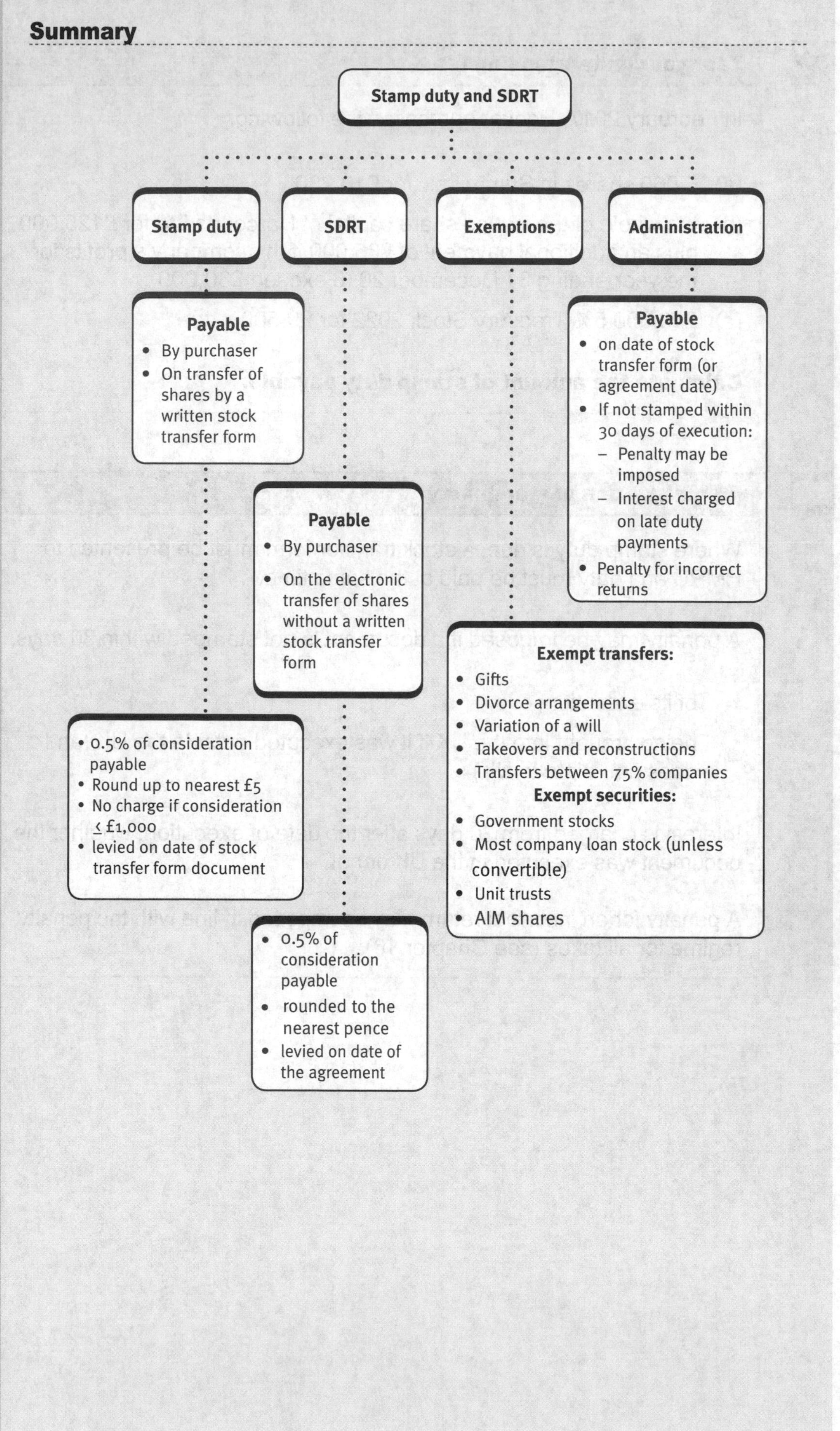
Stamp duty and SDRT
Stamp duty
SDRT
Exemptions
Administration
Payable
• By purchaser
• On transfer of shares by a written stock transfer form
Payable
• By purchaser
• On the electronic transfer of shares without a written stock transfer form
• 0.5% of consideration payable
• Round up to nearest £5
• No charge if consideration ≤ £1,000
• levied on date of stock transfer form document
• 0.5% of consideration payable
• rounded to the nearest pence
• levied on date of the agreement
Payable
• on date of stock transfer form (or agreement date)
• If not stamped within 30 days of execution:
– Penalty may be imposed
– Interest charged on late duty payments
• Penalty for incorrect returns
Exempt transfers:
• Gifts
• Divorce arrangements
• Variation of a will
• Takeovers and reconstructions
• Transfers between 75% companies
Exempt securities:
• Government stocks
• Most company loan stock (unless convertible)
• Unit trusts
• AIM shares

5 Chapter summary

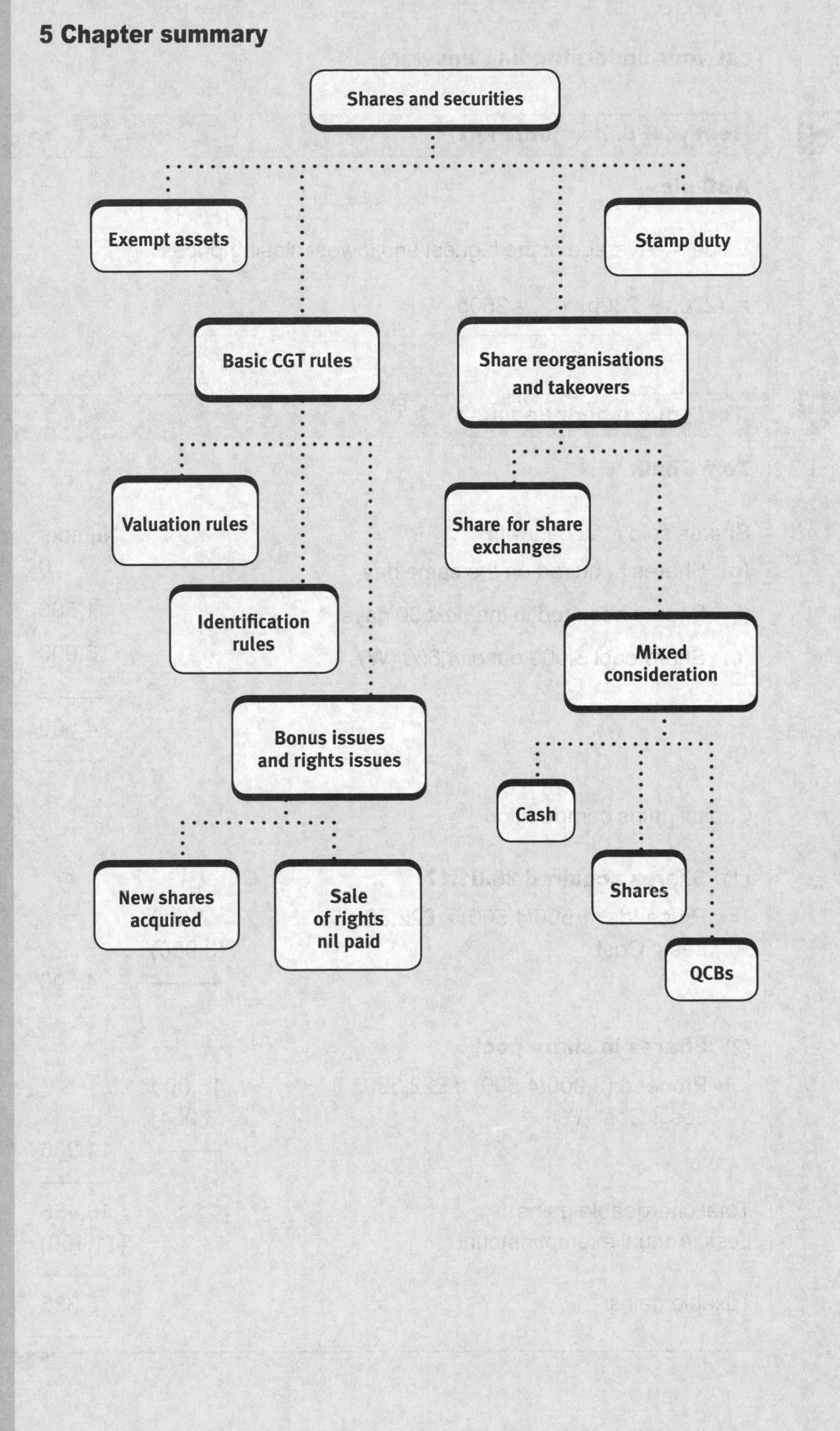

Test your understanding answers

Test your understanding 1

ABC plc

Value = Average of the highest and lowest closing prices

= (270p + 230p) × ½ = 250p

Test your understanding 2

Tom Chalk

Shares sold matched with:	Number
(a) Shares acquired on the same day	0
(b) Shares acquired in the next 30 days	1,500
(c) Share pool 3,000 out of 4,650 (W)	3,000
	4,500

Capital gains computation

	£	£
(1) **Shares acquired 28.01.17**		
Proceeds (1,500/4,500) × £22,500	7,500	
Less: Cost	(3,000)	
		4,500
(2) **Shares in share pool**		
Proceed (3,000/4,500) × £22,500	15,000	
Less: Cost (W)	(3,064)	
		11,936
Total chargeable gains		16,436
Less: Annual exempt amount		(11,100)
Taxable gains		5,336

Working: Share pool

		Number	Cost
			£
April 1994	Purchase	1,500	900
June 1997	Rights issue (1:3) × 70p	500	350
		2,000	1,250
May 2006	Purchase	1,000	2,000
		3,000	3,250
July 2006	Bonus issue (1:4)	750	0
		3,750	3,250
August 2010	Purchase	900	1,500
		4,650	4,750
December 2016	Sale	(3,000)	(3,064)
Balance c/f		1,650	1,686

Test your understanding 3

Ernest

(a) **Gain on the sale of rights nil paid – 25 August 2016**

Sale proceeds received = £6,000

Value of shares after rights issue = (£2.65 × 12,000) = £31,800
5% × £31,800 = £1,590

The sale proceeds are > £3,000 **and** > 5% of the value of the shares on which the rights are offered, therefore there is a part disposal of the original shares held:

	£
Sale proceeds	6,000
Less: Allowable cost (6,000/37,800 × £24,000)	(3,810)
Chargeable gain	2,190

Gain on the sale of the original shares – 23 June 2017

	£
Sale proceeds	37,000
Less: Allowable cost	
(10,000/12,000 × (£24,000 – £3,810))	(16,825)
Chargeable gain	20,175

(b) **Gain on the sale of rights nil paid – 25 August 2016**

Sale proceeds received = £1,500

The sale proceeds are < £3,000 therefore no gain arises on the sale of rights nil paid.

The sale proceeds are deducted from the cost of the original shares.

Note: There is no need to consider the 5% rule if the sale proceeds are < £3,000. Only one of the conditions need to be satisfied.

Gain on the sale of the original shares – 23 June 2017

	£
Sale proceeds	37,000
Less: Allowable cost (W)	(18,750)
Capital gain	18,250

Working: Share pool

		Number	Cost £
22.07.1996	Purchase	12,000	24,000
25.08.2016	Sale of rights nil paid		(1,500)
		12,000	22,500
23.06.2017	Sale of shares	(10,000)	(18,750)
Balance c/f		2,000	3,750

Test your understanding 4

Major

Disposal in December 2016

	£
Disposal proceeds	8,000
Less: Cost (W)	(4,000)
Chargeable gain	4,000

Working – cost of 'A' ordinary shares

July 2016 Major received:

4,000 'A' ordinary shares, valued at (4,000 × £2)	£8,000
2,000 preference shares, valued at (2,000 × £1)	£2,000

Cost attributable to the 'A' ordinary shares is therefore:

£5,000 × (£8,000/£10,000) = £4,000

Test your understanding 5

Victoria

	MV Jan 2017	Cost
Exchanged assets:	£	£
30,000 ordinary shares (£15,000 × 90/115)	90,000	11,739
10,000 preference shares (£15,000 × 15/115)	15,000	1,957
£10,000 cash (£15,000 × 10/115)	10,000	1,304
	115,000	15,000

Is the cash element material? = Yes

- The cash received is £10,000 which is > £3,000.
- The cash element also represents > 5% of the total value of exchanged assets (£115,000 × 5% = £5,750).

A chargeable gain is assessable in the tax year 2016/17 based on the part disposal of the shares as follows:

	£
Sale proceeds	10,000
Less: Cost	(1,304)
Chargeable gain	8,696

Victoria will have no CGT liability in the tax year 2016/17 as her chargeable gain is covered by her annual exempt amount of £11,100.

Test your understanding 6

Jasper

(a) **Chargeable gains – 2016/17**

Apportionment of cost of Cawte plc shares to the new securities and cash on 5 December 2016

For 12,000 Cawte plc ord shares:	Purchase consideration	Cost allocation
	£	£
12,000 Grasp £1 ord shs @ 350p	42,000	
£15,700 × (£42,000/£73,200)		9,008
24,000 Grasp 10% loan note @ 110p	26,400	
£15,700 × (£26,400/£73,200)		5,662
Cash (12,000 × 40p)	4,800	
£15,700 × (£4,800/£73,200)		1,030
	73,200	15,700

Cash consideration of £4,800 exceeds £3,000 and exceeds £3,660 (5% of £73,200). Therefore, cash consideration is not small and the part disposal rules apply.

	£	£
Disposal for cash		
Cash received		4,800
Less: Deemed cost		(1,030)
Chargeable gain		3,770
Disposal for QCBs (loan notes)		
Value of loan notes received	26,400	
Less: Deemed cost	(5,662)	
'Frozen' gain	20,738	
Taxable at time of takeover		0

Disposal of Grasp plc shares – 31 March 2017

Proceeds	3,600	
Less: Deemed cost (£9,008 × 400/12,000)	(300)	
		3,300
Total chargeable gains – 2016/17		7,070

(b) **Selling the QCBs (loan notes) – June 2018**

If Jasper were to sell the loan notes in June 2018 for £32,000, the increase in value of the loan notes of £5,600 (£32,000 – £26,400) is exempt from CGT as QCBs are exempt assets.

However, the disposal of the loan notes will crystallise the 'frozen' deferred gain of £20,738 in the tax year 2018/19.

Test your understanding 7

Bob

On the liquidation of the company, the shareholders are treated as having sold their shares for proceeds equal to the amount received on the liquidation and a normal capital gain/loss computation is required.

In this case, Bob will make a capital loss on the disposal of his shares.

Bob can make a negligible value claim as at 1 December 2016. This will give rise to a capital loss of £14,500 (£500 – £15,000) which will be deemed to arise in the tax year 2016/17.

As the capital loss arises on the disposal of unquoted trading company shares and Bob subscribed for the shares, relief against income is available.

Bob can relieve the loss against his total income for:

- 2016/17 (i.e. the year in which the loss arose); and/or
- 2015/16 (i.e. the previous tax year).

If losses are first relieved against current year income, any excess is available for offset against the prior year's income.

By making the claim, Bob's total income in the tax year 2016/17 will be reduced to £30,500 (£45,000 – £14,500).

Test your understanding 8

Hooker

	£
(a) Summit plc (0.5% × £10,230) = £51.15, round up to nearest £5	55
(b) Harcourts Ltd (0.5% × (£125,000 + £35,000))	800
(c) Treasury stock – Exempt	–
	——
Total stamp duty payable	855
	——

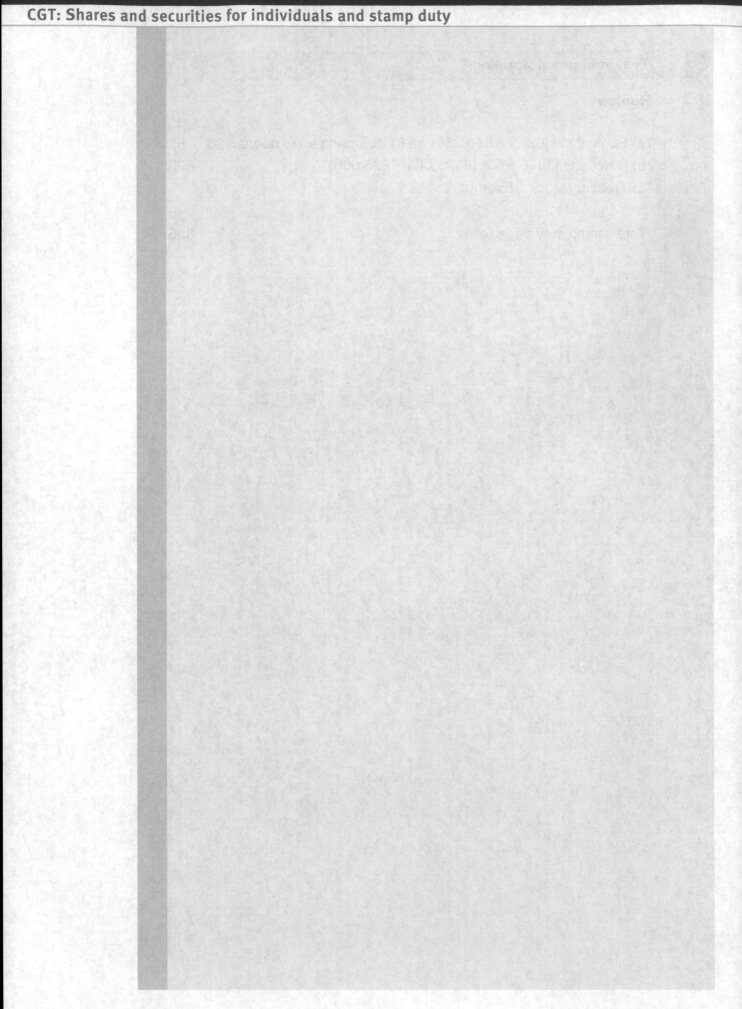

chapter

9

CGT: Reliefs for individuals

Chapter learning objectives

Upon completion of this chapter you will be able to:

- explain and calculate entrepreneurs' relief
- explain investors' relief
- identify the principal private residence exemption and letting relief available in a variety of circumstances on the disposal of an individual's main residence
- explain and apply rollover relief as it applies to individuals
- identify from a scenario when gift relief will be available, explain the conditions and show the application of gift relief in computations
- recognise and state the conditions for the availability of CGT deferral relief on the transfer of a business to a company
- calculate the relief where the consideration is wholly or partly in shares
- understand and apply enterprise investment scheme and seed enterprise investment scheme reinvestment relief ensuring that other available reliefs are maximised.

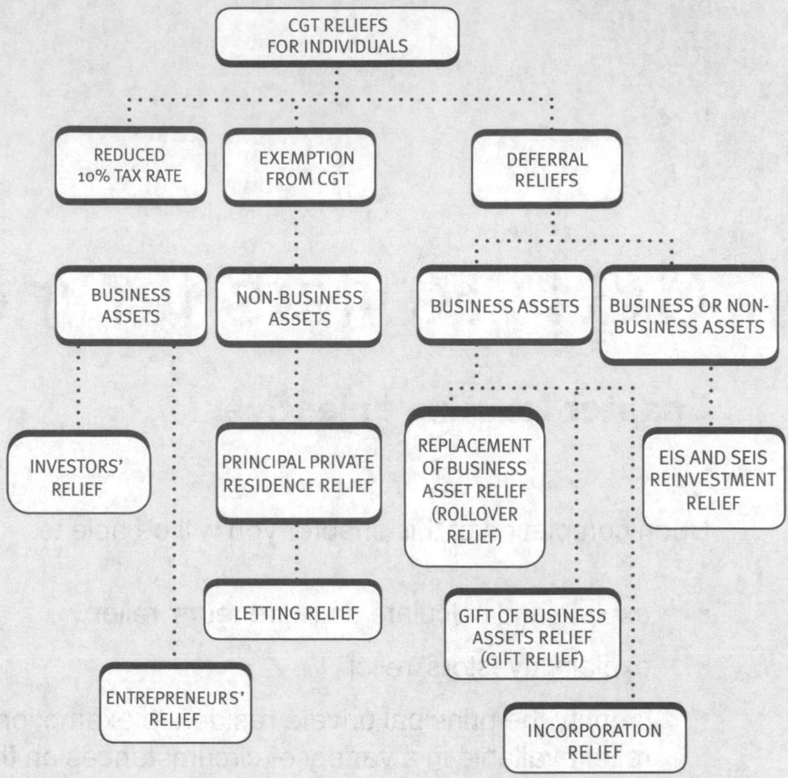

Introduction

After calculating the gains on disposals of individual assets, consideration must be given to the availability of CGT reliefs.

Much of this chapter is a revision of F6 knowledge with examples to check your retention of the required F6 knowledge. However, note that a greater depth of understanding is required at P6.

The reliefs feature regularly in the examinations and the main new reliefs introduced at P6 are incorporation relief, EIS and SEIS reinvestment relief. It is important to be able to calculate the amount of relief, to state the conditions that have to be satisfied and to explain the tax implications of claiming each relief.

1 Summary of reliefs

Entrepreneurs' relief (ER) and investors' relief (IR) tax certain gains at 10%. If ER or IR do not apply, gains are only taxed at 10% where they fall within the taxpayer's remaining basic rate band. Gains in excess of this are taxed at 20%.

The other reliefs either exempt, or defer to a later date, all or part of the gain.

Deferral reliefs	Exemptions
• Replacement of business asset relief (rollover relief) • Gift of business asset relief • Incorporation relief • EIS reinvestment relief	• Principal private residence (PPR) relief • Letting relief • SEIS reinvestment relief

2 Entrepreneurs' relief and investors' relief

Entrepreneurs' relief

Entrepreneurs' relief (ER) reduces the rate of CGT payable on certain qualifying business disposals to 10%.

A reminder of how the relief operates is given in expandable text and is summarised in the diagram at the end of this section.

Operation of the relief

- The first £10 million of gains on 'qualifying business disposals' will be taxed at 10%, regardless of the level of the taxpayer's income.
- Any gains above the £10 million limit are taxed in full at 10% or 20% (18% or 28% in the case of residential property) depending on the individual's taxable income.
- Gains qualifying for ER are set against any unused basic rate band (BRB) before non-qualifying gains.
- The 10% CGT rate is calculated after the deduction of:
  - allowable losses, and
  - the annual exempt amount (AEA).
- However, the taxpayer can choose to set losses (other than any losses on assets that are part of the disposal of the business) and the AEA against non-qualifying gains first, in order to maximise the relief.
- It is therefore helpful to keep gains that qualify for ER separate from those that do not qualify.

The relief must be claimed within 12 months of the 31 January following the end of the tax year in which the disposal is made.

For 2016/17 disposals, the relief must be claimed by 31 January 2019.

The £10 million limit is a lifetime limit which is diminished each time a claim for the relief is made.

Qualifying business disposals

The relief applies to the disposal of:

- the whole or substantial part of a business carried on by the individual either alone or in partnership
- assets of the individual's or partnership's trading business that has **now ceased**
- shares provided:
  - the shares are in the individual's 'personal trading company', **and**
  - the individual is an employee of the company (part time or full time).

An individual's 'personal trading company' is one in which the individual:

- owns at least 5% of the ordinary shares
- which carry at least 5% of the voting rights.

Note in particular that:

- the disposal of an individual business asset used for the purposes of a continuing trade does not qualify. There must be a disposal of the whole of the trading business or a substantial part (meaning part of the business which is capable of separate operation). The sale of an asset in isolation will not qualify.
- Where the disposal is a disposal of assets (i.e. not shares), relief is not available on gains arising from the disposal of those assets held for investment purposes.
- There is no requirement to restrict the gains qualifying for relief on shares by reference to any non-business assets held by the company.
- There are no rules about the minimum working hours of officers or employees; they just need to be an officer or employee throughout the one year qualifying period. Note also that non-executive directors and company secretaries will qualify as employees.
- For approved EMI share option schemes there is no requirement to hold ≥ 5% shareholding.

Restriction of ER in respect of goodwill

Gains in respect of goodwill will not qualify for ER if the goodwill is transferred to a close company (see Chapter 26) and the individual and the company are related, i.e. the individual is a shareholder in the company or an associate of a shareholder.

This restriction does not apply where the individual:

- holds less than 5% of the company's ordinary share capital or voting rights, or
- holds 5% or more of the company's ordinary share capital or voting rights, but sells the whole shareholding to another company within 28 days. The individual must hold less than 5% of the acquiring company's ordinary share capital and voting rights.

This restriction means that ER will be available on goodwill gains where an individual incorporates their business in order to sell the newly incorporated company.

The restriction also does not apply if the individual is a retiring partner.

Qualifying ownership period

In the case of the disposal of a business it must have been owned by the individual making the disposal for the 12 months prior to the disposal.

In the case of shares the individual must also have been an employee of the company and the company must have been their personal trading company for at least 12 months prior to the disposal.

Where the disposal is an asset of the individual's or partnership's trading business that has now ceased the disposal must also take place within three years of the cessation of trade.

For approved EMI share option schemes the 12 months ownership period can be counted from the date the option is granted (not when the shares are acquired).

Example 1 – Entrepreneurs' relief

In the tax year 2016/17, Kim sold her trading business which she set up in 1997 to Martha and realised the following gains/losses:

	£
Factory	275,000
Goodwill	330,000
Warehouse	(100,000)
Investment property	200,000

All of the assets have been owned for many years.

Kim also sold her shares in an unquoted trading company and realised a gain of £9,600,000. She owned 25% of the ordinary shares of the company which she purchased ten years ago. She has worked for the company on a part time basis for the last three years.

Kim has not made any other capital disposals in the tax year 2016/17, but she has capital losses brought forward of £9,000. She has never claimed any entrepreneurs' relief in the past.

Her only source of income is a trading profit of £40,000.

Calculate Kim's capital gains tax payable for the tax year 2016/17.

Solution

	Not qualifying for ER	**Qualifying for ER**
	£	£
Sale of investment property (Note 1)	200,000	
Sale of trading business:		
Factory		275,000
Goodwill		330,000
Warehouse (Note 2)		(100,000)
		505,000
Sale of trading company shares (Note 3)	105,000	9,495,000
	305,000	10,000,000
Less: Capital losses b/f (Note 4)	(9,000)	(0)
Less: AEA (Note 4)	(11,100)	(0)
Taxable gains	284,900	10,000,000

Capital gains tax: (Note 6)		
Qualifying gains	(£10,000,000 × 10%)	1,000,000
Non-qualifying gains	(£284,900 × 20%)	56,980
		1,056,980

Notes:

(1) Despite being part of the sale of the whole business, the gain arising on the investment property does not qualify for ER.

(2) The net chargeable gains on the disposal of an unincorporated business qualify for ER (i.e. the gains after netting off all losses arising on the disposal of the business, but excluding investment assets).

(3) After the first £10,000,000 of gains qualifying for ER have been taxed at 10%, any remaining gains do not qualify and are taxed at the appropriate rate depending on the individual's taxable income.

(4) Capital losses and the AEA are first set against gains not qualifying for ER.

(5) Kim's taxable income is £29,000 (£40,000 – £11,000 PA). Therefore, the BR band remaining is £3,000 (£32,000 – £29,000).

(6) The gains qualifying for ER are deemed to utilise the BR band first. Therefore the BR band remaining of £3,000 is set against the gains qualifying for ER leaving the remaining gains to be taxed at 20%.

Note: There is no need to calculate the BR band in this case because even if Kim had no taxable income, the gains qualifying for ER (£10,000,000) are > £32,000. Therefore the non-qualifying gains must be taxed at 20%.

Test your understanding 1

In the tax year 2016/17 Paul sold shares in Dual Ltd, an unquoted trading company, and realised a gain of £430,000. Paul has worked for Dual Ltd for many years and has owned 10% of the ordinary shares of the company for the last five years.

Paul set up a trading business in 2009 and in 2016/17 he sold a warehouse used in the business, realising a gain of £245,000.

Paul's trading income was £38,000 in 2016/17. He did not have any other source of income.

In the tax year 2017/18 Paul sold the rest of the business to another sole trader and realised the following gains:

Factory	£6,495,000
Goodwill	£130,000

All of the assets in the business have been owned for many years.

Paul also sold an antique table in 2017/18 and realised a gain of £5,325.

His trading profit in 2017/18 was £48,000 and prior to 2016/17 Paul has claimed entrepreneurs' relief of £3.5 million

Calculate Paul's CGT payable for the tax years 2016/17 and 2017/18.

Assume that the AEA for the tax year 2016/17 continues in the future.

Associated disposals

ER also applies to assets owned by the individual and used in their personal trading company or trading partnership **provided:**

- the individual also disposes of all or part of their partnership interest/shares
- as part of their withdrawal of involvement in the partnership/company business.

These disposals are referred to as associated disposals.

In order for relief to be available for associated disposals, the individual must not have charged rent to the business for the use of the assets.

Where a full market rent has been charged, the relief available is reduced to nil.

Where the rent paid is less than the market rate, the relief is restricted on a 'just and reasonable basis'.

Illustration

Lex has been a partner in the Luther partnership since 1 April 2010. Lex retires on 1 April 2016, selling his share of the partnership to the remaining partners. The gain arising on the disposal of Lex's partnership interest qualifies for ER.

Throughout the time Lex was a partner he allowed the Luther partnership to use a warehouse he owns personally as its business premises in return for a rent which is 75% of the market rate. The warehouse will be sold to the existing partners on 1 April 2016, resulting in a chargeable gain of £150,000.

The disposal of the warehouse will qualify for ER as an associated disposal, but relief will only be available for £37,500 (£150,000 × 25%) as Lex has charged rent at 75% of the market rate (100% – 75% = 25%).

Interaction with enterprise investment scheme (EIS)

Gains qualifying for ER that are deferred via an investment in EIS shares will still qualify for ER on becoming chargeable.

More detail is given in section 8.

Investors' relief

As explained above, ER is only available on a disposal of shares if the shares are in the individual's personal company (they hold 5% of the shares) and they are also an officer or employee of the company.

From 6 April 2016, investors' relief has been introduced which extends the benefits of ER to certain investors who would not meet the conditions for ER.

IR applies to the disposal of:

- unlisted ordinary shares in a trading company (including AIM shares)
- subscribed for (i.e. newly issued shares) on/after 17 March 2016
- which have been held for a minimum period of 3 years starting on 6 April 2016
- by an individual that is **not** an employee of the company.

IR is subject to a separate lifetime limit of £10 million of qualifying gains.

Note that claims for IR cannot be made before the tax year 2019/20 due to the 3 year minimum holding period. Therefore in the P6 examination you must not apply IR to gains arising before the tax year 2019/20.

Interaction with other reliefs

Note that other specific CGT reliefs (e.g. gift relief, rollover relief and incorporation relief) are given before considering ER or IR.

More detail on how the interaction between reliefs works is given later with the detail on the specific reliefs.

Interaction with takeovers

With a share for share exchange, it is possible that:

- the old shares would qualify for ER or IR if it were treated as a disposal
- but the new shareholding and so the later disposal of the shares would not qualify for relief.

However, where the share for share exchange takes place, the individual shareholder can:

- elect for the event to be treated as a disposal for CGT purposes, and
- claim ER or IR (i.e. tax the gain at 10%).

Summary

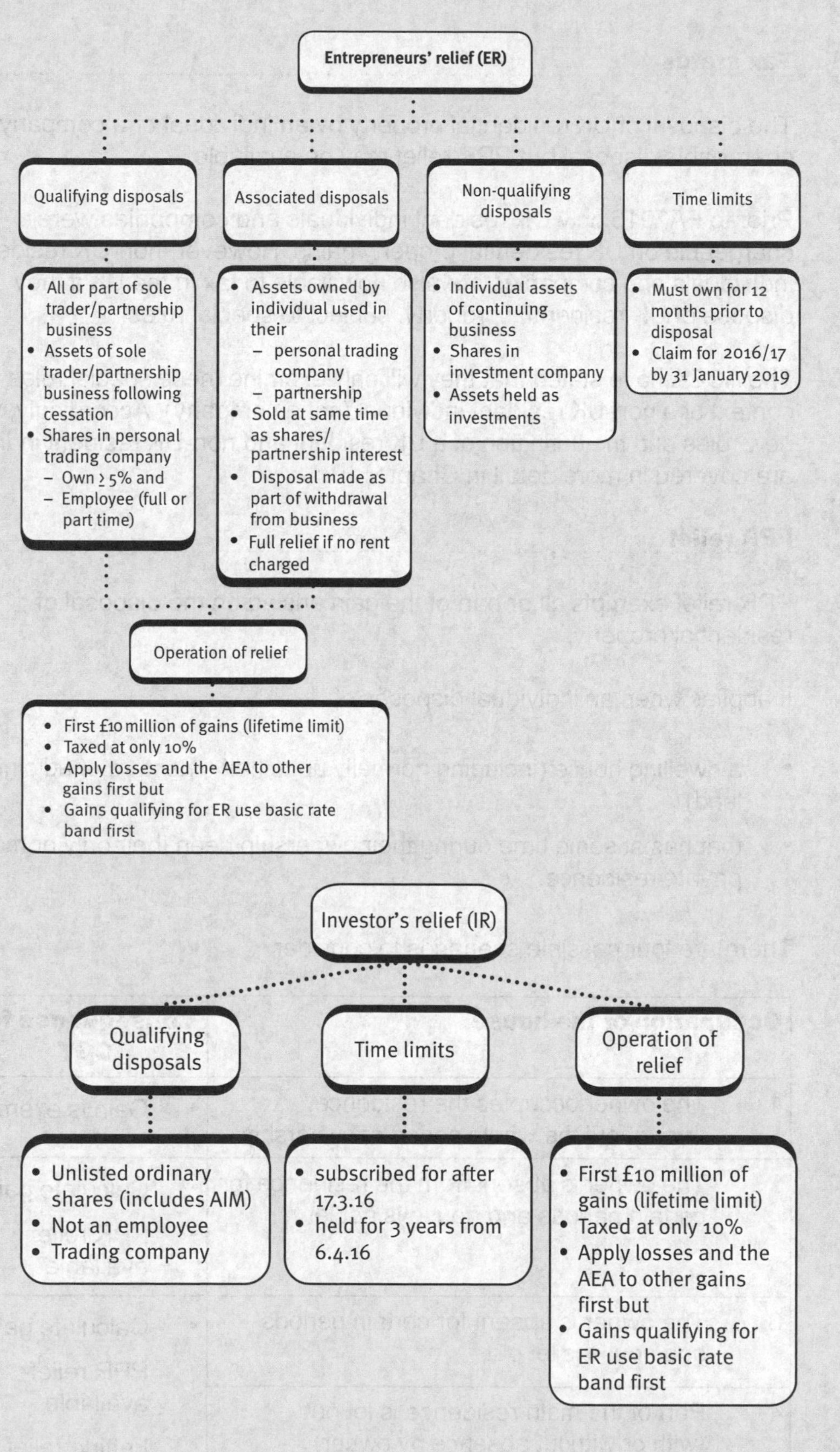

Entrepreneurs' relief (ER)
Qualifying disposals
Associated disposals
Non-qualifying disposals
Time limits
• All or part of sole trader/partnership business
• Assets of sole trader/partnership business following cessation
• Shares in personal trading company
– Own ≥ 5% and
– Employee (full or part time)
• Assets owned by individual used in their
– personal trading company
– partnership
• Sold at same time as shares/ partnership interest
• Disposal made as part of withdrawal from business
• Full relief if no rent charged
• Individual assets of continuing business
• Shares in investment company
• Assets held as investments
• Must own for 12 months prior to disposal
• Claim for 2016/17 by 31 January 2019
Operation of relief
• First £10 million of gains (lifetime limit)
• Taxed at only 10%
• Apply losses and the AEA to other gains first but
• Gains qualifying for ER use basic rate band first
Investor's relief (IR)
Qualifying disposals
Time limits
Operation of relief
• Unlisted ordinary shares (includes AIM)
• Not an employee
• Trading company
• subscribed for after 17.3.16
• held for 3 years from 6.4.16
• First £10 million of gains (lifetime limit)
• Taxed at only 10%
• Apply losses and the AEA to other gains first but
• Gains qualifying for ER use basic rate band first

3 Principal private residence (PPR) relief and letting relief

Tax status

The disposal of UK residential property by an individual or a company is a chargeable disposal but PPR relief may be available.

Prior to FA2015 only UK resident individuals and companies were chargeable on UK residential property gains. However, non-UK resident individuals and companies are also now liable to tax in the UK if they dispose of UK residential property, subject to special rules.

The ACCA have stated that they will only examine these special rules in the context of a non-UK resident individual (not a company). Accordingly, these new rules and the definition of a UK resident and non-UK resident individual are covered in more detail in Chapter 10.

PPR relief

PPR relief exempts all or part of the gain arising on the disposal of residential property.

It applies when an individual disposes of:

- a dwelling house (including normally up to half a hectare of adjoining land)
- that has at some time during their ownership been their only or main private residence.

There are four possible scenarios to consider:

<table>
<tr><th colspan="2">Occupation of the house</th><th>Consequence for CGT</th></tr>
<tr><td>1</td><td>The owner occupies the residence throughout the whole period of ownership</td><td>• Gain is exempt</td></tr>
<tr><td>2</td><td>The owner is absent from the residence for certain periods and house is not let</td><td>• Calculate gain
• PPR relief available</td></tr>
<tr><td>3</td><td>The owner is absent for certain periods and house is let out</td><td rowspan="2">• Calculate gain
• PPR relief available
• Letting relief</td></tr>
<tr><td>4</td><td>Part of the main residence is let out (with or without absence by owner)</td></tr>
</table>

The meaning of 'dwelling house'

The meaning of 'dwelling house' is not defined in the legislation and so it has been left to the courts to determine the limits of the expression.

A number of principles have emerged from decided cases:

- Caravans connected to mains services such as electricity and water qualify as dwellings.
- A taxpayer sold a bungalow and a small amount of land that was within the grounds of his house and which had been occupied by a part-time caretaker. It was held that the bungalow provided services for the benefit of the main house, was occupied by the taxpayer through his employee, and so qualified as part of the taxpayer's residence.

  A test resulting from this case is that buildings must together form an entity that can be regarded as a dwelling house, albeit divided into different buildings performing different functions.

- Where a taxpayer owns a large property which is divided into several self-contained units, only those parts that the taxpayer actually occupies qualify for exemption.
- A taxpayer first sold his house and part of his garden and then, about a year later, sold the remainder of the garden at a substantial profit. It was held that the PPR exemption applied only to the first disposal, because when the remainder of the land was sold, it no longer formed part of the individual's principal private residence. It is possible that if the order of sales were reversed, the land sold independently of the buildings may not qualify for relief, but is likely to depend on the facts of the case and the size and purpose of the land sold.

Ownership of more than one residence

Where an individual has more than one residence they can nominate which of them is to be treated as the principal residence for capital gains tax purposes by notifying HMRC in writing.

The election must be made within two years of acquiring an additional residence otherwise it is open to HMRC, as a question of fact, to decide which residence is the main residence.

Married couples/civil partners

Provided that they are not treated as being separated or divorced, a married couple (or civil partnership) is entitled to only one residence between them for the purposes of the PPR exemption.

The operation of the relief

Where there has been a period of absence from the PPR the procedure is:

(i) Calculate the gain on the disposal of the property.

(ii) Calculate the total period of ownership.

(iii) Calculate periods of occupation (see below).

(iv) Calculate the amount of PPR relief as follows:

Gain × (Periods of occupation ÷ Total period of ownership)

(v) If applicable, calculate the amount of letting relief available.

Periods of occupation

The 'periods of occupation' include:

- **any** period of **actual** occupation
- the **last 18 months** of ownership (always exempt, unconditionally)
- the following periods of **deemed occupation:**
  - (i) periods totalling up to **three years** of absence for any **reason**
  - (ii) **any** period spent living overseas due to employment.
  - (iii) periods totalling up to **four years** of absence in which the individual was **prevented from living in his UK property** because:
    - – their place of work was too far from the property, and their employer required them to live elsewhere in the UK, or
    - – they were self-employed, and their work required them to live elsewhere in the UK, or they were living overseas due to their self-employed business.

Note that:

- The periods of deemed occupation above must be preceded and followed by a period of actual occupation.

- The condition to actually reoccupy the property after the period of absence does not need to be satisfied for periods (ii) and (iii) above where the individual was unable to resume residence because the terms of employment required them to work elsewhere.

- FA2015 has introduced new rules relating to the definition of occupation and non-occupation where:
  - a non-UK resident individual has a property in the UK, or
  - a UK resident individual has a non-UK residential property
  - on which PPR relief is to be claimed.

  These rules are considered in more detail in Chapter 10. However, in this chapter it is assumed that all examples involve UK resident individuals disposing of UK residential properties, and therefore the 'periods of occupation' are as stated above.

Example 2 – PPR relief

On 1 May 1991 Mr Clint purchased a house in Southampton for £125,000, which he lived in until he moved to a rented flat on 1 July 1992.

He remained in the flat until 1 October 1994 when he accepted a year's secondment to his firm's New York office. He returned to the UK on 1 October 1995 and moved into a relative's house, where he stayed until he returned to his own home on 31 January 1996.

On 1 July 2006 he moved in with his girlfriend in Newcastle. Here he remained until he sold his Southampton house on 1 February 2017 for £350,000.

Calculate the chargeable gain, if any, arising on the disposal of the house on 1 February 2017.

Solution

	£
Disposal proceeds	350,000
Less: Cost	(125,000)
	225,000
Less: PPR relief (W)	(145,631)
Chargeable gain	79,369

Working – Chargeable and exempt periods of ownership

		Chargeable months	Exempt months
1.5.91 – 30.6.92	(actual occupation)	–	14
1.7.92 – 30.9.94	(absent – any reason)	–	27
1.10.94 – 30.9.95	(absent – employed abroad)	–	12
1.10.95 – 31.1.96	(absent – any reason)	–	4
1.2.96 – 30.6.06	(actual occupation)	–	125
1.7.06 – 31.7.15	(absent – see note (1))	109	–
1.8.15 – 31.1.17	(final 18 months)	–	18
		109	200

Total period of ownership = (109 + 200) = 309 months.
Exempt element of gain = (200/309) × £225,000 = £145,631

Notes:

(1) After Mr Clint left his house to live in Newcastle he never returned. Consequently the remaining 5 months (3 years – 27 months – 4 months) for any reason is not available for exemption as he did not meet the condition of actual occupation both before and after the period of absence.

(2) In contrast the exemption for the final 18 months of ownership has no such restriction and is therefore still available.

Letting relief

Letting relief is available where an individual's PPR is let for residential use.

It applies when:

- the owner is absent from the property and lets the house out, or
- the owner lets part of the property whilst still occupying the remainder.

It does not apply to let property that is not the owner's PPR (e.g. buy to let properties).

Letting relief is the lowest of:

(i) £40,000

(ii) the amount of the gain exempted by the normal PPR rules

(iii) the part of the gain **after PPR** relief attributable to the letting period.

Test your understanding 2

Mr Dearden bought a house on 1 April 1992. Occupation of the house has been as follows:

01.04.92 – 31.03.94	lived in the house as his PPR.
01.04.94 – 30.09.99	travels the world and lets the house.
01.10.99 – 31.03.08	lived in the house as his PPR.
01.04.08 – 31.03.17	house was left empty.

On 31 March 2017 Mr Dearden sells the house realising a gain before relief of £194,800.

Calculate the chargeable gain in the tax year 2016/17.

Business use

Where a house, or part of it, is used wholly and exclusively for business purposes, the part used for business purposes is not eligible for PPR relief.

Note that:

- the taxpayer cannot benefit from the rules of deemed occupation for any part of the property used for business purposes
- there is one exception:
  - if that part of the property used for business purposes was at any time used as the taxpayer's main residence, the exemption for the last 18 months still applies to that part
  - this exception does not apply to any part of the property used for business purposes throughout the whole period of ownership.

Test your understanding 3

On 31 July 2016 Alex sold his house for £125,000, resulting in a capital gain of £70,000. The house had been purchased on 1 July 2004, and one of the five rooms had been used for business purposes from 1 January 2007 to the date of sale.

Calculate the chargeable gain arising on the sale of the house.

Tax planning points

General advice

CGT planning concerning an individual's private residence focuses on two main areas:

- If the taxpayer's circumstances are such that any gain realised will be exempt they should ensure that this is maximised.
- Where the taxpayer is absent from the property they should attempt to structure their absences in such a way that they benefit as much as possible from the deemed occupation rules and the letting exemption.

For example, ensure:

- taxpayer reoccupies the property after the period of absence
- property let during periods of absence not covered by PPR relief.

Specific tax advice

Rate of tax

Any taxable gains arising on the sale of residential property (i.e. gains that are not covered by PPR or letting relief) will be subject to CGT at a rate of 18% (if the gains fall within any remaining basic rate band) or 28% rather than the normal rates of CGT.

If taxpayers have both chargeable gains arising from the sale of residential property and other chargeable gains, any capital losses and the AEA should be allocated first to the residential property gains as these will be taxed at higher rates than other gains.

More than one residence

Where the taxpayer has more than one residence they should ensure that they nominate the property with the greatest potential for gain as their main residence.

It should be noted, however, that any property subject to an election must be used by the taxpayer at some time as their residence. It is not acceptable to purchase a property as a financial investment, nominate it as the main residence of the taxpayer, and never set foot in it.

If an individual's finances permit, they should purchase a new residence before disposing of the old one. An election can be made for the new residence to be treated as the main residence for the CGT exemption but this does not prevent exemption being gained on the old residence for the final 18 months of ownership.

In this way the taxpayer can effectively gain exemption on two residences at once for a maximum of 18 months.

Business use of property

Subject to tax and other financial considerations, exclusive business use of the property should be avoided.

Where business use is necessary, thought should be given to the proportion of household expenses claimed under the income tax rules because these will be a material factor in determining the extent to which the PPR exemption is lost.

Letting the property

When the taxpayer is absent in circumstances that make the period ineligible for exemption under the deemed occupation rules, serious thought should be given to letting the property.

Whether this constitutes good tax planning will depend, on the one hand, at the rate the property is rising in value, and on the other hand, on the income and expenditure connected with the letting.

Summary

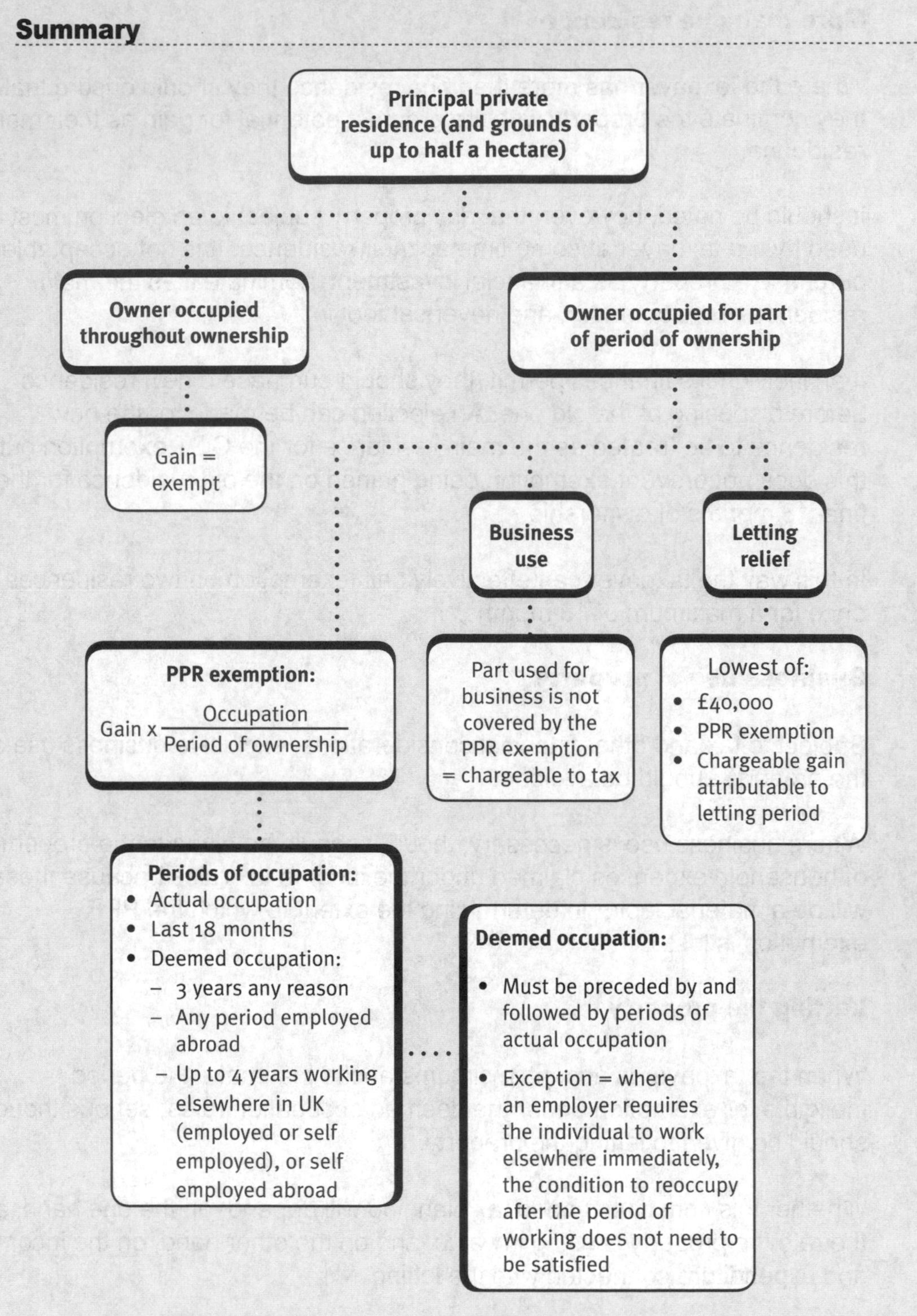

Principal private residence (and grounds of up to half a hectare)
Owner occupied throughout ownership
Owner occupied for part of period of ownership
Gain = exempt
Business use
Letting relief
PPR exemption:
Gain x Occupation / Period of ownership
Part used for business is not covered by the PPR exemption = chargeable to tax
Lowest of:
• £40,000
• PPR exemption
• Chargeable gain attributable to letting period
Periods of occupation:
• Actual occupation
• Last 18 months
• Deemed occupation:
– 3 years any reason
– Any period employed abroad
– Up to 4 years working elsewhere in UK (employed or self employed), or self employed abroad
Deemed occupation:
• Must be preceded by and followed by periods of actual occupation
• Exception = where an employer requires the individual to work elsewhere immediately, the condition to reoccupy after the period of working does not need to be satisfied

4 Comprehensive example

Test your understanding 4

Paul Opus disposed of the following assets during the tax year 2016/17:

(1) On 10 July 2016 Paul sold 5,000 £1 ordinary shares in Symphony Ltd, an unquoted trading company, for £23,600. He had originally purchased 40,000 shares in the company on 23 June 2012 for £110,400.

(2) On 15 July 2016 Paul made a gift of his entire shareholding of 10,000 £1 ordinary shares in Concerto plc to his daughter. On that date the shares were quoted on the Stock Exchange at £5.10 – £5.18. Paul's shareholding had been purchased on 29 April 1999 for £14,000. The shareholding is less than 1% of Concerto plc's issued share capital, and Paul has never been employed by Concerto plc.

(3) On 9 August 2016 Paul sold a motor car for £16,400. The motor car had been purchased on 21 January 2011 for £12,800.

(4) On 4 October 2016 Paul sold an antique vase for £12,400. The antique vase had been purchased on 19 January 2014 for £8,400.

(5) On 31 December 2016 Paul sold a house for £220,000. The house had been purchased on 1 April 2009 for £114,700. Paul occupied the house as his main residence from the date of purchase until 30 June 2012. The house was then unoccupied until it was sold on 31 December 2016.

(6) On 16 February 2017 Paul sold three acres of land for £285,000. He had originally purchased four acres of land on 17 July 2014 for £220,000. The market value of the unsold acre of land as at 16 February 2017 was £90,000. The land has never been used for business purposes.

(7) On 5 March 2017 Paul sold a freehold holiday cottage for £125,000. The cottage had originally been purchased on 28 July 2013 for £101,600 by Paul's wife. She transferred the cottage to Paul on 16 November 2015 when it was valued at £114,800.

(8) Paul has taxable income for the tax year 2016/17 of £25,000.

Compute Paul's CGT liability for the tax year 2016/17, and advise him by when this should be paid.

5 Replacement of business asset relief (rollover relief)

Rollover relief (ROR) is available to both individuals and companies.

This section deals with the rules as they apply to an individual with an unincorporated business. The rules for companies are very similar but the differences are explained in Chapter 23.

The operation of the relief

Where an individual:

- sells a qualifying business asset at a gain, and
- reinvests the sale proceeds in a replacement qualifying business asset
- within a qualifying time period

the individual may **make a claim** to defer the gain until the subsequent disposal of the replacement asset.

A reminder of how the relief operates and the conditions for the relief covered at F6 is given in expandable text, and is summarised in the diagram below.

Operation of the relief

The relief operates as follows:

- on the disposal of a business asset, the gain is 'rolled over' against (i.e. deducted from) the acquisition cost of the replacement asset
- provided the proceeds are fully reinvested, no tax is payable at the time of the disposal as the gain is deferred
- the relief effectively increases the gain arising on the disposal of the replacement asset, as its base cost has been reduced by ROR.
- ROR is not automatic, it must be claimed.

Note that:

- gains may be 'rolled over' a number of times provided a qualifying replacement business asset is purchased, therefore a tax liability will only arise when there is a disposal without replacement
- the relief is 'all or nothing' in that if the claim is made, the maximum gain possible must be deferred (i.e. a claim cannot be restricted to preserve the AEA)

- the relief is very flexible, where several assets are sold and several more acquired, the gains can be rolled over against the new assets in whatever order or proportion the individual chooses (but the full amount of gains must be deferred)
- making a ROR claim is optional. An individual may prefer to crystallise a gain in the current year if it is covered by their capital losses and AEA
- the base cost of the replacement asset is reduced for CGT purposes only.

Note that for income tax purposes, capital allowances (if applicable) are still available on the full cost of the replacement asset in the normal way.

Conditions for the relief

Qualifying business assets (QBAs)

There are many categories of QBAs, however for examination purposes, the main assets which qualify for ROR are:

- goodwill (for unincorporated businesses only)
- land and buildings (freehold and leasehold) occupied and used for trading purposes
- fixed plant and machinery (not movable).

Note that:

- shares are not qualifying assets for ROR purposes
- both the old and the replacement assets:
  - must be qualifying business assets, however they do not have to be the same category of qualifying asset
  - they do not have to be used in the same trade if the vendor has more than one trade.

Qualifying time period

The replacement assets must be acquired within a four year period beginning **one year before** and ending **three years after** the date of sale of the old asset.

Claim time period

Individuals must claim ROR within four years of the **later of** the end of the tax year in which the:

- disposal is made (i.e. by 5 April 2021 for a disposal in the tax year 2016/17)
- replacement asset is acquired.

Partial reinvestment of proceeds

If **all** of the net sale proceeds from the sale of the old asset are reinvested, full ROR is available (i.e. **all** of the gain is deferred).

However, where there is partial reinvestment of the proceeds:

- part of the gain will be chargeable at the time of the disposal
- the rest of the gain can be deferred with a ROR claim.

The gain which is **chargeable** at the time of the disposal is the **lower** of:

- the full gain, or
- the amount of the proceeds **not** reinvested.

This gain will be taxed at either 10% or 20% depending on the level of the individual's taxable income.

Note that entrepreneurs' relief is not available on the disposal of individual assets (unless the disposal is on the cessation of the business).

The deferred gain will be taxed at the rate applicable when the gain is crystallised in the future.

Test your understanding 5

In May 1991, Keith sold a freehold commercial building for £100,000 and realised a chargeable gain of £58,240.

In August 1991 Keith bought another freehold commercial building for £80,000 which he sold in July 2016 for £300,000. He did not replace this building with any other business assets.

Calculate the chargeable gain arising in the tax year 2016/17.

Non-business use

Adjustments need to be made to the calculation of the amount of relief available if there is an element of non-business use. Only the business use proportion of the gain can be considered for ROR.

This may occur because:

- an asset may be used partly for business purposes and partly for private use
- an asset is not used for business purposes for the whole of the period of ownership.

Reinvestment in depreciating assets

A depreciating asset is defined as:

- a wasting asset (i.e. with a predictable life of 50 years or less), or
- an asset that will become a wasting asset within ten years.

The most common examples of qualifying depreciating assets are:

- leasehold land and buildings with 60 years or less to run on the lease
- fixed plant and machinery.

The operation of the relief

The relief for depreciating assets operates in the following way.

- The capital gain is not 'rolled over' and deducted from the base cost of the replacement asset, instead it is deferred (i.e. 'frozen'), and becomes chargeable on the **earliest** of the following three events:
  (1) the **disposal** of replacement depreciating asset
  (2) the depreciating asset **ceases to be used** for the purposes of the trade
  (3) **ten years** from the date of acquisition of the replacement depreciating asset.
- However, if before the deferred gain crystallises, a non-depreciating asset is purchased, then the original deferred gain can be rolled over.

  This means that the deferred gain can be matched with the later purchase of a non-depreciating asset and the deferred gain will be deducted from the cost of the new asset.

Note that the partial reinvestment and non-business use rules apply in calculating the amount of the held over gain that can be deferred, in the same way as for rollover relief.

Example 3 – Reinvestment in depreciating assets

Smith purchased a factory in February 1995 for £195,000.

In August 2016 he sold the factory for £380,000 and acquired a lease of commercial property (with 55 years to expiry) in September 2016 for £385,000.

In April 2017 he purchased a new factory for £390,000 and he sold the lease for £430,000 in December 2017. In May 2019 he sold the second factory for £425,000.

Calculate the chargeable gain on:

(a) **the disposal of the first factory**

(b) **the disposal of the lease; and**

(c) **the disposal of the second factory.**

Solution

(a) **Gain on first factory – August 2016**

	£
Disposal proceeds	380,000
Less: Cost	(195,000)
Capital gain	185,000

As Smith reinvested the proceeds of the first factory in a depreciating asset (i.e. the lease), the gain on the first factory is held over.

The gain is therefore frozen until the earliest of three events.
Chargeable gain = £0

(b) **Disposal of the lease – December 2017**

Smith purchased another non-depreciating asset (i.e. the second factory) before the depreciating asset was sold. He could therefore rollover the gain on the first factory into the second, and a normal gain arises on the lease.

	£
Disposal proceeds	430,000
Less: Allowable expenditure (Note)	(385,000)
Chargeable gain	45,000

ER is not available as this is the disposal of an individual asset used for the purposes of a continuing trade.

The base cost of the second factory becomes:

	£
Cost	390,000
Less: ROR	(185,000)
Base cost	205,000

Note: The lease, although a depreciating asset for ROR purposes, is not a wasting asset because it had more than 50 years to expiry when it was sold. Its cost is therefore not wasted when computing the gain or loss on disposal.

(c) **Disposal of second factory – May 2019**

	£
Disposal proceeds	425,000
Less: Base cost	(205,000)
Chargeable gain	220,000

ER is not available as this is the disposal of an individual asset.

The gain will be taxed at the appropriate rate in the tax year 2019/20.

Assuming there is no change in rates for CGT, the gain will be taxed at 10% or 20%.

Interaction with entrepreneurs' relief

Entrepreneurs' relief is not available on the disposal of individual assets out of a business.

However, if the business is being sold and the proceeds are reinvested into new qualifying assets in another business, both ROR and ER are available.

- ROR is given before considering ER.
- On a subsequent disposal of the replacement assets (as part of the sale of the other business as a whole) ER will be available if the retention period of 12 months is met.

Effectively, the use of the lifetime relief of £10 million is also deferred.

However, ROR is optional and the taxpayer can choose **not to claim** ROR and utilise the available ER earlier if they want to.

Test your understanding 6

Sophie operates a business as a sole trader. The business has a 31 March year end.

Sophie purchased an office block in October 2005 for £70,000 and sold it in August 2011 for £120,000. She acquired fixed plant and machinery at a cost of £100,000 in April 2012. The maximum possible rollover relief was claimed, in respect of the gain arising on the office block, against the purchase of the fixed plant and machinery.

In November 2016 Sophie sold the fixed plant and machinery for £60,000.

Calculate the Sophie's chargeable gain in the tax year 2016/17.

Tax planning points

Much of tax planning for replacement of business assets involves taking care to ensure that the various conditions are met.

- Disposals and acquisitions need to be planned well in advance to ensure that the time limit for reinvestment is adhered to. It may be necessary to advance or delay capital expenditure (where commercially possible).
- It is not possible to choose to defer only part of a gain leaving sufficient to cover the AEA. However, it may be possible to reinvest all but £11,100 of proceeds in replacement assets to avoid wasting the AEA.
- The interaction between ROR and ER should also be considered carefully. It might not be advisable to defer gains on assets qualifying for ER, if the new business may be held for a period of less than twelve months.

Test your understanding 7

Your client, Medway, has been offered £160,000 for a freehold factory he owns and is considering disposing of it in early October 2016. He acquired the factory for £40,000 on 31 March 1989. The sale of the factory is part of a disposal of the entire business.

Medway has taxable income of £70,000 per annum.

(a) **Compute the capital gains tax that will arise if Medway disposes of the factory, and does not claim rollover relief.**

(b) **Indicate to Medway the capital gains consequences of each of the following alternative courses of action he is considering taking, following the sale, and give any advice you consider to be relevant.**

(i) **acquiring a new freehold factory as part of a new business in 2017 for £172,000.**

(ii) **acquiring a new freehold factory as part of a new business in 2017 for £150,000 and using the remainder of the proceeds as working capital.**

Summary

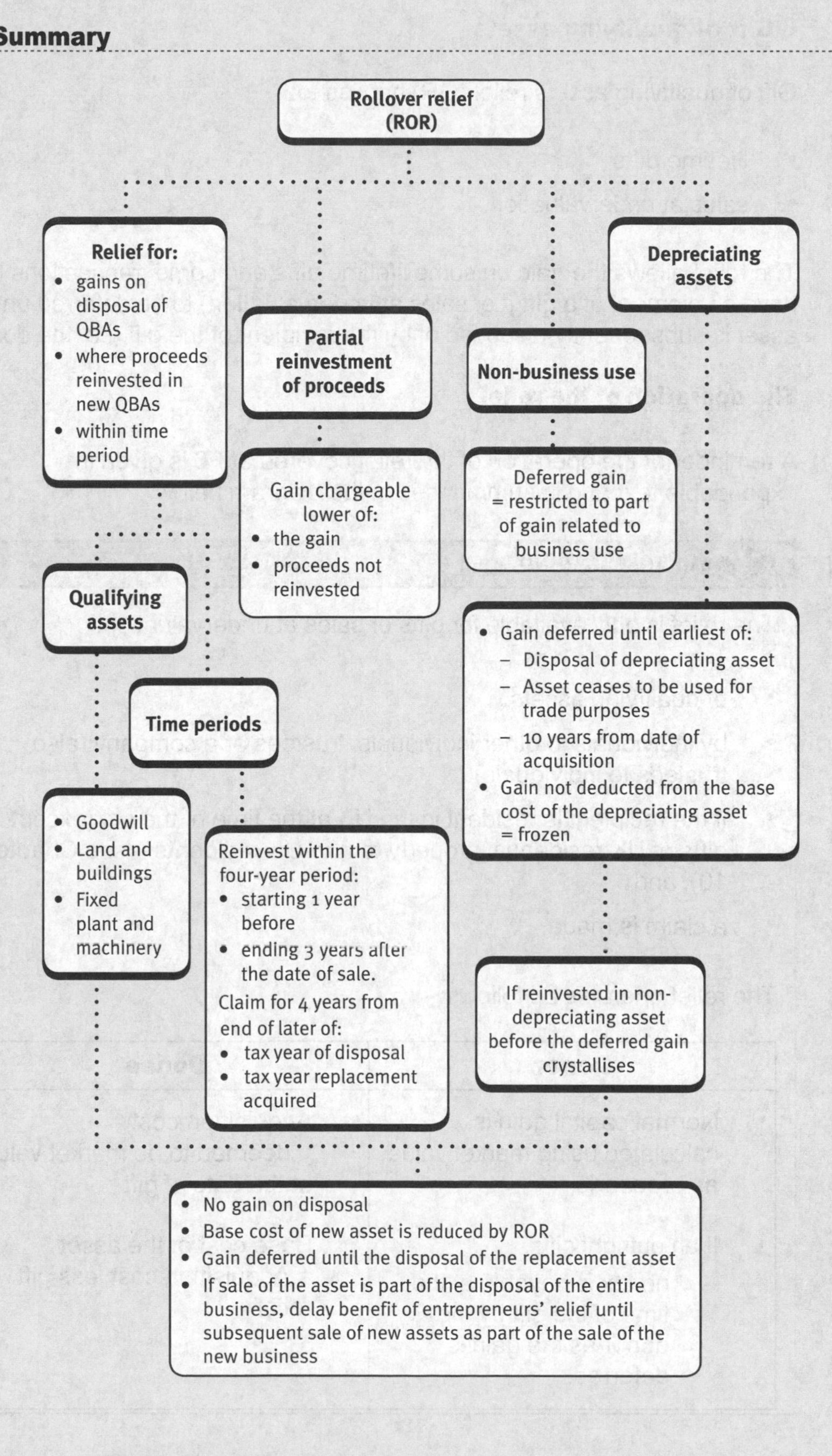
Rollover relief (ROR)
Relief for:
• gains on disposal of QBAs
• where proceeds reinvested in new QBAs
• within time period
Partial reinvestment of proceeds
Non-business use
Depreciating assets
Gain chargeable lower of:
• the gain
• proceeds not reinvested
Deferred gain = restricted to part of gain related to business use
Qualifying assets
Time periods
• Gain deferred until earliest of:
– Disposal of depreciating asset
– Asset ceases to be used for trade purposes
– 10 years from date of acquisition
• Gain not deducted from the base cost of the depreciating asset = frozen
• Goodwill
• Land and buildings
• Fixed plant and machinery
Reinvest within the four-year period:
• starting 1 year before
• ending 3 years after the date of sale.
Claim for 4 years from end of later of:
• tax year of disposal
• tax year replacement acquired
If reinvested in non-depreciating asset before the deferred gain crystallises
• No gain on disposal
• Base cost of new asset is reduced by ROR
• Gain deferred until the disposal of the replacement asset
• If sale of the asset is part of the disposal of the entire business, delay benefit of entrepreneurs' relief until subsequent sale of new assets as part of the sale of the new business

6 Gift of qualifying assets

Gift of qualifying assets relief (GR) applies to:

- lifetime gifts
- sales at undervaluation.

The relief allows the gain on some lifetime gifts and some transactions that have an element of a gift (i.e. sales at undervaluation) to be deferred until the asset is subsequently disposed of by the recipient of the gift (i.e. the donee).

The operation of the relief

A reminder of the operation of the relief covered at F6 is given in expandable text and is summarised in the diagram below.

Operation of the relief

The relief is only available for gifts or sales at undervaluation:

- of qualifying assets
- by individuals to other individuals, trustees or a company (also trustees to individuals)
- if the recipient is resident in the UK at the time of the gift (except for gifts of UK residential property to non-UK residents – see Chapter 10), and
- a claim is made.

The relief operates as follows:

Donor	Donee
• Normal capital gain is calculated using market value as proceeds.	• Acquisition cost = deemed to be market value at the date of gift.
• If an outright gift: – no tax is payable at the time of the gift by the donor as the gain is deferred.	• Base cost of the asset = Acquisition cost less gift relief

• If a sale at undervaluation: – a chargeable gain arises at the time of the sale if the actual sale proceeds received exceed the original cost of the asset – the balance of the gain is eligible for gift relief. – if the sale is part of a disposal of the entire business or qualifying shareholding, ER may also be available.	• On a subsequent disposal of the entire business or qualifying shareholding ER may be available if the donee has owned the asset for twelve months.

- Gift relief is not automatic, it must be claimed:
  - by both the donor and the donee (exception = gift into trust just needs to be signed by the donor)
  - by 5 April 2021 for gifts in the tax year 2016/17.

Qualifying assets

The main categories of qualifying assets for gift relief purposes are:

(1) Assets used in the trade of:
  - the donor (sole trader or partnership)
  - the donor's personal company.

(2) Unquoted shares and securities of any trading company.

(3) Quoted shares and securities of the individual donor's personal trading company.

(4) Any asset where there is an immediate charge to IHT (see Chapter 11).

(5) Agricultural property where APR is available (See Chapter 12).

Note that:

- a company qualifies as an individual's personal company if they own at least 5% of the voting rights
- no relief is available for business assets used in an investment business or shares in an investment company.

Interaction with entrepreneurs' relief

Gift relief is given **before** considering entrepreneurs' relief (ER).

If ER is applicable:

- the donee may be able to make his or her own claim to ER on a subsequent disposal if the conditions are satisfied
- the donor may choose not to claim GR in order to
  - crystallise a gain and utilise their AEA, and/or
  - claim ER instead so that the gain is taxed at 0% or 10% now rather than potentially at a higher rate later (i.e. if the donee will not qualify for the relief, for example if they would not satisfy the employment condition or one-year ownership rule).

Restrictions to gift relief

Non-business use

Adjustments need to be made to the calculation of the amount of gift relief available if there is an element of non-business use because the asset was:

- used partly for business purposes and partly for private use, or
- not used for business purposes for the whole of the period of ownership by the donor.

Where the asset has not been used entirely for business purposes, only the business portion of the gain is eligible for relief.

Shares in the donor's personal trading company

Gift relief is also restricted if:

- shares in the donor's personal trading company (quoted or unquoted) are gifted, and
- the company holds chargeable non-business assets (for example, investments in property or shares).

The portion of the gain that is eligible for GR is calculated as follows:

$$\text{Total gain} \times \frac{\text{MV of the chargeable business assets in the company (CBA)}}{\text{MV of the all chargeable assets in the company (CA)}}$$

Note the restriction only applies if the donor holds **at least 5%** of voting rights.

Where the donor holds **less than 5%** of the voting rights:

- for unquoted shares
  - there is no restriction to the relief, full relief is available.
- for quoted shares
  - GR is not available at all.

Chargeable assets (CA)

- A chargeable asset (CA) is one that, if sold by the company, would give rise to a chargeable gain (or an allowable loss).
- Exempt assets such as motor cars are therefore excluded.
- Inventory, receivables, cash etc, are also excluded as they are not capital assets and therefore not chargeable.

Chargeable business assets (CBA)

- Chargeable business assets (CBAs) are defined as chargeable assets used for the purposes of a trade.
- The definition therefore specifically excludes shares, securities or other assets held for investment purposes.

These definitions can be applied to most businesses to mean the following:

	Chargeable assets (CA)	**Chargeable business assets** (CBA)
Freehold/leasehold property used in trade	√	√
Goodwill	x	x
Motor cars	x	x
Plant and machinery (MV and cost £6,000 or less)	x	x
Investments (e.g. shares, investment property)	√	x
Net current assets	x	x

Consequences of restricting gift relief

Note that if the individual disposes of shares in a personal trading company:

- GR is available:
  - regardless of whether the individual works for the company
  - but may be subject to the (CBA/CA) restriction above.
- a chargeable gain will therefore arise at the time of the gift on the donor as not all of the gain can be deferred.
- the chargeable gain will be taxed on the donor at 0%, 10% or 20% depending on:
  - the availability of the donor's capital losses and AEA,
  - the availability of ER from the donor's point of view and, if not available,
  - the level of the donor's taxable income in that tax year.
- ER is available provided:
  - the donor works for the company, and
  - it has been the donor's personal trading company
  - for the 12 months prior to the disposal.
- IR is available provided:
  - the donor does not work for the company
  - the donor subscribed for newly issued ordinary shares in an unlisted trading company after 17 March 2016
  - the shares have been held for a minimum of 3 years starting on 6 April 2016.

Test your understanding 8

Fred is a sole trader. He gave his son, Ashley, a business asset on 1 July 2016 when its market value was £75,000. Fred paid £20,000 for the asset on 1 May 1995. Ashley sells the asset for £95,000 on 1 October 2017.

(a) **Compute the taxable gains arising on these disposals if gift relief is not claimed.**

(b) **Compute the taxable gains arising on these disposals if gift relief is claimed.**

(c) **If Ashley paid his father £53,000, what impact would this have.**

Test your understanding 9

Jack Jones gave 30,000 ordinary shares (representing his entire 30% holding) in Cross Ltd, an unquoted trading company, to his son Tom on 16 July 2016. The shares were valued at £450,000 on that date.

Jack purchased the shares on 16 October 2006, the day he became a full time director in the company. The shares cost Jack £200,000.

The company's issued share capital is 100,000 ordinary shares, and its net assets had the following market value on 16 July 2016:

	£
Freehold factory	1,140,000
Investments	60,000
Net current assets	370,000
	1,570,000

Calculate the chargeable gain for Jack and show the base cost for Tom, assuming all reliefs are claimed.

The emigration of the donee

Generally, to qualify for GR, the recipient must be resident in the UK at the time of the gift (except for gifts of UK residential property to non-UK residents – see Chapter 10).

If the recipient of a gift on which GR is given:

- emigrates from the UK within six years of the end of the tax year in which the gift was made
- the deferred gain at the time of the gift will crystallise and is chargeable on the donee the day before emigration.

Exception to the rule

Where the donee goes overseas to take up full time employment abroad a chargeable gain will not crystallise on his departure from the UK provided:

(i) they resume their status as UK resident within three years, and

(ii) they have not disposed of the asset whilst abroad.

Reasoning behind emigration rules

The overseas rules covered in Chapter 10 state that if an individual is not UK resident, capital disposals are usually exempt from CGT (except for disposal of UK residential property).

GR is generally not available in respect of gifts to a non-UK resident person as the non-UK resident could dispose of the asset whilst abroad and avoid CGT on the donor's original gain and any increase in value since the donee received the asset.

Therefore, to qualify for GR, the recipient must generally be resident in the UK at the time of the gift.

In addition, anti-avoidance legislation has been introduced to prevent individuals getting around the rules by:

- gifting assets to a UK resident person, and
- then the donee emigrates and disposes of the asset,
- to try and take advantage and avoid CGT on the donor's original gain and any increase in value since the donee received the asset.

Tax planning points

Much of tax planning for GR involves taking care to ensure that AEAs are utilised and gains are taxed at the lowest possible rates.

Rate of CGT

The outright gift of a qualifying asset results in:

- no chargeable gain arising on the donor at the time of the gift
- a higher gain arising on the donee on the subsequent disposal of the asset by the donee
- which is taxed at 0%, 10% or 20% depending on:
  - the availability of the donee's capital losses and AEA,
  - the availability of ER or IR from the donee's point of view or, if not available,
  - the level of the donee's taxable income in that tax year.

However, claiming GR is optional, and if it is not claimed:

- the gain arising at the time of the gift is assessed on the donor

- which is taxed at 0%, 10% or 20% depending on:
  - the availability of the donor's capital losses and AEA,
  - the availability of ER from the donor's point of view or, if not available,
  - the level of the donor's taxable income in that tax year.

Consequently:

- the donor may **choose not to claim** GR in order to:
  - crystallise a gain and utilise their capital losses and AEA, and/or
  - claim ER or IR
  - so that the gain is taxed at 0% or 10% now, rather than at a higher rate later.

For example, this may be advantageous if:

- the donor qualifies for ER or IR now but the donee will not qualify for the relief when they subsequently dispose of the asset (i.e. if they would not satisfy the employment condition and/or one-year ownership rule)
- the donor has capital losses, and/or has no other gains and therefore AEA available, and/or is a basic rate taxpayer whereas the donee is likely to be a higher rate taxpayer when the asset is disposed of.

Manipulating the chargeable gain

Note that if GR is claimed, all of the gain must be deferred; partial claims are not possible.

However, the individual could sell the asset at an undervaluation rather than making an outright gift to ensure that a GR claim will leave a gain to be taxed which utilises his capital losses and the AEA.

Impact of IHT

Lifetime gifts have both CGT and IHT consequences. Therefore, the impact of IHT must also be considered before giving advice. The interaction of CGT and IHT is covered in Chapter 13.

Summary

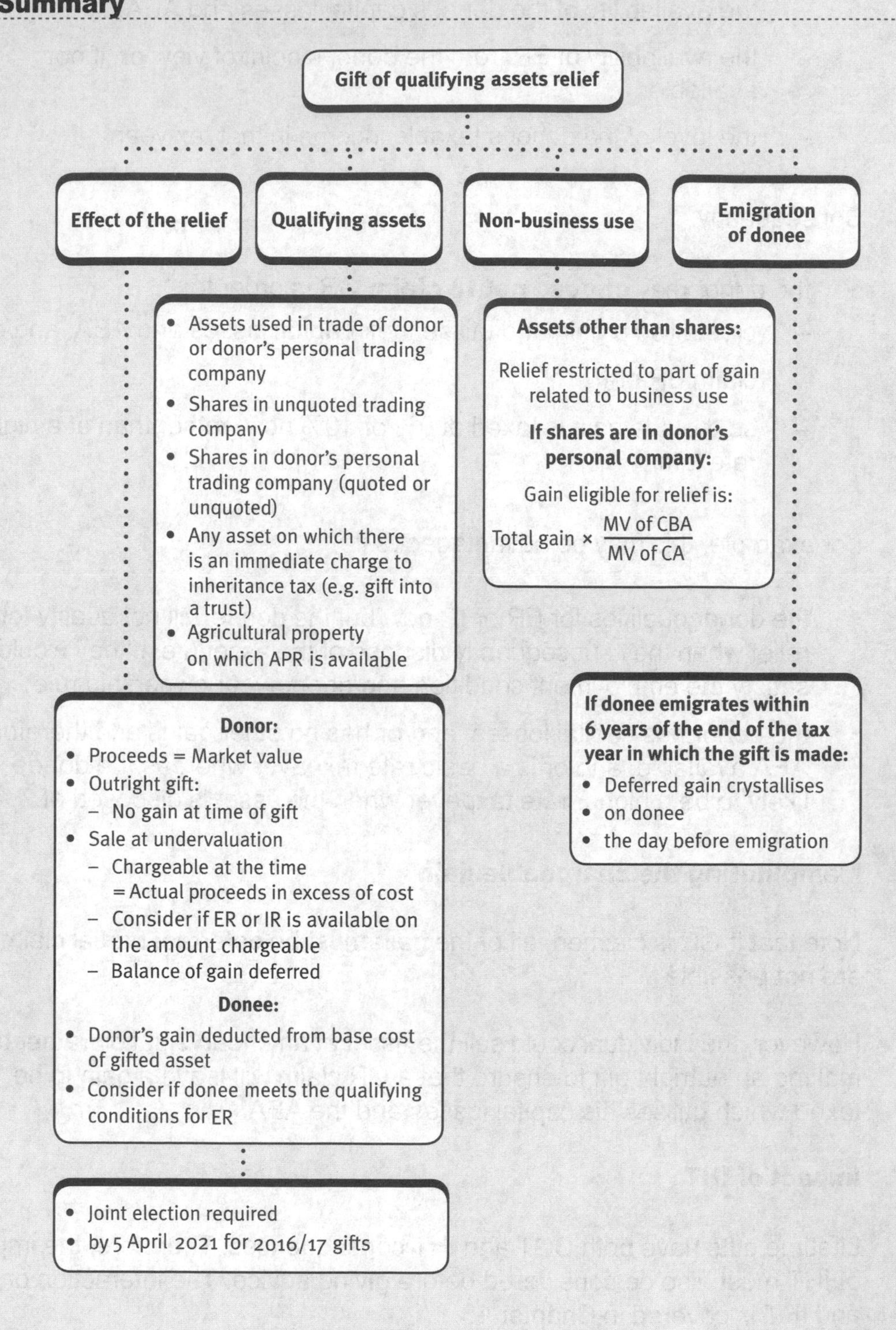
Gift of qualifying assets relief
Effect of the relief
Qualifying assets
Non-business use
Emigration of donee
Assets used in trade of donor or donor's personal trading company
Shares in unquoted trading company
Shares in donor's personal trading company (quoted or unquoted)
Any asset on which there is an immediate charge to inheritance tax (e.g. gift into a trust)
Agricultural property on which APR is available
Assets other than shares:
Relief restricted to part of gain related to business use
If shares are in donor's personal company:
Gain eligible for relief is:
Total gain × MV of CBA / MV of CA
If donee emigrates within 6 years of the end of the tax year in which the gift is made:
Deferred gain crystallises
on donee
the day before emigration
Donor:
Proceeds = Market value
Outright gift:
– No gain at time of gift
Sale at undervaluation
– Chargeable at the time = Actual proceeds in excess of cost
– Consider if ER or IR is available on the amount chargeable
– Balance of gain deferred
Donee:
Donor's gain deducted from base cost of gifted asset
Consider if donee meets the qualifying conditions for ER
Joint election required
by 5 April 2021 for 2016/17 gifts

7 Incorporation relief

Where an individual transfers their unincorporated business (i.e. a sole trader business or a partnership) to a company, the individual assets of the business are deemed to have been disposed of at market value to the company.

Incorporation relief is available to allow the gains arising on incorporation to be deferred until the shares in the company are disposed of.

The operation of the relief

Incorporation relief operates as follows:

- The total net chargeable gains arising on the deemed disposal of the individual assets are aggregated.
- The total net chargeable gains are deferred against the deemed acquisition cost of the shares in the company (i.e. deducted from the base cost of the shares).
- The deferred gain is deducted from the base cost of the shares.
- ER on the subsequent disposal of shares is based on the normal qualifying conditions.
- The relief is automatic provided certain conditions are met.

Conditions for the relief

All of the following conditions must be satisfied:

- The unincorporated business is transferred as a going concern.
- All of the assets of the business (other than cash) are transferred to a company (new or existing).
- The consideration received for the transfer of the business must be received wholly or partly in the form of shares in the company.

Where all of these conditions are met the relief is **automatic** and **mandatory.**

The calculation of the incorporation relief

The amount of the 'total gains' arising on incorporation that can be deferred depends on whether the transfer is wholly or partly for shares.

Transfer wholly for shares

Where the consideration for the transfer of the business to the company is wholly shares:

- the total net gains on the individual chargeable assets transferred to the company are deferred
- no chargeable gain arises at the time of the incorporation
- the market value of the shares acquired = the market value of the unincorporated business less the deferred gains.

Transfer partly for shares

Where part of the consideration for the transfer of the business is not in the form of shares (for example, cash and/or loan notes):

- incorporation relief

$$= \text{Total gains} \times \frac{\text{Market value of share consideration}}{\text{Market value of total consideration}}$$

- gain becomes chargeable at the time of incorporation

$$= \text{Total gains} \times \frac{\text{Market value of non-share consideration}}{\text{Market value of total consideration}}$$

Note that:

- cannot make a partial claim to defer only some of the gain
- however, the individual could choose to accept some cash or other non-share consideration to ensure that incorporation relief will leave a gain to be taxed which utilises their capital losses, ER and AEA.

Disapplying incorporation relief

- An individual can elect for incorporation relief not to apply (i.e. disapply the relief).
- This election may be useful if:
  - the gains on incorporation would be covered by the AEA and/or capital losses, or
  - it would be beneficial to take advantage of ER at the time of the transfer which may not be available on the eventual disposal of shares (see below).
- The election to disapply the incorporation relief rules must be made by 31 January 2020 for an incorporation that takes place in 2016/17.
- However, if the shares received are sold by the end of the tax year following the tax year of incorporation, this deadline is brought forward by one year (i.e. to 31 January 2019 for incorporation in 2016/17 with sale of shares during 2017/18).

Interaction with entrepreneurs' relief

If applicable, incorporation relief is given **before** considering ER. If the transaction is wholly for shares there will be no gain, and therefore, ER is not considered.

If full relief is not available using incorporation relief (e.g. if part of the consideration is in the form of cash), any remaining gain (with the possible exception of goodwill – see below) will usually qualify for ER as it relates to the disposal of an unincorporated business, provided the business has been owned for at least 12 months before incorporation. The chargeable gain after incorporation relief will therefore be taxed at 10%.

Rate of CGT – tax planning

It is important to note that:

- The subsequent disposal of the shares acquired at the time of incorporation should normally qualify for ER and any gain arising will be taxed at 0% or 10% depending on the availability of capital losses, AEA and provided the conditions for ER are satisfied.

- However, if this is unlikely (e.g. if the individual plans to dispose of the shares within one year and will fail the one-year ownership rule on the disposal), the individual may **choose to disapply** incorporation relief in order to crystallise a gain on incorporation so that they can claim ER now.

Note that gains in respect of goodwill may not qualify for ER where the business is transferred to a close company (see Chapter 26).

The circumstances in which gains in respect of goodwill will qualify for ER are covered in section 2 above.

Example 4 – Incorporation relief

Tristan, a higher rate taxpayer, bought a travel agency in Cornwall in April 2008 paying £11,500 for the goodwill.

On 15 July 2016 he sold the business as a going concern to Kareol Ltd, a large existing company, which took over all of the assets, except for cash, at the following agreed values:

	£
Freehold premises (cost £66,000 in May 2009)	284,000
Goodwill	44,000
Estate car	6,000
Inventory and receivables	6,000
	340,000

The consideration for the sale was settled by Kareol Ltd allotting to Tristan 70,000 ordinary shares of 20p each, valued at 350p per share, and paying him cash of £95,000. The shares are not quoted.

On 25 March 2017 Tristan sold 10,000 ordinary shares in Kareol Ltd for £22,664 to an unconnected person. On the same day Tristan gave a further 10,000 shares in Kareol Ltd to his daughter.

Calculate the CGT payable by Tristan as a result of the above disposals, assuming all available reliefs are claimed (where necessary).

Solution

Capital gains tax computation – 2016/17

	£	£
Gains not qualifying for ER		
Sale of Kareol Ltd shares (W2)	13,451	
Gift of Kareol Ltd shares (W3)	0	
Gains qualifying for ER		
Transfer of business to Kareol Ltd (W1)		69,993
Chargeable gains	13,451	69,993
Less: AEA (Note 1)	(11,100)	
Taxable gains	2,351	69,993

Capital gains tax:	£		£
Qualifying gains	69,993	× 10%	6,999
Non qualifying gains (Note 2)	2,351	× 20%	470
			7,469

Notes:

(1) The AEA is set against gains not qualifying for ER.

(2) After the gains qualifying for ER have been taxed at 10%, any remaining qualifying gains are taxed at the appropriate rate depending on the taxpayer's level of income.

Workings

(W1) **Transfer of business to Kareol Ltd – July 2016**

	£	£
Freehold premises		
Deemed proceeds (MV)	284,000	
Less: Cost	(66,000)	
		218,000
Goodwill		
Deemed proceeds (MV)	44,000	
Less: Cost	(11,500)	
		32,500
Estate car/inventory and receivables (exempt assets)		0
Total gains before reliefs		250,500
Less: Incorporation relief		
£250,500 × (£245,000/£340,000)		(180,507)
Gains qualifying for ER		69,993

Notes:

(1) Incorporation relief is given automatically and does not need to be claimed.

(2) If Kareol Ltd was a close company, the proportion of the remaining gain relating to goodwill would not qualify for ER.

(W2) **Sale of 10,000 Kareol Ltd shares**

	£	£
Sale proceeds		22,664
Shares acquired (July 2016)		
(70,000 × £3.50)	245,000	
Less: Incorporation relief	(180,507)	
Base cost of total shareholding	64,493	
Deemed cost of sale of 10,000 shares:		
(£64,493 × 10,000/70,000)	(9,213)	(9,213)
Deemed base cost of remaining shares	55,280	
Chargeable gain		13,451

Note: As Tristan owned the shares for less than 12 months, ER is not available.

Note that even if he had owned them for > 12 months, if he is not an employee of the company and/or owned ≤ 5%, ER would be denied.

(W3) **Gift of 10,000 Kareol Ltd shares**

	£
Capital gain (computed as above)	13,451
Less: Relief for gift of business assets (Note)	(13,451)
Chargeable gain	0

Note: The gift of unquoted trading company shares is an outright gift of qualifying shares for gift relief purposes. The base cost of the daughter's shares will be £9,213 (£22,664 – £13,451).

Test your understanding 10

On 31 January 2017, Stuart sold his business to a limited company for an agreed value of £1,100,000. He set up the business in August 2006.

All of the assets were transferred to the company with the exception of the cash.

The assets transferred were as follows:

	Date of Purchase	Market value 31 January 2017	Cost
		£	£
Freehold premises	August 2006	700,000	240,000
Goodwill	–	250,000	–
Inventory & receivables	–	150,000	–
		1,100,000	

(a) Calculate the gain immediately chargeable and the base cost of these shares assuming Stuart received:

(i) 100,000 £1 ordinary shares in the company.

(ii) 80,000 £1 ordinary shares plus £220,000 in cash.

(b) State the tax planning advice you would give to Stuart.

Alternative deferral using the gift relief provisions

One of the disadvantages of incorporation relief is that all of the assets (except cash) must be transferred to the company. If the trader wishes to retain any assets of the business other than cash, incorporation relief is denied and significant gains may crystallise on incorporation.

Alternatively, the trader may use gift relief to defer gains against the base cost of the assets for the company.

Alternative method of incorporation

An alternative, increasingly popular method of incorporation in recent years has been to sell the business (including goodwill) to the company for full market value in return for cash or a loan account in the company.

Gains would arise on disposal of the business assets, and would be fully chargeable. There would be no incorporation relief (as no shares were received) and no gift relief (as there was no gift). However, ER could be claimed so that CGT would only be payable at 10%.

One of the key benefits of this method was to extract cash from the company with a relatively low tax charge; any loan could be repaid by the company in future with no further tax liabilities (whereas extraction of funds as a bonus, for example, would result in tax charges).

In addition to the CGT benefit, advantageous corporation tax relief was then available to the company for the purchase cost of the goodwill acquired in the transaction (see Chapter 23). Generous double relief was therefore obtained on the value of goodwill which was usually a significant value and difficult to quantify and substantiate.

However, in FA2015, HMRC have stopped this double benefit by denying ER on the gain relating to goodwill, and disallowing corporation tax relief on the cost of the goodwill where these circumstances apply. This is considered in more detail in Chapter 18 where all of the tax implications of incorporating a business are covered.

Summary

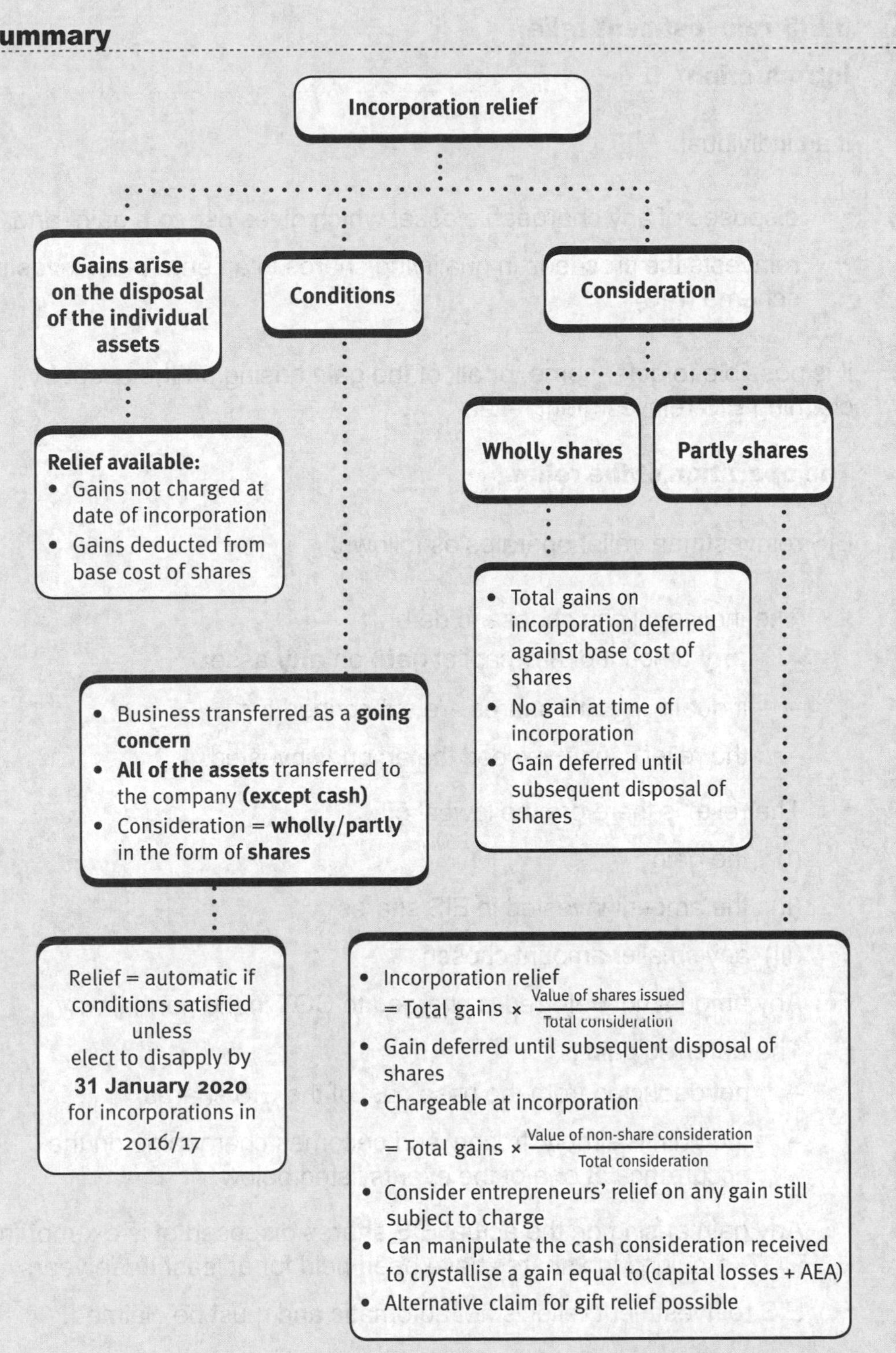
Incorporation relief
Gains arise on the disposal of the individual assets
Conditions
Consideration
Relief available:
• Gains not charged at date of incorporation
• Gains deducted from base cost of shares
Wholly shares
Partly shares
• Total gains on incorporation deferred against base cost of shares
• No gain at time of incorporation
• Gain deferred until subsequent disposal of shares
• Business transferred as a going concern
• All of the assets transferred to the company (except cash)
• Consideration = wholly/partly in the form of shares
Relief = automatic if conditions satisfied unless elect to disapply by 31 January 2020 for incorporations in 2016/17
• Incorporation relief = Total gains × Value of shares issued / Total consideration
• Gain deferred until subsequent disposal of shares
• Chargeable at incorporation = Total gains × Value of non-share consideration / Total consideration
• Consider entrepreneurs' relief on any gain still subject to charge
• Can manipulate the cash consideration received to crystallise a gain equal to (capital losses + AEA)
• Alternative claim for gift relief possible

8 EIS reinvestment relief

Introduction

If an individual:

- disposes of any chargeable asset which gives rise to a gain; and
- reinvests the proceeds in qualifying shares in an enterprise investment scheme (EIS)

it is possible to defer some, or all, of the gain arising on the asset by claiming EIS reinvestment relief.

The operation of the relief

EIS reinvestment relief operates as follows:

- The individual can choose to defer:
  - **any** amount of any capital **gain** on **any** asset
  - if qualifying EIS shares are subscribed for
  - the relief cannot exceed the amount invested.
- The relief is therefore the lowest of:
  - (i) the gain
  - (ii) the amount invested in EIS shares
  - (iii) any smaller amount chosen.
- Any amount not deferred is charged to CGT in the normal way.
- The deferred gain is
  - not deducted from the base cost of the EIS shares,
  - the gain is simply 'frozen' and becomes chargeable on the occurrence of one of the events listed below.
- Any gain arising on the actual EIS shares disposed of is exempt from CGT, provided the shares have been held for at least three years.
- EIS reinvestment relief is not automatic and must be claimed.

Occasions when the deferred gain becomes chargeable

Any of the following will cause the deferred gain to become chargeable:

- **EIS shares are disposed of** by:
  - the investor, or
  - the investor's spouse or civil partner (following a previous no gain/no loss transfer)
- **Within three years** of the issue of shares:
  - the investor, or
  - the investor's spouse or civil partner (following a previous no gain/no loss transfer)

  becomes non-UK resident (e.g. emigrates abroad) unless

  - working temporarily outside the UK (i.e. they resume UK residence within three years), and
  - they retain the shares throughout.

Conditions for EIS relief

To qualify for EIS relief:

- The individual must be UK resident when the gain arises and when the reinvestment is made.
- The reinvestment must be:
  - subscribing for new shares
  - wholly for cash
  - in an unquoted trading company trading wholly or mainly in the UK.
- The reinvestment must be made within a **four year** time period which runs from **12 months before** to **36 months after** the date the gain arose.
- The claim must be made by 31 January 2023 for 2016/17 disposals.

Note that:

- for EIS income tax relief there is a maximum investment of £1 million. However, there is no maximum amount for the purposes of this CGT reinvestment relief. The relief is effectively unlimited.
- the relief is flexible, any amount of reinvestment relief can be claimed. Therefore, the individual should choose an amount of relief so that the remaining gain is equal to any capital losses and AEA available.

Test your understanding 11

Alex sold a painting in November 2016 for £275,000 realising a capital gain of £150,000.

Alex subscribes for qualifying EIS shares in Milan Ltd, a trading company, the following month at a cost of £268,000. She has no other capital transactions for the tax year 2016/17, but has capital losses brought forward from 2013/14 of £6,000.

Three years later in the tax year 2019/20 Alex sells the EIS shares making a profit of £175,000.

(a) **Calculate the amount of reinvestment relief that Alex should claim.**

(b) **Explain the capital gains tax consequences of the sale of the EIS shares in the tax year 2019/20.**

Interaction with entrepreneurs' relief

If the asset disposed of does not qualify for ER, the deferred gain will be taxed at 10%/20% when it becomes chargeable.

If the asset qualifies for ER then the taxpayer may choose to either:

- claim ER at the time of disposal and pay tax on the eligible gain at 10% in the year of disposal, or
- claim EIS reinvestment relief and defer the gain until the EIS shares are sold (usually).

With effect from 2015/16, if ER would be available but is not claimed at the time of disposal and the gain is deferred:

- the deferred gain will **still be taxed at 10% when it becomes chargeable**
- provided a claim is made within 12 months of the 31 January following the end of the tax year in which the gain actually becomes chargeable.

The decision to claim ER at the time of the disposal or defer the gain and claim ER later will depend on the cash flow position of the taxpayer, but there is clearly a cash flow benefit to be gained from deferring the gain.

In addition, a further AEA may be available to set against the deferred gain when it becomes chargeable.

Test your understanding 12

Chris sold his 10% holding in Cracker Ltd in September 2016 for £750,000, realising a capital gain of £250,000.

He acquired the shares in July 2013 and has been a director of Cracker Ltd throughout his period of ownership.

In November 2016 he subscribed for qualifying EIS shares in Cream Ltd, a trading company, at a cost of £375,000.

Chris had no other capital transactions in the tax year 2016/17 but has capital losses brought forward of £50,000.

Calculate the amount of EIS reinvestment relief that Chris should claim in the tax year 2016/17 and discuss the interaction with entrepreneurs' relief.

Summary

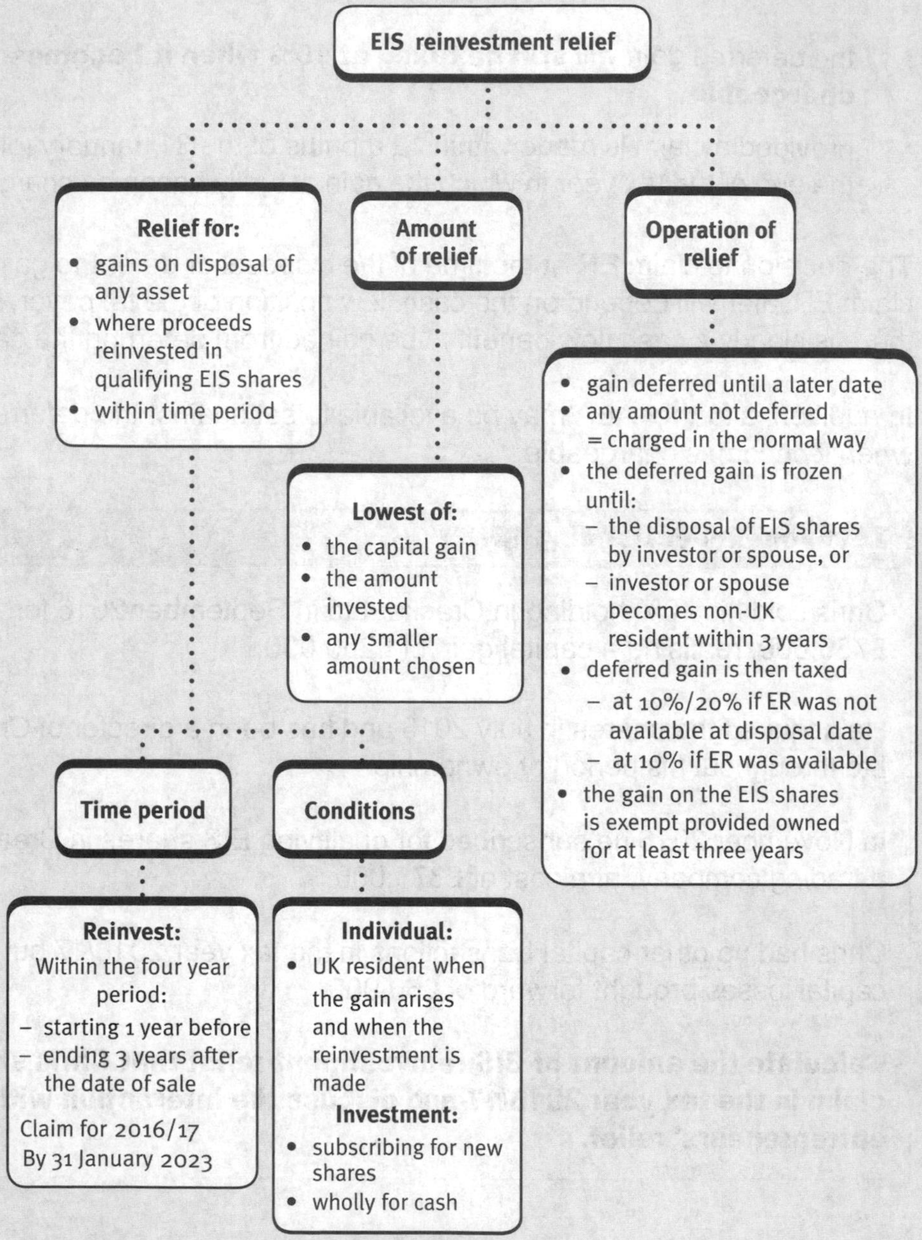

EIS reinvestment relief

Relief for:
- gains on disposal of any asset
- where proceeds reinvested in qualifying EIS shares
- within time period

Amount of relief

Lowest of:
- the capital gain
- the amount invested
- any smaller amount chosen

Operation of relief
- gain deferred until a later date
- any amount not deferred = charged in the normal way
- the deferred gain is frozen until:
  - the disposal of EIS shares by investor or spouse, or
  - investor or spouse becomes non-UK resident within 3 years
- deferred gain is then taxed
  - at 10%/20% if ER was not available at disposal date
  - at 10% if ER was available
- the gain on the EIS shares is exempt provided owned for at least three years

Time period

Reinvest:
Within the four year period:
- starting 1 year before
- ending 3 years after the date of sale

Claim for 2016/17
By 31 January 2023

Conditions

Individual:
- UK resident when the gain arises and when the reinvestment is made

Investment:
- subscribing for new shares
- wholly for cash

9 SEIS reinvestment relief

SEIS reinvestment relief works differently from EIS reinvestment relief, although in many respects it is the same.

If an individual:

- disposes of **any** chargeable asset which gives rise to a gain; and
- reinvests the proceeds in qualifying SEIS shares; and
- qualifies for SEIS income tax (IT) relief in the same tax year

some of the gain arising is **exempt** from capital gains tax (not deferred).

Any remaining gain is taxable in the normal way.

Note that if an investor elects to carry back the amount invested in SEIS shares to the previous tax year for the purposes of SEIS income tax relief, this will also apply for the purposes of SEIS reinvestment relief.

This means that:

- if an investment in SEIS shares was made in 2016/17, but
- a claim was made to carry back the investment and claim IT relief in 2015/16

reinvestment relief would be available in respect of gains made in 2015/16.

The operation of the relief

The maximum SEIS exemption = **50% of the lower of**:

(i) the amount of the gain

(ii) the amount reinvested in qualifying SEIS shares on which IT relief is claimed.

As the maximum amount that can qualify for IT relief is £100,000, the **maximum CGT exemption is £50,000.**

The relief must be claimed (it is not automatic), but is flexible, as any amount up to the maximum reinvestment relief can be claimed.

Therefore, if applicable, the individual should choose an amount of relief so that the remaining gain is equal to any capital losses and AEA available.

The time limits for making the claim are the same as for EIS reinvestment relief (i.e. by 31 January 2023 for 2016/17 disposals).

Test your understanding 13

Zosia sold an antique vase in June 2016 for £150,000 realising a capital gain of £75,000. In August 2016 she subscribed for qualifying SEIS shares in Browns Ltd.

She has no other capital transactions for 2016/17, but has a capital loss brought forward of £16,000.

(a) **Calculate Zosia's taxable gains for the tax year 2016/17 assuming the SEIS shares cost:**

(i) **£60,000**

(ii) **£125,000**

(b) **Explain the capital gains tax consequences if Zosia sells the SEIS shares in 2021.**

Withdrawal of SEIS relief

For the SEIS scheme, if the disposal within three years is:

	Not at arm's length	**At arm's length**
IT relief withdrawn (i.e. amount of IT that becomes payable)	**All** original IT relief given	Lower of: • original IT relief given • (50% × SP received for shares)
CGT relief withdrawn (i.e. previously exempted gain that becomes chargeable)	**All** of the gain previously exempted	• A proportion of the gain previously exempted • Proportion $= \frac{\text{Amount of IT relief withdrawn (above)}}{\text{Original IT relief given}}$

Test your understanding 14

Explain the capital gains tax consequences for Zosia (in Test Your Understanding 13) assuming that in 2018 she sells all of the SEIS shares for £65,000:

(a) **To her sister, not in an arm's length transaction.**

(b) **To her friend, in an arm's length transaction.**

Consider both of the scenarios where she originally subscribes for shares at a cost of £60,000, and at a cost of £125,000.

Summary

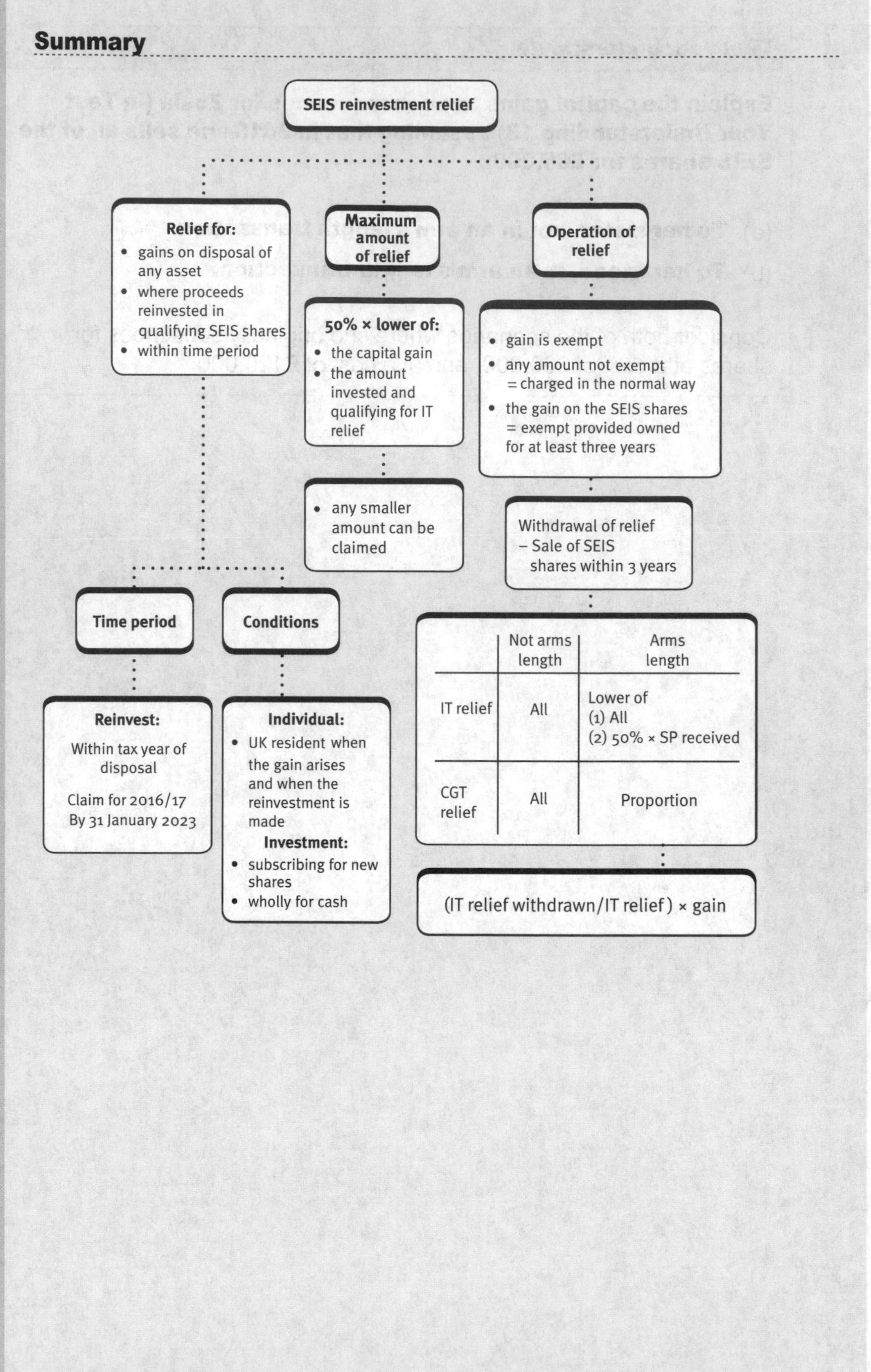
SEIS reinvestment relief
Relief for:
• gains on disposal of any asset
• where proceeds reinvested in qualifying SEIS shares
• within time period
Maximum amount of relief
50% × lower of:
• the capital gain
• the amount invested and qualifying for IT relief
• any smaller amount can be claimed
Operation of relief
• gain is exempt
• any amount not exempt = charged in the normal way
• the gain on the SEIS shares = exempt provided owned for at least three years
Withdrawal of relief – Sale of SEIS shares within 3 years
Not arms length
Arms length
IT relief
All
Lower of (1) All (2) 50% × SP received
CGT relief
All
Proportion
(IT relief withdrawn/IT relief) × gain
Time period
Reinvest:
Within tax year of disposal
Claim for 2016/17 By 31 January 2023
Conditions
Individual:
• UK resident when the gain arises and when the reinvestment is made
Investment:
• subscribing for new shares
• wholly for cash

10 Chapter summary

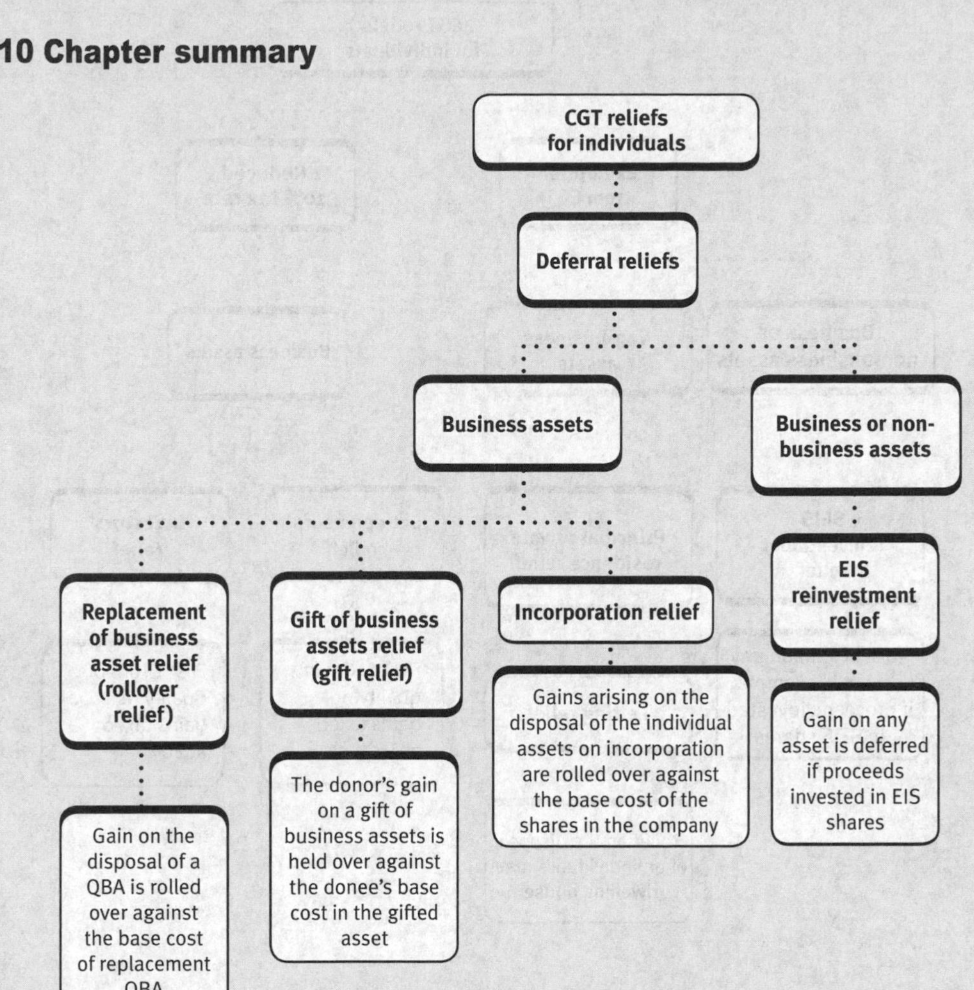

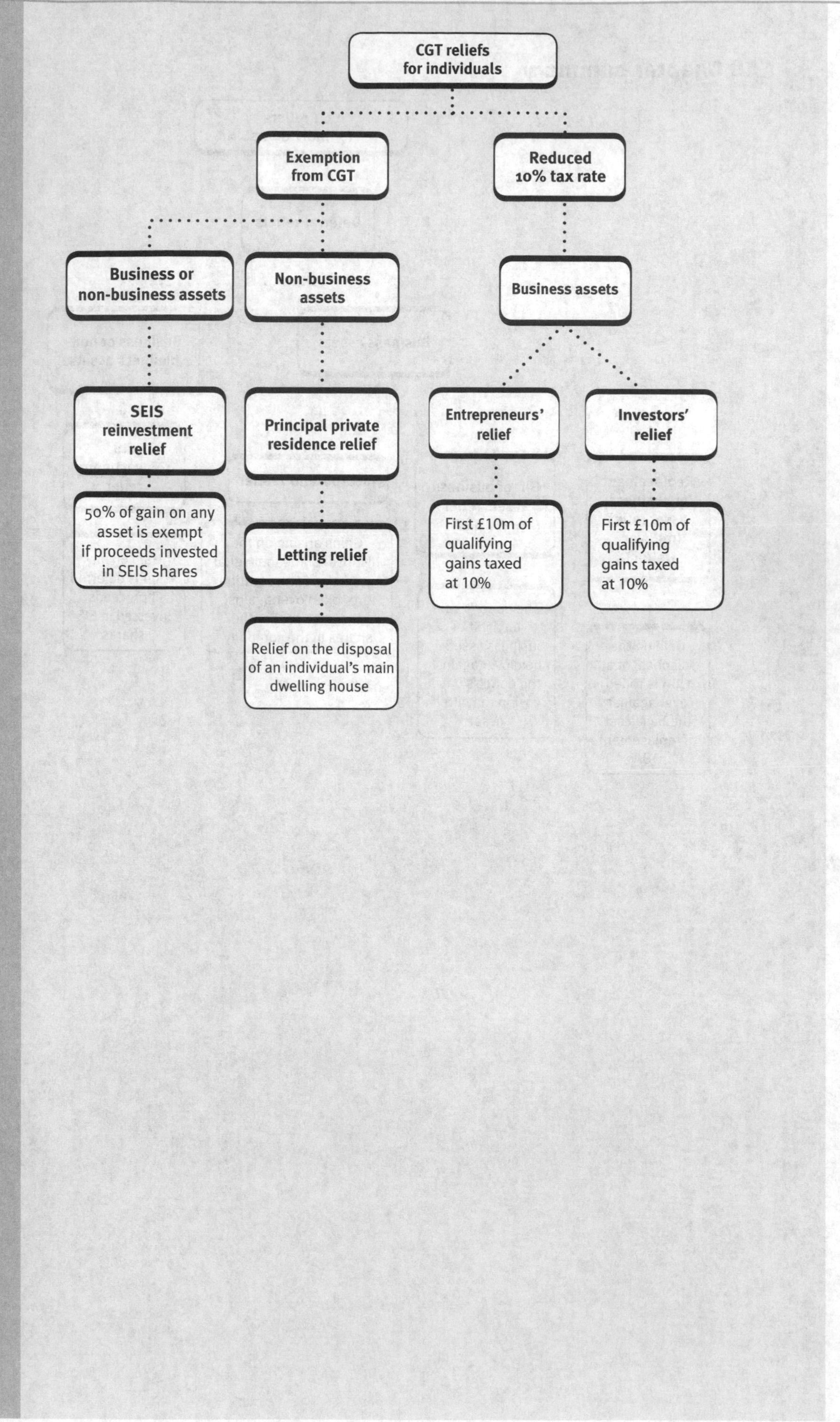

CGT reliefs for individuals
Exemption from CGT
Reduced 10% tax rate
Business or non-business assets
Non-business assets
Business assets
SEIS reinvestment relief
Principal private residence relief
Entrepreneurs' relief
Investors' relief
50% of gain on any asset is exempt if proceeds invested in SEIS shares
Letting relief
First £10m of qualifying gains taxed at 10%
First £10m of qualifying gains taxed at 10%
Relief on the disposal of an individual's main dwelling house

Test your understanding answers

Test your understanding 1

Paul

Capital gains tax

		Not qualifying for ER	Qualifying for ER
		£	£
2016/17			
Sale of warehouse (Note 1)		245,000	
Sale of company shares			430,000
Less: AEA (Note 2)		(11,100)	(0)
Taxable gains		233,900	430,000
Capital gains tax:			
Qualifying gains	(£430,000 × 10%)		43,000
Non qualifying gains	(£233,900 × 20%) (Note 3)		46,780
			89,780
Due date			31.1.2018

2017/18	£	£	£
Sale of antique table		5,325	
Sales of trading business:			
Factory	6,495,000		
Goodwill	130,000		
	6,625,000		
Qualifying for ER (W)	(6,070,000)	555,000	6,070,000
Chargeable gains		560,325	6,070,000
Less: AEA (Note 2)		(11,100)	(0)
Taxable gains		549,225	6,070,000

Capital gains tax:		£
Qualifying gains	(£6,070,000 × 10%) (Note 4)	607,000
Non-qualifying gains	(£549,225 × 20%) (Note 5)	109,845
		716,845
Due date		31.1.2019

Working: Qualifying gains in 2017/18

	£
Lifetime limit	10,000,000
Claims prior to 2016/17	(3,500,000)
Claim in 2016/17	(430,000)
Qualifying gains in 2017/18	6,070,000

Notes:

(1) The disposal of the warehouse in 2016/17 is the disposal of an individual business asset used for the purposes of a continuing trade. To qualify for ER, there must be a disposal of the whole or part of the trading business. The sale of an asset in isolation will not qualify.

(2) The AEA is set against gains not qualifying for ER, and any remaining AEA is then set against gains qualifying for ER.

(3) The gains qualifying for ER are deemed to utilise the BR band first. Paul's taxable income is £27,000 (£38,000 – £11,000 PA). Therefore the BR band remaining is £5,000 (£32,000 – £27,000). However, Paul's gains qualifying for ER (£430,000) exceed £32,000. Therefore, there is no need to calculate the BR band remaining in this case because even if Paul had no taxable income, and all of his BR band was available, it would be matched against these qualifying gains. Accordingly the gains not qualifying for ER will be taxed at 20%.

(4) After the first £10 million of gains qualifying for ER have been taxed at 10%, any remaining qualifying gains are taxed at the appropriate rate depending on the individual's taxable income.

(5) There is no BR band remaining in 2017/18 as Paul's taxable income of £37,000 (£48,000 – £11,000 PA) exceeds £32,000. Even if there were, the remaining BR band is set against gains qualifying for ER first leaving remaining gains to be taxed at 20%.

Test your understanding 2

Mr Dearden

	£
Capital gain before reliefs	194,800
Less: PPR relief (W1) (£194,800 × 180/300)	(116,880)
	77,920
Less: Letting relief (W2)	(19,480)
Chargeable gain	58,440

Workings

(W1) **Compute and analyse total period of ownership**

01.04.92 – 31.03.17 = 25 years (or 300 months)

	Exempt months	Chargeable months	Total months
01.04.92 – 31.03.94	24		24
01.04.94 – 30.09.99 (3 years any reason)	36	30	66
01.10.99 – 31.03.08	102		102
01.04.08 – 30.09.15 (Balance)		90	90
01.10.15 – 31.03.17 (last 18 months)	18		18
	180	120	300

(W2) **Letting relief**

The house was let for 66 months, from 01.04.94 – 30.09.99, but 36 months of that was exempted under the PPR rules therefore only 30 months is considered for letting relief.

Letting relief is the lowest of:

(1) £40,000

(2) PPR = £116,880

(3) Gain on letting = (£194,800 × 30/300) = £19,480

Test your understanding 3

Alex

Alex owned the house for 145 months and used 1/5th of the house (one of the five rooms) for business purposes for 115 months.

The last 18 months of ownership are exempt (the room had been used as part of the residence at some time).

The gain is therefore: £70,000 × 1/5 × (115 – 18)/145 = £9,366

Alternative approach:

	£	£
Capital gain before reliefs		70,000
Less: PPR relief		
£70,000 × 4/5	56,000	
£70,000 × 1/5 × (145 – (115 – 18))/145	4,634	
		(60,634)
Chargeable gain		9,366

Test your understanding 4

Paul Opus
Capital gains tax liability – 2016/17

		Total	Residential property	Other gains
	£	£	£	£
Ordinary shares in Symphony Ltd				
Disposal proceeds	23,600			
Less: Cost (£110,400 × 5,000/40,000) (Note 1)	(13,800)			
		9,800		9,800
Ordinary shares in Concerto plc				
Deemed proceeds (10,000 × £5.14) (Note 2)	51,400			
Less: Cost (Note 1)	(14,000)			
		37,400		37,400
Antique vase (Note 5)		4,000		4,000
House				
Disposal proceeds	220,000			
Less: Cost	(114,700)			
	105,300			
Less: PPR relief (Note 6)	(64,539)			
		40,761	40,761	
Land				
Disposal proceeds	285,000			
Less: Cost (Note 7)	(167,200)			
		117,800		117,800
Holiday cottage				
Disposal proceeds	125,000			
Less Cost (Note 8)	(101,600)			
		23,400	23,400	
Total chargeable gains		233,161	64,161	169,000
Annual exempt amount		(11,100)	(11,100)	
Taxable gains		222,061	53,061	169,000

Capital gains tax (Note 9)	£		
Basic rate			
(£32,000 – £25,000)	7,000 × 18%	(residential)	1,260
Higher rate			
(£53,061 – £7,000)	46,061 × 28%	(residential)	12,897
Higher rate	169,000 × 20%	(other gains)	33,800
	222,061		
Capital gains tax liability			47,957
Due date			31 January 2018

Notes:

(1) The shares are disposed of from the share pool.

(2) The shares in Concerto plc are valued at the mid-price quoted on the Stock Exchange
= (£5.10 + £5.18) × ½
= £5.14)

(3) ER is not available on the disposal of Symphony Ltd shares as Paul is not an employee of Symphony Ltd.

ER is not available on the disposal of the Concerto plc shares as the disposal is not from a personal trading company.
Gift relief is not available either as Paul's holding is ≤ 5%.

(4) Motor cars are exempt from CGT.

(5) The antique vase is a non-wasting chattel.
The gain is (£12,400 – £8,400) = £4,000.

(6) The total period of ownership of the house is 93 months, of which a total of 57 months (period of occupation plus final 18 months) qualify for exemption. The exemption is therefore £64,539 (£105,300 × 57/93).

(7) The cost relating to the three acres of land sold is £167,200 (£220,000 × £285,000/£375,000).

(8) The transfer of the holiday cottage between Paul and his wife is effectively ignored for CGT purposes, so the wife's original cost is used in calculating Paul's chargeable gain.

(9) The remaining basic rate band could be allocated instead to the 'other gains' first without making any difference to the overall capital gains tax liability.

Test your understanding 5

Keith

Not all of the sale proceeds have been reinvested therefore some of the gain will be taxable at the time of the disposal.

May 1991

The gain taxable in May 1991 was the lower of:

• the full gain	£58,240
• the amount of the proceeds not reinvested (£100,000 – £80,000)	£20,000
The gain rolled over was therefore (£58,240 – £20,000)	£38,240

July 2016

	£	£
Proceeds on sale of building 2		300,000
Less: Cost	80,000	
Gain rolled over	(38,240)	
Base cost		(41,760)
Chargeable gain		258,240

Note: The chargeable gain arising in 2016/17 will be taxed at 10% or 20% depending on the level of taxable income.

ER is not available. This is because the disposal of an individual asset used for the purposes of a continuing trade does not qualify. The trade itself is not being disposed of.

Test your understanding 6

Sophie

Disposal of office block – August 2011

	£
Sale proceeds	120,000
Less: Cost	(70,000)
	50,000
Cash retained (£120,000 – £100,000) = £20,000	
Deferred gains (£50,000 – £20,000)	(30,000)
Chargeable gain – 2011/12	20,000

The £30,000 gain is deferred until the earliest of:

(1) the disposal of replacement depreciating asset (November 2016)

(2) the depreciating asset ceases to be used for the purposes of the trade (November 2016)

(3) ten years from the date of acquisition of the replacement depreciating asset (April 2022).

Therefore, the deferred gain of £30,000 becomes chargeable in 2016/17.

Note: The chargeable gain arising in 2016/17 will be taxed at 10% or 20% depending on the level of taxable income.

ER is not available. This is because the disposal of an individual asset used for the purposes of a continuing trade does not qualify. The trade itself is not being disposed of.

Disposal of fixed plant and machinery – November 2016

Sophie has sold the machinery for a real loss of £40,000 (£100,000 – £60,000).

However, no allowable capital loss arises as relief for the £40,000 will have been given through the capital allowances system.

Test your understanding 7

Medway

(a) **Capital gain on the disposal of the factory**

	£
Proceeds	160,000
Less: Cost	(40,000)
Qualifying for ER	120,000
Less: AEA	(11,100)
Taxable gain	108,900
Capital gains tax @ 10%	10,890

(b) (i) **New factory cost £172,000**

All of the gain will be rolled over against the base cost of the new factory as all of the proceeds are reinvested

	£
Capital gain on factory (1)	120,000
Less: ROR	(120,000)
Chargeable gain	0

Base cost of new factory

Cost of new factory	172,000
Less: Gain deferred	(120,000)
Base cost of new factory	52,000

When Medway subsequently sells the replacement factory, as part of the sale of the whole of the new business, ER will be available if the conditions are satisfied.

(ii) **New factory cost £150,000**

As only part of the proceeds are reinvested, the gain that cannot be rolled over will be £10,000 (£160,000 – £150,000). The rest of the gain £110,000 (£120,000 – £10,000) can be deferred.

	£
Capital gain before reliefs	120,000
Less: ROR	(110,000)
Gain qualifying for ER	10,000
Less: AEA (part wasted)	(11,100)
Taxable gain	0

Base cost of new factory

Cost of new factory	150,000
Less: Gain deferred	(110,000)
Base cost of new factory	40,000

When Medway subsequently sells the replacement factory, as part of the sale of the whole of the new business, ER will be available if the conditions are satisfied.

The remaining relief available is the full £10,000,000, as there would be no point claiming relief for the original gain of £10,000 due to the availability of the AEA.

Test your understanding 8

Fred's taxable gains

2016/17	(a)	(b)	(c)
	£	£	£
Deemed proceeds (1 July 2016)	75,000	75,000	75,000
Less: Cost	(20,000)	(20,000)	(20,000)
	55,000	55,000	55,000
Less: Gift relief	0	(55,000)	(22,000)
Chargeable gain	55,000	0	33,000
Less: AEA	(11,100)		(11,100)
Taxable gain	43,900	0	21,900

Note: Under (c) Fred realises an actual profit of £33,000 (£53,000 – £20,000) and so this amount becomes chargeable leaving the balance to be deferred.

The taxable gains in (a) and (c) would be taxable at 10% or 20% depending on the level of taxable income. ER is not available as this is the disposal of an individual asset not the whole or substantial part of the business.

Base cost for Ashley	£	£	£
Deemed cost	75,000	75,000	75,000
Less: Gift relief	(0)	(55,000)	(22,000)
Base cost for future CGT disposal	75,000	20,000	53,000

Ashley's taxable gains	(a)	(b)	(c)
2017/18	£	£	£
Proceeds (1 October 2017)	95,000	95,000	95,000
Less: Base cost	(75,000)	(20,000)	(53,000)
Chargeable gain	20,000	75,000	42,000
Less: AEA	(11,100)	(11,100)	(11,100)
Taxable gain	8,900	63,900	30,900

Test your understanding 9

Jack Jones

Gift of shares – July 2016	£
Market value	450,000
Less: Cost	(200,000)
Capital gain before reliefs	250,000

As the gain is on shares in Tom's personal trading company, and the company holds investments, the amount eligible for gift relief is restricted as follows:

$$\text{Gift relief} = £250,000 \times \frac{£1,140,000}{£1,140,000 + £60,000} = £237,500$$

Note: Market values must be used in the CBA/CA fraction.

The chargeable gain at the time of the gift is therefore:

	£
Capital gain (as above)	250,000
Less: Gift relief	(237,500)
Gain qualifying for ER	12,500
Base cost of shares to Tom	
Market value	450,000
Less: Gift relief	(237,500)
Cost of shares	212,500

When Tom sells his entire holding, assuming he works for the company and owns the shares for 12 months, ER will be available.

Test your understanding 10

Stuart

(a) (i) **Chargeable gain on disposal of business – 2016/17**

	£	£
Premises: Proceeds	700,000	
Less: Cost	(240,000)	
		460,000
Goodwill: Proceeds	250,000	
Less: Cost	–	
		250,000
Total capital gains before reliefs		710,000
Less: Incorporation relief		(710,000)
Chargeable gain – 2016/17		0
Base cost of shares		
Market value of assets transferred		1,100,000
Less: Incorporation relief		(710,000)
Base cost		390,000

ER is delayed until a subsequent disposal of the shareholding provided the conditions are satisfied.

(ii) **Chargeable gain on disposal of business – 2016/17**

	£	£
Total capital gains before reliefs (as above)		710,000
Total consideration		
Cash	220,000	
Shares (balance)	880,000	
	1,100,000	
Less: Incorporation relief (deferred gain) (£710,000 × £880,000/£1,100,000)		(568,000)
Gain qualifying for ER		142,000
Base cost of shares		
MV of share consideration		880,000
Less: Incorporation relief		(568,000)
Base cost of shares		312,000

ER will be available on a subsequent disposal of the shares if the conditions are satisfied.

(b) **Tax advice for Stuart**

Assuming Stuart has no other capital gains in the year, Stuart should consider accepting non-share consideration (e.g. cash) to the value that would give rise to a chargeable gain which is covered by his AEA.

Gain required	£11,100
The deferred gains should be (£710,000 – £11,100) =	£698,900
Therefore the market value of the shares should be:	
£699,000 = MV of shares × (£710,000/£1,100,000)	
MV of shares =	£1,082,803
Therefore the cash should be:	
(£1,100,000 – £1,082,803) =	£17,197

Alternative calculation:

$$\frac{\text{Cash}}{\text{MV of business}} \times \text{Total net gains} = (\text{AEA} + \text{capital losses b/f})$$

$$\frac{\text{Cash}}{£1,100,000} \times £710,000 = £11,100$$

Cash = £17,197

Proof:

		£
Capital gain before reliefs		710,000
Less: Incorporation relief		
	$£710,000 \times \frac{£1,082,803}{£1,100,000}$	(698,900)
Chargeable gain		11,100
Less: AEA		(11,100)
Taxable gain		0

Test your understanding 11

Alex

(a) **Amount of reinvestment relief**

Alex can claim relief for any amount up to £150,000.

However, to claim this full amount will mean that she does not make full use of her AEA for 2016/17.

The EIS relief claim should therefore be calculated as follows:

	£	
Capital gain	150,000	
Less: EIS Reinvestment relief	(132,900)	Balancing figure
Chargeable gain	17,100	
Less: Capital loss b/f	(6,000)	
Less: AEA	(11,100)	
Taxable gain	0	

(b) **Sale of EIS shares**

When Alex disposes of the EIS shares in 2019/20, the gain of £132,900 will become chargeable.

The gain on the EIS shares of £175,000 will be exempt from CGT as the shares have been held for more than 3 years.

Test your understanding 12

The shares qualify for ER as Chris has had ≥ 5% interest in the company (a trading company) for more than 12 months and works for the company.

However, Chris does not have to claim ER and can defer the gain with an EIS claim as follows:

Chris

	£	
Capital gain	250,000	
Less: EIS reinvestment relief	(188,900)	Balancing figure
Chargeable gain	61,100	
Less: Capital loss b/f	(50,000)	
Net chargeable gain	11,100	
Less: AEA	(11,100)	
Taxable gain	0	

The deferred gain of £188,900 will become chargeable in the future (e.g. when the EIS shares are disposed of) and will be taxed at 10% as the gain would have qualified for ER if crystallised in 2016/17.

If the EIS shares are held for 3 years, any rise in value of the EIS shares will be exempt, any losses are always allowable.

Alternatively, Chris could choose not to claim EIS relief and claim ER in 2016/17 instead as follows:

	£
Gain qualifying for ER	250,000
Less: Capital loss b/f	(50,000)
Total chargeable gain	200,000
Less: AEA	(11,100)
Taxable gain	188,900
Capital gains tax @ 10%	18,890

The decision made by Chris will depend on his cash flow position in 2016/17, although there is no advantage to be gained from claiming ER and paying tax in 2016/17.

Test your understanding 13

Zosia

(a) **Taxable gains – 2016/17**

	(i)	(ii)
SEIS shares cost	£60,000	£125,000
	£	£
Capital gain	75,000	75,000
Less: SEIS reinvestment relief (W)	(30,000)	(37,500)
Chargeable gain	45,000	37,500
Less: Capital loss b/f	(16,000)	(16,000)
Less: AEA	(11,100)	(11,100)
Taxable gain	17,900	10,400

Working: SEIS reinvestment relief

	(i)	(ii)
	£	£
Maximum exemption = 50% × lower of		
(i) Gain	75,000	**75,000**
(ii) Amount invested in SEIS qualifying for IT relief	**60,000**	100,000 (max)
CGT exemption	**30,000**	**37,500**

Note: In scenario (ii), if Zosia's capital loss was more than £26,500, Zosia could claim up to £37,500 exemption but could choose instead to restrict the claim to preserve the use of the capital loss b/f and the AEA.

(b) **Sale of SEIS shares**

When Zosia sells the SEIS shares in 2021, there will be no gain.

The gain that was subject to reinvestment relief will not become chargeable, as the SEIS relief is an exemption rather than a deferral.

The gain on the SEIS shares will be exempt from CGT as the shares have been held for more than 3 years.

Test your understanding 14

Zosia

As the shares have been sold within three years, both income tax relief and capital gains tax relief will be withdrawn in both situations.

(a) **Sale to sister – not in an arm's length transaction**

Original investment	**£60,000**	**£125,000**
All IT relief claimed = withdrawn	£30,000	£50,000
All CGT exemption claimed = withdrawn	£30,000	£37,500

(b) **Sale to friend – in an arm's length transaction**

Original investment	**£60,000**	**£125,000**
IT relief claimed	£30,000	£50,000
CGT exemption claimed	£30,000	£37,500
IT relief withdrawn = Lower of: (i) IT relief given (ii) (50% × SP received for shares) = (50% × £65,000)	**£30,000** £32,500	£50,000 **£32,500**
CGT relief withdrawn = (% of IT relief withdrawn × gain exempt)	100% **£30,000**	(£32,500/£50,000) = 65% (65% × £37,500) = **£24,375**

chapter

10

Overseas aspects of income tax and capital gains tax

Chapter learning objectives

Upon completion of this chapter you will be able to:

- Explain and apply the concepts of residence and domicile
- Advise on the tax position of individuals coming to and leaving the UK
- Advise on the relevance of an individual's tax status to income tax and capital gains tax
- Advise on the availability of the remittance basis to UK resident individuals and non-UK domiciled individuals
- Determine the income tax treatment of overseas income
- Advise on the overseas aspects of income from employment, including travel and subsistence expenses
- Recognise the tax treatment of overseas trade travelling expenses
- Determine the UK taxation treatment of foreign gains
- Understand the relevance of the OECD model double tax treaty to given situations
- Calculate and advise on the double taxation relief available to individuals for income tax and capital gains tax
- Advise on the UK taxation of gains on the disposal of UK residential property owned by non-residents.

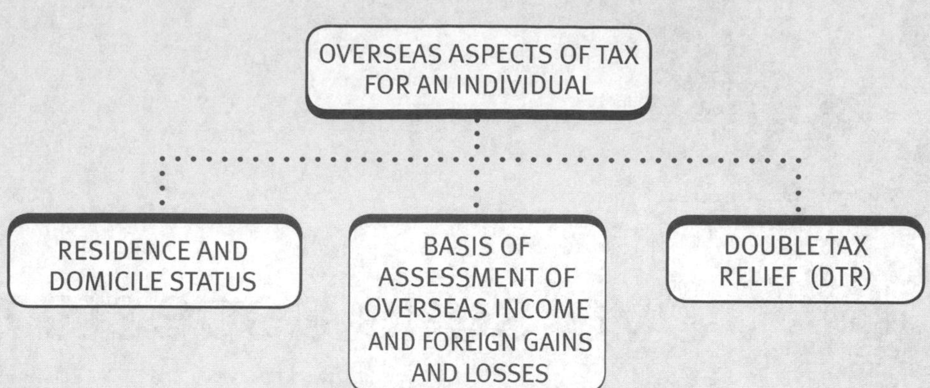

Introduction

This chapter explains the rules for determining the tax status of an individual and covers the overseas aspects of both income tax and capital gains tax. Much of the content in this chapter is new at P6.

1 The tax status of an individual

The tax status of an individual is fundamental in determining their basis of assessment to both income tax and capital gains tax.

Determining whether or not an individual has UK residence and domicile is therefore vital.

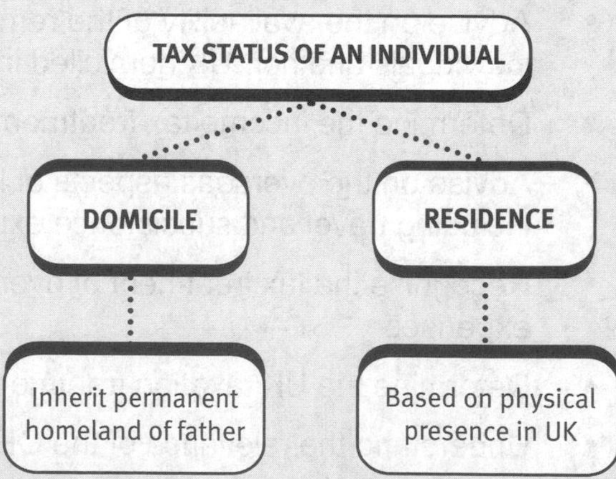

Domicile

The domicile status of an individual differs from the concepts of nationality and residence, it is based on the individual's permanent home. A person can only have one domicile at any one time.

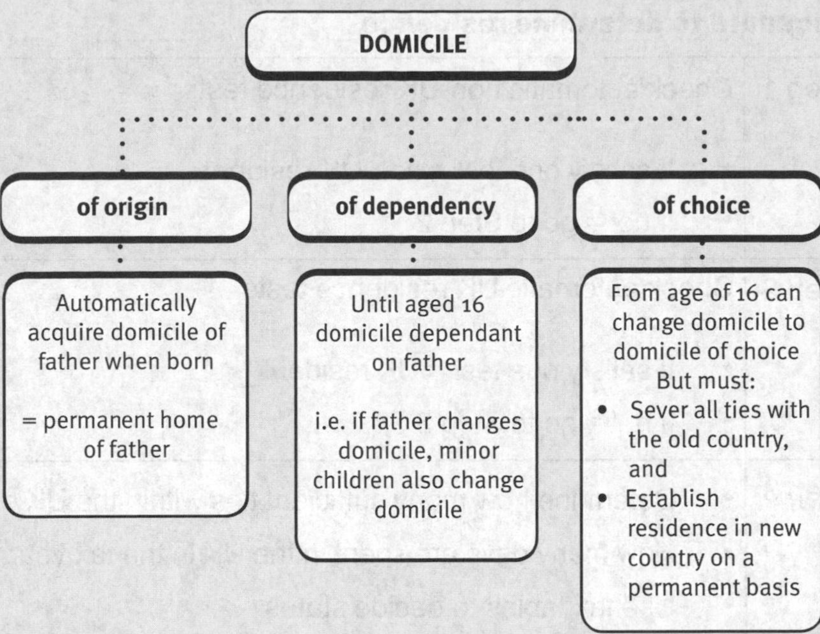

Residence

Definition of residence

An individual is UK resident in the tax year if they:

- do not meet one of the **automatic non-UK residence tests** (also referred to as automatic overseas residence tests), and
- meet one of the **automatic UK residence tests**, or
- meet one or more of the **sufficient ties tests** and have been in the UK for a sufficient length of time.

These rules are complex in practice. However, the P6 examining team have confirmed that the following simplified rules are to be applied in the P6 examination.

Note that under these rules an individual is either UK resident or non-UK resident for the whole of a tax year.

Procedure to determine residence

Step 1	Check automatic non-UK residence tests • If satisfy one test = non-UK resident • If not = go to Step 2
Step 2	Check automatic UK residence tests • If satisfy one test = UK resident • If not = go to Step 3
Step 3	• Determine how many sufficient ties within the UK exist, and • How many days are spent in the UK in the tax year, then • Use tax tables to decide status

The order of the procedure is important because it is possible for an individual to satisfy both one of the automatic non-UK residence tests and one of the automatic UK residence tests.

If this is the case, the non-UK residence test takes priority and the decision is made at Step 1. There is no need to continue on to Step 2.

Automatic non-UK residency tests

An individual is automatically **not** UK resident if they are 'in the UK' **in the tax year** for **less than**:

- **16 days**, and has been UK resident for one or more of the previous three tax years, or
- **46 days**, and has not been UK resident in any of the previous three tax years, or
- **91 days**, and works full time overseas.

Note that an individual is 'in the UK' if they are in the UK at midnight.

Automatic UK residency tests

An individual is automatically UK resident if they are in the UK for at least:

- **183 days** in the **tax year**, or
- **30 days** in the **tax year**, and their only home is in the UK, or
- **365 days continuously** working full time, some of which fall in the tax year.

These are the simplified rules which will be examinable. More detailed rules are given in expandable text.

More detail on second test

The second test requires that within a period of 91 consecutive days, **they spend at least 30 days in the tax year in their UK home** and if they also have an overseas home they spend fewer than 30 days in the tax year in that overseas home.

If the individual does not satisfy any of the automatic tests, the tax status is determined by:

- how many of the five 'sufficient ties tests' are satisfied, and
- the number of days spent in the UK.

Sufficient ties tests

To determine whether or not the individual is sufficiently connected to the UK to be considered UK resident, HMRC will look at the following five ties:

	This tie with the UK exists if the individual:
(1) Family	Has close family (a spouse/civil partner or minor children) in the UK that are UK resident
(2) Accommodation	Has a house in the UK which is made use of during the tax year and is available for at least 91 consecutive days during the tax year
(3) Work	Does substantive work in the UK (i.e. at least 40 days)
(4) Days in UK	Has spent more than 90 days in the UK in either, or both, of the previous two tax years
(5) Country	Spends more time in the UK than in any other country in the tax year

These are the simplified rules which will be examinable. More detailed rules are given in expandable text.

More detail on sufficient ties tests

Family: This tie with the UK exists if the individual has a

- spouse/civil partner (or is living with a partner as if married/civil partners), or children under 18 years old who are UK resident

Accommodation: This tie with the UK exists if the individual has a

- place in the UK available to live in for 91 consecutive days or more during the tax year and stays there in that tax year for:
  - at least one night, or
  - at least 16 nights (if it is the home of a close relative).

Note that the accommodation does not need to be owned by the individual.

Note that for an individual

- leaving the UK (previously resident)
  i.e. UK resident for one or more of the previous three tax years:
  - **all five ties** are relevant to decide the tax status
- arriving in the UK (not previously resident)
  i.e. **not** U.K resident for any of the previous three tax years:
  - only the **first four ties** are relevant (i.e. ignore the country tie).

Individuals leaving the UK and arriving in the UK

In summary, to determine the tax status of the individual, consideration is given to:

- the automatic 'non-UK residency' and 'UK residency tests', and then if none of the automatic tests are met
- how many of the 'sufficient ties tests' are satisfied, together with
- the number of days spent in the UK

as shown in the table on the following page.

Days in the UK	Previously resident	Not previously resident
Less than 16	Automatically **not** resident	Automatically **not** resident
16 to 45	Resident if 4 UK ties (or more)	Automatically **not** resident
46 to 90	Resident if 3 UK ties (or more)	Resident if 4 UK ties
91 to 120	Resident if 2 UK ties (or more)	Resident if 3 UK ties (or more)
121 to 182	Resident if 1 UK ties (or more)	Resident if 2 UK ties (or more)
183 or more	Automatically resident	Automatically resident

Note that this table will be given in the tax rates and allowances provided in the examination.

These rules mean it is more difficult for a person leaving the UK to lose UK residency status than it is for a person arriving in the UK to remain non-UK resident.

Test your understanding 1

Explain whether or not the following individuals are resident in the UK.

Ignore the impact of the leap year in counting days in the UK.

(i) Jean-Paul was born in France. He has lived in his home town in France until the tax year 2016/17 when he came to the UK to visit on 11 May 2016 until 17 December 2016.

(ii) Carmen who is retired, was born in Spain. She has lived in her home town in Spain until the tax year 2016/17 when she came to the UK to visit for a month.

(iii) Khalil, a bachelor, has always been UK resident until 5 April 2016 when he gave up work and on 1 May 2016 he left the UK for a year visiting his friends abroad, returning on 1 May 2017.

He did not spend more than a month in any other country whilst he was away, except for a 3 month stay (November to January inclusive) in his villa in Florida.

Whilst he was away he rented out his UK home.

(iv) On 6 April 2016 Bruce purchased a flat in London. He had previously visited the UK on holiday for a fortnight in each of the last four years and was treated as not UK resident in those years.

In the tax year 2016/17 he visited the UK and stayed in his flat in London for the summer from 25 May 2016 to 30 September 2016. He worked as a waiter for four weeks of that time.

The remainder of the year he worked in his home town of Brisbane in Australia and lived in his house in the suburbs of the town.

Summary of residency rules

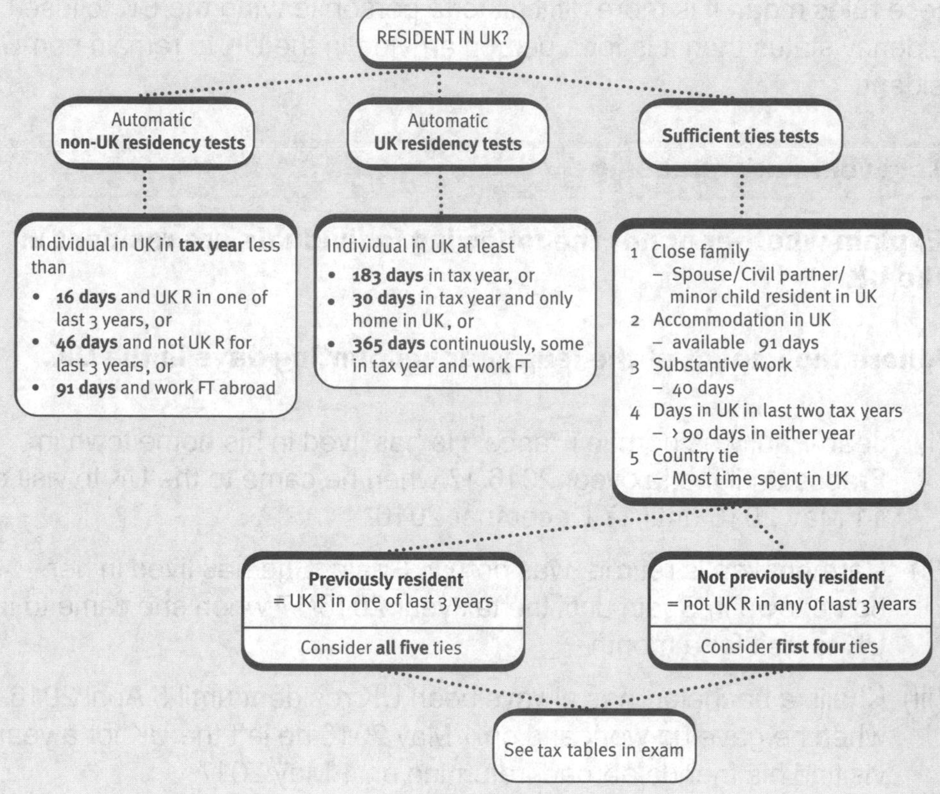

2 Splitting a tax year

Normally the **tax status of an individual is fixed for a whole tax year**.

However, there are some circumstances where **a tax year can be split** and an individual is deemed to be UK resident for only part of the year (UK part) and not UK resident for part of the year (overseas part).

Note that:

- the split year basis (SYB) applies automatically if conditions are satisfied; there is no claim to be made.
- it is not possible to disapply the SYB
- if an individual is non-UK resident for the tax year under the automatic tests or sufficient ties tests:
  - the SYB cannot apply to that year
  - the individual is non-UK resident for the whole year.

Accordingly, for the SYB to apply, **the individual must be UK resident in the tax year** under the automatic tests or the sufficient ties tests.

The way the SYB works depends on whether the individual is leaving the UK or arriving into the UK as follows:

<table>
<tr><th colspan="2">Leaving the UK</th></tr>
<tr><td colspan="2">SYB applies in the current tax year if the individual:
• is UK resident in previous year, and
• is UK resident in the current tax year, and
• is not UK resident in the following year, and
• leaves the UK part way through the current tax year for one of three reasons below.</td></tr>
<tr><td>Individual leaves the UK and:</td><td>Overseas part starts from:</td></tr>
<tr><td>(1) Begins working abroad
– Full time, and
– Does not spend more than a permitted number of days in the UK after departure (< 91 days per tax year, reduced proportionately in year of departure)</td><td>Date starts overseas work</td></tr>
</table>

(2) **Accompanies or later joins their partner abroad to continue to live with them** – As their partner leaves the UK and satisfies the full time working abroad situation 2 above in the current year or previous year – Provided does not spend more than a permitted number of days in the UK after departure (< 91 days per tax year, reduced proportionately in year of departure) – The partner is a spouse, civil partner or person with whom they have lived as if married/civil partners at some point during the current or previous tax year – Have no home in the UK or if they do, spend the greater part of the time in the overseas home	Later of date • partner starts overseas work • joins partner
(3) **Ceases to have any UK home** – After ceasing to have a UK home, spends minimal time in the UK (< 16 days), and – Establishes ties with the overseas country (e.g. buys a home abroad, becomes resident in overseas country, spends more than six months in overseas country)	Date cease to have a UK home

Note: Where the SYB can apply under more than one of the above situations, priority is given in the order above (i.e. Situation 1, 2 and then 3).

Test your understanding 2

Helen has been living in the UK since she was born and is UK resident for tax purposes. She has worked in the publishing industry for four years but leaves her job to take up a two year contract as a lecturer in Dubai.

She started work in Dubai on 1 November 2016, one week after she moved there, and has moved into a company provided flat for the duration of her contract.

She returns to visit her family in the UK over the New Year for two weeks, and does not work while she is there.

Helen remains working in Dubai throughout the tax year 2017/18, and only returns for two weeks in the summer.

Explain whether the split year basis will apply in the tax year 2016/17 and if so, define the UK part and overseas part of the tax year.

<table>
<tr><th colspan="2">Arriving in the UK</th></tr>
<tr><td colspan="2">SYB applies in the current tax year if the individual:
• is not UK resident in the previous year, and
• is UK resident in the current tax year
• arrives in the UK part way through the current tax year for one of four reasons below.</td></tr>
<tr><td>Individual arrives the UK and:</td><td>UK part starts from:</td></tr>
<tr><td>(1) Acquires a UK home
– Did not have sufficient ties in the UK to be UK resident prior to acquiring a UK home</td><td>Date acquires UK home</td></tr>
<tr><td>(2) Begins working in the UK
– Full time
– For ≥ 365 continuous days, and
– Did not have sufficient ties in the UK to be UK resident prior to entry</td><td>Date start work in UK</td></tr>
<tr><td>(3) Ceases work abroad and returns to the UK
– Following a period when the individual worked full time overseas, and
– Is resident in the UK in the following tax year</td><td>Date individual stops working overseas</td></tr>
<tr><td>(4) Accompanies or later joins their partner in UK to continue to live with them
– As their partner returns to the UK and satisfies the situation 3 above in the current year or previous year
– the partner is a spouse, civil partner or person with whom they have lived as if married/civil partners at some point during the current or previous tax year
– Is resident in the UK in the following tax year</td><td>Later of date
• partner stops overseas work
• joins partner in UK</td></tr>
</table>

Note: Where the SYB can apply under more than one of the above situations, priority is given to the situation which results in the smallest 'overseas part'.

Test your understanding 3

Bjorn has been working for his employer in Sweden for many years but on 1 July 2016 he came to the UK in search of alternative employment. He had no UK ties and has not been resident in the UK in the past.

In the UK he temporarily stayed with a friend until he secured a full time three year contract of employment and a house to rent in Nottingham. He signed a three year lease agreement, moved into the house on 1 August 2016 and started work on 22 August 2016.

Explain whether the split year basis will apply in the tax year 2016/17 and if so, define the UK part and overseas part of the tax year.

Summary of split year basis

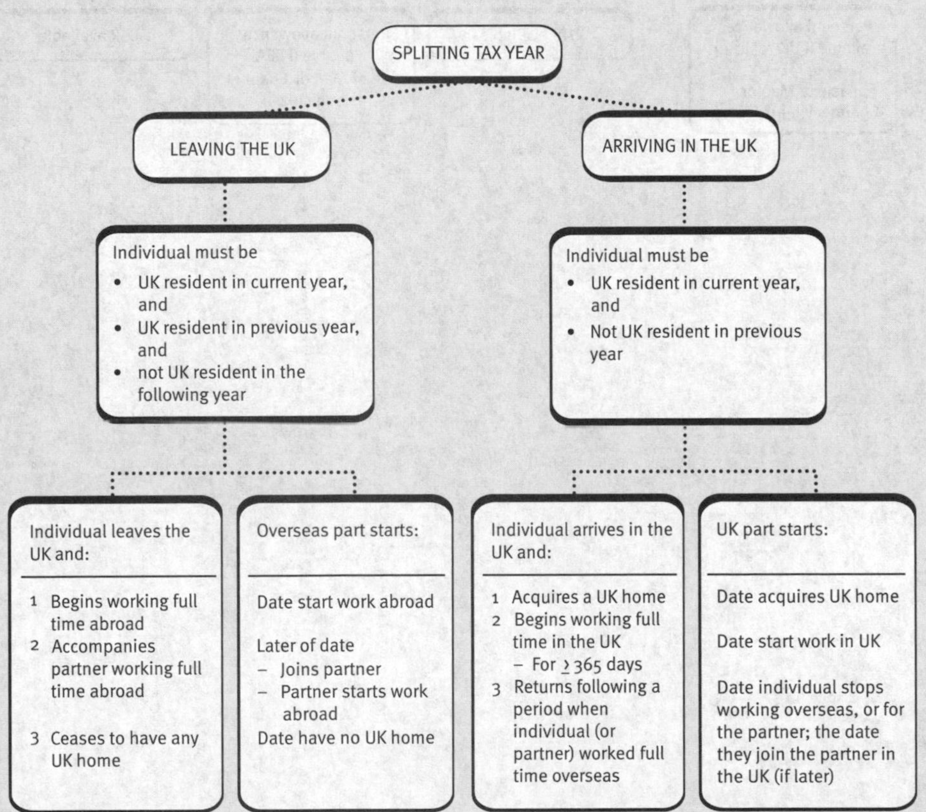

3 Overseas income – basis of assessment for income tax

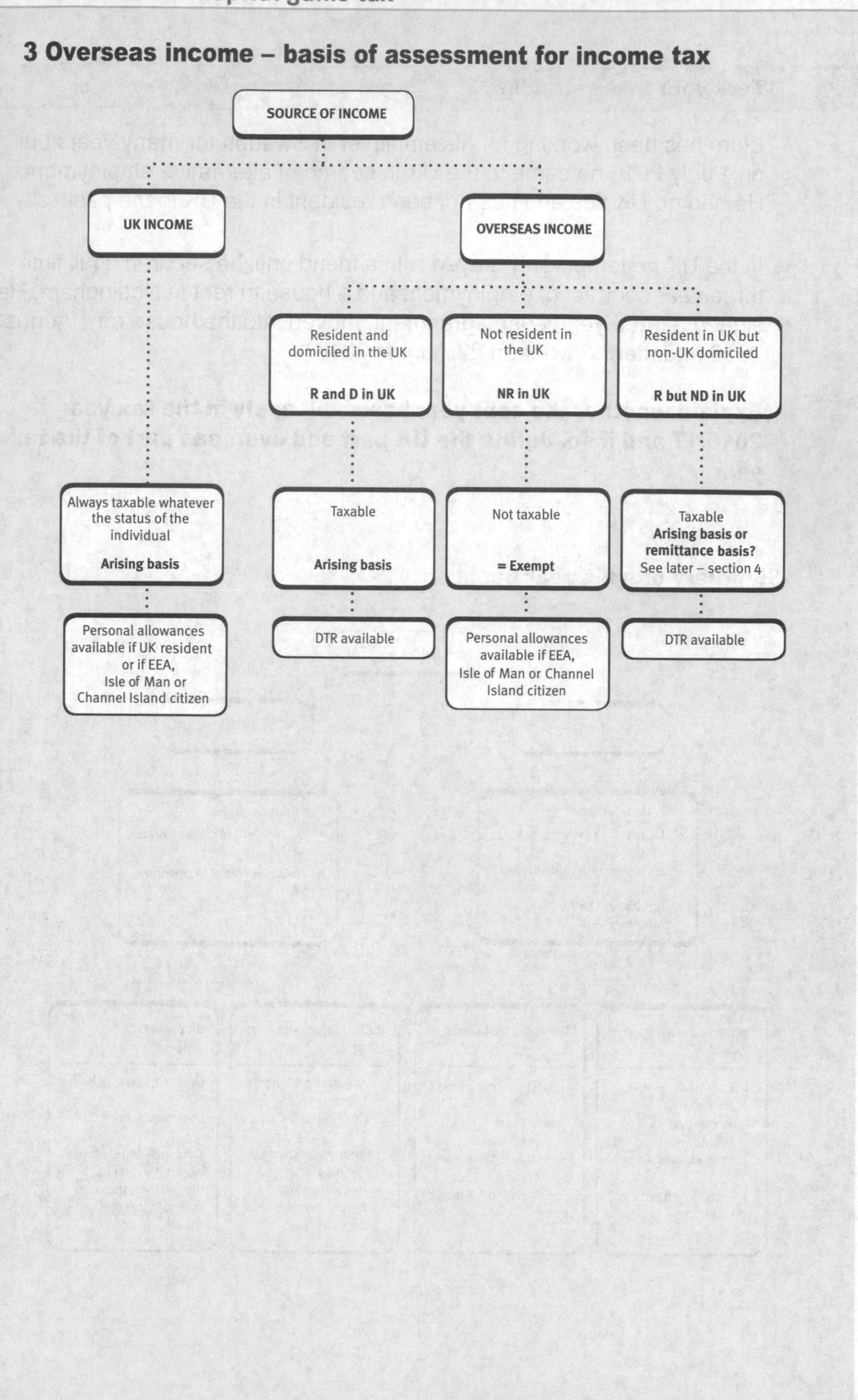

Types of overseas income

The following sources of overseas income may be included in an individual's UK income tax computation:

Source of overseas income	Basis of assessment
Dividends, rental income and interest	• Income grossed up for overseas tax suffered • UK residents owning shares in an overseas company will treat the grossed up overseas dividends like UK dividends • If overseas dividends or savings income are assessed on a remittance basis (see later), they are taxed at non-savings rates (and the savings and dividend nil rate bands do not apply) • DTR may be available
Trading income from business wholly abroad	• Calculate trading income as in the UK • Special rules apply for travelling expenses (see below) • Income grossed up for overseas tax suffered • DTR may be available
Pensions	• If assessed on an arising basis = 90% of pension is taxable • If assessed on a remittance basis = 100% of pension remitted • Income grossed up for overseas tax suffered • DTR may be available
Employment income	• Assessment rules are basically the same as for other overseas income • Some exceptions to the rule (see later)

Overseas travelling expenses relating to a trade

The following travelling and subsistence expenses will be allowable deductions when computing the adjusted trading profits:

- travelling to and from any place in the UK to the place where the trade is carried on overseas
- board and lodging at that overseas place
- the costs for the spouse/civil partner and children (under age 18) visiting the overseas place of work
  - up to two return trips in any year of assessment
  - once the individual has been absent from the UK for 60 or more continuous days.

The relief is only available to individuals who:

- carry on a trade, profession or vocation wholly overseas, and do not qualify for the remittance basis of assessment.

Overseas employment income

The basis of assessment for employment income basically follows the normal overseas income rules. However, technically the basis of assessment depends not only on the tax status of the individual, but also where the duties of the employment are performed.

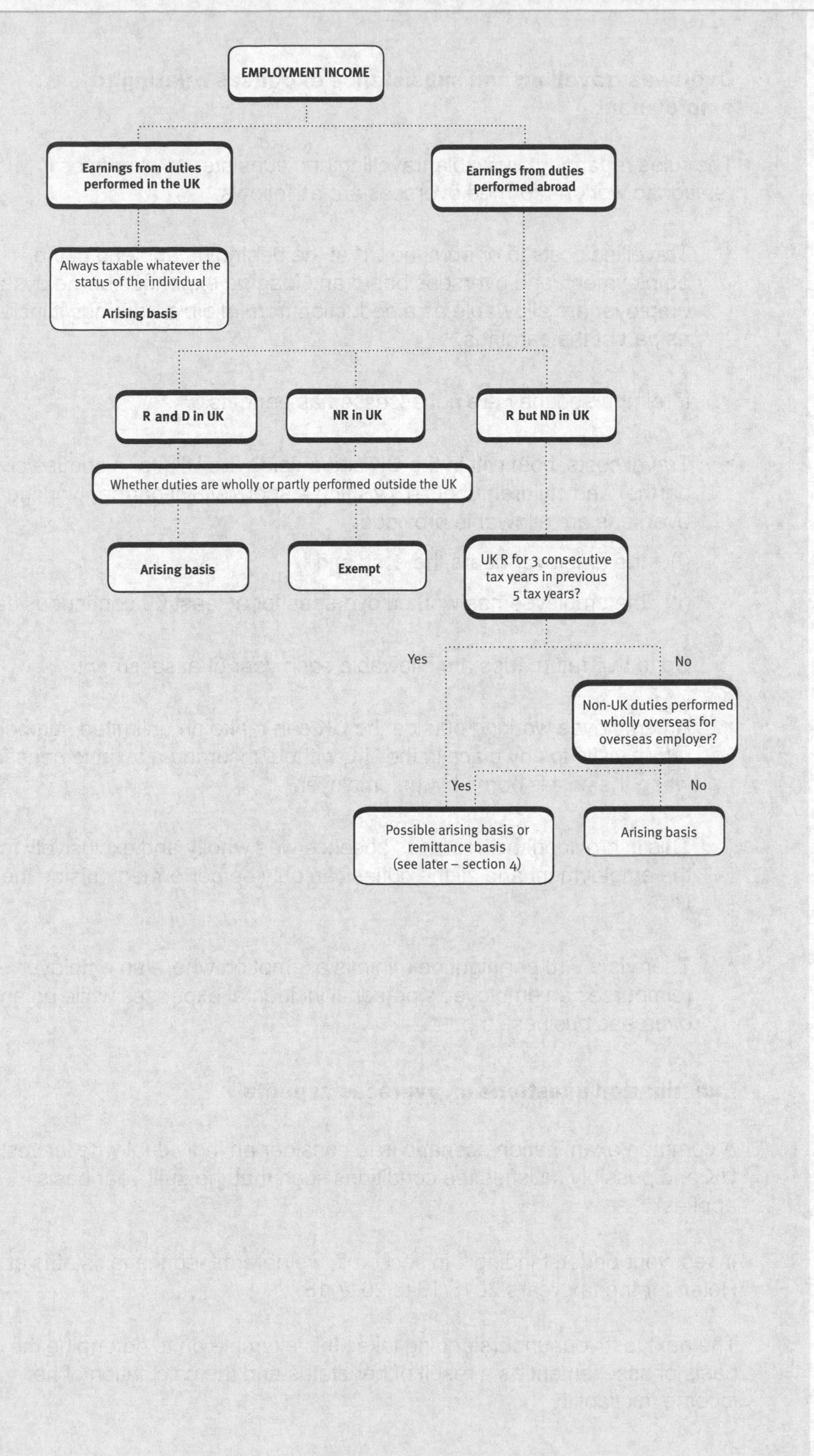
EMPLOYMENT INCOME
Earnings from duties performed in the UK
Earnings from duties performed abroad
Always taxable whatever the status of the individual
Arising basis
R and D in UK
NR in UK
R but ND in UK
Whether duties are wholly or partly performed outside the UK
Arising basis
Exempt
UK R for 3 consecutive tax years in previous 5 tax years?
Yes
No
Non-UK duties performed wholly overseas for overseas employer?
Yes
No
Possible arising basis or remittance basis (see later – section 4)
Arising basis

Overseas travelling and subsistence expenses relating to employment

The rules regarding allowable travelling and subsistence expenses in relation to work performed overseas are as follows:

- Travelling costs to or from the UK at the beginning and end of the employment, and overseas board and lodging expenses borne by the employer are allowable as a deduction from eligible earnings if included as part of the earnings.

  If reimbursed they are not assessed as benefits.

- Travel costs, both within the UK and outside the UK, for a spouse/civil partner and children under 18 visiting a spouse/civil partner working overseas are allowable provided:

  (i) the employer bears the cost; and

  (ii) the employee has worked overseas for at least 60 continuous days.

  Up to two return trips are allowable each year of assessment.

- An employee working outside the UK can make an unlimited number of return visits to any place in the UK, without incurring a taxable benefit when the cost is borne by the employer.

  This is provided the overseas absence was wholly and exclusively for the employment and all the duties can only be performed outside the UK.

- There is a £10 per night de minimis exemption where an employer reimburses an employee's personal incidental expenses while on an overseas business trip.

Examination questions on overseas aspects

A common examination scenario is to consider an individual who leaves the UK and possibly satisfies the conditions such that the split year basis applies.

In test your understanding 2 in section 2, we determined the tax status of Helen for the tax years 2015/16 to 2017/18.

The next test your understanding takes this example on to determine the basis of assessment as a result of her status and the calculation of her income tax liability.

Test your understanding 4

Assume that Helen (in test your understanding 2) actually finishes her contract in Dubai on 30 November 2018 and immediately returns to the UK and moves back into her home. She starts full time work for a UK publishing company on 1 December 2018.

Helen receives a salary of £48,000 each year, paid on a monthly basis, while she is in the UK and in Dubai. She also has a villa in Italy which generates rental income of £12,000 p.a. and during her time in Dubai Helen lets her home in the UK for £15,000 p.a.

(a) **Explain whether the split year basis will apply in the tax year 2018/19 and if so, define the UK part and overseas part of the tax year.**

(b) **Compute Helen's taxable income for all tax years she is in Dubai.**

(c) **Compute Helen's taxable income for all tax years she is in Dubai assuming the split year basis does not apply and she is treated as UK resident in the tax years 2016/17 and 2018/19, but not UK resident in 2017/18.**

4 The remittance basis of assessment for overseas income

In section 3 we see that if an individual is **resident** in the UK but is **not UK domiciled** they are assessed to tax on **either an arising or remittance basis**.

In some circumstances the individual will have no choice, however, in other circumstances they may be able to choose the basis on which they will be assessed to income tax and capital gains tax.

Consequences of being resident and non-UK domiciled

The rules depend on the level of unremitted income and gains in the tax year and the consequences are summarised as follows:

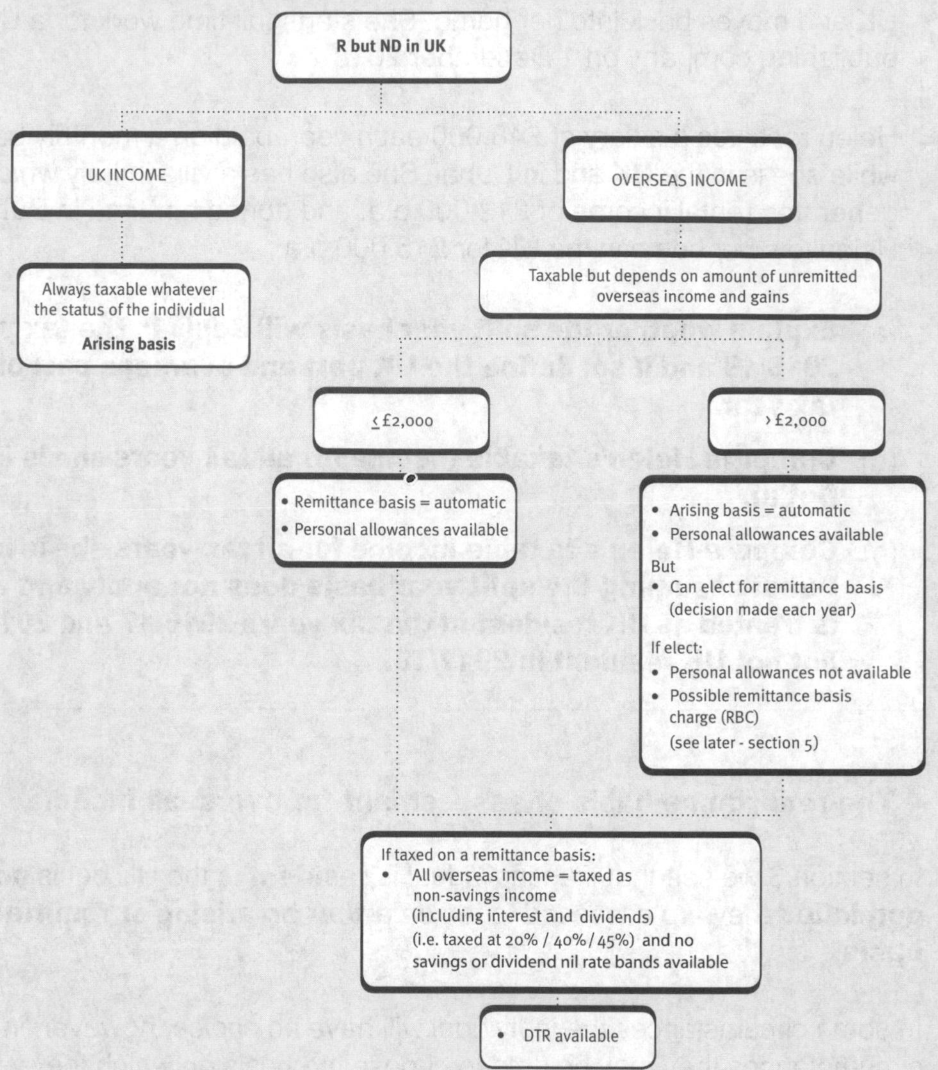

Test your understanding 5

Ewa Scott, a Polish national, has been resident in the UK for the last two years. She has her own self-employed hairdressing business and earns £25,000 in the UK. She also has £3,000 (gross) property income from Polish property that she does not remit to the UK.

Calculate Ewa's income tax liability for the tax year 2016/17 assuming that the election for the remittance basis

(a) **is not made**

(b) **is made.**

Definition of remittance

The term remittance includes

(1) Bringing overseas income directly into the UK with the exception of amounts remitted to the UK to:

- acquire shares in or make a loan to an unquoted trading company or member of a trading group
- pay the remittance basis charge (see below).

(2) Using overseas income to settle debts in the UK.

(3) Using overseas income to purchase goods and services which are subsequently brought into the UK with the exception of:

- personal items (e.g. clothes, shoes, jewellery, watches)
- items brought into the UK for repair
- items costing ≤ £1,000
- temporary importation rule (i.e. in UK for < 275 days) (e.g. works of art brought into the UK to exhibit).

5 The remittance basis charge (RBC)

The RBC was introduced to prevent long-term residents deliberately using the remittance basis rules to avoid paying UK income tax and capital gains tax by not remitting income and gains each year.

The RBC is an additional tax charge that is added to the individual's income tax liability and is paid under self-assessment.

Additional charge:	UK resident for:
£30,000 p.a.	7 out of last 9 tax years
£60,000 p.a.	12 out of last 14 tax years
£90,000 p.a.	17 out of last 20 tax years

Note that for this purpose a 'split year' (see section 2) counts as a tax year of UK residence.

However, note that the RBC aims to penalise **long-term UK residents** who are **not UK domiciled.**

It is therefore only levied if the individual:

- is aged ≥ 18 years old in the tax year
- is not UK domiciled

- is UK resident in the current year, and
- has been UK resident for at least 7 out of the last 9 tax years
- has unremitted income and gains > £2,000, and
- elects for the remittance basis to apply.

Test your understanding 6

The following details relate to four different individuals who are all non domiciled in the UK and are all taxed using the remittance basis.

	Ivor	Sasha	Juan	Pierre
Became resident in UK	2011/12	2000/01	2007/08	1995/96
Overseas income and gains not remitted to UK	£180,000	£220,000	£300,000	£1,900
Resident in UK	5 years	16 years	9 years	21 years

What RBC does each have to pay (if any) for the tax year 2016/17?

Example 1 – The remittance basis charge

Mr and Mrs Rich are domiciled in the USA but have been resident in the UK for the last 10 years. Their income for the tax year 2016/17 is as follows:

	Mr Rich	Mrs Rich
	£	£
Overseas income	300,000	40,000
Remitted to the UK	55,000	18,000

Decide whether or not Mr and Mrs Rich should elect for the remittance basis to apply. Assume they have no UK income.

Solution

Mr Rich will be better off if he claims the remittance basis and pays tax on £55,000 as well as paying the £30,000 charge:

	Arising basis	Remittance basis
	£	£
Income	300,000	55,000
Less: PA (Notes 1 and 2)	0	0
Taxable income	300,000	55,000

Income tax

£	£		£	£
32,000	32,000	at 20%	6,400	6,400
118,000	23,000	at 40%	47,200	9,200
150,000	–	at 45%	67,500	–
300,000	55,000			
Add: RBC				30,000
Total liability			121,100	45,600

Mrs Rich will be better off if she pays tax on the arising basis:

	Arising basis	Remittance basis
	£	£
Income	40,000	18,000
Less: PA	(11,000)	0
Taxable income	29,000	18,000
Income tax		
£29,000/£18,000 at 20%	5,800	3,600
Add: RBC		30,000
Total liability	5,800	33,600

Notes:

(1) Under the arising basis, Mr Rich's PA is reduced to £Nil as his adjusted net income is > £122,000.

(2) Under the remittance basis, the PA is not available.

Test your understanding 7

Gita Hoffheim, who is domiciled in Germany, has been resident in the UK since 2002.

In the tax year 2016/17 she earned a salary of £90,000 for which all duties were carried out in the UK. She also has significant overseas investments which generated gross interest of £63,000 and gross rental income of £95,000.

Gita remits £10,000 of overseas interest into the UK each year.

Calculate Gita's income tax liability for the tax year 2016/17 assuming:

(a) **she does not claim the remittance basis**

(b) **she does claim the remittance basis.**

Nominating income and gains

The RBC represents tax paid in advance on income/gains arising abroad but not yet remitted into the UK. The individual can choose which overseas income or gains the charge relates to.

When these nominated amounts are remitted, they are not taxed again. However, un-nominated income/gains are deemed to be remitted first.

6 Double taxation relief – income tax

As seen in section 3, an individual who is:

- R and D in the UK
  = taxed in the UK on their worldwide income
- R in the UK, but non-UK domiciled
  = taxed in the UK on their overseas income on either an arising or remittance basis

However, in addition, the overseas income may also be taxed to income tax overseas. To avoid a double charge to tax, double taxation relief (DTR) is available.

DTR is given in one of three ways:

- Under a DTR treaty agreement
- As a tax credit relief (known as 'unilateral relief')
- As an expense relief (only applicable where the individual has losses and unilateral relief is not available).

However, in computational **examination questions**, **unilateral relief** is to be applied. This is because expense relief is not examinable, and detailed knowledge of specific DTR agreements will not be examined.

You should have an awareness of standard treaty clauses and the importance of bilateral DTR agreements in practice, but you will not be expected to apply treaty provisions in the exam.

Further details of the principles behind DTR treaty agreements are given in expandable text. In addition, as DTR treaties are more relevant in the examination in a corporate scenario, more detail concerning standard treaty clauses is given in Chapter 28.

DTR treaties

- The two countries usually agree reciprocal arrangements to exempt certain types of income from tax in the overseas country so that there is no double taxation, and
- Allow 'unilateral relief' as a tax credit from the UK income tax liability for any overseas income that is still taxed twice.

Relief under the terms of a treaty is the usual method of relief in practice. The UK has over a hundred DTR treaties with different countries.

Unilateral relief

Where there is no DTR treaty agreement, DTR is normally allowed as a tax credit deduction against the UK income tax liability.

DOUBLE TAXATION RELIEF

Deduct from the individual's income tax liability
Lower of:
- Overseas tax withholding tax suffered
- UK income tax on that source of overseas income

UK income tax attributable to a source of overseas income = the reduction in the total income tax liability that would arise if that source of overseas income is excluded from taxable income

To calculate UK income tax on overseas income:
- Always treat overseas income as the 'top slice' of income type
- Calculate total income tax **including** that source of overseas income
- Calculate total income tax **without** that source of overseas income
- Difference = UK income tax on that source income

If more than one source of overseas income:
- Need separate DTR calculation for each source of overseas income
- Take out the source with the **highest rate of overseas tax** first

Example 2 – Double tax relief

Dean is resident and domiciled in the UK. In the tax year 2016/17 his only taxable income is an overseas dividend of £47,500 and UK property income of £20,000. The dividend is received after deduction of 5% foreign withholding tax.

Calculate Dean's UK income tax liability in the tax year 2016/17.

Solution

Income tax computation – 2016/17	£
Property income	20,000
Overseas dividend	
(£47,500 × 100/95)	50,000
Total income	70,000
Less: PA	(11,000)
Taxable income	59,000

Analysis of income

Dividends	**Non-savings income**
£50,000	(£59,000 – £50,000) = £9,000

Income tax:

£		£
9,000	× 20% (non-savings income)	1,800
5,000	× 0% (DNRB)	0
18,000	× 7.5% (dividend income)	1,350
32,000		
27,000	× 32.5% (dividend income)	8,775
59,000		11,925
Less: DTR		
Lower of		
(i)	Overseas tax = (£50,000 × 5%) = £2,500	(2,500)
(ii)	UK tax = (£1,350 + £8,775) = £10,125	
Income tax liability		9,425

Note: Dividends falling into the higher rate are taxed at 32.5% (not 40%) as Dean is assessed on an arising basis.

Example 3 – Double tax relief

Jeffrey has the following income:

	£	Overseas tax suffered
Employment income – UK	38,990	
Overseas rental income (1) (gross)	1,500	26%
Overseas rental income (2) (gross)	3,000	23%
	———	
Total income	43,490	
Less: PA	(11,000)	
	———	
Taxable income	32,490	
	———	

Analysis of income:

Non-savings income = £32,490

Income tax liability (before DTR) is:

£		£
32,000	× 20% (non-savings income)	6,400
490	× 40% (non-savings income)	196
———		
32,490		
———		———
Income tax liability (before DTR)		6,596
		———

Advise how much DTR is available on each source of overseas income.

Solution

The overseas rental income is charged in the UK partly at 40% and partly at 20%. To obtain the maximum DTR, the interest suffering the highest overseas rate of tax is considered first.

Overseas source (1) has the highest overseas tax rate, so the DTR on that source of income will be:

			£	£
(i) Overseas tax paid (£1,500 × 26%)				390
(ii) UK tax on the overseas income				
	490 (top slice)	@ 40%	196	
	1,010	@ 20%	202	
	1,500			398

DTR = lower amount = £390 (i.e. full credit for overseas tax paid)

The DTR on overseas source (2) will then be:

	£
(i) Overseas tax paid (£3,000 × 23%)	690
(ii) UK tax on overseas income (£3,000 × 20%)	600

DTR = lower amount = £600

Note: The unrelieved overseas tax of £90 on overseas source (2) is lost.

Test your understanding 8

Benny is UK domiciled and resident in the UK and has the following income assessable in the tax year 2016/17.

	£	
Salary from UK employment (PAYE £5,328)	37,640	(gross)
UK bank interest	3,085	
Utopian bank interest (50% Utopian tax paid)	1,100	(gross)
Ruritanian rent (15% Ruritanian tax paid)	600	(gross)

Calculate the income tax payable or repayable considering all available reliefs.

7 Overseas aspects of capital gains tax

As for income tax, the tax status of an individual is important in determining the gains on which they are assessed. The consequences of an individual's status are:

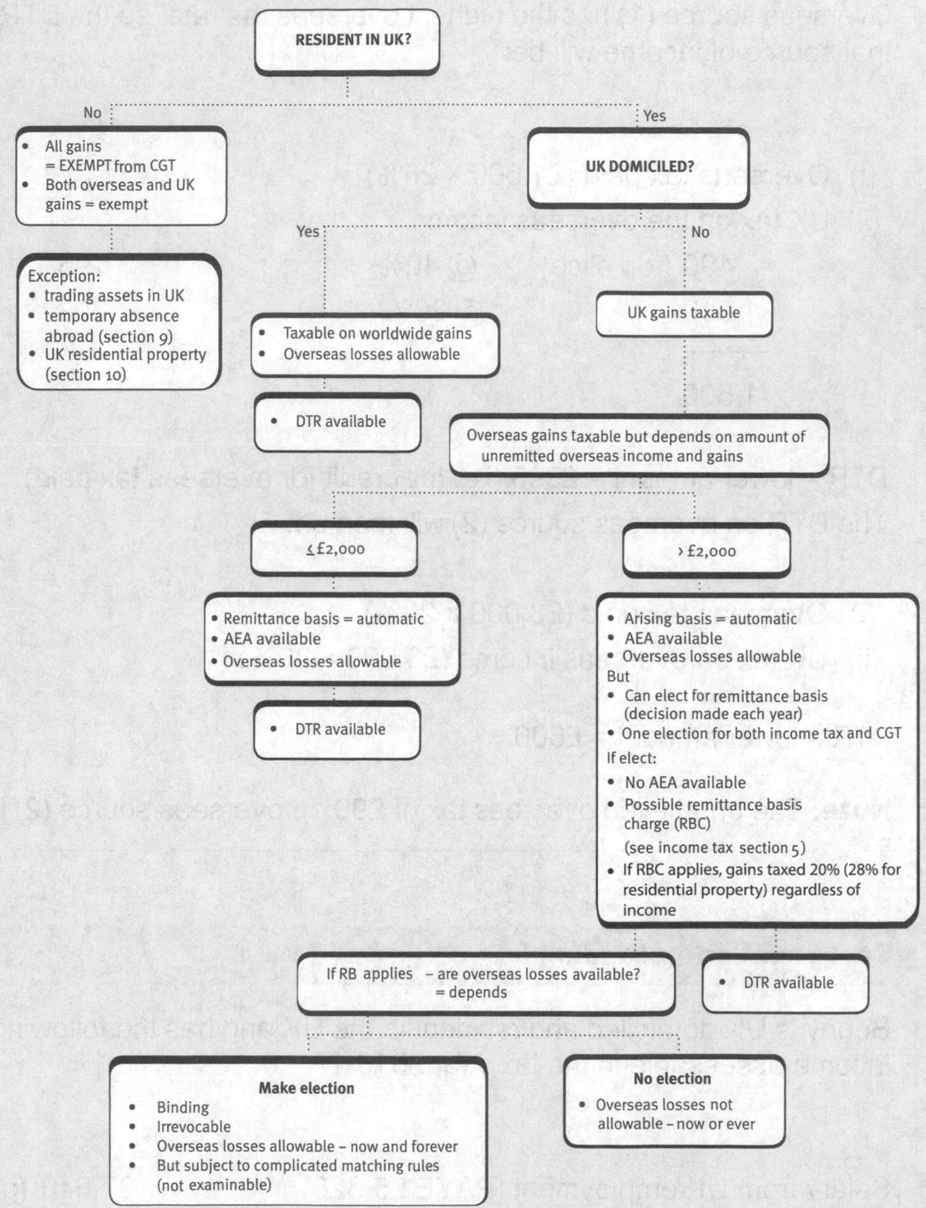

Notes:

- The individual will need to consider the remittance basis election each year separately as a large overseas gain in a year may make the remittance basis claim worthwhile in that year but not in others – but remember the election applies to both income and gains in that year.

- The capital loss election is a one-off election that had to be made the first time the individual elected for the remittance basis to apply whether or not the taxpayer had any capital losses at that time.

  As the capital loss election is binding, and the remittance basis election will probably have been claimed in the past by the taxpayer, in the examination question you need to find out whether or not the capital election was made at that time.

- Where proceeds from the sale of an overseas capital asset are remitted to the UK, that amount of the capital gain is deemed to be remitted first (not a proportion of the gain).

Exceptions to the exemption from CGT for non-UK residents

All gains (both UK and overseas gains) of an individual that is NR in the UK are exempt, except in three key circumstances:

- in the rare situation where the individual operates a trade, profession or vocation through a permanent establishment in the UK and disposes of an asset from the business
- where the temporary absence abroad conditions are satisfied (see section 9)
- where the individual disposes of UK residential property (see section 10).

Example 4 – Overseas aspects of capital gains tax

Jason sold a commercial investment property in Spain for £500,000 on 16 February 2017. Half of the proceeds were paid into his Spanish bank account and the other half into his UK bank account.

The gain on the disposal is £278,850. Jason purchased the property in August 1999.

Explain the CGT position assuming Jason is:

(a) **UK resident and domiciled in the UK**

(b) **UK resident for the previous 5 tax years but not UK domiciled and elected for the remittance basis**

(c) **UK resident for the previous 10 years but not UK domiciled and elected for the remittance basis**

(d) **not UK resident but UK domiciled.**

Solution

(a) **UK resident and domiciled in the UK**

Jason is liable to CGT on gains arising on his worldwide assets, regardless of whether or not the proceeds are remitted to the UK.

Chargeable gain	£278,850

The AEA is fully available.

(b) **UK resident for 5 tax years but not UK domiciled**

Jason is liable to CGT on gains arising on his overseas assets only to the extent that the proceeds are remitted to the UK as he has elected for the remittance basis.

As £250,000 (£500,000 ÷ 2) of the proceeds are remitted to the UK, this is deemed to be £250,000 worth of chargeable gain and will be assessed on Jason in the tax year 2016/17.

Chargeable gain	£250,000

No AEA is available.

Part of this gain may be taxed at 10% if Jason has any basic rate band remaining after taxing his income.

The remaining gain of £28,850 (£278,850 – £250,000) will be taxed when more of the proceeds are remitted.

(c) **UK resident for 10 tax years but not UK domiciled**

Jason is liable to CGT on gains arising on his overseas assets only to the extent they are remitted to the UK as he has elected for the remittance basis.

However, as he has been resident for 7 out of the last 9 tax years immediately preceding the current tax year, a £30,000 tax charge is payable.

This charge will be added to his CGT or income tax liability depending on whether Jason nominates income or gains to be covered by the charge.

In addition as half of the proceeds are remitted to the UK, £250,000 of the gain will be taxed in the tax year 2016/17.

No AEA is available.

All of this gain will be taxed at 20% regardless of the level of Jason's taxable income.

(d) **Not UK resident but UK domiciled**

Jason is exempt from CGT on both overseas and UK gains.

There are exceptions to this rule:

- Jason would be assessed to CGT if he disposes of an asset which is used in carrying on a trade, profession or vocation, through a permanent establishment in the UK.
- Jason is only temporarily absent abroad (section 9)
- the property is a UK residential property (not an overseas property or commerical property).

Test your understanding 9

Cecilia is domiciled in Austria, but has been resident in the UK for the last 4 years. For 2013/14 and 2014/15 she elected for the remittance basis to apply to her income and gains, but made no election in respect of capital losses as she did not have any in either of those tax years. Cecilia is a higher rate taxpayer.

In the tax year 2016/17, she sells the following assets:

(1) An asset in Austria for £220,000 and realised a capital gain of £55,000. She remitted £50,000 of the proceeds into the UK.

(2) An asset in Hungary for £80,000 and realised a capital loss of £35,000.

(3) A UK asset for £49,500 and realised a capital gain of £25,350.

(4) UK quoted shares for £30,100 and realised a capital loss of £18,000.

None of the assets disposed of are residential property.

Calculate Cecilia's CGT liability, assuming:

(a) **She does not claim the remittance basis for the tax year 2016/17**

(b) **She claims the remittance basis for the tax year 2016/17.**

8 Double taxation relief – capital gains tax

As seen in section 7, an individual who is:

- R in the UK and is D in the UK
  = taxed in the UK on their worldwide gains
- R in the UK, but is non-UK domiciled
  = taxed in the UK on their overseas gains on either an arising or remittance basis

However, the overseas gains may also be taxed overseas.

Double taxation relief (DTR) is available as follows:

(a) under a bilateral double taxation treaty agreement between the UK and the overseas country, or

(b) unilaterally as a tax credit relief.

Double taxation relief

Deduct from the individual's capital gains tax liability
lower of:
- Overseas capital gains tax suffered
- UK capital gains tax on the disposal of that overseas asset

When calculating the UK tax on overseas gains:

- the AEA is allocated against UK gains first
- the overseas gains are treated as the 'top slice' of taxable gains, giving the highest UK tax possible and maximising the DTR.

Example 5 – Double taxation relief

Julie is resident and domiciled in the UK. In December 2016 she sells assets which give rise to the following chargeable gains:

UK asset	£22,000
Overseas asset	£66,000

Overseas capital taxes of £14,000 are payable on the disposal of the overseas asset.

None of the assets disposed of are residential property.

Calculate Julie's CGT liability for the tax year 2016/17, assuming she is a higher rate taxpayer.

Solution

	£
UK asset	22,000
Overseas asset	66,000
Total chargeable gain	88,000
Less: AEA	(11,100)
Taxable gain	76,900
CGT liability (£76,900 × 20%)	15,380
Less: DTR (W)	13,200
CGT payable	2,180

Working: DTR

	£
Lower of	
(i) Overseas tax suffered (given)	14,000
(ii) UK tax on overseas gain:	
Overseas gain (£66,000 × 20%)	13,200
(AEA set against UK gain)	

Test your understanding 10

Diane is UK resident and domiciled in the UK. She disposed of the following assets in the tax year 2016/17:

(a) A UK asset was sold on 8 July 2016 giving rise to a gain of £22,000.

(b) An overseas investment asset was sold on 14 September 2016 giving rise to a gain of £12,760. Overseas CGT payable was £3,850.

(c) A UK asset was sold on 29 October 2016 giving rise to a gain of £29,000

Diane has taxable income for 2016/17 of £70,000.

None of the assets disposed of are residential property.

Calculate Diane's capital gains tax payable for the tax year 2016/17.

9 Temporary absence abroad

As for income tax, for capital gains tax, an individual normally retains their tax status for whole tax years.

However, the split year basis applies to capital gains tax in the same way as income tax (section 2).

For periods where an individual is not UK resident, they are effectively exempt from UK CGT on their worldwide gains (UK and overseas), apart from some exceptions.

However, to counter abuse of this rule, special rules apply for temporary absences abroad.

Special rules

When an individual returns to the UK after a period of 'temporary non UK residence', they will be **charged to tax on gains arising in that period of temporary non-UK residence** (i.e. the exemption from CGT does not apply) if conditions are satisfied.

Definition of 'temporary non-UK residence'

An individual will be regarded as temporarily non UK resident if:

- in **four** or more of the **seven tax years** immediately **preceding the tax year of departure** the individual was UK resident, and
- the **period of non-UK residence** is **five years or less**.

The way in which the capital gains are assessed is as follows:

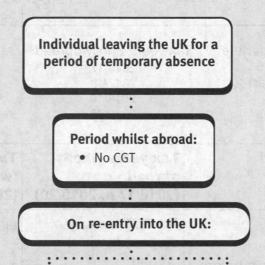

Individual leaving the UK for a period of temporary absence

Period whilst abroad:
- No CGT

On re-entry into the UK:

Return within five years

Liable on
- disposals of all assets whilst abroad, if the asset was owned before leaving the UK
- disposals after the date of return

Return after five years

Liable on
- disposals after the date of return only
- No CGT on disposals whilst abroad

Illustration

Joanna takes up a full time contract working abroad on 14 February 2016 and returns to the UK on 24 January 2021.

Assume that the split year basis applies in the tax year of departure and return.

As Joanna is abroad for less than five years, the gains arising whilst abroad are assessed to CGT.

The way in which the gains are assessed is as follows:

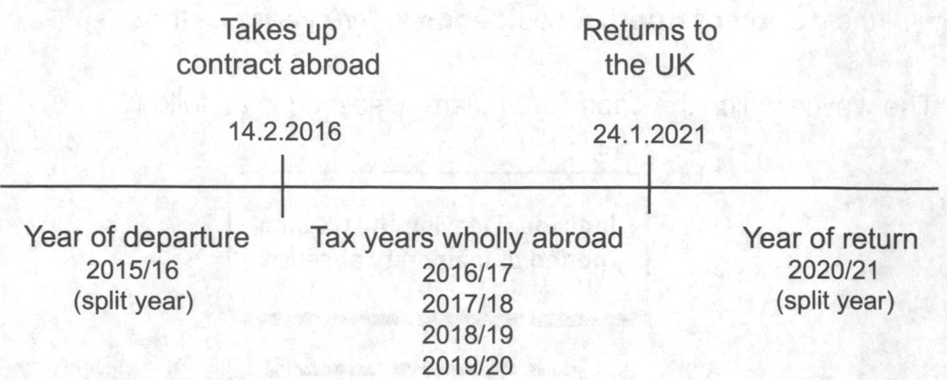

Tax year of departure (2015/16)	**Tax years wholly abroad (2016/17 to 2019/20)**	**Tax year of return (within 5 years) (2020/21)**
Liable on • disposals before the date of departure	**No CGT on any disposals** whilst abroad	Liable on • **all disposals of assets whilst abroad** if the assets were owned by the individual before leaving the UK (known as a 're-entry charge') • **any disposals made in the tax year of return**

Note that:

- Assets that the individual **acquired after leaving the UK** which she then sells whilst abroad are not liable to UK capital gains tax.
- In this example, if Joanna had stayed abroad for a further 21 days, she would be exempt from CGT on all disposals whilst abroad. This is because the period of absence from the UK would have spanned five years (14 February 2016 to 14 February 2021).

Example 6 – Temporary absence abroad

June has lived in the UK all her life and is planning to emigrate to Australia. On 31 December 2016, she will sell her UK home and plans to leave the UK on 6 January 2017.

Her home which is currently valued at £200,000 will give rise to a gain of £20,000.

She owns the following UK assets:

(1) 10,000 shares in Kestrel plc which she acquired for £6 each one year ago. The shares have a current value of £100,000 and if all of the shares were sold, a capital gain of £40,000 would arise.

(2) A painting which is worth £80,000. If it is sold it will crystallise an allowable loss of £10,000.

June wishes to sell as many assets as possible before she emigrates, but does not want to pay any capital gains tax.

Assume today's date is 10 December 2016 and that June has asked you for some advice.

(a) **Advise June of the assets she should sell before leaving the UK.**

(b) **Explain the consequences of selling the shares in Kestrel plc while she is abroad if:**

  (i) **she ceases to have a home in Australia, returns to the UK and acquires a UK home on 31 December 2020 as she is homesick**

  (ii) **she ceases to have a home in Australia, returns to the UK and acquires a UK home on 31 December 2024 as she is sick.**

Solution

(a) **Disposal of assets before leaving the UK**

Asset	Sell?	Reason
Home	Yes	An individual's principal private residence is exempt from CGT (see Note)
Painting	Yes	This is the disposal of a chargeable asset which generates an allowable capital loss of £10,000
Kestrel plc shares	Yes, but only some of the shares	June should dispose of sufficient shares to realise a gain of £21,100 which is covered by the allowable capital loss and her AEA. Therefore, June should dispose of 5,275 shares (see working below)

Note:

The sale of the UK home will trigger the split year in the tax year 2016/17 and the end of the UK part of that tax year. The period of temporary absence therefore starts on 1 January 2017.

Working: Optimum number of Kestrel plc shares to sell

	£
Sale proceeds for each share	10
Less: Cost of each share	(6)
Chargeable gain realised on disposal of each share	4

Therefore, to crystallise a chargeable gain of £21,100, June should dispose of 5,275 shares (£21,100 ÷ £4).

(b) **Consequences of selling the remaining shares whilst abroad**

	(i)	(ii)
End of UK residence	31.12.2016	31.12.2016
Start of UK residence	1.1.2021 = 4 years	1.2.2025 = 8 years
CGT on disposals of chargeable assets made while June is in Australia	As June is in Australia for less than 5 years, any gains made while in Australia will be subject to CGT in the tax year she returns to UK (2020/21).	As June is in Australia for more than 5 years, no CGT is payable on disposals made while she is in Australia.

Test your understanding 11

Yolanda, a UK national, has lived in the UK since birth. On 15 July 2016 she took up a full-time contract of employment in Columbia. She will not return to the UK during the contract period but will return to the UK at the end of the contract on 24 October 2019.

Her disposals during this period were as follows:

Asset	Date of purchase	Date of sale	Gain
			£
1	3 Sept 1999	17 July 2017	125,896
2	9 July 2011	18 Oct 2018	5,024
3	12 Aug 2016	27 Feb 2019	78,400

None of these assets were UK residential properties.

Explain which disposals will be chargeable and when any gains arising as a result of the disposals will be assessed.

10 Non-UK residents and UK residential property disposals

Non-UK residents are normally exempt from CGT on all asset disposals, however from 2015/16 non-UK resident individuals and companies disposing of UK residential property may be liable to tax (CGT or corporation tax), subject to special rules.

The ACCA have stated that they will only examine these special rules in the context of a non-UK resident individual (not a company).

Disposals by non-UK resident individuals

Prior to FA2015 only UK resident individuals were liable to CGT on UK residential property gains. Non-UK resident individuals were exempt, paid no CGT on such disposals, and PPR relief and the AEA were not a consideration.

However, from 2015/16, the disposal of UK residential property by a non-UK resident individual:

- is a chargeable disposal, and
- a liability to CGT will arise, but
- only on **gains accruing after 5 April 2015**
- to the extent that they are not covered by
  - reliefs (e.g. PPR relief, rollover relief or gift relief), or
  - the AEA.

Any **taxable gain** will be taxed according to the level of the individual's **UK taxable income** and consequential remaining basic rate band in the normal way.

HMRC must be notified of the disposal of any UK residential property by a non-UK resident individual within 30 days of the conveyance of the property, even if there is no CGT liability. If several disposals are made, each one should be reported separately.

Penalties will apply for late reporting, inaccurate returns and late payment as usual.

Methods of calculating the gain or loss

If the UK residential property is purchased after 5 April 2015, the gain (or loss) before considering reliefs is calculated in the normal way.

If the property was purchased before 5 April 2015, there are three methods of calculating the gain accruing since 5 April 2015 before the consideration of reliefs:

(1) rebasing the cost to market value at 5 April 2015 (automatic treatment without an election)

(2) electing for time apportionment of the gain pre and post 5 April 2015

(3) electing to be assessed on the whole gain or loss.

Test your understanding 12

Jim is domiciled in the UK and was UK resident until January 2014 when he emigrated to Portugal.

He purchased a cottage in the UK as an investment on 4 October 2006 for £420,000. He never lived in the property himself but has rented it out to tenants for the entire period of ownership.

On 6 June 2024 he plans to sell the UK cottage and hopes to receive sale proceeds of £780,000. The market value of the cottage on 5 April 2016 was £565,000.

(a) **Calculate the gain arising on Jim (before considering reliefs) in the tax year 2024/25 assuming:**

(i) **the gain is calculated using the automatic rebasing method**

(ii) **the election for time apportionment is made**

(iii) **the election for the whole gain is made.**

(b) **Calculate the allowable loss if the cottage is sold for £400,000 and had a market value on 5 April 2015 of £410,000, assuming:**

(i) **the loss is calculated using the automatic rebasing method**

(ii) **the election for time apportionment is made**

(iii) **the election for the whole loss is made.**

Assume that the 2016/17 rates and allowances apply throughout.

Allowable losses

Any losses arising are 'ring fenced' and can only be set against:

- gains from other UK residential property disposals in the same year, then
- carried forward against future UK residential property gains.

Brought forward losses can be restricted to preserve the AEA in the future year of set off.

If the individual changes his tax status and subsequently becomes UK resident:

- the unused losses will no longer be 'ring-fenced'
- they will become normal capital losses, and
- can be set against other chargeable gains.

Availability of CGT reliefs

There are three reliefs to consider in respect of the disposal of a UK residential property, each with special rules when applied to the disposal by a non-UK resident individual:

(1) **PPR relief**

If the property has at some time been the individual's principal private residence, PPR relief is available but is restricted and is subject to conditions (see below).

(2) **Rollover relief**

If the UK residential property is a business asset (e.g. furnished holiday lettings) and is sold, rollover relief is available but only if the replacement asset purchased is another UK residential property.

(3) **Gift relief**

Gift relief is normally only available on gifts of business assets by an individual to another individual, trustee or company that is resident in the UK at the time of the gift.

However, if the gift is

- UK residential property
- which is a business asset (e.g. furnished holiday lettings), and
- it is gifted to a non-UK resident individual, trustee or company,

gift relief is available.

PPR relief for non-UK resident individuals

PPR relief will be available as usual (see Chapter 9) for periods when the individual occupied the property as their main residence. However, as only the gain arising after 5 April 2015 is taxable, only the period of ownership from 6 April 2015 will be considered for PPR purposes.

With effect from 5 April 2015, non-UK resident individuals will only qualify for PPR on UK residential property in respect of periods of non-occupation if they (or their spouse or civil partner):

- were living in the UK for that tax year, or
- stayed in the property for a total of at least 90 nights in the tax year (the 90 day rule).

The 90 day rule is time apportioned if the property was not owned for the whole tax year.

The normal definition of periods of occupation and non-occupation and availability of letting relief is basically unchanged, except that for periods of non-occupation:

- if the 90 day rule above is not satisfied, the whole tax year is treated as a period of non-occupation for PPR purposes.

Provided the property qualified as the individual's PPR at some time during the period of ownership, PPR relief will be available for the last 18 months of ownership as for UK residents.

Test your understanding 13

Eric is domiciled in the UK and was UK resident throughout his life until 2011.

He purchased his home in the UK on 6 March 1991 for £250,000. He lived there until he retired on 5 April 2013 and went to live permanently in Australia. Since retiring he has rented the UK property.

Eric returns to the UK for a maximum of three weeks each year.

On 31 March 2021 he plans to sell the UK property and expects to receive sale proceeds of £600,000. The market value of the property on 5 April 2015 was £550,000.

Calculate the taxable gain arising on Eric in 2020/21 assuming:

(i) **the gain is calculated using the automatic rebasing method**

(ii) **the election for time apportionment is made**

(iii) **the election for the whole gain is made.**

Assume the 2016/17 rates and allowances apply using the two methods.

UK resident individuals with a property outside the UK

With effect from 5 April 2015, UK resident individuals with residential property outside the UK will qualify for PPR on that property in respect of periods of their non-residence in the other country provided they (or their spouse or civil partner):

- were living in that country for that tax year, or
- the 90 day rule is satisfied.

11 Chapter summary

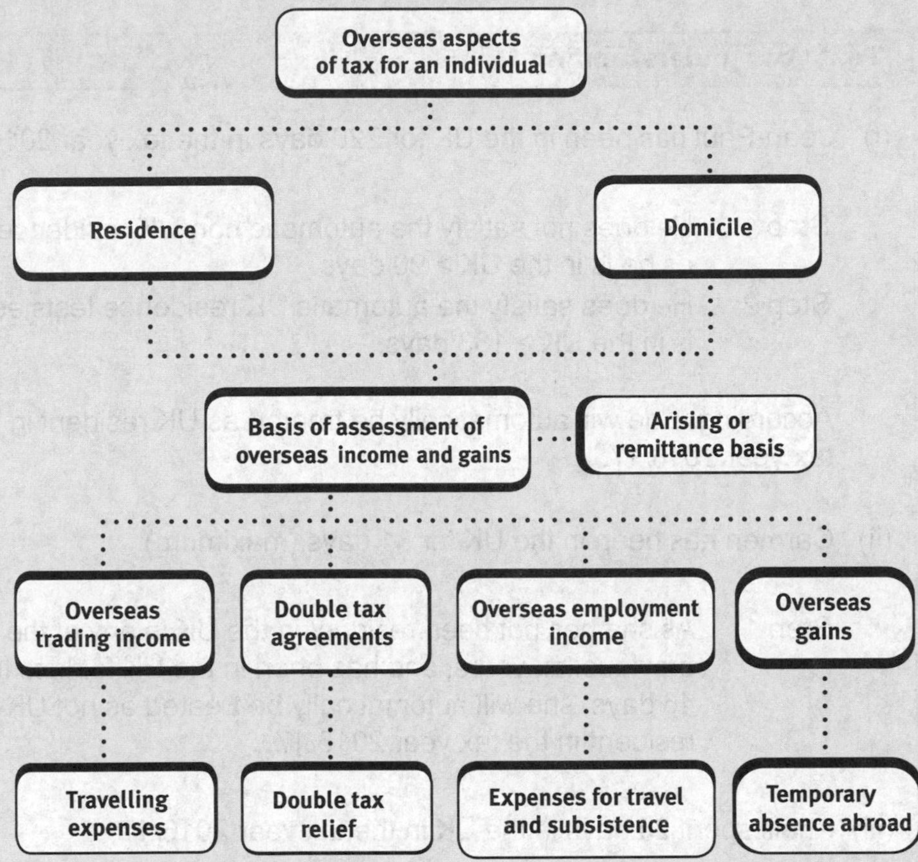

Test your understanding answers

Test your understanding 1

(i) Jean-Paul has been in the UK for 220 days in the tax year 2016/17.

Step 1: He does not satisfy the automatic non-UK residence tests as he is in the UK > 90 days.

Step 2: He does satisfy the automatic UK residence tests as he is in the UK > 183 days.

Accordingly, he will automatically be treated as UK resident in the tax year 2016/17.

(ii) Carmen has been in the UK for 31 days (maximum)

Step 1: As she has not been resident in the UK in any of the three previous tax years, and has been in the UK for less than 46 days, she will automatically be treated as not UK resident in the tax year 2016/17.

(iii) Khalil spent 25 days in the UK in the tax year 2016/17:

Step 1: He has spent too many days in the UK to be automatically not resident (i.e. > 16 days as previously resident in UK).

Step 2: He is not automatically resident as he has not been in the UK for sufficient days, has an overseas home and has not had full time work in the UK during the tax year 2016/17.

Step 3: Sufficient ties tests

Khalil has been UK resident during the three previous tax years.

He was in the UK in the tax year 2016/17 for between 16 and 45 days and must therefore meet at least four of the UK ties tests to be deemed UK resident.

Khalil meets the:

– days in UK tie (spent more than 90 days in UK in both of previous two tax years) only.

He does not meet the other ties as:

– he does not have a spouse/civil partner or minor children that are UK resident

– he does not have a house in the UK which was available for at least 91 days during the tax year
– does not work in the UK in the tax year 2016/17, and
– he spends three months (92 days) in Florida and therefore spends more time in U.S.A than he does in the UK in the tax year 2016/17.

As he only satisfies one sufficient ties test, not four, he is not UK resident in the tax year 2016/17.

(iv) Bruce spent 128 days in the UK in the tax year 2016/17.

Step 1: Bruce has spent too many days in the UK in the tax year 2016/17 to be automatically considered non-UK resident (i.e. > 90 days).

Step 2: He has not spent sufficient days in the UK (i.e. < 183 days) and has accommodation in Australia therefore he is not automatically UK resident.

Step 3: Sufficient ties tests

Bruce has not been UK resident in any of the previous three tax years.

As he has spent between 121 and 182 days in the UK in 2016/17 he must have two UK ties to be considered UK resident, and only the first four ties are considered.

Bruce meets the:

– accommodation tie (made use of a UK house) only.

He does not meet the other ties as:

– he does not have a spouse/civil partner or minor children that are UK resident
– he does not do substantive work in the UK tie (works less than 40 days)
– he has not spent more than 90 days in UK in either of previous two tax years.

As he meets only one UK tie he will be treated as not UK resident in the tax year 2016/17.

Test your understanding 2

Helen will be taxed on a split year basis for the tax year 2016/17 because:

- she was UK resident in 2015/16 and 2016/17 as she was in the UK for at least 183 days
- she is not UK resident for 2017/18
- she leaves the UK during 2016/17 to begin working abroad
- from 1 November 2016 until 5 April 2017 she:
  - works full time in Dubai
  - spends only 14 days in the UK, which is less than the permitted number of days.

For the tax year 2016/17, the year will be split as follows:

- UK part = 6 April 2016 to 31 October 2016
- Overseas part = 1 November 2016 to 5 April 2017

Test your understanding 3

Bjorn will be taxed on a split year basis for the tax year 2016/17 because:

- he is not UK resident for 2015/16
- he is resident for 2016/17 as he is in the UK for at least 183 days
- he acquired a home in the UK during the tax year and stayed there for the rest of the tax year
- he had no UK ties until acquiring his UK home on 1 August 2016.

For the tax year 2016/17, the year will be split as follows:

- Overseas part = 6 April 2016 to 31 July 2016
- UK part = 1 August 2016 to 5 April 2017

Note that Bjorn will also satisfy the conditions for split year basis as he begins 'working full time in the UK' – however under these rules his 'overseas part' will not end until 21 August 2016. However, where more than one of the situations applies, priority is given to the one that gives the shortest 'overseas part'.

Test your understanding 4

Helen

(a) **Reason for split year basis**

Helen will be taxed on a split year basis for the tax year 2018/19 because:

- she is not UK resident for 2017/18
- she is UK resident for 2018/19 (as she carries out full time work in the UK during a 365 day period, some of which falls within the tax year)
- she ceases working abroad and returns to the UK, having worked full time overseas
- she is resident in the UK in the following tax year (2019/20).

For 2018/19, the year will be split as follows:

- Overseas part = 6 April 2018 to 30 November 2018
- UK part = 1 December 2018 to 5 April 2019

(b) **Basis of assessment whilst in Dubai**

Tax year	**Status**	**Basis of assessment**
2016/17	**Split year basis applies:** R and D in UK up to 31 October 2016 (7 months) NR but D in UK for overseas part from 1 November 2016 (5 months)	Worldwide income = taxable on an arising basis All UK income = taxable on an arising basis Overseas income = exempt
2017/18	NR but D in UK for whole tax year	All UK income = taxable on an arising basis Overseas income = exempt
2018/19	**Split year basis applies:** NR but D in UK for overseas part up to 30 November 2018 (8 months) R and D in UK for UK part From 1 December 2018 (4 months)	All UK income = taxable on an arising basis Overseas income = exempt Worldwide income = taxable on an arising basis

Helen's taxable income

	2016/17	2017/18	2018/19
	£	£	£
Salary	28,000	0	16,000
(7/12 × £48,000)/(4/12 × £48,000)			
UK property income	6,250	15,000	10,000
(5/12 × £15,000)/full/(8/12 × £15,000)			
Foreign property income	7,000	0	4,000
(7/12 × £12,000)/(4/12 × £12,000)			
Total income	41,250	15,000	30,000
Less: PA	(11,000)	(11,000)	(11,000)
Taxable income	30,250	4,000	19,000

(c) **Helen's taxable income**

	2016/17	2017/18	2018/19
	£	£	£
Salary	48,000	0	48,000
UK property income (Note)	6,250	15,000	10,000
Overseas property income	12,000	0	12,000
Total income	66,250	15,000	70,000
Less: PA	(11,000)	(11,000)	(11,000)
Taxable income	55,250	4,000	59,000

Note: Helen's home is only rented when she is abroad and the income is UK income. Therefore it is always all taxable, but needs time apportioning in 2016/17 and 2018/19 because it is not rented for the whole of those years.

Test your understanding 5

Ewa Scott

Unremitted overseas income in the tax year 2016/17 is £3,000 which is > £2,000.

Therefore the arising basis will apply automatically and the personal allowance is available.

However, Ewa can elect for the remittance basis (RB) to apply. If the election is made, personal allowances will not be available.

Income tax computation – 2016/17

	No RB election	With RB election
	£	£
Trading profits in UK	25,000	25,000
Overseas property income (gross)	3,000	0
Total income	28,000	25,000
Less: PA	(11,000)	(0)
Taxable income	17,000	25,000
Income tax liability × 20%	3,400	5,000

Conclusion: Ewa should not claim the remittance basis in the tax year 2016/17.

Test your understanding 6

	Ivor	Sasha	Juan	Pierre
RBC	None	£60,000	£30,000	None

Note: Ivor has been in the UK for < 7 years so is not liable to the RBC.
Sasha has been in the UK for 12 out of the last 14 tax years, but not 17 out of the last 20 tax years.
Juan has been in the UK for 7 out of the last 9 tax years, but not 12 out of the last 14 tax years.
Pierre has unremitted income and gains of less than £2,000 and is not liable to the RBC. If his unremitted income and gains exceeded £2,000, his RBC would be £90,000.

Test your understanding 7

Gita Hoffheim

Income tax computation – 2016/17

	No RB election	With RB election
	£	£
Salary	90,000	90,000
Overseas interest (gross)	63,000	10,000
Overseas rent (gross)	95,000	0
Total income	248,000	100,000
Less: PA (Notes 1 and 2)	(0)	(0)
Taxable income	248,000	100,000
Income tax		
£32,000/£32,000 × 20% (non-savings)	6,400	6,400
£118,000/£68,000 × 40% (non-savings)	47,200	27,200
£35,000 × 45% (non-savings)	15,750	
£63,000 × 45% (savings)	28,350	0
	97,700	33,600
Plus: RBC (Note 3)	0	60,000
Income tax liability	97,700	93,600

Gita would be better off if she elects for the remittance basis to apply. The decision re-the remittance basis is made each year.

Notes:

(1) Under the arising basis, the PA is not available as adjusted net income is > £122,000.

(2) Under the remittance basis, the PA is not available.

(3) The remittance basis charge is £60,000 as Gita has been UK resident for 12 of the last 14 tax years.

(4) Without a remittance basis election, the savings nil rate band is not available as Gita is an additional rate taxpayer. With a remittance basis claim, Gita becomes a higher rate taxpayer. However, the savings nil rate band is still not available as all income is taxed at non-savings rates if the remittance basis is claimed.

Test your understanding 8

Benny

Income tax computation – 2016/17

	£
Employment income	37,640
Ruritanian rent	600
Utopian bank interest	1,100
Bank interest	3,085
Total income	42,425
Less: PA	(11,000)
Taxable income	31,425

Analysis of income:

Savings	Non-savings income
£4,185	(£31,425 – £4,185) = £27,240

Income tax:

£		£
27,240	× 20% (non-savings)	5,448
1,000	× 0% (SNRB)	0
3,185	× 20% (savings income)	637
31,425		
		6,085
Less: DTR	– Utopian tax (W1)	(220)
	– Ruritanian tax (W2)	(90)
Income tax liability		5,775
Less:	Tax credits	
	PAYE	(5,328)
Income tax payable		447

(W1) **DTR on Utopian income**

The Utopian income has suffered the higher rate of overseas tax and therefore relief is calculated in respect of this source of income first.

DTR = lower of

	£	£
(a) UK tax = £1,100 × 20%	220	
(b) Overseas tax = (50% × £1,100)		550

(W2) **DTR on Ruritanian income**

DTR = lower of

	£
(a) UK tax (20% × £600)	120
(b) Overseas tax (15% × £600)	90

Test your understanding 9

Cecilia

Capital gains tax computation – 2016/17

	(a) No RB election	(b) With RB election
	£	£
Asset in Austria	55,000	50,000
Asset in Hungary	0	0
UK asset	25,350	25,350
UK quoted shares	(18,000)	(18,000)
Total chargeable gains	62,350	57,350
Less: AEA	(11,100)	(0)
Taxable gains	51,250	57,350
Capital gains tax		
£51,250/£57,350 × 20%	10,250	11,470

Cecilia would be better off if she does not elect for remittance basis to apply in the tax year 2016/17.

Notes:

- The decision re-the remittance basis is made each year
- The decision re-the use of overseas losses must be made the first time the remittance basis is claimed, even if there are no overseas losses in that year, and the decision is irrevocable and binding on subsequent years

Test your understanding 10

Diane

Capital gains tax computation – 2016/17

		£
UK asset		22,000
Overseas asset		12,760
UK asset		29,000
		———
Total capital gains		63,760
Less: AEA		(11,100)
		———
Taxable gains		52,660
		———
Capital gains tax (£52,660 × 20%)		10,532
Less: DTR		
Lower of		
(i) Overseas CGT suffered	£3,850	
(ii) UK CGT applicable to overseas asset (W)	£2,552	(2,552)
		———
CGT payable		7,980
		———

Note: As Diane is UK resident and domiciled in the UK, she is liable on her worldwide asset gains on an arising basis. Full AEA is available. DTR is available.

Working: UK CGT on overseas asset

Overseas gain (Note) (£12,760 × 20%) = £2,552

Note: The AEA is set against the UK gains.

Test your understanding 11

Yolanda

End of UK residence:	15 July 2016
Start of UK residence:	24 October 2019
Years abroad:	3 years

Chargeable whilst abroad:

There is no CGT liability arising in the years whilst Yolanda is abroad.

However, the gains arising on the disposal of assets owned by Yolanda on 15 July 2016 become chargeable when she re-enters the UK in the tax year 2019/20.

Chargeable in the year of return to the UK: 2019/20

Assets 1 and 2: These assets were owned by Yolanda before she went abroad, therefore chargeable on return.

	£
Chargeable gain – Asset 1	125,896
Chargeable gain – Asset 2	5,024
	130,920

Asset 3: There is no CGT liability arising on the disposal of Asset 3 as the asset was not owned by Yolanda before she went abroad on 15 July 2016, and it was sold before she returned.

Test your understanding 12

(a) **Jim**

Chargeable gain before considering reliefs – 2024/25

At the time of disposal Jim is not resident in the UK and would normally be exempt on any gains arising in the UK and overseas. However, as he is disposing of UK residential property after 5 April 2015, a chargeable gain will arise as follows:

	(i) Rebasing to 5 April 2015	(ii) Time apportionment	(iii) Whole period
	£	£	£
Sale proceeds	780,000	780,000	780,000
Less: MV at 5 April 2015/Cost	(565,000)	(420,000)	(420,000)
Capital gain	215,000	360,000	360,000
Time apportionment (W)			
£360,000 × (110/212)		186,792	
Chargeable gain before considering reliefs	215,000	186,792	360,000

Jim would elect for the time apportionment basis to be applied.

(b) **Jim**

Allowable loss – 2024/25

If the property is sold for £400,000, an allowable loss would arise as follows:

	(i) Rebasing to 5 April 2015	(ii) Time apportionment	(iii) Whole period
	£	£	£
Sale proceeds	400,000	400,000	400,000
Less: MV at 5 April 2015/Cost	(410,000)	(420,000)	(420,000)
Capital loss	(10,000)	(20,000)	(20,000)
Time apportionment (W)			
£20,000 × (110/212)		(10,377)	
Allowable loss	(10,000)	(10,377)	(20,000)

Jim would elect for whole period of ownership basis to be applied.

Working: Time apportionment of gain/loss

Total period of ownership (4 October 2006 – 6 June 2024) = 17 years 8 months = 212 months
Period of ownership since 5 April 2015 = 9 years 2 months = 110 months

Test your understanding 13

Eric

Taxable gain – 2020/21

	(i) Rebasing to 5 April 2015	(ii) Time apportionment	(iii) Whole period
	£	£	£
Sale proceeds	600,000	600,000	600,000
Less: Cost/MV at 5 April 2015	(550,000)	(250,000)	(250,000)
Capital gain	50,000	350,000	350,000
Time apportionment (W)			
£350,000 × (72/361)		69,806	

Working: Time apportionment of gain

Total period of ownership (6 March 1991 – 31 March 2021) = 30 years 1 month = 361 months
Period of ownership since 5 April 2015 = 6 years = 72 months

Eric will not make an election and the gain before considering reliefs will be £50,000.

	£
Capital gain accruing since 5 April 2015 before reliefs	50,000
Less: PPR relief (W1)	(12,500)
	37,500
Less: Letting relief (W2)	(12,500)
Chargeable gain	25,000
Less: AEA	(11,100)
Taxable gain	13,900

Workings

(W1) PPR relief

Eric did not spend 90 nights in the UK property for any of the tax years 2016/17 to 2020/21 and therefore they are treated as years of non-occupation for PPR purposes.

However, PPR relief is available for the last 18 months unconditionally as the property has at some time been Eric's PPR.

Period of ownership since 5 April 2015 = 6 years = 72 months

PPR relief = £50,000 × (18/72) = £12,500

(W2) Letting relief

Lowest of:

(i)	PPR relief	**£12,500**
(ii)	Maximum	£40,000
(iii)	Chargeable gain after PPR relief that relates to a letting period	£37,500

chapter

11

An introduction to inheritance tax

Chapter learning objectives

Upon completion of this chapter you will be able to:

- outline the principal events for IHT
- explain the concept of 'transfer of value'
- consider 'excluded property'
- state which persons are chargeable to IHT
- recognise and explain the different types of lifetime gifts
- calculate the transfer of value for IHT
- identify when exemptions are available to reduce a lifetime transfer of value and apply them in the most beneficial way
- explain the annual exemption and demonstrate how it reduces the transfer of value
- explain the procedure and calculate the charge to IHT on a chargeable lifetime transfer during lifetime
- demonstrate the seven year cumulation period
- explain the procedure and calculate the charge to IHT on all lifetime transfers within 7 years of death
- recognise when taper relief is available to reduce the IHT charge
- recognise when a claim for fall in value on a lifetime gift can be made and demonstrate the effect
- calculate the IHT on the death estate where the value of the chargeable estate is provided.

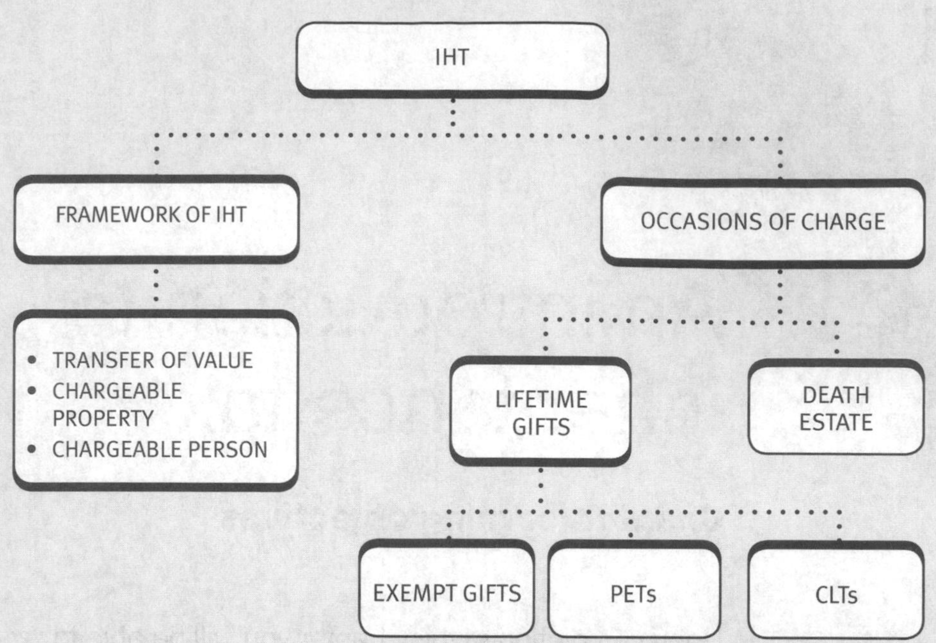

Introduction

This and the following two chapters deal with the way in which an individual is liable to inheritance tax (IHT).

This chapter is mainly a revision of the content covered at F6. It covers the principles that underpin IHT and considers the IHT payable calculations on lifetime gifts and on the death estate. A brief reminder of F6 content is given in expandable text and revision examples are provided to check your retention of the required F6 knowledge. Subsequent chapters cover more advanced aspects of the tax on lifetime gifts such as special valuation rules and reliefs and the detail of the computation of an individual's estate on death.

Lifetime gifts often feature in the examination as both the CGT and IHT implications of gifts can be tested. The two taxes are applicable where assets are gifted, but they work very differently. It is important to understand the distinction and interaction between the two taxes as the multi-tax aspects of capital transactions are frequently examined. Questions often require advice on how a transfer of assets could be organised more tax effectively.

The interaction of CGT and IHT is covered in Chapter 13, along with the tax implications and tax planning points to consider when planning to gift to the next generation either during your lifetime or on death in your will.

1 The charge to inheritance tax

Inheritance tax (IHT) is charged on:

- a **transfer of value**
- of **chargeable property**
- by a **chargeable person**.

A charge to IHT arises:

- on the death of an individual on their estate value
- on lifetime gifts where the donor dies within 7 years of date of gift
- on some lifetime gifts which are taxed at the date of the gift.

Transfer of value – diminution in value

A transfer of value is **a gift of any asset** which results in a reduction in the value of the donor's estate.

To be treated as a transfer of value the transfer must be a 'gratuitous disposition'. This basically means a gift.

A bad business deal will therefore not be liable to IHT, even though there is a fall in value of the estate, as it was not the donor's intention to give anything away.

To calculate the transfer of value for IHT purposes, the **loss to donor** principle is used (also referred to as the **diminution in value** concept).

The loss to the donor is the difference between the value of the donor's estate before and after the gift. This is the starting point for IHT calculations.

	£
Value of estate before gift	X
Less: Value of estate after gift	(X)
Diminution in value/Transfer of value	X

The loss to the donor is usually the **open market value** of the asset gifted.

However, in some circumstances, the transfer of value from the donor's point of view is not necessarily the same as the value of the asset received from the donee's point of view.

This is most common with unquoted shares, where a controlling shareholding has a higher value per share than a minority shareholding.

In addition, special valuation rules apply to gifts of certain assets. These rules are covered in Chapter 12.

Test your understanding 1

Linda owns 6,000 shares which represents a 60% holding in Loot Ltd. On 31 December 2016 she gifted a 20% holding in the company to her friend, Bob.

The values of shareholdings in Loot Ltd on 31 December 2016 have been agreed for IHT purposes as follows:

Holding	*Value per share*
Up to 25%	£9
26% to 50%	£15
51% to 74%	£26
75% or more	£45

Calculate the transfer of value relating to the gift of unquoted shares for IHT purposes.

Chargeable property

All property to which a person is beneficially entitled is chargeable property and is deemed to form part of their estate.

Therefore, a gift of any asset to which the person is beneficially entitled is a transfer of value, unless it is **excluded property**.

Excluded property is not chargeable to IHT and includes:

- property situated overseas where the owner is not UK domiciled
- reversionary interests in trust funds (see Chapter 14).

Chargeable persons

A chargeable person includes individuals and trustees of certain trusts. However, examination questions will focus on individuals.

Individuals

All individuals are potentially liable to IHT on their transfers of value.

- An individual who is domiciled in the UK is liable to IHT on transfers of their worldwide assets.
- If not UK domiciled, they are liable on transfers of UK assets only.

Domicile for IHT is discussed in more detail in Chapter 13.

Note that spouses and partners in a registered civil partnership are chargeable to IHT separately.

2 Occasions of charge

The main charge to IHT arises on the death of an individual as they become liable on the following:

- the value of all of their net assets in their estate at the date of death
- any lifetime gifts made in the seven years before their death, provided they are not exempt gifts.

However, IHT also arises on certain lifetime gifts at the date of the gift.

3 Lifetime gifts

There are three types of lifetime gifts by an individual for IHT purposes:

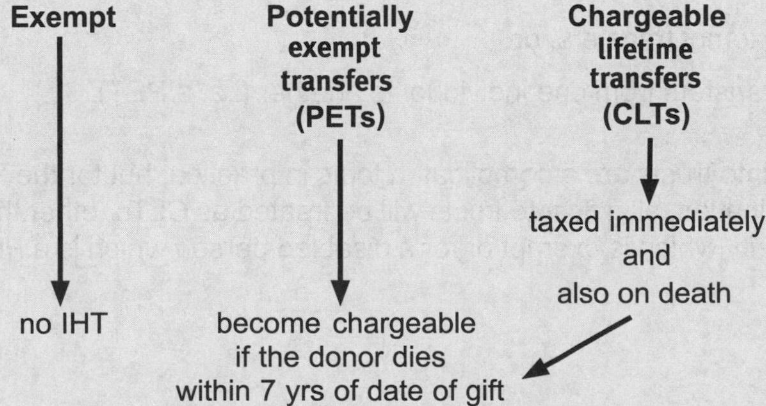

Types of lifetime gifts

Exempt transfers	Potentially exempt transfers (PETs)	Chargeable lifetime transfers (CLTs)
Definition		
A gift that is specifically deemed to be exempt from IHT (See below)	A gift by an individual • to another individual • into a disabled trust • into certain old trusts (not examinable)	No definition = residual category (i.e. a gift which is not exempt nor a PET) Main example: = gifts into trusts (except a charitable trust and those treated as PETs)
During lifetime		
No IHT payable	No IHT payable	IHT to pay calculated using the lifetime rates of tax
If Donor lives 7 years		
No IHT payable	No IHT payable Gift becomes exempt	No further IHT payable
If Donor dies within 7 years		
No IHT payable	The PET becomes chargeable on death for the first time	Possibly extra IHT payable, calculated using the death rates of tax

It is important to note that in practice, the majority of lifetime transfers made by individuals are:

- exempt transfers, or
- transfers from one individual to another (i.e. a PET).

Gifts into trusts are a complicated topic in practice, but for the P6 examination, all gifts into trusts will be treated as CLTs (other than a trust for a charity which is exempt or for a disabled person which is a PET).

Potentially exempt transfers (PETs)

PETs have derived their name from the fact that if the donor lives for more than seven years after making the gift, the transfer is exempt (i.e. free from IHT). Therefore, at the time of such transfer, it has the potential to be exempt.

However, if the donor dies within seven years of making the gift, then IHT may become chargeable on these gifts.

Note that transfers on death can never be PETs.

4 Exemptions and reliefs for IHT

The following table summarises all of the exemptions and reliefs available for IHT, some of which are covered in later chapters.

Exemptions and reliefs available against:		
Lifetime gifts only	**Lifetime gifts and death estate**	**Death estate only**
• Small gifts exemption – max £250 per recipient per tax year • Marriage exemption – £5,000 parent – £2,500 grandparent/party to marriage – £1,000 other • Normal expenditure out of income • Annual exemption – £3,000 per tax year – can c/f unused amount one year • Fall in value relief	• Inter spouse exemption • Charity exemption • Political party exemption • Agricultural property relief (APR) (see Chapter 12) • Business property relief (BPR) (see Chapter 12)	• Quick succession relief (QSR) (see Chapter 12) • Double taxation relief (DTR) (see Chapter 13)

5 Exemptions available for lifetime gifts only

A reminder of the detailed rules for exemptions covered at F6 is given in expandable text.

Note that the rules and limits for these exemptions are **not** given in the examination, and must be learnt.

Small gifts exemption

Lifetime gifts are exempt if they are:

- an outright gift of no more than £250
- per recipient
- per tax year.

The small gift exemption does not apply if the gift is in excess of £250.

Therefore, a gift of £300 will not qualify. Similarly, if an individual makes a gift of £240 to a person followed by another gift of £100 to the same person in the same tax year, neither gift will be exempt.

However, the donor can make gifts of up to £250 to any number of recipients and they will all be exempt.

Marriage exemption

A lifetime transfer made "in consideration of a marriage" (or registration of a civil partnership) is exempt up to the following maximum limits:

- £5,000 by a parent
- £2,500 by a grandparent or remoter ancestor
- £2,500 by a party to the marriage or civil partnership (e.g. from the groom to the bride)
- £1,000 by anyone else.

The exemption is conditional on the marriage taking place.

Normal expenditure out of income

IHT is levied on transfers of capital wealth.

Therefore, a lifetime transfer will be exempt if it can be shown that the gift:

- is made as part of a person's normal expenditure out of income, and
- does not affect the donor's standard of living.

To be treated as 'normal', gifts must be habitual (i.e. there is a regular pattern of giving). For example, payment of school fees for a grandchild or annual payments into a life assurance policy for the benefit of a child are usually exempted under this rule.

The annual exemption

The annual exemption (AE) is an exemption available against **lifetime** transfers and operates as follows:

- The AE:
  - exempts the **first £3,000** of lifetime transfers in any one tax year
  - is applied chronologically to the first gift in the tax year, then (if there is any left) the second gift and so on
  - must be applied to the first gift each year, even if the first gift is a PET and never becomes chargeable.
- Any unused AE:
  - may be carried forward to the next year
  - however, it can be carried forward for one year only, and
  - can only be used after the current year's AE.
- Other exemptions or reliefs, if available, are given before the AE.

Note that as the AE is used up by PETs as well as by CLTs, where more than one transfer is to be made during a tax year, CLTs should be made before PETs to ensure that the optimum use is made of the AE.

Test your understanding 2

Janet made the following lifetime gifts:

(a) 31 August 2013, £600, to her son

(b) 31 October 2013, £800, to a discretionary trust

(c) 31 May 2014, £2,100, to an interest in possession (IIP) trust

(d) 30 November 2014, £1,100, to a discretionary trust

(e) 30 April 2015, £5,000, to her daughter.

Calculate the transfer of value after AEs for each of the gifts.

6 Exemptions available for lifetime transfers and the death estate

Inter spouse exemption

Transfers between spouses and partners in a registered civil partnership are exempt whether they are made during the individual's lifetime or on death.

There is no maximum limit to this exemption **unless**

- the transferor is UK domiciled, and
- the transferee spouse or civil partner is non-UK domiciled.

In this case, the maximum exemption limit which is equal to the current nil rate band (NRB) (section 7) of **£325,000** can be deducted from the transfer of value.

However, an election is available whereby a non-UK domiciled individual with a UK domiciled spouse or civil partner can elect to be treated as domiciled in UK for IHT purposes.

This may be beneficial where assets of more than £325,000 are transferred to a non-UK domiciled spouse. This is because if the election is made, there would be no limit to the exempt amount and the whole transfer would be exempt. More detail on this election is given in Chapter 13.

Political party exemption

Gifts to qualifying political parties are exempt whether they are made during the individual's lifetime or on death.

There is no maximum limit to this exemption.

A donation to a political party qualifies for exemption if, at the last general election preceding the transfer of value either of the following conditions are met:

- two members were elected to the House of Commons, or
- one member was so elected and at least 150,000 votes were cast for the party.

Charity exemption

Gifts to recognised UK charities are exempt whether they are made during the individual's lifetime or on death.

There is no maximum limit to this exemption.

In addition, there is a reduced death rate of inheritance tax for estates in which at least 10% of the taxable estate is left to charity (Chapter 12).

Gifts for the public benefit or for national purposes

- Gifts to non-profit making institutions are, with Treasury approval, exempt.
- Examples could include land and buildings of outstanding beauty, or of historic interest.
- Undertakings are required concerning the use, preservation and public access of the property.

Gifts to a number of national institutions are also exempt.

These include:

- the British Museum
- the National Gallery
- approved museums, libraries and art galleries
- the National Trust.

Test your understanding 3

Margaret made the following lifetime transfers:

- Unquoted shares worth £525,000 in the family company to her husband on 1 June 2016.
- £15,000 to her son on 6 July 2016 as a wedding present.
- £20,000 to her nephew on 27 September 2016.
- £235 to her friend for her 40th birthday on 4th November 2016.
- £270,000 into a discretionary trust on 24 December 2016.
- £90,000 to the International Red Cross, a registered charity, on 1 January 2017.
- £20,000 to the Labour Party on 14 February 2017.

Calculate the transfer of value after exemptions for each of Margaret's gifts.

7 IHT payable during an individual's lifetime on CLTs

For P6, lifetime IHT is payable when an individual makes a gift into any trust (other than a trust for a charity which is exempt or for a disabled person which is a PET).

The procedure to calculate the lifetime IHT on a CLT

The lifetime tax should be calculated on each gift separately, in chronological order, as follows:

(1) First consider the specific exemptions, because if the gift is completely exempt, there is no need to quantify the gift (see notes below).

(2) Calculate the chargeable amount of the each CLT and PET:

	£
Value of estate before transfer	X
Less: Value of estate after transfer	(X)
	—
Transfer of value	X
Less: Business property relief and agricultural property relief	(X)
Marriage exemption	(X)
Annual exemptions	(X)
	—
Chargeable amount	X
	—

(3) Calculate the amount of nil rate band (NRB) available after deducting gross chargeable transfers (GCTs) in the previous 7 years (see below).

(4) Calculate the tax on the excess at either 20% or 25% depending on who has agreed to pay the tax; the donor or the donee (see below).

(5) Calculate the gross amount of the gift to carry forward for future computations.

(6) If required by the examination question, state the due date of payment of the IHT (see below).

Notes:

(i) If the gift is directly to, or into a trust for the benefit of:

– a charity

– a spouse or civil partner

– a qualifying political party

there is no need to compute a chargeable amount as the gift will be exempt.

(ii) There is no small gift exemption available for gifts into trusts.

The nil rate band (NRB)

All individuals are entitled to a NRB and are taxed on the value of gifts in excess of the NRB at different rates depending on who has agreed to pay the lifetime tax.

The NRB identifies the maximum value of lifetime and death gifts, which can be gifted without incurring any IHT liability.

The NRB has steadily increased each tax year in the past, although it has remained the same since 2009/10.

For lifetime calculations, the NRB applicable at **the time of the gift** should be used.

The NRBs for the tax year 2016/17 and previous tax years are provided in the tax rates and allowances in the examination.

The appropriate rate of tax

The appropriate rate of tax to apply to lifetime gifts depends on who has agreed to pay the tax due.

Trustees pay the tax

If the **trustees** of the trust (i.e. the donee) agree to **pay** the tax:

- the gift is referred to as a **gross gift**, and
- the appropriate rate of tax is 20%

Donor pays the tax

If the **donor** agrees to **pay** the tax:

- the gift is referred to as a **net gift**.
- As a result of the gift, their estate is being reduced by:
  - the value of the gift, **and**
  - the associated tax payable on the gift.
- Accordingly, to calculate the gross amount of the gift, it needs to be 'grossed up' to include the amount of tax that the donor has to pay.
- The appropriate rate of tax is 25% (i.e. 20/80ths of the net gift).
- The gross transfer to carry forward is the net chargeable amount of the gift plus any lifetime IHT paid by the donor. This amount remains fixed for all calculations, even if the NRB available at death differs from the amount available during the donor's lifetime.

In summary, the rate of tax on the value of CLTs in excess of the NRB is:

Payer:	*Chargeable amount represents:*	*Appropriate rate*
Trustees of the trust	Gross gift	20%
Donor	Net gift	25% (or 20/80)

Note that the tax due on a CLT is primarily the responsibility of the donor.

Therefore, where an examination question does not specify who has agreed to pay the tax, **always** assume that the **donor will pay** and that the gift is therefore **a net gift**.

The normal due date of payment of lifetime IHT

The date of payment of lifetime IHT depends on the date of the gift:

Date of CLT	*Due date of payment*
6 April to 30 September	30 April in the following year
1 October to 5 April	Six months after the end of the month of the CLT

Example 1 – IHT payable during lifetime

Charlotte makes a gift into a trust on 13 June 2016 of £366,000.

She has made no previous lifetime gifts.

Calculate the amount of lifetime IHT due on the gift into the trust and state the gross chargeable amount of the gift to carry forward for future computations, assuming:

(a) **the trustees of the trust have agreed to pay any IHT due.**

(b) **Charlotte has agreed to pay any IHT due.**

State the due date for payment of tax.

Solution

Charlotte

	(a) Trustees to pay IHT		(b) Charlotte to pay IHT	
	CLT 13.6.2016		CLT 13.6.2016	
		£		£
Transfer of value		366,000		366,000
Less: Annual exemption				
Current year	2016/17	(3,000)	2016/17	(3,000)
Previous year	2015/16 b/f	(3,000)	2015/16 b/f	(3,000)
Chargeable amount	Gross	360,000	Net	360,000
NRB @ date of gift	2016/17	(325,000)	2016/17	(325,000)
Taxable amount		35,000		35,000
IHT payable	@ 20%	7,000	@ 25%	8,750
Paid by		Trustees		Charlotte
Due date		30.4.2017		30.4.2017
Gross chargeable amount c/f		360,000	(£360,000 net + £8,750 tax)	368,750

In both parts of the example above, the individual had made no previous lifetime gifts and therefore all of the NRB was available to calculate the tax. However, the NRB is available for a **'seven year cumulation period'**.

Each time a CLT is made, in order to calculate the IHT liability, it is necessary to look back seven years and calculate how much NRB is available to set against that particular gift.

The seven year cumulation period

For lifetime calculations, to calculate the NRB available at any point in time, it is necessary to take account of the total of the **gross** amounts of all other **CLTs** made within the **previous seven years**.

- These CLTs in the seven year cumulation period are deemed to have utilised the NRB first.
- There will therefore only be NRB available to match against this latest gift if the total of the CLTs in the previous seven years is less than the NRB at the time of the gift.
- Note that although PETs may use the AE during the donor's lifetime, they do not affect the NRB as they are not yet chargeable.

Test your understanding 4

During his lifetime Alan had made the following gifts:

- 30 June 2007, £183,000 to a discretionary trust
- 30 June 2012, £150,000 to his daughter
- 30 June 2013, £191,000 to a discretionary trust
- 31 December 2016, £256,000 to a discretionary trust

The trustees of the first two trusts paid the IHT liabilities. Alan paid the tax on the last gift.

Calculate the IHT arising as a result of Alan's lifetime transfers.

State who will pay the tax, the due date of payment and the gross chargeable amount of each gift to carry forward to future computations.

Test your understanding 5

During his lifetime Simon had made the following cash gifts:

- 21 April 2008, £123,000 to a discretionary trust (trustees to pay tax)
- 15 April 2013, £140,000 to his son
- 19 March 2014, £221,000 to a discretionary trust (Simon to pay tax)
- 9 May 2016, £395,000 to a discretionary trust (trustees to pay tax)

Calculate the IHT arising as a result of Simon's lifetime transfers.

Summary of lifetime calculations

Remember to:

- only calculate IHT on CLTs
- consider the IHT position for each CLT separately and in chronological order
- use the valuation rules to calculate the chargeable amount
- use the NRB applicable for the tax year of the gift
- tax is due at 20% if the trustees pay, and 25% if the donor pays.

Also remember that PETs are not chargeable at this stage, but may use the annual exemptions.

8 IHT payable on lifetime gifts as a result of death

On the death of an individual, an IHT charge could arise in relation to lifetime gifts **within seven years of death** as follows:

- PETs become chargeable for the first time.
- Additional tax may be due on a CLT.

The IHT payable on lifetime gifts as a result of death is **always** paid by the recipient of the gift:

Type of gift:	*Paid by:*
CLT	Trustees of the trust
PET	Donee

Calculating the death IHT on lifetime gifts

The death tax should be calculated on each gift separately, in chronological order, as follows:

(1) Identify all gifts within seven years of death which are not exempt.

(2) Calculate the **gross chargeable amount** of each gift and any **lifetime tax paid.**

(3) Calculate the amount of NRB available after deducting **gross chargeable transfers** in the 7 years before the gift:
   - use the NRB on the date of **death** (rather than the date of the gift)
   - **include PETs** which have become chargeable (but not those that have become completely exempt).

(4) Calculate the death tax on the excess at **40%**.

(5) Calculate and deduct any **taper relief** available (see below).

(6) For CLTs, deduct any **lifetime IHT paid**.

(7) If required by the question, state who will pay the tax and the due date of payment (see below).

Further points regarding death tax calculations on lifetime gifts

Chargeable amount

- The **gross** chargeable amount of each gift is taxed on death.
- The gross amount of CLTs will have already been calculated in the lifetime IHT calculations.
- Remember to use the grossed up value of any CLTs where the tax is paid by the donor.
- The chargeable amount of a PET is calculated using the values at the time of the gift and PETs may use up the AEs, even though they only become chargeable if the donor dies within 7 years.

The nil rate band

- The NRB for the year of the gift is used against the lifetime calculations as seen above.
- The NRB for the year of death is then used to calculate the death tax but it is matched against **all** chargeable gifts (i.e. CLTs and PETs) in chronological order.

The seven year cumulation period

The seven year cumulation period for the NRB applies in a similar way as for the lifetime calculations.

However, note that:

- it is necessary to take into account the total of the **gross** amounts of **all chargeable gifts** made within the **previous seven years** (not just CLTs)
- therefore, to calculate the death IHT on each gift, it is necessary to look back seven years from the **date of each gift** and include the gross amount of:
  - all CLTs, **and**
  - PETs which have become chargeable due to the death of the individual.

This means that a CLT made more than 7 years before death may still affect the NRB when calculating death tax on lifetime gifts.

However, ignore any PETs made more than 7 years ago as they are not taxable.

The death rate of tax

The death rate of IHT is 40% on the excess over the NRB available.

Taper relief

Where IHT is chargeable on **any** lifetime transfer due to death, the amount of IHT payable on death will be reduced by taper relief:

- where more than 3 years have elapsed since the date of the gift
- by a percentage reduction according to the length of time between
  - the date of the gift, and
  - the date of the donor's death.

Note that:

- the relief applies to both CLTs and PETs
- for the first 3 years no taper relief is given

- then for each year after that, 20% relief is available, as follows:

Years before date of death:

Over	*Less than*	*Taper relief*
		%
0	3	0
3	4	20
4	5	40
5	6	60
6	7	80

For gifts made seven or more years before death there is no IHT payable on death, so taper relief is not relevant.

This table is provided in the tax rates and allowances in the examination.

Deduction of lifetime IHT paid

For CLTs, any lifetime IHT already paid can be deducted from the liability calculated on death.

However, no refund is made if the tax already paid is higher than the amount now due on death. At best, the deduction of lifetime tax paid will bring the liability on death down to £Nil.

The normal due date of payment of IHT on death

IHT as a result of death is due **six months** after the **end of the month of death**.

Example 2 – Death tax payable on lifetime gifts

Frank died on 30 June 2016. He made the following lifetime gifts:

- 31 July 2007, £80,000, to his son
- 30 November 2012, £110,000, to his daughter
- 30 April 2013, £235,000, to his son.

Calculate the IHT arising as a result of Frank's death on 30 June 2016. State who will pay the tax and the due date of payment.

Solution

Answer to example 1

IHT payable during lifetime

	PET 31.7.2007		PET 30.11.2012		PET 30.4.2013	
		£		£		£
Transfer of value		80,000		110,000		235,000
Less: Annual exemption						
Current year	2007/08	(3,000)	2012/13	(3,000)	2013/14	(3,000)
Previous year	2006/07 b/f	(3,000)	2011/12 b/f	(3,000)	2012/13 b/f	(0)
Chargeable amount		74,000		104,000		232,000
IHT payable (as all PETs)		0		0		0
Gross chargeable amount c/f		74,000		104,000		232,000

All gifts are PETs, therefore there is no lifetime tax to pay. However the gross chargeable amount of the PETs must be established at the time of the gift.

IHT payable on death

Date of death: 30 June 2016
7 years before: 30 June 2009

PET on 31.7.2007 is more than 7 years before death – therefore no IHT payable on death

	PET 30.11.2012		PET 30.4.2013	
	£	£	£	£
Gross chargeable amount b/f (as above)		104,000		232,000
NRB @ date of death – 2016/17	325,000		325,000	
Less: GCTs < 7 years before gift				
(30.11.2005 – 30.11.2012)	(0)			
(ignore 31.7.2007 PET as completely exempt)				
(30.4.2006 – 30.4.2013)			(104,000)	
(ignore 31.7.2007 PET as completely exempt, but include 30.11.2012 PET as became chargeable)				
NRB available		(325,000)		(221,000)
Taxable amount		0		11,000
IHT payable @ 40%		0		4,400
Less: Taper relief (30.4.2013 – 30.6.2016) (3-4 years before death) (20%)				(880)
Less: IHT paid in lifetime				(0)
IHT payable on death		0		3,520
Paid by (always the donee)				Son
Due date of payment (six months after end of month of death)				31.12.2016

Example 3 – Death tax payable on lifetime gifts

On 15 November 2009 Zandra made a transfer of £405,000 into a discretionary trust. She has made no other lifetime transfers. The IHT due in respect of this gift was paid by Zandra.

Zandra died on 30 September 2016.

Calculate the IHT arising on Zandra's lifetime gift, and the additional IHT arising as a result of her death.

State who will pay the tax and the due date of payment.

Solution

Lifetime IHT **15 November 2009 – CLT**	£	£
Transfer of value		405,000
Less: Annual exemption		
Current year – 2009/10		(3,000)
Previous year – 2008/09 b/f		(3,000)
Net chargeable amount		399,000
NRB @ date of gift – 2009/10	325,000	
Less: GCTs < 7 yrs before gift (15.11.02 to 15.11.09)	(0)	
NRB available		(325,000)
Taxable amount		74,000
IHT payable @ 25% (= net gift as Zandra paying the tax)		18,500
Payable by		Zandra
Due date (gift in second half of tax year)		31.5.10
Gross amount to carry forward for future computations (£399,000 + £18,500)		417,500

IHT payable on death

15 November 2009 – CLT	£	£
Gross chargeable amount (above)		417,500
NRB @ date of death – 2016/17	325,000	
Less: GCTs < 7 yrs before gift (15.11.02 – 15.11.09)	(0)	
NRB available		(325,000)
Taxable amount		92,500
IHT payable @ 40%		37,000
Less: Taper relief (15.11.09 to 30.09.16) (6 – 7 yrs) (80%)		(29,600)
Chargeable (40%)		7,400
Less: IHT paid in lifetime (CLT)		(18,500)
IHT payable on death		0

There is no repayment of lifetime IHT.

Example 4 – IHT payable on lifetime gifts as a result of death

Mark has made the following lifetime gifts:

- 1 September 2007, £120,000, to a discretionary trust.
- 1 May 2011, £262,000, to his son Alexander.
- 1 June 2012, £236,000, to a discretionary trust.
- 1 July 2014, £21,000, to his daughter Jayne.
- 1 August 2015, £93,000, to an interest in possession trust.

Mark had agreed to pay any IHT due on CLTs.

Mark died on 1 December 2016.

Calculate the IHT payable on the lifetime transfers during Mark's lifetime and on his death.

State who will pay the tax and the due date of payment.

Solution

Answer to example 4

IHT payable during lifetime

	CLT 1.9.2007		PET 1.5.2011		CLT 1.6.2012		PET 1.7.2014		CLT 1.8.2015	
		£		£		£		£		£
Transfer of value		120,000		262,000		236,000		21,000		93,000
Less: Annual exemption										
Current year	2007/08	(3,000)	2011/12	(3,000)	2012/13	(3,000)	2014/15	(3,000)	2015/16	(3,000)
Previous year	2006/07 b/f	(3,000)	2010/11 b/f	(3,000)	2011/12 b/f	(0)	2013/14 b/f	(3,000)	2014/15 b/f	(0)
Chargeable amount	Net	114,000		256,000	Net	233,000		15,000	Net	90,000
NRB @ date of gift	£				£				£	
– 2007/08	300,000									
– 2012/13					325,000					
– 2015/16									325,000	
Less: GCTs < 7 years before gift	(0)									
(1.9.2000 – 1.9.2007)					(114,000)					
(1.6.2005 – 1.6.2012) (ignore PET)									(238,500)	
(1.8.2008 – 1.8.2015) (ignore both PETs and gift on 1.9.2007 drops out as too old)										
NRB available		(300,000)				(211,000)				(86,500)
Taxable amount		0		0		22,000		0		3,500
IHT payable		0		0	@ 25%	5,500		0	@ 25%	875
Paid by						Mark				Mark
Due date of payment						30.4.13				30.4.16
Gross chargeable amount	(£114,000 net + £Nil tax)	114,000		256,000	(£233,000 net + £5,500 tax)	238,500		15,000	(£90,000 net + £875 tax	90,875

IHT payable on death

Date of death: 1 December 2016
7 years before: 1 December 2009
CLT on 1.9.2007 is more than 7 years before death – therefore no IHT payable on death

	PET 1.5.2011		CLT 1.6.2012		PET 1.7.2014		CLT 1.8.2015	
		£		£		£		£
Gross chargeable amount b/f (as above)		256,000		238,500		15,000		90,875
	£		£		£		£	
NRB @ date of death – 2016/17	325,000		325,000		325,000		325,000	
Less: GCTs < 7 years before gift								
(1.5.2004 – 1.5.2011) (always include CLTs)	(114,000)							
(1.6.2005 – 1.6.2012) (£114,000 + £256,000)			(370,000)					
(include 1.5.2011 PET as it became chargeable)								
(1.7.2007 – 1.7.2014) (£370,000 + £238,500)					(608,500)			
(include 1.5.2011 PET as it became chargeable)								
(1.8.2008 – 1.8.2015)								
(£256,000 + £238,500 + £15,000)							(509,500)	
(earliest CLT on 1.9.2007 drops out, include both PETs)								
NRB available		(211,000)		(0)		(0)		(0)
Taxable amount		45,000		238,500		15,000		90,875
IHT payable @ 40%		18,000		95,400		6,000		36,350
Less: Taper relief								
(1.5.2011 – 1.12.2016) (5 – 6 years before death)	(60%)	(10,800)						
(1.6.2012 – 1.12.2016) (4 – 5 years before death)			(40%)	(38,160)				
(1.7.2014 – 1.12.2016) (< 3 years before death)						(0)		
(1.8.2015 – 1.12.2016) (< 3 years before death)								(0)
Less: IHT paid in lifetime		(0)		(5,500)		(0)		(875)
IHT payable on death		7,200		51,740		6,000		35,475
Paid by (always the donee)		Alexander		Trustees		Jayne		Trustees
Due date of payment		30.6.2017		30.6.2017		30.6.2017		30.6.2017

Test your understanding 6

Mr Ambrose makes the following lifetime gifts:

1 May 2008	£205,000 to a discretionary trust, Mr Ambrose is to pay the IHT.
30 June 2009	£60,000 to his niece on the occasion of her 21st birthday.
11 June 2010	£134,000 to his nephew on the occasion of his marriage.
11 November 2014	£136,000 to a discretionary trust, the trustees are to pay the IHT.

(a) **Calculate the IHT liabilities arising as a result of the lifetime gifts.**

(b) **If Mr Ambrose dies on 14 February 2017, calculate the additional IHT on the lifetime gifts as a result of Mr Ambrose's death.**

(c) **Calculate the nil rate band left to set against the death estate.**

9 Fall in value (FIV) relief

The chargeable amount of a lifetime gift (CLT or PET) is calculated and fixed **at the time of the gift**.

If the gift becomes chargeable on the death of the donor:

- any **increase** in value between the date of the gift and the date of the donor's death is **ignored**
- if the asset **decreases** in value between the date of the gift and the date of the donor's death, **relief is available** to reduce the chargeable amount of this gift on death.

Conditions

To qualify for this relief, the asset must:

- either **still be owned** by the donee at the date of the donor's death, or
- it was **sold in an arm's length transaction** before the donor died.

Note that this relief is not available in respect of any property which is expected to fall in value over time, for example:

- plant and machinery
- wasting chattels (i.e. tangible movable property with a predictable useful life of less than 50 years).

Operation of the relief

The relief operates by **reducing the chargeable amount by the fall in value**, calculated from **the donee's point of view**.

The fall in value is the difference between:

- the value of the asset at the date of the gift
- the value of the asset at
  - the date of the donor's death, or
  - the date of the sale (if earlier).

Note that this relief:

- applies to both PETs and CLTs
- only affects the calculation of the IHT on that one gift
- has no effect on lifetime IHT already paid
- has no effect on the IHT payable on any subsequent gifts or the death estate.

Therefore, the **original gross chargeable amount** is accumulated and carried forward to calculate the NRB on subsequent events.

Test your understanding 7

Tim died on 30 June 2016.

On 30 April 2013 Tim had made a gift of 100,000 shares (a 1% holding) in ABC plc, a quoted company, into a discretionary trust. Tim paid the IHT arising on the gift. Tim had made no other lifetime gifts.

ABC plc's shares were worth £3.65 each on 30 April 2013, and £3.35 each when Tim died on 30 June 2016.

(a) **Calculate the IHT liability arising in respect of Tim's lifetime transfer on 30 April 2013, stating when it is due for payment.**

(b) **Calculate the gross chargeable amount to carry forward for the IHT on the death estate computation.**

10 IHT payable on the death estate

On the death of an individual, an IHT charge arises on the value of their estate at the date of death.

The detailed computation of a death estate is covered in Chapter 12. This section explains how the IHT charge is calculated once the estate value has been established.

The procedure to calculate the IHT on the death estate

The procedure to calculate the IHT on the death estate is as follows.

(1) Deal with the IHT on lifetime gifts within seven years of the date of death first **before** looking at the estate computation.

(2) Calculate the gross chargeable estate value (Chapter 12).

(3) Calculate the amount of NRB available after deducting GCTs in the previous 7 years (i.e. CLTs and PETs).

(4) Calculate the tax on the excess at 40% or 36% if at least 10% of the baseline amount is left to charity (see Chapter 12).

(5) Deduct quick succession relief (see Chapter 12) and double taxation relief (see Chapter 13), if applicable.

(6) If required by the question, state who will pay the tax (see Chapter 12) and the due date of payment (see below).

Further points regarding IHT payable on the death estate

The nil rate band

The NRB available to an individual on death of £325,000 is first used to calculate the death tax on lifetime gifts, then the estate after the lifetime gifts have been dealt with.

The seven year cumulation period

The seven year cumulation period applies in a similar way to the death calculations on lifetime gifts as follows:

- it is necessary to take into account the total of the gross amounts of all **chargeable gifts** made within the **previous seven years**
- therefore, look back seven years from the date of death and accumulate the gross amounts of:
  - **all** CLTs, **and**
  - **all** PETs (because all PETs within 7 years of death will have become chargeable on death).

The normal due date of payment of IHT on death

IHT as a result of death is due on the earlier of:

- **six months** after the end of the month of death, or
- on delivery of the account of the estate assets to HMRC.

Note that who pays the tax on the estate value depends on the composition of the estate. This is covered in detail in Chapter 12.

Example 5 – IHT payable on the death estate

Sally died on 15 June 2016 leaving a gross chargeable estate valued at £427,000 all of which was bequeathed to her brother.

(a) **Calculate the IHT liability arising on Sally's estate assuming she made no lifetime transfers**

(b) **What if Sally had gross chargeable transfers of £147,000 in the seven years prior to her death?**

Solution

(a) **No lifetime transfers**

	£	£
Gross chargeable estate value		427,000
NRB @ date of death – 2016/17	325,000	
Less: GCTs < 7 yrs before death (15.6.09 – 15.6.16)	(0)	
		(325,000)
Taxable amount		102,000
IHT payable @ 40%		40,800

(b) **Lifetime transfers = £147,000**

	£	£
Gross chargeable estate value		427,000
NRB @ date of death – 2016/17	325,000	
Less: GCTs < 7 yrs before death (15.6.09 – 15.6.16)	(147,000)	
		(178,000)
Taxable amount		249,000
IHT payable @ 40%		99,600

Test your understanding 8

Thomas died on 23 April 2016 leaving a gross chargeable estate valued at £627,560 which was bequeathed to his girlfriend.

Thomas had made the following lifetime gifts:

- 1 June 2007, £180,000, to a discretionary trust
- 16 March 2012, £228,000, to his cousin

Calculate the IHT liability arising on Thomas's estate and state the due date of payment.

Summary

Occasions of charge

Lifetime gifts

Death estate

CLTs

PETs

First computation = Lifetime IHT:

1. Consider exemptions:
   - spouse / charity / political party
   - small gifts
   - normal expenditure from income
2. Calculate the chargeable amount of the gifts which are not exempt
   - use diminution in value
   - consider ME, AE
3. Calculate the lifetime IHT at 20% or 25% on CLTs after taking account of:
   - whether a gross or net gift
   - the NRB available during lifetime
   - gross CLTs in the 7-year cumulation period
4. Calculate the gross amount to carry forward for future computations

Second computation = Death IHT on lifetime gifts:

1. Calculate the gross chargeable amount of gifts in the seven years before death
2. Consider fall in value relief
3. Calculate the tax at 40% after taking account of
   - the NRB available on death
   - gross CLTs and PETs which have become chargeable in the 7-year cumulation period
4. Calculate and deduct taper relief
5. For CLTs, deduct lifetime IHT paid

Last computation = Death IHT on estate value:

1. Calculate the gross chargeable estate value
2. Calculate the tax at 40%(or 36% if ≥ 10% left to charity) after taking account of
   - the NRB available on death
   - gross CLTs and PETs in the 7 years before death
3. Calculate and deduct QSR and DTR, if applicable

11 Chapter summary

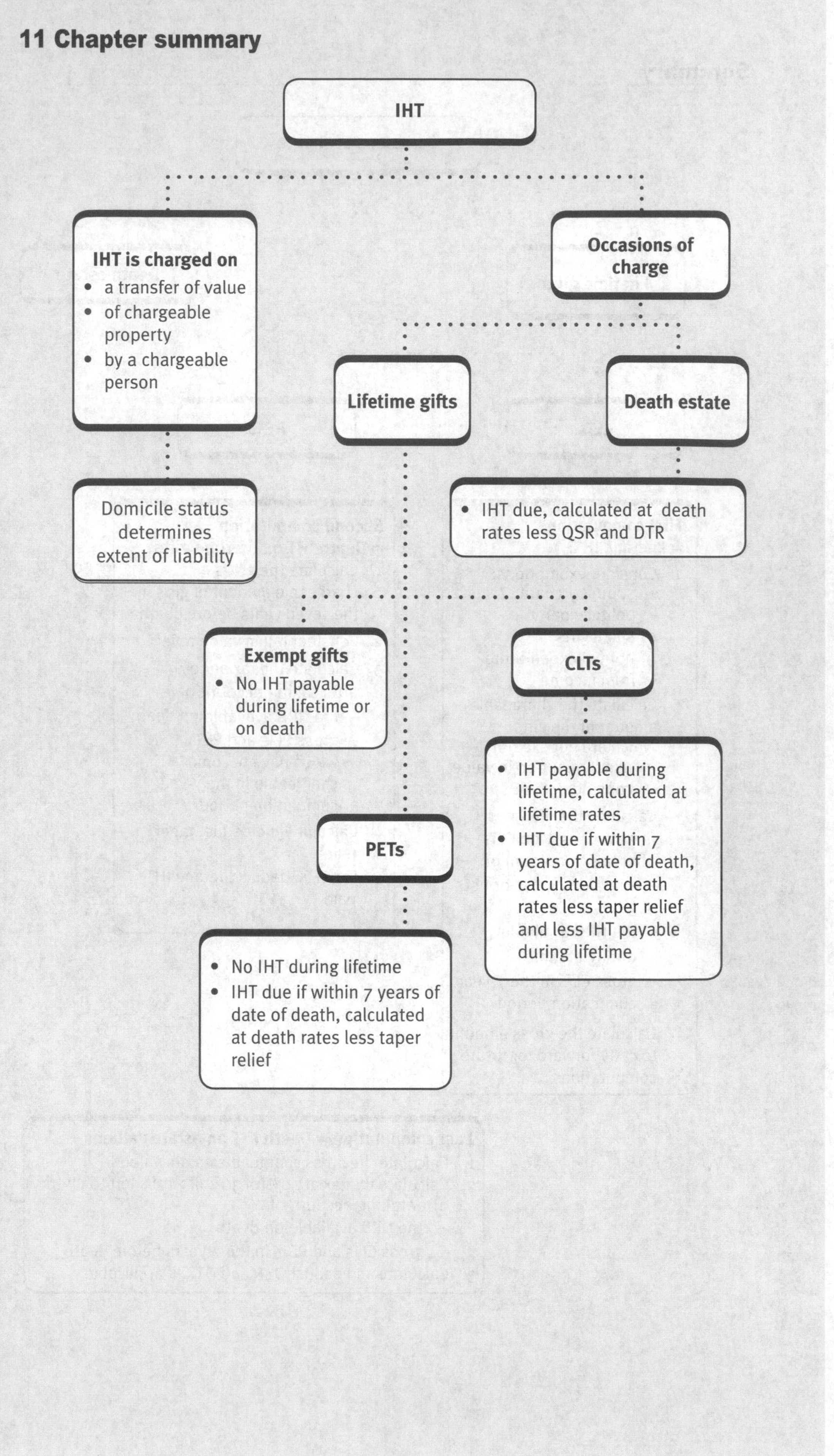

Test your understanding answers

Test your understanding 1

Linda

	£
Value of estate before transfer (6,000 × £26)	156,000
Less: Value of estate after transfer (4,000 × £15)	(60,000)
Transfer of value	96,000

Note that a lifetime gift will have both IHT and CGT consequences.

The diminution in value concept is very important but unique to IHT.

The value of the asset gifted, a 20% interest in these shares
= (2,000 × £9) = £18,000

This value:

- is not relevant for IHT purposes; it is the diminution in the value of the estate from the donor's point of view which is important, but
- is important for CGT purposes; the market value of the asset gifted is always the consideration used as the starting point of a chargeable gain computation.

Test your understanding 2

Janet

	PET 31.8.13	CLT 31.10.13	CLT 31.5.14	CLT 30.11.14	PET 30.4.15
Tax year of gift	2013/14	2013/14	2014/15	2014/15	2015/16
	£	£	£	£	£
Transfer of value	600	800	2,100	1,100	5,000
Less: Annual exemption					
2013/14	(600)	(800)			
2012/13 b/f (£3,000 avail)	(–)	(–)			
(all lost as not used and can only c/f for one year)					
2014/15			(2,100)	(900)	
2013/14 b/f (£1,600 avail)			(–)	(200)	
(remaining £1,400 lost as not used)					
2015/16					(3,000)
2014/15 b/f (none available – already used)					(0)
Chargeable amount	0	0	0	0	2,000

Test your understanding 3

Margaret

Exempt gifts

1.6.2016	Gift to husband = exempt inter-spouse transfer
4.11.2016	Gift to friend = small gift exemption applies as the gift is less than £250
1.1.2017	Gift to International Red Cross = exempt gift to charity
14.2.2017	Gift to Labour party = exempt gift to political party

Remaining gifts – chargeable amount

	PET **6.7.2016**	**PET** **27.9.2016**	**CLT** **24.12.2016**
Tax year of gift	2016/17	2016/17	2016/17
	£	£	£
Transfer of value	15,000	20,000	270,000
Less: Marriage exemption	(5,000)		
Less: Annual exemption			
2016/17	(3,000)	(0)	(0)
2015/16 b/f	(3,000)	(0)	(0)
Chargeable amount	4,000	20,000	270,000

The gifts to the son and nephew are PETs – therefore no tax is payable unless Margaret dies within 7 years.

The gift into trust is a CLT and is chargeable during Margaret's lifetime. However, as she has no chargeable gifts in the preceding seven years, there will be no IHT to pay as the gift is covered by the NRB of £325,000 (see later).

Test your understanding 4

Alan	CLT 30.6.2007		PET 30.6.2012		CLT 30.6.2013		CLT 31.12.2016	
		£		£		£		£
Transfer of value		183,000		150,000		191,000		256,000
Less: Annual exemption								
Current year	2007/08	(3,000)	2012/13	(3,000)	2013/14	(3,000)	2016/17	(3,000)
Previous year	2006/07 b/f	(3,000)	2011/12 b/f	(3,000)	2012/13 b/f	(0)	2015/16 b/f	(3,000)
Chargeable amount	Gross	177,000		144,000	Gross	188,000	Net	250,000
NRB @ date of gift	£				£		£	
– 2007/08	300,000							
– 2013/14					325,000			
– 2016/17							325,000	
Less: GCTs < 7 years before gift								
(30.6.2000 – 30.6.2007)	(0)							
(30.6.2006 – 30.6.2013) (ignore PET)					(177,000)			
(31.12.2009 – 31.12.2016) (ignore PET and CLT on 30.6.2007 drops out as too old)							(188,000)	
NRB available		(300,000)				(148,000)		(137,000)
Taxable amount		0		0		40,000		113,000
IHT payable		0		0	@ 20%	8,000	@ 25%	28,250
Paid by						Trustees		Alan
Due date of payment						30.4.2014		30.6.2017
Gross chargeable amount c/f		177,000		144,000		188,000	(£250,000 net + £28,250 tax)	278,250

Test your understanding 5

Simon	CLT 21.4.2008		PET 15.4.2013		CLT 19.3.2014		CLT 9.5.2016	
		£		£		£		£
Transfer of value		123,000		140,000		221,000		395,000
Less: Annual exemption								
Current year	2008/09	(3,000)	2013/14	(3,000)	2013/14	(0)	2016/17	(3,000)
Previous year	2007/08 b/f	(3,000)	2012/13 b/f	(3,000)	2012/13 b/f	(0)	2015/16 b/f	(3,000)
Chargeable amount	Gross	117,000		134,000	Net	221,000	Gross	389,000
NRB @ date of gift	£				£		£	
– 2008/09	312,000							
– 2013/14					325,000			
– 2016/17							325,000	
Less: GCTs < 7 years before gift								
(21.4.2001 – 21.4.2008)	(0)							
(19.3.2007 – 19.3.2014) (ignore PET)					(117,000)			
(9.5.2009 – 9.5.2016) (ignore PET and gift on 21.4.2008 drops out as too old)							(224,250)	
NRB available		(312,000)				(208,000)		(100,750)
Taxable amount		0		0		13,000		288,250
IHT payable		0		0	@ 25%	3,250	@ 20%	57,650
Paid by						Simon		Trustees
Due date of payment						30.9.2014		30.4.2017
Gross chargeable amount		117,000		134,000	(£221,000 net + £3,250 tax)	224,250		389,000

Test your understanding 6

Mr Ambrose

(a) IHT payable during lifetime

		CLT 1.5.2008		**PET 30.6.2009**		**PET 11.6.2010**		**CLT 11.11.2014**
		£		£		£		£
Transfer of value		205,000		60,000		134,000		136,000
Less: Marriage exemption						(1,000)		
Less: Annual exemption								
Current year	2008/09	(3,000)	2009/10	(3,000)	2010/11	(3,000)	2014/15	(3,000)
Previous year	2007/08 b/f	(3,000)	2008/09 b/f	(0)	2009/10 b/f	(0)	2013/14 b/f	(3,000)
Chargeable amount	Net	199,000		57,000		130,000	Gross	130,000
NRB @ date of gift	£						£	
– 2008/09	312,000							
– 2014/15							325,000	
Less: GCTs < 7 years before gift								
(1.5.2001 – 1.5.2008)	(0)							
(11.11.2007 – 11.11.2014)							(199,000)	
(ignore PETs)								
NRB available		(312,000)						(126,000)
Taxable amount		0		0		0		4,000
IHT payable		0		0		0	@ 20%	800
Paid by								Trustees
Due date of payment								31.5.2015
Gross chargeable amount	(£199,000 net + £Nil tax)	199,000		57,000		130,000		130,000

(b) **IHT payable on death**

Date of death: 14 February 2017
7 years before: 14 February 2010

CLT on 1.5.2008 and PET on 30.6.2009 are more than 7 years before death – therefore no IHT payable on death

	PET 11.6.2010		CLT 11.11.2014	
		£		£
Gross chargeable amount b/f (as above)		130,000		130,000
	£		£	
NRB @ date of death – 2016/17	325,000		325,000	
Less: GCTs < 7 years before gift				
(11.6.2003 – 11.6.2010)	(199,000)			
(exclude PET on 30.6.2009 as it became completely exempt)				
(11.11.2007 – 11.11.2014) (£199,000 + £130,000)			(329,000)	
(exclude PET on 30.6.2009 as it became completely exempt, but include 11.6.2010 PET as it became chargeable)				
NRB available		(126,000)		(0)
Taxable amount		4,000		130,000
IHT payable @ 40%		1,600		52,000
Less: Taper relief				
(11.6.2010 – 14.2.2017) (5 – 7 years before death)	(80%)	(1,280)		
(11.11.2014 – 14.2.2017) (< 3 years before death)				(0)
Less: IHT paid in lifetime		(0)		(800)
IHT payable on death		320		51,200
Paid by (always the donee)		Nephew		Trustees
Due date of payment		31.8.2017		31.8.2017

(c) **Nil rate band left to set against the death estate**

	£
NRB @ date of death – 2016/17	325,000
Less: GCTs < 7 yrs before death (14.2.10 to 14.2.17) (£130,000 + £130,000) (first two gifts = too old, include PET on 11.6.10 as it became chargeable on death)	(260,000)
NRB available against death estate	65,000

Test your understanding 7

Tim

(a) **IHT liability arising on the lifetime gift**

Lifetime IHT

30 April 2013 – CLT	£	£
Transfer of value (100,000 × £3.65)		365,000
Less: Annual exemption		
Current year – 2013/14		(3,000)
Previous year – 2012/13 b/f		(3,000)
Net chargeable amount (Tim agreed to pay)		359,000
NRB @ date of gift – 2013/14	325,000	
Less: GCTs in 7 years before gift (30.4.06 to 30.4.13)	(0)	
NRB available		(325,000)
Taxable amount		34,000
IHT payable @ 25%		8,500
Due date (gift in first half of tax year)		30.4.2014
GCT c/f (£359,000 + £8,500)		367,500

IHT payable on death

30 April 2013 – CLT	£	£
GCT b/f (above)		367,500
Less: Fall in value relief		
Value at gift (100,000 × £3.65)	365,000	
Value at Tim's death (100,000 × £3.35)	(335,000)	
Alternative calculation (100,000 × (£3.65 – £3.35))		(30,000)
Revised chargeable amount on death		337,500
NRB @ date of death – 2016/17	325,000	
Less: GCT < 7 years before gift (30.4.06 to 30.4.13)	(0)	
NRB available		(325,000)
Taxable amount		12,500
IHT payable @ 40%		5,000
Less: Taper relief (30.4.13 – 30.6.16) (3 – 4 years before death) (20%)		(1,000)
Less: IHT paid in lifetime (CLT)		(8,500)
IHT payable on death		0

There is no repayment of lifetime IHT paid

(b) **Gross chargeable amount to carry forward to the death estate computation**

Note that Tim's cumulative total to carry forward is the original gross chargeable amount per the lifetime IHT calculation.

Gross cumulative total to carry forward = £367,500

Test your understanding 8

Thomas

IHT payable during lifetime

		CLT 1.6.2007		**PET 16.3.2012**
		£		£
Transfer of value		180,000		228,000
Less: Annual exemption				
Current year	2007/08	(3,000)	2011/12	(3,000)
Previous year	2006/07 b/f	(3,000)	2010/11 b/f	(3,000)
Chargeable amount	Net	174,000		222,000
	£			
NRB @ date of gift – 2007/08	300,000			
Less: GCTs < 7 years before gift (1.6.2000 – 1.6.2007)	(0)			
NRB available		(300,000)		
Taxable amount		0		0
IHT payable		0		0
Gross chargeable amount c/f		174,000		222,000

IHT payable on death

Date of death: 23 April 2016
7 years before: 23 April 2009

CLT on 1.6.2007 is more than 7 years before death – therefore no IHT payable on death

	PET 16.3.2012		Estate value 23.4.2016	
		£		£
Gross chargeable amount		222,000		627,560
	£		£	
NRB @ date of death – 2016/17	325,000		325,000	
Less: GCTs < 7 years before gift (16.3.2005 – 16.3.2012)	(174,000)			
Less: GCTs < 7 years before death (23.4.2009 – 23.4.2016) (earliest CLT on 1.6.2007 drops out, include PET on 16.3.2012 as it became chargeable)			(222,000)	
NRB available		(151,000)		(103,000)
Taxable amount		71,000		524,560
IHT payable @ 40%		28,400		209,824
Less: Taper relief (16.3.2012 – 23.4.2016) (4 – 5 years before death)	(40%)	(11,360)		
Less: IHT paid in lifetime		(0)		
IHT payable on death		17,040		
Paid by		Cousin		Executors
Due date of payment		31.10.2016		31.10.2016

chapter

12

IHT: special valuation rules, reliefs, and the death estate

Chapter learning objectives

Upon completion of this chapter you will be able to:

- identify the basis of valuation for different types of assets
- consider the related party valuation rule, consider when this rule must be used and calculate the effect
- recognise the different types of reliefs available for lifetime and death transfers
- recognise the different types of business property for IHT and the rates of relief
- explain the conditions for business property relief to apply and calculate any restrictions
- recognise the different types of agricultural property for IHT and the rates of relief
- explain the conditions for agricultural property relief to apply
- prepare a death estate computation for IHT and calculate the IHT liability
- identify the relevant exemptions available to reduce the value of the chargeable estate at death
- compute the IHT on a death estate with substantial charitable legacies, when there is an exempt residue and with the transfer of unused nil rate band
- recognise when quick succession relief is available and calculate the effect.

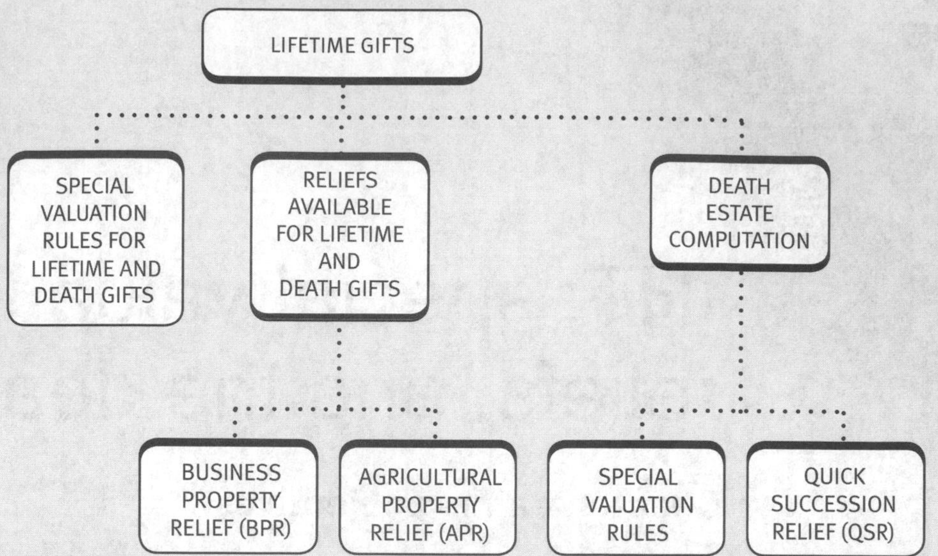

Introduction

This chapter covers further considerations which can affect the calculation of IHT on lifetime gifts, special valuation rules that apply to certain assets, reliefs, and the detailed death estate computation.

1 Special valuation rules for lifetime gifts and the death estate

As stated in the previous chapter, the transfer of value is normally the **open market value (OMV)** of the asset gifted.

However, there are special rules that apply to the valuation of some assets.

Quoted shares and securities

The value of quoted shares and securities for IHT purposes is computed as follows:

Value = Lower of:

(1) 'Quarter Up' method
(using the range of prices quoted on the stock exchange on that day)
= lower price + ¼ × (higher price – lower price).

(2) Average of the highest and lowest recorded bargains.

Note that these valuation rules applied to both IHT and CGT until 6 April 2015.

With effect from 6 April 2015, the rules for IHT remain the same but the rules for CGT lifetime gifts have changed (see Chapter 8).

The range of prices quoted is usually the 'cum dividend' values for shares and 'cum interest' values for securities.

In the examination, always assume shares and securities are quoted 'cum-dividend' and 'cum-interest' unless the question states otherwise.

Quoted ex-dividend or ex-interest

The capital value of shares and securities quoted ex-dividend or ex-interest is calculated as follows:

	Shares quoted ex-dividend	Securities quoted ex-interest
Value using 'lower of' rule	X	X
Plus: next dividend payment (amount received)	X	
Plus: next interest payment (amount received less 20% tax)		X
Capital value to include in the estate	X	X

Meaning of terminology

Quoted cum-dividend or cum-interest

When shares are quoted 'cum-dividend' this means that:

- if the shares are sold, they are sold '**with** the right to the next dividend payment'
- the shareholder buying the shares will therefore receive the next dividend payment.

Similarly, if securities are quoted 'cum-interest', the person buying the securities will receive the next interest payment.

Quoted ex-dividend or ex-interest

When shares are quoted 'ex-dividend' this means:

- if the shares are sold in this period, they are sold '**without** the right to the next dividend payment'
- the shareholder owning the shares on the date they went 'ex-dividend' will receive the next dividend payment.

Similarly, if securities are quoted 'ex-interest', the owners of the securities on the date they went 'ex-interest' will receive the next interest payment.

Therefore, if an individual dies when shares and securities are quoted 'ex-dividend' or 'ex-interest', that individual's estate will be entitled to the next dividend or interest payment which, in practice, is usually received a few weeks later.

Accrued interest to which the deceased was entitled is included in the death estate net of basic rate tax (20%). This is because the executors will be required to account for income tax at the basic rate to HMRC.

Test your understanding 1

Jeremy owns £100,000 of 10% loan notes in XY plc on the day he died. £100 of the loan notes were quoted at £94 – 98 ex-interest. Interest is paid on the loan notes every six months on 30 June and 31 December.

Calculate the value to include in Jeremy's estate in respect of the loan notes.

Valuation of quoted shares and securities

These valuation rules apply to all quoted shares and securities, including:

- investment trusts
- open ended investment companies (OEICs)
- gilt-edged securities
- venture capital trusts (VCTs)
- real estate investment trusts (REITs).

Unquoted shares and securities

The value of unquoted shares and securities to be used has to be agreed with the HMRC's Share Valuation Division.

In an examination question, the value of unquoted shares and securities to be used is given in the question.

For a lifetime gift, the diminution in value calculation will be required (as in Test your understanding 1 in Chapter 11).

Unit trusts

Unit trusts are valued at the lowest bid price (i.e. do not use the 1/4 up rule).

Test your understanding 2

Jimmy Harcourt owns 5,000 units in the Growbig Unit Trust.
At the time of his death they are quoted at 125p – 133p.

Calculate the value of the unit trusts for IHT purposes.

Related property

'Related property' is a concept unique to IHT.

Property is 'related' to the donor's property if it is **property of a similar kind owned by**:

- the **donor's spouse** (or civil partner)
- **an exempt body** as a result of a gift from that person or their spouse (or civil partner).

  An exempt body includes a charity, qualifying political party, national body or housing association.

  Property held by the exempt body is deemed to be related:

  – for as long as that body owns the asset, and

  – for five years after they have disposed of it.

In the examination, the most common related property is **property owned by the donor's spouse** (or civil partner).

Note that property of a similar kind owned by the donor's children or other family members is **not** related property.

The special valuation rules for related property

The related property valuation rules apply to the valuation of:

- unquoted shares
- collections of antiques and chattels
- adjacent plots of land.

However, in the examination, the related property rules normally apply to unquoted shares.

The related property valuation should be calculated as follows:

$$\frac{A}{A + B} \times \text{(Value of the total combined assets of a similar kind)}$$

The meaning of A and B in the formula is slightly different depending on whether the asset is shares or assets other than shares, as follows:

	Assets other than shares	Shares
A =	Value of the donor's asset	Number of shares held by the donor
B =	Value of the related parties' assets	Number of shares held by the related parties

Test your understanding 3

Sara owns two antique chairs which are part of a set of six. Her husband owns another three, and her daughter owns one.

Sara gifts one chair to her son on 23 April 2016.

The values of the chairs on that date are as follows:

1 chair	£5,000
2 chairs	£15,000
3 chairs	£25,000
4 chairs	£40,000
5 chairs	£60,000
6 chairs	£90,000

Calculate the transfer of value relating to the gift of one chair for IHT purposes.

Example 1 – Related property

Ordinary shares in Monsoon Ltd, an unquoted trading company, with an issued share capital of 100 shares of £1 each, are held as follows.

	% of shares (before the gift)
John	40
Geraldine – his wife	35
Jonathan – his son	15
Jennifer – his daughter	10
	100

John gave 5% of his shares to his daughter on 30 June 2016.

The value of the shares on 30 June 2016 was as follows:

	£
100%	150,000
75%	105,000
70%	80,000

Compute the value of the gift to the daughter for IHT purposes before exemptions and reliefs.

Solution	Before the gift % holding	After the gift % holding
John	40%	35%
Geraldine – wife	35%	35%
	75%	70%
Total value	£105,000	£80,000

	£
Value of John's shares before	
(40/75) × £105,000	56,000
Value of John's shares after	
(35/70) × £80,000	(40,000)
Transfer of value	16,000

Test your understanding 4

On 28 November 2016, James gave his son 6,000 ordinary shares in Simons Ltd, an unquoted trading company.

The company's share capital immediately before the transfer comprised 20,000 ordinary shares held as follows:

	Number
James	8,000
His wife	2,000
His brother	5,000
His sister	3,000
His father	2,000
	20,000

The agreed values for the shares are:

Holding	£
75% or more	10
50.01% – 74.99%	8
50% exactly	7
30% – 49.99%	6
10% – 29.99%	4
Under 10%	3

Calculate the transfer of value relating to the gift of shares for IHT purposes.

The need for special related property rules

The special related property valuation rules prevent a married couple (or civil partnership) from deliberately splitting the ownership of similar assets to avoid IHT.

Consider the following scenario:

(i) On 1 July 2016 Joe owned 60% of the share capital of XYZ Ltd, an unquoted company. This shareholding was valued at £600,000.

If Joe were to die on that day the £600,000 would be charged to IHT.

(ii) On 2 July 2016 Joe gave 30% of the XYZ Ltd shareholding to his wife. This transfer, being to a spouse, is exempt from IHT.

A 30% shareholding in XYZ Ltd valued in isolation is worth £200,000.

Without any special rules, if Joe and his wife were to die on that day only £400,000 (2 × £200,000) would be charged.

Two 30% shareholdings are worth less than a 60% shareholding because a 60% holding gives control, whilst a 30% holding is only a minority interest.

(iii) Assume that on 3 July 2016 both Joe and his wife died in a car crash.

Without the related property rules, the estates of Joe and his wife would each include shares valued at £200,000 based on 30% shareholdings and a total of £400,000 is subject to IHT.

However, if Joe had not made the inter-spouse transfer, the 60% interest valued at £600,000 would be chargeable. Therefore, without the special valuation rules, by splitting the interest between the couple, £200,000 of value would escape IHT.

Summary of special valuation rules

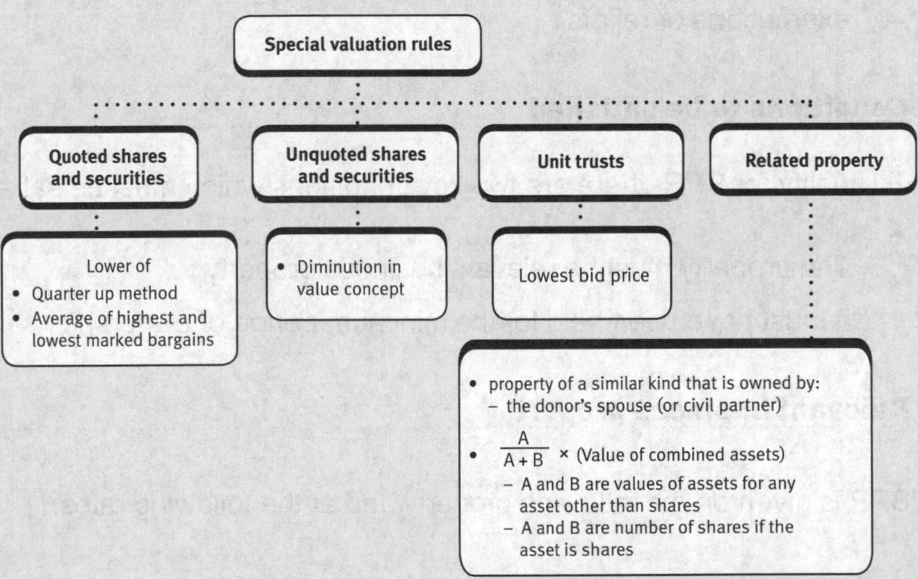

2 Key reliefs available for lifetime and death transfers

There are two key reliefs that are available for both lifetime gifts and transfers on death:

- Business property relief (BPR).
- Agricultural property relief (APR).

3 Business property relief

Business property relief (BPR) is a very important relief that significantly reduces the value of lifetime gifts and the value of an individual's death estate value if certain conditions are satisfied.

The relief:

- is given automatically if the conditions are satisfied, no claim is required
- reduces the transfer of value by either 50% or 100%, depending on the type of business property being transferred
- applies to worldwide relevant business property
- applies to both lifetime transfers and the death estate valuation
- on lifetime gifts, is deducted from the transfer of value **before** any other exemptions or reliefs.

Conditions to be satisfied

To qualify for BPR, there are two key conditions which must be satisfied:

- The property must be relevant business property.
- It must have been held for the minimum period of ownership.

Relevant business property

BPR is given on the following property and at the following rates:

Type of property		% relief
Unincorporated business	• e.g. sole trader or partnership interest	100%
Unquoted shares and securities	• including AIM listed shares and securities • relief on shares is available regardless of the number of shares held • relief is also available for securities in an unquoted company, but only if the individual has voting control of the company immediately before the transfer based on share ownership	100%
Quoted shares and securities	• relief is only available if the individual has voting control of the company immediately before the transfer	50%
Land, buildings, plant or machinery used in a business	• relief is only available if carried on by: – a company in which the donor has control – a partnership in which the donor is a partner	50%

Note that:

- to qualify, an unincorporated business must be a **trading** business and the companies in which the individual has shares must be **trading** companies.
- to determine control, **related property holdings** must be considered.
- BPR is not available if the asset concerned is subject to a **binding contract for sale** at the date of transfer.

  The most common example of where this happens is where a partnership agreement provides for the interest of a partner to be sold to the other partners in the event of death. As a binding contract of sale exists, no BPR is available.

  However, if the agreement provides an option for the other partners to purchase the interest, but not a binding obligation to do so, BPR would be available.

Test your understanding 5

David owns the following assets:

(1) 45% of the ordinary share capital of ABC plc, a quoted trading company.

(2) 15% of the ordinary share capital of DEF Ltd, an unquoted trading company.

(3) A factory owned personally by David, but used in a partnership of which David is not a partner.

(4) 35% of the ordinary share capital of GHI plc, a quoted trading company. David's wife also owns 12% of the share capital, and David's daughter owns a further 6%.

(5) A 25% shareholding in Green Ltd, an AIM listed trading company.

State whether David's assets qualify as relevant business property, and if so state the amount of BPR that will be given.

Minimum period of ownership

To qualify for BPR, the relevant business property must have been held for a minimum period of **two years** immediately preceding the transfer.

If the asset was inherited on the death of a spouse (or civil partner), the couple's combined ownership period is taken into account.

Example 2 – Business property relief

Peter inherited an unincorporated business from his wife on 1 January 2015. Peter died on 30 June 2016. Peter's wife had owned the property for one year.

State whether BPR is available on the unincorporated business on Peter's death.

Solution

Although Peter has owned the property for only 18 months, BPR will be available since his wife's one year period of ownership can be included to make a total combined period of ownership exceeding two years.

Exceptions to the two year qualifying rule

There are two key situations where the two year qualifying rule is not satisfied but BPR is still available. They are as follows:

- Replacement property.

  BPR is still available where

  - the relevant business property has not been held for two years because it **replaced** business property previously held, **and**
  - the individual owned some type of relevant business property for a combined period of ownership of at least **two out of the last five years**.

  BPR is given on the lower of the two property values (i.e. it cannot exceed the BPR that would have been given on the original property).

- Successive transfer.

  BPR is still available where

  - the relevant business property held was eligible for BPR **at the time it was acquired,** and
  - it was either acquired as a result of death, or is now chargeable as a result of death.

Test your understanding 6

On 31 December 2015, an unquoted trading company JKL Ltd was taken over by MNO Ltd, another unquoted trading company. Marsha had owned ordinary shares in JKL Ltd for four years before the takeover. The consideration on the takeover consisted of ordinary shares in MNO Ltd.

On 30 June 2016, Marsha gifted her shares in MNO Ltd to her sister. The shares in MNO Ltd were worth £160,000. She had made no other lifetime gifts.

Her shares in JKL Ltd had been worth £110,000 on 31 December 2015.

Calculate the gross chargeable amount of Marsha's lifetime gift to her sister.

Excepted assets

To qualify for BPR, an unincorporated business must be a **trading** business and the companies in which the individual has shares must be **trading** companies. There is no relief for interests in an investment business.

However, an individual may own an interest in a trading business but that business owns some investment assets (known as "excepted assets"). Where this is the case, BPR is available but the amount of relief is restricted.

Investment activities

The following investment activities prevent BPR from being available:

- dealing in securities, stocks and shares
- dealing in land and buildings
- making or holding investments, which includes the holding of land and buildings that are let.

Definition of excepted assets

An 'excepted asset' is an asset that:

- has not been used wholly or mainly for business purposes during the preceding two years, and
- is not likely to be required for future use in the business.

The main examples of excepted assets are:

- large cash balances in excess of reasonable business requirements
- investments in shares and securities
- investments in land and buildings which are let.

Restriction of BPR

On the transfer of an unincorporated business, BPR is only available on the business assets. No relief is available for excepted assets.

On the transfer of shares in a company that has excepted assets, BPR is only available on the business asset proportion of the total assets in the business, calculated as follows:

$$\text{Transfer of value} \times \frac{\text{Value of total assets less value of excepted assets}}{\text{Value of total assets}}$$

Test your understanding 7

On 31 May 2016, Wendy gifted 40,000 shares in STU Ltd, an unquoted trading company to her niece on the occasion of her marriage. Wendy had owned the shares since 2002 and on 31 May 2016 the shares were worth £180,000.

On that date, STU Ltd owned assets worth £500,000 which included an investment property valued at £50,000.

Wendy had made no other lifetime transfers.

Calculate the gross chargeable amount of Wendy's lifetime gift.

Withdrawal of BPR on death

If conditions are not satisfied at the date of death, BPR is withdrawn when calculating the IHT payable on lifetime gifts due to the death of the donor.

The detailed rules for the withdrawal of BPR are covered in expandable text.

Withdrawal of BPR on death

For lifetime gifts:

- The conditions for BPR are considered at the time of the gift and BPR is given at the appropriate rate when calculating the chargeable amount of a CLT or PET.
- If the gift becomes chargeable on death, BPR must be considered again at the time of death.
- BPR is available again on the death calculation provided:
  - the asset is still relevant business property at the date of death, and
  - the donee still owns the business property (or replacement business property) at the date of the donor's death (or the date of their death, if they predeceased the donor).
- If these two conditions are not satisfied, BPR is withdrawn and is not available in the death calculation.

4 Agricultural property relief

Agricultural property relief (APR) is very similar to BPR, but gives relief for transfers of agricultural property.

The relief:

- is given automatically if the conditions are satisfied, no claim is required
- reduces the transfer of value by 100%
- applies to both lifetime transfers and the death estate valuation
- on lifetime gifts, is deducted from the transfer of value first, **before** any other exemptions and before other reliefs (including BPR).

Conditions to be satisfied

To qualify for APR, there are two key conditions which must be satisfied:

- the property must be relevant agricultural property
- it must have been held for the minimum period of ownership.

Relevant agricultural property

APR is given at a rate of 100% on the **agricultural value** of **agricultural property**.

Agricultural value

The agricultural value is the value of the land and buildings assuming there is a perpetual covenant on the land preventing any other use of the land other than agriculture.

It is likely that the commercial value of the farming land and business will be considerably higher due to its development potential.

The difference between the market value of the business and the agricultural value is often referred to as the development value.

Agricultural property

Agricultural property is defined as the agricultural land and buildings.

Agricultural property therefore includes:

- farm land and pasture
- farm buildings, including the farmhouse, cottages, barns, pig sheds, milking parlours etc.

Unlike BPR, APR is not available on worldwide agricultural property. APR is only **available if** the property **is situated in the UK, the EEA, the Channel Islands or the Isle of Man.**

As with BPR, APR is not available if the asset concerned is subject to a **binding contract for sale** at the date of transfer.

APR at 50%

APR is available at 100% on most agricultural property.

However, only 50% relief is available if a farm is:

- a tenanted farm, and
- the lease was taken out before 1 September 1995, and
- at the date of transfer the owner does not have the right to obtain vacant possession within the next two years.

Minimum period of ownership

To qualify for APR, the agricultural property must have been held for the following minimum periods:

Agricultural property farmed by:	Minimum ownership period:
– the owner	**Two** years
– a tenant	**Seven** years

Exceptions to the minimum period

The same exceptions to the rule for BPR apply to APR (i.e. the replacement property provisions and successive transfers rule).

However, the replacement property rules are slightly different. APR is available where:

- the individual owned some type of relevant agricultural property for a combined period of ownership of:
  - at least **two** out of the last **five years** if farmed by the owner
  - at least **seven** out of the last **ten years** if farmed by a tenant.

The interaction of APR and BPR

Where agricultural property forms part of an unincorporated farming business, APR is given before BPR. Double relief is not available on the same value.

However, APR is only available on the agricultural value. Therefore, subject to the relevant conditions for BPR being met, BPR will then be available on any value of the remaining business assets that do not qualify for APR.

Note that if the farm is tenanted and it is not the owner's farming business, no BPR is available on the remaining business assets as they are investment assets, not the owner's trading assets.

Test your understanding 8

Zac plans to gift his farming business and £20,000 cash to his grandson on the occasion of his marriage in the tax year 2016/17. He has made no other lifetime gifts in the preceding seven years.

Zac lives on the farm and has owned and worked the business for the last seventeen years.

A surveyor has recently valued Zac's farm and its land as follows:

	£
Agricultural value	600,000
Development value	400,000
Market value of farm land and buildings	1,000,000
Animals and inventory	150,000
Plant and machinery and motor vehicles	80,000
Market value of farming business	1,230,000

Calculate the chargeable amount of Zac's gift to his grandson.

Shares in a farming company

APR is available in respect of shares in a farming company provided:

- the individual has control of the company
- the minimum period of ownership condition is satisfied.

Note that:

- to determine control, **related property holdings** must be considered (see above).
- APR is only given against the agricultural value that can be attributed to the shares. BPR may be due on some or all of the remainder.
- APR will be restricted where the farming company holds excepted assets in the same way as for BPR.

Example 3 – Agricultural property relief

Since 2003, John has owned a 75% shareholding in Arable Ltd, an unquoted trading company which owns farm land.

On 31 October 2016 John gifted the shares to his daughter when they were worth £375,000 and the accounts of Arable Ltd show:

	£
Farm land	350,000
Other assets	150,000
	500,000

The farm land has been let to tenants for the previous nine years.

The agricultural value of the farm land was £300,000. The other assets of £150,000 were all used in Arable Ltd's trade.

Calculate the gross chargeable amount of the gift to John's daughter.

Solution

APR is available as:

- Arable Ltd's farm land has been let out for the previous nine years
- John has a controlling shareholding in the company.

In addition, as the shareholding is in an unquoted company, BPR is available on any amount that does not qualify for APR, subject to the relevant BPR conditions being satisfied.

	£
Transfer of value – shares in farming company	375,000
Less: APR on agricultural value (Note)	
(£300,000/£500,000) × £375,000 × 100%	(225,000)
BPR on Arable Ltd's other assets	
(£150,000/£500,000) × £375,000 × 100%	(112,500)
Less: AE – 2016/17	(3,000)
– 2015/16 b/f	(3,000)
Gross chargeable amount	31,500

Note: APR is only available on the agricultural value of the farm land that can be attributed to the shares transferred.

BPR is available on the value that can be attributed to the business assets in Arable Ltd (i.e. the 'other assets'). BPR is not available on the development value of the farm land attributed to the shares as the farm is tenanted (i.e. not owned and farmed by Arable Ltd).

Withdrawal of APR on death

In the same way as for BPR, if conditions are not satisfied at the date of death, APR is withdrawn when calculating the IHT payable on lifetime gifts due to the death of the donor.

Withdrawal of APR on death

- For lifetime gifts, the conditions for APR are considered at the time of the gift and APR is given at the appropriate rate when calculating the chargeable amount of a CLT or PET.
- If the gift becomes chargeable on death, APR must be considered again at the time of death. APR is available again on the death calculation provided:
  - the asset is still relevant agricultural property at the date of death, and
  - the donee still owns the agricultural property (or replacement property) at the date of the donor's death (or at the date of their death, if they predeceased the donor).
- If these two conditions are not satisfied, APR is withdrawn and is not available in the death calculation.

5 Summary of reliefs available for lifetime and death transfers

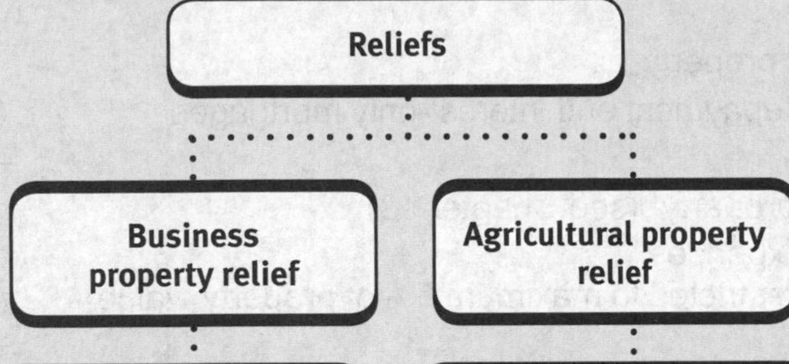

Business property relief

- Automatic
- Lifetime gifts and death estate
- Deduct 50% or 100% before exemptions and other reliefs
- Must be relevant business property held for at least two years
- Worldwide relevant business property qualifies
- Must be a trading business
- No relief for excepted assets
- BPR may be withdrawn if conditions not satisfied at death

Agricultural property relief

- Automatic
- Lifetime gifts and death estate
- Deduct 100% before exemptions and other reliefs
- Relief for agricultural value of agricultural property held for at least two years (seven years if tenanted farm)
- BPR may be available on the remaining value
- Available on agricultural property in the EEA, not worldwide
- APR may be withdrawn if conditions not satisfied at death

6 The death estate computation

The death estate includes all assets held at the date of death.

The value of assets brought into an individual's estate computation is normally the **open market value (OMV)** of the asset at the date of death (known as the probate value).

However, as we have seen, there are special rules that apply to the valuation of some assets.

The gross chargeable value of an individual's estate is calculated using the following pro forma:

Pro forma death estate computation

		£	£
Freehold property		x	
Less:	Repayment and interest-only mortgages	(x)	
		——	x
Foreign property* (see Chapter 13)		x	
Less:	Expenses (restricted to maximum 5% of property value)	(x)	
		——	x
Business owned by sole trader/partnership*			x
Farm*			x
Stocks and shares (including ISAs)*			x
Government securities			x
Insurance policy proceeds			x
Death in service policy			x
Leasehold property			x
Motor cars			x
Personal chattels			x
Debts due to the deceased			x
Interest and rent due to the deceased			x
Cash at bank and on deposit (including ISAs)			x
			——
			x
Less:	Debts due by the deceased	(x)	
	Outstanding taxes (e.g. IT, CGT due)	(x)	
	Funeral expenses	(x)	
		——	(x)
			——
			x
Less:	Exempt legacies (e.g. to spouse, charity, political party)		(x)
			——
Net free estate			x
Add:	Gift with reservation (GWR)		x
Add:	Settled property (interest in an IPDI trust) (Chapter 14)		x
			——
Gross chargeable estate			x
			——

Note that

- * These items may be reduced by BPR/APR if conditions are satisfied
- All net assets are included in the estate (including cars, ISAs etc) as there are no exempt assets for IHT.

The IHT liability on the estate value is then calculated as follows:

	£
IHT on chargeable estate (per Chapter 11)	x
Less: Quick succession relief (QSR) (section 11)	(x)
	X_A
Calculate the average estate rate (AER) = (X_A/chargeable estate) × 100	
Less: Double tax relief (DTR) (see Chapter 13)	
Lower of:	
(i) Overseas tax suffered	
(ii) AER × overseas property value in estate	(x)
IHT payable	X

Due date: Earlier of

- six months after end of month of death
- on delivery of estate accounts to HMRC

Allocation of IHT payable:

- The IHT payable on the estate is apportioned between different elements of the estate at the AER (after QSR).
- The tax on settled property is payable by the trustees.
- The tax on a GWR is payable by the beneficiary receiving the GWR.
- The remaining tax on death is initially paid by the executors.

  However, where there is overseas property, it is then apportioned between the UK and overseas element of the estate.
- The tax relating to the overseas property (after DTR) is recovered from the person inheriting the asset (i.e. the specific legatee).

  The gift of foreign property from an estate is therefore referred to as a 'tax bearing legacy'.
- The remainder of the tax relating to the UK assets is paid from the estate, and so is effectively borne by the person who inherits the residue of the assets after the specific legacies have been paid (known as the residuary legatee).

  Accordingly, specific legacies of UK assets do not bear any tax and are referred to as 'tax-free legacies'.

Allowable deductions in the death estate computation

Mortgages

Endowment mortgages are not deductible from the property value in the death estate computation. This is because the endowment element of the policy should cover the repayment of the mortgage on the owner's death and therefore there is no mortgage outstanding.

However, repayment and interest-only mortgages are still outstanding at the owner's death and are therefore deductible from the property value.

Funeral expenses

The costs of the individual's funeral are **allowable** providing they are reasonable, even though the cost is incurred after the date of death.

Reasonable costs of mourning clothes for the family and the cost of a tombstone are also allowable.

Costs of administering the estate

The cost of administering the estate by the executors/personal representatives is **not an allowable deduction** as it is for professional services carried out after the death.

Other allowable deductions

Debts are deductible if they:

- were outstanding at the date of death, and
- had been incurred for valuable consideration, or were imposed by law (i.e. legally enforceable debts).

Note that a 'promise' to pay a friend is not legally enforceable and therefore not deductible. Gambling debts are not incurred for valuable consideration and cannot be deducted.

This will include all outstanding taxes such as income tax, NICs and CGT, although not the IHT due on death itself.

If a debt is secured against specific property it is deducted from the value of that property. This will be the case with a repayment, or interest only mortgage secured against freehold property (see above).

Exempt legacies

The only exempt legacies that are allowable in the death estate are gifts to:

- the spouse or civil partner
- a charity
- a qualifying political party.

The detail of these exemptions has been covered in Chapter 11.

Reliefs

- BPR and APR may be available to reduce the value of an individual's death estate.

Transfer of ISA on death

Remember that on death, if ISA savings are left to the spouse/civil partner:

- the gift is an exempt legacy, and
- in addition, an ISA allowance equal to the deceased individual's ISA savings can be claimed by the surviving spouse/civil partner (Chapter 3).

As a result, the deceased individual's ISA savings will retain their beneficial tax treatment (i.e. exemption from income tax and capital gains tax) in the future, in the hands of the surviving spouse/civil partner.

Note however that the surviving spouse/civil partner is entitled to the allowance even if the ISA assets are left to someone else.

If this is the case, there will be no exempt legacy in the death estate computation, but the surviving spouse will be able to invest an additional amount of their own funds into an ISA to benefit from the ISA exemptions in the future.

Test your understanding 9

Tom died on 30 June 2016 leaving the following assets:

	£
House	200,000
Cottage	250,000
Unincorporated business	400,000
Bank account	75,000
Quoted shares in a trading company	100,000
Car	15,000

At the date of his death Tom owed £2,000 on his credit card, and £3,000 of income tax and CGT. Tom has owned the business for 20 years.

In Tom's will he left

- the business, the house and shares to his wife
- the cottage to his son
- the residue to his daughter.

Tom made a lifetime gift of £115,000 in cash to his son in August 2012.

Compute the IHT payable on Tom's death.

7 Special valuation rules affecting the death estate

Land and freehold property situated in the UK

When land and property is owned by two or more individuals, they own the property as either 'joint tenants' or 'tenants in common' which means that on the death of a tenant their share is inherited:

Joint tenants	Tenants in common
• automatically by the other tenant(s)	• in accordance with the terms of their will, or • in accordance with the rules of intestacy.

The valuation of the UK land and property to be included in the estate computation is the appropriate proportion of the value of the whole property for joint tenants. Usually this is one half of the whole as there are normally two joint tenants.

For tenants in common the value is negotiated and agreed with HMRC, but for the examination assume the value is 10% lower than the OMV.

Example 4 – Tenants in common

A brother and a sister jointly own a property as tenants in common worth £500,000.

Calculate the value of the brother and sister's share in the property for IHT purposes if they were to consider making a transfer of their share in the property.

Solution

The value of half the property would be on a 'stand-alone' basis. This is the OMV of the half share of the property on the open market which is unlikely to be 50% of the whole value.

However, who would buy half a house?

The Capital Taxes Division of HMRC accepts that a 'tenanted deduction' of between 5% to 15% from the OMV is appropriate for IHT valuation purposes.

For exam purposes, always assume a deduction of 10%.

	£
Half the value of the property (£500,000 × ½)	250,000
Less: 10% deduction	(25,000)
Value of the half share for IHT purposes	225,000

Life assurance policies

The IHT valuation of a life assurance policy (LAP) is as follows:

Terms of the policy	**Value to include in the estate**
LAP taken out on one's own life	Actual proceeds received by the estate
LAP written specifically for the benefit of a named beneficiary (e.g. the spouse and/or children) under a declaration of trust	Excluded from the estate

Note that:

- OMV is not necessarily the same as the surrender value.
- For a death in service policy (i.e. an insurance policy taken out by an employer on the life of an employee), in the event that the employee dies, the insurance company will pay out a lump sum to the beneficiaries of the estate. This lump sum forms part of the deceased's death estate.

Settled property

The beneficiary of an interest in possession (IIP) trust is known as the 'life tenant' of the trust.

The life tenant is entitled to an interest in the assets of the trust which is usually the right to the income generated by the assets in the trust fund.

For IHT purposes, the life tenant of an immediate post death interest (IPDI) trust is deemed to own the underlying assets in the trust fund.

For these types of IIP trusts, HMRC require the trust to pay an IHT liability on the death of the life tenant which is calculated as follows:

- The value of the trust fund is included in the individual life tenant's estate computation on death (this is known as 'settled property').
- The IHT on the whole estate is calculated and then the average rate of tax on the estate is calculated.
- The trustees pay the IHT relating to the value of the trust fund.
- The IHT is payable out of the trust assets.

The calculation of total IHT payable on an individual's death estate, including settled property, is examinable. However, the allocation of how much of the total IHT is payable by the trustees is not examinable.

On the death of the life tenant, the trust fund is usually wound up and the capital assets are distributed to the final beneficiary named in the trust deed, known as the 'remainderman' of the trust.

The remainderman therefore suffers the tax charge levied on the trust following the death of the life tenant.

The detailed rules concerning the different types of trusts and the appropriate treatment for IHT purposes are given in Chapter 14.

8 Factors affecting calculation of IHT liability on estate

Transfer of unused nil rate band

Any amount of NRB that has not been utilised at the time of a person's death can be transferred to their spouse or civil partner.

As a result, each spouse or civil partner can leave the whole of their estate to the surviving spouse or civil partner and the couple will not lose the benefit of the NRB.

- The surviving spouse or civil partner will have the benefit of
  - their own NRB, **and**
  - any unused proportion of their spouse's or civil partner's NRB.
- The increased amount can be used against any lifetime gifts taxable as a result of the donor's death and the death estate.
- The amount of the NRB that can be claimed is based on the **proportion** that was **unused by the first spouse** to die.
- The unused proportion is applied to the **NRB available on the second spouse's death**.
- The executors of the surviving spouse or civil partner must claim the transferred NRB by submitting the IHT return by the later of:
  - 2 years of the second death, or
  - 3 months of the executor starting to act.

Test your understanding 10

Joan was widowed on the death of her husband Neil on 21 June 2005.

Neil had a chargeable estate valued at £800,000, and this was left entirely to Joan.

Joan died on 23 May 2016 leaving an estate valued at £1 million, to her two children.

Joan has made no lifetime transfers.

Calculate the IHT liability due as a result of Joan's death assuming:

(a) **Neil made no lifetime transfers**

(b) **Neil gave £176,950 to his son on 16 March 2005.**

Reduced rate of IHT for substantial legacies to charity

A reduced death rate of 36% applies to estates in which 10% or more of the 'baseline amount' is left to a qualifying charity.

The 'baseline amount' is the taxable estate:

- after deducting exemptions, reliefs and available nil rate band, but
- before deducting the charitable legacies.

Method for calculating the appropriate rate of tax to apply:

(1) Add back the charitable legacies to the taxable estate = 'baseline amount'.

(2) Calculate 10% of the 'baseline amount' and compare to the amount of charitable legacies left on death.

(3) Tax the taxable estate at the following rate:
If charitable legacies ≥ 10% rule: 36%
If charitable legacies < 10% rule: 40%.

Test your understanding 11

Han died on 1 May 2016 leaving an estate consisting of:

House	£320,000
Quoted shares	£145,000
Cash	£67,000

Han owed tax of £3,200 at his death. In his will he left £215,000 to his wife and £40,000 to Oxfam, a UK registered charity.

Han had made one lifetime gift to his son of £310,000 on 10 April 2013.

Calculate the amount of IHT due as a result of Han's death.

Tax planning

IHT may be saved by increasing a charitable legacy, using a deed of variation (see Chapter 13), to ensure that:

- the charitable donations exceed the 10% rule, and
- thereby reduce the tax on the whole estate to 36%.

9 Comprehensive example – death estate

The following example involves a death estate computation using the special valuation rules.

Test your understanding 12

Wilma died in a car crash on 4 October 2016.

Under the terms of her will, the estate was left as follows:

- £120,000 to her husband
- £50,000 to the Conservative Party
- the residue of the estate to her son Joe.

At the date of her death, Wilma owned the following assets.

(i) Her main residence valued at £243,000.

(ii) A flat in London valued at £150,000. An endowment mortgage of £70,000 was secured on this property.

(iii) Four shops valued at £50,000 each. Wilma's husband Fred owns two adjacent shops valued at £60,000 each. The combined value of all six shops is £370,000.

(iv) A villa situated overseas worth $200,000. The exchange rate on 4 October 2016 was $10 to £1.

(v) A half share of partnership assets which are valued at £400,000 in total. The partnership trades in the UK. Wilma had been a partner for several years.

(vi) 20,000 shares in ZAM plc. The shares were quoted at 198p – 206p, with bargains of 196p, 199p and 208p.

(vii) 8,000 units in the CBA unit trust, valued at 130p – 136p.

(viii) Bank balances of £57,850.

Wilma is also the life tenant of an immediate post death interest trust. The value of the trust fund on 4 October 2016 was £260,000.

Wilma's outstanding income tax liability was £7,500, and her funeral expenses amounted to £2,000. She had made no lifetime gifts.

Calculate the IHT that will be payable as a result of Wilma's death.

Explain who will pay and who will suffer the IHT liability.

10 Reliefs available against the IHT liability on the death estate

There are two tax credit reliefs that **reduce the IHT liability on the death estate** as follows:

	£
IHT on chargeable estate	x
Less: **Quick succession relief (QSR)**	(x)
Double tax relief (DTR) (See Chapter 13)	(x)
	——
UK inheritance tax payable	x
	——

11 Quick succession relief

Quick succession relief (QSR) applies where an individual dies and **within the previous five years** they had:

- **inherited an asset** on someone else's death, and IHT was charged on the inheritance, or
- **received a lifetime gift,** and IHT was charged on the gift.

The most common situation is where two members of a family die within a five year period, the first person to die having made a bequest to the second person.

QSR is a **tax credit** against the IHT liability of an estate on the death of the individual receiving the asset.

The amount of QSR where two deaths occur within a five year period is calculated as follows:

QSR = (IHT on first death) × (Appropriate percentage)

The appropriate percentages are as follows:

Years between the two deaths		Appropriate percentage
More than	Not more than	used in formula above
0	1	100%
1	2	80%
2	3	60%
3	4	40%
4	5	20%

The IHT paid on the first death is either given in the question or can be calculated as follows:

$$\frac{\text{Total IHT paid on first death estate}}{\text{Gross chargeable estate value of first death}} \times \text{Value of asset gifted out of the first estate}$$

The following points should be noted:

- **The appropriate percentages are not given in the examination.** However, note that:
  - the closer the two deaths, the greater the percentage
  - each additional year between the gifts reduces the percentage by 20%.
- It is not necessary for the individual who received the asset to still own the property they received on date of their death. Even though the same asset is not subject to a double charge to IHT as it is not included in the second estate, QSR is still available. This is because the second person's estate will have a higher value following the gift to him whether the original property is retained, exchanged for other property or is converted into cash.
- QSR is given **before** DTR.

Test your understanding 13

Daisy died on 31 July 2016 leaving an estate of £340,000. She had made no lifetime gifts.

In June 2012, Daisy had been left £28,000 from her brother's estate. Inheritance tax of £75,000 was paid on a total chargeable estate of £450,000 as a consequence of her brother's death.

Calculate the IHT payable on Daisy's death.

Legacies left on death and single grossing up

The terms of a person's will are very important in determining the amount of IHT payable on death.

This section summarises rules already covered in relation to exempt legacies and gifts of specific UK assets to a chargeable person, but extends the situation to cover exempt residues where special rules apply.

Exempt legacy

Gifts to the following persons are exempt from IHT on death:

- Spouse or civil partner.
- Charity.
- Qualifying political party.

Where an exempt person is left a legacy in a will, the amount of the legacy is deducted in the calculation of the gross chargeable estate.

Specific gift of UK assets left to a chargeable person

Where a chargeable person is left a legacy of a specific UK asset, the IHT on the legacy is borne by the residuary legatee (i.e. the person who is left the residue of the estate in the will) not the specific legatee who receives the asset. The specific gift is a 'tax free' legacy.

For example, if you are left £100,000 in your grandfather's will, you will receive all £100,000. The IHT payable on the gift to you is borne by the person who is left the residue of your grandfather's estate.

This will cause no problems in the calculation of IHT where the residuary legatee is a chargeable person. However, where the residuary legatee is an exempt person, special rules apply to calculate the IHT on the estate.

Exempt residue

Special rules known as 'single grossing up' (SGU) are required where the terms of the deceased's will (or the rules of intestacy) leave gifts from the estate as follows:

- specific gift(s) of UK assets are left to a chargeable person(s), **and**
- the residue of the estate is left to an exempt person.

To find the IHT payable it is necessary to calculate the amount of chargeable assets that would be needed so that **after** the tax was paid, the amount left will pay the specific legacies.

The total of the specific gifts of UK assets is the **net** chargeable estate.

Accordingly, the IHT payable is calculated as:
(Net chargeable estate – NRB available) × 40/60

Note that the gross death rate of tax applied to the gross chargeable estate is 40% on the excess over the NRB available. Therefore the net rate of death tax is 40/60.

Once the IHT payable is calculated, the gross chargeable estate can be calculated as:
(Net chargeable estate **plus** IHT payable)

The amount allocated to the exempt residuary legatee will be the balancing amount.

Example 5 – Single grossing up

Edward Ager was a wealthy client of yours. His estate value is £900,000 and he had made no lifetime gifts.

By his will he left the following gifts:

- Holiday cottage £180,000 to his son.
- Legacies of £110,000 each in cash to his two daughters.
- Legacy of £50,000 cash to charity.
- Residue to his wife.

(a) **Compute the gross chargeable estate value, the IHT payable and the amount of residue which will pass to Edward's wife.**

(b) **Calculate how your answer would differ if Edward had made gross chargeable lifetime gifts of £267,000.**

Solution

(a) **Estate computation**

		£
Estate value		900,000
Less:	Exempt legacies	
	Charity	(50,000)
	Spouse (balancing figure)	(400,000)
Gross chargeable estate (W)		450,000
IHT liability on the estate value (W)		50,000

Distribution of the estate

	£
Residue to wife	400,000
Gift to charity	50,000
Cottage to son	180,000
Legacies to daughters (£110,000 × 2)	220,000
IHT on legacies to HMRC	50,000
	900,000

Working: Single grossing up

	£
Specific chargeable legacies	
Holiday cottage to the son	180,000
Legacies to the daughters (£110,000 × 2)	220,000
Net chargeable estate	400,000
IHT liability on estate:	
Net chargeable estate value	400,000
Less: NRB available	(325,000)
Taxable amount	75,000
IHT on death (£75,000 × 40/60)	50,000
Gross chargeable estate (£400,000 + £50,000)	450,000

(b) **Estate computation**

	£
Estate value	900,000
Less: Exempt legacies	
Charity	(50,000)
Spouse (balancing figure)	(222,000)
Gross chargeable estate (W)	628,000
IHT liability on the estate value (W)	228,000

Distribution of the estate

	£
Residue to wife	222,000
Gift to charity	50,000
Cottage to son	180,000
Legacies to daughters	220,000
IHT on legacies to HMRC	228,000
	900,000

Working: Single grossing up

		£
Specific chargeable legacies		£
Holiday cottage to the son		180,000
Legacies to the daughters (£110,000 × 2)		220,000
Net chargeable estate		400,000
IHT liability on estate:	£	£
Net chargeable estate value		400,000
NRB @ date of death	325,000	
Less: GCTs < 7 yrs before death	(267,000)	
NRB available		(58,000)
Taxable amount		342,000
IHT on death (£342,000 × 40/60)		228,000
Gross chargeable estate (£400,000 + £228,000)		628,000

Example 6 – Single grossing up

Alex died on 30 September 2016 leaving an estate valued at £664,000.

Under the terms of his will Alex left £331,000 to his son Raymond and the residue of the estate to his widow. Alex had made no lifetime gifts.

(a) **Calculate the IHT payable on Alex's death.**

(b) **Show how Alex's estate will be distributed between the beneficiaries.**

(c) **Show how the situation would change if Alex's widow was left £331,000 and Raymond was left the residue of the estate.**

Solution

(a) **Estate computation**

	£
Estate value	664,000
Less: Exempt legacies	
Spouse (balancing figure)	(329,000)
Gross chargeable estate (W)	335,000
IHT liability on the estate value (W)	4,000

Working: Single grossing up

	£
Specific chargeable legacies	
Cash to the son = Net chargeable estate	331,000

IHT liability on estate:	£
Net chargeable estate value	331,000
Less: NRB available	(325,000)
Taxable amount	6,000
IHT on death (£6,000 × 40/60)	4,000
Gross chargeable estate (£331,000 + £4,000)	335,000

(b) **Distribution of the estate**

	£
Residue to wife	329,000
Cash to son	331,000
IHT on Raymond's legacy to HMRC	4,000
	664,000

(c) **Estate computation**

	£
Estate value	664,000
Less: Exempt legacies	
Spouse	(331,000)
Gross chargeable estate	333,000
IHT liability on estate	
Gross chargeable estate value	333,000
Less: NRB available	(325,000)
Taxable amount	8,000
IHT on death (£8,000 × 40%)	3,200

Distribution of the estate	£
Residue to wife	331,000
Cash to son (£333,000 – £3,200)	329,800
IHT on Raymond's legacy to HMRC	3,200
	664,000

12 Summary of death estate

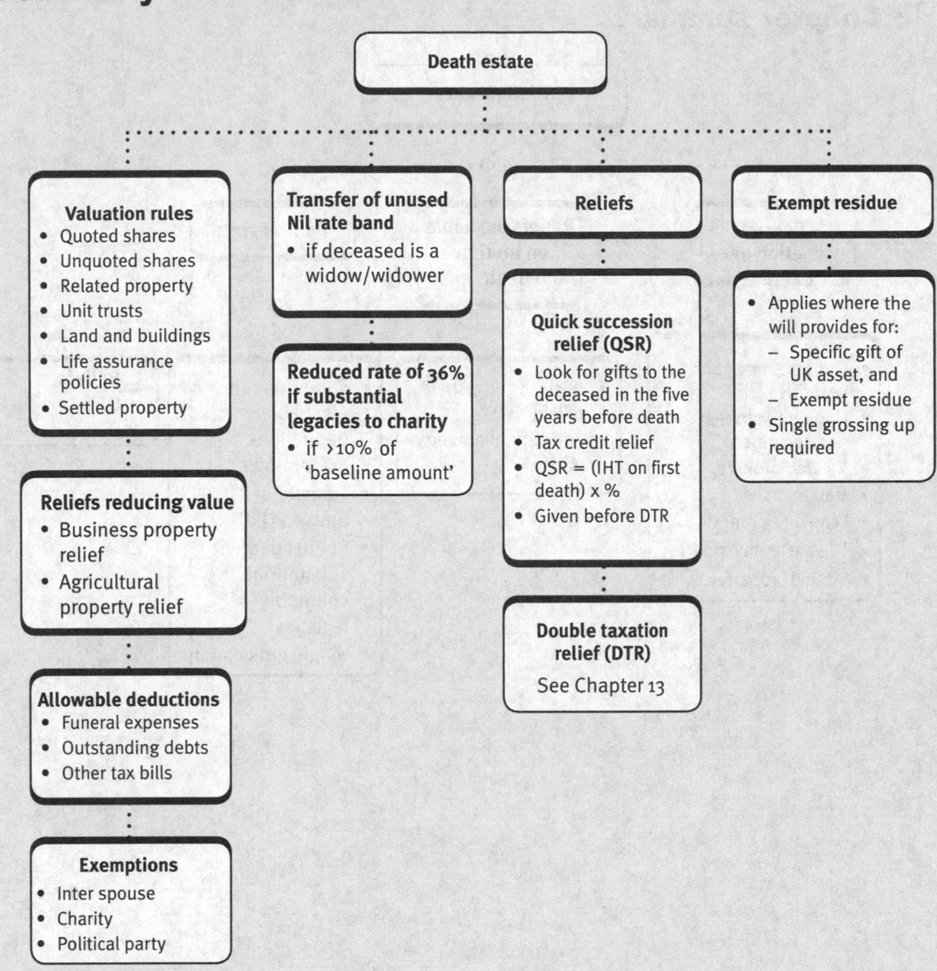
Death estate
Valuation rules
• Quoted shares
• Unquoted shares
• Related property
• Unit trusts
• Land and buildings
• Life assurance policies
• Settled property
Reliefs reducing value
• Business property relief
• Agricultural property relief
Allowable deductions
• Funeral expenses
• Outstanding debts
• Other tax bills
Exemptions
• Inter spouse
• Charity
• Political party
Transfer of unused Nil rate band
• if deceased is a widow/widower
Reduced rate of 36% if substantial legacies to charity
• if >10% of 'baseline amount'
Reliefs
Quick succession relief (QSR)
• Look for gifts to the deceased in the five years before death
• Tax credit relief
• QSR = (IHT on first death) x %
• Given before DTR
Double taxation relief (DTR)
See Chapter 13
Exempt residue
• Applies where the will provides for:
– Specific gift of UK asset, and
– Exempt residue
• Single grossing up required

13 Chapter summary

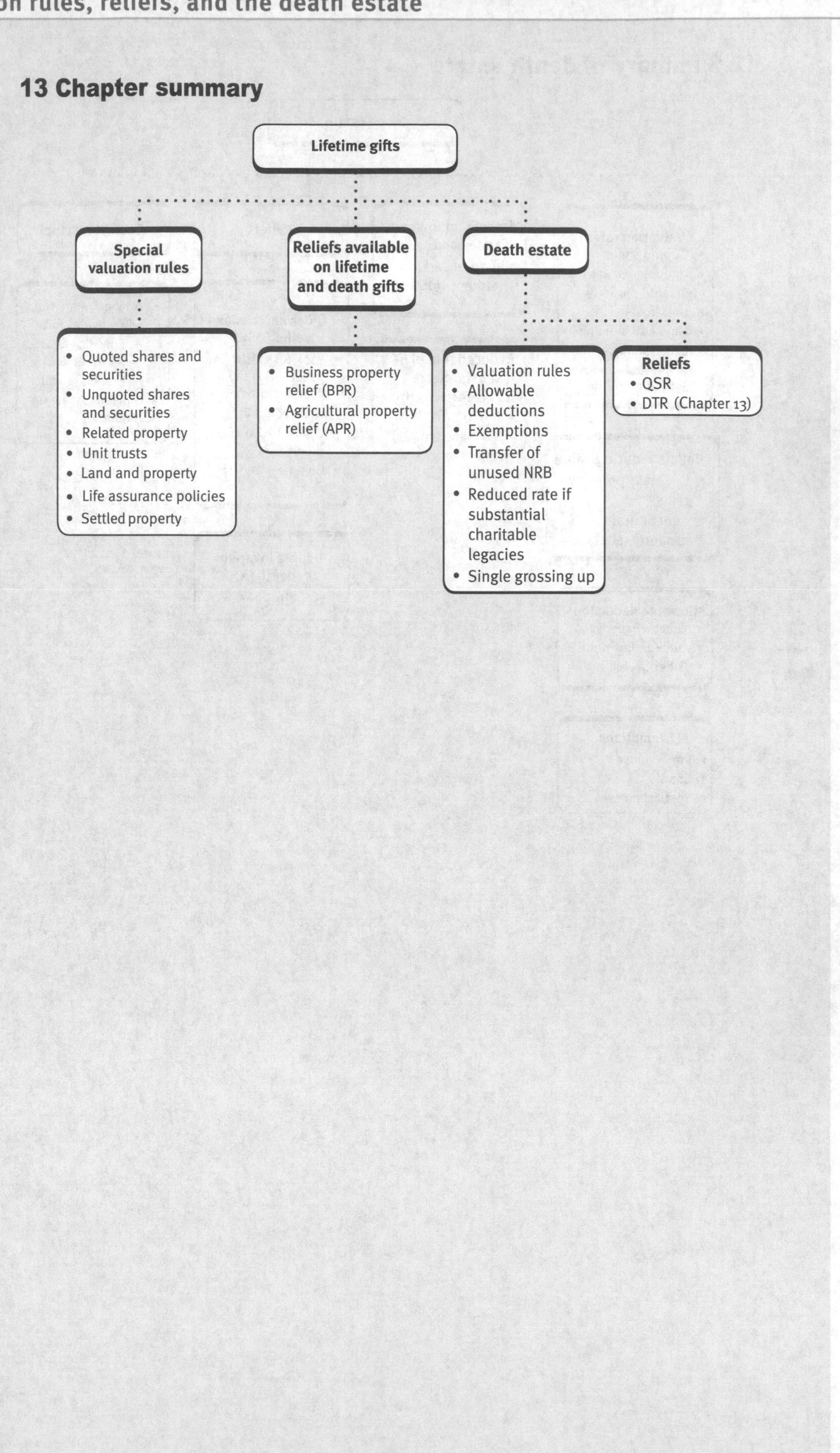

Test your understanding answers

Test your understanding 1

Jeremy

Company loan notes

Capital value = ¼ up method = 94 + (98 – 94) × ¼
= £95 per £100 of loan notes

Value of £100,000 loan notes:

	£
£100,000 × 95/100	95,000
Add: Next **net** interest payment	
£100,000 × **6/12** × 10% × 80%	4,000
Capital value	99,000

Test your understanding 2

Jimmy Harcourt

Value of 5,000 units = (5,000 × £1.25) = £6,250

Test your understanding 3

Sara

Before the gift, Sara and her husband own five chairs between them. After the gift, they own four chairs between them.

Note that the chair owned by the daughter is not related property.

The value of Sara's two chairs before the gift is:
[£15,000/(£15,000 + £25,000)] × £60,000 = £22,500

The value of Sara's one chair after the gift is:
[£5,000/(£5,000 + £25,000)] × £40,000 = £6,667

The transfer of value is therefore:

	£
Value of estate before transfer	22,500
Less: Value of estate after transfer	(6,667)
Transfer of value	15,833

Note that this value is significantly higher than the unrelated value of one chair = £5,000.

For CGT purposes, the MV of the asset gifted is used to start the computation (i.e. MV of one chair = £5,000).

Test your understanding 4

James

	Before the gift No. of shares	After the gift No. of shares
James	8,000	2,000
Wife	2,000	2,000
	10,000	4,000
% Holding	50%	20%
Value per share	£7	£4

The value of James' shares before the gift is:
(8,000 × £7) = £56,000

The value of James' shares after the gift is:
(2,000 × £4) = £8,000

The transfer of value is therefore:

	£
Value of Simons Ltd shares before the gift	56,000
Less: Value of Simons Ltd shares after the gift	(8,000)
Transfer of value	48,000

Test your understanding 5

David

(1) There is no entitlement to BPR as ABC plc is a quoted company and David does not have a controlling interest.

(2) BPR is available at the rate of 100% as DEF Ltd is an unquoted trading company.

(3) There is no entitlement to BPR as David is not a partner of the partnership. In this instance, the property is effectively held by David as an investment.

(4) There is no BPR since GHI plc is a quoted company, and David does not have a controlling interest even when taking account of his wife's shares.

(5) 100% BPR is given as Green Ltd is an AIM listed trading company.

Test your understanding 6

JKL Ltd

The shares in MNO Ltd have only been held for six months. However, BPR at 100% is available as Marsha has held relevant business property (MNO Ltd shares and JKL Ltd shares) for more than 2 years out of the last five years.

The amount of BPR will be restricted to £110,000 as it cannot exceed the amount of BPR that would have been given on the original property that was replaced.

Therefore, the gross chargeable amount of Marsha's PET to her sister:

	£
Transfer of value	160,000
Less: BPR	(110,000)
AE – 2016/17	(3,000)
– 2015/16 b/f	(3,000)
	–––––––
Gross chargeable amount	44,000
	–––––––

Test your understanding 7

Wendy

31 May 2016 Gift to her niece = PET

	£
Transfer of value	180,000
Less: BPR	
100% × £180,000 × (£450,000/£500,000)	(162,000)
ME	(1,000)
AE – 2016/17	(3,000)
– 2015/16 b/f	(3,000)
	–––––––
Gross chargeable amount	11,000
	–––––––

Test your understanding 8

Zac

		£
Transfer of value	– Farming business	1,230,000
	– Cash	20,0000
		1,250,000
Less:	APR on agricultural value	
	(£600,000 × 100%)	(600,000)
	BPR on remaining value	
	(£400,000 + £150,000 + £80,000) × 100%	(630,000)
	ME (grandparent to grandchild)	(2,500)
	AE – 2016/17	(3,000)
	– 2015/16 b/f	(3,000)
Gross chargeable amount		11,500

Note: Items such as the development value of the farm, the farm animals, inventory and farming equipment do not qualify for APR.

However, as it is Zac's unincorporated business and he has owned and worked the farm for more than 2 years, BPR is available.

If the farm was owned by Zac but let to tenants who worked the farm, APR would be available on the agricultural value but BPR would not be available on the remainder.

Test your understanding 9

Tom

Death estate – 30 June 2016

		£	£
House			200,000
Cottage			250,000
Unincorporated business		400,000	
Less: BPR (100%)		(400,000)	
			0
Bank account			75,000
Quoted shares (Note)			100,000
Car			15,000
Less: Allowable expenses	– Credit card		(2,000)
	– Income tax and CGT		(3,000)
			635,000
Less: Exempt legacy to wife	– house		(200,000)
	– quoted shares		(100,000)
	– business		(0)
Gross chargeable estate			335,000
IHT on chargeable estate (£335,000 – £216,000 (W)) = £119,000 × 40%			47,600

Note: The quoted shares do not qualify for BPR as it is assumed that Tom does not have a controlling interest in the company. Always assume that the individual does not have a controlling interest unless the question states otherwise.

Working: Lifetime gift to son

		£
Transfer of value		115,000
Less: AE	– 2012/13	(3,000)
	– 2011/12 b/f	(3,000)
PET		109,000

No lifetime tax was payable on this gift as it was a PET. At death, the current (2016/17) NRB of £325,000 is applied to the gift. The remaining NRB available for the estate = (£325,000 – £109,000) = £216,000

Test your understanding 10

(a) **Neil made no lifetime transfers**

On Neil's death:

- no lifetime gifts, so all NRB available for his death estate
- the transfer of his estate to Joan is an exempt legacy
- so, no IHT was due on his estate, and
- therefore none of his NRB was utilised (i.e. 100% unutilised).

Joan – Death estate

	£
Gross chargeable estate	1,000,000
Less: NRB at date of Joan's death	(325,000)
Less: NRB transferred from Neil (Note) (£325,000 × 100%)	(325,000)
Taxable amount	350,000
IHT payable on death (£350,000 × 40%)	140,000

This IHT is paid by the executors, but borne by Joan's children.

Note:

- Although the NRB available on Neil's death was only £275,000, the amount unused was 100% of the NRB. This percentage is applied to the current NRB of £325,000 to calculate the amount that can be transferred.
- Joan's executors must claim the transferred NRB on the submission of her IHT return within 2 years from her death, or 3 months after they start to act if later.

(b) **Neil made a lifetime gift to his son**

On Neil's death:

- Lifetime gift to son is a PET; therefore no lifetime IHT is due but the gift becomes chargeable on his death
- The PET is covered by the nil rate band available at death, therefore no death IHT is due

- However, the PET utilises £170,950 (£176,950 – (£3,000 × 2) AEs) of his nil rate band available at death
- The transfer of his estate to Joan is an exempt legacy
- Therefore, after taking account of his lifetime gifts, £104,050 (£275,000 – £170,950) of his nil rate band is unutilised
- The unutilised proportion is 38% ((£104,050/£275,000) × 100)

On Joan's death:

	£
Gross chargeable estate	1,000,000
Less: NRB at date of Joan's death	(325,000)
Less: NRB transferred from Neil (£325,000 × 38%)	(123,500)
Taxable amount	551,500
IHT payable on death (£551,500 × 40%)	220,600

Test your understanding 11

Han

Death estate – 1 May 2016

	£	£
House		320,000
Quoted shares		145,000
Cash		67,000
		532,000
Less: Debt due at death		(3,200)
		528,800
Less: Exempt legacies		
Spouse		(215,000)
Charity		(40,000)
Gross chargeable estate		273,800
IHT on chargeable estate:		
Gross chargeable estate		273,800
NRB @ date of death – 2016/17	325,000	
Less: GCTs < 7 years before death (1.5.09 to 1.5.16) (W1)	(304,000)	
NRB available		(21,000)
Taxable amount		252,800
IHT due on Han's death (£252,800 × 36% (W2))		91,008

Workings:

(W1) **Lifetime gift to son**

	£
Transfer of value	310,000
Less: AEs – 2013/14 and 2012/13 b/f	(6,000)
PET	304,000

This gift is a PET and falls below the value of the NRB at death.

No IHT is due on this gift but it reduces the NRB to set against the death estate.

(W2) **Rate of tax to use for the death estate**

	£
Taxable amount	252,800
Add back: Charitable legacy	40,000
Baseline amount	292,800
Apply 10% test (£292,800 × 10%)	29,280

As the charity legacy of £40,000 is more than £29,280, the reduced rate of 36% can be applied to calculate the tax on the estate.

Test your understanding 12

Wilma

Death estate – 4 October 2016

	£	£
Main residence		243,000
Flat (Note 1)		150,000
Shops (Note 2)		231,250
Villa ($200,000/10)		20,000
Partnership share (£400,000/2)	200,000	
Less: BPR (100%)	(200,000)	
		0
Shares in ZAM plc (20,000 @ 200p) (Note 3)		40,000
Units in CBA trust (8,000 @ 130p)		10,400
Bank balances		57,850
		752,500
Less: Income tax due	(7,500)	
Funeral expenses	(2,000)	
		(9,500)
		743,000
Less: Exempt legacies		
Husband	(120,000)	
Political party	(50,000)	
		(170,000)
Net free estate		573,000
Settled property		260,000
Gross chargeable estate		833,000

IHT liability on the estate value

Gross chargeable estate		833,000
NRB @ date of death – 2016/17	325,000	
Less: GCTs < 7 years before death (4.10.09 to 4.10.16)	(0)	
NRB available		(325,000)
Taxable amount		508,000
IHT due on Wilma's death (£508,000 × 40%)		203,200

Allocation of the IHT liability on the estate

The tax relating to the settled property is paid out of the trust assets by the trustees of the trust.

The rest of the tax is paid by the executors and is suffered by Joe, who inherits the residue of the estate.

Notes:

(1) Since the endowment mortgage would have been repaid upon Wilma's death, it is not deducted from the value of the flat.

(2) The shops are valued using the related property rules as follows:

$$\frac{£200{,}000\ (£50{,}000 \times 4)}{£200{,}000 + £120{,}000\ (£60{,}000 \times 2)} \times £370{,}000 = £231{,}250$$

(3) The shares in ZAM plc are valued at the lower of:

(i) Quarter up method = 198 + 1/4 (206 – 198) = 200p

(ii) Average of highest and lowest marked bargains = ½ × (196 + 208) = 202p

Test your understanding 13

Daisy

31 July 2016	£
Gross chargeable estate value	340,000
Less: NRB available	(325,000)
Taxable amount	15,000
IHT on death (£15,000 × 40%)	6,000
Less: QSR (W)	(933)
IHT payable on Daisy's estate	5,067

Working

QSR = (£75,000/£450,000) × £28,000 × 20% (Note) = £933

Note: June 2012 to July 2016 = 4 – 5 years

chapter

13

IHT: overseas, administration and tax planning

Chapter learning objectives

Upon completion of this chapter you will be able to:

- outline the effect for IHT of domicile status
- list the rules for identifying whether an asset is UK or overseas and determine whether an asset is chargeable to IHT
- calculate the availability of double taxation relief where there are overseas chargeable assets for IHT
- explain the advantages and disadvantages of lifetime giving compared to retention of assets until death
- state the conditions for there to be a valid variation of a will
- recognise the advantages of varying a will in a given situation and analyse the effect
- define a gift with reservation
- explain the taxation implications arising and how they may be mitigated
- identify and advise on the tax implications of associated operations.

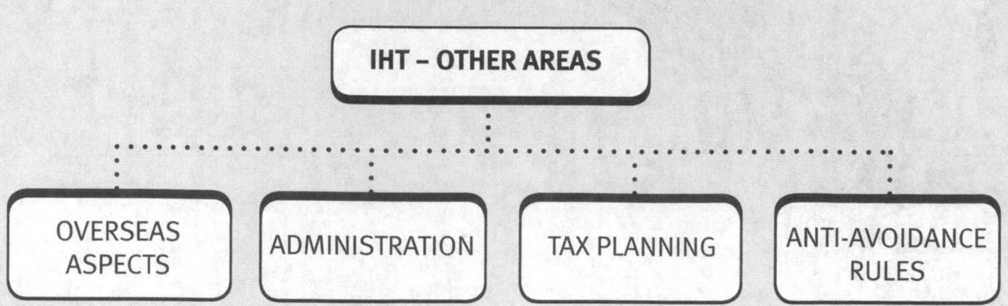

1 Overseas aspects of IHT

For IHT purposes, the individual's domicile status is key to determining the extent to which overseas assets will be liable to IHT.

Domicile and deemed domicile

The definition of domicile for IHT is the same as for income tax and capital gains tax (see Chapter 10).

However, the concept of **deemed domicile** only applies for IHT.

An individual:

- who has been domiciled in the UK, moves abroad and makes another country their permanent home, retains their UK domicile for three years.
- who has been resident in the UK for at least 17 out of the previous 20 tax years (ending with the tax year of the chargeable transfer) will be treated as UK domiciled from the start of the tax year.

The effect of an individual's domicile status for IHT

Individuals are assessed to IHT as follows:

Domicile status:	Charged to IHT on:
UK domiciled or deemed domiciled in the UK	Transfers of worldwide assets
Non-UK domiciled	Transfers of UK assets only

Test your understanding 1

Graham has been domiciled in the UK since birth.

On 1 June 2013, he emigrated to France with the intention of remaining there permanently and changed his domicile.

He died on 31 March 2016.

Explain the extent to which Graham will be liable to IHT.

Test your understanding 2

Jack is domiciled in Germany. He became UK resident on 1 May 1998 and died on 1 March 2017.

Explain the extent to which Jack will be liable to IHT.

Location of assets

UK domiciled individuals are charged to IHT regardless of the location of their assets. A non-UK domiciled individual is only liable to IHT on his UK assets.

It is therefore necessary to be able to identify where in the world an asset is deemed to be located for IHT purposes, as follows:

Type of asset	Location of asset
Land and buildings	Physical location
Registered shares and securities	Place of registration
Chattels	Location at time of transfer
Debts due to the individual	Where the debtor resides at the time of the transfer
Bank accounts	Location of the branch which maintains the account
Life assurance policies	Where the proceeds are payable
Business	Where the business is carried on

Test your understanding 3

Sam has lived in the UK for the last six years, however he is not UK domiciled and is not deemed to be domiciled in the UK. He owns the following property.

(i) Freehold property situated in the UK.

(ii) Leasehold property situated in the USA.

(iii) Shares in USA Inc., a company quoted and registered on the US stock exchange.

(iv) Antiques situated in Sam's US residence.

(v) A loan due to Sam by his sister who is resident in the USA. The sister used the loan to buy property situated in the UK.

(vi) A car that was bought in the USA, but is now situated in the UK.

(vii) Bank deposits in sterling with the UK Branch of a US Bank.

(viii) UK government stocks

(ix) US government stocks.

Explain whether Sam is liable to be charged to IHT if he transferred his property.

Election to be treated as UK domiciled

A non-UK domiciled individual with a UK domiciled spouse or civil partner can elect to be treated as domiciled in UK for IHT purposes.

The election:

- can be made any time during the non-UK domiciled spouse's lifetime (a 'lifetime election') and can apply from any date within the 7 years prior to the election, but cannot apply before 6 April 2014
- is irrevocable whilst the electing spouse is UK resident, but lapses if they become non-UK resident for four full consecutive tax years
- can be made within two years of the death (a 'death election') of either:
  - the UK domiciled spouse (where the non-UK domiciled spouse is still alive), or
  - the non-UK domiciled spouse (where their UK domiciled spouse has previously died), by the personal representatives

  and can specify that it is to take effect from any date within the 7 years prior to the deceased's death, but cannot apply before 6 April 2014

- only applies for the purposes of inheritance tax, and does not apply to any other taxes
- may be beneficial where assets of more than £325,000 are transferred to a non-UK domiciled spouse, as there would then be no limit to the exempt amount.

  However, this advantage must be weighed up against the fact that the non-UK domiciled spouse would then in the future be subject to UK IHT on their overseas assets, which would otherwise escape tax in the UK.

Test your understanding 4

Andrea, who is UK domiciled, and Lloyd, who is domiciled in Australia, married in June 2007. They have lived in South Wales since the marriage and have one child, Steven.

Andrea died in May 2016 leaving her entire estate consisting of UK assets valued at £950,000 to Lloyd. She had made no lifetime gifts.

Following Andrea's death, Lloyd is considering whether he should make the election to be treated as UK domiciled for IHT purposes. He intends to leave his entire estate to Steven and has made no lifetime gifts.

Lloyd owns UK assets worth £200,000 and overseas property valued at £250,000.

Advise Lloyd as to whether he should make the election.

Valuation of overseas assets

Overseas assets are valued at OMV on the same basis as assets situated in the UK. However, note that:

- where the value is provided in foreign currency it is converted into sterling at the exchange rate in force at the date of death which gives the lowest sterling valuation
- when valuing an overseas property to include in a death estate, additional expenses incurred in
  - administration relating to the overseas property, or
  - expenses relating to the sale of the overseas property

  may be deducted from the open market value of the property up to a maximum of 5% of the market value of the property
- if IHT is payable and overseas tax has been paid, double tax relief (DTR) may be due.

2 Double taxation relief

Double taxation relief (DTR) applies where an asset situated overseas is subject to both UK IHT and tax overseas.

DTR is a **tax credit** against the IHT liability of an estate on the death of the individual which is deducted **after** QSR, if any.

DTR is calculated as follows:

Lower of:
• the overseas tax suffered (given in the examination), and • the UK IHT payable on the overseas asset.

The UK IHT payable on the overseas asset is calculated at the average estate rate (AER) of IHT payable on the gross chargeable estate **after** QSR as follows:

$$\frac{\text{IHT on the estate after QSR}}{\text{Gross chargeable estate value}} \times \text{Value of asset in estate}$$

The value of the overseas asset brought into the estate is the value after deducting any additional expenses incurred in realising or managing the property (which may be subject to a maximum of 5%).

Example 1 – QSR and DTR

Peter died on 15 August 2016 leaving an estate valued at £375,000. The estate included property situated overseas valued at £60,000. Overseas IHT of £18,000 was paid on this property.

The estate also included a 4% interest in quoted shares that Peter inherited on the death of his mother on 10 November 2013. The shares were the total holding of shares held by his mother on her death.

At the time of her death the shares were worth £50,000, and on Peter's death they were worth £115,000. IHT of £80,000 was paid on a total estate of £400,000 on his mother's death.

Peter had made no lifetime gifts and he left his entire estate to his son.

Calculate the IHT payable as a result of Peter's death.

Solution

15 August 2016	£
Gross chargeable estate value	375,000
Less: NRB available	(325,000)
Taxable amount	50,000
	£
IHT due on death (£50,000 × 40%)	20,000
Less: QSR (W1)	(6,000)
	14,000
Less: DTR (W2)	(2,240)
IHT payable on Peter's estate	11,760

Workings

(W1) **QSR**

QSR = (£80,000/£400,000) × £50,000 × 60% (Note) = £6,000

Note: The appropriate percentage is 60% as there are between 2 – 3 years from the legacy and Peter's death.

The current value of the quoted shares is irrelevant to the calculation of QSR.

(W2) **DTR**

The rate of IHT on the estate after QSR is 3.733% (£14,000/ £375,000 × 100).

DTR is therefore the lower of:

(i)	Overseas tax suffered	£18,000
(ii)	UK IHT payable (£60,000 × 3.733%)	£2,240

Test your understanding 5

George died on 15 February 2017, leaving the following free estate.

A farm in Utopia rented out to tenant farmers	£45,000
Other assets after liabilities valued at	£303,250

The farm was left to his brother and the residue was left to his only son.

Additional costs of administering the Utopian farm were £3,500 and Utopian death duties payable amounted to £6,000.

George had made no lifetime transfers.

Compute the inheritance tax payable, showing clearly the amount payable by George's brother.

3 Payment of IHT

Normal dates of payment

IHT is payable as follows:

Transfer	Due Date
CLTs between 6 April and 30 September	30 April in the following year
CLTs between 1 October and 5 April	6 months after the end of the month in which the transfer is made
PETs chargeable as a result of death	6 months after the end of the month of death
Additional tax due on CLTs within 7 years before the death	6 months after the end of the month of death
Estate at death	Earlier of • 6 months after the end of the month of death, or • On delivery of the estate accounts to HMRC (unless tax is being paid in instalments, see below). Interest runs from 6 months after the end of the month of death.

Payment by instalments

IHT on land and buildings, a business or an interest in a business and certain shares can be paid in 10 equal annual instalments, starting on the normal due date for payment.

The asset must still be owned by the donee, and if it is sold the whole of the outstanding instalments become payable immediately.

Payment by instalments – detail

The tax must arise on any of the following:

- estate at death
- lifetime gifts made within 7 years before the death
- lifetime gifts where the donee has agreed to pay the tax arising.

The assets to which the instalment basis applies are:

- land wherever situated
- shares or securities in a company where the transferor controlled the company immediately before the transfer
- shares or securities in an unquoted company where the tax arises on death, and the amount of tax payable on all instalment assets is at least 20% of the total tax payable on the estate
- shares of an unquoted company with a value in excess of £20,000, which represent 10% or more of the nominal value of the company's shares
- a business or an interest in a business.

Note that a business or an interest in a business would usually qualify for 100% BPR – if so, no tax is due. If the transfer did not qualify e.g. the business had not been owned for 2 years, the instalment option could be considered for any tax due.

Interest is charged on instalments relating to the following assets:

- Land and buildings (unless qualify for APR)
- Shares in an investment company.
- Shares in a property dealing company.

Interest is only payable on other instalments where the instalment is paid late.

4 Comprehensive example

The following example involves a comprehensive death estate computation using the special valuation rules and reliefs.

Test your understanding 6

You have been asked by the chairman of your company for advice on the inheritance tax position on the death of his father. You ascertain that the chairman's father died on 1 March 2017, and his estate comprised of the following:

(i) Freehold house and land valued for probate at £630,000. This property was owned jointly by the deceased and his wife (who survived him) as joint tenants.

(ii) Overseas property with a sterling equivalent of £30,000, left to his daughter. Additional costs of administering the property were £1,800 and death duties payable overseas amounted to £6,500.

(iii) A property situated in Cornwall valued at £340,000.

(iv) £10,000 8% Corporate bonds valued at 82 – 86p. Interest is payable half yearly on 30 June and 31 December.

(v) £8,000 6% Treasury stock valued at 72 – 74p ex interest. Interest is payable half yearly on 31 March and 30 September.

(vi) Ordinary shares in Able Ltd, an unquoted trading company, worth £10,000. The shares have been owned for five years. 12% of the company's net assets are investments.

(vii) Bank deposit account £60,635.

(viii) Accrued interest £2,000 (net).

(ix) Personal chattels £10,000.

(x) Death in service £200,000. The death in service policy is expressed to be for the benefit of the spouse.

Debts and funeral expenses amounted to £2,665.

By his will apart from leaving the overseas property to his daughter, the chairman's father bequeathed legacies of £5,000 to each of two grandchildren, a legacy of £15,000 and the personal chattels to his widow and the residue to his son, your chairman.

The chairman's father had made one lifetime gift of £139,000 cash into a discretionary trust in November 2014. The chairman's father agreed to pay any IHT, if applicable.

The chairman's father is also the life tenant of an IPDI trust. The value of the trust fund on 1 March 2017 was £75,000.

Calculate the inheritance tax payable on the chairman's father's estate.

State who should pay the tax and who will suffer the tax.

5 Tax planning

Lifetime giving versus gifting on death

When advising a client of the advantages and disadvantages of lifetime giving versus gifting assets on death in a will, consideration should be given to the relationship between IHT and CGT as follows:

	CGT	**IHT**
Lifetime gift	• no CGT if asset is an exempt asset • chargeable gain/ allowable loss arises • calculated in normal way using **MV of the asset gifted** as consideration (see below) • gift relief may be available – applies to gifts of business assets, and – gifts of any asset where there is an immediate charge to IHT (i.e. a CLT) • on the subsequent disposal of the asset by the donee, IHT relief may be available (see below)	• no exempt assets for IHT • **diminution in value concept** applies to value the gift (see below) • if CLT – IHT payable during lifetime • if PET – no tax payable during lifetime but IHT payable if death within 7 years • valued at time of gift • exemptions available on lifetime gifts • BPR/APR available – lifetime and death • taper relief available if live for more than three years after the gift

Gift on death	• no CGT to pay on death	• asset forms part of death estate • IHT payable on the MV of the asset at the date of death unless the asset is – covered by reliefs (e.g. BPR/APR) – or is left to an exempt beneficiary (e.g. spouse, charity, qualifying political party) • no other exemptions available on death estate • taper relief not available

Starting point for calculations

It is important to appreciate that for lifetime gifts, the starting point for the computation of IHT and CGT is different.

- For IHT purposes, lifetime transfers are valued according to the **diminution in value** concept (i.e. the amount by which the donor's estate has diminished as a result of the gift) and the 'related property' rules must be taken into account.
- For CGT purposes, the value of a lifetime transfer (i.e. a gift) is the value of the asset actually gifted. The concept of 'related property' does not apply to CGT.
- If the asset gifted is quoted shares, different rules are used to value the shares.

Example 2 – Lifetime giving versus gifting assets on death

Eddy owns 100,000 shares (a 10% holding) in WXY Ltd. Eddy's wife owns 50,000 shares in WXY Ltd.

On 31 July 2016 he made a lifetime gift of 50,000 shares in WXY Ltd to his daughter.

The relevant values of WXY Ltd's shares at the time of the gift are:

	£
5%	8
10%	10
15%	13

(a) **Calculate the transfer of value for IHT purposes.**

(b) **Calculate the deemed sale proceeds for CGT purposes.**

Solution

(a) The transfer of value for IHT purposes will be calculated using the related property valuation rules as follows:

	£
Value of shares held before the transfer (based on a 15% holding) 100,000 × £13.00	1,300,000
Value of shares held after the transfer (based on a 10% holding) 50,000 × £10.00	(500,000)
Transfer of value	800,000

(b) For CGT purposes, a gift of a 5% shareholding has been made.

The deemed consideration is therefore £400,000 (50,000 × £8).

IHT deduction for CGT

Where an asset is gifted to another individual during the donor's lifetime both IHT and CGT need to be considered.

Where both:

- gift relief is claimed on the gift, and
- IHT is paid in relation to the gift

any IHT paid is allowed as a deduction when calculating the chargeable gain arising on the subsequent disposal of the asset by the donee.

Example 3 – Lifetime versus gifting assets on death

On 31 December 2013 Yaz made a gift of business property (not in relation to the disposal of the entire business) worth £341,000 to her daughter Jo. Yaz and Jo made a joint gift relief claim to defer the capital gain of £103,000 arising on the gift.

Assume that the business property did not qualify for BPR and that the IHT annual exemptions have already been used.

Yaz died on 30 April 2016 having made no other lifetime transfers except those to use her annual exemption each year.

Jo sold the business property for £368,000 on 31 August 2016. Jo is a higher rate taxpayer and makes no other disposals in the tax year 2016/17.

Calculate the CGT liability that will arise upon Jo's disposal of the business property on 31 August 2016.

Solution

When calculating her CGT liability, Jo will be able to deduct the IHT payable as a result of the PET becoming chargeable. It is therefore necessary to compute the IHT payable on the PET first.

IHT payable – during lifetime

31 December 2013 – PET	£
Transfer of value	341,000
Less: BPR (not applicable per question)	(0)
Less: AE (not available per question)	(0)
Potentially exempt	341,000
Lifetime IHT due (PET)	0

IHT payable – on death

	£
Gross chargeable amount (above)	341,000
NRB available at death	(325,000)
Taxable amount	16,000
IHT due on death (£16,000 × 40%)	6,400
Less: Taper relief (31.12.2013 to 30.4.2016) (< 3 years before death)	(0)
Less: IHT paid in lifetime (PET)	(0)
IHT payable on death	6,400

CGT liability – Disposal of asset gifted – 31 August 2016

	£	£
Sale proceeds		368,000
Base cost of asset to Jo:		
MV at date of gift	341,000	
Less: Gain held over	(103,000)	
		(238,000)
		130,000
Less: IHT paid on PET		(6,400)
Chargeable gain		123,600
Less: AEA		(11,100)
Taxable gain		112,500
CGT payable by Jo (£112,500 × 20%)		22,500

IHT planning

It is important for an individual to plan their lifetime gifts to be tax efficient and to make a will so that their estate is distributed in a tax efficient way.

There are a number of tax planning measures that can reduce an individual's liability to IHT which can be divided into three areas:

- lifetime tax planning
- death estate planning
- married couples and civil partners planning.

The overall objectives of all IHT tax planning measures are:

- to minimise the amount of tax payable
- to maximise the inheritance of the next generation.

IHT planning

Lifetime tax planning

IHT planning during an individual's lifetime involves making gifts of wealth as early as possible.

Advantages of lifetime gifts

- If the gift is a PET, no IHT will be payable if the donor survives seven years.
- If the gift is a CLT the tax is calculated at 20% and no additional IHT will be payable on death if the donor survives seven years.
- If the donor does not survive seven years, taper relief will be available after three years.
- A lifetime gift is valued at the time of the gift and the value is 'frozen'. This locks the value of an appreciating asset, so any increase in value up to the date of death will not be taxed.
- If the value of the asset decreases, fall in value relief may be available to reduce the chargeable amount on death.
- Exemptions such as normal gifts out of income, small gifts, marriage and AEs may reduce or eliminate the value of a lifetime gift.
- However, remember the CGT implications:
  - CGT may be payable on lifetime gifts of chargeable assets, but
  - CGT will not be payable on assets held at the date of death.
- An individual should therefore be advised to make lifetime gifts of assets that are:
  - appreciating in value, and
  - will not generate a significant liability to CGT.

  For example, gift assets that are exempt from CGT or assets that are deferred or exempted by available CGT reliefs.
- Note however that there is no IHT saving in gifting assets that qualify for BPR or APR at 100%.

Estate planning

An individual should be advised to draft a tax efficient will ensuring that:

- they fully utilise the NRB, and
- do not incur unnecessary charges to IHT on death.

Skipping a generation

Rather than leaving property directly to children, it may be more advantageous to miss out a generation and to leave the property to grandchildren instead.

There will be no immediate saving of IHT, but a charge to IHT on the death of the children will be avoided.

Such planning is particularly relevant if the children already have sufficient property in their own right.

The income tax benefits of this arrangement may also be attractive:

- If a parent sets up a source of income for a child, the parent is assessed on the income generated unless the amount is below the de minimis threshold of £100.
- However, if the grandparents set up the source of income, the income is assessed on the child regardless of the amount.

Married couples and civil partners

The following points should be considered by spouses and civil partners:

- Ensure elections are made to:
  - transfer unused NRB if a widow or widower (Chapter 12)
  - be treated as UK domiciled if beneficial (section 1).
- Choose carefully which assets to gift .
- Make use of a deed of variation to minimise IHT on death.

Choice of assets to gift

Advice that could be given to married couples or civil partnerships is:

- Where the couple own assets that qualify for BPR and/or APR these assets should not be left to the other spouse or civil partner. This is because the legacy would be covered by the inter-spouse exemption and the benefit of BPR/APR would be wasted.
- Therefore BPR and APR assets should be left to non-exempt beneficiaries and other assets left to the spouse or civil partner.

  As a result, the benefit of both the relief and inter-spouse exemption will be available to reduce the value of the chargeable estate.

Example 4 – IHT planning

Joan is 67 years old, and was widowed on the death of her husband on 21 June 2008. She has six grandchildren.

The husband had a chargeable estate valued at £800,000, and this was left entirely to Joan, he had made no lifetime transfers.

Joan now has an estate valued at £800,000, which will pass to her two children when she dies. Joan's children are both quite wealthy, and are concerned about the IHT liability that will arise upon Joan's death. Joan had made no lifetime transfers.

You are to advise Joan and her children of tax planning measures that they could take in order to minimise the impact of IHT.

Assume the current rate of NRB will apply when Joan dies.

Solution

Husband's death

On Joan's husband's death:

- the transfer to Joan is an exempt transfer
- no IHT is due on his estate, and
- therefore none of his NRB was utilised (i.e. 100% unutilised)

Joan – Death estate

	£
Gross chargeable estate	800,000
Less: NRB at Joan's death	(325,000)
Less: NRB transferred from her husband (Note) (£325,000 × 100%)	(325,000)
Taxable amount	150,000
IHT payable on death (£150,000 × 40%)	60,000

This IHT is paid by the executor, borne by Joan's children.

Note:

- Although the NRB available on Joan's husband's death in 2008/09 was only £312,000, the amount unused was 100% of the NRB. This percentage is applied to the current NRB of £325,000 to calculate the amount that can be transferred.
- Joan's executors must claim the transferred NRB on the submission of the IHT return within 2 years from her death.

Advice:

- Since Joan's children are already wealthy, it may be more beneficial for Joan to leave her estate to her grandchildren (possibly via use of a trust).

  Although this will not save IHT on Joan's death estate, by skipping a generation, IHT on the same wealth will not be due until transfers are made by the grandchildren.
- If Joan dies without considering the above, her children could alter Joan's will by a deed of variation within 2 years from Joan's death (see below).
- Joan should also consider making lifetime gifts to her grandchildren to utilise her AEs and to benefit from the advantages of making PETs.

Deed of variation

It is possible to change the terms of an individual's will after they have died by entering into a deed of variation (also known as a deed of family arrangement).

In practice, the main reason for entering into a deed of variation is to redistribute the deceased's estate on a fairer basis. However, a deed of variation can also be used as an effective tax planning tool for IHT and CGT purposes.

Changes can be made to make the provisions of a will more tax efficient in the following situations:

(i) Where an estate has been left to children who already have sufficient property of their own.
Part of the estate could be diverted to grandchildren, thus missing out a generation and therefore bypassing a potential charge to IHT on the death of the children.

(ii) Amounts left to charity could be increased to 10% or more of the 'baseline' estate to allow the rest of the estate to benefit from the 36% reduced rate of inheritance tax.

However, the revised terms of a will under a deed of variation will only be effective for tax purposes provided the following conditions are satisfied.

The deed must:

- be in writing and signed by all beneficiaries that are affected by the deed
- not be made for any consideration
- be executed within two years of death
- state that it is intended to be effective for tax (IHT and/or CGT) purposes.

Test your understanding 7

Faisal died on 8 August 2016 leaving his entire estate to his son. The estate is valued at £500,000 after deducting exemptions and reliefs, including a donation to charity of £18,000.

Faisal had made no lifetime gifts.

(a) **Assuming that a deed of variation is made after Faisal's death, calculate the minimum increase in the donation to charity that is required in order that Faisal's estate qualifies for the reduced rate of IHT.**

(b) **Calculate the net increase in the estate available for Faisal's son as a result of making this increased donation.**

6 Anti avoidance rules

The next sections cover the following anti-avoidance rules for IHT:

- Gifts with reservation
- Associated operations

7 Gifts with reservation

A 'gift with reservation of benefit' (GWR) is a lifetime gift where:

- the legal ownership of an asset is transferred, but
- the donor retains some benefit in the asset gifted.

Examples of a GWR include:

- the gift of a house, but the donor continues to live in it
- the gift of shares, but the donor retains the right to future dividends
- the gift of assets into a discretionary trust, but the donor is a potential beneficiary of the trust fund.

Special anti-avoidance rules apply to a GWR to ensure that these gifts do not escape from an IHT charge.

The treatment of GWR

When an asset is gifted but the donor retains the right to use it without payment of full rent, it falls into the GWR rules as follows:

Reservation still in place when donor dies	Reservation lifted before donor's death
(1) Original gift = GWR = PET or CLT @ MV of asset on date of gift	(1) Original gift = GWR = PET or CLT @ MV of asset on date of gift
(2) On death of donor: (donor still uses asset at date of death) = Asset put in donor's estate @ MV on date of death	(2) When reservation lifted: (donor no longer uses asset) = Deemed PET at that time @ MV of asset on date reservation lifted
A GWR therefore potentially gives rise to a double charge to IHT. However, HMRC have the right to charge: the **highest** tax liability arising from event (1) or (2) (known as double charges relief)	

Usually including the asset in the estate or treating as a PET when the reservation is lifted gives the higher IHT charge. This is because capital assets normally appreciate in value and no annual exemptions are available in the death estate or against the deemed PET.

Any tax arising is payable by the legal owner of the asset (i.e. the donee).

Example 5

Priya gave her house to her son Sushil on 1 April 2011 when it was worth £360,000. She had made no previous lifetime gifts.

Priya continued to live in the house and paid no rent to Sushil.

Priya died on 1 January 2017 leaving her estate of £700,000 (excluding the house) to Sushil. At this date the house was worth £475,000.

Calculate the IHT payable on Priya's death.

Solution

The transfer of the house is a gift with reservation of benefit.

(1) **Treat gift as a PET**

	£	£
1 April 2011 – PET		
Transfer of value		360,000
Less: Annual exemption		
Current year – 2010/11		(3,000)
Previous year – 2009/10		(3,000)
Gross chargeable amount		354,000
NRB @ date of death – 2016/17	325,000	
Less: GCT < 7 years before gift (1.4.04 to 1.4.11)	(0)	
NRB available		(325,000)
Taxable amount		29,000
IHT payable @ 40%		11,600
Less: Taper relief (1.4.11 to 1.1.17) (5 – 6 years) (60%)		(6,960)
IHT payable on death		4,640

1 January 2017 – Death estate	£	£
Gross chargeable estate value		700,000
NRB @ date of death	325,000	
Less: GCTs < 7 years before death (1.1.10 to 1.1.17)	(354,000)	
NRB available		0
Taxable amount		700,000
IHT payable @ 40%		280,000
Total IHT payable (£4,640 + £280,000)		284,640

(2) **Treat gift as part of death estate**

1 January 2017 – Death estate	£	£
Gross chargeable estate value (£700,000 + £475,000)		1,175,000
NRB @ date of death – 2016/17	325,000	
Less: GCTs < 7 years before death (1.1.10 to 1.1.17)	(0)	
NRB available		(325,000)
Taxable amount		850,000
IHT payable @ 40%		340,000

The higher amount of £340,000 will be chargeable on Priya's death

Exceptions to the GWR rules

The following gifts will not be treated as a GWR.

- Where full consideration is paid for the benefit derived from the use of the property.

  For example, where a house has been given away but the donor still lives in it, the payment of a commercial rent for the benefit of living in the house will avoid the GWR rules.

- Where the circumstances of the donor have changed in a way that was not foreseen at the time of the gift.

  This situation would be applicable where a house has been given away and the donor moves out of the house. Then, at a later date, the donor becomes ill. If the donor then returns to the house to stay with his or her family because he needs to be cared for, then this will not fall under the GWR rules.

8 Associated operations

Where there are **two or more transactions which affect the same property** and as a result tax is avoided, special rules may apply.

Associated operations

Two examples of associated operations are where:

- An asset is transferred piecemeal, so that the total value of the individual transactions is less than the value of the whole asset.
- A person transfers part of an asset which, although of little value, significantly reduces the value of the remainder. The remainder is then transferred at a reduced value thus allowing an asset to be given away at less than its full value.

Where tax is avoided by making a series of transactions and the associated operations rule is applied:

- the associated operations are treated as one transaction, and
- any resulting transfer of value is treated as being made at the time of the last associated operation.

However, note that the rules are not always applied:

- It is much more likely that the associated operations rule will be applied where transactions are with a connected person.
- The longer the length of time between the various transactions, the easier it will be to defend against an allegation of associated transactions.
- It may be possible to argue that there was no intention of making further transactions at the time of the first transaction.

Situations where the rules will not apply

The associated operations rules will specifically not apply in respect of:

- leases, where there is more than three years between the grant of a commercial lease and the subsequent transfer of the freehold
- transfers between spouses or civil partners, where property is transferred in order to utilise the AE or the ME provided the donee spouse acts from his or her own choice in making a gift.

  For example, where a son or daughter is to get married, both spouses may want to make use of the £5,000 ME. If the husband has no capital, and the wife makes a gift to him of £5,000 in order to make the gift to the son or daughter, then this will not normally be treated as an associated operation.

9 Summary of anti-avoidance rules

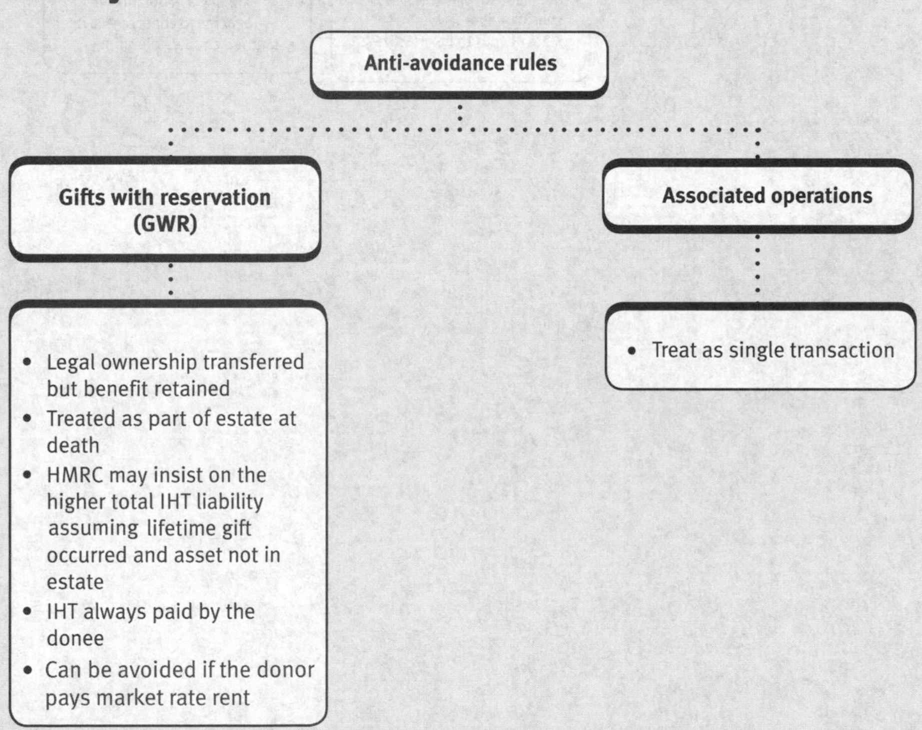

10 Chapter summary

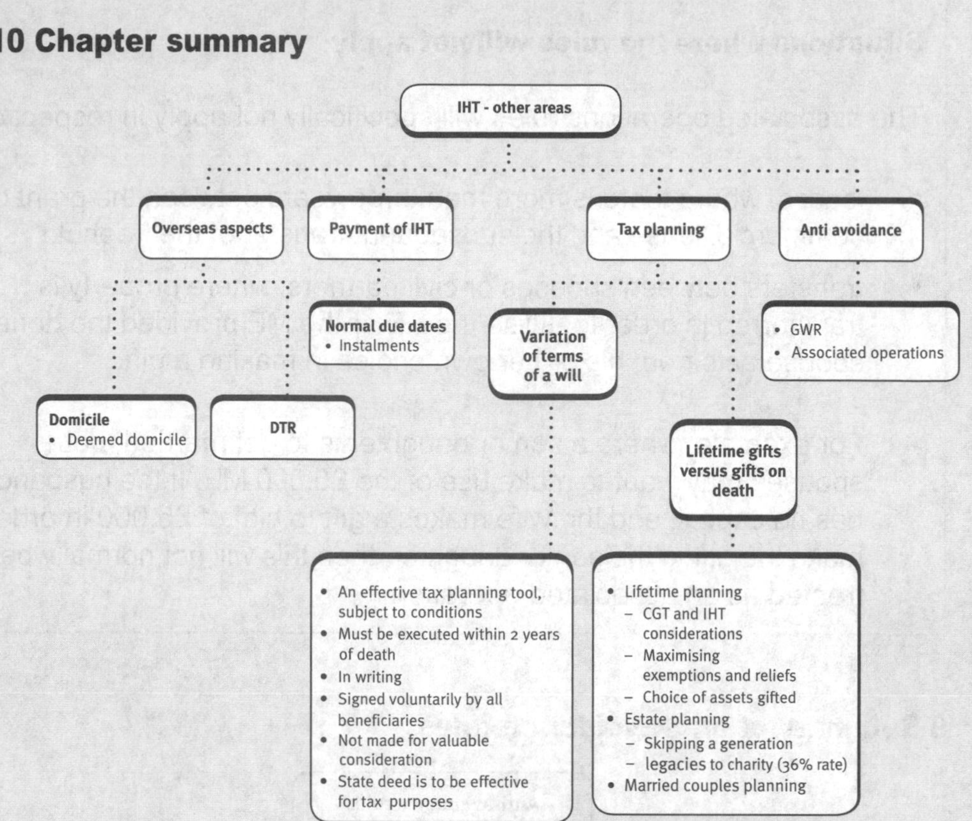

Test your understanding answers

Test your understanding 1

Graham

Graham ceased to be domiciled in the UK on 1 June 2013. For IHT purposes, he is deemed to be UK domiciled for a further three years until 31 May 2016.

As his death occurred before this date, he will be liable to UK IHT on his worldwide assets.

Test your understanding 2

Jack

Jack was resident in the UK for 19 tax years (1998/99 to 2016/17 inclusive).

He is therefore deemed to be domiciled in the UK, and will be liable to UK IHT on his worldwide assets.

Test your understanding 3

Sam

Sam is a non-UK domiciled individual and therefore he will only be chargeable to IHT on his assets located in the UK.

(i) The freehold property is situated in the UK and so is a chargeable asset for IHT.

(ii) The leasehold property situated in the USA is not in the UK and therefore not a chargeable asset.

(iii) The 20,000 shares in USA Inc. are registered in the US and therefore not a chargeable asset to Sam.

(iv) The antiques are in the US residence, so they are not chargeable to IHT at present. If Sam should bring them to the UK, then this would change their location for IHT to the UK.

(v) As Sam's sister lives in the USA, this is not an asset located in the UK but the USA. Therefore it is not a chargeable asset. The fact that the sister used the loan to buy property situated in the UK is irrelevant.

(vi) The motor car is now a UK located asset and therefore a chargeable asset.

(vii) Bank deposits in sterling with the UK branch of a US bank – located in the UK therefore chargeable.

(viii) The place of registration of the UK government stocks would have been the UK which makes this also a chargeable asset.

(ix) The US government stocks would have been registered in the US, which makes them an overseas asset and therefore not chargeable.

Test your understanding 4

Andrea and Lloyd

	If no election made		If election made	
	£	£	£	£
On Andrea's death (UK domiciled)				
Estate value		950,000		950,000
Less: Inter spouse exemption (Note 1)		(325,000)		(950,000)
Gross chargeable estate		625,000		0
NRB available	325,000			
GCTs in previous 7 years	0			
		(325,000)		
Taxable estate		300,000		
IHT payable @ 40%		120,000		0

On Lloyd's death (Non-UK domiciled)	£	£	£	£
UK assets:				
Owned personally		200,000		200,000
Inherited from Andrea				950,000
(£950,000 – £120,000)		830,000		
Overseas property (Note 2)		0		250,000
Gross chargeable estate		1,030,000		1,400,000
NRB available (Note 3)	325,000		650,000	
GCTs in previous 7 years	(0)		(0)	
		(325,000)		(650,000)
Taxable estate		705,000		750,000
IHT payable @ 40%		282,000		300,000
Total IHT payable		402,000		300,000

Notes

(1) If no election is made the inter spouse exemption is limited to £325,000, whereas with the election it is unlimited.

(2) The overseas property is only subject to UK IHT if Lloyd elects to become UK domiciled.

(3) Andrea's unused NRB can be transferred to Lloyd. If no election is made, all of Andrea's NRB is used on her death.

Advice:

Given the situation at the moment, it would be beneficial for Lloyd to make the election to be treated as UK domiciled in these circumstances.

However, the short term benefit of saving tax on the first death may not be ultimately beneficial if the overseas property increases significantly in value and has to be included in Lloyd's estate on death.

The decision must be taken carefully, and thankfully Lloyd can apply the election from any date within 7 years prior to making the election, therefore he can leave the decision for up to 7 years and back date its application.

Note that if Lloyd remains resident in the UK for more than 8 years he will be deemed to be UK domiciled for IHT purposes as he will have been resident in the UK for at least 17 out of the previous 20 tax years.

Test your understanding 5

George

Estate computation

	£
Farm in Utopia (Note below)	45,000
Less: Administration expenses (£3,500 but restrict to 5% of open market value i.e. £45,000)	(2,250)
	42,750
Other assets less liabilities	303,250
Gross chargeable estate	346,000

IHT liability on the estate value

	£
Gross chargeable estate value	346,000
Less: NRB available	(325,000)
Taxable amount	21,000
	£
IHT on death (£21,000 × 40%)	8,400
Less: QSR	(0)
IHT payable **after** QSR	8,400
(Estate rate = (£8,400/£346,000) × 100 = 2.428%)	
Less: DTR (W)	(1,038)
IHT payable on George's estate	7,362

Allocation of the IHT liability on the estate

IHT on:	£	£	Tax suffered by:
Foreign property	1,038		
Less: DTR	(1,038)		
		0	G's brother
Other net assets			
(£303,250 × 2.428%)		7,362	G's son
		7,362	

Working: DTR

DTR is the lower of:

(a) Overseas death duties suffered £6,000

(b) UK IHT attributable to overseas property (2.428% × £42,750) £1,038

Note:

- APR is not available because the land is not situated in the EEA, the Channel Islands or the Isle of Man.
- BPR is also not available because the farm is a tenanted farm, which is an investment asset.

Test your understanding 6

The chairman's father

Chargeable estate computation

	£	£
Freehold house	315,000	
Less: Spouse exemption	(315,000)	
		0
Overseas property	30,000	
Less: Administration expenses restricted to (5% × £30,000)	(1,500)	
		28,500
Property in Cornwall		340,000
Corporate Bonds [10,000 × (82 + ¼ × (86 – 82))]		8,300
Treasury stock [72 + ¼ × (74 – 72)] × 8,000	5,800	
Plus: interest (6% × £8,000 × 6/12)	240	
		6,040
Shares in Able Ltd	10,000	
Less: BPR (100% × £10,000 × 88%)	(8,800)	
		1,200
Bank account (including accrued interest)		62,635
Chattels		10,000
Death in service		200,000
Less: Funeral expenses		(2,665)
		654,010
Less: Specific spouse legacies		
Chattels		(10,000)
Cash		(15,000)
Death in service policy		(200,000)
Net free estate		429,010
Settled property		75,000
Gross chargeable estate		504,010

IHT liability on the estate

		£
Gross chargeable estate value		504,010
Less: NRB available (W)		(192,000)
Taxable amount		312,010
IHT on gross chargeable estate (£312,010 × 40%)		124,804
Less: QSR		(0)
IHT after QSR		124,804
AER = (£124,804/£504,010) × 100 = 24.762%		
Less: DTR = Lower of:		
(1) Overseas tax suffered	6,500	
(2) UK IHT on overseas asset (£28,500 × 24.762%)	7,057	(6,500)
IHT payable on estate		118,304

Working: NRB available

	£
NRB	325,000
Less: Lifetime CLT in previous 7 years (£139,000 – £3,000 (2014/15) – £3,000 (2013/14))	(133,000)
NRB available	192,000

IHT payment

The IHT due on the settled property will be payable by the trustees from the trust assets.

The rest of the IHT will be payable by the executors of the estate.

IHT suffered

The IHT on the overseas property will be recovered from the daughter.

The balance of the IHT will be taken from the residue of the estate, and will effectively be suffered by the son (i.e. residuary legatee).

No tax will be suffered by the grandchildren (specific legatee) or the widow (exempt legatee).

Test your understanding 7

Faisal

(a) **Increased charitable donation to charity required**

	£
Net estate after charitable legacy	500,000
Less: NRB available	(325,000)
Taxable estate	175,000
Add: Charitable legacy	18,000
Baseline amount	193,000
10% of 'baseline amount' (£193,000 × 10%)	19,300

In order to benefit from the reduced rate of 36%, the donation to charity must be increased by £1,300 (£19,300 – £18,000).

(b) **Net increase in the estate available for Faisal's son**

	£	£
Cost of extra charitable donation (part (a))		(1,300)
IHT on original taxable estate (without extra charitable donation) (40% × £175,000)	70,000	
IHT on revised taxable estate (with extra charitable donation) (36% × (£175,000 – £1,300))	(62,532)	
Reduction in IHT liability on estate		7,468
Net increase in estate for Faisal's son		6,168

chapter

14

The taxation of trusts

Chapter learning objectives

Upon completion of this chapter you will be able to:

- understand the nature of a trust and how it operates
- explain the main types of trust in existence and how they can be recognised
- understand in outline how income tax, capital gains tax and inheritance tax apply to transactions involving trusts
- explain the tax implications of creating a trust now or in the future
- outline the tax implications of property passing to a beneficiary
- explain the inheritance tax consequences of a settlor dying after creating a trust
- explain how trusts can be used in tax and financial planning.

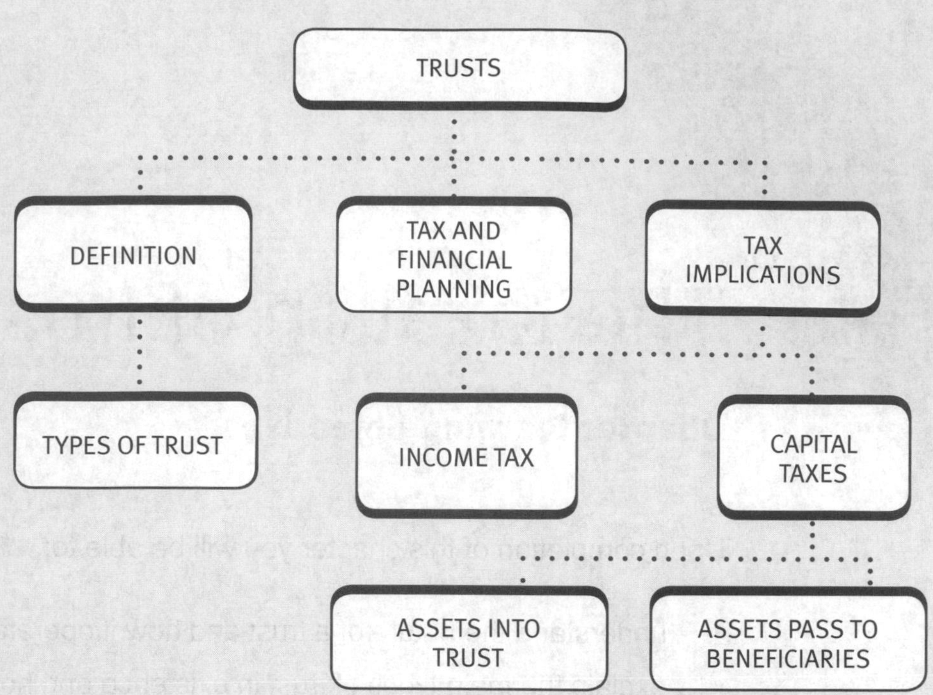

Introduction

Due to the complexity of the taxation of trusts, the ACCA has summarised the requirements in relation to trusts for the P6 and has excluded many aspects from the syllabus.

This chapter therefore just concentrates on the knowledge required by the P6 examining team.

A summary of the key topics that are examinable is as follows:

- Definition of a trust.
- Knowledge of some of the key types of trust (detailed knowledge of many specific trusts is excluded).
- An understanding of the income tax position of trust beneficiaries (Chapter 1).
- An overview of the income tax consequences of a trust on the trustees (but not calculations of the income tax payable by the trustees).
- Knowledge of the IHT and CGT consequences of transfers into and out of certain UK trusts and charges arising whilst assets are in a trust (but not the calculation of taxes payable by the trustees while the assets are in the trust).

1 The nature of a trust

A trust is an arrangement where:

- property (known as the trust assets or settled property)
- is transferred by a person (known as the settlor)
- to the trustees
- to be held for the benefit of one or more specified persons (known as the beneficiaries)
- on specified terms in the trust deed.

The trust must have more than one trustee and often in practice the settlor's lawyer or accountant will act as one of the trustees.

A trust (sometimes referred to as a settlement) can be created:

- during the settlor's lifetime, or
- on death under the provisions of the settlor's will, or
- following an individual's death under a deed of variation.

If the trust is a lifetime trust, the settlor can be a trustee and/or beneficiary of the trust.

The trust deed sets out the trustee's powers and duties.

The financial planning benefits of a trust arrangement

Trusts are useful arrangements as they allow an individual (the settlor) to give away the benefit arising from the ownership of property to others (the beneficiaries of the trust), whilst retaining some control over the property (as one of the trustees).

The trustees are the legal owners of the property, acting in a representative capacity in the best interests of the beneficiaries.

Separating the beneficial and legal ownership of assets provides financial planning benefits in setting up a trust which include the ability to:

- provide an income from the assets for one group of beneficiaries while preserving and protecting the capital for others
- provide a means for an older generation to protect and make financial provisions for the next generation, particularly where there are young children involved or it is thought that a recipient is financially imprudent
- transfer the benefits of owning property to minors while leaving the control over the assets, together with the responsibilities of managing and maintaining them, with the trustees.

2 Types of trust

There are two main types of trust examinable at P6:

- Discretionary trusts, and
- Interest in possession trusts (also known as life interest trusts).

Discretionary trusts

A discretionary trust is a flexible settlement where

- the beneficiaries have no legal right to benefit from the income or capital of the trust
- any distribution of income or capital out of the trust is at the complete discretion of the trustees.

The trustees can determine how to meet the needs of the beneficiaries as and when they arise.

In a typical discretionary trust the trustees may have power to decide:

- whether or not trust income is to be accumulated or distributed
- how the trust assets are managed and invested to generate income and capital growth
- how the trust income and the capital of the trust is to be shared amongst different beneficiaries.

Illustration – Discretionary trust

Imran owns a portfolio of shares and transfers them to a discretionary trust for the benefit of his grandchildren.

The trust is set up as follows:

Settlor:	Imran
Trustees:	Imran and Khalid (Imran's son)
Beneficiaries:	Imran's grandchildren
Trust property:	200,000 shares in ABC plc
Income:	Income may be accumulated for up to 20 years from the date of the trust settlement. Subject to the trustees' power to accumulate, the trustees shall each financial year distribute the income of the trust fund to the beneficiaries, and the trustees in their absolute discretion shall determine the proportion or amount of the income for that financial year to be distributed to the beneficiaries or any one or more of them to the exclusion of the others.
Capital:	The trustees may advance the capital of the trust to a beneficiary at any time, and shall have absolute discretion as to the proportion of the capital of the trust to be distributed to any such beneficiary.

Interest in possession trusts

An interest in possession (IIP trust) exists where:

- a beneficiary has an interest in the assets of the trust.

An IIP can be the legal right:

- to receive income generated by the trust assets, and/or
- to use a trust asset or live in a property owned by the trust.

The beneficiary who receives the right to income or use of an asset under an IIP is known as the 'life tenant' of the trust. The life tenant is said to have a 'life interest' in the trust.

The beneficiary who receives the capital assets in the trust when the life interest comes to an end is known as the remainderman.

The remainderman is said to have a 'reversionary interest' in the trust assets as the assets will only revert to them when the trust comes to an end.

IIP trusts are commonly used in a will where one spouse dies and there is a surviving spouse and children. The surviving spouse is usually named as the life tenant and is entitled to the income generated by the assets (and possibly the right to live in the family home for the rest of their life), but does not have access to the actual capital assets.

The children are usually the remaindermen and will receive the capital assets on the death of the surviving spouse.

This form of trust is a popular arrangement to protect the capital assets for the benefit of the children where, for example, the spouse remarries. The capital will eventually be transferred to the children of the first marriage and not to the new spouse and their family.

Illustration – Interest in possession trust

Felicity is married with two children, and is writing her will. Her main assets are a house and some cash deposits. Felicity would like to provide for her husband, Gerald, but wants to ensure that the capital value of her estate is eventually passed to her children, Olivia and Joe.

Felicity could set up an IIP trust with an immediate post-death interest for Gerald via her will.

The trust is set up as follows:

Settlor:	Felicity
Trustees:	Michael (Felicity's brother) and Arthur (solicitor)
Beneficiaries:	Gerald (life tenant), Olivia and Joe (remaindermen)
Trust property:	House and £350,000 cash
Income:	Payable to Gerald during his lifetime
Capital:	To be advanced to Olivia and Joe on the death of Gerald.

Summary

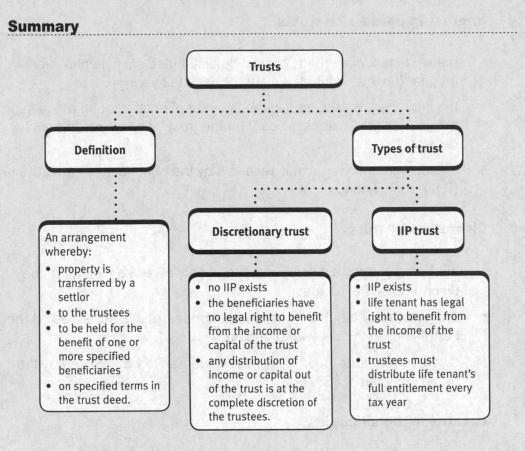

3 Income tax and trusts

The trust is a separate legal entity for income tax purposes. The body of trustees is a separate taxable person.

The trustees are subject to income tax on the income arising in respect of trust assets each tax year and they distribute income to the beneficiaries.

An understanding of the way in which trust income is taxed is required, however, the calculation of IT payable by the trustees is not examinable.

The taxation of the trust income operates as follows:

- the trustees account for income tax on the receipt of income by the trust each tax year under self-assessment
- trustees are taxed at different rates depending on the type of trust
- trustees distribute income to the beneficiaries according to the terms of the trust.

Interest in possession trusts

- the life tenant of an IIP trust must be distributed his full entitlement to income (i.e. his distributable share) each tax year
- the life tenant is assessed in the tax year of entitlement (i.e. the same tax year as the trustees account for the trust income), not in the year of receipt
- the income of an IIP trust is received by the beneficiary net of 20% tax (7.5% for dividends).

Discretionary trusts

- the beneficiary of a discretionary trust only receives income at the discretion of the trustees
- any income distributed from a discretionary trust is assessed on the beneficiary in the tax year of receipt
- discretionary trust income is always deemed to be received by the beneficiary net of 45% tax.

Taxation of beneficiaries

- the beneficiaries are taxed on the gross trust income in their personal income tax computations and they can deduct from their income tax liability the tax credit deducted at source by the trustees (see Chapter 1)
- the trustees must give the beneficiaries a certificate each tax year showing the amount of trust income the individual must be taxed on, and the associated tax credit
- trustees of a discretionary trust can choose to give income generated from the assets to the beneficiaries who are non-taxpayers so that a repayment of income tax paid by the trustees can be claimed.

4 The capital taxes and trusts

The P6 syllabus requires an understanding of the CGT and IHT consequences of:

- a settlor gifting assets **into** a trust, and
- trustees gifting assets **out of** a trust.

Whilst the assets are in the trust, further charges to capital taxes arise as:

- the trustees are subject to CGT:
  - on the gains arising in respect of managing the trust assets each tax year
  - at 20%
  - after deducting an annual exempt amount of £5,550 (i.e. half the normal annual exempt amount is available to a trust), and
- they may also be liable to pay IHT:
  - in respect of the property held in the trust every ten years (known as the principal charge), and
  - on transfer of assets out of the trust (known as exit charges).

The P6 syllabus requires knowledge of these charges to tax, however, the calculation of CGT and IHT payable by the trustees is not examinable.

Other types of trusts

There are several types of trusts available with different IHT consequences. However, the only trusts examinable at P6 are:

- Immediate post death interest (IPDI) trusts
- Relevant property trusts (RPTs).

An IPDI trust is a special type of IIP trust which can only be created on the death of the settlor. It is also sometimes referred to as a 'qualifying IIP trust'.

For the purposes of P6, RPTs are defined as all trusts (other than IPDI trusts) created on or after 22 March 2006.

Summary

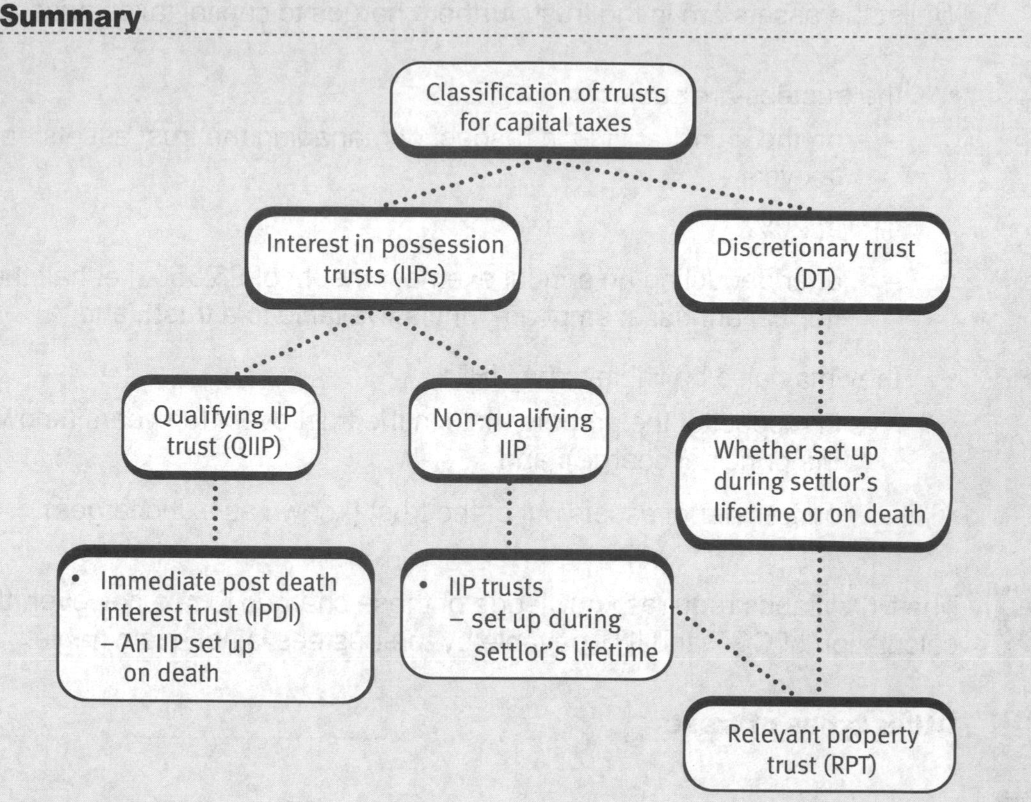

Gifts into a trust

A trust can be created:

- during the settlor's lifetime by means of a lifetime gift, and
- on death under the provisions of the settlor's will or under a deed of variation.

The capital tax consequences of a gift into a trust depends on the type of trust as summarised in the diagrams later in this section.

Capital tax charges whilst in trust

Whilst the assets are in the trust, the trustees are subject to CGT on the gains arising in respect of managing the trust assets each tax year.

Trustees may also be liable to a principal charge for IHT which is levied on RPTs only, every ten years following the creation of the trust.

The maximum rate of IHT payable on the principal charge is 6%.

The calculation of the CGT payable and the IHT principal charge payable by the trustees is not examinable.

Gifts out of a trust

Where a gift of assets is made out of a trust to a beneficiary, the gift is known as a 'capital distribution' and the property passes to the beneficiary 'absolutely' (i.e. the legal title of the property passes to the beneficiary).

The capital tax consequences of making capital distributions out of a trust to the beneficiaries depends on the type of trust as summarised in the diagrams later in this section.

Death of a life tenant of an IPDI trust

Settled property

For IHT purposes, the life tenant of an IPDI trust is deemed to own the underlying assets in the trust fund.

For these trusts, HMRC require the trust to pay an IHT liability on the death of the life tenant. As mentioned in Chapter 12, to calculate this tax, the value of the IPDI is included in the deceased life tenant's estate (known as settled property).

However, the calculation of the liability payable by the trustees on this value is not examinable.

Note that on the death of the life tenant, the trust fund is usually wound up and the capital assets are distributed to the remainderman of the trust.

The remainderman therefore suffers the IHT charge levied on the trust following the death of the life tenant.

Inheritance tax consequences

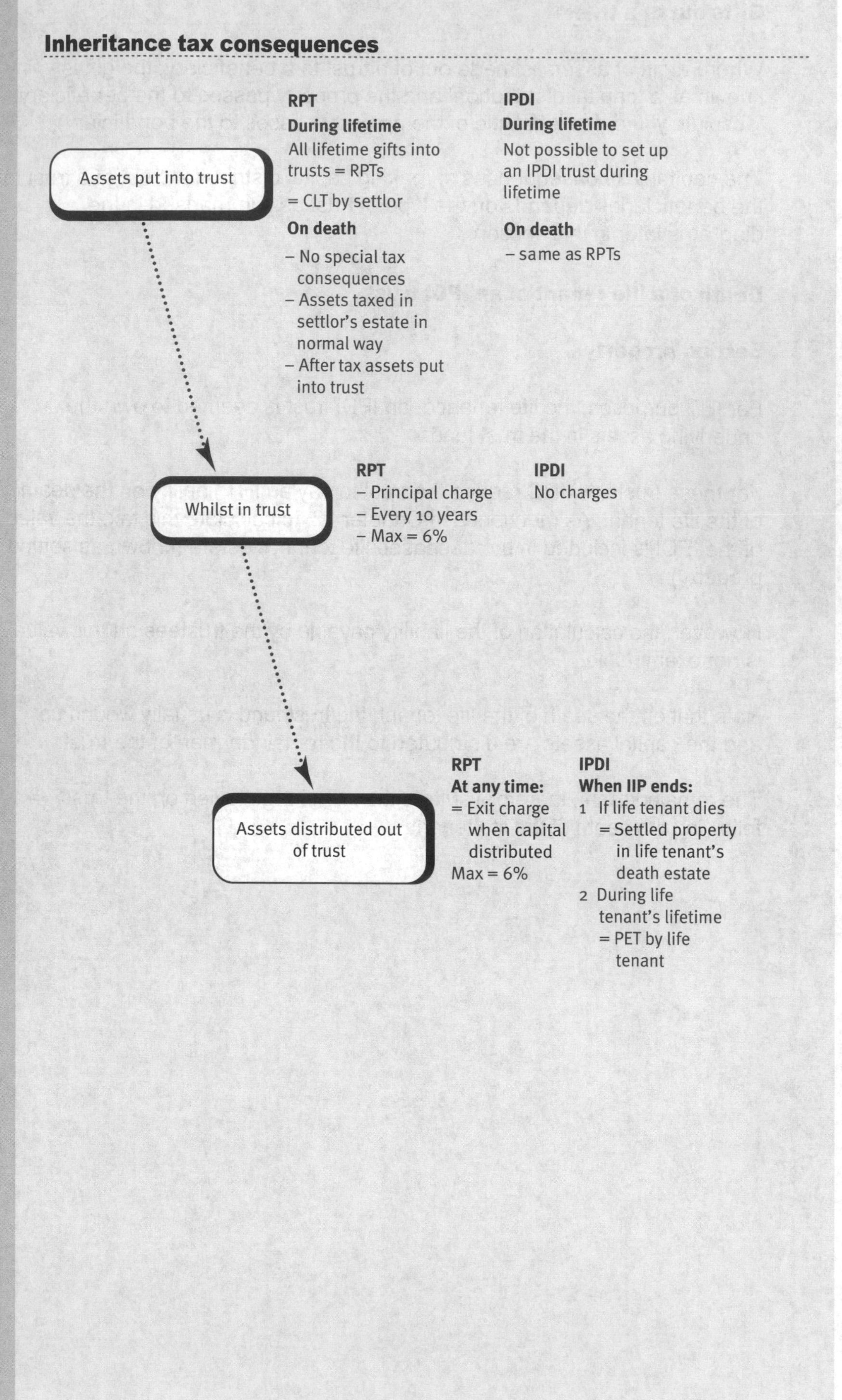
Assets put into trust
RPT
During lifetime
All lifetime gifts into trusts = RPTs
= CLT by settlor
On death
– No special tax consequences
– Assets taxed in settlor's estate in normal way
– After tax assets put into trust
IPDI
During lifetime
Not possible to set up an IPDI trust during lifetime
On death
– same as RPTs
Whilst in trust
RPT
– Principal charge
– Every 10 years
– Max = 6%
IPDI
No charges
Assets distributed out of trust
RPT
At any time:
= Exit charge when capital distributed
Max = 6%
IPDI
When IIP ends:
1 If life tenant dies
= Settled property in life tenant's death estate
2 During life tenant's lifetime
= PET by life tenant

Capital gains tax consequences

Assets put into trust

For all trusts
During lifetime
- Chargeable disposal of asset
- Calculate gain using MV as consideration
- Gift relief available on ANY asset as there is an immediate charge to IHT (but optional to claim)
- Trustees' base cost = MV less gift relief (if claimed)

On death
- No CGT consequences on death
- Not a chargeable disposal
- Trustees acquire assets at probate value

Whilst in trust

All trusts
- Chargeable gains on disposals by trustees
- AEA = half individual's AEA (£5,550 in 2016/17)
- Rate of tax = 20%
- Trustees pay out of trust fund
- Assessed under self-assessment rules

Assets distributed out of trust

IPDI ends
- **interest ends on death of a life tenant**
  = No CGT
  = Tax free uplift to MV

Remainderman receives assets at MV on life tenant's death

Any trust
- **in any other circumstances**
  = Chargeable disposal
- Gift relief on ANY assets as IHT charge
- unless IPDI
  = qualifying assets only

Example 1 – The capital taxes and trusts

Toppy died on 19 May 2016 leaving a widower and two children. She had made no lifetime gifts and her estate on death is valued at £422,000.

Under the terms of her will, she requested that a discretionary trust be set up for her children with £325,000 of her estate. The remainder is to go to her husband.

Calculate the IHT and CGT arising on Toppy's death and show how the estate is distributed between the beneficiaries.

Solution

Capital gains tax

- There is no CGT to pay on death.
- Any chargeable assets going into the trust have a base cost equal to the probate value.

Inheritance tax

Toppy: Estate computation

	£
Estate value	422,000
Less: Exempt legacies – Spouse	(97,000)
Gross chargeable estate	325,000
This is covered by the NRB available.	
IHT on death	0

Distribution of the estate

Residue to husband	97,000
Cash to trust	325,000
IHT to HMRC re: creation of trust	0
	422,000

Note: Use of discretionary trusts is advantageous if:

- The individual wants to control who the ultimate beneficiary of the trust will be, rather than leave the decision to the surviving spouse.
- The assets on the first death are likely to increase in value at a faster rate than the NRB. The growth of the assets will be in the trust fund and not be included in the surviving spouse or civil partner's estate.

Example 2 – Discretionary trust

Windy Miller, a wealthy farmer and landowner has decided to set up a discretionary trust for the benefit of various family members.

- On 6 May 2016 Windy put some shares in Windmill plc into the trust. He originally bought the shares for £20,000 on 1 May 2005. On 6 May 2016 the quoted shares have a market value of £50,000 for IHT purposes and £52,000 for CGT purposes.

  Windy has not made any previous lifetime gifts.

- On 30 November 2019, the trustees distributed the shares to Windy's grandson absolutely. Assume the market value of the quoted shares at that date will be £90,000 for IHT purposes and £95,000 for CGT purposes.

(a) **Explain an advantage for Windy of setting up a discretionary trust during his lifetime.**

(b) **Explain the capital tax consequences resulting from the creation of the discretionary trust on 6 May 2016.**

(c) **Explain the tax consequences arising during the life of the trust.**

(d) **Explain the capital tax consequences of distributing the property out of the trust to Windy's grandson absolutely on 30 November 2019.**

(e) **Explain the capital tax consequences of creating the trust and the distribution to the grandson assuming the discretionary trust had been set up on Windy's death in December 2017, rather than a lifetime gift. Assume the market value of the shares in December 2017 will be £60,000 for both IHT and CGT purposes.**

Assume the tax year 2016/17 tax rates and allowances apply throughout.

Solution

(a) **Advantages of setting up a discretionary trust during lifetime**

Assets placed in the trust can appreciate in value outside of both Windy's and his grandson's estates.

If the grandson is a non-taxpayer, a repayment of income tax paid by the trustees may be available.

(b) **Capital tax consequences of the creation of the trust**

Inheritance tax

– Lifetime gift into a RPT = a CLT by Windy Miller
– Based on £50,000 IHT value less exemptions
– Lifetime IHT payable
– Payable by Windy or trustees by agreement
– If Windy dies within 7 years: Additional IHT payable on death
– Death IHT payable by trustees from trust assets

Capital gains tax

– Chargeable disposal of asset at full MV of £52,000 for CGT purposes
– Gift relief available on any asset as there is an immediate charge to IHT
– Therefore no CGT payable when the assets are put into trust, the gain is held over against the base cost of the shares acquired by the trustees.

2016/17	£
MV of shares put into trust (May 2016)	52,000
Less: Cost (May 2005)	(20,000)
Capital gain before reliefs	32,000
Less: Gift relief	(32,000)
Chargeable gain	0

Base cost of the shares to the trustees	£
MV of shares put into trust (May 2016)	52,000
Less: Gain held over – gift relief	(32,000)
Base cost	20,000

(c) **Tax consequences during the life of the trust**

Income tax

The trustees will be subject to income tax on the income received from the trust assets.

The trustees account for income tax each tax year under self-assessment.

Inheritance tax

IHT at a maximum rate of 6% will be charged every ten years based on the value of the assets in trust on the principal charge date.

The first principal charge will be on 6 May 2026.

Capital gains tax

The trustees will manage the trust fund. They will buy and sell capital assets to maintain and grow the fund on behalf of the beneficiaries.

The sale of trust assets will give rise to capital gains which will be subject to CGT.

The trustees account for CGT each tax year under self-assessment.

(d) **Capital tax consequences of the distribution to the grandson**

Inheritance tax

- An exit charge arises
- Based on £90,000 IHT valuation
- Trustees pay a maximum of 6% of the value of the capital distribution

Capital gains tax

- Chargeable disposal of asset at full MV
- Gift relief available on any asset as there is an immediate charge to IHT
- Therefore no CGT payable when the assets are distributed out of the trust, the gain is held over against the base cost of the shares acquired by the grandson.

2019/20	£
MV of shares (Nov 2019)	95,000
Less: Base cost of shares	(20,000)
Capital gain before reliefs	75,000
Less: Gift relief	(75,000)
Chargeable gain	0

Base cost of shares acquired by the grandson

	£
MV of shares (Nov 2019)	95,000
Less: Gain held over	(75,000)
Base cost	20,000

(e) **If the discretionary trust is created on Windy's death**

Capital tax consequences of the creation of the trust

- **Inheritance tax**
  - Assets form part of Windy's estate
  - Included at a valuation of £60,000
  - Trust is established after the estate IHT has been paid (i.e. out of post-tax assets)

- **Capital gains tax**
  - No CGT consequences on death
  - Not a chargeable disposal, no CGT payable
  - Trustees acquire assets at IHT probate value of £60,000

Capital tax consequences of the distribution to the grandson

The same consequences as in part (d), with the exception of the CGT valuation

2019/20	£
MV of shares (Nov 2019)	95,000
Less: Cost of shares (probate value in Dec 2017)	(60,000)
Capital gain before reliefs	35,000
Less: Gift relief	(35,000)
Chargeable gain	0

Base cost of shares acquired by the grandson	
MV of shares (Nov 2019)	95,000
Less: Gain held over	(35,000)
Base cost	60,000

5 Tax planning opportunities

The following tax planning opportunities arise from creating a trust:

- By gifting assets into a trust during the individual's lifetime, the assets will no longer form part of the settlor's estate on death.
- Assets which appreciate in value can be transferred into the trust and will increase in value outside of both the settlor's and the beneficiaries estates.
- The exit charges and principal charges levied on some trusts are a maximum of 6% which may not be significant in the context of the financial planning requirements of the individual settlor.
- Trustees of a discretionary trust can choose to give income generated from the assets to the beneficiaries who are non-taxpayers so that a repayment of income tax paid by the trustees can be claimed.

6 Chapter summary

The taxation of trusts

Income tax

- Trustees account for IT on income generated by trust assets each tax year under self-assessment
- Beneficiary receives income net of tax:
  - IIP trust income: 20%/7.5% tax
  - DT income: 45% tax
- Include gross income in IT computation
- Deduct tax credit shown on certificate issued to beneficiary by trustees

Capital taxes

Gifts into trust

- **RPTs**
  During lifetime
  IHT
  = CLT by settlor
  CGT
  = Chargeable disposal at MV, gift relief available (RPTs)
  On settlor's death
  IHT
  = Assets taxed in estate, Trust set up out of post tax assets
  CGT
  = No CGT on death

- **IPDIs**
  During lifetime
  = Not possible as can only set up on death
- **On settlor's death**
  = same as RPTs for IHT and CGT

While assets in trust

- **CGT**
  = on capital disposals by trustees @ 20% (AEA = £5,550 p.a.)
- **IHT**
  = on RPTs only every ten years after the creation of the trust (max 6%)

Gifts out of trust

- **RPTs**
  IHT
  = Exit charge applies (max 6%)
  CGT
  = Chargeable disposal at MV, gift relief always available

- **IPDI trusts**
  IHT
  If due to death of life tenant
  = Settled property in life tenant's estate
  If distribution during life tenant's lifetime and is to an individual
  = PET by life tenant
  On any other occasion
  = CLT by life tenant
  CGT
  If due to death of life tenant
  = No CGT payable
  If distribution during life tenant's lifetime
  = Chargeable disposal at MV, gift relief may be available

chapter

15

Personal financial management

Chapter learning objectives

Upon completion of this chapter you will be able to:

- describe the principles underlying personal financial management
- compare and contrast the tax treatment of different investment products
- describe and contrast the different forms of finance that may be available to an individual
- calculate the receipts from a transaction, after tax, and compare the results of alternative scenarios and advise on the most efficient course of action.

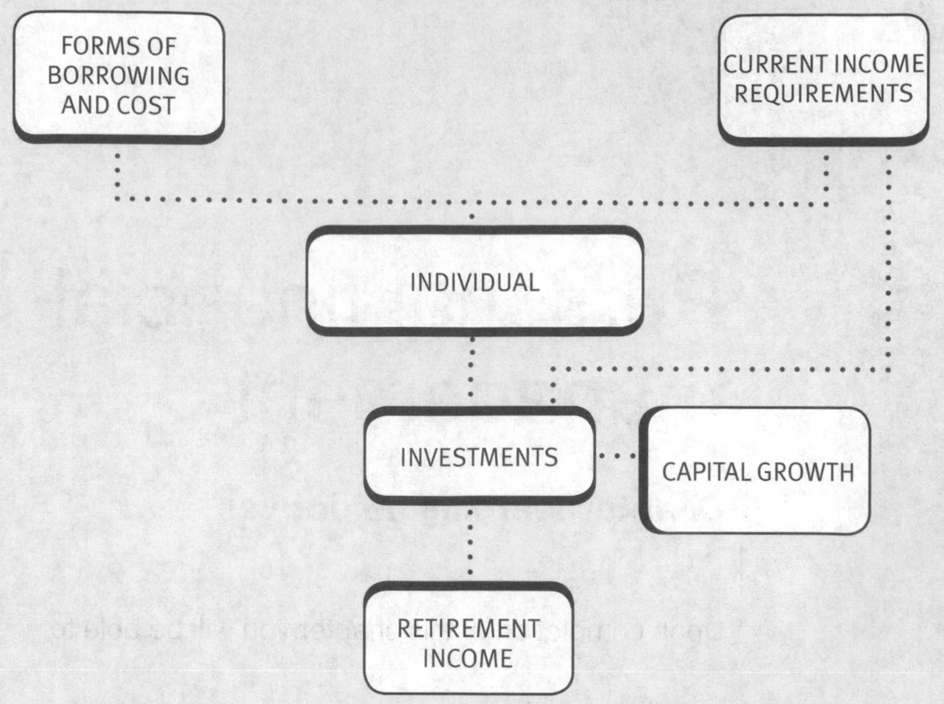

1 Personal financial management

The requirements of an individual when considering investments will change during their lifetime, partly as their lifestyle changes but also as their income increases.

When considering investments the main factors that need to be considered are usually:

- what income is available to invest after meeting the current outgoings from their existing income?
- does the taxpayer want to own their own home, and if so how should the purchase be financed?
- where the individual is responsible for children will they need money to fund school fees or university education, and how soon will this be needed?
- are they responsible for supporting their parents now or at some time in the future?
- ensuring there is sufficient income to fund their lifestyle after they have retired from employment or self-employment
- building a portfolio of investments that they may wish the children to inherit after death
- ensuring some investments are readily realisable if there is an unforeseen immediate need for cash (e.g. a cash ISA)

- if it is likely that they will inherit assets from family members at some time in the future, which could be used to fund asset purchases or living expenses during their retirement
- what is the individual's attitude to risk and ethical investment?

These considerations mean that in most cases it will be necessary to balance the requirement for income on an on-going basis, and investing for capital growth to be used to fund retirement.

An important issue is the tax treatment of any income or growth.

As a general rule:

- income will be liable to income tax
  - however, some income is exempt, or
  - could be tax-free if it is covered by the personal allowance or savings or dividends nil rate bands.
- capital growth will be liable to CGT
  - the AEA is a very important factor when deciding what the overall tax charge will be
  - some investments attract an exemption from CGT.

However, the taxpayer must not allow the tax treatment to cloud their judgement on the nature of the investments they make.

Individuals should also consider:

- the potential risks involved.

  For example, this could include a market crash affecting equities, property market reversals and future changes in interest rates.

- the timing of the investment.

  For example, a younger person should not tie up all their money in a pension fund if some of the money will be needed in the near future, as the pension cannot be accessed until the individual is 55.

2 Investments

Investment to generate income

An individual with low income will look to their investments to generate income. This will be the case for many pensioners.

The main examples of investments generating income are:

Investment	**Income**
Bank and building society accounts	Interest
Gilts	Interest
Corporate bonds	Interest
Government stock	Interest
Pensioners guaranteed income bonds	Interest
Shares/unit trusts, investment trusts, OEIC's	Dividends
Investment property	Rent

In some cases the income generated is exempt from tax (see Chapter 3).

Investment to generate capital growth

Some investments are more suitable when considering capital growth.

These would include:

- Unit trusts, investment trusts, Open ended investment companies (OEIC's) and shares where the profits are retained to generate growth instead of being distributed.
- Investment property.
- Capital bonds.

Choosing the investment

Some types of investment appear under both headings above, for example property. Many people invest in property for capital growth. However, some income is needed to cover the outgoings such as interest on borrowings and the cost of utilities.

For individuals who do not feel confident in their ability to choose the right properties to purchase, or who may wish to invest in a larger development the introduction of the Real estate investment trust (REIT) allows them to buy into property with whatever resources they have available.

Equities (i.e. shares) can be viewed as an income source or a capital investment. Companies will operate different dividend policies and the investor will need to consider these when deciding which shares to acquire.

There are some investment products that attract special tax relief. For example up to £15,240 may be invested each year in an individual savings account (ISA). Income and gains are then exempt.

Some shares in enterprise investment schemes (EIS), seed enterprise investment scheme (SEIS) and venture capital trusts (VCT) are exempt from CGT on disposal.

Not everyone will feel able to assess which investments are most suitable. In this case they may invest through a stockbroker or investment trust, relying on the fund manager to decide which investments should be made.

Many funds specialise in certain areas allowing the investor some element of choice. For example, specialising in property companies, overseas companies or technology companies.

Although the stockbroker or fund manager will charge a fee for their services the investor is being given the benefit of their investment expertise.

Tax efficient investments

There are a number of investments that give tax advantages.

The main ones to consider are:

- Personal pension contributions – Chapter 4.
- EIS and SEIS – Chapters 3 and 9.
- VCTs – Chapter 3.

Note however that although both EIS and VCT investments produce a reduction in an individual's income tax charge for the year of investment, they are both considered to be a relatively high risk investment.

There are other issues that need to be considered:

- An EIS or SEIS company will not normally pay a dividend. The profits are usually rolled up to give capital growth, on the assumption that the disposal of the shares will be exempt from CGT.
- EIS and SEIS companies are unquoted. It may be difficult to withdraw the investment as there is no ready market for the shares.
- These companies tend to be start-up companies, which is a particularly risky area for someone who cannot afford to lose their investment.
- To retain the income tax relief and obtain the CGT exemptions available the shares have to be retained for a minimum of 3 years (EIS and SEIS) and 5 years (VCT).

Key Investment products

	IT free	CGT free	Risk	Liquidity	Income/ capital growth
Bank/B Soc accounts	x	N/A	L	L1	I
NS&I accounts:					
– Investment	x	N/A	RF	L1	I
– Direct Saver	x	N/A	RF	L1	I
NS&I savings certificates	√	√	RF	L2	I
Premium bonds	√	√	RF	L1	I
Children's bonus bonds	√	√	L	L2	C
Qualifying life assurance policies	√	√	L	L3	C
EIS/SEIS (Note 1)	√	√	VH	L3	C
VCT scheme	√	√	H	L1	C
Pension schemes (Note 2)	√	√	M	L3	C
Qualifying corporate bonds	x	√	M	L1	C/I
Gilts	x	√	L	L1	I
'Real' property	x	x	M	L3	C/I
REIT	x	x	M	L1	C/I
Investment trusts, unit trusts and OEICs	x	x	M	L1	C
Quoted shares/ securities	x	x	M/H	L1	C
Unquoted shares/ securities	x	x	VH	L3	C/I
ISAs	√	√	L/M	L1	C/I

Key to terms:

I	Income	H	High risk
C	Capital growth	VH	Very high risk
x	Chargeable	L1	Immediate access
√	Tax-free	L2	Access possible but penalty
RF	Risk-free	L3	Non liquid
L	Low risk		
M	Medium risk	N/A	Not applicable

Notes:

(1) Tax relief on investment but income taxable

(2) Tax relief on payments

3 Raising finance for the individual

There are a number of different ways to raise finance as an individual borrower. A reminder of the key methods is given in expandable text.

Raising finance

Mortgages (long-term source of finance)

Mortgages are a good source of finance when interest rates are low.

If it is thought that the rates may rise it is possible to obtain a fixed rate mortgage, which provides certainty about the cost of the mortgage over the period for which the rate is fixed.

A fixed rate mortgage may at times be more expensive than an ordinary mortgage, however this may be preferable to obtain certainty of cash outflows.

Moving between providers can be expensive as lenders will often charge an early redemption penalty if the mortgage is repaid.

As property prices increase it may be possible to increase the mortgage on the property to use the funds for other purposes, such as starting a new business, buying property to let or to use as a holiday home.

Credit cards

Credit cards are an expensive source of finance, as the interest rates charged are very high. They should really only be considered for short term finance.

Many cards offer interest free periods on balance transfers and these can be used to minimise the cost of interest.

Bank overdraft (short to medium source of finance)

The interest rate on an overdraft tends to be lower than on a credit card, so this could be a better way to borrow for short or medium term.

Hire purchase agreements (short to medium source of finance)

This is often used as a method of purchasing household goods. Interest rates tend to be variable, and can be expensive.

4 Calculating the net return on an investment

It is difficult to compare the overall returns on different investments if they produce income and capital growth, as one may balance off against the other.

Where the individual needs an amount of income to meet their living expenses it is slightly easier to compare the investment return, as the net of tax return can be calculated for both a basic rate and higher rate taxpayer.

It is more difficult to predict capital growth for the different types of investments.

An elderly taxpayer may prefer a higher rate of income and lower long-term capital growth, as they have no realistic need for the value of their investments to increase during their remaining lifetime.

Example 1 – Net return

Tim has a bank overdraft of £2,000 and pays interest at 9% but has £5,000 in a deposit account earning interest at 4.7% gross.

Discuss the financial planning implications and suggest how Tim could increase his disposable income. Assume Tim is a basic rate tax payer and has taxable non-savings income in excess of £5,000.

Solution

- Tim is paying bank interest of £180 (9% × £2,000).
- Tim is receiving bank interest of £235 (4.7% × £5,000) which is tax-free, as he is a basic rate tax payer and therefore entitled to a savings nil rate band (SNRB) of £1,000.
- His net disposable income is £55 (£235 – £180).
- Tim should use £2,000 of the capital from his deposit account to repay his bank overdraft, thus saving him £180 of interest.
- Tim should, as far as is practical in accordance with living costs, build up his savings to fully utilise his SNRB of £1,000 (£500 if he becomes a higher rate taxpayer). If his savings income exceeds the available NRB in the future, sufficient capital should be transferred to a cash ISA to ensure that income in excess of the SNRB is received tax free.
- Interest received at (4.7% × £3,000) = £141.
- Tim has increased his disposal income by £86 (£141 – £55).

Example 2 – Net return

Jeremy has inherited £50,000 from his grandmother.

He has not yet decided what he should do with this money. He is currently in full time employment, and is a higher rate taxpayer.

He is considering investing in either shares or property, as he feels this would produce both income and capital growth.

As part of his considerations he has obtained the following information:

(1) If he bought shares in X plc there would be an annual dividend payment of £1,500 (approx).

(2) Shares in Y plc could be bought. Y plc is a REIT, and it is anticipated that the return would be in the region of £1,743 per annum.

(3) He could buy a small property and let it to students. The rental would be £150 per week with estimated outgoings of £80 per week.

(4) His bank is offering an internet deposit account paying gross interest of 5%.

Discuss the financial planning implications and consider the ways in which Jeremy's inheritance money could be invested.

Solution

X plc shares	Income tax treatment: The dividends will be received tax free as they will be covered by the dividend nil rate (DNRB) of £5,000. The DNRB is available irrespective of taxpayer's taxable income. Capital growth – possible over a period – subject to fluctuations of the stock market Easily realisable – yes – quoted shares can be sold on the stock exchange Risk – stock market crash

		£
Y plc shares	Net return after tax:	£
	Income (£1,743 × 100/80)	2,179
	Income tax at 40%	872
	Less: Tax credit (20% × £2,179)	(436)
	Income tax payable	436
	Net return (£1,743 – £436) (Note)	1,307
	Capital growth – possible over a period of time	
	Easily realisable – yes – quoted shares	
	Risk – property value crash	

Note: Alternative calculation using effective rate of tax on net interest received by a HR taxpayer:
(Net interest × 25%) = (£1,743 × 25%) = £436
Net return = (£1,743 × 75%) = £1,307

		£
Property	Net return after tax:	£
	Rent received (52 × £150)	7,800
	Less: Costs (52 × £80)	(4,160)
	Net rental income	3,640
	Less: Tax at 40%	(1,456)
	Net return	2,184
	Capital growth – yes depending on area	
	Easily realisable – no – dependent on property market, time to find buyer, process transactions	
	Risk – rent not paid but expenses still need to be met, property value crash	

Bank	Net return after tax:	£
	Interest (£50,000 × 5%)	2,500
	Less: Tax at 500 × 0%	(0)
	2,000 × 40%	(800)
	Net return	1,700

Capital growth – none
Easily realisable – yes
Risk – reduction in interest rates

5 Chapter summary

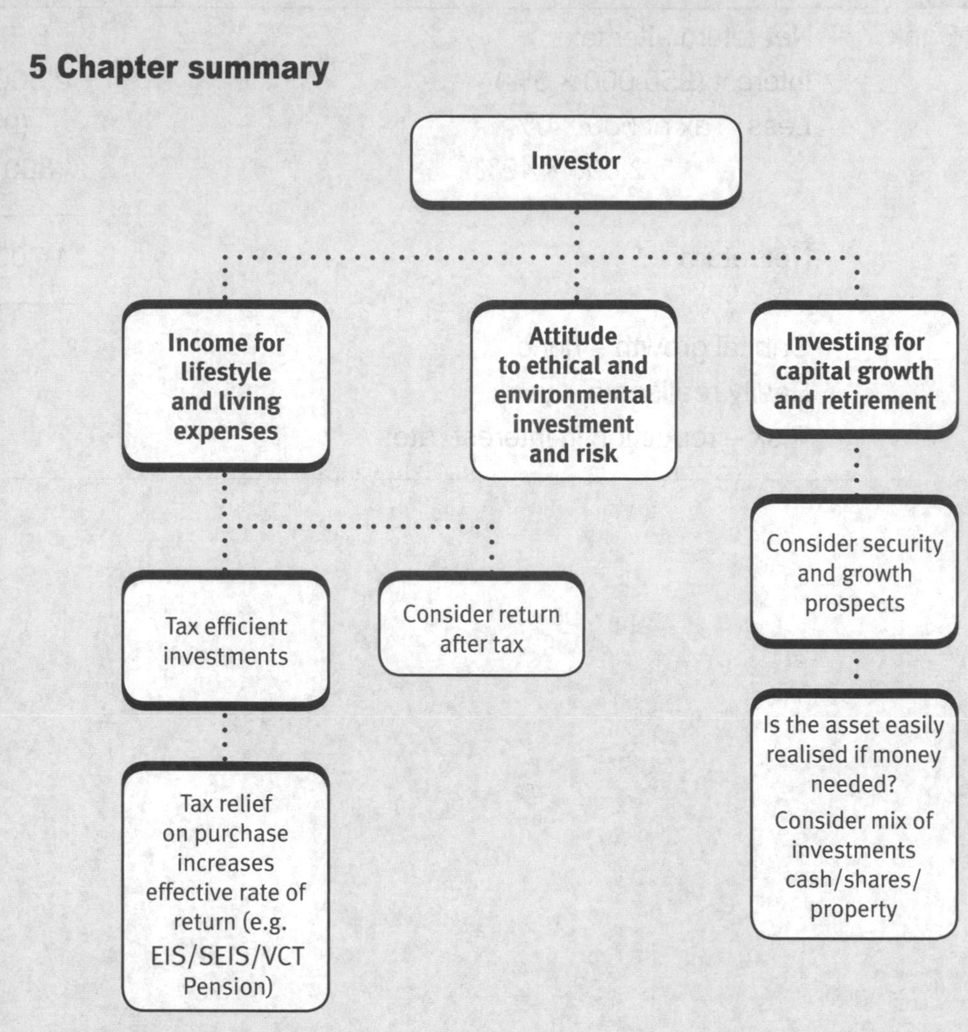

chapter

16

Ethics and personal tax administration

Chapter learning objectives

Upon completion of this chapter you will be able to:

- consider the effect of the Association's ethical guidelines when dealing with a client
- explain the principles of self-assessment for an individual including the time limits for notifying/filing returns and claims, due dates of payment and the penalties for non compliance
- list the information and records that taxpayers need to retain for tax purposes and consider the retention period
- explain the circumstances in which HM Revenue and Customs can perform a compliance check on a self-assessment tax return
- describe the procedures for dealing with appeals and disputes.

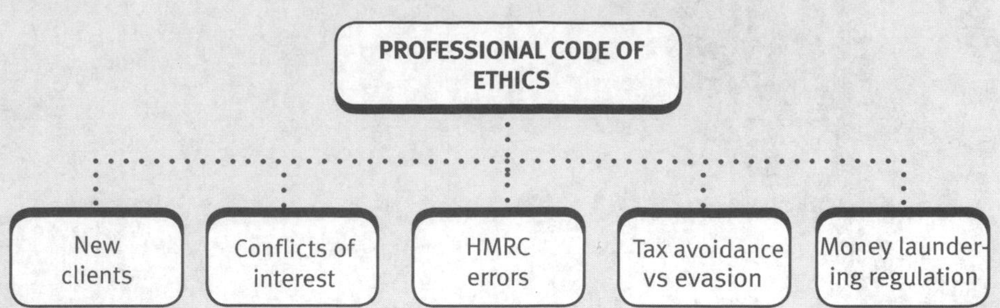

Introduction

This chapter covers the area of ethics and tax administration for individuals.

Professional ethics is an essential attribute required in practice and a topic which will appear for approximately 5 marks in every examination as part of a longer question. Much of the content has already been covered in earlier studies, however at P6 the principles must be learnt and applied to tax scenarios to provide advice to clients.

The personal tax administration in this chapter is also important to remember and apply. Much of the content is a revision of the rules covered in F6. A brief reminder is given and revision examples provided to check your retention of F6 knowledge.

1 Professional Code of Ethics

Overview

The ACCA 'Professional Code of Ethics and Conduct' sets out the standards of professional conduct expected from the members and students of the Association, and sets a framework of principles that should be applied. Guidance is also contained within the 'Professional Conduct in Relation to Taxation' provisions.

Failure to comply with this code could lead to disciplinary action.

THE FUNDAMENTAL PRINCIPLES

Objectivity
Professional behaviour
Professional competence and due care
Integrity
Confidentiality

Remember: OPPIC

A reminder of the definitions of the fundamental principles are as follows:

Objectivity (O)

- Members should not allow bias, conflicts of interest or the influence of others to override objectivity and to affect their business decisions.

Professional behaviour (P)

- Members must comply with relevant laws and avoid actions that may discredit the profession.

Professional competence and due care (P)

- Members have an ongoing duty to maintain professional knowledge and skills to ensure that a client/employer receives competent, professional service based on current developments.
- Members should be diligent and act in accordance with applicable technical and professional standards when providing professional services.

Integrity (I)

- Members should be straightforward and honest in all their professional and business relationships.

Confidentiality (C)

- Members should respect the confidentiality of information acquired as a result of professional and business relationships and should not disclose any such information to third parties unless:
  - they have proper and specific authority, or
  - there is a legal or professional right or duty to disclose (e.g. money laundering).
- Confidential information acquired as a result of professional and business relationships, should not be used for the personal advantage of members or third parties.

New clients

A member is required to exercise their professional expertise when dealing with clients.

Before taking on a new client the member should consider whether:

- acting for the client will pose any risk to the practice in terms of their integrity. This would include assessing the potential client's personal and business circumstances, and attitude to disclosure and compliance with tax law
- the member and their firm have the skills and competence to service the client's requirements
- the potential client is involved in any activity that could be considered as money laundering.

In the case of a limited company, the following information should be gathered:

- Proof of incorporation and primary business address and registered office.
- The structure, directors and shareholders of the company.
- The identities of those persons instructing the firm on behalf of the company and those persons that are authorised to do so.

In the case of an individual, the following information should be gathered:

- Proof of identity and residential address
- Any unincorporated business interests and if so details of the nature and structure and those persons that are authorised to act on behalf of the business (e.g. partners in a partnership)

Once it has been decided that the member can act for the client they should:

- ask permission to contact the old advisors to request the information necessary to decide whether they can act for the client (the old advisor should seek the client's permission before they discuss their situation with the new advisor)
- if the client does not give permission to contact the old advisors the member should give serious consideration as to whether they can act for them.

Assuming the situation is satisfactory and it is decided to act for the client the member should issue a letter of engagement setting out the terms and conditions of the arrangement, and other relevant items.

Example 1 – New clients

Where a member is asked to replace a client's existing advisors they must request the permission of the prospective client to contact the existing advisor.

What is the reason for this communication?

Solution

The main purpose of the communication is to ensure that the member:

(i) is aware of any factors that may be relevant to the decision as to whether they accept the work

(ii) is aware of any factors that may have a bearing on ensuring full disclosure of relevant items is made to HMRC

(iii) has the information with regard to filing deadline, elections and claims relating to the client so that no matters are overlooked during the period of the move to the new advisor.

Conflicts of interest

A member should not put themselves in the position where acting for two clients creates a conflict of interest.

If they become aware of a potential conflict they should act immediately to address it. Where no appropriate action can be taken to avoid the conflict the member should cease to act in the matter where the conflict arose.

Conflicts can occur in the following situations:

- where a member acts for a client and is then asked to act for another party in a transaction
- acting for both parties in a divorce
- acting for the employer and their employees
- where the advisor may benefit from the transaction.

It may be acceptable to act for both parties, as long as the following safeguards are put in place:

- the potential conflict should be pointed out to all of the relevant parties
- consent should be obtained to act for them
- the firm must have clear guidelines in relation to confidentiality; and
- should consider the need to use separate teams for each client.

Alternatively, the firm may consider acting for just one party, or not acting for either party.

Test your understanding 1

Steven has been asked to act for both parties to a transaction.

Describe the three courses of action open to Steven.

Test your understanding 2

Simon is about to give some tax advice to his client. If the client acts on this advice Simon will receive commission of £2,000 from a third party.

What action should Simon take?

Dealing with HMRC

It is important to ensure that information provided to HMRC is accurate and complete.

A member must not assist a client to plan or commit any offence.

If a member becomes aware that the client has committed a tax irregularity:

- they must discuss it with the client, and
- ensure that proper disclosure is made.

Examples would include:

- not declaring income that is taxable
- claiming reliefs to which they are not entitled
- not notifying HMRC where they have made a mistake giving rise to an underpayment of tax, or an increased repayment.

Where a client has made an error:

- it will be necessary to decide whether it was a genuine error or a deliberate or fraudulent act.

Once an error has been discovered:

- the member should explain to the client the requirement to notify HMRC as soon as possible, and the implications of their not doing so.

The letter of engagement may include a section with regard to disclosure of information to HMRC, if so it would be courteous to inform the client of the intention to disclose.

Should the client refuse to make a full and prompt disclosure to HMRC:

- the member must write and explain the potential consequences, and
- consider whether the amount is material, and if it is, whether they should continue to act for the client.

If the client still refuses to make a full disclosure, the member:

- should cease to act for the client
- must then also write to HMRC informing them that they have ceased to act for the client, but without disclosing the reason why
- must then consider their position under the Money Laundering Regulations.

Employees

Where the member is an employee they may become aware of irregularities in their employer's dealings with HMRC.

They should raise their concerns with the appropriate person.

If the employer refuses to take any appropriate action the employee should seek advice from the professional body. In addition they need to consider:

- the need to report to the employer's Money Laundering Officer
- whether they can continue in their current employment
- if it is necessary to disclose under the Public Interest Disclosure Act.

Where the employee is responsible for agreeing the employer's tax liabilities with HMRC they are in a similar position to members in practice.

If they discover an error, default or fraud they should bring it to the attention of the employer, and encourage them to disclose the relevant information.

Money Laundering Regulations

Money Laundering is the term used for offences including benefiting from or concealing the proceeds of a crime.

This includes tax evasion.

All businesses within regulated sectors must appoint a Money Laundering Reporting Officer (MLRO) within the firm.

The MLRO will decide whether a transaction should be reported to the National Crime Agency (NCA).

Where a report is made the client should not be informed as this may amount to 'tipping off', which is an offence.

A report to the NCA does not remove the requirement to disclose the information to HMRC.

Dishonest conduct of tax agents

- There is a civil penalty of up to £50,000 for dishonest conduct of tax agents.
- In cases where the penalty exceeds £5,000, HMRC may publish details of the penalised tax agent.
- With agreement of the Tax Tribunal, HMRC can access the working papers of a dishonest agent.

Tax avoidance or evasion

Tax evasion is unlawful. A taxpayer who dishonestly withholds or falsifies information for tax evasion purposes may be subject to criminal proceedings or suffer civil penalties.

A tax advisor who is a party to tax evasion is subject to the sanctions of the criminal law. Concealment of material facts may constitute tax evasion.

Tax avoidance is the use of legitimate means to reduce the incidence of tax. A tax advisor may properly advise or assist their clients to reduce their liability to tax. However, the courts are wary of schemes or arrangements the sole purpose of which is to avoid tax.

In recent years:

- The courts have taken an increasingly firm stance in finding that such schemes do not achieve their purpose.
- Specific anti-avoidance schemes have been targeted by HMRC with legislation to counter the **tax advantages** gained by the tax payer. Tax advantages include the reduction of tax liabilities, increase of tax deductions allowed, deferral of tax payments and acceleration of tax repayments.
- HMRC have also introduced:
  - disclosure obligations regarding anti-avoidance tax schemes requiring the declaration of the details of the scheme to HMRC
  - **a general anti-abuse rule (GAAR)** to counteract **tax advantages** arising from **abusive tax arrangements**.
- In FA2015 HMRC have increased measures to counter aggressive tax avoidance schemes and to penalise tax evasion.

General anti-abuse rule

- The meanings of the relevant terms are:
  - 'Tax advantages' include increased tax deductions, reduced tax liabilities, deferral of tax payments and advancement of tax repayments.
  - 'Tax arrangements' are arrangements with a main purpose of obtaining a tax advantage.
  - Arrangements are 'abusive' where they cannot be regarded as a reasonable course of action, for example, where they include contrived steps or are intended to take advantage of shortcomings in the tax legislation.
- If the GAAR applies, HMRC may respond by increasing the taxpayer's liability, accelerate tax payments or defer repayments and ignore artificial steps in a contrived abusive scheme.
- In FA2016, a new penalty of 60% of the tax advantage counteracted by the GAAR has been introduced.

Test your understanding 3

When you are checking a recent tax computation from HMRC you notice that they have made an error which has resulted in your client receiving a larger repayment than should have been made.

What actions should you take?

Example 2 – Employees

You have recently moved to work in the tax department of a medium sized trading company. You have been reviewing the recently submitted tax return and have identified several material errors.

You have brought this information to the head of the department but he refuses to adjust the figures as this will increase the tax payable for the year, and impact on his bonus.

What action should you take?

Solution

Taking no action is not permissible, so the following should be considered.

- Is there anyone else in the company with whom it may be appropriate to discuss these concerns?
- Consider taking advice from the ACCA or legal advice on the relevant course of action.
- Consider making a report to the company's money laundering reporting officer, if there is one and, if not, direct to the NCA.
- Consider looking for alternative employment.
- Consider whether disclosure should be made under the Public Interest Disclosure Act. Does the employer have in place any policies with regard to disclosures under this act? Consider taking legal advice before pursuing this course of action.

The member should keep a record of all action taken to demonstrate that they have acted properly throughout.

2 Personal tax administration

The collection of income tax

Employees have their income tax and national insurance liabilities on their employment income, and in some cases on small amounts of other income, collected at source through the PAYE system.

Self-assessment is the system for the collection of tax which is not deducted through the PAYE system.

Therefore, employees with more complicated tax affairs and other taxpayers (e.g. the self-employed) will normally be required to submit details of their taxable income and gains annually in a tax return, so that their tax liability can be calculated and collected through the self-assessment system.

Self-assessment

Under the self-assessment system the taxpayer will normally be required to provide HMRC with details of their taxable income in a tax return.

From 6 April 2016, certain taxpayers with relatively straightforward tax affairs may instead be issued with a simple assessment. However, the simple assessment system is not examinable.

Tax returns

Under the self-assessment system for the majority of individuals the onus is placed on the taxpayer to provide the information to calculate their tax liability.

- The taxpayer is sent a notice to complete a self-assessment tax return annually.
- The responsibility for providing information, calculating and accounting for income tax, class 2 and 4 NICs and CGT lies with the taxpayer.
- The taxpayer must complete and file (i.e. submit) a return with HMRC on paper or electronically.
- Different deadlines exist for filing paper and electronic (online) returns.

Return – filing deadline

The deadline for submitting the 2016/17 self-assessment tax return depends on how the return is filed.

The deadline for submitting the return is the **later** of:

- 31 October 2017 for a paper return
- 31 January 2018 for an electronic (online) return
- three months after a notice to file a return is issued by HMRC.

The 31 January following the end of the tax year is known as the **'filing date'**, regardless of whether the return is filed on paper or electronically.

This must be distinguished from the date on which the return is actually filed / submitted, which is the 'actual filing date'.

A reminder of other key aspects of self-assessment covered at F6 is given in expandable text and is summarised in the diagram in section 3.

The content of a tax return

The taxpayer completes the main tax return form (SA100) to give basic details including their name, address and certain types of investment income.

The taxpayer should then complete relevant supplementary pages to tell HMRC about all of their income and gains relating to the tax year. For example, income from employment, income from property, or capital gains.

If the taxpayer is completing their tax return online, these supplementary pages can be added as necessary. If the taxpayer is completing a paper tax return, the supplementary pages needed should be requested at the same time as the main tax return.

- **Self-employed people:** Should complete the self-employment supplementary pages.
- **Employees:** Generally pay their tax liability under PAYE and often a self-assessment tax return will not be required as there is no further tax liability. However, if they receive taxable income that is not fully taxed through the PAYE system, they will need to complete a tax return.

- **Partnerships:** Although partners are dealt with individually, a partnership return is required to aid self-assessment on the individual partners. This gives details of the partners, includes a partnership statement detailing the partnership's tax adjusted trading income and shows how it is allocated between the partners.

Return – calculation of tax

- Where a return is filed electronically:
  - a calculation of the tax liability is automatically provided as part of the online filing process.
- Where a paper return is submitted:
  - HMRC will calculate the tax liability on behalf of the taxpayer, provided the return is submitted by the 31 October deadline. The taxpayer has the option of calculating the tax himself.
  - the calculation by HMRC is treated as a self-assessment on behalf of the taxpayer.
- Where HMRC calculate the tax it makes no judgement of the accuracy of the figures included in the return, but merely calculates the tax liability based on the information submitted.
- HMRC normally communicate with the taxpayer by issuing a statement of account which is a reminder of amounts owing to HMRC.

Amendments to the return

Either party may amend the return:

- HMRC may correct any obvious errors or mistakes within **nine months** of the date that the return is filed with them.

  These would include arithmetical errors or errors of principle. However, this does not mean that HMRC has necessarily accepted the return as accurate.

- The taxpayer can amend the return within **12 months** of the 31 January filing date. For the tax year 2016/17, amendments must therefore be made by 31 January 2019.

  Note that the deadline is the same regardless of whether the return is filed on paper or electronically.

If an error is discovered at a later date then the taxpayer can make a claim for overpayment relief (see later) to recover any tax overpaid.

Notification of chargeability

Self-assessment places the onus on the taxpayer, therefore:

- Taxpayers who do not receive a notice to file a return are required to notify HMRC if they have income or chargeable gains on which tax is due.
- The time limit for notifying HMRC of chargeability is six months from the end of the tax year in which the liability arises (i.e. 5 October 2017 for the tax year 2016/17).
- Notification is not necessary if there is no actual tax liability. For example, if the income or capital gain is covered by allowances or exemptions.
- A standard penalty may arise for failure to notify chargeability (see section 8).

Penalties for failure to submit a return

HMRC can impose fixed penalties and tax-geared penalties for the failure to submit a return, depending on the length of delay.

See section 8 for the detail on the penalties that can be imposed.

Determination of tax due if no return is filed

Where a self-assessment tax return is not filed by the filing date, HMRC may determine the amount of tax due. The impact of this is:

- The determination is treated as a self-assessment by the taxpayer.
- The determination can only be replaced by the actual self-assessment when it is submitted by the taxpayer (i.e. the submission of a tax return).
- There is no appeal against a determination, which therefore encourages the taxpayer to displace it with the actual self-assessment.

A determination can be made at any time within **three years** of the filing date (i.e. by 31 January 2021 for 2016/17 tax return).

Claims

Wherever possible a claim for a relief, allowance or repayment can be made to HMRC usually by including it in the self-assessment tax return.

The amount of the claim must be quantified at the time that the claim is made. For example, if loss relief is claimed, then the amount of the loss must be stated.

Claims for earlier years

Certain claims will relate to earlier years. The most obvious example of this is the claiming of loss relief for earlier years.

The basic rule is that such a claim is:

- established in the later year
- calculated based on the tax liability of the earlier year.

The tax liability for the earlier year is not adjusted. Instead, the tax reduction resulting from the claim will be set off against the tax liability for the later year. The logic is that it avoids re-opening assessments for earlier years.

Alternatively if a separate claim is made HMRC will refund the tax due.

As the claim is only quantified by reference to the later year, POAs that are based on the relevant amount for the earlier year will not change.

Claim for overpayment relief

Where an assessment is excessive due to an error or mistake in a return, the taxpayer can claim relief. The claim must be made within four years of the end of the tax year concerned.

For the tax year 2016/17 the claim should be made by 5 April 2021.

A claim can be made in respect of errors made, and mistakes arising from not understanding the law.

Example 3 – Claims for earlier years

A taxpayer's relevant amount for the tax year 2015/16 is £4,400. In the tax year 2016/17 the taxpayer makes a trading loss of £1,000, and makes a claim to offset this against his total income of the tax year 2015/16.

Explain how the taxpayer will receive the tax refund arising as a result of the relief for the loss arising in the tax year 2016/17.

Solution

The taxpayer's POAs for the tax year 2016/17 are £2,200 (£4,400 × 1/2), and these will not change as a result of the loss relief claim.

The tax refund due will be calculated at the taxpayer's marginal income tax rate(s) for the tax year 2015/16.

The tax refund due will either be set off against the tax year 2016/17 tax liability, thereby affecting the balancing payment on 31 January 2018, or if there is insufficient tax left owing, HMRC will make a refund.

3 Summary

Self-assessment 2016/17 tax return

Responsibility placed on taxpayer

Format of the return

- Declare income
- Claim allowances and reliefs
- Calculate the tax (optional)

Notification of chargeability

- Within six months from end of tax year
- Penalty up to 100% of unpaid tax, depending on taxpayer's behaviour (section 8)

Filing dates

Paper return

- 31 October 2017
- i.e. 31 October following the end of the tax year

Electronic return

- 31 January 2018
- i.e. 31 January following the end of the tax year

If return not issued until after 31 October 2017

- must file within three months after the date of issue

Amendments to the return

- HMRC
  - obvious errors and mistakes
  - within 9 months of actual filing date
- Taxpayer
  - by 31 January 2019
  - i.e. within 12 months of filing date

If no return submitted by filing date

- HMRC can determine tax due within three years of filing date
- No appeal
- Taxpayer can displace determination with actual self assessment

Claims

- Must quantify amount of claims for reliefs, allowances, repayments
- Earlier year claims:
  - tax liability of earlier year not adjusted
  - tax reduction is set against current liability
  - does not affect POAs
- Taxpayer claim
  - for overpayment relief
  - must be made by 5 April 2021
  - i.e. within four years of end of tax year

Penalties (section 8)

- Late submission of return
  - initial penalty = £100 and if:
  - › 3 months late = £10 per day (max 90 days); and
  - › 6 months late = 5% of tax due (min £300); and
  - › 12 months late = further 5% tax due; more if failure deliberate

4 Payment of tax

Any tax due on income which is not deducted at source is payable by self-assessment as follows:

- Payment dates

First payment on account (POA)	–	31 January during the tax year.
Second payment on account (POA)	–	31 July following the tax year.
Balancing payment/repayment	–	31 January following the tax year.

- POAs are based on the previous tax year's 'relevant amount' (i.e. total income tax and class 4 NICs liabilities less amounts already taxed at source).
- Each POA is 50% of the 'relevant amount'.
- No POAs are ever required for CGT liabilities or class 2 NICs.
- Both CGT and class 2 NICs are due on 31 January following the end of the tax year and do not affect the POAs.

Test your understanding 4

Rebecca's tax payable for the tax year 2016/17 was as follows:

	£
Income tax	10,800
Less: Tax deducted at source	(2,500)
	8,300
Class 2 NICs	146
Class 4 NICs	800
CGT	4,454
Total tax liability	13,700

Two POAs have been paid on 31 January 2017 and 31 July 2017 of £4,000 each.

Calculate the amount payable on 31 January 2018.

A reminder of further rules relating to POAs covered at F6 are given in expandable text and are summarised in the diagram in section 5.

When POAs are not required

POAs are not required where:

- the relevant amount (i.e. income tax and Class 4 NIC liability less tax deducted at source) for the previous tax year is less than £1,000, or
- more than 80% of the income tax liability for the previous tax year was met by deduction of tax at source.

Accordingly, most employed people will not have to make POAs, since at least 80% of their tax liability is paid through PAYE.

Claims to reduce POAs

- A taxpayer can claim to reduce POAs, at any time before 31 January following the tax year, if they expect the actual income tax and class 4 NIC liability (net of tax deducted at source) for the tax year 2016/17 to be lower than in the tax year 2015/16.
- The claim must state the grounds for making the claim.

Following a claim:

- The POAs will be reduced.
- Each POA will be for half the reduced amount, unless the taxpayer claims that there is no tax liability at all.
- If POAs based on the prior year figures are paid before the claim, then HMRC will refund the overpayment.

In the event that the claim is incorrect and the actual tax liability for the current year turns out to be higher than the reduced POAs, then the following consequences arise:

- Interest will be charged on the tax underpaid.
- A penalty may be charged if a taxpayer fraudulently or negligently claims to reduce POAs. The maximum penalty is the difference between the amounts actually paid on account, and the amounts that should have been paid.
- A penalty will not be sought in cases of innocent error. The aim is to penalise taxpayers who claim large reductions in payments on account without any foundation to the claim.

Interest and penalties

A reminder of the rules for interest and penalties covered at F6 are given in expandable text and are summarised in the diagram in section 5.

Late payment interest

Interest will automatically be charged if **any** tax is paid late.

All interest is charged on a daily basis

- from: the date the tax was due to be paid
- to: the date of payment
- at a rate of 3% p.a. (rate given in tax rates and allowances).

However, in the examination, if required, calculations should be performed to the nearest month and £ unless indicated otherwise in the question.

Repayment interest

- Interest may be paid by HMRC on any overpayment of tax at a rate of 0.5% (rate given in tax rates and allowances).
- If applicable, interest runs from the later of:
  – the date the tax was due, or
  – the date HMRC actually received the tax.
- Interest runs to: the date of repayment
- Interest is only paid on the amount of tax that should have been paid (i.e. deliberate overpayments will not attract interest).

Penalties for late payments

Late payment interest is not a penalty, since it merely aims to compensate for the advantage of paying late.

Therefore, to further encourage compliance, penalties can also be imposed by HMRC where income tax, class 2 NICs, class 4 NICs or CGT is paid late.

Penalties do not apply to POAs.

Penalties are calculated as follows:

Tax paid	Penalty (% of tax due)
More than 1 month late	5%
More than 6 months late	Additional 5%
More than 12 months late	Additional 5%

Note that technically the penalties apply if tax is paid more than 30 days late, 5 months and 30 days late and 11 months and 30 days late, but the P6 examining team gives these time limits to the nearest month and it is acceptable to do so in the examination.

HMRC have the discretion to reduce a penalty in special circumstances, for example if they consider that the penalty would be inappropriate or disproportionate.

However, the inability to pay will not be classified as special circumstances.

Example 4 – Interest and penalties

Rowena's tax payable (after credits but before POAs) for 2016/17 is:

Income tax	£6,000
Capital gains tax	£3,000

POAs of £4,000 in total were made on the relevant dates. The balance of the tax due was paid as follows:

Income tax	28 February 2018
Capital gains tax	31 March 2018

Calculate the interest and penalties due on a monthly basis.

Solution

The relevant date for balancing payments is 31 January 2018.

No POAs are ever required for CGT.

The amounts due were therefore as follows:

31 January 2018	Income tax (£6,000 – £4,000)	£2,000
	Capital gains tax	£3,000

Interest will run as follows:

Income tax	£2,000 from 31 January 2018 to 28 February 2018, (1/12 × 3% × £2,000) = £5
CGT	£3,000 from 31 January 2018 to 31 March 2018, (2/12 × 3% × £3,000) = £15

In addition a penalty is due on the CGT (as it was more than one month late) of 5% of £3,000 = £150.

There is no penalty in respect of the late payment of income tax as it was paid within one month.

Total interest and penalties payable = (£5 + £15 + £150) = £170.

The penalty may be reduced if HMRC accept there were special circumstances.

5 Summary

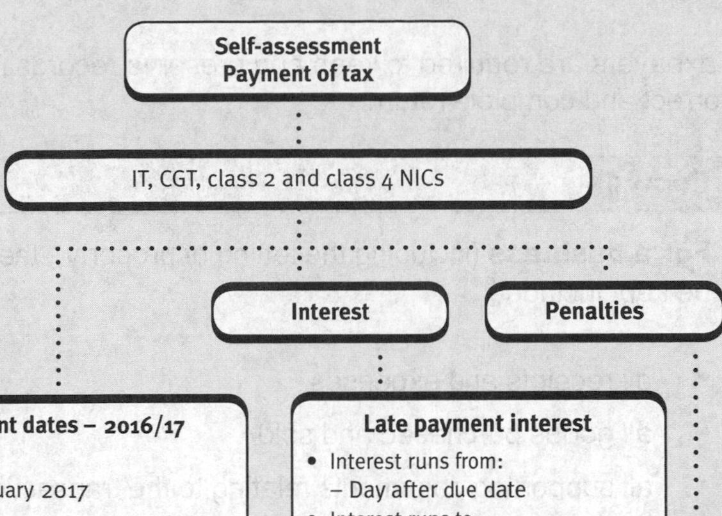

Payment dates – 2016/17

- POA 1
  - 31 January 2017
- POA 2
  - 31 July 2017
- Balancing payment
  - 31 January 2018
- POAs = 50% of relevant amount for previous tax year
- Relevant amount = IT and class 4 NICs net of tax deducted at source
- No POAs for class 2 NICs or CGT

POAs not required if

- IT payable for previous year < £1000 or
- > 80% of relevant amount for previous year deducted at source

Claim to reduce POAs

- Claim before 31 January following end of tax year
- Must state grounds
- If underestimate payments:
  - Interest charged from due date of POA to date of payment
  - Penalty payable if fraudulent or negligent
  - Maximum penalty = difference between amount paid and amount that should have been paid

Late payment interest

- Interest runs from:
  - Day after due date
- Interest runs to:
  - Day before payment made

Repayment interest

- Interest runs from later of:
  - Due date
  - Date received by HMRC
- Interest runs to:
  - Date repayment made

Penalties

- Payable in addition to unpaid tax and interest
- No late payment penalty on POA's
- If balancing payment not paid
  - Within 1 month of due date: 5%
  - Within 6 months: further 5%
  - Within 12 months: further 5%

6 Records

Taxpayers are required to keep and preserve records necessary to make a correct and complete return.

Records

For a business (including the letting of property), the records that must be kept include:

- all receipts and expenses
- all goods purchased and sold
- all supporting documents relating to the transactions of the business, such as accounts, books, contracts, vouchers and receipts.

Other taxpayers should keep evidence of income received such as:

- dividend vouchers
- P60s
- copies of P11Ds
- bank statements.

Retention periods

For taxpayers with a business (i.e. the self employed)

- All their records (not just those relating to the business) must be retained until **five years after the 31 January filing date**.
- For 2016/17 records must therefore be retained until 31 January 2023.

For other taxpayers

Records must be retained until the **latest** of:

- 12 months after the 31 January filing date (31 January 2019 for 2016/17)
- the date on which a compliance check into the return is completed
- the date on which it becomes impossible for a compliance check to be started.

Penalties for not keeping records

A penalty may be charged for failure to keep or retain adequate records.

The maximum penalty is only likely to be imposed in the most serious cases such as where a taxpayer deliberately destroys his records in order to obstruct an HMRC compliance check.

See section 8 for the detail on the penalties that may be imposed.

7 Compliance checks

HMRC have the right to enquire into the completeness and accuracy of any self assessment tax return under their compliance checks.

HMRC compliance checks

HMRC's right of enquiry

- HMRC must give written notice before commencing a compliance check (also known as an enquiry).
- The written notice must be issued within 12 months of the date the return is filed with HMRC. Once this deadline is passed, the taxpayer can normally consider the self-assessment for that year as final.

The compliance check may be made as a result of any of the following:

- a suspicion that income is undeclared
- deductions being incorrectly claimed
- other information in HMRC's possession
- being part of a random review process.

Additional points:

- HMRC do not have to state a reason for the compliance check and are unlikely to do so.
- A compliance check can be made even if HMRC calculated a taxpayer's tax liability.

Compliance check procedures

HMRC can demand that the taxpayer produces any or all of the following:

- documents
- accounts
- other written particulars
- full answers to specific questions.

The information requested by HMRC should be limited to that connected with the return.

An appeal can be made against the request.

The compliance check ends when HMRC gives written notice that it has been completed. The notice will state the outcome of the enquiry.

The closure notice must include either:

- confirmation that no amendments are required
- HMRC's amendments to the self-assessment.

The taxpayer has 30 days to appeal against any amendments by HMRC. The appeal must be in writing.

Discovery assessments

HMRC must normally begin compliance checks into a self-assessment return within 12 months of the date the return is filed, however a discovery assessment can be raised at a later date to prevent the loss of tax.

The use of a discovery assessment is restricted where a self-assessment has already been made:

- Unless the loss of tax was brought about carelessly or deliberately by the taxpayer, a discovery assessment cannot be raised where full disclosure was made in the return, even if this is found to be incorrect.
- HMRC will only accept that full disclosure has been made if any contentious items have been clearly brought to their attention – perhaps in a covering letter or in the 'white space' on the tax return.

- Information lying in the attached accounts will not constitute full disclosure if its significance is not emphasised.
- Only a taxpayer who makes full disclosure in the tax return has absolute finality 12 months after the date the return is filed.

The time limit for issuing a discovery assessment is:

	Time from end of tax year	For 2016/17
Basic time limit	Four years	5 April 2021
Careless error	Six years	5 April 2023
Deliberate error	Twenty years	5 April 2037

A discovery assessment may be appealed against.

Information and inspection powers

- HMRC has one set of powers to inspect business records, assets and premises.
- The regime covers all taxes in the P6 syllabus (i.e. income tax, NICs (collected through PAYE), capital gains tax, inheritance tax, stamp taxes, corporation tax and VAT.
- HMRC also have a single approach across all taxes to asking taxpayers for supplementary information, based on formal information notices with a right of appeal.

  They can also request information from third parties provided either the taxpayer or the new First-tier Tax Tribunal agrees (section 9).

  Collection of data from third party bulk data gatherers (e.g. banks, building societies and stockbrokers) are included in these powers.

8 Penalties

Standard penalties

HMRC has standardised penalties across taxes for different offences.

The standard penalty applies to two key areas:

- submission of incorrect returns – all taxes
- failure to notify liability to tax – income tax, CGT, corporation tax, VAT and NICs.

The penalty is calculated as a percentage of 'potential lost revenue' which is generally the tax unpaid as a result of the error or failure to notify.

Taxpayer behaviour	Maximum penalty (% of revenue lost)
Genuine mistake (for incorrect returns)	No Penalty
Careless/Failure to take reasonable care	30%
Deliberate but no concealment	70%
Deliberate with concealment	100%

An incorrect return:

- must result in an understatement of the taxpayer's liability, and
- no reasonable steps have been taken to notify HMRC of the error.
- Includes:
  - deliberately supplying false information
  - deliberately withholding information
  - inflating a loss and/or claims for allowances and reliefs
  - inflating a tax repayment claim
  - submitting incorrect accounts in relation to a liability.

If there is more than one error in a return, a separate penalty can be charged for each error.

Failure to notify liability to tax applies where:

- the taxpayer has a liability to tax, and notification is required
- but notification of chargeability is not made to HMRC.

The maximum penalties can be reduced where

- the taxpayer informs HMRC of the error (i.e. makes a disclosure), and
- co-operates with HMRC to establish the amount of tax unpaid
- with larger reductions given for unprompted disclosure.

There are minimum penalties that vary based on

- behaviour
- whether disclosure was prompted or unprompted.

An unprompted disclosure is where a taxpayer:

- makes a disclosure
- when they have no reason to believe that HMRC have, or are about to, discover the error.

An unprompted disclosure of a careless error can reduce the penalty to 0%.

A taxpayer can appeal to the first tier of the tax tribunal against

- a penalty being charged, and
- the amount of the penalty.

Penalties for late filing of returns

Standardised penalties are also being introduced for the late filing of tax returns in phases. However, for P6, in the June 2017, September 2017, December 2017 and March 2018 sittings, these rules apply for individuals only.

Date return is filed	**Penalty**
• after due date	• £100 fixed penalty
• 3 months late	• Daily penalties of £10 per day (maximum 90 days), in addition to £100 fixed penalty
• 6 months late	• 5% of tax due (minimum £300), plus above penalties
• more than 12 months after due date where withholding information was:	The above penalties plus:
– not deliberate	• Additional 5% of tax due (minimum £300)
– deliberate but no concealment	• 70% of tax due (minimum £300)
– deliberate with concealment	• 100% of tax due (minimum £300)

The tax geared penalties for submitting a return more than 12 months late can be reduced by prompted/unprompted disclosure.

Penalties for late payment of tax

Covered in section 4 of this chapter.

Other penalties

Offence	Penalty	
Penalty for fraud or negligence on claiming reduced payments on account		£
	POAs should have paid	X
	Less: POAs actually paid	(X)
		X
Failure to keep and retain required records	Up to £3,000 per tax year	

Example 5 – Penalties

A taxpayer was issued with a tax return in April 2017 which relates to the tax year 2016/17.

Unfortunately, he did not submit his return to HMRC until 10 October 2018. The tax due for the tax year 2016/17 amounts to £175.

Identify the penalties that will be charged.

Solution

A fixed penalty of £100 will be due as the return is not filed by 31 January 2018.

HMRC could also impose daily penalties of £10 for a maximum of 90 days, as the return was more than three months late.

In addition, as the return was more than six months late, a penalty of £300 will be due (as this is more than 5% × £175).

Penalties for offshore non-compliance

To counter **tax evasion** by taxpayers **deliberately** concealing taxable income, gains and assets **overseas** (i.e. outside of the UK):

- a higher tax-geared penalty regime applies
- in relation to errors concerning offshore income and capital gains.

This regime relates to:

- failures to notify liability or chargeability to tax
- failures to submit a return on time, and
- errors in a submitted return.

The regime applies to income tax, capital gains tax and inheritance tax.

The higher offshore non-compliance penalties apply if:

- HMRC discover that an asset has been moved overseas, and
- one of the above penalties applies, and
- the penalty for deliberate behaviour is due, and
- the asset move was a 'relevant offshore asset move'
- which took place in order to prevent or delay HMRC discovering about the asset.

There are four levels of penalty, the amount of which depends on:

- the overseas territory used
(four categories exist and have been defined by the Treasury), and
- the existence of, and degree of exchange of, information with HMRC.

In FA2016, the minimum penalties were increased and are applied to:

- the taxpayer, and
- anyone who assisted the taxpayer in committing the offence.

The P6 examining team do not expect you to know the detail in relation to the amount of the penalties or categorisation of overseas territories.

A 'relevant asset move' means that

- an asset has been moved from a country that exchanges information with the UK to one that does not, or
- the owner of the asset has ceased to be resident in a country that exchanges information with the UK and becomes resident in a country that does not.

Note that these penalties only impact on:

- non-compliant individuals
- who have carelessly or deliberately submitted inaccurate information, or
- failed to notify HMRC about income or gains from activities/sources or assets held abroad.

9 Appeals

A taxpayer can appeal against a decision made by HMRC, but they must do so within 30 days of the disputed decision.

Most appeals are then settled amicably by discussion between the taxpayer and HMRC.

However, if the taxpayer is not satisfied with the outcome of the discussions, they can proceed in one of two ways:

- request that their case is reviewed by another HMRC officer, or
- have their case referred to an independent tax tribunal.

If the taxpayer opts to have their case reviewed but disagrees with the outcome, they can still send their appeal to the Tax Tribunal.

The taxpayer must also apply to postpone all or part of the tax charged. Otherwise they will have to pay the disputed amount.

Tax Tribunals

The Tax Tribunal is an independent body administered by the Tribunals Service of the Ministry of Justice. Cases are heard by independently appointed tax judges and/or panel members. Each panel is appointed according to the needs of the case.

There are two tiers (layers) of the Tax Tribunal system:

- First-tier Tribunal, and
- Upper Tribunal.

First-tier Tribunal

The First-tier Tribunal will be the first tribunal for most issues. They deal with:

- *Default paper cases:* simple appeals (e.g. against a fixed penalty) – will usually be decided on without a hearing provided both sides agree.
- *Basic cases:* straightforward appeals involving a minimal exchange of paperwork in advance of a short hearing.
- *Standard cases:* appeals involving more detailed consideration of issues and a more formal hearing.
- *Complex cases:* some complex appeals may be heard by the First-tier Tribunal however they will usually be heard by the Upper Tribunal.

If the dispute is not resolved at the First-tier level then the appeal can go to the Upper Tribunal.

Upper Tribunal

The Upper Tribunal will mainly, but not exclusively, review and decide appeals from the First–tier Tribunal on a point of law.

In addition, they will also deal with complex cases requiring detailed specialist knowledge and a formal hearing (e.g. cases involving long and complicated issues, points of principle and large financial amounts).

Hearings are held in public and decisions are published.

A decision of the Upper Tribunal may be appealed to the Court of Appeal. However, the grounds of appeal must always relate to a point of law.

Publication of names of tax offenders

- HMRC will have power to publish the names and details of individuals and companies who are penalised for deliberate defaults leading to a loss of tax of more than £25,000.
- Names will not be published of those who make a full unprompted disclosure or a full prompted disclosure within the required time.

Monitoring of serious tax offenders

Those who incur a penalty for deliberate evasion in respect of tax of £5,000 or more will be required to submit returns for up to:

- the following 5 years
- showing more detailed business accounts information, and
- detailing the nature and value of any balancing adjustments within the accounts.

10 Chapter summary

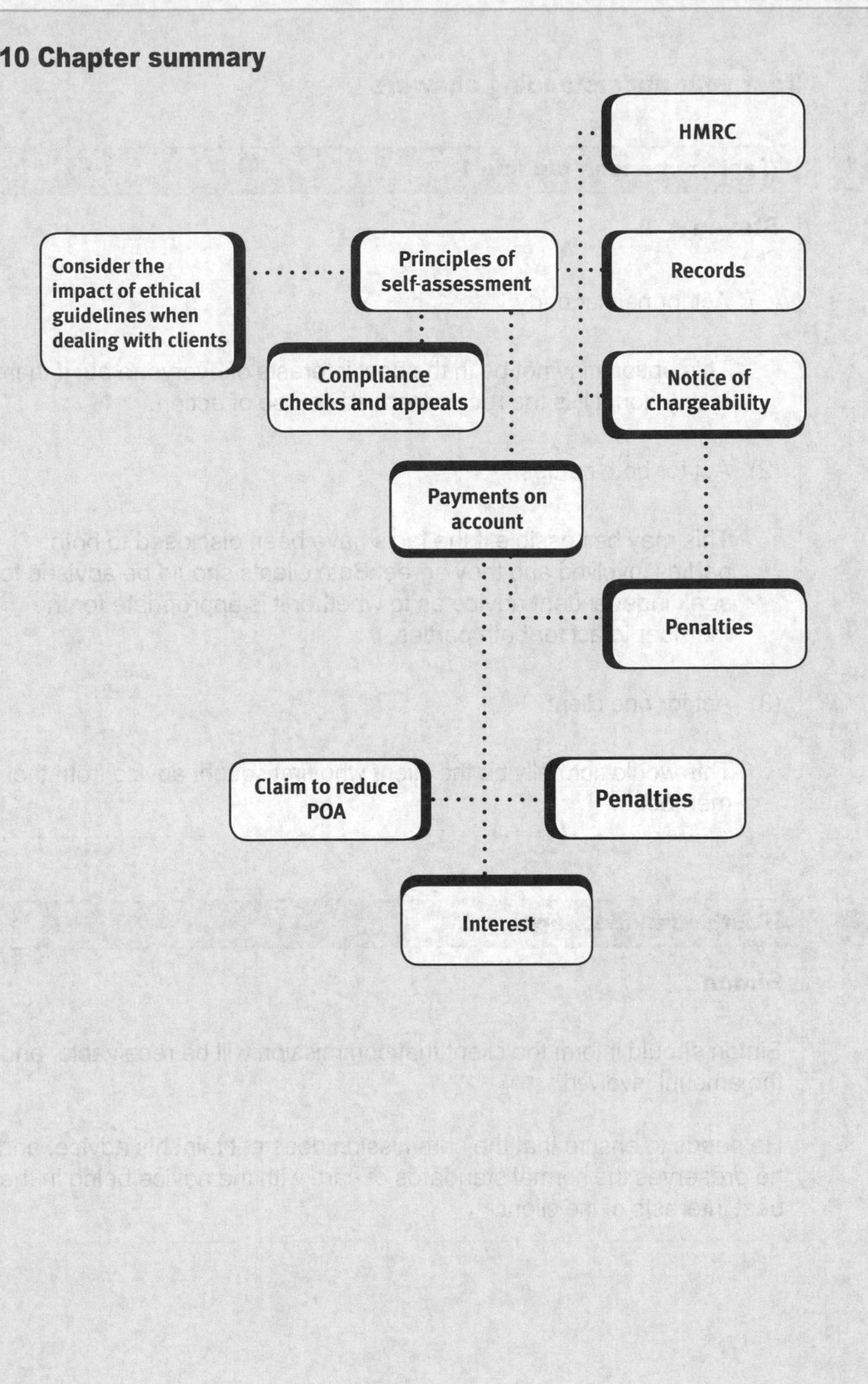

Test your understanding answers

Test your understanding 1

Steven

(1) Act for neither party

This option may not be in the best interests of everyone but if there is any doubt it is the recommended course of action.

(2) Act for both parties

This may be possible if the facts have been disclosed to both parties involved and they agree. Both clients should be advised to seek independent advice as to whether it is appropriate for the member to act for both parties.

(3) Act for one client

This would normally be the client who first sought advice from the member.

Test your understanding 2

Simon

Simon should inform the client that commission will be receivable, and the amount involved.

He needs to ensure that the commission does not taint his advice, and he preserves the normal standards of care with the advice being in the best interests of the client.

Test your understanding 3

HMRC error

The position should be reviewed carefully to confirm that an error has been made.

The client should be contacted for authority to disclose the error to HMRC, if this authority was not already given within the letter of engagement.

If the authority does not exist in the letter of engagement, the client should be told the consequences of not disclosing the error, including the implication for interest and penalties.

If the client refuses to allow the disclosure it would be necessary to consider whether the amount is material, and if it is, whether you can continue to act for the client.

If it is decided that it is not appropriate to continue acting, the client must be informed in writing. HMRC should also be notified that you have ceased to act, but not the reason why.

It may be necessary to make a report to the NCA under the Money Laundering Regulations.

Test your understanding 4

Rebecca

The balancing payment for 2016/17 due on 31 January 2018 will be:

	£
Total tax payable	13,700
Less: POAs	(8,000)
Balancing payment – 2016/17	5,700

The balancing payment comprises:

	£
Income tax and class 4 NICs (£8,300 + £800 – £8,000)	1,100
Class 2 NICs	146
CGT	4,454
Balancing payment – 2016/17	5,700

In addition, the first POA for 2017/18 will be due on 31 January 2018.

The first POA for the tax year 2017/18 will be 50% of the 'relevant amount' using the 2016/17 position.

	£
2016/17 – income tax payable (after deducting tax at source)	8,300
2016/17 – class 4 NICs	800
Relevant amount	9,100

First POA for 2017/18 = (£9,100 × 50%) = £4,550

Summary

	£
Balancing payment – 2016/17	5,700
First POA – 2017/18	4,550
Total payable by 31 January 2018	10,250

Note: Class 2 NICs and CGT have no impact on POAs.

chapter

17

New and ongoing unincorporated businesses

Chapter learning objectives

Upon completion of this chapter you will be able to:

- describe and apply the badges of trade
- prepare the tax adjusted profit/loss given a variety of situations
- compute plant and machinery capital allowances
- recognise the factors that will influence the choice of accounting date for a new business and compute the assessments
- state the conditions that must be met for a change of accounting date to be valid and compute the assessable profits
- understand how to calculate a trading loss for a tax year, explain how trading losses can be used for an ongoing business and can be relieved in the early years of a trade
- explain the limit on the amount of relief that can be deducted from total income in any tax year
- demonstrate the optimum use of trading loss reliefs
- state which businesses can use the cash basis and flat rate expenses and explain how tax adjusted trading profits are calculated using this method
- explain the NIC position and calculate the NIC liability for a self-employed individual
- calculate net receipts from a transaction, compare alternative scenarios and advise on the most tax efficient course of action
- identify and advise on the personal taxes applicable to a given course of action and their impact
- identify suitable tax planning measures in a given scenario to mitigate tax liabilities for an individual.

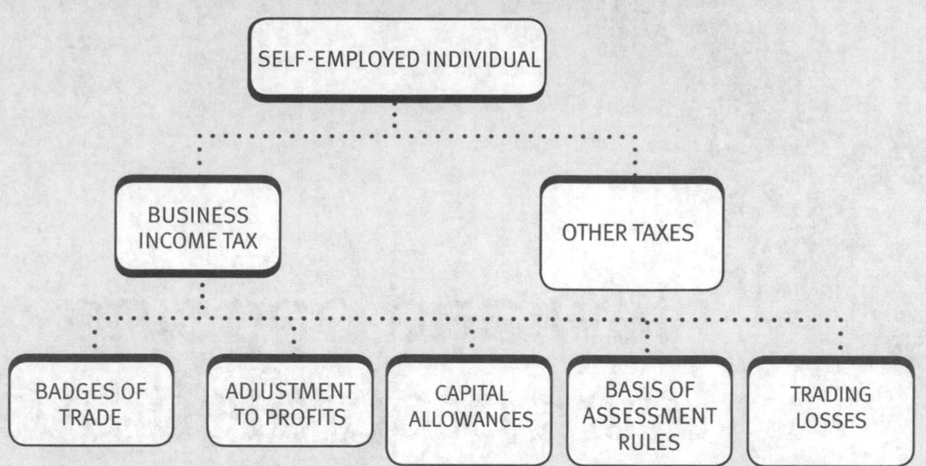

Introduction

This and the following two chapters deal with the way in which a self-employed individual is taxed on their income derived from an unincorporated business (i.e. a sole trader or partnership).

There is little new knowledge at P6 compared with F6, therefore much of this chapter is a revision of business tax rules. However, examination questions will bring many of the business tax topics together in a scenario and will test an in-depth understanding of the different taxes that apply.

Common scenarios are the opening years of a business, ongoing years where there is a change in the operations or closing years.

After studying this chapter you should be able to tackle examination questions involving all tax aspects of a new or ongoing business.

The key considerations are as follows:

- Badges of trade – is a trade being carried on?
- Income tax issues for new and ongoing businesses
- Loss reliefs
- NICs
- Expansion: taking on an employee or partner
- VAT
- Self-assessment

The new material is in respect of change of accounting date and the emphasis placed on tax planning issues arising from the basic rules.

1 A revision of basic income tax

The badges of trade

Income arising from a trade, profession or vocation is assessed as trading income in an individual's income tax computation.

In entering into a transaction, or series of transactions, it is not always clear whether an individual is:

- carrying on a trade, and therefore assessed to income tax, or
- making a capital disposal, which may be chargeable to capital gains tax (CGT) or is exempt from tax.

Example 1 – Trading income vs. gain

On 1 May 2016 Chow Tong bought a derelict property at an auction for £132,000. She paid cash of £42,000, and borrowed the remaining £90,000 from her bank at an interest rate of 8% pa.

On 15 July 2016 Chow obtained planning permission to convert the property into six holiday apartments, and entered into a contract with a builder to carry out the conversion. The work was completed on 30 September 2016 at a cost of £63,000, and Chow immediately put the six holiday apartments up for sale.

Five of the holiday apartments were sold during November 2016 for £85,000 each. On 30 November 2016 Chow paid her builder and repaid the bank loan. She decided to keep the remaining holiday apartment, valued at £85,000, for her own use. Legal fees of £750 were paid in respect of each of the five holiday apartments sold, and advertising costs amounted to £1,200.

Since the sale of the holiday apartments is an isolated transaction Chow believes that it should be treated as a capital gain rather than as a trade.

Chow has not disposed of any other assets during 2016/17. She has other taxable income of £155,000 for 2016/17.

Calculate Chow's net cash position arising from her property activities during 2016/17 if this is treated as:

(1) **trading income, and**

(2) **a capital transaction.**

You should ignore the implications of NIC and VAT.

Solution

Chow's net tax position treated as if trading income

If Chow is treated as trading she will be liable to income tax on the trading profit, including the holiday apartment retained by her which is treated as a disposal to her at its market value of £85,000.

Chow's income tax liability will be:

	Income tax	Net cash
	£	£
Sale proceeds (5 × £85,000)	425,000	425,000
Market value of property retained (Note 1)	85,000	–
Less: Cost of property	(132,000)	(132,000)
Less: Cost of conversion	(63,000)	(63,000)
Less: Loan interest		
(£90,000 × 8% × 7/12)	(4,200)	(4,200)
Less: Legal fees (5 × £750)	(3,750)	(3,750)
Less: Advertising	(1,200)	(1,200)
Taxable profit	305,850	
Income tax (45% × £305,850) (Note 2)	137,632	(137,632)
Net cash after tax		83,218

Note 1: The property retained must be taken into account for tax purposes, but is not real cash income.

Note 2: Income tax is at the additional rate of 45% as Chow's other taxable income is above £150,000.

Chow's net tax position if treated as capital

If Chow is treated as not trading, she will be subject to capital gains tax. The holiday apartment retained by her will not be charged to tax.

The disposal will be a part disposal, so the cost will be apportioned based on the formula:

Cost × (A/A+B)

where A is the value of the flats sold and B is the value of the remainder. As all of the six flats are valued at £85,000 in this case, the cost of the five flats sold can be simplified to (cost × 5/6).

Chow's CGT liability will be:

	CGT	Net cash
	£	£
Sale proceeds (5 × £85,000)	425,000	425,000
Less: Incidental costs of disposal (£3,750 + £1,200)	(4,950)	(4,950)
Net sale proceeds	420,050	
Less: Cost of property (£132,000 × 5/6)	(110,000)	(132,000)
Less: Cost of conversion (£63,000 × 5/6)	(52,500)	(63,000)
Chargeable gain	257,550	
Less: AEA	(11,100)	
Taxable gain	246,450	
CGT (28% × £246,450) (Note 3)	69,006	(69,006)
Less: Loan interest (£90,000 × 8% × 7/12) (Note 4)		(4,200)
Net cash after tax		151,844

Note 3: Entrepreneurs' relief is not available on the capital disposal as the business it is not a trading business and Chow owned the property for less than 12 months. CGT is charged at 28% as the gain relates to residential property.

Note 4: Interest is not an allowable deduction for CGT purposes, however must be paid out of 'after tax proceeds' to calculate the net cash after tax position.

Future position

Note that if treated as trading, Chow is deemed to have acquired the 6th apartment for £85,000 on the date it is appropriated from inventory.

If treated as capital, Chow is also deemed to have acquired the 6th apartment worth £85,000 on 1 May 2016 for a CGT cost of £32,500 ((£132,000 × 1/6) + (£63,000 × 1/6)). This treatment will therefore give rise to a bigger gain in the future.

What constitutes a trade is therefore very important in deciding how profits should be assessed.

The badges of trade produced by the Royal Commission are criteria used to determine whether or not the purchase and resale of property is to be treated as a trading transaction.

The key badges of trade are as follows:

- the subject matter of the transaction (S)
- the length of the period of ownership (O)
- the frequency or number of similar transactions by the same person (F)
- supplementary work, improvements and marketing (I)
- the circumstances responsible for the realisation (R)
- the motive (M).

The following additional badges should also be considered:

- Finance (F)
- Method of acquisition (A)
- Existence of similar trading transactions (ST).

The badges of trade – detail

It may be helpful to remember the badges of trade by the mnemonics: SOFIRM and FAST as denoted by the letters in the brackets in the main text above.

However, it is vital to appreciate that:

- no single badge of trade will be decisive
- it is necessary to consider all of the facts surrounding the transaction
- in any set of circumstances some badges may indicate trading whilst others may not
- it is the overall impression, taking into account all relevant factors, that is important.

The principles behind each badge of trade and some background information relating to decided cases are given below.

The subject matter of the transaction (S)

Property which does not yield an income nor gives personal enjoyment to its owner is likely to form the subject matter of a trading transaction.

Other property such as land, works of art and investments are more likely to be acquired for the income and/or personal enjoyment that they provide. The disposal of such items will more often give rise to a gain or loss of a capital nature, rather than a trading profit.

In a decided case, the taxpayer purchased one million rolls of toilet paper which were resold at a profit. This was held to be an adventure in the nature of a trade, since it was inconceivable that the rolls of toilet paper were acquired for any purpose other than realising a profit.

The length of ownership (O)

The sale of property within a short time of its acquisition is an indication of trading.

By itself, however, this is not a strong badge as, for example, stocks and shares will often be bought and sold on an active basis without giving rise to an adventure in the nature of a trade.

Frequency of similar transactions (F)

Repeated transactions in the same subject matter will be an indication of trading. This badge is of particular importance when an isolated transaction would not otherwise be treated as an adventure in the nature of a trade.

In a decided case, it was held that although the single purchase and resale of a cotton mill was capital in nature, a series of four such transactions amounted to trading.

Hence, subsequent transactions may trigger a trading profits liability in respect of earlier transactions.

Improvements to the property (I)

Carrying out work to the property in order to make it more marketable, or taking steps to find purchasers, will indicate a trading motive.

In a decided case, a syndicate was held to be trading when it purchased a quantity of brandy which was then blended, re-casked and sold in lots over an 18 month period.

However, a taxpayer is entitled to make an asset more attractive to potential purchasers, without this being an indication of trading.

Reason responsible for the realisation (R)

A forced sale to raise cash for an emergency will by presumption indicate that the transaction is not an adventure in the nature of a trade.

Motive (M)

If a transaction is undertaken with the motive of realising a profit, this will be a strong indication of trading. However, the absence of a profit motive does not prevent a person from being treated as trading.

In a decided case, the taxpayer was held to be trading when he bought some silver as a hedge against devaluation and later resold it at a profit.

Finance (F)

If the taxpayer takes out a loan to buy the asset which they expect to repay from the proceeds of sale, this is an indication of trading.

Existence of similar trading transactions (ST)

If the transactions are similar to those of an existing trade carried on by the taxpayer, this is also an indication of trading.

Method of acquisition (A)

If the taxpayer acquired the asset by way of purchase rather than receiving it as a gift or by inheritance, this suggests the transaction is more likely to be an adventure in the nature of a trade than not.

An overview of the trading income assessment for an individual

To calculate the trading income to include in a self-employed individual's income tax computation, the following procedure should be used:

(1) Calculate the tax adjusted trading profits.

(2) Calculate the capital allowances available on plant and machinery. Deduct capital allowances from the tax adjusted trading profits.

(3) Apply the basis of assessment rules to the tax adjusted trading profit figure after capital allowances have been deducted.

Pro forma tax adjusted trading profits computation

There are four key types of adjustment to be made to the accounting profit to calculate the tax adjusted trading profit as follows:

		£
Net profit per accounts		X
Add back:	Non-trading expenses (disallowable expenditure)	X
	Trading income not credited in the accounts	X
Deduct:	Non-trading income	(X)
	Trading expenses not charged in the accounts	(X)
Tax adjusted trading profits before capital allowances		X
Less:	Capital allowances:	
	Plant and machinery	(X)
Tax adjusted trading profits after capital allowances		X

Note that the detailed rules for adjusting the accounting profits were covered in F6. These are still examinable at P6. However, at P6 it is likely that only a few selected adjustments will be required, not a large adjustment to profits computation or a large capital allowances computation.

Basis of assessment rules

The basis of assessment rules determine in which tax year the adjusted trading profits will be assessed.

The normal basis of assessment will be the twelve month accounting period ending in the current tax year, known as the 'current year basis' (CYB) of assessment.

However, special rules apply:

- in the opening years
- in the closing years
- when an unincorporated business changes its accounting date.

2 The tax adjusted trading profits computation

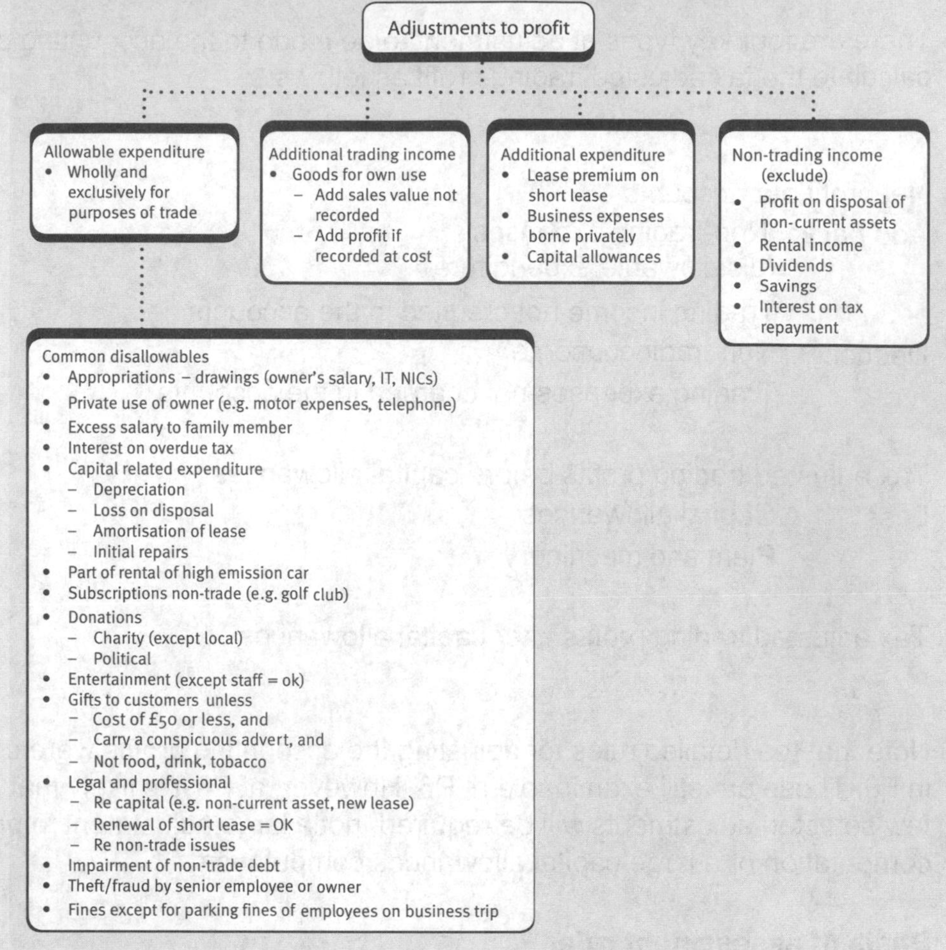

Adjustments to profit
Allowable expenditure
• Wholly and exclusively for purposes of trade
Additional trading income
• Goods for own use
– Add sales value not recorded
– Add profit if recorded at cost
Additional expenditure
• Lease premium on short lease
• Business expenses borne privately
• Capital allowances
Non-trading income (exclude)
• Profit on disposal of non-current assets
• Rental income
• Dividends
• Savings
• Interest on tax repayment
Common disallowables
• Appropriations – drawings (owner's salary, IT, NICs)
• Private use of owner (e.g. motor expenses, telephone)
• Excess salary to family member
• Interest on overdue tax
• Capital related expenditure
– Depreciation
– Loss on disposal
– Amortisation of lease
– Initial repairs
• Part of rental of high emission car
• Subscriptions non-trade (e.g. golf club)
• Donations
– Charity (except local)
– Political
• Entertainment (except staff = ok)
• Gifts to customers unless
– Cost of £50 or less, and
– Carry a conspicuous advert, and
– Not food, drink, tobacco
• Legal and professional
– Re capital (e.g. non-current asset, new lease)
– Renewal of short lease = OK
– Re non-trade issues
• Impairment of non-trade debt
• Theft/fraud by senior employee or owner
• Fines except for parking fines of employees on business trip

Hiring and leasing a car

There is no adjustment where the CO_2 emissions of a leased motor car do not exceed 130 g/km.

Where CO_2 emissions are more than 130 g/km then 15% of the leasing costs are disallowed in calculating taxable profits.

The motor car is the most common asset with private use by the owner. In this case, a further adjustment is required to reflect the private use.

Allowable element of short lease premiums

The adjustments required for a short lease are:

Add:	the amortisation charged in the accounts (capital)
Deduct:	(the property business income assessed on the landlord ÷ period of the lease)

Pre-trading expenditure

Any **revenue** expenditure incurred in the **seven years before a business commences** to trade (which is of the type that would normally be allowed if incurred whilst trading) is treated as an allowable deduction against trading profit on the **first day of trading**.

Capital expenditure incurred within **seven years** of the start of the trade:

- is treated as incurred on the **first day of trading** and may be eligible for capital allowances
- however, the actual date of acquisition determines the rate of FYAs and AIA available (if any).

Comprehensive example

The following example revises the key adjustments to profit covered at F6.

Test your understanding 1

Olive Green is self-employed running a health food shop. Her statement of profit and loss for the year ended 31 December 2016 is as follows:

	£	£
Gross profit		124,200
Expenses		
Depreciation	2,350	
Light and heat (note 1)	1,980	
Motor expenses (note 2)	4,700	
Rent and rates (note 1)	5,920	
Sundry expenses (note 3)	2,230	
Wages and salaries (note 4)	78,520	
		(95,700)
Net profit		28,500

Note 1 – Private accommodation

Olive lives in a flat that is situated above the health food shop. 30% of the expenditure included in the accounts for light, heat, rent and rates relates to the flat.

Note 2 – Motor expenses

During the year ended 31 December 2016 Olive drove a total of 20,000 miles, of which 8,000 were for business purposes.

Note 3 – Sundry expenses

The figure of £2,230 for sundry expenses includes £220 for a fine in respect of health and safety regulations, £180 for the theft of cash by an employee, £100 for a donation to a political party, and £140 for a trade subscription to the Health and Organic Association.

Note 4 – Wages and salaries

The figure of £78,520 for wages and salaries includes an annual salary of £14,000 paid to Olive's daughter. She works in the health food shop as a sales assistant. The other sales assistants doing the same job are paid an annual salary of £10,500.

Note 5 – Goods for own use

Each week Olive takes health food from the shop for her personal use without paying for it. The weekly cost of this food is £30, and it has a selling price of £45. No entry has been made in the accounts for these drawings.

Note 6 – Plant and machinery

The only item of plant and machinery is Olive's motor car, which has CO_2 emissions of 128 g/km. The tax written down value of this vehicle at 1 January 2016 was £16,667.

Note 7 – Patent royalties

Olive pays a patent royalty of £150 (gross) every quarter for the use of equipment that allows her to make her own organic breakfast cereal. This has not been accounted for in arriving at the net profit of £28,500.

Other income

(1) Olive has a part-time employment for which she was paid a salary of £6,000 during the tax year 2016/17. Income tax of £1,200 has been deducted from this figure under PAYE.

(2) During 2016/17 Olive received building society interest of £2,800 and dividends of £1,200.

(3) On 30 November 2016 Olive sold some investments, and this resulted in a chargeable gain of £12,500.

Other information

(1) During 2016/17 Olive paid interest of £220 (gross) on a loan taken out on 1 January 2014 to purchase equipment for use in her part-time employment.

(2) Olive contributed £5,000 (gross) into a personal pension scheme during 2016/17.

(3) Olive's payments on account of income tax in respect of 2016/17 totalled £4,559.

(a) **Calculate Olive's tax adjusted trading profit for the year ended 31 December 2016.**

(b) **Calculate:**

 (i) **the income tax and capital gains tax payable by Olive for the tax year 2016/17**

 (ii) **Olive's balancing payment for the tax year 2016/17 and her payments on account for the tax year 2017/18, stating the relevant due dates.**
 Ignore national insurance contributions.

(c) **Advise Olive of the consequences of not making the balancing payment for the tax year 2016/17 until 30 April 2018.**

3 Capital allowances for plant and machinery

The detailed rules for calculating capital allowances were covered in F6.

There is little new technical knowledge on capital allowances at P6 compared with F6. The only new areas introduced at P6 are tax planning, and the awareness that the AIA is split between related businesses.

Examination questions

Note that at P6:

- large capital allowance computations with many additions and disposals as seen at F6 are unlikely, less complicated computations will probably be required
- all of the knowledge in this chapter needs to be retained, however the computations are likely to focus on only a few aspects
- in some questions, it may be quicker and advisable to calculate allowances in single computations/workings rather than constructing a full pro forma.

Basis of the calculation

Capital allowances are calculated on an accounting period basis.

If the accounting period is not 12 months long, the AIA and WDA must be time apportioned. Note that FYAs are never time apportioned.

Pro forma capital allowances computation

The following pro forma computation should be used for unincorporated businesses:

Pro forma capital allowances computation – unincorporated businesses

	Notes		Main pool	Special rate pool	Short life asset	Private use asset (Note 2)	Allowances
		£	£	£	£	£	£
TWDV b/f			X	X	X		
Additions:							
Not qualifying for AIA or FYA:	(1)						
Second hand cars (up to 75 g/km)			X				
Cars (76 – 130 g/km)			X				
Cars (over 130 g/km)				X			
Car with private use						X	
Qualifying for AIA:							
Special rate pool expenditure		X					
Less: AIA (Max £200,000 in total)	(3)	(X)					X
Transfer balance to special rate pool				X			
Plant and machinery		X					
Less: AIA (Max £200,000 in total)		(X)					X
Transfer balance to main pool	(4)		X				
Disposals (lower of original cost or sale proceeds)			(X)		(X)		
			X	X	X	X	
BA / (BC)					X / (X)		X / (X)
Small pools WDA	(5)						
WDA at 18%			(X)				X
WDA at 8%				(X)			X
WDA at 8%/18% (depending on emissions)						(X) × BU%	X
Additions qualifying for FYAs:							
New low emission cars (up to 75 g/km)		X					
Less: FYA at 100%		(X)					X
			0				
TWDV c/f			X	X		X	
Total allowances							X

Notes to the pro forma capital allowances computation

(1) Cars are pooled according to their CO_2 emissions into either the 'main' pool (sometimes referred to as the 'general' pool) or 'special rate' pool (SRP).

New low emission cars receive 100% FYA.

(2) Cars with private use are depooled regardless of their CO_2 emissions, and only the business proportion of allowances can be claimed. However, the CO_2 emissions are important in determining the rate of WDA available.

(3) Allocate the AIA to the SRP expenditure in priority to main pool plant and machinery assets as a WDA of only 8% is available on the SRP pool as opposed to 18% available on main pool items.

(4) Expenditure qualifying for AIA in the main pool but exceeding the level of AIA available is eligible for a WDA of 18%.

(5) Small pools WDA: where the balance on the main pool and/or SRP before calculation of the WDA is ≤ £1,000, all of the balance can be claimed as a WDA.

(6) The taxpayer does not have to claim all or any of the AIA or WDA.

The procedure for calculating capital allowances

For plant and machinery capital allowances, adopt the following step-by-step approach if a full computation is required:

(1) Read the information in the question and decide how many columns/pools you will require.

(2) Draft the layout and insert the TWDV b/f (does not apply in a new trade).

(3) Insert additions not eligible for the AIA or FYAs into the appropriate column taking particular care to allocate cars into the correct column according to CO_2 emissions as relevant.

(4) Insert additions eligible for the AIA in the first column, then allocate the AIA to the additions.
Remember to time apportion if the period or account is not 12 months.
Allocate the AIA to SRP additions in priority to additions of plant and machinery in the main or other individual asset pools.

(5) Any SRP additions in excess of the AIA must be added to the SRP column to increase the balance available for 8% WDA.
Any main pool expenditure, in excess of the AIA, should be added to the main pool to increase the balance qualifying for 18% WDA.

(6) Deal with any disposal by deducting the lower of cost or sale proceeds.

(7) Work out any balancing charge / balancing allowance for assets in individual pools. Remember to adjust for any private use.

(8) Consider if the small pools WDA applies to the main pool and/or the SRP.

(9) Calculate the WDA on each of the pools at the appropriate rate (18% or 8%). Remember to:

- time apportion if the period of account is not 12 months
- adjust for any private use if an unincorporated business (not relevant for companies)

(10) Insert additions eligible for FYAs (i.e. any new cars with emissions of 75 g/km or less) which will get 100% FYA.
Remember the FYA is never time apportioned.

(11) Calculate the TWDV to carry forward to the next accounting period and add the allowances column.

(12) Deduct the total allowances from the adjusted profits.

The Annual Investment Allowance (AIA)

The Annual Investment Allowance (AIA) is a 100% allowance for the first £200,000 of expenditure incurred by a business on plant and machinery.

The key rules for the allowance are as follows:

- available to **all** businesses regardless of size
- available on acquisitions of plant and machinery in the main pool and acquisitions of SRP items (see later)
- **not** available on cars
- limited to a maximum of £200,000 expenditure incurred in each accounting period of 12 months in length
- for long and short accounting periods the allowance is increased/reduced to reflect the length of the accounting period
- not available in the accounting period in which trade ceases.

Where a business spends more than £200,000 in a 12 month accounting period on assets qualifying for the AIA:

- the expenditure above the £200,000 limit will qualify for writing down allowances (WDA) (see below).

Note also that:

- the taxpayer does not have to claim all/any of the AIA if he does not want to
- any unused AIA cannot be carried forward or carried back, the benefit of the allowance is just lost.

Expenditure on plant and machinery in the main pool/special rate pool not qualifying for AIA will qualify for WDAs.

The AIA amount of £200,000 is included in the tax rates and allowances provided to you in the examination.

AIA for related business

- The AIA must be split between related businesses.

  Businesses owned by the same individual are regarded as related where they:

  - engage in the same activities, or
  - share the same premises.

  In such circumstances the owner of the businesses can choose how to allocate a single AIA between them.

- Unrelated businesses owned by the same individual will each be entitled to the full AIA.

Other points to note

- If VAT registered, include:
  - all additions of plant and machinery at the VAT exclusive price
  - except cars which are included at the VAT inclusive price.
- If not VAT registered, include all additions at the VAT inclusive amounts.
- Pre-trading capital purchases:
  - include if incurred in the seven years before trade commenced
  - treated as acquired on the first day of trade at its market value on that day.

Summary of the capital allowances available for cars

The following table sets out the treatment of cars.

• Low emission – emissions ≤ 75 g/km – if new = FYA 100% – if second hand = as for standard emission
• Standard emission – emissions 76 – 130 g/km – put in main pool – WDA 18% for 12 month period
• High emission – emissions > 130 g/km – put in special rate pool – WDA 8% for 12 month period
• Private use cars – keep separate – WDA 18%/8% for 12 month period depending on emissions – BA or BC will arise on disposal

Note that:

- Cars are never eligible for AIAs
- Cars are not eligible for FYAs, unless a **new** low emission car

Special rate pool (SRP)

The SRP is a pool of qualifying expenditure that operates in the same way as the main pool except that:

- the WDA is 8% for a 12 month period (rather than 18%).

Note that:

- the AIA is available against this expenditure (except on high emission cars), and
- the business can choose the expenditure against which the AIA is allocated.

It will therefore be most beneficial for the AIA to be allocated against expenditure in the following order:

(1) the SRP (as assets in the SRP are only eligible for 8% WDA, whereas general plant and machinery is eligible for 18% WDA).

(2) the main pool

(3) short life assets

(4) private use assets.

Special rate pool – qualifying expenditure

The SRP groups together expenditure incurred on the following types of asset:

- long life assets
- integral features of a building or structure
- thermal insulation of a building
- high emission cars.

Qualifying expenditure includes

- initial cost, and
- replacement expenditure.

Qualifying replacement expenditure is expenditure which is more than 50% of the replacement cost of the integral feature at the time the expenditure is incurred.

It also includes situations where less than 50% is spent initially but further spending in the next twelve months takes the total over 50%.

This rule prevents businesses gradually replacing integral features and claiming the cost as a repair.

Long life assets

- Long life assets are defined as those with:
  - an expected working life of **25 years or more**
  - **total cost of £100,000** or more in a 12 month period of account (the limit is scaled down for periods of account of less than 12 months)
- If the definition is satisfied, the items **must** be treated as long life assets.
- Expected life:
  - from date first brought into use to the date it ceases to be capable of being used by anyone (i.e. not just the expected life in the hands of the current owner).
- Examples of long life assets:
  - aircraft, agricultural equipment, air conditioning units.
- Motor cars and plant and machinery situated in a building used as a retail shop, showroom, hotel or office can never be classified as a long-life asset.

Integral features of a building or structure and thermal insulation

Integral features of a building or structure include expenditure incurred on the following:

- electrical (including lighting) systems
- cold water systems
- space or water heating systems
- external solar shading
- powered systems of ventilation, air cooling or air purification
- lifts, escalators and moving walkways.

Thermal insulation in all business buildings (except residential buildings in a property business) is also included in the special rate pool.

The small pool WDA

Where the balance immediately before the calculation of the WDA on the main and/or special rate pool is **≤ £1,000** the balance can be claimed as a WDA and written off in that year.

The £1,000 limit is for a 12 month period of account, it is therefore increased/reduced to reflect the length of the accounting period.

The claim is optional. However, the taxpayer will normally want to claim the maximum available and reduce the balance on the pool to £Nil.

Hire purchase assets

For **hire purchase** contracts:

- the individual is treated **as if** they had purchased the asset outright
- when the contract was taken out (even though they do not legally own the asset until they make the final payment)
- the hire purchase interest is treated as an allowable trading expense of the period of account in which it accrues
- capital allowances are **based on the cash price** (excluding interest), regardless of the actual instalments paid in the period of account.

Comprehensive example

Example 2 – Capital allowances computation

Ashley runs a manufacturing business and prepares accounts to 31 December each year. During the year ending 31 December 2016 Ashley incurred the following expenditure:

1 May 2016	Spent £220,000 on a new air conditioning system for the factory which is expected to last 30 years.
1 June 2016	Purchased new machinery for £40,000.
3 June 2016	Purchased a new car with CO_2 emissions of 72 g/km for £17,000.
15 July 2016	Purchased a new car with CO_2 emissions of 123 g/km for £18,000.

In addition on 1 July 2016 Ashley sold an old machine for £10,000 (original cost £15,000) and the short life asset for £7,000, which had originally cost £15,000.

As at 1 January 2016 the tax written down values were as follows:

Main pool	£64,000
Short life asset	£9,000

Calculate Ashley's capital allowances for the y/e 31 December 2016.

Solution

Capital allowances computation – y/e 31 December 2016

		Main pool	Special rate pool	Short life asset	Allowances
	£	£	£	£	£
TWDV b/f		64,000	0	9,000	
Additions:					
Not qualifying for AIA or FYA:					
Car (CO_2 emissions 123 g/km)		18,000			
Qualifying for AIA:					
Long life asset	220,000				
Less: AIA (Max)	(200,000)				200,000
			20,000		
Qualifying for AIA:					
Plant and machinery	40,000				
Less: AIA (Max used)	(0)				
		40,000			
Disposal (lower of cost and SP)		(10,000)		(7,000)	
		112,000	20,000	2,000	
Balancing allowance				(2,000)	2,000
Less: WDA (18%)		(20,160)			20,160
WDA (8%)			(1,600)		1,600
Additions qualifying for FYA:					
Car (CO_2 < 75 g/km)	17,000				
Less: FYA (100%)	(17,000)				17,000
		0			
TWDV c/f		91,840	18,400	0	
Total allowances					240,760

Note: The AIA is allocated to the additions in the special rate pool (WDA 8%) in priority to the additions in the main pool (WDA 18%).

Tax planning measures to reduce tax liabilities

An individual has scope within the capital allowance rules to ensure that:

- the amount of and use of allowances, reliefs and losses are maximised
- the tax liabilities of an individual are minimised.

Key opportunities which may arise:

- the ability to claim some, or none, of the capital allowances available, to enable more capital allowances to be claimed in future
- the ability to accelerate capital allowances with a short life asset election.

Waiver of capital allowances

An individual does not have to claim the full capital allowances to which they are entitled if it would be advantageous not to do so.

A claim can be made in the self-assessment tax return for the whole or just part of the capital allowances available.

If a partial claim is made in one year:

- WDAs in subsequent years will be calculated on a higher TWDV figure than if the allowances had previously been claimed in full.
- Consequently, relief for the expenditure incurred will be delayed.
- However note any unused AIA cannot be carried forward or carried back, the benefit of the AIA is lost.

It may be advantageous to waive the right to capital allowances:

- to make full use of the individual's personal allowance
- to reduce a trading loss and claim higher allowances in the future, rather than having to waste losses against income already covered by the personal allowance.

Example 3 – Waiver of capital allowances

John has been trading for many years. His assessable trading income for the year ended 31 December 2016 is £11,200 before taking account any claim for capital allowances.

The TWDV of plant and machinery at 1 January 2016 is £12,000. He has made no additions or disposals in the year.

John is single and has no other income or outgoings.

Advise John on how much of his capital allowances he should claim for the year ended 31 December 2016.

Solution

John could claim a WDA of £2,160 (£12,000 × 18%), leaving a TWDV to carry forward of £9,840 (£12,000 – £2,160).

However, if he claimed the maximum allowance, his taxable income would be as follows:

	£
Trading income (£11,200 – £2,160)	9,040
Less: PA	(11,000)
Taxable income	0

He will have no taxable income, but will waste £1,960 (£11,000 – £9,040) of his PA. He should therefore restrict the claim for capital allowances to £200 to prevent the wastage of his PA.

His taxable income for 2016/17 will then be:

	£
Trading income (£11,200 – £200)	11,000
Less: PA	(11,000)
Taxable income	0

Although his taxable income is still £Nil, the TWDV carried forward is increased from £9,840 to £11,800 (£12,000 – £200), which will enable him to claim higher relief for capital allowances in subsequent periods.

The amount of capital allowances claimed is a particularly important tax planning tool in a trading loss situation. This is covered in more detail later in this chapter.

Accelerating capital allowances

The 'depooling' election to treat an asset as a short life asset enables a trader to accelerate capital allowances on certain types of short life plant or machinery, for example, computers.

However, if eligible for the AIA, there will be no expenditure left to 'depool' and the short life asset election will not be made. This means that there is no need to even consider the election unless the business has expenditure > £200,000 in a 12 month period.

Note that:

- If there is expenditure in excess of the maximum £200,000 on expenditure eligible for the AIA, it may be advantageous for the AIA to be allocated against the main pool expenditure rather than a short life asset and for the depooling election to be made.
- The depooling election is:
  - available on plant and machinery (except cars) where the intention is to sell or scrap the item **within eight years** of the end of the period of account in which the asset is acquired
  - beneficial if a BA arises on the disposal as it accelerates the capital allowances claim
  - not beneficial if it accelerates a balancing charge arising.
- The depooling election must be made within 12 months of 31 January following the end of the tax year in which the trading period of acquisition ends.
- If no disposal is made within eight years from the end of the accounting period in which the asset is acquired:
  - the balance on the separate short life asset column must be transferred back to the main pool
  - WDAs are claimed in the future in the normal way.

In order to determine whether making the election is beneficial, the trader must decide within two years whether they anticipate selling the asset for more or less than its TWDV.

As the election is irrevocable and binding, if they find that the disposal will crystallise a balancing charge, they should wait to dispose of the asset after eight years as it will then be included in the general pool and will not crystallise a charge.

Example 4 – Short life asset

Gina has traded for many years preparing accounts to 31 March each year. The TWDV on the main pool was £15,000 on 1 April 2016.

In May 2016, she acquired a new machine costing £10,000. She anticipated that the machine would last two years and she eventually sold it on 30 June 2018, for £1,750.

In August 2016, she acquired general plant and machinery for £202,000.

Calculate the allowances available for each year, illustrating whether or not an election to treat the new machine as a short life asset would be beneficial.

Assume the tax year 2016/17 rules apply throughout.

Solution

Capital allowances computation
– without making a short life asset election

		Main pool	Allowances
y/e 31 March 2017	£	£	£
TWDV b/f		15,000	
Additions qualifying for AIA:			
Plant and machinery (£202,000 + £10,000)	212,000		
Less: AIA	(200,000)		200,000
		12,000	
		27,000	
Less: WDA (18%)		(4,860)	4,860
TWDV c/f		22,140	
Total allowances			204,860
y/e 31 March 2018			
Less: WDA (18%)		(3,985)	3,985
TWDV c/f		18,155	
Total allowances			3,985

y/e 31 March 2019			
Disposal (lower of cost and SP)		(1,750)	
		16,405	
Less: WDA (18%)		(2,953)	2,953
TWDV c/f		13,452	
Total allowances			2,953

Capital allowances computation – with a short life asset election

		Main pool	Short life asset	Allowances
y/e 31 March 2017	£	£	£	£
TWDV b/f		15,000		
Additions qualifying for AIA:				
Plant and machinery	202,000		10,000	
Less: AIA	(200,000)		(0)	200,000
		2,000		
		17,000	10,000	
Less: WDA (18%)		(3,060)	(1,800)	4,860
TWDV c/f		13,940	8,200	
Total allowances				204,860
y/e 31 March 2018				
Less: WDA (18%)		(2,509)	(1,476)	3,985
TWDV c/f		11,431	6,724	
Total allowances				3,985
y/e 31 March 2019				
Disposal (lower of cost and SP)			(1,750)	
		11,431	4,974	
Balancing allowance			(4,974)	4,974
Less: WDA (18%)		(2,058)		2,058
TWDV c/f		9,373		
Total allowances				7,032

The total allowances claimed without making the election are £211,798 (£204,860 + £3,985 + £2,953). In the event Gina makes the election, the allowances available for the three years are £215,877 (£204,860 + £3,985 + £7,032)

Note that the election just accelerates the allowances available and only changes the timing of the allowances. The total allowances available will eventually be the same, however, without the election, it will take considerably longer to get the relief.

Therefore, if not covered by the AIA, it is recommended that the short life treatment is taken but only if it is expected that a balancing allowance can be accelerated. It is not advantageous to accelerate a balancing charge.

Test your understanding 2

On 1 January 2017, Gordon commenced in self-employment running a music recording studio. He prepared his first set of accounts for the 3 months to 31 March 2017.

The following information relates to the 3 months to 31 March 2017:

(1) The tax adjusted trading profit for the period is £149,340. This figure is before taking account of capital allowances.

(2) Gordon purchased the following assets:

		£
1 January 2017	Recording equipment	77,875
15 January 2017	Motor car with CO_2 emissions of 139 g/km (used by Gordon – 60% business use)	15,800
20 February 2017	Motor car with CO_2 emissions of 128 g/km (used by employee – 20% private use)	10,400
4 March 2017	Recording equipment (expected to be scrapped in 2 years)	3,250

Calculate Gordon's taxable trading income for the period ended 31 March 2017.

Summary of capital allowances for plant and machinery

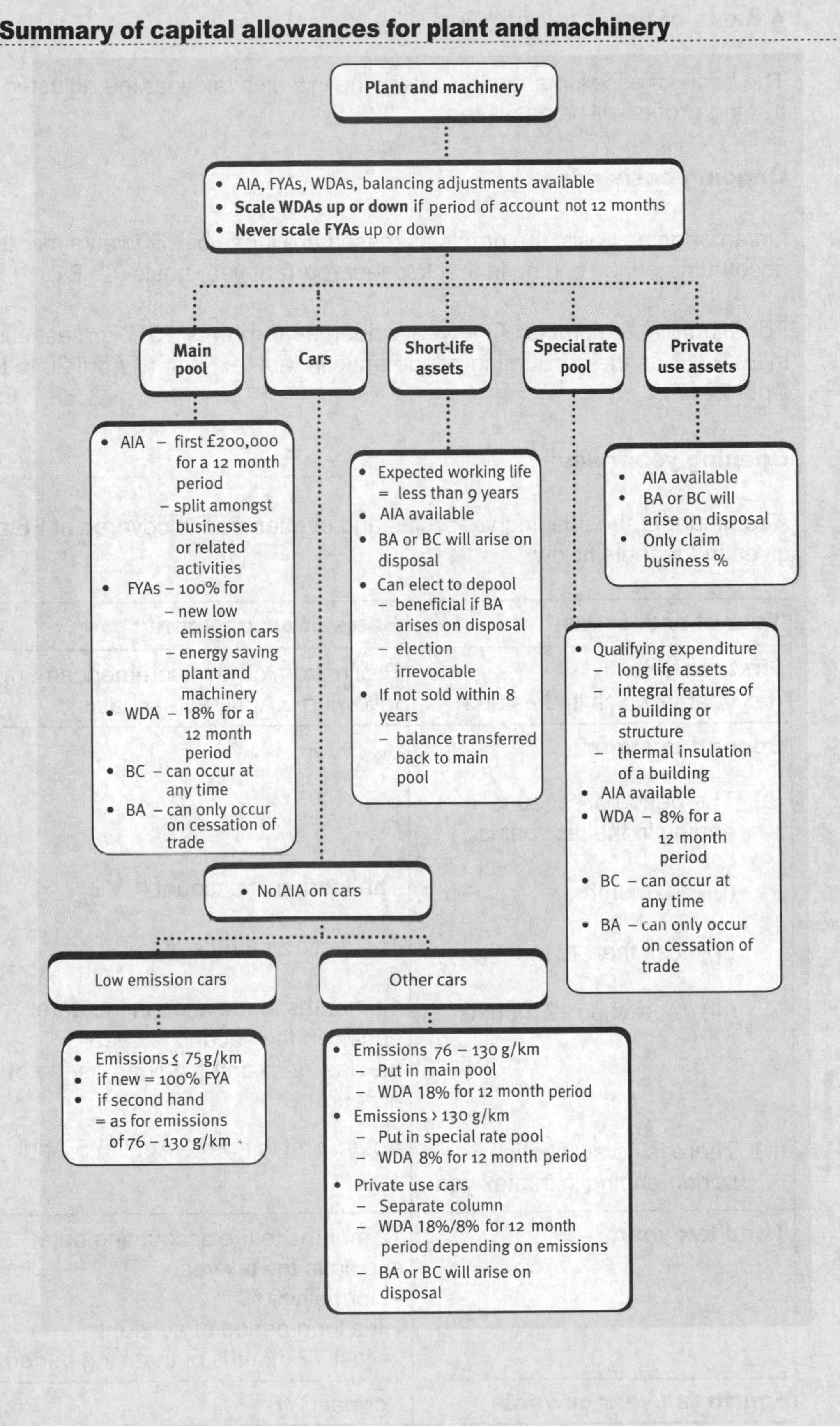

Plant and machinery
• AIA, FYAs, WDAs, balancing adjustments available
• Scale WDAs up or down if period of account not 12 months
• Never scale FYAs up or down
Main pool
Cars
Short-life assets
Special rate pool
Private use assets
• AIA – first £200,000 for a 12 month period
– split amongst businesses or related activities
• FYAs – 100% for
– new low emission cars
– energy saving plant and machinery
• WDA – 18% for a 12 month period
• BC – can occur at any time
• BA – can only occur on cessation of trade
• Expected working life = less than 9 years
• AIA available
• BA or BC will arise on disposal
• Can elect to depool
– beneficial if BA arises on disposal
– election irrevocable
• If not sold within 8 years
– balance transferred back to main pool
• AIA available
• BA or BC will arise on disposal
• Only claim business %
• Qualifying expenditure
– long life assets
– integral features of a building or structure
– thermal insulation of a building
• AIA available
• WDA – 8% for a 12 month period
• BC – can occur at any time
• BA – can only occur on cessation of trade
• No AIA on cars
Low emission cars
Other cars
• Emissions ≤ 75g/km
• if new = 100% FYA
• if second hand = as for emissions of 76 – 130 g/km
• Emissions 76 – 130 g/km
– Put in main pool
– WDA 18% for 12 month period
• Emissions > 130 g/km
– Put in special rate pool
– WDA 8% for 12 month period
• Private use cars
– Separate column
– WDA 18%/8% for 12 month period depending on emissions
– BA or BC will arise on disposal

4 Basis of assessment rules

The basis of assessment rules determine in which tax year the adjusted trading profits will be assessed.

Ongoing basis rules

On an ongoing basis, the profits assessed are those of the twelve month accounting period ending in that tax year (current year basis (CYB)).

For example, the profits of the year ended 28 February 2017 are assessed in 2016/17 as the accounting period ends in that tax year (6 April 2016 to 5 April 2017).

Opening year rules

A reminder of the opening year rules and overlap profits covered at F6 are given in the table below.

Year of assessment	Basis of assessment
First tax year (tax year in which trade starts)	Profits from date of commencement to following 5 April (actual basis)
Second tax year	
(a) The period of account ending in the tax year is:	
(i) 12 months	That period of account (CYB)
(ii) less than 12 months	The first 12 months of trade
(iii) more than 12 months	12 months to the accounting date ending in the second tax year (i.e. last 12 months of long period of account)
(b) There is no accounting period ending in the tax year	Actual profits from 6 April to 5 April
Third tax year	12 months to the accounting date ending in the tax year – normally CYB – if a long period of account = last 12 months of that long period
Fourth tax year onwards	Normal CYB

Note that where apportionment of trading profits is required, calculations should be performed to the nearest month.

Overlap profits

In the opening years, unless the trader has a 31 March or 5 April accounting end date, some of the profits are assessed in more than one tax year. These are known as 'overlap profits'.

Overlap profits:

- can arise in any of the first three tax years of assessment
- are carried forward, and are normally deducted from:
  - the assessment for the period in which the business ceases; or
  - possibly on an earlier change of accounting date.

Test your understanding 3

John started to trade on 1 July 2016. He prepared accounts with tax adjusted trading profits after capital allowances as follows.

Year ended 30 June 2017	£24,000
Year ended 30 June 2018	£30,000

Calculate the trading income assessments to include in John's income tax computations for the first three tax years of assessment and calculate the overlap profits to carry forward.

Test your understanding 4

Eric started to trade on 1 July 2016. He prepared accounts with tax adjusted trading profits as follows.

1 July 2016 to 30 April 2017	£20,000
Year ended 30 April 2018	£38,400

Calculate the trading income assessments to include in Eric's income tax computations for the first three tax years of assessment and calculate the overlap profits to carry forward.

Test your understanding 5

Edwina commenced trading on 1 July 2015. She prepared accounts to 31 March 2017 and annually thereafter.

Her adjusted trading profits for the first two periods were as follows:

21 months ended 31 March 2017	£42,000
Year ended 31 March 2018	£27,000

Calculate the trading income assessments to include in Edwina's income tax computations for the first three tax years of assessment and calculate the overlap profits to carry forward.

Choice of accounting date

This is an important consideration at P6 as choice of an appropriate accounting date at the commencement of a business can affect:

- the level of profits to be taxed in a particular tax year
- the overlap profits created
- the timing and amount of tax payments.

Over the life of the business, regardless of the accounting date chosen, the individual will be charged on all of the profits earned.

However, tax planning can have an advantageous impact on:

- cash flow
- can result in profits being assessed at a lower marginal rate of tax (depending on whether profits are increasing or declining, and the level of the individual's other income in each of the years).

Factors to consider

The following important factors should be considered when choosing the optimum accounting date.

Time lag between earning income and paying tax

- An accounting date of just after, rather than just before, 5 April (such as 30 April) will ensure the maximum interval between earning profits and having to pay the related tax liability.

- For example, the year ended 30 April 2016 will be assessed in the tax year 2016/17, with payments due on 31 January 2017, 31 July 2017 and 31 January 2018.
  However, the year ended 31 March 2016 would have been assessed in the tax year 2015/16, with payments due on 31 January 2016, 31 July 2016 and 31 January 2017.

Time to prepare accounts and calculate tax

- Under self-assessment, the tax return is generally due by 31 January following the tax year. Again, an accounting date of just after, rather than just before, 5 April (such as 30 April) will give more time to prepare accounts and calculate the tax due.
- For example, for the tax year 2016/17 the tax return is due by 31 January 2018. With a 30 April year end, this will be based on the year ended 30 April 2016, giving 21 months to prepare accounts. With a 31 March year end this will be based on the year ended 31 March 2017, giving only 10 months.

Avoiding overlap profits

- An accounting date just after 5 April will result in increased overlap profits upon the commencement of trading, whereas there are no overlap profits with a 31 March accounting date.
- For example, having a year end of 30 April will result in 11 months worth of overlap profits.
- However, this may be beneficial, depending on whether profits are rising or falling.

Profits rising or falling?

- If profits are rising, an accounting date of just after, rather than just before, 5 April (such as 30 April) will generally result in less tax payable in the opening years of the business, as the assessment each tax year will be based on earlier (lower) profits than with, say, a 31 March year end.
- The opposite would be true if profits were falling.

Note that the choice of an optimum accounting date depends on the implications of these factors in the given scenario. There is unlikely to be a clear cut recommendation. All of the facts have to be considered.

The common debate in examination questions is the choice between an accounting date ending early in the tax year (e.g. 30 April) or late in the tax year (e.g. 31 March).

A/cting period end	31 March 2016	30 April 2016
Time lag between earning income and paying tax	Assessed: 2015/16 Pay dates: 31.1.16, 31.7.16, 31.1.17	Assessed: 2016/17 Pay dates 31.1.17, 31.7.17, 31.1.18
	April year end means profits are assessed in the following tax year, and tax paid 12 months later	
Time to submit computations after a/cting end date	Submit: 31.1.2017 10 months to prepare	Submit: 31.1.2018 21 months to prepare
Overlap profits	None	11 months
Profits **increasing** in opening years	Assessments based on later (higher) profits	Assessments based on earlier (lower) profits
Profits **decreasing** in opening years	Assessments based on later (lower) profits	Assessments based on earlier (higher) profits

Having a 31 March year end is administratively the simplest solution, but having a 30 April year end can have significant tax advantages.

However, the commercial needs of the business should also be considered. For example, it may not be practical to have an accounting year-end falling during the busy trading period of a seasonal business.

Example 5 – Choice of accounting date

A trader commences to trade on 1 January 2016 and is considering preparing his first accounts to 31 March 2017 or 30 April 2017 and annually thereafter.

His estimated tax adjusted trading profits after capital allowances are:

£2,000 per month for the first 12 months
£3,000 per month for the second 12 months
£4,000 thereafter per month.

(a) **Calculate the assessable profits under each alternative for the first five tax years.**

(b) **Calculate the overlap profits.**

(c) **State when the income tax is due for payment for the accounts ending in 2018.**

Solution

Accounting periods: 31 March date

Periods ended 31 March:	2017	2018	2019	2020
Months:	(15)	(12)	(12)	(12)
	£	£	£	£
(£2,000 × 12) + (£3,000 × 3)	33,000			
(£3,000 × 9) + (£4,000 × 3)		39,000		
(£4,000 × 12)			48,000	48,000

Accounting periods: 30 April date

Periods ended 30 April:	2017	2018	2019
Months:	(16)	(12)	(12)
	£	£	£
(£2,000 × 12) + (£3,000 × 4)	36,000		
(£3,000 × 8) + (£4,000 × 4)		40,000	
(£4,000 × 12)			48,000

Basis periods	**31 March**	**30 April**
2015/16	1.1.16 – 5.4.16 (3/15 × £33,000) = £6,600	1.1.16 – 5.4.16 (3/16 × £36,000) = £6,750
2016/17	12m to 31.03.17 (12/15 × £33,000) = £26,400	No a/c period 6.4.16 – 5.4.17 (12/16 × £36,000) = £27,000
2017/18	y/e 31.3.18 £39,000	12m to 30.4.17 (12/16 × £36,000) = £27,000
2018/19	y/e 31.3.19 £48,000	y/e 30.4.18 £40,000
2019/20	y/e 31.3.20 £48,000	y/e 30.4.19 £48,000

Total assessable trading profits

	£	£
In first five tax years	168,000	148,750
Overlap profits (11/16 × £36,000)	0	24,750

Tax due for accounts ending in 2018	y/e 31.3.18	y/e 30.4.18
Assessed in	2017/18	2018/19
Tax due in instalment (1)	31.1.18	31.1.19
(2)	31.7.18	31.7.19
Final balance	31.1.19	31.1.20

Tax planning in opening years

It is usually beneficial to ensure that profits for the first period of trading, which are assessed more than once under the commencement rules, are kept to a minimum.

Profits can be minimised by increasing costs in the opening year, for example by:

- ensuring account is taken of any allowable pre-trading expenditure
- renting or leasing equipment for the first period of trading rather than purchasing it, if the rental / lease deduction exceeds the capital allowances available in the first year
- consider timing of purchases to bring forward revenue deductions or capital allowances.

These are all examples of acceptable common tax avoidance advice.

However, it is important to note that simply delaying the issue of sales invoices, or accruing non-bona fide expenses would not constitute normal tax avoidance. This would cross the boundary of tax evasion and is illegal.

5 Change of accounting date

Provided certain conditions are met, an unincorporated business is allowed to change its accounting date. There may be tax advantages in doing so, or the change may be made for commercial reasons. For example, it may be easier to perform an inventory check at certain times of the year.

The detailed conditions and consequences of failing to meet the conditions are covered in expandable text and are summarised in the diagram at the end of this section.

Conditions to be met for a valid change

All of the following conditions must be satisfied.

(1) The change of accounting date must be notified to HMRC on or before 31 January following the tax year in which the change is to be made.

(2) The first accounts to the new accounting date must not exceed 18 months in length.

If the period between the old accounting date and the proposed new accounting date is longer than 18 months; two sets of accounts will have to be prepared (12 months plus the balance).

(3) There must not have been another change of accounting date during the previous five tax years **unless** HMRC accept that the present change is made for genuine commercial reasons.

Not surprisingly, obtaining a tax advantage is not accepted as a genuine commercial reason.

If **all** of the above conditions are not met:

- the old accounting date will continue to apply for tax purposes
- if accounts are prepared to the new accounting date; the figures will have to be apportioned accordingly.

If the conditions are met, then the period of account for the tax year in which the change of accounting date is made, will either be less than or more than 12 months in length.

Change of accounting date – calculations

A trader has previously prepared accounts to 30 June. If he changes his accounting date to 30 September, the next set of accounts are going to be for either 3 or 15 months.

However, all basis of assessments other than for the first and final tax years must be of 12 months in duration.

As the period of account in which the accounting date changed will not be 12 months, the assessment in the tax year of change will either be:

- made up to 12 months, by creating further overlap profits, or
- reduced back to 12 months by relieving earlier overlap profits.

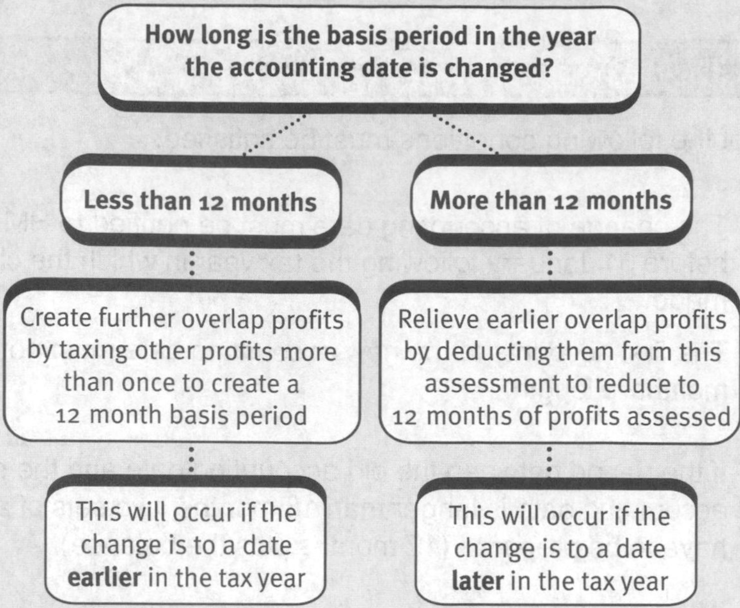

New date is earlier in the tax year

Where the new accounting date is earlier in the tax year than the old one, the basis period for the tax year of change will be the **12 month period ending with the new accounting date**.

This will result in some profits being assessed more than once. Overlap profits will therefore arise, which are treated in exactly the same way as overlap profits arising on the commencement of trade.

It is possible to have either a long or short period of account ending on the new date.

Test your understanding 6

(a) Andrea, a sole trader, has always prepared her accounts to 31 March. She decides to change her accounting date to 30 June by preparing accounts for the three-month period to 30 June 2016.

Andrea's tax adjusted profits after capital allowances are as follows:

	£
Year ended 31 March 2016	60,000
Three months to 30 June 2016	20,000
Year ended 30 June 2017	85,000

Calculate Andrea's trading income assessments for the tax years 2015/16 to 2017/18.

(b) Assume that instead of producing a three month set of accounts, Andrea had decided to change her accounting date to 30 June by preparing accounts for the fifteen month period to 30 June 2017 with tax adjusted profits of £105,000.

Calculate Andrea's trading income assessments for the tax years 2015/16 to 2017/18 and prove that the result would be virtually the same.

New date is later in the tax year

Where the new accounting date is later in the tax year than the old one the basis period for the tax year of change will be the period ending with the new accounting date.

As the resulting basis period may be more than 12 months, a corresponding proportion of any overlap profits that arose upon the commencement of trading are offset against the assessable profits.

Again, it is possible to have either a short accounting period creating the new date, or a long period.

Test your understanding 7

Peter, a sole trader, commenced trading on 1 July 2013, and has always prepared his accounts to 30 June.

He has now decided to change his accounting date to 30 September by preparing accounts for the 15 month period to 30 September 2016.

Peter's tax adjusted trading profits after capital allowances are:

	£
Year ended 30 June 2014	18,000
Year ended 30 June 2015	24,000
Period ended 30 September 2016	30,000
Year ended 30 September 2017	36,000

Calculate Peter's trading income assessments for all of the tax years affected by the results.

Summary of change of accounting date rules

Change of accounting date

Conditions:

- Accounts to new date **must not exceed 18 months**
- No other COAD in last five years unless genuine commercial reason
- Notify HMRC by **31 January following tax year** of change

Where the new accounting date is **earlier in the tax year** than the old accounting date

- The basis period must be for 12 months
- Assess: **12 months to the new accounting date**
- **Overlap profits** are **created**

Where the new accounting date is **later in the tax year** than the old accounting date

- The basis period must be for 12 months
- Assess: **Accounts not yet assessed up to the new accounting date**
- **Deduct** the appropriate number of months' worth of **overlap profits** to ensure that the equivalent of only 12 months' profits are assessed

6 Trading losses for new and ongoing business

There is little new technical knowledge in respect of trading loss reliefs at P6 compared with F6.

The key difference at P6 is that examination questions at this level will usually involve giving tax advice and recommending a particular course of action to ensure the optimum use of trading losses in a particular scenario.

Common scenarios are to look at losses in the opening years of business, the ongoing years, where there is a change in operations or the closing years (see Chapter 18).

It is necessary to have a firm grasp of the basic trading loss rules in order to:

- identify the suitable tax planning measures available
- be able to recognise the consequences, advantages and disadvantages of taking different courses of action.

The calculation of a trading loss

A trading loss occurs when the normal tax adjusted trading profit computation gives a negative result.

Where a trading loss occurs:

- the individual's trading income assessment will be £Nil
- a number of loss relief options are available to obtain relief for the loss.

Calculation of trading loss

	£	£
Tax adjusted trading profit/(loss) before capital allowances	X	(X)
Less: Capital allowances	(X)	(X)
Trading loss	(X)	(X)

Note that:

- capital allowances are taken into account in calculating the amount of the trading loss available for relief
- capital allowances:
  - can increase a tax adjusted trading loss; and
  - can turn a tax adjusted trading profit into a trading loss.

7 Loss relief options available

An individual trader has the following choice of options:

	Opening years	Ongoing years	Closing years
Relief against total income	√	√	√
Relief against chargeable gains	√	√	√
Carry forward of trading losses	√	√	x
Opening years loss relief	√	x	x
Terminal loss relief	x	x	√
Incorporation relief	x	x	√

Loss relief options in ongoing years

If an individual makes a trading loss in the ongoing years, they initially have to decide whether to claim relief against total income or carry forward all of the loss.

Where a claim against total income is made, any remaining loss is automatically carried forward unless the individual then makes a claim to set the loss against chargeable gains.

Note that a claim against gains can only be made after a claim against total income has been made. Any remaining loss is automatically carried forward.

The choices can be summarised as follows:

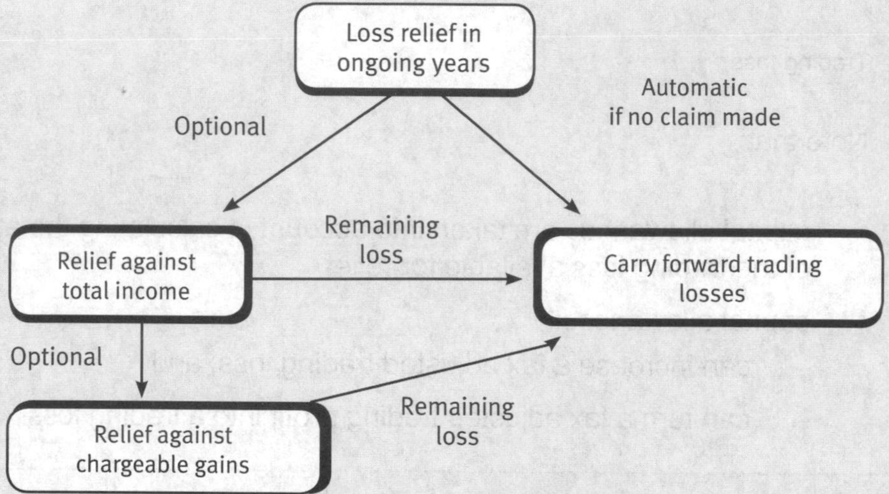

Relief against total income and carry forward

The key rules relating to the above reliefs are unchanged from F6 and are summarised as follows:

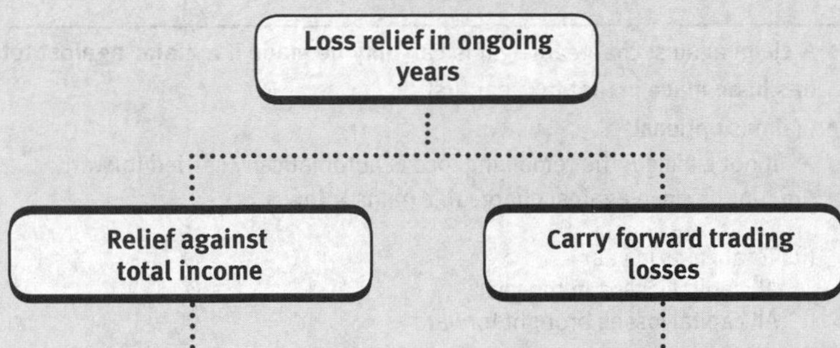

Relief against total income

- Claim is **optional**
- If claimed, set loss against **total income** in
  - the 'tax year of the loss', **and/or**
  - the preceding tax year
- 'Tax year of the loss' = tax year in which the loss making period ends
- Can set off
  - in either year in isolation
  - both years in any order
  - do not have to claim
- For example: loss in y/e 31.12.16
  - tax year of loss = 2016/17
  - can set off the loss in:
    1. 2015/16 only
    2. 2016/17 only
    3. 2015/16 first, then 2016/17
    4. 2016/17 first, then 2015/16
    5. make no claim and carry forward loss to 2017/18
- If claimed
  - must **set off maximum amount** possible
  - **cannot restrict** set-off to preserve the personal allowance
  - therefore the benefit of the personal allowance may be wasted if a claim is made
- Consecutive year losses: in any one year, total income is relieved by
  - the loss of that year first, then
  - the loss carried back from the following year
- Relief must be **claimed in writing**
- For 2016/17 loss, the claim must be made by **31 January 2019**

Carry forward trading losses

- **Automatic**
- **Carry forward** against
  - **First available**
  - **Trading profits**
  - Of the **same trade**
- Can carry forward indefinitely
- But must **set off maximum amount** possible each year
- If no claim against total income:
  - carry all loss forward
- If specific claim made (i.e. against total income or gains):
  - carry forward remaining unrelieved loss
- Claim must be made to **establish the amount of the loss** carried forward
- For a 2016/17 loss, the claim must be made **by 5 April 2021**

A revision of the rules for relief against chargeable gains

The key rules relating to relief against chargeable gains are unchanged from F6 and can be summarised as follows:

Relief against chargeable gains

- A claim against chargeable gains can **only be made if a claim against total income has been made** in that tax year first
- Claim is **optional**
  - if not claimed, the remaining loss is automatically carried forward.
- Amount of claim against chargeable gains = **lower** of:

	£
(i) Total gains in year	X
All capital losses in the year	(X)
All capital losses brought forward	(X)
	X
(ii) Remaining loss after claim against total income	X

- If claimed, treat the trading loss **as if** it is a **current year capital loss** in the capital gains tax computation
- **Claim** can be **made in the same tax years as a claim** against total income
- If claimed
  - must **set off maximum amount possible**
  - **cannot restrict set-off** to preserve the annual exempt amount
  - therefore the benefit of the annual exempt amount may be wasted if a claim is made
- Relief must be **claimed in writing**
- For 2016/17 loss, the claim must be made by **31 January 2019**

Note that utilising losses against gains will normally save tax at 10% or 20% (unless gain is in respect of residential property).

Example 6 – Relief against chargeable gains

Diana prepares her accounts to 31 December each year.

Her recent results have been as follows:

		£
y/e 31.12.2016	Tax adjusted trading profit	7,000
y/e 31.12.2017	Trading loss	(18,500)

Diana has received bank interest of £3,450 and dividends of £330 in 2016/17.

She realised the following chargeable gains in the year 2016/17:

	£
Asset 1	16,000
Asset 2	14,360

She has capital losses brought forward of £1,675.

Calculate Diana's taxable income and taxable gains for 2016/17, assuming that she decides to claim relief for her losses against her total income and against her gains in 2016/17 only.

Solution

- Diana's loss occurs in y/e 31 December 2017 = in 2017/18.
- She is entitled to claim relief against total income in 2017/18 and/or 2016/17.
- She has decided to claim relief in 2016/17 only.
- Therefore only allowed to claim relief against gains in 2016/17.

Income tax computation – 2016/17

	£
Trading income	7.000
Bank interest	3,450
Dividends	330
Total income	10,780
Less: Loss relief	(10,780)
Net income	0
Less: PA	(wasted)
Taxable income	0

Note that the PA, the savings and the dividend nil rate bands are wasted.

Claim against chargeable gains = lower of:

	£
(i) Total gains in year	30,360
All capital losses in the year	(0)
All capital losses brought forward	(1,675)
	28,685
(ii) Remaining loss after claim against total income (£18,500 – £10,780)	7,720

Therefore, claim £7,720 relief and treat it as if it is a current year capital loss in the capital gains computation as follows:

Capital gains tax computation – 2016/17

	£
Asset 1	16,000
Asset 2	14,360
Total chargeable gains	30,360
Less: Trading loss relief	(7,720)
Less: Capital loss b/f	(1,675)
Net chargeable gains	20,965
Less: AEA	(11,100)
Taxable gains	9,865

CGT saved will be £772 (£7,720 at 10%), as the gains offset against the losses would have fallen within the basic rate band.

Note: The trading loss is treated as a current year capital loss and therefore must be set off before capital losses brought forward.

Loss relief options in opening years

The options available in the opening years of trade are exactly the same as those available to an ongoing business, but with one extra option available: three year carry back against total income.

The choices can be summarised as follows:

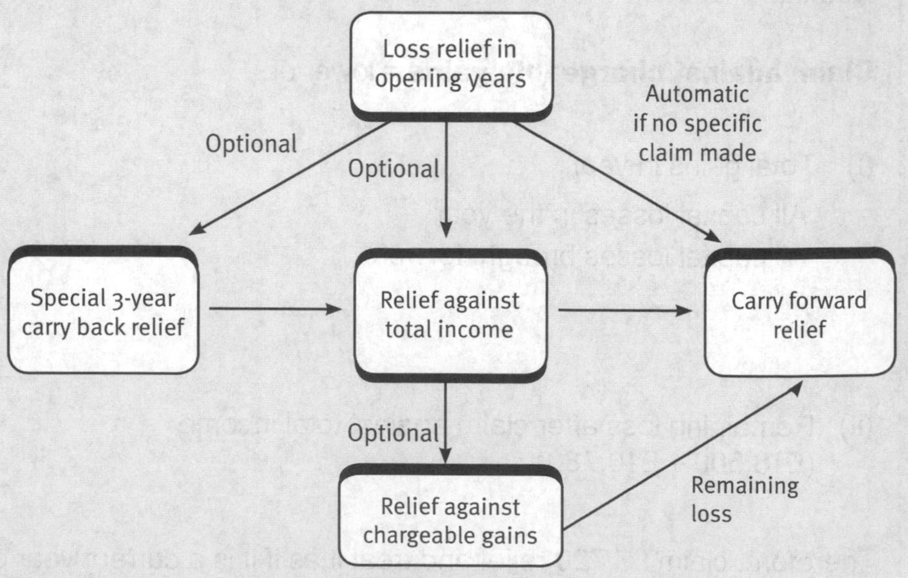

However, before a particular loss relief can be claimed it is necessary to determine the loss arising in each tax year.

Calculation of loss in opening years

The normal opening year basis of assessment rules apply regardless of whether the individual makes a profit or loss.

However, in calculating a loss in the opening years note that:

- It is vital to remember that a loss may only be relieved once.
- There is no such thing as overlap losses.
- If a loss is included in the computation in more than one tax year, then the amount taken into account in the first tax year cannot also be included in the second tax year.

Example 7 – Opening year loss

Germaine starts trading on 1 August 2015. His results, as adjusted for tax purposes, are:

10 months to 31 May 2016	Loss	(£20,000)
Year ended 31 May 2017	Profit	£48,000

Calculate Germaine's assessable profits for 2015/16 and 2016/17. State the amount of loss relief available in each year.

Solution	Assessable profits	Loss available
2015/16 (Actual basis)	£	£
1.8.15 – 5.4.16		
8/10 × (20,000) = (£16,000)	0	16,000
2016/17 (First 12 months)		
1.8.15 – 31.7.16		
Loss (10 m/e 31.5.16)	(20,000)	
Less: Taken into account in 2015/16	16,000	
	(4,000)	
2 months of y/e 31.5.17		
Profits (2/12 × 48,000)	8,000	
	4,000	
Loss relief claim (Note)		0

Note: The £4,000 loss relief is automatically given in 2016/17 by reducing the assessment from £8,000 to £4,000.

Choice of loss relief in opening years

If an individual makes a trading loss in the opening years, they have to decide whether to claim normal relief against total income, special opening year loss relief or carry forward all of the loss.

Where a normal claim against total income is made, any remaining loss is automatically carried forward unless the individual decides to make a claim against chargeable gains or special opening year claim.

Note that an individual can claim both normal relief against total income and opening year relief if there are sufficient losses. However, they must utilise the maximum amount of loss under one claim first, and can only make the other claim with the remaining loss.

Where a special opening year claim is made, any remaining loss is automatically carried forward unless the individual decides to make a normal claim against total income (and a possible extension against gains can then be considered).

Note that a claim against chargeable gains can only be made after a normal claim against total income has been made.

Special opening year loss relief

Special opening year relief against total income

- Optional claim
- Applies to loss arising in any of the **first 4 tax years** of trading
- If claimed, set loss against
  - **total income**
  - **in 3 tax years** before tax year of loss
  - on a FIFO basis (i.e. earliest year first)
- There is no need for the trade to have been carried on in the earlier years
- **One claim** covers all 3 years
- For example:
  Loss in y/e 31.12.16 (2016/17) will be set off in:
  1. 2013/14
  2. 2014/15
  3. 2015/16
- If claimed
  - Must set off **maximum amount possible**
  - Cannot restrict set-off to preserve the PA
  - Therefore, the benefit of the PA may be wasted if a claim is made
- For 2016/17 loss, the claim must be made by **31 January 2019**

The procedure for dealing with questions involving losses

The following procedure should be adopted when answering questions:

(1) Determine the tax adjusted profits and losses after capital allowances for each accounting period.

(2) Determine when losses arise and therefore when loss relief is available (i.e. in which tax years).

(3) Set up a pro forma income tax computation for each tax year side by side and leave spaces for the loss set off to be inserted later.

(4) Set up a loss memo working for each loss to show how it is utilised.

(5) If more than one loss – consider in chronological order.

(6) Consider each option – be prepared to explain the options, the consequences of making a claim, the advantages and disadvantages.

(7) Set off losses according to the requirements of the question, or in the most beneficial way if it is a tax planning question.

Pro forma income tax losses computation

For a new business starting in 2016/17 where loss arising in 2016/17

	2013/14	2014/15	2015/16	2016/17	2017/18
	£	£	£	£	£
Trading income				0	x
Less: Loss relief b/f					(x)
				0	x
Employment income	x	x	x	x	x
Other income	x	x	x	x	x
Total income	x	x	x	x	x
Standard loss relief			(x)	(x)	
Opening years relief	(x)	(x)	(x)		
Net income	x	x	x	x	x
Less: PA (if applicable)	(x)	(x)	(x)	(x)	(x)
Taxable income	x	x	x	x	x

Loss working	2016/17 £
Trading loss	x
Utilisation of loss:	
Opening years relief against total income (strict FIFO order)	(x)
Standard relief against total income (any order)	(x)
	——
C/f against future trading profits	x
	——

Tax planning with trading losses

The primary aims of tax planning for trading losses

When planning relief for trading losses, careful consideration needs to be given to the personal circumstances of the individual.

Tax advice should aim to satisfy the following goals of a taxpayer:

- Obtain tax relief at the highest marginal rate of tax.
- Obtain relief as soon as possible.
- Ensure that the taxpayer's PAs, savings and dividend nil rate bands are not wasted, if possible.

It may not be possible to satisfy all of these aims, for example:

- in order to get a higher rate of relief, the taxpayer may have to waste their PA and/or nil rate bands
- carrying losses forward may give a higher rate of relief, but the cash flow implications of claiming relief now rather than waiting for relief may be more important to the taxpayer.

In examination questions you will be given a scenario and the tax advice must address the specific facts of the situation presented.

Factors to consider

In understanding the position of the taxpayer, it is important to understand the key features of the reliefs available.

Test your understanding 8

Jeremy started in business on 1 July 2015 and decided to prepare accounts to 30 June.

The results for his first two trading periods are as follows:

	£
Year ended 30.6.2016 : Trading loss	(20,000)
Year ended 30.6.2017 : Trading profit	12,000

Prior to setting up in business he was employed and his employment income has been as follows:

	£
2012/13	13,000
2013/14	13,000
2014/15	14,000
2015/16	4,000

He had rental income of £1,000 for the years 2012/13 and 2016/17 only.

(a) **Show the loss claims if loss relief is claimed in the most beneficial way.**

(b) **Comment briefly on the result obtained under the alternative scenarios.**

Maximum deduction from total income

There is a limit on the amount of relief that can be deducted from total income in any tax year. The limit applies to trading losses and/or qualifying loan interest.

The **maximum deduction** from total income is the **greater of:**

- £50,000, or
- 25% of adjusted total income.

Adjusted total income (ATI) is calculated as follows:

	£
Total income	X
Add: Payroll deduction scheme contributions	X
	X
Less: Gross personal pension contributions	(X)
Adjusted total income	X

However, the P6 examining team has confirmed that only the personal pension contribution deduction will be required at P6.

Note that the restriction will be £50,000 unless the individual's ATI exceeds £200,000 (as £200,000 × 25% = £50,000).

The limit applies to trading losses set against:

- current year total income, and
- earlier years **if** set against income other than profits of the same trade.

It does not apply where the trading loss is set against profits from the same trade of an earlier year. Note that in this instance, trading losses are set against trading income from the same trade before income from other sources.

Any trade loss that cannot be set off against total income can be offset against chargeable gains of the same tax year in the usual way, or carried forward against future trade profits from the same trade.

However, note that the rules only restrict the loss that can be set off against total income, not chargeable gains.

As the reliefs against total income are 'all or nothing', it is possible that this restriction of the amount of the loss allowed to be deducted could be beneficial and prevent the wastage of personal allowances and nil rate bands.

Test your understanding 9

Luca is a sole trader and has adjusted trading results as follows:

Year ended 30 September 2015	£72,000
Year ended 30 September 2016	(£142,000)

He also has property income of £80,000 each year.

He does not make any charitable donations but contributes £5,000 cash to a personal pension scheme each year.

He wishes to offset his trading loss against his total income for 2016/17 and then 2015/16.

Calculate Luca's taxable income for 2015/16 and 2016/17.

Assume that the tax year 2016/17 rates and allowances apply throughout.

The above TYU considers the restriction of trading losses in the current and preceding year.

Note that the restriction is also relevant:

- when the special opening year loss relief rules are applied and the loss is carried back to earlier years, and
- where a claim is made to treat a capital loss on qualifying unquoted trading company shares as if it is a trading loss and is set against total income (Chapter 8).

Excess qualifying loan interest cannot be set off in any other year so if a taxpayer has both losses and qualifying loan interest they can choose to deduct the loan interest first.

8 Simplification of accounting and taxation for unincorporated businesses

Cash basis option for small businesses

Unincorporated businesses (i.e. sole traders and partnerships):

- can choose to calculate profits/losses on:
  - a cash basis (i.e. on the basis of cash received and expenses paid in the **period of account**), rather than
  - the normal accruals basis
- provided they have turnover under the VAT registration threshold (£83,000 with effect from 1 April 2016)

The cash basis option is not available to:

- companies, and
- limited liability partnerships (LLPs).

If an unincorporated business chooses the cash basis, it can continue to account on this basis until its annual turnover is twice the VAT registration threshold (i.e. £166,000 from 1 April 2016).

Note that the cash basis is optional and the detailed rules are complex, however, the P6 examining team has confirmed that:

- only the level of detail in this section is examinable, and
- it should be assumed in all questions involving sole traders and partnerships that the cash basis does not apply unless it is specifically referred to in the question.

Under the cash basis:

- the business accounts for cash receipts and payments in the period of account
- the business (like any other business) can prepare its accounts to any date in the year
- there is no distinction between capital and revenue expenditure in respect of plant, machinery and equipment for tax purposes, therefore:
  - purchases are allowable deductions when paid for, and
  - proceeds are treated as taxable cash receipts when an asset is sold
  - capital allowances remain available for expenditure on cars only; the capital cost is not an allowable deduction when paid
- in the P6 examination, the flat rate expense deduction for motor car expenses is claimed (see below) instead of capital allowances.

The key advantages of the cash basis are:

- simpler accounting requirements as there is no need to account for receivables, payables and inventory
- profit is not accounted for and taxed until it is realised and therefore cash is available to pay the associated tax liability.

However the main disadvantage is that:

- losses can only be carried forward to set against future trading profits, whereas under the accruals basis many more options for loss relief are available.

Flat rate expense deduction option for any unincorporated business

Any unincorporated business (whether or not they are using the cash basis) can:

- opt to use flat rate expense adjustments
- to replace the calculation of actual costs incurred in respect of certain expenses.

However, note that the P6 examining team has confirmed that:

- flat rate expenses will only be examined where the business has chosen the cash basis, and
- if the cash basis applies, the use of flat rate expenses should be assumed to also apply.

The flat rate expense adjustments that are examinable are as follows:

Type of expense	Flat rate expense adjustment
Motoring expenses = capital costs and running costs (e.g. insurance repairs, servicing and fuel)	Allowable deduction = amount using the AMAP rates of 45p and 25p per mile (i.e. same allowance as for employed individuals use of own car)
Private use of part of a commercial building = private accommodation in a guest house or small hotel (e.g. a bed and breakfast)	Private use adjustment re household goods and services, food and utilities = fixed amount based on the number of occupants Note that the private element of other expenses (e.g. mortgage interest and rates) must be adjusted for as normal.

In the P6 examination, if the flat rate expense adjustment for private use of a commercial building is required, it will be provided within the question.

The AMAP rates are included in the tax rates and allowances provided to you in the examination.

Note: When you are asked to calculate taxable profit using the cash basis, you should begin your calculation with revenue received, and make any necessary deductions or additions to this figure. It is possible to calculate the correct answer by adjusting the net profit as you would under the accruals basis. However, this method is likely to be more time consuming and complicated.

Test your understanding 10

Rosemarie opened a bed and breakfast on 1 August 2016 and has prepared her first set of accounts to 5 April 2017.

Her accountant prepared her statement of profit or loss for the period ended 5 April 2017 as follows:

	Notes	£	£
Revenue	(1)		48,035
Less: Food, utilities and other household goods	(2)		(15,670)
Gross profit			32,365
Depreciation	(3)	2,500	
Motor expenses	(4)	4,200	
Other expenses (all allowable)	(5)	14,500	
			(21,200)
Net profit			11,165

(1) Revenue includes £6,575 which is still receivable at 5 April 2017.

(2) Rosemarie paid for 80% of her purchases by 5 April 2017 and the remainder in June 2017. There is no closing inventory at 5 April 2017. Rosemarie lives with her husband at the bed and breakfast, and £4,900 of the costs relate to their personal use.

(3) The depreciation charge relates to the fixtures, fittings and equipment bought in the period for £9,000 and a motor car purchased on 1 August 2016. Rosemarie purchased the motor car with CO_2 emissions of 128 g/km for £9,600 and she uses the car 70% for business purposes.

(4) The motor expenses of £4,200 relate to Rosemarie's car and in the period she drove 11,000 business miles.

(5) The other expenses are all allowable for tax purposes, however Rosemarie paid for £460 of the expenses in June 2017.

The cash basis private use adjustment for two occupants in a business premises for 8 months is £4,000.

Calculate Rosemarie's tax adjusted trading profit for the year ended 5 April 2017 assuming:

(a) **She uses the normal accruals basis of accounting.**

(b) **She uses the cash basis.**

9 NICs payable in respect of self employed individuals

A reminder of the rules for class 2 and class 4 contributions covered at F6 is given in expandable text and are summarised in the diagram below.

Summary of total NICs payable

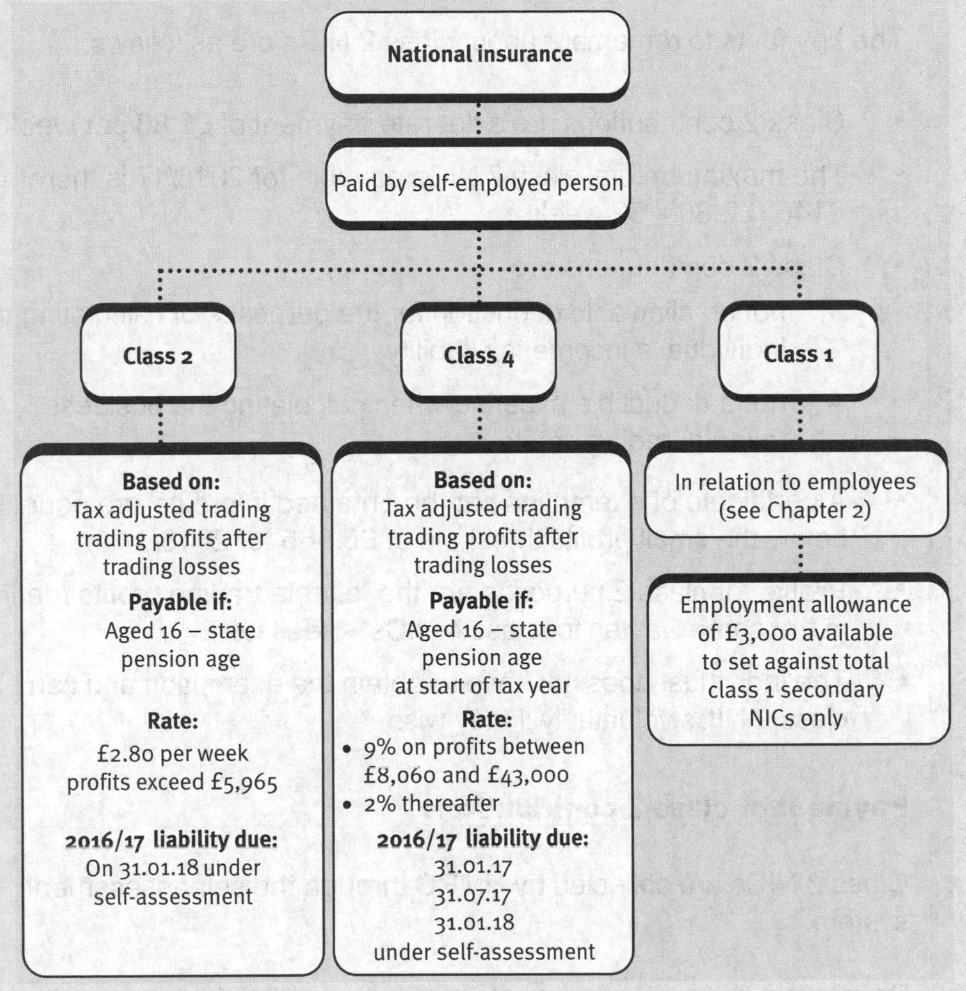

Class 2 contributions

Provided the individual does not have a certificate of exemption, class 2 contributions are payable by individuals:

- aged 16 or over **until** attaining state pension age.

The key facts to remember about class 2 NICs are as follows.

- Class 2 contributions are a flat rate payment of £2.80 per week.
- The maximum total class 2 NICs payable for 2016/17 is therefore £146 (£2.80 × 52 weeks).
- Class 2 contributions are
  - not an allowable deduction for the purposes of calculating the individual's income tax liability.
  - not a deductible expense when calculating the business' taxable trading profits.
- A certificate of exemption can be obtained if 'profits' are equal to or below the small profits threshold of £5,965 for 2016/17.
- Profits for class 2 purposes are the taxable trading profits (defined in the same way as for class 4 NICs – see later).
- The individual does not have to obtain the exemption and can pay class 2 NICs voluntarily if they wish.

Payment of class 2 contributions

Class 2 NICs are collected by HMRC through the self-assessment system.

Payment is due by 31 January following the end of the tax year, along with the balancing payment for income tax, class 4 NICs and capital gains tax.

State pension age

Up to 5 April 2010 the state pension age was 65 for men and 60 for women.

Between 2010 and 2018 the state pension age for women is gradually increasing to 65 and from 2018 onwards the state pension ages for both men and women are further increasing.

Class 4 contributions

In addition to class 2 NICs, a self-employed individual may also be liable to class 4 NICs.

Class 4 contributions are payable by self-employed individuals who:

- **at the start of the tax year**, are aged 16 or over.

They continue to pay until:

- **the end of the tax year** in which they reach state pension age.

The key facts to remember about class 4 NICs are:

- Class 4 NICs are a percentage-based contribution levied on the 'profits' of the individual in excess of £8,060 for 2016/17.
- Contributions payable are calculated as follows:
  - 9% on profits between £8,060 and £43,000 per annum
  - 2% on profits in excess of £43,000.
- Class 4 contributions are
  - not an allowable deduction for the purposes of calculating the individual's income tax liability
  - not a deductible expense when calculating the business' taxable trading profits.
- 'Profits' for the purposes of class 4 NICs consist of:
  - the taxable trading profits of the individual which are assessed to income tax
  - **after** deducting trading losses (if any).

  Note that 'profits' for class 4 NICs are **before** deducting the individual's PA which is available for income tax purposes.

- If the individual has more than one business, the aggregate of all profits from all self-employed occupations are used to calculate the class 4 NIC liability.

Payment of class 4 contributions

Class 4 contributions are paid to HMRC at the same time as the individual's income tax payments.

Income tax and class 4 NICs due are paid under self-assessment, as follows:

Payment	Due date	Amount
Payments on account	• 31 January in the tax year (i.e. 31.1.2017 for 2016/17) • 31 July following the end of the tax year (i.e. 31.7.2017 for 2016/17)	Two equal instalments of: • 50% of the amount paid by self-assessment in the preceding year
Balancing payment	• 31 January following the end of the tax year (i.e. 31.1.2018 for 2016/17)	Under or overpayment for the year

Test your understanding 11

James has been trading as a self-employed painter and decorator since 2002. His taxable trading profits for 2016/17 are £55,000 and he has trading losses brought forward of £10,000.

His wife, Poppy, is a part-time mobile hairdresser. Her taxable trading profits for 2016/17 are £8,330.

Calculate the class 2 and class 4 NICs payable by James and Poppy for 2016/17.

NICs: Self-employed individuals

A self-employed individual pays both class 2 and class 4 NICs in respect of tax adjusted trading profit.

In addition, if the self-employed individual employs staff, they will be required to account for:

- Class 2 and class 4 NICs in respect of their trading profits; and
- Class 1 primary, class 1 secondary and class 1A NICs in respect of earnings and benefits provided to employees.
  £3,000 relief is available for businesses to set off against their total employer's class 1 NIC bill, with the exception of a company where a director is the sole employee.

10 Employee versus partner

A popular scenario in the examination is the consideration of expanding the business and taking on an individual, often a spouse, as either an employee or a partner.

This section sets out a summary of the tax implications.

Employment of individuals in the business

- Employment costs (salaries, cost of providing benefits, employer's NICs) are tax deductible expenses for the employer.
- Employer's NICs can be avoided or reduced by taking on fewer full time staff and more part time staff because of the threshold at which NIC becomes payable.
- However, there is an increased administrative burden of employing staff.
- Alternatively, work could be subcontracted to self-employed individuals, avoiding the need to pay employer's NICs.

Employee

	Implications for sole trader	Implications for employee
Salary	• Allowable deduction from trading profits • Employer's class 1 NICs payable at 13.8% on earnings over £8,112 p.a. (allowable deduction from trading profits) £3,000 p.a. relief available • PAYE compliance burden	• Taxed on employment income – receipts basis • Employee's class 1 NICs payable at 12% (£8,060 – £43,000 p.a.) and 2% thereafter – deducted under PAYE

Provision of car	• Capital allowances 100% FYA or WDA of 18% or 8% depending on CO_2 emissions. • Allowable deduction from trading profits • No private use restriction for employee usage • Running costs allowable in full as deduction from trading profits • Employers class 1A NICs at 13.8% of assessable benefits (allowable deduction from trading profits)	• Benefit under employment income rules based on CO_2 emissions • Reduction in benefit for contribution toward private use

Setting up a partnership or taking on a partner

- Where two or more individuals are in partnership (rather than in the sole trader and employee relationship) then there is a NIC saving and a spreading of the tax burden.
- A partner
  - shares profit allocation
  - there is no employer's NIC to pay.

  Each partner is subject to the trading profit basis period rules and is responsible for their own income tax, class 2 and class 4 NICs.

  The detailed rules covering how partnerships are taxed are set out in Chapter 19.

Partner

	Implications for sole trader (existing partner)	Implication for new partner
Salary (profit share)	• Not allowable deduction from trading profits • Trading assessment on share of profits • No additional NICs	• Trading assessment on share of profits – opening year rules basis • Class 2 NICs payable – £2.80 per week • Class 4 NICs payable – 9% on share of profits (£8,060 – £43,000) and 2% thereafter • Tax and class 4 NICs payable under self-assessment
Provision of car	• Capital allowances for partners' cars = 100% FYA or WDA of 18% or 8% depending on emissions, based on cost • Allowable deduction from trading profits of the partnership • Private use restriction for partners' usage – only claim business use proportion • Running costs allowable as deduction from trading profits – business use proportion only • No NICs on cars (as no employment)	

Test your understanding 12

Henry has been in business as a sole trader for a number of years, and makes annual profits of £90,000.

He wants to involve his wife Mary in the business, either as an employee or as a partner, and is considering the following options:

(i) Employing Mary at a gross salary of £30,000 p.a.

(ii) Running the business in equal partnership with Mary.

Both Henry and Mary had rental income each year of £11,000.

(a) **Calculate the total annual tax payable by Henry as a sole trader**

(b) **Calculate the total annual tax saving for the couple under each of the suggested alternatives**

11 VAT

The key issues that may be relevant to a new or ongoing unincorporated business are:

- Registration
- Pre-registration input VAT
- Special accounting schemes.

These areas are all covered in detail in Chapter 20.

12 Self-assessment

Another important area in examination scenarios is likely to be advising the client on their duties under self-assessment, particularly:

- Notification of chargeability
- Payment of tax
- Submission of tax returns
- Record keeping.

These areas are all covered in detail in Chapter 16.

13 Chapter summary

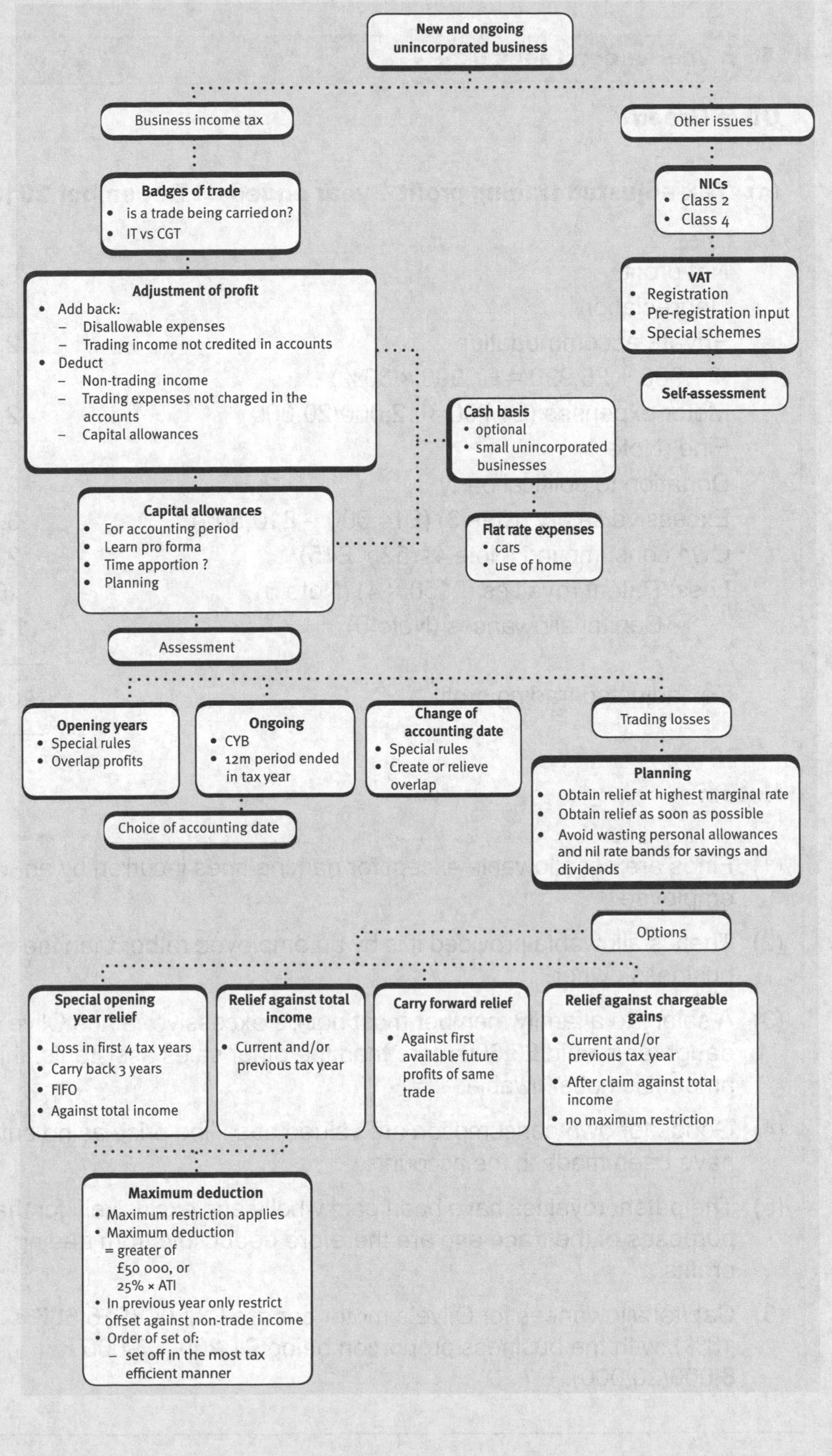
New and ongoing unincorporated business
Business income tax
Other issues
Badges of trade
• is a trade being carried on?
• IT vs CGT
NICs
• Class 2
• Class 4
VAT
• Registration
• Pre-registration input
• Special schemes
Self-assessment
Adjustment of profit
• Add back:
– Disallowable expenses
– Trading income not credited in accounts
• Deduct
– Non-trading income
– Trading expenses not charged in the accounts
– Capital allowances
Cash basis
• optional
• small unincorporated businesses
Flat rate expenses
• cars
• use of home
Capital allowances
• For accounting period
• Learn pro forma
• Time apportion ?
• Planning
Assessment
Opening years
• Special rules
• Overlap profits
Ongoing
• CYB
• 12m period ended in tax year
Change of accounting date
• Special rules
• Create or relieve overlap
Trading losses
Choice of accounting date
Planning
• Obtain relief at highest marginal rate
• Obtain relief as soon as possible
• Avoid wasting personal allowances and nil rate bands for savings and dividends
Options
Special opening year relief
• Loss in first 4 tax years
• Carry back 3 years
• FIFO
• Against total income
Relief against total income
• Current and/or previous tax year
Carry forward relief
• Against first available future profits of same trade
Relief against chargeable gains
• Current and/or previous tax year
• After claim against total income
• no maximum restriction
Maximum deduction
• Maximum restriction applies
• Maximum deduction
= greater of
£50 000, or
25% × ATI
• In previous year only restrict offset against non-trade income
• Order of set of:
– set off in the most tax efficient manner

Test your understanding answers

Test your understanding 1

Olive Green

(a) **Tax adjusted trading profit – year ended 31 December 2016**

	£
Net profit	28,500
Depreciation	2,350
Private accommodation (£1,980 + £5,920 = £7,900 × 30%)	2,370
Motor expenses (£4,700 × 12,000/20,000)	2,820
Fine (Note 1)	220
Donation to political party	100
Excessive salary (Note 3) (£14,000 – £10,500)	3,500
Own consumption (Note 4) (52 × £45)	2,340
Less: Patent royalties (£150 × 4) (Note 5)	(600)
Capital allowances (Note 6)	(1,200)
Tax adjusted trading profit	40,400

Notes:

(1) Fines are not allowable except for parking fines incurred by an employee.

(2) Theft is allowable provided it is by an employee rather than the business owner.

(3) A salary to a family member must not be excessive. Since Olive's daughter is paid £3,500 more than the other sales assistants, this amount is not allowable.

(4) Goods for own consumption are valued at selling price as no entries have been made in the accounts.

(5) The patent royalties have been paid wholly and exclusively for the purposes of the trade and are therefore deductible from trading profits.

(6) Capital allowances for Olive's motor car are £3,000 (£16,667 × 18%), with the business proportion being £1,200 (£3,000 × 8,000/20,000).

(b) **Income tax computation – 2016/17**

	Total income	Non-savings	Savings	Dividend
	£	£	£	£
Trading income	40,400	40,400		
Employment income	6,000	6,000		
Building society interest	2,800		2,800	
Dividend income	1,200			1,200
Total income	50,400	46,400	2,800	1,200
Less: Loan interest relief (Note 1)	(220)	(220)		
Net income	50,180	46,180	2,800	1,200
Less: PA (Note 1)	(11,000)	(11,000)		
Taxable income	39,180	35,180	2,800	1,200

Income tax £		
35,180	× 20% BR (Non-savings income)	7,036
500	× 0% SNRB (Savings income)	0
1,320	× 20% BR (Savings income)	264
37,000	Extended basic rate band (Note 2)	
980	× 40% HR (Savings income)	392
1,200	× 0% DNRB (Dividend income)	0
39,180		
Income tax liability		7,692
Less: Tax suffered at source		
PAYE		(1,200)
Income tax payable		6,492

Notes:

(1) The loan interest qualifies as a relief deductible from total income since the loan was used by Olive to finance expenditure for a qualifying purpose. It is paid gross.
Both the loan interest and the personal allowance are deducted from income in the most tax efficient manner. In this case, there is no advantage in setting these deductions against dividend income as this would waste the dividend nil rate band. They are therefore deducted from non-savings income.

(2) The personal pension contribution results in Olive's basic rate tax band threshold being extended to £37,000 (£32,000 + £5,000).

Olive's CGT liability for 2016/17

(£12,500 – £11,100) × 20% = £280

Balancing payment for 2016/17 due on 31 January 2018

(£6,492 + £280 – £4,559) = £2,213

Payments on account for 2017/18

Payments on account are not required for CGT, so the payments on account for 2017/18 will be £3,246 (£6,492 × 50%). These will be due on 31 January 2018 and 31 July 2018.

Consequences of paying balancing payment late

(1) Interest is charged where a balancing payment is paid late. This will run from 1 February 2018 to 30 April 2018.

(2) The interest charge will be £17 (£2,213 × 3% × 3/12).

(3) In addition, a 5% penalty of £111 (£2,213 at 5%) will be imposed as the balancing payment is not made within one month of the due date.

Test your understanding 2

Gordon

Period ended 31 March 2017

	£
Adjusted profit	149,340
Less: Capital allowances (W)	(52,058)
Trading profit	97,282

Working: Capital allowances computation

		Main pool	Short life asset	Private use car	Business use	Allow-ances
	£	£	£	£	%	£
Additions:						
Not qualifying for AIA or FYA:						
Car (CO_2 128 g/km) (Note 1)		10,400				
Private use car (CO_2 >130 g/km)				15,800		
Qualifying for AIA:						
Equipment	77,875		3,250			
Less: AIA (Max) (Note 2)	(50,000)		(0)			50,000
		27,875				
		38,275	3,250	15,800		
Less: WDA (18% × 3/12)		(1,722)	(146)			1,868
WDA (8% × 3/12) (CO_2 > 130 g/km)				(316)	× 60%	190
TWDV c/f		36,553	3,104	15,484		
Total allowances						52,058

Notes:

(1) Private use by an employee is not relevant. A separate private use asset column is only required where there is private use by the owner of the business.

(2) The AIA is pro-rated for the three month period. The maximum allowance is therefore £50,000 (£200,000 × 3/12). The AIA is allocated to the main plant and machinery in priority to the short life asset.

Test your understanding 3

John

Tax year	**Basis period**	**Trading income**
		£
2016/17	1 July 2016 to 5 April 2017 (9/12 × £24,000)	18,000
2017/18	Year ending 30 June 2017	24,000
2018/19	Year ending 30 June 2018	30,000

Overlap profits

1 July 2016 to 5 April 2017 (9/12 × £24,000)	£18,000

Test your understanding 4

Eric

Tax year	**Basis period**	**Trading income assessment**
		£
2016/17	1 July 2016 to 5 April 2017 (9/10 × £20,000)	18,000
2017/18	1 July 2016 to 30 June 2017 (£20,000 + 2/12 × £38,400)	26,400
2018/19	Year ending 30 April 2018	38,400

Overlap profits

	£
1 July 2016 to 5 April 2017 (9/10 × £20,000)	18,000
1 May 2017 to 30 June 2017 (2/12 × £38,400)	6,400
	24,400

Test your understanding 5

Edwina

Tax year	**Basis period**	**Trading income assessment**
		£
2015/16	1 July 2015 to 5 April 2016 (£42,000 × 9/21)	18,000
2016/17	Year ended 31 March 2017 (£42,000 × 12/21) (Note)	24,000
2017/18	Year ending 31 March 2018	27,000

Note: There is an accounting date in the second year of assessment so the assessment is the 12 months ending on that accounting date.

Overlap profits: There are no overlap profits.

Test your understanding 6

Andrea

(a) The accounting date has moved from March to June. The accounting date is moving to earlier in the tax year.

The tax year of change is the year in which accounts to the new accounting date are prepared (i.e. 2016/17).

The basis period for the tax year of change is the 12 months to the new accounting date.

Tax year	Basis period	Trading income
		£
2015/16	Year to 31.3.16 (Normal CYB)	60,000
2016/17	12-month period to new accounting date of 30.6.16	
	Year to 31.3.16: (£60,000 × 9/12)	45,000
	Period to 30.6.16	20,000
		65,000
2017/18	Year to 30.6.17	85,000

Note: The change in accounting date has created further overlap profits of £45,000, as the 9 months to March 2016 are assessed in both 2015/16 and 2016/17.

(b) The tax year of change is 2016/17 as Andrea does not adopt her normal 31 March year end here.

Because all the criteria are met, she is allowed to adopt the new accounting date in this year, and the profits assessed are those for the 12 months to the new accounting date – 30 June.

Tax year	Basis period	Trading income
		£
2015/16	Year to 31.3.16 (Normal CYB)	60,000
2016/17	12-month period to new accounting date of 30.6.16	
	Year to 31.03.16: (£60,000 × 9/12)	45,000
	Period to 30.06.16: (£105,000 × 3/15)	21,000
		66,000
2017/18	Year to 30.6.17 (£105,000 × 12/15)	84,000

Overlap profits still arise in respect of the 9 months to 31 March 2016 as before = £45,000.

Test your understanding 7

Peter

The tax year of change is the tax year in which accounts are prepared to the new accounting date (i.e. 2016/17).

As the new accounting date is later in the tax year, the basis period is the period ending with the new accounting date.

Tax year	Basis period	Trading income
		£
2013/14	1.7.13 to 5.4.14 (£18,000 × 9/12) (Actual)	13,500
2014/15	Year to 30.6.14 (CYB)	18,000
2015/16	Year to 30.6.15 (CYB)	24,000
2016/17	Period not yet assessed, ending on the new accounting date	
		£
	15 month period to 30.9.16	30,000
	Less: Overlap profits (£13,500 × 3/9)	(4,500)
		25,500
2017/18	Year to 30.9.17 (CYB)	36,000

The overlap profits in the opening years are £13,500, representing 9 months profits (1.7.13 to 5.4.14) that have been taxed twice.

In the tax year 2016/17 the period of account not yet assessed and ending with the new accounting date is 15 months. As no assessment can exceed 12 months, Peter is allowed to offset 3 months worth of his overlap profits.

The remaining 6 months of overlap profits are carried forward as normal and are available for relief, either on a further change in accounting date or on the cessation of trade.

Test your understanding 8

Jeremy

Step 1 Find the loss available, and the trading income assessments of the new business

		Trading income	Loss
		£	£
2015/16	1.7.15 – 5.4.16	0	
	9/12 × £20,000		15,000
2016/17	y/e 30.6.16	0	
	Loss is (£20,000 – £15,000)		5,000
2017/18	y/e 30.6.17	12,000	

Step 2 Set up income tax computations before loss reliefs

	2012/13	2013/14	2014/15	2015/16	2016/17	2017/18
Income:	£	£	£	£	£	£
Employment	13,000	13,000	14,000	4,000		
Trading				0	0	12,000
Rental	1,000				1,000	
Total	14,000	13,000	14,000	4,000	1,000	12,000

Step 3 Using special opening year relief only

(a) Loss in 2015/16 of £15,000 can be set against total income of 2012/13 – 2014/15 with earliest year first.

(b) Loss in 2016/17 of £5,000 can be used against total income of 2013/14 – 2015/16.

(c) No restrictions to preserve PA.

	2012/13	2013/14	2014/15	2015/16
	£	£	£	£
Total income	14,000	13,000	14,000	4,000
2015/16 loss	(14,000)	(1,000)		
2016/17 loss		(5,000)		
Net income	0	7,000	14,000	4,000
PA	Wasted	Part wasted		

Step 4 **Alternatively claim standard loss relief against total income and carry forward relief**

(a) Relief can be claimed against total income in the year of the loss and/or the previous year. For 2015/16 loss relief is available in 2015/16 and/or 2014/15. There is no point making 2015/16 claim as total income is covered by PA. Therefore use £14,000 in 2014/15 and then c/fwd £1,000 against trading income of 2017/18.

(b) The 2016/17 loss can be used in that year and/or 2015/16. In both years PA is available to cover total income. Therefore carry forward £5,000 against trading profit of 2017/18. This will still however result in some wastage of PA.

Step 5 **The effect is as follows**

	2014/15	2015/16	2016/17	2017/18
Income:	£	£	£	£
Employment	14,000	4,000	n/a	n/a
Trading	n/a	0	0	12,000
Less: Loss relief b/f				(1,000)
				(5,000)
Rental			1,000	
	14,000	4,000	1,000	6,000
Less: Loss relief	(14,000)			
Net income	0	4,000	1,000	6,000
PA	Wasted	Part Wasted	Part Wasted	Part Wasted

Using special opening year relief relieves the losses immediately as they were carried back. There is a wastage of PA in 2012/13 and partially in 2013/14 but repayments of tax at 20% will result.

Using standard loss relief against total income/carry forward wastes PA in 2014/15 and partially in other years. It does not relieve the loss immediately and tax saved is at 20% tax rates. Therefore on balance route (1) is preferred as loss is relieved quickly at a higher rate with minimum PA wastage.

Test your understanding 9

Luca

Loss relief offset

	2015/16	2016/17
	£	£
Trade profits	72,000	0
Property income	80,000	80,000
	152,000	80,000
Less: Loss relief		
Current year claim (restricted) (W1)		(50,000)
– Carry back claim (no restriction against profits from same trade)	(72,000)	
– Balance of loss against other income (not restricted as < £50,000)	(20,000)	
Net income	60,000	30,000
Less: PA	(11,000)	(11,000)
Taxable income	49,000	19,000

Note: The restriction in 2016/17 is useful as it prevents the wastage of Luca's PA.

Workings

(W1) **Maximum loss relief for 2016/17**

	£
Total income	80,000
Less: Gross personal pension contributions (£5,000 × 100/80)	(6,250)
Adjusted total income (ATI)	73,750
25% thereof	18,438

Maximum set off will be £50,000 as that is greater than £18,438.

Alternatively, it could be stated that as ATI < £200,000, the maximum set off is £50,000.

(W2) **Loss memorandum**

	£
Loss for 2016/17 (year ended 30 September 2016)	142,000
Used 2016/17	(50,000)
Used 2015/16 against profits from the same trade	(72,000)
Used 2015/16 against other income (within maximum £50,000)	(20,000)
Loss carried forward	0

Note: If the loss for 2016/17 were £175,000, relief against non-trading income in 2015/16 would be restricted to £50,000.

Test your understanding 10

Rosemarie

(a) **Normal accruals basis**

	£
Net profit	11,165
Food, utilities etc.	4,900
Depreciation	2,500
Motor expenses (£4,200 × 30%)	1,260
Other expenses	0
	19,825
Less: Capital allowances (W1)	(9,806)
Tax adjusted trading profit	10,019

Note:
The usual presentation of an adjustment of profits is produced above and must be used where accounts have been prepared and need adjustment.

However, an alternative method of calculating the same tax adjusted trading profit figure is to reproduce the accounts presentation but just deduct the expenses which are allowable, as opposed to adding back to net profit those that are not allowable.

This alternative presentation is given in (W3) as it provides a more direct comparison of the difference in the treatment when the cash basis is used.

(b) **Cash basis**

	£	£
Revenue (£48,035 – £6,575)		41,460
Less: Food, utilities etc. (£15,670 × 80%)		(12,536)
Less: Expenses		
Depreciation (Note 1)	0	
Capital expenditure (Note 1)	(9,000)	
Motor expenses (W2) (Note 2)	(4,750)	
Other expenses (£14,500 – £460)	(14,040)	
Plus: Private use adjustment (Note 3)	4,000	
		(23,790)
Tax adjusted trading profit		5,134

Notes:

(1) Depreciation is not allowable under the cash basis, the cost of the fixtures and fittings is allowable when paid for. The cost of the car is not however allowable, capital allowances are available – but see Note 2.

(2) Where the flat rate mileage allowance is claimed, capital allowances are not available on the cost of the car. The P6 examining team has stated that where the cash basis is used, you should assume that flat rate expenses will also be claimed.

(3) The private use adjustment of £4,000 relates to the private element of food and utility costs.

Workings

(W1) **Capital allowances**

		Main pool	Private use car		Allowances
	£	£	£		£
Additions:					
Car (CO_2 128 g/km)			9,600		
Fixtures and fittings	9,000				
Less: AIA	(9,000)				9,000
		0			
WDA (18% × 8/12)			(1,152)	× 70%	806
TWDV c/f		0	8,448		
Capital allowances					9,806

(W2) **Motor expenses – cash basis**

	£
10,000 × 45p	4,500
1,000 × 25p	250
	4,750

(W3) **Accruals basis – alternative presentation**

	£	£
Revenue		48,035
Less: Food, utilities etc. (£15,670 – £4,900)		(10,770)
Gross profit		37,265
Less: Expenses		
Depreciation (Note 1)	0	
Motor expenses (£4,200 × 70%)	(2,940)	
Other expenses	(14,500)	
Capital allowances (W1)	(9,806)	
		(27,246)
Tax adjusted trading profit		10,019

Note:

This question is for tutorial purposes. In practice it is unlikely that a business would prepare accounts on an accruals basis if they intend to use the cash basis for tax purposes.

Indeed such businesses may not even need an accountant to prepare cash accounts.

Test your understanding 11

James

Class 2 NICs	£
(£2.80 × 52 weeks)	146

James' profits for class 4 purposes are as follows:

	£
Taxable trading profits for 2016/17	55,000
Less: Trading losses b/f	(10,000)
Profits for class 4 purposes	45,000

Class 4 NICs	£
(£43,000 – £8,060) × 9%	3,145
(£45,000 – £43,000) × 2%	40
	3,185

Poppy

Class 2 NICs	
(£2.80 × 52 weeks)	146

Class 4 NICs	
(£8,330 – £8,060) × 9%	24

Test your understanding 12

Henry and Mary

Operating as a sole trader				**Total tax**
		£	£	£
Income tax on profit of £90,000				
(PA used by rental income)				
Basic rate band		32,000 @ 20%	6,400	
Higher rate band		58,000 @ 40%	23,200	
		90,000		
Income tax liability				29,600
NICs				
Class 2	(52 weeks @ £2.80 per week)			146
Class 4	(£43,000 – £8,060) × 9%		3,145	
	(£90,000 – £43,000) × 2%		940	
				4,085
Total tax and NIC liability				33,831

Employing Mary at a gross salary of £30,000 p.a.

	£	£	£
Employer's NICs re Mary payable by Henry			
Class 1 employer's contributions			
(£30,000 – £8,112) × 13.8%			3,021
Less: Employer allowance (Note)			(3,000)
			21
Tax payable by Henry on profits from the business			
Profits		90,000	
Adjustment to profits			
Mary's salary		(30,000)	
Employer's NICs		(21)	
Tax adjusted profits		59,979	
Income tax			
Basic rate band	32,000 @ 20%	6,400	
Higher rate band	27,979 @ 40%	11,192	
	59,979		
Income tax liability			17,592
NICs			
Class 2 As above			146
Class 4 (£43,000 – £8,060) × 9%		3,145	
(£59,979 – £43,000) × 2%		340	
			3,485
			21,244

Note: The employer allowance of £3,000 to set against the employer's class 1 contributions is available even if Mary is the sole employee. The allowance is only not available if it is a company where a director is the sole employee.

Tax payable by Mary re her salary

As rental income covers her PA, Mary will be assessed to tax on £30,000 taxable income (all other income):

	£	£	£
Income tax			
Basic rate band	30,000 @ 20%	6,000	
Income tax liability			6,000
NICs			
Employee's class 1 (£30,000 – £8,060) × 12%			2,633
			8,633
Total tax and NIC liability (£21,244 + £8,633)			29,877

Tax saved by employing Mary (£33,831 – £29,877) = £3,954

Running the business in equal partnership with Mary

Both Henry and Mary will be assessed to tax on £45,000 (£90,000 × 50%) taxable income (all other income) as follows:

		£	£	£
Income tax on profit of £45,000				
Basic rate band		32,000 @ 20%	6,400	
Higher rate band		13,000 @ 40%	5,200	
		45,000	11,600	
Income tax liability (£11,600 × 2)				23,200
NICs				
Class 2	(52 weeks @ £2.80 per week) × 2			291
Class 4	(£43,000 – £8,060) × 9%		3,145	
	(£45,000 – £43,000) × 2%		40	
			3,185	
Class 4 NIC liability (£3,185 × 2)				6,370
Total tax and NIC liability				29,861

Tax saved by taking Mary on as equal partner (£33,831 – £29,861) = £3,970

Note: If the examination question asks you to calculate 'total tax', you need to consider all the taxes that will apply (i.e. income tax and NICs in this question).

chapter

18

Cessation of an unincorporated business

Chapter learning objectives

Upon completion of this chapter you will be able to:

- recognise the factors that will influence the choice of cessation date and compute the assessments
- explain the range of loss reliefs available on the cessation of a business
- identify suitable tax planning measures in a given scenario to mitigate tax liabilities for an individual
- recognise that alternative courses of action have different tax consequences and assess the advantages and disadvantages
- demonstrate the optimum use of trading loss reliefs for an individual
- consider the tax implications of incorporating an existing business, and to advise on planning issue that may arise.

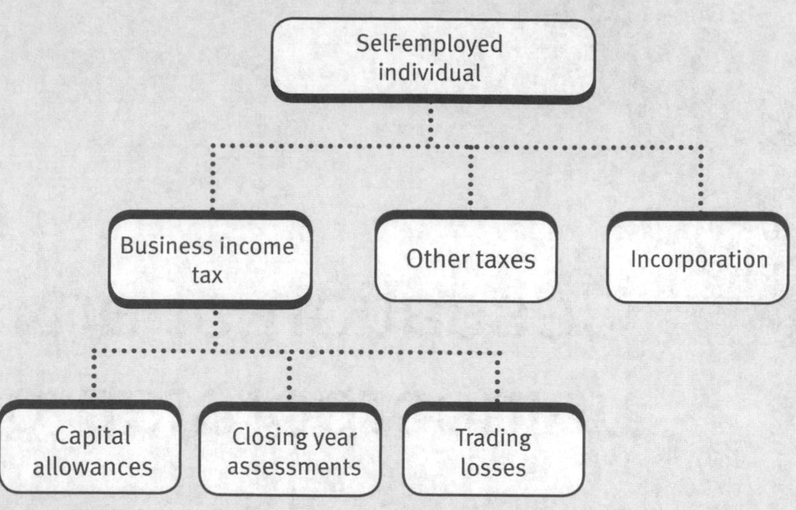

Introduction

This chapter covers the popular examination scenario of the cessation of an unincorporated business.

There is scope for a wide variety of questions due to the various ways in which an unincorporated business can cease:

- a sole trader sells his business to another sole trader
- a sole trader gifts his business
- a sole trader retires or dies
- a partner leaves the partnership
- a sole trader sells his business to a company (incorporation).

As in the previous chapter, we need to consider all of the possible tax implications of these scenarios.

The main considerations are as follows:

- income tax issues on cessation
- loss reliefs
- VAT issues on cessation
- capital gains tax issues on cessation
- incorporation of a business.

1 A revision of basic business income tax

If the business ceases to trade, the key differences in the calculation of taxable trading profits will be:

- calculating the capital allowances for the final accounting period
- applying the closing year rules for assessment of profits.

2 Capital allowances in the closing years

The final period of account before cessation is usually not 12 months in length, however there is no need for any time apportionment as:

- there are no WDAs, FYAs, or AIAs in the final period
- all additions are brought in, then disposals on cessation are dealt with
- if an owner takes over an asset, the disposal proceeds will be the market value
- the disposals will give rise to BCs and BAs
- the capital allowances computation is then closed off.

Successions to trade between connected persons

If the business is being transferred

- as a **going concern**
- to a **connected person**
- an **election** is available
- to **transfer the assets at their TWDV** (instead of market value) and thereby avoid BCs and BAs.

If the predecessor and successor to a trade are connected, and the election is made, the approach for capital allowances purposes is broadly to ignore the change of ownership:

- the actual sale price (if any)/transfer value is ignored
- the plant and machinery is deemed to have been sold for the predecessor's **opening written down value**
- consequently no balancing charge or allowance arises on the predecessor, and no WDAs are claimed in the period of transfer

- the successor uses the same written down value to begin his computation but it is treated as a transfer and not an acquisition.
- the successor claims WDA on the TWDV transferred
  - no AIA or FYA is available on this amount to the successor.

To be entitled to this privileged treatment, the following conditions must be satisfied:

- an election must be made jointly by the predecessor and successor within two years of the time the succession took place
- both parties must be within the charge to UK tax on the profits of the trade
- the assets must be in use in the trade immediately before and after the succession.

If no election is made assets are deemed to have been sold at market value as normal, and accordingly:

- balancing adjustments arise on the predecessor
- the successor is treated as having made an acquisition
  - however if the business is being transferred to a connected person, no AIA or FYA is available to the transferee.

Test your understanding 1

Julia has been trading as a sole trader since 2007 and has always prepared her accounts to 31 December. Her business is becoming more and more profitable, so she has decided to incorporate at the end of March 2017. She will transfer all her business assets to a new company to be formed, which is to be called Jules Ltd. Julia will be the sole shareholder of Jules Ltd.

The values of her plant and machinery are as follows:

	TWDV b/f at 1 January 2017	MV at 31 March 2017
	£	£
Main pool items	24,000	37,000

After incorporation, Julia will become a director and is the only employee of Jules Ltd. The company will prepare its accounts to 31 March.

The tax adjusted trading profits of the business are as follows:

	£
Year ended 31 December 2016 (after capital allowances)	62,300
Forecast for 3 months ended 31 March 2017 (before capital allowances)	20,250
Forecast for year ended 31 March 2018 (before capital allowances)	85,000

Explain the options available with regard to capital allowances. You should consider the effect on both Julia and Jules Ltd, including illustrative calculations, and advise on which alternative is best.

3 Basis of assessment rules

Closing year rules

Special rules are applied to the trading profits in the last tax year of assessment (i.e. the tax year in which the trade ceases).

The penultimate tax year is assessed on the current year basis as normal, however the rules for the final closing tax year ensure that in the final tax year:

- any profits not previously assessed are taxed
- any overlap profits from the commencement of trade are relieved.

Test your understanding 2

Michael ceased trading on 31 March 2017. His adjusted trading profits for the final three periods are as follows:

	£
Year ended 30 April 2015	40,000
Year ended 30 April 2016	42,000
Period ended 31 March 2017	38,000

Assume his overlap profits are £27,000.

Calculate Michael's taxable trading profit assessments for all of the tax years affected by the above results.

Choice of cessation date

If an individual dies, or a business is failing, the luxury of choosing a cessation date is not necessarily an available option.

However, where an individual is planning to:

- sell or gift the business to another person, or
- incorporate the business into a company

the choice of an appropriate cessation date is important and can affect:

- the level of profits to be taxed in a particular tax year, and
- the timing and amount of tax payments.

Tax planning can therefore have an advantageous impact on:

- cash flow, and
- can result in profits being assessed at a lower marginal rate of tax.

The appropriate advice will depend on whether profits are increasing or declining, and the level of the individual's other income.

Example 1 – Choice of cessation date

Susan starts trading on 1 June 2013 and prepares her first accounts to 31 May 2014.

Her tax adjusted trading profits after capital allowances are as follows:

Year ended 31 May 2014	£24,000
Year ended 31 May 2015	£31,000
Year ended 31 May 2016	£44,000

She is planning to retire in 2017 and has asked whether she should prepare her final accounts to 31 March 2017 or 30 April 2017.

From 1 June 2016 she estimates that her monthly tax adjusted profits will be £3,500.

Calculate Susan's taxable trading profit assessments for all of the tax years affected by the above results under the following alternative cessation dates:

(a) **She ceases trading on 31 March 2017**

(b) **She ceases trading on 30 April 2017.**

Solution

Susan's trading income assessable in the first three tax years is:

Tax year	Basis period	Trading income assessment
		£
2013/14	1 June 2013 – 5 April 2014 (10/12 × £24,000)	20,000
2014/15	Year ending 31 May 2014	24,000
2015/16	Year ending 31 May 2015	31,000

Overlap profits 1 June 2013 – 5 April 2014 (10/12 × £24,000)	£20,000

Ceases trading 31 March 2017 (2016/17)

		£
2016/17	1 June 2015 – 31 March 2017	
	Year ended 31 May 2016	44,000
	Period to 31 March 2017 (£3,500 × 10)	35,000
	Less: Overlap profits	(20,000)
		59,000

Ceases trading 30 April 2017 (2017/18)

		£
2016/17	Year ending 31 May 2016	44,000
2017/18	1 June 2016 – 30 April 2017 (£3,500 × 11)	38,500
	Less: Overlap profits	(20,000)
		18,500

By ceasing to trade one month later, a further £3,500 profits are assessed.

However, there is a lower assessment in 2016/17 and a small assessment in 2017/18, rather than all of the profits being assessed in 2016/17.

Depending on her level of other income in these years, she could save income tax by continuing to trade.

4 Trading losses

Loss relief options in closing years

The options available in the closing years of trade are exactly the same as those available to an ongoing business, except that:

- the option to carry forward losses is not available as there will be no further trading profits once the trade ceases
- an extra option for terminal loss relief is available
- an additional option for incorporation relief is available if the business is ceasing because it is being incorporated.

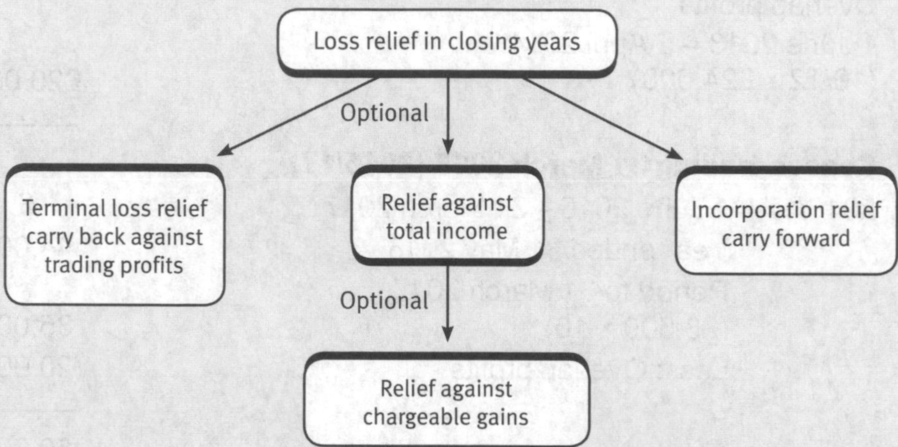

If an individual makes a trading loss in the closing years, they have to decide whether to claim relief against total income and then whether to extend the claim against their chargeable gains.

If there are remaining losses, the individual can claim terminal loss relief.

Relief against total income and terminal loss relief

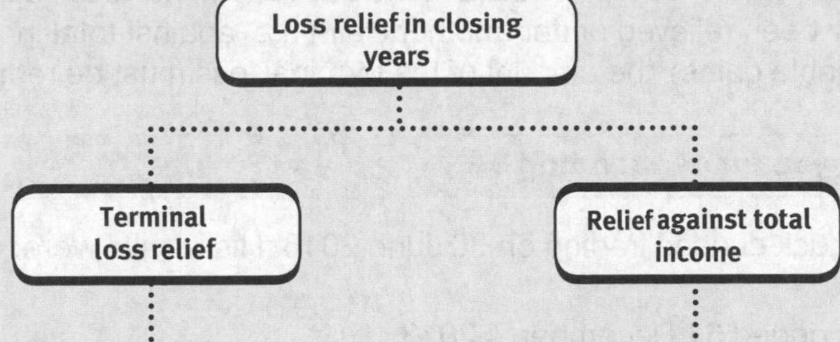

Terminal loss relief

- Claim is **optional**
  - however will normally be claimed
  - otherwise the benefit of the loss will be lost
- Relief is to set the **'terminal loss'** against **'trading income'**
  - of the **last tax year** (if any), and then
  - **carry back three tax years**
  - on a **LIFO basis**
- Terminal loss = **loss of the last 12 months** (see below)
- For 2016/17 loss, the claim must be made **by 5 April 2021**

Relief against total income

- Claim is **optional**
- Loss in the last tax year can be **set against total income** in
  - the last tax year **and/or**
  - the preceding tax year
- As for ongoing business
- For 2016/17 loss, the claim must be made **by 31 January 2019**

Extension of claim against chargeable gains

- Claim is **optional**
- Loss in the last tax year can be **set against chargeable gains** in
  - the last tax year, **and/or**
  - the preceding tax year
- As for ongoing business
- For 2016/17 loss, the claim must be made **by 31 January 2019**

The calculation of the terminal loss

The terminal loss is the loss of the **last 12 months of trading** and is calculated as follows:

	£
6 April before cessation to the date of cessation	
(1) Actual trading loss in this period (ignore if a profit)	X
(2) Overlap profits not yet relieved	X
12 months before cessation to 5 April before cessation	
(3) Actual trading loss in this period (ignore if a profit)	X
Terminal loss	X

Note that it is not compulsory to make a claim against total income before claiming terminal loss relief.

However, where losses included in the above terminal loss calculation have already been relieved under another claim (i.e. against total income or chargeable gains), the amount of the terminal loss must be reduced.

Test your understanding 3

Jim Luck ceased trading on 30 June 2016. His results were:

		£
Year ended 31 December	2013	30,000
	2014	24,000
	2015	20,000
Period to 30 June	2016 loss	(19,000)

Jim had overlap profits on commencement of the business of £11,500.

Calculate the terminal loss and show how it is relieved.

Rules for relief on incorporation

When an unincorporated business ceases, the individual will seek to obtain relief from any losses as soon as possible.

They will therefore consider relief against total income and against chargeable gains first, then claim terminal loss relief next. Normally, if there are any unrelieved losses remaining after these claims, the loss is lost.

However, where the business is ceasing due to incorporation, these unrelieved losses can be relieved against future income derived from the company.

The key rules relating to incorporation relief are as follows:

Incorporation relief against future income from the company

- Incorporation relief is available where an unincorporated business
  - is **transferred to a company**
  - **'wholly or mainly'** in exchange **for shares**
- 'Wholly or mainly' is usually taken to mean that **at least 80%** of the consideration received for the business from the company is in the form of shares
- The relief is to **carry the losses forward**
  - indefinitely
  - provided the owner retains the shares throughout the whole tax year in which the loss relief is given, and
  - provided the company continues to carry on the trade of the former unincorporated business
- Losses are **set against**
  - the **first available income** the individual derives **from the company** (e.g. salary, interest, dividends)
  - can set off against types of income from the company in any order
  - most beneficial order will be from employment income first, then savings income, then dividends
- Note that the losses cannot be set against the future profits of the company

Test your understanding 4

On 1 January 2016 Mr Percival transferred his business that he started on 1 May 1999 to a newly formed limited company, Atkinson Ltd, in exchange for shares. He had incurred trading losses in the opening years and £83,000 remained unrelieved at 1 January 2016.

Mr Percival owns all the share capital of Atkinson Ltd and plans to draw a salary of £20,000 p.a. from the company and pay himself a dividend of £10,000 in June each year.

His other income comprises dividends of £3,000 p.a. from other UK companies.

Calculate Mr Percival's net income after reliefs for all relevant years, showing how he will obtain incorporation relief against future income from the company for the losses from his business.

5 Capital gains tax

Whether a sole trader sells his business, gifts his business, incorporates as a going concern or sells off the assets to close the business down, this will represent a disposal for capital gains tax purposes.

Separate gains or losses will be calculated for each chargeable asset of the business, using market value as the proceeds where assets are either given or exchanged for shares in a company.

Typical examples of chargeable assets are:

- Goodwill (provided the business is transferred as a going concern)
- Land and buildings
- Investments

But not:

- Motor cars
- Plant and machinery falling under the £6,000 chattels exemption
- Plant and machinery sold at a loss (no capital loss if claimed capital allowances)

For basic calculation of chargeable gains/allowable capital losses see Chapters 6 and 7.

Reliefs available

There are a number of reliefs to consider, depending on the scenario:

- Rollover relief
- Gift relief
- Incorporation relief
- Entrepreneurs' relief
- EIS/SEIS reinvestment relief
- Investors' relief

All of these reliefs were covered in detail in Chapter 9.

Gains may also be reduced by:

- capital losses
- the annual exempt amount.

6 VAT

The key issues that may be relevant to a business which is ceasing are:

- deregistration
- transfer of a business as a going concern.

These areas are all covered in detail in Chapter 20.

7 Inheritance tax

If the sale of the business is at an arm's length price, then as there is no diminution in value of the owner's estate there are no IHT implications.

If there is a loss in value to the estate (i.e. the gift of the business or sale at undervalue), then there will be potential IHT implications:

- Gift to an individual – potentially exempt transfer (PET)
- Gift to a trust – chargeable lifetime transfer (CLT)
- Gift to spouse – exempt.

Reliefs

The key IHT relief to consider is business property relief (BPR). See Chapters 11 – 13 for a reminder of the IHT rules.

8 Incorporation

A sole trader or partnership may decide that they would be in a better position if they traded through a company, and therefore incorporate the business.

They may choose to:

- set up a new company for the purpose, or
- transfer the business to an existing company.

Whichever route is chosen, on incorporation, the individual trader (or partners) will own shares in the company which continues the trade of the unincorporated business.

Once the company has been targeted or set up, the assets and trade of the business will be transferred from the personal ownership of the individual to the company.

In most cases the proprietors receive shares in the company equal to the value of the assets transferred.

Note that if it is a new company that is set up with only a few shareholders (e.g. five or fewer shareholders), it is likely to be a close company (see Chapter 26).

Tax implications of transferring a business to a limited company

Transferring the assets to a limited company has the following tax consequences:

Income tax

- The business will cease at the date of the incorporation.
- The closing year rules will apply, and any overlap profit will be deducted.
- For capital allowances, incorporation is treated as an open market value disposal. However, as the trader and the company are connected, they may claim that the assets are transferred to the company at their opening tax written-down value (i.e. make the succession election).

  Which method is chosen will depend on whether a market value disposal would produce balancing charges or allowances.

  In either situation the company will then claim capital allowances, although no AIA or FYAs (if applicable) would be available.
- If the business had unrelieved losses at the time of the incorporation they can be relieved against future income derived from the company.

National insurance contributions

- As a sole trader the individual will have paid class 2 & 4 NICs.
- As a director/employee of the company the individual will have to pay employee class 1 NICs.
- The company also pays employer's class 1 NICs and class 1A NICs if benefits are provided.

  The company would not have the employment allowance if the individual is the sole director of the company.

Capital gains tax

- The assets of the business are treated as being sold to the company for their market value.
- There are two main ways in which relief can be given in respect of gains on incorporation depending on how the transaction is arranged:
  - transfer of trade and assets in return for shares (subject to conditions, see Chapter 9) = incorporation relief
  - assets gifted to the company (incorporation relief conditions are not satisfied or disapplied) = gift relief
- If full relief is not available using the incorporation relief or gift relief provisions, any remaining chargeable gain should qualify for entrepreneurs' relief (ER) and will therefore be charged to CGT at 10%.

- An alternative, increasingly popular method of incorporation in recent years has been to sell the business to the company for full market value in return for cash or a loan account in the company and to claim ER such that CGT would only be paid at 10% on the gains arising.

  In addition to the CGT benefit, advantageous corporation tax relief was then available to the company for the purchase cost of the goodwill acquired in the transaction (see Chapter 23).

  Generous double relief was therefore obtained on the value of goodwill which was usually a significant value and difficult to quantify and substantiate.

  However, anti avoidance legislation has stopped this double benefit by denying ER and disallowing corporation tax relief on goodwill where these circumstances apply.

  Accordingly, note that ER is not available on any gain arising in relation to goodwill where:

  - the company acquiring the goodwill is a close company (i.e. has five or fewer shareholders – see Chapter 26), and
  - the individual is or becomes a shareholder (or an associate of a shareholder) in the company acquiring the goodwill
  - unless the individual is a retiring partner.

  The taxable gain arising on such sales of goodwill to 'related companies' will be charged to CGT at 10% or 20%, and therefore this method of incorporation is likely to be less popular in future.

VAT

- Providing the company is registered for VAT the transfer of assets will be a transfer of a going concern, and so not a taxable supply.
- For ease of administration the company may take over the trader's VAT registration.

Stamp duty land tax

- Where there is a property involved, SDLT will be payable by the company, assuming the property is worth in excess of the SDLT threshold.
- This charge can be avoided by not transferring the property to the company, however CGT incorporation relief would not then be available (as it requires all assets to be transferred).
- In this case, the relevant assets could be gifted to the company, and a claim made to defer the gain under the gift relief provisions.

Corporation tax

- It is probable that the company will be a close company, and the implications of this are discussed in Chapter 26.

Inheritance tax

- There should be no IHT implications, as there is no gratuitous intent involved in an incorporation.
- Furthermore, the individual still owns the assets they did before but through a company, so there should be no fall in value in their estate.
- Consideration should be given as to the availability of BPR in the future. An unincorporated trading business is usually eligible for 100% BPR. However, going forward the individual will now own shares which may, or may not, be eligible for BPR.

Summary

Tax	Considerations
Income tax	Cessation of business Capital allowances and disposal value Trading losses
NIC	Change from classes 2 & 4 to class 1
CGT	Disposal at open market value Methods of deferring gain until later disposal Possible loss of ER on goodwill
VAT	Transfer of going concern
SDLT	Company liable if property transferred
CT	Company will probably be a close company
IHT	No IHT charge But watch out for BPR availability in future

Test your understanding 5

Isaac has owned a trading business for 4 years, and is considering transferring the business to a new limited company in exchange for shares.

Isaac will be the sole shareholder, director and employee of the company.

The gains before reliefs would be as follows:

Goodwill	£50,000
Freehold building	£80,000

It is anticipated that the property will increase in value by 50% in the next 2 years at which time it is likely to be sold and larger premises will then be rented.

Consider the alternative courses of action available to achieve the incorporation of the business and explain any immediate and future taxation impact including any advantages and disadvantages.

9 Comprehensive example

Test your understanding 6

Mavis has been trading for a number of years, but at the age of 55 decides that the time has come to retire, and sells the business.

She ceases trading on 31 March 2017, and has the following adjusted profits for her final accounting periods:

Year ended 30 June 2016 (after deducting capital allowances)	£45,250
9 months ended 31 March 2017 (before deducting capital allowances)	£35,187

The TWDVs at 1 July 2016 for capital allowances are:

	£
Main pool	15,637
Car (private use 40%)	12,700

No assets were purchased during the final accounting period, and on 31 March 2017 all assets in the pool were sold for £13,255, none for more than the original cost. Mavis decided to keep the car, which was worth £13,000.

Mavis's overlap profits from commencement were £10,800.

The following information is also available regarding the sale of the business on 31 March 2017:

Value of office	£170,000
Cost of office (January 1994)	£35,000
Value of goodwill	£200,000

After cessation, Mavis will receive a pension of £10,600 p.a.

(a)

(i) **Calculate Mavis's taxable profits for 2016/17.**

(ii) **Advise Mavis of the income tax implications of ceasing on 6 April 2017 (assume no profits are made between 31 March 2017 and 6 April 2017).**

(b)

(i) **Calculate the capital gains tax payable on the sale of the business**

(ii) **Explain the capital tax implications if Mavis were to give the business to her son instead.**

(c) Mavis has just received an offer from Jumbo plc to purchase her business for £400,000 broken down as follows:

	£
Office	170,000
Plant and machinery	13,255
Car	13,000
Net current assets	3,745
Goodwill	200,000
Market value of the business	400,000

Mavis would receive £150,000 in cash and £250,000 worth of shares in Jumbo plc.

Assume plant and machinery is sold at less than cost.

Calculate the CGT payable, assuming that all available reliefs are applied, and advise Mavis why it may be beneficial to elect to disapply incorporation relief.

Assume the 2016/17 rates and allowances apply throughout.

Chapter summary

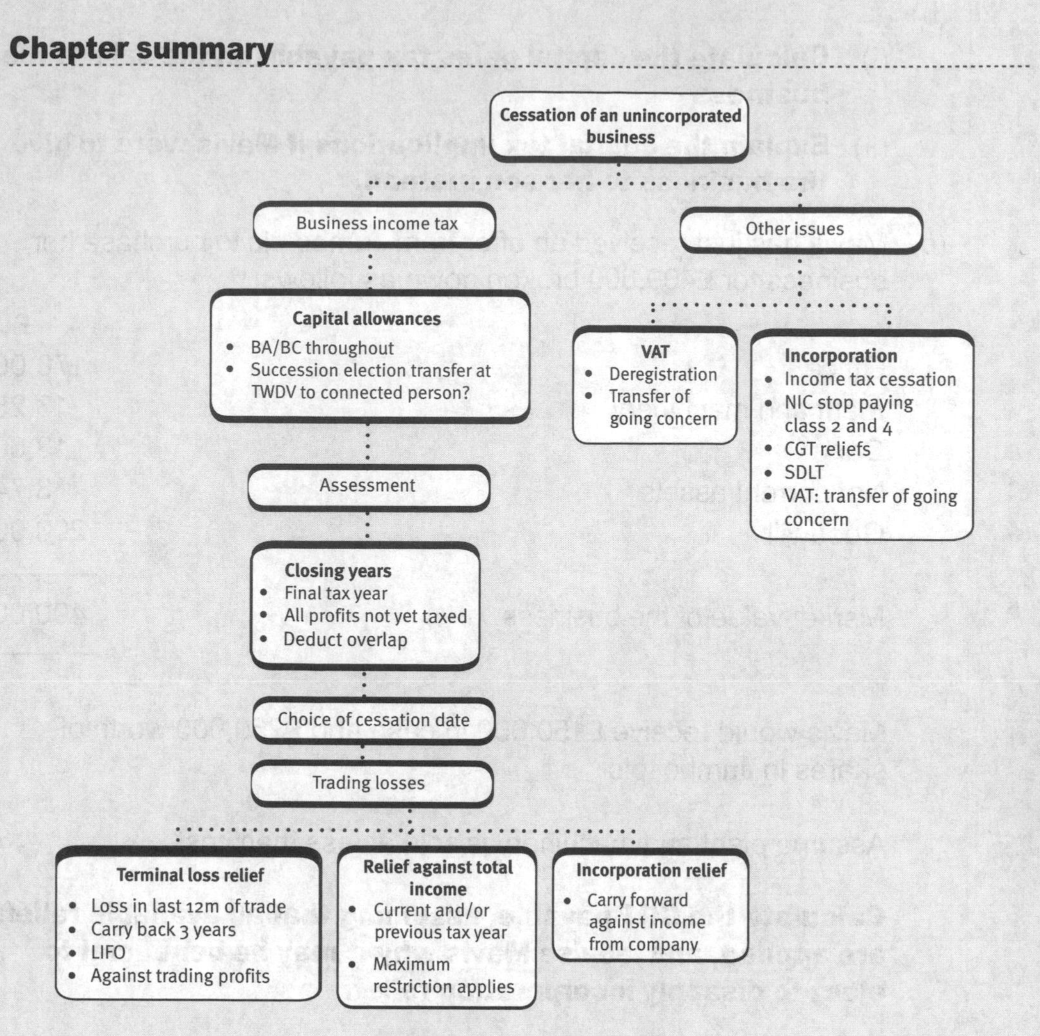

Test your understanding answers

Test your understanding 1

Capital allowances on incorporation

When Julia incorporates her business she has two options regarding capital allowances:

(1) **Option 1 – normal cessation of a business rules**

Balancing adjustments will arise in the final sole trader capital allowance computations. The adjustments are calculated by reference to the MV of the pool assets on incorporation (restricted to cost if lower), compared to the TWDV at that date.

The company can then claim an 18% WDA, on the reducing balance basis, based on the MV of the assets acquired. Note however that the AIA is not available on these assets, as they are acquired from a connected party.

If the business is incorporated on 31 March 2017, the taxable balancing charges will arise as follows:

	Main pool	Allowances/ (charges)
	£	£
TWDV b/f	24,000	
Disposal at MV	(37,000)	
Balancing charge	(13,000)	(13,000)

The allowances available to the company in the y/e 31 March 2018 will be:

	Main pool	Allowances/ (charges)
	£	£
Acquisition at MV	37,000	
Less: WDA (18%)	(6,660)	6,660
TWDV c/f	30,340	
Total allowances		6,660

(2) **Option 2 – succession election**

An election (known as the succession election) can be made for the assets in the main pool to be transferred to the company, Jules Ltd, at TWDV rather than the MV at the date of incorporation.

This is because the trade has passed between connected persons.

As a result, no balancing adjustments arise on the unincorporated business.

The company can then claim an 18% WDA, on the reducing balance basis, based on the TWDV of the assets acquired.

The allowances available to the company in the year ended 31 March 2017 will be:

	Main pool	Allowances/ (charges)
	£	£
Transfer at TWDV	24,000	
Less: WDA (18%)	(4,320)	4,320
TWDV c/f	19,680	
Total allowances		4,320

Note: Where a succession election is made, the assets are deemed to be transferred to the company at their TWDV at the end of the penultimate period of account.

There are no capital allowances available to Julia in the final period of account.

Recommendation

The succession election will be beneficial to Julia as:

- Without the election, the balancing charges of £13,000 would have the effect of increasing Julia's taxable trading profits. This would be avoided if the succession election is taken.
- Given her current level of profits, avoiding the increase in profits caused by the balancing charge would save income tax at 40% and class 4 NICs at 2%.
- The total saving by Julia would be £5,460 (£13,000 × 42%).

- However, the company would be able to claim £2,340 (£6,660 – £4,320) less capital allowances in the year ended 31 March 2018.
- Given the level projected profits of the business, this would result in an increase in corporation tax payable of £468 (£2,340 × 20%).
- The net tax saving is the succession election is made would be £4,992 (£5,460 – £468).

For this reason it would appear that a succession election would be beneficial to Julia.

The succession election will need to be made by 31 March 2019 (i.e. within two years of the date of incorporation).

Test your understanding 2

Michael

Tax year	Basis period	Trading income assessment
		£
2015/16	Year ended 30 April 2015	40,000
2016/17	23 months from 1 May 2015 to 31 March 2017	
	Year ended 30 April 2016	42,000
	Period ended 31 March 2017	38,000
		80,000
	Less: Overlap profits	(27,000)
		53,000

Test your understanding 3

Jim Luck

(a) **Terminal loss**

Loss of last 12 months (01.07.15 – 30.06.16)

	£	£
6 April 2016 – 30 June 2016		
(3 month period)		
Actual trading loss in this period		
(£19,000) × 3/6		(9,500)
Overlap profits		(11,500)
1 July 2015 to 5 April 2016		
Actual trading loss in this period		
(£19,000) × 3/6	(9,500) loss	
£20,000 × 6/12	10,000 profit	
Overall profit – ignore	500	0
Terminal loss		(21,000)

(b) **Terminal loss relief (TLR)**

	2013/14	2014/15	2015/16	2016/17
	£	£	£	£
Trading income	30,000	24,000	20,000	0
Less: TLR	–	(1,000)	(20,000)	(0)
Final assessments	30,000	23,000	0	0

Test your understanding 4

Mr Percival

	2015/16	2016/17	2017/18	2018/19
	£	£	£	£
Employment income	5,000	20,000	20,000	20,000
Less: Loss relief	(5,000)	(20,000)	(20,000)	(18,000)
Atkinson dividend	–	10,000	10,000	10,000
Less: Loss relief		(10,000)	(10,000)	
Other dividends	3,000	3,000	3,000	3,000
Net income	3,000	3,000	3,000	15,000

Loss working	£
Unrelieved losses b/f	83,000
Less: Incorporation relief	
2015/16	(5,000)
2016/17	(30,000)
2017/18	(30,000)
2018/19 (balance of loss)	(18,000)
	0

Test your understanding 5

Isaac

- As Isaac is transferring the whole business the gains will be automatically deferred against any share consideration he receives under incorporation relief.
- On a future disposal of the shares the CGT base cost (the market value of the shares at incorporation) will be reduced by the gains now deferred.
- Entrepreneurs' relief (ER) will be available on a future disposal of the shares, if Isaac owns ≥ 5%, is an employee of the limited company, and owns the shares for at least 12 months.
- There is a risk that if Isaac sells the shares within 12 months, he will lose the entitlement to ER.

- Isaac could consider disapplying incorporation relief with the effect that the gain of:
  - £80,000 relating to the freehold property will qualify for ER and will be taxed at 10%
  - £50,000 relating to goodwill (after deducting the AEA of £11,100) will not qualify for ER as the goodwill is transferred to a close company in which Isaac is a shareholder (a 'related company'). This gain will instead be taxed at 20%, as the gain on the freehold property will use up any of Isaac's basic rate band remaining.

  The total CGT payable immediately would be £15,780 (W).

  To disapply incorporation relief, an election must be made.

- Isaac could consider incorporating the business and receive consideration in the form of a mix of shares and loan account/cash. As a result, part of the gain is automatically chargeable on incorporation. With planning, the amount of cash consideration to take can be calculated to ensure the maximum use of any capital losses and the AEA.
- A more long term disadvantage of using incorporation relief is the fact that the property is transferred to the company. If the property continues to appreciate in value significantly, then on a sale by the company there will be an element of double taxation:
  - a corporation tax charge on the company, and
  - in extracting the profits a further income tax charge on the individual.
- If Isaac were to keep the property in personal ownership and not rent it to the company then he would be eligible for ER on a disposal of the property as long it was disposed of at the same time as the personal company shares.

  However incorporation relief would not then be available to defer the gain on the goodwill and ER would not be available on that gain as the transfer is to a 'related company'.

- An alternative would be to gift the goodwill (and other non-capital assets as relevant) to the company and claim gift relief to defer that gain so enabling the retention of the property outside the company.
- Alternatively the goodwill could remain within the charge to CGT but at 10% or 20% (as ER would not be available).

  Note that the company would not be able to claim relief for the cost of the goodwill for corporation tax purposes (see intangible assets in Chapter 23).

Working: Chargeable gain

	Not qualifying for ER		Qualifying for ER
	£		£
Gains on incorporation			
Freehold building			80,000
Goodwill	50,000		
Less: AEA	(11,100)		(0)
Taxable gains	38,900		80,000
		£	
CGT			
On qualifying gains (£80,000 × 10%)		8,000	
On non-qualifying gains (£38,900 × 20%)		7,780	
		15,780	

Test your understanding 6

Mavis

(a) (i) **Taxable profits – 2016/17**

Capital allowances computation – 9 m/e 31 March 2017

	Main pool	Private use car (B.U. 60%)		Allowances
	£	£		£
TWDV b/f	15,637	12,700		
Disposal	(13,255)	(13,000)		
	2,382	(300)		
Balancing allowance	(2,382)			2,382
Balancing charge		(300)	60%	(180)
TWDV c/f	0	0		
Total allowances				2,202

The capital allowances are then deducted from the profit for the 9 months ending 31 March 2017.

	£
Adjusted profit before capital allowances	35,187
Less: Capital allowances (W)	(2,202)
Adjusted profit for accounting period	32,985

Then the adjusted profits can be matched to tax years using the closing year rules.

Assessments

2016/17 (tax year of cessation)	£
Year ended 30 June 2016	45,250
Period ended 31 March 2017 (above)	32,985
Less: Overlap profits	(10,800)
Total taxable trading profit	67,435

(ii) **Cessation on 6 April 2017**

If Mavis ceased trading on 6 April 2017, her tax year of cessation would be 2017/18 giving the following assessments:

Assessments

	£
2016/17 (penultimate tax year)	
Year ended 30 June 2016	45,250
2017/18 (tax year of cessation)	
Period ended 6 April 2017 (above)	32,985
Less: Overlap profits	(10,800)
Total taxable trading profit	22,185

This would be beneficial for the following reasons:

- The £22,185 which is now taxable in 2017/18 will now fall into the basic rate band and will be taxed at 20% instead of 40%. This is assuming that Mavis has no other income apart from her pension (which is covered by her PA). This would save (£22,185 × 20%) = £4,437.
- There would, however, be an increase in class 4 NICs. Class 4 NIC would have been (£22,185 × 2%) = £444. Class 4 NIC is now (£22,185 – £8,060) × 9% = £1,271, giving an increase of (£1,271 – £444) = £827.
- The overall tax saving is as follows:

	£
Income tax saving	4,437
Less: Net increase in class 4 NIC	(827)
Tax saving	3,610

- There will also be an extra year to pay the tax due on the profit assessable in 2017/18, as the balancing payment will not be due until 31 January 2019.

(b) (i) **Capital gains tax payable on sale of the business**

Gains will arise only on the office and the goodwill as follows:

	£	£
Office		
Proceeds	170,000	
Less: Cost	(35,000)	
		135,000
Goodwill		
Proceeds	200,000	
Less: Cost	(0)	
		200,000
Chargeable gains – qualifying for ER		335,000
Less: AEA		(11,100)
Taxable gains		323,900
CGT payable (10% × £323,900)		32,390

Note: ER is available on the gain relating to goodwill as the business is not being transferred to a related company.

(ii) **Capital tax implications of gift of business**

Note that if the question asks you to talk about the 'capital taxes' this means not just CGT, but also IHT and stamp taxes.

Capital gains tax

- The assets would be deemed to be sold at market value
- Gains would arise as above
- However, Mavis and her son could jointly claim gift relief to defer the gains before ER
- The gains would then be deducted from the cost of the assets for Mavis's son, giving him bigger gains on the eventual sale

Inheritance tax

- The gift of the business would be a PET
- There would be no IHT payable during lifetime
- The gift would only become chargeable if Mavis were to die within 7 years
- As Mavis would be giving a whole business which she has owned for more than 2 years, 100% BPR would be available, leaving no IHT to pay
- However, if Mavis's son sold the business before Mavis's death, the BPR would be withdrawn

Stamp duty land tax

There would be no SDLT payable on the gift of the office as there would be no consideration.

(c) **CGT on transfer of business to Jumbo plc**

Again, the assets would be deemed to be sold for their market values and gains would arise on the chargeable assets as before.

As the business would be transferred to a company as a going concern, in exchange partly for shares, incorporation relief would automatically apply.

A proportion of the gain before ER would be deferred until the shares were sold.

	£
Total gains before reliefs (as above)	335,000
Less: Incorporation relief:	
Gains × $\frac{\text{Value of share consideration}}{\text{Total consideration}}$	
£335,000 × (£250,000/£400,000)	(209,375)
Chargeable gains – qualifying for ER	125,625
Less: AEA	(11,100)
Taxable gains	114,525
CGT payable (10% × £114,525)	11,452

It may be beneficial for Mavis to elect to disapply the incorporation relief in order to take advantage of ER on the office gain of £135,000 and on the goodwill gain of £188,900 (£200,000 – £11,100 AEA).

The reason for this is that as Mavis is receiving shares in a plc. Accordingly, it is unlikely to be a close company and therefore ER will be available on the goodwill gain now. It is also unlikely that she will own the 5% required to qualify for ER on the eventual sale of the shares, giving a higher tax charge on disposal.

chapter

19

Partnerships: income tax and capital gains tax

Chapter learning objectives

Upon completion of this chapter you will be able to:

- explain how a partnership is assessed to tax
- show the allocation of trading profits/losses between partners for the accounting period in a variety of business scenarios
- calculate the assessable profit for ongoing/new and ceasing partners
- describe the alternative loss relief claims that are available to partners
- explain the loss relief restriction that applies to the partners of a limited liability partnership
- identify the occasions when a capital gain will arise on a partner on the disposal of a partnership asset to a third party.

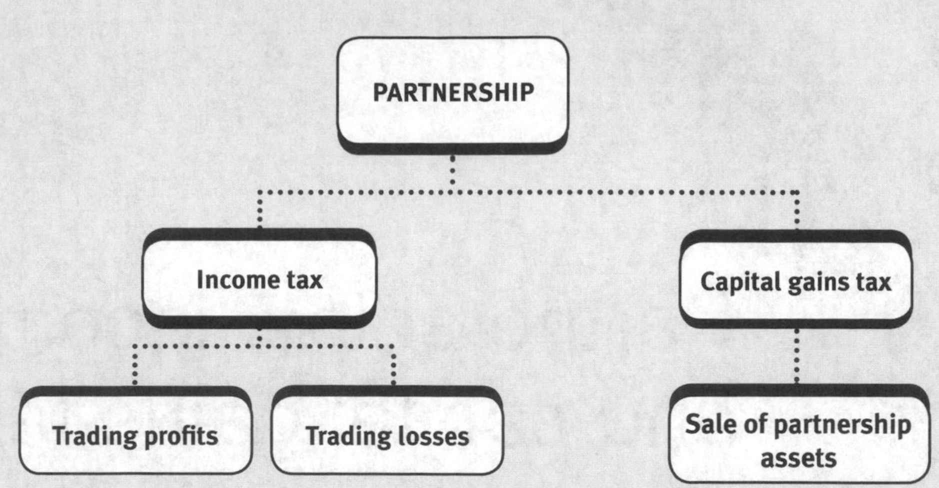

Introduction

This chapter starts with a revision of the treatment of partnerships. Much of the technical content in this section has been covered at F6.

A brief reminder of F6 content is given in expandable text and revision examples are provided to check your retention of F6 knowledge.

The new P6 topic introduced is the taxation of capital gains on the disposal of partnership assets to a third party.

1 Trading income assessments for partners

A partnership is a body of persons carrying on business together with a view to profit. Despite the fact that a partnership is a single trading entity, the partnership itself is not liable to tax.

For tax purposes, each partner is:

- treated as trading in their own right, as if they were a sole trader running their own business, and
- taxed individually on their share of the partnership profits and capital gains, and
- responsible for paying their own income tax, NICs and capital gains tax arising from their share of the partnership.

The partnership is therefore merely a collection of sole traders operating together.

Adjusted profits and allocation between partners

A reminder of the calculation of adjusted profits for a partnership and the allocation between partners covered at F6 is given in expandable text and is summarised in the diagram in section 4.

Partnership adjusted profits

The tax adjusted trading profits of a partnership are calculated in exactly the same way as for a sole trader:

- The accounting net profit is adjusted for disallowable expenditure, non-trading income, etc in the normal way.
- Capital allowances are calculated in the normal way and deducted from the tax adjusted profits.

Note that:

- Partners' salaries and interest on capital are often charged through the statement of profit or loss. These are not allowable deductions and need to be added back, as they are an appropriation of profit and not an expense of the business.
- Capital allowances can be claimed on assets owned personally by the partners if they are used in the partnership. However, the individual partners cannot claim the capital allowances on their own behalf. The capital allowances are an allowable expense against the partnership profits as a whole.

The allocation between partners

Profits are allocated:

- according to the **profit sharing arrangements** in force
- during the **accounting period** in which the profits are earned.

Once the partners have been allocated their share, each partner is assessed on their share of the trading profits according to the basis of assessment rules in the normal way, as if they were a sole trader.

Profit sharing arrangements (PSA) usually provide for a combination of three types of allocation:

- Salaries (a fixed allocation of profit).

- Interest on capital introduced into the business (a fixed percentage return on capital).
- Profit sharing ratio (PSR) (an agreed ratio to share the balance of profits).

The terms 'salaries' and 'interest' are just an allocation of profit, they are not assessed to income tax as employment income and savings income.

Whatever terms are used to describe the allocation method, the total amount allocated to each partner is assessed to income tax as trading income.

Test your understanding 1

Alan and Brian formed a partnership in June 2011. They agreed to share profits equally after charging interest of 10% p.a. on their fixed capital accounts of £8,000 and £5,000 respectively, and paying a salary to Alan of £5,000.

The tax adjusted trading profits for the y/e 31 December 2016 were £15,000.

Show the allocation of profits for the y/e 31 December 2016.

Change to profit sharing agreement

The profit sharing agreement between partners may change for a number of reasons:

- The existing partners may decide to allocate profits in a different way. This may be as a result of a change in duties, seniority or simply by agreement of the parties concerned.
- The membership of a partnership may change as the result of the admission, death or retirement of a partner.

Where there is a change in the PSA during the accounting period:

- The accounting period must be time apportioned into two or more parts (depending on the number of changes).
- Each part is then allocated separately between the partners according to the partnership agreement in place at that time.

Test your understanding 2

Xavier and Yvonne started in partnership on 1 January 2015 sharing profits equally, after allowing for a salary for Yvonne of £10,000 p.a. The partnership accounts are prepared to 31 December each year.

On 1 July 2016 Zack is admitted as a new partner, the profits continuing to be shared equally but with no salary allowance for Yvonne.

On 30 September 2017, Xavier retired from the partnership. Yvonne and Zack agreed to shares profits in the ratio of 3:2.

The tax adjusted trading profits for the first three accounting periods are:

Year ended 31 December 2015	£50,000
Year ended 31 December 2016	£90,000
Year ended 31 December 2017	£150,000

Show the allocation of profits between the partners for the three accounting periods.

The calculation of assessable trading income for each partner

Each partner is taxed on their share of the partnership profits as if they were a sole trader who runs a business that:

- starts when they join the partnership
- ceases when they leave the partnership, and
- has the same accounting periods as the partnership.

A brief reminder of the calculations required is given in expandable text and is summarised in the diagram in section 4.

Assessable trading income

To calculate the trading income assessments arising from the partnership allocations the following rules should be applied:

Event	Treatment
Commencement of the partnership.	• the opening year rules apply to all partners who set up the business • each partner has their own overlap profits arising.
New partner joins an existing partnership (Note 1).	• the existing partners continue to be assessed on a CYB basis • opening year rules apply to the new partner • new partner has their own overlap profits arising.
Partner leaves the partnership (Note 2).	• continuing partners continue to be assessed on a CYB basis • closing year rules apply to the partner leaving • leaving partner deducts their own overlap profits.

Notes:

(1) The same approach and rules apply if a sole trader takes on a partner and the business becomes a partnership.

(2) The same approach and rules apply if one partner leaves a two partner partnership so that the remaining individual now operates the business as a sole trader.

Test your understanding 3

Use the facts in test your understanding 2 for Xavier, Yvonne and Zack.

Calculate the trading income assessments arising for each partner for all of the tax years affected by the results.

Test your understanding 4

Alex, Arsene and Jose have been in partnership for a number of years. Their recent results and projected results into the future are as follows:

Year ended 30 September:	£
2015	103,500
2016	128,000
2017	140,000
2018	180,000
2019	210,000

The relationship is often fractious and there have been a number of disputes over the years. In an attempt to improve the dynamics, on 1 January 2016, Rafa was admitted to the partnership.

However, the disputes continued. Alex accepts that he is the cause of most of the arguments and has therefore agreed that he will leave the partnership at the end of March 2019. Alex has £15,000 of overlap profits from when he joined the partnership.

The profit sharing ratio prior to the admission of Rafa had been equal after allocating the following salaries and interest on capital.

Partner	Salary	Capital balance	Rate of interest on capital
Alex	£15,000	£100,000	5%
Arsene	£12,000	£80,000	5%
Jose	£10,000	£40,000	5%

Rafa's admission changed the profit sharing arrangements as follows:

Partner	Salary	Capital balance	Rate of interest on capital	Profit share
Alex	£20,000	£100,000	5%	35%
Arsene	£18,000	£80,000	5%	30%
Jose	£15,000	£40,000	5%	25%
Rafa	£10,000	Nil	n/a	10%

When Alex leaves the partnership, the salary and interest arrangements will remain in place, but the rest of the profit will then be split equally between the three remaining partners.

Calculate the assessable trading income for each of the partners for the tax years from 2015/16 to 2019/20.

2 Partnership trading losses

The calculation and allocation of partnership trading losses

Each partner is:

- allocated his share of the tax adjusted trading losses (including capital allowances)
- according to the **partnership agreement** in the **accounting period**
- in exactly the same way as profits.

Loss relief options available

Each partner is treated as a sole trader and can therefore utilise his share of the partnership loss:

- under the normal trading loss rules
- in the most tax efficient manner
- according to their own personal circumstances.

The options available can be summarised as follows:

Partner joining	Ongoing partners	Partner leaving
Relief against total income	Relief against total income	Relief against total income
Relief against gains	Relief against gains	Relief against gains
Carry forward	Carry forward	
In addition:		**In addition:**
Opening year relief		Terminal loss relief
		Incorporation relief

See Chapters 17 and 18 for a reminder of the loss relief rules.

Example 1 – Partnership losses

Peter, Paul and Mary are in partnership preparing accounts to 5 April.

During 2016/17 Paul left the partnership and Maggie joined in his place.

For the year ended 5 April 2017 the partnership made a tax adjusted trading loss (after taking account of capital allowances) of £20,000.

State the loss relief claims available to each of the partners.

Solution

Paul will be entitled to terminal loss relief since he has actually ceased trading.

Maggie will be entitled to claim opening years relief since she has actually commenced trading.

Peter and Mary will not be entitled to either of the above reliefs.

All the partners will be entitled to relief against total income and, if applicable, an extension of relief against chargeable gains in the current and/or previous tax years, provided a claim against total income is made first.

All the partners except Paul will be entitled to carry forward relief.

Limited liability partnerships (LLP)

An LLP is a special type of partnership where the amount that each partner contributes towards the partnership losses, debts and liabilities is limited by agreement.

The taxation implications of an LLP are as follows:

- generally taxed in the same way as other partnerships, and
- if applicable, the normal loss reliefs are available.

3 Partnership capital gains tax

The basis of assessment to CGT on partnership gains

Each partner:

- is deemed to own a fractional share of the partnership assets, and
- is assessed separately to CGT according to their own personal circumstances, if they dispose of some or all of their fractional share in a partnership asset.

The fractional share is determined by the agreed capital profit sharing ratio in the partnership agreement.

This ratio is usually taken as:

- the PSR used to allocate the balance of profits for income tax purposes as stated in the partnership agreement
- unless the agreement says otherwise.

Each partner will:

- include their share of the partnership gains in their CGT computation, along with gains from the disposals of other assets
- if the entire partnership share is being disposed of, entrepreneurs' relief will be available if the partnership business has been owned for at least 12 months
- deduct the AEA of £11,100 against the total chargeable gains of the individual in the normal way
- calculate the CGT at 10% or 20%.

Capital gains tax reliefs

As partnership assets are business assets, CGT reliefs are also available in the normal way, for example:

- rollover relief
- gift relief.

Note that with rollover relief and gift relief, each partner can decide independently whether or not they wish to make a claim.

If a partner decides to make a rollover relief claim:

- their share of a gain is rolled over (i.e. deferred)
- against their share of the cost of the replacement asset.

Disposal of a partnership asset to a third party

Strictly, each partner should have their own separate capital gains computation for each partnership disposal.

A separate gain computation should be calculated allocating the sale proceeds and cost of the asset between the partners.

However, it is usually acceptable to calculate the gain arising on the asset and then allocate this one figure between the partners.

Test your understanding 5

In January 2007, Paul and Phil commenced in partnership. They introduced capital into the business of £30,000 and £20,000 respectively and agreed to share profits in the ratio 60%:40%.

The partnership purchased freehold premises for £125,000 in January 2007. In September 2016 the partnership sold the premises for £495,000 and continued to trade in rented premises.

Calculate the chargeable gains arising on Paul and Phil in the tax year 2016/17 in respect of the partnership disposal.

4 Chapter summary

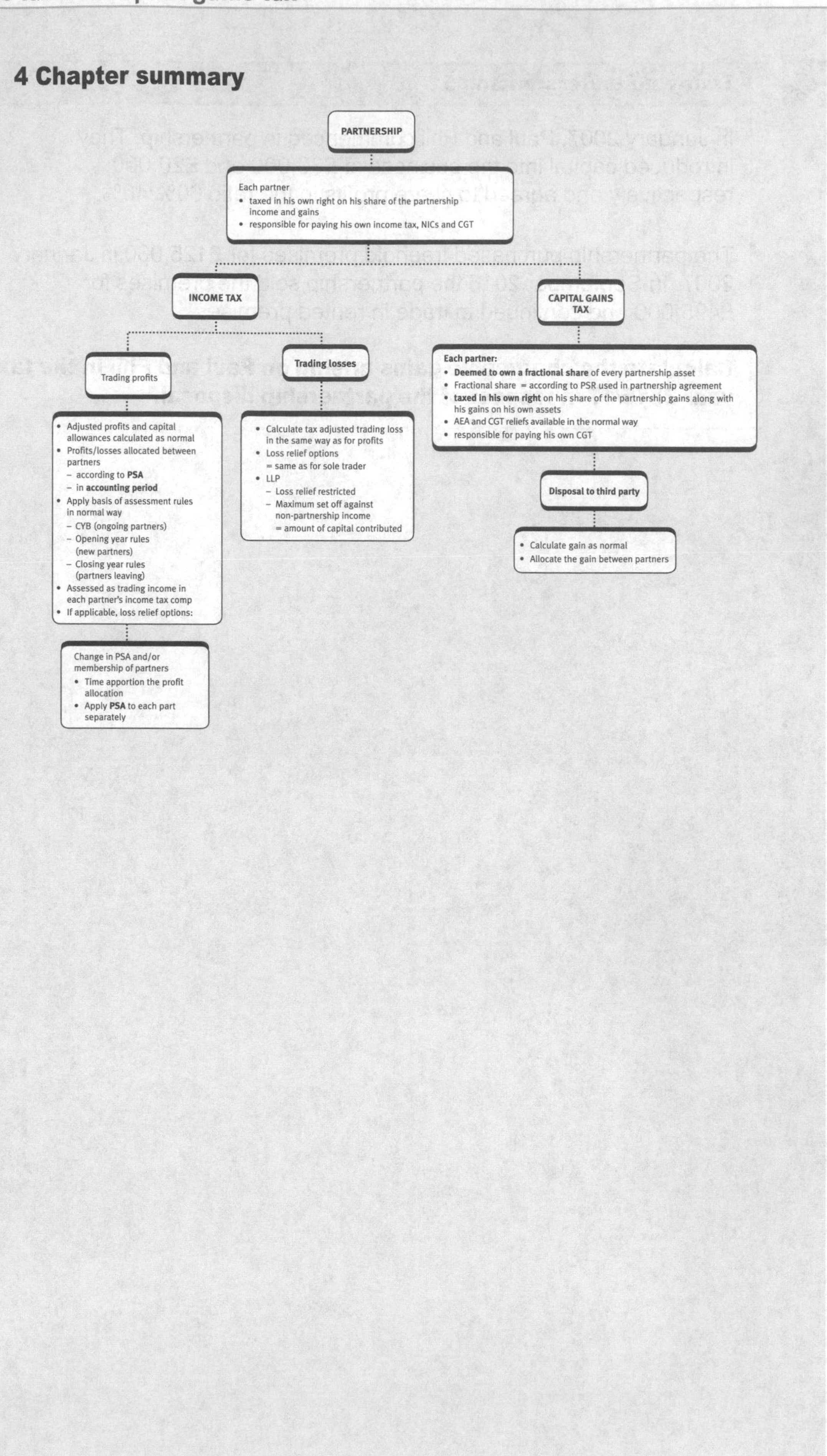

PARTNERSHIP
Each partner
• taxed in his own right on his share of the partnership income and gains
• responsible for paying his own income tax, NICs and CGT
INCOME TAX
CAPITAL GAINS TAX
Trading profits
Trading losses
• Adjusted profits and capital allowances calculated as normal
• Profits/losses allocated between partners
– according to PSA
– in accounting period
• Apply basis of assessment rules in normal way
– CYB (ongoing partners)
– Opening year rules (new partners)
– Closing year rules (partners leaving)
• Assessed as trading income in each partner's income tax comp
• If applicable, loss relief options:
Change in PSA and/or membership of partners
• Time apportion the profit allocation
• Apply PSA to each part separately
• Calculate tax adjusted trading loss in the same way as for profits
• Loss relief options = same as for sole trader
• LLP
– Loss relief restricted
– Maximum set off against non-partnership income = amount of capital contributed
Each partner:
• Deemed to own a fractional share of every partnership asset
• Fractional share = according to PSR used in partnership agreement
• taxed in his own right on his share of the partnership gains along with his gains on his own assets
• AEA and CGT reliefs available in the normal way
• responsible for paying his own CGT
Disposal to third party
• Calculate gain as normal
• Allocate the gain between partners

Test your understanding answers

Test your understanding 1

Alan and Brian

Y/e 31/12/2016	Alan	Brian	Total
	£	£	£
Interest on capital	800	500	1,300
Salary	5,000	0	5,000
Balance shared (1:1)	4,350	4,350	8,700
Allocation of profits	10,150	4,850	15,000

Test your understanding 2

Xavier and Yvonne

Y/e 31/12/15	Xavier	Yvonne	Zack	Total
	£	£	£	£
Salary	0	10,000	0	10,000
Balance shared (1:1)	20,000	20,000	0	40,000
Allocation of profits	20,000	30,000	0	50,000
Y/e 31/12/16				
01/01/16 – 30/06/16				
Salary	0	5,000	0	5,000
Balance shared (1:1)	20,000	20,000	0	40,000
				45,000
01/07/16 – 31/12/16				
Balance shared (1:1:1)	15,000	15,000	15,000	45,000
Total	35,000	40,000	15,000	90,000

Y/e 31/12/17	Xavier	Yvonne	Zack	Total
	£	£	£	£
01/01/17 – 30/09/17				
Balance shared (1:1:1)	37,500	37,500	37,500	112,500
01/10/17 – 31/12/17				
Balance shared (3:2)	0	22,500	15,000	37,500
Total	37,500	60,000	52,500	150,000

Test your understanding 3

Xavier

Xavier started to trade in partnership in 2014/15 and left the partnership in 2017/18. He will be assessed to the opening and closing year rules:

Tax year	Basis period		Trading income
		£	£
2014/15	1 January 2015 to 5 April 2015		
	(3/12 × £20,000)		5,000
2015/16	y/e 31 December 2015 (first 12 months)		20,000
2016/17	y/e 31 December 2016		35,000
2017/18	Profits not yet assessed	37,500	
	Less: Overlap profits (W)	(5,000)	
			32,500

Overlap profits:

1 January 2015 to 5 April 2015 (3/12 × £20,000) £5,000

Yvonne

Yvonne started to trade in partnership in 2014/15 and is still a partner. Her assessments will be as follows:

Tax year	Basis period	Trading income
		£
2014/15	1 January 2015 to 5 April 2015 (actual)	
	(3/12 × £30,000)	7,500
2015/16	y/e 31 December 2015 (first 12 months)	30,000
2016/17	y/e 31 December 2016	40,000
2017/18	y/e 31 December 2017	60,000

Overlap profits:

1 January 2015 to 5 April 2015 (3/12 × £30,000) £7,500

Zack

Zack joined the partnership in 2016/17 and is still a partner. The opening year rules apply to his shares of the profits assuming his first set of accounts run from 1 July 2016 to 31 December 2016.

Tax year	Basis period	Trading income £
2016/17	1 July 2016 to 5 April 2017 £15,000 + (3/12 × £52,500)	28,125
2017/18	y/e 31 December 2017 (12 months ending in 2nd year)	52,500
Overlap profits		
1 January 2017 to 5 April 2017 (3/12 × £52,500)		13,125

Test your understanding 4

Alex, Arsene and Jose

Allocate of profits between the partners:

	Total £	Alex £	Arsene £	Jose £	Rafa £
Y/e 30.09.15					
Salary	37,000	15,000	12,000	10,000	
Interest at 5%	11,000	5,000	4,000	2,000	
PSR (1:1:1)	55,500	18,500	18,500	18,500	
Total	**103,500**	**38,500**	**34,500**	**30,500**	

	Total	Alex	Arsene	Jose	Rafa
	£	£	£	£	£
Y/e 30.09.16					
01.10.15 – 31.12.15					
Salary (3/12)	9,250	3,750	3,000	2,500	
Interest at 5% (× 3/12)	2,750	1,250	1,000	500	
PSR (1:1:1)	20,000	6,667	6,667	6,666	
£128,000 × 3/12 = £32,000	32,000				
01.01.16 – 30.09.16					
Salary (9/12)	47,250	15,000	13,500	11,250	7,500
Interest at 5% (× 9/12)	8,250	3,750	3,000	1,500	0
PSR (35%:30%:25%:10%)	40,500	14,175	12,150	10,125	4,050
£128,000 × 9/12 = £96,000	96,000				
Total	**128,000**	**44,592**	**39,317**	**32,541**	**11,550**
Y/e 30.09.17					
Salary	63,000	20,000	18,000	15,000	10,000
Interest at 5%	11,000	5,000	4,000	2,000	0
PSR (35%:30%:25%:10%)	66,000	23,100	19,800	16,500	6,600
Total	**140,000**	**48,100**	**41,800**	**33,500**	**16,600**
Y/e 30.09.18					
Salary	63,000	20,000	18,000	15,000	10,000
Interest at 5%	11,000	5,000	4,000	2,000	0
PSR (35%:30%:25%:10%)	106,000	37,100	31,800	26,500	10,600
Total	**180,000**	**62,100**	**53,800**	**43,500**	**20,600**

	Total	Alex	Arsene	Jose	Rafa
	£	£	£	£	£
Y/e 30.09.19					
01.10.18 – 31.03.19					
Salary (6/12)	31,500	10,000	9,000	7,500	5,000
Interest at 5% (× 6/12)	5,500	2,500	2,000	1,000	0
PSR (35%:30%:25%:10%)	68,000	23,800	20,400	17,000	6,800
£210,000 × 6/12 = £105,000	105,000				
01.04.19 – 30.09.19					
Salary (6/12)	21,500		9,000	7,500	5,000
Interest at 5% (× 6/12)	3,000		2,000	1,000	0
PSR (1:1:1)	80,500		26,834	26,833	26,833
£210,000 × 6/12 = £105,000	105,000				
Total	**210,000**	**36,300**	**69,234**	**60,833**	**43,633**

Trading income assessments

Arsene and Jose will be assessed on a current year basis for each tax year. Their trading income assessments will be as follows:

Tax year	Basis period	Arsene	Jose
		£	£
2015/16	y/e 30 September 2015	34,500	30,500
2016/17	y/e 30 September 2016	39,317	32,541
2017/18	y/e 30 September 2017	41,800	33,500
2018/19	y/e 30 September 2018	53,800	43,500
2019/20	y/e 30 September 2019	69,234	60,833

Rafa will be treated as commencing on 1 January 2016, and will be assessed on his share of the partnership profits as follows:

Tax year	Basis period	Trading income
		£
2015/16	1 January 2016 to 5 April 2016 (£11,550 × 3/9)	3,850
2016/17	First 12 months trading £11,550 + (£16,600 × 3/12)	15,700
2017/18	y/e 30 September 2017	16,600
2018/19	y/e 30 September 2018	20,600
2019/20	y/e 30 September 2019	43,633

Rafa will carry forward overlap profits of £8,000 (£3,850 + £4,150).

Alex will be treated as ceasing to trade on 31 March 2019, he will be assessed on his share of partnership profits as follows:

Tax year	Basis period		Trading income
			£
2015/16	y/e 30 September 2015		38,500
2016/17	y/e 30 September 2016		44,592
2017/18	y/e September 2017		48,100
		£	
2018/19	y/e September 2018	62,100	
	p/e 31 March 2019	36,300	
		98,400	
	Less: Overlap profits	(15,000)	
			83,400

Test your understanding 5

Paul and Phil

	Paul	Phil	Total
	£	£	£
Sale proceeds (60%:40%)	297,000	198,000	495,000
Less: Cost (60%:40%)	(75,000)	(50,000)	(125,000)
Chargeable gain	222,000	148,000	370,000

The partnership asset is not part of the disposal of the entire business, so entrepreneurs' relief is not available.

Note: To save time in the examination, it is acceptable to compute the total gain of £370,000 and allocate it 60%:40% to the partners.

However, it is an important principle to appreciate that each partner technically owns a fractional share and that each partner should do their own capital gains computation.

chapter

20

VAT: outline

Chapter learning objectives

Upon completion of this chapter you will be able to:

- state the scope and nature of VAT
- explain the significance of the different types of supply for VAT
- list the principal zero rated and exempt supplies
- identify the two situations which require compulsory VAT registration
- discuss the advantages and disadvantages of voluntary registration
- identify when pre-registration VAT can be recovered
- explain when a person must compulsorily/may voluntarily deregister for VAT
- explain how VAT is accounted for under the special schemes available
- outline the alternative VAT treatments on the sale of a business
- identify the value of a supply and calculate the relevant VAT
- identify recoverable and non-recoverable input VAT on key purchases and expenses
- compute the relief that is available for impairment losses on trade debts
- advise on the meaning and impact of the disaggregation of business activities for VAT purposes
- advise on the VAT implications of the supply of land and buildings in the UK
- identify when partial exemption applies and calculate the impact
- state the purpose of the capital goods scheme and demonstrate how it operates.

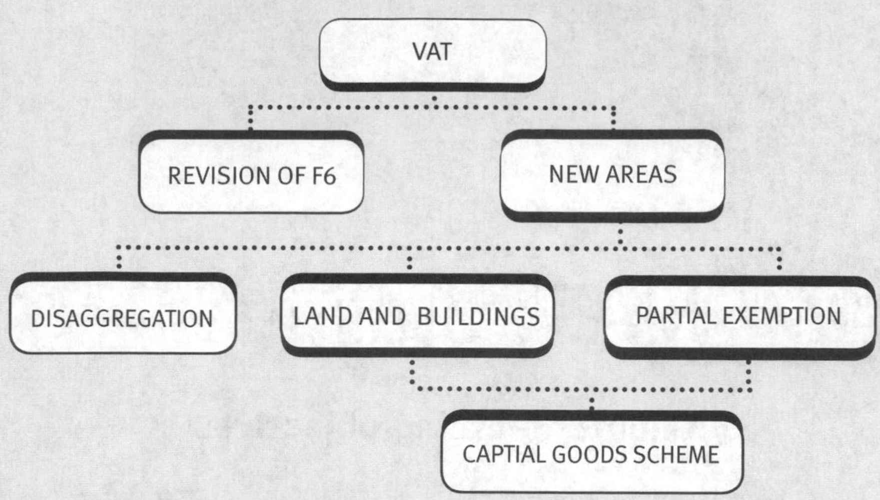

Introduction

This chapter and the next cover value added tax (VAT). The first part of this chapter revises the basic rules of VAT covered at F6.

The new topics introduced at P6 are shown in the diagram above.

1 A revision of basic VAT

The scope and nature of VAT

VAT is:

- an indirect tax on consumer spending
- charged on most goods and services supplied within the UK
- suffered by the final consumer, and
- collected by businesses on behalf of HM Revenue and Customs (HMRC).

Overview of how VAT works

VAT is collected by businesses at each stage in the production and distribution process of supplying goods and services as follows:

- businesses account to HMRC for the tax (known as output VAT) on sales
- if the customer is registered for VAT and uses the goods or services for business purposes, they can recover the tax they have paid on the purchase of the item or service (known as input VAT)

- accordingly, businesses actually account to HMRC for the tax on the 'value added' to the product at that stage of the process.

Businesses are merely acting as collectors of VAT on behalf of HMRC and they do not suffer any tax. It is only the final consumer who cannot recover the input VAT that suffers the tax.

How VAT works is shown in the illustration below.

Illustration – how VAT works

Assume that the rate of VAT throughout is 20%.

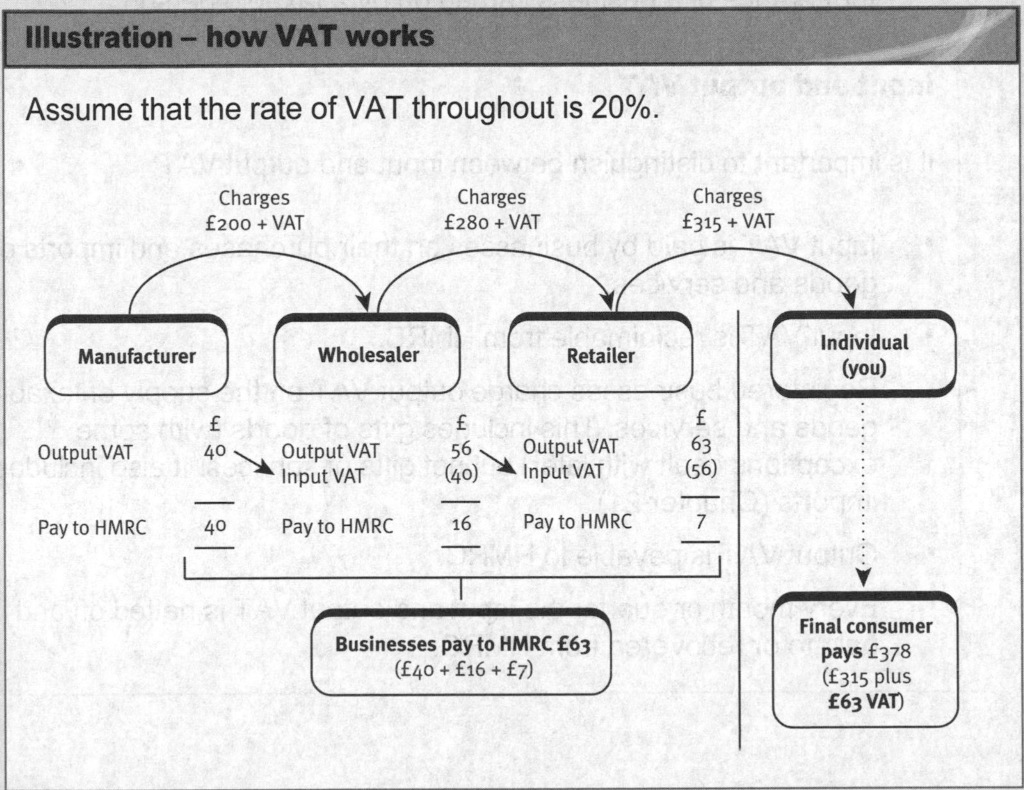

VAT is only charged

- by **taxable persons**
- when they make **taxable supplies** in the course of their business.

VAT is not generally charged on non-business transactions.

Key terms

- A **taxable person** is one who is or should be registered for VAT because they make taxable supplies. A person can be an individual or a legal person, such as a company.
- A **taxable supply** is any supply which is not exempt or outside of the scope of VAT. It includes sales of most goods and services, gifts and goods taken from the business for personal use.
- For VAT to apply, the taxable supply must be made in the course or furtherance of a business carried on by a taxable person.

Input and output VAT

It is important to distinguish between input and output VAT:

- Input VAT is paid by businesses on their purchases and imports of goods and services.
- Input VAT is reclaimable from HMRC.
- Registered businesses charge output VAT on the supply of taxable goods and services. This includes gifts of goods (with some exceptions dealt with later) but not gifts of services. It also includes imports (Chapter 21).
- Output VAT is payable to HMRC.
- Every month or quarter the input and output VAT is netted off and paid to or recovered from HMRC.

Types of supply

VAT is charged on taxable supplies, but not on exempt supplies or those outside the scope of VAT.

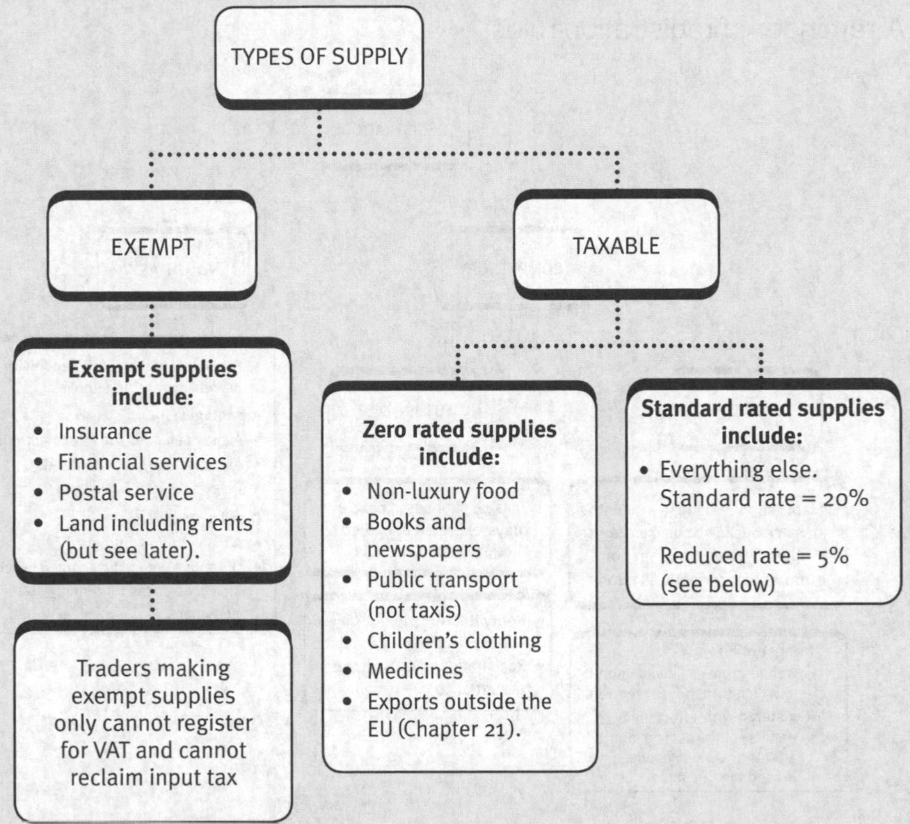

Note that:

- Some taxable supplies, mainly domestic or charitable use, are charged at the reduced rate. These are not important for the examination.
- Some supplies are outside the scope of VAT. These include wages, shares, dividends, other taxes (e.g. road fund licence) and sales between companies in a VAT group.

VAT registration

If a person's taxable supplies exceed the registration threshold, then registration is compulsory.

Taxable supplies in this context means:

- all standard, reduced and zero rated supplies (but not exempt supplies)
- excluding VAT, and
- excluding the sale of capital assets.

Voluntary registration is possible. This is particularly useful for businesses as it allows the recovery of input VAT.

However care should be taken when selling to the public as VAT will then be added to the selling price.

A reminder of registration rules:

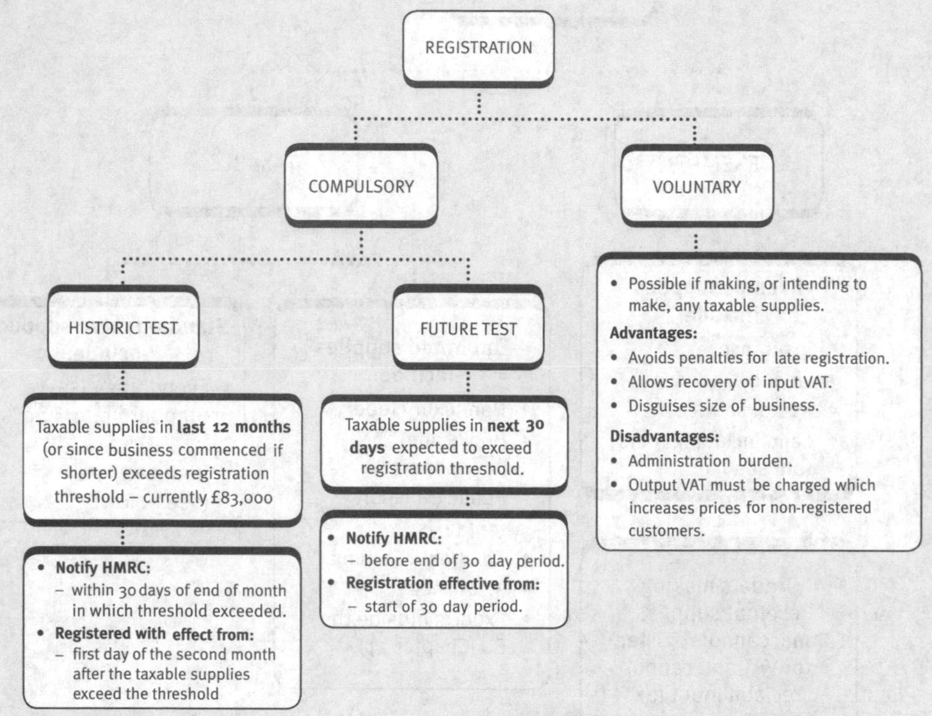

Note that:

- Registered traders are required to account for VAT.
- If a business fails to register in time, a penalty will be charged for late registration (see Chapter 21).
- A 'person' is registered for VAT (i.e. an individual, a partnership or a company).
- An individual sole trader has only one registration which covers all of the sole trader businesses that the individual carries on.
- A partnership is a separate person, therefore a partnership registration will cover all the businesses which are carried on by the same partners, but not any businesses they operate individually as sole traders.
- Companies are all registered individually, although it is possible to have a group registration (Chapter 27).
- It is possible to register, deregister and make variations to registration online. However, it is not compulsory to use the online service.

Pre-registration input VAT

Pre-registration input VAT can be recovered on the following:

- Goods (e.g. inventory and non-current assets):
  - if acquired for business purposes
  - in the last **four years**, and
  - goods are still in hand at the date of registration.
- Services:
  - if supplied for business purposes
  - in the **six months** prior to registration.

Deregistration

Deregistration is compulsory when a business:

- ceases, or
- is sold.

although it is possible, by joint election, to transfer a registration to a new owner who assumes all rights and obligations in respect of the registration.

Voluntary deregistration is also possible.

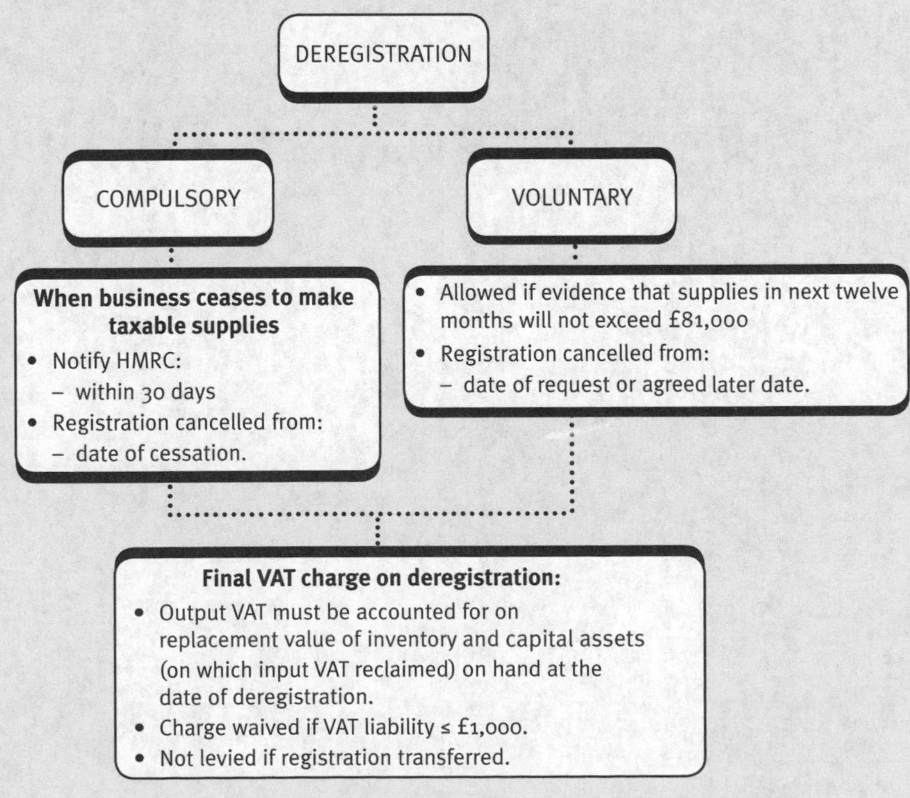

VAT on the sale of a business

When a business is sold it will be necessary to charge VAT on the sale proceeds. This is avoided if the transfer of going concern rules apply, in which case no VAT is charged (although see land and buildings below).

Conditions for transfer of going concern are as follows:

- The business is transferred as a going concern.
- There is no significant break in trading.
- The same type of trade is carried on after the transfer.
- The new owner is, or is liable to be, VAT registered immediately after the transfer.

Note that **all** of these conditions **must** be met.

Input and output VAT

This section deals with some of the special rules for determining the value of an output and reminds you of the purchases and expenses incurred by a business on which input VAT is not recoverable.

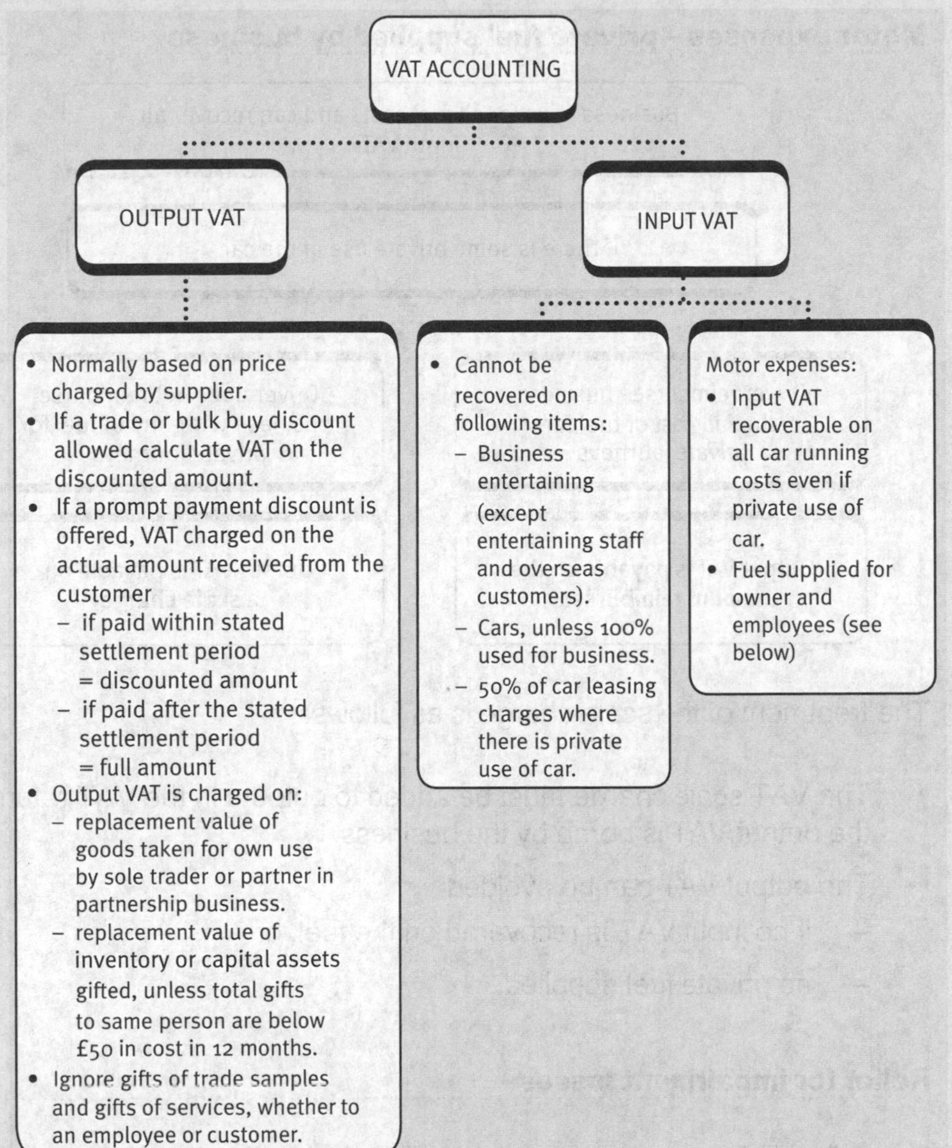
VAT ACCOUNTING
OUTPUT VAT
INPUT VAT
• Normally based on price charged by supplier.
• If a trade or bulk buy discount allowed calculate VAT on the discounted amount.
• If a prompt payment discount is offered, VAT charged on the actual amount received from the customer
– if paid within stated settlement period = discounted amount
– if paid after the stated settlement period = full amount
• Output VAT is charged on:
– replacement value of goods taken for own use by sole trader or partner in partnership business.
– replacement value of inventory or capital assets gifted, unless total gifts to same person are below £50 in cost in 12 months.
• Ignore gifts of trade samples and gifts of services, whether to an employee or customer.
• Cannot be recovered on following items:
– Business entertaining (except entertaining staff and overseas customers).
– Cars, unless 100% used for business.
– 50% of car leasing charges where there is private use of car.
Motor expenses:
• Input VAT recoverable on all car running costs even if private use of car.
• Fuel supplied for owner and employees (see below)

Note that output VAT is charged on the actual amount received from the customer if a prompt payment discount is offered.

Previously, VAT was always charged on the fully discounted amount, regardless of whether or not the discount was actually taken by the customer.

Remember there is **no distinction** between capital and revenue expenditure for VAT.

Input VAT is recoverable on the purchase of capital assets (i.e. purchase of plant and machinery, vans, equipment etc.) as well as revenue expenditure (except for the 'irrecoverable items' in the diagram above).

Motor expenses – private fuel supplied by business

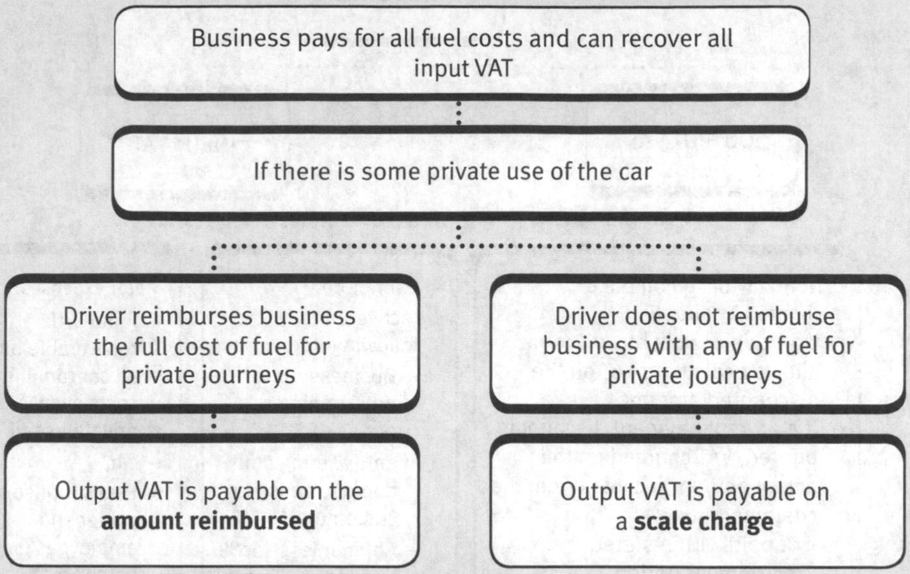

Business pays for all fuel costs and can recover all input VAT

If there is some private use of the car

Driver reimburses business the full cost of fuel for private journeys

Output VAT is payable on the **amount reimbursed**

Driver does not reimburse business with any of fuel for private journeys

Output VAT is payable on a **scale charge**

The treatment of the scale charge is as follows:

- The VAT scale charge must be added to outputs in the VAT return, and the output VAT is borne by the business
- The output VAT can be avoided
  - if no input VAT is recovered on the fuel, or
  - no private fuel supplied.

Relief for impairment losses

Normally, VAT output tax is accounted for when an invoice is issued. If the debt becomes irrecoverable, the seller has paid VAT to HMRC and never recovers this from the customer.

This position is addressed by the seller being able to claim VAT relief for impairment losses, provided the following conditions are satisfied:

- **At least six months** must have elapsed since the payment from the customer was due (or the date of supply if later).
- The debt must have been written off in the seller's VAT account.
- Claims for relief for irrecoverable debts must be made within **four years and six months** of the payment being due.

Relief is obtained by adding the VAT element of the irrecoverable debt to the input tax claimed.

If there has been a series of supplies, any payments made by the customer must be allocated on a FIFO basis unless the customer allocated a payment to a particular supply and paid in full.

Test your understanding 1

(1) Wilf Evans is a systems analyst who has recently started his own business. He has supplied you with the following information:

(a) His sales revenue for his first year ending 31 December 2016 is estimated to be £111,600 accruing evenly over the year. All Wilf's customers are VAT registered businesses and all Wilf's turnover is of taxable supplies.

(b) He purchased computer equipment for £3,150 including VAT on 14 January 2016.

(c) His business telephone bills are estimated to be £360 per quarter including VAT.

(d) He uses a room at his home as his office. His house has five main rooms and the electricity bill for the whole house for the year is estimated as £1,500 including VAT of £70.

(e) He has a petrol engine car which he uses 75% for business. Wilf bought the car in October 2015 for £15,000 including VAT. It was valued at £13,500 when he started his business on 1 January 2016. The car emits 190 g/km of CO_2 and annual running costs excluding petrol are £1,100 per year which includes £183 of VAT. He charges all his petrol costs through the business and these amount to £150 per month.

(f) Prior to starting in business, Wilf paid his accountant £350 plus VAT on 1 December 2015 for drawing up cash flow projections. His annual accountancy preparation costs are estimated to be £600 plus VAT.

Assume today's date is 1 February 2016.

Wilf has not yet registered for VAT. He wishes you to advise him when he will have to register compulsorily for VAT and whether it would be beneficial to register before that date.

(2) In his second year Wilf has problems collecting a debt from XYZ Ltd. He invoiced that company £3,500 including VAT, which was due for payment on 15 March 2017. In September 2017 he received £1,000 from XYZ Ltd in partial settlement of the debt but in October 2017 he wrote off the rest of the debt as irrecoverable.

Advise Wilf of the VAT position on this debt.

(3) In his third year of trading, Wilf decides to offer a trade discount of 5%.

Explain to Wilf what action he should take for VAT purposes when invoicing his customers.

(4) Assume that instead of offering a trade discount, Wilf offered a discount for prompt payment to try and improve his cash flow. The discount offered is 5% if invoices are paid within 14 days and 2.5% if paid within 30 days.

Explain how much output VAT should be charged if his customer pays after 21 days.

(5) In his fourth year of business Wilf receives an offer for his business of £450,000.

Wilf wants you to advise him whether VAT needs to be charged on this amount and whether there are any other actions he should take. The projected sale date for the business is 31 May 2020.

Assume the VAT rules for the VAT year to 31 March 2017 apply throughout.

The VAT scale charge for a car with 190 g/km of CO_2 emissions is £326 per quarter (inclusive of VAT).

VAT records

Records must be kept of all goods and services received and supplied in the course of a business. No particular form is specified, but they must be sufficient to allow the VAT return to be completed and to allow HMRC to check the return.

Records must be kept up-to-date and must be preserved for **six years**.

Records may be stored electronically.

In practice, the main records that must be kept are as follows:

- Copies of all VAT invoices issued.
- A record of all outputs (e.g. a sales day book).
- Evidence supporting claims for the recovery of input VAT (e.g. invoices).
- A record of all inputs (e.g. purchase day book).
- VAT account.

2 Special accounting schemes

There are three special VAT accounting schemes that are examinable and were covered at F6, namely:

- Cash accounting scheme
- Annual accounting scheme
- Flat rate scheme.

A brief reminder of these schemes is given in expandable text and is summarised in the diagram below.

The cash accounting scheme

Under this scheme VAT is accounted for on the basis of amounts received and paid in the VAT period rather than the normal basis.

To be eligible for cash accounting the following conditions must be satisfied:

- The trader must be up-to-date with VAT returns and must have committed no VAT offences in the previous 12 months.
- The trader's taxable turnover, including zero rated sales, but excluding VAT and excluding sales of capital assets, must not exceed £1,350,000 p.a.
- The trader must leave the scheme once their taxable turnover (excluding VAT) exceeds £1,600,000 p.a.
- The cash accounting scheme cannot be used for goods that are invoiced more than six months in advance of the payment date, or where an invoice is issued prior to the supply actually taking place.

The main advantages of cash accounting are:

- where customers are slow payers or there are irrecoverable debts no VAT is payable until the money is received (therefore automatic relief is obtained for irrecoverable debts)
- the information for the VAT return can be taken from the cash book, and no detailed cut-off procedures are required.

The main disadvantage is:

- the delay in the recoverability of input VAT which cannot be claimed until purchase invoices are paid.

The annual accounting scheme

This scheme alleviates the burden of administration of VAT and helps the cash flow of the business.

To be eligible to use the annual accounting scheme the same conditions as above must be satisfied.

The consequences of joining the scheme are as follows:

- Only **one VAT return** is submitted each year, but VAT payments must still be made regularly.
- Normally, **nine payments on account** of the VAT liability for the year are made at the **end of months 4 to 12** in that year.
- Each payment represents **10%** of the VAT liability of the previous year (or an estimated VAT liability for the year if a new business).
- A balancing payment (or repayment claim) is made at the same time as the annual return is filed, which must be **within two months** of the end of the annual return period.
- All payments must be made electronically (with no 7 day extension period allowed).
- The trader may apply to HMRC to agree quarterly payments on account instead of normal nine monthly payments.

Flat rate scheme

A trader with **taxable turnover (excluding VAT)** of **£150,000 or less**, may account for VAT using the flat rate scheme, provided they have committed no VAT offences in the previous 12 months.

The consequences of the scheme are as follows:

- Under the flat rate scheme, the VAT liability due to HMRC is calculated as:

  a flat rate percentage × total VAT inclusive turnover
  (i.e. taxable and exempt supplies)

- No input VAT is recovered (although a claim can be made to recover VAT on purchases of capital assets that cost more than £2,000).

  The need to calculate and record detailed output and input VAT information is therefore removed.

- The percentage varies according to the type of trade in which the business is involved and, if appropriate, will be given in the examination.

  In the first year in which a trader is registered for VAT, a 1% discount on the normal percentage is given.

- The flat rate scheme is **only** used to calculate the VAT due to HMRC. In other respects, VAT is dealt with in the normal way:
  - a **VAT invoice** must still be issued to customers and VAT charged at the appropriate rate (20% for standard rated supplies)
  - a **VAT account** must still be maintained.

- The flat rate scheme can be used together with the annual accounting scheme.

- It is not possible to join both the flat rate scheme and the cash accounting scheme, however it is possible to request that the flat rate scheme calculations are performed on a cash paid/receipts basis.

A trader may stay in the scheme until their **total VAT inclusive turnover** (i.e. taxable and exempt supplies) for the previous 12 months exceeds **£230,000**.

Summary

SMALL BUSINESS VAT SCHEMES

Cash accounting

- Same conditions as the annual accounting scheme
- Account on cash paid/cash received basis, not accruals
- Advantages
  - Automatic irrecoverable debt relief
  - Easier administration

Conditions:

- Annual taxable turnover (excluding VAT and capital sales) ≤ £1,350,000
- Up-to-date with returns and payments
- Leave scheme if taxable turnover (excluding VAT) > £1,600,000

Annual accounting

- Same conditions as the cash accounting scheme
- One VAT return for year
- Pay regularly electronically:
  - 9 monthly instalments of 10%, or
  - 3 quarterly instalments of 25%

  plus balancing payment
- First instalment = end of month 4
- Final payment = 2 months after year end
- Advantages
  - Regular cash outflows
  - Easier administration

Flat rate scheme

- VAT payment = (VAT inclusive total turnover × fixed %)
- Condition:
  - Taxable turnover (excluding VAT) ≤ £150,000
- Advantages
  - No need for detailed records of sales and purchases
  - Easier administration
- Leave scheme if VAT inclusive taxable turnover > £230,000 in previous 12 months

Comprehensive example

Test your understanding 2

Vector Ltd is registered for VAT, and is in the process of completing its VAT return for the quarter ended 31 March 2017. The following information is available.

(1) Sales invoices totalling £128,000 were issued in respect of standard rated sales. Vector Ltd offers its customers a trade discount of 2.5%.

(2) On 15 March 2017 Vector Ltd received an advance deposit of £4,500 in respect of a contract that is due to be completed during April 2017. The total value of the contract is £10,000. Both figures are inclusive of VAT.

(3) Standard rated expenses amounted to £74,800. This includes £4,200 for entertaining UK customers.

(4) On 31 March 2017 Vector Ltd wrote off £12,000 due from a customer as an irrecoverable debt. The debt was in respect of three invoices, each of £4,000, that were due for payment on 15 August, 15 September and 15 October 2016 respectively. No discounts were offered on these sales.

(5) On 1 January 2017 the company purchased a motor car costing £9,800 for the use of its sales manager. The sales manager is provided with free petrol for private mileage. The car has CO_2 emissions of 205 g/km and the relevant quarterly scale charge is £362. Both figures are inclusive of VAT.

Unless stated otherwise all of the above figures are exclusive of VAT.

(a) **Calculate the amount of VAT payable by Vector Ltd for the quarter ended 31 March 2017.**

(b) **State the conditions that Vector Ltd must satisfy before it will be permitted to use the cash accounting scheme, and advise the company of the implications of using the scheme.**

3 Disaggregation

There is a provision to prevent a business from being artificially split into small units thereby avoiding VAT registration because one or more units fall below the taxable turnover thresholds.

- Where HMRC are satisfied that persons are carrying on separate activities which could properly be regarded as part of a single business, then they will issue a direction.
- There is no requirement for HMRC to establish that the main reason for the separation of the activities was to avoid registration for VAT.
- The direction will state that the persons named therein are carrying on the activities listed together (i.e. a partnership is deemed to exist). However, a direction cannot have retrospective effect.
- For example, if a husband and wife run a pub together, but the wife operates the pub catering separately, both activities will be considered as one business if a direction is made. The taxable turnover from both activities will be taken into account for the registration thresholds.

4 Land and buildings

Types of supply
• Freehold sales, or leases of more than 21 years, of

Supplies of land and buildings in the UK can be either be zero rated, standard rated or exempt.

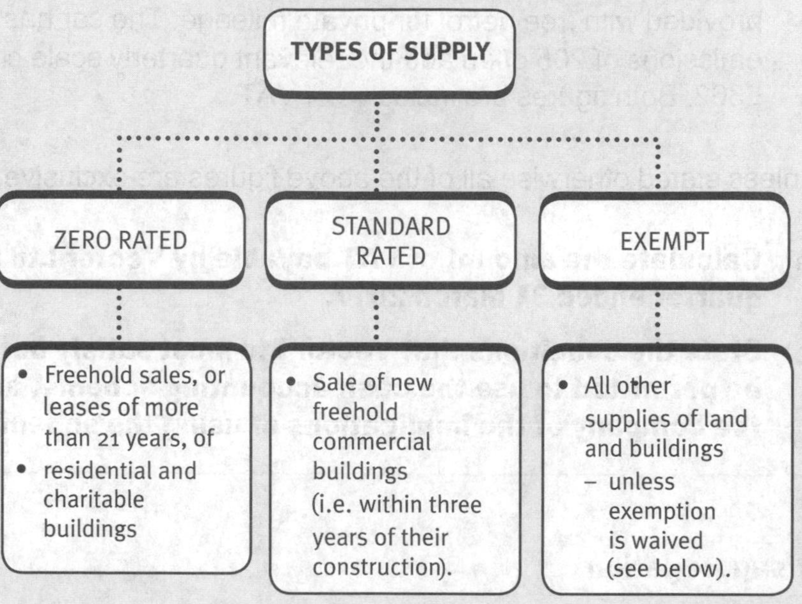

Opting to tax

A VAT registered vendor or lessor of a building can opt to waive the exemption of the building. This is usually referred to as 'opting to tax.'

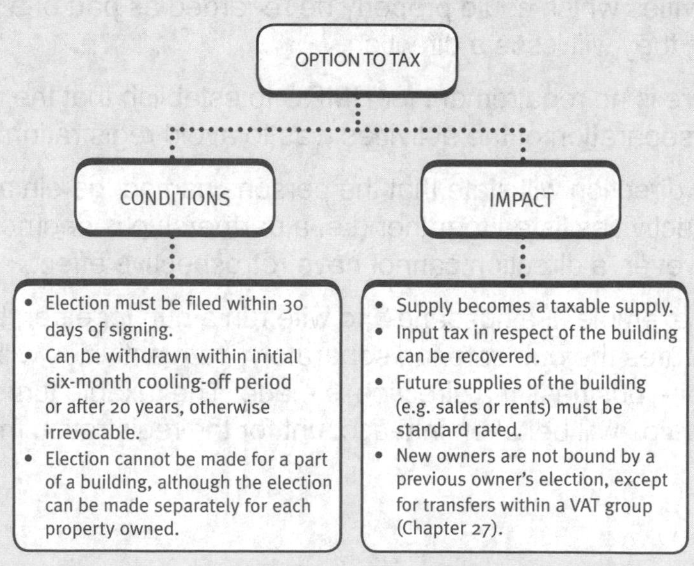

OPTION TO TAX
CONDITIONS
IMPACT
• Election must be filed within 30 days of signing.
• Can be withdrawn within initial six-month cooling-off period or after 20 years, otherwise irrevocable.
• Election cannot be made for a part of a building, although the election can be made separately for each property owned.
• Supply becomes a taxable supply.
• Input tax in respect of the building can be recovered.
• Future supplies of the building (e.g. sales or rents) must be standard rated.
• New owners are not bound by a previous owner's election, except for transfers within a VAT group (Chapter 27).

Note that opting to tax is particularly useful for landlords letting out commercial property which would normally be an exempt supply.

- By opting to tax the building, the landlord can recover any input tax on the purchase and running costs of the building.
- Tenants who are fully taxable traders will be able to recover any VAT charged to them on their rents.
- If tenants are exempt or partially exempt traders they will be disadvantaged by the landlord's election, as they will not be able to recover all the VAT charged on their rents. Such traders would prefer to have a tenancy in a building with no option to tax.

Transfer of going concern

Where an option to tax has been made on a building:

- That building can only be included as part of a transfer of a going concern (and therefore avoid VAT) if the new owner also opts to tax the building.
- If the new owner does not make the election, VAT must be charged by the vendor on the sale of the building.

Stamp duty land tax

SDLT is charged on

- the purchaser of the building
- on the consideration for the building **including VAT** (even if the purchaser can recover the VAT as input tax).

Example 1 – VAT on property

State whether the following statements are true or false:

(1) The waiver of exemption is the same thing as opting to tax.

(2) Once made, the waiver of exemption can never be revoked.

(3) If you buy a building which the previous owner has opted to tax, you are obliged to continue the option.

(4) The sale of second hand commercial buildings is always an exempt supply.

(5) The supply of new freehold buildings is always a standard rated supply.

Solution

(1) True.

(2) False – the waiver can be withdrawn within an initial six month cooling off period or after 20 years, otherwise it is irrevocable.

(3) False – the only time this is true is if the sale takes place within a VAT group.

(4) False – because the owner may have opted to tax the building.

(5) False – if the building is for residential or charitable use the sale will be zero rated.

Test your understanding 3

(1) X plc purchases a new factory building for use in its manufacturing trade from a builder, paying £700,000.

(2) Y plc is granted a 25 year lease on an office block which is intended for use in Y's trade.

(3) Z plc sells a 15 year old freehold building.

Assume that X, Y and Z plc are all registered traders and all transactions take place within the UK.

State the VAT implications of the above transactions.

5 Partial exemption

Traders who make both taxable and exempt supplies are given credit for only part of the input tax they incur. This section deals with the calculation of the recoverable input tax credit.

Methods of determining recoverable input tax

The standard method for determining the amount of recoverable input VAT is as follows:

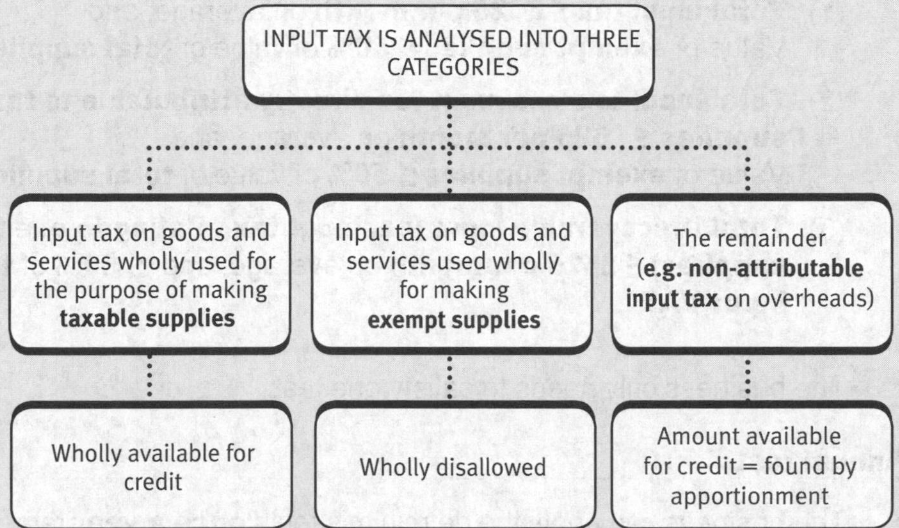

- The non-attributable input tax available for credit is the taxable proportion of total supplies (i.e. found by using the fraction):

$$\frac{\text{Total taxable supplies}}{\text{Total supplies}}$$

  Exclude VAT and supplies of capital goods when calculating this proportion.

- The ratio is computed as a percentage and, if not a whole number, it is rounded up to the next whole number.
- The percentage used during the year is generally the annual percentage **from the previous year**.

  Alternatively, the business can choose to calculate the percentage **each quarter** based on supplies for that quarter.

  Whichever method is used, it must be used consistently throughout the year.

  In either case, **an annual adjustment** will be made at the end of the accounting period.

- Any other reasonable method of apportionment can be agreed with HMRC.

De minimis limits

- All input tax (including that relating wholly or partly to exempt supplies) may be recovered if the business is below the de minimis limits. There are three tests to see whether a business is de minimis:

  (1) **Total input tax ≤ £625 per month** on average, and
  Value of **exempt supplies ≤ 50%** of value of **total supplies**

  (2) **Total input tax less input tax directly attributable to taxable supplies ≤ £625 per month** on average, and
  Value of **exempt supplies ≤ 50%** of value of **total supplies**

  (3) **Total irrecoverable input (i.e. input tax relating to exempt supplies) ≤ £625 per month** on average, and **≤ 50%** of **total input VAT**

  The business only needs to satisfy one test.

Annual test

- The business can apply the de minimis tests **once a year** rather than every return period if:
  - the business was **de minimis in the previous year**, and
  - the **annual test is applied consistently** throughout the current year, and
  - the **input VAT for the current year is not expected to exceed £1 million**.
- This means that the business can provisionally recover all input VAT relating to exempt supplies in each return period without having to perform de minimis calculations.
- At the end of the accounting period, the de minimis status must be reviewed based on the year as a whole and an annual adjustment made if necessary (see below).

Annual adjustment

The amount of recoverable input VAT is initially calculated for each VAT return period separately (i.e. usually for each quarterly return based on the supplies of the previous year, or the actual supplies for the quarter, or all of it is initially recoverable if the annual test is satisfied).

However, at the end of the accounting period, an annual adjustment calculation must be performed to ensure that the correct amount of input VAT is claimed for the year as a whole.

- Any under or over-declaration is then accounted for to HMRC, or reclaimed from them, on the first VAT return of the next year.
- Alternatively, the business can opt to bring forward the annual adjustment calculation to the last VAT return of the year (for example, if there was a repayment due).

Example 2 – Partial exemption

Arnold carries on activities which give rise to both taxable supplies and exempt supplies for which input tax is wholly disallowed.

Arnold prepares accounts to 31 December each year.

Relevant figures for the quarter ended 30 June 2016 are:

Activity	Attributable input tax
	£
Standard rated supplies (£96,000)	10,500
Zero rated supplies (£32,000)	3,500
Exempt supplies (£37,200)	4,000
	18,000
Overheads	5,000
Total input tax	23,000

Calculate the recoverable input tax for the quarter ended 30 June 2016, assuming Arnold chooses to calculate the percentage based on supplies for the quarter.

Solution

Quarter to 30 June 2016	Total	Recover	Disallow
	£	£	£
Relating to taxable supplies (£10,500 + £3,500)	14,000	14,000	
Relating to exempt supplies	4,000		4,000
Relating to overheads	5,000	3,900	1,100
	23,000	17,900	5,100

De minimis tests

(1) Total monthly input tax is £7,667 (£23,000 ÷ 3) on average.
As this exceeds £625, test 1 is not satisfied.

(2) Total input tax less input tax directly attributable to taxable supplies is £9,000 (£23,000 – £14,000). This gives a monthly average of £3,000 (£9,000 ÷ 3).
As this exceeds £625, test 2 is not satisfied.

(3) Monthly input tax relating to exempt supplies is £1,700 (£5,100 ÷ 3) on average.
As this exceeds £625, test 3 is not satisfied either.

Recoverable input VAT is therefore £17,900.

Annual adjustment

At the end of the year, when calculating the recoverable input VAT for the quarter ended 31 December 2016, the same calculation needs to be performed on an annual basis.

Any under or over claims for the previous quarters are made in this last return period, or in the first return period of the following year.

Working: Percentage apportionment of input VAT on overheads:

$$\frac{£96,000 + £32,000}{£96,000 + £32,000 + £37,200} \times 100 = 78\% \text{ (Note)}$$

Note: The percentage is rounded up to the nearest whole percentage.

Example 3 – Partial exemption annual adjustment

Arnold, from Example 2, continues to trade for the rest of the year ended 31 December 2016 and reclaims total input VAT of £82,500 over the year.

His final results for the year are as follows:

Activity	Attributable input VAT £
Standard rated supplies (£372,000)	39,500
Zero rated supplies (£131,000)	14,500
Exempt supplies (£151,700)	17,100
	71,100
Overheads	22,000
Total input tax	93,100

Calculate the annual adjustment required for the year ended 31 December 2016.

Solution

Year ended 31 December 2016

	Total £	Recover £	Disallow £
Relating to taxable supplies (£39,500 + £14,500)	54,000	54,000	
Relating to exempt supplies	17,100		17,100
Relating to overheads (W)	22,000	16,940	5,060
	93,100	70,940	22,160

De minimis tests

(1) Total monthly input tax is £7,758 (£93,100 ÷ 12) on average. As this exceeds £625, test 1 is not satisfied.

(2) Total input tax less input tax directly attributable to taxable supplies is £39,100 (£93,100 – £54,000). This gives a monthly average of £3,258 (£39,100 ÷ 12).
As this exceeds £625, test 2 is not satisfied.

(3) Monthly input tax relating to exempt supplies is £1,847 (£22,160 ÷ 12) on average.
As this exceeds £625, test 3 is not satisfied either.

Annual adjustment required

	£
Input VAT recoverable for the year	70,940
Less: Input VAT reclaimed	(82,500)
Amount payable	(11,560)

As the annual adjustment is an amount payable, it would be beneficial to make this adjustment in the quarter to 31 March 2017 rather than the quarter to 31 December 2016.

Working: Percentage apportionment of input VAT on overheads:

$$\frac{£372,000 + £131,000}{£372,000 + £131,000 + £151,700} \times 100 = 77\% \text{ (Note)}$$

Note: The percentage is rounded up to the nearest whole percentage.

Test your understanding 4

Toby's input tax and supplies made in the quarter to 31 December 2016 are analysed as follows:

	£
Input tax wholly re-taxable supplies	33,250
Input tax wholly re-exempt supplies	4,000
Non-attributable input tax	28,000
Value (excluding VAT) of taxable supplies	250,000
Value of exempt supplies	35,000

(a) **Calculate the deductible input tax assuming that Toby uses the standard method of attribution and chooses to calculate the percentage based on supplies for the quarter.**

(b) **Calculate the annual adjustment assuming the above figures are for the year to 31 December 2016, and the total input VAT recovery based on calculations for the four quarters separately is £53,625.**

6 The capital goods scheme

The capital goods scheme applies to partially exempt businesses that spend large sums on land and buildings or computers and computer equipment.

- Where the scheme applies, the initial deduction of input tax is made in the ordinary way and then reviewed over a set adjustment period.
- This is to stop businesses manipulating their proportion of taxable and exempt supplies in the period of purchase in order to reclaim more input tax.

Assets covered by the scheme

The assets dealt with by the scheme are as follows:

Item	Value	Adjustment period
Land and buildings	£250,000 or more	10 years (5 years where subject to a lease of less than 10 years at acquisition)
Computers and computer equipment	£50,000 or more	5 years

A trader making say 70% taxable supplies and 30% exempt supplies can initially reclaim 70% of the input VAT charged in respect of a building.

Adjustments are made over the next 10 (or 5) years if the proportion of exempt supplies changes.

The annual adjustment is:

$$\frac{\text{Total input tax}}{\text{10 (or 5) years}} \times (\text{\% now} - \text{\% in the original year})$$

Example 4 – Capital goods scheme

Confusion plc is a company that buys a new freehold building for £5,250,000 including VAT. 40% of the building is used in making exempt supplies and 60% taxable. After 7 years this changes to 50%: 50%.

Explain how Confusion plc can recover input VAT on the purchase of the building.

Solution

The purchase of the building is subject to the capital goods scheme as it is a building costing £250,000 or more. The adjustment period is 10 years as it is a freehold purchase.

The initial recovery of input tax is:

(60% × £5,250,000 × 20/120 (Note)) = £525,000

For years 1 – 7 of the adjustment period there is no need to make any adjustment.

For each of years 8, 9,10 the company will have part of its initial input tax recovery clawed back as follows:

£875,000 × 1/10 × (50% – 60%) = £8,750 owed to HMRC.

Note: The VAT element can be calculated using either 20/120 or 1/6.

Example 5 – Capital goods scheme

Delta plc is a partially exempt trader and makes 30% exempt and 70% taxable supplies.

On 1 March 2017 Delta plc buys a new freehold building for £2 million including VAT which is used in the same proportion. After two years Delta plc's percentages and use of the building change to 40% exempt and 60% taxable. After a further 3 years Delta plc ceases the exempt trade and makes only taxable supplies from thereon.

Calculate the input VAT relief that can be obtained by Delta plc.

Solution

The purchase of the building is subject to the capital goods scheme as it is a building costing £250,000 or more. The adjustment period is 10 years as it is a freehold purchase.

The initial recovery of VAT is:

(70% × 20/120 × £2,000,000) = £233,333.

There are no adjustments required for years 1 and 2 but for years 3 – 5 the company must repay part of its input tax relief as follows:

£2,000,000 × 20/120 × 1/10 × (60% – 70%)
= £3,333 due to HMRC for each of the years 3,4,5.

For years 6 – 10 the company will be able to reclaim further input tax relief as follows:

£2,000,000 × 20/120 × 1/10 × (100% – 70%)
= £10,000 due to Delta plc for each of years 6, 7, 8, 9, 10.

Adjustments for sale

On the disposal of an asset under the capital goods scheme during the adjustment period:

- The annual adjustment is made as normal in the year of disposal (as if the asset had been used for the full year).
- A further adjustment must be made to cover the remaining intervals. The adjustment for sale is as follows:
  - If the disposal was taxable (e.g. option to tax exists), we assume 100% taxable use for the remainder of the adjustment period, although note that the VAT recovery cannot exceed the VAT charged on the sale of the asset.
  - If the disposal was exempt (e.g. no option to tax exists), we assume 0% taxable use for the remainder of the adjustment period.

Example 6 – Capital goods scheme

Facts as in Example 5, except that Delta plc sells the building in year 6 for £2.5 million.

Calculate the adjustment for year 6 assuming that:

(a) **Delta plc does not opt to tax the sale**

(b) **Delta plc opts to tax the sale.**

Solution

(a) Adjustment for use: Year 6, £10,000 to be reclaimed from HMRC (as above).
Adjustment for sale: As the building is now over 3 years old the sale is exempt therefore an amount has to be repaid to HMRC as if the building will have 0% taxable use for the remaining intervals:

£2,000,000 × 20/120 × 1/10 × (0% – 70%) × 4 years
= £93,333 repaid to HMRC.

(b) Adjustment for use: Year 6, £10,000 to be reclaimed from HMRC (as above).
Adjustment for sale: Assume 100% taxable as the option to tax has been exercised:

£2,000,000 × 20/120 × 1/10 × (100% – 70%) × 4 years
= £40,000 reclaimed from HMRC.

7 Chapter summary

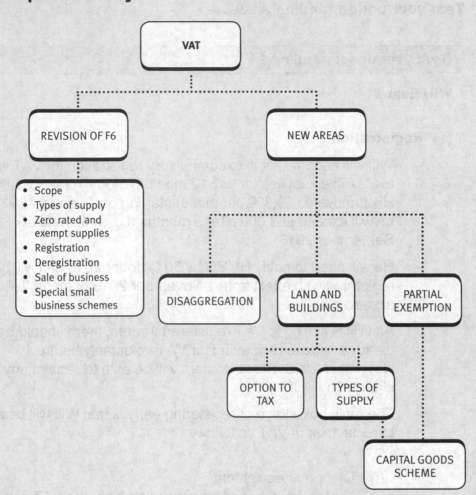

VAT

- REVISION OF F6
  - Scope
  - Types of supply
  - Zero rated and exempt supplies
  - Registration
  - Deregistration
  - Sale of business
  - Special small business schemes
- NEW AREAS
  - DISAGGREGATION
  - LAND AND BUILDINGS
    - OPTION TO TAX
    - TYPES OF SUPPLY
      - CAPITAL GOODS SCHEME
  - PARTIAL EXEMPTION
    - CAPITAL GOODS SCHEME

Test your understanding answers

Test your understanding 1

Wilf Evans

(1) **Registration**

- Wilf will become liable to compulsory registration for VAT when his taxable supplies for any 12 month period exceed £83,000. His turnover is £9,300 per month starting on 1 January 2016 so he will exceed £83,000 after 9 months (i.e. at the end of September 2016).
- He will need to notify HMRC by 30 October 2016 and will be registered with effect from 1 November 2016 or an earlier agreed date.
- As Wilf is selling to VAT registered traders, there should be no disadvantage to registering for VAT voluntarily before 1 November 2016. His customers will be able to reclaim any VAT charged by Wilf.
- The main advantage of registering early is that Wilf will be able to reclaim input VAT as follows:

  (i) Computer equipment
  – even if purchased before registration, the VAT can be recovered provided Wilf still owns the computer at the date of registration. Reclaim £525 (£3,150 × 1/6).

  (ii) Business telephone
  – reclaim £60 per quarter (£360 × 1/6).

  (iii) Use of home as office
  – Wilf can reclaim VAT on the business proportion of his electricity bills £14 (£70 × 1/5) for the year.

  (iv) Wilf cannot recover VAT on his car purchase.
  He can recover VAT on the running expenses of £183 and VAT on his petrol of £25 per month (£150 × 1/6).
  If he recovers input tax on the petrol, he will have to account for a VAT fuel charge.
  For a car with CO_2 emissions of 190 g/km, the amount VAT scale charge is £326 per quarter, which represents £54 of VAT (£326 × 1/6). This must be added to the output tax for each quarter.
  This fuel charge can be avoided if Wilf does not claim any VAT input tax in respect of fuel.

(v) If Wilf registers by 1 June 2016 he will be able to reclaim the input VAT on his accountant's fee for preparing his cash flow projections. This is because he can recover input VAT on services supplied in the six months prior to registration.

(2) **Irrecoverable debts**

In the quarter which includes October 2017 Wilf can make a claim for the VAT on his outstanding debt.

This will be £417 (£2,500 × 1/6). This is permitted because Wilf has written off the debt in his books and it is more than 6 months since the date payment was due.

(3) **Trade discount**

Wilf must charge VAT on the discounted amount. Hence for an invoice for £1,000 excluding VAT, the VAT charged should be:

(20% × 95% × £1,000) = £190

(4) **Prompt payment discount**

Wilf must charge VAT on the actual amount paid by the customer.

As the customer paid after 21 days, the discount allowed will be 2.5%.

Accordingly, for an invoice of £1,000 excluding VAT, the VAT charged should be:

(20% × 97.5% × £1,000) = £195

(5) **Sale of business**

There are two issues to consider here:

(i) No VAT needs to be charged if Wilf sells his business as a going concern provided:

- the new owner is, or is liable to be, VAT registered immediately after the transfer
- the assets sold are used in the same trade in the future, and
- there is no significant break in the trading.

Note that all of the above conditions must apply to avoid VAT, otherwise VAT must be charged on the assets that are sold.

(ii) Wilf must

– deregister unless his registration is transferred to the new owner. This is unlikely if they are unconnected third parties.

– notify HMRC that he has ceased to make taxable supplies. This notification must be within 30 days of cessation.

– account for VAT on the replacement values of his inventory (if any) and tangible non-current assets on hand at the date of deregistration unless the business is sold as a going concern as above. However there will be no charge as amounts below £1,000 are not collected.

Test your understanding 2

Vector Ltd

(a) **VAT Return – Quarter ended 31 March 2017**

	£
Output VAT:	
Sales (£128,000 × 97.5% × 20%)	24,960
Advance payment (£4,500 × 20/120)	750
Motor car scale charge (£362 × 20/120)	60
	25,770
Input VAT:	
Expenses (£74,800 – £4,200) × 20%	(14,120)
Irrecoverable debt relief (£4,000 + £4,000) × 20%	(1,600)
VAT payable	10,050

Notes:

(1) The calculation of output VAT on sales must take into account the trade discount. VAT is therefore calculated on 97.5% of the sales value.

(2) Input VAT on business entertainment is not recoverable, unless it relates to entertaining overseas customers.

(3) Relief for an irrecoverable debt is not given until six months from the time that payment is due. Therefore relief can only be claimed in respect of the invoices due for payment on 15 August and 15 September 2016.

(4) Input VAT cannot be recovered in respect of the motor car as it is not used exclusively for business purposes.

Note: Although the ACCA uses a VAT fraction of 20/120 it is equally valid to use a VAT fraction of 1/6.

Amounts due from customers are normally recorded inclusive of VAT. However, the question clearly states that all figures are VAT exclusive unless stated otherwise. Hence the two invoices of £4,000 due from a customer and written off as irrecoverable debts are treated as VAT exclusive.

(b) **Cash accounting scheme**

- Vector Ltd can use the cash accounting scheme if its expected taxable turnover (excluding VAT and sales of capital assets) for the next 12 months does not exceed £1,350,000.
- In addition, the company must be up-to-date with its VAT returns and VAT payments.
- The scheme will result in the tax point becoming the date that payment is received from customers.
- This will provide for automatic irrecoverable debt relief should a customer not pay.
- However, the recovery of input VAT on expenses will be delayed until payment is made.

Test your understanding 3

VAT on property

(1) **X plc**

The builder will charge VAT on the sale of a new commercial building. As it says that X plc paid £700,000 it can be assumed that this is the VAT inclusive price.

The VAT of £116,667 (20/120 × £700,000) can be reclaimed by X plc as they plan to use the building to make taxable supplies.

(2) **Y plc**

Unless the landlord has opted to tax the transaction, this will be an exempt supply. Y plc will not incur any input tax.

(3) **Z plc**

Normally the sale of a building more than 3 years old will be an exempt supply and no VAT will be charged. However, if Z plc has opted to tax the building then they will have to charge VAT on the disposal.

Test your understanding 4

(a) **Toby – Quarter ended 31 December 2016**

	Total	Recover	Disallow
	£	£	£
Relating to taxable supplies	33,250	33,250	
Relating to exempt supplies	4,000		4,000
Relating to overheads (W)	28,000	24,640	3,360
	65,250	57,890	7,360

De minimis test

The total input VAT, total input VAT less input VAT directly attributable to taxable supplies, and total irrecoverable input VAT (i.e. input VAT relating to exempt supplies), are all clearly greater than £625 per month on average for the 3 month period, therefore none of the de minimis tests are satisfied.

The recoverable input VAT is therefore £57,890.

Working: Allocate non-attributable VAT

Taxable % apportionment

$$= \frac{£250,000}{£250,000 + £35,000} \times 100 = 88\% \text{ (round up to whole \%)}$$

(b) **Annual adjustment**

If the above figures are annual figures, the apportionment would be the same but the de minimis tests need to be reconsidered:

– Total monthly input tax is £5,437 (£65,250 ÷ 12) on average.

  As this exceeds £625, test 1 is not satisfied.

– Total input tax less input tax directly attributable to taxable supplies is £32,000 (£65,250 – £33,250). This gives a monthly average of £2,667 (£32,000 ÷ 12).

  As this exceeds £625, test 2 is not satisfied.

– Monthly input tax relating to exempt supplies is £613 (£7,360 ÷ 12) on average. This is less than £625. The total irrecoverable VAT (i.e. input tax relating to exempt supplies) of £7,360 is also less than £32,625 (50% of total input VAT of £65,250).

  Test 3 is therefore satisfied.

Accordingly, all input VAT suffered for the year of £65,250 can be recovered.

The annual adjustment is therefore £11,625 (£65,250 – £53,625).

As this is a repayment of input VAT, Toby will claim to make the adjustment in the last quarter return to 31 December 2016 rather than wait until the first quarter of the following year.

chapter

21

VAT: administration and overseas aspects

Chapter learning objectives

Upon completion of this chapter you will be able to:

- identify how a default surcharge penalty arises and calculate it
- explain the procedure and effect when errors on earlier VAT returns are identified
- describe the penalty for submission of an incorrect VAT return and state the amount of the penalty
- describe the penalty regime for failure to notify liability for registration or change in nature of supplies by persons exempted from registration
- describe when a default interest charge will arise and calculate it
- advise on the VAT implications of imports and exports
- advise on the VAT implications of acquisitions and dispatches within the EU.

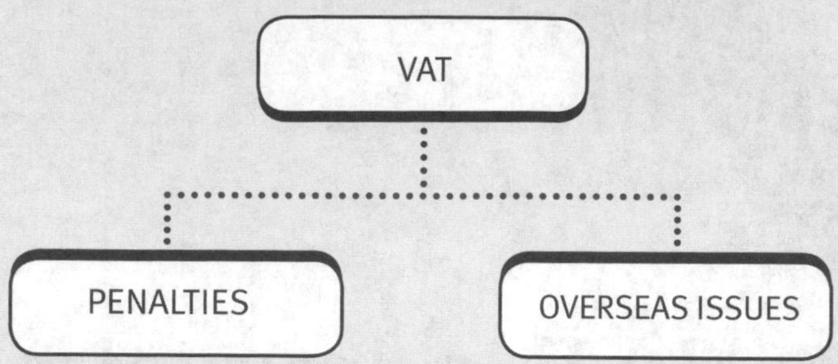

Introduction

This chapter revises the rules for penalties and interest covered at F6. The chapter also covers the main new topic at P6, namely some overseas aspects of VAT.

1 Electronic filing of VAT returns

All businesses must file the VAT return online and pay the VAT electronically:

- within **one month and seven days** of the end of the return period.

2 The default surcharge

The rules for default surcharges were covered at F6 and are unchanged. A brief reminder of the rules is given in expandable text and is summarised in the diagram below.

Default surcharge

A default occurs if a VAT return is not submitted on time or a payment is made late. The sequence for the default surcharge is as follows:

- On the first default, HMRC serve a surcharge liability notice on the trader.
- The notice specifies a surcharge period, starting on the date of the notice and ending on the 12 month anniversary of the end of the VAT period to which the default relates.
- If a trader defaults in the surcharge period, there are two consequences.
  - the surcharge period is extended to the 12 month anniversary of the VAT period to which the new default relates
  - if the default involves the late payment of VAT, the trader will be subject to a surcharge penalty.

- There is no surcharge penalty where a late VAT return involves the repayment of VAT, or if the VAT payable is £Nil.
- The rate of surcharge penalty depends on the number of defaults in the surcharge period:

Default in the surcharge period	Surcharge as a % of tax unpaid at the due date
First	**2%**
Second	**5%**
Third	**10%**
Fourth	**15%**

- Surcharge penalties at the rates of 2% and 5% are not issued for amounts of less than **£400.**
- Where the rate of surcharge is 10% or 15%, a surcharge penalty is the higher of:

  (i) £30, or

  (ii) the actual amount of the calculated surcharge.
- The surcharge liability period only ends when a trader submits four consecutive VAT quarterly returns on time, and pays any VAT due on time.

Example 1 – Default surcharge

Mark's VAT return for the quarter ended 30 June 2016 was submitted late, and the VAT due of £14,500 was not paid until 16 August 2016.

His return for the following quarter to 30 September 2016 was also submitted late and the VAT due of £16,200 was not paid until 9 November 2016.

Explain the consequences for Mark.

Solution

(1) **VAT return period ended 30 June 2016**
First default: surcharge liability notice issued.
The surcharge period runs from the date of the notice to 30 June 2017.

(2) **VAT return period ended 30 September 2016**
First default within the surcharge period.
Penalty of £324 (£16,200 × 2%) is due but as the amount is less than £400 an assessment will not be issued.
The surcharge period is extended to 30 September 2017.

3 Errors on a VAT return

VAT is a self-assessed tax. The trader calculates their own liability or repayment.

- HMRC make occasional control visits to check that returns are correct.
- HMRC have the power to enter business premises, inspect documents, including statements of profit or loss and statements of financial position, take samples, and inspect computer records (see Chapter 16 for HMRC information and inspection powers).

Errors on earlier VAT returns

If a trader realises that there is an error this may lead to a standard penalty as there has been a submission of an incorrect VAT return (see Chapter 16, section 8).

However, if the error is below the de minimis level and voluntarily disclosed, default interest will not be charged.

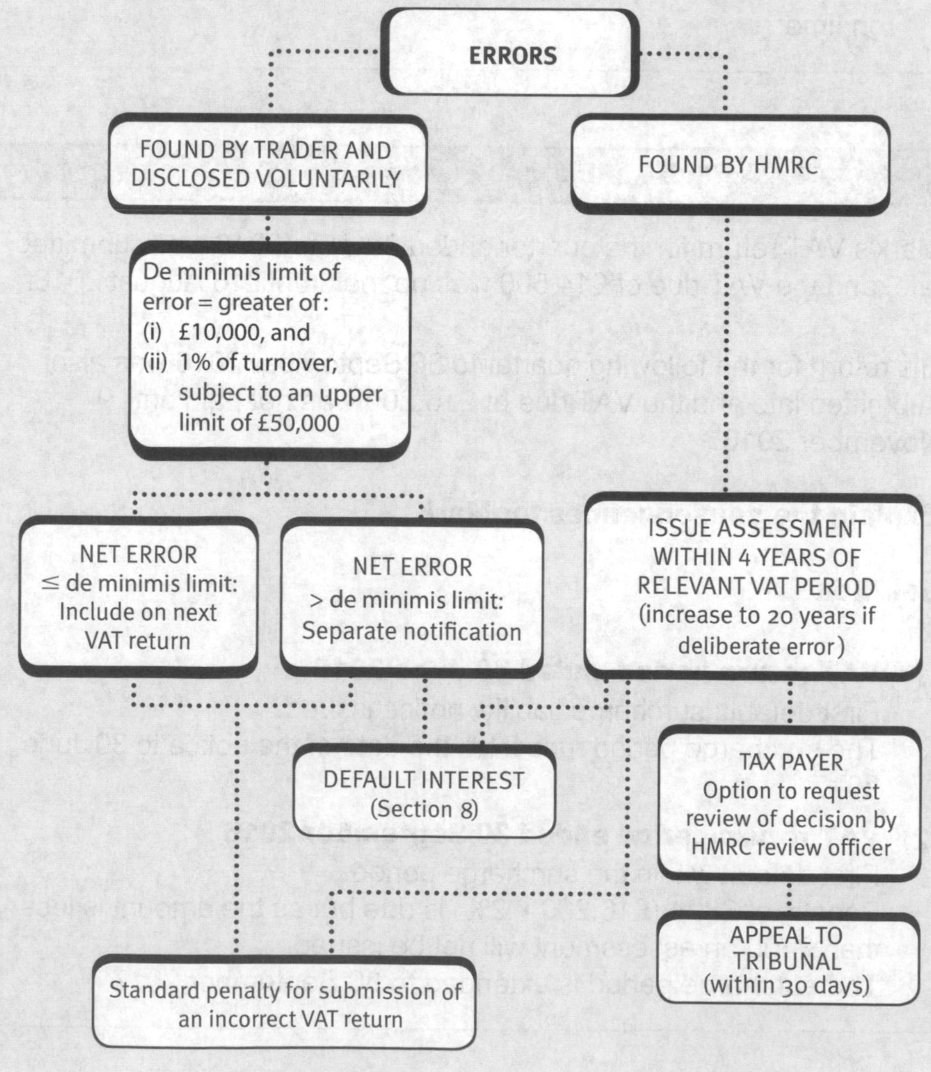

4 Default interest

Default interest (also known as penalty interest) is charged, if HMRC raise an assessment, or an error is voluntarily disclosed by the trader, as the net value of errors exceeds the de minimis limit.

Interest is charged:

from: – the date that the outstanding VAT should have been paid
to: – the actual date of payment.

Any interest charged by HMRC is limited to a **maximum of three years** prior to the date of the assessment or voluntary disclosure.

Example 2 – Penalties and interest

Hopeless Ltd has recently had a control visit from HMRC. During the visit it has been discovered that on their previous VAT return for the quarter to 31 March 2017, Hopeless Ltd forgot to include output VAT on £500,000 (VAT exclusive) of taxable supplies.

The actual output and input tax included in the return were as follows.

	£
Output tax	100,000
Input tax	30,000
Due to HMRC	70,000

Hopeless paid the underpaid VAT on 6 June 2017.

State whether a penalty for submission of an incorrect return will be levied on Hopeless Ltd and, if so, discuss the maximum penalty that will be imposed.

State the position with respect to default interest. Assume a rate of default interest of 3%.

Solution

The error Hopeless Ltd has made is to under declare output VAT of:

(20% × £500,000) = £100,000.

This means the VAT return for the quarter to 31 March 2017 is incorrect due to an understatement of the VAT liability.

The standard penalty therefore applies and is determined according to:

- The amount of tax understated.
- The reason for the understatement.
- The extent of disclosure by the taxpayer.

The level of the penalty is a percentage of the revenue lost as a result of the inaccuracy or under assessment and depends on the behaviour of the taxpayer as follows:

Taxpayer behaviour	Maximum penalty (% of revenue lost)
Genuine mistake.	No penalty
Careless/failure to take reasonable care.	30%
Deliberate but no concealment.	70%
Deliberate with concealment.	100%

The penalties may be reduced depending on the type of penalty and whether the taxpayer makes an unprompted disclosure of the understatement.

As Hopeless Ltd have not voluntarily disclosed the error (as it was discovered by HMRC), no reduction is likely to be made for unprompted disclosure.

Where the return is incorrect through deliberate intention of a third party, the penalty can be charged on the third party.

Default interest will also be charged from the day after the date the VAT should have been paid (7 May) until the day before the actual date of payment on 6 June (30 days), but calculate to the nearest month in the examination.

The charge will be: (1/12 × 3% × £100,000) = £250

Summary

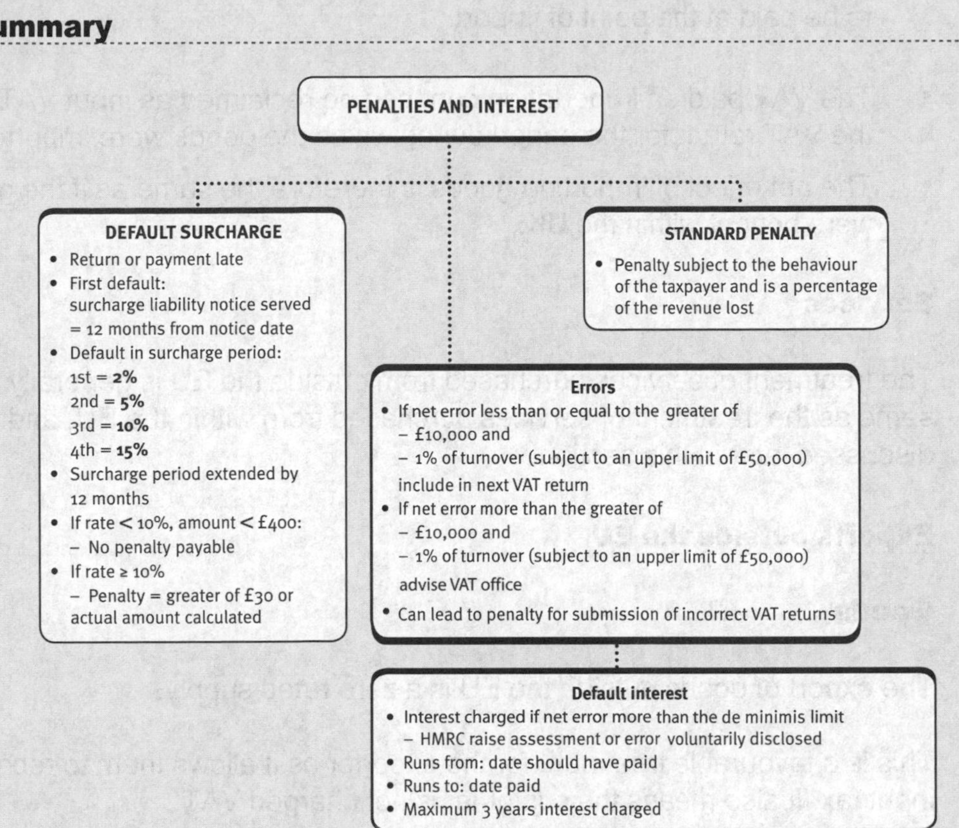

PENALTIES AND INTEREST
DEFAULT SURCHARGE
• Return or payment late
• First default: surcharge liability notice served = 12 months from notice date
• Default in surcharge period: 1st = 2% 2nd = 5% 3rd = 10% 4th = 15%
• Surcharge period extended by 12 months
• If rate < 10%, amount < £400: – No penalty payable
• If rate ≥ 10% – Penalty = greater of £30 or actual amount calculated
STANDARD PENALTY
• Penalty subject to the behaviour of the taxpayer and is a percentage of the revenue lost
Errors
• If net error less than or equal to the greater of – £10,000 and – 1% of turnover (subject to an upper limit of £50,000) include in next VAT return
• If net error more than the greater of – £10,000 and – 1% of turnover (subject to an upper limit of £50,000) advise VAT office
• Can lead to penalty for submission of incorrect VAT returns
Default interest
• Interest charged if net error more than the de minimis limit – HMRC raise assessment or error voluntarily disclosed
• Runs from: date should have paid
• Runs to: date paid
• Maximum 3 years interest charged

5 Overseas aspects of VAT

VAT is a tax levied within the European Union (EU) only. It is therefore necessary to distinguish imports and exports from outside the EU from transactions within the EU.

Imports from outside the EU

Goods

VAT is charged on goods imported from outside the EU as if it were a customs duty. It is normally collected direct from the importer at the place of importation, such as a port or airport.

- If the imported goods are immediately placed in a bonded warehouse or free zone, then VAT is postponed until the goods are removed from the warehouse or zone.
- Approved traders can pay all of their VAT on imports through the duty deferment system.

  In order to set up an account with HMRC the trader will need to arrange a bank guarantee. This allows all VAT on imports to be paid on the 15th of the month following the month of importation.

This assists the trader's cash flow and is more convenient than having to be paid at the point of import.

- The VAT paid on importation can then be reclaimed as input VAT on the VAT return for the period during which the goods were imported.
- The net effect of importing goods is therefore the same as if the goods were bought within the UK.

Services

The treatment of services purchased from outside the EU is generally the same as the treatment of services purchased from within the EU, and is discussed later in this section.

Exports outside the EU

Goods

The export of goods outside the EU is a zero rated supply.

This is a favourable treatment for the exporter as it allows them to recover input tax. It also means the customer is not charged VAT.

Services

The supply of services outside the EU is outside the scope of VAT.

Transactions within the EU

Goods

The following table summarises the two situations which can occur when trading between EU countries.

	Transactions	Accounting for VAT
Supplier and customer registered (i.e. Business to business (B2B)) (the destination system applies).	Supply is zero rated in country of origin. VAT chargeable at the appropriate rate in force in country of destination (reverse charge procedure).	(a) Supplier does not account for output VAT – supply zero rated. (b) Customer must account for output VAT on their VAT return at the rate in force in customer's country. (c) VAT suffered by customer may be reclaimed by them as input VAT in the appropriate quarter.
Supplier registered but not customer (i.e. Business to individual) (the origin system applies).	VAT chargeable at the appropriate rate in force in the country of origin.	(a) Supplier accounts for output VAT. (b) Where supplies to the destination country exceed an EU threshold, (the 'distance selling' threshold) the supplier will have to register for VAT in that country. (c) No input VAT recoverable by the customer (as not VAT registered).

The output VAT on purchases from the EU must be accounted for by the customer in their VAT return for the date of acquisition.

The date of acquisition is the date of the VAT invoice, which must be issued by the 15th day of the month following the month in which the goods came into the UK.

Both the output VAT and input VAT are therefore likely to be on the same VAT return and will cancel out, unless the business is partially exempt (see Chapter 20) or makes exempt supplies and therefore cannot reclaim input VAT.

VAT on purchases from within the EU and outside the EU is collected via different systems. However, both leave the UK business in the same overall financial position.

Test your understanding 1

Overseas Ltd is VAT registered and has been importing computers from Ruritania since 1 January 2017. Ruritania is not currently a member of the European Union but is expected to join in the near future.

Overseas Ltd makes only taxable supplies. For the quarter ended 31 March 2017 imports of £100,000 have been made. This amount excludes any VAT or duties.

Explain how Overseas Ltd will have to account for VAT on the computers imported from Ruritania.

State how this will change if Ruritania becomes a member of the European Union and show the entries required on Overseas Ltd's VAT return in this case.

Test your understanding 2

Foreign Ltd, a UK resident company registered for VAT, has the following international transactions.

(a) Sale of children's toys to a customer in Germany, who is VAT registered.

(b) Sale of ladies' handbags to Venezuela.

(c) Sale of men's ties to an Italian customer, who is not VAT registered.

(d) Purchase of silk fabric from Hong Kong.

Outline the VAT treatment in each case for Foreign Ltd.

Note that Germany and Italy are in the EU.

Supply of services

The rules governing VAT on the supply of services are complex. These notes just cover the basic principles needed for the P6 examination.

For services, VAT is generally charged at the place of supply.

The place of supply varies depending on whether the customer is a business or non-business customer.

Supply of service to	Place of supply
Business customer (B2B)	Where the customer is established
Non-business customer	Where the supplier is established

These rules can be applied to a UK business as follows:

<table>
<tr><th colspan="2">UK business</th><th>Accounting for VAT</th></tr>
<tr><td rowspan="2">Supplies services to</td><td>Overseas business customer (B2B)</td><td>• Place of supply is overseas
• Outside the scope of UK VAT</td></tr>
<tr><td>Overseas non-business customer</td><td>• Place of supply is UK.
• Output VAT charged at standard UK rate</td></tr>
<tr><td>Receives services from</td><td>Overseas business (B2B)</td><td>• Place of supply is UK
• Reverse charge procedure:
– UK business accounts for 'output VAT' at standard UK rate on VAT return.
– This VAT can then be reclaimed as input VAT.</td></tr>
</table>

Time of supply for cross border supplies of services

The rules are governed primarily by when a service is performed and a distinction is made between single and continuous supplies.

- For single supplies, the tax point will occur on the **earlier of**:
  - when the service is completed, or
  - when it is paid for.
- In the case of continuous supplies, the tax point will be the end of each billing or payment period.

6 Chapter summary

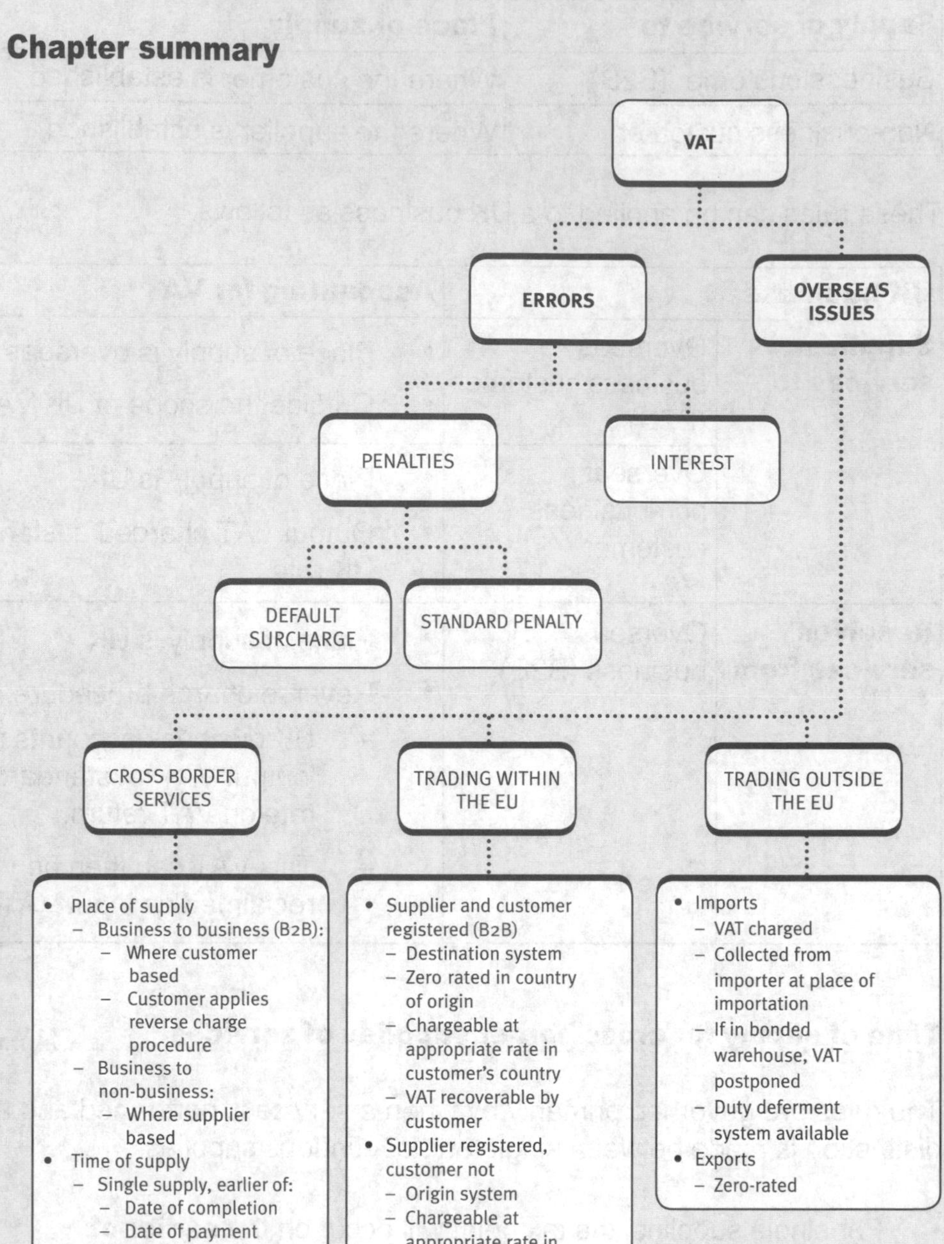

Test your understanding answers

Test your understanding 1

Overseas Ltd

(1) **Ruritania is not in the EU**

Overseas Ltd will have to account for VAT on the value of the computers (including any carriage and import charges) at the point of importation. This will amount to £20,000 (£100,000 × 20%). Overseas Ltd can then claim input tax relief of £20,000 on their next VAT return.

Overseas Ltd may be able to defer the payment of VAT on import under the duty deferment scheme and pay monthly on the 15th of the month following the month of importation.

(2) **Ruritania is in the EU**

The goods will be zero rated supplies in Ruritania and Overseas Ltd will be responsible for paying over the output VAT on the computers at the rate in force in the UK. This is essentially the same as if Ruritania were not in the EU, except that the VAT does not have to be paid over immediately at the date of importation.

The output VAT will be due on the date the invoice is issued which must be by the 15th of the month following that in which the goods are removed.

As before, Overseas Ltd will be able to reclaim the VAT as input VAT on their next VAT return which will therefore include the following:

Output tax	
On acquisition from Ruritania	£20,000
Input tax	
On acquisition from Ruritania	£20,000

Test your understanding 2

Foreign Ltd

(a) Foreign Ltd will charge VAT at the zero rate because it is an EU transaction, and the customer is VAT registered.

(b) The transaction is zero rated as an export outside the EU.

(c) The transaction must be charged in the UK at the standard rate as the customer is not VAT registered.

(d) VAT will be paid at the point of entry into the UK. Foreign Ltd will then recover the VAT through its VAT return.

chapter

22

Corporation tax: computations and administration

Chapter learning objectives

Upon completion of this chapter you will be able to:

- identify the accounting period rules and their significance for corporation tax
- prepare the corporation tax computation and liability for a UK resident company
- define related 51% group companies and recognise the effect for corporation tax
- state when corporation tax is due for non-large companies and define a large company and explain how they are required to pay corporation tax on a quarterly basis
- understand and explain the impact of taxation on the cash flows of a business
- explain the principles of company self-assessment including the time limits for notifying/filing returns and claims and the penalties for non compliance
- explain the penalties for late payment of corporation tax
- list the information and records that taxpayers need to retain for tax purposes together with the retention period.

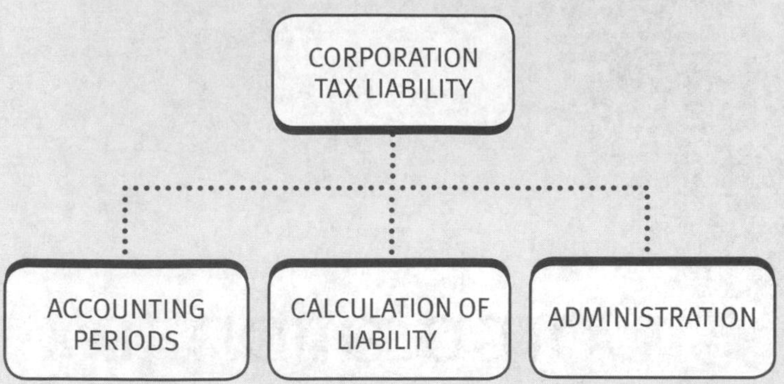

Introduction

This and the following two chapters deal with the way in which companies are subject to corporation tax.

This chapter sets out the basis of assessment and explains how a company's corporation tax liability is calculated. Much of this chapter is a revision of rules covered in F6.

1 Corporation tax computation

Basis of assessment

UK resident companies are assessed to corporation tax on their **taxable total profits** (TTP) arising in a **chargeable accounting period** (CAP).

TTP = income (excluding dividends received) **plus** net chargeable gains **less** qualifying charitable donations (QCDs).

Chargeable accounting period

- Chargeable accounting period (CAP) = the period for which a charge to corporation tax is made
  - usually = 12 months and is the same as the company's period of account
  - can be less than 12 months
  - cannot exceed 12 months.

Note that a company's period of account is the period for which the company prepares its financial statements. It is usually 12 months but can be shorter or longer than 12 months.

- If a company's period of account exceeds 12 months, it must be split into two corporation tax CAPs:
  - the first 12 months of the period of account
  - followed by the balance of the period of account = short CAP.
- A CAP **starts** when:
  - a company starts to trade, or
  - profits of a company first become liable to corporation tax, or
  - the previous CAP ends.
- A new company must notify HMRC of its establishment **within 3 months** of the start of its first CAP.
  There is a separate obligation to notify HMRC of chargeability to tax **within 12 months** from the end of its period of account.
- A CAP **ends** on the earliest of:
  - **12 months after it started**
  - the end of the period of account
  - when the company ceases to trade, to be UK resident or ceases to be liable to corporation tax
  - commences/ceases administration or winding up proceedings.

Example 1 – Chargeable accounting periods

AB Ltd was incorporated on 15 July 2016 and commenced to trade on 1 September 2016. The company chose 30 June as its accounting year end and prepared its first financial statements to 30 June 2017 and then for the twelve months to 30 June 2018.

State the dates of AB Ltd's first two CAPs.

Solution

First CAP:	1 September 2016 – 30 June 2017 (date of commencing trade until end of period of account).
Second CAP:	1 July 2017 – 30 June 2018 (immediately after the end of the previous CAP until the end of the period of account).

Note: A CAP does not start on the incorporation of the company.

Example 2 – Chargeable accounting periods

XY plc has been trading for many years, preparing its financial statements to 31 December each year. The board of directors decided to change the year end to 30 April.

State the chargeable accounting periods for XY plc if it prepared:

(a) **one set of financial statements covering the sixteen months to 30 April 2018, or**

(b) **two sets of financial statements covering the four months to 30 April 2017 and the twelve months to 30 April 2018.**

Solution

(a) If one set of financial statements is prepared covering sixteen months:

- it must be divided into:
  - a 12 month CAP to 31 December 2017, and
  - a 4 month CAP to 30 April 2018.

(b) If two sets of financial statements are prepared:

- the CAPs will be the same as the financial statements:
  - 4 months to 30 April 2017
  - 12 months to 30 April 2018

Example 3 – Chargeable accounting periods on cessation

ZW Ltd has been trading for many years with a 30 June year end. Due to recent financial difficulties, it was decided that the company should be wound up.

ZW Ltd ceased trading on 31 December 2015 and on 30 April 2016 the winding up commenced. The winding up was completed on 31 March 2017.

State the dates of ZW Ltd's chargeable accounting periods from 1 July 2015 onwards.

Solution

1.7.2015 – 31.12.2015	(immediately after the end of the previous CAP until cessation of trade)
1.1.2016 – 30.4.2016	(immediately after the end of the previous CAP until commencement of winding up proceedings)
1.5.2016 – 31.3.2017	(immediately after the end of the previous CAP until completion of winding up proceedings)

Note: the company's normal 30 June year end is ignored during the winding up process.

Pro forma corporation tax computation

Name of company
Corporation tax computation – for CAP ended:

	£
Trading profits	X
Interest income	X
Property business profits	X
Miscellaneous income	X
Net chargeable gains	X
Total profits	X
Less: Qualifying charitable donations (QCDs) (amount paid = gross amount)	(X)
Taxable total profits (TTP)	X
Corporation tax liability (TTP × 20%)	X
Less: Double taxation relief (DTR) (Chapter 28)	(X)
Corporation tax payable	X

Due date 9 months and one day after end of CAP (unless 'large company' which pays in instalments – section 4)

File date 12 months after end of period of account

Notes:

(1) Trading profits, interest income and property business profits includes income from overseas sources.

(2) All income is included in the computation **gross**.

(3) QCDs include **all** donations to charity by a company (except those allowed as a trading expense).

(4) The detailed rules for calculating TTP are in Chapter 23.

2 The corporation tax liability

A company's corporation tax liability is calculated by applying the appropriate rate of corporation tax to the company's taxable total profits.

Financial year

- The rate of corporation tax is fixed by reference to financial years.
- A financial year runs from 1 April to the following 31 March and is identified by the calendar year in which it begins.
- The year commencing 1 April 2016 and ending on 31 March 2017 is the financial year 2016 (FY2016).
- The rate of corporation tax applicable to FY2016 is 20%

Financial years should not be confused with tax years for personal taxes, which run from 6 April to the following 5 April.

- The rate of corporation tax is included in the tax rates and allowances provided to you in the examination.

Accounting periods straddling 31 March

When a company's CAP falls into two financial years, the corporation tax liability must be calculated for each financial year seperately if either of the following change:

- the corporation tax rate, or
- the rules governing the calculation of corporation tax.

However, in the P6 examination the rate of corporation tax will always be 20% and the rules governing the calculation of corporation tax have not changed. Therefore, it should be assumed that the FY2016 rules apply to all accounting periods.

3 Payment of tax

Due date

The payment date for corporation tax depends on the size of the company:

- For companies which are not 'large':
  - due date = **nine months and one day** after the end of the CAP.
- For 'large' companies:
  - the liability is settled through **quarterly instalment payments**, starting during the accounting period.

All companies must pay their corporation tax electronically.

Penalties for late payment are covered in section 5.

Definition of a large company

- A large company is one whose augmented profits for the accounting period in question are more than the profit threshold of £1.5 million.
- By definition, all other companies are not large and are therefore not required to pay corporation tax by instalments.

Augmented profits are calculated as follows:

	£
Taxable total profits (TTP)	X
Plus: Dividends received from non-group companies	X
Augmented profits	X

Dividends received

Although dividends received from UK and overseas companies are exempt from corporation tax, they can have an impact on whether a company is large and therefore whether corporation tax needs to be paid by instalments.

- The amount of cash dividends received are added to TTP in order to arrive at the augmented profits figure.

- Dividends received from an overseas company are included, but they may have been subject to tax in the overseas country. Any overseas tax suffered is ignored. Accordingly, only the actual cash received is included in this calculation (in the same way as UK dividends).
- Dividends received from related 51% group companies (see below) are also ignored in the calculation.

Remember that augmented profits determines the due date, but the corporation tax liability is **always** calculated on a company's **TTP** (not its augmented profits).

The £1.5 million threshold

- The £1.5 million threshold may need to be adjusted as follows:

– Short CAP:	time apportion
– Related 51% group companies (see below)	divide by the total number of group companies.

The threshold of £1.5 million is included within the tax rates and allowances provided to you in the examination.

Test your understanding 1

Beech Ltd has the following results for the 9 m/e 31 March 2017.

TTP	£330,000
Dividends received from UK companies	£20,000

Calculate the CT liability and state when it will be payable.

Related 51% group companies

Two companies are related 51% group companies if:

- One is a 51% subsidiary of the other, or
- Both are 51% subsidiaries of a third company.

A 51% subsidiary is one where more than 50% of the ordinary share capital is directly or indirectly owned.

Examples of each situation:

- One company is a 51% subsidiary of the other(s)

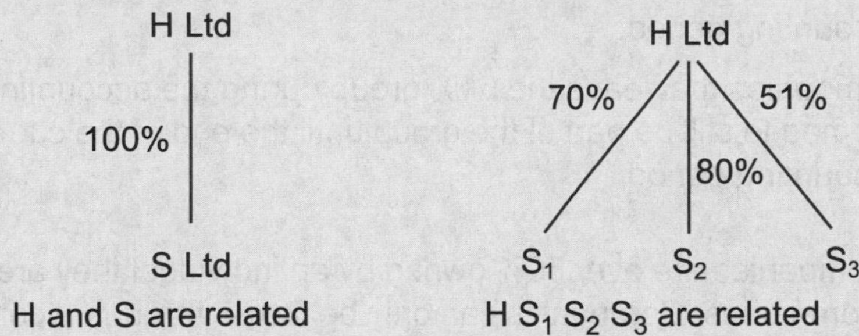

- Both are 51% subsidiaries of a third company.

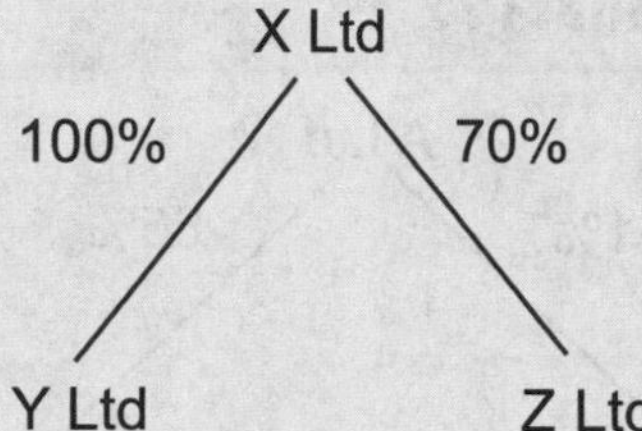

X Ltd, Y Ltd and Z Ltd are related.

Note that where shares are owned indirectly, the effective interest must be more than 50%:

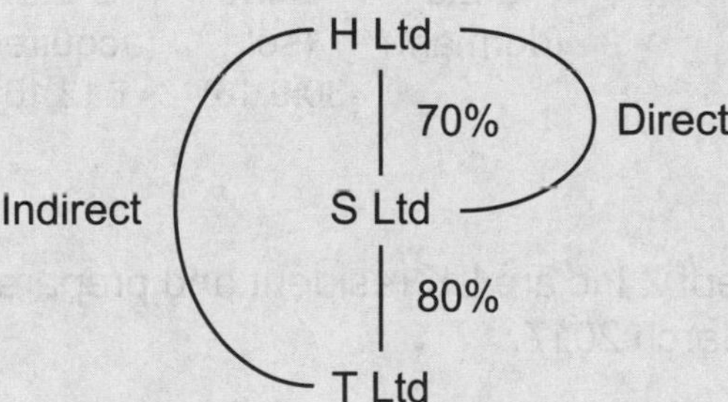

H Ltd has an effective interest in T Ltd of 56% (70% × 80%), therefore both S Ltd and T Ltd are 51% subsidiaries of H Ltd.

The definition of related 51% group companies (often abbreviated to 51% group comapnies) specifically **includes:**

- overseas resident companies

but **excludes:**

- dormant companies, and
- non-trading holding companies.

The number of 51% companies in a group for a CAP is determined at the end of the previous CAP. Therefore:

- Companies that join the 51% group during the accounting period are deemed to be part of the group from the beginning of the following accounting period.
- Companies that leave the 51% group during the accounting period are deemed to still be part of the group until the end of the current accounting period.

If two companies are over 50% owned by an individual they are not 51% group companies. Companies can only be linked through a corporate parent company.

Test your understanding 2

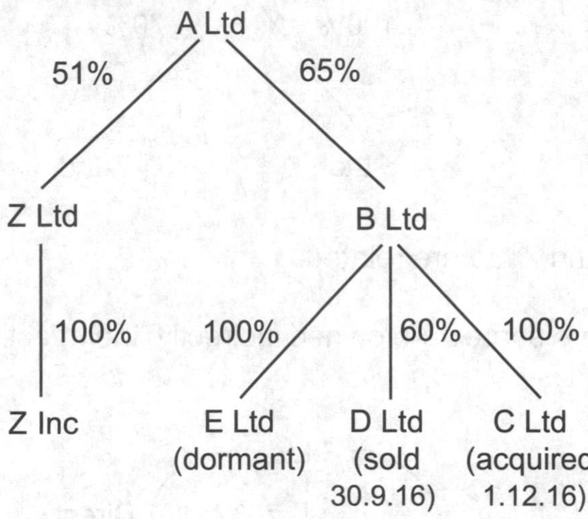

All companies except Z Inc are UK resident and prepare financial statements to 31 March 2017.

State which companies are 51% group companies of A Ltd and calculate the profit threshold that will apply in determining whether A Ltd will be required to pay corporation tax by instalments for the year ended 31 March 2017.

The consequences of 51% group companies

The consequences of having 51% group companies are:

- The £1.5m threshold used to determine whether the company is 'large' for the purposes of paying corporation tax quarterly instalments is **divided by the total number of 51% group companies.**
- **Dividends received** from 51% subsidiaries (UK and overseas) are **excluded from** the calculation of augmented profits for the purposes of deciding if corporation tax should be paid via quarterly instalments.

Quarterly instalments

Instalments paid by a 'large' company are based on the expected corporation tax liability for the **current** accounting period. It is therefore necessary for companies to produce an accurate forecast of their current period tax liability.

Companies will normally be able to obtain a refund if they subsequently find that instalments have been overpaid.

For a twelve month accounting period, four quarterly instalments are due:

- by on the **14th day**
- in months **7, 10, 13 and 16** following the **start** of the accounting period.

Exception to instalments

Large companies which do not have to pay by instalments are as follows:

- companies whose liability for the year is below **£10,000** (or a pro rata amount if the CAP is less than 12 months long)
- companies that have become large during the CAP provided:
  - (i) they were not large for the previous CAP, and
  - (ii) their augmented profits for the CAP do not exceed **£10 million** (reduced accordingly if there are related 51% group companies or a short CAP).

Test your understanding 3

Q plc is a single company with no 51% group companies.

On 1 February 2017 Q plc estimates that its taxable total profits will be £2,400,000 for the year ended 31 October 2017. Its taxable total profits for the year ended 31 October 2016 were £1,700,000 and for the year ended 31 October 2015 £1,200,000.

Q plc does not receive any dividends.

(a) **Calculate Q plc's corporation tax liabilities for the years ended 31 October 2016 and 31 October 2017 and explain how they will be paid. Assume you are writing in June 2017 and that the FY2016 rates apply throughout.**

(b) **In July 2017 the company revises its forecast taxable total profit figure to £2,640,000. State the difference, if any, this will make to their corporation tax payments.**

Special rules apply if the accounting period is less than 12 months.

Short accounting periods

Where the accounting period is less than 12 months:

- First instalment due by:
  14th day of 7th month after the start of the CAP (as normal)
- Subsequent instalments are due at 3 monthly intervals thereafter, until the date of the last instalment (see below) is reached.
- Last instalment due by:
  14th day of 4th month after the end of the accounting period.
- For an accounting period of 3 months or less applying the above instalment rules would result in the date of the first instalment being later than the last instalment. Therefore, in this situation the full tax due for the accounting period is due on the date of the last instalment, i.e 14th day of 4th month after the end of the accounting period.
- The amount of each instalment:
  = (estimated CT liability for CAP) × (n/length of CAP)

  Where n = 3 months for a full quarterly instalment
  But n = 2 or 1 for the last instalment if the period since the previous instalment is less than 3 months

Example 4 – Quarterly instalment payments for large companies

ABC plc prepared accounts for the 8 months ended 31 December 2016 and estimates its corporation liability will be £800,000.

Show when ABC plc's corporation tax liability will be due.

Answer to example 4

ABC plc's corporation tax liability is due by instalments:
£300,000 on 14 November 2016
£300,000 on 14 February 2017
£200,000 on 14 April 2017

Interest

Late payment interest:

- runs from: the normal due date on any tax paid late
- to: the date of payment, and

This interest is deducted from interest income in the corporation tax computation.

Any repayment of tax made by HMRC will attract interest:

- from the later of:
  - the day after the original due date, or
  - the actual date of payment
- to: the date of repayment.

This interest is taxable and is included in interest income in the corporation tax computation.

The interest rates will be provided in the tax rates and allowances provided in the examination.

Group payment arrangements

Group payment arrangements are **available** for **51% group companies** where at least one group company pays corporation tax by quarterly instalments.

The effect is as follows:

- **One group company pays** quarterly instalments of corporation tax on behalf of the group.
- This can **save interest**, as overpayments are effectively netted off against underpayments.

  Without a group payment arrangement, the interest charged on underpayments is likely to be more than the interest received on overpayments.

However, each company must still prepare a separate corporation tax computation at the end of the CAP.

Impact of taxation on the cash flows of a business

Companies need to take account of their tax payments when considering their cash flow forecasts for the year.

This will be a particular problem when the company changes to quarterly instalments for the first time.

4 Self-assessment for companies

Introduction

As for individuals, self-assessment applies for corporate taxpayers. Responsibility rests with the company to:

- calculate their own corporation tax liability for each CAP
- submit a self-assessment corporation tax return **within 12 months** after the end of the period of account
- pay any corporation tax due **within nine months and one day** after the end of the CAP or under the quarterly instalment system.

Given the timing of the due date for payment of tax, many companies will aim to complete the self-assessment tax return prior to the normal nine month deadline for paying the corporation tax to enable them to pay an accurate amount of tax and avoid interest charges on underpaid tax.

Notification of chargeability

A company coming within the scope of corporation tax for the first time must notify HMRC when its first accounting period begins, **within three months** of the start of its first accounting period.

Companies that do not receive a notice to file a corporation tax return are required to notify HMRC if they have income or chargeable gains on which tax is due.

The time limit for notifying HMRC of chargeability is **12 months** from the end of the accounting period in which the liability arises.

A standard penalty may be imposed for failure to notify HMRC of chargeability (see section 5).

The self-assessment tax return

The self-assessment tax return (Form CT600) must be submitted by the later of:

- **12 months** after the end of the accounting period; or
- **three months** after the issue of the notice to file a return.

The return must:

- contain all the information required to calculate the company's taxable total profits
- include a self-assessment of the amount of corporation tax payable for that accounting period
- be submitted online.

A company has to submit a copy of its financial accounts together with the self-assessment tax return.

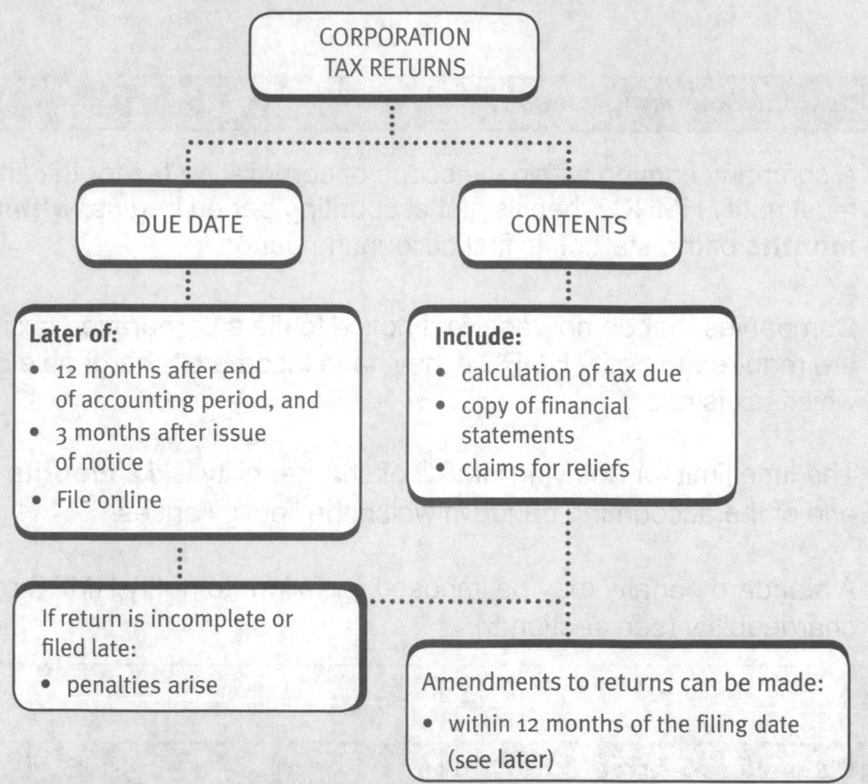

CORPORATION TAX RETURNS
DUE DATE
CONTENTS
Later of:
• 12 months after end of accounting period, and
• 3 months after issue of notice
• File online
Include:
• calculation of tax due
• copy of financial statements
• claims for reliefs
If return is incomplete or filed late:
• penalties arise
Amendments to returns can be made:
• within 12 months of the filing date (see later)

Determination assessments

To prevent companies deliberately delaying the submission of a return, HMRC have the following actions available if a return is not filed by the relevant due date:

- HMRC may determine the amount of corporation tax due by issuing a determination assessment.
- The determination assessment is treated as a self-assessment by the company, and will be replaced by the actual self-assessment when it is submitted by the company.
- There is no right of appeal against a determination assessment. Instead, the company must displace it with the actual self-assessment return.
- A determination assessment can be raised by HMRC at any time **within three years** of the filing date (i.e. four years from the end of the period of account).

Records

Companies are required to keep and preserve records necessary to make a correct and complete return.

The records that must be kept include records of:

- all receipts and expenses
- all goods purchased and sold
- all supporting documents relating to the transactions of the business, such as accounts, books, contracts and receipts.

The records must be retained until the later of:

- **six years** after the end of the accounting period to which they relate
- the date on which a compliance check into the return is completed
- the date on which it becomes impossible for a compliance check to be started.

A penalty may be charged for failure to keep or retain adequate records.

The maximum penalty is only likely to be imposed in the most serious cases, such as where a company deliberately destroys its records in order to obstruct a HMRC compliance check.

See section 5 for the detail of penalties that can be imposed.

Personal liability of senior accounting officers of large companies and groups

- A designated senior accounting officer (SAO) will have to:
  - ensure that the company's accounting systems will be adequate for the purposes of accurate tax reporting
  - certify annually that the accounting systems are adequate, or
  - specify the inadequacies and confirm that the auditors have been informed.
- These rules apply to a company, or a group of companies, with:
  - turnover of more than £200 million, and/or
  - a statement of financial position total of more than £2 billion.
- Penalties (personal and corporate) can be levied for careless or deliberate failure of these obligations.

Amendments and errors

Amendments to the return

- HMRC may correct any obvious errors or mistakes **within nine months** of the date that the return is filed. For example, they will correct arithmetical errors or errors of principle. This type of correction does not mean that HMRC has accepted the return as accurate.
- A company can amend the return **within 12 months** of the filing date. For a CAP ending on 31 March 2017, the filing date is 31 March 2018, and the company has until 31 March 2019 to make any amendments.
- If an error is discovered at a later date, then the company can make a claim for overpayment relief to recover any overpayments of corporation tax.

Claim for overpayment relief

- Where an assessment is excessive due to an error or mistake in a return, the company can claim relief.
- A claim can be made in respect of errors made, and mistakes arising from not understanding the law.
- The claim must be made **within four years** of the accounting period to which it relates.

Compliance checks into returns

HMRC have the right to check the completeness and accuracy of any self-assessment tax return and issue discovery assessments under their compliance check powers. The procedures and rules are similar to those for individuals.

The compliance check may be made as a result of any of the following:

- suspicion that income is undeclared
- suspicion that deductions are being incorrectly claimed
- other information in HMRC's possession
- being part of a random selection process.

Additional points:

- HMRC do not have to state a reason for the compliance check and are unlikely to do so.
- HMRC must give **written notice** before commencing an compliance check by the following dates:

If return filed:	Notice must be issued within 12 months of:
On time	the actual delivery of the tax return to HMRC
Late	the 31 January, 30 April, 31 July or 31 October next following the actual date of delivery of the tax return to HMRC

- Once this deadline is passed, the company can normally consider the self-assessment for that accounting period as final.

Compliance check procedure

HMRC can demand that the company produce any or all of the following:

- documents
- accounts
- other written particulars
- full answers to specific questions.

The information requested should be limited to that connected with the return.

- The company has 30 days to comply with the request. An appeal can be made against the request.
- The compliance check ends when HMRC give written notice that it has been completed.
- The notice will state the outcome of the compliance check and any HMRC amendments to the self assessment.
- A company has 30 days to appeal, in writing, against HMRC's amendment.
- Refer to Chapter 16 for more details about appeal procedures.

Discovery assessments

HMRC has the capacity to raise additional assessments, referred to as discovery assessments. The key points are:

- Although compliance checks must normally begin **within 12 months** of the actual submission date, a discovery assessment can be raised at a later date to prevent the loss of corporation tax.
- The use of a discovery assessment is restricted where a self-assessment return has already been made. Unless the loss of corporation tax was brought about carelessly or deliberately by the company, a discovery assessment cannot be raised where full disclosure was made in the return, even if this is found to be incorrect.
- HMRC will only accept that full disclosure has been made if any contentious items have been clearly brought to their attention – perhaps in a covering letter.
- Therefore, only a company that makes full disclosure in the self-assessment tax return, has absolute finality 12 months after the actual submission date.
- The time limit for making a discovery assessment is:

	Time from the end of the CAP
Basic time limit	four years
Careless error	six years
Deliberate error	twenty years

- A company may appeal against a discovery assessment.

5 Penalties

In addition to interest on the late payment of tax, HMRC can impose penalties.

Standard penalty

HMRC has standardised penalties across the taxes for the submission of incorrect returns and failure to notify liability to tax.

The rules are explained in Chapter 16, section 8.

The penalty is calculated as a percentage of 'potential lost revenue' which is generally the tax unpaid. The percentage charged can be reduced where the taxpayer makes a disclosure and co-operates with HMRC to establish the amount of tax unpaid.

Other penalties

Offence	Penalty
Late filing of corporation tax return:	
• within 3 months of filing date	• Fixed penalty = £100 (Note)
• more than 3 months after filing date	• Fixed penalty increased to £200 (Note)
Additional penalties:	
• 6 – 12 months after filing date	• Additional 10% of tax outstanding 6 months after filing date
• More than 12 months after filing date	• Additional penalty increased to 20%
	Note: Fixed penalties rise to £500 and £1,000 if persistently filed late (i.e. return for 2 preceding periods also late)
Failure to keep required records	Up to £3,000 per accounting period

6 Chapter summary

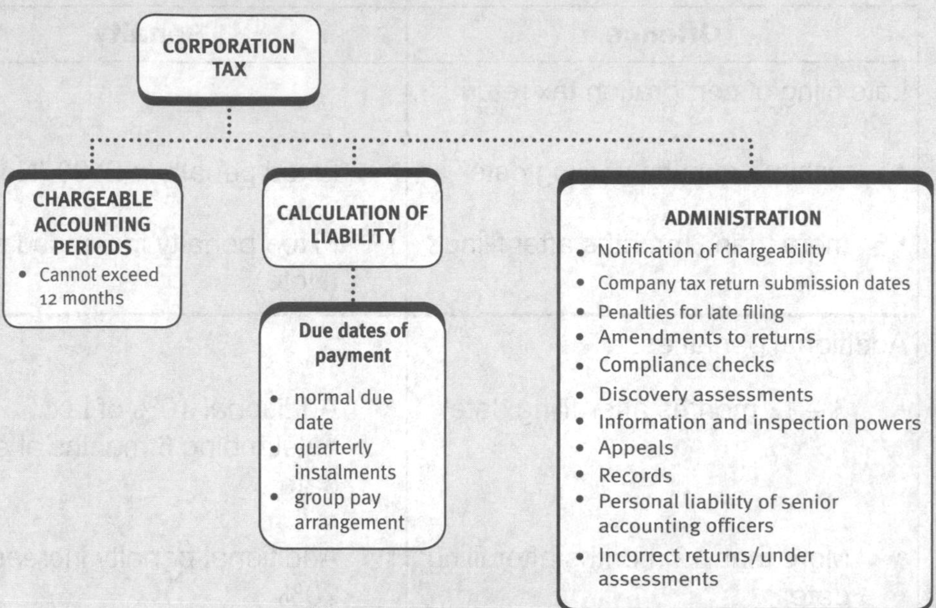
CORPORATION TAX
CHARGEABLE ACCOUNTING PERIODS
• Cannot exceed 12 months
CALCULATION OF LIABILITY
Due dates of payment
• normal due date
• quarterly instalments
• group pay arrangement
ADMINISTRATION
• Notification of chargeability
• Company tax return submission dates
• Penalties for late filing
• Amendments to returns
• Compliance checks
• Discovery assessments
• Information and inspection powers
• Appeals
• Records
• Personal liability of senior accounting officers
• Incorrect returns/under assessments

Test your understanding answers

Test your understanding 1

Beech Ltd

	£
TTP	330,000
Plus: Dividends received from non-group companies	20,000
Augmented profits	350,000

Corporation tax payment threshold must be scaled down as the CAP is only 9 months long.

Threshold (£1,500,000 × 9/12)	£1,125,000

Augmented profits fall below the threshold and therefore Beech Ltd is not large

Corporation tax on TTP (£330,000 × 20%)	£66,000
Due date	1.1.2018

Test your understanding 2

A Ltd

A Ltd has three 51% group companies: Z Ltd, Z Inc and B Ltd.

Z Inc is a 51% group company even though it is incorporated overseas.

D Ltd is not a 51% subsidiary of A Ltd as A Ltd only owns 39% (65% × 60%) of D Ltd. Note that D Ltd is a 51% subsidiary of B Ltd, but that is not relevant for this question.

C Ltd is deemed not to be a 51% group member for the year ended 31 March 2017 as it was purchased during the year. It will be included from 1 April 2017.

E Ltd is excluded from being a 51% group company as it is dormant throughout the accounting period.

As A Ltd has three 51% group companies, the profit threshold must be divided by four companies:

Threshold = (£1,500,000 ÷ 4) = £375,000

This means that if A Ltd's augmented profits exceed £375,000, it will be required to pay its corporation tax liability by quarterly instalment.

Test your understanding 3

Q plc

(a) **Corporation tax liabilities**

The company will be liable to corporation tax as follows:

Y/e 31 October 2016 (£1,700,000 × 20%)	£340,000
Y/e 31 October 2017 (£2,400,000 × 20%)	£480,000

Payment dates

Y/e 31 October 2016

As Q plc's augmented profit (TTP = augmented profit as no dividends received) for the y/e 31 October 2015 was less than the profits threshold of £1.5 million, the company was not large for corporation tax purposes in this CAP.

Q plc's augmented profit of £1.7 million for the y/e 31 October 2016 exceeds the profits threshold of £1,5 million, but quarterly instalment payments will not be due as the company was not large in the previous CAP (y/e 31 October 2015) and its augmented profit does not exceed £10 million.

Accordingly, the liability of £340,000 for the y/e 31 October 2016 will be due on 1 August 2017 (9 months and 1 day after the end of the CAP).

Y/e 31 October 2017

For the y/e 31 October 2017, as the company was large in the previous CAP, they will have to pay the £480,000 liability in quarterly instalments as follows:

Due date	£
14 May 2017	120,000
14 August 2017	120,000
14 November 2017	120,000
14 February 2018	120,000
	480,000

Note that interest will be charged from the due date until the date of payment for any instalments paid late (see section on interest later in chapter). This interest is an allowable deduction from interest income.

(b) **If Q plc revises its forecast**

If the profit forecast is revised upwards the company will have to revise its forecast tax payments.

The corporation tax liability will increase to £528,000 ((£2,640,000 × 20%).

Quarterly payments should therefore be £132,000 (£528,000 × 1/4).

Therefore an extra £12,000 (£132,000 – £120,000) will be due for each instalment.

As the instalment for May has already been paid, the additional £12,000 will attract interest from 14 May 2017 until it is paid (see section on interest later in chapter).

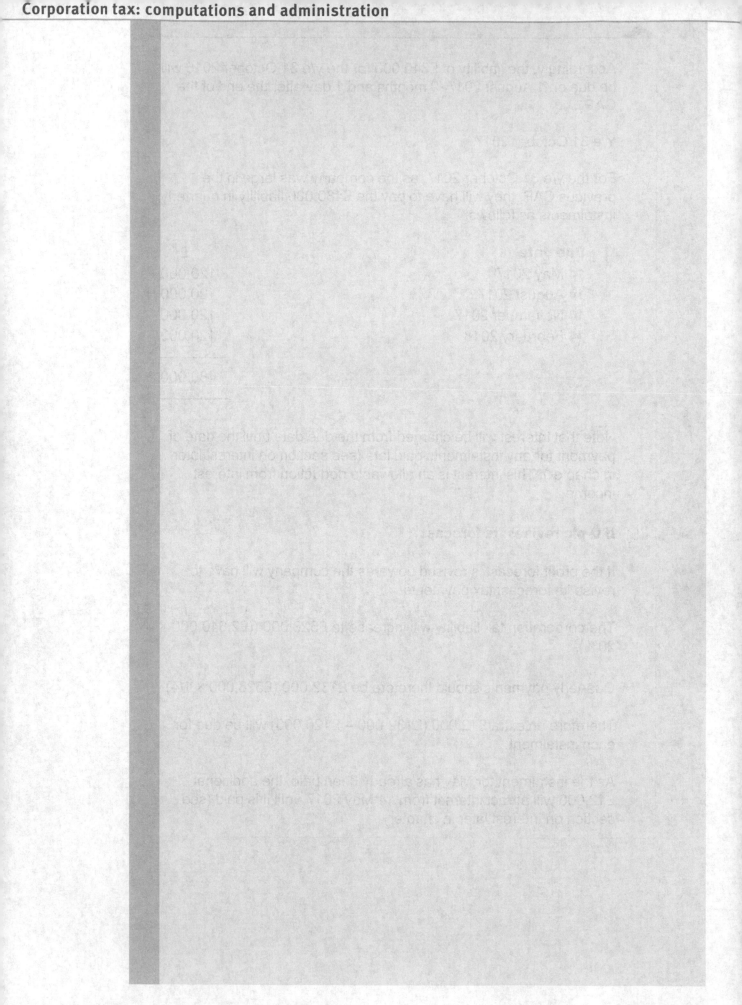

chapter

23

Calculation of corporation tax: income and gains

Chapter learning objectives

Upon completion of this chapter you will be able to:

- prepare a comprehensive computation of taxable total profits for a company
- distinguish the key differences in computing gains for a company
- explain the conditions required for the sale of shares by a company to be treated as an exempt transaction for capital gains
- identify qualifying research and development expenditure and determine the amount of relief by reference to the size of the individual company/group
- recognise the tax treatment of intangible assets and determine the appropriate treatment for a given company
- understand the purpose of transfer pricing rules and identify the companies/transactions where they will impact
- understand the issue of thin capitalisation and advise on the impact where a company is affected
- prepare a corporation tax computation for a company with investment business.

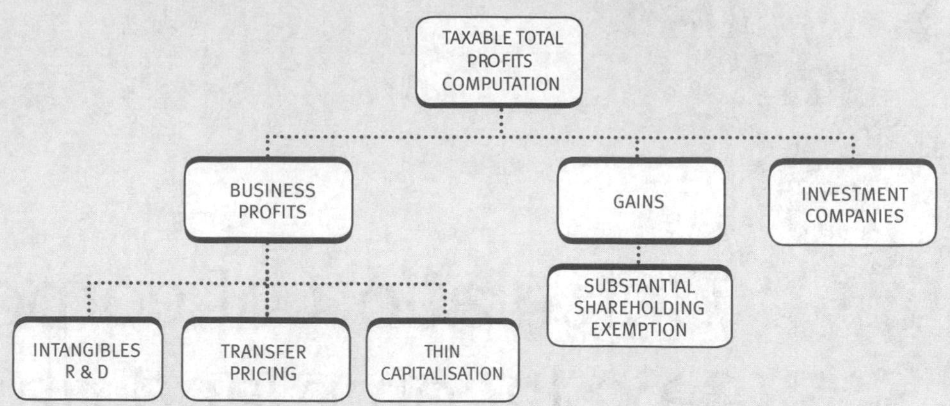

Introduction

This chapter revises the rules for computing a company's TTP and introduces the new topic areas at P6 shown in the diagram above.

A brief reminder of F6 content is given in expandable text and revision examples are provided to check your retention of the required F6 knowledge.

1 Computation of taxable total profit

Pro forma computation

Name of company
Corporation tax computation – for CAP ended:

	£
*Trading profits	X
*Interest income (non-trading loan relationships)	X
*Property income	X
Miscellaneous income	X
Net chargeable gains (chargeable gains less allowable losses)	X
Total profits	X
Less: Qualifying charitable donations (QCDs) (amount paid = gross amount)	(X)
Taxable total profits (TTP)	X

* Including overseas income (gross of overseas tax suffered)

Trading profits

As for a sole trader, the net profit per the accounts must be adjusted for tax purposes and capital allowances deducted.

The main adjustments are summarised in Chapter 17.

The key differences that apply to adjusting a company's profits are:

- There are no private use adjustments (including the capital allowances computation).
- Any interest receivable or payable for trading reasons is included in trading profit.
- If the interest is receivable or payable for a non-trading purpose then it is included in interest income (see below).
- Dividends payable are not an allowable trading expense.
- Enhanced deductions are available for research and development expenditure if conditions are satisfied (section 3).
- Adjustments may be required in respect of intangible assets (section 4), transfer pricing (section 5) and thin capitalisation (section 5)

Capital allowances

Capital allowances apply to companies in the same way as unincorporated businesses with the following additional points to note:

Annual investment allowance

- The maximum AIA for a 12 month accounting period is £200,000 (the same as for an unincorporated business (e.g. sole trader or partnership)).

The AIA amount of £200,000 is included in the tax rates and allowances provided to you in the examination.

- The AIA must be **split between 'related companies'**.

  A **group of companies** (i.e. parent company and subsidiaries) are 'related' for this purpose and the group is only entitled to **one AIA**.

  The group can choose how to allocate a **single AIA** between the group companies.

Note that:

– A 'group' for this purpose is defined by the Companies Act and essentially applies where a parent company holds a simple majority shareholding (> 50%) in another company or companies at the end of the accounting period.

– Therefore in an examination question related to capital allowances for a company within a group, the allocation of the AIA between the group members will need to be considered.

When allocating the AIA:

– the group members can allocate the maximum £200,000 AIA in any way across the group

– the AIA does not have to be divided equally between them

– all of the allowance can be given to one company, or any amount can be given to any number of companies within the group.

Companies owned by the **same individual** will also be regarded as 'related' for this purpose where they are:

– engaged in the **same activities**, or

– share the **same premises**.

For example, this could be the case if an individual runs two companies from home.

In such circumstances, the AIA will be split between the two companies and the owner of the companies can choose how to allocate a **single AIA** between them.

- **Unrelated companies** owned by the same individual will each be entitled to the **full AIA**.

Special rate pool

- The 8% special rate of writing down allowances in respect of plant and machinery that is integral to a building applies to both **initial and replacement** expenditure.

- Qualifying replacement expenditure is expenditure which is more than 50% of the replacement cost of the integral feature at the time the expenditure is incurred.
- It also includes situations where less than 50% is spent initially but further spending in the next twelve months takes the total over 50%.
- This rule prevents businesses gradually replacing integral features and claiming the cost as a repair.

Energy saving plant and machinery

- Expenditure on energy saving or environmentally beneficial plant and machinery qualifies for a 100% first year allowance.
- Where a company has made a loss, it may surrender that part of the loss that relates to such allowances in exchange for a payment from HMRC equal to 19% of the loss surrendered.

  This is similar to research and development expenditure loss credits (section 3).

  Such a claim can only be made where the company is unable to use the losses in the current CAP against its own profits or via group relief. The claim is made in the company's corporation tax return.

  The maximum payment that a company can claim is the higher of:

  - £250,000, and
  - its total PAYE and NIC liabilities for the relevant accounting period.

  Where any of the qualifying plant and machinery is sold within four years of the end of the relevant accounting period:

  - there will be a claw-back of an appropriate part of the payment made, and
  - a reinstatement of the loss.

Interest income – loan relationship rules

All income and expenses related to the borrowing and lending of money are dealt with under the loan relationship rules.

Expenses related to borrowing money

- interest paid on overdrafts, bank loans, corporate loan notes
- other costs such as arrangement fees, and other incidental costs incurred in raising loan finance
- write-off of impaired debt arising from lending money
- loss on disposal of corporate loan notes

Income received from lending money

- interest income (including interest from bank deposits, loans, government stocks and corporate loan notes)

Trade vs. non-trade purposes

In order to apply the loan relationship rules correctly, all income and expenses relating to borrowing and lending must be identified as either 'trading' or 'non-trading'.

	Income (e.g. interest receivable)	**Expenses (e.g. interest payable)**
Trade purpose	N/A (note 1)	• interest payable/expenses related to: – a loan taken out to purchase plant and machinery for the trade – a loan or overdraft to fund daily operations (i.e. working capital) – loan notes to fund trading operations • write-off of a trade related loan

Non-trade purpose	• interest receivable on bank accounts • interest receivable on investments such as gilts and loan notes • interest receivable from HMRC (note 2) • profit on disposal of corporate loan notes	• interest payable/expenses related to: – a loan to purchase a commercially-let property (where the rent would be taxable as property business income) – a loan to acquire shares of another company • interest payable to HMRC (note 2) • write off of a non-trade loan • loss on disposal of corporate loan notes

Notes:

(1) Generally, all interest received by a company is non-trade interest, unless it is a company's trade to lend money (e.g. a bank, which is not likely to be the case in the examination).

(2) Interest received from HMRC by a company is taxable as interest income. Interest paid to HMRC by a company is an allowable deduction from interest income.

Note that for individuals (e.g. sole traders), interest received from HMRC is exempt income and interest paid to HMRC is not deductible for income tax purposes.

Tax treatment – trade purpose

Amounts that are for trade purposes will be included as part of trading profits in the calculation of TTP.

If such amounts are already included in the accounting profit, no adjustment to profits is required for tax purposes.

Tax treatment – non-trade purpose

Amounts that are for non-trade purposes will be included under the 'Interest income (non-trade loan relationships)' heading in the calculation of TTP.

If these amounts are included in the accounting profit, they must be added back/deducted in the adjustment of profits computation and then shown separately under the 'Interest income (non-trade loan relationships)' heading.

Interest received and receivable is usually credited in the company accounts on the accruals basis. As interest receivable by companies is taxed on the accruals basis, the figure included in the accounts is the figure that should be taxed as interest income.

Generally, companies receive interest **gross** and the amount credited in the accounts is stated gross.

Most interest paid by companies is paid gross and interest paid and payable is usually debited in the company accounts on the accruals basis. As interest payable is taxed on the accruals basis, the figure included in the accounts is the figure that should be deducted in the calculation of interest income.

The **exception** to this rule is interest paid **to an individual** on **unquoted loan notes**, where a company is required to deduct 20% income tax from any interest paid to an individual. The company must account to HMRC for the income tax they deduct at source on behalf of the individual on a quarterly basis.

However, note that in the accounts of the company, the interest paid and payable charged against profit in the accounts will be the gross amount whether or not it is paid to another company or an individual.

If the non-trade expenses are more than the non-trade income, the excess is a deficit eligible for loss relief (Chapter 24).

Overseas income

- Any income from overseas (such as interest or rents) must be included in TTP under the appropriate heading.

  Dividends from overseas should be excluded as all dividends received by a company are exempt from corporation tax for the purposes of the P6 examination.
- Profits from overseas branches are included in trading profits unless the exemption election is made (Chapter 28).
- Overseas tax deducted must be added back to include the gross income in taxable total profits.
- Double tax relief may be available (Chapter 28).

Property income

Property income is calculated in the same way as for individuals (Chapter 3) except:

- a company is assessed on income in the accounting period, not the tax year

- interest on a loan to buy let property is treated as a deduction from interest income under the loan relationship rules, not property income
- losses can be relieved against other profits, not just property income (Chapter 24)
- Companies cannot have rent-a-room relief nor furnished holiday accommodation.

Note that the replacement furniture relief is unlikely to be applicable in a corporate question in an examination. This is because the relief only applies to furnished residential properties and companies in the examination usually rent commercial properties (e.g. warehouses, offices and factories).

Miscellaneous income

Miscellaneous income is uncommon. The most likely items are as follows:

- Patent royalties received/paid for a non-trading purpose (e.g. held as investments).

  If for a trade purpose then the amounts are included in trade profits and may be subject to a lower rate of tax if the company has elected to apply the patent box rules (section 4).

  In both cases the amounts are included on the accruals basis.

- Profits on the sale of goodwill and other intangible assets are included in miscellaneous income if (unusually) the asset is not held for trading purposes (section 4).

Chargeable gains

Chargeable gains are calculated in the same way as for individuals, with the following key differences:

- indexation allowance
- rollover relief
- capital losses
- annual exempt amount
- shares and secutities.

These important differences are covered in more detail in section 2.

Qualifying charitable donations (QCDs)

- All donations to charity by companies are allowable:
  - if a small local donation, as a trading expense
  - all other donations, as an allowable deduction from total profits.
- All charitable donations made by companies are **paid gross**.
- The amount **paid** in the accounting period is therefore allowable.
- If the QCDs paid exceed the total profits of the company:
  - no relief for the excess is given (i.e. it cannot be carried forward or carried back)
  - unless the company is part of a 75% group, in which case, group relief may be available (see Chapter 27).

Long period of account

A company requires permission from the Registrar of Companies if it wishes to extend its period of account beyond twelve months.

The accounting period cannot be more than 18 months long (unless the company is in administration).

- A chargeable accounting period (CAP) can never exceed 12 months.
- Therefore, if a company prepares accounts for a period which exceeds 12 months, the period must be split into two CAPs:
  - one for the first 12 months, the other for the balance of the time.

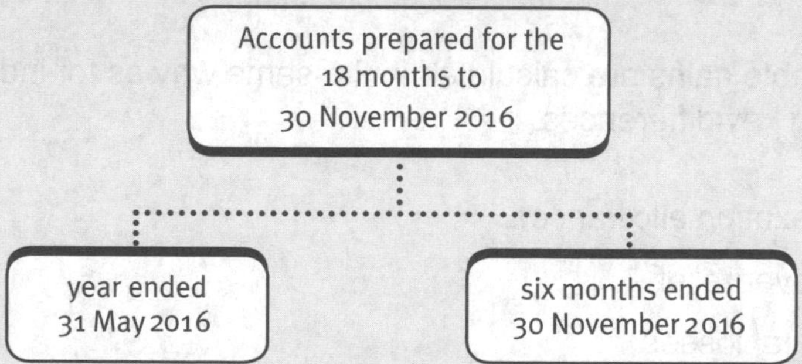

- Profits are split between the chargeable accounting periods as follows:

Income	Method of allocation
Tax adjusted trading profit before capital allowances	Adjust profit for the long period of account in the normal way then time apportion
Capital allowances	Separate computations for each CAP (In the short CAP, the WDA and AIA is reduced accordingly)
Interest and property income	Calculate accrued amount for each period separately (Note)
Chargeable gains	According to date of disposal
Qualifying charitable donations (QCDs)	According to date paid

Note: If information to apply the strict basis is not available: time apportion.

- Two separate corporation tax computations are then prepared, with two separate payment dates.

2 Chargeable gains for companies

Chargeable gains are calculated in the same way as for individuals, with the following key differences:

Indexation allowance

- An indexation allowance (IA) is available to companies.

  The IA gives a company some allowance for the effects of inflation in calculating a chargeable gain.

  The aim is to ensure that the capital gains subject to tax represent the true increase in capital value of the asset in real terms and to eliminate the effects of inflation.

- The rules for the IA are as follows:
  - the IA is based on the cost of the asset and the movement in the retail price index (RPI)
  - it is available:
    - from the month of purchase
    - to the month of disposal

- the IA is calculated separately for each item of expenditure (e.g. calculate a different IA for the original acquisition cost and any subsequent enhancement expenditure because they have different purchase dates).
- the IA cannot create or increase a capital loss.

- The IA is calculated as follows:

  IA = (indexation factor × allowable cost)

- The indexation factor is calculated as follows:

$$\frac{\text{RPI @ date of disposal} - \text{RPI @ date of expenditure}}{\text{RPI @ date of expenditure}}$$

  The indexation factor must be rounded to three decimal places.

  If the RPI falls between acquisition and disposal, the IA is £Nil.

- The relevant RPIs will be given in the question.

Rollover relief

- Rollover relief (including reinvestment in depreciating assets) is the only capital gains relief available for companies (see Chapter 9).
  - For companies, goodwill is not a qualifying asset for rollover relief purposes.

Test your understanding 1

Stella Limited has a 31 December year end. On 12 September 2016 Stella Ltd sold an office building for £3,500,000. The company had acquired the building on 3 June 1996 for £700,000 and an extension was built on 13 October 2002, costing £200,000.

The company reinvested £1,400,000 of the sale proceeds on 14 December 2016, purchasing a smaller office building for the purposes of its trade.

Assume the relevant RPIs are as follows:

June 1996	153.0
October 2002	177.9
September 2016	263.5

Calculate the chargeable gain to include in Stella Ltd's corporation tax computation for year ended 31 December 2016.

Capital losses

- All capital losses must be netted off against chargeable gains arising in the same CAP.
  - any net gain is chargeable as part of TTP
  - net capital losses are carried forward against the first available future net gains.
  - capital losses cannot be offset against other types of income, nor can they be carried back and set off against income or gains of a prior CAP.
- The following steps should be carried out to compute the chargeable gains to be included in a company's corporation tax computation:
  (1) Calculate the chargeable gains/capital loss arising on the disposal of each chargeable asset separately
  (2) Calculate the total net chargeable gains arising in the accounting period = (chargeable gains less capital losses)
  (3) Deduct capital losses brought forward = total net chargeable gains
  (4) Include in TTP computation.

Annual exempt amount

- Note that there is **no AEA** available to companies, the total net chargeable gain is simply included in the company's TTP computation.

Shares and securities

- The matching rules for the disposal of shares is different for companies. Disposals should be matched as follows:
  (1) Acquisitions on the **same day** as the disposal
  (2) Acquisitions during the **nine days before** the disposal (**FIFO basis**)
  (3) Acquisitions in the share pool.
- The share pool for companies is different as follows:
  - the pool contains shares in the same company, of the same class, purchased up to 9 days before the date of disposal.
  - the pool keeps a record of the:
    - number of shares acquired and sold
    - cost of the shares, and
    - indexed cost of the shares (i.e. cost plus IA).

- When shares are disposed of out of the share pool, the appropriate proportion of the cost and indexed cost which relates to the shares disposed of is calculated on an average cost basis.

- The calculation of cost and indexed cost in the share pool is not examinable.

Example 1 – Shares

ST Ltd sold 5,000 shares in JM Ltd for £50,000 on 12 January 2017. They had been acquired as follows:

Share pool	3,900 shares costing	£6,638
4 January 2017	2,000 shares costing	£4,500

The indexed cost of the share pool at 12 January 2017 is £9,345.

Calculate the chargeable gain to include in the corporation tax computation.

Solution

	Shares
(1) Same day acquisitions	0
(2) Previous 9 days: 4 Jan 2017	2,000
(3) Share pool	3,000
	5,000

Gain on shares acquired in last 9 days:	£
Proceeds (2,000/5,000 × £50,000)	20,000
Less: Cost	(4,500)
Chargeable gain	15,500

Gain on shares in share pool:	£
Proceeds (3,000/5,000 × £50,000)	30,000
Less: Cost	(5,106)
Less: Indexation allowance (£7,188 – £5,106)	(2,082)
Chargeable gain	22,812

Total chargeable gains on sale of 5,000 shares in JM Ltd:

	£
Previous nine days	15,500
Share pool	22,812
Total chargeable gains	38,312

Working: share pool	Number	Cost £	Indexed cost £
Pool per question	3,900	6,638	9,345
Sales: Jan 2017	(3,000)	(5,106)	(7,188)
Balance in share pool	900	1,532	2,157

- Remember that rollover relief is not available for gains on the disposal of shares.
- An exemption applies to the disposal of shares by a company out of a substantial shareholding (see below).

The conditions for the exemption often apply to disposals of shares by a company in the P6 examination such that it is usually not necessary to calculate a gain.

Substantial shareholding exemption

On the disposal by a company of shares **out of a substantial shareholding** in another company:

- **gains = exempt**
- **losses = not allowable.**

A substantial shareholding is defined as a holding:

- **of ≥ 10%**
- **owned for at least 12 months in the two years before the disposal.**

The conditions are as follows:

(i) The **disposing company** must be a **trading company** or a member of a **trading group**.

(ii) The **company disposed** of must be a **trading company** or the holding company of a **trading group** or sub group.

These conditions must also have been satisfied for at least 12 months out of the 24 months immediately prior to the disposal.

- The effect of this rule is to enable part disposals out of a substantial shareholding to continue to qualify for relief for 12 months after the vendor's holding falls below 10%.
- In deciding whether a substantial shareholding is held, shareholdings held by other group members are be taken into account.
- Where there has been a qualifying share-for-share exchange, the holding period of the original shares is effectively amalgamated with the holding period of the replacement shares in determining whether the '12 month' rule has been satisfied.

Shares owned for less than 12 months out of the previous 24 months

Where shares have been owned for less than 12 months, the ownership condition will still be satisfied if:

- the shares being disposed of are in a new company, and
- the new company received assets from another 75% group company, and
- the assets transferred were held and used in the trade of another group company for the 12 months before the transfer.

This this is particularly important when considering corporate reconstructions and reorganisations (Chapter 27).

Test your understanding 2

Omega Ltd owns 15% of the shares issued by Epsilon Ltd, a shareholding qualifying for the substantial shareholding exemption (SSE). The shares were acquired on 1 January 2010.

On 30 June 2016 Omega Ltd disposed of a 10% holding in Epsilon Ltd. The remaining 5% holding was disposed of on 31 December 2016.

For each disposal, explain whether the SSE applies.

Summary of key differences between individuals and companies

	Individuals	**Companies**
Gains subject to	Capital gains tax – tax separately from income	Corporation tax – include in TTP – tax with income
Annual exempt amount (AEA)	✓	×
Indexation allowance	×	✓
Matching rules for shares	Shares purchased: (1) on the same day (2) in the **following 30 days** (FIFO) (3) in the share pool	Shares purchased: (1) on the same day (2) in the **previous 9 days** (FIFO) (3) in the share pool
Gain/(loss) on shares	Chargeable/(allowable) regardless of size of holding	Exempt/(ignore) if disposal out of a substantial shareholding
Treatment of capital losses	• Offset against current year gains without restriction • Carry forward against future net gains but preserve AEA	• Offset against current year gains without restriction • Carry forward against future net gains without restriction (no AEA to preserve)
Entrepreneurs' relief, gift relief, PPR and investor's relief	✓	×
Rollover relief	✓	✓ (but not on goodwill)

Summary – Taxable total profits

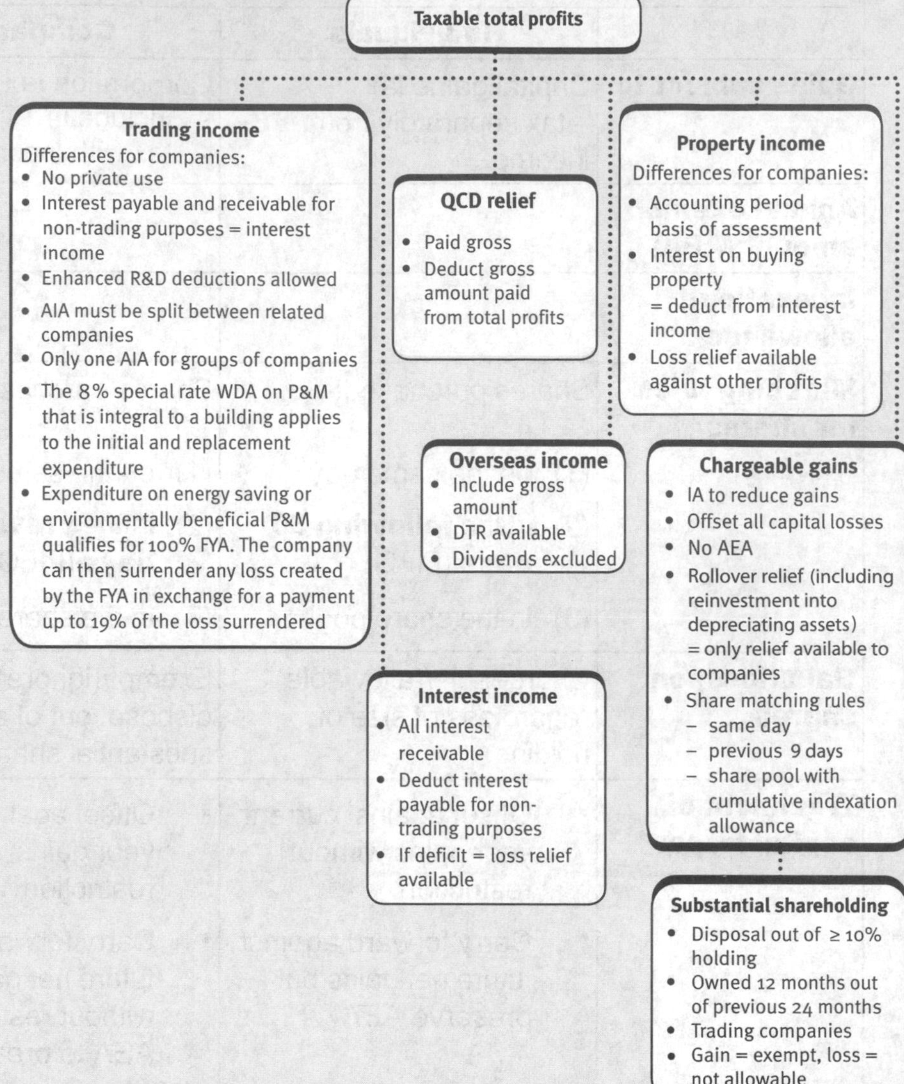

Taxable total profits
Trading income
Differences for companies:
• No private use
• Interest payable and receivable for non-trading purposes = interest income
• Enhanced R&D deductions allowed
• AIA must be split between related companies
• Only one AIA for groups of companies
• The 8% special rate WDA on P&M that is integral to a building applies to the initial and replacement expenditure
• Expenditure on energy saving or environmentally beneficial P&M qualifies for 100% FYA. The company can then surrender any loss created by the FYA in exchange for a payment up to 19% of the loss surrendered
QCD relief
• Paid gross
• Deduct gross amount paid from total profits
Property income
Differences for companies:
• Accounting period basis of assessment
• Interest on buying property = deduct from interest income
• Loss relief available against other profits
Overseas income
• Include gross amount
• DTR available
• Dividends excluded
Chargeable gains
• IA to reduce gains
• Offset all capital losses
• No AEA
• Rollover relief (including reinvestment into depreciating assets) = only relief available to companies
• Share matching rules
– same day
– previous 9 days
– share pool with cumulative indexation allowance
Interest income
• All interest receivable
• Deduct interest payable for non-trading purposes
• If deficit = loss relief available
Substantial shareholding
• Disposal out of ≥ 10% holding
• Owned 12 months out of previous 24 months
• Trading companies
• Gain = exempt, loss = not allowable

Comprehensive examples

Example 2 – Comprehensive example

PQR Ltd is a UK resident manufacturing company. Its statement of profit or loss for the accounting year ended 30 September 2016 shows a net profit before taxation of £331,700, after deducting the following expenses and including the following income:

Expenditure	£	
Loan note interest	12,000	Note 1
Long-term loan interest	6,000	Note 2
Depreciation	11,000	
Qualifying charitable donations made 1 August 2016	5,000	

Income

Loan interest	8,000	Note 3
Rents accrued	7,000	Note 4
Insurance recovery	6,800	Note 5
Profit on disposal of old headquarters building	100,000	Note 6
Dividend received	10,000	

Notes:

(1) This represents interest on loan notes issued by PQR Ltd in 2006 to provide funds to build a factory extension. The figure of £12,000 includes accrued interest of £3,000.

(2) This represents interest paid on a ten-year loan raised by PQR Ltd to purchase property which is currently let to another company.

(3) The loan interest receivable is in respect of a loan made by PQR Ltd to a supplier.

(4) The rents receivable relate to the property let by PQR Ltd.

(5) This represents an amount recovered from the company's insurers in respect of goods destroyed in a fire last year. The cost of these goods was written off and allowed as an expense last year.

(6) On 14 July 2016 the company sold an old building for £494,800. The building had been purchased in June 1992 for £150,000. At the time of its disposal, the building was held in the financial statements at a value of £394,800 due to a revaluation in 2008.

(7) Capital allowances of £34,700 are available.

(8) The RPI for June 1992 is 139.3 and for July 2016 is 262.7

Required

(a) **Compute the tax adjusted trading profit stating clearly your treatment of any interest paid or received.**

(b) **Compute the corporation tax liability of PQR Ltd for the year ended 30 September 2016.**

Solution

(a) **Tax adjusted trading profits – y/e 30 September 2016**

	£
Profit before tax	331,700
Add: Loan note interest payable	6,000
Depreciation	11,000
QCD payments	5,000
	353,700
Less: Rents receivable	(7,000)
Profit on disposal of building	(100,000)
Dividend	(10,000)
Loan interest receivable	(8,000)
Capital allowances	(34,700)
Adjusted trading profits	194,000

(b) **Corporation tax computation – y/e 30 September 2016**

	£
Tax adjusted trading profits (above)	194,000
Interest income (£8,000 – £6,000)	2,000
Property income	7,000
Chargeable gain (W)	211,900
	414,900
Less: QCDs	(5,000)
TTP	409,900
Corporation tax liability (£409,900 × 20%)	81,980

Working: Chargeable gain on headquarters building

	£
Proceeds	494,800
Less: Cost	(150,000)
Unindexed gain	344,800
Less: IA from June 1992 to July 2016	
(262.7 – 139.3)/139.3 = 0.886 × £150,000	(132,900)
Chargeable gain	211,900

Test your understanding 3

Arable Ltd commenced trading on 1 April 2016 as a manufacturer of farm equipment, preparing its first accounts for the nine month period ended 31 December 2016. The following information is available:

Trading profit

The tax adjusted trading profit is £315,326. This figure is before taking account of capital allowances and any deduction arising from the premiums paid in respect of leasehold property.

Plant and machinery

Arable Ltd purchased the following assets in respect of the nine month period ended 31 December 2016.

		£
15 April 2016	Machinery	69,500
18 April 2016	Building alterations necessary for the installation of the machinery	3,700
20 April 2016	Lorry	22,000
12 June 2016	Motor car (1) (emissions 125 g/km)	11,200
14 June 2016	Motor car (2) (emissions 171 g/km)	14,600
17 June 2016	Motor car (3) (emissions 74 g/km)	13,000
29 October 2016	Computer	4,400

The company will not make any short life asset elections.

Leasehold property

On 1 April 2016 Arable Ltd acquired a leasehold office building. A premium of £75,000 was paid for the grant of a 15 year lease.

The office building was used for business purposes by Arable Ltd throughout the period ended 31 December 2016.

Arable Ltd decided to let out an old warehouse. On 30 September 2016 Arable Ltd received a premium of £50,000 for the grant of a five year lease, and annual rent of £14,800 which was payable in advance.

Loan interest received

Loan interest of £6,000 was received on 30 September 2016, and £3,000 was accrued at 31 December 2016. The loan was made for non-trading purposes.

Dividends received

During the period ended 31 December 2016 Arable Ltd received dividends of £20,000 from Ranch plc, an unconnected company.

Profit on disposal of shares

On 5 December 2016 Arable Ltd sold 10,000 £1 ordinary shares in Ranch plc for £37,574. Arable Ltd had a share pool containing 20,000 shares in Ranch plc, with a total cost of £23,250. The indexed cost of the share pool at 5 December 2016 was £23,490. Arable Ltd's shareholding never represented more than a 1% interest in Ranch plc.

(a) **Calculate Arable Ltd's corporation tax liability for the nine month period ended 31 December 2016.**

(b) **State the date by which Arable Ltd's self-assessment corporation tax return for the period ended 31 December 2016 should be submitted, and explain how the company can correct the return if it is subsequently found to contain an error or mistake.**

3 Research and development expenditure

In order to encourage more spending on research and development (R&D), additional tax reliefs are given for qualifying revenue expenditure incurred by companies.

There are separate schemes for small or medium sized enterprises (SMEs) and large companies.

For R&D purposes, the question in the examination will state whether or not the company is a SME.

Scheme for SMEs

The scheme works as follows:

- Enhanced relief is available if the company spends money on qualifying R&D, as defined by generally accepted accounting principles (GAAP) and guidelines from the Department for Business Innovation and Skills.
- SMEs can deduct an **additional 130%** of qualifying expenditure for tax purposes.
- If the deduction creates a loss it may be surrendered in return for a cash payment from HMRC = 14.5% of the surrendered amount.
- If surrendered in return for cash, the loss cannot also be carried forward for future relief.

Qualifying R&D expenditure must be revenue expenditure on a project that seeks to achieve an advance in science or technology that is relevant to the company's trade.

It can include expenditure on the following:

- staffing costs, including NIC (class 1 and class 1A) and pension contributions but excluding assessable benefits
- agency staff for R&D
- materials, water, fuel and power for R&D
- software directly used in R&D
- payments to subcontractors (note that only 65% of this expenditure will be eligible for the enhanced tax credit).

It cannot include:

- contributions to other bodies for independent research
- expenditure covered by a grant or subsidy.

Test your understanding 4

Dax plc is a profitable company manufacturing audio visual equipment. Dax plc is a small enterprise for the purposes of R&D.

The company has recently decided to investigate the market for a new type of classroom projection equipment and has spent the following amounts in the year ended 31 December 2016 on the project:

	£
Market research	8,000
Staff directly involved in researching the project	20,000
Administrative support for the R&D department	5,000
Heat and light in the R&D department	9,000
New software	4,000
An agency for temporary R&D staff	10,000

Advise the company of any tax relief available in respect of its expenditure.

Scheme for large companies

The scheme for large companies is different to the scheme for SMEs. The key differences are as follows:

- large companies can opt to claim relief known as 'above the line tax credit' (see below)
- there is no option of surrendering losses for cash repayments for large companies, although they may receive a tax credit (see below)
- large companies cannot claim relief for payments made to SMEs
- large companies can claim relief for contributions made to a qualifying body such as a charity or a university for independent research provided the research is relevant to the company's trade.

Above the line tax credit

Large companies can opt to claim a tax credit for R&D expenditure against their corporation tax liability as follows:

- 11% of the qualifying R&D expenditure is:
  - included as taxable income in TTP and taxed at 20%, and
  - deducted from the corporation tax liability.

If the company is profitable, this alternative 'above the line tax credit' will give a net benefit of 8.8% of the qualifying expenditure.

	Qualifying expenditure = £10,000 **Tax saving**	
Tax credit		£
(11% of expenditure)	(£10,000 × 11%)	1,100
Less: (11% of expenditure taxed at 20%)	Less: (£10,000 × 11% × 20%)	(220)
= 8.8% relief		880

- if companies have no corporation tax liability or insufficient liability to net off all of the tax credit, the excess will be:
  - paid in cash, net of tax
  - up to a maximum amount = the company's PAYE/NIC liability for R&D employees for the relevant accounting period
- if the repayable tax credit exceeds the maximum cash repayment allowed, the remaining tax credit can be:
  - carried forward and offset against the first available future corporation tax liability, or
  - group relieved (Chapter 27).

Capital expenditure on research and development

Capital expenditure on R&D (excluding land) qualifies for a 100% R&D capital allowance in the year of purchase, so it is fully deductible as a trading expense.

It does not, however, qualify for any additional R&D relief.

When the capital assets are sold, the proceeds are treated as a balancing charge and are therefore taxed as trading income.

Test your understanding 5

(1) Gul Ltd is a small sized company for the purposes of R&D expenditure. In the year ended 31 December 2016 they spent £8,500 on qualifying R&D expenditure.

(2) Curzon plc is a large company for the purposes of R&D expenditure. In the year ended 31 March 2017 they have spent £60,000 on qualifying R&D expenditure.

Advise the companies of any tax relief available in respect of their expenditure.

4 Intangible assets

Intangible assets include the following items:

- purchased goodwill (not goodwill on consolidation)
- patents, copyrights and trademarks
- brands
- intellectual property and know-how.

Tax treatment of intangibles other than goodwill

The tax treatment of intangible assets other than goodwill broadly follows the accounting treatment. This is providing the accounting treatment is in accordance with GAAP (either UK or international).

Expenditure relating to intangibles which has been charged in the company's statement of profit or loss is allowable for tax purposes.

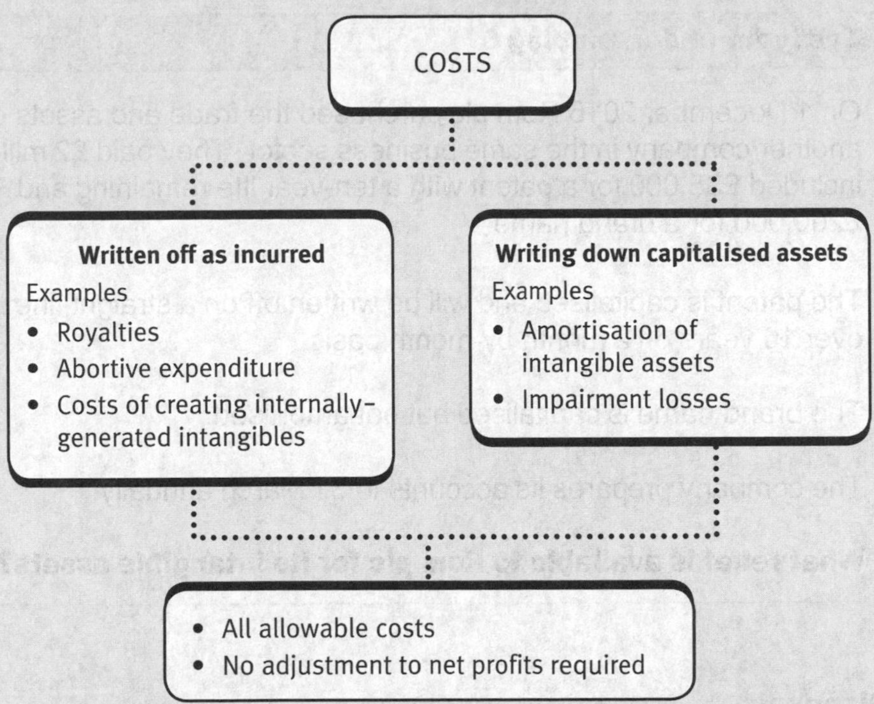

Election – alternative tax treatment

Instead of allowing the amounts charged in the accounts, an election can be made:

- to write off the cost of a capitalised intangible asset / intellectual property against profit for tax purposes at a rate of 4% per annum
- any accounting debits for amortisation or impairment losses would then be disallowed.

This is useful where:

(1) the asset is amortised at a rate of less than 4%, or

(2) the asset is not amortised in the accounts.

The allowable amount is calculated pro rata for accounting periods of less than twelve months.

The election is:

- irrevocable, and
- must be made within two years of the end of the accounting period in which the asset was acquired or created.

Test your understanding 6

On 1 December 2016 Rom plc purchased the trade and assets of another company in the same business sector. They paid £2 million that included £35,000 for a patent with a ten-year life remaining and £200,000 for a brand name.

The patent is capitalised and will be written off on a straight-line basis over 10 years on a month-by-month basis.

The brand name is capitalised but not amortised.

The company prepares its accounts to 31 March annually.

What relief is available to Rom plc for its intangible assets?

Disposals

On the disposal of an intangible asset, the proceeds of sale are compared with the tax written down value to give a profit/loss.

- Any profit or loss made on disposal of an intangible asset in the accounts:
  - will give rise to an identical tax profit or loss
  - unless the tax written down value at the time of disposal differs from the accounts value
  - this occurs when the 4% election has been made.

Test your understanding 7

Assume that Rom plc in the previous illustration decides to sell the business that it bought on 1 December 2016. The consideration includes £38,000 for the patent and £250,000 for the brand name. The sale is made on 1 April 2019.

State the effect for tax purposes of the disposal of the intangible assets.

Tax treatment of goodwill

Goodwill purchased is treated differently from other intangible assets.

Amortisation or impairment losses relating to goodwill are **not allowable** for tax purposes.

Disposals

On disposal of goodwill, the proceeds of sale are compared with the cost to give a profit/loss.

- Any **profit** will be treated as a **trading** profit
- However, any **loss** will be treated as a **non-trading debit** and can be:
  - set off against total profits of the current period
  - group relieved if part of a 75% group (Chapter 27)
  - carried forward and treated as a non-trading debit of the next period.
- There is no option to carry back non-trading debits arising on the sale of goodwill.

Special intangible rollover relief

- If a profit is made on disposal of any intangible asset and a new intangible asset is acquired within 12 months before or up to 36 months after disposal:
  - part of the taxable profit may be deferred.
- The maximum deferral
  = (Lower of disposal proceeds or amount reinvested)
  Less: Cost of the original intangible asset
- Special intangible rollover relief is available for goodwill as well as other types of intangible asset.

Patent box relief

This is a scheme that was introduced to encourage companies to:

- develop new innovative patented products, and
- retain and take advantage of existing patents.

Companies that own and hold patents for the purposes of their trade can elect for profits relating to those patents to be taxed at a lower rate of corporation tax.

Note that the scheme:

- is optional
- if claimed, must be claimed within **two years** of the end of the accounting period in which the patent profits arise

- applies to **all profits derived from patents such as:**
  - royalty income, and
  - a proportion of the profits made on goods or services where a patent has been used in the underlying production process.

In FY2016, 90% of the profits in the 'patent box' will be taxed at an effective 10% rate. In FY2017 all profits relating to patents will be taxed at 10%.

The relevant percentage will be given in the question if needed.

- The method of achieving the relief in the corporation tax computation is to reduce the company's total points by the patent box deduction. The revised profits are then taxed at the applicable corporation tax rate.

Steps to calculate the corporation tax liability

(1) Determine the profits attributable to patents (strictly these comprise income less certain deductions, but the calculation of these profits is not examinable)

(2) Calculate the patent box deduction using the formula:

Net patent profit × (main rate – 10%)/main rate

The 'main rate' in this formula is the 20% corporation tax rate in force for FY2016.

This formula will be included in the tax rates and allowances provided to you in the examination.

(3) For the year ended 31 March 2017, deduct **90%** of this amount from total profits of the company

(4) Tax the remaining profits as normal.

Test your understanding 8

Theta plc's has profits attributable to patents of £500,000 (after all relevant deductions have been made), and other trading profits of £2,000,000.

Calculate Theta plc's corporation tax payable for the year ended 31 March 2017, assuming an election has been made for the patent box rules to apply and the relevant patent profit percentage is 90%.

5 Transfer pricing

Aim of the legislation

Transfer pricing adjustments may be necessary for transactions between connected companies. Companies are connected if:

- one company directly or indirectly participates in the management, control or capital of the other company, or
- a third party directly or indirectly participates in the management, control or capital of both companies.

The transfer pricing rules apply to both transactions with non UK resident companies and UK transactions.

HMRC want to ensure that companies cannot manipulate total UK corporation tax by substituting a transfer price that is below or above an arm's length price.

- The transfer pricing legislation covers not only sales but also lettings/hiring of property and loan interest.
- Where transfer pricing policies are under review the basic aim is to **ensure transactions are recorded at an arm's length price.**
- Arm's length means the price which might have been expected if the parties had been independent persons dealing with each other in a normal commercial manner unaffected by any special relationship between them.
- An adjustment may be necessary to increase the profits of the advantaged company (i.e. the one gaining a tax advantage from the favourable price).
- A company must adjust its own profits under self-assessment, and must pay any additional tax due.
- Alternatively, the company may enter into an Advance Pricing Arrangement with HMRC, to agree that its transfer pricing policy is acceptable and avoid the need for subsequent adjustments.

Companies covered by the legislation

Not all companies are affected by the legislation. The following diagram summarises the position:

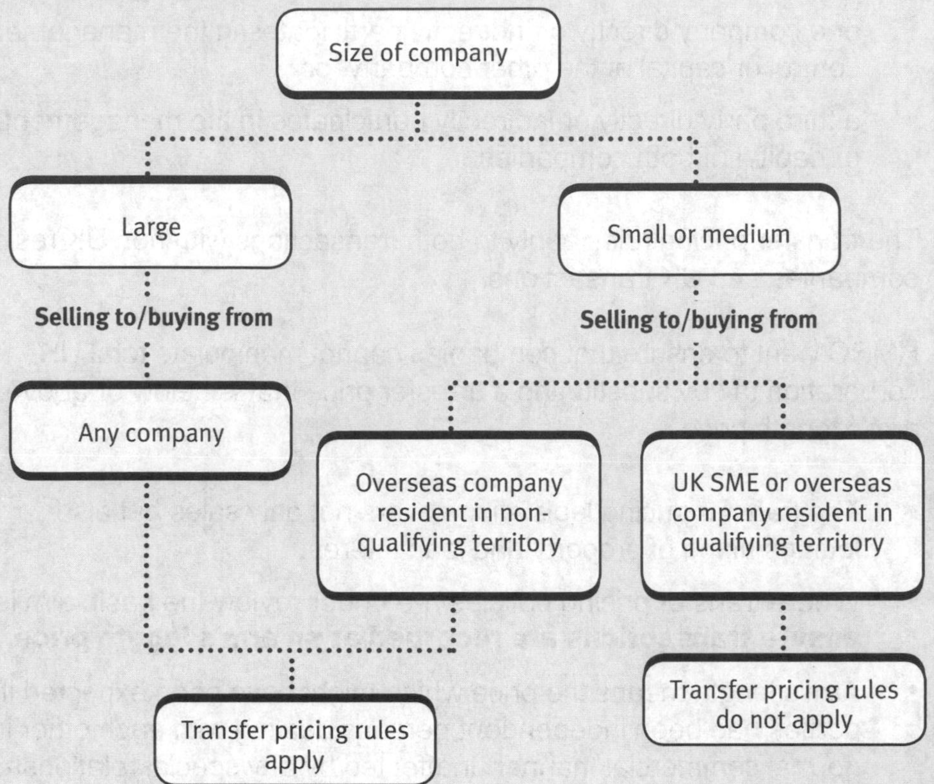

The definition of 'large' and 'small or medium' enterprises is the same as for research and development expenditure. The question in the exam will state if the company is 'large' or 'small' or 'medium'.

A medium sized company will be treated in the same way as a large company if there is 'manipulation' (for example, where there is a deliberate attempt to divert profits to a company paying at lower tax rate). If so, the transfer pricing rules will apply to that medium company on all transactions with any company.

A non-qualifying territory means one that is:

- not in the UK
- has no DTR agreement with the UK, or
- if it does have an agreement, that agreement does not have a non-discrimination clause.

It is also possible for the Treasury to designate countries as non-qualifying.

Test your understanding 9

Transaction		A Ltd	Subsidiary (B Ltd)
(1)	A Ltd sells 5,000 units to B Ltd at £1.50 each when the MV = £3 each	UK company (large)	Overseas company
(2)	As for (1)	UK company (medium/small)	UK company (medium/small)
(3)	As for (1)	UK company (large)	UK company
(4)	A Ltd makes a loan of £200,000 to B Ltd and charges interest at 2% when the commercial rate is 8%.	UK company (large)	Overseas company
(5)	As for (4)	UK company (medium/small)	UK company (medium/small)
(6)	As for (4)	UK company (large)	UK company

Explain the effect of the transfer pricing legislation on each transaction.

Thin capitalisation

When a UK company pays a dividend, there is no tax relief for the payment. When it pays loan interest, the interest is tax allowable. This means that companies may prefer to be financed through loans (debt) rather than through shares (equity).

The thin capitalisation rules aim:

- to stop UK companies from getting excessive tax relief on interest.

This occurs:

- usually because they have received a loan from a related party that exceeds the loan an independent lender would be prepared to lend.

The rules ensure that:

- **interest** on the part of the **loan that an independent third party would be prepared to lend** the company is **allowable.**
- the **excess is disallowed**.
- the borrowing capacity of the individual company and its subsidiaries is considered (but not the rest of the group).

Factors determining thin capitalisation

HMRC will usually look at two areas to determine whether they believe a company is thinly capitalised:

(1) Gearing:

- This is the relationship of debt to equity.
- In the UK this is usually around 50:50.
- A higher proportion of debt could cause thin capitalisation problems.

(2) Interest cover:

- This is the ratio of earnings before tax and interest to loan interest.
- It measures how risky the loan is for the lender.
- Many commercial lenders will look for a ratio of around 3.

Test your understanding 10

Archer plc is a wholly owned subsidiary of Berry Inc, a company resident in Babylonia. Archer borrows £100,000 from Berry Inc paying a market rate of interest of 8%. Archer had to borrow from Berry Inc as their UK bankers were not prepared to lend them more than £60,000.

Advise Archer plc of how much loan interest they are likely to have relieved for tax purposes.

6 Companies with investment business

A company with investment business is a company 'whose business consists wholly or partly in the making of investments'. This includes any company that makes and holds investments, regardless of whether or not it also carries on a trade.

The costs incurred by such a company in managing its investments are allowable when computing its corporation tax liability in accordance with the rules set out below.

Profits of a company with investment business

The taxable total profits of a company with investment business:

- are calculated in the same way as for a trading company
- the same rules for the various sources of income and capital gains apply (for example, that costs relevant to a property business will be deducted from the property income).

Management expenses

Management expenses are incurred in managing the company's investments and can be deducted from the company's 'total profits', subject to the normal rules regarding deductibility of expenditure.

Accordingly, expenses such as depreciation of office furniture would not be allowable but capital allowances would be calculated and allowed instead, and business entertaining expenses would not be allowable.

Expenses which the courts have allowed as management expenses include:

- directors' fees and commissions, provided they are not excessive
- salaries of management
- audit fees
- office rent and rates
- bank interest.

Excess management expenses can be:

- carried forward and treated as management expenses of the next accounting period
- group relieved if part of a 75% group (Chapter 27).

Test your understanding 11

Cheetah Ltd has the following results for the year ended 31 March 2017:

	£
Rental income	70,000
Deposit account interest receivable	20,000
Chargeable gains	3,000
Management expenses:	
Property management	35,000
Other	60,000
Capital allowances:	
Related to property business	2,300
Other	1,600
Loan stock interest payable (gross)	2,000
Directors' remuneration	3,000

Calculate Cheetah Ltd's CT liability for the y/e 31 March 2017.

7 Chapter summary

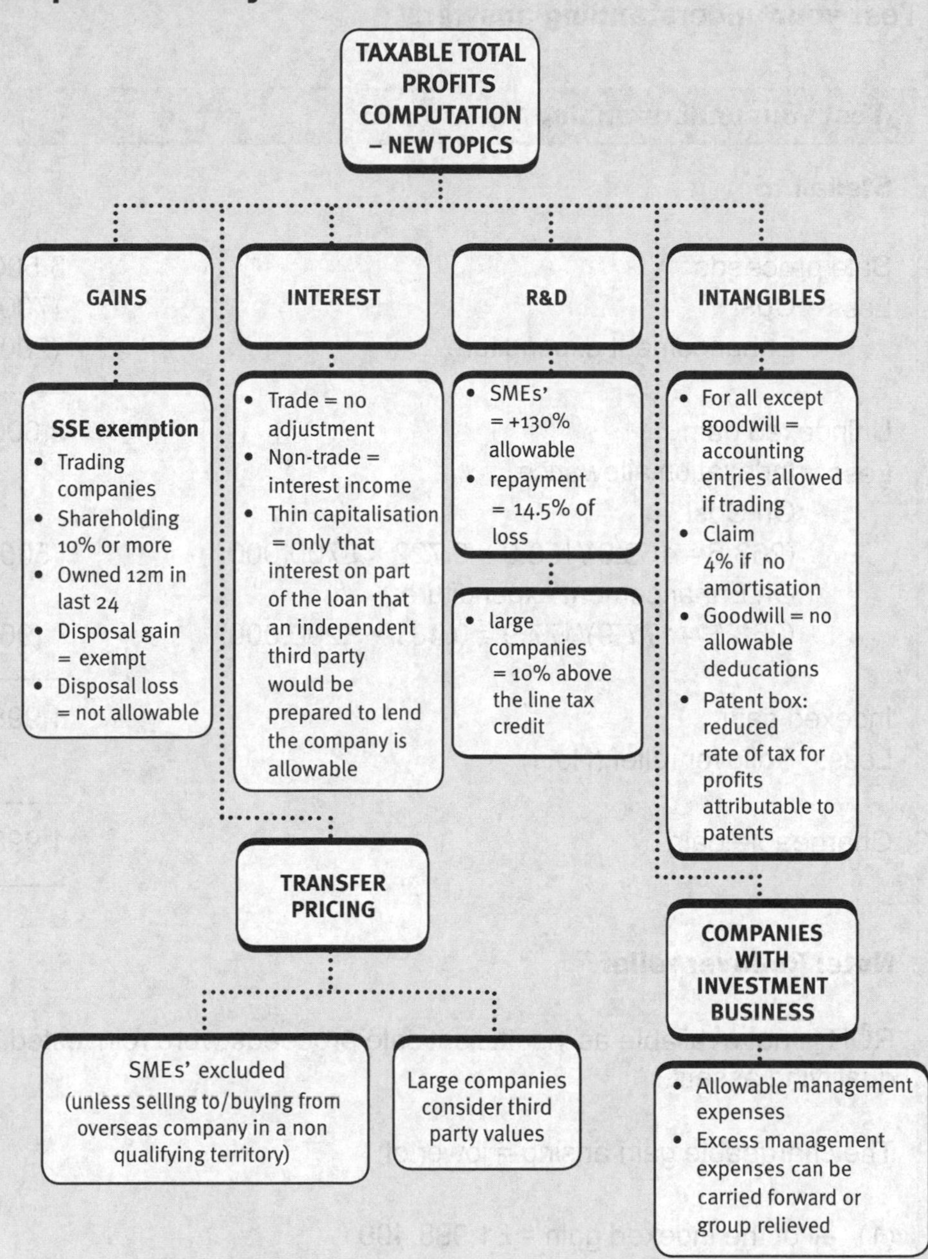

Test your understanding answers

Test your understanding 1

Stella Ltd

		£
Sale proceeds		3,500,000
Less:	Cost	(700,000)
	Enhancement expenditure	(200,000)
Unindexed gain		2,600,000
Less:	Indexation allowance	
	On Cost:	
	(263.5 – 153.0)/153.0 = 0.722 × £700,000	(505,400)
	On Enhancement expenditure:	
	(263.5 – 177.9)/177.9 = 0.481 × £200,000	(96,200)
Indexed gain		1,998,400
Less:	Rollover relief (Note)	(0)
Chargeable gain		1,998,400

Note: Rollover relief

ROR is not available as insufficient sale proceeds were reinvested in qualifying assets.

The chargeable gain arising = lower of:

(1) all of the indexed gain = £1,998,400

(2) sale proceeds not reinvested
= (£3,500,000 – £1,400,000) = £2,100,000

Test your understanding 2

Omega Ltd

Both of these disposals will qualify for the SSE.

- The first disposal of the 10% holding has been held for a 12 month period in the two years prior to disposal.
- The second disposal also qualifies, despite it being made out of only a 5% holding, because Omega Ltd held at least a 10% holding throughout a 12 month period during the two years prior to this second disposal.

Test your understanding 3

Arable Ltd

(a) **Corporation tax computation – p/e 31 December 2016**

	£
Trading profit	315,326
P & M – Capital allowances (W1)	(114,988)
Deduction for lease premium (W2)	(2,700)
Tax adjusted trading profit	197,638
Property income (W3)	49,700
Interest income (£6,000 + £3,000)	9,000
Chargeable gain (W4)	25,829
TTP	282,167
Corporation tax liability (£282,167 × 20%)	56,433

Note: The dividend received is exempt from corporation tax.

Workings

(W1) **Plant and machinery**

	£	Main pool £	Special rate pool £	Allowances £
p/e 31 December 2016				
Additions:				
Not qualifying for AIA or FYA:				
Cars (76 – 130 g/km)		11,200		
Cars (over 130 g/km)			14,600	
Qualifying for AIA:				
Plant and machinery (Note 1)	99,600			
Less: AIA (Note 2)	(99,600)			99,600
		0		
		11,200	14,600	
Less: WDA (18% × £11,200 × 9/12)		(1,512)		1,512
Less: WDA (8% × £14,600 × 9/12)			(876)	876
Low emission car	13,000			
Less: FYA (100%)	(13,000)			13,000
		0		
TWDV c/f		9,688	13,724	
Total allowances				114,988

Notes:

(1) Plant qualifying for AIA
= (£69,500 + £3,700 + £22,000 + £4,400) = £99,600

(2) The maximum AIA = (9/12 of £200,000) = £150,000 as the accounting period is only 9 months long.

(W2) **Deduction for lease premium**

The leasehold building has been used for business purposes, and so a proportion of the lease premium assessed on the landlord can be deducted.

The amount assessed on the landlord calculated as follows:
£75,000 × [(51 – 15)/50] = £54,000

This is deductible over the life of the lease, so the deduction for the nine-month period ended 31 December 2016 is:
(£54,000/15 = £3,600 × 9/12) = £2,700

(W3) **Property income**

	£
Old warehouse	
Premium assessed as property income	
£50,000 × [(51 – 5)/50]	46,000
Rent receivable (£14,800 × 3/12)	3,700
Property income	49,700

(W4) **Chargeable gain on the disposal of shares**

The substantial shareholding exemption does not apply as Arable Ltd's shareholdings never represented more than a 1% interest in Ranch plc

	£
Disposal proceeds	37,574
Less: Cost (see below)	(11,625)
Unindexed gain	25,949
Less: Indexation (£11,745 – £11,625) (see below)	(120)
Chargeable gain	25,829

Share pool	Number	Cost	Indexed cost
		£	£
Pool b/f	20,000	23,250	23,490
Disposal (December 2016)	(10,000)	(11,625)	(11,745)
Balance c/f	10,000	11,625	11,745

(b) **Self assessment corporation tax return**

Arable Ltd's self-assessment corporation tax return for the p/e 31 December 2016 must be submitted online by 31 December 2017.

It will be possible for Arable Ltd to amend its return at any time before 31 December 2018, being 12 months after the filing date.

If an error or mistake in a return is subsequently discovered, then Arable Ltd can make a claim for relief before 31 December 2020, being four years from the end of the accounting period.

Test your understanding 4

Dax plc

Dax plc is an SME; they can claim an additional R&D deduction against their taxable profits as follows:

	£
Allowable expenses but not qualifying for additional relief:	
Market research	8,000
Administrative staff	5,000
	13,000
Allowable expenses qualifying for additional relief:	
Staff	20,000
Heat and light	9,000
Software	4,000
Agency staff	10,000
	43,000
× 230%	98,900
Allowable amount (£98,900 + £13,000)	111,900

Note: £111,900 is the total allowable amount, but the actual expenses of £56,000 (£43,000 + £13,000) will already have been charged in the statement of profit or loss. Therefore an additional £55,900 (£111,900 – £56,000) is deducted in the adjustment to profits computation.

Test your understanding 5

(1) **Gul Ltd**

Normal relief for R&D expenditure

The normal R&D expenditure allowable deduction already charged in the accounts of £8,500 will give a tax saving of £1,700 (£8,500 × 20%).

Extra deduction

Gul Ltd can claim an extra deduction of 130% on their £8,500 qualifying expenditure giving an additional tax saving as follows:

	£
Allowable R&D deduction (130% × £8,500)	11,050
Corporation tax saving (20% × £11,050)	2,210

Total tax saving = (£1,700 + £2,210) = £3,910

(2) **Curzon plc**

Normal relief for R&D expenditure

The normal R&D expenditure allowable deduction charged in the accounts will give a tax saving of:

(£60,000 × 20%) = £12,000

Election for tax credit

Curzon plc can elect to receive a taxable 'above the line' tax credit of 11%.

The net effect of this is as follows:

	£	£
Tax credit deduction in CT liability computation (11% × £60,000)		6,600
Include in TTP as taxable income (£60,000 × 11%)	6,600	
Increase in CT liability (£6,600 × 20%)		(1,320)
Net corporation tax saving		5,280

Alternative calculation = (£60,000 × 8.8%) = £5,280

Total tax saving = (£12,000 + £5,280) = £17,280

Test your understanding 6

Rom plc

(1) Patent

- This is being amortised at 10% per annum.
- The accounting treatment = tax allowable amount.
- Therefore £3,500 p.a. (£35,000 × 10%) will be the amortisation and tax allowable amount, and no adjustment to profits is required.
- The allowable amount is £1,167 (4/12 × £3,500) in the year ended 31.3.2017 as amortisation is calculated on a monthly basis and the patent was acquired on 1.12.2016.
- A 4% election should not be made as the tax allowable amount would be less than the amortisation available.

(2) Brand name

- This is not being amortised.
- It will therefore be beneficial for the company to elect to write this off for tax purposes at 4% per annum.
- An allowance of £8,000 (£200,000 × 4%) will be available.
- Therefore £8,000 should be deducted in the adjustment of profits computation.

Note: The full annual allowance is available in the year ended 31.3.2017 as the accounting period is 12 months in length. It is irrelevant when in the accounting period the brand name was purchased.

Test your understanding 7

Rom plc continued

Patent		£
Original cost		35,000
Less:	Amounts written off	
	Year ended 31.3.2017	(1,167)
	Year ended 31.3.2018	(3,500)
	Year ended 31.3.2019	(3,500)
TWDV at 1 April 2019		26,833
Proceeds		38,000
Profit (included in taxable trading profits)		11,167

Brand name

As the 4% election has been made, the company cannot follow the accounts in relation to the profit arising on the brand name.

Any accounting profit is deducted for tax purposes in the adjustment of profits computation and is replaced with the following taxable profit.

		£
Original cost		200,000
Less:	Amounts written off	
	Year ended 31.3.2017	(8,000)
	Year ended 31.3.2018	(8,000)
	Year ended 31.3.2019	(8,000)
TWDV at 1 April 2019		176,000
Proceeds		250,000
Profit (included in taxable trading profits)		74,000

Test your understanding 8

Theta plc

Corporation tax computation – y/e 31 March 2017

	£
Trading profits	2,000,000
Profits attributable to patents	500,000
Less: Patent box deduction	
(£500,000 × ((20% –10%)/20%) × 90% (Note)	(225,000)
TTP	2,275,000
Corporation tax at 20%	455,000

To prove that this method achieves the desired effect:

	£
Net patent profits (90% to be taxed at 10%)	
(£500,000 × 90% × 10%)	45,000
Remaining profits taxed at main rate	
((£500,000 × 10%) + £2,000,000) × 20%	410,000
	455,000

Test your understanding 9

A Ltd and B Ltd

(1) The transfer pricing legislation applies.

A Ltd must increase its taxable total profits by £7,500 (£1.50 × 5,000).

(2) The transfer pricing legislation does not apply, unless a medium company and HMRC consider profits are being manipulated.

(3) The transfer pricing legislation applies.

A Ltd must increase its taxable total profits by £7,500 and B Ltd may make an equal and opposite adjustment to its taxable total profits as it is UK resident.

(4) The transfer pricing legislation applies.

A Ltd must increase its taxable total profits by £12,000 (6% × £200,000).

(5) The transfer pricing legislation does not apply.

(6) The transfer pricing legislation applies.

A Ltd must increase its taxable total profits by £12,000 and B Ltd may make an equal and opposite adjustment to its taxable total profits as it is UK resident.

Test your understanding 10

Archer plc

A third party was only prepared to lend Archer plc £60,000.

As they have borrowed £100,000 from their parent company, it is likely that interest on the excess £40,000 will be disallowed for tax purposes.

Of the £8,000 interest they pay to Berry Inc, only £4,800 is likely to be allowed for tax.

Test your understanding 11

Cheetah Ltd

Corporation tax computation – year ended 31 March 2017

	£
Property income (W1)	32,700
Interest income (£20,000 – £2,000)	18,000
Chargeable gains	3,000
Total profits	53,700
Less: Management expenses (restricted) (W2)	(53,700)
TTP	0
Corporation tax liability	0

Workings

(W1) **Property income**

	£
Rents	70,000
Less: Capital allowances	(2,300)
Property management expenses	(35,000)
Property income	32,700

(W2) **Management expenses**

	£
General management expenses	60,000
Directors' remuneration	3,000
Capital allowances	1,600
	64,600
Less: Total profits	(53,700)
Excess management expenses	10,900

Excess management expenses are carried forward and treated as management expenses of the y/e 31 March 2018.

chapter

24

Corporation tax losses

Chapter learning objectives

Upon completion of this chapter you will be able to:

- explain and show the alternative methods for relieving a range of losses in a single company
- identify the factors that influence the choice of a loss relief claim and advise on the effect of alternative courses of action
- recognise the circumstances when the use of losses may be restricted on a change of ownership of a company and state the effect.

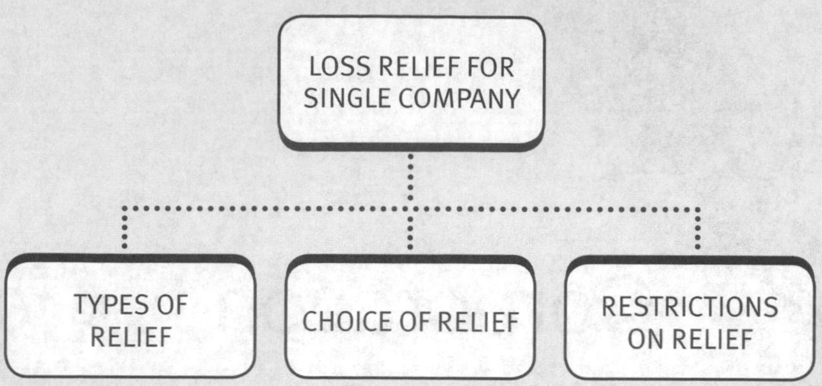

Introduction

This chapter covers the rules for loss reliefs available to a single company.

Much of this chapter is a revision of rules covered at F6. A brief reminder of F6 content is given in expandable text and revision examples are provided to check your retention of the required F6 knowledge.

The new areas at P6 are

- the treatment of non-trading loan relationship (NTLR) deficits, and
- the restrictions for the use of some losses.

There is also a much greater emphasis at P6 on choosing the most tax efficient use of loss reliefs available and tax planning for companies with losses.

1 Loss reliefs for a single company

A revision of trading loss reliefs available

The following diagram summarises the trading loss relief options to a single company covered at F6:

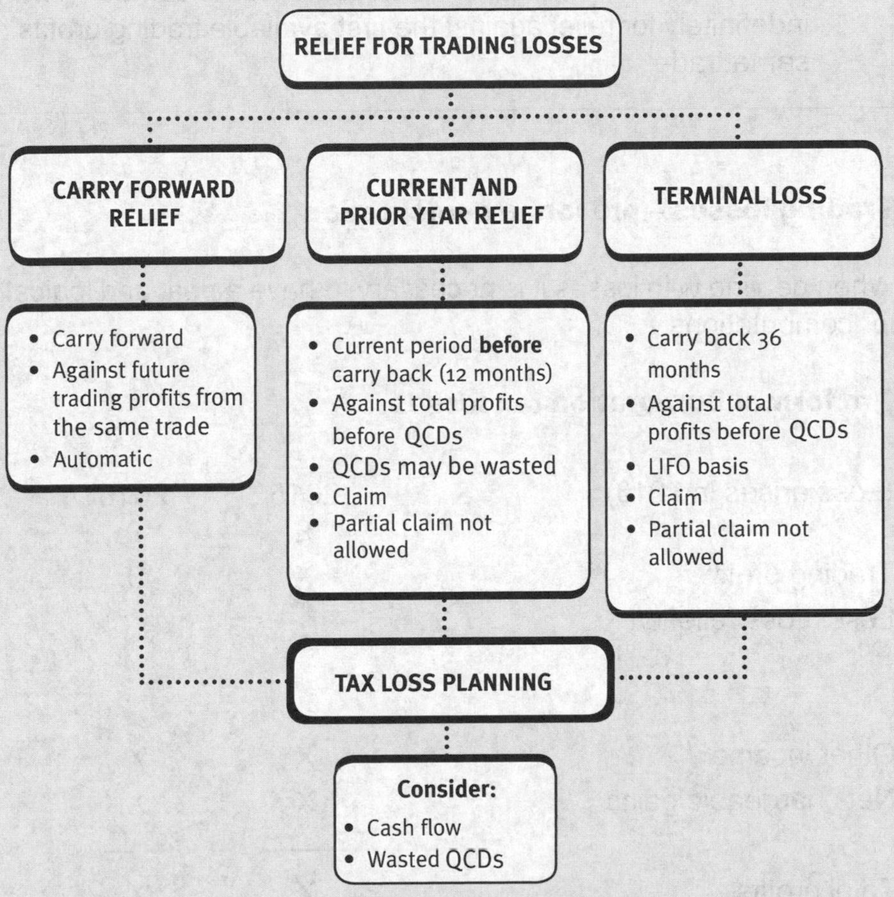

Trading losses

- The current year and carry back reliefs need to be claimed within 2 years of the end of the CAP in which the trading loss occurred.
- For carry forward relief, although there is no limit on the time within which the loss may be offset, a claim to establish the amount of the loss must be made within four years of the end of the CAP in which the loss was made.
- The carry back option can only be considered after claiming in the current period.

- Any trading loss remaining after a current year claim can be carried back against total profits before qualifying charitable donations (QCDs) of the preceding 12 months. The carry back is optional.
- On cessation of trade only, the trading loss of the last 12 months can be carried back 36 months on a LIFO basis.
- If there are trading losses remaining after a current year/carry back claim, or no such claims are made, the loss is carried forward indefinitely for relief against the first available trading profits of the same trade.

Trading losses – pro forma computation

When dealing with losses it is necessary to have a neat and logical layout for computations.

Pro forma: Corporation tax losses

(Loss arises in 2016)	2015	2016	2017
	£	£	£
Trading profit	X	0	X
Less: Loss relief b/f			(X)
			X
Other income	X	X	X
Net chargeable gains	X	X	X
Total profits	X	X	X
Less: Loss relief			
– Current year offset		(X)	
– 12 month c/back	(X)		
	0	0	X
Less: QCDs	Wasted	Wasted	(X)
Taxable total profits	0	0	X

Note: Unlike income tax, for companies there is no maximum deduction for current period and carry back losses (as in section 6 of Chapter 17).

Loss-making period of less than 12 months

The length of the loss-making period is not important:

- Full relief is given against the current period total profits before QCDs.
- The remaining loss can be carried back in full in the normal way.

Short accounting periods prior to year of loss

If any of the accounting periods falling in the carry back period are less than 12 months:

- The profits of the accounting period that falls partly into the carry back period must be time apportioned.
- The loss can only be offset against those profits which fall within the carry back period.
- Remember, the loss is offset on a LIFO basis (i.e. against the later accounting period first).

Illustration 1 – Short accounting period prior to the loss

If the CAP immediately preceding the loss making y/e 31 December 2017 is the 8 m/e 31 December 2016, then the loss can be carried back:

- Against the 8 m/e 31 December 2016, and then if sufficient loss;
- Against 4/12 of the total profits before QCDs of the 12 months to 30 April 2016.

Non-trading losses

In addition to trading losses three other types of loss can occur.

The following diagram summarises the non-trading loss relief options to a single company:

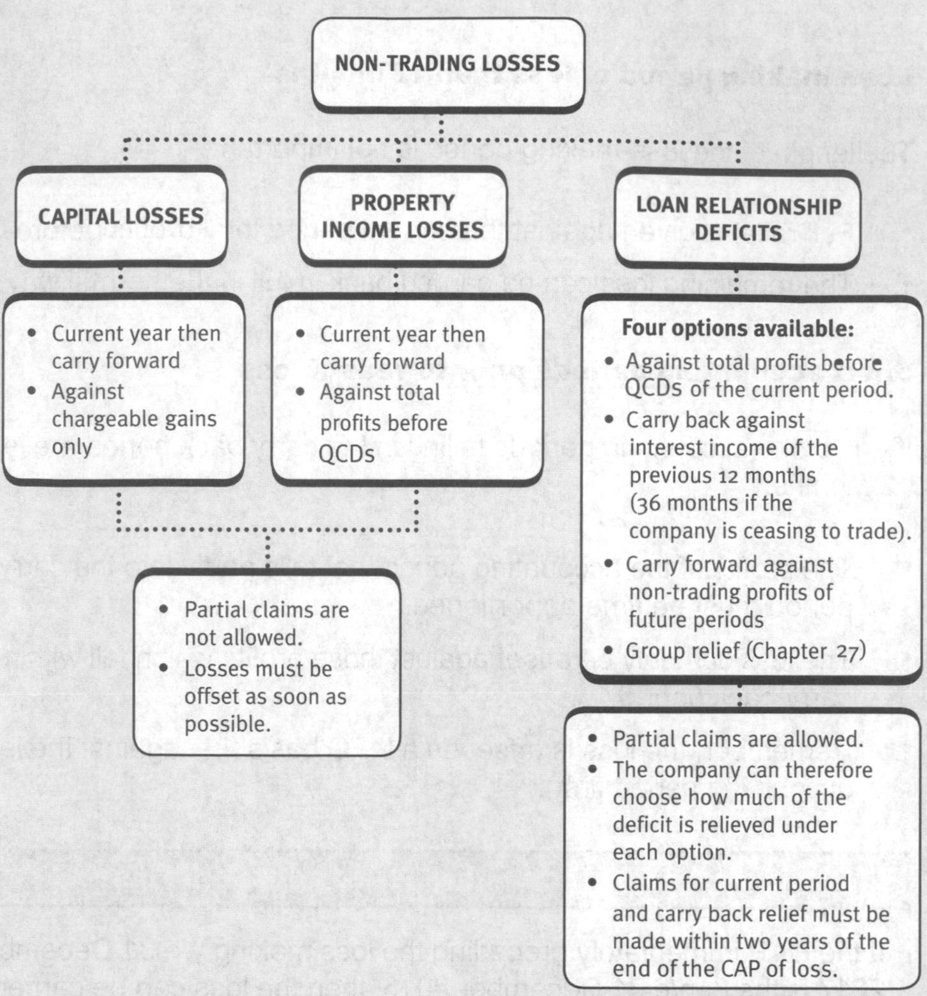

Example 1 – Loan relationship deficits

Lily Ltd has the following results for the year ended 31 March 2017:

	£
Trading profits (before taking account of interest)	105,000
Property income	62,000
Interest receivable on building society deposit	21,000
Interest payable on loan stock used to purchase rental property	42,000
Legal fees payable in respect of above issue of loan stock	6,000
Interest payable on loan to fund working capital	8,000

Calculate Lily Ltd's taxable total profits for the year ended 31 March 2017, showing clearly how the loan relationship deficit may be relieved.

Solution

Corporation tax computation – year ended 31 March 2017

	£
Trading profits	105,000
Less: Interest payable on loan to fund working capital	(8,000)
Adjusted trading profit	97,000
Property income	62,000
	159,000
Less: Deficit on NTLR (W)	(27,000)
TTP	132,000

Working: Deficit on non-trading loan relationship

	£
Interest receivable	21,000
Interest payable on loan to purchase rental property	(42,000)
Fees payable on loan to purchase rental property	(6,000)
Deficit on NTLR	(27,000)

Approach for loss computations

A question involving company losses often covers several years and may include one or more of property, NTLR and capital losses as well as trading losses. Therefore, a methodical approach is important.

Step 1: Write out the skeleton TTP pro forma, remembering to leave space for loss relief claims, and setting out the years side by side.

Step 2: Fill in the pro forma with the TTP information provided, ignoring loss relief.

Step 3: If there are any 'non-trading' losses identify each separately, in a separate loss working, and show the amounts used and carried forward. Deal with property losses and NTLR deficits before using the trading loss.

Step 4: In the year of the trading loss, the trading income is £Nil. Keep a separate working for the trading loss. If there are losses in more than one CAP, keep a separate loss working for each loss and update the workings as the loss is relieved.

Step 5: Consider the alternative loss relief options available, reading carefully any guidance given in the requirement on the loss reliefs to consider or the objectives of the company.

- If a question states 'relief is to be obtained as early as possible', the order of set-off is:
  - Current year claim followed by a carry back claim to the previous 12 months (or 36 months for a terminal loss).
  - Carry forward any remaining loss and offset against future trading profits (not an option in a terminal loss question).
- Where there is more than one loss to offset:
  - Deal with the earliest loss first.
  - Losses brought forward are offset in priority to current year and carry back claims.
- Identify the QCD relief and cash flow implications under each option and conclude as to which option is preferable based on the requirement.

Step 6: Calculate the revised TTP after the appropriate loss reliefs have been applied.

Example 2 – Loss computation

Daffodil Ltd has the following results for the four accounting periods ended 31 March 2017.

Year ended:	31.03.14	31.03.15	31.03.16	31.03.17
	£	£	£	£
Trading profit/(loss)	14,000	10,000	23,500	(25,000)
Interest income	2,200	1,800	2,000	2,400
Property income	800	1,100	(800)	800
Chargeable gains	0	(700)	Nil	2,600
QCDs	200	200	200	200

There was a trading loss brought forward at 1 April 2013 of £7,000. Daffodil continues to trade after 31.03.17.

Calculate Daffodil Ltd's taxable total profits, assuming that loss relief is claimed as early as possible.

Solution

- There are two trading losses to consider:
  – £7,000 brought forward at 1 April 2013
  – £25,000 in the year ended 31 March 2017

  The phrase "as early as possible" in the requirement means that a current year claim should be made, then a carry back claim, for the loss of £25,000. Relief should be given for earlier trading losses before relief is given for later losses.

- The capital loss can only be carried forward and used against future gains.
- The property loss should be deducted from total profits before QCDs of the accounting period of the loss.
- As each loss is relieved the loss working should be completed.

Corporation tax computations

Year to:	31.03.14	31.03.15	31.03.16	31.03.17
	£	£	£	£
Trading profit	14,000	10,000	23,500	0
Less: Trading loss b/f	(7,000)			
	7,000			
Interest income	2,200	1,800	2,000	2,400
Property income	800	1,100	0	800
Chargeable gains (£2,600 – £700)	0	0	0	1,900
Total profits	10,000	12,900	25,500	5,100
Property loss relief			(800)	
Less: Trading loss relief				
– current CAP				(5,100)
– carry back			(19,900)	
	10,000	12,900	4,800	0
Less: QCDs	(200)	(200)	(200)	Wasted
TTP	9,800	12,700	4,600	0

Loss working – trading losses

	£
Loss carried forward at 01.04.13	7,000
Less: Used in y/e 31.03.14	(7,000)
	0
Loss for y/e 31.03.17	25,000
Less: Used in current CAP – y/e 31.03.17	(5,100)
Used in 12 month carry back – y/e 31.03.16	(19,900)
	0

Loss working – non-trading losses

	£
Capital loss for y/e 31.03.15	700
Less: Deducted from chargeable gains for y/e 31.03.17	(700)
	0
Property business income loss for y/e 31.03.16	800
Less: Used against total profits of y/e 31.03.16	(800)
	0

Test your understanding 1

Lost Ltd's results for the three accounting periods to 31 March 2017 are:

	y/e 30.06.15	p/e 31.03.16	y/e 31.03.17
	£	£	£
Trading profit/(loss)	88,600	20,800	(78,300)
Property income	0	4,500	5,600
Chargeable gain/(capital loss)	(3,000)	0	9,500
QCDs	(1,400)	(800)	(1,100)

There was a trading loss brought forward at 1 July 2014 of £2,000.

(a) **Assuming that Lost Ltd claims relief for its losses as early as possible, compute the company's taxable total profits for the three accounting periods to 31 March 2017.**

Your answer should clearly identify the amount of any losses that are unrelieved.

(b) **Explain how your answer to (a) above would have differed if Lost Ltd had ceased trading on 31 March 2017.**

2 Choice of loss reliefs

Factors that influence choice of loss relief

Where there is a choice of loss reliefs available, the following factors will influence the loss relief chosen:

- Tax saving
- Cash flow
- Wastage of relief for QCDs.

Tax saving

The company will want to save (or obtain a refund at) the highest possible rate of tax.

In previous financial years, the main rate of corporation tax was higher than 20%. However, the rates applicable to past financial years are not examinable.

You should therefore assume in examination questions that all tax saved will be at a rate of 20%.

Cash flow

A company's cash flow position may affect its choice of loss relief.

Note that when a loss is carried back, it will probably result in a repayment of corporation tax for the earlier period, whereas carrying the loss forward will only result in a reduction of a future liability. Therefore, for cash flow purposes it will be better to make a current year claim and then carry losses back.

3 Restrictions on loss relief

In order to prevent tax avoidance there are restrictions on the carry forward or carry back of trading losses when there is a change in the ownership of a company.

Change in ownership

A change in ownership means that **more than one half** of the ordinary share capital of a company is acquired by a person or persons, ignoring any person acquiring 5% or less. A person could be an individual or a company.

For example, an individual shareholder owns 10% of a company's shares and purchases a further 60%, making his total holding 70%. As more than half (in this case 60%) of the shares have changed hands, this is a change in ownership.

Restrictions

The restrictions apply in two situations:

- where there is **both** a **change in ownership** and a **major change** in the **nature or conduct of the trade** within **three years before or after** the change in ownership, or
- when **at any time** after the scale of **activities** of the trade has become **small or negligible**, and before any considerable revival of the trade, there is a change in the ownership of the company.

The restrictions prevent:

- losses from before the change in ownership being carried forward against profits arising after the change in ownership, and
- losses incurred after the change of ownership being carried back before the change of ownership.

Major change in the nature or conduct of the trade

It is important to understand that the trade itself has not changed, just the nature or conduct of trade. Major changes include:

- a major change in the type of property dealt in or services provided; and
- a major change in customers, outlets or markets.

Test your understanding 2

All the share capital of H Ltd has recently been acquired by Richard.

H Ltd manufactures mobile phone accessories which it sells to large retailers. H Ltd has made heavy losses for the last two years.

Richard wants to make the following changes to the company over the next three years:

- Relocate most of the manufacturing activity overseas.
- Expand the company's product range.
- Start to sell direct to the public over the internet.
- Appoint two new sales directors.

State the effect these changes are likely to have on the company's corporation tax loss position.

Changes to a trade without a change in ownership

Remember that trading losses can only be carried forward against future trading profits from the **same trade**.

Therefore, even without a change of ownership, if a company's trade changes so greatly that it is considered to be a different trade from the one which generated the losses, it will not be possible to offset the losses against profits from the new trade.

4 Chapter summary

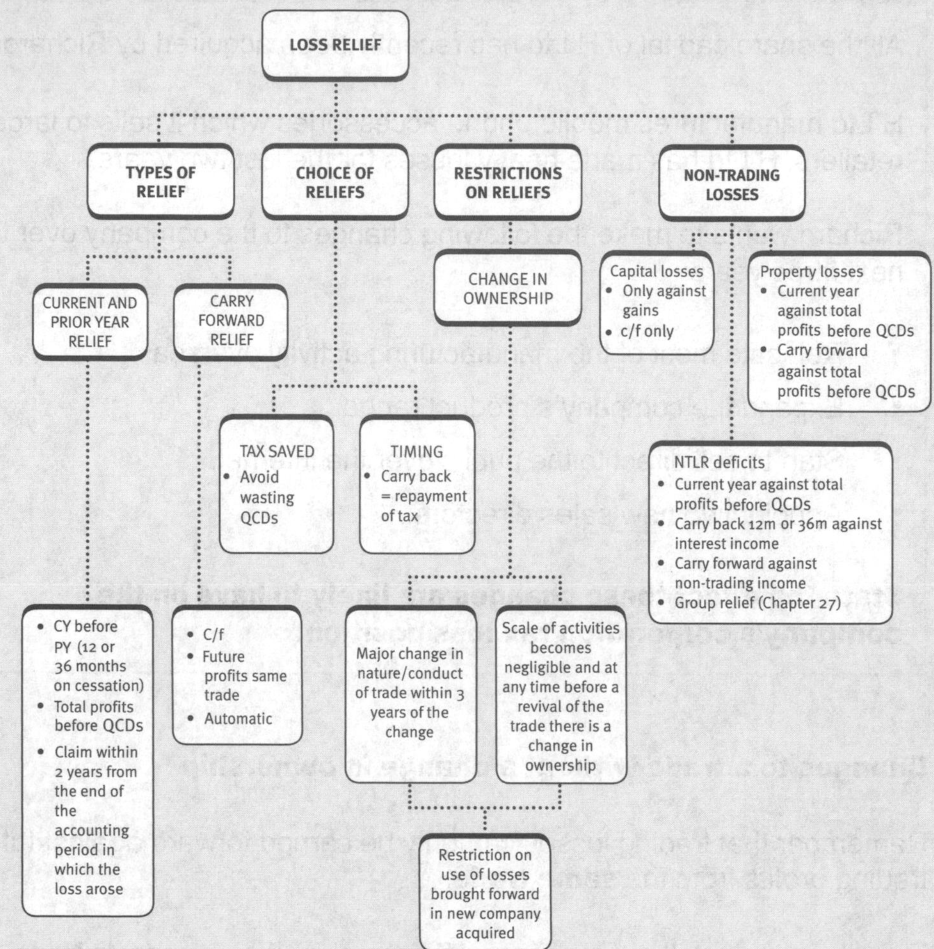

Test your understanding answers

Test your understanding 1

Lost Ltd

(a) **Lost Ltd – Taxable total profits**

	y/e 30.06.15	p/e 31.03.16	y/e 31.03.17
	£	£	£
Trading profit	88,600	20,800	0
Less: Loss b/f	(2,000)	(0)	(0)
	86,600	20,800	0
Property income	0	4,500	5,600
Net chargeable gain (£9,500 – £3,000)	0	0	6,500
Total profits	86,600	25,300	12,100
Less: Loss relief			
– Current year			(12,100)
– Carry back 12 mths	(21,650)	(25,300)	
	64,950	0	0
Less: QCDs	(1,400)	Wasted	Wasted
TTP	63,550	0	0

Loss working

	£
Trading loss y/e 31.03.17	78,300
Less: Used in current year claim – y/e 31.03.17	(12,100)
	66,200
Less: Used in 12 month carry back	
– 9 m/e 31.03.16	(25,300)
	40,900
– y/e 30.06.15: Maximum = (3/12 × £86,600)	(21,650)
Loss remaining to carry forward	19,250

(b) **If Lost Ltd ceased to trade on 31 March 2017**

- The trading loss of the final 12 months could be relieved against total profits for the previous 36 months.
- Therefore the unrelieved losses of £19,250 could have been carried back and fully set off in the year ended 30 June 2015.

Test your understanding 2

H Ltd

The changes that Richard proposes are likely to be taken by HMRC as a major change in the nature or conduct of H Ltd's trade.

As the changes occur within three years of Richard buying the company (a change in ownership) they will have the result of disallowing H Ltd's loss relief.

Losses will no longer be available to carry forward against trading profits arising after the change in ownership.

chapter

25

Business financial management

Chapter learning objectives

Upon completion of this chapter you will be able to:

- discuss the methods of financing a business by means of investment by individuals and other corporate bodies, and explain the impact for tax of these various methods, including the effect on the investor and the business that is raising the finance
- compare the different methods of financing the non-current assets of a business from a tax and commercial viewpoint
- describe the various methods available to defer or reduce tax liabilities for an individual or a business.

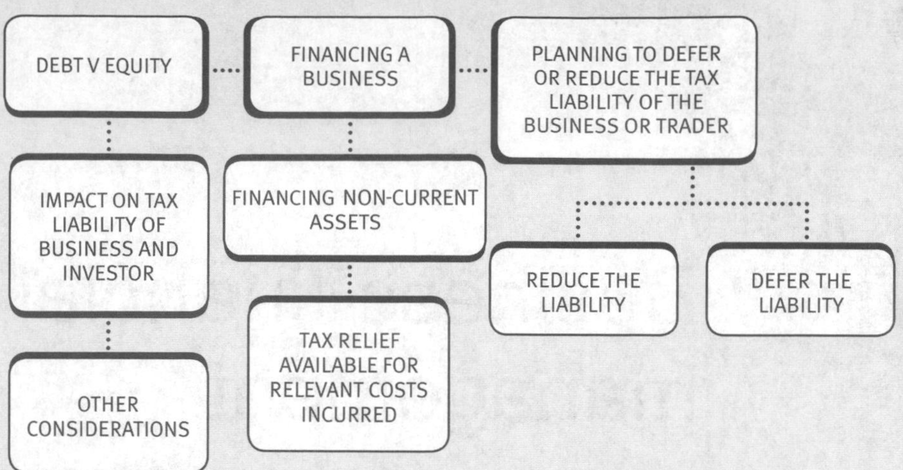

Introduction

This chapter deals with the way in which sole traders or partnerships, and companies can raise finance. Non-current asset financing is also considered.

The tax implications and other commercial considerations that should be borne in mind when deciding how to finance the business are discussed.

1 Business finance

Financing a company – long-term finance

A company can raise long-term finance to fund its activities from:

- Shareholders (equity).
- Third party loan finance, sometimes by way of an issue of loan notes (debt).

The effect of each of these is different from the company's perspective.

However, the requirements of the investors also need to be taken into account, and these will vary depending on whether they are individuals or other companies.

The main considerations for the company raising the finance will be:

- funding the interest payments or dividends that will result
- the security required by the lenders – they may require a charge on company assets which would be exercised if the company failed to meet its obligations with regard to income and/or capital repayments.

Comparison between the use of equity or debt

A summary of the main differences between using these two methods of finance is as follows:

	Equity	**Debt**
Amount	The maximum issued share capital is • specified in the Articles when the company is formed • usually well in excess of what it is anticipated the company will need.	There is no limit to the amount of finance that can be raised in debt, other than the amount the investors are prepared to invest.
Return	Dividends • The company must have distributable profits to pay a dividend. • The dividend payment is not allowable for corporation tax.	Interest • Interest must be paid irrespective of the company's profitability. • It is deductible on an accruals basis. • Interest is paid net of 20% tax if it is paid to an individual in respect of an unquoted loan note. • Companies receive interest gross.
Corporate Investors	• No CT on dividends received.	• Interest income (on an accruals basis) = part of TTP

	Equity	Debt
Individual Investors	• A basic rate taxpayer – 7.5% IT liability on UK dividends received if not covered by £5,000 dividend nil rate band. • A higher rate or additional rate taxpayer – 32.5% or 38.1% liability if not covered by £5,000 dividend nil rate band.	• A basic rate tax payer – 20% liability on gross interest received if not covered by £1,000 savings nil rate band (but interest paid net of 20% tax if in respect of an unquoted loan note). • A higher rate taxpayer – 40% liability if not covered by £500 savings nil rate band. • An additional rate taxpayer – 45% liability (note: no savings nil rate band).
Other points	• Companies that are not listed on the Stock Exchange may find it difficult to raise finance with a new issue of shares. • For an owner managed business the existing shareholders may not be prepared to accept outside shareholders that could dilute their control of the company. In this case new share issues will probably be to existing shareholders and their family members.	• A lender may require a charge on assets as security for the debt. • If the company defaults on either the interest or the capital that charge can be called in, and the assets of the company sold to finance the outstanding amounts.

Example 1 – Debt vs. Equity

M Ltd is an unquoted trading company set up a number of years ago with 1,000 £1 ordinary shares issued at par. In order to expand the production facilities it needs to raise a further £50,000.

There are **two** possibilities:

(1) The company will issue a further 50,000 5% preference shares, which have a nominal value of £1 and a market value of £1 each.

(2) £50,000 loan notes will be issued at par. This will carry interest of 5% payable annually.

Required:

(a) **Calculate the retained profit for the year ended 31 March 2017 on the assumption that:**

- **the shares or loan notes will be issued on 1 April 2016**
- **a full year's preference dividend will be paid in the year**
- **no dividend is paid on the ordinary shares in the year**
- **the profit before interest, tax and dividends is £150,000.**

(b) **Calculate the net return for the investor on the assumption that:**

- **the investor is an individual who is a higher rate taxpayer and does not receive any other dividends or savings income**
- **the investor is a company.**

Solution

(a) **Retained profit – y/e 31 March 2017**

	Equity	Debt
	£	£
Profit	150,000	150,000
Less: Interest (5% × £50,000)		(2,500)
	150,000	147,500
Less: CT at 20%	(30,000)	(29,500)
	120,000	118,000
Less: Dividend (5% × £50,000)	(2,500)	
Retained profit	117,500	118,000

(b) **Return**

Individual investor

	Equity	Debt
Dividend received	2,500	
Interest received (£2,000 × 100/80) (Note)		2,500
IT at 0% on dividend (DNRB) (<£5,000)	0	
IT at 0% on savings (SNRB) (first £500)		0
IT at 40% on interest (remaining £2,000)		800
IT credit (20% × £2,500)		(500)
IT payable	0	300
Net income:		
Dividend (£2,500 – £0)	2,500	
Interest (£2,000 – £300)		1,700

Note: Companies deduct 20% income tax at source when they pay interest to an individual in respect of an unquoted loan note.

Corporate investor

	Equity	Debt
Dividend received	2,500	
Interest received		2,500
CT at 20%	0	(500)
After tax income	2,500	2,000

Incentives to invest in shares

HMRC offer tax-advantaged schemes where the issuing company meets certain conditions. These schemes allow the investor tax relief on the investment, and/or when the shares are sold and may therefore make the share issue more attractive to potential investors.

The most important of these schemes are:

<table>
<tr><th></th><th></th><th>Chapter</th><th>Applies to</th></tr>
<tr><td>Enterprise Investment Scheme</td><td>EIS</td><td rowspan="2">3 and 9</td><td rowspan="3">Individual investors</td></tr>
<tr><td>Seed Enterprise Investment Scheme</td><td>SEIS</td></tr>
<tr><td>Venture Capital Trusts</td><td>VCT</td><td>3</td></tr>
<tr><td>Substantial Shareholding Exemption</td><td>SSE</td><td>23</td><td>Corporate investors</td></tr>
</table>

Drawbacks of investing in shares

If the investment is wholly by way of equity, no return can be received by the investor until the company becomes profitable, whereas interest must always be paid irrespective of the company's profitability. Therefore, investors may prefer purchasing loan notes to shares as they have more certainty of a return. However, interest returns tend to be fixed, whereas, dividends could increase substantially with profits.

As a result an investor may wish to invest using a mix of debt and equity, especially where they are investing in a new company, which may not yet have distributable profits.

Financing a sole trader or partnership

There are two main sources of finance for unincorporated businesses (i.e. where the business is owned by the individual sole trader or partners in a partnership):

- the individuals themselves
- loans from banks and other financial institutions.

Financing by the individuals:

- An individual may have funds that they can invest in the business.

- If they are sole traders there is no interest charged to the business by the individual, as the individual is entitled to all of the profits of the business.
- In a partnership the profit sharing arrangements would reflect the amount invested by each partner in the business. However, any interest paid to partners is not deducted from trading profits.

Financing from a loan:

- A bank may be prepared to lend money to an individual to invest in their business. Interest relief against total income is available on this borrowing where the individual borrows money:
  - to invest in a partnership, of which they are a partner
  - to buy plant and machinery for use by a partnership of which they are a partner. In this case, relief is available in the tax year of purchase and the following three years.
- Many sole traders rely on short term financing such as bank overdrafts. The interest is deducted from the business profits as an expense.
- Most lenders will require some form of personal guarantee before they will lend money or allow an overdraft facility to a sole trader or partnership. If the business fails, the individual will then be responsible for repaying the debt from their personal resources.

Short term finance

Sources of short-term finance are:

- bank overdraft – interest allowed as a deduction from trading profits
- short term loans – as for debt except interest is always paid gross to both individuals and companies
- trade credit – not utilising cash balances to pay for purchases increases a credit balance or reduces the overdraft
- invoice discounting
- debt factoring
- hire purchase and leasing.

Invoice discounting is where a company sells its receivables to a third party who pays them an amount after deducting a service charge. The company will have to reimburse the money if the debt becomes irrecoverable.

Debt factoring is where the company sells its debt outright, and the debt factors take the risk of irrecoverable debts. The cost charged to the company is usually higher than where they use invoice discounting.

Summary

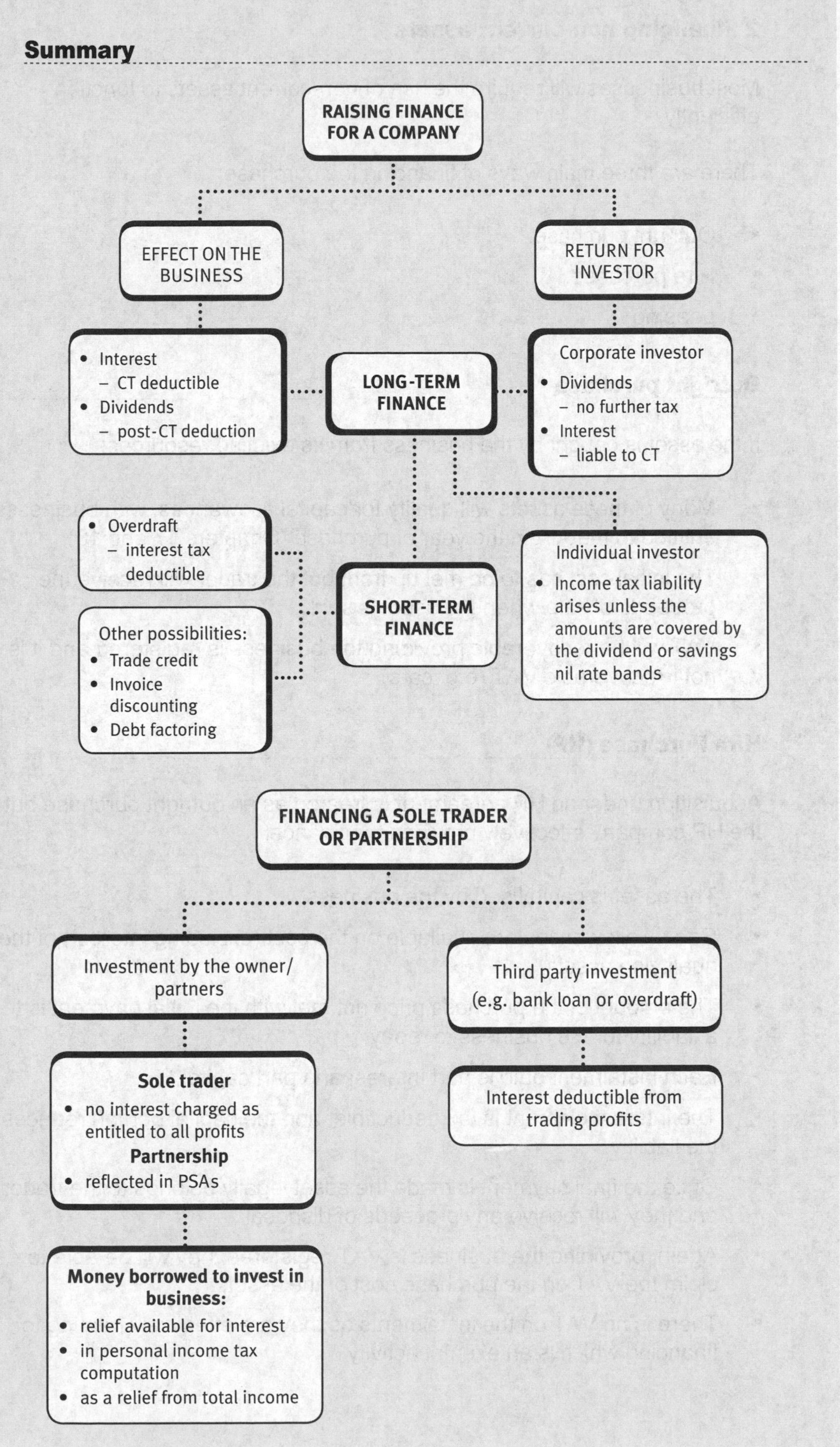
RAISING FINANCE FOR A COMPANY
EFFECT ON THE BUSINESS
RETURN FOR INVESTOR
• Interest
– CT deductible
• Dividends
– post-CT deduction
LONG-TERM FINANCE
Corporate investor
• Dividends
– no further tax
• Interest
– liable to CT
• Overdraft
– interest tax deductible
Other possibilities:
• Trade credit
• Invoice discounting
• Debt factoring
SHORT-TERM FINANCE
Individual investor
• Income tax liability arises unless the amounts are covered by the dividend or savings nil rate bands
FINANCING A SOLE TRADER OR PARTNERSHIP
Investment by the owner/ partners
Third party investment (e.g. bank loan or overdraft)
Sole trader
• no interest charged as entitled to all profits
Partnership
• reflected in PSAs
Interest deductible from trading profits
Money borrowed to invest in business:
• relief available for interest
• in personal income tax computation
• as a relief from total income

2 Financing non-current assets

Most businesses will require the use of non-current assets to function efficiently.

There are three main ways of financing the purchase:

- Outright purchase.
- Hire purchase.
- Leasing.

Outright purchase

If the asset is bought by the business from its existing resources:

- Many of these assets will qualify for capital allowances, with businesses entitled to the AIA in the year of purchase (Chapters 17 and 18).
- The initial cost has to be met up front but the trader will receive the proceeds of sale when the asset is sold.
- VAT will be recoverable providing the business is registered and it is not irrecoverable VAT (e.g. cars).

Hire Purchase (HP)

Acquisition under an HP agreement is treated as an outright purchase but the HP company effectively provides the finance.

- The asset is capitalised by the business.
- Capital allowances are available on the cost (excluding interest) of the qualifying assets.
- The amount of the purchase price not met with the initial payment is then a liability for the business to repay.
- Each instalment paid is part interest and part capital.
- The interest element is tax deductible, and the capital portion reduces the liability.
- Once the final payment is made the asset legally belongs to the trader, and they will receive any proceeds of disposal.
- Again, providing the business is VAT registered they will be able to claim the VAT on the purchase cost of the asset.
- There is no VAT on the instalments as they are effectively relating to financing which is an exempt activity.

HP therefore achieves the same outright ownership of the asset but without the up-front cost. The overall cost will be greater as the interest has to be paid but it is spread over the period of the HP contract.

Leasing

Where an asset is leased:

- The business pays a rent, which is deductible for tax purposes.
- Tax relief is given when the payments are debited to the statement of profit or loss, and these are spread using the normal accounting principles.
- The asset returns to the leasing company at the end of the lease. Accordingly, there are
  - no proceeds of sale
  - no problems trying to find a buyer when the asset is no longer required.
- VAT is recovered by a VAT registered business.
- Where the asset is a high emission car there is a restriction on the tax relief available on the rental payments. In addition, usually only 50% of the VAT can be reclaimed on any car lease payments.

Summary

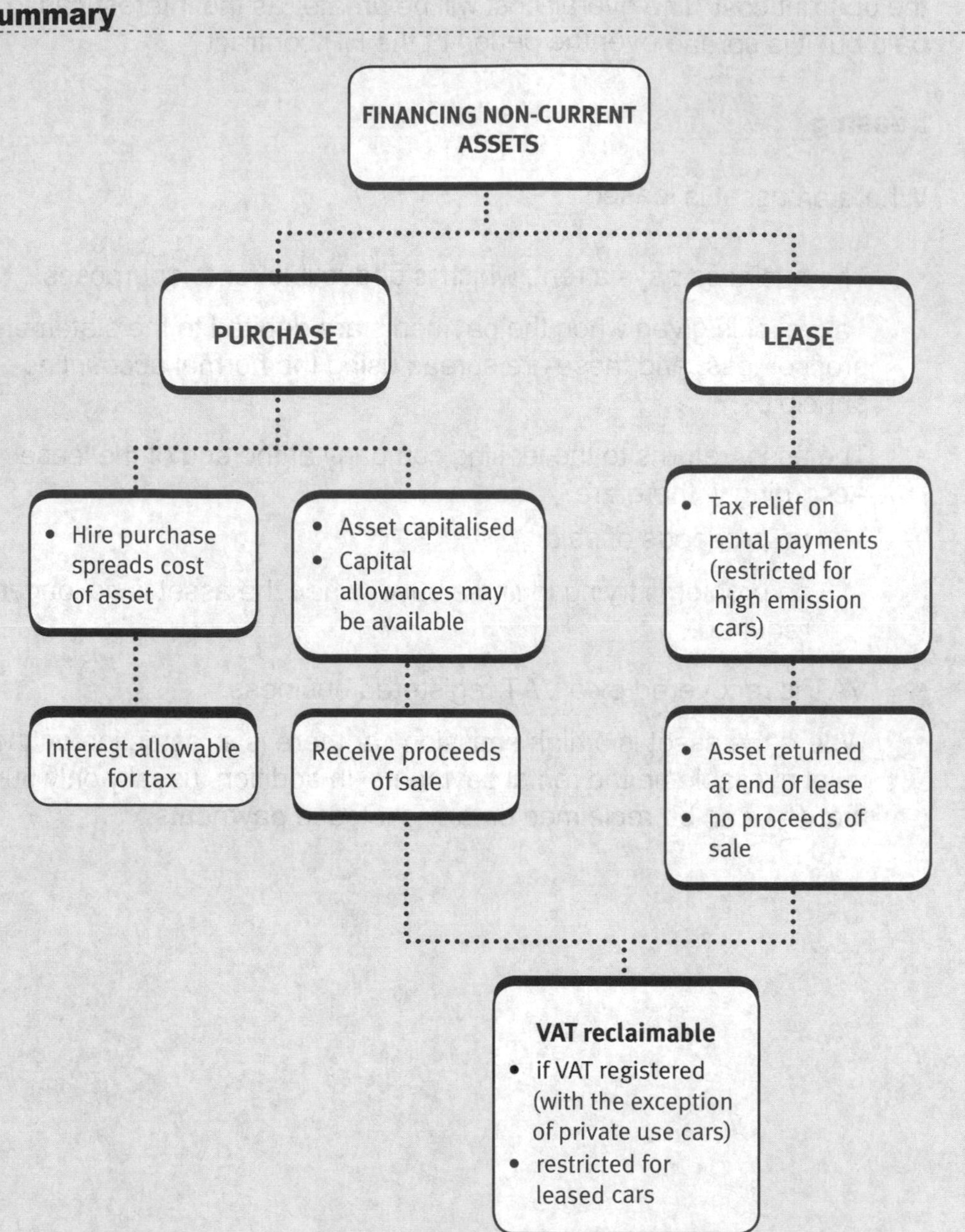

3 Deferring or reducing the tax liability of a business

There are a number of ways of reducing or deferring a tax liability incurred by a business.

For a quoted company it is necessary to consider the effect of these measures on the company's net profit as this will affect their ability to pay dividends, and possibly their share price.

Factors to consider have been covered in detail in earlier chapters. A reminder of the key factors to consider is given in expandable text and the considerations are summarised in the chapter summary.

Key factors

The following factors may be considered:

- The disposal of non-current assets may create a balancing allowance (BA) or charge (BC). The timing of the disposal should be considered to see whether a BA can be accelerated into the current year and a BC delayed until the next.
- Similarly there may be a capital gain or loss. Will the timing of the disposal affect the date on which the tax is payable or any loss relieved?
- Where the capital disposal is by an individual they need to consider the availability of the AEA. If they have a gain in the year, and there is to be a disposal that will create a capital loss, there is no point in crystallising the loss if the gain is already below the AEA and so no tax is payable.
- Where an individual has low income in a year they may waste PAs. In this situation they could consider not claiming all their capital allowances entitlement. If the full amount is not claimed the pool balance carried forward will be higher, and so greater allowances will be available in subsequent years. However, any entitlement to AIA or FYA not claimed, cannot be claimed in a subsequent year.
- Where the business sells an asset will there be a qualifying replacement purchased within the required time limit? If so, the gain can be deferred using rollover relief. Where the business is part of a group of companies the replacement can be made by any member of the gains group.
- Similar considerations apply where a company sells an intangible asset (other than goodwill) and replaces it with a further intangible asset.
- EIS and SEIS investment relief reduces the current year's income tax liability. However, it is difficult to withdraw from an EIS/SEIS investment as they are unquoted shares. In addition, EIS/SEIS companies tend not to pay dividends and retain their profits to increase the gain on disposal, as the gain should be exempt if the conditions are met.
- An investment in EIS shares may allow a gain on another disposal to be deferred. It will become chargeable when the EIS shares are sold.
- An investment in SEIS shares may exempt up to 50% of the gain.

- VCTs are a better investment in this context as they will pay dividends (exempt income), and because they are quoted companies it should be possible to realise the investment when needed. However, they are considered to be a risky investment and should not be used by someone who cannot afford to lose their investment.

4 Chapter summary

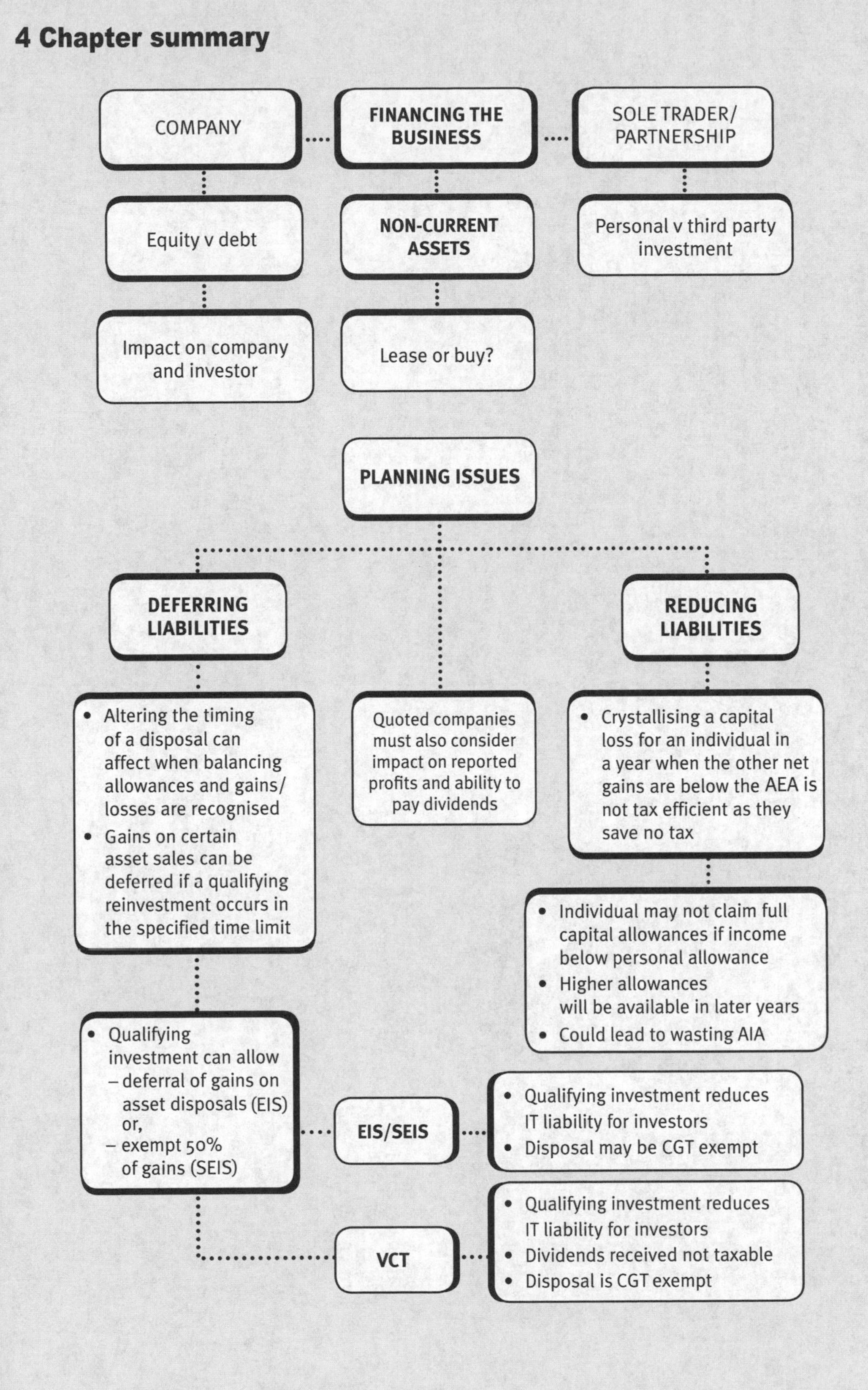
COMPANY
FINANCING THE BUSINESS
SOLE TRADER/ PARTNERSHIP
Equity v debt
NON-CURRENT ASSETS
Personal v third party investment
Impact on company and investor
Lease or buy?
PLANNING ISSUES
DEFERRING LIABILITIES
REDUCING LIABILITIES
• Altering the timing of a disposal can affect when balancing allowances and gains/ losses are recognised
• Gains on certain asset sales can be deferred if a qualifying reinvestment occurs in the specified time limit
Quoted companies must also consider impact on reported profits and ability to pay dividends
• Crystallising a capital loss for an individual in a year when the other net gains are below the AEA is not tax efficient as they save no tax
• Individual may not claim full capital allowances if income below personal allowance
• Higher allowances will be available in later years
• Could lead to wasting AIA
• Qualifying investment can allow
– deferral of gains on asset disposals (EIS) or,
– exempt 50% of gains (SEIS)
EIS/SEIS
• Qualifying investment reduces IT liability for investors
• Disposal may be CGT exempt
VCT
• Qualifying investment reduces IT liability for investors
• Dividends received not taxable
• Disposal is CGT exempt

chapter

26

Family companies and related planning scenarios

Chapter learning objectives

Upon completion of this chapter you will be able to:

- describe the various business vehicles available to individuals who want to start their own business
- identify companies that may fall within the close company regime, and set out the implications for the company and its shareholders
- discuss the different ways of extracting profits from a company, identifying the various tax issues that may arise
- identify personal service companies (PSC) and advise on the tax consequences of the company being treated as a PSC
- advise on the availability of, and the application of, disincorporation relief
- discuss the various methods available to shareholders who wish to withdraw their investment from a company.

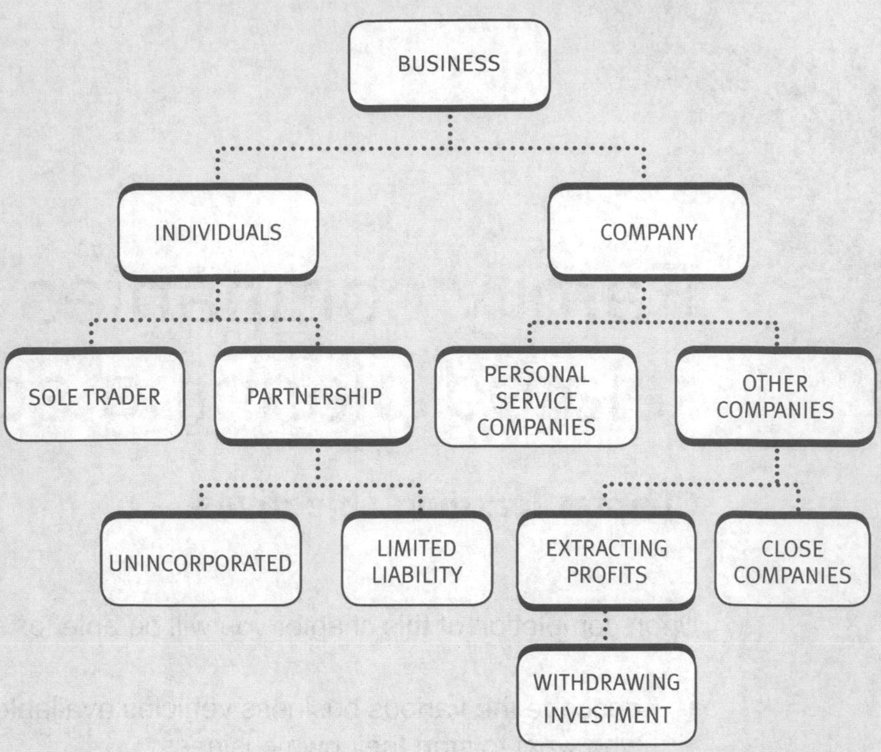

Introduction

This chapter considers multi-tax scenarios from a business perspective and introduces tax planning measures to minimise tax liabilities.

Much of the content of this chapter is covered in more detail in other chapters. However, this chapter aims to show how various ideas and taxes interact and form the basis of multi-tax scenario examination questions.

Areas covered in this chapter which primarily draw from previous knowledge include:

- Choosing the appropriate business vehicle when starting to trade.
- Extracting profits from a company.

The new areas at P6 introduced in this chapter include:

- Close companies.
- Personal service companies.
- Disincorporation relief.
- Exit strategies such as the purchase of own shares by a company and putting a company into liquidation.

1 Business vehicle

When an individual decides to start their own business, one of the most important factors they have to consider is how they should own it.

Direct ownership will be as a sole trader, or if there is more than one person involved, a partnership.

The alternative is to set up a limited company, and own the assets through the company. The individuals involved will then be shareholders and (probably) directors of the company.

Each method has its own tax implications.

The main areas that need to be considered are:

- What amounts does the individual pay tax on?
- Is there a liability to NIC?
- When is any tax payable?
- Commercial considerations.

Summary of differences

The main differences between operating as an unincorporated business or as a company can broadly be summarised as follows:

	Sole trader	**Company**
Taxation of profits	Trading profit assessed on a current year basis under income tax rules.	Corporation tax on TTP – after the individual has paid themselves a salary.
	Adjustments for private use when calculating trading profit.	No adjustments for private use when calculating trading profit – instead the individual is taxed on benefits received.
	Capital allowances with private use adjustments.	Capital allowances in full (no private use adjustments).
	Personal allowance.	No personal allowance for the company (although the individual will have a personal allowance to set against their income).
	Income tax at: 20%/40%/45%	Corporation tax at 20%
	Class 4 NICs = 9% of profits (£8,060 to £43,000) and 2% thereafter.	
	Class 2 NICs = £2.80 per week.	

	Sole trader	**Company**
Relief for losses	Relief available against total income of individual. Opening years relief – loss in any of first four tax years, set against total income of 3 preceding tax years (FIFO). Relief against total income of current/previous tax year. Extension against chargeable gains in same years. C/fwd against trading profit of same trade.	Loss relieved against company's total profits (income and gains) only. No opening years relief available. Current year – set against total profits (income and gains) of current CAP. Prior year – set against total profits (income and gains) of previous 12 months. C/fwd – against trading profit of same trade.

	Sole trader	**Company**
Withdrawal of funds	No tax implications – all profits already assessed to tax on the individual as trading profit.	Salary/Bonus • Employment income for individual. • Allowable deduction for the company. • Employee class 1 NICs. • Employer's class 1 NICs for company (allowable deduction). Dividend • Assessed on a cash receipts basis • Taxed as top slice of income • First £5,000 covered by the dividend nil rate band • Excess taxed at 7.5%/32.5%/38.1%. • Dividends not an allowable deduction from trading profit for a company. • Company must have distributable profit.
VAT	Individual registers	Company registers

	Sole trader	Company
Disposal of business	Gains on individual chargeable assets: • Gains are business assets: – for gift relief – for entrepreneurs' relief if disposal of the entire business. IHT – 100% BPR on gift/legacy.	Gain on shares: • Shares in an unquoted trading company will usually be business assets. • Gift relief if shares gifted. • Entrepreneurs' relief or investors' relief on disposal. IHT – 100% BPR on gift/legacy.

Considerations when choosing the relevant structure

Intention to withdraw **profits**:

- A sole trader is required to pay tax on the profits made, not the amount drawn out of the business.
- Where it is not intended to withdraw all the profits, it will probably be more advantageous to operate as a company, as the company pays tax at 20% allowing the retained profits to be taxed at the lower rate (although the future extraction of funds will potentially have further tax consequences).

Initial losses

- If the business will start with losses it may be preferable to structure it initially as a sole trade, allowing the losses to be used against the owner's total income and take advantage of opening years loss relief, which is only available to individuals, not companies.
- Once the business becomes profitable, it may be incorporated if a company is the preferred structure.

Liability

- Where liability is an issue, a company will probably be preferred as a corporate structure will limit the individual's potential liability.
- However, it should be remembered that some businesses are not allowed to incorporate. In this case a Limited Liability Partnership (LLP) may be used.

Limited liability partnership

- A LLP is taxed in the same way as an unincorporated partnership, with each partner paying tax on their share of the profits.
- Each partner's liability is limited to their investment in the LLP. However, each partner has no limit to their liability for the work that they are personally responsible for.

Summary

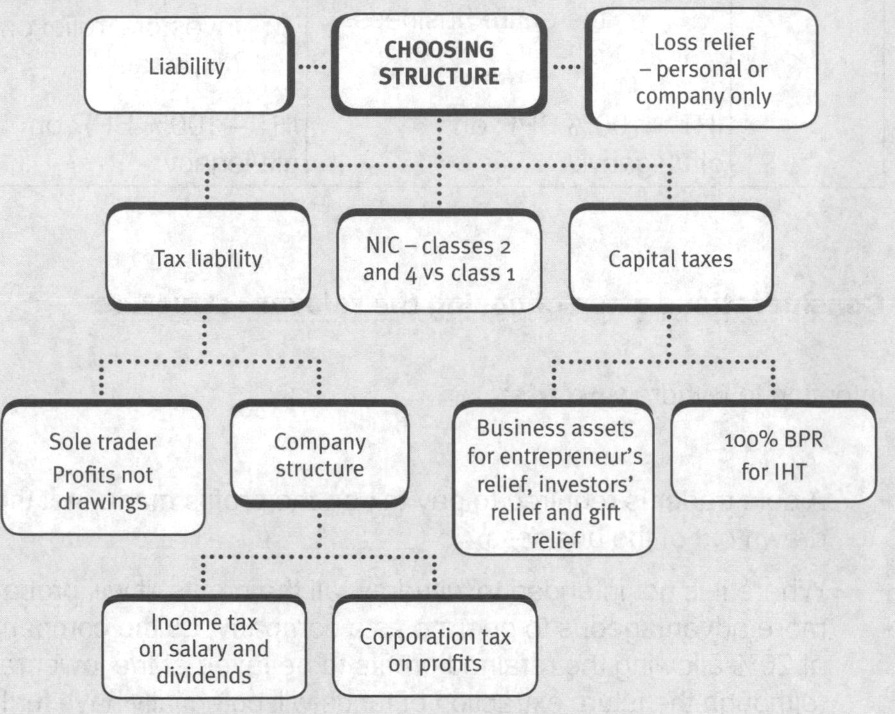

2 Close companies

Definition of a close company

Many 'owner managed' businesses will be close companies.

A close company is a company controlled by:

- any number of directors; or
- five or fewer participators.

'Control' means holding > 50% of:

- the issued share capital of the company, **or**
- the voting power, **or**
- the right to receive distributable profits, **or**
- the right to receive the net assets in the event of a winding up.

A participator is primarily a shareholder.

To decide whether a group of individuals has control of the company it is necessary to include the shares of their associates.

Associates are taken to be the spouse (or civil partner), children and issue, parents and remoter ancestors, brothers and sisters and business partners.

A company which is a subsidiary takes its status from the parent company.

So, if the parent company of a group is a close company, the subsidiary is also a close company.

If the parent company is not a close company, the subsidiary will not be close either, even if it is a wholly-owned subsidiary.

Test your understanding 1

Shares in La Famille Ltd are owned as follows:

	% shares
Jeanette	12
Arthur (Jeanette's husband)	6
Louis (Jeanette's son)	5
Cecile (Jeanette's cousin)	5
Hugo (unconnected) (the only director)	20
Felicity (unconnected)	4
24 other unconnected shareholders, each with 2%	48
	100

Explain whether or not La Famille Ltd is a close company.

An examination question may require you to identify that a company is close. Therefore you need to be able to spot a close company scenario, even if you are not told there is one!

Implications of close company status

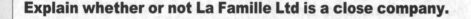

In close companies, shareholders (who may also be directors) may have significant influence over company resources and decisions. There are anti avoidance measures in place to prevent these shareholders benefiting unfairly from their significant influence over a close company.

The principal measures cover:

- the provision of benefits to shareholders, and
- the provision of loans to or from shareholders.

In considering the measures, the status of the individual must be identified:

- the individual may be a shareholder only, or
- they may be both a shareholder and an employee/director.

The provision of benefits to shareholders

The provision of a benefit to an individual who is an employee/director is subject to the employment income provisions.

- For the company, the cost of providing the benefit is an allowable expense and reduces trading profits.
- For the individual, the taxable benefit is calculated using employment income rules.

The tax implications for the company and the individual shareholder of the provision of a benefit to a shareholder (or their associate) who is **not** an employee/director are as follows:

Company	Individual (shareholder)
The company is deemed to have paid a dividend. There is no need for the company to have sufficient distributable profits as the provision of the benefit is not a genuine dividend.	No employment income charge possible as no office or employment.
The **amount** (i.e. value) of the dividend is determined using the benefit rules.	The value of the benefit is treated as a dividend.
No trading profit deduction for the cost of providing the benefit as it is treated as a dividend.	This will be taxed in the year the benefit is provided. The first £5,000 of dividend income is covered by the nil rate band and the excess is taxed at the rate of 7.5% if the individual is a basic rate taxpayer, 32.5% if higher rate, or 38.1% if additional rate.

Test your understanding 2

Malcolm and Helen are shareholders of Houghton Ltd, a close company. Malcolm is also a director of the company.

Houghton Ltd provided each of them during the current accounting period with a petrol engine company car, list price £20,000 and a CO_2 emission rate of 146 g/km. They each travel 5,000 miles; 3,000 miles of Malcolm's mileage is on company business. The company does not pay for private petrol for either Malcolm or Helen.

Houghton Ltd is a profitable company.

Malcolm and Helen are both higher rate taxpayers.

Explain the tax implications for the company and the individuals of the provision of the company cars.

The provision of a loan to a shareholder

The provision of a loan to a shareholder, irrespective of employment status, has the following implications:

For the company

- There is a tax charge of 32.5% of the amount of the loan.
- This charge is paid at the same time as the corporation tax liability (i.e. either 9 months and one day after the end of the accounting period or the charge is built into the company's quarterly instalment payments).
- No tax is payable if the loan has been repaid before 9 months and one day after the end of the accounting period.
- Where the tax charge has been paid, it becomes repayable when:
  (1) the loan is repaid:
    – where part of the loan is repaid the same proportion of the tax is repayable
  (2) the loan is written off:
    – the company can reclaim the tax paid when the loan was made
    – there is no deduction for the write-off against the company's profits for CT purposes
    – at this point the individual becomes liable for income tax (see below).

- No tax is payable by the company where the loan fulfils three requirements:
  - (1) The amount of the loan is less than or equal to £15,000, and
  - (2) The individual is a full-time working employee, and
  - (3) The individual (including associates' interests) owns 5% of the shares or less.

For the shareholder

- There are no immediate tax implications for the individual when the company makes them a loan.
- If the loan is written off, they then become subject to income tax on the amount written off as though it was a dividend received at the date of the write-off.

Interest

Where the company does not charge interest of at least the official rate (currently 3%), there will be a taxable benefit. The rules for the provision of benefits apply (see above).

- For an employee, this benefit will be taxed as earnings.
- Where the individual is not an employee, the benefit will be treated as a dividend distribution.

Test your understanding 3

Sally and Claire are both shareholders and full time employees in White Ltd, a close company. The company prepares its accounts to 31 March annually and is not a large company for quarterly instalment purposes.

Sally owns 15% of the company, whilst Claire owns 3%. They are not connected with each other. The company lends each of them £12,000, on 6 April 2016. Claire repays £4,000 on 31 December 2016. Interest of 2% is charged on the loans.

Explain the tax implications for both White Ltd and its employees Sally and Claire of the loans made by the company.

The provision of loans from shareholders to the close company

A shareholder may take out a personal loan in order to make a loan to or buy shares in a close company.

Income tax relief on interest paid on such borrowing is available as a relief deducted from total income, provided the company is not a close investment company (see below).

The conditions are that the individual:

- has a material interest (more than 5%) in the company, or
- is a full-time working officer or employee involved in the management of the company.

The maximum deduction allowed from total income includes this type of qualifying interest (Chapter 1).

Close investment holding company (CIC)

All close companies are close investment companies (CIC) unless their main activity is trading, or letting property to unconnected persons.

The tax consequences of a CIC are as follows:

- The shares will not be treated as business assets for IHT nor CGT.
- Tax relief will not be available to an individual if they borrow money to invest in a CIC.

Summary

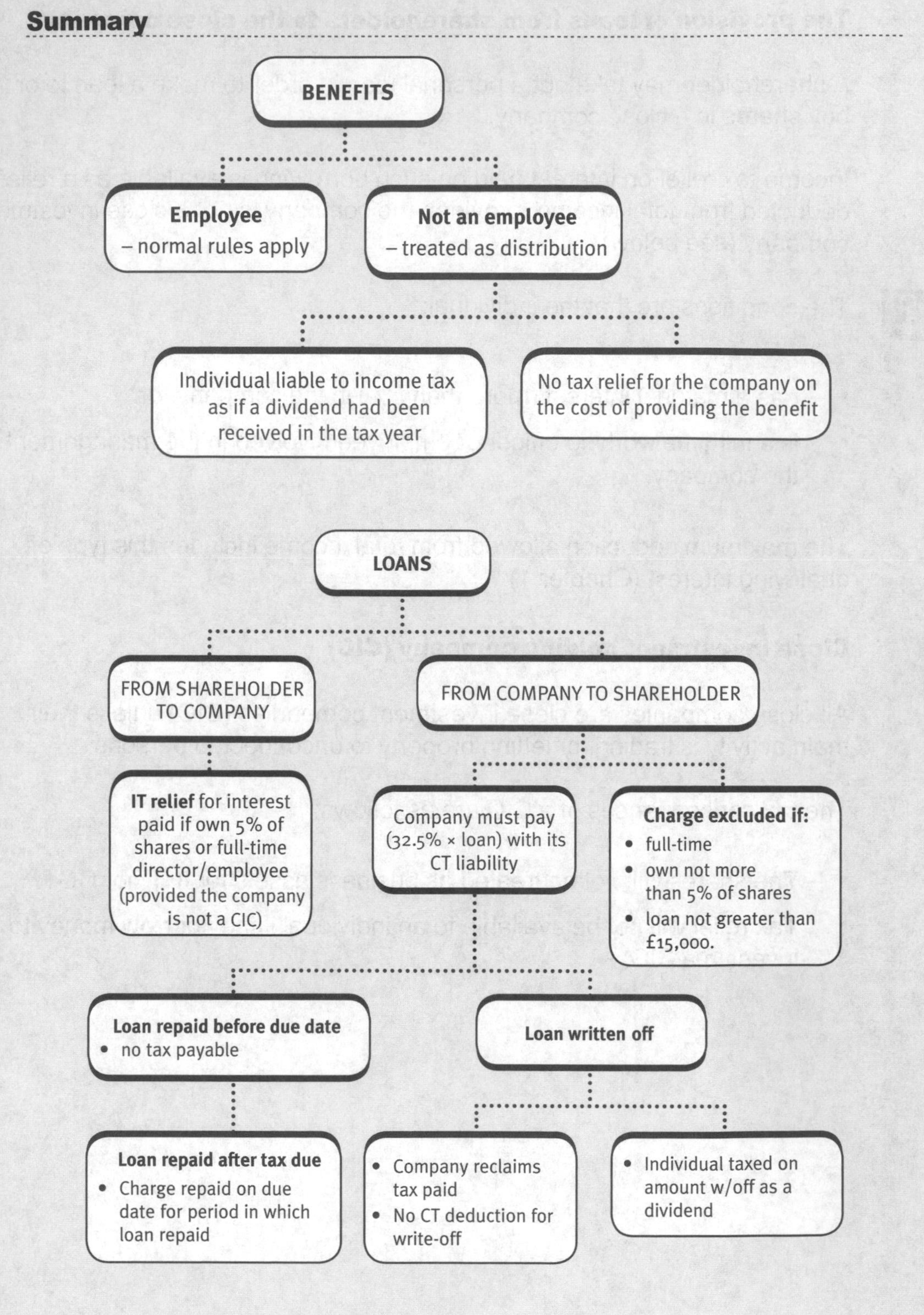
BENEFITS
Employee – normal rules apply
Not an employee – treated as distribution
Individual liable to income tax as if a dividend had been received in the tax year
No tax relief for the company on the cost of providing the benefit
LOANS
FROM SHAREHOLDER TO COMPANY
FROM COMPANY TO SHAREHOLDER
IT relief for interest paid if own 5% of shares or full-time director/employee (provided the company is not a CIC)
Company must pay (32.5% × loan) with its CT liability
Charge excluded if:
• full-time
• own not more than 5% of shares
• loan not greater than £15,000.
Loan repaid before due date
• no tax payable
Loan written off
Loan repaid after tax due
• Charge repaid on due date for period in which loan repaid
• Company reclaims tax paid
• No CT deduction for write-off
• Individual taxed on amount w/off as a dividend

CLOSE INVESTMENT COMPANY

- All close companies – unless trading or let property to third parties
- Shares not business assets
- No IT relief for loan from shareholder

3 Extracting profits from a company

Many UK companies are small trading companies, and consideration is often given to tax efficient means of extracting profits in either an income or capital form.

This section considers the methods of extracting profits from a company and the implications for both the company and the individual shareholder and/or director.

Salary v dividend

	Salary	**Dividend**
Rates of IT	20%/40%/45%	7.5%/32.5%/38.1%
NICs paid by individual	Individual must pay class 1 NICs on the salary at 12% or 2%.	No NICs payable on dividends.
NICs paid by Company	Employer must pay class 1 NIC on the salary at 13.8%. Note that the employers £3,000 NIC allowance is not available where the director is the sole employee.	No NICs is payable on dividends.
CT implications for company	The salary paid to the employee and the NICs paid by the company are treated as staff costs. This reduces the trading profit of the company and the CT payable.	None.

Pension contributions	Salary is earned income and is relevant earnings for pension tax relief purposes.	Dividends are not earned income and are not relevant earnings for pension tax relief purposes.
Formalities	If a bonus is accrued at the end of the accounting period it must: • be paid within 9 months of the end of the accounting period; and • comply with IAS 37.	The company must have distributable profits to be able to pay a dividend.

Test your understanding 4

Norman is the only shareholder and employee/director of Fletcher Ltd. He has been paid a salary of £48,000.

It has been decided that there are £50,000 of profits before corporation tax that can be used to either pay a bonus to Norman, or a dividend. The £50,000 is to include any employer's NIC liability.

Calculate the amount Norman will receive after all taxes have been paid and the overall tax cost of the additional profit extraction.

Other possibilities

There are a number of other possible ways of extracting profits, depending on the individual situation which include:

- charging rent,
- charging interest, and
- funding a pension scheme.

Further details of these extraction methods are given in expandable text.

Rent

- Where property is to be bought for the use of the company it may be preferable to consider owning it personally and charging the company rent for its use.
- The rent would be an allowable deduction for corporation tax, providing it was at no more than a commercial rent.
- When the individual retires they may sell the property with the shares or might consider retaining it so that the rent received would supplement their pension income.
- A further advantage of direct ownership is that if the company owns the asset there will be two charges to tax before the individual receives the proceeds of a sale of the property:

  (1) The company pays corporation tax on any gain arising.

  (2) The individual would then be taxable when the profits were extracted from the company.
- A slight drawback of holding the property outside the company is that if IHT became an issue, BPR would only be available at 50%. However, if the business is sold before the individual dies this would not create a problem. If there was a concern about a charge, insurance could be taken to cover any liability that may arise on death.
- Further, on the disposal of the property it would not qualify for entrepreneurs' relief even if sold at the same time as the disposal of the company shares. This is because the associated disposal rules do not apply where a market rent is charged to the company by the individual for the use of the asset (see Chapter 9).

Interest

- Where the individual has lent money to the company, interest may be paid by the company to the individual. The rate applied cannot be in excess of a commercial rate.
- There may be a timing advantage as the company will deduct the interest on an accruals basis but the individual is not taxed until it is received:
  - Consider a company with a year ended 31 March 2017. Interest can be accrued within the accounts for that period but providing it is not paid until 6 April 2017 it will only be taxed on the individual in 2017/18.

- The individual will be taxed on the interest received in excess of the savings nil rate band at 20%/40%/45% depending on whether they are a basic/higher/additional rate taxpayer. The savings nil rate band is £1,000/£500/£Nil depending on the level of their taxable income.
- Where the individual and the company are connected, the interest must be paid within 12 months of the end of the accounting period to be allowable as a deduction for the period in which it is accrued. If it is not, it only becomes an allowable deduction for corporation tax when it is paid.

Pension contributions

- The company may make contributions to a pension scheme on behalf of the individual. Providing they fall within the approved limits there would be no income tax or NIC liability.
- The main drawback of this method of extraction is that the pension funds cannot be accessed until the individual is at least 55.

Summary

Type of payment	Liable to IT?	NIC	Pensionable income	CT deductible?
Salary	Yes	Class 1	Yes	Yes – providing paid within 9 months of end of the AP and complies with IAS 37
Dividend	Yes	No	No	No
Rent	Yes	No	No	Yes – providing at commercial rate
Interest	Yes	No	No	Yes – providing not at > commercial rate and paid < 12 months of end of CAP
Pension contributions	No	No	No	Yes when paid

4 Personal service companies (PSC)

The purpose of the PSC legislation

The purpose of the legislation on personal service companies (PSC) is to counter practices of tax avoidance which were becoming widespread.

Reference is sometimes made to these rules as the IR35 legislation, which is the name of the original HMRC press release issued that set out the objectives of the legislation.

The schemes that the legislation aims to combat are as follows:

- Many businesses have been reluctant to pay an individual for their services directly as a self-employed individual because if HMRC reclassify them as employees there can be substantial costs and penalties incurred by both the self-employed business and the business employing their services (the client).
- As a result:
  - individuals who were self-employed have been encouraged to set up companies which the client would then contract with, and pay the company for the individual's services. Where the client is paying a company it would be more difficult to argue that the individual was a direct employee of that client.
  - companies have encouraged existing employees to resign, set up a company, and the client would then use their services through that company, resulting in a major saving of NIC for that client.
- The company owned by the individual worker is referred to as a Personal Service Company (PSC).

Advantages to the individuals

Individuals realised that operating through a company could have advantages as follows:

(1) The PSC invoices for the individual's services (plus VAT, if appropriate) and

- the client pays the invoices gross without having to apply the PAYE regulations
- there are no employer's NIC contributions payable.

(2) The PSC pays CT at only 20% on profits net of any expenses wholly and exclusively incurred for the trade.

(3) The individual is an employee of the PSC, or better still, a director without a contract of employment thereby side-stepping the National Minimum Wage regulations.

(4) The individual could draw sufficient remuneration (or director's fees)

- to exceed the lower earnings limit for NIC purposes thereby creating entitlement to benefits
- but below the primary threshold so that no class 1 liabilities arise.

The individual can then draw out the rest of the profits of the business as dividends.

(5) There is scope for dividing the shareholding of the PSC with a spouse so that two basic rate bands are utilised before higher rate income tax is payable.

(6) Income could be rolled up indefinitely net of a 20% CT charge so that good and bad years can be evened out and the individual need never pay higher rate tax unless they so choose.

As a result of such schemes HMRC introduced rules to combat what they perceived was a loss of tax/NIC arising where individuals used a company to bill their services to a client.

What makes a company a PSC?

HMRC look at the relationship between the client and the worker.

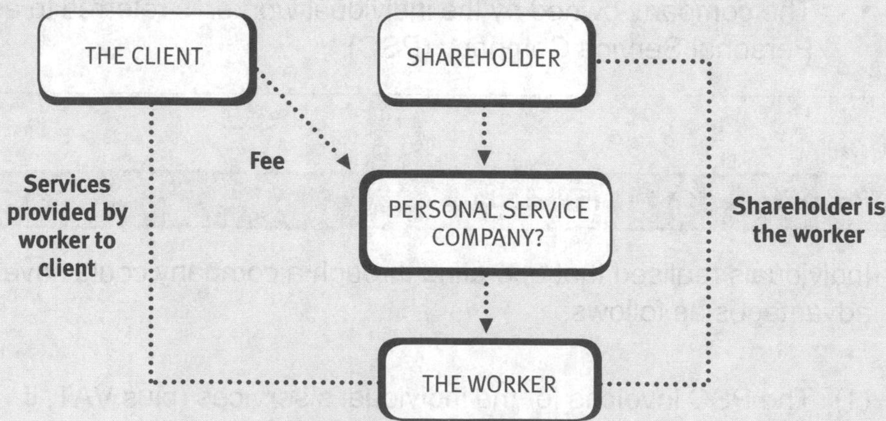

HMRC will ask the question: if the company was not there, would the worker be an employee of the client or self-employed? The normal rules for deciding employment or self-employment are used (see Chapter 2).

If the situation is considered to be one of employment the company owned by the worker is a PSC, and the special legislation applies.

The scope of PSC rules

The rules only apply to 'relevant engagements'. These are contracts between the company and the client which would have been a contract of employment in the absence of the PSC.

Although the client of the PSC is a significant beneficiary of the abuse, they are not the focus of the provisions.

The PSC has to:

- treat the income from relevant engagements arising in a tax year **as if it were paid out as salary** to the employee, and
- account for the notional income tax and NIC on 19 April following the end of the tax year.

This **notional** salary is deemed paid at the end of the tax year.

Notional salary

The notional salary is the income from the relevant engagements, reduced by the following:

- any actual salary and benefits received in the year
- expenses incurred by the company which would have been deductible under the employment income rules if the individual had incurred them personally
- contributions made by the company to an occupational pension scheme
- employer's NIC paid during the year on actual salary and on the notional salary
- 5% of gross payments from relevant engagements as a flat rate deduction to cover such things as overheads and training, whether or not the money is spent.

Pro forma for notional salary calculation

		£
Amount received in tax year from relevant engagements		X_A
Less:	Statutory deduction (5% × X_A)	(X)
	Employer's NICs paid by PSC	(X)
	Pension contributions by PSC	(X)
	Salary paid by PSC	(X)
	Allowable expenses	(X)
Deemed salary including PSC's deemed employer's NICs		X_B
Less: PSC's employer's NICs [X_B × (13.8/113.8)]		(X)
Notional salary		X

To avoid a double charge to tax:

- The notional salary and NIC is allowable for calculating corporation tax profits.
- Where dividends are subsequently paid out of this income they are ignored as part of the individual's taxable income.

Test your understanding 5

Brian is a consultant trading through a personal service company, Conrad Ltd. He is the only director/employee and owns all of the shares of the company.

During the tax year 2016/17 Brian was occupied almost full-time under a contract Conrad Ltd had with Wilson Ltd. Wilson Ltd paid Conrad Ltd £70,000 in fees for Brian's services.

Brian drew a salary of £25,000 from Conrad Ltd in the tax year 2016/17 which is taxed via PAYE and employer's NICs of £2,331 were paid.

(a) **Calculate the deemed employment income arising from the relevant engagement with Wilson Ltd and the income tax and the employer's NIC payable in respect of the relevant engagement.**

(b) **Calculate the corporation tax payable by Conrad Ltd in the year ending 31 March 2017, assuming the personal service company legislation applies.**

Summary

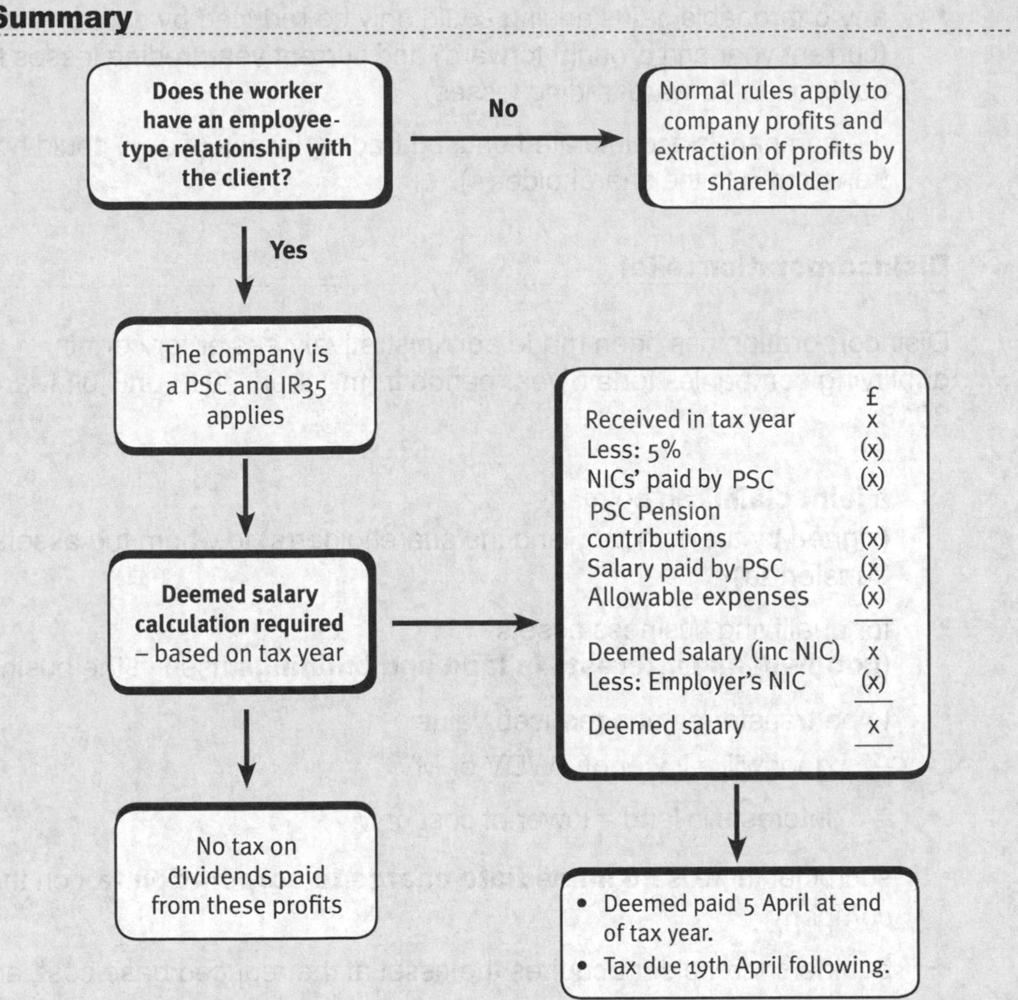
Does the worker have an employee-type relationship with the client?
No
Normal rules apply to company profits and extraction of profits by shareholder
Yes
The company is a PSC and IR35 applies
Deemed salary calculation required – based on tax year
No tax on dividends paid from these profits
£
Received in tax year x
Less: 5% (x)
NICs' paid by PSC (x)
PSC Pension contributions (x)
Salary paid by PSC (x)
Allowable expenses (x)
Deemed salary (inc NIC) x
Less: Employer's NIC (x)
Deemed salary x
• Deemed paid 5 April at end of tax year.
• Tax due 19th April following.

5 Disincorporation

The term disincorporation means the transfer of a company's trade and assets as a going concern to one or more of its shareholders, who wind up the company and continue the business as a sole trader/partnership.

In the past, despite many small companies wanting to disincorporate and to operate as an unincorporated business (sole trader or partnership), disincorporation was administratively difficult and did not attract any tax reliefs.

It was therefore an unattractive, expensive transaction in terms of tax cost, professional and administrative fees as, for example:

- the company's assets (tangible and intangible) had to be transferred to the shareholder(s) at market value giving rise to potentially large chargeable gains and income gains for the company which were subjected to corporation tax

- any chargeable gains arising could only be reduced by capital losses (current year and brought forward) and current year trading losses (but not brought forward trading losses)
- the company's accumulated unused trading losses (if any) could not be transferred to the shareholder(s).

Disincorporation relief

Disincorporation has been made administratively easier for certain qualifying companies for a 5 year period from 1 April 2013 until 31 March 2018:

- a **joint claim** can be made (signed by the company and the shareholder(s) to whom the assets are transferred)
- for qualifying business assets (**goodwill and interests in land and buildings** used in the business)
- to be transferred at a reduced value
  - goodwill = lower of TWDV or MV
  - interests in land = lower of cost or MV
- such that there is **no immediate charge to corporation tax** on the company
- but the shareholder acquires the asset at the reduced base cost, and
- therefore the **gains are effectively deferred** until the shareholder(s) disposes of the asset transferred.

To qualify, **all** of the following conditions must be satisfied:

- the whole business must be transferred as a going concern
- all of the business assets (with the exception of cash) must be transferred to the shareholder(s)
- all of the shares in the company must be held by individuals
- the shareholder(s) must have held their shares throughout the 12 months preceding the transfer
- the total market value of the **qualifying assets** must not exceed £100,000
- the claim must be made within two years of the transfer of the business assets.

Test your understanding 6

Rupert has owned shares in Bear Ltd for 7 years, but now plans to transfer the business back to himself and carry on trading as a sole trader.

The values of Bear Ltd's assets at 31 March 2017 are:

	£
Land and buildings (cost £25,000)	71,000
Goodwill (not recognised in accounts)	18,000
Inventory (at cost)	9,000
Receivables	3,000
	101,000

Calculate the taxable profits (if any) arising in Bear Ltd as a result of the disincorporation, and the base cost of the land and buildings and goodwill for Rupert, if a joint claim for disincorporation relief is made.

6 Withdrawing investment from a company

Overview

When a shareholder wishes to withdraw their investment from a company there are a number of exit strategies available.

- They could sell their shares.
- The company could purchase the shares back from the shareholder.
- The company could be put into liquidation.

Sale of shares

The simplest method of withdrawing investment in a company is to sell the shares:

- This may not be as easy as it sounds as there is no ready market for shares in unquoted companies. They can usually only be sold to the other shareholders, or with their permission to a third party.

- If the shares are sold the main tax to consider will be CGT, and the availability of entrepreneurs' relief (ER).

  Most shares in unquoted trading companies will be qualifying assets if the individual has been a full-time employee or director of the company. Therefore, if the shares have been owned for at least 12 months, ER would apply.

  Note that investors' relief may be available on the disposal of shares in the future

  – but not until 6 April 2019 (as the shares must be held for 3 years post 6 April 2016), and

  – provided the shareholder is not an employee.

- Before the shares are sold it may be possible to pay a dividend (assuming the company has distributable profits). This would reduce the value of the shares on sale.

  To decide if this is worthwhile it will be necessary to consider the tax rates that apply to the amounts received by the shareholder.

  – Dividends are taxed at 0% on the first £5,000 and then 7.5%/32.5%/38.1% depending on whether they are a basic/higher/additional rate taxpayer.

- Where ER is relevant (ignoring the AEA) CGT will be payable at 10% on the first £10 million of gains for a taxpayer. After the first £10 million of gains the effective rate is 10% or 20%.

  Therefore, a BR taxpayer may benefit from a dividend being paid before the shares are sold, but a higher or additional rate taxpayer with dividends in excess of £5,000 would not.

Purchase of own shares

Where it is not possible to sell the shares to another person, it may be possible for them to be bought by the company.

Depending on how the transaction is structured the amount received for the shares will be treated:

- **as an income distribution (dividend), or**
- **a capital payment.**

The income distribution will trigger a tax liability for an individual who has dividends in excess of £5,000. Assuming ER is available it may be better structured as a capital disposal, where the rate of capital gains tax is 10%.

Conditions for treatment as a CGT disposal

(1) The company must be an unquoted trading company (companies quoted on the AIM are treated as unquoted).

(2) The shareholder must be resident in the UK.

(3) The shares must normally have been owned by the shareholder for at least five years (three years if inherited, including the ownership of the deceased person). If acquired from the spouse or civil partner, the combined length of ownership is considered.

(4) The shareholder must either dispose of their entire interest in the company or their interest must be substantially reduced. This means they own less than 75% of their holding from before the purchase once the shares have been bought back.

(5) The shareholder must not immediately after the purchase be connected with the company (i.e. be able to control it or be in possession of > 30% of the voting power).

(6) The purchase must be for the benefit of the trade and not part of a scheme to avoid tax, for example:

- buying out retiring directors
- buying out dissident (disruptive) shareholders
- a shareholder has died and the beneficiaries do not want the shares
- a venture capitalist withdrawing their investment.

If **any** of the above provisions do not apply the payment will be treated as a distribution.

Companies may seek HMRC clearance to ensure that the capital treatment applies.

Note that the taxpayer cannot choose which treatment is to apply. If the specified conditions are fulfilled it **must** be treated as a capital disposal, and if not it **will be** an income distribution.

Tax treatment

If treated as a capital disposal, a normal CGT computation applies.

If treated as an income distribution, the amount of the distribution is the excess of the payment over the amount originally subscribed for the shares.

Where the person whose shares are being purchased is a company HMRC will always treat the event as a capital disposal.

Note that any legal costs and other expenditure incurred by the company in purchasing its own shares will **not** be allowable against the company's profits for corporation tax.

Test your understanding 7

You act as tax advisor for Bliss Ltd (which operates a successful marriage bureau) and its managing director, Mr Crippen.

The company has made tax-adjusted trading profits in excess of £250,000 p.a. over the previous five years. It has now built up a substantial reserve of cash, since its policy has been not to pay out any dividends. The company has not made any chargeable gains in recent years and has always prepared accounts to 30 April.

Mr Crippen informs you that he and Mr Bluebeard, his fellow shareholder, are in serious disagreement about the future strategy of the company and that this is having a very harmful effect on the running of the business.

It has therefore been decided that Mr Bluebeard should no longer be involved in the management of the company and that the company will purchase all of his shares from him.

Further relevant information

(1) Mr Bluebeard has worked in the company as a full-time director since it was incorporated on 1 June 2004, when he acquired 10% of the ordinary shares for £3,000.

(2) Mr Bluebeard has taxable income of £50,000 per annum after deducting his personal allowance. He received no other income in the tax year.

(3) The company has agreed to buy back Mr Bluebeard's shares at market value of £600,000 on 1 April 2017.

(4) All of Bliss Ltd's assets are in use for the purposes of the trade.

Set out the tax implications for Mr Bluebeard if the:

(a) **income treatment applies.**

(b) **capital treatment applies.**

Liquidation

Many people associate liquidation with a company that has gone bankrupt. This is not always the case. A liquidation can be an effective way of extracting the final value from the company where:

- the net assets of the company are worth more than the shares on a going concern basis, or
- no one wishes to buy the shares in the company as it stands.

The process of liquidation is normally as follows:

(1) The liquidator is appointed, and the trade ceases.

(2) The assets of the company are sold, the outstanding debts collected, and the liabilities paid.

(3) There will be corporation tax due on any profits and gains made on the disposal of the assets, and this must be paid.

(4) The liquidator pays out the balance of the funds to the shareholders, and the shares are cancelled.

(5) The shareholders pay any tax due on the amounts received.

If payments are made to the shareholders:

- **before** the **liquidator is appointed** they are taxed as **dividends**
- **after** the **liquidator is appointed** they are treated as **capital receipts** for the disposal of the shares.

Whichever of these two the taxpayer prefers will, again, depend on their relevant income tax rates, and CGT position.

Test your understanding 8

Simon set up an unquoted trading company on 1 July 2009, and acquired 100% of the shares for £1,000.

The business has been successful but he has decided that now is the time to retire.

A liquidator will be appointed on 1 January 2017, to oversee the disposal of the assets and the winding-up of the company.

It is anticipated that after the assets have been sold the statement of financial position will be as follows:

	£
Bank and cash	840,000
Liabilities (incl. corporation tax due on profit)	(120,000)
	720,000
Share capital	1,000
Retained profits	719,000
	720,000

Simon is a an additional rate taxpayer, but has not received any dividends in the tax year and has realised substantial gains already in the current year.

Calculate the impact of extracting the profits as follows:

(i) **£180,000 before the liquidation commences, with the remaining £540,000 paid on 1 April 2017.**

(ii) **The whole £720,000 is paid out on 1 April 2017.**

Winding-up

The costs of appointing and paying a liquidator can be high.

Where the business is profitable it is possible to wind-up the company without the formal appointment of a liquidator.

HMRC will allow payments made to shareholders to be treated as capital, even though no liquidator has been appointed, providing:

- the company is being wound-up, and
- all liabilities are agreed and subsequently paid (including the individual's personal liability on any distribution by the company).
- the total payment is no more than £25,000.

If the payment is more than £25,000, the whole amount will be treated as a distribution.

A major element in the planning of a liquidation is deciding whether the investment should be withdrawn in a form treated as income, or capital.

For an individual who is a higher rate taxpayer the capital route would normally be preferred if they are eligible for entrepreneurs' relief, as this gives a tax rate of 10% on the first £10 million of capital gains.

Summary

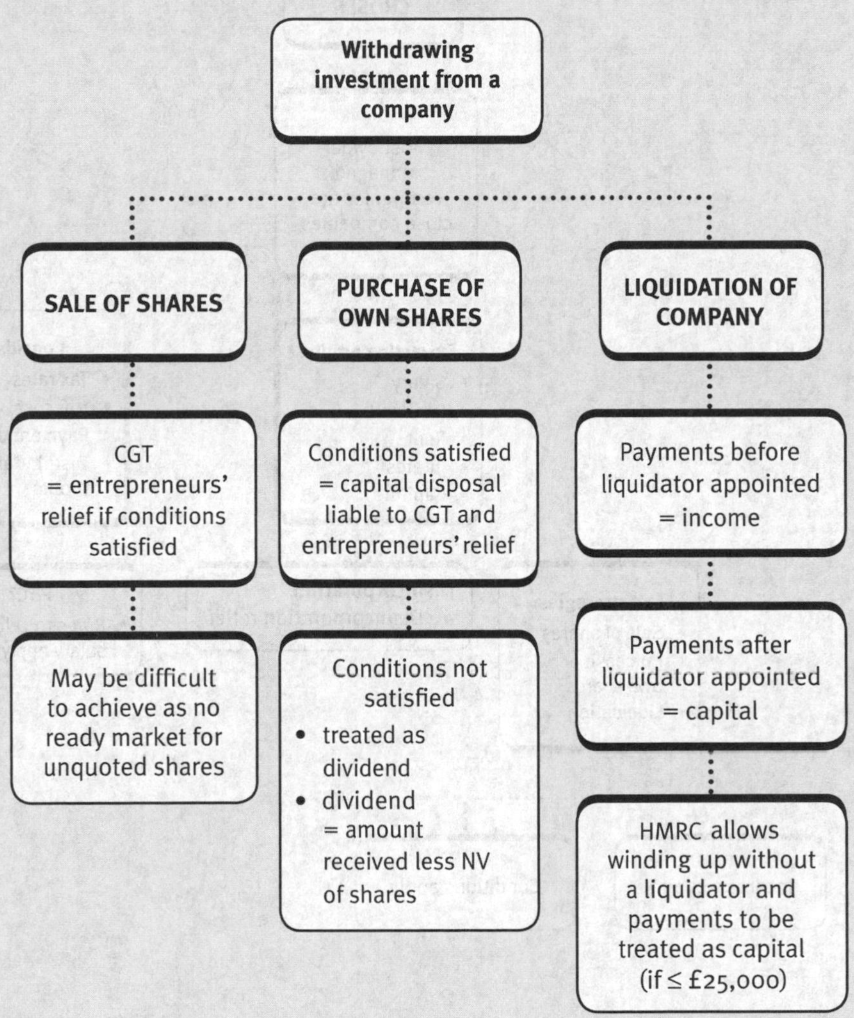

7 Chapter summary

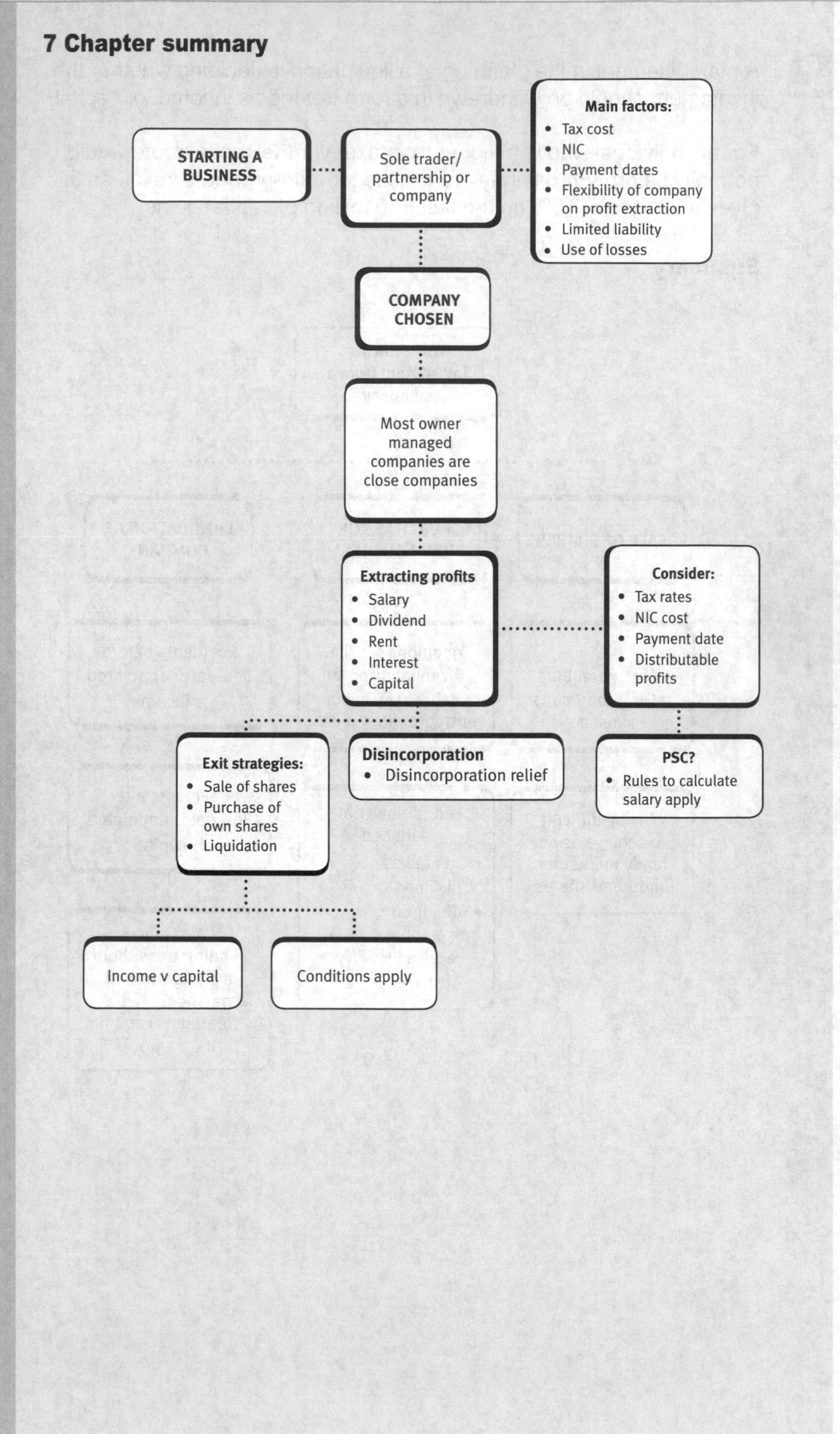

Test your understanding answers

Test your understanding 1

La Famille Ltd

The company is not controlled by its directors, as Hugo is the only director and only has 20% of the shares.

It is, however, controlled by 5 or fewer shareholders, as follows:

		% shares
(1)	Jeanette (plus associates Arthur and Louis)	23
(2)	Hugo	20
(3)	Cecile	5
(4)	Felicity	4
		52

Between them, the 4 largest shareholders (including their associates) own more than 50% of the shares, therefore La Famille Ltd is a close company.

If the shareholders were unconnected, the company would not be a close company as the 5 largest shareholders would only hold 48% (20% + 12% + 6% + 5% + 5%).

Test your understanding 2

Malcolm and Helen

The provision of the company car to Malcolm, who is a director as well as a shareholder, has the following consequences:

- For Malcolm, there is an employment benefit, calculated as follows:
  Appropriate% = 16% + (145 – 95) × 1/5 = 26%
  Car benefit = (£20,000 × 26%) = £5,200.
- As Malcolm is a 40% taxpayer, this benefit will result in additional income tax of £2,080 (£5,200 × 40%), which will be collected through the PAYE system by adjusting his tax code.
  There are no employees' NICs payable on benefits.
- For Houghton Ltd, a capital allowance is available: (£20,000 × 8%) = £1,600, as emissions exceed 130 g/km. Tax relief at 20% means that corporation tax will be reduced by £320.
- In addition Houghton Ltd is liable to employers' NICs. The car benefit is subject to class 1A, on which the company gets tax relief. The class 1A charge is £718 (£5,200 × 13.8%). Tax relief at 20% means that corporation tax will be reduced by £144.

The provision of the company car to Helen, who is not a director but who is a shareholder, has the following consequences:

Houghton Ltd	**Helen**
• No tax relief under the capital allowances system • Dividend is deemed to be made • Value of dividend is £5,200 (£20,000 × 26%)	• No assessable benefit as she is not an employee or director • Dividend of £5,200 is taxed in 2016/17. Further charges will arise in subsequent tax years as long as a benefit continues • The first £5,000 is covered by the dividend nil rate band • As she is a higher rate taxpayer, £65 (£200 × 32.5%) tax is due on the remaining dividends.

Test your understanding 3

Sally and Claire

	Sally	Claire
Is the amount loaned less than or equal to £15,000?	Yes	Yes
Is the individual is a full-time working employee?	Yes	Yes
Does the individual own 5% or less of the shares?	No	Yes
Therefore, is the loan caught by the close company provisions?	Yes	No

Sally

She has received the benefit of a low interest loan, for which under the employment income rules there is a benefit charge of £120 (£12,000 × (3% – 2%)). This is the difference between the interest paid by Sally and the interest that would have been payable at the official rate of interest, based on the average loan outstanding during the tax year.

The loan to Sally is caught by the provisions as she has 5% or more of the company's shares. Therefore White Ltd will be required to pay a £3,900 (£12,000 × 32.5%) tax charge on 1 January 2018. If any part of the loan is repaid before 1 January 2018 then the tax charge is reduced accordingly.

The £3,900 will be recoverable by White Ltd when the loan is repaid, or written off.

Claire

The loan is not caught by the close company provisions (see above), but it will still be caught by the employment income benefit provisions.

Using the average method the benefit is calculated as:

Average loan = (£12,000 + £8,000) × 1/2 = £10,000

	£
Interest on average loan (3% × £10,000)	300
Less: Interest actually paid (£12,000 × 2% × 9/12) + (£8,000 × 2% × 3/12)	(220)
Loan benefit	80

Claire may elect for the precise method to be used if the benefit is lower.

HMRC also have the right to impose the precise method but would only do so if the repayment pattern was not commercial or designed to reduce the benefit. This does not appear to be the case here.

Test your understanding 4

Fletcher Ltd

		Salary	Dividend
	£	£	£
Profit available for Norman		50,000	50,000
Salary	43,937		
Employer's NIC			
(13.8/113.8 × £50,000)	6,063		
		(50,000)	
TTP		0	50,000
Corporation tax at 20%		0	10,000
Profit available if dividend is paid			40,000

Note that the employers £3,000 NIC allowance is not available if Norman is the sole employee. However, even if he is not, in this example it is assumed that if the allowance were available, it has already been claimed.

Norman

Norman is a higher rate (HR) taxpayer having already received a salary of £48,000.

	Salary	Dividend
	£	£
Additional salary	43,937	
Dividend		40,000
Income tax		
£43,937 × 40%	17,575	
£5,000 × 0% (dividend nil rate band)		0
£35,000 × 32.5%		11,375
Class 1 NIC (£43,937 × 2%)	879	0
	18,454	11,375
Net after tax income for Norman		(Note)
Salary (£43,937 – £18,454)	25,483	
Dividend (£40,000 – £11,375)		28,625

Total overall tax cost of the additional profit extraction

	Bonus	Dividend
	£	£
Additional income tax	17,575	11,375
Additional employee NICs	879	0
Additional cost to Norman	18,454	11,375
Additional employer NICs	6,063	0
Additional corporation tax saving	(10,701)	(0)
Net saving for company	(4,638)	0
Total net tax cost/(saving) of the additional profit extraction	13,816	11,375

Note: Alternative calculations

The after-tax income in each scenario can be calculated much quicker if you work 'in the margin' using marginal rates of tax. As a higher rate taxpayer:

- Additional salary will be taxed at 42% (40% IT and 2% NICs) therefore Norman will receive 58% after tax

  = (£43,937 × 58%) = £25,483

- Additional dividend in excess of the first £5,000 will be taxed at 32.5% therefore Norman will receive 67.5% after tax plus £5,000

  = (£35,000 × 67.5%) = £23,625 + £5,000 = £28,625

Test your understanding 5

Brian

(a) **Employment income, income tax and employer's NICs**

	£
Total contract value earned	70,000
Less: Statutory deduction (5%)	(3,500)
	66,500
Less: Salary	(25,000)
Employer's NICs	(2,331)
Deemed salary including employer's NICs	39,169
Less: Employer's NICs (£39,169 × 13.8/113.8)	(4,750)
Deemed employment income	34,419

Income tax:

£		£
18,000	× 20% (W)	3,600
16,419	× 40%	6,568
34,419		
Income tax on deemed employment income		10,168

Working: Basic rate band remaining

	£
BR band	32,000
Less: Taxable income (£25,000 – £11,000)	(14,000)
BR band remaining	18,000

(b) **Conrad Ltd**

Corporation tax liability – year ending 31 March 2017

	£
Trading profit	70,000
Less: Staff costs (£25,000 + £2,331)	(27,331)
IR35 costs (£34,419 + £4,750)	(39,169)
TTP	3,500
Corporation tax at 20%	700

Test your understanding 6

Bear Ltd

In the corporation tax computation of Bear Ltd the taxable profit on each asset is calculated as follows:

Land and buildings

	£
Proceeds (lower of MV or cost)	25,000
Less: Cost	(25,000)
Chargeable gain	0

Goodwill

	£
Proceeds (lower of MV or TWDV)	0
Less: Cost	0
Trading profit	0

There will be no taxable trading profit on the transfer of inventory or receivables.

Rupert

For Rupert, the base cost of the assets for calculation of future gains on disposal are:

Land and buildings	£25,000
Goodwill	£Nil

The effect of disincorporation relief is that the gains are deferred until the shareholder disposes of the assets.

If the business is disposed of as a whole, ER should be available.

If so, after allowing for the AEA, the gains will be taxed at 10%.

Test your understanding 7

Bliss Ltd

(a) **The income treatment applies**

Mr Bluebeard will be treated as receiving a dividend on 1 April 2017 and will be subject to income tax in the tax year 2016/17 as follows:

		£
Cash received		600,000
Less: Original subscription price		(3,000)
Net distribution = deemed dividend received		597,000
Income tax	first £5,000	0
	= £84,000 × 32.5% (Note 2)	27,300
	(£597,000 – £89,000) × 38.1%	193,548
Plus: Loss of PA (£11,000 × 40%) (Note 1)		4,400
Total tax payable		225,248
Due date		31.1.2018

Notes:

(1) The PA will also be restricted to £Nil as ANI exceeds £122,000, therefore other taxable income will increase by £11,000 to £61,000, and the loss of the PA will affect the total tax implications of the deemed dividend received.

(2) The first £5,000 of dividends is taxed at 0%, but uses part of the higher rate band. Therefore, the remaining higher rate band is:

	£
HR band limit	150,000
Other taxable income (Note 1)	(61,000)
First £5,000 dividends	(5,000)
	84,000

(b) **The capital treatment applies**

Mr Bluebeard will be liable to capital gains tax as follows:

	£
Sale proceeds	600,000
Less: Cost	(3,000)
Gain qualifying for entrepreneurs' relief	597,000
Less: AEA	(11,100)
Taxable gain	585,900
Capital gains tax (£585,900 × 10%)	58,590
Due date	31 Jan 2018

Test your understanding 8

Simon

(i) **Option 1**
Pre-liquidation dividend – Income tax

	£	£
Dividend received	180,000	
Income tax: (First £5,000 × 0%)	0	
(£175,000 × 38.1%)	66,675	
	66,675	66,675
Post-liquidation distribution – CGT		
Proceeds	540,000	
Less: Cost	(1,000)	
Gain qualifying for entrepreneurs' relief	539,000	
Less: AEA (already used)	(0)	
Taxable gain	539,000	
CGT payable (10% × £539,000)		53,900
Total tax payable		120,575

(ii) **Option 2 – CGT**

	£
Proceeds	720,000
Less: Cost	(1,000)
Gain qualifying for entrepreneurs' relief	719,000
CGT payable (10% × £719,000)	71,900

chapter

27

Groups and consortia

Chapter learning objectives

Upon completion of this chapter you will be able to:

- distinguish the different 75% group relationships which exist for corporation tax and gains purposes and identify the relevant groups from the information provided
- recognise the reliefs available when provided with a group scenario and advise on the effect of alternative courses of action
- determine the effects on loss relief availability where arrangements exist for a company to leave a group and recognise when relief is available for trading losses incurred by an overseas company
- define a consortium and recognise how consortium loss relief operates
- advise on the tax consequences of a transfer of tangible and intangible assets within a group and advise on the tax consequences of a transfer of trade and assets where there is common control; recognise when a degrouping charge will arise in connection with asset transfers
- determine pre-entry losses and understand their tax treatment
- identify the availability of any stamp duties exemption/relief in connection with group transactions; explain the taxation implications for a company of a scheme of reconstruction
- define the relationship required for group VAT registration, explain the effects and outline any advantages or disadvantages of group VAT registration and explain the purpose of divisional registration for VAT.

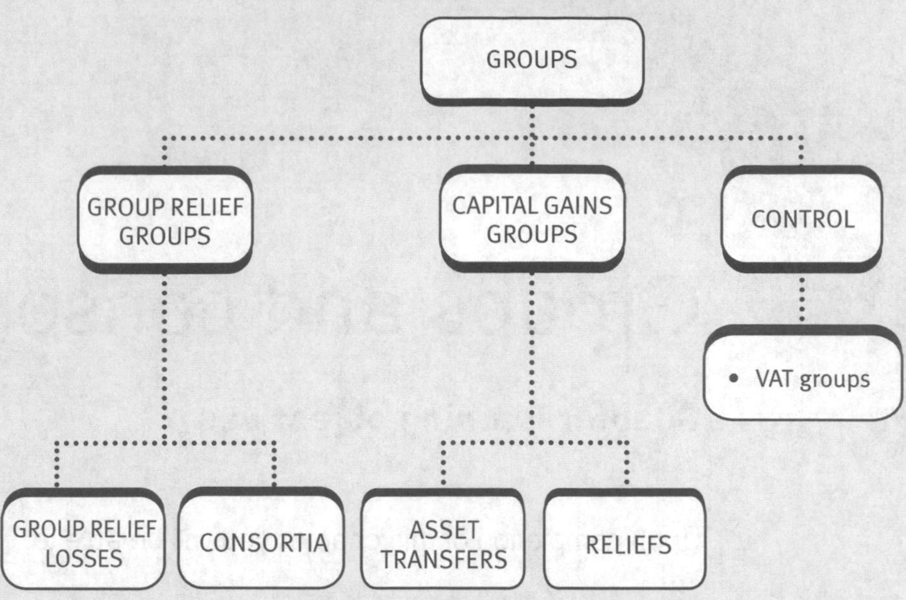

Introduction

This chapter deals with the tax position of groups of companies, where one company owns shares in another.

Remember that for corporation tax purposes:

- each company within the group is treated as a separate entity
- each company is required to submit its own individual tax return
- but being a member of a group provides opportunities for tax planning, to save tax and improve the cash flow of the group.

Much of this chapter is a revision of the rules covered in F6, however there is a much greater emphasis at P6 on tax planning aspects:

- choosing the most tax efficient group structure for the business
- effective use of loss reliefs
- effective crystallisation or deferral of chargeable gains, and
- giving tax advice on proposed strategies.

The new areas at P6 are:

- Consortium relief
- Degrouping charges
- Pre-entry capital losses
- Transfers of a trade and assets.

1 75% groups

Identification of 75% groups

The identification of the appropriate 75% groups for corporation tax purposes is essential before any tax planning advice can be given.

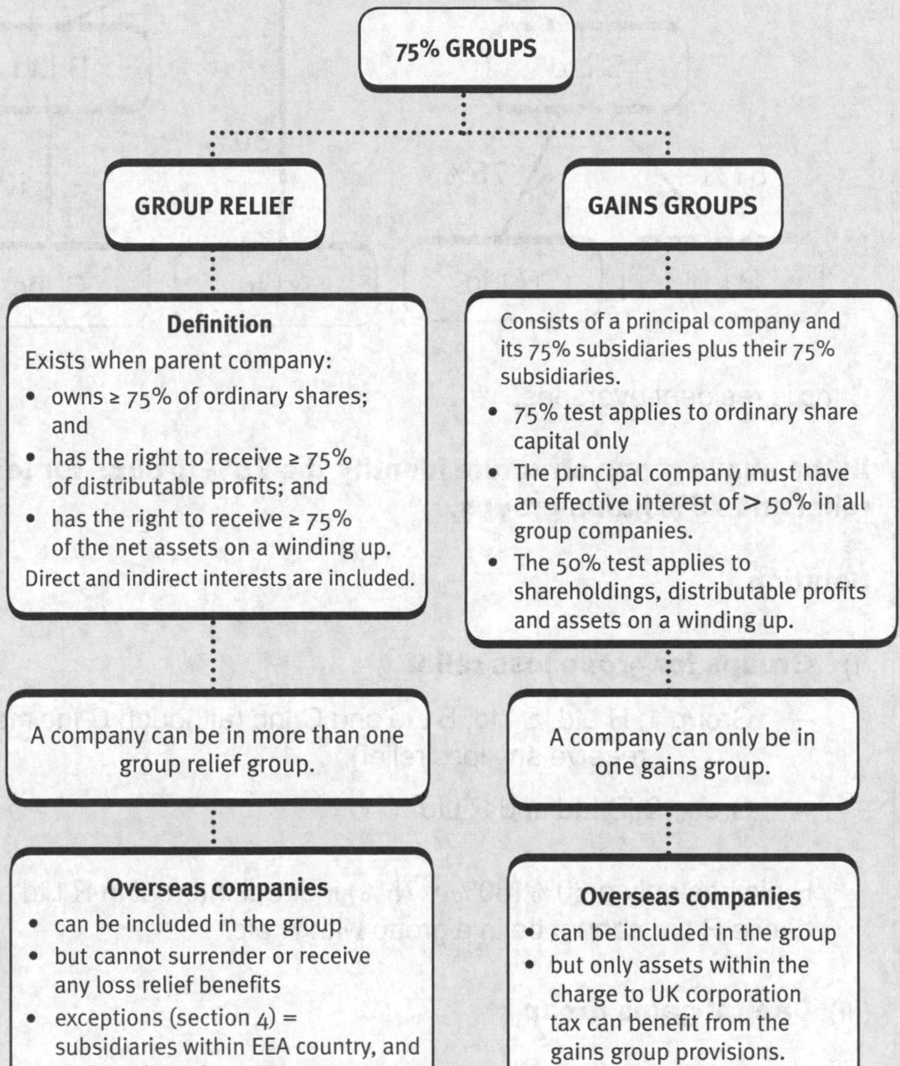

75% GROUPS
GROUP RELIEF
GAINS GROUPS
Definition
Exists when parent company:
• owns ≥ 75% of ordinary shares; and
• has the right to receive ≥ 75% of distributable profits; and
• has the right to receive ≥ 75% of the net assets on a winding up.
Direct and indirect interests are included.
Consists of a principal company and its 75% subsidiaries plus their 75% subsidiaries.
• 75% test applies to ordinary share capital only
• The principal company must have an effective interest of > 50% in all group companies.
• The 50% test applies to shareholdings, distributable profits and assets on a winding up.
A company can be in more than one group relief group.
A company can only be in one gains group.
Overseas companies
• can be included in the group
• but cannot surrender or receive any loss relief benefits
• exceptions (section 4) = subsidiaries within EEA country, and UK branches of an EEA company
Overseas companies
• can be included in the group
• but only assets within the charge to UK corporation tax can benefit from the gains group provisions.

Example 1 – 75% groups

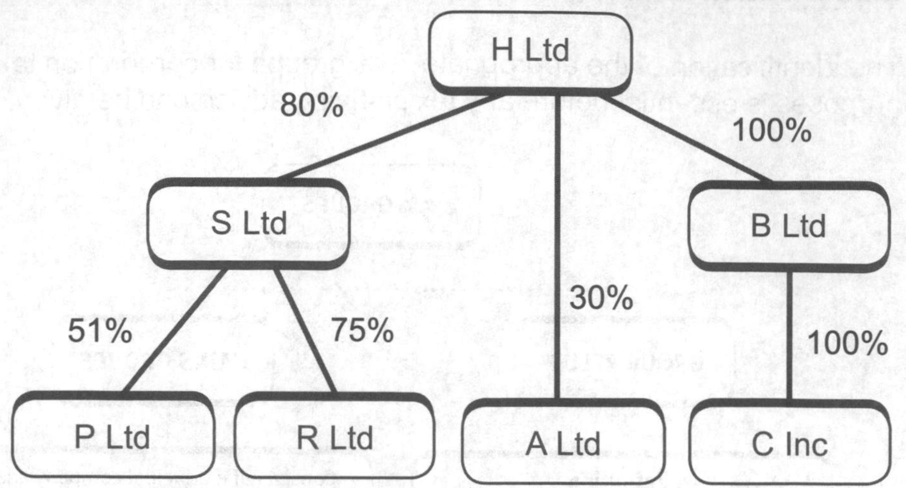

C Inc is resident overseas.

In the above group structure identify the 75% groups for loss relief and 75% gains groups.

Solution

(i) **Groups for group loss relief**

- Group 1: H Ltd, S Ltd, B Ltd and C Inc (although C Inc may not receive any loss relief).
- Group 2: S Ltd and R Ltd

H plc has only a 60% (80% × 75%) indirect interest in R Ltd and hence R Ltd cannot be in a group with H plc.

(iii) **Capital gains group**

R Ltd can be included in the main group which now consists of H Ltd, S Ltd, R Ltd, B Ltd and C Inc (although the reliefs only apply to assets within the charge to UK corporation tax).

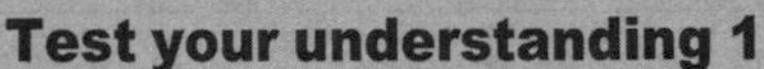

Test your understanding 1

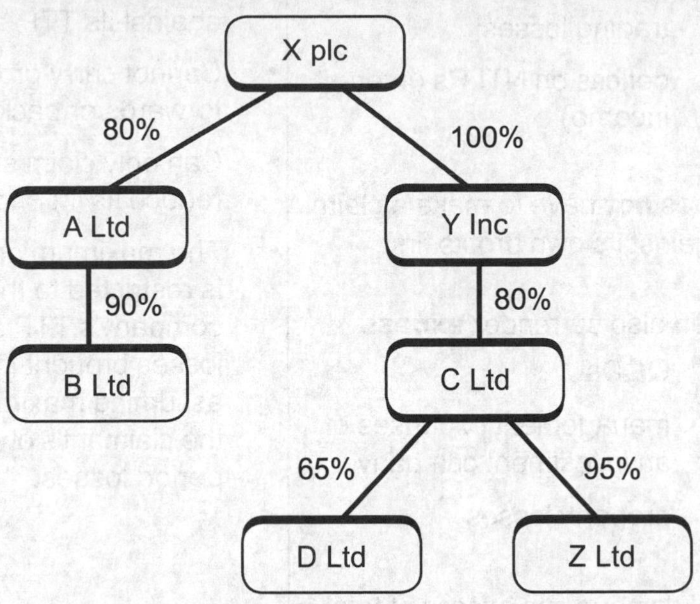

Y Inc is resident in Canada.

In the above group structure identify the 75% groups for loss relief and 75% gains groups.

2 Group relief

- Members of a group relief group may surrender losses to profitable group members for corresponding accounting periods.
- Losses surrendered must be set against the claimant company's taxable total profits of a 'corresponding' accounting period.

  A corresponding accounting period = any accounting period falling wholly or partly within the surrendering company's accounting period.

  Where the companies do not have coterminous (same) year ends, the available profits and losses must be time apportioned to find the relevant amounts falling within the corresponding accounting period.

- Rules apply to both the surrendering and the claimant companies as follows:

Surrendering company	Claimant company
• Can surrender **current period**: – trading losses – deficits on NTLRs (interest income) does **not** have to make a claim against its own profits first. • Can also surrender **excess** – QCDs – management expenses of an investment company – property losses only amounts in excess of total profits (before loss relief) can be surrendered. • Can surrender to one or more companies within the group. • Can surrender **any amount** desired provided the claimant company can utilise the loss. • Can only surrender current period amounts, not brought forward or carried back losses.	• Offsets the surrendered loss against its TTP • Cannot carry group relief forwards or backwards. • Can only claim sufficient to reduce its TTP to £Nil. • The maximum group relief claim is restricted to the claimant company's TTP after deducting losses brought forward and assuming maximum set off of the claimant's own current period losses.

- Group relief is claimed
  - by the **claimant company** on its corporation tax return
  - within **two years of the end of its CAP**
  - but requires a notice of consent from the surrendering company.

Test your understanding 2

A Ltd and B Ltd are members of the same 75% loss relief group.

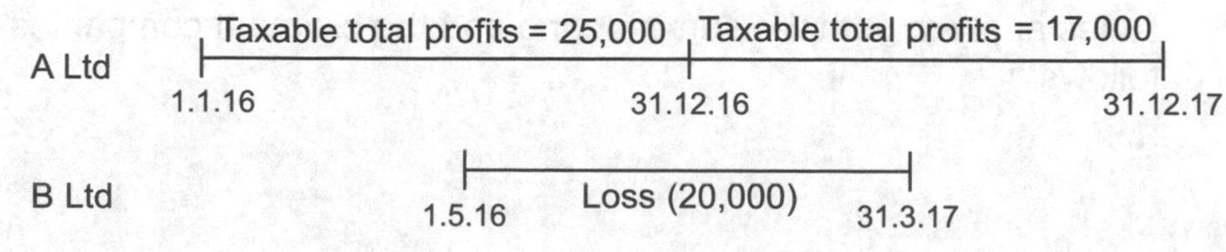

(a) **Calculate the maximum amount of loss that B Ltd can surrender to A Ltd for use in year ended 31.12.16 and compute the revised taxable total profits of A Ltd assuming B Ltd surrenders the maximum amount of loss.**

(b) **Calculate the maximum amount of loss that B Ltd can surrender to A Ltd for use in year ended 31.12.17 and compute the revised taxable total profits of A Ltd assuming B Ltd surrenders the maximum amount of loss.**

- The surrendering company can choose to surrender less than the maximum amount and utilise the rest of the loss against its own profits.
- If it has paid QCDs, it should ensure that the losses retained will reduce total profits before deduction of QCDs to the amount of any QCDs paid. This will allow the QCDs to be deducted in full without any corporation tax becoming due and will also maximise the losses remaining to be carried forward (if any).
- If the surrendering company was profitable in the previous period, it may be beneficial to retain enough losses to make a carry back claim and generate a refund of corporation tax already paid. However, in order to make a prior year claim, an 'all or nothing' current year claim must first be made, which may waste QCDs in the current year.
- As a claim against the company's own profits is 'all or nothing' it is important that the optimum group relief surrender is made first, leaving the desired amount of loss available to offset against the company's own profits.

Payment for group relief

- It is usual, particularly where there is a minority shareholder, for the claimant company to pay for group relief. Such payments subject to a maximum of £1 per £1 of loss claimed, are ignored for tax purposes.

3 Effect on group relief of changes in group structures

Companies joining a group

There are several areas to consider:

- Group relief is only available for losses and profits generated after a company joins a group.
- It is not possible to have group relief for pre-acquisition losses or to relieve pre-acquisition profits.
- A corresponding accounting period begins when a company joins a group.

- When a loss making company joins a group there is a 'change in ownership' of that company, and consequently there may be a restriction on the use of its brought forward losses against its own profits if there is also a major change in the nature or conduct of trade (Chapter 24).

Companies leaving a group

Group relief ceases to be available once **arrangements are in place** to **sell the shares** of a company. This will usually occur sometime before the actual legal sale of the shares.

- HMRC consider that arrangements come into existence once there is agreement in principle between the parties that the transaction will proceed. This is so even though such agreement is still subject to contract and not finally binding on either party.
- HMRC will look at correspondence and details of the negotiations to determine the date of any arrangements coming into force.
- For computational examination questions you should be given the date on which a company is deemed to leave a group.

Test your understanding 3

Romeo Ltd owns 80% of the ordinary share capital of Juliet Ltd. These shares were acquired many years ago. Both companies are UK resident for tax purposes. Their most recent results have been:

	Romeo Ltd	Juliet Ltd
	12 m/e	9 m/e
	31.12.16	31.03.17
	£	£
Tax adjusted trading profit	890,000	
Tax adjusted trading losses		(102,000)
Capital gains		15,000
Bank interest receivable	6,000	4,000
Property income	2,000	8,000
Dividends from other UK companies		32,000
Dividend from Juliet Ltd	27,000	
Qualifying charitable donation	4,000	5,000

Compute the corporation tax payable by each company for the above accounting periods, on the assumption that maximum possible group relief is claimed by Romeo Ltd.

Assume that the FY2016 rates and rules apply throughout.

4 Losses of overseas companies

Group relief is normally only allowed between UK resident group companies.

However, there are two exceptions:

- Overseas company losses can be group relieved to the UK, but only if:
  - (i) the overseas subsidiary is either resident in, or has a permanent establishment (e.g. branch) in, the European Economic Area (EEA), and
  - (ii) losses **cannot** be relieved in any other way.

  Note that losses may only be surrendered by an EEA subsidiary to a UK parent and not from the parent to the subsidiary.

  The P6 examining team has stated that if an overseas subsidiary sustains a trading loss, the question will state whether the company is, or is not, resident in an EEA country. You are not expected to know which countries are in the EEA.

- Losses of a UK permanent establishment (e.g. branch) can be group relieved in the UK to a UK company, but only if:
  - (i) the UK permanent establishment is owned by an EEA company, and
  - (ii) the loss **has not been** utilised in any other way.

  However, note that the relief is based on whether the losses **are** relieved in another country, rather than whether the losses **could be** relieved elsewhere.

5 Consortia

Introduction

Further loss relief is available if companies are structured as a consortium.

The tax reliefs available between qualifying companies where a consortium is involved are more limited than for a 75% loss group.

Definition of a consortium

There are several elements to the definition:

- A consortium exists where two or more companies (UK or overseas) between them own at least 75% of another company.
- Each company must own at least 5% but less than 75%.
- Ownership includes ordinary shares and assets and profits as for a 75% group.
- The investing company is known as a consortium member.
- The target company is known as a consortium company.

Test your understanding 4

(i)

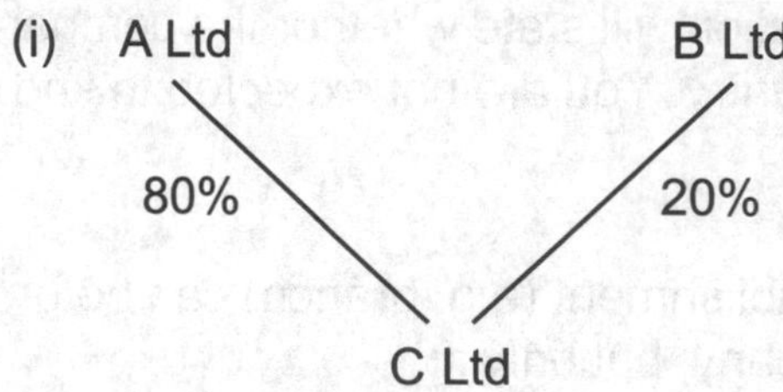

(ii)

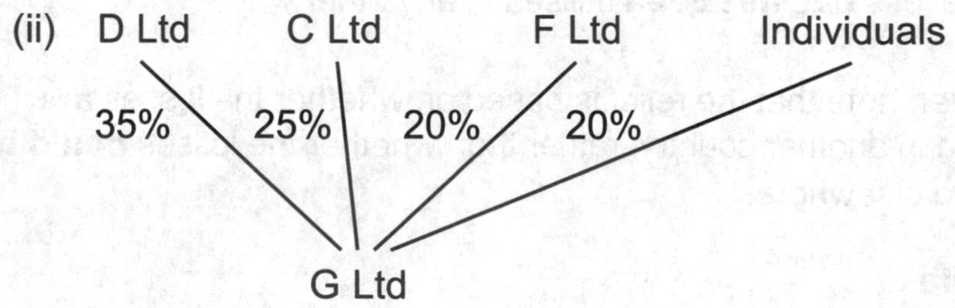

Explain whether the above structures are a consortium for tax purposes.

Effect of being in a consortium

Consortium relief (a form of loss relief) is available between a UK consortium company and its UK members, for current period qualifying losses.

Corresponding accounting period rules apply as they do for group relief.

- Losses can be **surrendered upwards** from the consortium company to the consortium members:
  - But only up to the percentage interest that the consortium member has in the consortium company.
  - The loss must first be relieved against current period total profits before QCDs in the consortium company.
- Losses can also be **surrendered downwards** from consortium members to the consortium company to relieve
  - up to their percentage of the consortium company's TTP.
  - the loss does not have to be relieved in the consortium members computation first.
- The maximum consortium loss relief available for surrender is the lower of:
  (i) the results of the consortium member
  (ii) the consortium members' percentage entitlement to the results of the consortium company.
- Losses cannot be exchanged between consortium members.
- Consortium members can be resident anywhere in the world but only a UK resident consortium member can claim or surrender losses.

Test your understanding 5

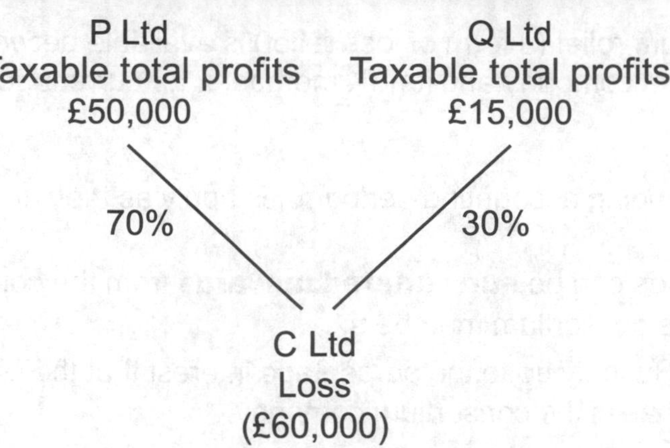

Calculate the maximum consortium relief available for P Ltd and Q Ltd. Assume all companies have coterminous year end dates.

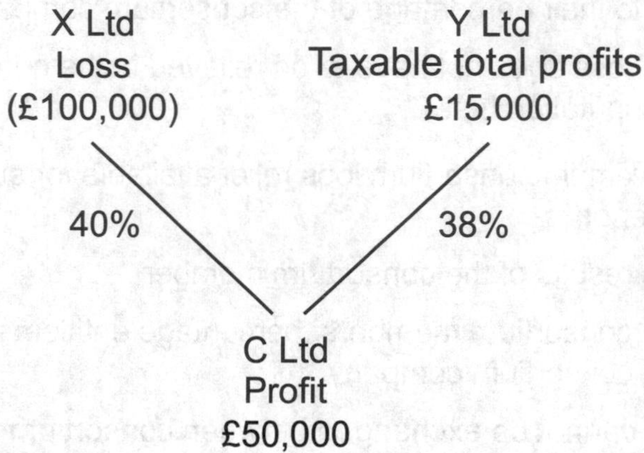

Explain how X Ltd can relieve its loss within the consortium. Assume all companies shown have coterminous year end dates.

As for group relief, consortium relief must be claimed:

- by the **claimant company** on its corporation tax return
- within **two years of the end of its CAP**.

Test your understanding 6

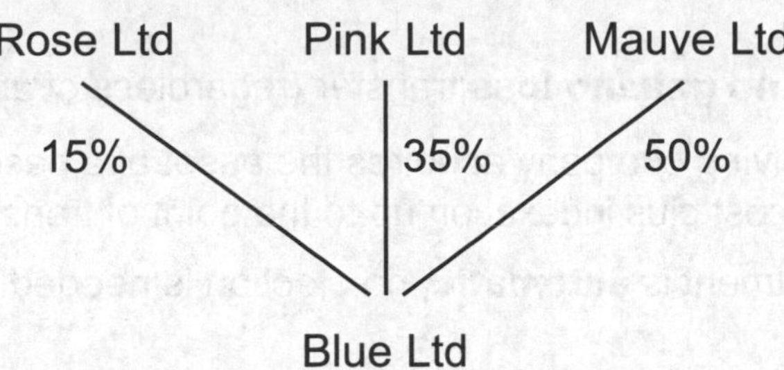

In the year ended 31 March 2017 their results were:

		£
Rose Ltd	Trading loss	(90,000)
Pink Ltd	Trading loss	(126,000)
Mauve Ltd	Taxable total profit	55,000
Blue Ltd	Taxable total profit	300,000

(i) **Calculate the corporation tax liabilities of all companies, on the assumption that the maximum amount of consortium relief is claimed.**

(ii) **Explain how your answer would differ if Rose Ltd owned 80% of Blue Ltd, with Pink Ltd and Mauve Ltd owning 10% each. Do not recalculate the liabilities.**

6 Capital gains groups

Introduction

There are various special tax rules to consider within a capital gains group:

- Transfer of assets within the group and subsequent disposal
- Degrouping charges for companies leaving a group
- Reallocation of gains or losses
- Rollover relief

Transfer of assets

When an asset is sold to another gains group member:

- this is a **no gain/no loss** transfer (regardless of any actual price paid)
- the receiving company acquires the asset at a base cost equal to its original cost plus indexation up to the point of transfer
- this treatment is **automatic**, no election is needed.

No gain arises until either:

- the receiving company sells the asset outside the group, or
- the group company receiving the asset leaves the group (degrouping charge).

Disposals of assets outside the group

A normal capital gain or loss is calculated.

Test your understanding 7

Green Ltd acquired an office building on 1 April 1995 for £100,000. The office building is transferred to Jade Ltd, a wholly owned subsidiary on 1 October 2005 for £120,000, when it was worth £180,000.

On 1 December 2016 Jade Ltd sells the office building outside the group for £350,000.

Assume the relevant RPIs are as follows:

April 1995	149.0
October 2005	193.3
December 2016	264.7

Calculate any chargeable gains arising on the disposals.

Degrouping charge

A degrouping charge arises when a group company:

- leaves a group
- still owning an asset that it had received via a no gain/no loss transfer from a fellow group company
- within the last **six years**.

Calculation of degrouping charge

- The company leaving the group is deemed to have:
  - sold and repurchased any assets acquired from other group members
  - at their MV on the day of intra-group transfer (not the MV when it leaves the group).

	£
Proceeds (MV at date of intra-group transfer)	x
Less: Cost to group	(x)
Less: Indexation to date of intra-group transfer	(x)
	——
Degrouping charge	x
	——

- The degrouping charge is added to the consideration received by the vendor company selling the shares in the company leaving the group.

  Note that if there is a degrouping loss, this is deducted from the consideration.
- This additional consideration is unlikely to be taxable:
  - as the company selling the shares is likely to benefit from the substantial shareholding exemption (SSE)
  - in respect of any gain or loss on disposal of the shares, including the degrouping charge.
- If not covered by SSE:
  - the company can elect to reallocate the gain to another group member in the original group (see later)
  - however group rollover relief is not available for a gain on shares (as shares are not qualifying assets).

Other points

- If the company leaves the group within **three years** of the original transfer:
  - the original exemption for SDLT is withdrawn, with duty becoming payable.
- A similar charge arises when a company leaves the group:
  - still owning an **intangible asset** acquired
  - in the previous **six years** from another group company.

  This charge arises in the company leaving the group, although it can be reallocated within the old capital gains group.

Example 2 – Degrouping charge

Shelley plc bought a freehold office block on 15 May 1996 for £350,000. On 10 June 2011 Shelley sold the office block to its wholly owned subsidiary Wordsworth Ltd, for £400,000 when the true market value of the office block was £620,000.

On 1 March 2017 Wordsworth Ltd sold the office block for £800,000.

Both companies prepare financial statements to 31 March each year.

Assume the relevant RPIs are as follows:

May 1996	152.9
June 2011	235.2
March 2017	265.9

(i) **Calculate the gain realised by Wordsworth Ltd in March 2017.**

(ii) **Rather than have Wordsworth Ltd sell its office block, Shelley plc sells its entire shareholding in Wordsworth Ltd for £5 million on 1 March 2017. Advise the group of the gains (if any) that will arise as a result of this sale and any reliefs available.**

Solution

Inter group transfer: nil gain/nil loss:	£
Cost	350,000
Plus: IA (May 1996 to June 2011)	
(235.2 – 152.9)/152.9 = 0.538 × £350,000	188,300
Base cost to Wordsworth Ltd	538,300

Sale of asset outside the group

	£
Proceeds	800,000
Less: Base Cost	(538,300)
Unindexed gain	261,700
Less: IA (June 2011 to March 2017)	
(265.9 – 235.2)/235.2 = 0.131 × £538,300	(70,517)
Chargeable gain	191,183

Sale of Wordsworth Ltd

- Degrouping charge arises.
- Wordsworth Ltd is treated as if it had sold the building on 10 June 2011 at its MV, and then immediately reacquired it.

	£
Proceeds	620,000
Less: Base cost to Wordsworth Ltd (as above)	(538,300)
Degrouping charge	81,700

- The degrouping charge is added to the £5m proceeds on the sale of the shares in Wordsworth Ltd.
- However any gain is likely to be exempt under the substantial shareholding rules as Shelley plc has owned 10% of the shares for 12 months out of the previous 24 months.
- SDLT would not have been charged when the office block was sold between the group companies.
- It is not charged retrospectively when Wordsworth leaves the group as this is more than three years after the original transfer.

Test your understanding 8

Yellow Ltd sold its wholly owned subsidiary, Orange Ltd, on 15 April 2016. Yellow Ltd had purchased a building on 1 August 1996 for £180,000. On 1 December 2010, the building was transferred to Orange Ltd for £230,000. Its market value on the date of the transfer was £375,000. Orange Ltd still owned the building on 15 April 2016.

Both companies prepare accounts to 31 March each year.

Assume the relevant RPIs are as follows:

August 1996	153.1
December 2010	228.4
April 2016	261.5

Explain the tax implications of the sale of Orange Ltd.

Reallocation of gains or losses

Companies within a gains group can make a joint election to reallocate chargeable gains/allowable losses between group companies.

This election allows groups to achieve the following:

- Chargeable gains and allowable capital losses can be matched together within one company.
- Gains can be transferred to the group company/companies with capital losses brought forward (but beware of the restrictions on pre-entry capital losses).

The joint election:

- is available provided both companies are members of the gains group at the time the gain or loss arose
- must be made within two years of the end of the accounting period of disposal outside of the group
- must specify which company in the group is to be treated as having disposed of the asset.

Remember that only **current year** chargeable gains or allowable losses can be transferred (not brought forward capital losses).

Benefits of the joint transfer election

- As no actual transfer of assets is taking place within the gains group, there will be savings in legal and administrative costs.
- The two year time limit for making the election, means that tax planning can be undertaken retrospectively.
- An election can specify the amount of gain or loss to be transferred (i.e. it does not need to be the whole chargeable gain/allowable loss arising on a disposal). This gives increased flexibility with tax planning.

Test your understanding 9

During the year ended 31 March 2017 Violet Ltd is to dispose of a factory that will result in a capital loss of £75,000. Mauve Ltd, a 100% subsidiary of Violet Ltd, is to dispose of a warehouse that will result in a capital gain of £100,000.

The results of Mauve Ltd and Violet Ltd for the y/e 31 March 2017 are:

	Mauve Ltd	Violet Ltd
Trading profits	£30,000	£250,000

Show the taxable total profits for the year ended 31 March 2017 for each group company assuming the group wants to minimise the corporation tax of the group as a whole.

Group rollover relief

For the purposes of rollover relief, the gains group is treated as a single trade.

This means that a gain on the disposal of a qualifying asset in one group company can be rolled over against the purchase of qualifying assets, within the permitted time period, by another group company.

7 Comprehensive example

Test your understanding 10

Anvil Ltd owns the following shares:

- 80% of the shares in Bench Ltd, which itself owns 80% of the shares in Chair Ltd
- 90% of the shares in Desk Ltd, and
- 60% of the shares in Fork Ltd

Desk Ltd acquired 90% of the shares in Easel Ltd on 1 January 2017.

All other shares are held by individuals.

The companies have the following tax adjusted results for the year ended 31 March 2017:

	Anvil Ltd	Bench Ltd	Chair Ltd	Desk Ltd	Easel Ltd	Fork Ltd
	£	£	£	£	£	£
Trading profit/loss	500,000	0	0	(665,000)	0	(50,000)
Interest Income	0	100,000	0	30,000	140,000	0
Chargeable gain/loss	(10,000)	0	20,000	0	0	0
QCDs				(10,000)		

In addition to the above, Easel Ltd also has a trading loss brought forward of £20,000.

Required:

(a) (i) Explain the group relationship that must exist for trading losses to be surrendered between group companies.

Distinguish this from the relationship that must exist for chargeable assets to be transferred between two companies in a group without incurring a chargeable gain or an allowable loss.

Identify which of the above companies form a losses group and which companies form a gains group.

(ii) Explain the factors that should be taken into account by the Anvil Ltd group when deciding how to use the trading losses within the group.

(b) (i) Calculate the taxable total profits for each of the companies in the Anvil Ltd group for the year ended 31 March 2017 assuming that reliefs are claimed as efficiently as possible.

(ii) Give an explanation of why you have chosen the reliefs as applied above in (b)(i), and explain how any unrelieved amounts may be used.

8 Pre-entry capital losses

Identification of pre-entry capital losses

The rules on pre-entry capital losses (PECL) are designed to prevent a group from purchasing a company in order to use its capital losses incurred in the period before it joins a gains group, via a nil gain/nil loss transfer.

Where a company joins a gains group it must identify its capital losses at the point of entry.

Pre-entry capital losses are **realised losses only**.

(i.e. losses **already crystallised** on **disposals made** by the company **before** it **joined the gains group**).

Unrealised capital losses are not pre-entry capital losses (i.e. any losses that result from the sale of capital assets owned when the company joined the group are not subject to the following restrictions).

Using the loss

Pre-entry capital losses can only be used by the company that joins the group.

They can use them to relieve chargeable gains on assets:

- sold before joining the group (but in the same AP as the loss)
- owned when joining the group and sold later
- bought after joining the group from third parties (i.e. not other group members) and used in their own business.

9 Transfers of assets within a group

No gain/no loss transfer

As seen before, generally a transfer between companies would be a chargeable event giving rise to an allowable loss or a chargeable gain.

However, companies in a 75% capital gains group:

- Make intra-group transfers of chargeable assets at nil gain/nil loss.
- This is regardless of any price actually paid.
- The transferee company takes over the asset at cost plus indexation to the date of transfer.
- This treatment is automatic, no election is needed.

Transfers of intangible assets

Intangible assets, such as goodwill, fall outside the capital gains regime.

However, various reliefs which apply to capital gains groups are mirrored in the rules for intangible assets held within groups. Groups in this case are defined in the same way as capital gains groups.

Transfers of intangible assets between companies within groups are made on a 'tax neutral' basis. This means that the acquiring company is treated as if it has always owned the assets and takes it over as its tax written down value (cost less any amounts deducted).

Stamp taxes

Three key points to remember in relation to stamp taxes and groups:

- There is no charge to stamp duty or SDLT where assets are transferred between two gains group companies.
- This relief is not available where, at the time the assets are transferred, arrangements exist for the purchasing company to leave the group.
- Any relief given in respect of SDLT is withdrawn, with duty becoming payable, if the transferee company leaves the group within **three years** of the transfer whilst still owning the land transferred.

Transfer of trade within a group

Special reliefs apply when a company sells its trade and assets to another company that is under 75% common control.

Transfers between gains group members will meet this condition, as will transfers between companies with the same shareholders as follows:

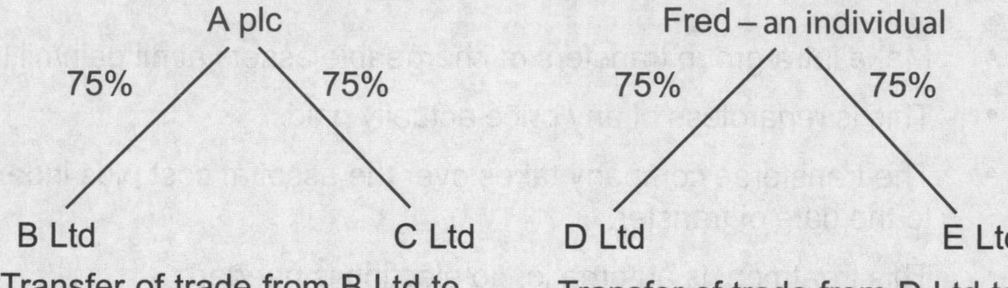

The same person or persons must have owned at least 75% of the trade:

- at some time within one year before the transfer of the trade, and
- on or at any time within two years after that transfer.

Normally when the trade and assets of a company are transferred to another company:

- any losses remain with the original company
- assets are transferred at market value, therefore:
  - balancing adjustments arise for capital allowances
  - capital gains arise.

However, if the special rule applies, the following reliefs apply:

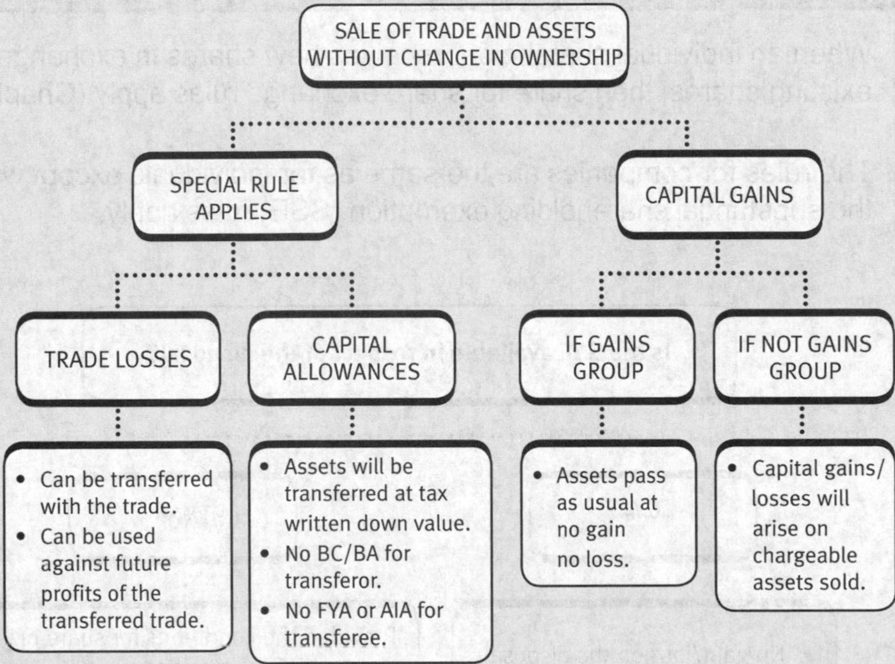

It may be that a company wishes to separate a particular business by transferring it to a newly created subsidiary company. This is often referred to as a **'hive down'**.

Note that although the holding company of the new subsidiary will not have owned the shareholding in the new company for at least 12 of the previous 24 months:

- the substantial shareholding exemption (SSE) will be available on the sale of the shares in the new subsidiary.
- as long as the assets owned by the new subsidiary have been used within a trade carried on by the group for at least 12 of the previous 24 months.

In such a situation the above tax reliefs will also be available if all relevant conditions are satisfied.

10 Reconstructions and reorganisations

The term reconstruction is used to describe a number of situations. In general terms these are transactions in which:

- one company takes over another company, or
- one company takes over the business of another company.

However, because shares or loan notes are issued to the original shareholders they retain an interest in the company or its business.

Share for share exchange

When an individual shareholder receives new shares in exchange for existing shares, then share for share exchange rules apply (Chapter 8).

The rules for companies are the same as for individuals except where the substantial shareholding exemption (SSE) rules apply.

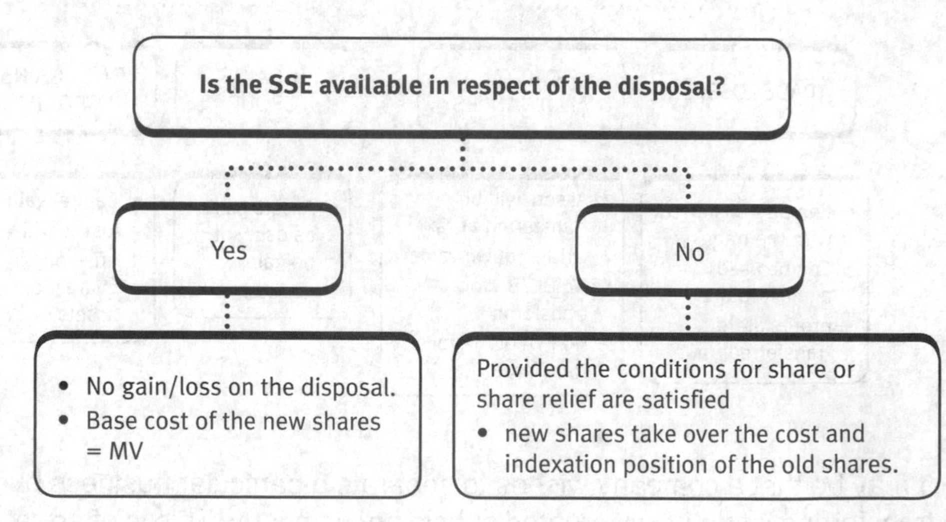

Sale of shares or assets

A group may also choose to reorganise its business by selling its shares in a subsidiary, or simply by selling the trade and assets of the subsidiary, to a third party.

The main implications of company A selling its shares in company B as opposed to company B selling its trade and assets are summarised in the following tables:

	SALE OF SHARES	SALE OF TRADE AND ASSETS
Chargeable gains	• Chargeable gain / capital loss on the disposal of shares in the company – but ignore if SSE applies (gain = exempt, loss = not allowable)	• Chargeable gain / allowable capital loss arises on disposal of every single chargeable asset in the business transferred to the new group company – e.g. Land and buildings, investments etc – but not cars, P&M with value and cost < £6,000, net current assets – ROR may be available • Taxable trading profit / allowable trading expense on disposal of intangible assets – e.g. Goodwill, licences, franchises etc (except loss on disposal of goodwill = non-trading debit) – Intangible ROR may be available
Stamp Duty	• Stamp duty payable at 0.5% by purchaser of shares	• Stamp duty land tax payable by purchaser of land and buildings
Number of related 51% group companies	• Company leaving group – related for whole of CAP when leaves group but not related to companies in new group until next CAP – decrease in number of related companies in old group next CAP	• Company does not leave the group – related for whole of CAP – but if company sells its only trade = will become dormant – decrease in number of related companies in old group next CAP
Degrouping charge?	• Degrouping charge arises if the company leaving the group – is in a capital gains group, and – received an asset via a NGNL transfer – in the six years prior to leaving the group – added to sale proceeds received on disposal of shares and increases gain on those shares – but ignore if SSE applies	• No degrouping charge – only arises on the sale of shares in a company NOT on the sale of trade and assets
Value of assets transferred	• Assets transferred with the company at TWDV – no balancing charges or balancing allowances arise – capital allowances continue to be claimed by the company on TWDV in future, and – base cost of assets for chargeable gain purposes unchanged	• Assets transferred to new group company at market value – balancing charges and balancing allowances arise in old company – capital allowances to be claimed by new group company on MV, and – base cost of assets for chargeable gain purposes = MV
CAP	• CAP unchanged	• If company sells its only trade – it will cease to trade and a CAP will end

<table>
<tr><th></th><th colspan="2">SALE OF SHARES</th><th colspan="2">SALE OF TRADE AND ASSETS</th></tr>
<tr><td>VAT</td><td colspan="2">• No VAT arises on the sale of shares
– outside the scope of VAT</td><td colspan="2">• For VAT – transfer as a going concern rules will probably apply
– not a taxable supply
– no VAT arises on sale
– unless transfer land and buildings on which there is an option to tax</td></tr>
<tr><td>Losses</td><td colspan="2">• If company leaving group = loss-making
– time apportion trading losses for CAP
– group relief possible to old group up to the date an arrangement is in place to sell the company
– no group relief from date of arrangement to date of actual sale
– group relief possible to new group from date of change in ownership
– normal loss relief within the company itself available throughout
– unrelieved trading losses at date of sale
– go with the company to the new group
– trading losses b/f that go with the company
– can be used by that company in the future
– but watch out for major change in nature or conduct of trade within three years either side of the change in ownership
– trading losses b/f can only be used by that company in the future
– cannot be group relieved</td><td colspan="2">• If company whose trade and assets are sold = loss-making
– trading losses stay with the old company
– not transferred to the new group company
– trading losses have limited use:
– possible claims:
current period claim against total profits before QCD relief
group relief to old group
– remaining loss
= useless as there will be no future profits from the same trade
– if sells its only trade and ceases to trade:
– terminal loss carry back for three years against total profits before QCD relief</td></tr>
<tr><td></td><th>Advantages</th><th>Disadvantages</th><th>Advantages</th><th>Disadvantages</th></tr>
<tr><td></td><td>• No tax on disposal if SSE applies
• No BAs or BCs arise
• Loss relief goes with the company to the new group</td><td>• All of the company is transferred
– assets and liabilities</td><td>• Can transfer just the assets the purchaser wants</td><td>• Gains = taxable (may be deferred but not exempt)
• BAs and BCs arise
• Losses do not go to the new group</td></tr>
</table>

Example 3 – Sale of a company

X Ltd has been a 100% subsidiary of Y plc since 2001. To streamline its businesses, Y plc wants to sell X Ltd and is considering either selling the shares or the trade and the assets on 1 April 2017 to Z plc.

X Ltd has some losses brought forward from previous years:

Trading losses	(£225,000)
Capital losses	(£50,000)

Y plc is confident that X Ltd will be profitable again in future.

The main asset owned by X Ltd is an office, purchased from Y plc for its market value of £160,000 on 1 June 2014. The office is currently worth £300,000, and originally cost Y plc £100,000.

X Ltd and Y plc prepare accounts to 31 December each year and both companies are trading.

(a) **Set out the key tax implications of a:**

(i) **sale of the shares in X Ltd**

(ii) **sale of the trade and assets of X Ltd**

(b) **Explain the tax implications and benefits to a potential purchaser of transferring the trade and assets of X Ltd to a newly formed subsidiary, Newco Ltd, (a hive down) followed by the sale of Newco Ltd to the purchaser.**

You should ignore indexation allowance.

Solution

(a) (i) **Sale of shares in X Ltd**

Y plc

There will be no chargeable gain on the disposal of the shares in X Ltd as the substantial shareholding exemption (SSE) will apply. Y plc has held 10% of the X Ltd shares for at least 12 months out of the previous 24 months, and both companies are trading.

There will be a degrouping charge, as X Ltd will be leaving the Y plc group less than 6 years after the no gain, no loss transfer of the office building, with the asset.

Ignoring indexation allowance, the degrouping charge will be the market value of the office on 1 June 2014 of £160,000 less the original cost to the group of £100,000, giving a charge of £60,000.

However, this degrouping charge will be added to the proceeds for the sale of shares by Y plc and will be covered by the SSE.

X Ltd

X Ltd will continue to trade as before, and will continue to carry its trading and capital losses forwards.

However, as X Ltd will change its owners, if there is a major change in the nature or conduct of its trade within 3 years, the trading losses will not be available to set against future trading profits after 1 April 2017.

The capital losses will be pre-entry capital losses. These capital losses will only be available for use in X Ltd and cannot be set against gains from the sale of existing Z plc (or its group) assets.

Any plant and machinery will remain in X Ltd at its TWDV, and capital allowances will be unaffected by the change in ownership.

The base cost of the office building within X Ltd will be its market value on 1 June 2014 of £160,000.

X Ltd will still be a related 51% group company of Y plc in the year ended 31 December 2017.

Z plc

Z plc will pay stamp duty at 0.5% on the purchase of the shares in X Ltd.

As Z plc is purchasing an existing company, it may be exposed to contingent liabilities arising from events taking place prior to 1 April 2017.

(ii) **Sale of trade and assets of X Ltd**

X Ltd

X Ltd will have a chargeable gain on the disposal of the office. Ignoring indexation allowance, this gain will be the current value of £300,000 less the original cost to the group of £100,000, giving a gain of £200,000. The capital losses of £50,000 can be set against this gain, but this will still leave a taxable gain in X Ltd.

If X Ltd has any plant and machinery, balancing allowances or charges may arise on disposal. The trading loss brought forward could be set off against any balancing charge.

After the sale, X Ltd will cease trading, and any unused trading losses will be wasted.

X Ltd will still be a related 51% group company of Y plc in the year ended 31 December 2017, but will then be a dormant company in the following year and will no longer be counted as a related 51% group company.

There will be no VAT on the sale, assuming that the business is transferred as a going concern and Z plc is VAT registered, unless X Ltd has opted to tax the office building.

Z plc

Z plc must pay SDLT of £4,500 (W) on the purchase of the office building.

The base cost of the office for future disposals will be £300,000, as at 1 April 2017, giving a smaller gain on a future sale than if Z plc buys the shares in X Ltd.

If Z plc acquires plant and machinery from X Ltd, capital allowances (including the AIA) will be available based on the market value at 1 April 2017. This will give higher allowances for Z plc than if the shares in X Ltd are purchased.

Z plc will not acquire any losses, as these remain within X Ltd.

Working: Stamp duty land tax

	£	£
	150,000 × 0%	0
	100,000 × 2%	2,000
	50,000 × 5%	2,500
	300,000	4,500

(b) **Hive down**

X Ltd

The transfer of trade and assets to Newco Ltd will be a no gain, no loss transfer.

As Newco Ltd and X Ltd are under the same 75% ownership, the trading losses of £225,000 will be transferred with the trade, and any plant and machinery will be transferred at TWDV.

The capital loss brought forward will remain in X Ltd.

There will be no SDLT at the time of the transfer, but SDLT will be charged when Newco Ltd leaves the group within less than 3 years.

There will be no gain on the sale of the shares in Newco Ltd. The SSE will apply as the assets of Newco Ltd will have been used for the purposes of the trade within the 75% group for at least 12 months in the 2 years pre sale.

Z plc

The key advantage for Z plc is that it will acquire the trading loss as well as the trade and assets of Newco Ltd.

However, as Newco Ltd will change ownership, if there is a major change in the nature or conduct of its trade within 3 years, the trading losses will not be available to set against trading profits after the change in ownership.

Also, Z plc will acquire a 'clean' company, with no latent contingent liabilities.

11 VAT

VAT groups

UK companies that are under common control can elect for a group VAT registration, provided that all the companies are trading in the UK via a permanent establishment.

Definition of common control

The definition of common control is similar to the definition of related 51% subsidiaries (see chapter 22), in that common control exists if:

- a company controls another company or companies

  however the key difference is that for VAT purposes:

- common control is also established if two or more companies are controlled by the **same person** (which could be a company or **an individual**), and
- where there is indirect control, the effective indirect interest does **not** need to be > 50%, there just needs to be > 50% interest at each link.

Examples

- Both are controlled by the same person (in this case an individual)

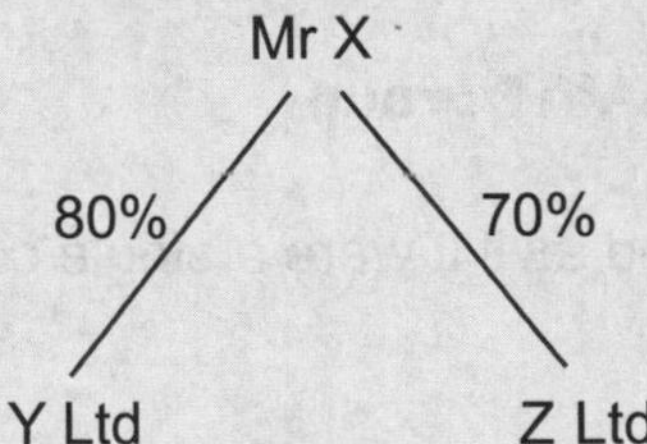

Y Ltd and Z Ltd can form a VAT group.

Mr X is the controlling link, although as an individual he cannot be included in the VAT group.

- Indirect control

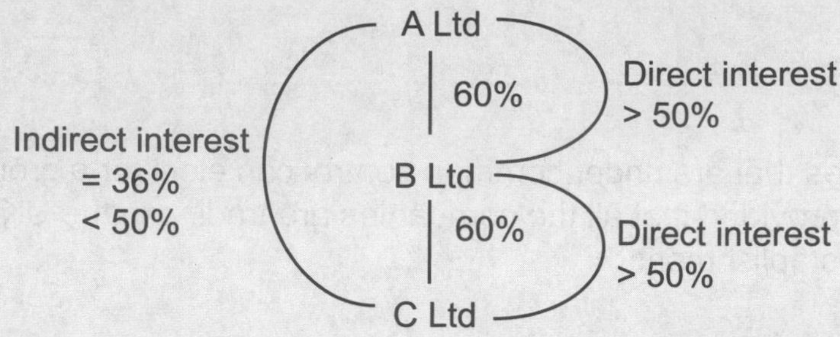

A Ltd has an effective interest in C Ltd of 36% (60% × 60%) which is <50%.

However, as A Ltd has a >50% direct interest in B Ltd and B Ltd has a >50% direct interest in C Ltd, all three companies could form a VAT group.

Control

Control is determined by company law and means the ability to control >50% of the:

- issued share capital, or
- voting power, or
- right to receive distributable profits, or
- right to receive the net assets on a winding up.

Consequences of a VAT group

A VAT group is treated as if it were a single company for the purposes of VAT.

Group registration is optional and not all members under common control have to join.

The effect of a group VAT registration is as follows:

- Goods and services supplied by one group company to another within the group registration are disregarded for the purposes of VAT. Therefore there is **no need to account for VAT on intra group supplies**.
- The VAT group appoints one company as a **representative member** which is responsible for accounting for all input and output VAT for the group.

- The representative member submits **a single VAT return** covering all group members, but all companies are jointly and severally liable for the VAT payable.
- The normal time limits apply for submission of VAT returns.
- An application for group VAT registration has immediate effect, although HMRC has 90 days during which they can refuse the application.

Overseas companies with no UK permanent establishment cannot be part of a group VAT registration.

Transactions with such companies would be treated as imports/exports (see Chapter 21).

Advantages and disadvantages of group VAT registration

Advantages	Disadvantages
• VAT on intra-group supplies eliminated. • Only one VAT return required which should save administrative costs. • Flexible: do not have to include all group companies. • Companies which make exempt supplies can be included, which may allow recovery of input tax that would otherwise be irrecoverable (but see disadvantages).	• All members remain jointly and severally liable. • A single return may cause administrative difficulties collecting and collating information. • The inclusion of a net repayment company (i.e. a company making wholly or mainly zero rated supplies) would result in loss of monthly repayments. • Inclusion of an exempt company would cause the group to become partially exempt. This may restrict input tax recovery. • The limits for joining the cash accounting scheme (Chapter 20) are applied to the whole group rather than the individual companies. • The other VAT schemes for small businesses are not available to companies registered as a group.

Test your understanding 11

Stewart plc owns 100% of the share capital of Enterprise Ltd. Both companies are UK resident trading companies.

All of Stewart's supplies for VAT purposes are taxable. Only 25% of the supplies of Enterprise are taxable and 75% exempt.

Their VAT details for the year ended 31 March 2017 are as follows:

		£
Stewart plc	Total supplies excluding VAT	600,000
	Input tax:	
	Relating to taxable supplies	60,000
	Relating to share of group overheads	5,000
Enterprise Ltd		
	Total supplies excluding VAT	950,000
	Input tax:	
	Relating to taxable supplies	40,000
	Relating to exempt supplies	115,000
	Relating to share of group overheads	18,000

Explain whether a group VAT registration would be worthwhile.

Divisional registration

In some cases a large enterprise operates not as a group of companies but as a single company with a number of divisions.

If the divisions are largely autonomous units dealing in different products and having separate accounting systems, it may be difficult to produce one VAT return for the whole company.

In these circumstances the company can apply to be registered in the name of its separate divisions.

12 Chapter summary

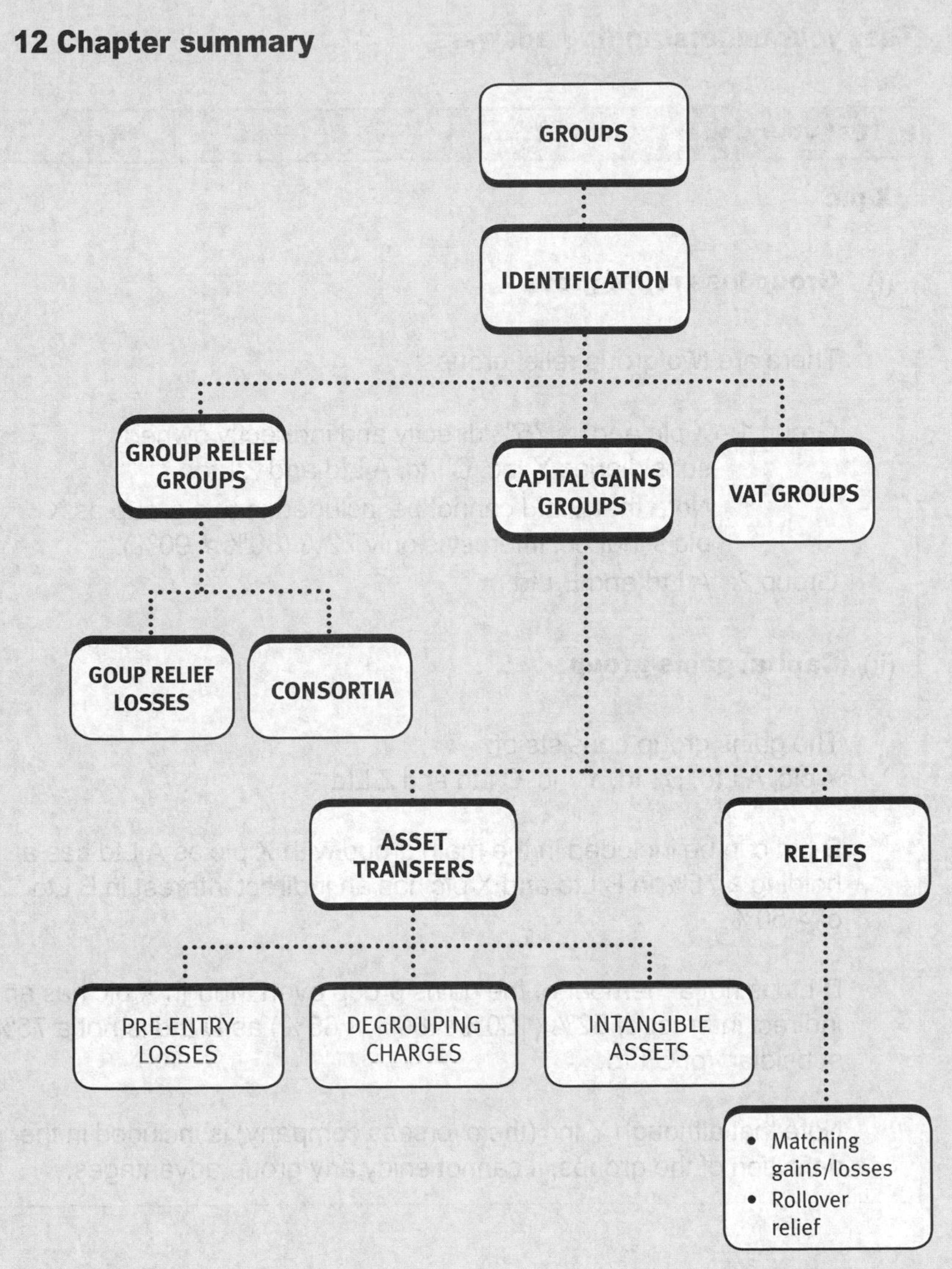

Test your understanding answers

Test your understanding 1

X plc

(i) **Group loss relief group**

There are two group relief groups:

Group 1: X plc and its 75% directly and indirectly owned subsidiaries Y Inc, C Ltd, A Ltd and Z Ltd.
Note that B Ltd cannot be included in this group as X plc's indirect interest is only 72% (80% × 90%).

Group 2: A Ltd and B Ltd.

(ii) **Capital gains group**

The gains group consists of:
X plc, A Ltd, B Ltd, Y Inc, C Ltd and Z Ltd.

B Ltd can be included in the main group with X plc as A Ltd has a holding ≥ 75% in B Ltd and X plc has an indirect interest in B Ltd of > 50%.

D Ltd is not a member of the gains group even though X plc has an indirect interest of 52% (100% × 80% × 65%) as D Ltd is not a 75% subsidiary of C Ltd.

Note that although Y Inc (the overseas company) is included in the definition of the groups, it cannot enjoy any group advantages.

Test your understanding 2

A Ltd and B Ltd

(a) **Maximum group relief – y/e 31.12.16**

Lower of:

(1) A Ltd's TTP in corresponding period
8/12 × £25,000 = £16,667

(2) B Ltd's loss in corresponding period
8/11 × £20,000 = £14,545

Y/e 31.12.16 – A Ltd's revised TTP calculation

	£
TTP	25,000
Less: Group relief	(14,545)
Revised TTP	10,455

(b) **Maximum group relief – y/e 31.12.17**

Lower of:

(1) A Ltd's TTP in corresponding period
3/12 × £17,000 = £4,250

(2) B Ltd's loss in corresponding period
3/11 × £20,000 = £5,455

Y/e 31.12.17 – A Ltd's revised TTP calculation

	£
TTP	17,000
Less: Group relief	(4,250)
Revised TTP	12,750

Test your understanding 3

Romeo Ltd

Corporation tax computations	Romeo Ltd	Juliet Ltd
	12 months to 31.12.16	9 months to 31.3.17
	£	£
Trading profit	890,000	0
Interest income	6,000	4,000
Property income	2,000	8,000
Chargeable gains		15,000
Total profits	898,000	27,000
Less: Loss relief		(27,000)
QCD relief	(4,000)	(Wasted)
	894,000	0
Less: Group relief (W)	(68,000)	
TTP	826,000	0
Corporation tax (20% × £826,000)	165,200	0

Note: The dividends received are exempt from corporation tax and have no impact on the corporation tax payable.

Working:

Loss available for group relief

The corresponding accounting period, is 6 months to 31 December 2016 (1.7.16 to 31.12.16).

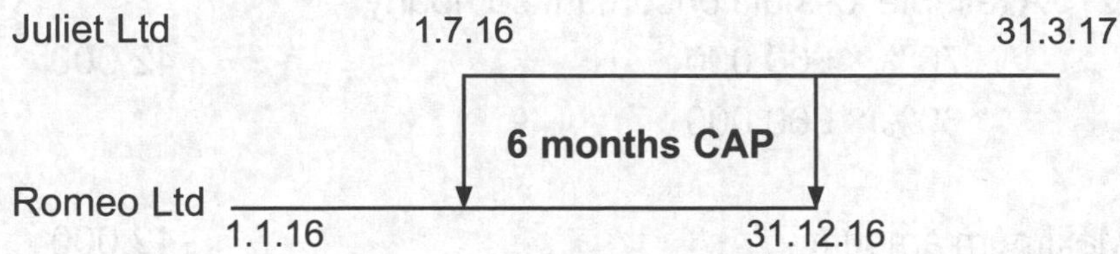

Therefore, maximum group relief = lower of:

(a) Loss of Juliet Ltd (£102,000 × 6/9) = £68,000

(b) Romeo Ltd's TTP (£894,000 × 6/12) = £447,000

Test your understanding 4

A Ltd and B Ltd

(i) This is not a consortium.

A Ltd has ≥ 75% of C Ltd so this is a 75% group.

(ii) This is a consortium.

D Ltd, C Ltd and F Ltd own ≥ 75% of G Ltd and each own ≥ 5%.

G Ltd is the consortium company and D Ltd, C Ltd and F Ltd are consortium members.

Test your understanding 5

P Ltd and Q Ltd	P Ltd	Q Ltd
	£	£
Maximum CR = lower of		
(1) Available TTP of members	50,000	15,000
(2) Available loss of consortium company		
70% × £60,000	42,000	
30% × £60,000		18,000
Maximum amount	42,000	15,000

X Ltd and Y Ltd

X Ltd can use part of its loss to relieve up to 40% of C Ltd's TTP = £20,000.
X Ltd cannot surrender any of its loss to Y Ltd.

Test your understanding 6

Blue Ltd, Rose Ltd, Pink Ltd and Mauve Ltd

(i) **Corporation tax computations**

Blue Ltd	£
TTP	300,000
Consortium relief (W):	
– From Rose Ltd	(45,000)
– From Pink Ltd	(105,000)
TTP	150,000
CT Liability (£150,000 × 20%)	30,000
Rose Ltd	
CT liability	0
Loss carried forward (W)	45,000
Pink Ltd	
CT liability	0
Loss carried forward (W)	21,000

Mauve Ltd

	£
TTP	55,000
CT liability (£55,000 × 20%)	11,000

Working: Maximum consortium relief

	Rose Ltd	Pink Ltd
	£	£
Lower of:		
(i) Consortium member loss	90,000	126,000
(ii) % of consortium company TTP		
15% × £300,000	45,000	
35% × £300,000		105,000
Loss left to c/f	45,000	21,000

(ii) **If Rose Ltd owned 80% of Blue Ltd**

The two companies would form a group relief group.

The whole of Rose Ltd's loss would be available as group relief to reduce the TTP of Blue Ltd to £210,000 (£300,000 – £90,000).

Pink's loss would no longer be available to Blue Ltd and would have to be used by Pink Ltd only.

Mauve Ltd would be unaffected.

Test your understanding 7

Green Ltd

Intergroup transfer:	£
Cost	100,000
Plus: IA: (April 1995 to October 2005)	
(193.3 – 149.0)/149.0 = 0.297 × £100,000	29,700
Base cost	129,700

Sale outside the group:

	£
Proceeds	350,000
Less: Base cost	(129,700)
Unindexed gain	220,300
Less: IA (October 2005 to December 2016)	
(264.7 – 193.3)/193.3 = 0.369 × £129,700	(47,859)
Chargeable gain	172,441

Test your understanding 8

Orange Ltd

When Orange Ltd leaves the group, the company still owns an asset which it had acquired from Yellow Ltd in the six years preceding Orange Ltd's departure.

Orange Ltd is treated as if it had sold the building on 1 December 2010 at its market value on that date, and then immediately reacquired it.

	£
Proceeds	375,000
Less: Base Cost: (Note):	
Cost to Yellow Ltd	(180,000)
IA (Aug 1996 – Dec 2010)	
(228.4 – 153.1)/153.1 = 0.492 × £180,000	(88,560)
Degrouping charge	106,440

The degrouping charge is added to the consideration received by Yellow Ltd on sale of the shares in Orange Ltd. However, any gain is likely to be exempt under the substantial shareholding exemption rules as Yellow Ltd has owned 10% of the shares for 12 out of the previous 24 months.

Note: Orange Ltd's cost is the original cost to Yellow Ltd plus the indexation allowance from the date of purchase by Yellow Ltd to the date of transfer to Orange Ltd.

Test your understanding 9

Mauve Ltd and Violet Ltd

Year ended 31 March 2017 – taxable total profits computation

To minimise tax for the group as a whole:

- Violet Ltd and Mauve Ltd should dispose of their chargeable assets realising their chargeable gain and allowable capital loss.
- The group should then make an election by 31.3.19 to reallocate the capital loss in Violet Ltd to Mauve Ltd.
- As a result the chargeable gain and capital loss are treated as being realised by Mauve Ltd.

	Mauve Ltd	Violet Ltd
	£	£
Trading profits	30,000	250,000
Net chargeable gain (£100,000 – £75,000)	25,000	
TTP	55,000	250,000

Note: The same result could be achieved by transferring Mauve Ltd's chargeable gain to Violet Ltd. As both companies are subject to corporation tax at 20% it makes no difference to the overall tax liability which company the net gain of £25,000 is taxed on.

Test your understanding 10

(a) (i) **Group relationships**

The group structure of the Anvil group is as follows:

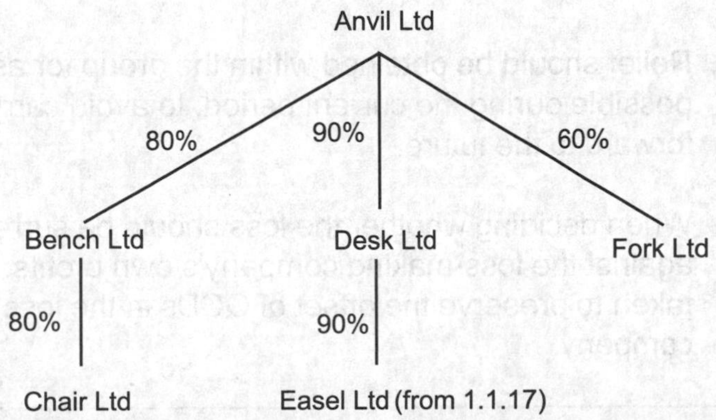

Group relief

For group relief purposes, two companies are members of a 75% group where one of them is a 75% subsidiary of the other, or both of them are 75% subsidiaries of the parent company.

To qualify as a 75% subsidiary, the parent company must hold 75% or more of the subsidiary's ordinary share capital, and have the right to receive 75% or more of its distributable profits and net assets (were it to be wound up). The 75% holding must be an effective interest that is held directly or indirectly.

Capital gains

For the purposes of transferring chargeable assets between two companies without incurring a chargeable gain or an allowable loss, the definition of a 75% subsidiary is 'less rigorous' than for group relief. The 75% holding must only be met at each level in the group structure, subject to the principal company having an effective interest of over 50%.

The 75% losses groups are as follows:

– Anvil Ltd, Bench Ltd, Desk Ltd, Easel Ltd (from 1.1.17) NOT Chair Ltd as the effective holding is only 64% (80% × 80%); NOT Fork Ltd as the direct share is only 60%.
– Bench Ltd and Chair Ltd form a separate losses group.

The 75% gains group is as follows:

– Anvil Ltd, Bench Ltd, Chair Ltd, Desk Ltd, Easel Ltd (from 1.1.17)
NOT Fork Ltd as the direct share is only 60%.

(ii) **Surrender of trading losses**

Relief should be obtained within the group for as much loss as possible during the current period, to avoid carrying losses forward to the future.

When deciding whether the loss should be surrendered or used against the loss-making company's own profits, care should be taken to preserve the offset of QCDs in the loss making company.

Any QCDs that are not offset during the current period will be wasted, whereas unrelieved losses could be carried forward.

The ability of companies with minority interests to compensate for group relief surrenders will be another factor.

(b) (i) **Corporation tax computations – y/e 31 March 2017**

	Anvil Ltd	Bench Ltd	Chair Ltd	Desk Ltd	Easel Ltd	Fork Ltd
	£	£	£	£	£	£
Trading profit	500,000	0	0	0	0	0
Interest income	0	100,000	0	30,000	140,000	0
Net gains (Note 1)	10,000	0	0	0	0	0
Total profits before loss relief	510,000	100,000	0	30,000	140,000	0
Current year loss (Note 2)				(20,000)		
Total profits	510,000	100,000	0	10,000	140,000	0
Less: QCDs				(10,000)		
Group relief (Note 2)	(510,000)	(100,000)	0	0	(35,000)	0
TTP	0	0	0	0	105,000	0

(ii) **Explanation of reliefs**

(1) **Capital gains**

An election should be made to reallocate Chair Ltd's chargeable gain to Anvil Ltd.

Anvil Ltd's capital loss can be set against the gain, and the remaining gain can be relieved by claiming group relief from Desk Ltd (Note 2).

If the remaining gain was left in Chair Ltd, it would remain chargeable, as Chair Ltd is not part of the same 75% losses group as Desk Ltd and cannot claim group relief.

(2) **Relief for trading losses**

Fork Ltd's loss

Fork Ltd is not part of a losses group, so its loss cannot be surrendered.

This loss could be carried back for 12 months against total profits of Fork Ltd, or otherwise will be carried forward against Fork Ltd's future trading profits of the same trade.

Easel Ltd's loss

As Easel Ltd's loss is brought forward from an earlier accounting period, it cannot be surrendered.

This loss will be carried forward against future profits of the same trade in Easel Ltd.

However, Easel Ltd has been subject to a change in ownership. If there is a major trade in the nature or conduct of Easel Ltd's trade within 3 years of the change in ownership (1 January 2017), the loss will not be carried forward past the date the ownership changed.

Desk Ltd's loss

The aim in setting off Desk Ltd's loss of £665,000 is to relieve as much loss as possible but avoid wasting Desk Ltd's QCDs.

The surrender to Easel Ltd is restricted, as Easel Ltd has only been part of the group since 1 January 2017:

Maximum surrender by Desk Ltd
(3/12 × £665,000) = £166,250
Maximum claim by Easel Ltd against profits for the corresponding period: (3/12 × £140,000) = £35,000

The maximum surrender to Easel Ltd is therefore £35,000.

The loss should be used as follows:

	£
Total loss	665,000
Surrender to Anvil Ltd; reduce profits to £Nil	(510,000)
Surrender to Bench Ltd; reduce profits to £Nil	(100,000)
Surrender to Easel Ltd (see above)	(35,000)
Claim in Desk Ltd (Note)	(20,000)
	0

Note: The claim to set the trading loss against Desk Ltd's own profits is an all or nothing claim, and cannot be restricted.
In order to leave £10,000 profit in Desk Ltd to off Desk Ltd's QCDs, the group relief surrenders should be made first, leaving just £20,000 loss to set off in Desk Ltd.

Test your understanding 11

Stewart plc

Without a group registration:

Both companies account for VAT separately and the input tax recovery would be as follows:

	£
Stewart plc (can recover all input VAT)	65,000
Enterprise Ltd (W1)	44,500
Recoverable input VAT	109,500

With a group VAT registration:

	£
Stewart plc and Enterprise Ltd (W2)	
– Relating to taxable supplies	100,000
– Relating to group overheads	12,650
	112,650

Conclusion

It is worthwhile for Stewart plc and Enterprise Ltd to form a VAT group as it allows a higher recovery of input VAT of £3,150 (£112,650 – £109,500).

Working

(W1) **Enterprise Ltd**	Total	Recover	Disallow
	£	£	£
Relating to taxable supplies	40,000	40,000	
Relating to exempt supplies	115,000		115,000
Relating to overheads (25%/75%)	18,000	4,500	13,500
	173,000	44,500	128,500

De minimis test

The total input VAT, total input VAT less input VAT directly attributable to taxable supplies, and input VAT relating to exempt supplies, are all clearly greater than £625 per month on average, therefore none of the de minimis tests are satisfied.

(W2) **Group position**	Total	Recover	Disallow
	£	£	£
Relating to taxable supplies (£60,000 + £40,000)	100,000	100,000	
Relating to exempt supplies	115,000		115,000
Relating to overheads (£5,000 + £18,000) (see below for split) (55%/45%)	23,000	12,650	10,350
	238,000	112,650	125,350

Split of non-attributable VAT

Taxable supplies = £600,000 + (25% × £950,000) = £837,500

Total supplies = (£600,000 + £950,000) = £1,550,000

Taxable % apportionment

(£837,500 ÷ £1,550,000) × 100 = 55% (rounded up to whole %)

De minimis test

The total input VAT, total input VAT less input VAT directly attributable to taxable supplies, and input VAT relating to exempt supplies, are all clearly greater than £625 per month on average, therefore none of the de minimis tests are satisfied.

chapter

28

Overseas aspects of corporation tax

Chapter learning objectives

Upon completion of this chapter you will be able to:

- explain how the residence of a company is determined and state the impact
- recognise the impact of the OECD model double tax treaty on corporation tax
- explain the meaning of and implications of a permanent establishment
- advise on the tax position of a non UK resident company trading in the UK
- determine the corporation tax liability when a UK company has overseas chargeable profits and calculate the double taxation relief available
- identify and advise on the tax implications of controlled foreign companies.

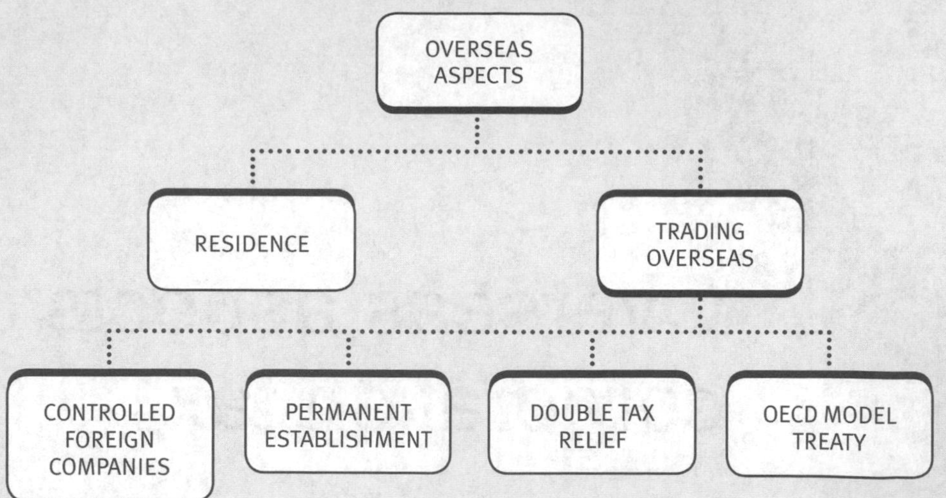

Introduction

This chapter considers the overseas aspects of corporation tax. Much of the content of this chapter is new, apart from the definition of residence for a company.

This chapter aims to show the impact of:

- UK resident companies trading overseas via a branch or an overseas company set up for the purpose, and
- overseas companies trading in the UK.

1 Company residence

Determining UK residence

Under UK law, a company is resident in the UK if it is:

- **incorporated** in the UK, or
- incorporated elsewhere, but has its place of **central management and control** in the UK.

The centre of management and control is where the key operational and financial decisions are made. HMRC will look at factors such as:

- the location of the board meetings
- where the effective day-to-day management decisions are made, and
- the residence status of the directors.

No one factor is conclusive in determining the centre of management and control.

Note that other countries may have different definitions to determine residency status. Therefore, it is possible for a company to have dual residence status.

For example, a company incorporated in another country may be treated as resident there, but if it were centrally managed and controlled in the UK it would also be treated as resident in the UK.

Implications of UK residence

A UK resident company is chargeable to corporation tax on its worldwide profits. This includes:

- all UK profits
- overseas branch profits (unless exemption election made – section 3)
- other overseas income (e.g. rental income and interest income), and
- chargeable gains.

2 OECD model tax treaty

The OECD (Organisation for Economic Cooperation and Development) is an organisation of developed countries whose main purpose is to maintain financial stability and the expansion of world trade.

In order to help avoid double taxation between countries, the OECD has published a model Double Taxation Convention with an accompanying commentary.

Significance of the OECD model tax treaty

The UK has a large number of tax treaties with other countries. Whenever a new treaty is drawn up or an old treaty is renegotiated, the OECD model is used as a guide.

Detailed knowledge of treaties is not required in your examination but you are required to understand the impact of the OECD model tax treaty on corporation tax.

The main function of any treaty is to avoid double taxation and to decide which country shall have the right to tax income (the 'primary taxing rights').

Contents of the model treaty

Some of the main areas covered in the treaty are as follows:

Article 1:	states that companies which are covered by the treaty are those resident in one or both of the countries involved.
Article 4:	explains that residence is determined by the laws of a state (i.e. not by the model treaty itself). It includes a 'tie breaker' clause to be applied when a company appears to be resident in two countries. In this case, residence is where the place of 'effective management' is situated. This is usually where the head office, main company records and senior staff are located.
Article 5:	deals with the meaning of 'permanent establishment' (section 3).
Articles 6 to 22:	deal with the treatment of different types of income.
Article 23:	explains the two methods of giving relief for double taxation • exempting the income in one state and taxing it only in the other, or • the credit method which gives credit in one state for the tax levied by the other. The credit method (also known as unilateral relief) is covered in section 4.

3 Trading overseas

The taxation of overseas trading income

The normal provision in tax treaties (based on the OECD model tax treaty) is that a foreign country will usually only tax income arising in its country from the commercial operation of a UK resident company if:

(a) a trade is carried on **within its boundaries**, and

(b) the profits are derived from a **permanent establishment** set up for that purpose.

The term 'within a country's boundaries' is important, as trading **with**, as opposed to **within**, another country will avoid any liability to overseas revenue taxes.

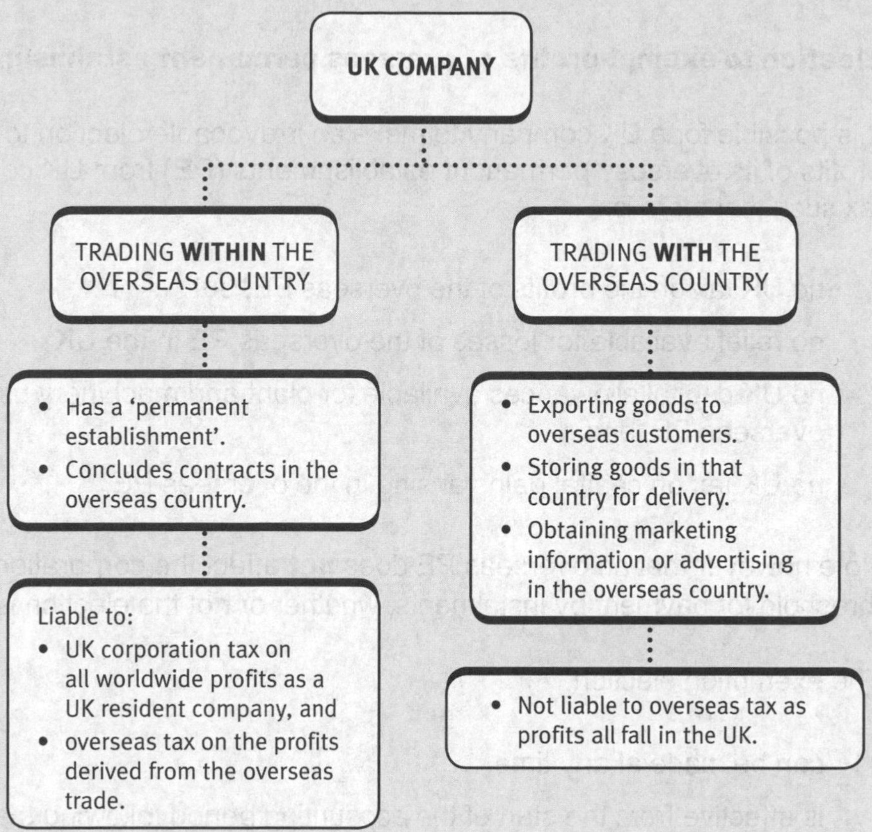
UK COMPANY
TRADING WITHIN THE OVERSEAS COUNTRY
TRADING WITH THE OVERSEAS COUNTRY
• Has a 'permanent establishment'.
• Concludes contracts in the overseas country.
• Exporting goods to overseas customers.
• Storing goods in that country for delivery.
• Obtaining marketing information or advertising in the overseas country.
Liable to:
• UK corporation tax on all worldwide profits as a UK resident company, and
• overseas tax on the profits derived from the overseas trade.
• Not liable to overseas tax as profits all fall in the UK.

Permanent establishment

The term 'permanent establishment' within an overseas country includes:

- a place of management
- a branch
- an office
- a factory, a workshop or any mine or other place of extraction of natural resources.

A UK resident company that has a permanent establishment trading within an overseas country will normally:

- be charged to tax on its overseas profits arising,
- by both HMRC under the UK residence rule, and
- the overseas tax authority under their own tax code.

Double taxation relief (DTR) will be available (section 4).

Election to exempt profits of overseas permanent establishment

It is possible for a UK company to make an irrevocable election to exempt profits of its overseas permanent establishments (PE) from UK corporation tax such that there is:

- no UK tax on the profits of the overseas PE, but
- no relief available for losses of the overseas PE in the UK
- no UK capital allowances available for plant and machinery used by the overseas PE, and
- no UK tax on capital gains arising in the overseas PE.

Note however that an overseas PE does **not** affect the corporation tax threshold for payment by instalments, whether or not the election is made.

The exemption election:

- can be made at any time,
- is effective from the start of the accounting period following that in which the election is made, and
- once made, applies to all overseas PEs of that company.

Tax planning

It may not be beneficial to make the election if:

(i) double tax relief means that there is little or no UK corporation tax payable, and/or

(ii) losses are possible or anticipated in any overseas branch in the future, as the election applies to all branches of the company, current and future.

Alternative overseas investment structures

Companies have the option of structuring their business operations and investments in various ways.

The two principal methods of setting up a permanent place of business overseas are:

(i) setting up a branch (or division), or

(ii) incorporating a new subsidiary (i.e. setting up an overseas resident company).

Note that:

- The branch or division will probably be regarded as a permanent establishment and hence may be subject to both UK and local taxes.
- The new subsidiary will be incorporated overseas. Provided that it is centrally managed and controlled in the overseas country, it will be resident there for tax purposes and not in the UK.
- There are fundamental differences for tax purposes between the two structures.

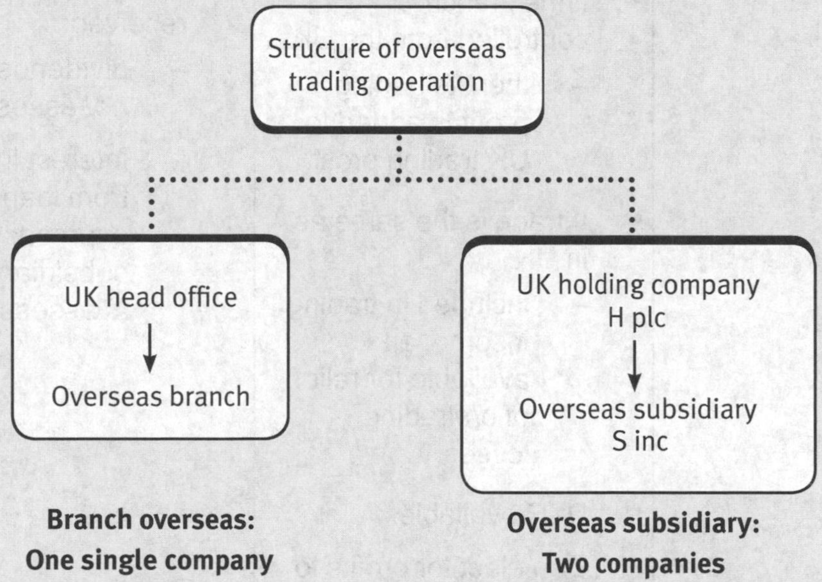

Overseas dividends

Overseas dividends are treated in the same way as UK dividends:

- They are exempt from corporation tax.
- They are included for the purposes of determining if the company is liable to pay tax by quarterly instalment, unless the dividends are received from 51% group companies, in which case they are ignored completely for corporation tax purposes.

The tax implications of both structures:

	Overseas branch	Overseas subsidiary
Scope and basis of charge	• Extension of UK operations. • All profits arising assessed on UK company. • If the branch is controlled from the UK: – then its trading profit is added to UK trading profit. • If trade is the same as in UK: – included in trading income, and available for relief of b/f trading losses. • DTR available. • Can elect for profits to be exempt.	• Overseas profits not assessed in UK if left in overseas subsidiary. • Profits remitted to UK parent company may be chargeable when received: – dividends *not* assessable – interest income from loan to overseas subsidiary *is* assessable.
Trading loss relief	• Can relieve trading losses of overseas PE against UK profits: – unless the loss can be relieved in the country in which it arose. • UK losses can be relieved against overseas PE profits. • No relief if election for branch exemption made.	• UK trading loss – cannot be surrendered to overseas subsidiary. • Overseas loss from 75% subsidiary in EEA – can be surrendered to UK parent if no alternative relief in overseas country.
Capital allowances	• Available on overseas located assets purchased and used by overseas branch, unless election for branch exemption made.	• Not available under UK tax rules.

	Overseas branch	Overseas subsidiary
Chargeable gains	• Capital gains computed using UK rules • Rollover relief is available on reinvestment • Capital losses can be utilised. • No capital gains or utilisation of capital losses if branch exemption election made.	• Not assessed in UK.
Impact on tax payments	• None (as not a separate entity).	• As a related 51% group company, the corporation tax threshold for payment by instalment is reduced.

Tax planning

Where a new overseas operation is expected to make losses initially, it may be advantageous to set it up as a branch.

Once the overseas operation expects to be profitable, its trade can be transferred to an overseas resident subsidiary company so that its profits are not taxable in the UK (if paid as dividends).

- Starting as a branch would enable the UK company to offset the losses against its other profits.
- The transfer of the trade represents a disposal of the assets of the branch at MV which may lead to:
  - balancing adjustments in respect of assets qualifying for capital allowances, and
  - chargeable gains.
- Where all of the assets of the branch (excluding cash) are transferred to the overseas company in exchange for shares:
  - an election is available
  - to defer any gains arising until the overseas company is sold.
- The deferred gains will also be charged if the overseas company disposes of the assets transferred to it within six years of acquisition.

- Consideration should be given as to whether or not it is necessary to obtain the consent of the Treasury for the transfer of the trade to the overseas company. This is because it is generally illegal for a UK resident company to permit a non-UK resident company over which it has control to create or issue shares.

Alternatively, an election could be made to exempt the profits and gains of the branch once profitable. However, as this election applies to all overseas permanent establishments and is irrevocable, this would require careful consideration.

Example 1 – Branch vs. subsidiary

Explain the advantages for taxation purposes of operating overseas through a branch rather than through an overseas subsidiary, assuming that a branch exemption election has not been made.

Solution

Advantages of operating through an overseas branch

(1) Relief is usually available in the UK for trading losses if incurred by an overseas branch, but no UK relief is available for trading losses incurred by an overseas subsidiary unless the overseas subsidiary is resident in the EEA and no relief is possible in the overseas country.

(2) UK capital allowances are available in respect of plant and machinery purchased by an overseas branch.

(3) Unlike an overseas subsidiary, an overseas branch cannot be a related 51% group company. The UK corporation tax threshold for payment by instalment will therefore not be reduced.

Worldwide debt cap

There is a potential restriction on the amount of finance expense (i.e. interest relief) that UK group members of a worldwide group can deduct, known as the 'worldwide debt cap'.

Broadly speaking, it will be limited to the consolidated gross finance expense. However, you are not expected to know any further details for this examination.

Foreign companies trading in the UK

A non-UK resident company can be liable to UK corporation tax on trading profits if it trades **within** the UK, but not for trading **with** the UK.

- Trading within the UK means either trading through a permanent establishment or concluding contracts in the UK.
- Trading with the UK means activities such as exporting goods to UK customers, storing goods in the UK for customers and advertising and marketing activities in the UK.

Corporation tax is generally charged at the UK rate of 20% unless there is a double taxation treaty specifying a lower rate.

If a UK PE owned by an EEA company makes a loss, the loss can be group relieved in the UK if it has not been relieved in another country (even if it could be).

Example 2 – Trading in the UK

Morn Inc is a large company resident in the country of Shortland. Morn Inc manufactures mobile telephones in Shortland, and has been selling these in the UK since 1 September 2016.

Initially, Morn Inc sold the telephones through a UK based agent and stored the telephones in a rented warehouse. On 1 February 2017 Morn Inc rented an office and showroom in London which were staffed initially by two sales managers and an administrator from Shortland.

Morn Inc intends to incorporate a UK subsidiary company on 31 December 2017 to operate the UK business.

There is no double tax treaty between the UK and Shortland.

Advise Morn Inc of its liability to UK corporation tax during the period from 1 September 2016 to 31 December 2017.

Solution

Morn Inc will be liable to UK corporation tax (CT) if it is trading through a permanent establishment in the UK (i.e. trading within the UK). The company will not be liable to UK CT if it is merely trading with the UK.

From 1 September 2016 to 31 January 2017, Morn Inc employed a UK agent, and maintained an inventory of telephones in the UK. Provided that contracts for the sale of the telephones are concluded in Shortland, Morn Inc will probably not be liable to UK CT on profits made during this period.

On 1 February 2017, Morn Inc would appear to have opened a permanent establishment in the UK by renting an office and showroom, and it is likely that the sales managers will be empowered to conclude contracts in the UK.

Morn Inc will therefore be liable to UK CT on the profits made in the UK during the period from 1 February 2017 to the date that the trade is transferred to the new company (presumably 31 December 2017).

CT will be charged at the UK rate of 20%, since there is no double taxation treaty between the UK and Shortland.

4 Double taxation relief

UK resident companies can get relief for overseas taxes suffered in the following ways:

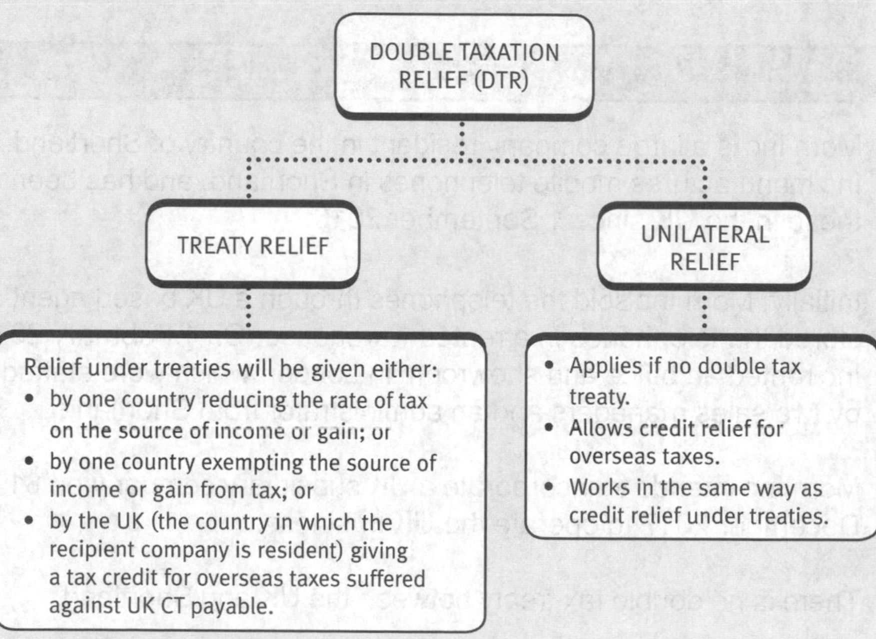

DOUBLE TAXATION RELIEF (DTR)
TREATY RELIEF
UNILATERAL RELIEF
Relief under treaties will be given either:
• by one country reducing the rate of tax on the source of income or gain; or
• by one country exempting the source of income or gain from tax; or
• by the UK (the country in which the recipient company is resident) giving a tax credit for overseas taxes suffered against UK CT payable.
• Applies if no double tax treaty.
• Allows credit relief for overseas taxes.
• Works in the same way as credit relief under treaties.

Calculation of unilateral (credit) relief

All overseas income must be included in the corporation tax computation gross (i.e. including any overseas taxation suffered).

Relief is available for overseas withholding tax (WHT) as follows:

- WHT = any overseas tax deducted at source from foreign income.

- If the **amount** of WHT is given
  - simply add it back to the net income to give the gross amount.

- If the **rate** of WHT is given
  - gross up as normal.

DTR is the **lower of:**

(i) overseas tax suffered, and

(ii) UK CT attributable to the overseas income.

Example 3 – DTR

UK Ltd is a UK resident company. The company's UK trading profit for the y/e 31 March 2017 is £355,000. UK Ltd has an overseas branch and an overseas subsidiary, and has not elected for overseas branch profits to be exempt.

Overseas branch

The branch is controlled from overseas. It has a trading profit of £65,000 for the y/e 31 March 2017. The overseas corporation tax on these profits is £26,000.

Overseas subsidiary

UK Ltd owns 80% of the share capital of Overseas Inc, a company that is resident overseas. UK Ltd received a dividend of £80,750 during the y/e 31 March 2017. This dividend was net of withholding tax of £4,250.

Calculate UK Ltd's CT liability for the y/e 31 March 2017.

Solution

	Total	UK	Branch
	£	£	£
Trading profits = TTP	420,000	355,000	65,000
CT @ 20%	84,000	71,000	13,000
Less: DTR (W)	(13,000)		(13,000)
CT liability	71,000	71,000	0

Working: DTR

Lower of:	£
(i) Overseas tax	26,000
(ii) UK CT (20% × £65,000)	13,000

Note: There is no DTR for the withholding tax suffered on the dividend received, as the dividend is not taxable in the UK.

Test your understanding 1

R plc has received rent of £119,000 in the year ended 31 March 2017 from an overseas property.

A WHT rate of 15% has been applied to the rent received by R plc.

Compute the CT payable by R plc, on the assumption that R plc has trading profits of £900,000 in the year ended 31 March 2017 in addition to the overseas income but no other income or gains.

Further aspects of DTR

If there is more than one source of foreign income, basic DTR is computed on each overseas source separately.

- A columnar approach is recommended in computations.
- In computing the UK CT attributable to an overseas source, general loss reliefs (current year, carry back, group relief) and QCD relief can be set off in the most beneficial manner as follows:
  - first against UK sources
  - then against the source suffering the **lowest rate** of overseas tax.

Example 4 – DTR with losses

London Ltd, a UK resident trading company, owns two overseas branches, one in Paris and one in Rome.

It also owns 4% of the share capital of Berlin GmbH, an overseas company and owns an overseas property from which it receives rental income.

The following information relates to London Ltd's y/e 31 March 2017:

	£
Tax adjusted trading profits	38,000
Overseas income:	
Paris branch profits	
– after deduction of withholding tax of 40%	54,000
Rome branch loss	(50,200)
Rental income	
– after deduction of withholding tax of 15%	43,435
Dividend from Berlin GmbH	
– After deduction of withholding tax of 27%	2,700

Compute London Ltd's UK corporation tax payable for the y/e 31 March 2017 assuming the overseas branch exemption election:

(a) **has not been made**

(b) **has been made.**

Solution

(a) **Overseas branch exemption election has not been made**
Corporation tax computation – y/e 31 March 2017

	Total	UK income	Paris profits	Rental income
	£	£	£	£
Trading profit	38,000	38,000		
Overseas income (W1)	141,100		90,000	51,100
Overseas branch loss (Note)	(50,200)	(38,000)		(12,200)
Total profits = TTP	128,900	0	90,000	38,900
Corporation tax				
£128,900 @ 20%	25,780	0	18,000	7,780
Less: DTR (W2)	(25,665)	0	(18,000)	(7,665)
Corporation tax payable	115	0	0	115

Notes:

(1) The overseas branch loss is offset against the UK income first, then against the overseas income with the lowest overseas tax rate, in order to maximise the DTR.

(2) The overseas dividend from Berlin GmbH is exempt.

(b) **Overseas branch exemption election has been made**
Corporation tax computation – y/e 31 March 2017

	Total	UK income	Rental income
	£	£	£
Trading profit	38,000	38,000	
Overseas income (W1)	51,100		51,100
Total profits = TTP	89,100	38,000	51,100
Corporation tax			
£89,100 @ 20%	17,820	7,600	10,220
Less: DTR (W3)	(7,665)	0	(7,665)
Corporation tax payable	10,155	7,600	2,555

Less corporation tax is payable if the election is not made, because:

- relief for the overseas branch loss is not available,
- there is no UK tax due on the Paris branch profits anyway as this is fully covered by the DTR, and
- the corporation tax liability is correspondingly £10,040 higher (£10,155 – £115).

Alternative calculation of the difference
= (£50,200 branch loss × 20%) = £10,040

Note: It is not possible to make the exemption election for the current accounting period, only future periods. Therefore, London Ltd would have had to make the election before the current period began, when the results would not be known.

Workings

(W1) Grossing up the overseas income

	Paris profits	Rental income
	£	£
Income received	54,000	43,435
Add: WHT (40/60)/(15/85)	36,000	7,665
Gross income	90,000	51,100

(W2) DTR – without election

	Paris profits	Rental income
	£	£
Lower of:		
UK CT on overseas profits	18,000	7,780
Overseas taxed suffered (W1)	36,000	7,665
Lower amount	18,000	7,665

(W3) DTR – with election

	Rental income
	£
Lower of:	
UK CT on overseas profits	10,220
Overseas tax suffered (W1)	7,665
Lower amount	7,665

Test your understanding 2

Z plc has the following income for the year ended 31 March 2017:

Trading profit	£200,000
Foreign dividends received 1 March 2017 (net of 29% WHT)	£5,680
Foreign rents received (net of 17% WHT)	£4,980

Z plc paid a qualifying charitable donation of £100,000 in the year ended 31 March 2017.

Compute Z plc's UK corporation tax payable for the year ended 31 March 2017.

Unrelieved overseas tax

Initially DTR is dealt with on a source by source basis. This can lead to overseas tax being only partly relieved.

Utilise the excess overseas taxes according to the following:

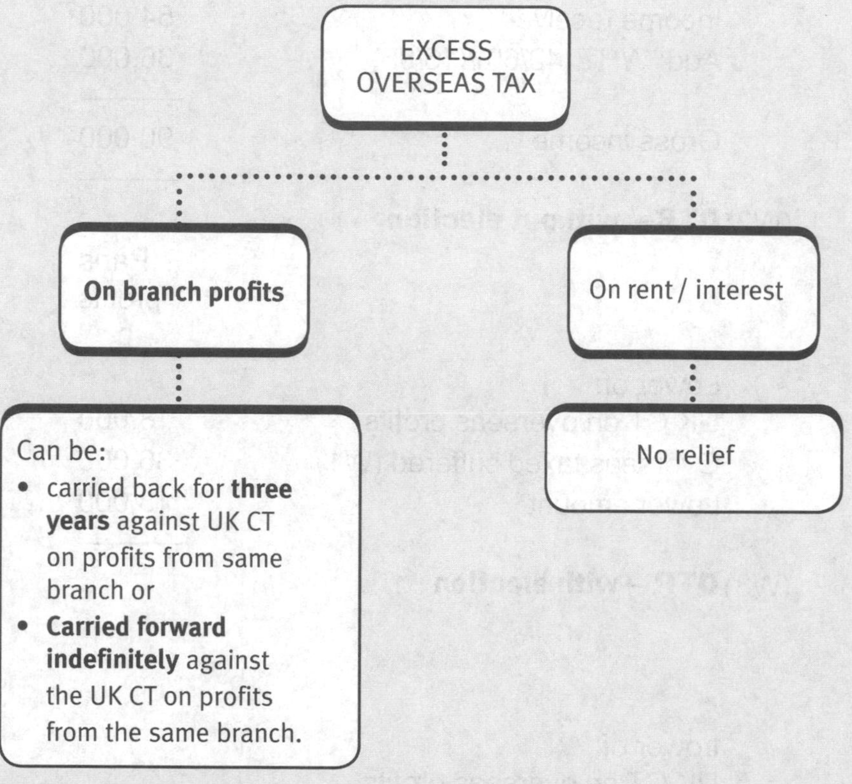

5 Controlled foreign companies

Introduction

- If a company is considering setting up an overseas subsidiary, it will be attracted to countries with low rates of tax (known as tax havens) so that it can divert profits from the UK to countries charging a lower rate of tax.
- However, there is anti avoidance legislation in place to prevent the use of overseas companies (known as Controlled Foreign Companies (CFCs)) for this purpose.

For the P6 examination, a CFC is defined as:

- a **non UK resident company**
- that is **controlled by UK resident** companies and/or individuals, and
- that has **artificially diverted profits** from the UK.

The CFC regime

As with most anti avoidance legislation, the rules are complex, but in overview the regime operates as follows:

- a **CFC charge** (i.e. a charge to UK corporation tax) will arise based on the **chargeable profits** of the UK company shareholders if:
  - the **UK company owns at least a 25% interest** in the CFC
  - unless an exemption, or restriction on the profits apportioned, applies (see below)
- note that no CFC charge arises on individual shareholders
- **chargeable profits** = the income of the CFC (but not chargeable gains) that are artificially diverted from the UK, calculated using the UK tax rules
- CFCs are regarded as having **no chargeable profits** (and therefore no CFC charge) if any of the following conditions are satisfied:
  - the CFC does not hold any assets or bear any risks under any arrangements/tax planning schemes intended to reduce UK tax
  - the CFC does not hold any assets or bear any risks that are managed in the UK
  - the CFC would continue in business if the UK management of its assets and risks were to cease
- if applicable, **the CFC charge** is calculated as:

	£
(UK company's share of the CFC profits × UK rate of corporation tax) (see note below)	X
Less: Creditable tax	
DTR that would be available if the CFC were UK resident	(X)
UK corporation tax on income of CFC that is taxable in UK (if any)	(X)
Income tax suffered by the CFC on its income	(X)
CFC charge	X

Note: The UK company's share of profits is usually **apportioned based on the percentage of shares held.**

- Prior to 8 July 2015, UK losses and excess management expenses could be offset against the profits taxable in a CFC charge.

  However, for CAPs commencing on/after 8 July 2015, the offset of losses and excess expenses in the calculation of the CFC charge is no longer possible.

This applies to losses and excess expenses that are:

- Brought forward from previous years
- Generated in the current period, and
- Group relieved from other group companies.

- UK companies are required to self assess their liability to the CFC charge
- a clearance procedure exists for companies to check with HMRC how the rules will be applied in specific cases.

Test your understanding 3

Zetec Ltd, a UK company with taxable profits of £20,000 for the year to 31 March 2017, holds 90% of an overseas subsidiary resident in Maxia. The subsidiary falls within the definition of a CFC.

The overseas subsidiary has £600,000 of profits for the period, 75% of which are caught by the CFC legislation and stand to be charged. The tax payable in Maxia is 5%.

Show the effect of the CFC on Zetec Ltd's corporation tax payable for the year ended 31 March 2017.

Exemptions to CFC charge

Even if a CFC has chargeable profits, it is rare for a CFC charge to arise due to the availability of exemptions to the charge.

The CFC charge is not applied if any **one** of the following exemptions apply:

(1) **Exempt period**

The first 12 months of the overseas company coming under the control of UK residents will be exempt from a CFC charge provided:

- it continues to be a CFC in the following accounting period, and
- it is not subject to a CFC charge in that accounting period (i.e. one of the other exemptions available now applies).

This exemption is intended to provide a period of time for companies to restructure to avoid the charge applying. It does **not** apply to newly incorporated companies.

(2) **Excluded territories**

HMRC provide a list of territories where rates of tax are sufficiently high to avoid a CFC charge arising.

If the CFC is resident in an excluded territory, no CFC charge arises.

(3) **Low profits**

The CFC's TTP are:

- £500,000 or less
- of which no more than £50,000 comprises non-trading profits.

(4) **Low profit margin**

The CFC's accounting profits are no more than 10% of relevant operating expenditure.

(5) **Tax exemption**

The tax paid in the overseas country is at least 75% of the UK corporation tax which would be due if the CFC were a UK resident company.

It can be difficult to remember these exemptions; you may find the following mnemonic helpful:

Energetic (**E**xempt period)

Elephants (**E**xcluded territories)

Love (**L**ow profits)

Lifting (**L**ow profit margin)

Trees (**T**ax)

Example 5 – Controlled foreign companies

X plc is a large UK company with annual profits of £10 million. They are considering investing overseas and have identified two possible alternative investments in Farland where the corporate tax rate is 10%.

X plc plans to buy a 70% stake in Dorn Inc, an investment company resident in Farland. Dorn Inc makes regular annual profits of £2 million. Alternatively, they could invest in Burton Inc which is a trading company but only produces profits of £400,000.

It is anticipated that Burton Inc could make losses in the future due to significant investment required to develop new products.

There is no double tax treaty between the UK and Farland.

Advise the tax considerations that X plc should take into account before making their investment.

Solution

Dividends

- Any dividends paid by the foreign companies to X plc will be exempt for X plc.

Controlled foreign companies

- Both of the potential investments will be classed as CFCs. They are:
  - (i) resident outside the UK
  - (ii) controlled by persons resident in the UK
- This means that X plc could have an additional tax charge at 20% on their 70% share of profits, less a tax credit for the overseas tax suffered.
- The investment in Dorn Inc does not appear to satisfy any of the exemptions, so there is very likely to be a tax charge if there are chargeable profits in the CFC (i.e. income profits artificially diverted from the UK).
- The exemption for the first 12 months of the company coming under the control of UK residents may apply, but only if there is no CFC charge in the following period.
- Burton Inc has total profits of less than £500,000, all of which are apparently from trading, so will be covered by the low profits exemption.

Loss relief

It is not possible for losses to be surrendered from an overseas company to a UK company unless:

(i) the UK company has at least 75% interest in the overseas company's shares

(ii) no other method of relieving the loss exists

(iii) the company is resident in the EEA.

In this case there cannot be any UK relief for losses made in Farland as the company proposes to buy only a 70% stake.

Test your understanding 4

Wordsworth Ltd, a UK resident company, has three wholly owned overseas subsidiaries.

Explain which of the companies are likely to be exempt from the CFC rules:

(1) Alcock Inc – resident in Ruritania where the CT rate is 8%. Alcock Inc is an investment company producing taxable profits of £40,000 p.a.

(2) Barbauld SA – resident in Narnia where the CT rate is 20%. Barbauld SA is an investment company producing profits of £2 million p.a.

(3) Blake Inc – resident in Albion where the CT rate is 5%. Blake Inc makes nursery accessories and has profits of £750,000 p.a.

6 Chapter summary

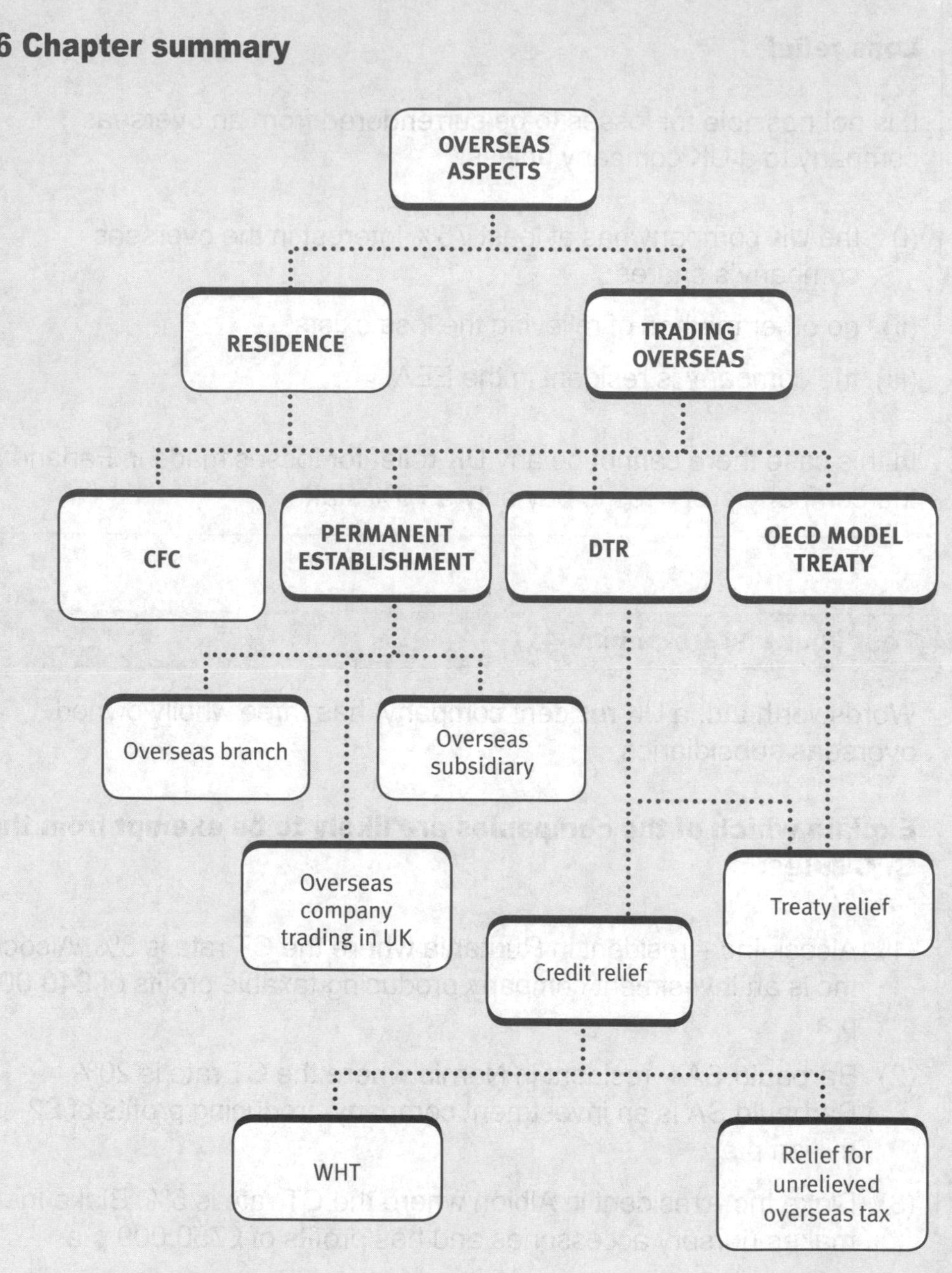

Test your understanding answers

Test your understanding 1

R plc

Corporation tax computation – year ended 31 March 2017

	UK	Foreign Income	Total
	£	£	£
Trading profit	900,000		900,000
Overseas rent (W1)		140,000	140,000
TTP	900,000	140,000	1,040,000
CT @ 20%	180,000	28,000	208,000
Less: DTR (W2)		(21,000)	(21,000)
CT liability	180,000	7,000	187,000

Workings

(W1) **Gross overseas rent**

	£
Rent received	119,000
Add: WHT (15/85 × £119,000)	21,000
Overseas rent	140,000

(W2) **DTR**

	£
Lower of (i) Overseas tax suffered (W1)	21,000
(ii) UK CT (20% × £140,000)	28,000

Test your understanding 2

Z plc

Corporation tax computation – year ended 31 March 2017

	UK income	Foreign rent	Total
	£	£	£
Income (W1)	200,000	6,000	206,000
Less: QCDs	(100,000)	0	(100,000)
TTP	100,000	6,000	106,000
CT @ 20%	20,000	1,200	21,200
Less: DTR (W2)	0	(1,020)	(1,020)
CT liability	20,000	180	20,180

Workings

(W1) **Gross overseas rental income**

	£
Amounts received	4,980
Add: WHT (£4,980 × 17/83)	1,020
Gross overseas income	6,000

(W2) **DTR on overseas rental income**

	£
Lower of:	
(i) Overseas tax suffered (W1)	1,020
(ii) UK CT on overseas income	1,200

Test your understanding 3

Zetec Ltd

The UK corporation tax payable by Zetec Ltd is:

		£
Taxable total profits		20,000
Corporation tax (20% × £20,000)		4,000
Extra UK tax on CFC profits:		
UK tax on apportioned profits		
(20% × 90% × 75% × £600,000)	81,000	
Less: DTR for tax suffered in Maxia		
(5% × 90% × 75% × £600,000)	(20,250)	
		60,750
Total UK corporation tax payable		64,750

Test your understanding 4

Wordsworth Ltd

All the companies should be exempt from the CFC charge as:

(1) Alcock Inc has taxable profits below £50,000 (the low profits limit for non-trading profits).

(2) Barbauld SA is resident in a country where the CT payable is likely to be at least 75% of the tax that would be payable in the UK if the company were UK resident (tax exemption).

(3) Blake Inc may not satisfy any of the exemptions, but its trading profits will not fall within the charge to UK tax unless they are dependent on an activity provided from the UK and only arise in Blake Inc for the purposes of avoiding UK tax.

chapter

29

Planning for companies

Chapter learning objectives

Upon completion of this chapter you will be able to:

- identify and advise on the taxes applicable to a given course of action and their impact on a business scenario
- identify and advise on the types of investment and other expenditure that will result in a reduction of tax liabilities for a business
- recognise that alternative courses of action have different tax consequences and assess the advantages and disadvantages
- identify suitable tax planning measures in a given scenario to mitigate tax liabilities for a company
- identify relevant procedures, time limits and claims for transactions with a tax impact.

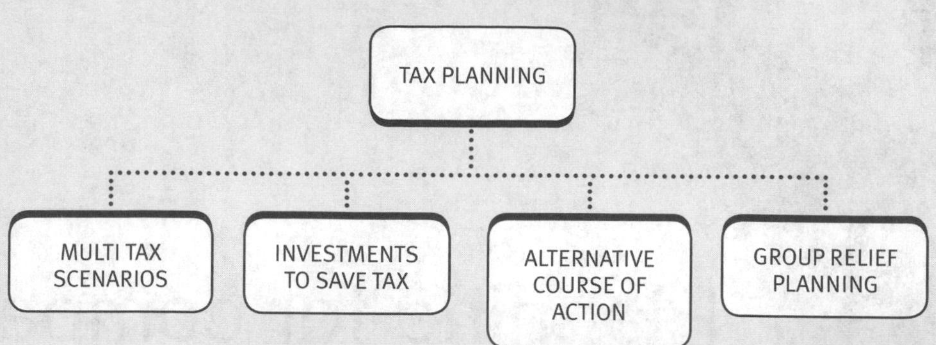

Introduction

The purpose of this chapter is to consider tax planning in the context of multi tax corporate scenarios.

It concentrates on corporate aspects of planning, the most likely taxes to consider being corporation tax, VAT and stamp taxes. However, the income tax and NIC implications of employing staff can also feature in an examination question.

None of the content in this chapter is new. However, the chapter aims to show how to advise clients and deal with a selection of corporate taxation scenarios that may form the basis for an examination question.

1 Purchase of a building

Companies often need to buy buildings. These can be bought freehold or leasehold and there are a number of tax implications to consider:

	Freehold	**Leasehold**
VAT	• Charged if: – building less than 3 years old, or – if previous owner opted to tax building. • Otherwise an exempt supply. • Recoverable by registered purchaser using the building to make taxable supplies (or opting to tax).	• Charged if previous owner opted to tax • Otherwise an exempt supply. • Recoverable by registered trader using the building to make taxable supplies (or opting to tax).

	Freehold	Leasehold
Tax relief on cost	• Capital asset. • Price paid is the cost for future capital disposals.	• Tax relief on: – rents paid, and – a portion of premium if lease is less than 50 years.
Rollover relief	• Qualifying asset if used for the trade.	• If lease has less than 60 years to run when purchased = depreciating asset: – gains not deducted from cost of replacement – gains are frozen and deferred for up to 10 years
SDLT	• Payable on cost by the purchaser.	• Payable on lease premium by the purchaser (note stamp duty on leases is not examinable).

Test your understanding 1

Ariel Ltd is an unquoted company which manufactures refrigerators. The company was set up five years ago, has been expanding rapidly ever since and is registered for VAT. It now requires a new factory building.

Two alternative options have been identified as follows:

(i) A suitable factory is available for rent. The owners of the factory are prepared to grant a 30 year lease for a premium of £600,000. The annual rent payable will be £42,600. The owners have opted to tax the factory and therefore the grant of the lease will be standard rated. Both figures are inclusive of VAT at 20% where applicable.

(ii) A new factory can be purchased from a building company. This will cost £600,000 excluding SDLT as follows:

	£
Land and legal fees	185,300
Central heating	20,000
Fire alarm	8,400
Factory and offices	296,938
VAT	89,362
	600,000

In order to finance the purchase of either the lease or the freehold building it is necessary for the company to raise funds.

The company will borrow £274,000 from the bank on a 10 year loan at a fixed rate of 8% and will sell its old factory for £350,000 which includes £50,000 for land. The old factory was bought new 5 years ago for £200,000 plus £40,000 for land.

Use an RPI factor of 0.220 for this disposal.

Advise Ariel Ltd of the tax implications of the two alternatives, and from the financing of whichever alternative is chosen.

Ignore stamp duty land tax.

2 Expenditure that reduces tax

Certain types of investment and other expenditure can result in a reduction of tax liabilities for a company. The detailed tax rules in respect of these types of expenditure are dealt with in earlier chapters. The main points are mentioned below.

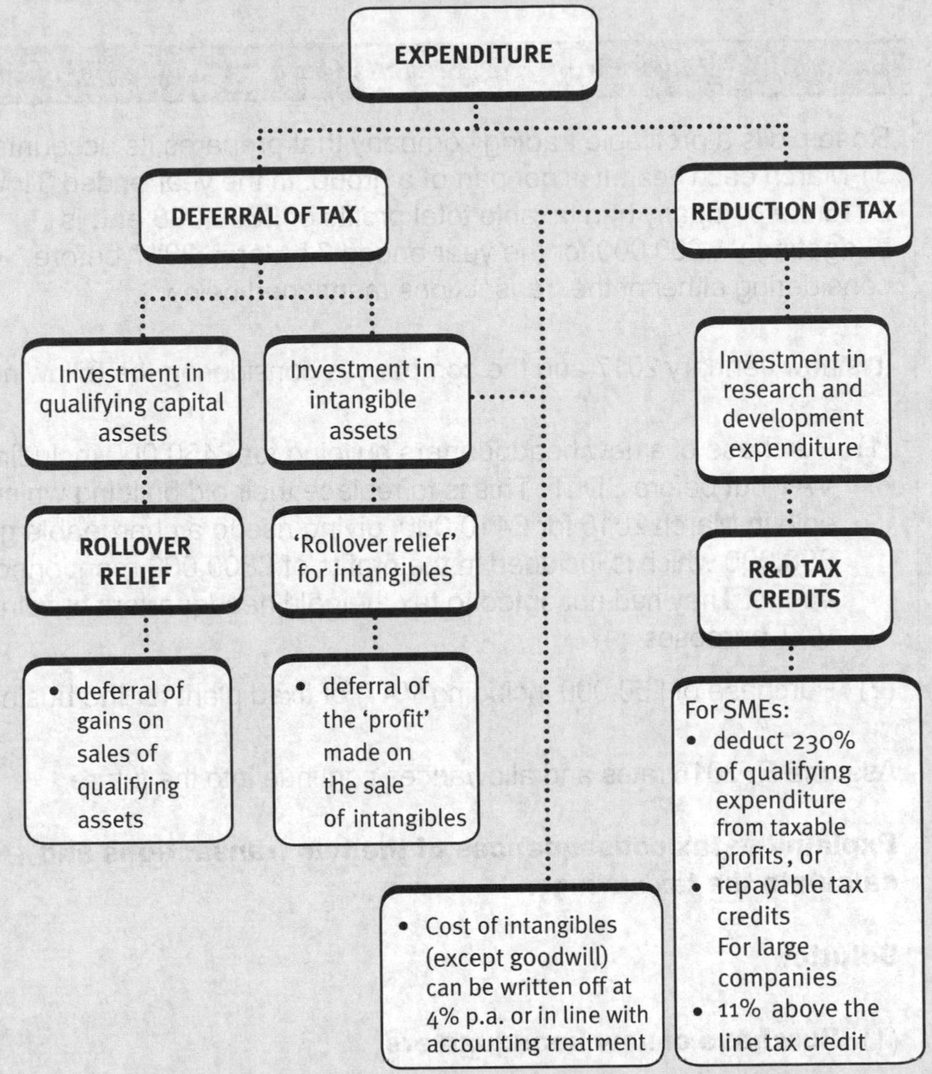

Note that capital allowances on plant and machinery can also reduce tax liabilities but are not considered further here.

Example 1 – Expenditure that reduces tax

Rose plc is a profitable trading company that prepares its accounts to 31 March each year. It is not part of a group. In the year ended 31 March 2016 the company had taxable total profits of £800,000 and is budgeting £1,200,000 for the year ended 31 March 2017 before considering either of the transactions mentioned below.

It is now January 2017 and the company is considering the following:

(1) Purchase of a new headquarters building for £450,000 including VAT but before SDLT. This is to replace their old building which they sold in March 2016 for £410,000, giving rise to a chargeable gain of £90,000 which is included in the profits of £800,000 mentioned above. They had not opted to tax their old headquarters building for VAT purposes.

(2) Purchase of £50,000 including VAT, of fixed plant for the business.

Assume FY2016 rates and allowances continue into the future.

Explain the tax consequences of the two transactions and calculate the tax savings.

Solution

(1) **Purchase of new headquarters**

The company made a gain of £90,000 in March 2016 which was included in their TTP of £800,000. As the company has made an investment in a new building there is a possible ROR claim.

Providing the company is using the building to make taxable supplies it should be able to recover the VAT charged of £75,000 (20/120 of £450,000).

SDLT will be £12,000 (W).

Hence the overall cost of the building is £387,000 (£450,000 – £75,000 + £12,000).

Working: SDLT

£		£
150,000	× 0%	0
100,000	× 2%	2,000
250,000		
200,000	× 5%	10,000
450,000		12,000

Chargeable gain now

	£
Proceeds of sale of old building	410,000
Less: Cost of new building	(387,000)
Proceeds not reinvested	23,000

	£
Gain on old building	90,000
Less: ROR (bal. fig.) (£90,000 – £23,000)	(67,000)
Gain remaining (= proceeds not spent)	23,000

Base cost of new building:	£
Original cost	387,000
Less: Gain rolled over	(67,000)
	320,000

This claim will reduce the total profits for the y/e 31 March 2017 by £67,000 which will save the company tax at 20%.

Therefore, Rose plc will have £13,400 (£67,000 × 20%) less to pay at the normal payment date for the y/e 31 March 2017 of 1 January 2018.

The ROR claim must be made within 4 years from 31 March 2017.

(2) **Purchase of fixed plant**

The purchase of fixed plant has two tax consequences:

- The cost net of recoverable VAT is £41,667 (100/120 × £50,000).
- The company may claim the AIA (subject to other acquisitions) on up to £200,000. Otherwise a WDA at 18% can be claimed. This will save the company tax at 20% for the y/e 31 March 2017.

  The tax saving is therefore:
  (£41,667 × 20%) = £8,333, if the AIA is available.

In addition, the company has made a purchase of fixed plant which is eligible for rollover deferral relief. In excess of £23,000 has been spent on the fixed plant, which allows the balance of the gain of £23,000 on the old headquarters building to be deferred until the earliest of three events:

- The plant ceases to be used in the trade.
- The plant is sold.
- 10 years after the plant is purchased.

This will save the company tax of £4,600 (20% × £23,000) in y/e 31 March 2017.

The ROR claim must be made within 4 years from 31 March 2017.

3 Investment in companies

This section looks at the different levels of investment that can be made in other companies and the tax effects.

Stake purchased in UK company	< 50%	> 50% but < 75%	≥ 75%
Related 51% group company	No	Yes	Yes
Can join VAT group	No	Yes	Yes
Group relief group	No	No	Yes
Consortium relief	Possible (1)	Possible (1)	No
Gains group	No	No	Possible (2)
Other issues (1) Losses b/f can be used	Yes	Possible loss of b/f losses if: major change in nature/conduct of trade, or revival of negligible activities	
(2) Stamp duty	½% on share purchases		

Notes: (1) It depends on ownership of remaining shares. For a consortium at least 75% of the shares in the consortium company must be owned by companies, each of whom has at least a 5% stake.

(2) It depends on the group structure. For a new subsidiary to participate in gains group reliefs it must be a 75% subsidiary of its direct parent company, and a 51% subsidiary of the ultimate parent company.

	Joining a 75% group	Leaving a 75% group
Related 51% group company	• Not related in CAP in which purchase takes place.	• Related for whole of CAP in which sale takes place.
Group relief	• Only possible from date of joining group. • No relief for pre acquisition losses.	• Ceases from date 'arrangements' come into force for company to leave group.
Capital losses	• Pre acquisition capital losses cannot be used to relieve gains in other group companies.	• No relief against group gains for capital losses realised after leaving group.
Degrouping charge	• Not applicable.	• Arises if company leaves gains group still owning asset which it received from another gains group member on a NGNL transfer within the last 6 years. • Degrouping gain added to parent company share proceeds. • SSE may be available.
VAT	• No VAT on share sales or purchases. • Can join a VAT group but is optional.	• No VAT on share sales or purchases. • Will leave VAT group unless parent company still owns > 50%.
Stamp duty levied	• Purchaser pays ½% on share purchases.	• No stamp duty for vendor.
Stamp taxes 'group transfers'	• Transfers of property between gains group members exempt from stamp taxes.	• Stamp taxes may be payable if leave group owning an asset transferred in by another group member with SD/SDLT exemption within last 3 years.

Example 2 – Investments in companies

You act as a tax advisor to Northanger Ltd, a UK company specialising in the manufacture and sale of kitchen appliances. Northanger Ltd has a 31 March year end and is registered for VAT making solely taxable supplies for VAT purposes.

The company has been very successful since its formation seven years ago and now has taxable total profits of £1 million each year. The board of directors are considering several opportunities for expansion. They have asked you to report on the taxation consequences of both of the possible projects they have under review.

The details of the two projects are as follows:

(1) **Buy a stake in Fridgco Ltd**

This is a small company which has developed a new food storage product. At present, Fridgco Ltd is wholly owned by Mrs Austin who is willing to sell Northanger Ltd a 60% stake in Fridgco Ltd for £350,000 although she is prepared to consider offers for a higher stake. Mrs Austin will continue to own the shares that she does not sell to Northanger Ltd.

Fridgco Ltd has made losses in the past although it is expected to be profitable in future. At 1 April 2017, the company had trading losses brought forward of £70,000, and a capital loss of £55,000 on the sale of its headquarters building on 1 June 2017.

Since that sale, the company has used rented office space in addition to its manufacturing plant. For the year to 31 March 2018, the company expects to make a trading loss of £48,000.

Mrs Austin is considering increasing the asking price of £350,000 to take account of the value of these losses.

Assume any share purchase will take place on 1 February 2018.

(2) **Set up a new branch to expand sales**

This branch could be located in the UK but as the directors are keen to expand exports, they feel it would be better to locate it overseas in the country of Bajoria, a country outside the EU which has no double tax treaty with the UK.

The branch operation is expected to be loss making initially and then produce profits of £200,000 per annum. Components would be shipped from the UK and sold through the branch. The Bajorian tax system operates in a similar way to the UK and levies tax on branch profits at 18%.

One of the directors has raised the possibility of operating in Bajoria through a company rather than a branch.

Write a report to the board of directors which covers the tax consequences of these two projects. Include any suggestions that you consider would improve the company's tax position.

Assume that FY 2016 rates and allowances continue into the future.

Solution

Report

To: The board of directors
From: An Advisor
Subject: Tax consequences of two new investments

Buy stake in Fridgco Ltd

(1) **Buy a 60% stake in Fridgco Ltd**

This will have the following tax consequences:

The company will be a related 51% group company from the start of the following accounting period (i.e. the year ended 31 March 2019).

The £1.5m corporation tax profits threshold will then be halved to £750,000. With profits of £1m, Northanger Ltd will have to start paying tax by instalments but not until year ended 31 March 2020.

Northanger Ltd and Fridgco Ltd can join a VAT group. This will be useful if there is to be much trading between the two companies, as supplies within the group are ignored for VAT.

Any dividends paid by Fridgco Ltd to Northanger Ltd will be classed as intra group income and ignored.

No group relief or capital gain advantages are available with a 60% stake. A consortium does not exist because this requires at least 75% of the shares to be owned by companies. Mrs Austin could incorporate a company to hold her shares and then a consortium would exist allowing Northanger Ltd to claim 60% of Fridgco Ltd's loss from 1 February 2018 onwards.

The purchase represents a change of ownership for Fridgco Ltd (more than half the shares have changed hands). If this is followed (or preceded) within 3 years by major changes to the nature and conduct of the trade, then the trading losses of £70,000 brought forward plus £40,000 losses accruing from 1 April 2017 to 1 February 2018 (10/12 of £48,000) will lapse and will not be available to carry forward against future profits.

Provided Northanger Ltd holds the shares in Fridgco Ltd for at least 12 months, any capital gain on the sale of the shares will be exempt under the substantial shareholding rules.

(2) **Increase purchase to at least 75%**

If Northanger Ltd buys at least 75% of Fridgco Ltd, then all of the above consequences will occur but it will also be possible to create a group relief and capital gains group. This would enable group relief to be claimed by Northanger Ltd for Fridgco Ltd's losses from 1 February 2018.

£8,000 (2/12 × £48,000) could be surrendered to use against Northanger Ltd's TTP for the year ended 31 March 2018.

It is not possible for Northanger Ltd to make use of Fridgco Ltd's trading losses brought forward as group relief, nor can they make use of the capital losses brought forward. These are designated as pre entry losses and can only be used by Fridgco Ltd against gains on assets it owned when it joined the group or purchased subsequently from third parties.

Although in gains groups it is possible to roll gains made by one company on land and buildings used for the trade over against qualifying assets purchased in another gains group company, this is not possible for Fridgco Ltd's gain as it was incurred before it joined the gains group.

Advice – the company should negotiate with Mrs Austin to buy at least 75% of Fridgco Ltd. Any increased price as a result of the available losses should only be considered if there will be no major changes to the trade within three years of the sale (and there hasn't been any major change in the three preceding years).

Set up new branch to expand sales

(1) **Set up overseas branch**

The profits of an overseas branch are taxed in the UK as part of trading profits. The initial losses will be relievable against UK profits of Northanger Ltd.

The extra £200,000 profits that are expected would be subject to tax at 20% in the UK although credit would be given for the 18% tax payable in Bajoria.

Alternatively, once the branch is profitable, Northanger Ltd could make an irrevocable election to exempt branch profits in the UK. This would avoid the extra 2% tax in the UK (20% – 18%), but would mean that if further branch losses were made in the future they could not be used in the UK.

Bajoria is outside the EU therefore no VAT is charged in that country. Any goods shipped from the UK to sell in Bajoria will be zero rated supplies in the UK.

(2) **Set up an overseas company instead of branch**

If a company is set up instead of a branch then there will be no relief for the initial losses. They will remain in Bajoria.

When profitable, any profits paid up to the parent company will be in the form of a dividend and will be exempt in Northanger Ltd's computation of taxable profits. As Northanger Ltd will own 100% of the shares, the dividend will not be included as FII for the purposes of determining if the company is liable to pay tax by quarterly instalment.

Although the tax rate in Bajoria is lower, this should not cause any problems under the CFC rules as tax payable in Bajoria is more than 75% of the UK equivalent tax.

A subsidiary in Bajoria will be a related 51% group company, which will further reduce the corporation tax payment threshold.

As the UK has no double tax treaty with Bajoria, any trading between UK companies of any size, and related companies in Bajoria may be subject to the transfer pricing rules. Northanger Ltd will have to ensure that any goods sold to the new subsidiary are sold at an arm's length price.

Advice – start the overseas operation as a branch to obtain relief for its expected losses. Once profitable it could be transferred to a company, or an election could be made to exempt branch profits in the UK.

4 Complex group planning

Approach to a complex group losses question

Where there are qualifying losses for group relief, they need to be allocated for the benefit of the **group** as a whole (i.e. to save as much tax as possible).

The approach (as a general rule) to complex group questions should be:

(i) Prepare a diagram of the group structure.

(ii) Determine the 75% group(s) and consortia.

(iii) Set up a tabular pro forma for TTP.
May need to calculate gains, consider ROR and reallocation of gains in a gains group to calculate TTP.
Do this before dealing with losses.

(iv) Complete the computations down to TTP, separating out any losses to loss workings.

(v) Determine the best use of any qualifying losses.

(vi) Where there are a number of losses in a question, deal with the losses with the most restricted set off first.

(vii) Compute CT liability on revised TTP.

(viii) Show CT payable and any losses or surpluses to be carried forward.

Factors to consider:

- Cash flow.
- Wastage of QCDs.
- Another factor that should be taken into account is whether a group company has **double taxation relief** available as the surrender of losses to such a company may waste the DTR credit available (as UK tax on the overseas income may be reduced).

Test your understanding 2

The MN Group has the following structure:

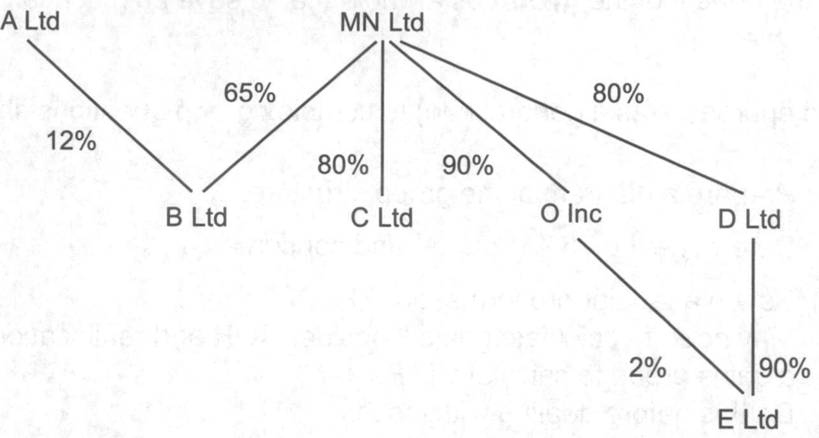

O Inc is resident in a non EEA country. All other companies are UK resident.

No company had any other source of income or gains.

The trading results for the y/e 31 March 2017 were as follows:

		£
A Ltd	Loss	60,000
B Ltd	Profit	58,000
MN Ltd	Profit	53,000
C Ltd	Loss	10,000
D Ltd	Profit	293,000
E Ltd	Loss	300,000
O Inc	Loss	12,000

Assuming the maximum possible relief is claimed for the above losses, compute the corporation tax payable by each of the above companies for the 12 months ended 31 March 2017.

5 Chapter summary

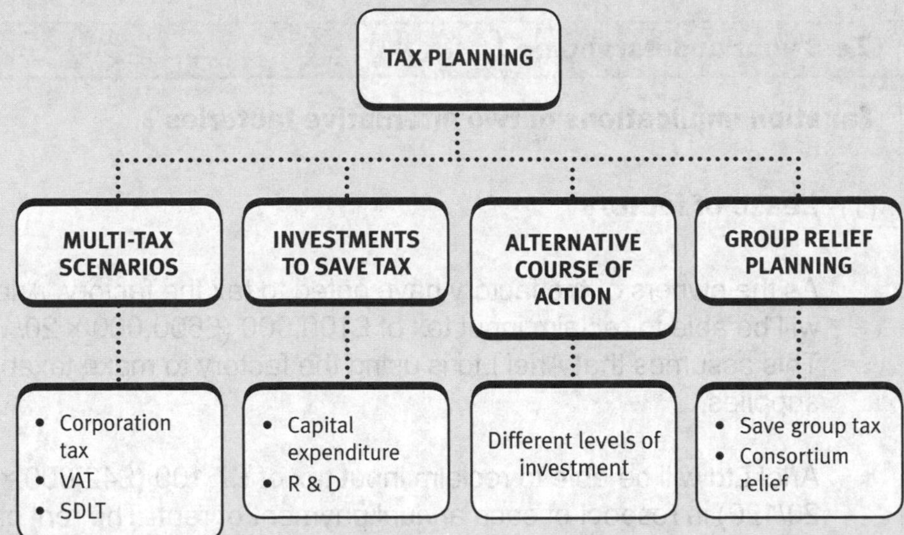

Test your understanding answers

Test your understanding 1

Taxation implications of two alternative factories

(1) **Lease of factory**

As the owners of the factory have opted to tax the factory, Ariel Ltd will be able to reclaim input tax of £100,000 (£600,000 × 20/120). This assumes that Ariel Ltd is using the factory to make taxable supplies.

Ariel Ltd will be able to reclaim input tax of £7,100 (£42,600 × 20/120) in respect of each annual payment of rent. The rent paid of £35,500 (£42,600 – £7,100) will be deductible for corporation tax purposes.

The proportion of the premium assessed on the owners as property income will be deductible for CT purposes spread over the period of the lease, as follows:

Property income assessment on the landlord = £600,000 × 100/120 × [(51 – 30)/50]	£210,000
Relief available to the payer of the premium: (£210,000 × 1/30)	£7,000 p.a.

The deduction of £7,000 will be restricted for the CAP in which it is paid according to the length of the period from the date of payment to the end of that CAP.

(2) **Purchase of new factory**

The VAT of £89,362 will be fully recoverable.

The central heating and fire alarm are eligible for plant and machinery capital allowances. Subject to other acquisitions, the AIA of £200,000 p.a. may be used against the acquisitions.

If the AIA is not available (e.g. already allocated to other purchases), a WDA at 8% for the central heating (an integral feature) and 18% for the fire alarm will be available.

However, if the AIA is available, it will be used against the central heating first, and is sufficient to cover the fire alarm cost as well, giving total allowances of £28,400.

There will be no immediate tax relief for the remaining cost of the factory.

(3) **Bank loan**

Loan interest is deducted from trading profits on the accruals basis as the loan is raised for a trading purpose.

The annual deduction will therefore be £21,920 (£274,000 at 8%).

(4) **Sale of old factory**

	£
Sale proceeds (including land)	350,000
Less: Cost	(240,000)
Unindexed gain	110,000
Less: Indexation (£240,000 × 0.220)	(52,800)
Chargeable gain	57,200

Replacement of business asset:

- **If the new factory is bought:**
  - The gain on sale of the old factory can be rolled over against the base cost of the new factory.
  - There is no restriction on the amount of the gain that can be rolled over, as the full proceeds of £350,000 will be reinvested.
  - This is provided that the new factory is purchased within the reinvestment period of 12 months before and up to three years after the disposal of the old factory.
- **If the factory is leased:**
  - The gain can only be held over for a maximum of 10 years from the date of purchase.
  - This is because the replacement asset will be a depreciating asset with a life of less than 60 years.
  - The gain will crystallise in 10 years time unless the asset is sold or ceases to be used in the business within the next 10 years.

Test your understanding 2

Corporation tax computations – Year ended 31 March 2017

	A Ltd	B Ltd	MN Ltd	C Ltd	D Ltd	E Ltd
	£	£	£	£	£	£
Trading profits	0	58,000	53,000	0	293,000	0
Consortium relief (W3)		(6,960)				
Group relief						
(1)					(293,000)	
(2)			(10,000)			
TTP	0	51,040	43,000	0	0	0
Corporation tax @ 20%	0	10,208	8,600	0	0	0

Generally claims should be made within 2 years of the end of the CAP of claim (i.e. by 31 March 2019).

Workings

(1) **Analysis of group structure**

75% Groups

Group 1	=	MN Ltd, C Ltd, D Ltd, O Inc (but O Inc resident overseas, therefore no loss relief)
Group 2	=	D Ltd, E Ltd
Consortium		
Members	=	A Ltd, MN Ltd
Consortium company	=	B Ltd

(2) **Loss working**

	A Ltd	C Ltd	E Ltd
	£	£	£
Loss	60,000	10,000	300,000
Group relief			
– to D Ltd			(293,000)
– to MN Ltd		(10,000)	
Consortium relief (W3)	(6,960)		
Loss to c/f	53,040	0	7,000

O Inc is an overseas company, therefore its loss cannot be surrendered.

E Ltd can only surrender its loss to D Ltd.

A Ltd can only surrender its loss to B Ltd as consortium relief. The surrender is restricted to A Ltd's share of B Ltd's TTP.

C Ltd's loss can be surrendered to MN Ltd or D Ltd.

D Ltd has no profits remaining after claiming losses from E Ltd.

Therefore, losses should be surrendered to MN Ltd.

(3) **Consortium relief to B Ltd**

Lower of:	£
(1) A Ltd's loss	60,000
(2) % of B's TTP (12% × £58,000)	6,960

chapter

30

Questions and Answers

1 Income tax: Computation

Danny

Question 1

Danny has the following income and outgoings in 2016/17.

	£
Salary and commission from his employer 'Flyhigh Ltd' (PAYE of £3,501 collected)	28,505
Benefits, assessable as employment income	2,100
Building society interest received	2,500
UK dividends received	2,300
Qualifying loan interest paid to buy shares in 'Flyhigh Ltd'	1,500

On 15 November 2016 Danny and his civil partner, Ben, jointly bought a property that has been let out as unfurnished accommodation. The assessable property income for 2016/17 is £4,300. No declaration has been made in respect of this source of income.

From 6 April 2017 Danny's salary will increase to £40,000.

Ben utilises his personal allowance and is a basic rate taxpayer.

Required:

(a) Calculate the income tax payable by Danny for 2016/17.

(5 marks)

(b) Explain how Danny's salary increase will affect the amount of income tax due on his savings income in 2017/18 and future years.

(3 marks)

Assume tax rates and allowances for 2016/17 apply in the future.

(Total 8 marks)

2 Employment income and related NIC

Mr Darcy

Question 1

Mr F Darcy, MD of the Pemberley Trading Co Ltd, is paid a salary of £37,000 p.a. and also bonuses based on the company's performance.

Mr Darcy pays 7% of his basic salary to a registered occupational pension scheme.

Pemberley's accounting year ends on 31 December each year and the bonuses are normally determined and paid on 31 May thereafter.

In recent years bonuses have been:

	£
Year to 31 December 2014	4,000
Year to 31 December 2015	8,000
Year to 31 December 2016	4,000

He uses a company car purchased in 2013 at its list price of £20,000, for 25,000 miles during 2016/17, of which 25% is for non-business use. Running expenses, including petrol paid by the company, were £4,600 in the year and the car has a carbon dioxide emission rating of 197 g/km.

Under the terms of the company's approved all employee share scheme Mr Darcy was allotted 1,000 ordinary £1 shares of the company, the market value of which is £3 per share, on 21 January 2017. He purchased 375 partnership shares during the year, £125 being deducted from his salary each month for 9 months, starting from 21 January 2017, to pay for the shares. The company allotted him a further 750 matching shares with a value of £2,250.

Mr Darcy is not married but lives with Sonia as if they are a married couple. Sonia earns £4,500 in 2016/17.

Required:

Compute Mr Darcy's income tax liability for 2016/17.

Briefly give reasons for your treatment of items included or excluded in arriving at Mr Darcy's taxable income.

Explain how the benefit of receiving the approved all employee share scheme shares will be taxed on Mr Darcy in 2016/17.

(8 marks)

Hubert

Question 2

Hubert, a bachelor, received the following income in 2016/17:

	£	
Salary	23,000	PAYE £4,500
Pension from former employer	5,000	PAYE £1,000
Profits from a partnership interest	9,194	
Treasury stock interest received	250	
Bank deposit account interest received	2,100	
Building society interest received	115	
UK dividends received	642	
Foreign property income (gross) (no overseas tax suffered)	1,200	

The following information is also available:

(1) In March 2006, Hubert was granted unapproved share options to buy 25,000 shares at £7. The shares were worth £7.50 at that time. In January 2017, Hubert exercised his options, bought 25,000 shares and sold them on the same day for £200,000.

(2) Hubert paid subscriptions of £360 to the Institute of Builders. He worked for an unquoted property development company.

(3) He also received the following benefits of employment:

- A company car was provided for the whole year. The car has a list price of £20,000 and CO_2 emissions of 155 g/km.
- Petrol for private use of the company car was paid for by the employer.
- The employer reimbursed expenses of £1,960. Hubert had incurred the expenses on accommodation while on business trips abroad.
- Hubert uses his employer's tools occasionally during the course of his work. During 2016/17 he used one of his employer's cement mixers throughout the whole year whilst building his property overseas. The cement mixer cost the company £1,200 two years ago.

Required:

Calculate the tax payable by Hubert for 2016/17.

(15 marks)

Benny Korere

Question 3

Assume today's date is 1 June 2017.

Benny Korere has been employed as the sales director of Golden Tan plc since 2002. He earns an annual salary of £32,000 and is provided with a petrol-driven company car, which has a CO_2 emission rate of 147 g/km and had a list price when new of £22,360. In August 2014, when he was first provided with the car, Benny paid the company £6,100 towards the capital cost of the car.

Golden Tan plc does not pay for any of Benny's private petrol and he is also required to pay his employer £18 per month as a condition of being able to use the car for private purposes.

On 1 December 2016, Golden Tan plc notified Benny that he would be made redundant on 28 February 2017. On that day, the company paid him his final month's salary together with a payment of £8,000 in lieu of the three remaining months of his six-month notice period in accordance with his employment contract. In addition, the company paid him £17,500 in return for agreeing not to work for any of its competitors for the six-month period ending 31 August 2017.

On receiving notification of his redundancy, Benny immediately contacted Joe Egmont, the managing director of Summer Glow plc, who offered him a senior management position leading the company's expansion into Eastern Europe. Summer Glow plc is one of Golden Tan plc's competitors and one of the most innovative companies in the industry, although not all of its strategies have been successful.

Benny has agreed to join Summer Glow plc on 1 September 2017 for an annual salary of £39,000. On the day he joins the company, Summer Glow plc will grant him an option to purchase 10,000 ordinary shares in the company for £2.20 per share under an unapproved share option scheme. Benny can exercise the option once he has been employed for six months but must hold the shares for at least a year before he sells them.

The new job will require Benny to spend a considerable amount of time in London. Summer Glow plc has offered Benny the exclusive use of a flat that the company purchased on 1 June 2014 for £165,000; the flat is currently rented out. The flat will be made available from 1 September 2017. The company will pay all of the utility bills relating to the flat as well as furnishing and maintaining it. Summer Glow plc has also suggested that if Benny would rather live in a more central part of the city, the company could sell the existing flat and buy a more centrally located one, of the same value, with the proceeds.

Required:

(a) Calculate Benny's employment income for 2016/17.

(4 marks)

(b) (i) Advise Benny of the income tax implications of the grant and exercise of the share options in Summer Glow plc on the assumption that the share price on 1 September 2017 and on the day he exercises the options is £3.35 per share.

Explain why the share option scheme is not free from risk by reference to the rules of the scheme and the circumstances surrounding the company.

(4 marks)

(ii) List the additional information required in order to calculate the employment income benefit in respect of the provision of the furnished flat for 2017/18.

Advise Benny of the potential income tax implications of requesting a more centrally located flat in accordance with the company's offer.

(4 marks)

You should assume that the rates and allowances for the tax year 2016/17 apply throughout this question.

(Total: 12 marks)

3 Property and investment income

Muriel Grand

Question 1

On 31 December 2016 Muriel Grand made a gift of a house in London to her brother Bertie.

Bertie is to rent out the house in London, either unfurnished or as furnished holiday accommodation. In either case, the roof of the house must be repaired at a cost of £24,000 before it will be possible to let the house. The roof was badly damaged by a gale on 5 December 2016.

If the house is let unfurnished, then Bertie will have to decorate it at a cost of £3,600. The forecast rental income is £28,000 p.a.

If the house is let as furnished holiday accommodation, then the house will be converted into two separate units at a cost of £41,000. The total cost of furnishing the two units will be £9,000.

This expenditure will be financed by a £50,000 bank loan at an interest rate of 8% p.a. The total forecast rental income is £45,000 p.a., although 22.5% of this will be deducted by the letting agency. Other running costs, such as cleaning, will amount to £3,500 p.a. in total.

Bertie is a higher rate taxpayer and plans to sell the house when he retires at age 60, and anticipates making a substantial capital gain.

Required:

Advise Bertie of the tax implications of letting out the house in London either

(i) unfurnished, or

(ii) as furnished holiday accommodation.

Your answer should include details of the tax advantages of letting the house as furnished holiday accommodation.

(10 marks)

Anthony & Cleopatra

Question 2

Anthony has the following income and outgoings in 2016/17.

	£
Salary from 'Roma publications' (PAYE £19,700)	50,000
Rental income from an apartment in Bath	11,979
Building society interest received	52,650
UK dividends received (Note 6)	75,433
Qualifying loan interest paid to buy equipment for Roma publications	(550)

The following information is also available for the y/e 5 April 2017:

(1) Anthony is the sales manager of Roma publications and is entitled to an annual bonus based on the company's results for each year ending 31 December. The bonuses are determined at the April board meetings following the end of the year and are paid on 30 April each year.

Bonuses were as follows:

y/e 31 December 2015	£2,000
y/e 31 December 2016	£2,100

(2) One of Anthony's clients, Julius, gave him a cash tip of £1,000 after Anthony arranged for his assignment to be dealt with as a priority.

(3) Anthony had the use of a company computer. The state of the art laptop and accessories cost the company £3,000 on 31 May 2016. Anthony uses the laptop at home and lets his children use the computer as much as possible to help with their studies.

(4) Anthony had the use of a company car, which was imported to the UK from Rome at a cost of £25,000. The list price of this car is £30,000 and CO_2 emissions are 108 g/km. The car has a diesel powered engine and all fuel was paid for by the company on a company credit card. Anthony makes no payment for any private use of the vehicle.

(5) Roma publications own a villa in Italy which cost the company £65,000. The villa has an annual value of £2,250. The family are allowed to use the villa at any time during the year. Anthony pays the company £120 per month for this privilege.

(6) On 6 April 2016 Anthony has invested £20,000 in an unquoted trading company, in the UK, that qualifies for relief under the enterprise investment scheme. Of the £75,433 dividends received by Anthony, £2,700 relates to the EIS shares.

Cleopatra has the following income and outgoings in 2016/17.

	£
Salary from her part-time employment with 'The Spa'	12,500
Allowable subscriptions to the 'Institute of Beauty'	(400)
Interest from an ISA account	500

Cleopatra has inherited some cash from her father and decided to invest £20,000 in a Venture Capital Trust company. She received dividends of £1,000 from the VCT company during 2016/17.

Required:

(a) Calculate Anthony and Cleopatra's income tax payable (or repayable) for 2016/17.

(b) Advise Anthony and Cleopatra of any tax planning they may wish to use to reduce future tax liabilities assuming their income remains the same in the future.

(20 marks)

4 Pensions

Enid, Tom and Norman

Question 1

(a) Enid is the sole shareholder and director of Enid Limited, a trading company which prepares accounts to 31 March each year.

Enid has had a successful year to date the company's tax adjusted trading profits for the year ended 31 March 2017 have been forecast at £85,000 after paying a gross salary to Enid of £25,000. Apart from this salary, Enid currently has no other income.

Assume that today's date is 2 April 2017 and Enid has not yet made any pension contributions in 2016/17.

She is contemplating making a lump sum payment into her personal pension scheme and is also arranging for the company, Enid Limited, to make a lump sum premium of £14,000 into the same scheme for her benefit.

Required:

Write brief notes advising Enid of the taxation implications of the proposed lump sum pension scheme contributions in 2016/17.

(5 marks)

(b) Tom is a self-employed computer consultant and has just inherited £150,000.

He has decided to invest some of his inheritance into his personal pension scheme and to use the balance to pay off his mortgage. Tom has never made any contributions to a pension scheme before.

Assume today's date is 14 January 2017 and Tom's trading profits for 2016/17 are £40,000.

Required:

Calculate the maximum gross amount that Tom can contribute into his personal pension plan on which tax relief can be obtained in 2016/17.

Explain how Tom will obtain tax relief for any contributions paid.

(4 marks)

(c) Norman has inherited £125,000 and decided to invest some of the proceeds to provide for an additional entitlement to a pension.

From 6 April 2016 Norman has been employed at an annual salary of £20,000. He was also provided with a petrol engine car with CO_2 emissions of 139 g/km and a list price of £30,000. He drives a total of 12,000 miles. Norman's employer pays for all of the fuel for the car and Norman contributes £50 per month towards the car (£10 of which is towards the fuel).

Norman pays 6% of his salary into his employer's registered company pension scheme. The company contributes a further 5%.

Required:

Advise Norman as to the additional contribution he should make into the registered company pension scheme in 2016/17.

(5 marks)

(Total: 14 marks)

Clive Scott

Question 2

Assume today's date is 1 January 2017.

Clive Scott has approached you for some advice concerning pensions. He is single and has no children and informs you that he owns all of the shares in Scott Engineering Limited, a company which has been trading since April 2002.

The company prepares its accounts to 31 March each year.

Whilst the profits in the earlier years of the business have been reinvested back into the firm, Scott Engineering Limited is now more established and over the last few years Clive has been withdrawing more funds from the business.

He is now keen to put money aside for his retirement in ten to twelve years time and wants to know more about the options open to him.

Clive's expected income from the company for 2016/17 is a salary of £15,000 and dividends of £51,500. Clive has no income other than from Scott Engineering Limited.

Required:

(a) Assuming Clive wishes to set up a personal pension scheme in 2016/17 advise him of:

(i) The maximum pension contributions that he can make in 2016/17 and by when these should be paid to obtain relief.

(3 marks)

(ii) The way in which tax relief will be given if he pays the pension contributions personally.

Your answer to this part should include a calculation of the effect of making such contributions on his 2016/17 income tax liability.

(3 marks)

(iii) The tax implications of Scott Engineering Limited making contributions into his personal pension scheme and the factors to be considered in deciding whether he or the company should pay these contributions.

Detailed calculations are not required for this question part.

(6 marks)

(b) Briefly advise Clive of any alternative HMRC registered pension arrangements that could be made.

You are not required to comment on the benefits that may ultimately be received under such arrangements.

(3 marks)

(Total: 15 marks)

5 Income tax planning

Ethel Jones

Question 1

Assume today's date is 30 June 2017.

Ethel Jones is married to George, who is independently wealthy in his own right. They have one child, Simone.

Ethel owns the following assets:

(1) 10,000 ordinary £1 shares in Bluebird plc, a quoted UK resident trading company with an issued share capital of 1 million ordinary shares. The company prepares its accounts to 31 March each year.

Ethel was a director of this company for many years until she had to retire for health reasons on 31 May 2016. During 2016/17 she earned £14,500 in director's fees from Bluebird plc.

The company has paid the following dividends in recent years:

Year ended	Dividend	Payment date
31 March 2016	27.8 pence per share	30 April 2016
31 March 2017	30 pence per share	30 April 2017

(2) A 25% beneficial interest in £100,000 10% loan stock in Chaffinch plc, which is quoted on the UK stock exchange. This loan stock is held jointly with George who has always owned the remaining 75% beneficial interest in it.

The couple has not made a declaration of beneficial interest to HMRC in respect of this asset. This loan stock is a qualifying corporate bond.

(3) Cash deposits amount to £145,000, which generated gross interest receipts in 2016/17 of £5,250.

Required:

(a) Calculate Ethel's 2016/17 income tax liability.

(5 marks)

(b) Advise Ethel and George whether it would be beneficial to make a declaration of beneficial interest to HMRC in respect of the loan stock held in Chaffinch plc.

Detailed calculations are not required for this part of the question.

(3 marks)

(Total: 8 marks)

6 CGT: Computations and stamp duty land tax

Julie

Question 1

Julie made the following disposals in 2016/17:

(1) On 29 June 2016 she sold a concert grand piano for £12,500. She bought the piano in September 2003 for £8,750. She uses the piano to play at home purely for pleasure.

(2) On 23 September 2016 she sold her car, a Renault Espace for £8,700. She bought the car for £18,000 in March 2010.

(3) On 25 December 2016 she sold a commercial property, held as a investment for £485,000. She bought the property for £156,000 in August 2009. Legal costs, estate agent fees and stamp duty land tax totalled £2,700 at the time of purchase and £4,075 on the sale of the property.

(4) On 4 January 2017 she sold a business asset for £37,000. She purchased the asset for £4,000 in October 2013. The asset had been used for the purposes of her self-employed business for the whole period of ownership. The disposal was not part of a disposal of the whole of the business.

Julie has capital losses brought forward at 6 April 2016 of £3,250.

She has taxable income for 2016/17 of £80,000.

Required:
Calculate Julie's after tax sales proceeds realised from the above disposals.

(10 marks)

7 CGT: Variations to computations

Dangle

Question 1

Dangle had the following capital transactions during 2016/17.

(1) He gave away a greyhound on 1 May 2016, which he had bought assuming that it had a good pedigree for £8,000 in 2005. It had come last in every race it had been entered in and had no value when he gave it away.

(2) Dangle had some unquoted shares which he sold for £6,000 on 2 August 2016. These had been left to him in his uncle's will in July 1991 when the probate value was £7,500.

(3) Dangle purchased a lease with 39 years to run on 12 February 2009 for £200,000. Dangle used the property wholly for the purposes of his trade until 19 October 2016 when he sold the lease for £275,000. This was not part of the disposal of the whole of the business.

(4) He purchased a painting for £9,000 on 14 May 2000 which was destroyed in a flood on 25 December 2016. He received insurance proceeds of £50,000 and decided not to buy more paintings.

(5) After the shock of losing the painting, Dangle gifted his only other antique, a ring worth £1,000 to his mother on Boxing Day, 26 December 2016. He had acquired this from a flea market in the summer (July) of 2011 for £5.

(6) Dangle bought a 24 acre plot of land for £130,000 in March 2008 for investment purposes. In June 2014, Dangle sold four acres of the land for £30,000. The remaining 20 acres were worth £150,000. On 28 March 2017 Dangle sold the remaining 20 acres for £205,000.

Dangle's only income is employment income of £35,000. He has no plans to sell any other assets in the near future.

Dangle paid £4,000 into his personal pension scheme in 2016/17.

Required:

(a) Calculate the capital gains tax payable by Dangle for 2016/17 and state the due date of payment.

(15 marks)

(b) Explain, with supporting calculations, why it would have been preferable for CGT purposes if Dangle had delayed the sale of the plot of land until 6 April 2017 (assuming the sale proceeds remained the same).

(5 marks)

You should assume that the rates and allowances for 2016/17 continue to apply in future years.

(Total: 20 marks)

Relevant lease percentages are:

39 years	94.842
32 years	89.354
31 years	88.371

8 Shares and securities for individuals and stamp duty

Emma

Question 1

Emma made the following disposals during the year ended 5 April 2017:

(1) On 9 February 2017 she sold 1,050 shares in Apple plc for net proceeds of £95,000.

The history of this shareholding is as follows:

March 2013	purchased 400 shares for £10,000
January 2014	took up 1 for 4 rights issue at £30 per share
December 2015	purchased a further 200 shares for £8,000
January 2016	Bonus issue of 1 for every 2 shares

Emma does not work for the company and her shares are a very small percentage of the shares in issue.

(2) On 19 March 2017 she gifted to her sister three out of her shareholding of ten shares in Willow Ltd, her unquoted personal trading company. The value of the three shares gifted was £50,000.

Emma acquired the shares at a cost of £100 per share when she set up the company in February 1993. Emma had never worked for the company. Gift relief will not be claimed.

(3) On 15 September 2016, she sold National Savings Certificates worth £600. Emma acquired the certificates from her grandfather's estate following his death in August 2012. The shares were valued at £500 at that time.

(4) Emma had acquired 100 ordinary shares in Bridge plc for £9,200 in June 2004. She had never worked for Bridge plc. In January 2017, Bridge plc was subject to a takeover.

In return for each share Emma received the following: £350 cash, and a loan note in Poker plc worth £50.

Emma has taxable income of £160,000 for 2016/17.

Required:

Calculate Emma's capital gains tax payable for 2016/17.

(15 marks)

9 CGT: Reliefs for individuals

Mr Harry and Mr Leonard

Question 1

(a) Mr Harry owns 60 per cent of the ordinary share capital of X Ltd, an unquoted trading company.

He acquired his holding on 1 January 2001 for £70,000 and since that date he has been a full-time working director of the company.

The following information has been extracted from the accounts of X Ltd at 30 November 2016.

	£
Buildings	480,000
Investments in other companies (not in the same industry)	80,000
Plant and machinery	16,000
Net current assets	32,333

The plant and machinery consists entirely of movable plant with no single item costing, or having a current value of, more than £6,000.

Assume today's date is 1 December 2016.

On 1 January 2017 Mr Harry intends to retire from the company, and plans to gift his entire share holding to his daughter. The market value of the shareholding is estimated to be worth £365,000.

In November 2016 Mr Harry sold his house for net proceeds of £503,000. The house cost £38,000 in September 1994. He intends to use the proceeds received from the sale of his house to build a new flat in Spain.

Mr Harry lived in the house throughout his ownership except for a period of one year, six years ago. He moved out and let the property while he lived and worked as the manager of the local pub. He returned to his house one year later.

Both Harry and his daughter are higher rate taxpayers.

Required:

Compute the expected capital gains tax payable for 2016/17 assuming Mr Harry gifts the shares to his daughter and assuming all available reliefs are claimed, which are beneficial.

(6 marks)

(b) The building owned by X Ltd was originally purchased by Mr Leonard for use in his unincorporated business. He sold it to the company on 1 April 2016 after ceasing to trade. Mr Leonard has already paid the capital gains tax liability for 2015/16 arising on the disposal.

Mr Leonard is now considering buying some commercial property with a view to setting up a new business. He would like to know if there are any CGT advantages in purchasing new property and setting up a new business.

Required:

Prepare notes for a meeting with Mr Leonard covering the CGT advantages of his proposal and any conditions he should consider.

(10 marks)

(Total: 16 marks)

Bangle

Question 2

Barbara Bangle is a higher rate taxpayer. She has carried on her retail jewellery business as a sole trader since April 1988. On 1 July 2016 she transferred the business as a going concern to Bangle Ltd, an unquoted company she formed for that purpose. Bangle Ltd allotted 200,000 £1 ordinary shares, valued at par, in settlement of the consideration for the transfer.

The net assets transferred to the company were as follows:

	Cost/MV	Acquisition date	Market value 1 July 2016
	£		£
Freehold trade premises	65,000	(1.4.1988)	165,000
Shop fittings	6,000	(1.4.1988)	5,000
Shop front and canopy	13,165	(1.7.1989)	8,000
Inventory			109,000
Bank/cash			3,000
			290,000
Less: Current liabilities			(90,000)
Net assets transferred			200,000

Required:

(a) (i) Compute the chargeable gain arising after incorporation relief as a result of the transfer, and the base cost of the shares received by Barbara.

(5 marks)

(ii) Compute the capital gains tax payable in 2016/17 if, in March 2017, Barbara sold 80,000 of her new shares for net proceeds of £90,000.

(3 marks)

(iii) Calculate the increase in tax in 2016/17 if Barbara disapplied incorporation relief on the transfer of her business. and sold her shares as above.

(4 marks)

(b) Calculate the chargeable gains arising

- Had the consideration for the transfer been settled by
  - the allocation of 150,000 £1 ordinary shares at par, and
  - the balance being left on loan account, and
- Barbara had, in March 2017, sold 80,000 shares to her sister for £81,000 when their true value was, as before, £90,000.

Assume that incorporation relief is not disapplied, and that a joint claim for gift relief is made.

(5 marks)

(c) Assuming that Barbara intends to keep her shares in Bangle Ltd for several years, briefly explain any alternative tax efficient method of transferring the chargeable assets of her business to Bangle Ltd.

You are not to consider the possibility of Bangle Ltd registering as an enterprise investment scheme company.

(4 marks)

(Total: 21 marks)

10 Overseas aspects of income tax and capital gains tax

Mr and Mrs Posh

Question 1

Mr and Mrs Posh are domiciled in Switzerland but have been resident in the UK for the last 9 years. Their income for 2016/17 is as follows:

	Mr Posh	Mrs Posh
	£	£
Overseas rental income	39,500	423,000
Remitted to the UK	15,640	108,900

Required:
Advise Mr and Mrs Posh as to whether they should elect for the remittance basis to apply in 2016/17 and justify your reasons.

(10 marks)

Darwin

Question 2

Darwin, a UK domiciled and UK resident individual, received the following income in 2016/17.

	£
Salary from Darwin's personal company (PAYE deducted £8,702)	34,700
Bank interest received from UK bank	3,550
Erewhon bank interest (45% Erewhon tax paid) (gross amount)	1,265
Narnia rental income (15% Narnian tax paid) (gross amount)	690

Other relevant information for 2016/17 is as follows:

(1) Darwin's company provided him with a company car and diesel fuel for private use. The car has a list price of £32,000 and CO_2 emissions of 183 g/km.

(2) Darwin received goods from his company when a new shipment came in. If sold to a customer they would be valued at £500 but the cost of the goods was £300.

(3) Darwin paid £9,840 into a personal pension scheme on 13 May 2016.

Required:

Calculate Darwin's income tax payable for 2016/17.

(13 marks)

Peter Singer

Question 3

Peter Singer was born and lived in Portugal all of his life. He moved to the UK to work full time at his company's headquarters in Manchester on 6 January 2017 and started work on 13 January 2017.

His contract is for three years and during that time he plans to stay in the UK and will only return to Portugal for the occasional short break. He plans to return to his company's Lisbon office in Portugal at the end of the contract in the UK.

Peter will be paid £44,000 salary p.a. by the UK company. He will also receive rental income of £28,000 p.a. (UK equivalent) on one of his two Portuguese homes while he is in the UK. This rent will be retained in his Portuguese bank account.

Peter's employment package includes the following:

(1) Company car – costing £28,000 with CO_2 emissions of 168 g/km. All petrol will be provided by the company.

(2) Private medical insurance – costing £1,874.

(3) The company has bought a flat for his use, costing £187,000. The rateable value of the property is £4,500. The company will meet all the expenses of running the flat which are estimated to be in the region of £5,700 per annum. The company have furnished the flat at a cost of £49,000. Peter will pay rent of £1,300 per month to the company for the use of the flat.

(4) The company has arranged for Peter's daughter to attend a local private school starting on 5 September 2017. The cost will be £1,500 per month.

(5) Peter is provided with a mobile phone, and it is estimated that he spends about £135 per month on calls.

(6) Employees of the company are allowed to use a corporate membership at the local health club costing £220 per month.

Peter also has a number of investments in the UK and overseas which have yielded income as follows:

		Remitted to the UK
	£	£
UK dividends	4,000	
Portuguese dividends	3,150	2,500
Portuguese bank interest	2,900	1,300
UK bank interest	1,100	

The figures for the Portuguese income are shown before the deduction of withholding tax at 10%.

Required:

(a) Discuss the factors HMRC will use to decide whether Peter is resident and domiciled in the UK in 2016/17 and 2017/18 and explain the impact of this on his income tax computation.

(9 marks)

(b) Calculate Peter's income tax liability for 2017/18, on the basis of the information given above, assuming that the 2016/17 tax rates and allowances continue to apply.

(16 marks)
(Total: 25 marks)

Roberta

Question 4

Roberta has always lived in the UK until December 2016 when she left the UK to take up a full time contract working abroad. She started work on 2 January 2017 and plans to return to the UK in June 2020 as her contract is due to end on 31 May 2020.

She intends to travel elsewhere in the world on her holidays from work and does not plan to return to the UK until the end of her contract. Once she returns to the UK however she does not plan to leave again other than for short holiday breaks and will permanently settle in the UK.

Whilst she is working abroad she plans to sell the following two assets:

In May 2017 she sold an asset for £195,000 that she bought in June 2010 for £76,000.

In July 2017 she plans to sell another asset for £26,500. She bought the asset in February 2010 for £54,000.

Required:

(a) Explain Roberta's tax status in tax years 2016/17 to 2020/21.

(8 marks)

(b) Explain how Roberta will be assessed on her chargeable gains arising in 2017/18.

(5 marks)
(Total: 13 marks)

11 An introduction to inheritance tax

There are no questions for this chapter.

12 IHT – special valuation rules, reliefs, and the death estate

Gary Genius

Question 1

Gary Genius is a wealthy individual aged 57, married to Jane, aged 54. The couple have two children, Jack, aged 34 and Jill, aged 37, who both have children of their own.

Gary currently owns 60% of the issued share capital of GG Limited, a UK resident trading company, which he set up in 1988. The remaining shares are held, 20% by his daughter Jill and 20% by unconnected third parties.

Gary has made the following gifts during his lifetime. Gary agreed that he would pay any inheritance tax arising on these gifts.

4 June 2008	£376,000 cash gift to a discretionary trust.	
4 March 2012	£10,000 cash as a wedding gift to his son Jack.	
4 March 2012	20% of the shares in GG Limited to his daughter Jill. At this time the GG Limited shares were valued as follows:	
		£
	20%	100,000
	60%	450,000
	80%	600,000
	100%	800,000
4 June 2014	A further £100,000 cash gift to the discretionary trust created on 4 June 2007.	

Required:

Explain the IHT implications arising from the lifetime gifts made between 4 June 2008 and 4 June 2014.

Your answer should include a calculation of any IHT payable and an explanation of any exemptions or reliefs available.

You are not required to explain the implications for the trustees of the discretionary trust.

(12 marks)

13 IHT overseas, administration and tax planning

Mary Day

Question 1

Mary Day is a wealthy widow who has asked for your advice in respect of a number of gifts that she is planning to make in the near future.

Her only previous gift was a gross chargeable transfer of £335,000 into a discretionary trust two years ago.

The proposed gifts are as follows:

(a) A gift of a holiday cottage worth £100,000 to her nephew Paul.

As a condition of the gift, Mary would have the free use of the cottage for six months each year.

(b) A gift of an antique clock worth £10,000 to her granddaughter Jane in respect of her forthcoming wedding.

(c) A gift of 20,000 £1 ordinary shares in DEF Ltd into a discretionary trust for the benefit of her nieces and nephews.

Mary currently holds 30,000 shares in the company. She acquired the shares one year ago.

DEF Ltd is an unquoted trading company with a share capital of 200,000 £1 ordinary shares.

A 5% holding is worth £10 per share, whilst 10% and 15% holdings are worth £13 and £16 per share respectively.

(d) A gift of agricultural land and buildings with an agricultural value of £160,000 to her son David.

The land was bought ten years ago, and has always been let out to tenants.

The most recent tenancy agreement commenced in 2011, and comes to an end in six months' time. Mary has obtained planning permission to build ten houses on the land.

The value of the land with planning permission is £280,000.

David owns the neighbouring land, and the value of this will increase from £200,000 to £250,000 as a result of the gift.

Mary will pay the inheritance tax arising from the gift into the discretionary trust. Any inheritance tax arising on the other gifts will be paid for by the respective donee.

Required:

Advise Mary of the inheritance tax implications arising from the above gifts, ignoring annual exemptions.

(12 marks)

Jenny Cambeth

Question 2

(a) Jenny Cambeth died on 20 November 2016. At the date of her death Jenny owned the following assets:

(1) A main residence valued at £235,000. This has an outstanding repayment mortgage of £40,000.

(2) Building society deposits of £87,000.

(3) 10,000 £1 ordinary shares in Banquo plc. On 20 November 2016 the shares were quoted at 945p – 957p, with bargains on that day of 937p, 961p and 939p.

Jenny inherited the shares as a specific gift on the death of her sister on 10 August 2014 when they were valued at £68,000. The sister's executors paid IHT of £54,000 on an estate valued at £360,000.

(4) A life assurance policy on her own life. Immediately prior to the date of Jenny's death, the policy had an open market value of £86,000. Proceeds of £104,000 were received following her death.

(5) Agricultural land valued at £168,000, but with an agricultural value of £110,000. The land was purchased during 1997, and it has always been let to tenant farmers. The most recent tenancy commenced on 1 January 2011.

Jenny made the following gifts during her lifetime (any IHT arising was paid by Jenny):

(1) On 28 November 2007 she made a cash gift of £90,000 into a discretionary trust.

(2) On 15 April 2011 she made a gift of 50,000 shares in Shakespeare Ltd, an unquoted trading company, to her son as a wedding gift. The shares were valued at £155,000, and were originally acquired by Jenny in 1997.

Her son still owned the shares on 20 November 2016. Shakespeare Ltd has 20% of the value of its total assets invested in quoted shares.

(3) On 10 March 2012 she made a cash gift of £283,000 into a discretionary trust.

Jenny's husband Duncan is wealthy in his own right. Under the terms of her will Jenny has therefore left a specific gift of £100,000 to her brother, with the residue of the estate being left to her children.

Required:

(i) Calculate the IHT that will be payable as a result of Jenny's death.

(15 marks)

(ii) State who is primarily liable for the tax, the due dates of the IHT liabilities, the amount of IHT that can be paid under the instalment option, and the amount of inheritance that will be received by Jenny's children.

(4 marks)

(b) Jenny's husband Duncan is in good health, and expects to live for at least ten more years.

The Cambeth family appreciate that Jane's estate may not have been distributed in a tax efficient manner. They have therefore agreed that the terms of her will are to be varied so that the entire estate is left to Duncan.

Duncan will then make gifts totalling £500,000 to the children and Jenny's brother during 2017 and 2018.

Required:

(i) State the conditions that must be met in order that the variation of the terms of Jenny's will is valid for IHT purposes.

(2 marks)

(ii) Advise the Cambeth family of the IHT implications of the proposed plan.

You are not expected to calculate the revised IHT liability or to consider anti-avoidance legislation.

(4 marks)

(Total: 25 marks)

Paul

Question 3

Paul, due to ill health, is expected to die in the near future. You should assume that today's date is 31 December 2016.

The current value of his estate, and forecast value for 12 months time, is:

	Present value	Forecast value
	£	£
20,000 shares (1% holding) in BCD plc	50,000	45,000
8,000 shares (2% holding) in GHI plc	70,000	85,000
30,000 shares (10% holding) in NOP Ltd	65,000	60,000
Main residence	330,000	350,000
Holiday cottage	130,000	110,000
	645,000	650,000

All of these assets have been owned for at least two years. The above companies are all trading companies.

Under the terms of his will, Paul has left all of his assets to his son. His son has two children.

Paul's wife is also ill, and is not expected to live for more than three months. She does not have any assets of her own, but Paul is confident that his son will look after her upon his death.

Paul has made the following transfers of value during his lifetime:

(i) On 1 November 2007, he made a gift of £203,000 into a discretionary trust. The trust paid any IHT arising on the gift.

(ii) On 1 October 2012, he gave his son £150,000 as a wedding gift.

(iii) On 1 November 2012, he gave his son a business valued at £250,000. Paul had run the business for 10 years, and his son has continued to run it since.

Required:

(a) Calculate the IHT liabilities that would arise if Paul were to die on 31 December 2016. Your answer should show the relevant due dates of payment.

(8 marks)

(b) Explain why it might be beneficial to change the terms of Paul's will.

If the changes were not made by Paul, explain whether it would be possible for his son to subsequently make the changes after the date of Paul's death.

(4 marks)

(c) Paul's son is considering selling the business that was given to him by Paul for its current value of £175,000.

Explain the IHT implications if the sale was before Paul's death.

(2 marks)

(d) Explain:

(i) The main advantages in lifetime giving for IHT purposes.

(ii) The main factors that need to be considered in deciding which assets to gift.

(6 marks)

(Total: 20 marks)

Henry

Question 4

Henry died on 5 October 2016. He was survived by his wife, Sally and two children, Cecil and Ida.

Sally is herself in a frail condition and not expected to live for much longer. Both Cecil and Ida have children of their own and are relatively wealthy in their own right.

Henry owned the following assets:

(1) 100,000 £1 ordinary shares in Peel plc a quoted company with an issued share capital of 10,000,000 £1 ordinary shares.

On 5 October 2016 these shares were quoted at 200 – 208p per share with marked bargains of 201p, 204p and 207p.

A dividend of 10p per share had been paid on 30 September 2016.

(2) £20,000 10% Government Stock quoted at 95p – 97p ex interest. Interest is payable half yearly on 30 April and 31 October.

(3) The following capital deposits both of which have been held for several years:

– £25,000 deposited with a building society.

– £18,000 invested in an ISA account.

The following interest was received during 2016/17.

Building society	£400 on 30 June 2016 with a further £380 on 31 December 2016.
ISA	£350 on 30 June 2016 with a further £358 on 31 December 2016.

All interest figures relate to the actual amount received.

(4) A house valued on 5 October 2016 at £450,000. This property was his and Sally's family home but was owned outright by Henry.

Under the terms of his will Henry has left £20,000 each to Cecil and Ida with the remainder of his estate left to his wife. Sally's will currently leaves her estate equally to their two children.

The only gifts made by Henry during his lifetime were cash gifts of £231,000 on 1 January 2008 and £164,000 on 1 January 2011 respectively. Both gifts were made to a discretionary trust. Henry had agreed to pay any inheritance tax arising on these lifetime gifts.

The only other taxable income Henry received during the period 6 April 2016 to 5 October 2016 was a state retirement pension of £6,030 and gross annuity income of £10,300. Basic rate income tax at the rate of 20% was deducted from the annuity income. The annuity did not have any capital value on Henry's death.

Required:

(a) Explain how Henry's income will be taxed in 2016/17, the tax year of his death, and calculate the income tax payable for this tax year.

(7 marks)

(b) Calculate the inheritance tax liabilities arising:

(i) from the lifetime gifts of cash to the discretionary trust; and

(ii) arising as a consequence of Henry's death on 5 October 2016.

(10 marks)

(c) Explain any action that could be taken following Henry's death to reduce or defer any inheritance tax liability that may become payable upon the future death of his wife, Sally.

(8 marks)

(Total: 25 marks)

Thelma

Question 5

Assume today's date is 30 June 2017.

Thelma is aged 78 years and a higher rate taxpayer. She is married to Gordon, who is independently wealthy in his own right. They have one child, Louise.

Thelma has unfortunately recently become terminally ill and is expected to live for only another four years.

She owns the following assets:

(1) 10,000 ordinary £1 shares in Blackbird plc, a quoted UK resident trading company with an issued share capital of 1 million ordinary shares. The company prepares its accounts to 31 March each year.

The shares are currently quoted at 1460p – 1468p. Thelma acquired 5,000 of her shares in June 2001 for £25,000. The remainder of the shares were acquired by way of a rights issue in June 2007 for a further £50,000.

Thelma was a director of this company for many years until she had to retire for health reasons on 31 May 2016.

(2) A 25% beneficial interest in £100,000 10% loan stock in Robin plc, a quoted UK resident trading company.

This loan stock is currently quoted at 102p – 106p and is held jointly with Gordon who has always owned the remaining 75% beneficial interest in it. This loan stock was acquired in June 2009 for £90,000.

(3) Main residence valued at £500,000.

(4) Three antique plates which are part of a set of six. Thelma bought her three plates in June 2009 for £2,500. On the same day Gordon bought two of the plates for £1,500 whilst Louise bought the remaining plate for £750. The value of the plates are currently:

	£
1 plate	1,000
2 plates	2,200
3 plates	3,800
4 plates	6,000
5 plates	10,000
6 plates	20,000

(5) Cash deposits amount to £145,000.

(6) Sundry personal chattels collectively worth £20,000 with no individual asset worth more than £5,000.

Under the terms of Thelma's will, all of her assets are to be left to Louise with the exception of the house and her sundry personal chattels which are bequeathed to Gordon.

Due to her failing health, Thelma and her family are currently considering whether she should either:

(i) gift all of her assets, with the exception of the house and her sundry personal chattels, to Louise upon her death in four years time, or

(ii) make these gifts to Louise now.

In four years time her assets are expected to be valued at the following amounts for inheritance tax purposes:

	£
Blackbird plc shareholding	200,000
100% of the Robin plc loan stock	100,000
Residence	600,000
Antique plates	10,000
Cash deposits	160,000
Sundry personal chattels	20,000
	1,090,000

The only previous gift made by Thelma was a cash gift, net of annual exemptions, of £360,000 made to Louise in September 2015.

Required:

Advise Thelma whether she should make the transfers of the selected assets to Louise:

(i) upon her death in four years' time, or

(ii) 6 July 2017.

Your answer should consider the likely IHT and CGT implications and should include a calculation of any capital taxes likely to arise under each option.

Stamp duty and stamp duty land tax should be ignored.

You should assume that the rates and allowances for 2016/17 continue to apply.

(18 marks)

14 The taxation of trusts

The Wood Discretionary Trust

Question 1

You are a member of the tax team in the firm 'Tax & Co'. In a few days time you have a meeting set up with potential new clients.

The clients are about to become the trustees of 'The Wood Discretionary Trust' which is to be set up under the terms of Tom Wood's will following his recent death.

Required:

Make brief notes for the meeting with the potential trustees detailing.

(a) The income tax implications of distributing income to the beneficiaries

(b) The CGT and IHT implications of distributing capital to the beneficiaries.

(15 marks)

15 Personal financial management

There are no questions for this chapter.

16 Ethics and personal tax administration

Fred Foyle

Question 1

Fred was employed until 31 March 2016. He purchased an existing business on 1 June 2016. Accounts have been prepared for the ten-month period to 5 April 2017. The results show a marked decline compared to the results of the previous owner for the y/e 31 May 2016.

	Previous owner y/e 31 May 2016	Fred p/e 5 April 2017
	£	£
Sales – Cash	600,000	400,000
– Credit	120,000	100,000
Gross profit	300,000	150,000
Net profit	216,000	80,000

Fred included the figures in his self-assessment tax return for 2016/17 which was submitted on 31 January 2018.

HMRC proceeded to carry out a compliance check into Fred's 2016/17 return, and have stated that they consider the sales shown in the accounts to be understated by £100,000.

HMRC gave written notice that the compliance check was complete on 31 July 2017 and amended Fred's self-assessment. Fred did not raise an appeal, and paid the additional tax due on 31 August 2018.

Fred is single, and has no other income or outgoings.

Required:

(a) State the likely reasons why HMRC have investigated Fred's 2016/17 tax return.

State possible criteria that he could put forward in order to justify the fall in profits from those of the previous owner. **(5 marks)**

(b) Calculate the late payment interest, assuming that tax is payable on the understated amount at 40%.

(2 marks)

(c) State the maximum amount of penalty that HMRC can charge Fred, and state the factors that will be taken into account in deciding if this maximum amount should be mitigated.

(2 marks)

(Total: 9 marks)

17 New and ongoing unincorporated businesses

Ali

Question 1

Ali has been in business as a sole trader for many years as a publisher.

He had an illness at the end of 2016 which resulted in his profits falling unexpectedly. The results for the last few years, and the projected profits for the next accounts, are as follows:

Year ended:		£
31 December 2015	Profit	55,000
31 December 2016	Loss	(18,000)
31 December 2017 (forecast estimate)	Profit	26,000

Ali also had other income and outgoings as follows:

	2015/16	2016/17	2017/18
	£	£	£
Bank interest received	8,690	5,050	0
Income from residential property	9,200	6,820	6,840

During 2016/17, to realise some cash funds, he sold one of the properties, an appartment, that he let and made a chargeable gain of £20,000. The property was purchased in 1995.

Ali had unused capital losses of £8,750 at the beginning of 2016/17.

Required:

Advise Ali of the best method of utilising the loss for the year ended 31 December 2016 and calculate the taxable income and taxable gains for all relevant tax years assuming your advice is taken.

Assume rules, rates and allowances for 2016/17 apply throughout.

(10 marks)

David and Patricia

Question 2

(a) Assume that today's date is 1 December 2016.

David is married to Patricia and the couple have one child who is six years old.

David has been employed since 2004 earning £3,750 per month (monthly PAYE deducted £970). He will have no other income in the tax year 2016/17. From 6 April 2017 he will have a source of property business income of £45,000 per year.

David intends to cease his current employment on 31 December 2016, and start trading as a self-employed businessman on 1 January 2017 preparing accounts to 31 March each year. His business plan shows profits in the region of £60,000 per year, before any payment to his wife, Patricia.

Patricia has been employed as a bookkeeper since 2006, earning £1,100 per month (monthly PAYE deducted £37). She will also cease her current employment on 31 December 2016 and will keep the books and prepare the accounts for David's business from 1 January 2017. She will continue to work the same number of hours per week as she does in her current employment.

David would like some advice on the taxation implications of involving his wife, Patricia, in his business either as an employee, or, alternatively, by taking her into partnership as an equal partner.

David has never previously had dealings with HMRC, so would also like details as to when he should notify HMRC about his new business for income tax purposes; when his 2016/17 self-assessment income tax return is due; and how he should pay the income tax due on the profits made by the business in both the first and subsequent years.

Required:

(i) Evaluate the taxation implications for the couple of:

(1) David employing his wife Patricia, and

(2) taking her into partnership as an equal partner.

Support your answer with calculations of the income tax (IT) and national insurance contributions (NIC) payable, based on the expected trading results for a full year of operation and the tax rates and allowances for 2016/17.

(11 marks)

(ii) State the information David requires concerning tax administration.

(4 marks)

(b) Assume that today's date is 1 May 2017.

David decided to form a partnership with his wife, Patricia, sharing profits and losses equally, and to adopt a 31 March year end for accounting purposes.

The business in fact showed a loss of £40,000 in the three month period to 31 March 2017, but profits of £60,000 per annum are still anticipated for future years.

Required:

Identify the loss reliefs available to David and explain which of the available reliefs would be most beneficial for him to claim.

Support your answer with calculations of the income tax (IT) saving achieved in each case.

(10 marks)

Assume that the tax rates and allowances for 2016/17 apply throughout this question.

(Total: 25 marks)

Angela

Question 3

Angela opened a guest house on 1 July 2016. She lives at the guest house with her dog.

She has been keeping her business records for the year ended 30 June 2017 in a folder during the year and has summarised them for you:

	£
Revenue This is the amount of invoices billed, however at 30 June 2017 she is still owed £4,560 from customers.	57,640
Guest house furniture – payments for furniture purchased.	5,300
Food and household expenses (cleaning and utilities) – all paid at 30 June 2017. Personal living costs account for 40% of the food and household expenses.	16,200
Motor car On 20 July 2016 Angela purchased a car (paid for by cheque) with CO_2 emissions of 120 g/km. She uses the car approximately 80% for business purposes	18,500
Motor expenses During the year ended 30 June 2017 she incurred petrol, servicing and MOT costs (all paid at 30 June 2017). She drove 10,800 business miles.	5,720
Other expenses (all allowable) This is the amount of bills payable, however she has not paid £850 of them by 30 June 2017.	4,960

The cash basis private use adjustment for one occupant in a business premises for 12 months is £4,200.

Calculate Angela's tax adjusted trading profit for the year ended 30 June 2017 assuming she:

(a) **Uses the cash basis**

(b) **Uses the accruals basis.**

18 Cessation of an unincorporated business

Jane Seemore

Question 1

You should assume today's date is 1 March 2017.

Jane Seemore has been running a small restaurant business as a sole trader since 1 September 2004. She has decided to sell her business, and needs some advice concerning the tax implications.

Offer for sale of business:

- Jane has accepted an offer from Hollywood Ltd, an unconnected company quoted on the Alternative Investment Market, to purchase her business.
- Hollywood Ltd would like to complete the purchase on 31 March 2017.
- The purchase consideration will consist of either cash or ordinary shares in Hollywood Ltd, or a mixture of cash and shares.
- Jane will become an employee of Hollywood Ltd from 1 April 2017 on an annual salary of £30,000.
- If the consideration is taken wholly in the form of shares in Hollywood Ltd, then Jane's holding will represent 7.5% of the company's total share capital.

Trading results:

- Jane's trading profits and losses are as follows:

	£
Year ended 31 August 2013	15,000
Year ended 31 August 2014	6,000
Year ended 31 August 2015	15,000
Year ended 31 August 2016	10,000
Period ended 31 March 2017 (before adjustments for capital allowances and sale of inventory)	(21,500)

- Jane has overlap profits brought forward of £2,815.

Forecast market values of Jane's business assets:

- The market values of the assets to be sold, at 31 March 2017 are:

	£
Premises (bought for £335,000 in 2012)	365,000
Goodwill	50,000
Inventory (cost plus 5%)	8,300
Shelving and restaurant fittings (all below cost)	10,000
Van (used 85% for business purposes)	4,700
Total value	438,000

Capital allowances:

- The tax written down value on capital allowances main pool at 31 August 2016 was £15,050.
- Jane purchased equipment for £820 in November 2016.
- The written down value of the van at 31 August 2016 was £4,130.

Other income:

- Jane currently has no other income. Her savings and dividend income will exceed £40,000 p.a. for 2017/18 onwards, regardless of whether the consideration is taken as cash or shares.

Required:

(a) (i) Explain the capital allowances implications for Jane on the transfer of the business, with supporting calculations.

(3 marks)

(ii) Calculate Jane's trading income assessments for all relevant tax years, and calculate the amount of the trading loss.

(3 marks)

(iii) Outline briefly the loss relief options available and explain their relative merits in Jane's situation.

(6 marks)

(b) Explain why there would be no capital gains tax liability on the transfer of Jane's business in exchange for shares.

Calculate the maximum cash proceeds that Jane could receive without giving rise to a capital gains tax liability, and suggest how much cash Jane should actually receive.

(6 marks)

You should assume that the tax rates and allowances for 2016/17 apply throughout.

(Total: 18 marks)

19 Partnerships – income tax and capital gains tax

Alf and Bob

Question 1

Alf and Bob have been in partnership together since 1 December 2003.

The partners sold their business on 30 November 2016 for its market value of £520,000.

The partnership assets at 30 November 2016, and the capital gains arising on the disposal, were as follows:

	Market value	Capital gain
	£	£
Freehold property	322,000	97,000
Goodwill	100,000	100,000
Plant and machinery	58,000	0
Net current assets	40,000	0
	520,000	197,000

The assessable trading income for the final four tax years, before allocation between the partners, was as follows:

			£
2013/14	Y/e 30.11.13	Profit	19,000
2014/15	Y/e 30.11.14	Profit	19,500
2015/16	Y/e 30.11.15	Profit	15,200
2016/17	Y/e 30.11.16	Loss	(37,000)

Profits and losses have always been shared 40% to Alf and 60% to Bob.

Alf is single and had employment income from a part time job as follows:

	£
2013/14	7,000
2014/15	11,000
2015/16	12,500

He has capital losses brought forward at 6 April 2016 of £25,000.

Bob is single and also has no other income or outgoings apart from bank interest received of £3,850 on 1 December 2016 from investing the proceeds of sale of his holiday cottage. The cottage had been sold in June 2016, and the chargeable gain was £5,500.

Assume the 2016/17 rates and allowances apply to all years.

Ignore overlap relief.

Required:

(a) Calculate the chargeable gains in respect of the partnership that will be assessed on Alf and Bob for 2016/17.

(3 marks)

(b) (i) Advise the partners of the possible ways of relieving the partnership loss for 2016/17 and which loss relief claims would be the most beneficial.

(5 marks)

(ii) After taking into account the advice in (i), calculate the partners' taxable income for 2013/14 to 2016/17 and their taxable gains for 2016/17.

(5 marks)

(Total: 13 marks)

20 VAT: outline

Ken and Cindy

Question 1

(a) Ken has a market stall selling clocks and watches.

He started trading on 1 March 2016, and his turnover has accrued evenly over time as follows:

	£
One month ended 31 March 2016	36,800
Quarter ended 30 June 2016	72,600
Quarter ended 30 September 2016	63,000
Quarter ended 31 December 2016	60,000

Required:

(i) Advise Ken if he should register for VAT and, if so, when HMRC should be notified.

(3 marks)

(ii) Explain the impact on Ken's customers of Ken registering for VAT.

(2 marks)

(iii) Explain, with reasons, whether any of the VAT special accounting schemes would be suitable for Ken.

(6 marks)

(b) Cindy's input tax and supplies made in the quarter to 31 December 2016 are analysed as follows:

	£
Input tax wholly re-taxable supplies	25,575
Input tax wholly re-exempt supplies	15,400
Non-attributable input tax	30,800
Value (excluding VAT) of taxable supplies	275,000
Value of exempt supplies	120,000

Required:

Calculate the deductible input tax assuming that Cindy uses supplies for the current quarter for attributing input tax.

(3 marks)

(Total: 14 marks)

Sandy Brick

Question 2

Sandy Brick has been a self-employed builder since 2008. He registered for VAT on 1 January 2017, and is in the process of completing his VAT return for the quarter ended 31 March 2017.

The following information is relevant to the completion of this VAT return:

(1) Sales invoices totalling £44,000 (excluding VAT) were issued to VAT registered customers in respect of standard rated sales. Sandy offers his VAT registered customers a 5% discount for prompt payment within 30 days.

This discount was taken up by customers whose invoices (pre-discount) totalled £26,400 as they paid within the specified time.

(2) Sales invoices totalling £16,920 were issued to customers that were not registered for VAT. Of this figure, £5,170 was in respect of zero-rated sales with the balances being in respect of standard rated sales. Standard rated sales are inclusive of VAT.

(3) Standard rated materials amounted to £11,200, of which £800 were used in constructing Sandy's private residence.

(4) Since 1 December 2015 Sandy has paid £120 per month for the lease of office equipment. This expense is standard rated.

(5) During the quarter ended 31 March 2017 £400 was spent on mobile telephone calls, of which 30% relates to private calls. This expense is standard rated.

(6) On 20 February 2017 £920 was spent on repairs to a motor car. The motor car is used by Sandy in his business, although 20% of the mileage is for private journeys. This expense is standard rated.

(7) On 15 March 2017 equipment was purchased for £6,000. The purchase was partly financed by a bank loan of £5,000. This purchase is standard rated.

Unless stated otherwise all of the above figures are exclusive of VAT.

Required:

(a) State the circumstances in which Sandy is required to issue a VAT invoice, and the period during which such an invoice should be issued.

(2 marks)

(b) Calculate the amount of VAT payable by Sandy for the quarter ended 31 March 2017.

(10 marks)

(Total: 12 marks)

21 VAT: administration and overseas aspects

There are no questions for this chapter.

22 Corporation tax: computations and administration

There are no questions for this chapter.

23 Calculation of corporation tax income and gains

Lowland Ltd

Question 1

Lowland Ltd is a small unquoted trading company. Lowland Ltd has always had an accounting date of 31 December, with its most recent accounts being prepared to 31 December 2015. However, the company now plans to change its accounting date to 30 June 2017.

Lowland Ltd has forecast that its results for the 18 month period to 30 June 2017 will be as follows:

(1) Tax adjusted trading profits, before capital allowances, per six monthly periods will be:

	£
Six months to 30 June 2016	155,000
Six months to 31 December 2016	139,000
Six months to 30 June 2017	145,000

(2) The tax written-down value of plant and machinery at 1 January 2016 is £22,000. On 31 January 2016 Lowland Ltd will purchase plant costing £40,000.

(3) Lowland Ltd owns two freehold office buildings that have always been rented out unfurnished. These are both to be sold. The first building in Reading will be sold on 30 June 2016 resulting in a chargeable gain of £46,000, whilst the second building in Guildford will be sold on 30 November 2016 resulting in an allowable capital loss of £28,000.

(4) The building in Reading is currently let at £53,000 p.a., rent being due quarterly in advance on 1 January, 1 April etc. The building in Guildford was let until 30 September 2015, but has been empty since then. It will be decorated at a cost of £10,000 during November 2016 prior to its disposal. Both lettings are at a full rent and Lowland Ltd is responsible for all repairs.

(5) A dividend of £55,000 (net) will be paid on 15 April 2016.

(6) Lowland Ltd has a 20% shareholding in Mini Ltd, an unquoted trading company. A dividend of £13,750 will be received from Mini Ltd on 16 December 2016.

Required:

Advise Lowland Ltd of whether it would be beneficial to:

(i) prepare one set of accounts for the 18 month period to 30 June 2017, or

(ii) prepare separate accounts for the 6 month period to 30 June 2016 and for the year ended 30 June 2017.

Your answer should include a calculation of Lowland Ltd's total corporation tax liability for the 18 month period to 30 June 2017 under each alternative.

You should assume that the current rates of capital allowances apply throughout and that the tax rates for FY2016 continue to apply in future.

(17 marks)

24 Corporation tax losses

Iris Ltd

Question 1

Iris Ltd has the following results for the periods to 31 August 2017:

	y/e 31.12.15	8 m/e 31.8.16	y/e 31.8.17
	£	£	£
Trading profit/(loss)	170,000	78,000	(176,100)
Property income	10,000	11,000	12,000
Interest income	2,500	3,600	4,100
Qualifying charitable donation	3,000	3,000	3,000

Required:

Calculate the taxable total profits for all three periods, assuming that as much of the loss as possible is relieved against total profits.

State the amount of unrelieved loss at 1 September 2017.

(8 marks)

Cosmet Ltd

Question 2

(a) Cosmet Ltd is a company that manufactures cosmetics. The recent results of Cosmet Ltd are as follows:

	y/e 31.5.14	y/e 31.5.15	p/e 31.12.15	y/e 31.12.16
	£	£	£	£
Trading profit	750,250	500,500	101,999	
Trading loss				(232,790)
Property income	10,000	10,000	10,000	11,000
Bank interest receivable	8,460	7,526	5,076	5,275
Capital (loss)/gain	1,622	(4,000)	2,990	60,400

Required:

(i) Calculate the taxable total profits for all four periods, assuming that relief is obtained for the loss against total profits.

(6 marks)

(ii) Calculate the tax repayments arising from the claim. You should assume that the tax rates for FY2016 apply throughout.

(2 marks)

(b) The company director is thinking about the company's options and has arranged a meeting with you and your tax partner.

He is considering one of the following two options:

(1) merging with another company which will buy the shares in Cosmet Ltd. The acquiring company is keen to acquire the goodwill and clients of Cosmet Ltd and utilise the losses, or

(2) changing the products that Cosmet Ltd currently make, and moving into the more lucrative market of making beauty products for Spa Hotels.

Required:

Make brief notes for your meeting with the director on the effect on trading losses of the two options being considered.

(6 marks)

(Total: 14 marks)

25 Business Financial Management

There are no questions for this chapter.

26 Family companies and related planning scenarios

Bream

Question 1

Bream is a participator in, but not an employee of, Test Valley Ltd, a close trading company that prepares accounts to 31 December each year. Test Valley Ltd does not pay corporation tax by instalments.

In June 2014 the company loaned Bream £72,000 for the purchase of a yacht. In January 2016 Bream repaid £20,000 and in March 2017 the company waived the outstanding amount of the loan.

Bream has taxable income of £50,000 p.a. but has not received any dividends in 2016/17.

Required:

Show the effect of these transactions on Test Valley Ltd and on Bream.

(5 marks)

Assume that the current rates of tax apply throughout.

Joe

Question 2

Joe subscribes for 100,000 £1 shares in his family company, Grange Ltd, at par in November 1992. This represents a 25% holding in the company. Joe is not an employee of Grange Ltd.

In August 2016 Joe sells the shares back to the company at £7.30 per share, as he is aged 58 and ready to retire, and the family do not want the shares to go to outsiders.

Joe has earned income of £160,000 in 2016/17 but has received no dividends and made no other capital disposals during the year. Grange Ltd is an unquoted trading company.

Required:

Advise Joe of how the sale of shares will affect his tax liability for 2016/17 if:

(a) the transaction is treated as a distribution, and

(b) the transaction is not treated as a distribution.

(c) Explain the effect of satisfying the conditions for treatment as a capital event.

(6 marks)

John

Question 3

Assume that today's date is 1 March 2016.

John will resign from his job, in which he has been employed since 2002, earning a salary of £6,000 per month, on 31 March 2016.

John intends to start trading on 1 April 2016 producing VAT exempt goods. His business plan shows expected profits of £90,000 per annum net of wages to his employees. He is undecided whether he should incorporate or not as he does not understand the differences in the taxation of a sole trader and a company.

The business needs funds in the order of £100,000 to start up, but John does not want to use his own capital.

He expects that funds will be easier to raise if he incorporates, but is confused about the taxation implications of equity versus loan finance.

John estimates that he needs £20,000 per year to cover his living expenses, in addition to the £11,000 property business income that he receives annually. John has not made any pension provision to date.

He has no other employees.

Required:

(a) Identify the main differences between the taxation of John as a sole trader and the taxation of John's company and John as an employee and shareholder.

Calculate the income tax (IT), corporation tax (CT) and national insurance contributions (NIC) payable by John and (where applicable) John's company for the tax year 2016/17 or for the year ended 31 March 2017, under each of the following options:

(i) John trades as a sole trader,

(ii) John incorporates and takes a dividend of £21,216 as his only income from the company, and

(iii) John incorporates and takes a gross annual salary of £27,990 as his only income from the company.

Ignore the odd five days at the start of the accounting period (i.e. assume that it matches the tax year 2016/17). **(8 marks)**

(b) Describe the taxation implications of both equity and loan finance from the point of view of:

(i) a company, and

(ii) an individual investor. **(6 marks)**

(c) Assuming that John decides to incorporate on 1 April 2016, taking an annual salary of £25,000 and annual dividends of £9,000, briefly describe the options available to John for investing in a pension.

Indicate which of the options identified is preferable in his case and calculate the maximum contributions he could make before 31 December 2016.

(8 marks)

(Total: 22 marks)

27 Groups and consortia

Longbow Ltd

Question 1

Longbow Ltd wishes to acquire Minnow Ltd and has made an offer to the shareholders of that company which it would like to finalise on 1 October 2016. The share capital of Minnow Ltd is owned equally by A Ltd, B Ltd and C Ltd.

The forecast results of Longbow Ltd and Minnow Ltd for the year ended 31 March 2017 are as follows:

	Longbow Ltd	Minnow Ltd
	£	£
Adjusted trading profit/(loss)	220,000	(140,000)
Trading losses brought forward	–	(9,000)
Capital gain	–	50,000
Interest received on loan notes (gross)	5,250	–

Longbow Ltd purchased £150,000 of 7% loan notes issued by an unrelated company on 1 August 2016. On 30 April 2017 the company is to purchase a new freehold factory for £120,000.

Minnow Ltd's capital gain is in respect of the proposed sale of a freehold office building for £150,000 on 10 February 2017. One-quarter of the building has never been used for the purposes of the company's trade.

Required:

Calculate the corporation tax liability for both Longbow Ltd and Minnow Ltd for the year ended 31 March 2017 if:

(a) Longbow Ltd acquires one-third of Minnow Ltd's share capital from A Ltd on 1 October 2016.

(4 marks)

(b) Longbow Ltd acquires two-thirds of Minnow Ltd's share capital from A Ltd and B Ltd on 1 October 2016.

(3 marks)

(c) Longbow Ltd acquires all of Minnow Ltd's share capital from A Ltd, B Ltd and C Ltd on 1 October 2016.

(4 marks)

(Total: 11 marks)

Willow Group

Question 2

Willow Ltd, a UK resident company, has holdings of ordinary shares in other companies, which, apart from Beech Inc, are all UK resident.

90% in Beech Inc (an overseas resident company not in EEA)
90% in Fig Ltd
85% in Oak Ltd
55% in Pine Ltd

Fig Ltd holds 75% of the ordinary shares of Cherry Ltd, Ash Ltd holds 45% of the shares in Pine Ltd and Beech Inc holds 5% of the shares in Cherry Ltd.

Trading results for each company for the year ended 31 March 2017:

		£
Ash Ltd	Loss	(160,000)
Pine Ltd	Profit	158,000
Willow Ltd	Profit	153,000
Oak Ltd	Loss	(107,000)
Fig Ltd	Profit	294,000
Cherry Ltd	Loss	(310,000)
Beech Inc	Loss	(110,000)

No company had any other source of income or gains.

Required:

Assuming the maximum possible relief is claimed for the above losses, calculate the UK corporation tax payable by each of the UK companies for the year ended 31 March 2017.

(10 marks)

28 Overseas aspects of corporation tax

X Ltd

Question 1

X Ltd is a UK resident company which has, to date, traded only in the UK. The directors have decided to establish a factory overseas and seek advice on the taxation implications of this proposal.

In particular, they wish to know whether the overseas trade should be conducted through a foreign-based subsidiary or simply as a branch of the UK company.

Required:

Draft an appropriate memorandum to the board of the company highlighting the taxation implications of each of the two alternatives.

Assume today's date is 10 July 2016.

(6 marks)

Bertie Overseas

Question 2

You have recently met with Bertie, a UK resident individual, who requires some preliminary advice concerning setting up an overseas operation.

You ascertain during the course of the meeting that Bertie owns 30% of the share capital and is the managing director of Bertie Ltd a successful UK resident trading company which manufactures lawnmowers in the UK. The remaining shares are held by other third party individuals.

Bertie Ltd operates on a wholesale basis and currently only sells products in the UK. Bertie, however, believes the time is right for overseas expansion and is considering setting up a distribution operation in the country of Picea (a non EEA country) ('Bertie Overseas') which will be wholly owned by Bertie Ltd. It is planned that Bertie Overseas will also operate on a wholesale basis and will only buy lawnmowers from Bertie Ltd.

The following additional information is available:

(1) The rate of Picean corporation tax is 10%, irrespective of whether the trading entity is a branch or a company incorporated in Picea. Picean tax law only allows the offset of trading losses generated against other profits earned in the same period. Under Picean tax law no withholding tax is deductible on overseas profits remittances. There is no double tax treaty between the UK and Picea.

(2) The mark up currently achieved by Bertie Ltd, after all selling and distribution costs, on sales to its UK customers is 100%. The mark up on sales to Bertie Overseas will be 80%. Bertie Overseas will be responsible for all of its own selling and distribution costs including meeting carriage costs from the UK. Bertie believes that, in the absence of Bertie Overseas, Bertie Ltd would achieve a comparable mark up on sales to Picea of 85%.

(3) Setting up the Picean operation will involve the acquisition of some freehold premises as well as necessary vehicles and equipment.

(4) Local Picean management will be appointed to run the day to day operations of Bertie Overseas. Bertie is considering retaining a high level of ultimate control over Bertie Overseas.

(5) Bertie Ltd is planning to charge Bertie Overseas interest on any loan finance provided at the rate of 4% per year. If Bertie Overseas were to arrange its own loan finance via an independent bank it would have been charged 6% per year.

(6) The business plans produced indicate that Bertie Overseas is likely to make a loss for its first trading period and will then produce progressively stronger profits. Once profits are being generated it is planned to remit 25% of these to Bertie Ltd.

Bertie has asked that you write to him setting out the principal business tax issues that need to be considered in advance of a future meeting where these issues will be discussed in more detail.

Required:

Write a letter to Bertie identifying the principal business tax issues that can be identified from the above information regarding the setting up of Bertie Overseas.

You are not required to discuss any employee or VAT issues.

The points covered should include (but not be restricted to) an analysis of whether Bertie Overseas should be set up as a branch or a limited company, the anti-avoidance legislation that HMRC could use to tax the overseas profits in the UK and whether relief will be available in the UK for any Picean taxes paid.

Marks will be awarded for presentation, structure and format.

(25 marks)

29 Planning for companies

North and South

Question 1

Bertrand owns 100% of the issued share capital of two UK resident trading companies, North Limited and South Limited. Both companies operate in the retail sector and commenced trading on 1 April 2016.

The actual and forecast results for both companies are as follows:

	Trading profit/(Loss)
	£
North Limited	
Actual for the year ended 31 March 2017	10,000
Forecast for the year ended 31 March 2018	(114,000)
South Limited	
Actual for the year ended 31 March 2017	160,000
Forecast for the year ended 31 March 2018	200,000

Due to the losses forecast for North Limited some restructuring of the two companies is required. This is planned to take place on 1 April 2017.

The forecast figures given above for both companies are stated before the effects of this proposed restructuring, which will comprise:

(1) North Limited selling one of its retail outlets to a third party for £160,000 with the consideration allocated as follows:

	£
Freehold property	120,000
Inventory (cost £6,000)	10,000
	130,000

At the date of sale the freehold property will have an indexed cost of £80,000.

(2) As South Limited has sufficient cash resources it will acquire a replacement retail outlet costing £120,000 with the consideration allocated as follows:

	£
Freehold property	100,000
Inventory	20,000
	120,000

Required:

(a) Calculate the actual and forecast corporation tax liabilities of North Limited and South Limited for the years ended 31 March 2017 and 31 March 2018 assuming that the objective is to minimise the total tax liability for these years.

Your answer should clearly identify any unrelieved losses carried forward at 31 March 2018.

(4 marks)

(b) Explain the weaknesses of the above group structure and advise as to how this position could be improved by making one company a wholly owned subsidiary of the other company.

Your answer should include a summary of the procedures involved in altering the group structure to a more tax efficient basis together with an explanation of any relieving provisions which can be used in this group restructuring.

(8 marks)

(c) Recalculate the corporation tax liabilities of North Limited and South Limited for the years ended 31 March 2017 and 31 March 2018 assuming that the group restructuring identified at part (b) had been implemented with effect from 1 April 2017 and the objective is again to minimise the total tax liability for these years.

(5 marks)

You should assume that the rates and allowances for the financial year 2016 apply throughout.

(Total: 17 marks)

Test your understanding answers

Danny

Answer 1 – Chapter 1

(a) **Income tax computation – 2016/17**

	£
Employment income (£28,505 + £2,100)	30,605
Building society interest	2,500
Property income (Note)	2,150
UK dividends received	2,300
Total income	37,555
Less: Relief – Qualifying loan interest	(1,500)
Net income	36,055
Less: PA	(11,000)
Taxable income	25,055

Analysis of income:

Dividends	**Savings**	**Non-savings income**
£2,300	£2,500	(£25,055 – £2,300 – £2,500) = £20,255

£		£
20,255 × 20%	Non-savings income	4,051
1,000 × 0%	Savings NRB	0
1,500 × 20%	Savings	300
2,300 × 7.5%	Dividends	172
25,055		
Income tax liability		4,523
Less: Tax credits – PAYE		(3,501)
Income tax payable		1,022

Note: The property income, being joint income received by civil partners, is divided between Danny and Ben on a 50:50 basis (£4,300 ÷ 2 = £2,150).

As Ben and Danny both use their PA and Ben is a HR taxpayer, it is not possible to claim the marriage allowance.

(b) Currently, in 2016/17, Danny is a basic rate taxpayer. Accordingly, he is entitled to a £1,000 savings nil rate band.

In 2017/18 and future years Danny's taxable income will exceed £32,000 and consequently his savings nil rate band will be £500, the amount available to higher rate taxpayer.

The remaining £2,000 of savings income will be taxed at 40%, resulting in £800 of income tax payable.

This is £500 higher (£800 – £300) than the tax currently payable by Danny.

Mr Darcy

Answer 1 – Chapter 2

Income tax computation – 2016/17

	£
Salary	37,000
Bonus (Note 1)	8,000
Car benefit (Note 2)	7,200
Fuel benefit (Note 2)	7,992
	60,192
Less: Pension contributions (7% × £37,000)	(2,590)
Partnership shares (3 × £125) (Note 3)	(375)
Employment income	57,227
Less: PA	(11,000)
Taxable income (all 'non-savings income')	46,227

Income tax:

£		
32,000	× 20%	6,400
14,227	× 40%	5,691
46,227		
Income tax liability		12,091

Note: Even though Sonia does not utilise all of her PA, it is not possible to claim the MA as Mr Darcy and Sonia are not legally married.

Even if they were married it would still not be possible, as Mr Darcy is a higher rate taxpayer.

Notes:

(1) Under the receipts basis for directors the bonus is treated as received, and therefore taxed, when it is determined. Thus the bonus determined in May 2016 is taxable in 2016/17.

(2) Car and fuel benefit

CO_2 emissions 197 g/km, available all year

Appropriate percentage:

(195 – 95) ÷ 5 = 20% + 16% (petrol car) = 36%

Car benefit = (36% × £20,000)	£7,200
Fuel benefit = (36% × £22,200)	£7,992

(3) The cost of partnership shares in the approved SIP is an allowable deduction against employment income (and would have been deducted before applying PAYE). The cost of the shares purchased is less than 10% of his salary, therefore there is no restriction in the allowable deduction.

Taxation in 2016/17 of SIP shares received

The free shares and the matching shares are allotted tax free under the approved all employee share scheme (SIP scheme).

There is therefore no taxable benefit assessed on Mr Darcy in 2016/17 in respect of these shares.

Hubert

Answer 2 – Chapter 2

The requirement asks for the 'tax payable' (not just 'income tax payable').

Consideration must therefore be given to income tax, capital gains tax and NICs.

Income tax computation – 2016/17

	£	£
Employment income (W1)		59,696
Pension		5,000
Trading income		9,194
		73,890
Bank interest	2,100	
Building society interest	115	
Treasury stock interest	250	
		2,465
Foreign property income (gross)		1,200
UK dividends received		642
Total income		78,197
Less: PA		(11,000)
Taxable income		67,197

Analysis of income:

Dividends	Savings	Non-savings income
£642	£2,465	(£67,197 – £642 – £2,465) = £64,090

Income tax:

£			£
32,000	× 20%	(non-savings income)	6,400
32,090	× 40%	(non-savings income)	12,836
64,090			
500	× 0%	(savings NRB)	0
1,965	× 40%	(savings)	786
642	× 0%	(dividend NRB)	0
67,197			
Income tax liability			20,022
Less: Tax credits			
PAYE (£4,500 + £1,000)			(5,500)
Income tax payable			14,522

Capital gains tax

No capital gain arises on the disposal of the shares as the sale proceeds received are equal to the base cost of the shares acquired.

National insurance contributions

Class 1 primary contributions – payable by Hubert

(£23,000 – £8,060) × 12% = £1,793

Note: There are no allowable deductions in the calculation of class 1 NICs, and there is no NIC liability arising on an employee for any employment benefit received.

Class 1 NIC would be payable by Hubert on the amount subject to income tax when quoted share options are exercised. If the shares were unquoted, class 1A NIC would be payable but this is an employer only charge. Class 2 and class 4 NIC would be payable on Hubert's trading income. However, as class 1 NIC is also payable by Hubert, the calculation of total NICs due would be subject to an 'annual maxima' calculation which is excluded from the P6 syllabus.

Workings

(W1) **Employment income**

	£
Salary	23,000
Car benefit (W2)	5,600
Fuel benefit (W2)	6,216
Business expenses (Note)	0
Use of assets (W3)	240
	35,056
Less: Professional subscriptions	(360)
	34,696
Plus: Unapproved share options (W4)	25,000
Employment income	59,696

Note: The business expenses reimbursed by the employer are exempt.

(W2) **Car and fuel benefit**

CO_2 emission 155 g/km, available all year

Appropriate percentage:

(155 – 95) ÷ 5 = 12% + 16% (petrol car) = 28%

Car benefit = 28% × £20,000	£5,600
Fuel benefit = 28% × £22,200	£6,216

(W3) **Use of assets**

Use of cement mixer (20% × £1,200)	£240

(W4) **Unapproved share options**

	£
Charge on exercise (MV at that time)	200,000
Less: Price paid (25,000 × £7)	(175,000)
Employment income	25,000

Benny Korere

Answer 3 – Chapter 2

(a) **Employment income – 2016/17**

	£
Salary (£32,000 × 11/12)	29,333
Payment in lieu of notice (Note)	8,000
Payment for agreeing not to work for competitors	17,500
Car benefit (W1)	3,939
Employment income	58,772

As the payment in lieu of notice is made in accordance with Benny's contractual arrangements with Golden Tan plc, it will be treated as a payment in respect of services provided and will be taxable in 2016/17, the year in which it is received.

The payment for agreeing not to work for competitors is a restrictive covenant payment and is specifically taxable as earnings in the year received.

Working: Car benefit

CO_2 emissions 147 g/km, available for 11 months in 2016/17

	%
Petrol	16
Plus: (145 – 95) × 1/5	10
Appropriate percentage	26

Employment income

	£
List price (£22,360 – £5,000)	17,360
Car benefit (£17,360 × 26% × 11/12)	4,137
Less: Contributions for private use (£18 × 11)	(198)
Assessable benefits	3,939

(b) (i) **The share options**

There are no income tax implications on the grant of the share options.

In the tax year in which Benny exercises the options and acquires the shares, the excess of the market value of the shares over the price paid, i.e. £11,500 ((£3.35 – £2.20) × 10,000) will be subject to income tax.

Benny's financial exposure is caused by the rule within the share option scheme obliging him to hold the shares for a year before he can sell them.

If the company's expansion into Eastern Europe fails, such that its share price subsequently falls to less than £2.20 before Benny has the chance to sell the shares, Benny's financial position may be summarised as follows:

- Benny will have paid £22,000 (£2.20 × 10,000) for shares which are now worth less than that.
- He will also have paid income tax of £4,600 (£11,500 × 40%).

(ii) **The flat**

The following additional information is required in order to calculate the employment income benefit in respect of the flat.

- The flat's annual value.
- The cost of any improvements made to the flat prior to 6 April 2017.
- The cost of power, water, repairs and maintenance, etc. borne by Summer Glow plc.
- The cost of the furniture provided by Summer Glow plc.
- Any use of the flat by Benny wholly, exclusively and necessarily for the purposes of his employment.

The market value of the flat is not required as Summer Glow plc has owned it for less than six years.

Income tax consequences of requesting a more centrally located flat

One element of the employment income benefit in respect of the flat is calculated by reference to its original cost plus the cost of any capital improvements prior to 6 April 2017.

If Benny requests a flat in a different location, this element of the benefit will be computed instead by reference to the cost of the new flat, which in turn equals the proceeds of sale of the old flat.

Accordingly, if, as is likely, the value of the flat has increased since it was purchased, Benny's employment income benefit will also increase. The increase in the employment income benefit will be the flat's sales proceeds less its original cost less the cost of any capital improvements prior to 6 April 2017 multiplied by 3%.

Muriel Grand

Answer 1 – Chapter 3

Tax implications of letting property

In either case, Bertie will be assessed on the profits of a business of letting property. The assessment will be on an actual basis from 6 April to 5 April, and will be calculated in accordance with most of the rules used in calculating assessable trading profits.

Repairs to roof

The roof was damaged before Muriel transferred the house to Bertie. Since the roof must be repaired before the house can be let, the house would not appear to be usable at the time of the transfer. The cost of repair of £24,000 is therefore likely to be classed as capital expenditure as it is pre-acquisition expenditure. This will increase Bertie's base cost for CGT purposes.

Let as unfurnished accommodation

The cost of decoration would normally be a revenue expense. However, some of the expenditure may be classed as capital if the house was in a bad state of repair on 31 December 2016. The decoration will presumably be carried out before letting commences, and so will be pre-trading expenditure. This will be allowed as an expense on the first day of business.

Any capital gain arising on the disposal of the house when Bertie retires at 60, will be fully chargeable.

Let as furnished holiday accommodation

The cost of converting the house into two separate units will be mainly capital expenditure, and this will increase Bertie's base cost for CGT purposes. The figure of £41,000 may include some revenue expenditure, such as decorating costs, and this will be treated as above. The £9,000 cost of furnishing the two units will be capital expenditure.

Bertie will be able to claim the following deductions from his annual gross rents of £45,000:

(1) the loan interest of £4,000 (£50,000 at 8%)

(2) capital allowances in the form of the annual investment allowance of £9,000.

(3) the letting agency fees of £10,125 (£45,000 at 22.5%)

(4) the other running costs of £3,500.

Expenses will be restricted if Bertie occupies the house for his own use.

Given Bertie's level of rental income the letting is likely to qualify for the special rules applicable to furnished holiday lettings.

This will mean that:

- capital allowances will be available on plant and machinery, such as furniture and kitchen equipment
- the property business profit will qualify as relevant earnings for personal pension purposes
- entrepreneurs' relief will be available provided that all qualifying conditions are met
- rollover relief will be available on disposal
- gift relief will be available if the property is gifted or sold at undervalue.

The letting of holiday accommodation is standard rated for VAT purposes. The forecast rental income of £45,000 is below the VAT registration limit of £83,000, but the impact of VAT will have to be considered if Bertie is already registered for VAT, or if there is an increase in rental income.

Conclusion

Letting the house as a furnished holiday letting will produce annual income of approximately £18,375 (£45,000 – £4,000 – £10,125 – £9,000 – £3,500), compared to £28,000 (given in the question) if the house is let unfurnished.

It will also be necessary to incur additional expenditure of £46,400 (£41,000 + £9,000 – £3,600).

This must be compared against the potential CGT saving upon the disposal of the house arising from entrepreneurs' relief available for furnished holiday letting which is not available for unfurnished property.

Anthony & Cleopatra

Answer 2 – Chapter 3

(a) **Income tax payable computations**

Anthony
Income tax computation – 2016/17

	£
Employment income (W1)	65,272
Building society interest	52,650
Rental income (gross)	11,979
UK dividends received (Note 1)	75,433
Total income	205,334
Less: Reliefs – Qualifying loan interest	(550)
Net income	204,784
Less: PA (Note 2)	(0)
Taxable income	204,784

Analysis of income:

Dividends	Savings	Non-savings income
£75,433	£52,650	(£204,784 – £75,433 – £52,650) = £76,701

Notes:
1. EIS dividends are normal taxable dividends.
2. As Anthony's ANI exceeds £122,000, no PA is available.
3. The savings nil rate band is not available to additional rate taxpayers.

£		£
32,000	× 20% (non-savings income)	6,400
44,701	× 40% (non-savings income)	17,880
76,701		
52,650	× 40% (savings)	21,060
5,000	× 0% (dividend NRB)	0
15,649	× 32.5% (dividends)	5,086
150,000		
54,784	× 38.1% (dividends)	20,873
204,784		
		71,299
	Less: EIS investment relief (30% × £20,000)	(6,000)
	Income tax liability	65,299
	Less: Tax credits	
	PAYE	(19,700)
	Income tax payable	45,599

Cleopatra

Income tax computation – 2016/17

	£
Employment income (£12,500 – £400)	12,100
ISA interest (exempt)	0
VCT dividends (exempt)	0
Total income	12,100
Less: PA	(11,000)
Taxable income (all non-savings income)	1,100

	£
£1,100 × 20%	220
Less: VCT investment relief (30% × £20,000 = £6,000) (part wasted)	(220)
Income tax liability	0
Less: Tax credits	(0)
Income tax payable	0

Note: VCT investment relief is restricted to the income tax liability, the remaining relief is wasted. It cannot be paid in cash, nor carried forward or back to other years.

(b) **Tax planning**

Transferring capital assets to Cleopatra

Anthony is an additional rate taxpayer, however Cleopatra is a basic rate taxpayer. The couple should be advised to transfer capital assets from Anthony to Cleopatra, to ensure that her personal allowance, savings and dividends nil rate bands and basic rate band are used each year.

Transferring cash from the bank and building society accounts will save income tax at 40% on the first £1,000 of interest, which will fall into Cleopatra's savings nil rate band (assuming she is a basic rate taxpayer). Income tax will be saved at 20% (40% – 20%) on any excess.

Transferring the property giving rise to the rental income will also save the couple 20% income tax (40% – 20%), and in addition, less of Anthony's dividends will be taxed at 38.1% as they will fall into the 32.5% band.

Transferring shares giving rise to the dividend income will save the couple income tax at 37.5% on the first £5,000 falling into Cleopatra's nil rate band and at 30.6% (38.1% – 7.5%) to the extent that the dividend falls into Cleopatra's basic rate band.

In addition, Anthony is currently not entitled to any personal allowance as his income is greater than £122,000. Reducing his adjusted net income below £100,000 would give him a full personal allowance, which would save tax at 45.6% (tax saving at 40%, plus part of the dividend would fall from the 38.1% band to the 32.5% band).

Note: The transfer of capital assets will not give rise to CGT as inter spouse transfers are at nil gain/nil loss, and no IHT arises as inter spouse transfers are exempt from IHT.

Workings

(W1) **Employment income**

	£
Salary	50,000
Bonus (W2)	2,000
Gift from client (W3)	1,000
Computer benefit (W4)	500
Company car benefit (W5)	6,300
Fuel benefit (W5)	4,662
Accommodation benefit (W6)	810
Employment income	65,272

(W2) **Bonus**

The bonus for the year ended 31 December 2015 was determined at the Board meeting in April and paid on 30 April 2016. It is therefore assessed in 2016/17.

(W3) **Gift from a client**

Any form of payment including tips and gratuities whilst in the course of carrying out one's employment duties will be taxable as earnings, if they can be converted into cash.

(W4) **Computer benefit**

(£3,000 × 20% × 10/12)	£500

Note: The laptop was only available for private use for 10 months in 2016/17.

(W5) **Car and fuel benefit**

CO_2 emission 108 g/km, available all year

Appropriate percentage:

(105 – 95) ÷ 5 = 2% + 19% (diesel car) = 21%

Car benefit (21% × £30,000)	£6,300
Fuel benefit (21% × £22,200)	£4,662

(W6) **Accommodation benefit**

	£
Annual value	2,250
Less: Contributions made by Anthony (£120 × 12)	(1,440)
Assessable benefit	810

Enid, Tom and Norman

Answer 1 – Chapter 4

(a) **Enid – Brief notes on the tax implications of lump sum pension contributions**

The tax treatment of making lump sum contributions into an occupational pension scheme will depend upon whether or not the scheme is a registered scheme with HMRC.

If the scheme is a registered scheme, significant tax advantages can accrue:

– The employer's payment made on Enid's behalf will be an exempt benefit.

– Enid Limited will obtain a tax deduction at its marginal corporation tax rate on the contribution paid.

– Enid will be able to make and obtain income tax relief on additional employee contributions of up to 100% of her earned income. Such contributions will not, however, attract relief from class 1 NIC.

– If Enid contributes 100% of her earnings (£25,000) and the company contributes £14,000, the total contributions (£39,000) will not exceed the annual allowance of £40,000. Therefore full relief is available for both contributions and no further tax consequences arise.

– The funds will be invested in a tax free environment.

– Upon retirement Enid will be able to take a tax free lump sum payment of up to 25% of the lower of the fund value at that time and the lifetime allowance (£1,000,000 for 2016/17).

Such advantages will not accrue if the scheme is not a registered scheme with HMRC.

(b) **Tom – Maximum gross contribution into a private pension**

The maximum gross amount Tom can contribute into a private pension in 2016/17 and obtain tax relief is:

Greater of:
- £3,600
- 100% × relevant earnings of the tax year = £40,000

To obtain tax relief for £40,000 in 2016/17, Tom would need to have paid £32,000 (80% × £40,000) into the pension scheme before 6 April 2017.

Basic rate tax relief (20%) is given at source and HMRC will give the pension scheme £8,000 (£40,000 × 20%).

Higher rate relief is given by extending Tom's basic rate band in his income tax computation by £40,000 from £32,000 to £72,000.

(c) **Norman – Additional contributions payable by employee**

Norman is in pensionable employment. He therefore has a number of choices if he wants to make an additional contribution to a registered pension scheme.

He can either contribute an additional voluntary contribution (AVC) into the company scheme run by his employer, or make a free standing AVC into a scheme run by an insurance company.

The maximum additional amount that Norman can contribute into a registered pension plan is:

	£
100% × Employment income (W)	32,048
Less: Amount already contributing (6% × £20,000)	(1,200)
Maximum additional contributions	30,848

Working: Employment income

Car and fuel benefit:

CO_2 emission 139 g/km, available all year

Appropriate % = (135 – 95) ÷ 5 + 16% (petrol car) = 24%

Benefits:	Car	Fuel
	£	£
(£30,000 × 24%)	7,200	
(£22,200 × 24%)		5,328
Less: Contribution from Norman (£40 × 12) (Note)	(480)	
	6,720	5,328

Employment income = (£20,000 + £6,720 + £5,328) = £32,048

Note: No deduction from the fuel benefit for partial contributions towards the cost of the fuel provided for private use.

Clive Scott

Answer 2 – Chapter 4

(a) (i) **Maximum pension contributions – 2016/17**

If Clive sets up a personal pension scheme in 2016/17 the maximum gross pension contributions that Clive can make into the scheme are restricted to the higher of:

- £3,600, or
- 100% of his earned income = £15,000.

Note that the dividend income does not count as earnings and is not relevant in determining the level of pension contribution.

To obtain relief in the current 2016/17 tax year the contributions need to be paid by 5 April 2017.

This will mean that Clive can make a maximum gross contribution of £15,000 by 5 April 2017.

(ii) **Method of obtaining tax relief**

Tax relief for contributions into pension schemes is given as follows.

- Basic rate tax relief is given at source. Assuming the maximum contribution possible is paid, Clive will actually pay £12,000 (£15,000 × 80%) to the pension provider.
- Higher rate tax relief is given by extending his basic rate and higher rate tax bands by £15,000 (i.e. the gross amount of the pension contribution paid).

The effect of making such contributions on his 2016/17 income tax liability will be a £15,000 reduction in his dividend income liable to the higher 32.5% tax rate applicable to dividend income. As a result his income tax liability will be reduced by £3,750 (W).

(iii) **Tax implications of the company pension contributions**

It is possible to set up the scheme such that Scott Engineering Limited pays all or some of the pension contributions. If this is the case the total combined contributions that may be paid by the employee and his employer on which tax relief can be obtained is restricted to the annual allowance of £40,000 for 2016/17. The annual allowance may not be brought forward from the previous three tax years, 2013/14 to 2015/16, as Clive was not a member of a registered pension scheme.

If Scott Engineering Limited pays any contributions, these will be paid gross and the company will obtain corporation tax relief on the contributions at its marginal tax rate.

Providing the personal scheme is a registered scheme, these contributions will not be treated as employee benefits or be liable to class 1 NICs.

If total contributions in excess of the annual allowance are made, Clive will be liable to income tax at his marginal rate on the excess.

Whether direct contributions by Scott Engineering Limited are more beneficial than personal contributions by Clive will depend upon several factors, such as:

(1) whether Clive's income is reduced to reflect the contributions paid by the company

(2) if income is so reduced whether this is the dividend income (for which no corporation tax deduction is available) or his salary (which already obtains corporation tax relief and is liable to employer's class 1 NIC), and

(3) the marginal tax rates of Clive and the company.

(b) **Alternative registered pension arrangements**

As Clive is an employee of Scott Engineering Limited the principal alternative pension arrangement that could be made would be for the company to set up an occupational pension scheme.

This is usually set up in the form of an irrevocable trust to ensure that the scheme assets are held independently of the employer.

The amount of tax relief that can be obtained is the same under either a personal pension scheme or an occupational scheme. However the method of obtaining the tax relief is different.

The method of relief for such schemes is as follows:

– employee contributions are deducted from employment income and tax relief is given at both the basic and higher rates via the PAYE system.

– employer contributions are tax deductible for corporation tax purposes and are not regarded as employee benefits nor are they liable to class 1 NICs.

Working: Income tax relief via the income tax computation

	£
Employment income	15,000
UK dividends received	51,500
Total income	66,500
Less: PA	(11,000)
Taxable income	55,500

Analysis of income:

Dividends	**Savings**	**Non-savings income**
£51,500	£0	(£55,500 – £51,500) = £4,000

Income tax before pension contribution

£		£
4,000 × 20% (Non-savings income)		800
5,000 × 0% (dividends NRB)		0
23,000 × 7.5% (dividends)		1,725
32,000		
23,500 × 32.5% (dividends)		7,637
55,500		
Income tax liability		10,162

Income tax after pension contribution

£		£
4,000 × 20% (Non-savings income)		800
5,000 × 0% (dividends NRB)		0
38,000 × 7.5% (dividends)		2,850
47,000 (Extended basic rate band) (W)		
8,500 × 32.5% (dividends)		2,762
55,500		
Income tax liability		6,412
Income tax reduction = (£10,162 – £6,412)		3,750

Alternative calculation: £15,000 × (32.5% – 7.5%) = £3,750

Working: Extended basic rate band

	£
Basic rate band	32,000
Plus: Gross PPCs	15,000
	47,000

Ethel Jones

Answer 1 – Chapter 5

(a) **Income tax computation – 2016/17**

	£	£
Employment income		14,500
Loan stock interest		
(£100,000 × 10% × ½) (Note)	5,000	
Interest on cash deposits	5,250	
		10,250
UK dividends received (10,000 × 27.8p)		2,780
Total income		27,530
Less: PA		(11,000)
Taxable income		16,530

Analysis of income:

Dividends	**Savings**	**Non-savings income**
£2,780	£10,250	(£16,530 – £2,780 – £10,250) = £3,500

Income tax:

£		£
3,500	× 20% (non-savings income)	700
1,500	× 0% (savings)	0
5,000		
1,000	× 0% (savings NRB)	0
7,750	× 20% (savings)	1,550
2,780	× 0% (dividends NRB)	0
16,530		
Income tax liability		2,250

Note: In the absence of a declaration of beneficial entitlement, the interest income on the Chaffinch plc loan stock will be shared equally between Ethel and George.

(b) **Declaration of beneficial interest**

The effect of making a declaration of beneficial interest in respect of the loan stock in Chaffinch plc would be that Ethel would only be taxed upon her 25% beneficial entitlement with her husband George being taxed on the remaining 75%.

This would reduce Ethel's taxable income from this source to £2,500 and hence her total income for 2016/17 would reduce to £25,030 (£27,530 – £2,500). This would save tax at 20% on £2,500.

However, the effect for George would also need to be considered. If he is a higher rate or additional rate taxpayer the effect of the declaration would increase his income tax payable by 40% or 45% of the gross income transferred, which would negate the benefit of lower tax payable by Ethel.

Julie

Answer 1 – Chapter 6

Capital gains tax – 2016/17

	£
Piano (W1)	3,750
Car (Exempt asset)	0
Property (W2)	322,225
Business asset (W3)	33,000
Less: Capital loss b/f	(3,250)
Total net chargeable gains	355,725
Less: AEA	(11,100)
Taxable gains	344,625
Capital gains tax liability (£344,625 × 20%)	68,925

Note: Capital losses b/f are offset against the capital gains in 2016/17

Net cash received from sale of assets

Proceeds received:	£
Piano	12,500
Car	8,700
Property (£485,000 – £4,075)	480,925
Business asset	37,000
Less: CGT payable	(68,925)
Net cash received	470,200

Workings

(W1) **Piano**

	£
Sale proceeds	12,500
Less: Cost	(8,750)
Chargeable gain	3,750

(W2) **Property**

	£
Sale proceeds	485,000
Less: Costs of sale	(4,075)
Net sale proceeds	480,925
Less: Cost	(156,000)
Costs of acquisition	(2,700)
Chargeable gain	322,225

(W3) **Business asset**

	£
Sale proceeds	37,000
Less: Cost	(4,000)
Chargeable gain	33,000

The asset does not qualify for entrepreneurs' relief as it is not part of the sale of the whole of the business.

Dangle

Answer 1 – Chapter 7

(a) **Capital gains tax – 2016/17**

	£
Greyhound (W1)	0
Lease (W3)	87,954
Painting (W5)	41,000
Ring (exempt)(W6)	0
Land (W7)	96,667
Less: Capital loss (W2)	(1,500)
Total chargeable gains	224,121
Less: AEA	(11,100)
Taxable gains	213,021

	£	£
Basic rate (W9)	13,000 × 10%	1,300
Higher rate	200,021 × 20%	40,004
	213,021	
Capital gains tax liability		41,304
Due date for payment		31 January 2018

Workings

(W1) **Greyhound**

A greyhound is a wasting chattel which is exempt from CGT.

(W2) **Unquoted shares**

	£
Proceeds	6,000
Less: Probate value	(7,500)
Allowable loss	(1,500)

(W3) **Short lease**

	£
Proceeds	275,000
Less: Deemed cost (W4)	(187,046)
Chargeable gain	87,954

Entrepreneurs' relief is not available as this is not a disposal of the entire business.

(W4) **Deemed lease cost**

Years left to run at acquisition	39 years	12.02.09
Years left to run at disposal	31 years 4 months	19.10.16

The percentage for 31 years 4 months is

88.371 + ((89.354 – 88.371) × 4/12) = 88.699

The allowable cost to deduct in the computation is therefore deemed to be:

(% for life of the lease left on disposal date ÷ % for life of the lease left on acquisition date) × Cost

= (88.699 (% for 31 years 4 months) ÷ 94.842 (% for 39 years)) × £200,000
= £187,046

(W5) **Painting**

	£
Proceeds	50,000
Less: Cost	(9,000)
Chargeable gain	41,000

(W6) **Antique ring**

The antique ring is a chattel. As it was sold for less than £6,000, and cost less than £6,000, the gain is exempt.

(W7) **Remaining interest in land**

	£
Proceeds	205,000
Less: Deemed cost (W8)	(108,333)
Chargeable gain	96,667

(W8) **Deemed cost of part disposal**

Disposal in June 2014 – Deemed cost Cost (4 acres of 24 acres) = £130,000 × (£30,000/£180,000)	£21,667
Disposal on 28 March 2017 – Deemed cost (£130,000 – £21,667)	£108,333

(W9) **Remaining basic rate band**

	£	£
Basic rate band		32,000
Add: Gross PPCs (£4,000 × 100/80)		5,000
Extended basic rate band		37,000
Employment income	35,000	
Less: PA	(11,000)	
Taxable income		(24,000)
Remaining basic rate band for CGT purposes		13,000

(b) **Effect of delaying the sale of the plot of land**

If the sale of the land took place on 6 April 2017, the gain of £96,667 would not be taxed until 2017/18.

This would save CGT, as a further AEA would be available to match against this gain, and part of the gain would now fall into Dangle's remaining basic rate band and be taxed at 10% instead of 20%.

The tax saved would be as follows:

	£
Saving from AEA (£11,100 × 20%)	2,220
Part of gain now in BR band (£13,000 × (20% – 10%))	1,300
Total tax saved by delaying sale	3,520

In addition, the tax payable on the gain on disposal of land would not be due until 31 January 2019, which would represent a cash flow benefit to Dangle.

Emma

Answer 1 – Chapter 8

Capital gains tax – 2016/17

	£
Apple plc shares (W1)	74,000
Willow Ltd shares (W2)	49,700
NS certificates (Exempt)	0
Bridge plc takeover (W3)	26,950
Total chargeable gains	150,650
Less: AEA	(11,100)
Taxable gains	139,550
Capital gains tax liability (£139,550 × 20%)	27,910

Workings

(W1) **Shares in Apple plc**

Share pool		Number	Cost
			£
March 2013:	Purchase	400	10,000
January 2014:	Rights issue		
	1:4 @ £30 per share	100	3,000
December 2015:	Purchase	200	8,000
January 2016:	Bonus issue 1:2	350	0
		1,050	21,000
Disposal		(1,050)	(21,000)
Balance to c/f		0	0

	£
Disposal proceeds	95,000
Less: Cost	(21,000)
Chargeable gain	74,000

(W2) **Willow Ltd**

	£
Proceeds	50,000
Less: Cost (see below)	(300)
Chargeable gain	49,700

Share Pool	Number	Cost
		£
February 1993: Purchase	10	1,000
Disposal	(3)	(300)
Balance c/f	7	700

(W3) **Bridge plc takeover**

For 100 Bridge plc shares:	January 2017
	£
Loan notes in Poker plc (100 × £50)	5,000
Cash (100 × £350)	35,000
Consideration received	40,000

The loan notes are qualifying corporate bonds (QCBs).

Where a QCB is received in exchange for shares, the gain attributable to these shares is computed as if the bond were cash and this gain is frozen until the corporate bond is disposed of at a later date.

The only gain chargeable in 2016/17 is the gain attributable to the cash received.

The cash consideration is not small and therefore the part disposal rules apply.

Allocation of cost:		£
Loan notes	(£9,200 × 5/40)	1,150
Cash consideration	(£9,200 × 35/40)	8,050
		9,200

Gain re cash consideration:	
	£
Cash proceeds	35,000
Less: Deemed cost (above)	(8,050)
Chargeable gain	26,950

Mr Harry and Mr Leonard

Answer 1 – Chapter 9

(a) **Capital gains tax – 2016/17**

With gift relief claim	£
X Ltd shares (W1)	42,143
House (W3)	0
Total chargeable gains	42,143
Less: AEA	(11,100)
Taxable gains qualifying for ER	31,043
Capital gains tax (£31,043 × 10%)	3,104

Without gift relief claim	£
X Ltd shares (W1)	295,000
House (W3)	0
Total chargeable gains	295,000
Less: AEA	(11,100)
Taxable gains qualifying for ER	283,900
Capital gains tax (£283,900 × 10%)	28,390

The decision to claim gift relief depends on the intention of Mr Harry's daughter in the future.

On the subsequent disposal of the shares by the daughter she will be entitled to ER provided she satisfies the conditions. Mr Harry and his daughter will therefore benefit from both gift relief and ER.

If, however, she does not intend to own the shares for at least 12 months and/or not work for the company, ER will not be available to her. In this case it would be beneficial for Mr Harry and his daughter not to claim gift relief on the original gift as (assuming the capital gains tax rates remain unchanged) she will be liable to tax at 20% on the gain, but Mr Harry would only be liable at a rate of 10% on the gain arising now.

(b) **Notes for meeting with Mr Leonard**

- Rollover relief (ROR) may be available to Mr Leonard.
- This means that he can make a claim to defer the gain on the building he sold to X Ltd in April 2016, against the base cost of the new commercial property.
- As a result, he will
  - obtain a repayment of the CGT paid in respect of the building, and
  - defer the gain until the new commercial property is sold.
- However, conditions must be satisfied to obtain the relief.
- Mr Leonard has disposed of a freehold property which is a qualifying business asset (QBA) for ROR purposes.
- The replacement commercial building can be either freehold or leasehold, but must be occupied and used for trading purposes.
- The replacement property must be acquired before 1 April 2019 (i.e. within the four year qualifying period beginning one year before, and ending three years after the date of sale of the old asset).
- A claim needs to be made for ROR by the later of 5 April 2020 (i.e. within 4 years from the end of the tax year in which the disposal occurred (2015/16 disposal), or 4 years from the end of the tax year in which the replacement is acquired).
- If all of the proceeds from the sale of the old asset are reinvested, full ROR is available (i.e. all of the gain is deferred).

However, where there is partial reinvestment of the proceeds only part of the gain may be deferred.

- Mr Leonard could plan his reinvestment to ensure that a ROR claim will leave a gain to be taxed which utilises his capital losses and the AEA.
- If the new commercial property is a leasehold interest in land and buildings with 60 years or less to run on the lease, the gain will be taxable ten years after the date of acquisition of the leasehold property or earlier if the replacement building is sold or ceases to be used in the trade before then.
- Adjustments need to be made to the calculation of the amount of deferral relief available if there is an element of non-business use.

- ER would be available on any remaining gain on the sale of the building to X Ltd in 2015/16. This is because Mr Leonard sold the building when he ceased trading, and as long as the building was sold within three years of cessation the relief is available. However, if Mr Leonard had carried on trading there would be no ER as the disposal was the sale of a single asset.

Workings

(W1) **X Ltd shares**

	£
Market value	365,000
Less: Cost	(70,000)
Capital gain before reliefs	295,000
Less: Gift relief (W2)	(252,857)
Gain qualifying for ER	42,143

ER is available as Mr Harry is disposing of a shareholding in a personal trading company. The relief is not restricted for investments in the company accounts.

If Mr Harry and his daughter do not claim gift relief then Mr Harry will have the following capital gain:

	£
Capital gain qualifying for ER	295,000

(W2) **Gift relief**

Proportion of gain eligible for gift relief

= (MV of total CBA/MV of total CA) × £295,000

= [£480,000/(£480,000 + £80,000)] × £295,000 = £252,857

(W3) **Principal private residence**

The sale of the home is fully covered by the PPR relief.

Although Mr Harry did not live in the house for one year, any period or periods which together do not total more than three years is exempt under the PPR rules provided the property was owner occupied at some time both before and after the period of absence.

Bangle

Answer 2 – Chapter 9

(a) (i) **Chargeable gain on the disposal of the business**

	£	Gains/(losses) £
Freehold premises:		
Deemed proceeds (MV)	165,000	
Less: Cost	(65,000)	
Chargeable gain		100,000
Shop fittings – exempt		0
Shop front and canopy:		
Deemed proceeds (MV)	8,000	
Less: Cost	(13,165)	
Allowable loss		(5,165)
Net chargeable gains before reliefs		94,835
Less: Incorporation relief		(94,835)
Chargeable gain – 2016/17		0

Note 1: As all of the consideration is received in the form of shares, all of the net gains can be deferred with incorporation relief.

Note 2: The net chargeable gains are deferred. ER is postponed until the sale of the shares providing the conditions are met when the shares are sold.

Base cost of shares received by Barbara Bangle

	£
Market value of 200,000 shares allotted	200,000
Less: Incorporation relief	(94,835)
Base cost	105,165

(ii) **Sale of shares in Bangle Ltd**

Share pool	Number	Cost
		£
Shares acquired	200,000	105,165
Disposal	(80,000)	(42,066)
Balance carried forward	120,000	63,099

	£
Sale proceeds	90,000
Less: Cost (see above)	(42,066)
Chargeable gain	47,934
Less: AEA	(11,100)
Taxable gain	36,834
Capital gains tax (£36,834 × 20%)	7,367

As the shares have been held for less than 12 months, there is no ER available.

(iii) **Chargeable gain on disposal of the business**

Net chargeable gains before reliefs (as before)	£94,835

Base cost of shares received by Barbara Bangle

Market value of 200,000 shares allotted = base cost	£200,000

Sale of shares in Bangle Ltd

Share pool	Number	Cost
		£
Shares acquired	200,000	200,000
Disposal	(80,000)	(80,000)
Balance carried forward	120,000	120,000

	£
Sale proceeds	90,000
Less: Cost (see above)	(80,000)
Chargeable gain	10,000

As the shares have been held for less than 12 months, there is no ER available.

Capital gains tax payable – 2016/17

	£	£
Not qualifying for ER		
Sales of Bangle Ltd shares	10,000	
Gains qualifying ER		
Incorporation of Bangle Ltd (Note 1)		94,835
Less: AEA (Note 2)	(10,000)	(1,100)
Taxable gains	0	93,735
Capital gains tax:		
Qualifying gains (£93,735 × 10%)		9,373
Non-qualifying gains (£Nil × 20%)		0
		9,373

Tax increase if incorporation relief is disapplied:	
(£7,367 (per (a)(ii)) less £9,373 (above))	£2,006

Notes:

(1) As Barbara owned her business for more than 12 months, the gain qualifies for ER. Had any of the gain related to goodwill, that part of the gain would not qualify for ER as Bangle Ltd will be a close company (Chapter 26).

(2) The AEA is set against gains not qualifying for ER first.

(3) After the gains qualifying for ER have been taxed at 10%, any remaining qualifying gains are taxed at the appropriate rate depending on the individual's taxable income.

(b) **Chargeable gain on disposal of the business**

	£
Net chargeable gains before reliefs (as before)	94,835
Less: Incorporation relief	
– limited to proportion of consideration received in the form of shares: (£94,835 × £150,000/£200,000)	(71,126)
Gain qualifying for ER	23,709

Base cost of shares received by Barbara Bangle

	£
Market value of 150,000 shares allotted	150,000
Less: Incorporation relief	(71,126)
Base cost	78,874

Sale of shares in Bangle Ltd

Share pool	Number	Cost £
Shares acquired	150,000	78,874
Disposal	(80,000)	(42,066)
Balance c/f	70,000	36,808

	£
Market value (as sale at under-value to connected person)	90,000
Less: Cost	(42,066)
	47,934
Less: Gift relief (balancing figure)	(9,000)
Chargeable gain (W) not qualifying for ER	38,934

Working: Sale of shares

If there is a sale at undervaluation, a gain arises at the time if the actual consideration received is in excess of the original cost.

	£
Actual consideration	81,000
Less: Original cost	(42,066)
Gain after gift relief	38,934

(c) **Alternative method of deferring gains on incorporation**

Barbara can defer gains on incorporation by using the gift relief provisions instead of incorporation relief.

She can do so by either:

– ensuring she does not satisfy the conditions for incorporation relief, or

– she can satisfy the conditions and elect to disapply incorporation relief.

If the gift relief route is taken, Barbara can gift the individual business assets to the company.

The gain on the freehold premises could be deferred against the market value of the freehold premises at acquisition. The gain on the shop-fitting is exempt. There is an allowable loss on the shop front and canopy which would be set against other gains.

The property could be retained by Barbara personally, to avoid double charges to CGT in the future, but should not be rented to the company as this will deny ER on a future disposal of the property if sold as part of the disposal of the company shares.

Mr and Mrs Posh

Answer 1 – Chapter 10

Mr Posh will be better off if he pays tax on the arising basis:

	Arising basis	Remittance basis
	£	£
Income	39,500	15,640
Less: PA	(11,000)	0
Taxable income	28,500	15,640
Income tax		
£28,500/£15,640 × 20%	5,700	3,128
Plus: RBC		30,000
Income tax liability	5,700	33,128

Mrs Posh will be better off if she claims the remittance basis and pays tax on £108,900 as well as paying the £30,000 charge:

	Arising basis	Remittance basis
	£	£
Income	423,000	108,900
Less: PA (Note)	0	0
Taxable income	423,000	108,900

Income tax:

£	£		£	£
32,000	32,000	× 20%	6,400	6,400
118,000	76,900	× 40%	47,200	30,760
273,000	–	× 45%	122,850	
423,000	108,900			
Plus: RBC				30,000
Income tax liability			176,450	67,160

Note: Under the arising basis the PA is fully withdrawn as total income exceeds £100,000 by more than double the personal allowance.

Darwin

Answer 2 – Chapter 10

Income tax computation – 2016/17

	£	£
Employment income (W1)		54,512
Bank interest	3,550	
Foreign interest (gross)	1,265	
		4,815
Foreign property income (gross)		690
Total income		60,017
Less: PA		(11,000)
Taxable income		49,017

Analysis of income:

Dividends	**Savings**	**Non-savings income**
£Nil	£4,815	(£49,017 – £4,815) = £44,202

£			£
44,202	× 20%	(Non-savings income) (W3)	8,840
44,202			
402	× 0%	(savings NRB)	0
44,300			
98	× 0%	(savings NRB) (Note)	0
4,315	× 40%	(savings)	1,726
49,017			
			10,566
Less: Double taxation relief (W4) (£506 + £104)			(610)
Income tax liability			9,956
Less: Tax credits			
PAYE			(8,702)
Income tax payable			1,254

Note: As Darwin is a higher rate taxpayer, his savings nil rate band is £500. This uses part of his extended basic rate band.

Workings

(W1) **Employment income**

	£
Salary	34,700
Company car benefit (W2)	11,520
Fuel benefit (W2)	7,992
Goods (Cost to employer)	300
Employment income	54,512

(W2) **Car and fuel benefit**

CO_2 emission 183 g/km, available all year

Appropriate percentage:

(180 – 95) ÷ 5 = 17% + 19% (diesel car) = 36%

Car benefit = 36% × £32,000	£11,520
Fuel benefit = 36% × £22,200	£7,992

(W3) **Extension of basic rate band**

	£
Basic rate band threshold	32,000
Add: Personal pension premium (£9,840 × 100/80)	12,300
Extended basic rate band threshold	44,300

(W4) **Double taxation relief**

DTR on Erewhon income

The Erewhon income has suffered the higher rate of overseas tax and therefore relief is calculated in respect of this source of income first. The amount of credit cannot exceed the UK tax attributable.

DTR = lower of

(a) UK tax	(£1,265 × 40%)	= £506
(b) Overseas tax	(£1,265 × 45%)	= £569

DTR on Narnian income

The relief for overseas tax is computed on a source by source basis, therefore the relief for Narnian tax must be separately computed, treating it as the next slice of income.

DTR = lower of

		£
(a) UK tax:		
Narnian income in BR band	£690 × 20%	138
Savings income in BR band after Narnian income omitted	(£690 – £402) = £288 × (40% – 20%)	58
		196
(b) Overseas tax	(£690 × 15%)	104

Peter Singer

Answer 3 – Chapter 10

(a) **Tax status of Peter**

Residence (R)

In 2016/17 Peter is automatically UK resident as he will be working in the UK for at least 365 days continuously, some of which falls into this tax year.

He will also be:

– UK resident in the following year, 2017/18

– but has not been UK resident prior to arriving in the UK, and

– arrives in the UK part way through the current tax year.

Accordingly the split year basis applies in 2016/17, and the UK part starts the day he starts work in the UK (13 January 2017).

In 2017/18 Peter will be automatically UK resident as he will be in the UK for more than 183 days in the tax year.

Domicile

Domicile is the place a person regards as their permanent home. As Peter was born and lived in Portugal until his move to England this will be his domicile of origin.

It appears that Peter intends to return there, and so will retain his Portuguese domicile for UK tax purposes.

Effect on tax computation

All Peter's UK income will be taxable. With regard to his overseas income the amount taxable in the UK will depend on his tax status.

His investment income and overseas rent will be taxable on an arising basis if he acquired UK domicile as well.

However, if, as appears likely here, he remains non-UK domiciled, he can elect to be taxed on the remittance basis for his overseas income as his unremitted income is in excess of £2,000 (unremitted dividends of £650, bank interest of £1,600 and rental income of £28,000 paid into his Portuguese bank account).

The election will result in Peter only being assessed on overseas investment income remitted to the UK, but with the loss of his personal allowance.

Note that he will not be subject to the £30,000 remittance basis charge as he has not been resident in the UK for more than 7 years.

Basis of taxation

Where overseas income is taxed on a remittance basis, regardless of the source of income, it is treated as 'non-savings income' for the purposes of identifying how much UK tax is payable and for calculating the DTR available.

(b) **Income tax computation – 2017/18**

Peter will elect to be taxed on the remittance basis as the saving from omitting the unremitted foreign income (£30,250) outweighs the loss of the personal allowance (£11,000).

	£
Salary – UK	44,000
Benefits (W1)	37,834
Employment income	81,834
Rental income – overseas (none remitted)	0
UK dividends	4,000
UK bank interest	1,100
Overseas dividends (amount remitted)	2,500
Overseas bank interest (amount remitted)	1,300
Total income	90,734
Less: PA (none as remittance basis claimed)	(0)
Taxable income	90,734

Analysis of income:	£
Savings income (UK)	1,100
Savings income (overseas)	1,300
Dividends (UK)	4,000
Dividends (overseas)	2,500
Non-savings income	81,834

Income tax	£
£32,000 × 20% (non-savings income)	6,400
£49,834 × 40% (non-savings income)	19,934
£500 × 0% (UK savings – NRB)	0
£600 × 40% (UK savings)	240
£1,300 × 40% (overseas savings)	520
£4,000 × 0% (UK dividend income – NRB)	0
£2,500 × 40% (overseas dividends remitted)	1,000
	28,094
Plus: Remittance basis charge (not applicable)	0
	28,094
Less: DTR (£2,500 + £1,300 × 10%) (W2)	(380)
Income tax liability	27,714

Workings

(W1) **Benefits**

		£
Company car		
Appropriate percentage = (165 – 95) × 1/5 + 16 = 30%		
Car benefit (£28,000 × 30%)		8,400
Fuel benefit (£22,200 × 30%)		6,660
Medical insurance		1,874
Living accommodation		
Rateable value	4,500	
Expensive accommodation charge (£187,000 – £75,000) × 3%	3,360	
Running costs	5,700	
Use of furniture (£49,000 × 20%)	9,800	
	23,360	
Less: Rent paid (£1,300 × 12)	(15,600)	
		7,760
School costs (£1,500 × 7)		10,500
Mobile phone – exempt		0
Health club (£220 × 12)		2,640
Total benefits		37,834

(W2) **DTR**

For the purposes of DTR each source of overseas income must be dealt with separately.

The tax on the overseas income is then compared with the UK tax on that source, and relief given for the lower of the two.

In this example both sources of income had 10% overseas tax deducted at source, and the UK rate is clearly higher, therefore the computation has taken the shortcut of just deducting DTR as the 10% overseas tax suffered.

Where the UK tax rate is clearly in excess of the overseas tax rate, an approach like this would be acceptable in the exam providing the answer is suitably annotated to explain the approach.

Roberta

Answer 4 – Chapter 10

(a) **Roberta's tax status**

2016/17

In 2016/17, Roberta is automatically UK resident as she is in the UK for at least 183 days in the tax year.

She was also:

– UK resident in the previous year 2015/16

– is not UK resident in 2017/18 (see below)

– leaves part way through the year because she begins working abroad on a full-time contract, and

– does not return to the UK for more than the permitted number of days in the UK after departure.

Accordingly the split year basis will apply and the overseas part starts the date she starts her overseas work (2 January 2017).

2017/18 to 2019/20 inclusive

Roberta will be automatically non-UK resident as she does not intend to visit the UK at all in the tax year.

2020/21

In 2020/21, Roberta is automatically UK resident as she is in the UK for at least 183 days in the tax year.

She was also:

- not UK resident in the previous year 2019/20
- arrives in the UK part way through the year because she ceases to work abroad on a full-time contract
- returns to the UK, and
- is resident in the following year.

Accordingly the split year basis will apply and the UK part starts the date she ceases to work overseas (31 May 2020).

(b) **Roberta's assessment to chargeable gains**

Temporary non-UK residence starts from the start of the overseas part in the split year of departure = 2 January 2017

Temporary non-UK residence ends from the start of the UK part in the split year of return
= 31 May 2020

Roberta's period of temporary non-UK residence is therefore less than 5 years.

Therefore the gains are assessed as follows:

2016/17 = Split year

- taxable on worldwide gains
- on disposals before the date of departure

2017/18 to 2019/20 inclusive = abroad

- not taxable on any gains at the time (except on UK residential property)

2020/21 = Year of return = split year

- on re-entry into the UK within 5 years = taxable on any gains arising whilst abroad relating to assets owned before departure from the UK, and
- gains in that year arising after the return to the UK

Therefore the gains on the disposal in both May 2017 and July 2017 will become chargeable in 2020/21 when Roberta returns to the UK.

Disposals:	May 2017		July 2017
	£		£
Sale proceeds	195,000		26,500
Less: Cost	(76,000)		(54,000)
Chargeable gain/(Allowable loss)	119,000		(27,500)
Net chargeable gains – taxed in 2020/21		91,500	

Gary Genius

Answer 1 – Chapter 12

IHT payable during lifetime

	CLT 4.6.2008		PET 4.3.2012		PET 4.3.2012		CLT 4.6.2014	
		£		£		£		£
Value of estate before gift					(80% shs)	600,000		
Value of estate after gift					(60% shs)	(450,000)		
Transfer of value		376,000		10,000		150,000		100,000
Less: BPR					(100%)	(150,000)		
Less: Marriage exemption				(5,000)				
Less: Annual exemption								
Current year	2008/09	(3,000)	2011/12	(3,000)	2011/12	(0)	2014/15	(3,000)
Previous year	2007/08 b/f	(3,000)	2010/11 b/f	(2,000)	2010/11 b/f	(0)	2013/14 b/f	(3,000)
Chargeable amount	Net	370,000		0		0	Net	94,000
NRB @ date of gift	£						£	
– 2008/09	312,000							
– 2014/15							325,000	
Less: GCTs ‹ 7 years before gift								
(4.6.2001 – 4.6.2008)	(0)							
(4.6.2007 – 4.6.2014)							(384,500)	
(ignore PETs)								
NRB available		(312,000)						(0)
Taxable amount		58,000		0		0		94,000
IHT payable	@ 25%	14,500		0		0	@ 25%	23,500
Paid by		Gary						Gary
Due date of payment		30.4.2009						30.4.2015
Gross chargeable amount c/f	(£370,000 net + £14,500 tax)	384,500		0		0	(£94,000 net + £23,500 tax)	117,500

Notes:

CLT – 4.6.2008 No further IHT is due in respect of the first CLT as Gary has survived the gift by more than 7 years.

CLT – 4.6.2014 Should Gary die before 4 June 2021, additional IHT at death rates of 40% may become payable on the last CLT. Taper relief may be available and the lifetime tax paid is an allowable deduction.

4 March 2012 – Gift to son – explanation

The wedding gift of £10,000 to Jack, being made from one individual to another, will be a PET. There is no IHT payable during Gary's lifetime and providing Gary survives until 4 March 2019 no IHT will arise in relation to this gift.

However, if Gary dies before 4 March 2019, the PET will become chargeable.

As the gift was made in consideration of marriage, a marriage exemption of £5,000 will be available for gifts from a parent to their child. As there is another gift on the same day (see below) Gary's 2011/12 AE may need to be apportioned by reference to the value of the gifts made on the same day. The AE is, however, only used after other exemptions and reliefs.

The gift of shares in GG Ltd made on the same day to Jill is likely to qualify for 100% BPR (see below). It is likely therefore that the entire AE for 2011/12 will be allocated against the wedding gift to the son.

The PET is therefore valued at nil. There will be no IHT payable, even if Gary does not survive 7 years after making the gift.

4 March 2012 – Gift to daughter – explanation

The gift of shares to Jill, being made from one individual to another, will also be a PET. As mentioned above, this gift would have been entitled to a share of the AE. It wasn't necessary to apportion the AE in this case due to the availability of BPR.

The shares will be valued applying the loss to the donor's estate principle. Before the gift Gary owned an 80% holding (see tutorial note) and after the gift Gary owned a 60% holding. The value of the transfer is therefore £150,000 (£600,000 – £450,000).

As the GG Ltd shares are unquoted trading company shares and Gary owned the shares for the minimum qualifying period of two years prior to the gift, BPR at the rate of 100% is likely to be available. Therefore no IHT is payable on this PET at the time of the gift.

In addition, IHT is not payable on the death of Gary within seven years unless, upon Gary's death before 4 March 2019, Jill has ceased to own the shares gifted to her or GG Ltd has ceased to be a qualifying company.

Note: The question says Gary currently (in 2017) owns a 60% holding. At the time of the gift in March 2012, he must therefore have had an 80% holding.

Mary Day

Answer 1 – Chapter 13

Mary's previous chargeable lifetime transfer for £335,000 will have fully utilised her nil rate band of £325,000.

(a) **Holiday cottage**

Where an individual makes a gift of property but reserves a benefit, the special gift with reservation (GWR) rules will apply.

Short holiday visits to the cottage would not be caught by the rules, however six months free use would make the gift a GWR.

The gift of the cottage will be a PET of £100,000, ignoring AEs per question but Mary will still be treated as beneficially entitled to the cottage.

It will therefore be included as part of her estate when she dies, and will be included at its value on the date of death.

This might give rise to a double charge to IHT, since the cottage is a PET and also part of Mary's estate.

Relief for the double charges will be given if this is the case, by only considering the treatment (PET or inclusion in death estate) that gives the higher IHT payable.

Mary could avoid the GWR rules by paying a commercial rent for the use of the cottage.

(b) **Antique clock**

The gift of the clock is in consideration of marriage by a grandparent to a grandchild. It will therefore qualify for a wedding gift exemption of £2,500.

The balance of the gift will be a PET of £7,500 (ignoring AEs per question).

(c) **DEF Ltd shares**

The gift of 20,000 shares in DEF Ltd out of an existing shareholding of 30,000 shares into a discretionary trust will be a CLT.

	£
Value of estate before the gift:	
30,000 shares valued at £16 each	480,000
Value of estate after the gift:	
10,000 shares valued at £10 each	(100,000)
Transfer of value	380,000

BPR is not available because Mary has owned the shares for less than two years. Therefore the chargeable amount of the CLT is £380,000 (ignoring AEs per question).

As Mary is to pay the lifetime IHT liability and there is no nil rate band available, she will have to pay IHT of £95,000 (£380,000 × 25%).

The gross chargeable amount of the transfer is therefore £475,000 (£380,000 + £95,000).

(d) **Agricultural land**

The gift of agricultural land will be a PET with a transfer of value of £280,000.

The increase in the value of David's land is irrelevant.

If the PET becomes chargeable as a result of Mary dying within seven years, APR at the rate of 100% should be available as Mary has owned the land for seven years.

However, APR will only be available on the agricultural value of £160,000.

The relief will only be available if David still owns the land, and it is still agricultural property, at the date of Mary's death.

Jenny Cambeth

Answer 2 – Chapter 13

Jenny Cambeth

(a) (i) IHT payable during lifetime

	CLT 28.11.2007		PET 15.4.2011		CLT 10.3.2012	
		£		£		£
Transfer of value		90,000		155,000		283,000
Less: BPR (100% × 80%) (Note)				(124,000)		
Less: Marriage exemption				(5,000)		
Less: Annual exemption						
Current year	2007/08	(3,000)	2011/12	(3,000)	2011/12	(0)
Previous year	2006/07 b/f	(3,000)	2010/11 b/f	(3,000)	2010/11 b/f	(0)
Chargeable amount	Net	84,000		20,000	Net	283,000
NRB @ date of gift	£				£	
– 2007/08	300,000					
– 2011/12					325,000	
Less: GCTs < 7 years before gift						
(28.11.2000 – 28.11.2007)	(0)					
(10.3.2005 – 10.3.2012)					(84,000)	
(ignore PET)						
NRB available		(300,000)				(241,000)
Taxable amount		0		0		42,000
IHT payable		0		0	@ 25%	10,500
Paid by						Jenny
Due date of payment						30.9.12
Gross chargeable amount	(£84,000 net + £Nil tax)	84,000		20,000	(£283,000 net + £10,500 tax)	293,500

Note: As Shakespeare Ltd owns quoted shares (i.e. excepted assets), BPR is only available on 80% (100% – 20%) of the value of the shares.

IHT payable on death

Date of death: 20 November 2016
7 years before: 20 November 2009

CLT on 28.11.2007 is more than 7 years before death – therefore no IHT payable on death

	PET 15.4.2011		CLT 10.3.2012	
		£		£
Gross chargeable amount b/f (as above)		20,000		293,500
	£		£	
NRB @ date of death – 2016/17	325,000		325,000	
Less: GCTs < 7 years before gift				
(15.4.2004 – 15.4.2011)	(84,000)			
(10.3.2005 – 10.3.2012) (£84,000 + £20,000)			(104,000)	
(include 15.4.2011 PET as it became chargeable)				
NRB available		(241,000)		(221,000)
Taxable amount		0		72,500
IHT payable @ 40%		0		29,000
Less: Taper relief				
(10.3.2012 – 20.11.2016) (4 – 5 years before death)			(40%)	(11,600)
Less: IHT paid in lifetime		(0)		(10,500)
IHT payable on death		0		6,900
Paid by (always the donee)				Trustees
Due date of payment				31.5.2017

IHT on Estate at death – 20 November 2016

	£	£
Main residence		235,000
Less: Mortgage		(40,000)
		195,000
Agricultural land	168,000	
Less: APR (Note 1)	(110,000)	
		58,000
Building society deposits		87,000
Ordinary shares in Banquo plc (W1)		94,800
Life assurance policy		104,000
Gross chargeable estate		538,800
NRB at death	325,000	
GCTs in 7 yrs pre-death (20.11.09 – 20.11.16) (£20,000 + £293,500) (first gift is too old, Include PET as chargeable on death)	(313,500)	
NRB available		(11,500)
Taxable amount		527,300

	£
IHT due on death (£527,300 × 40%)	210,920
Less: QSR	
(£68,000 × £54,000/£360,000 × 60%) (Note 2)	(6,120)
IHT payable on estate	204,800

Note: 1 APR is available since the property is let out for the purposes of agriculture, and has been owned for at least seven years.

2 The appropriate percentage for QSR is 60% as there is 2–3 years between the death of Jenny and her sister.

(ii) **Payment of IHT liability**

The additional IHT respect of the gift made on 10 March 2012 is payable by the trustees of the discretionary trust by 31 May 2017.

The IHT liability of the estate will (in practice) be payable by the executors of Jenny's estate on the earlier of 31 May 2017 or the delivery of their account.

It will be possible to pay IHT of £96,165 (W2) in respect of the main residence and agricultural land in ten equal instalments commencing on 31 May 2017.

Inheritance received by Jenny's children

Jenny's children will inherit £344,000 (W3).

Workings:

(W1) **Value of Banquo plc shares**

Lower of

(1) Quarter up method = 945 + (957 – 945) × ¼ = 948p

(2) Average of marked bargains = (937 + 961) × ½ = 949p

Value of 10,000 £1 ordinary shares
= (10,000 × 948p) = £94,800

(W2) **Payment by instalments**

Average estate rate
= (£204,800/£538,800) × 100 = 38.010%

	£
Main residence	195,000
Agricultural property	58,000
Land and buildings in estate	253,000
Payment by instalments (£253,000 × 38.010%)	96,165

(W3) **Inheritance to children**

	£
Chargeable estate	538,800
Plus: APR	110,000
Value of assets in estate	648,800
Less: Specific gift to brother	(100,000)
IHT payable on the estate (Note)	(204,800)
Estate value to be shared between the children	344,000

(b) **Variation of the terms of Jenny's will**

Conditions to be met

Jenny's will can be varied by a deed of variation within two years of the date of her death.

The deed must be in writing, and be signed by Duncan, the children, and Jenny's brother (i.e. those who benefit from the original will and the revised variations).

It must include a declaration that the will should be treated as being effective for IHT purposes.

The children could not enter into the deed of variation if they were still minors.

Proposed plan

Under the revised terms of Jenny's will, the entire estate is left to Duncan. This will be an exempt transfer, and so the IHT liability of £204,800 will no longer be payable.

The gifts from Duncan to the children and Jenny's brother will be PETs, and these will be completely exempt if Duncan lives for seven years after making the gifts.

Should the PETs become chargeable, taper relief will be available after three years.

Duncan's annual exemptions of £3,000 for 2015/16 to 2018/19 may also be available.

Even if Duncan dies within three years of the gift, the IHT liability should not be greater than £204,800 (subject to APR being available), and the IHT liability will be postponed until six months after the end of the month of his death. As a result tax savings will be achieved.

The transfer to Duncan will mean that £11,500 of NRB will not be utilised against Jenny's death estate, which is 3.538%.

This unused proportion can be used on Duncan's death estate, in addition to his own NRB available, on his subsequent death.

Paul

Answer 3 – Chapter 13

(a) IHT liabilities if Paul dies on 31 December 2016

IHT payable during lifetime

		CLT 1.11.2007		PET 1.10.2012		PET 1.11.2012
		£		£		£
Transfer of value		203,000		150,000		250,000
Less: BPR (100%)						(250,000)
Less: Marriage exemption				(5,000)		
Less: Annual exemption						
Current year	2007/08	(3,000)	2012/13	(3,000)	2012/13	(0)
Previous year	2006/07 b/f	(3,000)	2011/12 b/f	(3,000)	2011/12 b/f	(0)
Chargeable amount	Gross	197,000		139,000		0
NRB @ date of gift	£					
– 2007/08	300,000					
Less: GCTs ‹ 7 years before gift (1.11.2000 – 1.11.2007)	(0)					
NRB available		(300,000)				
Taxable amount		0		0		0
IHT payable		0		0		0
Gross chargeable amount	(£197,000 net + £Nil tax)	197,000		139,000		0

IHT payable on death

Date of death: 31 December 2016
7 years before: 31 December 2009

CLT on 1.11.2007 is more than 7 years before death – therefore no IHT payable on death

		PET 1.10.2012		PET 1.11.2012
	£	£		£
Gross chargeable amount b/f (as above)		139,000	(Note)	0
NRB @ date of death – 2016/17	325,000			
Less: GCTs < 7 years before gift (1.10.2005 – 1.10.2012)	(197,000)			
NRB available		(128,000)		
Taxable amount		11,000		0
IHT payable @ 40%		4,400		0
Less: Taper relief (1.10.2012 – 31.12.2016) (4 – 5 years before death)	(40%)	(1,760)		
Less: IHT paid in lifetime		(0)		
IHT payable on death		2,640		0
Paid by (always the donee)		Son		
Due date of payment		30.6.2017		

Note: The business is still owned by his son at the date of Paul's death, therefore BPR is still available on the death calculation. If the son had disposed of the business before his father's death, the PET would have become chargeable and BPR would not be available.
The taxable amount would therefore be £250,000.

Estate at death

	£	£
Value of estate		645,000
Less: BPR (£65,000 × 100%)		(65,000)
Gross chargeable estate		580,000
NRB at death	325,000	
GCTs in 7 yrs pre-death (31.12.09 – 31.12.16) (first gift is too old, but include PET as chargeable on death)	(139,000)	
		(186,000)
Taxable amount		394,000
IHT due on death (£394,000 × 40%)		157,600
Due date		30.6.2017

(b) **Advice relating to changing the terms of Paul's will**

At present, Paul has left all of his estate to his son.

The following tax planning points should be considered:

(1) Paul should leave £325,000 of his estate to his wife. In due course this will utilise her NRB which would otherwise be wasted, and will save IHT of £130,000 (£325,000 × 40%). It would only be transferable to Paul if his wife were to die first.

(2) If Paul left an additional amount to his wife, then she could use her AEs of £3,000 by making gifts to the son or grandchildren.

(3) Paul could leave some property to his grandchildren, and thus miss out a generation.

It would also be possible to put this tax planning into effect after Paul's death by making a deed of variation.

This must be made within two years of the date of death and must be signed by all the beneficiaries affected (probably just Paul's son).

(c) **Implications of selling the business**

If the business was sold before the date of Paul's death, it would no longer qualify for business property relief.

On Paul's death, the gift would become chargeable, with the charge being based on the sale proceeds of £175,000. This is because relief can be claimed for the fall in the value of a lifetime gift.

The IHT liability will be £42,000 (£175,000 × 40% × 60% (after 40% taper relief)). The NRB would have been utilised as Gross chargeable transfers in the previous 7 years amount to £336,000 (£197,000 + £139,000)

Additional IHT of £74,400 (£186,000 × 40%) will also be due on Paul's estate, since none of the NRB would then be available.

(d) (i) **Main advantages in lifetime giving for IHT purposes**

Possible advantages of lifetime giving include:

- Making use of lifetime IHT exemptions in reducing a taxpayer's chargeable estate at death. In particular, gifts between individuals will not become liable to IHT unless the donor dies within seven years of making the gift.
- If the donor does die prematurely there may still be an IHT advantage in lifetime giving because:
  - The value of the asset for calculating any additional IHT arising upon death is fixed at the time the gift is made.
  - Possible availability of taper relief (providing the donor survives at least three years) may help reduce the effective IHT rate.

(ii) **Main factors to consider in choosing assets to gift**

The main factors to consider include:

– Whether or not a significant CGT liability will arise upon making the gift.

Lifetime gifting therefore needs to be balanced against the fact that no CGT liability will arise upon death (which results in the 'tax free' uplift of the chargeable assets included in the deceased's estate).

The availability of CGT reliefs (primarily gift relief for business assets or if there is an immediate charge to IHT) and CGT exemptions (e.g. AEA) is therefore relevant in selecting assets.

– Whether an asset is appreciating in value.

Because any additional IHT arising as a result of death will be based on the (lower) value of the asset at the date of gift it may be advantageous to select assets that are likely to significantly appreciate in value.

– Whether the donor can afford to make the gift.

Whilst lifetime gifting can result in significant IHT savings this should not be at the expense of the taxpayer's ability to live comfortably, particularly in old age.

– The availability of significant IHT reliefs, particularly BPR. There may be little point in selecting an asset that already qualifies for 100% relief.

Henry

Answer 4 – Chapter 13

(a) **Income tax in the year of death**

The basic rule determining the taxation of an individual's taxable income in the tax year of death is that only income due and payable up to the date of death will be included in the deceased's income tax computation.

This will include Henry's retirement pension and annuity income as well as the investment income actually received prior to his death. Apportionments of investment income are not generally required.

However, the following should be noted:

- The accrued income scheme will not apply to the 10% Government stock as the transfer results from Henry's death.
- Interest received on the ISA account is exempt from income tax.

Henry will therefore only be taxed on the following interest:

	Date received
10% Government stock	30 April 2016
Building Society	30 June 2016

Income tax computation: 2016/17 (date of death 5.10.2016)

	£	£
State pension		6,030
Gross annuity		10,300
Building society interest	400	
Government interest (£20,000 × 10% × 6/12)	1,000	
		1,400
UK dividends (100,000 × 10p)		10,000
Total income		27,730
Less: PA		(11,000)
Taxable income		16,730

Analysis of income:

Dividends Savings Non-savings income

£10,000 £1,400 (£16,730 – £10,000 – £1,400) = £5,330

£		£
5,330	× 20% (non-savings income)	1,066
1,000	× 0% (savings NRB)	0
400	× 20% (savings)	80
5,000	× 0% (dividend NRB)	0
5,000	× 7.5% (dividends)	375
16,730		
Income tax liability		1,521
Less: Tax credits		
Annuity (20% × £10,300)		(2,060)
Income tax repayable		(539)

(b) Inheritance tax liabilities

IHT payable during lifetime

	CLT 1.1.2008		CLT 1.1.2011	
		£		£
Transfer of value		231,000		164,000
Less: Annual exemption				
Current year	2007/08	(3,000)	2010/11	(3,000)
Previous year	2006/07 b/f	(3,000)	2009/10 b/f	(3,000)
Chargeable amount	Net	225,000	Net	158,000
	£		£	
NRB @ date of gift				
– 2007/08	300,000			
– 2010/11			325,000	
Less: GCTs < 7 years before gift				
(1.1.2001 – 1.1.2008)	(0)			
(1.1.2004 – 1.1.2011)			(225,000)	
NRB available		(300,000)		(100,000)
Taxable amount		0		58,000
IHT payable		0	(@ 25%)	14,500
Gross chargeable amount c/f	(£225,000 net + £Nil tax)	225,000	(£158,000 net + £14,500 tax)	172,500

IHT payable on death

Date of death: 5 October 2016
7 years before: 5 October 2009

CLT on 1.1.2008 is more than 7 years before death – therefore no IHT payable on death

		CLT 1.1.2011
	£	£
Gross chargeable amount		172,500
NRB @ date of death – 2016/17	325,000	
Less: GCTs < 7 years before gift (1.1.2004 – 1.1.2011)	(225,000)	
NRB available		(100,000)
Taxable amount		72,500
IHT payable @ 40%		29,000
Less: Taper relief (1.1.2011 – 5.10.2016) (5 – 6 years before death)	(60%)	(17,400)
Less: IHT paid in lifetime		(14,500)
IHT payable on death	(Note)	0

Note: Lifetime IHT cannot be repaid, at best the deduction brings the liability on death down to £Nil.

Henry's estate computation

	Workings	£
Shares – Peel plc	(1)	202,000
Government stock	(2)	20,100
Cash (£25,000 + £18,000)		43,000
Income tax refund due (part (a))		539
Accrued interest	(3)	331
Home		450,000
		715,970
Less: Exempt legacy to spouse (balancing figure)		(675,970)
Gross chargeable estate (£20,000 × 2)		40,000
NRB at death	325,000	
GCTs in 7 yrs pre-death (5.10.09 – 5.10.16) (first gift is too old)	(172,500)	
		(152,500)
Taxable amount		0
IHT due on death		0

Workings:

(W1) **Value of Peel plc shares**

Lower of

(1) Quarter up method = 200 + ((208 – 200) × ¼) = 202p
(2) Average of recorded bargains = (201 + 207) × ½ = 204p

Value of 100,000 shares = (100,000 × £2.02) = £202,000

BPR is not available on these shares as they are quoted shares and Henry does not have a controlling interest.

(W2) **Value of Government stock**

Quarter up method = 95 + (97 – 95) × ¼ = 95.5p

	£
20,000 × 95.5p	19,100
Next interest receipt due (20,000 × 10% × 6/12)	1,000
Value of stock	20,100

(W3) **Accrued interest**

Accrued interest arises on the building society account and ISA deposit as follows:

(£304 + £358) × 3/6 = £331

(c) **Action to reduce or defer IHT liabilities**

Henry's will resulted in the balance of the estate above £40,000 being an exempt transfer to his wife. This has left £112,500 (£152,500 – £40,000) of his NRB unused, which is 34.615%.

This unused proportion can be transferred to Sally and utilised against her death estate, in addition to her own available NRB. The executors of Sally's estate must claim the transferable NRB on submission of Sally's IHT return within 2 years of her death.

As Henry's children are already reasonably wealthy, consideration might have been given to transferring the £40,000 directly to Henry's grandchildren. The idea here is to avoid a charge to IHT arising on any transfers that Cecil and Ida may make to their children.

Deed of variation

Providing various conditions are satisfied it is possible to vary a will after the individual's death and make more tax efficient provisions as outlined above by entering into a deed of variation.

The main conditions to be satisfied as follows:

(i) The deed of variation must be in writing.

(ii) It must be signed by all the beneficiaries that are affected.

(iii) It must be executed within two years of the date of death.

(iv) It must not be made for a consideration.

(v) The deed should include a statement that the variation is to be effective for IHT (and/or CGT) purposes.

The effect of making such a variation is that for IHT purposes the deceased's will is treated as rewritten. In this particular case an appropriate deed variation needs to be drafted by 5 October 2018.

Lifetime gifts by Sally

Sally could make lifetime gifts to her children or grandchildren (for the reason outlined above) to reduce the IHT payable on her death.

If she survives seven years, the gifts will be exempt. However, she is in a frail condition and is possibly not likely to live seven years. Nevertheless, if she survives at least three years taper relief will be available to at least partially mitigate any IHT arising on potentially exempt transfers becoming chargeable within seven years of death.

If she does not survive seven years, the PETs will become chargeable, however PETs are valued at the time of the gift and AEs are available. Therefore, the chargeable amount will be less than valuing the assets in Sally's estate (assuming the assets will appreciate in value between the date of the gift and Sally's death). The IHT position would certainly be no worse than if she had not made any lifetime transfers.

Sally should also make use of her IHT exemptions as follows:

– immediate gifts of £6,000 could be made in 2016/17 (to make use of her two AEs) which would potentially save £2,400 (£6,000 × 40%)

– thereafter annual gifts of £3,000 would save £1,200 (£3,000 × 40%) for each tax year that she survives.

Consideration should be given to personal circumstances. She may wish to gift her main asset (i.e. her home) to her children, but still live in it. However, this will give rise to 'gift with reservation of benefit' problems unless she pays full market rent while living in the house.

Substantial lifetime giving and paying full market rent for living in her home may not be desirable as she may wish to retain sufficient income bearing assets to maintain herself during her lifetime.

Thelma

Answer 5 – Chapter 13

(i) **Thelma retains assets until death**

IHT implications

Cash gift – September 2015

The cash gift made to Louise in September 2015 is a PET which will become chargeable if Thelma dies within seven years of making the gift. There are no other lifetime gifts.

If Thelma therefore dies within four years time (i.e. on or before 30 June 2021) IHT will become payable on the PET as follows:

	£	£
Gross chargeable amount (after exemptions per question)		360,000
NRB at death	325,000	
GCTs in 7 yrs pre-gift (Sept 2008 – Sept 2015)	(0)	
		(325,000)
Taxable amount		35,000
		£
IHT due on death (£35,000 × 40%)		14,000
Less: Taper relief (Sept 2015 to June 2021) (5 – 6 years) (60%)		(8,400)
Chargeable (40%)		5,600
Less: IHT paid in lifetime (PET)		(0)
IHT payable on death		5,600

Estate on death – 30 June 2021

	£	£
Residence		600,000
Blackbird plc shares		200,000
Robin plc loan stock – Thelma's share (£100,000 × 25%)		25,000
Cash deposits		160,000
Antique plates		10,000
Other chattels		20,000
		1,015,000
Less: Exempt estate (£600,000 + £20,000)		(620,000)
Gross chargeable estate		395,000
NRB at death	325,000	
GCTs in 7 yrs pre-death (30.6.14 – 30.6.21) (Include PET as chargeable on death)	(360,000)	
		(0)
Taxable amount		395,000
IHT due on death (£395,000 × 40%)		158,000

CGT implications

Death is not a chargeable event for the purposes of CGT. Therefore there is no CGT payable if Thelma retains the assets and gifts them in her will.

The recipients of the assets will receive them at their probate value which will form their base cost for future CGT purposes.

(ii) **Thelma gifts selected assets to Louise now (6 July 2017)**

IHT implications

Cash gift – September 2015

The implications for the PET made in September 2015 are as above with £5,600 of IHT becoming payable as a result of Thelma's expected death in four years' time.

Gifts to Louise on 6 July 2017

The gifts of assets to Louise will be further PETs likely to become chargeable on Thelma's death, with further IHT arising as follows:

	Notes	£	£
Blackbird plc shares	(1)		146,200
Robin plc loan stock	(2)		25,750
Antique plates	(3)		6,333
Cash deposits			145,000
			323,283
Less: AE – 2017/18			(3,000)
– 2016/17 b/f			(3,000)
Gross chargeable amount			317,283
NRB at death		325,000	
GCTs in 7 yrs pre-death (30.6.14 – 30.6.21) (Include PET as chargeable on death)		(360,000)	
			(0)
Taxable amount			317,283
IHT due on death (£317,283 × 40%)			126,913
Less: Taper relief (6.7.17 to 30.6.21) (3 – 4 years) (20%)			(25,383)
Chargeable (80%)			101,530
Less: IHT paid in lifetime (PET)			(0)
IHT payable on death			101,530

Notes:

(1) Blackbird plc shares

Quarter up method = (1,460p + (1,468p – 1,460p) × ¼) = £14.62 per share

Value of 10,000 shares = (10,000 × £14.62) = £146,200

There is no BPR available as the shares are quoted shares and Thelma does not have a controlling interest.

(2) Robin plc loan stock

Quarter up method = (102p + (106p – 102p) × ¼)
= 103p per share

Value of loan stock = (£100,000 × £1.03 × 25%) = £25,750

(3) Value of the plates

Valued under related party valuation rules, taking account of the fact that Thelma and Gordon own five plates between them (the daughter Louise's plate does not count as related property).

Value of 3 plates/Value of 3 + 2 plates
= [£3,800/(£3,800 + £2,200)] × £10,000 = £6,333

Estate on death

When Thelma dies the transfers of the house and personal chattels to Gordon will be exempt under the inter-spouse provisions.

Therefore there is no IHT payable on the estate at death.

CGT implications

Gift of cash and loan stock

The gifts of cash deposits and loan stock (a qualifying corporate bond) are exempt from CGT.

Gift of plates

Whilst the plates form a set, because Thelma has never in the past owned the plates which are owned by her husband and daughter there is no need to treat the gift of her plates to Louise as a part disposal nor to amalgamate the gift with any previous gifts.

The value of the consideration for CGT purposes will simply be the market value of the three plates gifted by Thelma (i.e. £3,800). As their value is less than £6,000 and they cost less than £6,000, any gain arising will also be exempt under the CGT chattels rules.

Gift of Blackbird plc shares

The gift of these shares will, however, give rise to a chargeable gain. Assuming the gift is made on 6 July 2017, the CGT will be:

	£
Market value (connected persons) (Note)	146,400
Less: Cost (£25,000 + £50,000)	(75,000)
Chargeable gain	71,400

Entrepreneurs' relief is not available as Thelma owns 1% of the shareholding. Gift relief is not available as the shares are quoted and Thelma has a < 5% interest in the company.

	£
Total chargeable gains	71,400
Less: AEA	(11,100)
Taxable gains	60,300
CGT (£60,300 × 20%)	12,060

Conclusion

The tax payable under both options is as follows:

	IHT	CGT	Total
	£	£	£
Retention of assets (£5,600 + £158,000)	163,600	0	163,600
Gifting assets now (£5,600 + £101,530)	107,130	12,060	119,190

It would therefore appear that, providing the key assumptions hold (i.e. asset values in four years, Thelma survives four years), it is preferable to make the gifts to Louise now giving a tax saving of £44,410 (£163,600 – £119,190).

Note: The valuation for CGT is different from the IHT valuation used for the PET calculation above.

For CGT, quoted shares are valued at the average of the highest and lowest prices:
= (1,468p + 1,460p) × ½ = 1,464p per share
Value of 10,000 shares = (10,000 × £14.64) = £146,400

The Wood Discretionary Trust

Answer 1 – Chapter 14

Notes for meeting with trustees

Income tax in relation to the Wood Discretionary Trusts

(1) **Basis of assessment**

- All trusts are assessed to income tax on trust income received on a tax year basis.
- Trustees of all trusts are subject to self-assessment under the same system applying to individuals.
- When income payments are made to a beneficiary, the trustees pay the income net of 45% tax credit.

(2) **Payment of income made to a beneficiary**

If a discretionary payment is made in the tax year:

- The beneficiary is taxed on the gross income actually received in the tax year.
- The income received is grossed up at 100/55, and included in the beneficiary's IT computation.
- A tax credit of 45% is deducted in the beneficiary's IT liability computation.
- A 'statement of trust income' form must be completed for HMRC to show the gross, tax and net amounts distributed to the beneficiary in that tax year.

CGT in relation to the Wood Discretionary Trust

(1) **Occasions of charge**

Trustees are chargeable persons for the purposes of CGT and therefore a liability to tax may arise where a trustee makes a chargeable disposal of a chargeable asset.

There are three main occasions of charge to CGT:

- When assets are put into trust (this is a charge on the individual settlor, not the trust itself)
- Disposals of trust assets by the trustees to persons other than the beneficiaries when they are managing the trust assets
- When capital assets are distributed to the beneficiaries.

(2) **Assets put into trust on death**

- Not a chargeable disposal as trust set up on death in a will.
- No CGT payable.
- Trustees acquire assets at probate value.

(3) **Disposals of trust assets by trustees to persons other than the beneficiaries**

- Chargeable disposals of chargeable assets give rise to chargeable gains.
- CGT payable by the trustees on a tax year basis under self-assessment.

(4) **Distribution of capital assets out of the trust to beneficiaries**

- Chargeable disposal of asset at full market value
- Gift relief available on any asset as there is an immediate charge to IHT
- Beneficiary acquires the assets at base cost = market value less gift relief.

IHT in relation to The Wood Discretionary trust

(1) **Basis of assessment**

- Taxed as a separate entity with its own nil rate band.

(2) **Occasions of charge**

There will be three key occasions of charge to IHT as follows:

- When assets are put into trust
- The principal charge every ten years following the creation of the trust
- When capital assets are distributed out of the trust to the beneficiaries.

(3) **Assets put into trust on death**

- Assets form part of the settlor's estate on death
- IHT payable on the estate

  Note there is no difference in IHT payable on the estate if an individual puts his estate into a trust on death or leaves the estate directly to another individual
- Trust established after the estate IHT has been paid (i.e. out of post-tax assets).

(4) **The principal charge**

– An anniversary charge every tenth anniversary of the creation of the trust is levied on the market value of all of the assets in the trust on the anniversary date

– The maximum rate of IHT is 6%.

(5) **Distribution of capital assets out of the trust to beneficiaries**

– Exit charge arises

– The maximum rate of IHT is 6%.

Fred Foyle

Answer 1 – Chapter 16

(a) **Reasons for investigation**

HMRC will probably have investigated into Fred's 2016/17 return because of the fall in the gross profit (GP%) and turnover compared to the accounts of the previous owner.

Fred's GP% is 30% (£150,000/(£400,000 + £100,000) × 100), compared to 41.7% (£300,000/(£600,000 + £120,000) × 100) for the previous owner.

The fall in the GP% has arisen because Fred's cash sales are £400,000 compared to an expected £500,000 (£600,000 × 10/12), which is a shortfall of £100,000.

HMRC will therefore assume that cash sales of £100,000 have not been recorded. The adjustment will increase Fred's GP% to the required 41.7%.

Fred could put forward the following points to justify the fall in GP%:

(1) He may be selling goods at a lower margin than the previous owner.

(2) He may be selling a different mix of goods.

(3) He may have suffered an increase in theft or wastage.

(b) **Late payment interest**

Interest will run from 1 February 2018 to 30 August 2018, and will be as follows:

£100,000 @ 40% = (£40,000 × 3% × 7/12) = £700

(c) **Maximum penalty**

The penalty is determined in the same way as penalties on incorrect income tax and corporation tax returns, according to:

– The amount of tax understated
– The reason for the understatement
– The extent of disclosure by the taxpayer.

The level of the penalty is a percentage of the revenue lost as a result of the inaccuracy or under assessment and depends on the behaviour of the taxpayer as follows:

Taxpayer behaviour	Maximum penalty (% of revenue lost)
Genuine mistake	No penalty
Careless/Failure to take reasonable care	30%
Deliberate but no concealment	70%
Deliberate with concealment	100%

The penalties may be reduced depending on the type of penalty and whether the taxpayer makes an unprompted disclosure.

Where the return is incorrect through deliberate intention of a third party, the penalty can be charged on the third party.

Ali

Answer 1 – Chapter 17

Loss relief options available:

- **Relief against total income**

  This relief allows trading losses to be set against the total income of the current and /or the previous tax year.

- **Relief against gains**

  This relief is allowed after a claim against total income has been made. It allows relief to be claimed against chargeable gains. The trading loss is 'converted' into a current year capital loss.

- **Carry forward relief**

  This relief is automatic if no other claim is made. It allows trading losses to be carried forward and set against the first available trading profits of the same trade.

Optimum use of losses:

- **If relief against total income and gains is claimed:**

  If relief is claimed against total income and gains, the trading loss incurred in 2016 (£18,000 relating to y/e 31.12.16) can be set against total income and gains in 2016/17 and/or 2015/16.

  Allocated against the current year – 2016/17

  If the trading loss of £18,000 is set against the interest and property income of 2016/17 (£11,870 see below), this would utilise most of the loss but the PA and savings nil rate band would be wasted. As the loss would be set against the non-savings income in preference to the savings income, there would be no tax saved on the savings income. This is because the rate of tax on savings income is 0% where it falls within the first £5,000 of taxable income.

  There would be £6,130 of loss left (£18,000 – £11,870) to allocate against the chargeable gain. However, when considering whether to allocate a loss against the chargeable gain, consideration should be given to the other reliefs that may be wasted such as the AEA of £11,100 and the rate of CGT applicable.

Before considering relief against gains, it should be noted that the chargeable gain is almost covered by the capital losses brought forward and the AEA (£20,000 – £8,750 = £11,250).

A claim against gains is an 'all or nothing' relief. This means that you cannot choose how much of the loss can be utilised. If a claim is made, the maximum amount possible must be used, therefore all £6,130 of the loss would be utilised.

As a result, a small amount of tax is saved £27 (£150 see below × 18%). Note that the tax saving is at 18% as Ali is a basic rate taxpayer and the gain is in respect of a residential property.

Accordingly claims against total income and gains in 2016/17 are not an attractive option.

Allocated against the previous year – 2015/16

If the loss was to be set against the interest and property income of the previous year (£72,890 see below) the loss and PA would be set against the non-savings income in preference to the saving income to preserve the savings nil rate band. The loss would therefore give income tax relief at 40% and would not waste the PA nor the savings nil rate band.

The tax saving is £7,200 (£18,000 × 40%).

This method utilises the loss as quickly as possible and will help Ali's cash flow position.

- **If losses are carried forward:**

If the loss is carried forward, the loss of £18,000 would be set against the next available profits from the same trade of £26,000 in 2017/18.

The total income for the year would be £14,840 (£26,000 – £18,000 + £6,840). The PA would not be wasted, however the rate of tax relief is only £3,600 (£18,000 × 20%).

- **Conclusion:**

Ali should claim relief against his total income of 2015/16 and an income tax saving of £7,200 will be achieved.

Taxable income computations

	2015/16	2016/17	2017/18
	£	£	£
Trading income	55,000	0	26,000
Less: Loss relief b/f	(0)	(0)	(0)
	55,000	0	26,000
Bank interest	8,690	5,050	0
Property income	9,200	6,820	6,840
Total income before reliefs	72,890	11,870	32,840
Less: Loss relief	(18,000)	(0)	
Net income after reliefs	54,890	11,870	32,840
Less: PA	(11,000)	(11,000)	(11,000)
Taxable income	43,890	870	21,840

Taxable gain computation – 2016/17

	£
Gain in the year	20,000
Less: Trading loss relief	(0)
	20,000
Less: Capital loss b/f	(8,750)
Net chargeable gain	11,250
Less: AEA	(11,100)
Taxable gain	150

David and Patricia

Answer 2 – Chapter 17

(a) (i) **Taxation implications for David of involving his wife in the business**

Employing Patricia

If David employs his wife, he is only able to claim a tax deduction for the salary paid if he pays her the market rate. As she was earning £13,200 (£1,100 × 12) as a bookkeeper previously, this would appear to be the market rate.

The business must pay employers' NICs at 13.8% on her gross salary in excess of £8,112 p.a. However, there is an allowance of £3,000 available for employers to set against the liability.

The salary and NICs will both be tax deductible expenses for the business.

Patricia will have to pay NICs at 12% as an employee on her salary in excess of £8,060 and will be taxed on her salary under PAYE.

Note: The employer's allowance is available even though Patricia is the only employee. The allowance is only not available if it is a company and a director is the sole employee.

Setting up a partnership

If David and Patricia are in equal partnership, they will each be assessed to income tax on half of the partnership profits.

In addition, Patricia will pay class 4 NIC at a maximum rate of 9% and class 2 at a fixed rate of £146 for the year. This is compared to employee class 1 NICs of 12% for Patricia and employer's class 1 NICs of 13.8% for the business, as an employee.

Calculation of income tax and NICs under each option assuming a full year of operation

(1) **Patricia as an employee**

Employment costs relating to Patricia

	£	£
Salary		13,200
Employers' NIC	702	
(£13,200 – £8,112) × 13.8%		
Less: Employer NIC allowance (max £3,000)	(702)	
		0
Employment costs		13,200

This amount is tax deductible for the business.

Income tax and NIC payable by David

	£	£
Trading income (£60,000 – £13,200)		46,800
Income tax (£46,800 × 40%)		18,720
Class 2 NIC (52 × £2.80)		146
Class 4 NIC (£43,000 – £8,060) × 9%	3,145	
(£46,800 – £43,000) × 2%	76	
		3,221
Total income tax and NIC		22,087

Note: In addition David will have property income which will utilise his PA. The above calculation is just isolating the impact of his trading profits on his IT and NIC position.

Income tax and NIC payable by Patricia

	£
Salary	13,200
Less: Personal allowance	(11,000)
Taxable income	2,200
Income tax (£2,200 × 20%)	440
Class 1 NICs (£13,200 – £8,060) × 12%	617
Total income tax and NIC	1,057
Total tax payable by the couple (£22,087 + £1,057)	23,144

(2) **Patricia as a partner, sharing profits 50:50 (David: Patricia)**

The profits for a full year will be allocated £30,000 (£60,000 × 50%) each to David and Patricia.

Income tax and NIC payable by David

	£
Income tax (£30,000 × 40%)	12,000
Class 2 NIC (52 × £2.80)	146
Class 4 NIC (£30,000 – £8,060) × 9%	1,975
Total income tax and NIC	14,121

Note: In addition David will have property income which will utilise his PA. The above calculation is just isolating the impact of his trading profits on his IT and NIC position.

Income tax and NIC payable by Patricia

	£
Trading income	30,000
Less: Personal allowance	(11,000)
Taxable income	19,000
	£
Income tax (£19,000 × 20%)	3,800
Class 2 NIC (52 × £2.80)	146
Class 4 NIC (£30,000 – £8,060) × 9%	1,975
Total income tax and NIC	5,921
Total tax payable by the couple (£14,121 + £5,921)	20,042

Conclusion

By operating as an equal partnership the couple can achieve a tax saving of £3,102 (£23,144 – £20,042).

Note

If David and Patricia are in partnership, then the profit sharing ratios can be in any proportion they decide. The ratio does not have to reflect their respective input to the business provided there is a proper partnership agreement and Patricia takes an active part in the business.

The ratio can therefore be chosen so as to reduce their overall tax liability, and may even be changed at a later date if their circumstances change.

David has property business income of £45,000 from 2017/18 onwards and so he will be a higher rate taxpayer. Patricia has no other income. The maximum income tax saving will therefore be generated where Patricia's share equates to £43,000 (i.e. equivalent to the PA of £11,000 plus the basic rate band of £32,000).

This would imply a profit sharing ratio of 3:7 (David: Patricia) as £43,000 is approximately 72% of £60,000.

However, the question told you that David would take Patricia on as an equal partner.

(ii) **Tax administration**

Notification of new source of income in 2016/17

For income tax purposes HMRC should be notified by 5 October 2017 (i.e. within six months from the end of the tax year in which the liability on the new source of income arises).

Submission of tax return

David's self-assessment return due filing date for 2016/17 depends upon whether he intends to file electronically or in paper format.

If he decides to file in paper format it is due on the later of:

(1) 31 October 2017
(2) 3 months after the notice to file the return is issued.

If he files electronically it is due on the later of:

(1) 31 January 2018
(2) 3 months after the notice to file the return is issued

Payment dates

Income tax is normally payable as follows:

31 January in the tax year	Payment on account
31 July following the tax year	Payment on account
31 January following the tax year	Balancing payment

However, as the payments on account are each based on 50% of the previous year's income tax and NIC liability, this is not possible in the first tax year.

Thus, if the business starts to trade on 1 January 2017, the first payment on account is due on 31 January 2017, but no payment will be made, as trade has just commenced. The second payment on account is due on 31 July 2017, but again, it is unlikely that any payments will be made as there was no liability in the prior year. The balancing payment is due on 31 January 2018, and the total liability will be paid on that date.

(b) **Loss reliefs available to David**

The loss relief options available to David are as follows:

(1) Relief against total income of the previous three tax years on a first in first out (FIFO) basis.

(2) Relief against total income (and gains, if required) of the current tax year and/or the previous tax year.

(3) Relief by carrying forward against future trading profits of the same trade.

When deciding which loss relief to take, consideration should be given to the rate of tax saved, to the timing of any relief/repayment and to avoiding the loss of personal allowances.

Note: In this question there is no savings income or dividends, therefore the preservation of the nil rate bands is not a consideration.

The profit sharing ratio is 50:50, so the loss arising to David (and Patricia) in 2016/17 is £20,000 each.

David – the most beneficial claim

David has had employment income of £45,000 p.a. since 2004, with £33,750 (£3,750 × 9 months) in 2016/17. David will also have total income of £75,000 (£45,000 property income + £30,000 equal share of trading profits) from 2017/18 onwards.

The tax saving achieved under each option is as follows:

(1) Carry the loss back three years to the tax year 2013/14 and receive a repayment of income tax of £4,400 (W1)

(2) Use the loss against total income in 2016/17 resulting in a tax saving of £4,000 (W2) or against total income in 2015/16 resulting in a tax saving of £4,400 (W1); or

(3) Carry forward the loss against trading profits in 2017/18 saving tax of £8,000 (W3).

Ignoring the timing of tax saving, the greatest tax is saved if the loss is carried forward to 2017/18.

Workings

(W1) **Using the loss in 2013/14 or 2015/16**

	Before loss relief	After loss relief
	£	£
Employment income	45,000	45,000
Less: Loss relief	0	(20,000)
Net income	45,000	25,000
Less: Personal allowance	(11,000)	(11,000)
Taxable income	34,000	14,000
Tax saving: loss of £20,000		
Relief at higher rate		
(£34,000 – £32,000)	2,000 × 40%	800
Remainder at basic rate		
(£20,000 – £2,000)	18,000 × 20%	3,600
Total loss	20,000	
Tax saved		4,400

(W2) **Using the loss in 2016/17**

	Before loss relief	After loss relief
	£	£
Employment income (9 × £3,750)	33,750	33,750
Trading profit	0	0
	33,750	33,750
Less: Loss relief	0	(20,000)
Net income	33,750	13,750
Less: Personal allowance	(11,000)	(11,000)
Taxable income	22,750	2,750
Tax saved: (£20,000 × 20%)		4,000

(W3) **Using the loss in 2017/18**

	Before loss relief	After loss relief
	£	£
Trading profit (£60,000 × 50%)	30,000	30,000
Less: Loss relief	0	(20,000)
	30,000	10,000
Property income	45,000	45,000
Net income	75,000	55,000
Less: Personal allowance	(11,000)	(11,000)
Taxable income	64,000	44,000
Tax saved: (£20,000 × 40%)		8,000

Angela

Answer 3 – Chapter 17

(a) **Cash basis – year ended 30 June 2017**

	£	£
Revenue (£57,640 – £4,560)		53,080
Less: Guest house furniture	5,300	
Food and household expenses (£16,200 – £4,200)	12,000	
Motor expenses (W) (Note)	4,700	
Other expenses (£4,960 – £850)	4,110	
		(26,110)
Tax adjusted trading profit		26,970

Note: The cost of the car is not allowable under the cash basis. Capital allowances are available instead for expenditure on cars, but are not available where the flat rate mileage allowance is claimed.

The P6 examining team has stated that where the cash basis is used, you should assume that the flat rate expenses will be claimed.

Working: Motor expenses – cash basis

	£
10,000 × 45p	4,500
800 × 25p	200
	4,700

(b) **Accruals basis – year ended 30 June 2017**

	£	£
Revenue		57,640
Less: Food and household expenses		
(£16,200 × 60%)	9,720	
Motor expenses (£5,720 × 80%)	4,576	
Other expenses	4,960	
Capital allowances (W)	7,964	
		(27,220)
Tax adjusted trading profit		30,420

Working: Capital allowances

		Private use car	Allowances
	£	£	£
Additions – no AIA or FYA:			
Private use car			
(CO_2 emissions < 130 g/km)		18,500	
Additions – with AIA			
Equipment	5,300		
Less: AIA	(5,300)		5,300
		0	
		18,500	
Less: WDA (18% × £18,500)		(3,330) × 80%	2,664
TWDV c/f		15,170	
Total allowances			7,964

Jane Seemore

Answer 1 – Chapter 18

(a) (i) **Capital allowance implications on transfer of business**

If Jane incorporates her business, balancing adjustments will be made in the final capital allowance computations, calculated by reference to the market value (restricted to cost if lower) of the assets at cessation compared to the tax WDV at that date.

There is no possibility of making an election to transfer the assets at their tax written down values in this case, as Jane will not control Hollywood Ltd.

The capital allowances for the final accounting period are:

1.9.16 – 31.3.17	Main pool	Van		Allowances
	£	£		£
TWDV b/f	15,050	4,130		
Additions	820			
Disposals	(10,000)	(4,700)		
	5,870	(570)		
Balancing allowance	(5,870)			5,870
Balancing charge		570	× 85%	(484)
Net balancing allowance				5,386

(ii) **Trading income assessments**

Trading loss – period to 31 March 2017

	£
Trading loss before adjustment	(21,500)
Add: Profit on sale of inventory (£8,300 × 5/105)	395
Less: Capital allowances (from (i))	(5,386)
Trading loss	(26,491)

		Trading loss	Income assessment
		£	£
2013/14	y/e 31.8.13		15,000
2014/15	y/e 31.8.14		6,000
2015/16	y/e 31.8.15		15,000
2016/17	1.9.15 – 31.3.17		
	y/e 31.8.16	10,000	
	p/e 31.3.17	(26,491)	
	Less:		
	Overlap profits	(2,815)	
		(19,306)	0

(iii) **Options available for relief of loss**

Jane has made a trading loss in 2016/17 which is at the end of her trading cycle. The following represent the possible ways she can relieve this loss.

Relief against total income

The trading loss can be used in 2016/17 and/or 2015/16 against Jane's total income.

	2015/16	2016/17
Total income	£15,000	£Nil

By using the loss in 2015/16, Jane will waste her personal allowance. The rest of the loss will save tax at 20%, but part of the loss will remain unrelieved.

Relief against chargeable gains

After making a claim against total income in a particular tax year, it is also possible to make a further claim in the same year to reduce capital gains tax.

Depending on the consideration received, Jane may have a chargeable gain in 2016/17 realised on the disposal of the business and can use the loss to reduce this gain.

However, this will only save capital gains tax at 10%, as the disposal of the business qualifies for entrepreneurs' relief.

Terminal loss relief

As the loss arises in the last 12 months of trading, it can be carried back for three years on a LIFO basis and reduce trading profits of the previous three tax years.

	2013/14	2014/15	2015/16
Trading profits	£15,000	£6,000	£15,000

The loss would be used in 2015/16, then 2014/15, wasting two PAs and saving tax on the balance of the loss at 20%.

Incorporation relief

Special incorporation loss relief will be available if the consideration for the business is at least 80% in the form of shares.

The trading loss can be carried forward to 2017/18 and offset against the first available future income that Jane receives from the company.

	£
Employment income	30,000
Savings and dividend income	40,000
Total income in 2017/18	70,000

In Jane's case, the loss will be offset against her employment income of £30,000 from the company, Hollywood Ltd, saving tax at 40% with no wasted PA and no wastage of the savings and dividend nil rate bands.

Conclusion

The most tax efficient use of the loss would be to carry it forward against Jane's employment income to save tax at 40%, although there would be a slight cash flow disadvantage as relief would not be obtained until 2017/18.

(b) **Capital gains implications of incorporation**

Where all of the assets of Jane's business are transferred to Hollywood Ltd as a going concern wholly in exchange for shares, any capital gains arising are relieved via incorporation relief such that no capital gains tax liability arises.

However, where part of the payment received from the company is in the form of cash, Jane will have chargeable gains arising.

For Jane to have no liability to capital gains tax in 2017/18, assuming she has no other capital gains in the year, her chargeable gains must be covered by her AEA of £11,100.

	£
Gain on premises (£365,000 – £335,000)	30,000
Gain on goodwill	50,000
Total capital gains before reliefs	80,000
Chargeable gains required:	11,100
Incorporation relief should therefore be: (£80,000 – £11,100)	68,900

Therefore the MV of the shares to be accepted should be:

£68,900 = £80,000 × (MV of shares/£438,000)
MV of shares = £377,227

Therefore the cash to accept as part of the consideration can be up to the value of £60,773 (£438,000 – £377,227) and there will be no capital gains tax arising on the transfer.

Alternative calculation:
(Cash/£438,000) × £80,000 = £11,100
Cash = £60,773

The shares will have a capital gains tax base cost of:

	£
MV of shares (see above)	377,227
Less: Incorporation relief	(68,900)
Base cost of shares	308,327

If Jane wants to carry forward her losses, as explained above, then she must take at least 80% of the value as shares.

She should therefore take cash of no more than £87,600 (20% × £438,000) if she wants to be able to carry her losses forward to obtain maximum relief.

Cash of £60,773 would be well within this limit, therefore both CGT incorporation relief and incorporation loss relief would be available.

Alf and Bob

Answer 1 – Chapter 19

(a) **Chargeable gains assessed on the partners**

The capital gains of £197,000 arising on the disposal of the business will be split between the partners in their PSR:

	£
Alf (40%)	78,800
Bob (60%)	118,200

Chargeable gains for 2016/17 are as follows:

Alf – gains qualifying for entrepreneurs' relief	£78,800
Bob – gains qualifying for entrepreneurs' relief	£118,200

(b) **Loss relief options**

There are two possible ways that the partnership loss can be relieved.

(i) A claim can be made against total income for 2016/17 and/or 2015/16.

Subject to this claim being made, it would then be possible to extend the claim against chargeable gains of the same year.

(ii) Terminal loss relief (TLR) can be claimed.

The final trading income assessments will be split between the partners as follows:

	Alf 40%	Bob 60%
	£	£
2013/14	7,600	11,400
2014/15	7,800	11,700
2015/16	6,080	9,120
2016/17	(14,800)	(22,200)

The most beneficial loss relief claim available to Alf would appear to be a terminal loss claim to carry back the loss on a LIFO basis against trading income only in 2015/16 first, then 2014/15 and the balance in 2013/14.

This would save income tax at 20% in each year and not waste the PA.

He could make a claim against his total income of £18,580 (£6,080 + £12,500) for 2015/16, but this would waste some of his PA.

A claim against his chargeable gains for 2016/17 would only save 10% tax, as the gains qualify for entrepreneurs' relief.

Bob could also make a terminal loss claim, but this would waste his PAs for several years and save very little tax.

He would be advised to make a claim against his total income of £3,850 (bank interest) for 2016/17. This saves no tax, as the income is covered by his PA, however it allows him to then claim loss relief of £18,350 (£22,200 – £3,850) against his chargeable gains for 2016/17 (i.e. £5,500 cottage and £118,200 partnership share).

Alf – taxable income and taxable gains

	2013/14	2014/15	2015/16	2016/17
	£	£	£	£
Trading income	7,600	7,800	6,080	0
Less: TLR	(920)	(7,800)	(6,080)	(0)
	6,680	0	0	0
Employment income	7,000	11,000	12,500	0
	13,680	11,000	12,500	0
Less: PA	(11,000)	(11,000)	(11,000)	0
Taxable income	2,680	0	1,500	0
Chargeable gains				78,800
Less: Capital loss b/f				(25,000)
Net chargeable gains				53,800
Less: AEA				(11,100)
Taxable gains				42,700

Bob – taxable income and taxable gain

	2013/14	2014/15	2015/16	2016/17
	£	£	£	£
Trading income	11,400	11,700	9,120	0
Bank interest	0	0	0	3,850
	11,400	11,700	9,120	3,850
Less: Loss relief				(3,850)
Less: PA	(11,000)	(11,000)	(11,000)	(wasted)
Taxable income	400	700	0	0

Chargeable gains in 2016/17

	£	£
Gains not qualifying for ER:		
Gain on cottage	5,500	
Gains qualifying for ER:		
Gain on partnership		118,200
Less: Balance of trading loss		
((£22,200 – £3,850) = £18,350)	(5,500)	(12,850)
AEA	(0)	(11,100)
Taxable gain	0	94,250

The taxable gain is subject to 10% CGT.

Note: The trading loss is set off against gains not qualifying for ER first.

Ken and Cindy

Answer 1 – Chapter 20

(a) (i) **Ken's VAT registration**

Traders become liable to register for VAT at the end of any month if the value of taxable supplies in the previous 12 months > £83,000.

Month to	£
31 March 2016	36,800
30 April 2016 (£72,600 ÷ 3)	24,200
31 May 2016 (£72,600 ÷ 3)	24,200
	85,200

Ken will therefore be liable to register for VAT from 31 May 2016, and he must notify HMRC by 30 June 2016.

Ken will be registered from 1 July 2016.

(ii) **Effect of VAT registration on Ken's customers**

Once Ken is registered, he will have to charge output VAT on his sales.

If his customers are not VAT registered, which seems likely given that he trades from a market stall, then this VAT will represent an extra cost for them.

Ken may be forced to reduce his prices if this makes his business uncompetitive.

Any customers who are VAT registered will be able to claim back the VAT charged by Ken.

(iii) **Suitability of special accounting schemes**

Flat rate scheme

Based on his current levels of sales, Ken will be unable to join the flat rate scheme, as he will have annual sales revenue of more than £150,000.

Cash accounting scheme

Ken would be eligible to join the cash accounting scheme, as his taxable turnover will not exceed £1,350,000 p.a.

However, the cash accounting scheme is most suited to businesses that have a high level of credit sales, as it avoids the need to pay VAT before cash is received from customers.

As Ken's sales are likely to be cash sales, there would be no benefit from joining the cash accounting scheme.

Annual accounting scheme

Ken could join the annual accounting scheme, as his taxable turnover will not exceed £1,350,000 p.a.

This scheme is likely to be beneficial, as it will mean that Ken will only have to submit one VAT return every year, thus reducing the administrative burden of being VAT registered.

VAT will be payable by instalment during the year, with a balancing payment due with the VAT return 2 months after the year end.

(b) **Cindy**

	Total	Recoverable	Irrecoverable
	£	£	£
Relating to taxable supplies	25,575	25,575	
Relating to exempt supplies	15,400		15,400
Relating to overheads (W)	30,800	21,560	9,240
	71,775	47,135	24,640

Cindy's deductible input VAT is therefore £47,135.

Working: split of non-attributable VAT

Taxable % apportionment
= £275,000 ÷ (£275,000 + £120,000) × 100
= 70% (rounded up to whole %)

De minimis test

The total input VAT, (total input VAT less input VAT directly attributable to taxable supplies), and (input VAT relating to exempt supplies), are all greater than £625 per month on average, therefore none of the de minimis tests are satisfied.

Sandy Brick

Answer 2 – Chapter 20

(a) **VAT invoices**

- A VAT invoice must be issued when a standard rated supply is made to a VAT registered person.
- A VAT invoice should be issued within 30 days of the date that the taxable supply of services is treated as being made.

(b) **VAT returns – Quarter ended 31 March 2017**

	£	£
Output VAT		
Sales to VAT registered customers (Note 1)		
(£26,400 × 95% × 20%)		5,016
£17,600 × 20%		3,520
Sales to non-VAT registered customers		
(£16,920 – £5,170 = £11,750 × 20/120)		1,958
		10,494
Input VAT		
Materials (£11,200 – £800 = £10,400 × 20%)	2,080	
Office equipment (Note 3)		
(£120 × 9 = £1,080 × 20%)	216	
Telephone (Note 4)		
(£400 × 70% × 20%)	56	
Motor repairs (Note 5) (£920 × 20%)	184	
Equipment (£6,000 × 20%)	1,200	
		(3,736)
VAT payable		6,758

Notes:

(1) The calculation of output VAT on sales must take account of the discount for prompt payment for those customers who paid within the specified time.

(2) Input VAT cannot be claimed in respect of the materials used in constructing Sandy's private residence since the goods are not used for business purposes.

(3) Input VAT can be recovered on services supplied in the six months prior to registration, so the office equipment claim can be backdated to July 2016.

(4) An apportionment is made where a service such as the use of a telephone is partly for business purposes and partly for private purposes.

(5) However, no apportionment is necessary for motor expenses provided there is some business use.

Lowland Ltd

Answer 1 – Chapter 23

(i) **One set of accounts for the 18 month period to 30 June 2017**

Lowland Ltd's 18 month period of account will be split into two chargeable accounting periods as follows:

	Year ended 31.12.2016	Period ended 30.6.2017
	£	£
Trading profits (W1)	292,667	146,333
Less: Capital allowances (W2)	(43,960)	(1,624)
	248,707	144,709
Property income (W3)	16,500	0
Chargeable gain (£46,000 – £28,000)	18,000	0
TTP	283,207	144,709
Corporation tax		
(£283,207 × 20%)	56,641	
(£144,709 × 20%)		28,942
Due date (W4)	1 Oct 2017	1 Apr 2018
Total liability (£56,641 + £28,942)	£85,583	

(ii) **Preparing separate accounts for the six month period to 30 June 2016 and for the year ended 30 June 2017**

	Period ended 30.6.2016	Year ended 30.6.2017
	£	£
Trading profits (W5)	155,000	284,000
Less: Capital allowances (W6)	(41,980)	(3,604)
	113,020	280,396
Property business profit/(loss) (W7)	26,500	(10,000)
Chargeable gain (see note below)	46,000	0
TTP	185,520	270,396
Corporation tax		
(£185,520 × 20%)	37,104	
(£270,396 × 20%)		54,079
Due date (W8)	1 Apr 2017	1 Apr 2018
Total liability (£37,104 + £54,079)	£91,183	

Note: The capital loss occurs in the y/e 30 June 2017. It can only be carried forward and set against future chargeable gains.

Conclusion

Preparing one set of accounts for the 18 month period to 30 June 2017 appears to be beneficial, as it results in an overall tax saving of £5,600 (£91,183 – £85,583).

It also results in a later due date for some of the corporation tax liability (1 October 2017 compared to 1 April 2017).

This can be reconciled by the fact that, under the lower tax option the capital loss of £28,000 has been utilised saving tax of £5,600 (£28,000 × 20%).

Workings

(W1) **Trading profits – 18 month accounts**

	£
Total trading profits	
(£155,000 + £139,000 + £145,000)	439,000
Year ended 31 December 2016 (£439,000 × 12/18)	292,667
Period ended 30 June 2017 (£439,000 × 6/18)	146,333

(W2) **Capital allowances – 18 month accounts**

		Pool	Allowance
Year ended 31 December 2016		£	£
TWDV b/f		22,000	
Addition qualifying for AIA			
31 January 2016	40,000		
Less: AIA	(40,000)		40,000
		0	
		22,000	
WDA (18% × £22,000)		(3,960)	3,960
TWDV c/f		18,040	
Total allowances			43,960
Period ended 30 June 2017			
WDA (18% × 6/12)		(1,624)	1,624
TWDV c/f		16,416	

(W3) **Property income – 18 month accounts**

	£
Year ended 31 December 2016	
Reading – rental income (£53,000 × 6/12))	26,500
Guildford – allowable loss	(10,000)
Property income assessment	16,500

The cost of decorating the Guildford building is allowable on 'business' expense principles. The allowable loss is automatically set off against the rental income from the Reading building as all lettings are treated as a single business.

(W4) **Corporation tax due dates – 18 month accounts**

Year ended 31 December 2016:

Augmented profits = (£283,207 TTP + £13,750 dividends received) = £296,957
Augmented profits are below the threshold of £1,500,000

Period ended 30 June 2017

Augmented profits = £144,709 TTP + £Nil dividends received) = £144,709

The threshold is pro-rated for the length of the accounting period:

(£1,500,000 × 6/12) = £750,000

Augmented profits are still below the threshold.

Therefore, for both periods, tax is due 9 months and 1 day after the end of the CAP.

(W5) **Trading profits – Separate accounts**

	£
Period ended 30 June 2016	155,000
Year ended 30 June 2017 (£139,000 + £145,000)	284,000

(W6) **Capital allowances – Separate accounts**

		Pool	Allowance
Period ended 30 June 2016		£	£
TWDV b/f		22,000	
Additions qualifying for AIA			
31 January 2016	40,000		
Less: AIA (Max £200,000 × 6/12)	(40,000)		40,000
		0	
		22,000	
WDA (18% × 6/12)		(1,980)	1,980
TWDV c/f		20,020	
Total allowances			41,980
Year ended 30 June 2017			
WDA (18%)		(3,604)	3,604
TWDV c/f		16,416	

(W7) **Property business loss – Separate accounts**

The cost of decorating the Guildford building is allowable on 'business' expense principles.

The allowable loss is automatically set off against Lowland Ltd's other income for the year ended 30 June 2017.

(W8) **Corporation tax due dates – Separate accounts**

Six months to 30 June 2016

Augmented profits = (£185,520 TTP + £Nil dividends received) = £185,520

The threshold = (£1,500,000 × 6/12) = £750,000

The augmented profits are less than £750,000.

Year ended 30 June 2017

Augmented profits = (£270,396 TTP + £13,750 dividends received) = £284,146

For the year ended 30 June 2017 the augmented profits are less than £1,500,000.

Therefore, for both periods, corporation tax is due 9 months and 1 day after the end of the CAP.

Iris Ltd

Answer 1 – Chapter 24

Taxable total profits computations

	Year to 31.12.15	8 m/e 31.08.16	Year to 31.08.17
	£	£	£
Trading profit	170,000	78,000	0
Less: Loss relief b/f	(0)	(0)	(0)
	170,000	78,000	0
Property income	10,000	11,000	12,000
Interest income	2,500	3,600	4,100
Total profits	182,500	92,600	16,100
Less: Loss relief	(60,833)	(92,600)	(16,100)
	121,667	0	0
Less: QCDs	(3,000)	(wasted)	(wasted)
TTP	118,667	0	0
Unrelieved QCDs	0	3,000	3,000

Loss memorandum

	£
Loss for y/e 31.08.17	176,100
Less: Loss relief:	
y/e 31.08.17	(16,100)
Eight months to 31.08.16	(92,600)
y/e 31.12.15 (£182,500 × 4/12)	(60,833)
Loss available to carry forward	6,567

Note: The loss may be carried back against profits of the 12 months before 1 September 2016.

The loss may therefore be set against all of the total profits (before QCDs) for the 8 m/e 31.08.16 and 4/12 of the total profits (before QCDs) for the y/e 31.12.15.

Cosmet Ltd

Answer 2 – Chapter 24

(a) (i) **Corporation tax payable – after loss relief**

	y/e 31.5.14	y/e 31.5.15	p/e 31.12.15	y/e 31.12.16
	£	£	£	£
Trading profit	750,250	500,500	101,999	0
Property income	10,000	10,000	10,000	11,000
Bank interest	8,460	7,526	5,076	5,275
Net chargeable gains (W)	1,622	0	0	59,390
	770,332	518,026	117,075	75,665
Less: Loss relief	0	(40,050)	(117,075)	(75,665)
TTP	770,332	477,976	0	0

Loss memorandum	£
Loss for y/e 31.12.16	232,790
Less: Loss relief:	
Current period claim: y/e 31.12.16	(75,665)
Carry back 12 months: 7 m/e 31.12.15	(117,075)
y/e 31.5.15 (max £518,026 × 5/12 = £215,844)	
restricted to amount of loss left	(40,050)
Loss available to carry forward	0

(ii) **Tax repayments:**

P/e 31.12.15 (20% × £117,075)	£23,415
Y/e 31.5.15 (20% × £40,050)	£8,010

Working: Net chargeable gains

y/e 31.5.15:	Capital loss to carry forward £4,000
p/e 31.12.15:	Net chargeable gain = (£2,990 – £2,990 capital loss b/f) = £Nil Capital loss remaining to c/f = (£4,000 – £2,990) = £1,010
y/e 31.12.16:	Net chargeable gain = (£60,440 – £1,010 capital loss b/f) = £59,390

(b) **Notes for meeting**

(1) **Merging with another company**

- There are anti-avoidance provisions that restrict the carry forward of trading losses when there is both a change in the ownership and a major change in the nature and conduct of trade within a three year period.
- The three year period can be either before or after the change of ownership.
- Trading losses arising before the change in ownership cannot be carried forward to periods after the change, nor can losses arising after a change in ownership be carried back to periods before the change.
- A change in ownership means that more than one half of the ordinary share capital of the company is acquired by a person or persons, ignoring any person acquiring 5% or less.

- A major change in the nature or conduct of the trade includes:
  - a major change in the type of property dealt in or services provided; and
  - a major change in customers, outlets or markets.

(2) **Changing the products and trading in a more lucrative market**

- Carry forward relief is only available against future trading income of the same trade.
- If the nature of the trade changes to such an extent that the original trade ceases and a new trade commences, carry forward relief is denied for losses of the original trade.

Bream

Answer 1 – Chapter 26

The effect of the transactions on Test Valley Ltd:

June 2014 (y/e 31.12.14)	• Company liable to pay tax equal to 32.5% of the loan outstanding on corporation tax due date	
	• within 9 months of the end of the AP (i.e. on 1.10.15)	
	• (£72,000 × 32.5%)	£23,400
January 2016 (y/e 31.12.16)	• Company becomes entitled to repayment of tax	
	• to extent loan repaid (i.e. £20,000 × 32.5%)	
	• repayment is due on 1 October 2017	£6,500
March 2017 (y/e 31.12.17)	• Company becomes entitled to repayment of tax	
	• on the loan w/off (i.e. £52,000 × 32.5%)	
	• repayment is due 1 October 2018	£16,900

The effect of the transactions on Bream:

June 2014
- If interest is charged at less than the official rate of 3%, the difference is treated as a dividend. The interest at 3% will be calculated on the outstanding balance as for employment income.

March 2017
- Loan waived = treated as dividend payment in 2016/17

	£
• Include in income tax computation as dividends	52,000
• First £5,000 tax at 0%	0
• Remaining £47,000 tax at 32.5%	15,275
Income tax payable	15,275

Note: In addition, the personal allowance in 2016/17 will be restricted as Bream's adjusted net income will exceed £100,000.

Joe

Answer 2 – Chapter 26

(a) **Transaction treated as a distribution**

	£
Dividend	630,000
Income tax	
First £5,000 × 0%	0
Remaining £625,000 × 38.1%	238,125
	238,125

The amount to be treated as a dividend is the difference between the sale proceeds and the amount originally subscribed.

The dividend is therefore £630,000 (100,000 × £7.30 = £730,000 – £100,000).

(b) **Transaction not treated as a distribution**

	£
Proceeds	730,000
Less: Cost	(100,000)
Capital gain (Note)	630,000
Less: AEA	(11,100)
Taxable amount	618,900
Capital gains tax @ 20%	123,780

Note: As Joe did not work for the company, entrepreneurs' relief is not available.

(c) **Effect of satisfying the capital treatment conditions**

The purchase of a company's own shares is always treated as a distribution unless all of the capital conditions are satisfied.

The taxpayer cannot choose which method applies.

If all of the conditions are satisfied, the effect is that income converts into a capital gain.

As can be seen by the question, this is advantageous as CGT is only charged at 20% compared to 38.1% for income tax (on all but the first £5,000 of dividends).

In an exam question, consider the effects of both situations.

John

Answer 3 – Chapter 26

(a) (i) **Taxation as a sole trader**

		£
John's income tax:		
Trading income		90,000
Income tax		
£	£	£
32,000 × 20%		6,400
58,000 × 40%		23,200
90,000		29,600
John's national insurance contributions:		
Class 2 (52 × £2.80)		146
Class 4		
(£43,000 – £8,060) × 9%	3,145	
(£90,000 – £43,000) × 2%	940	
		4,085
John's total IT and NIC payable		33,831

Note: The personal allowance is offset against John's property business income of £11,000.

(ii) **Taxation as a company, drawing a dividend of £21,216**

Company's corporation tax	£	£
TTP	90,000	
Corporation tax at 20%		18,000
John's income tax:		
Dividend income	21,216	
Income tax first £5,000 × 0%	0	
(£16,216 × 7.5%)	1,216	
Income tax payable		1,216
Total tax payable		19,216

National insurance:
No NICs is payable on dividends

(iii) **Taxation as a company, drawing gross salary of £27,990**

Company's corporation tax:

	£	£
Trading income	90,000	
Less: Salary	(27,990)	
Employer's NIC		
(£27,990 – £8,112) × 13.8% (Note)	(2,743)	2,743
TTP	59,267	
Corporation tax at 20%		11,853
John's income tax:		
Employment income	27,990	
Income tax (£27,990 × 20%)		5,598
John's National Insurance:		
Class 1 (£27,990 – £8,060) × 12%		2,392
Total tax payable		22,586

Comparison of taxation

The main difference between the taxation of a sole trader and a company is that income tax and NICs are due on all of the profits of a sole trader, whereas although all of the profits of a company are charged to corporation tax, only profits withdrawn from the company are charged to income tax.

Additionally, NICs are only payable on salary, not on dividends.

Tutorial note

John will need to take a dividend of £21,216 to receive a net cash receipt of £20,000.

This is because the dividend will suffer no income tax on the first £5,000, but thereafter suffers tax at 7.5% as John will be a basic rate taxpayer.

Therefore the dividend required is calculated as follows:

$D - ((D - 35,000) \times 7.5\%) = £20,000$

$D - 0.075D - £375 = £20,000$

$0.925D = £19,625$

$D = £21,216$

Note: The question gives the amount of dividend to be paid, therefore the above calculation is for tutorial purposes only to prove that John's net income will be £20,000.

John will need to take a gross salary of £27,990 to receive a net salary of £20,000.

This is because the net salary is after deducting income tax of 20% on the gross salary (G) and after deducting NICs of 12% on (G – £8,060).

Therefore the gross salary is calculated as follows:

G – (G × 20%) – ((G – £8,060) × 12%)) = £20,000

G – 0.2G – 0.12G + £967 = £20,000

0.68G = £19,033

G = £27,990 (£19,033 ÷ 0.68)

Note: The question gives you the gross salary to use in the computation. The above computation is for tutorial purposes only to prove that the net income John will receive is £20,000 (i.e. the same as the net income received if a dividend of £21,216 is paid).

(b) **Implications of equity and loan finance**

(i) **From the company's point of view**

Equity

- Fees incurred in issuing share capital are not an allowable deduction against trading profits.
- The cost of making distributions to shareholders are disallowable.
- The dividends themselves are not allowable.

Loan finance

- Interest on loans taken out to finance the business is deductible from trading profits.
- Capital costs, for example loans issued at a discount, are deductible from trading profits, where the loan finance is used for trade purposes.
- Incidental costs of obtaining medium or long term business loans and for issuing loan stock where the funds are used for trade purposes are deductible from trading profits.

(ii) **From an individual investor's point view**

Equity

- If the investor is an individual, the dividends received are taxed on the excess over the first £5,000 at 7.5%/32.5%/38.1% depending on whether they are a basic/higher/additional rate taxpayer.
- There will be a chargeable gain or loss on the disposal of the shareholding.

Loan finance

- If the investor is an individual, interest received will be charged to income tax at 40%/45%, to the extent that the individual is a higher/additional rate taxpayer.
- Usually the original creditor will not realise a gain or loss when the debt is disposed of, however a debt on a security can result in a capital gain or a capital loss.

(c) **Pension options available**

- John could invest in a personal pension. He can invest up to a maximum of £25,000 (100% of earnings) in 2016/17 and obtain tax relief.

  This amount is paid net of basic rate tax, and the basic rate band is extended by the gross payment when calculating his income tax liability to obtain higher rate relief.
- The company could set up a small self administered scheme (SSAS). Loans may be made to the company from the funds. Property can be purchased from the fund. However the costs of setting up and administering the scheme would probably cancel any advantages this option may have.
- John could set up a self invested personal pension scheme (SIPPS). It is possible to purchase commercial property with the fund. Again the costs of setting up and administering the scheme would probably cancel any advantages this option may have.

Longbow Ltd

Answer 1 – Chapter 27

(a) **One-third of Minnow Ltd's share capital acquired**

Minnow Ltd	£
Chargeable gain	50,000
Less: Loss relief	(50,000)
TTP	0

Longbow Ltd	£
Trading profit	220,000
Interest income (£150,000 @ 7% × 8/12)	7,000
	227,000
Less: Consortium relief (£140,000 – £50,000) = £90,000 × 1/3 × 6/12	(15,000)
TTP	212,000
Corporation tax liability (£212,000 × 20%)	42,400

Note:

(1) Minnow Ltd is a consortium company, and one-third of its trading loss can therefore be surrendered to Longbow Ltd. Minnow Ltd must take into account its own current year profits when calculating the loss to surrender, and this is restricted to the overlapping period of 1 October 2016 to 31 March 2017.

(2) Minnow Ltd's brought forward trading loss will be carried forward, as will the trading loss not used in y/e 31 March 2017 of £75,000 (£140,000 – £50,000 – £15,000) against the first available trading profits arising in Minnow Ltd.

(b) **Two-thirds of Minnow Ltd's share capital acquired**

Minnow Ltd

The company's TTP will be the same as above.

Longbow Ltd

	£
Trading profit	220,000
Interest income	7,000
	227,000
Less: Consortium relief (£140,000 – £50,000 = £90,000 × 2/3 × 6/12)	(30,000)
TTP	197,000
Corporation tax liability (£197,000 × 20%)	39,400

Note:

(1) Minnow Ltd is a 51% group company, and so the threshold for payment of corporation tax by instalment is to £750,000 (£1,500,000 ÷ 2).

(2) The remaining loss of £60,000 and the trading loss b/f of £9,000 will be carried forward in Minnow Ltd for use against first available trading profit subject to no major change in the nature and conduct of trade following the change in ownership.

(c) **All of Minnow Ltd's share capital acquired**

Minnow Ltd

	£
Chargeable gain (Note 2)	12,500
Less: Loss relief	(12,500)
TTP	0

Longbow Ltd

	£
Trading profit	220,000
Interest income	7,000
	227,000
Less: Group relief (£140,000 × 6/12)	(70,000)
TTP	157,000
Corporation tax liability (£157,000 × 20%)	31,400

Notes:

(1) Minnow Ltd is a 75% subsidiary.

(2) Rollover relief could be claimed based on the freehold factory to be purchased by Longbow Ltd.
As all of the sale proceeds relating to the business use is reinvested (i.e. £120,000 > 75% × £150,000 = £112,500), all of the business proportion of the gain can be rolled over.
The gain rolled over would be £37,500 (75% × £50,000).
Chargeable gain = (£50,000 – £37,500) = £12,500

A rollover claim is likely to be beneficial, as the deferred gain is only chargeable when Longbow Ltd sells the new asset, and may be rolled over again if further reinvestment is made in qualifying assets.

Relief for the trading loss carried forward in Minnow Ltd will be against the first available trading profits arriving in Minnow Ltd, subject to no major change in the nature and conduct of trade following the change in ownership.

An alternative to the rollover claim would be to leave the £50,000 gain chargeable in Minnow Ltd and offset £50,000 of Minnow Ltd's trading losses against it in the current year. This would leave a smaller loss to carry forward in Minnow Ltd, and may avoid a higher tax charge on the deferred gain in future when there may not be losses available to set against it.

Assuming the rollover claim is made, the trade loss to carry forward in Minnow Ltd will be:

	£
Trading loss arising y/e 31.3.17	140,000
Less: Group relief	(70,000)
Less: Current year offset	(12,500)
Available to c/f	57,500
Add: Trading loss b/f	9,000
Total available to c/f	66,500

Willow Group

Answer 2 – Chapter 27

Corporation tax computations – y/e 31 March 2017

	Ash Ltd	Pine Ltd	Willow Ltd	Oak Ltd	Fig Ltd	Cherry Ltd
	£	£	£	£	£	£
Trading profits	0	158,000	153,000	0	294,000	0
Consortium relief (W3)		(71,100)				
Group relief (W2)			(107,000)		(294,000)	
TTP	0	86,900	46,000	0	0	0
Corporation tax @ 20%	0	17,380	9,200	0	0	0

Workings

(1) **Analysis of group structure**

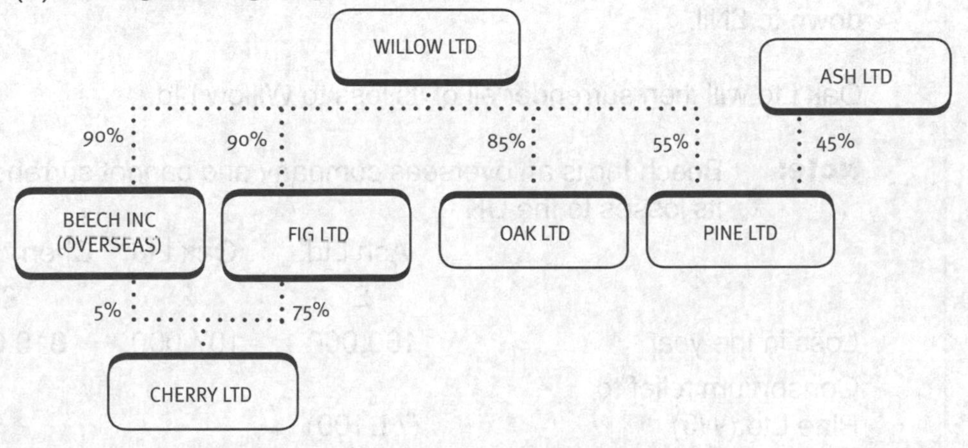

75% groups

Group 1	= Willow Ltd, Beech Inc, Fig Ltd, Oak Ltd (but Beech Inc is an overseas company and cannot surrender its losses to the UK)
Group 2	= Fig Ltd, Cherry Ltd
Consortium members	= Ash Ltd, Willow Ltd
Consortium owned company	= Pine Ltd

(2) **Losses working**

Deal with the most restricted losses first:

(i)	Consortium relief	Ash Ltd can only give its loss to Pine Ltd
(ii)	Group relief	Cherry Ltd can only give its loss to Fig Ltd
(iii)	Group relief	Oak Ltd can give its loss to Fig Ltd and Willow Ltd

Aim of loss relief: to use as much loss as possible.

Therefore, Cherry Ltd will give its loss to Fig Ltd to reduce its profits down to £Nil.

Oak Ltd will then surrender all of its loss to Willow Ltd.

Note: Beech Inc is an overseas company and cannot surrender its losses to the UK

	Ash Ltd	Oak Ltd	Cherry Ltd
	£	£	£
Loss in the year	160,000	107,000	310,000
Consortium relief to Pine Ltd (W3)	(71,100)		
Group relief to Fig Ltd			(294,000)
Group relief to Willow Ltd		(107,000)	
Loss to carry forward	88,900	0	16,000

(3) **Consortium relief**

Lower of:	£
(1) Available loss of Ash Ltd	160,000
(2) Percentage of Pine Ltd's TTP/(loss) (45% × £158,000)	71,100

X Ltd

Answer 1 – Chapter 28

To: Board of Directors
From: Tax advisor
Date: 10 July 2016
Subject: Taxation implications of establishing a factory overseas

If no elections are made, the factory will be a 'permanent establishment' overseas and the profits will suffer foreign tax. DTR will be given for the overseas tax suffered up to the full amount of UK corporation tax on that income.

Overseas branch of UK company – no election made

(1) The company would be liable to UK corporation tax on all profits of the branch.

(2) Since the branch is considered as part of the UK company, UK capital allowances are available and any branch losses would automatically be relieved.

(3) Chargeable gains arising would be subject to UK corporation tax.

(4) The overseas branch would not affect the upper and lower limits for deciding the rate of corporation tax.

Overseas branch of UK company – election made

It is possible for the company to make an irrevocable election to exempt profits of overseas permanent establishments. If this election is made, the tax treatment of the overseas branch will be as follows:

(1) The profits of the branch would be exempt in the UK.

(2) There would be no relief for branch losses in the UK.

(3) There would be no UK capital allowances available for plant and machinery used by the overseas branch.

(4) Chargeable gains arising in the overseas branch would not be subject to UK corporation tax.

(5) The overseas branch would still not affect the threshold for payment of corporation tax by instalment.

Overseas based subsidiary

(1) The parent company will only be liable to UK corporation tax on amounts received as interest from the subsidiary, but not dividends.

(2) Capital allowances and relief for losses would not be available between the parent and a non-UK resident subsidiary, unless the company is established in an EEA country and the losses cannot be utilised in the overseas subsidiary.

(3) Chargeable gains arising in a non-UK resident subsidiary would not be subject to UK corporation tax.

(4) Management control must be exercised overseas for the subsidiary to be accepted as a non-UK resident.

(5) The overseas company will be a related 51% group company and therefore will affect the threshold for payment of corporation tax by instalment.

Bertie Overseas

Answer 2 – Chapter 28

Client Address — Firm address

Date

Dear Bertie,

Re: Overseas Expansion

Further to our recent meeting I am writing to set out the principal business tax issues regarding the setting up of Bertie Overseas in the country of Picea.

These would appear to be as follows:

- The basis of taxation of overseas profits and relief for overseas losses.
- Whether Bertie Overseas should take the form of an overseas branch or a limited company.

- Whether relief can be obtained in the UK for any overseas taxes paid.
- Whether there is any relevant anti-avoidance legislation which may apply.

Dealing with each of these in turn.

Basis of taxation and the branch v limited company decision

Subject to the anti-avoidance measures detailed below, when Bertie Overseas starts making profits the 'usual' rules are as follows:

If Bertie Overseas takes the form of a non-UK resident limited company then dividends payable to Bertie Ltd will not be assessable in the UK.

This will be beneficial as corporate taxes in Picea are only 10%.

On the other hand if Bertie Overseas is set up as an overseas branch of Bertie Ltd, which is controlled from the UK, the automatic position is that all of the overseas profits generated (whether or not they are remitted to the UK) will be treated as part of the profits of Bertie Ltd and therefore entirely taxable in the UK. In these circumstances, however, the vehicles and equipment acquired will qualify for UK capital allowances.

Alternatively, it is possible for Bertie Ltd to make an irrevocable election to exempt the profits of overseas permanent establishments. If this election is made, the overseas branch profits will not be taxable in the UK so there will be very little difference between the tax treatment of the branch compared to the non-UK resident limited company.

However, if the election is made then there will be no relief for losses in the UK, and no UK capital allowances may be claimed.

It should be noted that these rules could be used to your advantage.

Your business plan anticipates that Bertie Overseas will make a loss in its first year of operation which will then be followed by progressively stronger profits.

If Bertie Overseas takes the form of a non-UK resident limited company in year one then it is unlikely that Bertie Ltd will be able to offset the losses generated against its own profits. The use of these losses will therefore be determined by Picean tax law. It is stated that Picea has no facility to carry losses backwards or forwards and presumably therefore these losses would remain unrelieved.

If, however, Bertie Overseas takes the form of an overseas branch this is effectively regarded by UK tax law as an extension of the UK trade. Any overseas losses generated are likely therefore to be automatically offset against UK source profits generated by Bertie Ltd. As Bertie Ltd is a successful company, it seems probable that these will therefore all be relieved as incurred.

This would only be of benefit in year one of the overseas operations. To prevent 100% of eventual overseas profits being taxed in the UK after year one the overseas branch could then be incorporated as a non-UK resident limited company, or the election to exempt the profits of overseas permanent establishments could then be made.

Some relevant points to note here are:

(a) If the incorporation route is chosen it may be necessary to secure the consent of the Treasury for the incorporation to proceed. It is generally illegal for a UK resident company to permit a non-UK resident company over which it has control to create or issue any shares.

However, providing full market value consideration is given, this transaction may be covered by published Treasury General Consents and so, in these circumstances, specific consent may not be required.

(b) The conversion will be a disposal of the branch assets at market value.

(i) In the case of the equipment and vehicles this will give rise to a balancing adjustment which (if a balancing charge) may increase the profits subject to UK corporation tax.

If the Picean Limited company is not chargeable to UK corporation tax after the incorporation, a succession election, which is normally possible where such assets are passed between connected persons, will not be possible.

(ii) In the case of the freehold premises a chargeable gain may arise. It is possible, by election, to defer this in circumstances where all the branch assets (with the exception of cash) are transferred to the Picean Limited company in return for ordinary shares.

If such an election is made the deferred gain will become taxable when the shares in the overseas company are sold or the overseas company disposes of any chargeable assets within six years of the incorporation.

Relief for overseas taxes paid on branch profits

To prevent the taxation of overseas income twice (once in the UK and once in the overseas territory) UK legislation allows for double tax relief.

In the absence of a double tax treaty this works by allowing any Picean corporation tax paid on branch profits from Bertie Overseas to be credited against Bertie Ltd's UK corporation tax.

Double tax relief is, however, restricted to the lower of the overseas corporation tax paid and the UK corporation tax on the taxable profits from the overseas source.

As Picean corporation tax rates are 10% which is lower than the rate of UK corporation tax currently being paid (i.e. 20%), all of the Picean tax should be available as a credit against Bertie Ltd's corporation tax liability.

Anti-avoidance legislation

The fact that the use of an overseas subsidiary paying dividends allows companies to avoid UK corporation tax on remittances to the UK is of concern to HMRC. As a result a variety of anti-avoidance legislation exists to protect the UK Treasury position.

The principal pieces of such legislation are as follows:

Transfer pricing

In circumstances where sales are made by a large UK resident company to another company which it controls, at an undervalue (thus depressing UK profits), HMRC can substitute a market value price. This is known as transfer pricing.

Assuming that Bertie Ltd is classified as a large company under the transfer pricing legislation it would appear that this legislation is in point.

This is because the proposed mark up to Bertie Overseas is lower than HMRC might expect (80% compared to 85%). We are aware that Bertie Overseas will be responsible for all of its sale and distribution costs therefore it may be possible to explain the reduction in mark up if Bertie Overseas is required to undertake further responsibilities. This is an area that can be further explored at our next meeting.

It is likely that a transfer pricing liability may also exist relating to the differential in interest rates that will be charged of 2%.

Bertie Ltd must self assess its liability under transfer pricing within its corporation tax return. Penalties can be levied if HMRC are successful in arguing that adjustments should have been made but were not.

For this reason it is recommended that Bertie Ltd sets out in advance its proposed transfer pricing arrangements to HMRC under a statutory procedure known as Advance Pricing Arrangements and negotiate their acceptance with them.

Residence status of overseas limited company

The exemption from the UK corporation tax will only apply to dividends received from non-UK resident companies. If HMRC can successfully argue that Bertie Overseas is in fact UK resident then all of its profits will be subject to UK corporation tax (with double tax relief available for tax paid in Picea).

A company will be UK resident if it is incorporated in the UK or it is managed and controlled from the UK. Clearly the former is not a problem but the latter may be. This is because the test is not where day to day control is exercised but rather the highest level of strategic control. If this is exercised by the UK Board of Bertie Ltd it is likely that HMRC will regard control as being UK based thus making Bertie Overseas UK resident.

This is something that will need to be explored in greater depth when we next meet.

Controlled foreign company

In certain circumstances HMRC have powers to apportion profits of controlled foreign companies ('CFC') to a UK resident company.

A CFC exists where a foreign company under UK control is resident in a low tax area (tax is less than 75% of UK corporation tax that would be payable) and is set up with a view to avoid UK tax.

On the face of it, it would appear that Bertie Overseas will be caught by this legislation but this is considered unlikely as various exemptions exist.

In the short term, Bertie Overseas will be covered by the low profits exemption. This applies if the overseas company's TTP is £500,000 or less in a 12 month period, of which no more than £50,000 comprises non-trading profits.

Even if profits increase above this level, trading profits of the CFC will only fall within the charge to the extent that the profits are dependent on an activity provided from the UK which the CFC would be incapable of doing for itself, and the profits are only arising in the CFC for the purpose of avoiding UK tax.

This does not seem to be the case, as Bertie Overseas is considered to have a genuine commercial presence in Picea, and is therefore not considered further.

I hope the above adequately summarises the position but should you have any queries please do not hesitate to contact me.

Meanwhile I look forward to hearing from you further in the near future.

Yours sincerely,

A Accountant

North and South

Answer 1 – Chapter 29

(a) **Corporation tax computations**

North Limited

Year ended 31 March	2017	2018
	£	£
Trading profit	10,000	
Chargeable gain (£120,000 – £80,000)		40,000
Less: Loss relief – current year		(40,000)
– carried back	(10,000)	
TTP	0	0
Corporation tax liability	0	0

Loss working:	£
Loss per question	(114,000)
Less: Profit on sale of inventory	
(£10,000 – £6,000)	4,000
Revised loss	(110,000)
Current year offset	40,000
Carry back relief	10,000
Carried forward as at 31 March 2018	(60,000)

South Limited

Year ended 31 March	2017	2018
	£	£
Trading profit = TTP	160,000	200,000
	£	£
Corporation tax liability:		
(£160,000 × 20%) (£200,000 × 20%)	32,000	40,000

Total corporation tax payable by South Limited is therefore £72,000 (£32,000 + £40,000).

(b) **Weaknesses of the group structure**

North and South Limited are owned personally by Bertrand and do not therefore form a 75% group for both group relief and chargeable gains purposes.

As a consequence:

(i) The forecast trading losses of North Limited for the y/e 31 March 2018 cannot be relieved against the profits made by South Limited for this accounting period.

(ii) The group rollover relief provisions are not available. As a result, North Limited is unable to relieve its gain of £40,000 by rolling this (at least partially) into the proposed acquisition of the freehold property by South Limited in the y/e 31 March 2018.

Improvement of group structure

To improve the group structure a 75% relationship therefore needs to be established for North Limited and South Limited. This could be achieved either by placing North Limited and South Limited beneath a holding company or (more simply) by placing North Limited beneath South Limited (or vice versa).

Procedures to alter the group structure

Either route would involve Bertrand making a disposal of (at least some of) his shares. For example if South Limited becomes the holding company of North Limited this would involve Bertrand transferring his shares in North Limited to South Limited.

This transfer is a chargeable disposal for capital gains tax purposes. However, providing the conditions for a 'paper for paper' share exchange are satisfied this gain will not be taxable.

The main conditions are that the:

(a) consideration received for the shares transferred is shares,

(b) acquiring company acquires more than a 25% interest as a result of the transaction, and

(c) transaction is undertaken for bona fide commercial purposes.

It is possible (and advisable) that Bertrand obtains a clearance from HMRC that this transaction will be relieved under these provisions. Providing Bertrand can provide a sound commercial reason this should not prove too difficult. If the provisions apply the original base cost for capital gains purposes of the shares that Bertrand transfers will become the base cost of the new shares that he acquires.

The transaction should be exempt from stamp duty under the 'group reconstruction relief' provisions.

This is because:

(a) it is likely that the whole of the share capital of North Limited will be acquired by South Limited, and

(b) there is unlikely to be a change in the ultimate ownership after the reconstruction.

It should be noted, however, that this relief will only apply if the transaction is undertaken for bona fide commercial purposes.

If desired, following this group restructuring the shop acquired by South Limited could be transferred on a no gain/no loss basis to North Limited.

(c) **Revised corporation tax computations**

North Limited

Year ended 31 March	2017	2018
	£	£
Trading profit	10,000	0
Chargeable gain (Note 1)		20,000
Less: Loss relief – current year (Note 2)	0	(20,000)
– carried back (Note 2)	(10,000)	0
TTP	0	0
Corporation tax	0	0

Loss working

	£
Loss per question	(114,000)
Less: Profit on inventory	4,000
Revised loss	(110,000)
Current year offset	20,000
Carry back offset	10,000
Group relief	80,000
Carried forward as at 31 March 2018	0

South Limited

Year ended 31 March	2017	2018
	£	£
Trading profit	160,000	200,000
Group relief (Note 2)		(80,000)
TTP	160,000	120,000
Corporation tax liability: (as before)/(£120,000 × 20%)	32,000	24,000

Total corporation tax payable by South Limited and North Limited is therefore £56,000 (£32,000 + £24,000) a saving of £16,000 (£72,000 – £56,000).

Notes:

(1) Group rollover relief will be available as follows:

	£
Original gain on freehold property	40,000
Less: Rollover relief (balancing figure)	(20,000)
Taxable now = proceeds not reinvested	20,000

(2) In order to minimise the tax liability of the group, the excess loss of North Ltd (after setting off against its own profits) can be surrendered to South Ltd. Further a carry back in North Limited to y/e 31 March 2017 will be beneficial from a cash flow perspective as this will result in a repayment of tax.

Index

51% group companies.....802
75% groups.....945

A

Above the line tax credit.....844
Accommodation.....52
Accrued income scheme.....111
Additional rate.....5
Adjusted income.....142
Adjusted net income.....13
Adjustments to profit.....615
Agricultural property relief (APR).....464
Allowable expenditure
– Capital gains tax.....179
– Employment income.....43
– Property income.....99
– Trading income.....616, 660
Amendments to tax return.....581, 812
Annual allowance for pension contributions.....139
Annual accounting scheme.....756
Annual exempt amount for capital gains tax.....181
Annual exemption for inheritance tax.....411
Annual investment allowance.....622, 823
Annual value – living accommodation.....52
Appeals.....600
Approved Mileage Allowance Payments.....46
Approved share option schemes.....67, 69
Arising basis for overseas income.....354
Asset damaged.....216
Asset lost or destroyed.....214
Assignment of leases.....210
Associated disposals for entrepreneurs' relief....268
Associated operations.....526
Augmented profits.....801
Automatic residency tests – individuals.....344

B

Badges of trade.....609
Balancing payments.....586
Basic rate band.....5
Basis of assessment of trading profits.....615, 636, 695
Beneficial loans.....60
Benefits of employment.....48
Benefits to shareholders.....910
Bond washing.....112
Bonus issues.....230
Branch vs. subsidiary.....998
Business finance.....886
Business property relief (BPR).....458

C

Capital allowances – Plant and machinery
– Accelerating capital allowances.....631
– Annual investment allowance.....622, 823
– Approach to computational questions.....621
– Cars.....624
– Closing years.....693
– Companies.....823
– Energy saving plant and machinery.....825
– First year allowance.....624
– Groups of companies.....823
– Hire purchase assets.....627
– Integral features.....626
– Long life assets.....626
– Low emission cars.....624
– Pro forma computation.....620
– Related businesses.....623, 823
– Short life assets.....631
– Small pool WDA.....627
– Special rate pool.....625, 824
– Successions to trade.....693
– Thermal insulation.....625
– Waiver of capital allowances.....629
Capital gains group.....945, 955
Capital gains tax (CGT)
– Annual exempt amount.....181
– Asset damaged.....216
– Asset lost or destroyed.....214
– Calculation of individual gains/losses.....179
– Capital gains tax payable.....181
– Capital losses.....180, 245, 833, 874, 962
– Capital losses in year of death.....186
– Chargeable assets.....177
– Chargeable disposal.....177
– Chargeable person.....176
– Chattels.....206
– Compensation and insurance.....213
– Connected persons.....200
– Date of disposal.....178
– Death of an individual.....185
– Exempt assets.....177, 228
– Exempt disposal.....177
– Husband and wife/civil partnership.....201
– Leases.....210
– Loss relief against income.....245
– Negligible value claims.....181
– Overseas aspects.....370
– Part disposals.....205

– Partnerships.....731
– Payment.....184
– Payment by instalments.....184
– Qualifying corporate bond (QCB) 229
– Rates of CGT.....182
– Reliefs.....see 'Reliefs for capital gains'
– Residential property disposals by non-UK residents.....382
– Shares and securities.....see 'Shares and securities'
– Small part disposals.....205
– Transfers to trust.....187
– Wasting assets.....207

Capital goods scheme.....769
Capital losses.....180, 245, 833, 874, 962
Car benefit.....56
Carry forward of trading losses.....649, 871
Cars – capital allowances.....624
Cash accounting scheme.....755
Cash basis for unincorporated businesses.....659
Cash vouchers.....43
Change in ownership.....880
Change in partnership agreement.....726
Change of accounting date.....642
Chargeable accounting period (CAP).....796
Chargeable assets for capital gains tax.....177
Chargeable disposal for capital gains tax.....177
Chargeable gains/losses for a company.....829
Chargeable lifetime transfers (CLTs).....407
Chargeable persons for capital gains tax.....176
Chargeable persons for inheritance tax.....407
Chargeable property for inheritance tax.....406
Charity exemption for inheritance tax.....413
Chattels.....206
Child benefit charge.....21
Children's bonus bonds.....562
Children's income.....20
Choice of accounting date.....638
Choice of cessation date.....696
Choice of loss reliefs.....656, 879
Civil partnerships.....17, 160, 201, 274, 412, 519
Claimant company.....948
Claim for overpayment relief.....582, 812
Claims to reduce POAs.....587
Close companies.....908
Close investment holding company (CIC).....913
Closing year loss reliefs.....698
Closing year rules.....695
Company car benefit.....56
Company share option plan (CSOP).....69, 71
Company residence.....994
Company van benefit.....59
Compensation and insurance.....213
Compliance checks.....593, 812
Compulsory registration.....748
Conflicts of interest.....573
Connected persons.....200
Consortia.....951
Controlled foreign companies (CFCs).....1010
Copyright royalties.....12
Corporation tax liability.....800
Credit cards.....51, 563

D

Date of disposal for capital gains tax.....178
Death estate.....469
Death tax on lifetime gifts.....420
Debt finance.....887
Debt vs. equity.....887
Deed of variation.....521
Deemed domicile.....504
Deemed occupation.....274
Deemed salary.....922
Default interest.....785
Default surcharge.....782
Degrouping charge.....956
Depreciating assets.....285
Deregistration.....749
Destination system.....789
Determination assessments.....582, 810
Diminution in value.....405
Disaggregation.....759
Discovery assessments.....594, 814
Discretionary trusts.....540
Dishonest conduct of tax agents.....576
Disincorporation.....923
Disincorporation relief.....924
Disposal date.....178
Dividend income – individuals.....4, 9
Dividends received by companies.....801, 999
Divisional VAT registration.....976
Domicile.....342, 504
Double tax relief (DTR)
– Capital gains tax.....374
– Corporation tax.....1004
– DTR treaties.....365, 995, 1004
– Income tax..... 364

Index

– Inheritance tax.....508

– Unilateral relief.....365, 1004

Due dates for payment of tax.....see 'Payment of tax'

E

Earned income.....3

EIS reinvestment relief.....310

Electronic filing of VAT return......782

Employee pension contributions.....43

Employee shareholder shares.....78

Employer pension contributions.....48, 143

Employment benefits.....48

Employment income.....43

Employed vs. self-employed.....40

Employee vs. partner.....667

Energy saving plant and machinery.....825

Enterprise investment scheme (EIS)...113, 310, 561

Enterprise management incentive (EMI).....69, 72

Entrepreneurs' relief.....263

Equalisation of income.....160

Equity finance.....887

Errors on VAT returns.....784

Estate rate.....471

Ethical code.....570

Ex gratia payments.....80

Excepted assets.....462

Exempt assets.....177, 228

Exempt disposal.....177

Exempt benefits.....48

Exempt income.....4

Exempt legacies.....473, 482

Exempt residue.....483

Exempt supplies.....747

Exempt transfers for inheritance tax.....409

Exit charge.....545

Expenses from employment income.....43

Expensive living accommodation benefit.....52

Exports.....788

Extracting profits from a company.....915

F

Fall in value relief.....430

Filing date.....579, 799

Finance for the individual.....558, 891

Financing a company.....887

Financing non-current assets.....894

First year allowance.....624

Flat rate expenses.....661

Flat rate scheme (VAT).....757

Foreign assets for inheritance tax.....505

Fuel benefit.....58

Furnished holiday accommodation.....101

Future test.....748

G

General anti-abuse rule (GAAR).....577

Gift aid.....6

Gifts of assets benefit.....55

Gift of qualifying assets.....292

Gift relief for capital gains.....292

Gifts into trust.....546

Gifts out of trust.....547

Gifts with reservation.....523

Goodwill.....848

Groups of companies

– Approach to questions.....1035

– Capital allowances.....823

– Capital gains group.....945, 955

– Companies joining.....949, 1030

– Companies leaving.....950, 1030

– Consortia.....951

– Degrouping charge.....956

– Group payment arrangements.....808

– Group relief.....947

– Group relief group.....945

– Losses of overseas subsidiaries.....951

– Matching election.....960

– Payment for group relief.....949

– Pre-entry capital losses.....962

– Reallocation of gains and losses.....960

– Reconstructions.....966

– Related 51% group companies.....802

– Rollover relief.....961

– Transfer of trade.....964

– VAT groups.....973

Group relief.....947

Group VAT registration.....973

H

Higher rate band.....5

Hire purchase.....627, 894

Historic test.....748

Holdover relief for reinvestment in depreciating assets.....285

Husband and wife.....17, 160, 201, 274, 412, 519

I

Identification rules for shares.....230, 833

Index

Immediate post death interest trusts.....545

Impairment losses.....752

Imports.....787

Income tax computation.....2

Income tax liability.....3

Income tax payable.....3

Incorporation

- Loss relief.....700
- Tax implications.....704
- Relief for capital gains.....301

Indexation allowance.....831

Individual savings accounts (ISAs).....109, 187, 473, 562

Information and inspection powers.....595

Inheritance tax

- Agricultural property relief (APR).....464
- Annual exemption.....411
- Associated operations.....526
- Business property relief (BPR).....458
- Chargeable lifetime transfers (CLTs).....407
- Chargeable persons.....407
- Chargeable property....406
- Charity exemption.....413
- Civil partnerships.....412, 519
- Death estate.....469
- Death tax on lifetime gifts.....420
- Deed of variation.....521
- Deemed domicile.....504
- Diminution in value.....405
- Domicile.....504
- Double taxation relief.....508
- Excepted assets.....462
- Exempt transfers.....409
- Fall in value relief.....430
- Foreign assets.....505
- Gifts with reservation.....523
- Husband and wife.....412
- Instalments.....511
- Joint tenants.....474
- Life assurance policies.....476
- Lifetime gifts.....407
- Lifetime tax on CLTs.....414
- Location of assets.....505
- Marriage exemption.....410
- Married couples.....412, 519
- Nil rate band.....415
- Occasions of charge.....407
- Payment.....417, 423, 433, 510
- Planning.....513
- Political party exemption.....412
- Potentially exempt transfers (PETs).....407
- Quick succession relief.....481
- Reduced rate for legacies to charity.....478
- Related property.....453
- Settled property.....476, 547
- Single grossing up.....482
- Small gifts.....410
- Taper relief.....422
- Tenants in common.....475
- Transfer of nil rate band.....477
- Transfer of value...405
- Valuation of shares.....450, 452
- Unit trusts.....453

Input VAT.....746

Instalments for capital gains tax.....184

Instalments for corporation tax.....805

Instalments for inheritance tax.....511

Intangible assets.....846, 957

Intangible rollover relief.....849

Integral features.....625

Interest.....588, 807

Interest in possession trusts.....541

Interest income for companies.....825

Interest income for individuals.....4

Interest received gross.....4

Interest received net.....4

Investment companies.....854

Investment products.....562

Investors' relief.....269

IR35.....919

J

Job related accommodation.....53

Joint income.....17

Joint tenants.....474

K

Key investment products.....562

L

Land and buildings – VAT.....760

Late payment interest.....588

Leases.....210

Lease premiums.....106, 616

Leasing of assets.....895

Leasing of cars.....616, 895

Letting relief.....276

Life assurance policies.....476, 505

Life tenant.....476, 541

Index

Lifetime allowance for pensions.....147
Lifetime gifts for inheritance tax.....407
Lifetime tax on CLTs.....414
Limited liability partnerships.....731, 908
Liquidation of a company.....245, 929
Living accommodation benefit.....52
Loan relationship deficits.....874
Loan relationships.....825
Loan to shareholder.....911
Location of assets.....505
Long life assets.....626
Long period of account.....830
Loss relief.....see 'Trading loss reliefs'
Low emission cars.....624
Lump sum payments.....80

M

Major change in nature or conduct of trade.....880
Management expenses.....855
Marriage allowance.....17
Marriage exemption.....410
Married couples..... 17, 160, 201, 274, 412, 519
Matching election for gains groups.....960
Matching rules for shares.....230, 833
Mileage allowances.....46
Miscellaneous income.....829
Money laundering.....576
Motor expenses – VAT.....752
Mortgages.....472, 543, 563

N

N S & I interest.....4, 562
N S & I savings certificates 4, 562
National insurance contributions
– Class 1 NICs.....82
– Class 1A NICs.....85
– Class 2 NICs.....663
– Class 4 NICs.....663
– Directors.....86
– Persons with more than one job.....86
Negligible value claim.....181
Net return on investment.....564
New clients.....572
Nil rate band for inheritance tax.....415
Non-cash vouchers.....51
Non-trading losses....873
Normal expenditure out of income.....411
Notification of chargeability.....582, 809
Notional salary.....922

O

Occupational pension schemes.....133
OECD model tax treaty.....995
Opening year rules.....636, 728
Option to tax.....760
Origin system.....789
Output VAT.....746
Overlap profits.....637
Overseas aspects of capital gains tax.....370
Overseas aspects of corporation tax
– Branch vs. subsidiary.....998
– Controlled foreign companies (CFCs).....1010
– Dividends.....999
– Double tax relief.....1004
– Overseas income.....828
– Permanent establishment.....997
– Treaty relief.....1004
– Trading income.....996
– Unilateral relief.....1004
– Unrelieved overseas tax.....1010
– Worldwide debt cap.....1002
Overseas aspects of VAT.....787
Overseas income for individuals
– Basis of assessment.....354
– Dividends.....355
– Double tax relief.....364
– Employment income.....355, 356
– Pensions.....355
– Remittance basis.....359
– Remittance basis charge.....361
– Trading income.....355
Overseas income for companies.....828
Overseas permanent establishment.....997
Overseas travelling expenses re: trade.....356
Overseas travelling expenses re: employment.....358

P

Part disposals.....205
Partial exemption.....762
Partnerships
– Allocation of partnership profits/losses.....725
– Capital gains tax.....731
– Change in profit sharing agreement.....726
– Limited liability partnerships.....731, 908
– Loss relief.....730
– Partner joining.....728
– Partner leaving.....728
Patent box relief.....849
Patent royalties.....12

Index

Payment of tax
- Capital gains tax.....184
- Corporation tax.....801
- Income tax – self-assessment.....579
- Inheritance tax.....417, 423, 433, 510
- National insurance contributions.....82, 663

Payment on account.....586
Penalties.....582, 588, 595, 814
Pensions
- Adjusted income.....142
- Annual allowance.....139
- Benefits on death.....147
- Benefits on retirement.....146
- Contributions by individual.....135
- Employer contributions.....137
- Lifetime allowance.....147
- Maximum annual amount.....135
- Method of obtaining relief.....136
- Occupational pension schemes.....133
- Personal pension schemes.....134
- Planning.....163
- Relevant earnings.....135
- Relief for contributions.....135
- Restriction of AA.....141
- Spreading of employer contributions.....143
- Threshold income.....142
- Types of registered scheme.....133

Permanent establishment.....997
Personal allowances.....5, 12
Personal financial management.....558
Personal pension schemes.....134
Personal liability of senior accounting officers.....811
Personal service companies.....919
Political party exemption.....412
Potentially exempt transfers (PETs).....407
Premium bonds.....4, 562
Premiums received on the grant of a lease.....106
Pre-entry capital losses.....962
Pre-registration input VAT.....749
Pre-trading expenditure.....617
Principal charge.....545
Principal private residence relief.....272, 384
Private fuel benefit.....58
Private use assets.....625
Professional code of ethics.....570
Pro forma computations
- Adjustment of profits.....615
- Capital allowances.....620
- Capital gain/loss for individuals.....179
- Capital gains tax payable.....181
- Corporation tax liability.....799
- Death estate.....469
- Income tax.....3
- Income tax losses.....655
- Personal service companies.....922
- Taxable total profits.....799, 822
- Trading losses for companies.....872

Property income.....98, 828
Property income losses.....103, 874
Purchase of own shares.....926

Q

Qualifying charitable donations (QCD) relief.....830
Qualifying corporate bond (QCB).....229, 562
Qualifying loan interest.....11
Quarterly instalments.....805
Quick succession relief.....481

R

Rates of income tax.....5
Real estate investment trusts (REITs).....108, 562
Receipts basis.....43
Reconstructions and reorganisations.....966
Records.....592, 811
Redundancy payments.....80
Registration for VAT.....747
Related 51% group companies.....802
Related businesses AIA.....623, 823
Related property.....453
Relief against total income.....3, 649, 699
Relief against chargeable gains.....650
Relief in closing years.....698
Relief in opening years.....652
Reliefs for capital gains
- EIS reinvestment relief.....310
- Entrepreneurs' relief.....263
- Gift relief.....292
- Holdover relief for reinvestment in depreciating assets.....285
- Incorporation relief.....301
- Investors' relief.....269
- Principal private residence relief...272, 384
- Letting relief.....276
- Replacement of business asset relief.....282, 961
- Rollover relief.....282, 832, 961
- SEIS reinvestment relief....314

Relief for pension contributions.....135, 136, 137

Index

Remittance basis.....359

Remittance basis charge.....361

Rent a room relief.....103

Rental income.....98

Reorganisations and takeovers.....235

Repayment interest.....588

Replacement furniture relief.....100

Replacement of business asset relief.....282, 961

Research and development.....843

Residence – company.....994

Residence – individuals.....342

Rights issues.....230

Rollover relief.....282, 832, 961

S

Salary vs. dividend.....915

Sale of a business – VAT.....761

Sale of shares vs. assets.....966

Sale of rights nil paid.....232

Save as you earn (SAYE) scheme.....69

Savings income.....6

Savings income nil rate band.....6

Scholarships.....62

Seed enterprise investment scheme (SEIS).....116, 562

SEIS reinvestment relief....314

Self-assessment

– Appeals....600
– Amendments to tax return.....581, 812
– Balancing payments.....586
– Claim for overpayment relief.....582, 812
– Claims to reduce POAs.....587
– Compliance checks.....593, 812
– Determination assessments.....582, 810
– Discovery assessments.....594, 814
– Filing date.....579, 799
– Information and inspection powers.....595
– Interest.....588
– Notification of chargeability.....582, 809
– Payment of tax.....586
– Payments on account (POAs).....586
– Penalties.....582, 588, 814
– Quarterly instalments.....805
– Records.....592, 811
– Tax return.....580, 809
– Tax tribunals.....601

Senior accounting officers.....811

Services – VAT.....790

Settled property.....476, 547

Share for share exchange.....235, 966

Share incentives.....68

Share incentive plan.....70, 73

Share options.....67

Share schemes.....66

Shares and securities

– Bonus issues.....230
– Exempt shares and securities.....228
– Identification rules for companies.....833
– Identification rules for individuals.....230
– Matching rules for companies.....833
– Matching rules for individuals.....230
– Reorganisations.....235
– Rights issues.....230
– Sale of rights nil paid.....232
– Share for share exchange.....235, 966
– Share pool for companies.....833
– Share pool for individuals.....230
– Takeovers.....235
– Valuation rules for shares.....186, 229, 450

Short lease.....106, 210

Short life assets.....631

Short term finance.....892

Single grossing up.....482

Small gifts exemption.....410

Small part disposals.....205

Small pool WDA.....627

Sole trader vs. company.....904

Special rate pool.....625, 824

Splitting the tax year.....349

Stamp duty land tax.....187, 706, 761

Stamp duty.....246

Stamp duty reserve tax.....246

Standard rated supplies.....747

Starting rate for savings income.....6

State pension age.....85, 664

Substantial shareholding exemption.....835

Successions to trade.....693

Sufficient ties test.....345

Surrendering company.....948

T

Takeovers.....235

Taper relief.....422

Tax avoidance.....576

Tax efficient investments.....158, 561

Tax evasion.....576

Tax tribunals.....601

Index

Taxable income.....2
Taxable supplies.....745
Taxable total profits...799, 822
Temporary absence abroad.....376
Temporary place of work.....46
Tenants in common.....474
Terminal loss relief.....699
Termination payment.....80
Thin capitalisation.....853
Threshold income.....142
Trading losses
- Adjusted total income.....658
- Approach to losses questions.....655, 875
- Carry forward of losses.....649, 871
- Change in ownership.....880
- Choice of loss reliefs.....656, 879
- Closing year loss options....698
- Computation of losses.....647, 653
- Incorporation loss relief.....700
- Major change in nature or conduct of trade.....880
- Maximum deduction from total income.....657
- Options for companies.....871
- Options for individuals....647
- Ongoing year loss options.....646
- Opening year loss relief.....653
- Partnership losses.....730
- Procedure for losses questions.....655, 875
- Pro forma for income tax.....655
- Pro forma for corporation tax.....872
- Relief against total income.....649, 699
- Relief against total profits.....871
- Relief against chargeable gains.....650
- Relief in opening years.....652
- Restrictions on loss relief.....880
- Tax planning.....656
- Terminal loss relief.....699

Trading profit.....614, 823
Transfer of going concern.....761
Transfer of trade.....964
Transfer of value for inheritance tax.....405
Transfer pricing.....851
Travel expenditure.....45
Treaties (DTR).....365, 995, 1004
Trivial benefits.....49
Trusts
- Capital gains tax..... 549
- Discretionary trust.....540
- Immediate post death interest trusts.....545
- Income tax.....543
- Inheritance tax.....548
- Interest in possession trust.....541
- Types of trust.....540

U

Unapproved retirement benefits.....81
Unapproved share schemes.....67
Unilateral relief.....365, 1004
Unit trusts.....453, 560
Unrelieved overseas tax.....1010
Use of assets benefit.....54

V

VAT
- Annual accounting scheme.....756
- Capital goods scheme.....769
- Cash accounting scheme.....755
- Compulsory registration.....748
- Default interest.....785
- Default surcharge.....782
- Deregistration.....749
- Destination system.....789
- Disaggregation.....759
- Divisional registration.....976
- Electronic filing.....782
- Errors on VAT returns.....784
- Exempt supplies.....747
- Exports.....788
- Flat rate scheme.....757
- Group registration.....973
- Impairment losses.....752
- Imports.....787
- Input VAT.....746
- Land and buildings.....760
- Motor expenses.....752
- Option to tax.....760
- Origin system.....789
- Output VAT.....746
- Overseas aspects.....787
- Partial exemption.....762
- Penalties.....782
- Pre-registration input VAT.....749
- Records.....754
- Registration.....747
- Sale of a business.....761
- Services.....790
- Taxable supplies.....747
- Transfer of going concern.....761

– Types of supply.....747
– Voluntary registration.....748
– Zero-rated supplies.....747
Valuation rules for shares.....186, 229, 450
Van benefit.....59
Venture capital trusts (VCTs).....118, 562
Voluntary registration.....748
Vouchers.....43

W

Waiver of capital allowances.....629
Wasting assets.....207
Winding up.....930
Withdrawing investment from company.....925
Withholding tax.....1004
Worldwide debt cap.....1002
Writing down allowance.....623

Z

Zero rated supplies.....747